# New Trends in Criminal Investigation and Evidence

## Volume II

# New Trends in Criminal Investigation and Evidence

## Volume II

Editors:
C.M. Breur
M.M. Kommer
J.F. Nijboer
J.M. Reijntjes

INTERSENTIA
Antwerpen – Groningen – Oxford

J.F. Nijboer & J.M. Reijntjes (eds.)
*Proceedings of the First World Conference on New Trends in Criminal Investigation and Evidence (Volume I)*
ISBN 90-5458-431-9

C.M. Breur, M.M. Kommer, J.F. Nijboer, J.M. Reijntjes (eds.)
New Trends in Criminal Investigation and Evidence – Volume II

© 2000 INTERSENTIA
Antwerpen – Groningen – Oxford
http://www.intersentia.be

ISBN 90-5095-133-3
D/2000/7849/44
NUGI 694

Hoewel bij deze uitgave de uiterste zorg is nagestreefd, kan voor de afwezigheid van eventuele (druk)fouten en onvolledigheden niet worden ingestaan en aanvaarden auteur(s), redacteur(en) en uitgever deswege geen aansprakelijkheid.

# Contents

Contents

Contents

# Preface

This volume contains a representative selection from the papers, delivered at the Second World Conference on New Trends in Criminal Investigation and Evidence. This conference was held in Amsterdam, 10-15 December 1999. It attracted over 200 delegates. They were a mixture of scholars and professionals, involved in the field of investigation and adjudication of criminal cases. Many of them were lawyers by education, also many were not. But what they shared was their lively and active interest in exchanging information and experience, crossing professional, disciplinary, and national borders.

The selection for this volume was not easy, given the abundance of materials. We tried to publish as much as possible a representative selection. Papers published elsewhere are not included. As a consequence the papers delivered at the series of workshops, set up by Peter Tillers, on Artificial Intelligence and Proof, are left out: they will be published in the Cardozo Law Review. However, one (general) article about Artificial Intelligence, written by E. Nissan, has been enclosed in this book.

The papers in this volume are presented in alphabetical order of authors. It was very difficult to find clear common denominators that would enable us to divide the materials in chapters, apart from the problem of the 'logical' order of such chapters. The topics covered by the various authors often touch upon others in many ways. Therefore, we finally decided – unlike in the proceedings of the First World Conference on New Trends in Criminal Investigation and Evidence – to use the alphabetical order. It is clear and at least seems democratic. The only undemocratic exception is that the book opens with the plenary address by Hans Nijboer, the conference president. The reason for this is that in this piece some headlines of the conference are discussed. We, the editors, thought that it might be helpful to readers to read this article first in order to get a better view on the scope of the conference. For the rest, we hope that the table of contents is sufficient to guide you through the volume.

Finally, we would like to thank those who made the publication of this book possible: the Dutch Ministry of Justice (WODC), the Netherlands Organisation for Scientific Research (NWO) and the International Network for Research on the Law of Evidence and Procedure (INREP). Also, we would like to thank Ian Freckelton, Janneke Metz and Reino Rustige for their work and support.

We hope that the readers will enjoy it and that it shows to be useful to the further developments in the field of criminal investigation and evidence, in theory and practice!

The editors,

Caroline Breur
(Junior researcher, Universiteit Leiden, Seminarium voor Bewijsrecht)

Max Kommer
(Senior advisor to the Dutch Minister of Justice, The Hague)

Hans Nijboer
(Director Seminarium voor Bewijsrecht/INREP, Universiteit Leiden and president of the conference)

Jan Reijntjes
(Professor of criminal law at the Open Universiteit, Heerlen, and co-president of the conference)

# Challenges for the Law of Evidence

*J.F. Nijboer*

### Introduction: Evidence and the Law of Evidence

Fact finding in the criminal process can be seen as a legal species of a far more general form of human activity. In the modern Western world most important decisions are made on the basis of factual information as thorough as possible. We like 'warranted' knowledge; we prefer choices between evidence based options. In science and other scholarly fields establishment of facts is subject to empirical research (*e.g.* psychological research on human inference). But it is also subject to 'norms'. Most of these norms have a methodological/logical background, some are derived from ethical considerations. This is not different in law; except for the circumstance that a small part of the norms have gained legal status as legal (binding) rules. Therefore the system of the legal rules of evidence can be mentioned an incomplete system. It is incomplete from both, the methodological/logical and the ethical perspectives.

In the tradition of common law countries the system of the legal rules of evidence take the form of presentation rules.[1] Departing from the 'theory' of free proof, all (means of) evidence can be introduced except for some. Thus it basically can be depicted as an incomplete system of exclusion rules with regard to the introduction of evidence. Exclusion of evidence usually has one of two rationales: unreliability or illegality. In continental law countries the tradition is not very different. The same 'theory' is the point of departure. The 'theory' is based on the assumption that human observation and experience, combined with rational thinking guarantee sound fact finding. The most important difference is that the legal rules of evidence tend to take the form of decision rules rather than presentation rules, but the two rationales are the same. And here too, the system can best be perceived as an incomplete system of exclusionary rules. This being the case, it is also arguable that the standards of proof correspond. In criminal procedure the presumption of innocence requires that the burden of proof, that is the obligation to prove beyond reasonable doubt that the accused committed the alleged crime, lies with the prosecution. There is no reason to suggest that continental expressions for the standard to which the proof must be delivered (like *conviction raisonnée, conviction intime, overtuiging* or *Überzeugung*) are different from the criterion beyond reasonable doubt.

By depicting the law of evidence as an incomplete system of rules, one admits that the law cannot completely regulate 'proof'. The same goes for 'investigation'. In fact, it is the opposite: most aspects of investigation and proof are not legally regulated. Therefore it is erroneous to confuse 'proof' with 'the law of proof'. Where we define procedural law as the law regulating

---

[1] There are also attribution rules, like the ones concerning the allocation of burdens of proof.

the process, the process 'itself' can be seen as the social object of such regulation. In the case of the law of proof, however, this is more complex: the law of proof regulates 'proof', which is not primarily factual, but normative in itself. We say 'valid' proof, not 'true' proof. This is the case, disregarding the fact that in most settings the claimed result of a valid proof will be a true state of affairs.

Better said: true statement about real state of affairs. This is the case in almost all fields of human knowledge. Only in very formal fields like deductive (proposition) logic and theoretical mathematics we do not directly refer to empirical knowledge. But in all the other fields from archaeology to zoology as well as in non-academic fields of experience we refer to such real state of affairs, al be it that they might consist in historical (past) facts (events). A consequence of the above mentioned incompleteness is that new problems or new challenges for (the law of) proof do not always require legal solutions in the form of adding more rules to the law of evidence or refining it by creating sub-rules. Sometimes it might be better when the law of evidence stays silent about such problems, especially in fast developing fields. For instance this country, the Netherlands, was pretty much in the forefront by statutorily regulating DNA profiling in 1994. The then developed regulation was clearly inspired by the technical possibilities of that moment, when it was not yet possible to multiply cell-materials. Presently the technical possibilities are much higher, much larger and the techniques have enormously changed. Therefore again it turned out to be necessary to totally revise the still pretty young regulation on this topic. I am not sure that it is the best way to do when trying to be to much ahead compared to practice in regulating subjects in the field of investigation and evidence.

The dominant idea that can be found in most treaties on evidence in relation to legal context is the freedom of proof, either as a principle for the introduction of evidence (common law) or for the evaluation of evidence (continental law). This idea is based on the assumption of general or even universal human capacities. And it is exactly this assumption that nowadays has become the object of serious criticism from the side of cognitive psychology. In experimental situations it turns out that human observation and human inference are matters that can be done in a better or a worse way and that the capacities of human beings are not equal at all when it comes to fact finding in general, including fact finding in legal situations.

The free proof principle in fact is founded on this outdated assumption of equal capacities in relation to a general idea of the very nature of the process of fact finding. This idea is best summarised as fact finding based upon observation and rationality. This paradigm can be labelled as an 'empirical rational model'. My impression is that this paradigm has lost much of its impact. For the moment we realise ourselves much better the flaws/fallibility of testimony as form of evidence. Testimony is the result of process of observation, perception, retention and reproduction. All these four tasks can be done in a better or worse form. Even the best form is far from perfect. And it is exactly this insight that leads to a lesser appreciation of evidence which exists in statements from observation (of witnesses or other participants). On the other side we can observe the fast development of forensic techniques and forensic specialities in the broader sense. Between archaeology or accountancy in its forensic form and the forensic zoology we indeed see over hundred different forensic disciplines, of which some are well-established (like forensic psychiatry) and some have just started in developing 'objective' standards (shoe-print comparison). The increasing number of such fields combined with the increasing number of experts in investigation and evidence leads to the suggestion that a new paradigm is upcoming: forensic expertise as the dominant form of fact finding in legal settings. And forensic expertise brings in statistics and probability theory, central basis of its kind of 'knowledge'.

**Stock Taking**

At least from the 16th century on, treatises on evidence in the law always have been interdisciplinary in certain sense: they are hardly restricted to the law only, but usually somewhere in the beginning start discussing other than legal insights as well. The only main group of exceptions are handbooks and commentaries in the so-called expository tradition,[2] that are confined to the explanation of rules in the law of evidence. The main non-legal fields that historically are involved in evidence-theory are logic, epistemology, linguistics, mathematics and physics. At present the situation is not very different, except that far more specialised fields often are referred to. I already touched upon the importance of legal psychology for knowledge about human observation and human inference. But we might also think of the just mentioned probability theory which plays a major role in many discussions on evidence and the law of evidence nowadays.

It is interesting to see that the fields we are discussing here recently have been discovered by legal comparatists. Today there is much attention given to the procedural law in action as a subject of comparative study. Let me just mention the classical work of M.R. Damaška with regard to the practice of the trial in relation to matters of evidence in common law countries as supposed to continental law countries.[3] Within the European Union the project *Corpus Iuris*,[4] the proposal with regard to Union criminal law and criminal procedure, has articulated the differences amongst the different European countries with regard to procedure especially in practice. The idea expressed in *Corpus Iuris* is that investigation and related rules in the sphere of evidence should be

---

[2] W.L. Twining, *Rethinking evidence*, Oxford 1989.
[3] *See* M.R. Damaška, *The faces of justice and state authority*, New Haven 1986; *Evidence law adrift*, New Haven 1997.
[4] M. Delmas-Marty *et al.*, *Corpus Iuris*, Paris 1997.

matters of domestic law, usually the domestic law of the country where the actual investigative activity takes place. This should lead to mutual recognition of results of investigation, including forensic information (products of forensic expertise). These subjects have become highlights in actual comparative discussions. But another issue that has attracted much attention in the already mentioned fast development of DNA profiling and related genetical research.

The last issue that I only want to mention is the creation of international criminal tribunals and future international criminal courts which have own rules of evidence and procedure which also have drawn interest of the professional scholars in evidence.

## The Conference Programme (Amsterdam, 10-15 December 1999)

This Second World Conference on New Trends on Criminal Investigation and Evidence shares with the first conference (which took place in 1995) that it covers a large area of topics of interest for the legal professions for forensic experts, and for theoretical, legal, philosophical, etc. scholarship. The conference however also differs in a decisive way from the first: in 1995 we devoted whole day programmes or half-day programmes to simultaneous workshops on related themes. Looking back this was felt as a shortcoming, since delegates were not able to follow all sessions on their field of interest, because these sessions were simultaneously held. Therefore we now choose for the sequential format with the result that sessions on related subjects can be consequently attended. Furthermore the scheme provides for three parallel programmes on other locations, where we offer the possibility to be better informed about certain aspects of the Netherlands legal system:
-    forensic psychiatric clinic De Kijvelanden (Rotterdam);
-    Customs and Excises in the Rotterdam harbour;
-    the inner city programme of Amsterdam.

Also, a special theoretical part of the conference set up by Peter Tillers is added to the program.[5] This stream starts as a plenary session on Artificial Intelligence and proof in a more general sense. It will be followed by various related topics for specialised workshops.

## Practice(s)

In many modern countries developments can be observed which widely reflect changes in scientific and technical fields. Upcoming forensic specialties seek their way to forensic fields, such as forensic accountancy. Sometimes novel techniques in the very end can influence legal norms, even in substantive fields. After techniques became available to reliably testing blood-alcohol and breath-alcohol levels, in many countries finally laws were introduced in which driving with a

---

[5] The papers of that theoretical part will be published elsewhere.

certain measured degree of alcohol in the blood or in the breath was penalised. Analysing this example in steps: first the parting point is that there was no specific rule. Serious incidents were prosecuted on the basis of for instance man- slaughter, homicide or causing harm by negligence or recklessness. Subsequently a rule was introduced in which specifically endangering the traffic on public roads was formulated as an offence in itself. Proving this specific offence turned out to be difficult on the basis of for instance witness evidence. Then, more objective tests became available, at first for blood analysis, secondly for breath analysis. The idea was that by developing such techniques, more objective test procedures could be implemented in the actual law enforcement practice. The results were available as expert evidence. Once admitted in evidence, the actual way the offence was proven implicitly was build upon generalisations, more refined statistical information of the kind that there is a large risk of accidents when someone drives a car with the promillage of 1,0. Not all courts were happy with this kind of reasoning in order to proof the offence. And in many countries the subsequent step was that the crime definition was changed in percentage definition. Here the legislator by definition declares that it is dangerous to drive with a blood alcohol level that exceeds a certain limit. Not always substantive law is influenced by developments in terms of technical and scientific investigation of evidence. Classical issues of proof, like identity of persons, are the field where new biometric knowledge and experience is brought in. When we in this way compare the different countries and their 'law in action', it may become clear that modern legal life is unthinkable without including the work of forensic experts. There is an ever increasing number of relations between the activities of the legal actors in the legal system and their scientific and technical counterparts in the broad field of what we call forensic expertise.

One further explanation can be given with regard to the fields where novel technical and scientific developments are introduced without directly effecting substantive law. Sometimes the legal system is eager to issue legislation. The reasons therefore can be many but an important role probably is the protection of human rights. And it is especially important to develop clear rules when the use of certain technical or scientific forms of investigation necessarily have an impact on the classical rights and liberties of a person such as the integrity of a body and the privacy. And this exactly reflects the reasons why initially DNA legislation is given so much priority in the Netherlands. In order to develop clear legal rules it is necessary to create statutory provisions. Courts can produce rules which can be the same as statutory regulation, especially when its origin lies in the case law of a superior court. An example from the Netherlands: in the so-called *Shoemakers decision* the Court of Cassation *(Hoge Raad)* formulated number of criteria that meant to be met a lower court, our court when it uses contested results of expertise.[6]

---

[6] HR 27 January 1998, *NJ* 1998, 403.

## Procedural Reforms and Court Reforms

Continuing the comparative approach, we can also observe the changes with regard to fact finding in relation to forensic expertise and developments here. Such developments are often embedded in a general climate of procedural reform. In many countries reforms of procedural law (codes of procedure) have been adopted or still are underway in parliamentary proceedings.

Types of procedures are developed and introduced. And often the organisation of legal institutes is under review as well. One interesting development at this moment is that we see the effects of the introduction of quality management and quality systems. Attention to this is given on a large scale, both primarily in the actual organisation of police, prosecutorial, and court services and (secondly) in the world of forensic expertise. So we see changes on both sides, the legal side of the legal actors and the professional side of the forensic experts. As an example I mention the almost simultaneous reorganisation and introduction of quality systems in forensic laboratories and in prosecutorial systems. And on both sides we see the same types of concepts emerge such as the primary process, the primary products or essential products or key products, key actors, strategical advantages and disadvantages, norms and procedures labelled with SOTA (State Of The Art).

In essence as a consequence, professional, normative settings tend to become more explicit, more articulated. At the same time this kind of observations reveal that it is not only the formal legal rules that thoroughly effect the actual work of the legal actors and forensic experts. In fact, much of the normative framework in which they work is not even formulated in the legal way, but is nevertheless essential to a sound functioning of the legal system as a whole. Elsewhere I contended that the open spaces that are left to for instance experts by formal law (statutes, case law, policies) do not mean that they work in a normative vacuum. Rules as developed in codes of practice, desk top manuals, disciplinary jurisdiction, etc. in fact determine the results of forensic and legal practice to a much higher degree than usually is thought of.[7]

## The General and the Specific: the Emergence of Forensic Expertise

Let us go back some steps in time for a moment. In the 19th century some forms of applied expertise was not unknown. But it lasted to the 20th century where firstly slow and later on with much more speed different forensic specialties came up and became institutionalised. As said before, at the moment over 100 different fields can be found. And there is no *a priori* reason to assume that this development will stop. As a consequence, especially in complex cases, the influence and effects will become clearer and clearer. Especially the case of DNA

---

[7] J.F. Nijboer, 'De gedisciplineerdheid van de deskundige', in: K. Boonen *et al. Criminalistiek, forensische deskundigen en strafrechtspleging*, Deventer 2000, pp. 19-28.

research and its forensic applications have triggered wide discussions between experts and jurist about standards of sound forensic investigation and evidence. It has become clear that DNA based techniques are in fact not perfect but they are not too weak. But at the same time it was discovered that many techniques and methods lack a sound basis in a broader scientific sense. Very often objective standards and information about the validity and reliability of specific forensic techniques are simply unknown. Scales of reference are not made explicit. And the theoretical frameworks in many cases at the best stay not clear but often are very, very vague. This all indicates that there is a real and continuous need for thorough discussion and evaluation. We, as organisers, hope that this conference offers opportunities in that direction.

## Three Examples of Challenges

The challenges are related to the quest of sound legal answers and professional answers in terms of rules, standards, SOTA-practises. And if possible such answers should not be only local or national but international as well. Let me illustrate the difficulty of some problems with three examples.

The first one is the case of Mr Dekwaadsteniet. Mr Dekwaadsteniet is a scientist who works at an institute RIVM that is active in different environment studies. It is a Dutch State institute. The message of Dekwaadsteniet, which he firstly communicated to his superiors, but finally as a whistle blower seeking publicity, is this: when preparing reports to governmental instances and other organisations about the effects of certain measures in terms of infrastructure (harbours, railways and airports), the instance he works with (RIVM) uses statistical models to a much higher level than he thinks that it is justified. In fact his message is that there is only 1% of measuring and observations and 99% of 'speculation' based upon statistical assumptions within the basis of their inferential conclusions. No reality; only mathematics. If Mr Dekwaadsteniet is right, and I think that he is, this has much relevance to our fields as well. Many forensic techniques and methods can probably be compared with the kind of reports Mr Dekwaadsteniet points to. In the case of the RIVM, decisions about the future are made upon expectations but the techniques used in the underlying type of investigation or research is not very different from the ones used in forensic environmental investigations. And what goes for forensic environmental investigation probably for other forms of forensic expertise as well. The superiors of Mr Dekwaadsteniet were not pleased with his message and did not change their instructions how the work should be carried out. Finally after seeking publicity, Mr Dekwaadsteniet received official warnings, from the Ministry for the Environment that he should not disclose opinions that were contrary to the interest of State organisations. Till today whistle-blowers, even when day firstly have tried to convince their superiors of the need for change, have no easy life. As soon as a Nobel Price for legal practice and forensic expertise will be introduced, Mr Dekwaadsteniet should be nominated.

I turn to my second example, which can be pointed out very briefly, because it was already mentioned before. It is the issue of the legal relevance and the legal status of professional norms in forensic expertise. It is unpractical and probably unthinkable to give a formal legal status to all the often fluent rules and standards on all different fields of expertise. Nevertheless, on the other side the law can not eternally stay silent about such norms, especially when it turns out that in a remarkable number of cases the accurateness of the methods used is far from good. In my opinion the developments in professional standards and the ways of certifying and monitoring the quality of forensic work is not only the task of the relevant technical or scientific applied discipline. Discussion and the articulation of norms should be open for the legal actors and also for general public. This requires much more debate on these issues. And in order to illustrate the problematic nature of the field I just refer to the habit in the medical world to internally solve differences in insights in the application of certain treatments and in diagnostic and prognostic tests.

I come to my third example. This example was an issue at the first conference, four years ago, as well. What I would like to draw your attention to is the increasing importance of 'risk management' and 'risk assessment' in all kind of societal domains, including the criminal justice system. New tools are developed in terms of assessing risks with regard to certain groups or individuals in society. The basis of the criminal law is shifting from causing harm and fear and so on to causing danger or simply increasing risk. Different methods of strategical techniques in which societal sectors, like the financial, are monitored, such as what the Germans call *Rasterfahndung*, become important. They help to identify goals for further investigation, actually far before classical crimes in fact occur. Especially the change is substantive in which more and more crime definitions are introduced in terms of danger and risk. Such crimes create tension with the classical 'principle of guilt' and its procedural counterpart the 'presumption of innocence'. This can be easily illustrated: if it is punishable to introduce to the natural environment products that *can be* dangerous for the environment, the burden of proof for the prosecution is simply to establish that the defendant brought some material in the environment which usually is assumed to be potentially harmful for that environment. Consequently, it is up to the defence to proof that in this case what the defendant did was not endangering the environment. The difficulty of this position of the defence here, is that he has to contest statistics, whereas the prosecution simply can use results of measurements and so long combined with federal populations statistics (epidemiological dates).

I think that these three examples sufficiently illustrate the difficulty of the problems that we encounter in the field of evidence and the law of evidence.

**The Human Factor**

Let me conclude. Forensic psychology has told us that the human factor is important, when we like to base our decisions on for instance witness observations and estatements about their observations. The fallibility of human observation, human memory, human reproduction of past observations is large. Therefore we have to be very careful when we rely on human observation (as is the case in witness' testimony). The same goes for human inferences from in itself reasonably reliable data. It turns out that we are not very good at reasoning. What strikes me is the combination of human factors when we look at forensic expertise, how large the risks are that we take when we base our decisions upon human observations that form the basis for forensic investigations carried out with weak techniques by humans, after which the results are used by courts composed of humans. There is a lot to do.

# The Uncertain 'Revolution' in the Canadian Law of Evidentiary Privilege: what Principles take us where?*

*B.P. Archibald*

## 1.    Introduction

The past quarter century has seen something of a revolution in the manner in which Canadian lawmakers deal with evidentiary privilege.[1] The principles governing this revolution, which continues to this day,[2] are far from clear, as is the ultimate destination to which the courts and legislatures are taking us. The general subject here is evidentiary privileges: that is, the rules which exclude from civil or criminal cases relevant information, not because the evidence would not help get at the truth, but because some principle or value other than truth finding is deemed more important in the circumstances.[3] The focus of concern in this paper is personal or relational privilege – that is, claims that otherwise helpful statements or information are to be excluded on the grounds that confidential, inter-personal relations or private interests ought to be protected above the concerns of 'rectitude of decision' seen from an empirical perspective.[4] Thus, the discussion will not include reference to governmental privilege or 'public interest immunity' which may lead to exclusion of relevant information from litigation for reasons of state,[5] nor will it address the so-called 'privilege against self-

---

* The author would like to thank colleagues Shalin Sugunasiri and Rollie Thompson of Dalhousie University and Louise Viau of the University of Montreal for helpful comments on an earlier draft of this paper. Their generously given advice was not always followed to the letter, however, and errors are clearly the responsibility of the author.

[1] For purposes of this article it may be said that this quiet revolution began with the case of *Slavutych* v. *Baker* [1976] 1 *S.C.R.* 254 (Wigmore's criteria for privileged confidential communications were advanced to explain the exclusion of university tenure and promotions documents). For an early comment on this case and its significance *see* B. McLachlin, 'Confidential Communication and the Law of Privilege' (1977), 11 *U.B.C.L. Rev.* 266.

[2] For most recent manifestation is *L.C. and Attorney General of Alberta* v. *Mills*, unreported Supreme Court of Canada, November 25, 1999. Hereafter referred to simply as *Mills*.

[3] Standard Canadian sources on this topic include: J. Sopinka, S.M. Lederman & A.W. Bryant, *The Law of Evidence in Canada* (2nd ed.), Toronto: Butterworths 1999, pp. 709-819; D. Paccioco & L. Stuesser, *The Law of Evidence* (2nd ed.), Toronto: Irwin Law 1999; R.J. Delisle, *Evidence: Principles and Problems*, Toronto: Carswell/Thomson Publishing 1999; S.A. Schiff, *Evidence in the Litigation Process* (Master Edition), Toronto: Carswell 1993; J. Fortin, *Preuve pénale*, Montréal: Les Editions Themis 1984; J. Bellemare & L. Viau, *Droit de la preuve pénal*, Montréal: Mementos Thémis 1991; G. Boilard, *Guide to Criminal Evidence*, Cowansville: Editions Yvan Blais 1991; and R.D. Manes & M.P. Silver, *The Law of Confidential Communications in Canada*, Toronto: Butterworths 1996.

[4] On the expansion of 'truth finding' to encompass a broader notion of 'rectitude of decision', *see* W. Twining, *Rethinking Evidence: Exploratory Essays*, Oxford: Basil Blackwell 1990, pp. 71-82 and 185-186.

[5] Canadian terminology in this area is in a state of flux. The historical label 'Crown privilege' seems a thing of the past. While some writers and courts cling to the appellation 'government privilege' (*see* Delisle, *supra*, footnote 3, at pp. 687-690), most seem to be adopting the more inclusive 'public

(to be continued)

11

incrimination' which balances state interests in truth finding against the interests of accused (or potentially accused) persons or other witnesses in litigation.[6] However, the right to silence and privilege against self-incrimination will form an ver present backdrop, to the extent that in criminal matters the personal privileges of witnesses other than the accused interfere with the right to full answer and defence. This is particularly the case when the right to full answer and defence is in some measure equated with full access by an accused to absolutely all relevant evidence which may possibly assist in raising a reasonable doubt about guilt.

It is commonly assumed by members of the general public that the only concern of civil and criminal litigation is 'finding the truth' so that 'justice can be done'. Indeed, many rules of evidence in common law jurisdictions are primarily oriented to ensuring the reliability and probative value of evidence. Rules in relation to hearsay, opinion, similar fact and character are often contrasted with rules of privilege on this ground.[7] While this rectitude of decision is clearly an important value for judges, lawyers and legislators, these professionals generally understand that adjudication involves compromising among a number of potentially conflicting values: truth finding, procedural fairness as between litigating parties, concerns of cost and efficiency, and public

---

interest immunity' (*see* Sopinka, Lederman & Bryant, *supra*, footnote 3, pp. 853-891; and Paciocco & Stuesser, pp. 172-176). The latter approach has the merit of including both 'governmental' and 'judicial' privilege/immunity under a common analytical framework.

[6] Many argue that the 'privilege' against self-incrimination should be viewed as a 'principle' of procedural law rather than a doctrine of evidence: *see* S. Sugunasiri, 'Contextualism: The Supreme Court's New Standard of Judicial Analysis and Accountability' (1999), 22 *Dal Law J.* 154, at footnote 127. In Canada the 'privilege' or 'principle' against self-incrimination can be said to comprehend a number of constitutional statutory and common law protections for an accused person, including a constitutionally entrenched pre-trial right to silence (based on *Charter of Rights and Freedoms*, Section 7), common law confessions rules as strengthened by constitutional principles (*see R.* v. *Hebert*, [1990] *S.C.R.* 151), the constitutional right not to be compelled to testify in criminal proceedings against one (*Charter*, Section 11(c)), and the constitutional and statutory protections against the use of a witness testimony to incriminate or open civil liability in subsequent proceedings other than those for perjury (*Charter*, Section 13, *Canada Evidence Act, R.S.C.* 1985, c. C-5 as amended, Section 5, and cognate provincial evidence act sections). In this latter connection it may be helpful to note that the Canada statutory tradition going back a century, reinforced by *Charter* Section 13, differs from common law and American constitutional doctrine. Canadian witnesses cannot 'plead the fifth' in the sense of refusing to answer questions. Protection is given against subsequent incriminating use of answers to questions or of derivative evidence obtained from such answers; *see R.* v. *S.(R.J.)*, [1995] 1 *S.C.R.* 451; *British Columbia (Securities Commission)* v. *Branch*, [1995] 2 *S.C.R.* 3, and *Phillip* v. *Nova Scotia (Commission of Inquiry into the Westray Mine Tragedy)*, [1995] 2 *S.C.R.* 97. Recent constitutional doctrine may, however, be pushing Canadian courts beyond the 'subsequent use immunity' notion where these principles provide inadequate protection against self-incrimination: *see R.* v. *S.(R.J.)* (1995), 36 *C.R.* (4th) 1 (S.C.C.); *British Columbia (Securities Commission)* v. *Branch* (1995), 38 *C.R.* (4th) 133 (S.C.C.); *R.* v. *Jobin* (1995) 38 *C.R.* (4th) 176 (S.C.C.) and *R.* v. *Primeau* (1995) 38 *C.R.* (4th) 189 (S.C.C.).

[7] *See* Delisle, *supra*, footnote 3, at p. 663; also D. Watt, *Watt's Manual of Criminal Evidence* (1999), Toronto: Carswell/Thomson Publishing, at p. 99.

confidence in the reliability and fairness of the adjudicative system.[8] This balancing of competing values in adjudication can be demonstrated in many areas of the law of evidence.[9] However, in relation to evidentiary privileges which exclude highly probative and trustworthy information from the court's decisional database, delineation of the principles and values for this balancing exercise becomes a particularly acute problem.[10] When and why should concerns about protecting confidential, inter-personal relations or private individual interests trump truth finding in the litigation process? Exploring Canadian experience in relation to answering this question is the purpose of this paper.

This discussion of personal or relational evidentiary privileges is divided into three parts. The first will describe in general terms the scope of the Canadian evidence rules dealing with these privileges. The second part will analyze the range of rationales employed in Canada to advance personal or relational privilege claims: herein of principles, values, rights and politics. The third part will assess the present state of what can only be described as an uncertain revolution in the Canadian law of evidentiary privileges, and attempt to evaluate the emerging foundations for further developments in this area.

## 2. Canadian Rules on Personal or Relational Evidentiary Privileges

It is helpful to adopt the Supreme Court of Canada's distinction between traditional 'class' privilege claims on the one hand, and 'case-by-case' privilege claims on the other, for the purpose of the following description.[11] The essential distinction is that information covered by a 'class' privilege claim is presumptively excluded once the existence of the communication within a

---

[8] See Schiff, supra, footnote 3, pp. 13-18.

[9] See, for example, B.P. Archibald, 'The Canadian Hearsay Revolution: Is Half a Loaf Better Than No Loaf at All?', (1999) 25 Queen's Law Journal 1-63, for an analysis of how this balancing process occurs in relation to hearsay doctrine.

[10] A helpful and comprehensive over-view of American doctrine in this field is the note 'Developments in the Law: Privileged Communications' (1985), 98 Harv. L. Rev. 1450-1666. For a short but pithy American overview, see D.J. Capra, 'The Federal Law of Privileges' (1989), 16 Litigation 32. For a comparative insight into the subject of privilege in continental or civilian legal systems, see H.A. Hammelman, 'Professional Privilege: A Comparative Study' (1950), 28 Can. Bar. Rev. 750-758. However, on the dangers of over-broad generalizations about continental procedure in relation to evidence, see J.F. Nijboer, 'Common Law Tradition in Evidence Scholarship Observed from a Continental Perspective' (1993), 41 Am. J. of Comp. L. 299-338.

[11] This distinction was articulated in R. v. Gruenke [1991] 3 S.C.R. 263 by Lamer, C.J.C. It may be helpful at this point to indicate the extent of applicability of such common law precedent in Canada. The common law acts as a general source of evidential law throughout the common law provinces and the federal jurisdiction where common law rules have not been altered by a statutory rule, such as in the Canada Evidence Act, or a provincial evidence act: see Beach, infra, footnote 26. However, in the Province of Quebec where private law has its origins in the civilian tradition and is codified, the common law has no direct application in that private sphere although it applies in relation to federal matters such as criminal law. See Fortin, supra, footnote 3, pp. 16-18 and 158-160; and Bellemare & Viau, supra, footnote 3, pp. 12-15.

protected relationship is established, while information sought to be excluded by operation of 'case-by-case' privilege analysis is presumptively admitted until the nature and benefit of the privilege are demonstrated to the satisfaction of the court, largely in its discretion. The presentation of these two categories of privilege will be followed by a discussion of the recent Canadian controversy concerning production of the personal records of sexual assault victims, since it may signal a new direction in the analysis of personal privilege claims.

## 2.1    Traditional 'Class' Privilege Claims

Under this heading can be said to fall communications between solicitor and client, certain communications between spouses, and communications in furtherance of dispute settlement. The Canadian doctrine also brings police informer privilege under this heading, although in some measure the latter may also be thought a sub-set of public interest immunity.

### 2.1.1  Solicitor-Client Privilege

The most firmly entrenched evidentiary privilege in Canadian law is that in relation to communications between solicitor and client. While courts pay lip service to the English roots of the privilege in the 16th century[12] and its 19th century English reformulation,[13] the *locus classicus* of Canadian judicial analysis now seems to be Wigmore's enunciation of the rule: "Where legal advice of any kind is sought from a professional legal adviser in his capacity as such, the communications relating to that purpose, made in confidence by the client, are at his instance permanently protected from disclosure by himself or by the legal adviser, except the protection be waived."[14]

As one would expect, this common law rule has spawned a voluminous case law, which cannot be rehearsed here.[15] Certain propositions concerning the Canadian law of solicitor client privilege, however, merit emphasis for the purposes of this analysis.

---

[12] *Berd* v. *Lovelace* (1577), *Cary* 62, 21 *E.R.* 33 (Ch.) and *Dennis* v. *Coderington* (1579), *Cary* 100, 21 *E.R.* 53 (Ch.).

[13] *Greenough* v. *Gaskell* (1833), 1 *My. & K.* 98, 39 *E.R.* 618.

[14] J.H. Wigmore, *Evidence in Trials at Common Law* (Vol. 8)(J.T. McNaughton, rev.), Toronto: Little Brown, 1961, § 2292, p. 554. This passage is cited with approval as having "framed the modern principle of privilege for solicitor client communications" by Dickson, J. in *Solosky* v. *R.* (1979), 16 *C.R.* (3d) 294 (S.C.C.), at p. 307.

[15] For helpful treatments of the case law *see* Sopinka, Lederman & Bryant, *supra*, footnote 3, pp. 728-770; Paciocco & Stuesser, *supra*, footnote 3, pp. 153-160; Delisle, *supra*, footnote 3, pp. 663-675; Watt, *supra*, footnote 8, pp. 102-108; G. Watson & F. Au, 'Solicitor-Client Privilege and Litigation Privilege in Civil Litigation' (1998), 77 *Can. Bar. Rev.* 315; and R.D. Manes & M.P. Silver, *Solicitor Client Privilege in Canadian Law*, Markham: Butterworths 1993.

First, the rules governing solicitor-client privilege are not simply rules of evidence which preclude admission of communications at the point of trial. They are substantive rules which will have application prior to litigation and outside the courtroom to prevent or limit searches of solicitor's offices.[16]

Secondly, the rules have been extended to provide a 'litigation privilege'[17] or 'work product privilege'[18] extending beyond solicitor client privilege to cover communications between solicitors and third persons for the purpose of conducting litigation on behalf of a client.

Thirdly, the solicitor-client privilege rules, with their litigation extension, are commonly said to be subject to three exceptions:[19]

1. the right of an accused to information so as to make full answer and defence to a criminal charge;[20]
2. communications which are in themselves criminal or intended to further the commission of an offence;[21] and
3. in the interests of public safety, where there is a clear risk to an identifiable person or group of persons of serious, imminent bodily harm or death.[22]

A number of observations are pertinent in relation to the above-described rules. First, the solicitor-client communication is an absolute 'class' privilege in the sense that it is composed of firm rules, subject to exceptions, which are to be enforced by the courts once the facts of the case are brought within the ambit of the rule. This is not a case of the exercise of judicial discretion in relation to factors to be 'weighted' in accordance with the court's appreciation of them. Secondly, the major justification for the rules which may exclude relevant and reliable information is largely an instrumental one: to promote a relationship which is critical to the fair operation of the legal system. Litigation is too complex to be conducted without expert legal advice,[24] and lawyers cannot properly advise their clients without being informed in a candid manner of all the relevant circumstances. In other words, truth finding is sacrificed for the maintenance of a relationship which will promote fair procedures as between parties to the

---

[16] *Descoteaux et al.* v. *Mierzwinski and A.G. Que.* (1982), 141 *D.L.R.* (3d) 590 (S.C.C.).

[17] *Smith* v. *Jones* (1999), 132 *C.C.C.* (3d) 225 (S.C.C.)(extension to a psychiatric referral, subject to exceptions). There are those who would assert that a clear distinction ought to be made between solicitor-client privilege and litigation privilege, despite the apparent willingness of the Supreme Court of Canada to countenance apparent conflation of the two in *Smith* v. *Jones. See* R.J. Sharpe, 'Claiming Privilege in the Discovery Process', in: *Law in Transition: Evidence*, L.S.U.C. Special Lectures, DeBoo, Toronto 1984, as cited with approval in *General Accident Insurance Co.* v. *Chrusz* [1999] *O.J. No.* 3291 (Ont. C.A.). *See also* Sopinka, Lederman & Bryant, *supra*, footnote 3, pp. 745-750.

[18] The American label: *Hickman* v. *Taylor* 67 *S. Ct.* 385; 329 *U.S.* 495 (1947).

[19] *See Smith* v. *Jones, supra*, footnote 17, pp. 242-243, per Cory, J.

[20] *R.* v. *Dunbar and Logan* (1982), 68 *C.C.C.* (2d) 13 (Ont. C.A.), cited with approval in *Smith* v. *Jones, ibid.*

[21] *R.* v. *Cox and Railton* (1884), 14 *Q.B.D.* 153 (per Stephen, J.) cited with approval in *Descouteaux et. al.* v. *Mierzwinaki et al., supra*, footnote 16, p. 609.

[22] *Smith* v. *Jones, supra*, footnote 17, pp. 249-252, per Cory, J.

litigation, and may contribute to public confidence in the system of adjudication, to the extent that the public may appreciate the significance of the role of counsel in litigation.[25]

### 2.1.2 Spousal Communication Privilege

While solicitor-client privilege is governed by the common law in Canada, spousal privilege is a product of statutory rules.[26] The rules state: "No husband is compellable to disclose any communication made to him by his wife during their marriage, and no wife is compellable to disclose any communication made to her by her husband during their marriage."[27]

The rules have their origin in late 19th century reforms which rendered spouses competent and compellable witnesses in circumstances where they had previously been disqualified.[28] By comparison with solicitor client privilege, the privilege relating to spousal communications seems anomalous in several respects: the literal wording of the rule frames it in terms of 'compellability' rather than 'privilege'; the privilege is controlled by the testifying recipient spouse and cannot be enforced by the originating spouse;[29] it covers communications only (not observations),[30] but communications are protected whether or not they were intended to be confidential.[31] On the other hand, communications revealed to others may be admissible.[32] To these quirks are added the uncertainties of how to apply these provisions in an era when there is

---

[25] There is a perception, of course, that solicitor-client privilege may erode public confidence in justice, to the extent that the public generally has a low opinion of lawyers who are often suspected of manipulation of 'technicalities' for dubious purposes which undermine truth-finding.

[26] *See Canada Evidence Act, R.S.C.* 1985 c. C-5 as amended, Section 4(3) and cognate provisions in the provincial evidence acts which are virtually identical; *see* D.E. Beach, *The 1996 Annotated Canadian Evidence Acts*, Toronto: Carswell/Thomson Publishing 1995.

[27] *Ibid.*; there is also, in many provincial evidence acts a rule of privilege respecting evidence of sexual intercourse between spouses which arose out of a perceived need in the late 1940s to reverse the possible effects of the English case *Russell* v. *Russell* [1924] *A.C.* 687 (H.L.). This rule shall not be the subject of comment here. *See* generally, Sopinka, Lederman & Bryant, *supra*, footnote 3, pp. 782-783.

[28] For a full discussion *see* Sopinka, Lederman & Bryant, *supra*, footnote 3, pp. 770-783; Delisle, *supra*, footnote 3, pp. 675-681; Paciocco & Stuesser, *supra*, footnote 3, pp. 160-163; and Watt, *supra*, footnote 8, pp. 109-111.

[29] *Rumping* v. *Director of Public Prosecutions*, [1962] 2 *All E.R.* 256 (H.L.), at p. 275, per Lord Morris of Borth-Y-Gest.

[30] *Gosslin* v. *R.* (1903), 33 *S.C.R.* 255 (where a spouse was required to disclose the condition of her husband's clothing where he was charged with murder); and *R.* v. *McKinnon* (1989), 70 *C.R.* (3d) 10 (Ont. C.A.) (where evidence of spouse's presence at discovery of body by police was admitted).

[31] *MacDonald* v. *Bublitz* (1960), 31 *W.W.R.* 478 (B.C.S.C.).

[32] *Rumping* v. *D.P.P.*, *supra*, note 29 (where letter from one spouse to another which had been given to and opened by a third person was admitted in evidence). Cf. *R.* v. *Lloyd* [1981] 2 *S.C.R.* 645, whereby a conversation between spouses recorded in an authorized police wiretap was excluded on the grounds that *Criminal Code* Section 189(6) covering 'privileged communications' was applicable.

little stability in marital relations, or even agreement as to what constitutes a marital union: pre-marriage and post marriage communications are excluded on the face of the rule; co-habiting partners who are not formally married have been excluded from the rule;[33] but the spousal competence rule has been lifted recently in relation to formally married spouses who are irreconcilably separated;[34] and there is confusion in the case law concerning whether the privilege terminates with the death of a spouse.[35] How the 'rule' should be applied in the context of recent judicial decisions founded upon constitutional equality provisions giving spousal status to gay and lesbian couples in social welfare contexts is a matter of speculation.[36]

Some observations on the nature and rationale of the spousal communication privilege are necessary to ground subsequent discussion concerning the policy basis for claims of privilege in general. In terms of its form, the statutory spousal communication rule is an absolute privilege which brooks no alteration via judicial discretion, where it is applicable.[37] The modern purposes of the privilege are said to be protection of marital harmony, candour and frankness in marital relations and the maintenance of the institution of marriage generally.[38] While there is professional scepticism about the value of the rules in Canada,[39] and a harkening to England where the rules have been abolished,[40] there is currently no indication that Canadian politicians or the general public share this view. Spousal privilege, such as it is, seems likely to remain undisturbed for the foreseeable future.

---

[33] *R.* v. *Coffin* (1954), 19 *C.R.* 222 (Que. Q.B.); *R.* v. *Andrew* (1986), 26 *C.C.C.* (3d) 11 (B.C.S.C.); *Wells* v. *Fisher* (1831), 1 *M. & Rob.* 99, 174 *E.R.* 34 (N.P.); and *R.* v. *Thompson* (1994), 90 *C.C.C.* (3d) 519 (Alta. C.A.).

[34] *R.* v. *Salituro*, [1991] 3 *S.C.R.* 654 in tune with jurisprudence removing the privilege for divorced spouses; *see R.* v. *Kanester* [1966] *S.C.R.* v. *A fortiori* for divorced spouses: *see R.* v. *Marchand* (1980), 55 *C.C.C.* (2d) 77 (N.S.C.A.).

[35] *Connolly* v. *Murrell* (1891), 14 *P.R.* 187 (Ont. Practice Court) affd. (1891), 14 *P.R.* 270 (Ont. C.A.)(privilege continues after death), and *Layden* v. *North American Life Assurance Co.* (1970), 74 *W.W.R.* 266 (Alta. Master)(wife required to answer questions in relation to spousal communications which might shed light on her husband's alleged suicide).

[36] *See Vriend* v. *Alberta* (1998), 224 *N.R.* 1 (S.C.C.); *see also Miron* v. *Trudel*, [1995] 2 *S.C.R.* 418.

[37] This contrasts, for example, with the proposed but never enacted recommendation of the Law Reform Commission of Canada which advocated the creation of a *discretionary* 'family member privilege'; *see* Law Reform Commission of Canada, *Report on Evidence*, Ottawa: Information Canada 1975, pp. 29 and 79.

[38] Much of the discussion concerning the justification for the spousal communication privilege is rooted in the history of the spousal incompetency rules, the demise of which occasioned the advent of the privilege rules: *see R.* v. *Salituro*, *supra*, footnote 34.

[39] *See* Paciocco & Stuesser, *supra*, footnote 3, p. 161, and Sopinka, Lederman & Bryant, *supra*, footnote 3, pp. 780-781.

[40] *Civil Evidence Act 1968* (UK), 1968 c. 34, subsection 16(3), and *Police and Criminal Evidence Act 1984* (UK), subsection 80(4), cited with approval by Paciocco & Stuesser, *ibid.*, *The Report of the Federal/Provincial Task Force in the Law of Evidence*, Toronto: Carswell 1982, also advocated abolition of spousal privilege (*see* p. 416). As indicated, *supra*, footnote 37, the Law Reform Commission of Canada in 1975 was willing to move in the direction of expanding marital privilege.

### 2.1.3 Communications Furthering Dispute Settlement

Canadian courts have recognised a robust common law privilege in relation to communications in furtherance of dispute settlement.[41] This is true for both civil and criminal litigation.[42, 43] Moreover, the concept has been extended by statute in certain circumstances to mediation discussions.[44] The common law privilege applies when a litigious dispute exists or is within contemplation, when good faith negotiations are made to effect a settlement, and when it is expressly or impliedly understood that the communications will not be revealed to the court in the event that negotiations fail.[45] Although the proposition is not without controversy, the rule probably applies to privileged discussions if they are sought to be disclosed in subsequent proceedings between third parties.[46] There are exceptions which, in some measure, appear to be inverse statements of the general rule. Thus, threatening or simply prejudicial communications do not fall within the rubric of peaceable dispute resolution,[47] and communications can be put in evidence where the purpose is to prove they form the content of a successfully concluded agreement.[48]

The foregoing discussion demonstrates that the privilege recognised by Canadian courts in relation to communications in furtherance of dispute resolution is indeed cast as a 'class' or 'absolute' rule, applicable when the relevant conditions are properly invoked. It is not a matter of the exercise of judicial discretion. As to the rationale for the rule, there is some judicial support for Wigmore's notion that settlement negotiations are hypothetical or conditional only, and therefore evidence in relation to them is both irrelevant and unreliable.[49]

---

[41] Generally, see Sopinka, Lederman & Bryant, *supra*, footnote 3, pp. 807-820; and Delisle, *supra*, footnote 3, pp. 681-687.

[42] For an early Canadian example *see Pirie* v. *Wyld* (1886), 11 *O.R.* 422 (Ont. C.A.).

[43] *R.* v. *Pabani* (1994), 17 *O.R.* (3d) 659 (Ont. C.A.) leave to appeal refused (1994), 91 *C.C.C.* (3d) vi; *R.* v. *Bernardo*, [1994] *O.J. No.* 1718 (Gen. Div.); *R.* v. *Lake*, [1997] *O.J. No.* 5447 (Gen. Div.); *R.* v. *L.N.* (1998), 124 *C.C.C.* (3d) 564 (Ont. Gen. Div.), all of which uphold the privilege in relation to plea bargaining discussions between Crown and accused.

[44] *Divorce Act, R.S.C.* 1985 c. 3 (2nd Supp.) Sections 10(4) and (5); and *Children's Law Reform Act, R.S.O.* 1990, c. C-12, Section 31. Mediation, however, will not always lead to a successfully recognized privilege. *See*, for example, *R.* v. *Pabani*, *supra*, footnote 43, where private mediation between spouses under guidance of a spiritual advisor was held not to be privileged in a subsequent criminal prosecution against the husband in relation to the death of his wife.

[45] This is the general formulation from Sopinka, Lederman & Bryant, *supra*, footnote 3, p. 810.

[46] *Middlekamp* v. *Fraser Valley Real Estate Board* (1992), 71 *B.C.L.R.* (2d) 276 (B.C.C.A.); *I. Waxman and sons Ltd.* v. *Texaco Canada Ltd.* [1968] 1 *O.R.* 642 (H.C.J.), and *Ed Miller Sales and Rentals Ltd.* v. *Caterpillar Tractor Co.* (1990), 74 *Alta. L.R.* (2d) 271 (C.A.) But cf. *contra Derco Industries Ltd.* v. *A.R. Grimwood Ltd.* (1984), 57 *B.C.L.R.* 395 (C.A.).

[47] *Greenwood* v. *Fitts* (1961), 29 *D.L.R.* (2d) 260 (B.C.C.A.); *Re Daintrey: ex parte Holt*, [1893] 2 *Q.B.* 116 (C.A.).

[48] *Begg* v. *East Hants (Municipality)* (1986), 75 *N.S.R.* (2d) 431 (N.S.S.C., App. Div.); *Thibodeau* v. *Thibodeau* (1984), 65 *N.S.R.* (2d) 422 (N.S.S.C., T.D.), and *Ed Miller Sales and Rentals, Ltd*, *supra*, footnote 46.

[49] *See* 4 Wigmore, *supra*, note 14, (Chadbourn rev. § 1061 at 33-47 as cited in *Derco Industries Ltd.* (to be continued)

However, the predominant view is that the settlement privilege is based on a public policy intended to encourage peaceful and efficient dispute resolution rather than encouraging costly and unnecessary litigation.[50]

### 2.1.4 Police Informer Privilege

The common law as applied in Canada prevents disclosure of the identity of police informers, or of any information which would reveal their identity, in a civil or criminal proceeding.[51] The rule is applicable to genuine, private citizen informers and cannot be relied on by accused persons to shield them from prosecution,[52] nor can it be relied on by police officers who are under a public duty to enforce the law.[53] The rule is subject to one broad exception: the evidence is admissible where the identity of the informer is critical to demonstrating the innocence of the accused.[54] This exception has arisen in a number of guises: where the accused is a material witness to the offence; where an agent provocateur is *in issue;*[55] or where the informer's information has become the basis for a search warrant[56] or wire-tap.[57] The procedure adopted is for the court to examine the basis for the accused's claim that 'innocence is at stake', and when convinced that this is the case, only to reveal as much information as is required to allow proof of innocence. In such circumstances the Crown is to be given the

---

v. *A.R. Grimwood Ltd.*, *supra*, note 46, in reliance on *Schetky* v. *Cochrane* (1917), 24 *B.C.R.* 496 (C.A.).

[50] *Middlekamp* v. *Fraser Valley Real Estate Board*, *supra*, footnote 46; *Pirie* v. *Wyld*, *supra*, footnote 42; *I. Waxman and Sons Ltd.* v. *Texaco Canada Ltd.*, *supra*, footnote 46; and *Thibodeau* v. *Thibodeau*, *supra*, footnote 48, *inter alia*. For an excellent scholarly treatment of the subject, *see* D. Vaver, 'Without Prejudice Communications – Their Admissibility and Effect', (1974) 9 *U.B.C. L. Rev.* 85.

[51] *R.* v. *Leipert* [1997] 1 *S.C.R.* 281; 143 *DLR* (4th) 38 is the Supreme Court of Canada's most recent and most comprehensive pronouncement on the topic. *See also* Sopinka, Lederman & Bryant, *supra*, note 3, pp. 882-892; Delisle, *supra*, footnote 3, pp. 707-714; Paciocco & Stuesser, footnote 3, pp. 176-177; Watt, *supra*, footnote 8, pp. 117-122; L.E. Lawlor, 'Police Informer Privilege: A Study for the Law Reform Commission of Canada' (1985-86), 28 *C.L.Q.* 91; and D.B. Evison, 'The Development and Power of Police Informer Privilege: The Health Records Inquiry' (1983), 9 *Queen's L.J.* 207.

[52] *R.* v. *Hiscock* (1992), 72 *C.C.C.* (3d) 303 (Que. C.A.) leave to appeal refused (1993), 77 *C.C.C.* (3d) vi.

[53] *R.* v. *Samson* (1977), 35 *C.C.C.* (2d) 258 (Que. C.A.).

[54] *See R.* v. *Leipert*, *supra*, footnote 51. The implication here, of course, is that the rule is subject to no exceptions in the *civil* context. Moreover, as a criminal law doctrine, it cannot be over-ruled in Canada by provincial legislation: *see Bisaillon* v. *Keable*, [1983] 2 *S.C.R.* 60; 7 *C.C.C.* (3d) 385.

[55] *See* discussion in *R.* v. *Scott* (1990), 2 *C.R.* (4th) 153 (S.C.C.) and *R.* v. *Davies* (1982), 1 *C.C.C.* (3d) 299 (Ont. C.A.).

[56] *R.* v. *MacIntyre* v. *Nova Scotia (Attorney General)* [1982] 1 *S.C.R.* 175; *R.* v. *Hunter* (1987), 34 *C.C.C.* (3d) 14 (Ont. C.A.); but cf. *R.* v. *Archer* (1989), 47 *C.C.C.* (3d) 567 (Alta. C.A.).

[57] *Dersch* v. *Canada (Attorney General)*, [1990] 2 *S.C.R.* 1505; 60 *C.C.C.* (3d) 132.

option whether it wishes to stay the proceedings or continue the prosecution upon revelation of the informer's identity.[58]

Canadian courts have rejected the notion that police informer privilege is simply a form of public interest immunity which the government can waive.[59] In *Leipert* the Supreme Court of Canada says: "[T]he Crown cannot, without the informer's consent, waive the privilege either expressly or by implication by not waiving it."[60] This is because the privilege is said to be a matter of vital importance to law enforcement, protecting citizens who assist in this endeavour and thereby encouraging others to do the same. The court in *Leipert* is explicit in contrasting police informer privilege with the discretionary balancing which characterises public interest immunity[61] or case-by-case privileges of confidentiality.[62] Indeed it is said that "[o]nce established neither the police nor the court possess the discretion to abridge it."[63] However, the practical implication of the 'innocence at stake' exception is that in criminal cases, if not civil ones, the Crown can *de facto* waive the informer's privilege by a decision to pursue a prosecution following the court's ruling that informer identity must be disclosed for reasons of full answer and defence. While the court may treat the matter as a rule-based class privilege, the Crown may exercise its discretion such that continuation of a prosecution trumps secrecy of the informer's identity.

## 2.2 New 'Case-by-Case' Discretionary Privileges

The conceptual starting point for this analysis of 'case-by-case' privilege is a famous passage from Wigmore, which has been picked up by Canadian courts. It is therefore necessary here to examine the Wigmore doctrine itself, and to look at some examples of how this 'new' doctrine has been applied.

### 2.2.1 Wigmore's Analysis of Privilege

In *Slavutych* v. *Baker*,[64] the Supreme Court of Canada, *in obiter*, cited with approval the proposition of Wigmore[65] that four fundamental conditions are recognised as necessary for the establishment of a privilege against the disclosure of confidential communications. They are:

1. the communications must originate in a *confidence* that they will not be disclosed;

---

[58] *R.* v. *Leipert, supra,* footnote 51.
[59] *R.* v. *Leipert, supra,* footnote 51; *R.* v. *Scott, supra,* footnote 55.
[60] *Leipert, supra,* footnote 51, para 15.
[61] *Carey* v. *Ontario* [1984] 2 *S.C.R.* 637.
[62] *Leipert, supra,* footnote 51 para 12.
[63] *Ibid.,* para 14.
[64] *Supra,* footnote 1.
[65] 8 Wigmore § 2285, p. 527, *supra,* footnote 14, cited by Spence, J. *ibid.,* p. 260.

2. this element of *confidentiality must essential* to the full and satisfactory maintenance of the relations between the parties;
3. the *relation* must be one which in the opinion of the community ought to be sedulously *fostered*;
4. the *injury* that would inure to the relation by the disclosure of the communications must be *greater than the benefit* thereby gained for the correct disposal of the litigation.[66]

One reading of the original Wigmore text is that these 'fundamental conditions' were proffered as an explanation or rationalisation for the *existing* class privileges, and certainly not as a jumping-off point for case-by-case judicial discretion. Thus, while some Canadian judges have suggested that Wigmore intended his 'fundamental conditions' as the basis for a case-by-case analysis of privilege based on judicial discretion,[67] the original text supports the view that Wigmore was opposed to the expansion of categories of privilege on the theory that courts of justice are entitled to 'everyman's evidence'.[68] The pages in the treatise which follow upon the enunciation of Wigmore's conditions evince a clear scepticism about the proliferation of statutory privileges in American state jurisdictions,[69] and McNaughton's 1961 revision of Wigmore's volume on privilege reports with a certain satisfaction that respected American law reform proposals "excluded all of the so-called novel privileges".[70] Nonetheless, the Supreme Court of Canada has promulgated and acted upon the notion that case-by-case privilege directly applying the Wigmore conditions to the facts of each individual case is the order of the day.[71] Indeed, Chief Justice Lamer speaking for a majority of the Supreme Court of Canada opined, in a case which involved a claim of privilege for religious communications, "[u]nless it can be said that the policy reasons to support a class privilege for religious communications are as compelling as the policy reasons which underlay the privilege for solicitor client communications, there is no basis for departing from the fundamental 'first principle' that all relevant evidence is admissible until proven otherwise."[72] Finding that religious communications were, unlike solicitor client communications, not necessary for the effective operation of the legal system, the former were denied the protection of a 'class' privilege and relegated to analysis on a case-by-case basis in accordance with Wigmore's 'fundamental conditions'.

In converting Wigmore's policy analysis for class privileges into a standard for recognising privileges in individual cases, the Supreme Court of Canada

---

[66] Wigmore, *ibid.*
[67] *See* L'Heureux-Dubé, J. in *R. v. Gruenke*, [1991] 3 *S.C.R.* 263, pp. 309-310.
[68] 8 Wigmore § 2192, p. 70.
[69] 8 Wigmore § 2286 and § 2287, pp. 528-540.
[70] 8 Wigmore § 2286, p. 537, concludes: "Significantly, both the Model Code of Evidence, adopted in 1942, by the American Law Institute, and the Uniform Rules of Evidence, approved in 1953 by the National Conference on Uniform State Laws, excluded all of the so-called novel privileges."
[71] *R. v. Gruenke, supra*, footnote 11.
[72] *Ibid.*, pp. 288-289.

appears to have made a conscious choice in favour of flexibility over certainty and predictability. L'Heureux-Dubé, J. warned of the dangers of uncertainty in *R. v. Gruenke* when she stated: "One danger of the ad hoc approach to privileges, however, is its tendency to focus on the palpable need for evidence in the individual case, and to neglect more tangible and long-term interests."[73] She preferred the certainty and predictability of a class privilege in the priest-penitent context. However, the Court majority's preference for the case-by-case approach was confirmed in *M.(A.) v. Ryan*.[74] In that case the Court was urged to follow the lead of the US Supreme Court[75] and create a class privilege in relation to communications between sexual assault complainants and psychiatrists or psychotherapists. The court refused to do so, and citing concerns about the 'occasional injustice' to which the class privilege approach may give rise where relevant evidence is excluded because it falls within the scope of an inflexible rule.[76] Indeed, the court reinforced the principle of flexibility by moving from 'case-by-case' approach to a virtual 'document-by-document' approach which it described as a 'partial privilege'.[77] The prescribed procedure is now for the court to determine the existence of privilege by considering documents "individually or by sub-groups in a 'case-by-case' basis".[78] Broad procedural discretion appears to be open to trial judges on evidence hearings or *voir dires*: they may simply decide on the basis of general evidence and argument without viewing the documents, or do so after an *ex parte* inspection of the document. If a decision is made to produce documents (or edited versions thereof) to counsel for the opposing party, this may be accompanied by conditions limiting the circulation and use of the documents, even including prohibition on access by the applicant party (as opposed to his solicitor or expert witnesses).[79]

### 2.2.2 Doctor and Patient Communications

Canadian courts have until recently been faithful to the English common law position[80] that recognises no privilege in communications between doctor and

---

[73] *Ibid.*, p. 311, quoting from Mitchell, 'Must The Clergy Tell?' (1987), 71 *Minn. L. Rev.* 723.

[74] *M.(A.) v. Ryan*, [1997] 1 *S.C.R.* 157; 143 *D.L.R.* (4th) 1.

[75] *Jaffee v. Redmond*, 116 *S.Ct.* 1923 (1996).

[76] *M.(A.) v. Ryan, supra*, note 74, per McLachlin, J. citing in support the dissent of Scalia, J. in *Jaffee v. Redmond, ibid.*

[77] *Ibid.*

[78] *Ibid.*

[79] *Ibid.*; the plaintiff M.(A.) alleged the defendant Dr Ryan had sexually abused her during therapy. The latter then sought access to the records in the hands of the plaintiff's subsequent therapist. The Supreme Court of Canada upheld a Court of Appeal ruling which denied access entirely to the second psychiatrist's personal notes, and gave access to other documents by Dr Ryan's solicitor and experts, but denying direct access to them by Dr Ryan.

[80] *R. v. Kingston* (Duchess) (1776), 20 *State Tr.* 355; *Garner v. Garner* (1920), 36 *T.L.R.* 196 (Div. Ct.); *Hunter v. Mann*, [1974] *Q.B.* 767 (D.C.).

patient.[81] Only one province (Quebec) has abrogated this common law rule by legislation establishing a general physician-patient communication privilege,[82] though some provinces have enacted a limited privilege in relation to communications for medical research.[83] However, communications in the course of psychiatric examinations have developed as an exception to the rule. This development occurred prior to the Supreme Court's enunciation of its Wigmorean case-by-case approach,[84] and indeed the latter may have slowed or stopped the evolution of a class privilege in this context. While the recent case of *M.(A.)* v. *Ryan*[85] may have upheld a partial privilege for certain patient-psychiatrist communications, the limitations on the privilege mean it is far more restrictive than some of the dicta in previous cases.[86] Moreover, the recent Canadian controversy over defence access to sexual assault complainants' medical records[87] is all premised on the assumption that there is no class privilege protecting patient-doctor communications, and that even the psychiatrist-patient or doctor-patient privilege, which may be recognised on a case-by-case basis, is not sufficient in the eyes of many to protect the privacy of sexual assault victims.

It has been suggested that the reasons why provinces other than Quebec have not, and/or should not, establish a class privilege for doctor patient communications are at least threefold:

1. the existence of the privilege is unlikely of its own to increase candour in relations between doctor and patient, and thus have no perceptible impact on treatment;[88]
2. a high percentage of civil litigation, whether in the context of life insurance claims, personal injury claims, probate claims and the like, may depend for accurate resolution on access to medical evidence;[89] and
3. such claims cannot oust concerns about the liberty of subject and full answer and defence in criminal matters.[90]

Thus, while the advent of a general class privilege for physician-patient communications in Canada is unlikely, the extent to which constant resort by the

---

[81] *Halls* v. *Mitchell*, [1928] *S.C.R.* 125; and *Frenette* v. *Metropolitan Life Ins. Co.* [1992], 1 *S.C.R.* 647. *See also* Friedman, 'Medical Privilege' (1954), 32 *Can. Bar. Rev.* 1; and Sopinka, Lederman & Bryant, *supra*, footnote 3, pp. 798-807.

[82] *Medical Act, R.S.Q.* 1977 c. M-9 s. 42. *See also* the *Code for Professions, R.S.Q.* 1977 c. C-26, and the *Quebec Charter of Human Rights and Freedoms, R.S.Q.* 1977, c. C-12, s. 9.

[83] *See* for example, British Columbia, *R.S.B.C.* 1996, c. 124, s. 51(4).

[84] *Dembie* v. *Dembie* (1963), 21 *R.F.L.* 46 (Ont. S.C.), *G.* v. *G.*, [1964]) *O.R.* 361 (H.C.J.).

[85] *Supra*, footnote 71.

[86] Stewart, J. in *Dembie* v. *Dembie*, *supra*, footnote 81, stated at p. 50: "(...) I think it inimical to fair trial process to force a psychiatrist to disclose the things he heard from a patient (...)."

[87] *See* discussion *infra*.

[88] (McRuer Commission) *Report of the Royal Commission into Civil Rights in Ontario*, Toronto: Ministry of the Attorney General 1968, p. 822.

[89] 8 Wigmore § 2380(a), pp. 831-832, *supra*, footnote 8.

[90] *R.* v. *Burgess*, [1974] 4 *W.W.R.* 310 (B.C.Co. Ct.).

courts to a case-by-case psychiatrist-patient protection may allow the latter to harden into a *de facto* class privilege has yet to be seen.

### 2.2.3 Priest-Penitent or Spiritual Advisor Privilege

As noted above, the Supreme Court of Canada has recently reaffirmed the traditional common law view that there is no class privilege to prohibit priests or spiritual advisors from being compelled to testify about what their parishioners or adepts may have told them.[91] Two provinces, however, have enacted statutory privileges in this context. Newfoundland only protects communications made during confession,[92] while Quebec permits clergy to refuse to divulge information generally received by virtue of their clerical status.[93] It is interesting to note that in the application of the Wigmorean 'case-by-case' approach,[94] there have been no reported successful exclusions of statements to ministers.[95] However, the true reason for the apparent lack of case-by-case success is that courts in Canada, as in England, have been unwilling as a matter of practice (even in the absence of a class privilege) to *force* priests or spiritual advisors to disclose confidential communications.[96] Therefore the claim of privilege needs rarely to be put to the test.

The few recent cases which have dealt with the case-by-case privilege claims for religious communications are interesting in terms of their analysis. While they focus on the instrumental policy matters raised by the Wigmore fundamental conditions (especially expectations of confidentiality, and the relative importance of the religious relationship in comparison to the need for 'truth' at the trial), reference is also made to constitutional rights.[97] Section 2 of the Canadian *Charter of Rights and Freedoms* protects freedom of religion, and Section 27 requires that the *Charter* "shall be interpreted in a manner consistent with the preservation and enhancement of the multi-cultural heritage of Canadians". These constitutional rights *per se* have not been sufficient to persuade the courts to raise communications between spiritual advisors and followers to the level of a class privilege. These freedoms are not absolute,[98] and must be balanced with other

---

[91] *R.* v. *Gruenke, supra*, footnote 68.

[92] *Newfoundland Evidence Act, R.S.N.* 1990, c. E-16, s. 8.

[93] *Quebec Charter of Human Rights and Freedoms, R.S.Q.* 1977, e. C-12, s. 9.

[94] First advocated in its context by the Ontario courts: *R.* v. *Church of Scientology* (1987), 31 *C.C.C.* (3d)(449).

[95] For example, in both *R.* v. *Gruenke, supra*, footnote 68, and in *R.* v. *Medina* [1988] *O.J. No.* 2348 (H.C.J.), the courts held that the Wigmorean fundamental conditions had not been met because they did not originate in an understanding that they would not be disclosed.

[96] *See* Sopinka, Lederman & Bryant, *supra*, footnote 321, p. 784 suggesting that the English case of *R.* v. *Hay* (1860), 2F and F4, P75 *E.R.* 933 (N.P.) is the only recorded example in England or Canada of a priest being found in contempt for failure to disclose a confidence when required to do so.

[97] *See* both *Gruenke, supra*, note 68, and *R.* v. *Church of Scientology, supra*, note 91 on this point.

[98] *R.* v. *Church of Scientology, supra*, footnote 91.

rights, such as an accused's constitutionalised right to full answer and defence.[99] However, the constitutionalised religious and cultural rights, and attendant 'Charter values', are to inform the interpretation and application of the Wigmore criteria.[100] Thus, any restriction of the notion of 'protected relationship' to, for instance, the Roman Catholic or analogous Christian churches, which have a 'confession' doctrine, would appear to be constitutionally suspect on grounds of multi-culturalism.[101] Indeed, even the naming of the privilege is now problematic on this constitutional basis. On the other hand, the reference to freedom of religion and multiculturalism as relevant constitutional values does point the way beyond Wigmore's instrumentalism as a basis for the analysis of privileges in general.

### 2.2.4  Journalist-Source Privilege

Canadian courts generally adopted the common law position that there is no class privilege to protect communications between journalists and confidential sources from the requirement that they be revealed in court.[102] There has for some time been controversy as to whether there exists a limited exception to the general common law approach to protect the names of journalistic sources at the discovery stage in civil defamation actions against publishers.[103] However, the certainty of the older common law approach is now undermined by the case-by-case Wigmorean analysis. Indeed, in an Alberta case, the province's Labour Relations Board considered Wigmore's four fundamental conditions in response to a reporter's claim that she not be required to disclose sources which could provide evidence for the union in an unfair labour practice dispute.[104] On the facts it was held that there had been no promise of confidentiality, and that maintenance of the relationship would not outweigh the importance of truth-finding in the circumstances.

Of significance for the purposes of this article is that recent Canadian cases dealing with journalistic privilege have generally involved the invocation of constitutional rights in addition to Wigmore's instrumentalist criteria. *Charter* Section 2(b) protects: "freedom of thought, belief, opinion and expression, *including freedom of the press and other media of communication.*" (Emphasis

---

[99] The 'right to full answer and defense' has been read into *Charter* Section 7: "Everyone has the right not to be deprived of life, liberty or security of the person, except in accordance with the principles of fundamental justice." See *R.* v. *Rose*, [1998] 3 *S.C.R.* 262; 129 *C.C.C.* (3d) 449.

[100] *R.* v. *Gruenke, supra*, footnote 68. On the distinction between '*Charter* rights' and '*Charter* values', *see* text, *infra*.

[101] This topic will be revisited *infra*.

[102] *Attorney-General* v. *Clough* [1963], *All E.R.* 420 (Q.B.C.); *A.G.* v. *Mulholland*; *A.G.* v. *Foster* [1963] 2 *Q.B.* 477 (C.A.); *Crown Trust Co.* v. *Rosenberg* (1983), 38 *C.P.C.* 109 (Ont. H.C.J.).

[103] *See* Sopinka, Lederman & Bryant, *supra*, footnote 3, pp. 790-795, under the heading 'the newspaper rule'.

[104] *Moysa v. Alberta (Labour Relations)*, [1989] 1 *S.C.R.* 1572.

added.)[105] The Supreme Court of Canada has thus far been able to duck grappling with the full nature and extent of journalistic privilege. However, the court has indicated that in subsequent cases it wants evidence on the issue of whether "compulsion would detrimentally affect the journalist's ability to gather information".[106]

### 2.2.5 Miscellaneous Examples of Case-by-Case Privilege

The application of Wigmore's fundamental conditions on a case-by-case basis is very open-ended. Major litigation thus far has concentrated on the standard examples cited above: doctor-patient; priest-penitent; and journalist-source. However, there are some interesting side-lights. The initial case of *Slavutych* v. *Baker*[107] involved a situation where privilege was sought in relation to communications exchanged in the course of a university tenure and promotions process. The outcome which protected the communications in that case caused something of a stir at the time.[108] The most curious example to date would seem to be the privilege granted, purportedly on the basis of Wigmore's conditions, to protect from production the diaries of a sexual assault victim.[109] Her assailant stepfather had been convicted criminally of sexual assault. In a civil action against him the defendant sought production of the diaries. The refusal to order this was dressed in the language of Wigmore's conditions, but clearly rooted in an assessment that production would violate the victims' right to privacy. There was no 'relationship' to protect, other than perhaps that between the victim and her alter ego 'Dear Diary', and the implications of the courts approach are potentially far-reaching.[110]

### 2.3    Personal Records of Sexual Assault Complainants

The question of the principles underlying personal or relational privileges in Canadian law cannot be appreciated fully in the absence of an understanding of a recent controversy concerning the protection of the personal records of complainants in sexual assault cases. In a high profile decision, the Supreme Court of Canada promulgated a new set of rules, purportedly as a matter of 'common law', limiting access by accused persons to the personal therapeutic

---

[105] *Moysa* v. *Alberta, ibid.*; *Coates* v. *The Citizen* (1986), 72 *N.S.r.* (2d) 116 (T.D.) Affd. in part (1986), 74 *N.S.R.* (2d) 143 (N.S.S.C. App. Div.); and Canadian *Broadcasting Corporation* v. *Lessard* [1991] 3 *S.C.R.* 421; 67 *C.C.C.* (3d) 517.
[106] *C.B.C.* v. *Lessard, ibid.*, p. 433 *(S.C.R.)*, per La Forest, J.
[107] *Slavutych* v. *Baker* [1976] 1 *S.C.R.* 254.
[108] *See* B. MacLachlin, *supra*, footnote 1; and J. Arvay, '*Slavutych* v. *Baker*: Privilege, Confidence and Illegally Obtained Evidence', (1977) 15 *Osgoode Hall L.J.* 456.
[109] *V(K.L.)* v. *R(D.G.)*, [1994] 10 *W.W.R.* 105 (B.C.C.A.) leave to appeal was granted but the case settled. *See* discussion in Paciocco & Stuesser, *supra*, footnote 3, p. 149.
[110] These implications will be addressed *infra*.

records of sexual assault victims.[111] Parliament responded with legislation designed to give further protection to sexual assault victims, containing rules in some measure based on the dissent from the court decision which sparked the controversy.[112] Recently the Supreme Court upheld the constitutionality of the legislation which overturned its previous majority's point of view.[113] The common law and statutory regimes will be explained briefly below, since they have much to say about the principles underpinning the law of privilege.

### 2.3.1 The Common Law

The procedural origins of the *O'Connor* decision rest in an application by the defence for a judicial stay of proceedings based on a claim that the Crown had failed to comply with its constitutional duty to disclose in a timely way all evidence likely to be relevant to the defence and not covered by privilege.[114] O'Connor was a Roman Catholic bishop charged with a number of sexual offences which were alleged to have occurred some 25 years earlier when he was a priest at a residential school. The defence sought production to the Crown, and ultimately to the defence, of all files relating to the complainants in the hands of all therapists, psychologists and psychiatrists who had ever treated the complainants. The Crown only complied reluctantly, fitfully and belatedly. While the Supreme Court of Canada refused to grant a stay under the circumstances, it went on to enunciate new rules governing access by the defence to the therapeutic records of Crown witnesses.

The majority of the court firstly opined that therapeutic records in the hands of the Crown were already subject of a *de facto* waiver, and must be produced to the defence. With respect to therapeutic records in the possession of third persons, the court set out a two step process: first, evidence is to be produced for inspection by the judge if there is a reasonable possibility that the information sought may be logically relevant to substantive matters in issue in the case, credibility of a witness, or the reliability of other evidence; secondly, evidence thus provided to the court will be produced to the defence if upon inspection the judge concludes that disclosure is necessary after weighing:

1. the extent to which the record is necessary to the accused's full answer the defence;

---

[111] *R.* v. *O'Connor* (1995), 130 *D.L.R.* (4th) 235 (S.C.C.). Hereafter simply referred to as *O'Connor*.
[112] *Stats. Canada 1997*, c. 30, s. 1 introducing what are now *Criminal Code* Sections 278.1 to 278.9. *See* H. Holmes, 'An Analysis of Bill C-46: Production of Records in Sexual Assault Proceedings', (1997) 2 *Can. Crim. L. Rev.* 71; K. Busby, 'Discriminatory Uses of Personal Records in Sexual Violence Cases', (1997) 9 *C.J.W.L.* 148; and D. Paciocco, 'Bill C-46 Should Not Survive Constitutional Challenge', (1996) 3 *S.O.L.R.* 185.
[113] *L.C. and Alberta (A.G.)* v. *Mills, supra,* footnote 2.
[114] *See R.* v. *Stinchombe* (1995), 96 *C.C.C.* (3d) 318 (S.C.C.) and cased which provide a class in it such as *R.* v. *O'Connor, supra,* footnote 108; *R.* v. *La* (1997), 116 *C.C.C.* (3d) 7 (S.C.C.) and *R.* v. *Dixon* (1998), 122 *C.C.C.* (3d) 1 (S.C.C.).

2. the probative value of the record;
3. the nature and extent of the complainant's reasonable expectations of privacy vested in the record;
4. whether the production would be premised on any discriminatory belief or bias; and
5. the potential prejudice to the complainant's dignity, privacy or security of the person that would be occasioned by the production of the record in question.[115]

The minority would have added two more factors:

1. society's interest in the reporting of sexual offences; and
2. the integrity of the trial process.

### 2.3.2 The Statutory Regime

The statutory regime, as mentioned above, is based primarily in an adoption of the minority position in *O'Connor*. However, it does go farther. It protects against simple production on demand "any form of record that contains personal information for which there is a reasonable expectation of privacy (...)", excluding investigatory or prosecutorial records,[116] in relation to a long list of sexual offences.[117] Defence can obtain access to such records only pursuant to the procedures set out in the legislation.[118] Unlike the common law position in *O'Connor*, the legislation protects records in the possession of the Crown as well as third parties, although the former is under a duty to give notice to the defence of the existence of such a record without disclosing its contents.[119]

Like the common law regime, the statutory procedure sets up a two stage process for production of records: first to the judge for inspection, and secondly to the defence if warranted by the judge. However, the seven 'O'Connor minority factors' described above, with the addition of one requiring reference to society's interest in encouraging the obtaining of treatment by complainants of sexual offences, now do double duty. These eight factors are relevant at the threshold stage of production to the judge as well as at the second stage of production to the defence.[120] Moreover, at the threshold stage, the legislation makes clear that the court is not to rely on mere assertions or speculation that the records are "likely relevant to an issue at trial or to the competence of a witness to testify", and lists a number of "insufficient grounds" for ordering production even to the judge.[121]

---

[115] *O'Connor, supra*, per Lamer, C.J.C., Sopinka, J., Cory, J., Iaccobucci, J. & Major, J.
[116] *Criminal Code* Section 278.1.
[117] *Criminal Code* Section 278.2. This arguably goes well beyond the therapeutic records protected by the common law in *O'Connor*.
[118] *Criminal Code* Section 278.2.
[119] *Criminal Code* Section 278.2(3).
[120] *Criminal Code* Section 278.5(2).
[121] *Criminal Code* Section 278.3(4). Note: the Supreme Court in *Mills* read this to mean, not that these grounds are 'insufficient' *per se* but that they are insufficient if based merely in an assertion (to be continued)

### 2.3.3  O'Connor, Mills and Privilege

On its face *O'Connor*, and the companion case of *Behariell*[122] are not cases about a personal or relational privilege, but cases concerning the production and disclosure of records. Indeed, the Supreme Court of Canada explicitly states that it is not deciding the former on the grounds of privilege, which is said to have been waived on the facts.[123] While this distinction may be credibly drawn in relation to the view of the majority in *O'Connor* which could be characterized as deciding about record production primarily in relation to relevance and probative value, even that majority is weighing truth finding (full answer and defence) against privacy interests in the record, and the dignity, privacy and security of the person of the complainant.[124] The *O'Connor* minority and Parliament expanded the number of concerns which are to weighed against rectitude of decision (as seen in the narrow sense of defence access to relevant information) by looking to encouragement of the reporting of sexual offences and treatment of sexual complainants, and to the integrity of the trial process (read acquittals on specious grounds involving unjustified attacks on female complainants rooted in improper gender stereotypes).[125] This reasoning bears all the hallmarks of privilege: exclusion of evidence which may be relevant on grounds unrelated to truth finding in the individual case, but rather embodying other concerns of public policy.

The decision in *Mills* confirms the privilege analysis by upholding the constitutionality of a legislative scheme that may result in the exclusion of evidence relevant to the defence for reasons which trump truth-finding in the discretionary judicial 'weighing' process. What results is not a 'class' privilege in relation to all personal records of sexual assault complainants, but rather a 'case-by-case' protection of such records weighing factors deemed relevant by Parliament. Surely, this is simply a privilege by another name. The Supreme Court in *Mills* recognises that what it is doing is reviewing the constitutionality of this scheme in a process which is not unlike the weighing of factors in the case-by-case analysis of privileged confidential relationships using 'the Wigmore test'.[126]

Thus, for assessing the principles underlying personal and relational privileges, the *Mills* analysis is very interesting. While this is not the place for a full comment on the Mills case, the following observations may be pertinent.

---

lacking any evidentiary foundation (*see* para 120).

[122] *A.(L.L.)* v. *B.(A.)*, [1995] 4 *S.C.R.* 536, hereinafter called *Behariell*.

[123] *O'Connor*, 130 *D.L.R.* (4th) 235, pp. 248-249. The waiver of any privilege was said to have occurred when the documents were 'shared' with the Crown prosecutors.

[124] *O'Connor, supra.*

[125] *O'Connor, supra*, and *Criminal Code* Section 278.3.

[126] *Mills*, paras 83 and 84, referring directly to Wigmore and *M.(A.)* v. *Ryan, supra.*

Firstly, the majority states explicitly that "the scope of the right to make full answer and defence must be determined in the light of privacy and equality rights of complainants and witnesses."[127] Then the court states that "the right to full answer and defence is *not* engaged where the accused seeks information that will *only* serve to distort the truth seeking purpose of the trial."[128] Later the Court elaborates that "(…) it is constitutionally permissible for the Crown (…) to end up with documents that the accused has not seen, as long as the accused can make full answer and defence and the trial is fundamentally fair."[129] On the problem of the 'Catch-22' at the threshold step of production to the judge, the court states: "Where there is a danger that the accused's right to make full answer and defence will be violated, the trial judge should err on the side of production to the court."[130]

Secondly, the key to the decision, of course, is the court's somewhat ambiguous analysis of the operation of the balancing of factors in *Criminal Code* Section 278.5(2), and in particular those factors relating to privacy and equality interests of complainants, and to the equality interests of potential complainants (those targeted by the 'encouraging reporting' factor). The court states that there may be clear cases where interests of full answer and defence are paramount (where the information in the record bears directly on the case as part of the case to meet or where its probative value is high), and others where privacy and equality interests are paramount (where 'only distorting the truth' is at issue).[131] It is the hard cases in the middle, of course, which are of real interest. On these the court, somewhat surprisingly, seems content to say: "Trial judges are not required to rule conclusively on each of the factors nor are they required to determine whether the factors relating to the privacy or equality of the complainant or a witness 'outweigh' factors relating to the accused's right to full answer and defence. To repeat, trial judges are only asked to 'take into account' all the factors listed in Section 278.5(2) when determining whether production of part or all of the impugned record to the accused is necessary in the interests of justice."[132]

To the extent that relevant evidence (though not information necessary to full answer and defence) may be excluded by weighing privacy and equality factors on a 'case-by-case' basis, it is hard not to conclude that the Court has approved the constitutionality of a statutory privilege relating to personal records of sexual assault complainants. It is not a class privilege, but surely it may operate as a privilege nonetheless in those cases where relevant records excluded are not

---

[127] *Mills*, *supra*, footnote 2, para 94.

[128] *Mills*, *ibid.*, para 94.

[129] *Mills*, *ibid.*, para 112.

[130] *Mills*, *ibid.*, para 137.

[131] *Mills*, *ibid.*, para 94.

[132] *Mills*, *ibid.*, para 141. This seems perilously close to authorizing trial judges to invoke the operation of a privilege, while directing them not to give reasons for their decision – on the grounds that they might be controversial(?).

deemed essential to full answer and defence. Treating the matter simply as a procedural mechanism established by statute to limit disclosure cannot hide what is really going on. Regardless of how narrow the scope of the privilege for exclusion of sexual assault complainant records may be, it is still a 'case-by-case' privilege where it excludes relevant evidence.

### 3. The Rationales for Personal or Relational Privileges: Principles, Rights, Values and Politics

The rationales advanced for the existence of personal or relational privileges occupy different practical and intellectual planes. Some are utilitarian justifications in the guise of legal principles, while others are social values dressed in the garb of constitutional rights. Finally, some of these privileges may be analysed in terms of important political concepts central to the functioning of democracy, while finding their daily articulation in the world of partisan *real politik*. This part of the paper is intended to explore the Canadian experience with the evidentiary privileges described above, in order to determine whether one can tease out of the common law, statutory and constitutional morass the beginning of a general theory of privileges. The tendency among Canadian jurists in the past, following the pragmatic English lead, has been to simply describe privilege as a matter of heterogeneous 'public policy'[133] or 'extrinsic social policies',[134] or to place the doctrine under the all encompassing and over inclusive phrase "excluding evidence for purposes other than promotion of the truth".[135] The Canadian law, however, is now ripe for an infusion of some of the theoretical debate which currently animates American evidence scholarship on the topic,[136]

---

[133] For an example of this English approach *see* C. Tapper, *Cross and Tapper on Evidence*, London: Butterworths 1999.

[134] Schiff, *supra*, footnote 3, Ch. 15 'Exclusion of Evidence under Extrinsic Social Policies'.

[135] Delisle, *supra*, footnote 3, Ch. 6.

[136] The American post-Wigmore debate began with D.W. Louisell, 'Confidentiality, Conformity and Confusion: Privileges in Federal Court Today', (1956) 31 *Tulane Law Review* 101, and took on new dimensions in the privilege controversy which stalled the adoption of the American *Federal Rules*: *see* T.G. Krattenmaker, 'Testimonial Privileges in Federal Courts: An Alternative to the Proposed Federal Rules of Evidence', (1973) 62 *Georgetown L. Rev.* 61; and E.J. Imwinkelried, 'An Hegelian Approach to Privileges Under the Federal Rule of Evidence 501: The Restrictive Thesis, the Expansive Antithesis and the Contextual Synthesis', (1994) 75 *Nebraska L. Rev.* 511. This discussion was advanced by a couple of helpful notes: 'Developments in the Law: Privileged Communications' (1985), *supra*, footnote 10, and 'Making Sense of the Rules of Privilege under the Structural (Il) logic of the Federal Rules of Evidence', (1992) 105 *Harv. L. Rev.* 1339. A spate of recent stimulating articles include: Christopher B. Mueller, 'The Federal Psychotherapist-Patient Privilege After *Jaffee*: Truth and Other Values in a Therapeutic Age', (1998) 49 *Hastings L.J.* 945; E.J. Imwinkelried, 'The Rivalry Between Truth and Privilege: The Weakness of the Supreme Court's Instrumental Reasoning in *Jaffee* v. *Redmond* 518 *U.S.* 1 (1996)', (1998) 49 *Hastings L.J.* 969; M.S. Raeder, 'The Social Worker's Privilege, Victim's Rights and Contextualized Truth', (1998) 49 *Hastings L.J.* 991; and G. Weissenberger, 'The Psychotherapist's Privilege and the Supreme Court's Misplaced Reliance on State Legislatures', (1998) 49 *Hastings L.J.* 999.

and of the insights of European political-legal theory.[137] This segment of the paper is an initial sketch of such an approach.

## 3.1    The Limits of Wigmore's Instrumental Conditions

Wigmore's four fundamental conditions for the existence of a privilege[138] are all problematic from the perspective of legislative policy and are doubly so as a basis for judicial law-making. The confidentiality requirement does not seem to work across the board. While it has been the basis for solicitor-client and informer privilege,[139] it has never been critical to spousal privilege.[140] In terms of emerging law, confidentiality may be important in the journalist-source privilege,[141] but has been rejected by Parliament in relation to the disclosure of sexual assault complainants' personal records.[142] As a minimum condition for development of privilege, then, the requirement that communications originate in a confidence that they will not be disclosed is evidently over-inclusive. For some forms of privilege, the expectation of confidence is simply not the key in terms of explaining the precedents.

The requirement that confidentiality must be essential to the full and satisfactory relation between the parties is often criticised on empirical grounds.[143] It is suggested that in relation to most of the relational privileges there is simply no evidence that participants even know of the existence of an evidential privilege attaching to their 'confidential' communications, or that the behaviour of those involved would change one whit with the knowledge that a privilege has either been granted or taken away.[144] Where the essential nature of confidentiality seems 'self-evident', such as in solicitor-client or informer privilege, the point may not be critical. However, before granting or withholding privilege on these grounds, courts or legislatures should demand evidence on these matters. It is heartening that the Supreme Court of Canada has given an indication, at least in relation to the possible granting of journalist-source privilege on a case-by-case basis, that it will be seeking an empirical foundation when litigation next brings the matter forward.[145] Loose-footed acceptance of "judicial notice of legislative fact" in this context ought not to be good enough.[146]

---

[137] Especially J. Habermas, *Between Facts and Norms: Contributions to a Discourse Theory of Law and Democracy*, Cambridge: MIT Press 1999.

[138] *See* text, *supra*, corresponding to footnotes 62-76.

[139] *See* text, *supra*, corresponding to footnotes 12-25 and 51-63.

[140] *See* text, *supra*, corresponding to footnotes 26-40.

[141] *See* text, *supra*, corresponding to footnotes 116-121.

[142] *Criminal Code* Section 278.1 applies no such restriction to the records covered.

[143] 'Developments in the Law – Privileged Communications', *supra*, footnote 10; *see also* articles by Imwinkelried and Raeder, *supra*, footnote 135.

[144] *See* J.W. Strong *et al.*, *McCormick on Evidence* (5th ed.), St. Paul: West Group 1999, p. 398, discussing the point in the context of doctor-patient privilege. Hereafter referred to as *McCormick*.

[145] *C.B.C.* v. *Lessard*, *supra*, footnote 105.

[146] On the problems of 'legislative fact/social context' analysis in relation to judicial notice, *see* (to be continued)

As to whether the relation is one which in the opinion of the community ought to be sedulously fostered, this is a question which the courts are particularly ill-suited to answer. While Canadian courts have sometimes accepted public opinion poll evidence on community standards,[147] they have rejected its admissibility in others.[148] The question is often fudged by the courts through taking judicial notice of the importance of the relationship, a procedure which, with alarming regularity, appears to be based on information found in law review articles.[149] This sort of analysis is surely a matter of politics for legislatures and not 'law' for judges.

The 'cost-benefit analysis' in Wigmore's final condition is equally problematic. Whether the injury caused to confidential relations, either in the short or the long run, is greater than the costs to civil litigants or accused persons of losing the evidence, would seem to be largely a matter of opinion. While the Supreme Court of Canada struggled with this problem in *Mills*, it was certainly not treated as a matter capable of empirical resolution. The court was explicitly balancing values and conflicting rights in that case, rather than adjudicating upon facts, since the litigation was cast in constitutional terms. Moreover, the process is the same when the courts are called upon to apply Wigmore's condition four. For class privileges, at least hypothetically, there is no cost in recognising the privilege if one assumes that the 'communicant' would have said nothing in the absence of knowledge that the communication is privileged. The outcome is uncertain in case-by-case policy choices.

However, the methodology adopted by the Supreme Court of Canada[150] based on Wigmore gives preference to truth finding over the potential development of privilege.[151] 'Class' privileges are to be rarely, if ever, accorded, and case-by-case privilege will be recognised only where the proponent of the privilege meets the burden to 'prove' the fundamental conditions one way or another.[152] Costs of a privilege are thus assumed normally to be greater than the benefits in the normal

---

Sopinka, Lederman & Bryant, *supra*, footnote 3, p. 1064.

[147] Particularly in the context of what constitutes a community standard of tolerance in matters of criminally prohibited obscenity: *see Town Cinema Theatres Ltd.* v. *R.* (1985), 45 *C.R.* (3d) 1 (S.C.C.).

[148] For example, determining what 'brings the administration of justice into disrepute' for purposes of applying the exclusionary rule of evidence under *Charter*, Section 24(2): *see Collins* v. *R.* (1987), 56 *C.R.* (3d) 193 (S.C.C.).

[149] Often American ones. *See* for example *R.* v. *Lavallée* (1990), 76 *C.R.* (3d) 329 (S.C.C.) in another context or *M.(A.)* v. *Ryan*, *supra*, footnote 74 in relation to privilege.

[150] *R.* v. *Gruenke*, *supra*, footnote 67.

[151] This point is noted in the US as well. *See* 'Developments in Law-Privileged Communications', *supra*, footnote 10, pp. 1479-1480.

[152] Separating burdens of proof in relation to legislative and adjudicative fact in this context is somewhat awkward. This matter was not addressed in *Mills* directly, although it is addressed in a less than satisfactory way in *R.* v. *Oakes* (1986), 50 *C.R.* (3d) 1 (S.C.C.) dealing with Section 1 notifications under the *Charter of Rights*.

course of things. Truth-finding, and particularly full answer and defence in the criminal context, seems likely to win out.

## 3.2 The Impact of Constitutional Freedoms, Rights and Values

The distinctions between constitutional freedoms, rights and values are not entirely clear in Canadian law.[153] However, for the purposes of this analysis it can be said that constitutional freedoms (such as those of religion, conscience, expression)[154] and constitutional rights[155] (such as protection from unreasonable search and seizure) are explicitly entrenched in the language of the *Charter*. On the other hand, constitutional values are general propositions which can be derived from the context and structure of such rights and freedoms, even though they may not constitute explicitly applicable constitutional rules. Constitutional rights and freedoms are enforceable in relation to public litigation involving state actors.[156] Thus, privileges rooted in constitutional freedoms and rights will in principle have mandatory application in criminal matters.[157] However, the *Charter* may not be applicable to private litigation,[158] though the courts are now tending to elaborate common law rules with an eye to '*Charter* values' where appropriate.[159] These distinctions have application in the area of relational or personal privileges as the discussion below will indicate.

### 3.2.1 Freedoms of Conscience, Religion, Thought, Belief, Opinion and Expression (including Freedom of the Press and other Media)

The freedoms of conscience, religion, thought, belief, opinion and expression (including freedom of the press and other media of communication) in *Charter* Section 2 have not yet been found to be the direct source of privilege in Canadian litigation. However, cases in the area of priest-penitent[160] and journalistic[161]

---

[153] *See* generally, P. Hogg, *Constitutional Law of Canada* (4th ed.), Scarborough: Carswell 1997.

[154] *Charter of Rights* Section 2.

[155] *Charter of Rights* Sections 7-15.

[156] *Charter*, Section 32 ensures that its provisions apply to both federal and provincial governments. For example: statutory tribunals are bound by *Charter* rules: *Mooring* v. *Canada (National Parole Board)*, [1996] 192 *N.R.* 1 (S.C.C.). In a curious case, however, *R.* v. *Carosella* (1997), 4 *C.R.* (5th) 139 (S.C.C.) extended the *Charter* application to a sexual assault centre, and provided a constitutional stay of proceedings where the centre destroyed sexual assault complainant's records rather than allowing them to fall into the hands of the Crown for purposes of disclosure to the accused.

[157] *See* cases on the privilege against self-incrimination, *supra*, footnote 6.

[158] *Schreiber* v. *Canada (Attorney General)*, [1998] 1 *S.C.R.* 841.

[159] The process seems to have its genesis in *R.* v. *Hebert* (1990), 77 *C.R.* (3d) 145 (S.C.C.) where common law confessions rules were said to be subject to re-consideration in light of '*Charter* values'.

[160] Text, *supra*, corresponding to footnotes 91-101.

[161] Text, *supra*, corresponding to footnotes 102-106.

privilege have indicated that these freedoms are to be taken into account in the 'Wigmore analysis' for recognising the existence of a case-by-case privilege. Whether this is as an application of the freedom directly or as a *'Charter* value' will depend on the context of the particular litigation. In either case, however, the process lends weight to the observation that the application of Wigmore's conditions is not an empirical matter, but rather one concerning judgement about values, in this case constitutional values.

### 3.2.2  The Right to Privacy

The right to privacy has been at the forefront of litigation in the most contested subject area testing the limits of privilege in Canada: sexual assault and complainants' records. The way in which this constitutional right has been interpreted and applied in these cases may tell us much about the developing theoretical bases for personal and relational privileges.

American critics of the Wigmore approach to personal or relational privileges have largely turned to the concept of privacy as their doctrinal justification for these privileges.[162] Canadian *Charter* jurisprudence primarily locates the entrenchment of privacy interests in the protection against unreasonable search and seizure.[163] The case law provides that 'reasonable expectations of privacy' will be protected in relation to person and bodily integrity[164] in ways that will vary with the circumstances. None of the traditional 'class' privileges discussed above were generally justified by reference to privacy. Solicitor client,[165] police informer[166] and dispute resolution[167] privileges all have their basis in the efficient operation of some aspect of the justice system which requires confidentiality. However, even spousal privilege is justified on the basis of marital harmony, candour and support for the institution of marriage rather than on a broad concept of privacy *per se*.[168] It is therefore of significant note that *O'Connor*,[169] *M.(A.)* v. *Ryan*[170] and *Mills*[171] all to some degree discuss the justification of limitations on access to records of sexual assault complainants in terms of privacy. In these

---

[162] Krattenmaker, *supra*, footnote 135; McCormick *supra*, footnote 143 , p. 300. A. Weston, *Privacy and Freedom* as cited in 'Development of Law-Privileged Communications', *supra*, footnote 10. J. Rachels, 'Why is Privacy Important', (1975) 4 *Philosophy and Public Affairs* 323, as cited in *Mills*. Also Ch. Fried, 'Privacy', (1967-68) 77 *Yale L.J.* 475.

[163] *Charter*, Section 8, which reads simply: "Everyone has the right to be secure against unreasonable search or seizure".

[164] *R.* v. *M.(M.R.)* [1998] 3 *S.C.R.* 393.

[165] *See* text, *supra*, at footnotes 12-25.

[166] *See* text, *supra*, at footnotes 51-63.

[167] *See* text, *supra*, at footnotes 41-50.

[168] *See* text, *supra*, at footnotes 37-40.

[169] *See* text, *supra*, at footnote 114.

[170] *See* text, *supra*, at footnotes 74-79.

[171] *See* text, *supra*, at footnotes 2 and 126-132.

cases privacy is not the sole basis for the limitation on access to the record. However, it is treated as a significant one.

In *Mills*, the Court's rhetoric about privacy is strong. Privacy is defined as "the right to be free from intrusion or interference."[172] Approval is given to the view that "every man has a right to keep his own sentiments, if he pleases: he has certainly a right to judge whether he will make them public (...).".[173] It is said that "privacy concerns are strongest where aspects of one's individual identity are at stake (...).".[174] In full flight, the court then cites Charles Fried: "To respect, love, trust, feel affection for others and to regard ourselves as objects of love trust and affection is at the heart of our notions of ourselves as persons, and privacy is the necessary atmosphere for these attitudes and actions, as oxygen is for combustion."[175]

Coming back to earth, the court states that privacy must nonetheless yield to full answer and defence because "the threat of convicting an innocent individual strikes at the hear of the principles of fundamental justice."[176] However, the section on privacy concludes: "The values protected by privacy rights will be most directly at stake where confidential information contained in a record concerns aspects of one's individual identity or where the maintenance of confidentiality is crucial to a therapeutic or other trust-like relationship."[177]

Regardless of the court's final attempt to bring the record production issue back to a Wigmore-style instrumentalism rooted in confidential relationships, it would appear that the privacy genie is out of the bottle. Privacy must now be taken very seriously as part of the quest for case-by-case privilege, as indeed was explicitly recognised by the Court in *M.(A.)* v. *Ryan*[178] (in the absence of the flamboyant language of *Mills*). The case of privilege for the sexual assault victim's diary in the civil action against the perpetrator seems peculiar if the instrumentalism of Wigmore's 'confidential communications' analysis is relied upon to justify the result. However, it does not seem anomalous in the context of privacy analysis. Quite the reverse.

### 3.2.3 Rights to Equality

To those steeped in a due process model of justice, where the weak accused is thought to need protection against the overwhelming power of the state in its capacity to muster witnesses and resources,[179] the notion that privilege could be

---

[172] *Mills, supra*, at para 79 citing *R.* v. *Edwards*, [1996] 1 *S.C.R.* 128 per Cory, J.

[173] Quoting Yates, J. in *Miller* v. *Taylor* (1769), 4 *Burr.* 2303, 98 *E.R.* 201.

[174] *Mills*, para 80.

[175] Ch. Fried, *supra*, footnote 162, as cited in Mills at para 81.

[176] *Mills, supra*, para 89.

[177] *Mills, ibid.*

[178] *Supra*, footnote 71.

[179] For a full description of 'due process' as opposed to 'crime control' models of justice *see* H. Packer, *The Limits of the Criminal Sanction*, Stanford C.A.: Stanford U. Press 1968.

founded upon equality rights may seem strange. For the due process advocate 'full answer and defence' is the essence of the adjudicative process, at least on the criminal law side. However, the legal battles centred on sexual assault and male abuse of women and children, and the new emphasis on victims' rights, have wrought a paradigm shift in Canadian criminal law.[180] This is more than new pressure toward crime control by merely reinforcing the role of police and prosecution. Victims, and particularly sexual assault complainants, are no longer viewed simply as important Crown witnesses in the adversarial confrontation between state and accused.[181] The apparent unfairness of defence tactics, which sought an acquittal chiefly by challenging the credibility of the complainant, humiliating her and 'putting her on trial', generated a reaction among women's groups and feminist lawyers.[182] After two decades of struggle Canadian criminal law has been transformed: victims are consulted in the exercise of prosecutorial discretion;[183] rape shield legislation[184] and changes in evidentiary rules relating to treatment of sexual assault complainants[185] have come about; substantive law limiting claims of 'honest but mistaken belief in consent' has been changed;[186] victim impact statements are presented on sentencing[187] and at parole hearings;[188] and victim fine surcharges raise funds to aid victims.[189]

The upshot of the foregoing changes is that victims of violent crime, especially sexual assault, are now treated as virtual parties to a criminal proceeding rather than as mere Crown witnesses. Official statements do not acknowledge this state of affairs in such a bold fashion. However, the extent to which this alternate paradigm of criminal justice has penetrated judicial circles is exemplified by the fact that an out of court statement by a sexual assault

---

[180] *See* K. Roach, *Due Process and Victims Rights: The New Law and Politics of Criminal Justice*, Toronto: U. of T. Press 1999.

[181] *See* Chr. Boyle, M.A. Betrand, C. Lacerte-Lamontagne & R. Sahmai, *A Feminists Review of Criminal Law*, Ottawa: Minister of Supply and Services 1985.

[182] *See* the helpful charter and bibliography on this topic in Roach, *supra*, footnote 181, and M. McCrimmon 'Trial by Ordeal?', (1996) 1 *Can. Crim. L. Rev.* 3.

[183] *Crown Guidelines* have been altered across Canada in this regard.

[184] *Criminal Code* Section 176. This section is Parliament's third effort as two previous attempts were found to be unconstitutional. The constitutionality of the present section is now under challenge. *R. v. Darrach* (1998), 13 *C.R.* (3d) 283 (Ont. C.A.) on appeal to the Supreme Court of Canada.

[185] *Criminal Code* Section 277 now provides that evidence of sexual reputation is not admissible for the purpose of challenging or supporting the credibility of the complainant. Moreover, Section 274 provides that corroboration of a complainant's testimony is not required for a conviction in sexual assault matters; and Section 275 abrogates the evidentiary rules on recent complaint (although to uncertain effect).

[186] *Criminal Code* Section 273(2) provides that it is no defense to sexual assault that the accused believed the complainant consent where "the accused did not take reasonable steps, in the circumstances known to the accused at the time, to ascertain that the complainant was consenting."

[187] *Criminal Code* Section 722.

[188] *Corrections and Conditional Release Act*, *S.C.*1992, c. 20, in force November 1, 1992.

[189] *Criminal Code* Section 737.

complainant has been treated as a *party admission* for the purposes of the hearsay rule, and found to be admissible on those grounds.[190] Accused persons in sexual assault cases and their alleged victim/complainants are perceived as the primary combatants at the trial by persons inside and outside the criminal justice system. While Crown prosecutors have not yet been relegated simply to the role of counsel for the victim and clearly still represent the public interest,[191] the worm has turned several degrees and tightened the vice. This is the broad context for the Supreme Court of Canada's most recent pronouncements on equality rights as a basis for the protection of sexual assault records from production to the accused.

The *Charter* guarantees that "every individual is equal before the law and under the law and has the right to the equal protection and equal benefit of the law without discrimination (...)."[192] Furthermore, it also states explicitly (perhaps redundantly) that all *Charter* rights "are guaranteed equally to male and female persons."[193] In *Mills* the Supreme Court of Canada refers to these provisions, and then states the accused is not entitled to information which would "distort the truth seeking goal of the trial process (...)" and in particular the accused is "not permitted to 'whack the complainant' through the use of stereotypes regarding victims of sexual assault."[194] The Court then goes on to quote from *M.(A.) v. Ryan*: "A rule of privilege which fails to protect doctor patient communications in the context of an action arising out of sexual assault perpetuates the disadvantage felt by victims of sexual assault, often women. The intimate nature of sexual assault heightens the privacy concerns of the victim and may increase, if automatic disclosure is the rule, the difficulty of obtaining redress for the wrong. The victim of a sexual assault is thus placed in a disadvantaged position as compared with the victim of a different wrong. The result may be that the victim of a sexual assault does not obtain the equal benefit of the law to which Section 15 of the *Charter* entitles her. She is doubly victimised, initially by the sexual assault and later by the price she must pay to claim redress – redress which in some cases may be part of her program of therapy."[195]

This paragraph does not go far enough to satisfy certain intervenors in the Mills case who hoped for a stronger affirmation of the equality principle, and indeed in on this basis sought an absolute privilege with respect to the personal

---

[190] *R.* v. *Grant* (1989), 49 *C.C.C.* (3d) 410 (Man. C.A.). The complainant was said not to be a formal party, but the evidentiary rule was clearly applied as if she was – with results which are potentially inimical to victims' interests.

[191] On the role of the Crown generally, *see* B.P. Archibald, 'The Politics of Prosecutorial Discretion: Institutional Structures and the Tensions between Punitive and Restorative Paradigms of Justice', (1998) 3 *Can. Crim. L. Rev.* 69.

[192] *Charter* Section 15(1) goes on to enumerate certain prohibited grounds of discrimination, in particular race, national or ethnic origin, color, religion, sex, age or mutual or physical disability. Subsection (2) authorizes affirmative action programs.

[193] *Charter* Section 28.

[194] *Mills, supra*, para 90.

[195] *Mills, supra*, para 91.

records of sexual assault victims.[196] On the other hand, the Chief Justice dissenting in *Mills* concludes that "the risk of suppressing relevant evidence and convicting an innocent person outweighs the salutary effect on the impugned provisions on privacy and equality rights."[197] This echoes the views of most defence counsel.

Equality rights, then, as a basis for privilege in civil and criminal adjudication take us well beyond the domain of confidential relationships. The context for the remarks from *M.(A.)* v. *Ryan* quoted above in *Mills* was an application of equality analysis to determine whether the psychiatrist sexual assault patient/complainant relationship ought to be sedulously fostered, and whether the Wigmorean cost/benefit analysis should be informed by equality concerns as '*Charter* values'. This could be characterised as a narrow and limited privilege. However, it can be argued that equality analysis pushed to the limit could raise personal or relational evidentiary privilege to the level of an instrument of affirmative action for certain classes of persons suffering from discrimination. The court in *Mills* is far from such an analysis because of its concerns for conviction of the innocent and for rights to full answer and defence. Will the same reluctance to ground privilege in equality rights characterise civil litigation where 'only money' is at stake? What are the implications of equality analysis for discovery and trial in Canadian civil proceedings?

### 3.3    Autonomy, Political/Legal Theory and *Real Politik*

Neither Wigmore's instrumentalism nor various constitutional rights and freedoms in their strict sense provide complete explanations for the many personal or relational privileges under discussion. However, it has been suggested that political/legal theory may provide a unifying rationale. On the other hand, the cynic may argue that the only credible understanding of privilege lies with power politics.

### 3.3.1  Autonomy and Law in a Democracy

Habermas provides a convincing modern analysis of the necessity for and the nature of the rule of law in complex democratic societies.[198] As societies develop both social stratification and sub-cultural differentiation, traditional shared values no longer provide the glue that can bind a society together in a coherent,

---

[196] *See* the Factum of Women's Legal Education and Action Fund (LEAF) prepared by counsel A.S. Derrick and P. Kobly of Buchan, Derrick and Ring, Halifax, NS. Ms Derrick, it should be noted, is no stranger to the need for full answer and defense. She represented one of Canada's most celebrated victims of a wrongful conviction: *see Royal Commission on the Donald Marshall, Jr. Prosecution*, Halifax: Province of Nova Scotia 1989.

[197] *Mills*, *supra*, para 11, per Lamer, C.J.C.

[198] *Between Facts and Norms*, *supra*, footnote 137, pp. 132-193.

functional way. Political-legal discourse and political-legal institutions provide the normative and structural means to resolve value conflict and to set the conditions which enable social and economic interaction to occur on a predictable basis. This all occurs in a historical context in which law is a product of social, economic and political interaction, while also having a reflexive impact on these phenomena.[199] Individuals in a democracy may be enthusiastically committed to the norms and institutions in the society of which they form a part, or they may simply be coerced participants, responding to political-legal dictates of this normative and institutional order.[200] The point for this discussion of legal privilege, however, is that modern democratic societies governed by the rule of law as understood in this way are extremely complex, confusing and potentially alienating social environments.

The notion of autonomy as a basis for evidentiary privilege, by preference to the notion of privacy, may be helpful in this context. Edward Imwinkelried suggests: "[Autonomy] is conceived as an ultimate value in a liberal democratic system such as ours. In a pluralist society, the person has a substantial degree of autonomy to determine the content of his or her life plan. In a liberal democratic society, the individual is a chooser, and he or she has the right to select the preferences which define his or her life plan."[201]

For Imwinkelried, moreover, privacy is essential to the exercise of autonomy and in that sense, privacy is subsidiary to autonomy in a society which respects such individual autonomy. In any community, however, individual choices may collide with one another. In democracies governed by the rule of law, litigation is the ultimate mechanism for peaceably resolving these conflicts between individuals. Moreover, many choices, even of the non-conflictive sort, are difficult to make and require expert advice of varying kinds. This advances us to the question of personal or relational evidentiary privileges.

In order to make enlightened choices, the autonomous individual living in the complex society must turn to consultants. If the consultation is to be effective the chooser must make him or herself vulnerable by sharing information with the consultant and breaching privacy. Legal choices may require consultation with counsel, medical choices with physicians, spiritual choices with enlightened advisors, and family choices with significant others. As Imwinkelried concludes: "[T]he creation of a private, intimate enclave for the person and the consultant will enhance the person's ability to make intelligent, independent life preference

---

[199] *Ibid.*, pp. 388-446; *see also* G. Teubner, 'Substantive and Reflexive Elements in Modern Law', (1983) 17 *Law and Society Rev.* 239-285.

[200] Habermas, *supra*, footnote 137, pp. 287-315. On the importance of Habermas' view to procedural matters, *see* P. Bal, 'Discourse Ethics and Human Rights in Criminal Procedure', in: M. Deflem (ed.), *Habermas, Modernity and Law*, London: Sage Publications 1996.

[201] Imwinkelried, 'The Rivalry between Truth and Privilege...', *supra*, footnote 136, p. 985. For an application of the autonomy theory to the analysis of solicitor/client privilege *see* R.C. Wydick, 'The Attorney-Client Privilege: Does It Really Have Life Everlasting?', (1998-99) 87 *Kentucky L.J.* 1165-1190.

choices."[202] In this light, personal and relational privileges are a "means to creating the necessary enclave"[203] and a legitimate aspect of adjudication in a democratic society characterised by the rule of law.

Acceptance of this 'autonomy analysis' in the inchoate form described, clearly does not provide automatic answers to such questions as 'what kind of consultations should be fostered to promote intelligent participation in complex democratic societies?' or 'what should be the boundaries of the privileged private sphere or consultative relationship?'[204] It has the benefit, however, of providing a unifying set of principles for analysis connected to the nature of democratic society,[205] and not merely those associated with the narrow and often isolated sphere of adjudication and self-serving legal discourse. More importantly, it may serve to put the present 'privacy' and 'equality' discussions of the Supreme Court of Canada in a more balanced perspective.

### 3.3.2 Privilege and *Real Politik*

The foregoing discussion, which attempts to place the subject of evidentiary privilege in the broad context of political/legal theory, may represent the theoretical high road to politics. The cynic or realist may argue that the politics of evidentiary privilege is a far cruder phenomenon. Solicitor client privilege, and priest-penitent or doctor-patient privileges where they exist, may be seen as simply the product of the political power and influence of those elite groups, which enable them to shield themselves and their activities from judicial scrutiny. Certainly those who do not benefit from such protection may be forgiven the sceptical observation that legal counsel and judges benefit from privileges, while proclaiming that the legal system which they control can compel 'everyman's evidence'.

Aside from those jaundiced observations, however, the politics of evidentiary privilege does provide the stuff of sobering reflection. The American experience demonstrates that legislative adoption of individual evidentiary privileges is often a response to powerful political lobbying.[206] This arguably is demonstrated in Canada as well by the priest-penitent privileges in Quebec and Newfoundland,[207]

---

[202] *Ibid.*, p. 987.

[203] *Ibid.*, p. 988.

[204] Imwinkelried admits that "the linkage between privacy and the primary good of autonomy unquestionably requires more extended analysis and bemoans the absence of full discussion of this topic in philosophic literature", *ibid.* p. 988.

[205] It is interesting that there are few if any Canadian attempts to relate legal rights, fundamental freedoms and democratic rights under the Canadian *Charter* which have entered the sphere of professional legal discourse.

[206] *See* 'Developments in the Law-Privileged Communications', *supra*, footnote 10; and Wigmore, *supra*, footnote, § 2285 and § 527.

[207] Text, *supra*, corresponding to footnotes 91 to 93.

or the process which led to the new Canadian *Criminal Code* provisions on the protection of personal records of sexual assault victims.[208]

On the other hand, an absence of consensus in modern democracies concerning which privileges, based on what values and protecting which relationships should be recognised, may form an insuperable barrier to comprehensive law reform in this area. Here again the American experience is instructive. It was controversy over privileges proposed in the draft American Federal Rules which delayed their approval for over two years.[209] The rules only received Congressional approval when the US Supreme Court's specific proposed rules on privilege were abandoned in favour of a proposition that privilege would be "governed by the principles of the common law as they may be interpreted by the courts of the US in the light of reason and experience."[210] An extraordinary retreat! Privilege rules, despite the elegant and attractive unifying force of the autonomy theory, have the potential to split society along professional, class, religious and gender lines which defy the capacity of politicians to transcend.[211]

## 4    Assessing the Canadian Privilege Revolution

An assessment of the recent privilege revolution in Canadian evidentiary law can usefully include three components:
1. placing the privilege developments in the context of contrasting developments in relation to other exclusionary rules;
2. evaluating the values at stake and their institutional impact; and
3. reflecting on the challenges to adjudication in many democratic societies and the role of evidence in such controversies.

### 4.1    Privilege and Trends in Exclusionary Rules

The move toward a 'case-by-case' analysis of privilege claims in Canadian litigation has the potential to lead to more frequent exclusion of relevant, probative and reliable information. This trend might be thought contrary to what is occurring in other areas of evidence law in Canada. For example, admission of hearsay has been expanded in Canada through the judicial development of a residual exception grounded in Wigmore's twin notions of necessity and reliability.[212] In a parallel development, the rules governing admission of similar

---

[208] *See* text, *supra*, corresponding to footnotes 111-132.

[209] *See* Imwinkelried, 'An Hegelian Approach to Privileges...', *supra*, footnote 136.

[210] *American Federal Rule of Evidence* 501, as cited by McCormick, *supra*, p. 314.

[211] The fate of the Law Reform Commission of Canada's proposed Evidence Code, and the Uniformity Commissioners Task Force *'Uniform Evidence Act'* fall squarely within this trend of analysis – they seem to be consigned to political oblivion.

[212] Once again the Supreme Court of Canada employed a conceptual framework designed by Wigmore as an explanation for the contours of existing law (patterns of hearsay exceptions), and used it as the basis for the creation of a discretionary rule applicable to govern the admissibility of (to be continued)

fact evidence have been loosened to allow greater use of this controversial type of information.[213] Following Bentham's anti-nomian thesis (eliminate exclusionary rules and admit all relevant evidence),[214] these developments in the area of similar fact and hearsay have expanded the field of admissibility. The trend in personal and relational privilege is the opposite: more relevant evidence will be excluded at a cost to the principle of rectitude of decision.

On the other hand, the form (if not the content) of the developments in the area of privilege is identical to what is happening in other areas of the law of evidence. That is to say, apparently firm exclusionary rules (albeit with exceptions) are giving way to balancing tests and discretionary exclusion based on judicial assessment of the circumstances of the individual case.[215] This is the case with hearsay and similar fact, as well as privilege – both case-by-case personal and relational privileges and public interest immunity.[216] Moreover, the Supreme Court of Canada has now asserted on many occasions that any decisions on admissibility pursuant to individual exclusionary rules are subject to an over-riding discretion on the part of the trial judge to exclude otherwise admissible evidence where "prejudice outweighs probative value".[217] Of course, this sort of balancing act is now also familiar to Canadian criminal courts in the process exclusion of unconstitutionally obtained evidence which "could bring the administration of justice into disrepute".[218] The ultimate result is to sacrifice certainty and predictability in the interests of flexibility and justice in individual cases. While this may seem a laudable endeavour in principle, it may have the effect in practice of favouring those who have the financial means to litigate, since almost any trial decision can be plausibly challenged on appeal in such a system. Equality may be the casualty in the long run.

---

evidence in individual cases (admission of evidence which is 'reasonably necessary' where there exist 'circumstantial guarantees of trustworthiness'); *R.* v. *Khan* (1990), 79 *C.R.* (3d) 1 (S.C.C.); *R.* v. *Smith*, [1992] 2 *S.C.R.* 915; *R.* v. *B.(K.G.)* (1993), 19 *C.R.* (4th) 1 (S.C.C.). For a discussion of these and related developments, *see* Archibald, *supra*, footnote 9.

[213] *See R.* v. *Arp* (1998), 20 *C.R.* (5th) 1 (S.C.C.). This proposition may be controversial. *Arp*, and the recent line of similar fact cases in the Supreme Court of Canada of which it is one exemplar, may be thought to have streamlined similar fact doctrine without altering its substance. Without firm empirical support to back the proposition, I would nonetheless argue that the net effect of these cases has been to increase admissibility of 'similar facts', particularly in sexual assault cased. *See* Sopinka, Lederman & Bryant, *supra*, footnote 3, pp. 521-602; Watt, *supra*, footnote 9, pp. 395-422.

[214] *See* W. Twining, *Theories of Evidence: Bentham and Wigmore*, London: Weedenfield and Nicholson 1985.

[215] *See* Twining, *Rethinking Evidence*, *supra*, footnote 4, and A. Stein, 'The Refoundation of Evidence Law', (1996) 9 *Canadian Journal of Law and Jurisprudence* 279-342.

[216] *See* text, *supra*, corresponding to footnotes 64 to 110, and in relation to public interest immunity the approach taken by the Supreme Court of Canada in *Carey* v. *Ontario*, [1986] 2 *S.C.R.* 637.

[217] *R.* v. *Potvin* (1989), 68 *C.R.* (3d) 193 (S.C.C.) and more recently *R.* v. *L.(D.O.)*, [1993] 4 *S.C.R.* 419 are helpful examples of this.

[218] *Charter*, Section 24(2). *See* for example, *Collins* v. *R.* (1987), 56 *C.R.* (3d) 193 (S.C.C.) and *R.* v. *Stillman*, [1997] 1 *S.C.R.* 607.

## 4.2    Privilege, Lawyer's Values and Public Values

The law of evidentiary privilege is clearly a potential focal point for value conflict in the legal system. Lawyers may tend to concentrate on the values intrinsic to the adjudicative system, while members of the general public may have other concerns. As noted at the outset of this article, adjudication involves a compromise among competing values: truth finding; fairness as between adversarial parties; considerations of cost and efficiency; and public confidence in the administration of justice.[219] Privileges obviously inhibit truth finding. However, the values upheld by traditional privileges have tended to maintain the intrinsic integrity of the adjudication process from a lawyer's perspective: hence, the existence of solicitor client privilege, police informer privilege, dispute resolution discussion privilege, and a general disposition to be suspicious of other forms of privilege. It would appear that concerns extrinsic to the formal values of adjudication are driving other developments in the law of privilege. Some of these concerns may fall within the rubric of public confidence in the administration of justice. It could be argued that any case-by-case privilege tied to in notions of privacy, equality or autonomy could fall within that proposition. The general public seems generally responsive to both principled and rhetorical claims based on these broader values. However, other privileges for professional groups can simply be the result of power politics – extrinsic to lawyers values concerning fair adjudication, and potentially inimical to public values in the broadest sense.

Another aspect of the tension between lawyers values and broader public values in the area of privilege is the potential conflict between the legislative and judicial institutions where these tensions get played out. Mention has been made of the institutional interplay between the US Supreme Court and Congress over the adoption of the American Federal Rules.[220] The recent developments in the Canadian law dealing with production of personal records of sexual assault records present another interesting example. Lawyer's values predominated the Supreme Court's assessment of the problem in *O'Connor*.[221] Parliament responded with legislation which reflected a broader range of public concerns and a different hierarchy of values.[222] In *Mills* the Supreme Court of Canada, despite expectations that it might interpret the *Charter* to reassert the lawyers values in full answer and defence as it had done in *O'Connor*, accepted the constitutionality of the new parliamentary regime. In doing so, the court engaged in a fascinating discussion of the institutional relationship between a final appellate court and parliament in a constitutional democracy where the legislature

---

[219] Text, *supra*, corresponding to footnotes 8-10.
[220] Text, *supra*, corresponding to footnotes 209 and 210.
[221] *Supra*, footnotes 114-130.
[222] Text, *supra*, corresponding to footnotes 126-131.

has chosen explicitly to reverse a judicial decision.[223] The court reiterated pronouncements that a "dialogue between and accountability of the [legislative and judicial] branches have [sic] the effect of enhancing the democratic process, not denying it."[224] In relation to privilege, it appears that this dialogue may result in the vindication of public values as opposed to lawyers' values, at least when there emerges a public consensus or politically saleable position.

## 4.3 Adversarial Adjudication and its Rivals

The foregoing discussion about privilege assumes the centrality of adjudication as the predominant dispute resolution mechanism in democratic societies and also the importance of exclusionary rules of evidence related thereto. This, of course, is an exercise characterised by a high degree of cultural bias. While complex rules of evidence may be normal in common law tradition, the justice systems of European democracies in the civilian tradition do not have such a labyrinthine approach to the admissibility of proof.[225] By and large, European courts decide cases on the principle of relevance with few exclusionary rules and no regard to a discipline of 'evidence law'.[226]

Interestingly enough, however, among the few formal rules of evidence found in European systems are rules of privilege, including forms of confidential communication not always excluded in common law jurisdictions.[227] The European level of comfort with the absence of exclusionary rules relates, of course, not only to judge-centred as opposed to party-centred presentation of proof, but also to the phenomenon of 'trial de novo' as a widespread form of appeal as contrasted with common law appellate deference to trial level findings of fact.[228] However, the existence of this firmly entrenched alternative tradition has provoked introspection among common law jurists looking at evidence in general, and privileges in particular, since the time of Wigmore.[229]

In many common law jurisdictions there is emerging a widespread dissatisfaction with formal adjudication as a means of dispute resolution. The complexity and cost of litigation has led to a search for alternative forms of dispute resolution in both civil[230] and criminal[231] contexts. A.D.R. is now an

---

[223] *Mills, supra*, paras 43-60. This is not the only recent example where the Canadian Parliament has reversed a judicial decision from the Supreme Court of Canada in short order: *see R. v. Daviault* (1994), 33 *C.R.* (4th) 165 (S.C.C.) leading to *Criminal Code* Section 33.1 dealing with intoxication as a defense.

[224] *Mills, supra*, para 57, citing the remarks of Iacobacci, J. in *Vriend, supra*, footnote 36, para 139.

[225] *See* J.F. Nijboer, 'The Common Law Tradition in Evidence Scholarship Seen from a Continental Perspective', *supra*, footnote 10.

[226] Evidence rules are generally studied and described as a part of civil, criminal or administrative procedure, *ibid.*

[227] *See* Hammelman, *supra*, footnote 10.

[228] M.R. Damaška, *Evidence Law Adrift*, New Haven: Yale University Press 1997.

[229] J.H. Wigmore, *A Panorama of the World's Legal Systems*, St. Paul: West Publishing 1928.

[230] R.H. McLaren & J.P. Sanderson, *Innovative Dispute Resolution: The Alternative*, Toronto: (to be continued)

adjunct to the publicly funded judicial system for civil trials and is central to emerging private systems of mediation/arbitration.[232] Similarly, restorative justice and transformative justice are on the agenda in Canadian criminal law circles, and indeed the *Criminal Code* has recently been amended to allow for establishment of systems of 'alternative measures'.[233] One cannot avoid the perception that complex evidentiary rules and the problems and delays occasioned by them are part of the public's dissatisfaction with civil and criminal adjudication in Canada and other common law jurisdictions. Controversy over the rules relating to privilege may play a part in this malaise. Comparative analysis of common law adjudication with its domestic and foreign rivals will shed light on this situation. In such comparative perspective, the Canadian revolution in the law of privilege may not seem so revolutionary, and the potential directions for post-revolutionary development may seem less murky.

---

Carswell/Thomson Publishing 1995.

[231] J. Braithwaite, *Crime, Shame and Re-integration*, Cambridge: Cambridge U. Press 1989; B.P. Archibald, 'A Comprehensive Canadian Approach to Restorative Justice: The Prospects for Fair Alternative Measures in Response to Crimes', in: D. Stuart, R.J. Delisle & A. Manson, *Toward a Clear, and Just Criminal Law: A Criminal Reports Forum*, Toronto: Carswell/Thomson Publishing 1999.

[232] J. MacFarlane, *Dispute Resolution: Readings and Case Studies*, Toronto: Emond Montgomery 1999.

[233] *Criminal Code* Section 717. Even the formal principles of sentencing in *Criminal Code* Sections 718(1) and 718(2) are to be implemented with an eye to restorative justice: *see R.* v. *Gladue*, [1999] 1 *S.C.R.* 688, and Judge M.E. Turpel-Lafond, 'Sentencing within a Restorative Justice Paradigm: Procedural Implications of *R.* v. *Gladue*', (1999) 43 *Crim. L.Q.* 34-50.

# The Offence of Money Laundering – Polish Penal Regulations vis-à-vis the European Norms

*J.B. Banach*

## Introduction

Money laundering is said to be one of the major activities of organised crime. Much of the money comes from drug trafficking, whereas other forms of transnational crime may account for around 25% of all the illegal proceeds that enter the global financial system.

The money, which derives from illicit proceeds, has somehow to be made legitimate. This procedure is called money laundering and usually involves three main stages. The first stage is the placement of cash proceeds into the financial system through banks or other financial institutions. It is most often done through a large number of small transactions ('smurfing'). Another possibility is smuggling large amounts of cash out of the country to deposit it where the reporting requirements are less stringent.

At the second stage of money laundering the so-called 'layering' is involved, which separates the funds from their source and is designed to disguise the audit trial. The third stage is integration, which involves the "introduction of criminally derived wealth into the legitimate economy without arousing suspicion and with some apparent legitimacy for its source". It may involve such actions as the purchase of real estate or simply the complicity of banks in countries, which lack money laundering legislation.[1]

Money laundering is a relatively new kind of crime. First, it was noticed and called as a socially dangerous in the US, in the sixties. Soon then, this phenomenon occurred in Europe. At the end of the eighties, the European states started to take legislative action in combating money laundering.

In recent years two approaches towards money laundering have been developed, *i.e.*, the preventive approach and the repressive approach. The former deals with prevention of financial institutions from being used for purposes of money laundering, while the latter one aims at the suppression of the behaviour in question.[2] The Polish legislator following both of these tendencies introduced Article 299 into a new *Penal Code* of 1997 (it entered into force in 1998) and some other regulations to prevent money laundering, the adopted legal remedies may be recognised as compatible with the principal requirements of the European norms. However, its effectiveness in practice still remains a disputable issue among Polish criminal lawyers.

---

[1] HEUNI Papers No. 6/1995, *Organised Crime across the Borders*, pp. 5-7.
[2] C. Fijnaut, J. Goethals, T. Peters & L. Walgrave, *Changes in Society, Crime and Criminal Justice in Europe: a challenge for criminological education and research, Vol. II*, Kluwer Law International 1995, p. 168.

## The Definition and Practice of Money Laundering

As to the definition of 'money laundering' one may say that it is generally treated as using the bank's or financial system for 'conversion' of money gained from criminal activities into legal funds – in this way 'the dirty money' are becoming 'clean'. This world's problem is particularly important in the case of financial systems of the post-communist countries, like Poland overcoming the transformation process in the sphere of economy. There is a searching for new possibilities of money laundering.[3]

Money laundering, the most often, is connected with activity of organised criminal groups and its purpose is to conceal the illegal origin of the money by introducing the gathered gains into the legal order. Illegal funds usually come from trafficking in drugs and other forms of transnational crime.

In the opinion of Professor E. Pływaczewski, the practice of money laundering includes varied techniques, procedures and mechanisms for changing illegally gained financial funds (so-called 'dirty money') or funds coming, indeed, from legal sources, but having to avoid taxes, into other forms of actives. The actions undertaken by offender aim at concealing the original sources of the funds or their owner, and consequently to make possible a safety inclusion of certain funds into the legal economic and financial system.[4]

Thus, money coming from illegal gains must be in any way 'legitimated', this process is called, generally as a 'money laundering' or 'laundering of the dirty money'.

The cases registered in recent years on money laundering by Polish Prosecutor's Offices have concerned, mainly the banking sector. Taking into account, the basic techniques which are applied by offenders through banks. The Prosecutor W. Huba states that effectiveness of each operation of money laundering may be achieved using three stadiums, namely:

1. 'location'-investment, that is changing cash into financial instruments or instrumental goods;
2. 'disguise', that is disguising of undertaken operation of money laundering by doing quite complicated financial transactions and making longer the way, the money is going through;
3. the financial legislation (legitimisation) of the funds by getting the documents certifying their legal source of origin.[5] As it was already mentioned, money laundering is connected directly with organised crime. Great gaines flowing from crime may cause some suspicious of law

---

[3] 'Unia chce ukrócić pranie pieniędzy (Union wants to stop money laundering)', in: *European Dialogue*, September/October 1996/5, pp. 6-7 (Polish).

[4] E. Pływaczewski, *Pranie pieniędzy (Money laundering)*, Toruń 1993, p. 33; quoted after W. Huba, 'Przestępstwo prania piniędzy w świetle prawa I praktyki prokuratorskiej (The offence of money laundering in the light of laws and public prosecutor's practice)', in: *Prokuratora i Prawo* 11/1996, p. 7.

[5] W. Huba, *op. cit.*, pp. 8-9.

enforcement agencies, thus, they need to be 'disguised' in any way or 'converted' into other activities (material goods) for concealing the trials of their criminal origin.

Generally speaking, the action of 'money launder' (the process of money laundering) is aimed at making it impossible to find out the offences committed by him by concealing the evidentiary trials of their existence and at having to ensure the enjoyment of the gained funds. While, the purpose of the fight against money laundering is to punish the offender and to take over his illegally gathered gains. This kind of sanction may be achieved by the confiscation of the proceeds of crime. Actually, there has been recently evaluated a term on fighting against money laundering in a preventive sense and a repressive sense. The fight, on one hand shall be aimed at prevention of the financial institutions from using them for money laundering, and on the other hand at imposing certain sanctions on the offender.[6]

## The European Legal Instruments in the Fight against Money Laundering

It is recognised that if the international community takes seriously the problem of money laundering, international co-operation is to be a *conditio sine qua non*.

Most of the money laundering operations are carried out on a transnational basis. It is a result of the internationalisation of organised crime, and internationalisation of the economy and society in general (so-called 'global village').

The *European Convention on Laundering, Search, Seizure and Confiscation of the Proceeds of Crime of November 8, 1990 (Laundering Convention)*[7] relates to establishment of inter-state so-operation in combating money laundering. Its purpose is to create a judicial assistance in this matter and to harmonise the substantive criminal law. There is also stresses a need of undertaking certain measures at the level of national and international legal order.[8]

Article 2 of the Laundering Convention obliges the parties to "adopt such legislative and other measures as may be necessary to enable it to confiscate instrumentalities and proceeds or property the value of which corresponds to such proceeds". The term "confiscation" should be understood as "a penalty or a measure, ordered by a court following proceedings in relation to a criminal

---

[6] C. Fijnaut *et al.*, *op. cit.*, p. 168.

[7] E.T.S. No. 141, *see also* Chr. van den Wyngaert, *International Criminal Law, A Collection of International and European Instruments*, Kluwer Law International 1996, pp. 107-121. Note: the first international instrument on fighting money laundering is considered the *UN Convention against Illicit Traffic in Narcotic Drugs and Psychotropic Substances of December 19, 1988 (Vienna Convention)*. As to the European instruments of the most important are said to be the *Convention of the Council of Europe* and the *EC Directive No. 308/91*.

[8] C. Fijnaut *et al.*, *op. cit.*, pp. 171-174.

offence or criminal offences resulting in final deprivation of property". "Property" is relating to property of any description (corporeal or incorporeal, movable or immovable, legal documents or instruments evidencing title to, or interest in such property). "Proceeds" in turn means, any economic advantage from criminal offences.

The parties are also obliged to penalise money laundering under its domestic law, when committed intentionally according to the definition included in Article 6(1). These are such activities as: "(a) the conversion or transfer of property knowing that such property is proceeds, for the purpose of concealing or disguising the illicit origin of the property or of assisting any person who is involved in the commission of the predicate offence to evade the legal consequences of his actions; (b) the concealment or disguise of the true nature, source, location, disposition, movement, rights with respect to, or ownership of property, knowing that such property is proceeds; (…)."

It is worth noticing that the *Laundering Convention* regulates the inter-state co-operation during all stages of the procedure: the pre-trial, trial and post-trial stage. It is said that in the past inter-state co-operation in criminal matters was exclusively modelled towards immobilising the suspect. Its purpose was mainly to detect and arrest the suspect, to collect the evidence and finally to convict the offender. Today, much more attention is focused on an additional aspect, *i.e.*, confiscating the proceeds of crime. This is called a second goal of the criminal justice system.[9]

In its provision, the Convention lays down an obligation to provide investigative assistance. Article 8 obligates the Parties to take "the widest possible measures of assistance in the identification and tracing of instrumentalities, proceeds and other property liable to confiscation (…)." The assistance should be "carried out as permitted by and in accordance with the domestic law of the requested Party and, to the extent not incompatible with such law, in accordance with the procedures specified in the request."[10] The Convention also allows for "spontaneous information".[11]

An important aspect of the investigation of money laundering is the legal possibility to seize the property, which is suspected to be the proceeds from crime. Otherwise, the owner of the property may try to remove the property in order to avoid its confiscation. According to Article 11 the Parties have to take provisional measures such as "freezing or seizing, to prevent and dealing in, transfer or disposal of property which, at a later stage, may be the subject of a request for confiscation or which might be such as to satisfy the request."[12]

It is argued that 'classical' mutual assistance in criminal matters aims mainly at collecting evidence for the purpose of using it in a criminal proceeding abroad, *i.e.*, during the trial stage. While the Convention, in

---

[9] *Ibid.*
[10] Article 9 *Laundering Convention* – the *locus regit actum* principle.
[11] Article 10 *Laundering Convention*.
[12] *See* footnote 8.

question, goes beyond this, namely its provisions allow for enforcement of specific sentence of confiscation. As a rule the ulterior confiscation is pronounced by the judicial authorities of the state, which instituted the criminal proceedings. The property, which has to be a subject of confiscation, may be, however, situated in another state.

In such situation Article 13 is applied, stating that: "(1) A Party, which has received a request made by another Party for confiscation concerning instrumentalities or proceeds, situated in its territory, shall: (a) enforce a confiscation order made by a court of a requesting Party in relation to such instrumentalities or proceeds; or (b) submit the request to its competent authorities for the purpose of obtaining an order of confiscation and, if such order is granted, enforce it."

These two models of carrying out a foreign confiscation request correspond with the following forms of judicial co-operation: the enforcement of a foreign criminal judgement and the transfer of proceedings.[13]

One may also distinguish two types of confiscation: property and value confiscation. In the first case the confiscation sentence relates to specific property which is somehow related to the offence for which the confiscation is pronounced. The latter term covers the confiscation which is pronounced as a debt which can be enforced on any property available for that purpose.

The Convention provides also regulations concerning the execution of confiscation, grounds for refusal or postponement of co-operation, protection of the third parties' rights, procedural and other rules. Worth mentioning is Article 18(7), which excludes bank secrecy as a possible ground to refuse co-operation.[14]

The *Directive on Prevention of Use of the Financial System for the Purpose of Money Laundering, 1991* is mostly addressed to the EU Member States,[15] it is a pattern, which should be accepted by the applicant states. It requires the implementation of prescribed regulations in order to prevent of use the financial system for money laundering. However, the penalisation of this procedure was left for each member state.

The EU is afraid that occurrence of organised crime in the applicant states, and in consequence the procedure of money laundering might be a threat for a stability of the European financial system, laws and public order. Therefore, it was established through the European Agreements, that the implementation of the Directive shall be a condition for obtaining full membership by the candidate states. An important role is played by the programme Phare, assisting them in the process of integration and in the fight with drugs and organised crime.

---

[13] *Ibid.*

[14] *Ibid.*

[15] O.J.L. 166, 28 June 1991; *see also* Chr. van den Wyngaert, *op. cit.*, pp. 125-131.

Although the Directive does not oblige the EU Member States to impose penal sanctions, they "shall take appropriate measures to ensure full application of all the provisions of this Directive and shall in particular determine the penalties to be applied for infringement of the measures adopted pursuant to this Directive."[16] It also allows for adopting or retaining in force stricter provisions in the field covered by the directive to prevent money laundering.

In accordance with its provisions the credit and financial institutions shall require identification of their customers and all the persons which have rights to the questionable property. They shall also pay attention to the transactions, where is suspicion of money laundering and inform about this fact the competent authorities. The latter obligation imposed on banks is an exception of bank secrecy.

The credit and financial institutions are also obliged to: "(1) establish adequate procedures of internal control and communication in order to forestall and prevent operations related to money laundering; (2) take appropriate measures so that their employees are aware of the provisions contained in this Directive. These measures shall include participation of their relevant employees in special training programmes to help them recognise operations which may be related to money laundering as well as to instruct them as to how to proceed in such cases."[17]

The definition of money laundering covered in the Directive is rather general. By this procedure is meant the following conduct when committed intentionally: "the conversion of transfer of property, knowing that such property is derived from criminal activity or from an act of participation in such activity, for the purpose of concealing or disguising the illicit origin of the property or of assisting any person who is involved in the commission of such activity to evade the legal consequences of his action; the concealment or disguise of the true nature source, location, disposition, movement, rights with respect to, or ownership of property (…); the *acquis*ition, possession or use of property (…); participation in, association to commit, attempts to commit and aiding, abetting, facilitating and counselling the commission of any of the actions mentioned in the foregoing paragraphs."[18] Knowledge, intent and purpose are the required elements of the above-mentioned activities.

Also, the definition of "property" is quite wide and it means assets of every kind, whether corporeal or incorporeal, movable or immovable, tangible or intangible and legal documents or instruments evidencing title to or interests in such assets. According to the directive money laundering defined as such above takes place even where the activities which generated the property to be

---

[16] Article 14 Directive.
[17] Article 11 Directive.
[18] Article 1 Directive.

laundered were perpetrated in the territory of another Member State or in that of a third country.

The Directive obliges the EU Member States to bring into force the laws, regulations and administrative decisions necessary to comply with its provisions before January 1, 1993 at the latest. An important aspect of this document is the preventive approach, which complements the penal approach.

It is also worth mentioning that the Directive allows distinguishing *ratione materiae* and *ratione personae*.[19] In the first case, its provisions are applied to the laundering of money derived from drug trafficking. But, Member States may extend the application filed to other predicate offences. In the second case, the obligations created by the Directive only apply to financial institutions and credit institutions.

The duties instituted by the Directive relates *inter alia* to the identification of customers. Article 3 of the Directive states that in the EC law financial institutions shall require identification from their customers in three situations:
1. when entering into business relations (*e.g.*, by opening a bank account);[20]
2. for all transactions involving a sum amounting more than ECU 15,000;[21] and
3. whenever there is a suspicion of money laundering.[22]

According to Article 4, the credit and financial institutions shall "keep the following for use as evidence in any investigation into money laundering:
- in the case of identification, a copy or the references of the evidence required, for a period of at least five years after relationship with their customers has ended;
- in the case of transactions, the supporting evidence and records, consisting of the original documents or copies admissible in court proceedings under the applicable national legislation for a period of at least five years following execution of the transactions."

To conclude one may agree with a statement that provisions of the Directive have imposed on credit and financial institutions law obligations for preventing money laundering, through for example a constant control above them in the application of the established rules.[23]

Next to the EC Council Directive No. 308/91, the provisions relating to money laundering has been adopted in the *Action plan to combat organised crime 1997*.[24] In Part II ('Political Guidelines') it declares that "the European Council stresses the importance for each Member State of having well-

---

[19] *Ibid.*
[20] Para 1.
[21] Para 2.
[22] Para 6.
[23] Chr. van den Wyngaert, *op. cit.*, pp. 125-131. *See also* C. Fijnaut *et al.*, *op. cit.*, pp. 169-171.
[24] O.J.C. 251, 15 August 1997.

developed and wide ranging legislation in the field of confiscation of the proceeds from crime and the laundering of such proceeds."[25]

The legislation of the EU Member States shall be particularly aimed at:

- introducing special procedures for tracing, seizure and confiscation of proceeds from crime;
- preventing an excessive use of cash payments and cash currency exchanges by natural and legal persons from serving to cover up the conversion of the proceeds from crime into other property;
- extending the scope of laundering provisions to the proceeds form all forms of serious crime, and making a failure to comply with the obligation to report suspicions financial transactions liable to dissuasive sanctions;
- addressing the issue of money laundering on the Internet and via electronic money products.

Furthermore, the *Action plan* obliges the Member States to rapid ratification and full implementation of both the international legal instruments and the EU Conventions in the fight against money laundering. These are the following:

1. Recommendation 13:
   1. *European Convention on Extradition*, Paris 1957;
   2. *Second Protocol to the European Convention on Extradition*, Strasbourg 1978;
   3. *Protocol to the European Convention on Mutual Assistance in Criminal Matters*, Strasbourg 1978;
   4. *Convention on Laundering, Search, Seizure and confiscation of the Proceeds of Crime*, Strasbourg 1990;
   5. *Convention on Mutual Assistance between Customs, Administrations and Protocol thereto*, Naples 1967;
   6. *Agreement on Illicit Traffic by Sea, implementing Article 17 of the United Nations Convention against Illicit Traffic in Narcotic Drugs and Psychotropic Substances*, Strasbourg 1995;
   7. *Convention on the Fight against Illicit Traffic in Narcotic Drugs and Psychotropic Substances*, Vienna 1988;
   8. *European Convention on the Suppression of Terrorism*, Strasbourg 1977;

2. Recommendation 14 – the EU Conventions:
   1. *Convention on simplified Extradition Procedure between the Member States of the European Nation*;
   2. *Europol Convention*;
   3. *Convention on the Protection of the European Communities' Financial Interests*;
   4. *Convention on the Use of Information Technology for Customs Purposes*;

---

[25] *Ibid.*, Part II, p. 8(11).

5. *Convention relating to Extradition between the Member States of the European Union;*
6. *Protocols to the Convention on the Protection of the European Communities' Financial Interests.*

It is also worth noticing that the Pre-accession Pact on Organised Crime about which is stated in the *Action Plan* has been adopted in 1998.[26] Its provisions confirm the intention of candidate states to co-operate fully with the EU Member States "in fighting all kinds of organised crime and other forms of serious crime" and to implement the EU *acquis*. A special emphasis is placed on the Recommendations 13 and 14 mentioned above. Its implementation into the national systems is also relating to the candidate states.[27]

Another Action of the of the European Union dealing with money laundering is the *Joint Action of December 3, 1998 on Money Laundering, the Identification, tracing, freezing, seizing and Confiscation of Instrumentalities and the Proceeds from Crime.*[28] It promotes the closer co-operation of law enforcement agencies in the implementation of the Council of Europe Convention on Laundering, Search, Seizure and Confiscation of the Proceeds from Crime 1990 and the legal instruments of the EU. It may be done for example by the European Judicial Network, establishment appropriate measures in domestic proceedings and direct contact between investigators, investigating magistrates and prosecutors, as well as training programmes.

### The Impact of the European Legislation on Polish Penal Law

A quite important instrument, in respect to Poland, is the *European Agreement*, *i.e.*, the *European Agreement between the European Communities and Poland* of 1991.[29] In accordance with Article 85 of this Agreement, "[t]he Parties agree on the necessity of making every effort and co-operation in order to prevent the use of their financial systems for laundering of proceeds from criminal activities in general and drug offences in particular." They also declared that "co-operation in this area shall include administrative and technical assistance with the purpose of establishing suitable standards against money laundering equivalent to those adopted by the Community and international for a in this field, in particular the Financial Action Task Force (FATF)."

One may say, in fact, we have the two most important European legal instruments in regard to money laundering in Europe. The first instrument is

---

[26] Pre-accession Pact on Organised Crime between the Member States of the European Union and the applicant countries of Central and Eastern Europe and Cyprus, O.J.C. 220, 15 July 1998.
[27] As to the European Conventions in penal law adopted by Poland, see the Annex.
[28] O.J.L. 333, December 9, 1998.
[29] The *European Agreement between the European Communities and their Member States*, of the one part, and the Republic of Poland, of the other part, was signed in Brussels on December 16, 1993. For the decision of the Council and the Commission on its conclusion see O.J.L. 348, December 31, 1993.

the European Convention on Laundering, Search, Seizure and Confiscation of the Proceeds from Crime and the second one is the EC Council Directive No. 91/308 on Prevention of the Use of the Financial System for Purpose of Money Laundering.

As to the former instrument Poland signed it on November 5, 1998. While the provisions of the EC Directive were adopted by majority via Regulation No. 16/1992 issued by the President of the Polish National Bank.[30]

In accordance with the EC Directive, each Member State shall take appropriate measures to ensure full application of all its provisions, and in particular, determine the penalties to be applied for the infringement of measures adopted pursuant to this Directive. It is, however, within the competence of each Member State to penalise the practice of money laundering under their national legal order.

The Regulation has imposed on the Polish banks in particular the following duties:

1. identification of their customers, especially in the event of cash transactions which involve sums of money over 20,000 of Polish zlotych (ECU 5,000)[31] or its equivalent in foreign currency, and save this information along with the supporting evidence for a period of five years;
2. providing the records of the operations defined above which should include among others *(inter alia)* the identification and address of the customer, the number of the bank accounts related to the transaction if such ones exist, the nature of the transaction, identification of the banks participating in the transaction, the date of the transaction (on which date it was made) and the amount of the transaction;
3. in the event of reasoned suspicious that is carried out an operation relating to money laundering, the bank shall inform about this fact a competent *ratione loci* the Public Prosecutors Office;
4. banks also have to establish the internal programmes for the prevention of the operations which could be related to money laundering.[32]

The practice of money laundering was penalised in the next Polish Act, *I.e.*, in the *Act for the Protection of Economic Relations* (1994). Article 5(1) of this Act defines the criminal offence of money laundering as legalisation of the proceeds from organised crime;[33] however not from every crime. The basic legal property which shall be protected are regular economic relations. The

---

[30] This Regulation in fact lost its validity on January 1, 1998 on the base of Article 182 Section 1 of the *Banking Law* of 1997 (Prawo bankowe z 1997r. Dz.U. Nr. 140, poz. 939). A. Zoll (ed.), *Kodeks karny – czesc szczególna, kommentarz do art. 278-363* (The Criminal Code – a special part, commentary to the Articles 278-363), Zakamycze 1999, pp. 353-354.

[31] In the original text it is said of 200 millions of the old Polish zlotych. As I was informed by the bank's official the present sum of money shall be ECU 5,000.

[32] Zarządzenie Nr 16/1992 Prezesa NBP – Regulation No. 16/1992 of the Polish National Bank, October 1, 1992 (Dz.Urzędowy NBP No. 9, poz. 20).

[33] The term of organised crime for the first time was used in Article 5 of this Act. However, its definition has not been precised.

main weakness of this Act was cataloguing of organised crime limited to the four categories traffic in narcotic drugs, forgery of money and securities, traffic in arms and extortation of ransom.[34]

It is regarded that such an enumeration made the fight against money laundering ineffective. Another barrier was Polish banking law, including a rigorous interpretation of bank secrecy. Consequently, both of these legal remedies resulted in the dismissal of the majority of criminal proceedings, which were conducted in the years 1995-1997. Even as soon as it was instituted, it was discontinued because the committed act lacked the features of the criminal offence *ex lege, i.e.*, in understanding of the Act in question.[35]

The Prosecutor W. Huba in his analytical paper of 1997 evaluated the cases on money laundering conducted in Public Prosecutor's Offices as to their effectiveness on the basis of Article 5 of the *Act for the Protection of Economic Relations* and some other penal regulations. He proved that most of the criminal proceedings were instituted on the base of the bank's announcement. The data may be presented as follows:

Grounds of Proceedings in Public Prosecutor's Office: Years 1995-1996

| Total amount: 52 cases | |
| --- | --- |
| Bank's announcements | 42 |
| Announcement by other objects | 4 |
| Material excluded from other cases | 3 |
| Operational actions taken by police forces | 3 |

In some of the cases the proceedings were well reasoned and a suspect was brought into charge of the committing of the offence of money laundering. Out of 52 cases, 10 were not instituted, 11 were discontinued, five were suspended, four ended in another way, two prosecuted by indictment and 20 were still continued. The amount of 'laundered' money in those two years was estimated as at least about:
-   5.821.172.000 PLN;
-   70.237.000 DM;
-   66.950.000 $.

The often applied method by the offenders were for instance exchange in 'change kantoor' or using the bank's accounts of fictitious existing companies. Moreover, according to the Prosecutor W. Huba, as the main reasons which had a negative influence on the effectiveness of the prosecutor's trials shall be mentioned:
1. not precisely expressed the contents of some banking law provisions and executive regulations;

---

[34] The *Act for Protection of Economic Relations*, October 12, 1994 (Dz.U. Nr. 126, poz. 615/94), note that it was replaced with the new penal regulations – Article 299 of the *Polish Penal Code* of 1997.
[35] W. Huba, *op. cit.*, pp. 7-22.

2. necessity of request for foreign legal assistance that makes the trial longer, negatively influencing its final result (it was used in 19 cases out of 52);
3. necessity to order a fiscal control (in 16 cases out of 52 Public Prosecutor applied for fiscal control).[36]

## Amendments introduced by *Polish Banking Law* and *Penal Code* of 1997

In consequence to a harsh critique of the legal gaps in Polish regulations made not only by lawyers, but also by the public, new remedies were adopted, these being:
- a new *Polish Banking Act* of 1997, which enables the Public Prosecutor a wider access to the information otherwise blocked by the bank secrecy;
- a new *Polish Penal Code (PPC)* of 1997 which includes Article 299 regarding criminal liability in the cases of all categories of organised crimes; thus, we do not have a specific listing as it was outlined earlier.

The same Article also imposes certain obligations upon banks and financial institutions including the criminal liability of their employees. Article 299 of the *PPC* provides, in particular:
- if the employee of the bank, financial or credit institution being responsible for informing the competent internal organs (administration or supervision board) about carrying out financial operations, he or she does not do it immediately, although its circumstances support the suspicious (suspicion) of its illicit origin defined in Article 299 Section 1, he or she is liable to a penalty of liberty deprivation up to three years;[37]
- if the offender is involved in the criminal activities defined in Article 299 Sections 1 or 2, in co-operation with the other persons, the prescribed penalty is from one year up to 10 years; the same penalty is prescribed for the offender who is involved in the criminal activities defined in Article 299 Sections 1 or 2 if he has required a great property profit;[38]
- in the event of conviction for the offence defined in Article 299 Sections 1 or 2, the court shall adjudge a forfeiture of the instruments (objects) flowing directly or indirectly from the crime, even though the offender is not their owner;
- there is no criminal liability if the offender voluntarily reveals to the competent authority established for the prosecution of crime, information concerning the persons which participated in the commission of the

---

[36] Not published.

[37] In accordance with Article 299 Section 1 illicit origin may concern all categories of organised crime. It also prescribes penalty of liberty deprivation for offenders involved in money laundering from three up to five years.

[38] Article 299 Section 2 imposes a criminal liability upon the employee of banks, credit and financial institutions which accepts in cash, against the regulations, money or other currency, carrying out its transfer or conversion, or when he accepts it in other circumstances of reasoned suspicious that it may be derived from disguise its illicit origin. The prescribed penalty in this event is the same as in Section 1 of this Article.

criminal act and its circumstances, if he has prevented another criminal act; the court may adjudge also the extraordinary mitigation of punishment if the offender has undertaken his effort in order to reveal the information and circumstances.

In the opinion of the Police services, new penal regulations still do not create an effective system in fighting money laundering. The main reason is 'bank secrecy'. Namely, pursuant to the banking law police does not have inspection into the bank documents (Article 105). Such a right is only given to the Public Prosecutor's Office (Article 106). In other words, the bank is obliged to inform the Public Prosecutor's Office about any suspicious transactions which in its view might be used for money laundering. The prosecutor, in return may require from the bank to send the appropriate documentation concerning transactions. This legal solution is regarded is not sufficient enough, as it has a negative influence on preliminary investigation that results in not finding grounds for criminal proceedings. The Police argue that 'bank secrecy' is against international regulations for example 40 recommendations of FATF and *Vienna Convention* of 1988. Another barrier for more effective police actions is also lack of the access to customs, insurance and fiscal information. Certain remedy for improving the present legal system is seen in the future establishment of General Inspector on Financial Information by the Act of Parliament, that is actually taken under discussion.[39]

Also, the National Public Prosecutor's Office points out a low level of effectiveness in regard to money laundering on the base of recent penal law (compare tables 1 and 2). It suggests therefore a necessity of making further analyses of such a state and working on the new remedies in a proposed Draft of the Act on prevention of introducing into financial system property values from illicit or not revealed origin sources.[40]

As it was mentioned, the Directive has imposed on the Member States a duty to introduce appropriate laws, regulations and administrative decisions for prevention of money laundering and being complied with its provisions. The above obligations are concerned also the associated countries, that is the states applying for admission to the EU, like Poland. Thus, undertaking effective measures in prevention and suppression of money laundering is one of the conditions to achieve a membership in the EU for the candidate countries.

The changes made in Polish domestic legal regulations on combating money laundering, which leads to harmonisation with the European norms, may be recognised as a positive approach. Although, they cause also some doubts. There may arise for example two questions: first, the lack of the 'confiscation penalty', second, the term of 'organised crime' in the Polish penal law.

---

[39] Source: the Main Police Office, Warsaw 1999.
[40] Source: the National Public Prosecutor's Office, Warsaw 1999.

The international and European community requires application in the national legal order of the states the penalty of 'confiscation' (that is to be understood as 'confiscation of property' in reference to the proceeds of crime). Whereas the legislator has resigned in the latest *Polish Penal Code* of 1997 from this kind of penalty, replacing it by the 'forfeiture' (Articles 299(7), 39, 44 and 45).

The question as to the 'confiscation of property' is quite disputable in the present Polish legal literature. The authors of the commentary to the *PPC* of 1997 Professors K. Buchata and A. Zoll, maintain that penalty of confiscation was unknown under the *PPC* of 1932. And, it is also unknown under the *Penal Codes* of the states being members of the EU. In accordance with the amendments introduced in 1990 this type of penal sanction was quashed in the Polish *Penal Code*.

As a new remedy, which in the opinion of Professors K. Bichata and A. Zoll, is supposed to be effective, was introduced a judgement of the forfeiture of objects (Article 44 *PPC*) and achieve profits (Article 45 *PPC*). The forfeiture of objects contains three groups: those coming from the crime, those using for its commission or serving for such a purpose, and those as to which production, possession, traffic or transport is prohibited.[41]

### Combating Organised Crime in the Light of European Standards – Polish Case

The new penal regulations introduced into the Polish legal order should have a positive effect on combating organised crime in Poland. One may argue that Polish law has taken a big step toward approximating to the European standards.

In the 90s, Poland became a Party to such international agreements as the *European Convention on Extradition, the European Convention on Mutual Assistance in Criminal Matters* and the *Convention on the Transfer of Sentenced Persons*. Also, some important modifications were effected, namely there is a higher criminal liability for the offenders involved in 'organised crime' (Article 65 *PPC*), the institution of 'incognito witness' was adopted (Article 184 *Polish Code of Criminal Procedure*), there is a separate Act concerning a 'crown witness' of 1997 and the Police Act includes a 'control delivery'. *PPC* also penalised participation in 'organised criminal group' or 'criminal association' (Article 258 *PPC*).[42]

Poland has signed some bilateral agreements, like with Germany, that makes it possible to send the requests for judicial assistance directly to the

---

[41] K. Buchała & A. Zoll, *Kodeks karny – czesc ogólna* (The *Penal Code* – a general part), Zakamycze 1998.

[42] Further details on the Polish penal provisions relating to organised crime *see* B. Kunicka-Michalska, 'Les systèmes de Justice Pénale á l'Épreuve de Crime Organisée', in: *International Review of Penal Law*, Topic II, Special Part, Alexandrie November 8-12, 1997 , pp. 463-484.

appropriate courts of public prosecutor's offices, omitting in this way, the ministerial level. Stable relationships have been established between Poland and the US Government in combating organised crime, Poland is also active in the UN (*e.g.*, the *UN Convention on Combating Organised Crime* was a subject of the Conference held in Warsaw, 1998) and in the framework of the Task Group on organised crime in the Baltic Region.

Polish Police co-operates with the police forces from many countries of the entire world on the basis of bi- and multilateral agreements (*e.g.*, Germany, the Netherlands, Interpol). Since January 1994, in Police Offices have been operating special Units established for the fight against organised crime. The similar Units – so-called Investigation Departments on organised crime work in the Public Prosecutor's Offices in Poland.

However, as it was earlier said the term of 'organised crime' has not been precised by any normative Polish Act. Although, it functions in practice. The *PPC* is just passing over this term. In the Polish legal literature, there is a view that about organised crime one may say in 'functional sense' ('organised offence') or 'structural sense' ('criminal organisation'), *i.e.*, as a way of committing offences or as a criminal structure, within which the offences are committed. It is argued that by organised crime shall be understood both of the above meanings.[43]

In the opinion of Professor E. Pływaczewski, organised crime shall be understood as committing at least few offences within organised structure, which links larger amount of persons, characterised by hierarchy, planning and division of functions, as well as aimed at longer or lasting action and applying the internal sanctions.[44]

Assisting character to determine the term of organised crime is provided by the Directives of the Polish Supreme Court of 1962, which refer to the definition of 'organised criminal group'. According to its provisions the action is committed in the organised criminal group, if it is a result of arrangement among at least three participants, which are linked (joined) by the structural element, based on division of roles and co-ordination of activities.[45]

The present definitions of organised crime are quite different, but they share some common elements. According to the EU criminal group may be defined as organised crime, when the following characteristics are present: collaboration between more than two people, suspected of serious criminal offences and determined by the pursuit of profit and/or power. The next ones among which, at least three must be included are:
- each person having their own appointed tasks;

---

[43] K. Buchała, P. Kardas, J. Majewski & W. Wróbel, *Komentarz do ustawy o ochronie obrotu gospodarczego (A commentary of the Act for protection of economic relations)*, Warszawa 1995, pp. 86-87.
[44] E. Pływaczewski, cited after: Buchała, Kardas & Majewski, *op. cit.*, pp. 86-87.
[45] H. Pracki, Nowe rodzaje przestępstw gospodarczych (The new kinds of economic crimes), Prokuratura i Prawo 2/1995, p. 35.

- action for a prolonged or indefinite period of time;
- using some form of internal discipline and control;
- operating at an international level;
- using violence or other means suitable for intimidation;
- using commercial or business-like structures;
- engaged in money laundering;
- exerting influence on politics, media, public administration, judicial authorities or economy.[46]

The *PPC* applies the terms of 'organised criminal group' and 'association having for its purpose committing offences'. In practice, however, there exists the term 'organised crime'. Both in Police and in the Public Prosecutor's Offices operate special Units established for fight against organised crime. From the perspective of future Poland's membership in the European Union and judicial and police co-operation in criminal matters, it would be reasonable to implement the term of organised crime to Polish Penal system and its precising. Such an implementations of 'organised crime' into penal law would afford for distinguishing the particular forms of crime, in its structural meaning.

Introducing 'organised crime' into penal terminology seems quite important, taking into account the present legislation of the European Union, and international efforts for fighting this wide spreading phenomenon.

## Actions taken by the European Union

The Actions taken by the EU have, in particular, to improve judicial and police co-operation in preventing and fighting all forms of international organised crime. The more detailed provisions on combating organised crime are covered in the *Action Plan* of 1997.[47]

In reference to Poland, an important shall be Political Guideline No. 5 and Recommendation No. 3, concerning a Pre-accession Pact on co-operation against organised crime. This Pact shall be based on "the *acquis* of the Union and may include provisions for close co-operation" between the candidate countries of Central and Eastern Europe, including the Baltic States, and Europol and "undertakings by those countries to rapid ratification and full implementation of the Council of Europe instruments which are essential to the fight against organised crime". The text of such a Pact as a set of principles was approved by J.H.A. Council in May 1998.[48]

---

[46] Ibid. *See also* C.H. Ulrich, 'Transnational Organised Crime and Law Enforcement Co-operation in the Baltic States', in: *Transnational Organized Crime, Vol. 3*, No. 2, summer 1997, pp. 115-134, London.
[47] O.J.C. 251, August 15, 1997.
[48] O.J.C. 220, July 15, 1998.

The states have declared to "co-operate fully in fighting all kinds of organised crime and other forms of serious crime", and the applicant countries have to "implement the EU *acquis* before entering the European Union".

So, the candidate states have to adopt the European Convention on Mutual Assistance in Criminal Matters of 1959, as well as other Conventions mentioned in Recommendations No. 13 and 14 of the EU Action Plan to combat organised crime. The co-operation in the fight against organised crime shall be based on the operation of central law enforcement and judicial bodies at the national level, assistance of Europol, the judicial contact points, the mutual exchange of law enforcement intelligence, the mutual practical support for investigations and operations (*e.g.*, training and equipment assistance, joint investigative activities and special operations, mutual exchange of law enforcement officers and judicial authorities for traineeships).

There is also stressed an importance of working on bi- or multilateral joint law enforcement projects, implementation of the Joint Action on good practices in mutual legal assistance in criminal matters of June 1998, ratification of the Extradition Conventions of the EU of 1995 and 1996, and some programmes established in the field of justice and home affairs (*e.g.*, OISIN, Grotius, STOP, Odysseus or Falcone).

The most important Joint Actions and Resolutions on combating organised crime adopted by the EU concern such matters as:

- establishing a mechanism for evaluating the application and implementation at the national level of international undertakings in the fight against organised crime;[49]
- making it a criminal offence to participate in a criminal organisation in the Member States of the EU. Article 1 of this Joint Action provides that: "a criminal organisation shall mean a structured association, established over a period of time, of more than two persons, acting in concert with a view to committing offences which are punishable by deprivation of liberty or detention order of a maximum of at least four years or a more serious penalty, whether such offences are an end in themselves or a means of obtaining material benefits and, where appropriate, of improperly influencing the operation of public authorities (...)";[50]
- the protection of witnesses and/or individuals who co-operate with the judicial process in the fight against international organised crime;[51]
- the prevention of organised crime with reference to the establishment of a comprehensive strategy for combating it;[52]
- the common framework for the initiatives of the Member States concerning laison officers;[53]

---

[49] O.J.L. 344, December 15, 1997.
[50] O.J.L. 351, December 29, 1998.
[51] O.J.C. 327, December 7, 1995; O.J.C. 10, January 11, 1997.
[52] O.J.C. 408, December 29, 1998.
[53] O.J.L. 268, October 19, 1996.

- the creation and maintenance of a directory of specialised crime, in order to facilitate law enforcement co-operation between the Member States of the EU.[54]

**Final Conclusions**

Combating money laundering and organised crime, as such from the legal point of view despite of some weaknesses, may be recognised as progressing in Poland. Polish judicial and police authorities are still searching for more effective measures in the fight against all forms of organised crime and try to elaborate the most efficient methods to prevent money laundering. They are active in establishing the closer co-operation with its contrapartners in other countries. The Polish law enforcement agencies (judges, prosecutors or police officers) participate in the held Conferences and seminars both at national and international level. They also take part in the exchange of programmes, including training that facilitate their co-operation on criminal matters. Some cases have even been already conducted with the help of 'foreign colleagues' (legal and operational assistance). Worth mentioning, at this point, is well-established co-operation with the Dutch and German agencies. The Polish practitioners highly appreciate the direct contacts with their colleagues from abroad, because it allows for avoiding a long way of official procedure at ministerial level. Moreover, one must consider that money laundering is a problem to be solved not only in Poland. It is a common problem arising before the European states. Therefore, it causes a necessity of their close co-operation and implementation of already existing European legal instruments into national systems.

---

[54] O.J.L. 342, December 31, 1996.

# The Law of Confessions in Israel – Trends of Reform

*D. Bein*

In the past there used to be a saying that a confession of an accused in his or her interrogation is the 'Queen of all Evidential Material'. This saying was based on the assumption that no one takes the blame on him or herself if not guilty. However, experience has shown that there is no justification in seeing the confession as having any special weight in comparison to other forms of evidence.

There are various situations where it turns out that confessions may be false. For this phenomenon there may be various reasons:

1. psychological problems stemming from the accused person's personality, family history, mental illness or retardation, guilt feelings, desire for publicity, etc.;
2. the exertion of force by the police;
3. use by the police of more subtle means of duress (such as isolation or lack of sleep) or of deceit or the use of promises of early release or immunity from prosecution;
4. the wish of the accused to protect a friend or family member by taking the guilt upon himself or herself.

A false confession may lead to a false conviction while the real culprit is still at large. Any law relating to confessions must strike a fair balance between the following interests:

1. ascertainment of truth;
2. the protection of the right of the suspect to remain silent;
3. the protection of human dignity;
4. the regulation of police conduct during interrogation.

The first interest exists in relation to any kind of confession - even to those made before another citizen not in position of authority - while the other three interests come into play mainly when the confession was made during police investigation.

The law as to confessions in Israel is laid down in Section 12 of the *Evidence Ordinance (New Version)* enacted during the British mandate of Palestine (now Israel). This section lays down the rule that for a confession to be admissible in evidence, it must be free and voluntary. A confession not freely made is excluded. The question of admissibility is decided in a 'trial-within-a-trial'. The exclusion of a confession does not lead to inadmissibility of material evidence (*e.g.* drugs or stolen property) obtained through such confession. This Section 12 rule is based on the following assumptions:

1. an involuntary confession infringes the right to remain silent;
2. there is a rebuttable presumption that an involuntary confession may be untrue.

The Supreme Court of Israel laid down the rule that in order to convict the accused upon his or her confession the prosecution must adduce an additional evidential 'something' which need not amount to corroboration. This piece of evidence must add to the reliability of the confession.

In the leading case of *Muadi* v. *State of Israel*,[1] the Supreme Court decided, after a long line of conflicting decisions, that in a case where brutal and inhuman means were used by the police, the confession will not be accepted as evidence without having recourse to the question whether these means negatived the free will of the accused. However, if more subtle means of coercion or enticements were being used the court still has to ask itself whether the use of such means negativated the accused's free will.

Since the *Muadi* case, the *Basic Law: Human Dignity and Liberty* has been enacted and there are opinions to the effect that according to the principles of this basic law a confession must be disqualified whenever any unlawful means were used, even means which are subtle (*e.g.* use of moderate force or the use of tricks) and without recourse to the question whether if nevertheless the confession was made freely.

This stand is to be preferred since in 1986 Israel has joined the *Convention against Torture and Other Cruel Inhuman or Degrading Treatment and Punishment 1984*. This Convention was ratified by Israel on 4 August 1991 and came into force on 2 November 1991. Article 15 of this Convention states that any member country shall ensure that any statement, which has been exerted by torture, shall not be invoked as evidence.

"Torture" is defined in Article 1 of the Convention as "any act by which severe pain or suffering whether physical or mental is inflicted (...)."

On the other hand, the general direction of reform in the law of evidence in Israel is to move from rules of admissibility towards rules of reliability, and this trend may lead to a position that disfavours a wider use of rules of exclusion.

The problem of involuntary confessions has caused much public concern in many countries. In Israel a special public committee headed by Justice Goldberg of the Supreme Court was nominated by the Minister of Justice to deal with convictions based solely on confession and causes for re-trial (1994).

The majority of the Goldberg Committee has recommended that the use of means amounting to 'torture' as defined by the Convention previously referred should exclude confessions so obtained but where subtler unlawful means have been used no exclusionary rule should be applied and the court should consider the weight of the confessions at the end of the trial taking into account all the circumstances.

In the opinion of the committee too wide an exclusionary rule may infringe the delicate balance between the exigencies of law enforcement and human

---

[1] 38[1] *P.D.* 197.

rights considerations. In the opinion of the majority of the Goldberg Committee, other means than the application of a wide exclusionary rule should be used, in order to fight the use of improper techniques during police investigation, which do not amount to torture.

Three members of the Goldberg Committee recommended that generally the additional evidential 'something' should amount to an independent corroboration and only in special circumstances, and with reasons which must be recorded, should a court convict without corroboration provided the evidence furnished to the court includes additional external evidence which in the circumstances may strengthen the accused's confession. However, the majority was of the opinion that the existing law as to the evidential 'something' should be retained though it was stressed that the weight of the additional evidence may change according to the circumstances. They recommended that in any case it should negate any reasonable doubt as to the trustworthiness of the confession.

In order to ensure that investigators will refrain from using unlawful means in obtaining confessions, use should be made of penal and disciplinary sanctions against such investigators.

There is no doubt that the ordinary criminal offences such as assault, threats, fraud, etc. apply to investigators and they do not enjoy any special immunity. As to disciplinary transgressions, it is not enough to define them in general terms, but a 'Code of Practice' (like the *Code of Practice* enacted in Britain in 1985 according to the *Police and Criminal Evidence Act 1984*) should be adopted in Israel. Such a Code is a very important tool to prevent the use of improper means in order to obtain a confession. The Goldberg Committee stated that the presence of a lawyer during investigation, even if only as a spectator without a right of active interference, is of the utmost importance in ensuring free and trustworthy confessions.

This right is still not enshrined under existing law, although an arrested person has a right to confer with a lawyer upon arrest. However, such a conference is not a pre-condition for the commencement of the interrogation of the suspect.

The fact that as of late a new law relating to Public Defenders has been enacted, which enables poor defendants to get the service of a lawyer without paying fees, is a good opportunity to lay down a new rule according to which a suspect may demand the presence of lawyer during all the process of investigation, at least as a passive spectator, as recommended.

To a lesser degree the recording of at least all interrogations of the suspect on videotape is also an effective tool in achieving the goal that confessions may be obtained only by legitimate means. The shortcomings of this tool are due to the following, first that its mere presence may deter the suspect from admitting his or her guilt, and second that videotapes may be mishandled (*e.g.* by omitting certain parts of the interrogation). The system of videotaping is already applied in certain serious offences, especially murder.

The Goldberg Committee also recommended that the police erect an inner body headed by a senior officer which will control and review the systems and methods of investigation and review and follow the process of investigation by various police departments.

An important role should also be played by the judges before whom the arrested suspect is brought (generally 24 hours after arrest), in order to prolong the period of arrest. They should be open to hear, record and act on complaints by suspects about improper methods of investigation used during arrest.

# International Tribunals

*G.T. Blewitt*

## Introduction

The last decade of this century has been designated by the United Nations as the 'Decade of International Law'. Soon this Decade, along with the millennium, will come to an end. The latter will go out with considerable fanfare, the other with hardly a murmur.

Some may wonder whether international law has benefited from the Decade. I have no doubt that it has. The past ten years have seen advances in international law which had previously been unimaginable, or at least only dreams. Probably one real failure of the Decade is that it was incorrectly named. The past ten years have really been the 'Decade of International *Criminal* Law'.

The 1990s have seen the explosive development of international criminal law. The results achieved were believed unrealistic a mere ten years ago. The world has witnessed the creation of the International Criminal Tribunal for the former Yugoslavia (ICTY), the International Criminal Tribunal for Rwanda (ICTR) and the successful negotiation of the Statute of the Permanent International Criminal Court (ICC) in Rome.

The two *ad hoc* Tribunals have served, in their short existence, as laboratories for the development of procedures to effectively investigate and prosecute serious crimes, which are of concern to the international community as a whole. These crimes are of such major proportions that investigation and prosecution procedures under domestic jurisdictions are generally rendered unsuitable for application within the Tribunals. The Tribunals have therefore had to develop their own unique set of practice and procedures. The sources of these are found in the basic tenets of justice as contained in the major legal systems of the world, and as formulated in international instruments regarding fair trials. The jurists who populate the Tribunals come from these varying systems, and their interpretations of these principles through the glasses of their own legal training and experience, create the synergy from which effective and efficient procedures are evolved for the Tribunals.

And it does not stop there. The new techniques and practices in criminal investigation and prosecution at the international level which are being evolved by the ICTY, and our sister, the ICTR, are being directly utilized to develop the *Rules of Procedure and Evidence* of the ICC. In short, all those involved in this process are currently the pioneers in the ongoing quest to establish international rule of law at the level of individual responsibility.

The Second World Conference on New Trends in Criminal Investigation and Evidence provides an excellent opportunity to focus on the importance of the rule of law at all levels of society, including at the final frontier which is international criminal law. I want to whet your appetite for this highly stimulating and exciting field by briefly highlighting some of the most important problems, and lessons that have been learnt by the ICTY. Much of what we have learnt through experience has already been incorporated into the law being developed for the ICC, and represents realities that that court will also one day be confronted with. I will focus first on investigations, and thereafter on prosecutions.

## Investigations

International crimes of concern to the international community as a whole are crimes that have been committed on a vast scale. These crimes are not committed in isolation, and must be seen against the background of the culture, history and politics of the region in which they have been committed. In order to deal adequately with such crimes, the Prosecutor must master this background.

This means that when embarking upon the investigation, the Prosecutor is likely to start off with an inadequate knowledge of the basis giving rise to the conflict in which the crimes were or are being committed. To bring those responsible for crimes at the highest level to justice, requires in the first place the laying of that basis. Without this basis, it will be virtually impossible to link political and military leaders to physical crimes committed on the ground.

You will see this in the ICTY's approach. When we started our investigations, we could not immediately commence indicting the prominent military and political leaders. It made sense to initially focus on lower level perpetrators. This allowed for a gradual build-up of knowledge relevant to understanding the conflict. As these investigations progressed, they automatically started to lead up the ladder of responsibility. Our history of indictments makes for interesting reading. They show a steady upward progression through the ranks, and ultimately go right to the top. A few years ago we started off with a lowly camp guard, and this year we have indicted a sitting Head of State. The lesson learnt from this is that bringing persons to justice under international criminal law cannot be instant justice.

A second problem facing international tribunals is that they do not have a police force at their disposal, which will automatically execute all warrants and orders of the court. This hampers investigations in various ways. The obvious disadvantages are that tribunal investigators are sometimes denied access to crime scenes by national authorities, or access to vital witnesses.

A further aspect in this regard bears mentioning. Consider the fact that the situations and events that international tribunals investigate have often been the focus of undivided international attention. The recent Kosovo conflict is a good example. For months we survived on a media diet reporting blow by blow on NATO bombings and gross human rights abuses, and an incessant analysis of the events. Parallel to this, national intelligence services were also quietly collecting intelligence on all aspects of the unfolding drama, also by means of probing satellite surveillance of the conflict area. The inescapable conclusion is that such conflicts these days are generally extremely well documented.

Logic dictates that later, when an international tribunal undertakes its investigation into the crimes committed, it will inevitably approach those governments and organizations that have documented the conflict, for access to their information.

And this could and does present problems. The objection that can be anticipated from states is that information cannot be provided due to overriding national security considerations in the requested state. In the case of the ICTY, it is only in the last two years that we have been able to establish really effective co-operative ties with governments and organizations that have resulted in regular access to meaningful material. Even so, we still do not have unlimited access to such material and there are serious and important gaps, which in many cases means the difference of being able to bring an indictment or not.

This leads to a further interesting development in investigations – the potential of using new technology. For example, where we have been able to gain access to high resolution satellite imagery, this has sometimes led our investigations in particular directions. To illustrate, we have had instances where we were able, through satellite pictures, to determine not only the location of mass graves, but also when they actually appeared. This was done through comparing images from successive satellite passes, and spotting differences in ground features.

Following through with the same technique has shown how and when certain mass graves were subsequently re-opened to remove the bodies, in an attempt to hide the fact of the mass killings by re-burying bodies in numerous smaller graves. Such images, while not always depicting the actual activity, have pointed to earth disturbances, and the presence of earth-moving equipment.

Such information can lead investigators on the ground to search for evidence of military orders to move military units, with earth moving equipment, into the vicinity at the time of the appearance of the graves. If specific military orders can be traced, this could off course lead to proving responsibility of leaders.

Worth mentioning is the effect that the magnitude of the crimes themselves or the extent of separate crimes scenes have on how the investigative task is often approached. Once again Kosovo provides a good example. The ICTY simply did not have enough resources to cope with the investigative tasks that confronted it after the cessation of the NATO air strikes. Governments were approached and forensic teams from fourteen countries ultimately provided teams to assist us. This led to the forensic investigation of roughly a third of the 600 identified crime sites in Kosovo. Through this method we were able to augment our resources by 300 experts for a period of five months.

Moving away from actual investigations, one other issue which is also relevant to the absence of having our own police force, is the important question of the arrest of indicted persons. In the early days of the ICTY, when the international community was demanding results, it was seen as an achievement to merely produce an indictment in which suspects were named. Some were perhaps naively confident that arrests would automatically follow. Some did indeed, but many of the indictees merely went underground and out of reach.

This was when we had to rethink our strategy, which resulted in the practice of keeping our indictments sealed. This merely entails producing indictments in a confidential manner. Upon confirmation, the confirming Judge is requested to order that the indictment and the arrest warrant remain confidential until the arrest of the accused is effected.

Persons indicted under sealed indictments, therefore, remain oblivious of the fact that they have been indicted until the moment they are arrested. This creates potential opportunities for their arrest. General Momir Talic, Chief of Staff of the Bosnian Serb Army, is a prime example of this system yielding successful results. Even though he should have suspected that he was a target for indictment, he calmly traveled to Vienna for a seminar. The Austrian authorities, also oblivious of the existence of an indictment, allowed him to enter their territory. Once he was there, we revealed the existence of the indictment to the Austrian authorities for the first time. They were handed the arrest warrant, which they then promptly executed.

A number of indictees are now in detention as a direct result of this system. We would of course be prepared to reconsider this procedure if countries, which currently still shield publicly indicted persons on their territory, showed a real commitment to surrender such persons to the Tribunal for trial. International Tribunals will, however, continue to have difficulty in securing the arrest of indicted persons.

**Prosecutions**

Turning to prosecutions, as indicated earlier, the ICTY is in a continuing process to develop Rules of Procedure and Evidence, which will allow for the most effective and fair conduct of prosecutions and trials. The law and procedures developed must accord with the highest international standards of justice.

The major problem complicating this effort is the tension that exists between the common law and civil law systems. The Tribunal's Statute and its Rules of Procedure and Evidence are based on the adversarial common law approach. Many jurists involved in the work of the Tribunal, including judges, prosecutors and defense lawyers, come from the civil law background and are initially not at total ease with the common law content of the Statute and Rules.

As an example, consider the procedure of requiring the accused to enter a plea of guilty, or not guilty, upon first appearance. Civil law lawyers are horrified at the prospect of a court convicting someone merely on his or her plea of guilty. They view this as contrary to the principle that an accused is deemed innocent until *proven* otherwise.

With time and experience, however, lawyers from all persuasions become more comfortable with the law of the Tribunal, and become more open to utilizing principles drawn from other legal systems. This allows for the best possible law to be distilled for the Tribunal, taking the best from various systems and adapting them to the needs of the Tribunal. This process of cross-pollination of principles and interpretations from various legal systems makes the development of the Tribunal's law a vibrant and healthy process. One recurring problem is of course that, every time a new lawyer appears at the Tribunal, the syndrome of 'legal imperialism of one's own system' reappears, until that lawyer realizes that his or her domestic law is not the only valid system in the world.

The bottom line is that the current system applied by the ICTY is working, and is to a large extent being adopted for the ICC. Less reliance, however, is being placed on the actual label that should be attached to a particular principle. Ultimately it is irrelevant whether a specific principle is common law or civil law in its origin. What is more important is whether the application of that principle is effective and corresponds to international standards of justice.

We are gradually progressing beyond labeling principles and procedures as common law or civil law, and forging ahead on the basis of what works best for this new law being created. Perhaps we should call it 'Tribunal Law'. When we achieve this, and truly mean it, international criminal law will indeed have come of age.

Turning briefly to a few problems concerning prosecution of cases, one of the most worrying factors is currently the length of trials. This is due to various factors such as:
- volume of evidence and the resultant magnitude of disclosure obligations;
- the amount of pre-trial and other motions brought by the defense in many cases;
- the unwillingness of the defense to narrowing the facts at issue, which if done, could vastly limit the scope of proceedings;
- the fragmentation of cases through the arrest of persons on the same indictment at different times. This has already resulted in the same trial having to be conducted more than once. It is not always possible, or fair, to wait until all those on the indictment have been arrested before commencing a trial against those already in custody;

- the restraint by judges in asserting their authority in the courtroom in the interest of speeding up proceedings. It would help, for example, if judges would clamp down on time-consuming irrelevant cross-examination or on the leading of irrelevant evidence at length.

Efforts are, however, afoot from the side of the judges, prosecution, registry and defense to streamline procedures and practices so as to speed up trials. The responsibility to achieve this is a shared one, with improvements and adjustments to their own attitudes and approaches having to be made in good faith by all parties. This is currently the project that bears the highest priority in the Tribunal.

Also of concern are the long periods that accused remain in detention in the pre-trial and trial phases. In view of the difficulty of obtaining the presence of these persons in the first place, as already pointed out earlier, and of the nature of the crimes they are charged with, provisional release on bail or otherwise cannot be a standard option that an international tribunal will exercise. The solution here also lies in the speeding up of the trials. The maxim that 'justice delayed is justice denied' applies in international criminal law as well. Standards used at the domestic level to measure what would constitute an acceptable delay should, however, not be applied unchanged at the level of international tribunals. They are simply not applicable. New standards need to be developed that will take into account the unique circumstances at that level, carefully balancing the interests of the accused against those of victims, the requirements of justice, and the need to build a solid platform for the creating a lasting peace.

## Conclusion

This has indeed been the Decade of International Criminal Law. We are at present still out of breath from the roller-coaster ride. In some circles there is still apprehension as to whether these developments are desirable.

This apprehension is, however, due to the fact that we are judging a new development against dated opinions and predictions. Once we have been able to catch our breath again, we are going to realize that international criminal law is a reality.

Then we will slowly realize, and come to accept, the beneficial effects of this law. The world is going to gradually become a very small place for international criminals, in particular the pariah leaders of the world.

In ten years from now, international criminal law will be a natural and accepted part of the legal order of the world. The international tribunals applying that law will be accepted as part of everyday life. And the world will be so much the better because of it.

# Undercover Policing in the Netherlands

*J. Boek & A.M. van Hoorn*[*]

## Introduction

In this paper we will discuss 20 cases of undercover policing in the Netherlands during 1996. The cases were thoroughly researched by the Dutch Research and Documentation Centre of the Ministry of Justice on a parliamentary request. In the Netherlands several years ago, a large scale political discussion evolved concerning the use of special investigative methods (such as observation/surveillance, the participation of civilians in criminal investigations as confidential informers, undercover policing, etc.) Although undercover policing was considered an important investigative method, little was known about its effectiveness. This was the main reason for starting the research.

One of the results of the research that struck us the most was the fact that undercover policing was, apart from the one big case, so very common. Taking an overview of all the cases that we studied, we noticed that most cases were quite ordinary. Undercover operations are used rarely in the Netherlands because the main opinion is that such operations should not be carried out lightly. Undercover operations are considered to be very intrusive. For this reason, we expected that undercover operations would be carried out only in special criminal investigations, focusing on the *crème de la crème* of the Dutch criminals. But this is hardly the case, at least not as far as the study shows.

Another result that struck us was the fact that most of the undercover operations failed. Only in a few cases a considerable amount of relevant information was gathered as a result of the undercover operation and in even fewer cases the goals that were set in advance were reached. We must appreciate the fact that in some cases these goals were very ambitious, in order to get approval for the undercover operation. Apart from that, a major problem appeared to be the creation of a relationship between the target of the undercover activities and the undercover officer.

We underline that we must be careful in our conclusions and generalisations, because the study was very limited (it only involved 19 cases). But some of the things we found are important and may be of useful application.

---

[*] The authors were seconded to the Dutch Research and Documentation Centre of the ministry of justice in 1998-1999. Together with M. Kruissink they wrote *Undercover policing in the Netherlands, in law and practice* (in Dutch) published by the Dutch Research and Documentation Centre of the Ministry of Justice.

## The Research and some of its Results

In 1995, the Public Prosecutors Office, which is a national organisation with local branches, introduced a review committee, composed of both experienced public prosecutors and high-ranking police officers. This committee must give its approval for the use of some of the special investigative powers, among which are some undercover activities and all of the undercover operations. This review committee was the starting point for the data collection in our research.

In 1996, 22 cases in which an undercover operation or single undercover activities were planned were admitted to this committee. Nineteen of these cases were studied intensively during our research. We were given access to the files of the review committee and to the dossier of the criminal case itself. We also talked to the prosecutors, police officers and judges who were involved in the different cases.

In two of the 1996 cases the public safety was at risk and in one case the undercover operation was still ongoing at the time of our research. These cases could not be included in the research. Today some of the results of one of these three cases are made public, so we can include that one in our paper.

In four cases permission to carry out the intended undercover operations was refused. We will not talk about these cases. That leaves us with 15 cases and the one that was finished late 1999.

Before we go into the cases, there are two things we have to point out: first, no deep cover operations are carried out in the Netherlands, at least that is what police officers tell us, and second, civilians co-operating with the police sometimes play an active role in criminal investigations. For instance, a civilian buys drugs from the suspect on the directions of the police and public prosecutor, which leads to the suspect's arrest. When a civilian assists in a criminal investigation like this, it is perceived as an *undercover activity*. Not that the identity of the civilian is covered – the identity of this person often is known to the suspect – but because of the fact that the suspect is *being misled on the true intentions* of the person he or she is dealing with.

Now we will focus on the cases we have studied.

We found out that in most of the undercover operations more or less the same strategy was used:

1. the undercover officer has to make contact with the suspect or with somebody close to him or her: a relative or a friend;
2. the undercover officer tries to make contact in a bar, gym or somewhere else and tries to build up a relationship with the target;
3. then the suspect must turn the contact into a criminal contact. This is very difficult, especially since entrapment must be avoided. Some incitement is allowed, but the suspect may not be provoked into committing a crime when he or she had no intention of committing a crime in general. In other words, the undercover police officer or co-operating civilian may not

induce a person to commit an offence other than the one he or she was already intending to commit;

4. This contact must result into criminal actions that can be proven in a court of law.

In theory the most difficult part is the beginning: to win someone's confidence so he or she will do criminal business with the undercover officer. It is clear that things would be a lot easier if a contact between the suspect and the undercover officer already existed at the start of an undercover operation. Therefore we can distinguish two categories of cases:

1. cases in which a (criminal) contact already existed before the undercover operations actually started;

2. cases in which there was no such contact.

From these two categories we have to distinguish the (what we will simply call) international cases, the cases in which undercover activities in the Netherlands take place on the request of a foreign police department. These cases appeared to have special problems, which we will explain later on.

**Cases with no Prior Contact**

There are several problems for an undercover officer who must make contact with the target. Often it is not possible or sensible to approach the suspect directly (a so-called *cold approach*), for instance, lest the suspect is supposedly very violent or only does business with people he or she knows well. Therefore, somebody close to the person, someone whom the police thinks can be approached relatively easy, will be chosen as the target of the undercover officer. However, a lot of things can go wrong.

In case #1 for instance, the main suspect was the central figure of a small gang in one of Holland's major cities. The members of the gang were allegedly involved in drug trafficking, fraud and violence. During the investigation the use of what we call the more traditional investigative methods, like wiretapping and observation, failed because the suspects were very careful on the phone and police officers were easily spotted in the neighbourhood where the suspects were living. It is one of those places where everybody knows everybody. Also because there was political pressure to put an end to the criminal activities of this gang, the police decided to start undercover activities against the main suspect. This man was a violent man. (He was arrested several times for beating up somebody.) Therefore, the police decided to try to make contact with a friend who was close to the gang. He was considered a good target, because he frequently visited the same café. Several undercover officers in different groups visited this place dozens of times and in the end one of them succeeded in making contact with this friend. When the conversations were brought round to the main suspect, this friend became detached. After a while the undercover officers found out that this friend was no longer a friend of the main suspect. He was no longer part of the gang and he had differences of opinion with the main suspect. Considering the suspect's violent reputation it was understandable that the friend was not very keen on introducing the undercover officers to him. Finally, the operation was called off. The main suspect was arrested and convicted due to the use of more traditional police tactics.

Case #2 was a relative success, but dealt with common thugs. The major problem in this case was that one of the four suspects got himself arrested all the time for the use of violence against people or small time drug-dealing, while the police were trying to prove with undercover activities that he was a major drug dealer. The fact that the suspect was in police custody all the time did not help.

As we said before, this was a group of several suspects. Two were frequent visitors of a specific bar. They were quite violent in this small town and harassed people who were having a night out. An undercover officer visited the bar regularly and succeeded in making contact with the two frequent visitors. He managed to buy 100-gr. cocaine on two different occasions. He also tried to buy a kilo of cocaine but the police called off this deal, because they were afraid the deal would end up in a 'rip deal'. Shortly after the failed attempt to buy one kilo of cocaine, one of the suspects was arrested by uniformed police officers, suspected of committing a violent crime and the possession of drugs and a side arm. The undercover operation was cancelled. Two of the suspects were sentenced to 18 months imprisonment for several crimes, including the selling of drugs to the undercover police officers.

Case #3 is quite typical. The police carried out an undercover operation against two brothers, who had a violent reputation. The undercover police officer planned to make contact with a friend of the brothers, but they were unable to find him. After a while it turned out that this friend and one of the brothers were having a quarrel and the friend was in hiding. Then the police carried out 'Plan B' and tried to make contact with one of the brothers, but the first undercover officer and the brother could not get along, so a second undercover officer was introduced. He made contact with the brother. They met frequently, but the brother evidently was not interested in doing criminal business with the undercover officer. After a year the operation was cancelled because of lack of results.

In case #4 the undercover police officers also failed to get the main suspect to trust them.

In case #5 the police was investigating a group of computer robbers. The plan was to make contact with one of the main suspects of this group in a bar he supposedly frequented, but he never showed up. In the meantime, by means of wiretapping, the identity of the fence of the group was disclosed. The police found out that this fence was putting ads in the paper, in which he offered computers for sale. An undercover officer reflected on one of these ads, bought one computer and then ordered a lot. On the day of the delivery police raided the fence's house and everybody was arrested. The police managed to relate several of these computers to reported robberies and the members of the group were convicted.

In case #6 the undercover officers could not find the suspect in the bars he was supposed to be in. In case #7 they did not find the suspect on a campground. They thought the suspect would be there because his girlfriend and her family were there, but the suspect and the girl had broken up. The police did stumble into a criminal contact with the girl's father though. He happened to be a suspect in a totally different criminal investigation (see case #14).

In case #8 the suspect disappeared before the undercover operation started. Word has it that he had a heart attack and spent some time in a hospital abroad.

In case #9 the police worked on a sting operation for several years to arrest a family that was suspected of drug trafficking. The undercover police officers did manage to get involved in the criminal business of a close friend to the family. But the best they did with the members of the family was waving once at the oldest brother from a distance. In the end the group was arrested. Evidence was gathered by the use of common police tactics: one member of the group was caught red-handed; the police questioned him; and; he started talking and on the basis of this information wiretapped phone conversations could be analysed. The main figure of the group (the oldest brother of the family) was sentenced to 9 years imprisonment.

The last case we mention here is case #10. We did not thoroughly research this case because it was ongoing at the time of our research, but from the reports in the paper we know that it is concerned with a major undercover operation that lasted several years, involving an Israeli undercover officer, and that it was a success. A group of drug traffickers was arrested and a lot of illegal drugs were confiscated.

To conclude: in eight cases (case #1, #3, #5, #6, #7, #8, #9) the undercover officers failed to make contact with the initial suspects, while in one case (case #4) the police did make contact, but failed to turn this into a criminal contact. In case #4 the police made a criminal contact with two of several suspects and in case #5 they changed the operation towards a person who was easy to get in touch with. In case #7 they only managed to get in touch with the father of the former girlfriend of the main suspect, who was not a very clever man and offered drugs to the undercover officer. The only successful case is #10, which was an investigation of several years.

## Cases with a Prior Contact

We now turn to some of the more successful undercover operations. What we will see is that it is more likely that an undercover operation will come to a successful conclusion in cases in which contact between the co-operating civilian and the suspect already exists, than in the cases described before, in which there were no already existing contacts.

For instance, in case #11 a police informer stated to the police that he was offered confidential police information. This information was offered to him by an apparently corrupt police officer. The police and the public prosecutor in charge of the investigation decided that the informer should either introduce a third party to the corrupt police officer who would buy the information or buy the information himself. Because of the fact that the suspect was a police officer, capable of checking the identity of any third party, the risks of the first scenario were considered too big, and the police decided that the buy and bust operation would be carried out by the informer himself. The informer made an appointment with the suspect and pretended he was willing and able to buy the information. The informer met with the suspect, bringing a couple of thousand guilders and carrying a listening device, so that the police were able to listen in to the conversation and to monitor the actions of the informer. Immediately after the deal was closed, the suspect was arrested. He confessed to the selling of confidential police information to criminals. He was sentenced by the district court to two years of imprisonment.

Now, this was a successful operation, but the fact that the civilian co-operating with the police already is in touch with the suspect is obviously not a guarantee for success. In case #12 the participation of a civilian in a large scale drug trafficking case turned out to be a failure, because of the fact that in the course of the operation the civilian got into an argument with the suspect and their contact was broken off. In case #13 the main suspect approached a police informer. The latter should help with the trafficking of drugs. But before the informer could participate the main suspect suffered a heart attack and the undercover operation was cancelled.

As we stated before, a strategy used by the undercover police team is not to seek contact with the suspect himself, but to get acquainted with a friend or somebody else close to the suspect. The case which was in our opinion the most successful of those we studied, considering the amount and the quality of the criminal information which was retrieved during the operation, was case #14. This case is a sequel to another investigation, in which the police approached the father of the (former) girlfriend of the suspect. (See #7.) During the investigation it appeared to the police that the father himself was involved in drug trafficking. The father apparently liked and trusted the undercover police officer and soon he started talking about his involvement in the trafficking of cocaine. The undercover operation continued, now focusing on the suspected criminal behaviour of the father. The father introduced the undercover police officer to two people. A meeting between these people and the undercover police officers was videotaped.

This videotape, on which the suspects appear talking about the importation into the Netherlands of hundreds of kilos of cocaine, was shown in court, but was excluded as evidence on the basis that at the relevant time there was no provision in the law, allowing police investigators to videotape the suspect's actions for the purpose of using the tape as evidence in court. Such legal basis is required, since videotaping the suspect and using the videotape as evidence in court is considered a serious breach of a person's right to a private life. Such interference on a person's private life can only be made "in accordance with the law", as the European Court of Human Rights put it.

The court *did* use the written and verbal statements of the undercover police officers as evidence. The suspects were convicted by both the district court and the Court of Appeal for the participation in a criminal organisation, the preparation of the importation of a large amount of cocaine as well as for the actual importation of a couple of kilos of cocaine into the Netherlands. They were sentenced to up to seven years of imprisonment. The father was sentenced to two years and nine months of imprisonment. His case is admitted to the Dutch Supreme Court and has to be decided on.

### International Co-operation

As we mentioned earlier, undercover operations in the Netherlands carried out on behalf of the authorities of another state for the purpose of providing legal assistance to that state constitute special problems. Most of these problems result from the fact that it is not the Dutch police and public prosecutor's own decision to carry out the undercover operation. They act on behalf of the foreign authorities, and for the most part they have to go along with the strategy chosen by these foreign authorities. This means for example that the Dutch undercover police team has to work with a participating foreign civilian, who they consider not to be very reliable and solid. If this were a fully Dutch case they would have chosen not to work with this particular person (#15).

Another problem which was pointed out to us was the fact that the foreign authorities sometimes do not provide the Dutch police and the Dutch public prosecutor with enough information on the criminal investigation and the goals and objectives of the operation to be carried on Dutch territory. The police officer and public prosecutor we interviewed told us that it is hard to give your full co-operation when you do not have all the information on the goals of the operation and of the criminal investigation. In this case the Dutch public prosecutor received the impression that he was co-operating in a fishing expedition instead of in a systematic criminal investigation with pre-set fixed goals. The lack of information in this case led to a (fortunately, now solved) dispute between the Dutch and the foreign authorities involved and to the premature ending of the operation (#16). Although the lack of information was a problem in only one of the cases we studied, there is reason to believe that this is a more generally experienced problem when it comes to requests for legal assistance from foreign countries. Since an undercover operation in the Netherlands is considered to be a very special investigative method which should not be used easily, the problem of the lack of information in these kinds of cases is a major problem.

## Concluding Remarks

The results of the study on the effectiveness of undercover policing seem a bit disappointing, looking at the few cases in which a substantial amount of relevant information was gathered as a result of the undercover operation and in which the goals which were set in advance were fully reached. The statement of one of the public prosecutors we interviewed can explain these disappointing results. To the question why a particular case had failed, he answered: *"The reason of failure was exactly the same as the reason for starting the undercover operation*: the case was very complex and the suspect acted like a professional criminal."

Although they do not usually involve the biggest criminals, the cases are often complicated – involving organised drug crime on a (inter)national level – and traditional investigative methods sometimes have been applied in vain. Consequently, in these cases the probability of failure is very high, right from the beginning of the undercover operation.

As we have seen, the chances on a successful completion of the case are bigger when contact between the undercover police officer or co-operating witness and the suspect already exists. The hard part of the undercover operation is to make contact with the suspect and to enter into criminal business with the suspect.

In case these obstacles are already overcome, for example in the case of the co-operating civilian who bought confidential police information from a corrupt police officer, success still is not guaranteed, because of the fact that you are dealing with people, or, to be more specific, people who are suspected to be criminals. Their behaviour and actions just cannot be predicted.

Our final conclusion: undercover operations can be fruitful where traditional investigative methods have failed. However, success is not guaranteed, because of the nature of both the cases involved and the method itself. When there is no prior contact within the criminal group, undercover operations are probably not the best means to turn to when a quick solution is needed. Without prior contact patience is needed. Given enough time, an undercover operation can be successful.

# Speech as a Biometric: separating the Goats from the Sheep?

*A.P.A. Broeders*

### Introduction

Probably the earliest recorded example of speaker identification in a forensic context occurs in the Bible. A brief reminder of the case may be in order here. Jacob, the son of Isaac and Rebecca, has found his elder brother Esau prepared to part with his birthright in exchange for a plate of lintel soup. One day, Rebecca tells Jacob, who is her favourite son, that Isaac, who feels that his end is drawing near, is about to give *his* favourite and firstborn son Esau his blessing. Since Esau has sold his birthright to him, Jacob, aided and abetted by Rebecca, decides to trick his father Isaac into giving him the blessing instead of Esau. Now, while the Bible tells us that Isaac is old and that his eyes are dim, it does not report any hearing loss on the part of Isaac. In fact, when Jacob goes up to his father and calls out to him, "My father". Isaac, who is of course expecting to hear Esau rather than Jacob, is clearly puzzled. "Here am I; who art thou, my son?", is Isaac's answer. When Jacob responds with "I am Esau thy firstborn", his answer apparently does little to dispel Isaac's suspicion, because he answers: "Come near, I pray thee, that I may feel thee, my son, whether thou be my very son Esau or not". And when Jacob steps forward so that Isaac can feel him, Isaac says: "The voice is Jacob's voice, but the hands are the hands of Esau", at which point Isaac makes the fatal mistake of putting more trust in his sense of touch than in his sense of hearing. Or, as it says in Genesis 25:23: "And he discerned him not, because his hands were hairy, as his brother Esau's hands: so he blessed him. And he said, Art thou my very son Esau? And he said, I am." What Isaac did not know of course – but the reader of Genesis does – is that, on the advice of his mother Rebecca, prior to presenting himself to his father, Jacob has covered his hands and neck with the skin of a lamb and has even stooped to wearing his brother's clothes.

Although the relevance of this story to the theme of the present conference, the Second World Conference on New Trends in Criminal Investigation and Evidence, may not be immediately obvious, a modest attempt at exegesis may reveal that there are nevertheless a number of interesting lessons to be learnt for anyone involved in this particular sphere of human endeavour.

The first point to note is that Isaac does quite well in the speaker identification department, in spite of the fact that Esau and Jacob are twins. Perhaps we should not stretch the exegesis at this point because their very different physical build makes it unclear whether or not we are meant to think of them as identical twins. What it does suggest is that even close relatives of the same sex can be distinguished by the sound of their voices.

The second point is that they are of course both of them familiar speakers to their father Isaac. There is indeed some support for the notion that humans are better at recognising familiar speakers than unfamiliar speakers. What is more, there is experimental evidence now to suggest that not only humans but even baboons are capable of recognising individual members of their clan and distinguishing them from non-members.[1]

A final point worth noting is that if Isaac is taken in by the second biometric measure he decides to use, the skin test, it is probably primarily because, being blind, he is unable to efficiently guard against foul play and not because the test is intrinsically unreliable.

### Speaker Recognition, Speaker Identification and Speaker Verification

The term 'speaker recognition' is generally used as a cover term for the wide variety of procedures in which people are differentiated on the basis of the sound of their voices. 'Speaker identification' and 'speaker verification' are normally used to refer to two distinct subsets of these types of tasks. In the majority of practical forensic applications, the question that needs to be answered is whether or not the suspect is the person who made a particular recorded telephone call. This is in fact a speaker verification task, involving a comparison of the speech of the suspect with the recorded speech of the anonymous speaker making the questioned call. In the speaker verification task it is customary to set a threshold for the degree of similarity beyond which the speaker of a test utterance is accepted as the target speaker.

In the forensic context, the speaker verification task may be used as evidence for or against the involvement of the suspect in the commission of a crime, and since the relation between the speaker and the crime is typically beyond question, it may be used as evidence for and against the suspect's guilt. There is however, certainly in an investigative as opposed to an evidential context, a second application of speaker recognition techniques, where the task is to establish whether a particular anonymous speech sample is produced by any one of a number of speakers. This amounts to a speaker identification task, involving $N$ comparisons of the anonymous sample with each of those of the $N$ relevant known speakers. In this type of application, the performance of a system can be measured in terms of the number of times the speaker of a test utterance comes up with the smallest distance measure – or the highest similarity score – to the target speaker.

Alternatively, though, performance may also be measured in terms of the number of times a target speaker is listed within the top 10 or top 50 most similar speakers. This performance measure clearly resembles the type of database search that is routinely undertaken for fingerprints, handwriting

---

[1] Cheney & Seyfarth (1999).

analysis or firearms analysis and which results in a ranking of potential matches in descending order of similarity to the test sample.

## Speaker Recognition in the Forensic Context

The performance of automatic speaker recognition systems, as of other biometric devices, is often expressed in terms of the system's Equal Error Rate (EER), *i.e.*, the performance level where false acceptance and false rejection figures are equal. For any practical application, this is not a terribly meaningful measure, since the severity of the two types of error is not in practice of the same magnitude. In a banking application we might be particularly highly motivated to avoid false rejection of our customers even if this means a modest loss of capital through cash withdrawals by falsely accepted non-clients. In the forensic context, there is traditionally a firm bias against the conviction of even a single innocent suspect. False acceptance should therefore be avoided at all costs, which in practice can only be achieved by raising the number of false rejects, thus allowing guilty suspects to go free.

## Recent Developments in the Interpretation of Forensic Evidence

The discussion of the value of speaker identification evidence, and indeed of other types of forensic evidence has recently been placed in a somewhat different perspective. Although the arguments can be traced back at least a 100 years,[2] the discussion of the role of the forensic expert has clearly gained fresh impetus in the last decade under the influence of a number of different developments. One of these has been the increasing prominence of DNA evidence and of the conceptual framework associated with it.

In countries with what is traditionally described as an adversarial criminal law system like the US and the UK, questions surrounding the admissibility of forensic evidence have clearly accelerated the discussion.[3] The use of expert scientific testimony in personal injury litigation in the US has come under attack in Huber's *Galileo's Revenge: Junk Science in the Courtroom* (1991) and the role of expert evidence in general in influential books by Robertson & Vigneaux (1995) and Foster & Huber (1997). Finally, following a series of highly publicised miscarriages of justice in which forensic expertise sometimes played a crucial role, even traditionally firmly established forensic disciplines like fingerprint identification have come under severe attack, in the sense that their scientific status has been called into question.[4] While there are clearly fundamental differences in the way expert evidence is treated in inquisitorial as

---

[2] Champod, Taroni & Margot (1999).
[3] *Daubert* v. *Merrell Dow Pharmaceuticals Inc.* (1993), *US* v. *Starzecpyzel* (1995), *Kuhmo Tire Inc.* v. *Carmichael* (1999).
[4] Saks (1998).

opposed to adversarial criminal law systems,[5] the effects of these developments are also beginning to make themselves felt in the predominantly inquisitorial, continental European countries, if only under the influence of the decisions of the European Court of Human Rights.

## The Use of 'Transposed Conditionals'

Even in fields where the degree of quantification of the frequency of the relevant characteristics is not even remotely comparable to that in DNA evidence, as in handwriting analysis, toolmark, fibre or firearms analysis, the conceptual framework that is associated with this type of evidence is rapidly gaining ground. One of its key features relates to the type of statement the expert is permitted to make. Whereas forensic experts have traditionally been prepared, and indeed frequently been encouraged by judges, to make statements about the probability of the prosecution hypothesis given the evidence, the use of such transposed conditionals has been severely criticised as logically incorrect.[6] The increasing awareness among forensic experts of the problem posed by transposed conditionals has led to attempts to express the evidential value of their forensic expertise in different terms.[7]

A central notion here is that of the Likelihood Ratio (LR). The LR may be looked upon as a measure of the strength of the forensic evidence, which is independent of the prior probability of the prosecution hypothesis.[8] It is defined as the ratio between the probability of the evidence given the hypothesis that the suspect is the perpetrator and the probability of the evidence under the hypothesis that perpetrator is somebody other than the suspect. If the LR is greater than one, it supports the prosecution hypothesis; if it is smaller than one it weakens the prosecution hypothesis. In this type of framework, frequently referred to as Bayesian (after the 18th-century Scottish minister and mathematician Thomas Bayes who developed the theorem), expert opinion is therefore not expressed in terms of a statement about the probability of the hypothesis that the suspect did or did not leave the mark, write the letter or fire the gun. Instead, the expert states the probability of the evidence arising under two or more rival hypotheses: one that the suspect did produce the utterance or leave the stain, the other hypothesis being that the utterance was made or the stain left by somebody other than the suspect. It is worth noting that a high LR is not in itself necessarily very damaging for the suspect. If the prior probability of the suspect being the perpetrator is very low, this may largely cancel out the effect of the forensic evidence.

---

[5] Van Kampen (1998), Broeders (1999b).
[6] Evett (1995).
[7] Evett (1991), Aitken (1995), Taroni & Aitken (1999).
[8] Aitken (1995), Evett (1995), Royall (1997).

There is an interesting parallel here in the use of large scale screening tests for certain medical conditions. A positive result on an HIV-test is not itself meaningful, even if we know the false alarm rate of the test is low, *i.e.*, even if we know the LR of the test is high. The reason is that even a test which is both highly sensitive in the sense that it will tend to detect a very high percentage of those infected, and highly specific in the sense that it will indicate a very low percentage of infection among those who are not infected, will generate far more false alarms than true positives if the base rate or prevalence of the particular condition in the relevant population is extremely low, as for HIV-infection or, to a lesser extent, breast cancer. In more formal terms, the predictive value of a test crucially depends on the prior probability of the hypothesis being tested. So in this sense a LR which is greater than 1 says no more about the suspect's involvement than a positive result in a health test. In both cases we need to know the prior probability of the hypothesis being correct in order to make a meaningful estimate of the actual probability of either guilt or infection?

What is interesting in this context is that whereas both automatic speaker verification and identification techniques tended to use thresholds and thus produce binary yes/no decisions, some of the more recent approaches using Gaussian mixture models, like those proposed by Meuwly *et al.* (1998), Koolwaaij & Boves (1999) and Marescal (1999), use LRs, which, in theory anyway, comfortably meet the type of norm set by the Bayesian framework.[9]

## Speech: a Behavioural Biometric

Speech has some powerful things going for it as a biometric. In most applications its user acceptance is probably vastly superior to that of other biometrics such as fingerprints and to a lesser extent hand, body or iris scans. People are accustomed to being recognised by their voices. Speech is not difficult to elicit, it is easy to record and many types of disguise are easy to detect, even in automatic systems. And last but not least, people's linguistic behaviour is unique and this uniqueness manifests itself most obviously in people's speech. Although speakers may sound very similar to each other, given enough material, they will invariably be able to be distinguished from each other, even if only by those who know them very well. As I indicated earlier, there is now evidence that this may even apply to baboons.

What makes speech decidedly less attractive as a biometric is its behavioural dimension, which it shares with handwriting. It means that the physical nature of speech may vary importantly with the communicative context in which it is used. It also means that in certain circumstances speakers may deliberately or also involuntarily produce speech, which is unrepresentative of their usual repertoire. Boves (1998) even goes so far as to

---

[9] Champod & Meuwly (1998).

say that, precisely because speech is a behavioural biometric, near error-free performance is a theoretical impossibility.

An even more fundamental problem concerns the inherent temporal variability of speech. This has enormous implications for its use in human identification. As Doddington puts it,[10] the challenge in speaker recognition is *variance*, not similarity. In physical terms, speech may be thought of as a sequence of air pressure variations created by the organs of speech which are propagated in all directions and may be picked up by the ear of a listener. The signal that serves as input for an automatic speaker recognition system is a highly complex and continuously varying vibration. The crucial question in speaker recognition is where in this complex, continually varying signal the speaker-specific information may be found.

## The State-of-the-Art in Automatic Speaker Verification

The answer to the question posed above is that, so far, we do not really know. The performance of existing automatic speaker identification algorithms may be quite high in laboratory conditions, in real-world applications, especially in a forensic context, it is still a long way removed from what would be desirable. With EERs of 5% to 1%, it is substantially below the theoretical error rates that can be obtained with four of five digit PIN codes.[11] Prominent observers of the scene[12] believe that in order for the performance of automatic speaker recognition techniques to improve significantly a better understanding of the speaker-specific element in the speech signal will be necessary. In recent years, what progress has been made, has been the result of an increasingly more effective exploitation of the information contained in the parameters extracted from the speech signal. The more fundamental type of research into what parameters truly capture speaker-specific information in the signal has received comparatively little attention, partly because the research is largely funded by application-oriented organisations and industries.

One of the best indications of the present performance of the various automatic speaker recognition techniques is provided within the framework of the American National Institute of Standards and Technology (NIST).[13] It provides regular evaluations to encourage research and develop state-of-the-art systems in core technology areas such as speaker recognition. NIST runs a series of annual tests based on a common speech corpus of American English speakers. An excellent survey of the various State-of-the-Art speaker recognition methods and techniques as well as a brief description of the history of forensic speaker identification is provided by Meuwly (2000).

---

[10] 1998: 61.
[11] Boves (1998).
[12] Boves (1998), Doddington (1998), Meuwly (1999).
[13] Przybocki & Martin (1998).

**Animal Farm**

The world of automatic speaker recognition research is increasingly dominated by members of the animal kingdom. Essentially, what this reflects is the existence of a considerable lack of homogeneity in the performance of speakers in a particular population. In other words, it would appear that in any population a disproportionate number of errors is accounted for by a relatively small number of speakers.

In a statistical analysis of the 1998 NIST Speaker Recognition Evaluation, Doddington *et al.* (1998) distinguish four types of animal: sheep, goats, lambs and wolves. Sheep are the default speakers for whom the system performs well. Goats are those speakers who are particularly difficult to identify; speakers with goatlike features would cause major problems in entry control systems or banking because they would be likely to be erroneously rejected. In this sense then, it would be essential to separate the goats from the sheep. But goats are not the only problem animals. Lambs and wolves collectively are responsible for a disproportionate amount of false alarms, albeit in different capacities. Lambs are those speakers who are particularly easy to imitate, in the sense that another speaker's speech may be falsely accepted as theirs.

Finally, wolves are speakers who are particularly likely to be accepted as other speakers. Doddington *et al.* (1998) observe that if lambs and wolves can be identified and recruited to defeat speaker recognition systems, this would obviously pose a real threat to the viability of the system as such. At the same time though it is still too early to tell whether the observed effects are in fact speaker-based or whether they are partly or wholly the result of the failure of present speaker recognition techniques to adequately capture the speaker-specific information in the signal and are therefore ultimately due to non speaker-based variables. There is however, apart from anecdotal, also independent experimental evidence that some voices may indeed be more difficult to remember and recognise than others.[14]

**Successful Applications of Automatic Speaker Recognition Techniques**

Boves (1998) points out that successful applications seem to share a number of key features:
- false accept and false reject risks are small to moderate but never high;
- multi-session enrolment is no problem;
- the method is combined with other types of protection.

In the forensic context, probably the most frequently used application is home detention. In view of recent reports that the alternative localisation method, the use of ankle-band transmitters has caused major problems due to the failure of the transmitters to respond in urban and hi-rise environments

---

[14] Yarmey (1991); Orchard & Yarmey (1995).

causing prisoners to be placed back in prison detention – thereby turning the 'outmates' into inmates again – this particular application may be a serious alternative

### Speaker Identification in the Forensic Context: the Present

In some countries forensic speaker identification is still somewhat controversial. This is no doubt partly due to the exaggerated claims made by those who were once responsible for the introduction of the so-called voiceprint technique, which some decades ago enjoyed considerable prestige in parts of the US and some other countries. A voiceprint is essentially a spectrographic representation of a speech signal. From a physical point of view, a speech signal is a highly time-variant complex vibration. A spectrogram is a time by frequency by intensity plot of the speech signal showing the relative intensity of the frequency components making up this complex vibration with time. The voice print technique essentially amounts to a visual comparison of spectrograms of linguistically identical utterances to determine whether they originated from a single speaker.

Spectrograms may provide forensically interesting information about speech signals but there is little justification for the use of the term voiceprint, suggesting as it does that there is an important parallel between the voiceprint and the fingerprint and thereby implying that the status of voiceprint evidence is somehow comparable to that of fingerprint evidence. Despite the publication of a critical review of the use of sound spectrograms for the purposes of forensic speaker identification carried out by a National Research Council committee of the American National Academy of Sciences in 1979,[15] testimony based on modified forms of the voiceprint technique as practised by members of the Voice Identification and Acoustic Analysis Subcommittee (VIAAS) of the International Association for Identification (IAI) and others continues to be admitted as evidence.

Saks (1998) reports that by his last count it is admissible in six states, excluded in eight, admissible in four federal courts and excluded in one. In addition to VIAAS, whose membership is predominantly American and is open only to those who are certified IAI members, there are currently two more international organisations whose members are in one way or another involved in forensic speaker identification. One is the International Association for Forensic Phonetics (IAFP), which was formally established in 1991 with the aim of providing a forum for those working in the field of forensic phonetics as well as ensuring professional standards and good practice in this area. Its membership is predominantly European.

Also in Europe, the Working Group for Forensic Speech and Audio Analysis had its inaugural meeting in Voorburg, the Netherlands in July 1998

---

[15] Bolt *et al.* (1979).

and has since met in June 1999 in Madrid, Spain. It forms part of the European Network of Forensic Science Institutes (ENFSI), which was founded in 1991, currently has 40 member laboratories from 25 countries and has been the driving force behind the establishment of Working Groups for the various forensic disciplines. The Forensic Speech and Audio Analysis Working Group's membership includes experts from some 16 European countries, as well as Turkey. One of the first priorities the Working Group has set itself is to collect information about the various procedures that are used in the member laboratories.

In addition to voiceprint evidence, forensic speaker identification in general has also come in for considerable criticism not only in the survey by Saks (1998), which I had occasion to refer to earlier, but also from the Groupe Francophone de la Communication Parlée of the Société Française d'Acoustique (SFA), a group of French speech scientists, most of them with an engineering background, who are active in the field of speech technology. In response to a recent, highly publicised court case in France, the group is currently circulating a petition on the Internet demanding that voice expertise is no longer used by the legal system until such time as it is scientifically validated.[16] It has earlier gone on record as arguing that it is unethical for anyone to be active in the field of forensic speaker identification without first demonstrating his or her competence in the field.[17] Both Braun & Künzel (1998) and earlier Broeders (1991) have argued that while there is a real concern that voice evidence is presented in an irresponsible and incompetent manner, the charge of unethical conduct is unfounded and the call for speech experts to dissociate themselves from forensic examinations is will ultimately only result in an increased danger that phonetically uninformed testimony will go unchallenged. Essential of course is that those who are involved in deciding issues of guilt, *i.e.*, judges and juries are made aware of the limitations of the methodology employed.

## Conclusion

As a behavioural biometric, speaker verification is not in the best of positions to compete with non-behavioural, time-invariant biometrics like fingerprints, hand geometry and iris scans. In spite of a gradual improvement in performance under laboratory conditions,[18] there is a clear need for a more fundamental approach to research in this area to identify parameters, which will more accurately capture the speaker-specific information in the signal. Failing this, automatic speaker identification is unlikely to make a serious impact as a commercially viable identification technique. There is, however,

---

[16] GFCP (1999).
[17] GFCP (1991).
[18] Przybocki & Martin (1998).

one distinct advantage to speaker verification over other biometrics, which is its suitability for identification over telephone lines. Unfortunately, this advantage in practice brings its own drawback in that existing speaker recognition algorithms are extremely sensitive to transmission conditions, including the use of different handsets, microphones, the presence of noise and the like.

Although the use of LRs lends an initial attraction to the applicability of automatic speaker verification in a forensic context, there is as yet insufficient knowledge of the external validity of the results of the types of technique proposed by Marescal (1999), Meuwly (1999) and Koolwaaij & Boves (1999) for these to be assigned anything but limited evidential value. Alternatively, automatic speaker identification techniques may be used profitably for investigative purposes, as in large-scale telephone tapping operations.[19] What is clear is that the need for forensic phoneticians, speech scientists and engineers working in automatic speaker recognition to collaborate on common research projects is today as great as it was four years ago.[20]

Meanwhile, many practising forensic experts will continue to rely on the largely subjective methods they have been using in the last decade, combining the results of phonetic-linguistic analyses with measurements of electro-acoustic parameters.[21] As I have argued elsewhere,[22] the verbal probability scales used by forensic experts in speech and handwriting analysis effectively amount to subjective categorical judgements. Whether they are subjective or objective is far less important than whether they are correct. There is however, only one way to even begin to find out whether they are correct and that is by the introduction of a system of validation. The frequently voiced excuse that realistic validation exercises are hard to design cannot convincingly continue to be used in justification of their absence.

## References

**Aitken, C.G.G.** (1995), *Statistics and the Evaluation of Evidence for Forensic Scientists*, Wiley: Chichester.
**Bouten, J.S. & Broeders, A.P.A.** (1999), 'Text-Independent Forensic Speaker Identification Using Telephone Speech', in: *Proceedings of the XIVth International Congress of Phonetic Sciences*, San Francisco, pp. 1377-1379.
**Boves, L.** (1998), 'Commercial Applications of Speaker Verification: Overview and Critical Success Factors', in: *Proceedings of RLA2C Workshop on Speaker Recognition and its Commercial and Forensic Applications*, Avignon, pp. 150-159.
**Braun, A.** (1998), 'Voice Analysis', report for the 12th Triennial Interpol Conference on Forensic Sciences, Internal report Interpol: Lyon.

---

[19] Bouten & Broeders (1999).
[20] Broeders (1995).
[21] Braun (1998).
[22] Broeders (1999a).

**Braun, A. & Künzel, H.J.** (1998), 'Is Forensic Speaker Identification Unethical – Or Can It Be Unethical Not to Do It?', in: *Proceedings of RLA2C Workshop on Speaker Recognition and its Commercial and Forensic Applications*, Avignon, pp. 145-148.

**Broeders, A.P.A.** (1991), 'Great Debate on...', in: *Nesca – The ESCA Newsletter*, No. 4, pp. 50-51.

**Broeders, A.P.A.** (1995), 'The Role of Automatic Speaker Recognition Techniques in Forensic Investigations', in: *Proceedings of the XIIIth International Congress of Phonetic Sciences*, Stockholm, Vol. 3, pp. 154-161.

**Broeders, A.P.A.** (1999a), 'Some Observations on the Use of Probability Scales in Forensic Identification, in: *Forensic Linguistics* 6(2), pp. 228-241.

**Broeders, A.P.A.** (1999b), 'The Role of the Forensic Expert in the Inquisitorial System', paper presented as part of the 'Dublin Trial' at the International Congress on Psychology and Law, July 1999, Dublin.

**Champod, C. & Meuwly, D.** (1998), 'The Inference of Identity in forensic Speaker Recognition', in: *Proceedings of RLA2C Workshop on Speaker Recognition and its Commercial and Forensic Applications*, Avignon, pp. 125-166.

**Champod, C., Taroni, F & Margot, P.-A.** (1999), 'The Dreyfus Case – an Early Debate on Experts' Conclusions', in: *International Journal of Forensic Document Examiners* 5, pp. 446-459.

**Cheney, D.L. & Seyfarth, R.M.** (1999), 'Recognition of Other Individuals' Social Relationships by Female Baboons', in: *Animal Behavior* 58 (1), pp. 67-76.

***Daubert* v. *Merrell Dow Pharmaceuticals Inc.*** (113 S.Ct. 2786 1993).

**Doddington, G.R.** (1998), 'Speaker Recognition Evaluation Methodology: An Overview and Perspective', in: *Proceedings of RLA2C Workshop on Speaker Recognition and its Commercial and Forensic Applications*, Avignon, pp. 60-66.

**Doddington, G.R. et al.** (1998), 'Sheep, Goats, Lambs and Wolves: A Statistical Analysis of Speaker Performance in the NIST 1998 Speaker Recognition Evaluation', in: *ICSLP*, pp. 608-611.

**Evett, I.W.** (1991), 'Interpretation: A Personal Odyssey', in: Aitken, C.G.G. & D.A. Stoney, *The Use of Statistics in Forensic Science*, Ellis Horwood: New York.

**Evett, I.W.** (1995), 'Avoiding the Transposed Conditional', in: *Science & Justice* 35(2), pp. 127-131.

**Foster, K.R. & Huber, P.W.** (1997), *Judging Science: Scientific Knowledge and the Federal Courts*, MIT Press: Cambridge MA.

**GFCP** (1991), 'About the Ethics of Speaker Identification', in: *Proceedings of the XIIth International Congress of Phonetic Sciences*, Aix-en-Provence, Vol. 1, p. 397.

**GFCP** (1999), 'Petition pour l'Arrêt des Expertises Vocales (sans Validations Scientifiques)', http://www.lapetition.com.

**Huber, P.W.** (1991), *Galileo's Revenge: Junk Science in the Courtroom*, Basic Books: New York.

**Kampen, P.T.C. van** (1998), *Expert Evidence Compared*, Intersentia: Antwerp and Groningen.

***Kuhmo Tire Inc.* v. *Carmichael*** (119 S.Ct. 1167 1999).

**Koolwaaij, J. & Boves, L.** (1999), 'On Decision Making in Forensic Casework', in: *Forensic Linguistics* 6(2), pp. 242-264.

**Marescal, F.** (1999), 'The Forensic Speaker Recognition Method Used in the French Gendarmerie', internal publication, IRCGN: Paris.

**Meuwly, D. et al.** (1998), 'Forensic Speaker Recognition Using Gaussian Mixture Models and a Bayesian Framework', in: *Proceedings of the 8th COST Workshop on Speaker Identification by Man and Machine: Directions for Future Applications*, Ankara, pp. 52-55.

**Meuwly, D.** (2000), *Reconnaissance des Locuteurs en Sciences Forensiques: l'Apport d'une Approche Automatique*, doctoral dissertation, University of Lausanne.

**Orchard, T.L. & Yarmey, A.D.** (1995), 'The Effects of Whispers, Voice-Sample Durations and Voice Distinctiveness on Criminal Speaker Identification', in: *Applied Cognitive Psychology* Vol. 9, pp. 249-260.

**Przybocki, M. & Martin, A.F.** (1998), 'NIST Speaker Recognition Evaluations', in: *Proceedings of LREC*, Granada, pp. 331-335.

**Robertson, B. & Vigneaux, G.A.** (1995), *Interpreting Evidence: Evaluating Forensic Science in the Courtroom*, Wiley: Chichester.

93

A.P.A. Broeders

**Royall, R.M.** (1997), *Statistical Evidence: A Likelihood Paradigm*, Chapman Hall: London.
**Saks, M.J.** (1998), 'Merlin and Solomon: Lessons from the Law's Formative Encounters with Forensic Identification Science', in: *Hastings Law Journal* 49(4), pp. 1069-1141.
**Taroni, F. & Aitken, C.G.G.** (1998), 'Probabilistic Reasoning in the Law (I): Assessment of Probabilities and Explanations of the Value of DNA Evidence', in: *Science & Justice* 38(3), pp. 79-189.
*US* v. *Starzecpyzel* (880 *F.Supp.* 1027; *S.D.N.Y.* 1995).
**Yarmey, A.D.** (1991), 'Descriptions of Distinctive and Non-Distinctive Voices over Time', in: *Journal of the Forensic Science Society* 31, pp. 412-428.

# The Relationship between International Law and Criminal Procedure – a UK Perspective

*A.N. Brown*

## Introduction

That transnational crime is of increasing importance has not been a novel proposition for over a century. As long ago as 1874, Sir Edward Clarke was able to write, in his *Treatise upon the Law of Extradition* that "the complexity of business transactions, the vast extension of credit, the general use of paper money of various kinds, all make it easy for a modern criminal to commit a fraud which may cause far more widespread misery than a similar act could formerly have produced, and to insure at least a few hours concealment of his guilt. And other improvements – the use of steam, the multiplication of means of locomotion – make it easy for him in those few hours to effect his escape to a foreign country".[1]

In an introduction to a German legal text-book published in 1893, Von Liszt made a similar point, writing that "(…) the professional thief or swindler feels equally at home in Paris, Vienna or London (…) counterfeit roubles are produced in France or England and passed in Germany (…) gangs of criminals operate continuously over several countries".[2] In the final month of the 20th century such words are as true as ever. Substitute a reference to the electronic transfer of funds for that to paper money, replace "steam" with "air travel" and either comment could have been made by a modern commentator.

In the last 150 years or so there has been a series of developments by which states have sought to respond to and cope with this increasing internationalisation of crime. In the last two to three decades in particular, they have resulted in a wide range of instruments designed to attack aspects of transnational crime[3] and to secure international co-operation against such crime. As a result, Judge Haentjens and Professor Swart have written (in a criminal law context) of a developing "osmosis between international law and domestic law".[4]

---

[1] E. Clarke, *A Treatise upon The Law of Extradition*, Stevens and Haynes, 1874, p. 12.

[2] F. von Liszt, quoted without more precise reference in F. Bresler, *Interpol*, Sinclair Stevenson, 1992, p. 11.

[3] There were in 1991, according to Bassiouni, "315 international instruments, elaborated mostly on an *ad hoc* basis between 1815 and 1988, which cover 22 categories of offences" (M Cherif Bassiouni, 'Policy Considerations on Inter-State Co-operation', in: A. Eser & O. Lagodny, *Principles and Procedures for a New Transnational Criminal Law*, Society for the Reform of Criminal Law and Max Planck Institute for Foreign and International Criminal Law 1992, p. 807).

[4] R. Haentjens & B. Swart, 'Substantive Criminal Law', in: B. Swart & A. Klip (eds.), *International Criminal Law in the Netherlands*, Max Planck Institute for Foreign and International (to be continued)

It is surprising, therefore, that, although the relationship between international law and municipal law in general is well trodden ground, the relationship between international law and criminal law in particular has, until recently, received relatively little attention from scholars. Professor Nadelmann has said that "(...) US foreign policy and criminal justice (...) have had remarkably little to do with one another. The vast majority of criminal justice scholars have extended their attention no further than their nations' borders (...). Among students of US foreign policy (...) almost no one has paid much attention to issues of crime and law enforcement (...). Whatever arguments might once have justified this disengagement of the two disciplines can no longer be sustained. The interpenetration of foreign policy and criminal justice institutions and concerns have simply become too substantial to be ignored by scholars any longer."[5]

What Professor Nadelmann wrote about the US could be written with equal force about the UK. The relationship between international law and the criminal law of the UK jurisdictions remains largely unexamined. For the last six years, I have been engaged in research which seeks to begin to remedy that state of affairs, at least so far as extradition and mutual legal assistance law are concerned. The research has, therefore, been about the relationship between international law and aspects of criminal procedure; hence the title of this paper.

**The Phases**

I think we can identify three phases in the relationship. The first, which subsisted until about 1985, was one in which domestic law and practice had overwhelming dominance and the UK had a well deserved reputation for being unco-operative. The second phase lasted from the middle 1980s until very recently. During this second phase the UK was vocal in its support for the principle of international co-operation against crime, entered into numerous treaties on the subject and amended its domestic legislation so as to make provision for such co-operation. Upon examination of that legislation, however, it becomes clear that, for all its rhetoric, the UK was still determined to preserve its existing domestic practice to the greatest extent possible and that certain reservations made to treaties and certain provisions in the legislation can best be explained by a continuing deep seated distrust of

---

Criminal Law 1997, p. 28.

[5] E.A. Nadelmann, *Cops Across Borders: The Internationalization of US Criminal Law Enforcement*, Pennsylvania State University Press 1993, p. xiii. A similar observation was made by Currie, who wrote: "(...) criminal cases having foreign aspects tend to fall between two stools, in the academic world at least" (B. Currie, *Selected Essays on the Conflict of Laws*, 1963, quoted in J.J. Murphy, 'Revising Domestic Extradition Law', 131 *University of Pennsylvania Law Review* 1063, 1065 [1983]).

foreign criminal justice systems and a determination to maintain priority for domestic law.

We have only just embarked on the third phase. Certain recent developments suggest that there is now a readiness to accept that foreign criminal justice systems, at least within the European Union, can be trusted and that the present Government is now willing to allow European human rights law to play a significant part in the UK criminal justice process. It may be that we are entering upon an era in which the UK will move away from its determined Anglocentricity and accept the rather more relaxed and positive approach to international and European criminal law initiatives which seems to outside eyes to characterise Dutch practice; though it is as yet too soon to predict that with any certainty.

## The First Phase – Introduction

As many of those attending a conference such as this well know, until the middle 1980s, the UK saw no particular need to co-operate with other countries in international criminal justice matters. For over 100 years, from 1870 until 1989, such limited co-operation as there was with jurisdictions other than those in the Commonwealth was governed primarily by the *Extradition Act 1870*, which, Mr Alan Harding of the Home Office observed in 1992, epitomised the 'essentially 19th century view' that "as a common law jurisdiction, with well established mechanisms for ensuring the fairness and effectiveness of criminal proceedings, it was neither right nor possible to take much cognisance of other countries' judicial processes".[6] Professor Warbrick noted that the *1870 Act* reflected the fact that the UK was "protected by the sea from extensive traffic in fugitive criminals, its Parliament infected with a Dicyean suspicion of things continental and legal and its public opinion firmly resolved to protect fugitives waging revolution against continental despotisms."[7]

## The First Phase – Extradition

We can get some evidence of the continuing prevalence of this view at the Public Record Office in London. It is possible there to consult the draft brief for the UK representative for the Council of Europe meeting in October 1953

---

[6] A. Harding, 'Treaty Making in the Field of International Co-operation: The United Kingdom Experience', in: A. Eser & O. Lagodny (eds.), *Principles and Procedures for a New Transnational Criminal Law*, Society for the Reform of Criminal Law and Max Planck Institute for Foreign and International Criminal Law 1992, pp. 235-236.

[7] C. Warbrick, 'The Criminal Justice Act 1988 (1) The New Law on Extradition', [1989] *Crim. L.R.* 4.

to consider extradition principles acceptable to all Member States,[8] with a view to negotiating what was to become the *European Convention on Extradition 1957 (ECE)*. The introduction to the draft brief, having offered the opinion that "[i]t seems unlikely that (...) general agreement will be reached on many principles", concluded with the remark that "[w]e have no desire to hasten the work on this subject and it would be an advantage if this meeting did no more than undertake some preliminary discussion and determine what principles should be further examined". It is difficult to interpret this as anything other than an elegantly framed instruction to be obstructive. Since in fact a considerable measure of agreement was reached it appears that the UK misread the situation quite seriously.

Although nowhere stated explicitly, there seems to have been a fear underlying the brief that the whole exercise would result in continental approaches to extradition being imposed on the UK. The most obvious example of this relates to the question of the non-extradition of nationals, a principle entrenched in the constitutions of certain countries (such as Germany).[9] The UK delegate[10] was instructed to maintain the strong preference of the UK for the principle of surrender of nationals. He was instructed that the *aut dedere aut judicare* principle (now found in many multilateral instruments) could not be accepted as compensation for refusal to surrender nationals and was instructed to advance in support of that position arguments which related entirely to the inability of English criminal procedure to deal with the extraterritorial criminal jurisdiction which such an approach necessitates and which failed completely to recognise either that other countries approach jurisdiction in a different way[11] or that change in English criminal procedure might be considered. It should be said that there is no reason to suppose that Scots law would have been any better equipped to deal with bases of jurisdiction other than the territorial one but there is no evidence in the draft brief that the Scottish position was considered.

---

[8] FO 371/108050, WU 1591/10.

[9] *See* the declarations and reservations set out in Schedule 3 to *the European Convention on Extradition Order 1990* (SI 1990 No 1507).

[10] He was Mr F.L.T. Graham-Harrison, Assistant Secretary at the Home Office (Public Records Office, Foreign Office Doc 371/108050 1591/13A, *Report of the Committee of Experts on Extradition*, CM (53) 129, 15).

[11] For a summary of the different bases of jurisdiction used by Council of Europe member States, *see* European Committee on Crime Problems, *Extraterritorial criminal jurisdiction*, Council of Europe 1990. *See also* P.J. Slot & E. Grabandt, 'Extraterritoriality and Jurisdiction' (1986), 23 *CMLR* 545. Some things do not change. On 24 March 1999, Kate Hoey, Under-Secretary of State at the Home Office, who manifested no understanding whatever of the issues involved in the bases of jurisdiction, said in public that the refusal of civilian jurisdictions to extradite their own nationals was "eminently unreasonable" (House of Lords Select Committee on the European Communities, *Prosecuting Fraud on the Communities' Finances-the Corpus Juris*, HL Paper 62, 1999, 106). *See* the writer's attempt at damage limitation *(ibid.)*.

The inescapable conclusion from the draft brief and the related material is that the UK had a deep antipathy to the whole idea of a multilateral convention and had no intention of allowing its extradition practice to be modified so as to reflect any treaty which did not itself conform to the parameters set by the *1870 Act*. The UK did not at that time sign *ECE*.

### The First Phase – Mutual Legal Assistance

So far as other forms of mutual assistance were concerned, the picture was very similar. The UK did not even participate in the negotiation of the *European Convention on Mutual Assistance in Criminal Matters 1959 (ECMA)* and its domestic law made very little provision for either giving or receiving such assistance. As an inter-departmental working group put it in 1987, there was a belief that mutual legal assistance treaties ('MLATs') "were in general unlikely to be of significant use to us because the insistence of our law on oral testimony left little scope for the admission of witness statements and other documents, which form the bulk of the traffic".[12] This, of course, ignored the possibility of the *provision* of assistance to foreign states which sought to obtain evidence within the UK. Although it seems that by 1975 at the latest the Crown Office in Scotland was arranging for the evidence of witnesses resident in Scotland to be obtained for foreign criminal proceedings[13], this was not done as a matter of obligation, was *ad hoc* and somewhat informal and, in the absence of legislation giving power to carry out searches on behalf of foreign authorities, cannot have extended to compulsory measures.

### The Second Phase – Introduction

Reconsideration of this position was forced in 1978 when Spain denounced its extradition treaty with the UK as a result of the difficulties it experienced over the *prima facie* case requirement.[14] The Interdepartmental Working Party on Extradition, which had originally reported in 1974, was reconvened in 1982 and their Report noted that developments in the nature of international crime and in the measures taken by states to deal with it demanded a complete re-examination of the subject. The growth of transnational crime associated with

---

[12] *International Mutual Assistance in Criminal Matters: Report to Ministers from the Inter-Departmental Working Group*, July 1987 (not yet in the public domain)(hereafter, 'Working Group').

[13] *Criminal Procedure in Scotland (Second Report)*, Cmnd 6218, 1975, para 43.27.

[14] *Extradition*, Cmnd 9421, 1985, 5. It may be noted that history has a way of repeating itself. In 1865, France terminated its extradition treaty with the UK on the ground that the *prima facie* case requirement insisted on by the UK was an insuperable obstacle to extradition. By doing so, France prompted the overhaul of the law which resulted in the *1870 Act*.

increased freedom of movement within Europe was in particular regarded as a development which required attention.[15] It dawned gradually upon the UK that the difficulties arising from the differences between the English common law system and the civilian systems "may have meant in some cases that criminals have escaped justice".[16]

This view became firmer as the 1980s progressed (and was to affect the UK attitude to other forms of mutual assistance too), until in Lords Committee on Part I of the Bill which became the *Criminal Justice Act 1988*, the Earl of Caithness was to say that the fact that the UK was not party to *ECE* had become "a major stumbling block in our negotiations throughout Western Europe to get a more comprehensive agreement on crime where people who are committing crimes can easily hop from one country to another".[17] A little later in the same debate, he said that the clear implication of the decisions of certain countries not to even try to obtain extradition from the UK was that serious offenders were known to be in the UK but no attempt was being made to extradite them.[18] Evidently it had finally been realised by the Government that it was denying itself the opportunity which extradition requests present to be rid of foreign criminals. There seems also to have been a realisation that the UK's own approach to extradition was inconsistent with the Government's developing general international criminal law policy, which was that "international crimes can only be dealt with in an international framework"[19] and that what was needed was "practical means of co-operation which will prevent criminals from using jurisdictional barriers to evade justice".[20]

There was, at the same time, a recognition that the UK was 'seriously hampered' in providing mutual assistance because of the inadequacy of existing legislative provisions. This, it was said, had earned the UK a bad reputation for negative responses to reasonable requests for assistance and had "caused serious problems for our own prosecution authorities as a result of other States refusing to render us assistance because of lack of reciprocity". Moreover, the continued reliance by the UK on what the Mutual Assistance Working Group called "antiquated and limited powers to give assistance to foreign courts" amounted to an obstacle to assisting in investigations. The Working Group noted that this had "caused considerable difficulties and has been a point of friction with the US. The effect is that the UK is isolated through its inability to offer other countries reciprocal treatment. We have a good reputation for co-operation in the exchange of information already

---

[15] 1982 Working Party, para 1.9.
[16] *Ibid.*, para 1.11.
[17] HL Debs Vol 489 (No 1369) Col 22 (20 October 1987).
[18] *Ibid.*, col 44.
[19] Sir Michael Havers, 'Legal Co-operation: A Matter of Necessity', in: 21 *International Lawyer* 185 (1987).
[20] *Ibid.*, 193.

available to our investigatory agencies, but a bad reputation in terms of the provision of hard evidence for criminal prosecutions." The Working Group also reported that "foreign countries, including some of our European partners and the US, are privately highly critical of the UK's performance".[21] The Working Group concluded that there were "strong arguments in favour of reform of UK mutual assistance law with a view to participation in formal mutual assistance arrangements" and suggested consultation followed by the introduction of legislation in the 1988/89 session.[22]

## The Second Phase – Extradition

The scene was set, then, for an overhaul of UK extradition and mutual assistance law so as to enable the UK to participate fully and effectively in these forms of international co-operation. On the face of it, that is what was done by the UK's accession to *ECE* and *ECMA* and by legislation in *the Extradition Act 1989* (the *1989 Act*) and the *Criminal Justice (International Co-operation) Act 1990* (the *1990 Act*). On examination, however, it can be seen that these accessions and pieces of legislation, although representing a significant advance, were actually rather heavily qualified by reservations and by reliance on domestic law models. It could also be shown – although space does not permit elaboration here – that the UK courts have consistently approached questions in these areas on the basis of domestic law assumptions.

Many points could be made about the treaty accessions and the legislation. Here, I take only a few as examples.

The *1989 Act* was meant to make it possible for the UK to accede to *ECE* and participate more effectively in other international extradition arrangements. There is no doubt that it has significantly eased the extradition relationship between the UK and its European partners. Nevertheless, in that Act the UK actually reinforced the dominance of municipal law. Section 4(2) of the Act provides that extradition arrangements cannot be given effect in UK domestic law unless they are in conformity with the provisions of the Act. This re-enacts an identical provision in the *1870 Act* and gives legislative expression to the approach which the UK has taken to extradition treaty-making. The starting point has always been municipal law, so that in 1958 Lord Parker CJ was correct when he said in *R* v. *Governor of Brixton Prison ex p Minervini*[23] (referring to the *1873 Treaty* with Norway and justifying the interpretation of that treaty in light of the municipal legislation), that "the two contracting parties in 1873 must have had in mind the Act of 1870 and the fact

---

[21] *Working Group Report*, para 5.
[22] *Working Group Report*, para 20.
[23] [1958] 3 *W.L.R.* 559.

that an Order in Council[24] would be made referring to the treaty and applying to it the provisions of the Act".[25] By contrast, the Dutch position has been described by Professor Swart. The *Extradition Act* of 1967, he says, "limits the power of Government to freely negotiate the terms of an extradition treaty. However (…) it does not completely rule out the possibility that Government conclude a treaty that, in some way or other, does not conform to the provisions of the Act. Allowing that this may, on occasion, be necessary or desirable, Article 3 of the Act obliges the Government to submit a Bill to amend the Act in order to re-establish a close correspondence between the terms of the treaty and the provisions of the Act."[26] In practice, of course, the UK Government has it in its power to amend the *1989 Act* if it becomes desirable to agree a treaty provision which is inconsistent with the Act. Extradition treaty negotiators from both the Netherlands and the UK are, therefore, constrained by domestic legislation but both Governments can, if necessary, amend that legislation. The difference, which might well reflect differences in attitude to the relationship between treaties and national law, is that Dutch law specifically contemplates legislation to bring the national instrument into line with the international one. UK law declines to contemplate any such thing. The UK approach, which gives pre-eminence to domestic law, indicates that Professor Gilbert's remark that "domestic [extradition] legislation reflects treaty provisions"[27] does not describe UK practice entirely satisfactorily.

That conclusion is reinforced when one examines the UK's reservations to *ECE*. What the UK did in the *1989 Act* was to legislate in terms which were compatible with *ECE* but which did not directly apply *ECE*. On accession, reservations were made and these were the subject of a dialogue between the UK and the Council of Europe's Committee of Experts on the operation of European Conventions in the Penal Field ('PC-OC') recorded in Council of Europe Secretariat Memorandum PC-OC (91)1 (the 'PC-OC Memorandum'). We have space to examine only one aspect of them.

Article 2 *ECE* defines the offences which are extraditable. They are those "punishable under the laws of the requesting Party and of the requested Party by deprivation of liberty or under a detention order for a maximum period of at least one year or by a more severe penalty." The UK reservation provides that it "may decide to grant extradition in respect of any offences which under the

---

[24] An Order in Council is a species of subordinate legislation which does not require full Parliamentary scrutiny.
[25] At 563. It is not obvious why Norway would have had UK municipal primary legislation in mind, or why Norway should have been expected to understand the subtleties of UK secondary legislation.
[26] B. Swart, 'Extradition', in: B. Swart & A. Klip (eds.), *International Criminal Law in the Netherlands*, Max Planck Institute for Foreign and International Criminal Law, 1997, pp. 89-90.
[27] G. Gilbert, *Aspects of Extradition Law*, Martinus Nijhoff Publishers 1991, p. 2.

law of the requesting state and the law of the UK are punishable by a sentence of imprisonment for a term of 12 months or any greater sentence, whether or not such a sentence has in fact been imposed." A further reservation permits the UK to refuse extradition "if it appears, in relation to the offence or each of the offences in respect of which (...) return is sought that, by reason of its trivial nature or because the accusation is not made in good faith in the interests of justice, it would in all the circumstances be unjust or oppressive to return him."

The UK explained to PC-OC that both of these reservations are designed to reflect the terminology of the UK legislation.[28] The 'trivial offence' reservation repeats, almost verbatim, Section 11(3)(a) and (c) of the *1989 Act*. That Section is derived from the *Fugitive Offenders Act 1967* Section 8(3), which itself was a response to paragraph 9(3) of the *Commonwealth Rendition Scheme* and derived from the *Fugitive Offenders Act 1881* Section 10 (but is not traceable to the *1870 Act*). In a Commonwealth setting, the provision makes sense, because both the Imperial legislation and the Scheme which succeeded it proceeded (until the Scheme was revised) by the enumerative method. The eliminative method is intrinsically more apt to weed out trivial offences, especially in the legal systems of civilian states where the sentences available for particular offences fall generally within tighter bands than those in any of the UK systems.[29] The breadth of the sentencing bands available in the UK might well have meant that some sort of reservation in respect of trivial offences would have been required anyway; but the particular reservation made represents the application to late 20th century Europe of law developed to deal with rendition within the 19th century British Empire. That was not explained to PC-OC, though the UK did hasten to assure it that it was thought unlikely that the safeguard for accusations not made in good faith in the interests of justice would be relevant in the context of requests made by parties to *ECE*.[30]

It was explained to PC-OC that the reservation about the definition of extraditable offences reflects the terminology of the *1989 Act* and it was said that the Act was framed so as to enable the UK to accept the *ECE* definition.[31] The obvious question is why the *1989 Act* definition was so different from the *ECE* definition as to require clarification by reservation. Indeed PC-OC had some concern that the reservation amounted to a derogation.[32] What the UK might have explained, but did not, was that the definition of extradition crime in the *1989 Act* is intended to satisfy all those extradition arrangements which are within Part III of the Act and not only *ECE*. The *Commonwealth Rendition*

---

[28] *PC-OC Memorandum*, paras 10 and 11.
[29] *See 1974 Working Party Report*, 23 para 41c.
[30] *PC-OC Memorandum*, para 11.
[31] *Ibid*.
[32] *Ibid*.

*Scheme* is the other obvious example. That Scheme is "not a treaty; it is a basis agreed among the member states for national legislation conforming substantially[33] thereto in order to achieve reciprocity and similarity of procedures".[34] That approach works because the Commonwealth countries all have legal systems which are to a significant extent derived from English law. Indeed, the Scheme might almost be said to represent the erection of aspects of English criminal procedure into an international instrument.

### The Second Phase – Mutual Legal Assistance

If we consider mutual legal assistance, we can find similar evidence that, even after enactment of the *1990 Act*, domestic law had a clear priority. For example, Article 3 *ECMA* provides that the requested Party shall execute requests "in the manner provided for by its law". This formula leaves open the possibility that municipal law in the requested state will permit execution according to the procedures of the requesting state, a course Dutch law takes in relation to requests under its bilateral MLATs with the USA and Canada.[35] US law provides a similar facility by permitting the person appointed by the court dealing with the request to apply "in whole or in part the practice and procedure of the foreign country".[36] The UK, however, "reserves the right not to take the evidence of witnesses or require the production of records or other documents where its law recognises in relation thereto privilege, non-compellability or other exemption from giving evidence." This, on one view, is consistent with a continuing deep-seated distrust of foreign process.

So is the UK legislative approach, which is to apply UK municipal procedures to the collection of evidence for a foreign authority, albeit with some relaxation as regards the compellability of witnesses.[37] The kind of difficulties which can result from this approach may be illustrated by a Norwegian case[38] in which English police officers had, for the purposes of a case pending before Norwegian courts, given evidence before English courts without stating their true identities. This was permissible in English law. The evidence was, however, held to be inadmissible in Norway, where the law

---

[33] In 1989 the Commonwealth Secretariat published a revised version of its *Survey of Extradition and Fugitive Offenders Legislation as Between Commonwealth Jurisdictions*, listing all of the relevant legislation in Commonwealth countries as it then stood.

[34] I.A. Shearer, *op. cit.*, 217.

[35] R. Haentjens, 'Mutual Assistance in Criminal Matters', in: B. Swart & A. Klip (eds.), *International Criminal Law in the Netherlands*, Max Planck Institute for Foreign and International Criminal Law 1997, 123 at 134.

[36] 28 *USC* 1782.

[37] *Criminal Justice (International Co-operation) Act 1990* Schedule 1.

[38] Hyesterett (39B/1997) May 27, 1997 [1997] *Rt* 869, [1997] 12 *Euro CL* 138 (para 132).

seems to be that police officers are only able to give evidence anonymously in exceptional circumstances.[39]

It is important to recognise that the UK reservation to Article 3, both in its terms and in its subject matter, has to do with the law of evidence. It refers to privilege and non-compellability as exemptions from giving evidence. It does not address or seek to protect property rights in records and documents or to make any exception on the basis of contractual arrangements as to the confidentiality of the information which such records and documents contain.

The argument which may be put in favour of applying this somewhat complex branch of UK evidence law to a request for assistance in connection with an investigation in another European jurisdiction is that the UK rules have a public policy foundation and that to take the evidence of the witness or seize the documents or records would defeat that policy even if they were never used in evidence. Against that, however, it may be said that the rules about privilege and non-compellability are not there to protect a person's secrets for their own sake. They do not relate to any kind of property interests. Rather, they relate specifically to the law of evidence. Moreover, the reservation in terms relates to exemptions from giving evidence, not to the protection of property rights of any kind, nor to any privilege of the witness founded on public policy. Where the UK is the requested state and a witness claims that the evidence which he is being required to give is evidence which he could not be compelled to give in the requesting state, Schedule 1 paragraph 4 to the *1990 Act* requires that the evidence be taken but not transmitted if the court in the requesting state upholds the witness's claim. Rules on privilege and compellability equivalent to, and sometimes wider than, UK rules do apply in other legal systems. The scheme provided by Schedule 1 paragraph 4 of the *1990 Act* would, it is suggested, be sufficient to meet the real interests in the case. The reservation made by the UK to Article 3 gives UK domestic law a priority which is not necessary.

**The Third Phase**

There are some signs that the UK's attitude is changing. In March 1999 the UK submitted to the EU K4 Committee a paper entitled *Mutual Recognition of Judicial Decisions and Judgements in Criminal Matters*. In it, the UK proposes that "the EU should agree in principle on the objective of abolition of dual criminality restrictions on granting mutual legal assistance. This would be consistent with the principle of the recognition of the validity of the legal systems of EU partners." It notes that public opinion is not always ready to

---

[39] The principles developed by the European Court of Human Rights are somewhat similar to the Norwegian position – *see* the summary of *ECHR* law in Karen Reid, *A Practitioner's Guide to the European Convention on Human Rights*, Sweet & Maxwell 1998.

accept that the procedures of other member States are equivalent to their own and asserts that Governments will have to inform and educate public opinion. The clear implication is that the UK Government does accept that it is possible to have confidence in the criminal justice systems of other EU countries. We have come a long way from the attitude described by Harding.

Not only that but we are now in the period between the enactment and the entry into force of the *Human Rights Act 1998 (HRA)*. According to the White Paper, *Rights Brought Home: The Human Rights Bill*,[40] "the essential feature of the [Act] is that the UK will not be bound to give effect to the Convention rights merely as a matter of international law, but will also give them further effect directly in our domestic law."[41] One of the ways in which *HRA* seeks to achieve its objective is to require, by Section 3, that "so far as it is possible to do so, primary legislation and subordinate legislation must be read and given effect in a way which is compatible with the Convention rights." Moreover, Section 2(1) *HRA* requires, that "a court or tribunal determining a question which has arisen in connection with a Convention right must take into account" the Convention case law, including the case law of the European Court of Human Rights (ECrtHR). Ashworth has noted that "the Convention text should not be read as it stands, without reference to the jurisprudence of the European Court."[42] *HRA* therefore requires that UK courts should interpret a statute in a way which is in conformity with a treaty and should, in so doing, have regard to the case law of an international court whose task it is to interpret that treaty. It follows that UK courts will henceforth require to work within a framework, which includes international law in a way they have not previously had to do.

There is considerable force in Ovey's assertion that "no Article of the Convention is without implications for criminal law, if only to the extent that the existence or non existence of criminal sanctions may give rise to a violation of the right safeguarded."[43] Even if it is correct to maintain that the fact that Article 6 *European Convention for the Protection of Human Rights and Fundamental Freedoms (ECHR)* (for example) is focused narrowly on the trial process rather than on criminal justice as a whole, and is therefore relatively limited in its impact,[44] the emphasis must be on the word 'relatively'. A very large part of the jurisprudence of the ECrtHR and of the European Commission of Human Rights (EComHR) has related to Articles 5, 6, 7 and 8 as they affect criminal cases. Dennis has argued that the increasing

---

[40] Cm 3782, October 1997.

[41] Para 2.1.

[42] A. Ashworth, 'Article 6 and the Fairness of Trials', in: [1999] *Crim. L.R.* 261, 271.

[43] C. Ovey, 'The European Convention on Human Rights and the Criminal Lawyer: An Introduction', in: [1998] *Crim. L.R.* 4, 6. *See also* D. Feldman, 'The Developing Scope of Article 8 of the European Convention on Human Rights', in: [1997] *E.H.R.L.R.* 265.

[44] *See* S. Sharpe, 'The European Convention: A Suspect's Charter?', in: [1997] *Crim. L.R.* 848.

willingness of the Court and the Commission to pronounce on matters of criminal evidence and procedure "indicates the arrival of more detailed pan-European norms of criminal process".[45] The effect of *HRA* in relation to criminal law will be at least as significant as its effect in any other area of law.

This does not, however, mean that international law will have a dominant position. It was the Government's clear policy, in enacting *HRA*, not to interfere with the doctrine of Parliamentary sovereignty. The Government's expectation when a court finds it impossible to find an interpretation of a piece of legislation which is consistent with the Convention rights is clear. At Second Reading of the Human Rights Bill in the House of Lords, the Lord Chancellor said that "the Bill does not allow the courts to set aside or ignore Acts of Parliament" and that Section 3 "preserves the effect of primary legislation which is incompatible with the Convention".[46] Later in the same debate, he said that the intention of the legislation was to maximise the protection to individuals "while retaining the fundamental principle of Parliamentary sovereignty". [47] The remedy provided for the situation in which a court cannot find a way to construe legislation compatibly with the Convention rights is the declaration of incompatibility, which will not affect the validity, continuing operation or enforcement of the provision in respect of which it is given and which will not bind the parties to the proceedings in which it is made.[48] Such a declaration might well prompt the Government to make legislative change but will not oblige it to do so. That having been said, the Convention rights have undergone a limited incorporation for Scotland by Section 57(2) of the *Scotland Act 1998*, which disables the prosecutor from doing any act which is incompatible with the Convention rights. That provision is in its earliest days and its effect cannot yet be said to have stabilised. There are, however, some indications that the courts are not well disposed to the parliamentary sovereignty argument and are inclined to construe statutes to which it might apply very narrowly indeed, so as to limit its ambit.

**Conclusion**

There is overwhelming evidence that, until the mid 1980s, the UK was apathetic and sometimes even obstructive about international co-operation. There is strong evidence that the detail of the UK's reservations to the

---

[45] I.H. Dennis, 'Human Rights and Evidence in Adversarial Criminal Procedure: The Advancement of International Standards', in: J.F. Nijboer & J.M. Reijntjes (eds.), *Proceedings of the First World Conference on New Trends in Criminal Investigation and Evidence*, Koninklijke Vermande bv/Open University of the Netherlands 1997, p. 523.
[46] H.L. Debs, 3 November 1997, cols 1230-1231.
[47] H.L. Debs, 3 November 1997, col 1294.
[48] *Human Rights Act 1998* Section 4(6).

international instruments and of its legislation shows that in the last decade it has been less whole-hearted about engagement in international co-operation than the Government s rhetoric might have suggested. But there is now some evidence that it might be moving into a time of more constructive engagement. The train is still moving very quickly and how far it will go is uncertain. Against the background of the first and second phases of the UK's attitude to international co-operation, one should be cautious about making large claims for what the UK might do in the future. After all, it remains true that the content of international law is very largely within the control of states[49] and that control over the content of criminal law is typically regarded by states as a matter of sovereignty. It tends, therefore, to be guarded quite jealously.[50] By accepting an international obligation with which existing domestic criminal law is inconsistent, a state commits itself to changing that criminal law. Its willingness to accept such obligations must therefore (and obviously) depend in large measure on its willingness to change its criminal law. The critical question will always be how anxious a state is, as a matter of policy, to achieve the objective of the treaty in question. The Home Office has continued to stress the importance of national sovereignty[51] and there is no reason at present to suppose that the Government is considering changing that position. That being so, municipal law seems likely to retain some priority. Nevertheless, the Government's agenda for the immediate future was made clear to the House of Lords Select Committee on the European Communities in a Home Office memorandum as recently as 24 March 1999[52] and was an ambitious one. The Government proposes the development of the concept of the mutual recognition of court decisions, which "might in due course lead to fast-track extradition (similar to backing of warrants); abolition of dual criminality restrictions on extradition and MLA requests; and the ability for member states to freeze suspect assets and certain types of evidence more quickly to prevent their being dispersed."

The relationship between international law and criminal law in the UK is not, in the final analysis, a matter of legal principle. It is, rather, a matter of the working out in the law of political priorities. One may identify and describe trends in the relationship but the conclusion must be a positivist one. There are no immutable principles. The relationship between international law and UK criminal law is entirely a matter of Governmental choice as expressed in treaties and legislation; no more and no less. Policy priorities shift over time. One may await developments with considerable interest.

---

[49] A. Cassese, *International Law in a Divided World*, Oxford: Clarendon Press 1986, pp. 169-199.

[50] *See* Chr. van den Wyngaert, 'Foreword', in: Chr. van den Wyngaert *et al.* (eds.), *Criminal Procedure Systems in the European Community*, Butterworths 1993, i.

[51] House of Lords Select Committee on the European Communities, *Prosecuting Fraud...*, 99, para 297, evidence of Kate Hoey, Parliamentary Under-Secretary of State at the Home Office.

[52] House of Lords Select Committee on the European Communities, *Prosecuting Fraud...*, 98.

# Forensic Accountancy and Fraud Auditing: the Case of the Indian Securities Scam

*P. Chattopadhyay*

The present paper underscores the distinction between forensic accountancy and fraud auditing insofar as the former has the major concern of laying down policies, procedures and practices of recording, coding and classifying transactions in a fool-proof manner of purposes of faithful reporting and transparency while the latter stresses on finding out what happened with particular reference to whether any fraudulent transactions had taken place in the corporate. The dimensions of forensic accountancy and fraud auditing are thus different. This is not always kept in view and the two are often used as synonyms. The nature of economic offences and the complexities involved in each of these offences require appreciation. On the other hand, when fraud has been reported, the series of events and steps that follow also call for consideration. Charts I and II seek to show the economic offences and the steps that accompany the detection of fraud. The first part of this paper deals with the general issues concerning forensic accountancy and the second part highlights the Securities Scam, which took place in India in the early 90s with far reaching consequences.

## General Issues

Traditionally, accountants have not been called upon to present expert views in court except where misfeasance, embezzlement, different financial irregularities and fraudulent transactions have been alleged *against* parties embracing individuals, groups and managers of bodies corporate. In recent years, cases have been reported from different countries about *large-scale* fraudulent transactions in terms of both number and amounts involved. Many such cases have been reported in different publications, notably books, journals, newspapers and reports, emanating from the US, UK, the Netherlands, Germany, Australia, France, Japan and India. Though the nature of fraudulent transactions has been variegated, the focus of forensic accounting has remained the same in all cases, in the sense that both proactive and reactive strategies could be adopted by accountants and auditors to prevent such transactions. The question that arises is basically, whether the accountants and auditors have the jurisdiction of *raising* objection, either by way of laying down a procedure aimed at minimising such frauds in the first place, or by way of detecting such fraudulent transactions before it was too late for application of correctives.

The collusion of officials and non-officials, of corporate managers and politicians, or of each of these categories *inter se*, has been a factor in all this.

Thus, proceeding, on the assumption that in the absence of suspicion the auditor is a gentleman, but when suspicion is aroused, the auditor acts like a bloodhound, may not appear enough. The axiom remains somewhat underplayed in modern times. All this is mentioned because of the fact that the legal position is that companies are not owned by individuals, they are owned by themselves as long as they are going concerns. Corporate property is public property, not private property of shareholders. Corporate body is a singular entity and discrete from other entities.

This means that a company has an interest in healthy perpetuity, which may be totally distinct from either the entire body of shareholders or a section thereof, *i.e.*, those having control. This being the position, independence of auditors is automatically underlined. While, as an employee, an accountant can bring to book any perpetrator of fraudulent transactions or other delinquencies even when such a perpetrator is his boss, because his appointment is with the company, his bosses, though they may be appointing authorities, are not his employers. This position puts a burden on the accountant that he does not always recognise.

In India, the last several years have witnessed such fraudulent transactions at multifarious levels and involving huge sums of money, which could have been prevented. Even now, all the culprits do not appear to have been brought to book. The great Indian Securities Scam had a large number of players on a countrywide scale and the *dramatis personae* included banks, mutual funds, brokers and powerful executives in different organisations and even government officials. The *modus operandi* was complex but, given the opportunity, the accountant could have detailed out the entire procedure including the fraudulent transactions of securities and *de facto* transfers of document and false entries in the Subsidiary General Ledger in the Public Deposit Office in the Reserve Bank of India. The rigmarole of inquiries by journalists, by the officials and lastly by representatives of Parliament could trace only half of the total money involved. The other half remains untraced even now. This was quickly followed by other scams like the Fodder Scam in Bihar and the Letter of Credit Scam in Assam, both notable Indian states in the East and the Northeast. In such cases even an ordinary, public accountant employed by a company, could have initiated public interest petitions because a company is a social institution and has some stake in the successful operation of all these companies which comprised the major part of economic activities of any country. Even the law operating in most of these countries has many escape routes which the forensic accountant can chalk out in the course of his submissions before the Court of Law seeking justice against misuses of public funds and properties. Companies being *de facto* public institutions and large bodies of evidence exist to corroborate this stand; the focus of the forensic accountant is primarily for protection of public interest.

Naturally, there are three aspects in the approaches of forensic accountants, namely:

1. the lessons of the past and bringing into account the modus operandi of fraudulent transactions of any kind in public institutions including government;
2. initiating proceedings against the guilty in Courts of Law and making presentations before the courts as expert interpreters of accounts and accounting procedures;
3. laying down procedures and practices, especially methods of internal cheek and external vigilance, to ensure that fraudulent transactions cannot be committed without collusion of a large number of individuals and that, when committed, it is brought to light in no time before any large scale damage is caused.

In this respect, along with forensic accounting, some authors have suggested forensic auditing also, but since auditing is done by qualified accountants in practice, auditors are not separately mentioned. Moreover, forensic accounting and auditing comprise two sides of the same coin. Their functions are as if they remained on two sides of the fence – one makes the entries and the other checks them.

*Post facto* investigations into the methods adopted, the nature of the damage caused and the remedial actions, may all be relevant for making the atmosphere fraud-free and taking steps to prove guilt of those concerned on the basis of conscionable evidence. It is possible that forensic accounting be recognised as a way to minimise the risks of large-scale transactions of a fraudulent nature causing huge losses either to the country's exchequer, or to the coffers of individual companies, or even to individuals. Methods of inquiry and recording of findings along with preservation of the documents would call for expert handling, which forensic accountants could provide.

Large-scale computer-based frauds have been reported recently and they would require not only expert knowledge and literacy in handling computers but also unearthing the codes and passwords hiding the actual details in such cases. While the Internet and the web site have truly brought large possibilities, the negative impacts have also not been insignificant. Forensic accountants would have to train themselves more sensitively. However, even now they are in a position to call forth skills that could lay bare many hideous, insidious practices. This growing discipline of forensic accountancy has immense possibilities in bringing to book errant and fraudulent activities and transactions having *mala fide* intentions and impacts on business and individual wealth.

P. Chattopadhyay

*Chart I: Economic Offences*

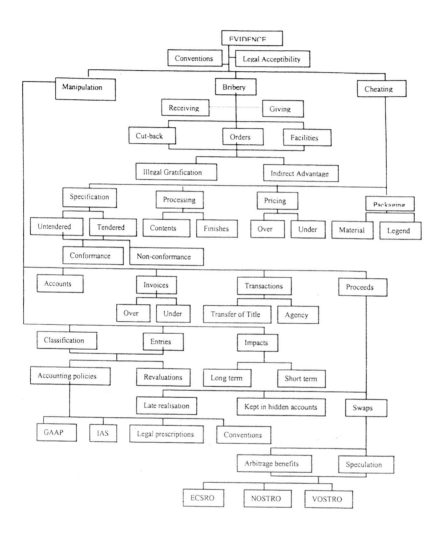

*Chart II: Fraud finding Modalities*

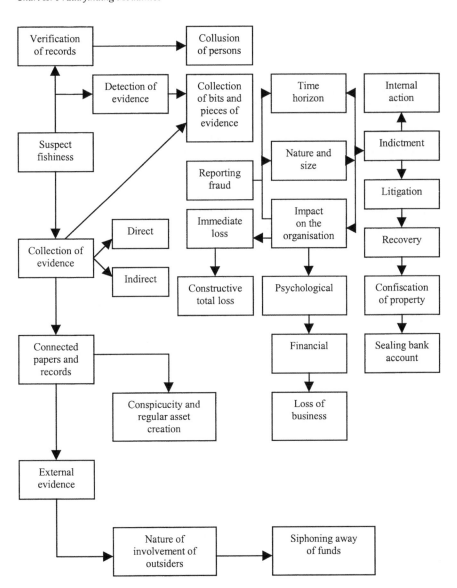

## The Securities Scam

The Securities Scam took the country by storm, as it ravaged the capital market in a whirlwind of fake transactions of gargantuan magnitude. In a way the Securities Scam may be directly related to the aura of liberalisation and deregulation initiated by the P.V. Narasimha Rao Government since July 1991. The upsurge of transactions in the primary and secondary stock market, as also in the securities transactions, has been unprecedented, both in terms of the volumes of trade and in value. Many thought these were a natural outcome of opening of floodgates. The upsurge noticed in the stock exchanges caught everyone by surprise and during the year from July 1991 to June 1992, the transactional volumes and features defied all rhymes and reasons. Speculation was at its peak and many types of operators reaped huge profits, at the cost of others. It was, however, ultimately a multi-person, zero-sum game, so that those who lost had their counterparts in those who gained. Chart III indicates the *dramatis personae*, an assortment of institutions and individuals. The year-long struts and frets of these characters: ultimately subsided when the authorities woke up for action. When the scam surfaced in mid 1992, it created a lot of hullabaloo, in the press, in parliament and also outside. Since then much has been written and spoken about the scam. Janakiraman Committee, appointed by the Reserve Bank of India to inquire into the irregularities, submitted six reports dealing with different transactional areas involved in the scam and suggested various measures to be taken by the Reserve Bank of India, on the one hand, and the banks and other parties, on the other. The six reports submitted by the committee provide some insight into the systemic details and is of some value to the students of banking at large. The Joint Parliamentary Committee, appointed for the purpose of determining the roles of various parties in the scam, submitted its report in two volumes. In the meantime, books have also appeared dealing with different aspects of the scam. In all this, beating-out-the-bush exercises in shielding the culprits and diluting the effects and the banking system, nay, the financial sector, have been common, as the issue took on some *political* colour.

In a more significant way the scam can *also* be taken as a failure of the vogue surveillance system, especially reporting, and actions thereupon by the highest ups in the RBI and the Banking Division of the Union Finance Ministry. This paper concentrates on the Janakiraman Committee Report as a view on the mechanism of securities transfer and the flaws that existed including the delays that took place.

In acting upon the reports of the inspection conducted by the RBI, the impact of the scam has been highlighted at the end, embracing the funds involved and the erring officials concerned. The gaps in the whole process are taken into view and corrective measures suggested for avoiding recurrence. Incidentally, most of the books are authored by journalists with focus of attention on the operational mechanisms adopted by the *dramatis personae*. The more serious side of the story, the impact of the scam and the fundamental flaws in the system have yet remained untraced. The journalistic tinge of some of the authors of these books becomes apparent when the scam is defied as an Americanism. It is, in fact, an American slang, as given in Webster's New World Dictionary of the American Language, second edition, meaning swindling in a confidence game. Appropriately, therefore, the scam can be called The Great Indian Swindle. On the other hand, the total involvement of funds in the cam, estimated by the Jan Raman Committee as about Rs. 5,000 crore, is small as a proportion to the total transactions in the stock exchanges and the total market capitalisation. Apparently the characters involved directly into this have attracted a lot more attention to the system that could give rise to such a swindle of this magnitude. It is in this context that an attempt has been made in the following paragraphs to examine the character and content of the scam with particular reference to whether failures were involved or the systems were respected in the negative even though, as laid down, they were quite sensitive.

The Janakiraman Committee in its final report contended that for understanding the nature and extent of the irregularities in the securities transactions of banks it would be necessary to understand the environment in which these irregularities took place. The committee delineated the following significant features of the related environmental issues:

1. there were large investible funds with the corporate sector, particularly with public sector units. With the gradual withdrawal of budgetary support from the government, the Public Sector Undertakings (PSUs) alone raised Rs. 20,700 crore by the issue of bonds between 1 April 1986 and 31 March 1992. An effective, worthwhile channel for these funds was not immediately visible;

2. the large public issues made by the PSUs did not find a ready market. These PSUs, therefore, made arrangements with banks whereby the banks subscribed for a significantpart of the issues and in turn, the PSUs placed the funds raises by A issues with the banks who subscribed to the issues. For example, Canfina subscribed to PSU bands on ten occasions during 1991-92 for an aggregate amount of Rs. 2182 crore an private placement basis, and of this, Rs. 2122.80 crore was placed with the PSUs. UCO Bank had subscribed an amount of Rs. 150 crore to Power Finance Corporation bonds in March 1992 which was placed by PFC with UCC Bank for portfolio management. There was nothing wrong with this practice as such, but for the motives behind, yet not objectionable on the surface;

3. as many of the bonds issues by PSU were tax free, they along with Units under the Unit-64 scheme of the Unit Trust of India, which *also* provided tax benefits under Section 80M of the Income Tax Act, were mainly held by corporate entities including banks. Thus, as on 30 June 1992 the total funds invested by banks alone, both on their own account and on behalf of

115

PMS clients in PSU bonds and units, aggregated almost Rs. 11,583 crores (face value). This was a gargantuan sum;

4. however, while these large investible funds were available with the corporate sector, the opportunities for short-term investment of these funds were restricted. There did not exist a significant money market in which these funds could be effectively invested and the call money market was restricted to banks and specified financial institutions. This pointer calls for particular consideration;

5. while companies in the private sector could invest in inter-corporate deposits, these were perceived as a risky form of investment for large amounts. PSUs were generally prohibited by administrative guidelines from investing in inter-corporate deposits. For deposits with banks there were ceilings on the rates of interest which varies according to monetary policy, the maximum rate of interest which banks were allowed to pay being 13% since April 1992 on deposits beyond 46 days and to three years or more. Though the ceiling on interest rates did not apply to Certificates of Deposit issued by banks, each deposit had to be for a minimum value of Rs. 1 crore (lowered to Rs. 50 lakh in 1990) and there was a monetary ceiling on the aggregate amount of CD which could be issued by a bank;

6. on the other hand, the stock market was booming. The sensitive index of the Bombay Stock Exchange had risen from 956.11 on 25 January 1991 to 4467.32 on 22 April 1992 and the average *'badla'* rates at which stock brokers borrowed funds had during that period ranged from 7.8% to 59.1%. A whopping rise by all counts;

7. banks, particularly the foreign banks, were, therefore, quick to identify 'arbitrage' opportunities whereby funds could be borrowed cheap and lent dear. This was the nub of the whole matter that created provocations.

To exploit these arbitrage opportunities, banks needed to circumvent existing regulations. The most significant of these regulations were:

1. as noted earlier, banks were not permitted to offer rates of interest which were in excess of the stipulated rates. On the other hand, PSUs needed to service the bonds issued, and therefore needed a return on the funds placed with the bank at a rate higher than the coupon rate on the bonds. This created a compulsion in PSUs to seek avenues that would meet the requirement;

2. banks were required to maintain a significant portion of their deposits in or in specified securities or with RBI. During most of the relevant time, the Cash Reserve Ratio was 25% of the incremental deposits and the Statutory Liquidity Ratio was 38.5% of the deposits. Thus, 63.5% of the deposits earned either no interest or interest which was considerably lower than the market rates, and only 36.5% of the deposits was available for commercial lending. Even out of this, almost 40% in respect of nationalised banks and private sector banks and a lower percentage for foreign banks was required to be lent to the priority sector earning only a concessional rate of interest.

One has to name a rope tighter than all this on which the banks were asked to walk;

3. banks were required to maintain reserve requirements (CRR and SLR) on call and notice money borrowings, which added significantly to the cost of borrowing such funds. Banks were caught in the noose, so were the PSUs with no escape routes discernible;

4. banks were permitted to accept funds from the corporate sector under protfolio management schemes where the depositor could earn higher returns but the acceptance of these funds was subject to the following restrictions:
   - there was a minimum 'lock-in' period of one year;
   - the bank was to act as an agent of the depositor to make investments on his behalf and the risk of the investments was to remain with the depositors;
   - the bank could not share in the profits or losses made by the depositor out of the investment of the funds and could only charge a fee (fixed or as a percentage);

5. banks could enter into ready forward transactions in securities only with other banks and only in respect of government and other approved securities;

6. the yield on bank's investments in government securities under the SLR prescription was much below the prevailing market rates on long-term debt instruments, and banks felt the need to improve the yield both through trading in these securities (at artificial rates) and through the mechanism of ready forward transactions.

A widely and hotly discussed instrument used in the securities transactions was the Bank Receipt (BR). The conditions and circumstances in which the BR figured as a key document of manoeuvre had been several, of which the following are significant. BR, in fact, did occupy the centre stage. The use of the BR acquired high significance for reasons as stated below:

1. in respect of sale and purchase transactions in government securities, normally the sale would be supported by delivery of SGL transfer forms. These are orders issued on the PDO to transfer the securities from the account of the seller to the account of the purchaser. However, the incidence of dishonour of SGL transfer forms had increased due to a number of reasons. The PDO records were maintained manually and on some occasions there was delay in intimating the fact of dishonour. Therefore for ready forward transactions, banks increasingly resorted to the issue of BRs rather than SGL transfer forms;

2. SGL account facilities in the PDOs were granted region wise. Thus, if the securities were held in the SGL account with one regional PDO and the sale was made in another region, it was not possible to issue a SGL transfer form without first transferring the securities from one PDO to the other. Although the transfers could be effected by telegram/telex, in these

circumstances a BR needed to be issued even for transactions in government securities;

3. SGL facilities were restricted to government securities. For purchase and sale of other securities, *e.g.* Units or PSU bonds, it was necessary to effect physical delivery of the bonds, along with transfer forms. In many cases of PSU bonds, the actual issue of scrips was delayed for several years and the holders' evidence of ownership was only an 'allotment letter'. The seller therefore could not make delivery of parts of the bonds covered by the 'allotment letter' until the scrips were issued. Even where bonds were available, exact delivery could not be made if the scrips were not available in denominations which permitted exact delivery. Finally, for large transactions, physical delivery could be cumbersome in respect of ready forward transactions, which were intended to be reserved within a short period of time. Therefore, in all such cases BRs were increasingly resorted to. Thus, the stage was set for an aura of irregular dealings in money disguised as securities transactions. There was a triple coincidence of wants; first, the PSUs who, after the withdrawal of the government budgetary support, had to raise funds massively in the market and had short term liquidity on their hands, wanted an avenue of investment yielding more than the coupon rates on the bonds they had issued. Secondly, the stock market was booming and the 'bulls' desperately needed funds to finance their overbought positions, in the face of the high *'badla'* rates. Thirdly, bankers who had accepted high cost funds from PSUs saw that the only avenue that yielded anticipated high returns were financing the stockbrokers in a booming market. What was needed was to devise some 'innovative' techniques to circumvent the regulation in the prevailing conditions and goaded by the compulsions of high returns, 'innovative' bordered on the 'irregular', in the use of the mechanisms found. To circumvent the regulations banks needed the assistance of brokers and, therefore, a close nexus had developed between certain brokers and certain banks. This aggravated by the fact that operating managers were under pressure to greatly increase the profitability of banks. While in the case of foreign banks this arose out of the growth of intense competition, in the case of nationalised banks there was a growing awareness that their overall performance compared very unfavourably with the performance of foreign banks and steps were needed to improve the 'bottom line' of their published results;

4. brokers had directly been financed by banks through the discounting of bills not supported by genuine transactions or by purchase of shares by the bank under 'ready forward' terms, and appeared to be an attempt to bypass RBI directives to banks governing direct advances by banks to brokers. They suffered from the further disadvantage that brokers got access to bank funds without complying with margin requirements as was the case when direct loans were given. Since the transactions had been on a 'ready forward'

basis, there was no need to permanently transfer the underlying securities and therefore under several excuses, banks had been resorting to the indiscriminate issue of BRs. On reversal of the transaction these BRs were returned. There had also been cases where SGLs issued had been returned without being deposited with the PDOs;

5. the use of BRs had been justified on the grounds that there was delay in recording of transactions at the PDOs and also that there was undue delay in the issue of scrips after allotment by PSUs. However, a large number of BRs had also been issued for units;

6. cheques issued in the names of banks by the purchasing banks had been collected and credited to the individual accounts of brokers without any such instruction by the issuing bank. *This* had enabled brokers to collect monies from purchasing banks under contracts, which were ostensibly with banking counterparts;

7. banks had lent their names to transactions, which were not on their own account. Thus banks had issued BRs at the request of brokers against BRs received or to be received in their favour in respect of transactions where they were neither purchasing nor selling investments. These facilities had been provided to earn a fee but without disclosing to the counter parties that the concerned bank was not entering the transaction on its own account;

8. through the portfolio Management scheme, corporate funds had been used to finance brokers in the manner of *'vyaj badla'* but at much lower rates than the prevailing *'vyaj badla'* rates;

9. merchant banking subsidiaries of banks had accepted substantial amounts by way of intercorporate deposits at high rates of interest and had been under compulsion to earn higher returns. These had been obtained through 'ready forward transactions';

10. in the case of some merchant banking subsidiaries of banks, the deals were made by the subsidiaries but the actual transactions for receipt/delivery of scrips, BRs, etc. and receipt/payment of monies payable/due were arranged by the parent bank. The subsidiary, therefore, was not able to effectively monitor the transaction;

11. special facilities had been made available to select brokers whereby bank cheques drawn in favour of the bank had been credited to brokers' accounts and against these cheques the bank had issued its own banker's cheques in favour of parties nominated by the broker. These had helped to hide the true nature of transactions from counter parties;

12. in a number of cases there had been total lack or a breakdown of essential discipline regarding the issue and recording of BRs, the scrutiny for genuineness of signatures, the receipt and delivery of securities and the receipt and payment for settlement of transactions;

13. there had been no periodical reconciliation by banks of the investment accounts with the SGL accounts maintained by the PDO and in several cases this reconciliation was in arrears for long periods. If such

reconciliation had been regularly done the investments periodically verified by the internal auditors, the non-availability of BRs would have been immediately detected;

14. in the PDO, the records were not computerised. Separate manual accounts were maintained for each scrip held by each bank and a minimum of information was available in the ledger where these accounts were maintained. It had, therefore, not been the practice not did it appear feasible (in the absence of computerisation) for a statement of transactions in the individual bank's account to be sent to the bank. If such a statement was available with the bank, it would have the means of regularly reconciling its investment account. Balance confirmation certificates were also not issued periodically and appeared to be an attempt to bypass RBI directives to banks governing direct advances by banks to brokers. They suffered from the further disadvantage that brokers got access to bank funds without complying with margin requirements as was the case when direct loans were given.

The Janakiraman Committee in their interim report submitted in May 1992 noticed that there had been a systematic diversion of funds from the banking system to the individual accounts of certain brokers and this diversion was presumably represented by the transactions for which the banks and subsidiaries were not holding BRs or were holding BRs of doubtful values. Three devices employed in this context for effecting diversion of funds, as noted by the Committee, are:

1. purchases had been made by banks and subsidiaries of securities and other instruments where the counter party is ostensibly another bank but in reality the proceeds had been directly or indirectly credited to brokers' accounts;
2. readyforward transactions had been entered into by banks either on their own account or on constituents' accounts with brokers which had provided funds to broker at rates which presumably were lower than the ruling *'vyaj badla'* rates in the stock market; and
3. brokers were directly financed by banks through the discounting of bills not supported by genuine transactions or by purchase of shares by the banks under ready forward terms. Some of the ready forward deals by banks were not completed and in consequence the banks might be holding investments whose market value might be considerably lower than the amount paid for the purchase of the investments.

Cheques issued in the names of banks by the purchasing banks have been collected and credited to the individual accounts of brokers without any such instructions by the issuing banks. This has enabled brokers to collect monies from purchasing banks under contracts which were ostensibly with banking counterparts. The diversion of funds was also made possible by a number of other factors:

1. there was a significant increase in the volume of transactions in securities and capital investments since July 1991. Thus, in the State Bank of India

alone the volume of transactions increased from about Rs. 10.000 million to Rs. 87.000 million in March 1992;

2. these transactions were mainly for the ready forward deals between banks, between banks and brokers and under portfolio management schemes. These were purely financing transactions though they took the form of purchase and sale of investments and appeared to be an attempt to bypass the RBI directives to banks governing direct advances by banks to brokers. They suffered from the further disadvantage that a broker got access to bank funds without complying with margin requirements as would be the case when direct loans were given;

3. since the transactions had been on a 'ready forward' basis, there was no need to permanently transfer the underlying securities and, therefore, under several excuses, banks had been resorting to the indiscriminate issue of BRs. On reversal of the transaction these BRs were returned. There had also been cases where SGLs issued had been returned without being deposited with the PDOs.

It has been acknowledged that a key element in the perpetration of the irregularities was the BR. On the heels of a close nexus between brokers and the banks, BRs were issued for generating transactions, which had no security backing. In fact, BRs acquired the status of negotiable instruments in the matter in which they were dealt with, as they were transferred from bank to bank and third party. BRs were accepted by banks. A complete breakdown of the internal control systems in a number of banks also played a key part in perpetrating irregularities of the dimension and import that the scam entailed. Perhaps flouting of the internal control system would be a better way to describe the phenomenon. The system was indeed there: it was not respected in practice. Banks developed a practice in which there were no independent contracts between counterpart banks and in many cases, deliveries of securities, BRs and SGL transfer forms were made to, and received from, brokers and even cheques for settlement of dues were given to, or received from the brokers. This invariably resulted in brokers delaying delivery of securities, BRs and SGL transfer forms as also cheques for settlement. Furthermore, irregularities were also perpetrated by the fact that brokers started dealing with their own account and causing differences between the rates at which the same contract was booked by the counterpart banks and the large differences paid to or received from brokers. Holes naturally developed in the investment portfolio of banks, remaining undetected because the portfolio was supported by SGL transfer forms or BRs. The Janakiraman Committee named individual banks and brokers and unearthed the mechanism that banks and brokers employed in close relationship with each other. Senior managers in the banks saw the treasury departments making huge profits, thus opted for choosing not to inquire too deeply as to how these profits were earned. They avoided rocking the boat, a phrase used by the Janakiraman Committee in its sixth and final report. Large sums of monies were diverted out of the country or to accounts of individuals not coming within the identifiable nets easily. Those who lost had to face a hopeless situation. Those who gained had to hide sources from which the gains accrued. The game of hide and seek has many ramifications when it is played on high stakes.

There are certain deeper issues that should not escape notice. Since nationalisation took place, commercial banks under the control of the Central Government were forced to pursue different tenets of social banking yielding practically no return, on the one hand, and creating grave doubts about realisation even of the principal amounts, on the other. Secondly, as if to add salt to injury, government and Parliament became increasingly vocal to the effect that the banks should earn profits whereas the discretion allowed to the banks to deploy funds in profitable channels remained a small fraction of total. Thirdly, being subordinate to administrative ministries, in this case the Union Ministry of Finance, banks could hardly object either to the dictates of the administrative ministries or the criticisms in Parliament. While, on the one hand loan melas, social banking, differential rates of interest and so on, bled them literally white, asking them to yield returns created an atmosphere of desperation. Banks, therefore, had to seek ways in which they could boost their earnings. It is not that the Reserve Bank did not know that irregularities on a large scale were being perpetrated through the machinations of brokers and banks; the Reserve Bank, in fact dragged its feet on the issue. Moreover, the Reserve Bank offers an example of *imperium in imperio*.

The functioning of the Reserve Bank of India and the hush hush that envelopes, several of its operational systems and procedures created an aura of disbelief. It has been widely held that the RBI must have had skeletons in its cupboard. Though all this may not be true, it does raise some fundamental questions as to why the country's central bank should remain outside a system of formal surveillance of its operations. The audit done or for that matter inspection system that operates hardly brings to light details which the powers that be do not want disclosed or brought in the open. In the context of the irregularities, for instance, the period involved since the irregularities were reported was quite considerable so as to attract proper attention for providing the stitch in time. The authorities, however, chose to turn a Nelson's eye to the whole issue and moved so leisurely that they could not stop perpetration of the irregularities, as the Janakiraman Committee stresses. It is in this context that one finds good enough reasons to underline that there is no valid ground why commercial banks as the Reserve Bank should not be audited by the Comptroller and Auditor General of India. Right from the days of nationalisation I, for one, have been shouting at the top of my voice about the logic of introducing CAG's audit both for commercial banks and the development financing institutions. CAG audited the banks and the Reserve Bank, the lackadaisical attitudes of these bodies could be immediately brought to the fore for necessary action by Parliament and Government. A discussion in Parliament on the basis of CAG's findings could have nailed the culprits in proper time. In fact, CAG could initiate the practice of cost audit of banks with issue of detailed guidelines in consultation with the Company Law Board on the basis of the experience of MADCARC. It was appropriate that the note appended to the Narasimham Committee Report on the financial system by Professor M. Datta Chowdhury and M.R. Shroff underlined that "it is important to move further to make the autonomy of these institutions credible and that the government should not appoint its officials on the boards of public sector banks and financial institutions. The banking division of the Ministry of Finance, as at present constituted, should consequently be abolished", for avoidance of duality of control between the Reserve Bank and the banking division. With the withdrawal of the bureaucratic breathing over the shoulders of banks cost audit could bring to light different aspects of financial performance of the banks on the basis of which the Reserve Bank and the government could decide on various related issues. The Institute of Cost and Works Accountants of India, incidentally, brought out a research publication on *Cost Accounting in Commercial Banking Industry*, the recommendations of which could be usefully applied to the banking sector in this country.

Dr. P.R. Brahmananda holds the view that the scam took place in the money market more than in the stock exchanges. In his V.K.R.V. Rao Memorial lecture under the aegis of the Indian Economic Association, Dr. P.R. Brahmananda underlined that large-scale transfer of funds from the money market to the stock market due to arbitrage potential was at the back of the securities scam. The failure of monetary policy and not any failure of the system were the cause for the scam. The low interest rate in the call money market had caused a large flow of funds into the stock market. The cost of fund generation through BR had been close to the coupon rates of the Government bonds and as such, provided a source for the scam. Loans obtained from the commercial banks also gravitated to the stock market, Dr. Brahmananda asserted. He further opined that the scam could be linked to the skyrocketing share price throughout 1992, but the Janakiraman Committee and the JPC focused only on the period from April 1991, to June 1992, missing the eye of the storm that ensued.

Last but not the least, during the liberalisation regime and government's allowing public sector banks to raise capital from the market, it would be essential that a regular and systematic review and appraisal of the total transactions of these banks should be made in the light of the objectives of these banks. The machinations of the banks, brokers and development financial institutions can hardly be called sophisticated; they were fraudulent from the beginning to the end. The details that provided meat to journalists are only the outer manifestations. The shield that Janakiraman Committee provided in these reports to give to the Reserve Bank of India systems and procedures can also be debated on several counts. The Finance Minister called the scam a 'systems failure'. It was not. Apart from the fact that a system is only as good as the people behind it desire of it, there are two aspects that call for particular consideration in the present context. First, because the system itself was inadequate in terms of depth and comprehension; the question of failure was irrelevant. Secondly, because the irregularities were known from the inspection reports of the Reserve Bank much earlier than the scam was reported in the press, what was needed was immediate corrective action, which was not taken due to procrastination of the authorities, to say the least.

*Chart III*

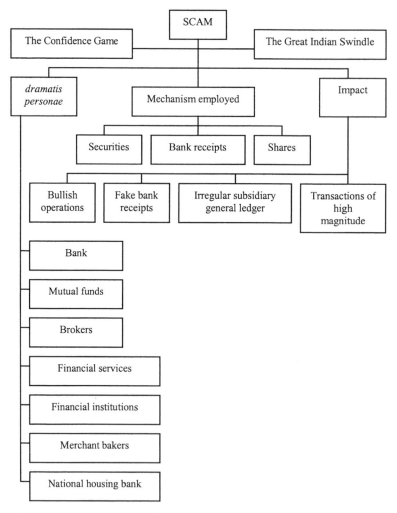

N.B. The *modus operandi* was not sophisticated at all. Seriousness of purpose was missing all along the line. RBI and the authorities dragged their feet to make all this happen. The scam in fact made it imperative on the part of the authorities that be to track down case by case the sources and uses of funds.

## Scam Glossary

| | |
|---|---|
| Call Money | Inter-bank deals, lending or borrowing money for periods as short as a day or three days to meet the cash reserve ratio stipulated by the RBI. |
| Coupon Rate | Interest rate fixed to the bond. |
| CRR | Cash Reserve Ratio is a percentage of deposits that banks are supposed to maintain in liquid assets. |
| Double ready forward | The sale of securities between two operators, each conducting a ready forward deal. |
| Gilts | Government securities like central loans and state loans. Includes government guaranteed bonds like that of Industrial Development Bank of India (IDBI). Gilts is the short form of gilt-edged securities – so called because they carry no risk at all. |
| PDO | The Public Debt Office of the Reserve Bank of India (RBI). In ledgers earmarked for each bank, the PDO records transactions are recorded separately. |
| Money Markets | Covering all short-term financial products directly linked to the interest rate like treasury bills, certificates of deposit and commercial paper. Includes inter-bank call money as well. In many cases, even capital market instruments like bonds and units are included in the ambit of money market as they are often converted into synthetic short-term assets through buy back deals. |
| Roll over | Buying time. When the National Housing Bank (NHB) faced a cash crunch, it had no alternative but to ask the lender (Bank of India (BOI) Mutual Fund and Canfin) to roll over its debts till it arranged for funds. |
| SGL Form | Subsidiary General Ledger, a RBI form that verifies ownership of security. |
| Securities | Instruments for State's loans. |
| Ready Forward | The sale of securities, with a fixed buy rate and date. |
| SLR | Statutory Liquidity Ratio is a percentage of their deposits that banks are supposed to mandatorily invest in approved securities. |

P. Chattopadhyay

## References

**Barua, S.K. & Verna, J.R.**, *The Great Indian Scam*.

**Basu, D. & Dalal, S.** (1993), *THE SCAM: Who Won, Who Lost and Who Got Away*, New Delhi: UBS Publishers' Distributers Ltd.

**Dasgupta, G.** (1993), *The Securities Scandal*, New Delhi: Peoples' Publishing House.

**Ramachandranm, K.S.**, *Scanning the SCAM*.

*Interim Report of the Committee to Enquire into the Securities Transactions of the Banks and Financial Institutions*, Reserve Bank of India, Mumbai, May 1992.

*Second Interim Report of the Committee to Enquire into the Securities Transactions of the Banks and Financial Institutions*, July 1992.

*Report No. 3 of the Committee to Enquire into the Securities Transactions of the Banks and Financial Institutions*, August 1992.

*Report No. 4 of the Committee to Enquire into the Securities Transactions of the Banks and Financial Institutions*, March 1993.

*Report No. 5 of the Committee to Enquire into the Securities Transactions of the Banks and Financial Institutions*, April 1993.

*Report No. 6 – Final Report of the Committee to Enquire into the Securities Transactions of the Banks and Financial Institutions*, April 1993.

*Report of the Joint Committee to Enquire into Irregularities in Securities and Banking Transactions*, Vol. I and II, New Delhi: Lok Sabha Secretariat, December 1993.

# The Exclusion of Improperly Obtained Evidence in England & Wales: a Continuing Saga[*]

*A.L.-T. Choo & S. Nash*

## Introduction

This paper discusses the approach of the courts in England & Wales to excluding prosecution evidence, which has been obtained illegally or improperly by the police. We considered this topic a suitable one for an international conference in view of the very different approaches, which have been taken to the issue in different jurisdictions. Furthermore, the English position is of particular interest at present because England is in the process of 'incorporating' the *European Convention for the Protection of Human Rights and Fundamental Freedoms (ECHR)* into its domestic law.

For well over a decade now, there has been in existence in England a statutory provision, Section 78(1) of the *Police and Criminal Evidence Act 1984 (PACE)*, which states: "In any proceedings the court may refuse to allow evidence on which the prosecution proposes to rely to be given if it appears to the court that, having regard to all the circumstances, *including the circumstances in which the evidence was obtained*, the admission of the evidence would have such an adverse effect on the fairness of the proceedings that the court ought not to admit it."[1]

This provision "is by now known almost by heart by most people who have anything to do with the law,"[2] and is by far the most cited provision of the Act.[3] Yet the extent to which the senior judiciary in England is willing to sanction the use of Section 78(1) of *PACE* to secure the exclusion of improperly obtained *but reliable* evidence remains unclear. This paper[4] has been prompted by a recent line of Court of Appeal authority suggesting that it is only in very exceptional circumstances that such evidence can be excluded in English law. Our argument is that, in so suggesting, the Court of Appeal has taken a wrong turn. Far better, it is submitted, if the Court had not sought to sideline but instead had learnt valuable lessons from a number of important developments in English law, particularly those relating to the discretionary exclusion of confession evidence and the doctrine of abuse of process.

---

[*] This paper is based on the authors' article, 'What's the Matter with Section 78?' (1999), *Crim. L.R.* 929.

[1] Italics added.

[2] *Hudson* v. *D.P.P.* [1992] *R.T.R.* 27, 34, per Hodgson J.

[3] K. Grevling, 'Fairness and the Exclusion of Evidence under Section 78(1) of the Police and Criminal Evidence Act' (1997), 113 *L.Q.R.* 667, 667.

[4] *See also*, for a recent sustained discussion of improperly obtained evidence, P. Mirfield, *Silence, Confessions and Improperly Obtained Evidence* (1997).

## Early Promise

The common law position – at least as it appeared from the decision of the House of Lords in *Sang*[5] – was effectively that improperly obtained evidence could be excluded only in the exercise of the court's discretion to ensure a *fair trial*, and in the exercise of this discretion such evidence could be excluded only if the impropriety affected the reliability of the evidence or constituted an infringement of the accused's right against self-incrimination. Evidence could not be regarded as having been obtained in violation of the accused's right against self-incrimination unless it had been obtained *from the accused after the offence*. The extent to which Section 78(1) of *PACE* would affect the common law was initially a matter of speculation. The ordinary principles of statutory interpretation, requiring as they do a consideration of the plain meaning of the words of the provision, would seem to have permitted courts to develop a fresh approach unencumbered by the common law: the reference to "the circumstances in which the evidence was obtained" is a general one which does not in any way imply that courts are restricted to a consideration of circumstances which cast doubt on the reliability of the evidence obtained, or circumstances involving the obtaining of evidence from the accused after the offence.

Certainly, a number of landmark cases on confession evidence in the late 1980s saw the Court of Appeal making strong statements about the utility of Section 78(1) in addressing the issue of breaches of the rules of police investigation. Although exclusion under Section 78(1) must not be used directly to discipline the police,[6] "significant and substantial" breaches would be taken seriously in the sense that they would weigh heavily in favour of the exclusion of evidence obtained as a result of the breaches.[7] Also evident from the cases is the notion that a breach may, by its very nature, be significant and substantial – in other words, it will be significant and substantial even if the police acted in good faith – but that bad faith can effectively convert a breach which is not otherwise significant and substantial into one which is.[8]

The cases provide instances of strongly worded judicial condemnations of improper police practices. In *Mason* the Court of Appeal, in holding that the confession evidence ought to have been excluded under Section 78(1), observed: "It is obvious from the undisputed evidence that the police practised a deceit not only upon the appellant, which is bad enough, but also upon the solicitor whose duty it was to advise him. In effect, they hoodwinked both solicitor and client. That was a most reprehensible thing to do."[9] In *Samuel* the

---

[5] [1980] *A.C.* 402.
[6] *Mason* [1988] 1 *W.L.R.* 139; *Delaney* (1988) 88 *Cr. App. R.* 338.
[7] *See, e.g., Keenan* [1990] 2 *Q.B.* 54.
[8] *See, e.g., Walsh* (1989) 91 *Cr. App. R.* 161.
[9] [1988] 1 *W.L.R.* 139, 144.

Court stated: "In this case the appellant was denied improperly one of the most important and fundamental rights of a citizen."[10] In *Dunn* the Court "stress[ed] yet again the importance of the police complying strictly with the Codes of Practice. There were serious breaches in this case."[11] Again, the breaches in *Canale* were described by the Court as "flagrant", "deliberate" and "cynical";[12] the police conduct "demonstrate[d] a lamentable attitude towards the *1984 Act* and the codes made thereunder. (…) If, which we find it hard to believe, police officers still do not appreciate the importance of *[PACE]* and the accompanying Codes, then it is time that they did."[13]

Unsurprisingly, the confession cases gave rise to the expectation that Section 78(1) would also prove a useful vehicle for securing the exclusion of improperly obtained real evidence. Certainly, initial indications were that this might well be the view taken by the courts. In the early 1990s, decisions of the Divisional Court in road traffic prosecutions appeared to advocate an approach in relation to evidence of breath specimens which was analogous to that taken in relation to confession evidence.[14] Thus an impropriety could be considered "significant and substantial", and hence strong grounds for exclusion under Section 78(1), in the absence of bad faith on the part of the police, and simply because it constituted a breach of an important right of the accused. In one case, for example, the Court declined, despite the absence of bad faith, to interfere with the justices' decision to exclude evidence of a positive breath specimen provided after an unlawful arrest: "The justices were entitled to conclude that the substantial breach by the constable [meant that] the protection afforded to members of the public by Section 6 [of the *Road Traffic Act 1988*] was denied to the defendant, that as a result the prosecutor obtained evidence which he would not otherwise have obtained, and that as a result the defendant was prejudiced in a significant manner in resisting the charge against him."[15]

The decision of the Court of Appeal in *Smurthwaite* also provided those hoping that the courts would embrace a wide interpretation of Section 78(1) with good reasons to be cheerful. In *Sang*, the House of Lords had held that entrapment (that is, the inducement of the commission of an offence which would not otherwise have been committed) was not a factor which could be considered at common law in determining whether evidence ought to be excluded in the exercise of discretion.[16] In *Smurthwaite*, however, the Court of

---

[10] [1988] *Q.B.* 615, 630.

[11] (1990) 91 *Cr. App. R.* 237, 243.

[12] [1990] 2 *All E.R.* 187, 192.

[13] *Ibid.*, 190.

[14] *D.P.P.* v. *McGladrigan* [1991] *R.T.R.* 297; *D.P.P.* v. *Godwin* [1991] *R.T.R.* 303. *See also* *D.P.P.* v. *Kay* [1999] *R.T.R.* 109.

[15] *D.P.P.* v. *Godwin* [1991] *R.T.R.* 303, 308.

[16] The argument that evidence obtained by entrapment could not be excluded in the exercise of discretion proceeded on the following (rather tenuous) basis. If entrapment evidence were (to be continued)

Appeal, in holding that evidence obtained in undercover police operations can be excluded under Section 78(1) if the circumstances warrant it, provided the following non-exhaustive list of factors which may be considered by a court in deciding whether to exercise its exclusionary discretion: "Was the officer acting as an agent provocateur in the sense that he was enticing the defendant to commit an offence he would not otherwise have committed? What was the nature of any entrapment? Does the evidence consist of admissions to a completed offence, or does it consist of the actual commission of an offence? How active or passive was the officer's role in obtaining the evidence? Is there an unassailable record of what occurred, or is it strongly corroborated? (...) A further consideration for the judge in deciding whether to admit an undercover officer's evidence is whether he has abused his role to ask questions which ought properly to have been asked as a police officer and in accordance with the codes."[17] The very first factor mentioned by the Court clearly turns the common law position on its head.

Finally, the 1990s saw a marked expansion of the doctrine of abuse of process.[18] The House of Lords confirmed in *R. v. Horseferry Road Magistrates' Court, ex p. Bennett*[19] that criminal proceedings could be stayed as an abuse of process on account of improper police or prosecutorial conduct at the pre-trial stage.[20] Thus, a stay would be appropriate if it was shown that a defendant had been forcibly abducted and brought to the UK to face trial in disregard of the extradition laws.[21] The doctrine was refined by the House of Lords in *Latif*,[22] which concerned a claim by Shahzad, whose appeal was conjoined with Latif's, that his prosecution for being knowingly concerned in the importation of heroin should have been stayed as an abuse of process because of the involvement and assistance of Honi, an informer, and officers of the Customs and Excise. The House of Lords acknowledged[23] that "Shahzad would probably not have committed the particular offence of which he was

---

excluded and the evidence were the only prosecution evidence, or perhaps a crucial part of the prosecution evidence, the case against the accused would collapse. This would be tantamount to a recognition of a defense of entrapment, which does not exist in England, through the back door.

[17] [1994] 1 *All E.R.* 898, 903.

[18] *See generally* A.L.-T. Choo, 'Halting Criminal Prosecutions: The Abuse of Process Doctrine Revisited', [1995] *Crim. L.R.* 864.

[19] [1994] 1 *A.C.* 42.

[20] For further discussion *see* C. Gane & S. Nash, 'Illegal Extradition: The Irregular Return of Fugitive Offenders' (1996), 1 *Scottish Law & Practice Quarterly* 277.

[21] *See also Mullen* [1999] 2 *Cr. App. R.* 143, discussed below. Cf. *R. v. Staines Magistrates' Court, ex p. Westfallen* [1998] 4 *All E.R.* 210; *see generally* S. O'Doherty, 'Home Thoughts from Abroad' (1998), 148 *N.L.J.* 1802.

[22] [1996] 1 *W.L.R.* 104. *See generally* A.J. Ashworth, 'Should the Police be Allowed to Use Deceptive Practices?' (1998), 114 *L.Q.R.* 108, 119-20; K. Grevling, 'Undercover Operations: Balancing the Public Interest?' (1996), 112 *L.Q.R.* 401; S. Sharpe, 'Judicial Discretion and Investigative Impropriety' (1997), 1(2) *E. & P.* 149.

[23] *Ibid.*, 111-13.

convicted, but for the conduct of Honi and customs officers, which included criminal conduct." If, however, a court were always to stay the proceedings in such cases, it would "incur the reproach that it is failing to protect the public from serious crime". If, on the other hand, the proceedings were never to be stayed, "the perception will be that the court condones criminal conduct and malpractice by law enforcement agencies. That would undermine public confidence in the criminal justice system and bring it into disrepute." It would be inappropriate, therefore, to adopt either extreme position. The approach, rather, should be as follows.

First, if the court concludes that the impugned conduct would make a *fair trial* impossible, the proceedings must automatically be stayed. What is envisaged here, clearly, is the unlikely possibility of the conduct affecting trial fairness in the sense of compromising the ability of the trial to determine guilt or innocence properly. In the present case, it was "plain that a fair trial was possible and that such a trial took place."

In such a situation it would be necessary to proceed to the second question, which is whether, despite a fair trial being possible, the judge ought nevertheless to stay the proceedings on the basis that it would be contrary to the public interest in the integrity of the criminal justice system for the trial to proceed. In other words, "it is for the judge in the exercise of his discretion to decide whether there has been an abuse of process, which amounts to an affront to the public conscience and requires the criminal proceedings to be stayed". In exercising this discretion, the court must perform a balancing exercise: "in a case such as the present the judge must weigh in the balance the public interest in ensuring that those that are charged with grave crimes should be tried and the competing public interest in not conveying the impression that the court will adopt the approach that the end justified any means."[24]

The willingness of the House of Lords to breathe life into the abuse of process doctrine may be viewed as an expression of its recognition that it is now completely outdated to regard judicial responsibility as being confined to ensuring the non-conviction of an innocent person. There are, as the House put it simply in *Latif*, "broader considerations of the integrity of the criminal justice system."[25] Considerations of extrinsic policy are as much a concern as considerations of intrinsic policy. Even if there is no danger of the conviction of an innocent person, a court has the duty to act if failure to do so would compromise the legitimacy of the adjudicative process and the moral authority of a guilty verdict if such a verdict were to ensue.[26] It would therefore be

---

[24] It would seem, therefore, that where undercover police operations are concerned, either the exclusion of evidence *(Smurthwaite)* or a stay of the proceedings as a whole *(Latif)* may be ordered by the trial judge in the exercise of his or her discretion. Unfortunately, the precise relationship between these alternative judicial measures has yet to be properly clarified.

[25] [1996] 1 *W.L.R.* 104, 112.

[26] *See generally* I.H. Dennis, *The Law of Evidence* (1999), pp. 36-43.

anomalous if a court were to be permitted to act by staying 'tainted' proceedings (a fairly drastic measure), but were not to be permitted to act by simply excluding an item of 'tainted' evidence (a potentially less drastic measure)[27]. As will be seen shortly, however, this is precisely the effect of the recent decision of the Court of Appeal in *Chalkley*.[28]

## Subsequent Disappointment

Recent decisions of the Court of Appeal on improperly obtained evidence appear to have signalled a move away from the approach, taken in the confession cases referred to above, of focusing on the *nature of the breach*, and towards an approach which takes the *nature of the evidence* as its central consideration. The fact that non-confession evidence is often of undoubted reliability is considered a strong factor in favour of not exercising the exclusionary discretion. At issue in *Cooke*,[29] a prosecution for rape and kidnapping, was evidence of a DNA profile obtained from hair roots and sheaths plucked from the accused's head. The Court of Appeal held that this evidence had not been obtained illegally,[30] but even assuming that it had been, the trial judge had not erred in failing to exclude the evidence under Section 78(1). The Court noted that "the vast majority of cases in which the court has ruled such evidence inadmissible have been cases in which what was challenged was an alleged confession obtained from the defendant in breach of one of the *Police and Criminal Evidence Act Codes of Practice*."[31] In this case the DNA profile constituted very strong evidence that Cooke had had sexual intercourse with the complainant. Any illegality involved in the way in which the evidence was obtained would not have "in any way cast doubt upon the accuracy or strength of the evidence. In this way evidence of this kind differs from, for example, a disputed confession, where the truth of the confession may well itself be in issue."

In *Chalkley*,[32] Chalkley and Jeffries were charged with conspiracy to commit robbery. The prosecution proposed to adduce evidence of covertly obtained tape recordings of highly incriminating conversations between the defendants. The Regional Crime Squad had obtained the necessary authorisation, under the Home Office guidelines, to place a listening device in

---

[27] Of course, if the evidence were the only prosecution evidence, or perhaps a crucial part of the prosecution evidence, then its exclusion would be tantamount to a complete stay of the proceedings.

[28] [1998] 2 *All E.R.* 155.

[29] [1995] 1 *Cr. App. R.* 318.

[30] Hair plucked from the scalp constituted a non-intimate sample under Section 65 of *PACE* and could therefore be taken without consent under Section 63(3).

[31] *Ibid.*, 328.

[32] [1998] 2 *All E.R.* 155.

Chalkley's home.[33] In order to install the device, they arrested Chalkley in connection with crimes about which no action had previously been taken, seized his house key, and used it to enter the house. They also arranged the cutting of a copy of the key, which was later used on two occasions to enter the house to renew the battery on the device. The Court of Appeal held that the arrest of Chalkley had not been unlawful,[34] but that even if it had been, the trial judge's decision not to exclude the evidence under Section 78(1) should stand. The Court suggested, in effect, that the discretion to exclude evidence on the ground that it had been obtained improperly was applicable only in relation to:

1. evidence of a confession obtained from the accused;
2. other evidence obtained *from the accused* after the commission of the offence;
3. evidence excludable under the *Smurthwaite* principles; and
4. evidence the quality of which had been, or might have been, affected by the way in which it had been obtained.

As for the evidence in this case, "there was no dispute as to its authenticity, content or effect; it was relevant, highly probative of the appellants' involvement in the conspiracy and otherwise admissible; it did not result from incitement, entrapment or inducement or any other conduct of that sort; and none of the unlawful conduct of the police or other of their conduct of which complaint is made affects the quality of the evidence."[35]

The Court referred to the decisions of the House of Lords in *Ex p. Bennett* and *Latif*, but took the view that Section 78(1) could not be used to "exclude [evidence] as a mark of disapproval of the way in which it had been obtained", since Section 78(1) and the abuse of process doctrine did not share the same juridical basis. "The determination of the fairness or otherwise of admitting evidence under s. 78 is distinct from the exercise of discretion in determining whether to stay criminal proceedings as an abuse of process."[36] A balancing approach is accordingly not appropriate to a determination of whether improperly obtained evidence should be excluded under Section 78(1).

The decision in *Chalkley* is thus potentially far-reaching. It suggests that evidence of the type in *Chalkley*, and real evidence not obtained from the accused, such as evidence obtained as a result of a search, must be admitted if it is reliable; such evidence *cannot* be excluded on the ground that it was

---

[33] There were, at the time, no statutory provisions governing the use of such devices. *See* now *Police Act 1997*, Pt III, on which *see generally* M. Colvin, 'Part III Police Act 1997' (1999), 149 *N.L.J.* 311; S. Uglow & V. Telford, *The Police Act 1997* (1997), Ch. 3.
[34] "A collateral motive for an arrest on otherwise good and stated grounds does not necessarily make it unlawful. It depends on the motive."([1998] 2 *All E.R.* 155, 176).
[35] *Ibid.*, 180.
[36] *Ibid.*, 178.

obtained improperly.[37] Real evidence obtained from the accused, on the other hand, is subject to discretionary exclusion, although *Cooke* suggests that courts generally *will not* exclude such evidence, given its inherent reliability. Such a narrow approach seems contrary to the plain meaning of the words of Section 78(1), discussed earlier. It also appears inconsistent with the endorsement in *Chalkley* of the *Smurthwaite* principles: these principles, as we have seen, permit the exclusion of evidence simply because of the manner in which it was obtained, and irrespective of its quality in terms of its cogency in implicating the accused in the commission of the offence. That *Chalkley* is not a mere aberration, however, is demonstrated by a subsequent decision where, in approving *Chalkley*, the Court of Appeal held in very clear terms: "Here the quality of the evidence is simply unaffected by the (...) illegality and in our judgment the decision under Section 78 therefore *had to go in favour of the prosecution.*"[38]

The decision in *Chalkley* may be compared with the earlier decision of the House of Lords in *Khan (Sultan).*[39] On the day after his arrival from Pakistan, Khan, on being interviewed at a police station, denied any offence and declined to answer most of the questions put to him. He was released without charge. Some six months later, he visited the home of a person whom the police suspected of being involved in the supply of heroin on a large scale. As a result of these suspicions, the police had installed an aural surveillance device on the exterior of the property, without the knowledge or consent of the owner or occupier of the property. The police obtained a tape recording of a conversation which took place between Khan and others in the house, during which Khan said things which plainly demonstrated his involvement in the importation of heroin. The House of Lords held that, in considering whether evidence of the taped conversation should be excluded under Section 78(1), a court could take into account any apparent or probable breach of Article 8 of the *ECHR*, which guarantees the right to privacy: "If evidence has been obtained in circumstances which involve an apparent breach of art. 8, or, for that matter an apparent breach of the law of a foreign country, that is a matter which may be relevant to the exercise of the s. 78 power."[40]

---

[37] Cf., however, *Stewart* [1995] *Crim. L.R.* 499 and *McCarthy* [1996] *Crim. L.R.* 818, in which the Court of Appeal appeared to suggest that evidence obtained as a result of an illegal search *is* subject to discretionary exclusion, although the discretion is unlikely to be exercised because of the inherent reliability of such evidence.

[38] *Bray*, unrep., C.A., 31 July 1998 (italics added).

[39] [1996] 3 *All E.R.* 289. *See generally* P.B. Carter, 'Evidence Obtained by Use of a Covert Listening Device' (1997), 113 *L.Q.R.* 468; S. Sharpe, 'Electronic Eavesdropping: A Chance for Accountability?' (1996), 146 *N.L.J.* 1088; J.R. Spencer, 'Bugging and Burglary by the Police', [1997] *C.L.J.* 6; P. Tain, 'Covert Surveillance, *R.* v. *Khan* and the European Convention' (1996), 140 *S.J.* 785; C.F.H. Tapper, 'Overhearing and Oversight' (1997), 1(2) *E. & P.* 162.

[40] *Ibid.*, 301. *See also R.* v. *Governor of Pentonville Prison, ex p. Chinoy* [1992] 1 *All E.R.* 317; M. Mackarel & C. Gane, 'Admitting Irregularly or Illegally Obtained Evidence from Abroad into Criminal Proceedings – A Common Law Approach', [1997] *Crim. L.R.* 720.

The House of Lords concluded that the trial judge in this case had been entitled to hold that, even if there had been a breach of Article 8, the Section 78(1) discretion ought not to have been exercised. Rather disappointingly, and especially in view of the fact that this has been the only real opportunity which the House of Lords has had to discuss Section 78(1), no explanation was provided of precisely *why* the trial judge had not erred. Tellingly, however, the observation was made that the conclusion was reached "not only quite firmly as a matter of law, but also with relief. It would be a strange reflection on our law if a man who has admitted his participation in the illegal importation of a large quantity of heroin should have his conviction set aside on the grounds that his privacy has been invaded."[41] A possible difference between *Khan* and *Chalkley* lies in the fact that the House of Lords in the former case appeared to acknowledge that such evidence *could* be excluded in the exercise of discretion, albeit probably only in very limited circumstances, while the Court of Appeal in the latter case appeared to suggest that such evidence *could not* be excluded in the exercise of discretion. Be that as it may, the commitment to a reliability principle in both cases seems abundantly clear.[42]

## Missed Opportunities

By effectively treating improperly obtained but reliable evidence as belonging in a special category which cannot be touched by considerations drawn from other areas of the law of evidence and procedure, the Court of Appeal has missed valuable opportunities to learn from a number of these areas. The most obvious of these is the abuse of process doctrine. As has been seen, the House of Lords endorsed in two recent cases a wide conception of the scope of the doctrine. The Court of Appeal in a post-*Chalkley* decision similarly took a wide view of the doctrine. In *Mullen*, the appellant was convicted of conspiracy to cause explosions and sentenced to 30 years imprisonment. In the Court of Appeal it was argued that his trial should not have proceeded, primarily on the basis that "the British authorities initiated and subsequently assisted in and procured the deportation of the appellant, by unlawful means, in circumstances in which there were specific extradition facilities between this country and Zimbabwe. In so acting they were not only encouraging unlawful conduct in Zimbabwe, but they were also acting in breach of public international law."[43] The Court acknowledged that this was not a case in which there had been any danger of an unfair trial: "(...) [I]t seems to us that *Bennett*-type abuse, where it would be offensive to justice and propriety to try the defendant at all, is different (...) from the type of abuse which renders a

---

[41] *Ibid.*, 302.
[42] *See also Aujla* [1998] 2 *Cr. App. R.* 16; *see generally* J.R. Spencer, 'Electronic Eavesdropping and Anomalies in the Law of Evidence', [1999] *C.L.J.* 43.
[43] [1999] 2 *Cr. App. R.* 143, 156.

fair trial impossible. (...) It arises not from the relationship between the prosecution and the defendant, but from the relationship between the prosecution and the Court. It arises from the Court's need to exercise control over executive involvement in the whole prosecution process, not limited to the trial itself."[44]

Significantly, the Court noted that "certainty of guilt cannot displace the essential feature of this kind of abuse of process, namely the degradation of the lawful administration of justice."[45]

On the facts of the case: "This Court recognises the immense degree of public revulsion which has, quite properly, attached to the activities of those who have assisted and furthered the violent operations of the IRA and other terrorist organisations. In the discretionary exercise, great weight must therefore be attached to the nature of the offence involved in this case. Against that, however, the conduct of the security services and police in procuring the unlawful deportation of the appellant in the manner which has been described, represents, in the view of this Court, a blatant and extremely serious failure to adhere to the rule of law with regard to the production of a defendant for prosecution in the English courts. The need to discourage such conduct on the part of those who are responsible for criminal prosecutions is a matter of public policy, to which (...) very considerable weight must be attached."[46]

The Court's conclusion was that "we have no doubt that the discretionary balance comes down decisively against the prosecution of this offence."[47] It is difficult to imagine a greater contrast between the approach taken here and the approach to Section 78(1) in *Chalkley*. Particularly notable is the acknowledgement in *Mullen* that the 'balance' came down in favour of a stay despite the seriousness of the offence in question.

Whether one is considering the possibility of excluding evidence on account of pre-trial police impropriety, or the possibility of staying the proceedings as a whole on account of such impropriety, what is at stake is surely the same fundamental question: should the prosecution be deprived of the fruits of the pre-trial police impropriety? English law has already accepted that proceedings may be stayed on account of pre-trial impropriety even if there is no danger of the trial being 'unreliable' in terms of being unable to determine guilt or innocence accurately. Consistency dictates, therefore, that, by analogy, improperly obtained but reliable evidence should be capable of being excluded. Yet this is diametrically opposed to the approach taken in *Chalkley*. The peremptory dismissal in *Chalkley* of considerations drawn from the law of abuse of process is therefore particularly disappointing as it introduces a glaring anomaly into the law.

---

[44] *Ibid.*, 158.
[45] *Ibid.*, 155.
[46] *Ibid.*, 156-7.
[47] *Ibid.*, 157.

Turning to confession evidence, it is doubtless true that such evidence may well be of questionable reliability; the possibility that false confessions to crime may be made is now well recognised.[48] But *Chalkley* is surely wrong in implying that reliability is the sole concern in confessions cases. The strong statements made in decisions on the exclusion of confession evidence under Section 78(1), referred to above, demonstrate that the Court of Appeal was focusing rather more on the police breaches themselves than on the nature of the evidence yielded by those breaches. Such statements suggest that the Court considered the breaches to be capable of leading to exclusion *regardless of the type of evidence in question*. It is therefore inappropriate for the Court of Appeal in cases like *Chalkley* to attempt to explain away the discretionary exclusion of confession evidence solely in terms of exclusion *because of* potential unreliability.

Relatedly, the Court of Appeal has acknowledged on several occasions that identification evidence obtained in breach of Code D of *PACE* may be excluded under Section 78(1).[49] Again, a court taking the *Chalkley* line would attempt to rationalise these decisions by reasoning that, like confession evidence, identification evidence may be of doubtful reliability given the possibility of misidentification.[50] Yet this would be to ignore the fact that in such cases the Court of Appeal may be as much concerned with the failure to comply with procedures as with the potential unreliability of the resulting evidence. For example, in *Quinn*, a case on identification evidence, the Court stated: "The function of the judge is (...) to *protect the fairness of the proceedings*, and normally proceedings are fair if a jury hears *all* relevant evidence which either side wishes to place before it, but proceedings may become unfair if, for example, one side is allowed to adduce relevant evidence which, for one reason or another, the other side cannot properly challenge or meet, <u>or where there has been an abuse of process, *e.g.* because evidence has been obtained in deliberate breach of procedures laid down in an official code of practice.</u>"[51]

Valuable insights can also be gained from a somewhat unlikely source, the recent decision of the Court of Appeal in *Radak*.[52] The question in this case was whether, although evidence of a witness statement constituted hearsay evidence which was technically admissible under Section 23 of the *Criminal*

---

[48] *See* G.H. Gudjonsson, *The Psychology of Interrogations, Confessions and Testimony* (1992), 226-8.

[49] *See, e.g., Nagah* (1990) 155 *J.P.* 229; *Tiplady* (1995) 159 *J.P.* 548; *Willoughby* [1999] 2 *Cr. App. R.* 82.

[50] *See generally* B.L. Cutler & S. D. Penrod, *Mistaken Identification: The Eyewitness, Psychology and the Law* (1995), Chapters 6 and 7.

[51] [1990] *Crim. L.R.* 581, quoted in *R.* v. *King's Lynn Magistrates, ex p. Holland* [1993] 2 *All E.R.* 377, 379 (italics in original; underlining added).

[52] [1999] 1 *Cr. App. R.* 187. *See generally* S. Nash, 'The Admissibility of Witness Statements Obtained Abroad: *R.* v. *Radak*' (1999), 3 *E. & P.* 195.

*Justice Act 1988*, the evidence should nevertheless not be admitted on the basis that the prosecution had failed to make use of available mutual legal assistance mechanisms. Although they had been aware from the outset that an important prosecution witness was reluctant to leave the US to attend to give oral evidence, they had failed to obtain his written statement in accordance with Section 3 of the *Criminal Justice (International Co-operation) Act 1990*. The Court of Appeal held that the statement ought not to have been admitted in evidence. Once again, the tenor of the judgement suggests that the Court's central concern was the failure to respect the accused's procedural rights. The focus was on the culpability of the executive rather than on the quality of the impugned evidence; no reference was made to the fact that the status of this evidence as hearsay evidence cast doubts on its reliability. Indeed, the Court acknowledged that the statement, having been "made by the only person qualified to make it", was "unambiguous and plausible".[53]

If we look at a recent major decision of the European Court of Human Rights, we find, too, a focus on the impugned pre-trial conduct rather than on the nature of the resulting evidence. While the European Court does not "as a matter of principle and in the abstract"[54] lay down rules on the exclusion of irregularly obtained evidence, its willingness to subject the pre-trial actions of investigative authorities to close scrutiny is evident from *Saunders* v. *UK*.[55] In *Saunders*, the Court was prepared to accept that the use of evidence obtained in breach of internationally recognised procedural safeguards could violate basic principles of fair procedure inherent in Article 6 of the *ECHR*. The Court held that the applicant's right to a fair trial under Article 6 had been violated because statements obtained from him in the exercise of compulsory powers were then admitted as evidence against him. The Court emphasised that, *regardless of whether the statements were of a self-incriminatory or of an exculpatory nature*, the fact that the authorities used them in evidence after obtaining them in such a manner constituted a violation of the accused's human rights. This holding must be regarded as one of vital importance, given the current 'incorporation' of the *ECHR* into English law by the *Human Rights Act 1998*.

It is also of note that, while acknowledging more recently in *Teixeira de Castro* v. *Portugal* that the fight against organised crime may require "appropriate measures [to] be taken", the Court was firmly of the view that "the right to a fair administration of justice nevertheless holds such a prominent place that it cannot be sacrificed for the sake of expedience".[56] Of interest, too, is the fact that the Court has recently declared admissible an

---

[53] *Ibid.*, 199.
[54] *Schenk* v. *Switzerland* (1988) 13 *E.H.R.R.* 242, para 46.
[55] (1996) 23 *E.H.R.R.* 313.
[56] (1998) 28 *E.H.R.R.* 101, para 36.

application to have the case of Sultan Khan, discussed earlier, heard by the Court.[57]

## Where do we go from here?

One of the main themes of this paper has been that the Court of Appeal has *already* embraced the view that evidence can, irrespective of its reliability, be excluded on account of pre-trial irregularities. It is of course possible to rationalise the confessions cases, identification cases and *Radak* as sanctioning exclusion for reasons of intrinsic policy alone. To do so would, however, be to put forward an explanation not inherent in the cases themselves.

The abuse of process doctrine points the way forward. The trial process is concerned with more than ensuring factually accurate verdicts; there is also the crucial consideration of the adverse effect which the admission of improperly obtained evidence may have on the legitimacy of the adjudicative process and on the moral authority of a guilty verdict should such a verdict ensue. The problem with Section 78(1) is that its reliance on the concept of "the fairness of the proceedings" has enabled courts to give effect to their natural discomfort about excluding evidence on account of extrinsic policy considerations alone. While the European Court suggests that the right to a fair trial under the Convention can be denied as a result of the admission of irregularly obtained evidence, whatever the nature of that evidence, the notion of a *fair trial* in English law is much narrower. It connotes a trial in which the right not to be convicted if innocent, and possibly the right not to be convicted on the basis of evidence obtained in breach of the right against self-incrimination, are adequately protected. In cases like *Chalkley*, the word "proceedings" in Section 78(1) is effectively being interpreted by the Court of Appeal to mean "trial". Even at a purely technical level this interpretation is by no means foolproof; both Sections 77 and 79 of *PACE* use the word "trial" rather than "proceedings", and thus the concept of the fairness of the proceedings in Section 78(1), read in the context of *PACE* as a whole, connotes something broader than trial fairness.[58] Like the abuse of process doctrine, therefore, Section 78(1) should be interpreted as safeguarding not only the fairness of the trial, *but also* broader notions of the fairness of the entire process. "The fairness of the proceedings as a whole," Dennis has written, "may be adversely affected if admission of the prosecution evidence in question means that the prosecution have an advantage which is inconsistent with the fundamental moral and political values of the criminal justice system. This advantage may be the use of evidence which is unreliable and prejudicial,

---

[57] 20 April 1999, Application No. 35394/97. *See* [1999] *Crim. L.R.* 666.

[58] "The suggestion that the words are intended only to refer to the proceedings of a trial cannot be sustained when contrasted with the words of ss. 77 and 79": *R. v. King's Lynn Magistrates, ex p. Holland* [1993] 2 *All E.R.* 377, 379.

or it may be the use of evidence obtained in violation of the accused's human rights, or it may be evidence obtained by deliberate abuse of process, and so on. Section 78 enables the trial judge to calculate whether the extent of the unfair advantage is such as to require the exclusion of the evidence."[59]

Perhaps the essence of this quotation could be encapsulated in a new provision, such as Section 78(1A). By merely clarifying the law in this way, and without even expanding the narrow concept of trial fairness in English law, we will be able to achieve a result that is not only justifiable in principle but is also in harmony with the requirements of the *ECHR*. If the Court of Appeal's decision on abuse of process in *Mullen* is anything to go by, there is every reason to expect that our modest suggestions will result in a significant change in judicial attitudes to the issue of the exclusion of improperly obtained but reliable evidence.

---

[59] I.H. Dennis, *The Law of Evidence* (1999), 81-2.

# European Criminal Law[1]

*G.J.M. Corstens*

## Introduction

European criminal law is composed of a collection of criminal standards (substantive, procedural, penological) which are common to various European States with the aim of better combating criminal activities and, in particular, organised transnational criminal activities. This definition immediately throws up obstacles to such a law, but it also invites the question of whether a European criminal law is in fact a necessity.

## Obstacles

To ponder over the obstacles to constructing a European criminal law is to question whether this task is actually possible.

An initial obstacle is represented by the notion of sovereignty: administering justice – and criminal justice in particular – is an attribute of sovereignty, like the management of foreign policy, but, in an associated way, the peoples of Europe frown upon any attempt at European unification as an affront to their own culture.

A second obstacle stems from national peculiarities in criminal law – particularly with regard to fraud committed to the detriment of the European Community – and indeed in criminal procedure. It is known that two major systems exist in Europe; continental 'criminal law' stemming largely from Roman law, and common law represented mainly in England. A rapprochement between these two systems is clearly discernible today.

The second obstacle (national particularities) is not however a determining factor. Firstly, because there are entire aspects which, though well delineated, could nevertheless be unified, for instance in general criminal law (such as the grounds for non-liability) and even in special criminal law. At this level, one may think mainly in terms of community fraud, where it is essential to have a procedure for bringing offences to light in order to protect the Community's financial interests. Whilst certain domestic legislative systems already have procedures for bringing Community fraud to light – Germany and Italy for instance – many others do not: thus, in France and the Netherlands, prosecution is only possible on the basis of general law offences like fraud, forgery, deception, or indeed customs fraud, which often leads to settlements meaning that the offender escapes criminal justice. We may think in terms of

---

[1] This text is based on the introduction of J. Pradel & G.J.M. Corstens, *Droit pénal européen*, *Dalloz*, Paris 1999. References can be found there.

creating a specific criminal offence, for instance as proposed in *Corpus Iuris* for suppressing Community fraud. The problems are the same with respect to the environment and, more generally, for offences concerning matters for which there is no (or still no) national legal tradition. It is not, of course, being suggested that such cases would be judged by a supra-national European court. It would be more appropriate to envisage uniform rules being integrated into national laws and applied by national judges.

On the other hand, there is another possibility to overcome this obstacle for the development of a European law; namely that it is often quite sufficient to provide for harmonisation between laws, where European law is then composed of mutual assistance agreements and guiding principles. We should, in this respect, highlight the determining role of the Council of Europe with regard to the harmonisation of criminal legislation.

**A Necessity**

It would appear, in truth, that a European criminal law, essentially limited to an ideal for harmonisation, represents an imperious necessity. Such necessity stems from a simple, though very real and fundamental, fact: the increase in and internationalisation of criminal activities. More specifically, such crime is becoming increasingly threatening and is the result of perpetrators of various nationalities who are active in different countries: we are talking more and more about organised crime, particularly in the areas of drug trafficking, terrorism, the Mafia, and also the illegal trade in works of art or vehicles that are stolen and then sold on, not forgetting corruption amongst officials. Since crime is becoming international, so too must criminal law. An internationalised fight against crime, if it is to be organised on a global scale, is very difficult to implement and risks becoming merely a token promise. Nevertheless, there is every chance the fight against crime will be more effective at a regional level. Hence the justification for a European criminal law. Europe is, above all, a geographical area, which implies "criminal intervention at a European level and justifies the inclusion of criminal matters at the heart of the rapprochement process of the existing legal systems".[2] Currently, people no longer have any doubts about its legitimacy and necessity and this is why favourable studies are growing in number.

---

[2] L.H. Labayle, 'L'application du titre VI du traité sur l'Union européenne à la matière pénale', *Rev. sc. crim.* 1995, p. 48 *et seq.* This author also recalls that jurisprudence often justifies the existence of a European body of criminal law by the necessity to compensate for 'the security loophole' resulting from the disappearance of frontiers. But he does not believe that this disappearance encouraged criminality, which always managed to use frontiers to its own advantage.

## The Diversity of European Criminal Law

We may, however, discern that such a European criminal law, whilst it does exhibit a certain unity, is fundamentally characterised as being diverse. In simple terms, we might refer to a bipolar Europe since, schematically, it is possible to distinguish two different Europes: the Council of Europe's Europe (with 40 States) and Community Europe of the *Treaties of Rome* of 1957 and the *Maastricht Treaty* of 1992 establishing the European Union (15 States), these treaties having themselves been amended by the *Amsterdam Treaty* signed on 2 October 1997 and entered into force on the first of May 1999. The first Europe is the Europe of human rights (a notion which extends, moreover, beyond criminal law) and police and legal co-operation, whilst the second Europe is the Europe of Community law (which is not, relatively speaking, centred to any appreciable degree on criminal law and which supposes a more forceful integration).

It would therefore be tempting, at first sight, to make a distinction between two overall categories within European criminal law. In real terms though, such a broad picture skirts over police and legal co-operation – formerly a monopoly of the Council of Europe – which is now also taken into consideration by the European Union. The *Treaty on European Union*, as amended by the *Amsterdam Treaty*, and already mentioned, does in fact contain an entire section – Section 6 – which deals with co-operation in criminal matters.

In this respect, it may be accepted that European criminal law contains three overall categories: inter-State co-operation in criminal matters, human rights and, finally, Community law. These three categories, which are different from a geographical perspective, constitute aspects of this "European legal area", a term that is frequently employed in legal theory since Mr Giscard d'Estaing, former president of the French Republic, coined this expression in 1977 during the European Council of Brussels.

## European Co-operation in Criminal Matters

Over the centuries, a large number of States have experienced the need to become contractually affiliated to one another with a view to facilitating the fight against crime. This has given birth to international criminal law, founded on the notion of co-operation or mutual assistance; in short, on the ideal of trust. To fight crime more effectively, such co-operation is essential and we could even have talked in terms of the 'advantages' of international co-operation.

This co-operation is particularly well developed at a European level and especially emanating from the Council of Europe. In this light, a European criminal law of co-operation emerged – and is still developing – which has its own specificity, whilst still constituting a part of the international criminal law of co-operation.

The collection of Conventions, emanating from the Council of Europe, is now – as has been stated – supplemented by the provisions of the *Maastricht Treaty*, known as the *European Union Treaty* of 1992 as amended by the *Amsterdam Treaty*. Thanks to the concept of co-operation, a dual European legal area is emerging: that of the Council of Europe and that of the European Union on a more limited scale. In both cases, we are witnessing the internationalisation of criminal law, which serves to dilute two principles: the territorial aspect of law and the sovereignty of legislators. Within Europe, moreover, co-operation also exists between certain neighbouring States. In this respect, a Nordic Committee on criminal law was set up in 1960, a permanent body incorporating a representative from each of the five States (Denmark, Iceland, Norway, Finland and Sweden), whose mission is to prepare co-operation in criminal matters. The aforementioned *Amsterdam Treaty* also expressly indicates "that it constitutes no obstacle to developing closer co-operation between two or more Member States at a bilateral level within the framework of the Western European Union and the Atlantic Alliance, provided that such co-operation does not contravene or impede the provisions in this section";[3] this was also incorporated in the former Article J.7 of the *Maastricht Treaty*.

## The European System of Protection of Human Rights

The idea of a European Convention for the Protection of Human Rights and Fundamental Freedoms was suggested by the European Movement following a conference held in The Hague in 1948. The project was to be embodied within the framework of the Council of Europe.

The European Convention – more precisely, *European Convention for the Protection of Human Rights and Fundamental Freedoms (ECHR)* – was signed in Rome on 4 November 1950 by the founding States of the Council of Europe. It has eleven additional protocols. It was 'closed', in the sense that it was solely open to signature and ratification by the members of the Council of Europe. It may be considered that its 'closed' nature was not due to the first sentence of Article 59 of the Convention ("This Convention is open only to signature by the members of the Council of Europe"), but due to the absence of a disposition allowing States which were not members of the Council of Europe to participate. We will restrict our scope for the present time to that of the broad outlines of this major text.

The Convention affirms the existence of rights. These are not created by the Convention, but are solely recognised by it: in fact, according to Article 1 of the Convention: "The High Contracting Parties recognise that all persons under their jurisdiction have the rights and liberties defined under Title I of this

---

[3] Article 17-4 *Amsterdam Treaty*.

Convention". This means that these rights are protolegal, have a permanent value and pre-exist the Convention, which has a declarative and not a constituent function.

These rights are not social or economic rights, which are highly contingent by nature because they are linked to the socio-economic context. These are civil and political rights, which are universal by nature. These rights, which will be examined in detail below, are concerned with:

- the physical individual (the right to life, the right not to be subjected to torture or pain or to inhumane or degrading treatment; the right not to be subjected to forced or mandatory labour; the right to liberty and security);
- the mind of the individual (freedom of thought, of conscience, of opinion, of religion);
- the individual in his or her private or family life; and
- the individual in the legal system (the right to fair trial).

Thus "the Convention embodies the current requirements of a European public human rights order"[4] and forms "the human rights backbone for the whole body of human rights".[5]

The result was a convention that contains a catalogue of human rights that is reminiscent of that contained in the *New York Pact* and the *San José Convention*. It does not deal exclusively with criminal law and criminal procedure although it is true to say that criminal law is frequently covered. Whilst not entirely dedicated to criminal law, the *ECHR* is primarily criminal: approximately two out of every three cases judged in Strasbourg are criminal cases.

The rights contained in the *ECHR* are all the more interesting because the authors have instituted legal controls, which are intended to ensure that these rights are respected. After having exhausted all available national remedies, citizens can refer their case to the European Court of Human Rights. In this way, the authors of *ECHR* have created a system of 'justiciability' for the standards it contains, which grants persons who believe their rights have been violated the possibility of referring matters to a body with international jurisdiction, *i.e.*, the Court. Nevertheless, it is true to say that there are subtle restrictions on the extent to which the principle of national sovereignty can be undermined. Whilst the Court is able to decide that a certain State has breached a provision of the Convention (through the actions of its own bodies, judges, administrators, police force, etc.), its judgements are referred to the Council of Europe's Ministerial Committee which monitors their execution.

---

[4] S. Marcus-Helmons, 'La contribution de la consécration internationale des droits de l'homme au développement du droit', *Mélanges Levasseur*, abstr., p. 230. *See also* F. Sudre, 'Existe-t-il un ordre public européen?', in: *Quelle Europe pour les droits de l'homme? La Cour de Strasbourg et la réalisation d'une "Union plus étroite"*, under the direction of P. Tavernier, Brussels: Bruylant 1996, pp. 44-46.
[5] G. Cohen-Jonathan, *Quelques considérations sur l'autorité des arrêts de la Cour européenne des droits de l'homme*, Liber amicorum Marc-André Eissen, Bruylant and LGDJ 1995, p. 39.

And whilst the Court is able to order a State to pay the victim "just satisfaction" (Article 41 *ECHR*), that is, a sum of money, it cannot force the States to execute its decision. In fact, its decisions are not enforceable and the State in question can put an end to the observed breach and settle the consequences in any way it sees fit.

## European Criminal Law and Community Law

The idea of turning Europe into a single economic entity dates back to 1950. This was the year when R. Schuman, French Minister for Foreign Affairs, presented his partners in neighbouring States with a plan (at the time still a modest plan) which resulted in the signing of a Treaty founding the European Coal and Steel Community (ECSC) in Paris on 18 April 1950. This new entity comprised a number of bodies: a High Authority, a special Council of Ministers and a Court of Justice. This was the first step towards the present European construction.

On 25 March 1957, two Treaties were signed in Rome. One founded a European Atomic Energy Community (EAEC or Euratom) and the other, of much greater importance, a European Economic Community (EEC or common market). The preamble to this second treaty is extremely enlightening. The signatories declare that they are "determined to establish the foundations for an increasingly close Union between the people of Europe" and "determined to ensure, through common action, the economic and social advancement of their countries whilst breaking down the barriers which divide Europe". In order to achieve these aims this treaty, which would become known as the *Treaty of Rome*, created a common, or single, market, corresponding to the territories of the six signatory States. Within these territories, the States established the free movement of goods, which implied the suppression of customs laws (Article 3), and also the free movement of persons, services and capital, whilst respecting the principle of free competition. At an institutional level they created a European Parliament, a Council, a Commission, a Court of Justice and a Court of Auditors.

The *Treaty of Rome* which founded the EEC is absolutely fundamental since the Community which it founded "constitutes a new system of international law, for the purpose of which the States have established limits on their sovereignty, albeit in a restricted number of areas, and the subjects of which are not only the Member States themselves, but also their nationals".

A number of years later the Treaty was extended several times. Now the European Community has 15 members.

The *Treaty on European Union* is very important. It was signed on 7 February 1992 in Maastricht by the Ministers for Foreign Affairs and Finance of the European Economic Community's Member States.

On the negative side, the *Maastricht Treaty* does not transform the Communities into a union. Whilst Article A, the first provision of the first

Section (first Article, *Amsterdam Treaty on European Union*) clearly states: "With this treaty the high contracting parties form between them a European Union", this formulation is misleading. In reality the new Union has no legal character. It is not a new structure as it is devoid of legal personality, a budget and its own financial means. In this light, the Union created at Maastricht has no more than a political existence. Furthermore, on the negative side, the Union has no federal vocation. This was eventually discarded after having been retained in a succession of provisional versions.

On the positive side, the Treaty does form a Union, as according to the preamble the authors are "determined to reach a new stage in the process of European integration, which was started with the creation of the European Communities". With this in mind, the Treaty both amends the basic treaties (EEC, EAEC and ECSC) and contains new provisions intended to realise this political union. According to the first Article, paragraph 3 of the *Amsterdam Treaty on European Union*, "the Union is founded on the basis of the European Communities plus the policies and forms of co-operation established in this Treaty. Its mission is to organise, in a coherent and interdependent manner, the relationships between the Member States and their peoples." More specifically, the *Maastricht Treaty* comprises three aspects, or three 'pillars' as they are often known.

The first pillar relates to the Community (Titles 1 to 4 of the Treaty), the second to external policy and Community security (Title 5) and the third, and by far the most important for us, to justice and internal affairs (policing) (Title 6). Within Title 6, the key article is the former Article K.1 which stated: "In order to realise the Union's objectives, in particular the free movement of persons, and without prejudice to the competencies of the European Community, the Member States consider the following areas as matters of common interest: (...) (4) The fight against drug addiction, (5) The fight against international fraud, (...) (7) Legal co-operation in criminal matters, (...) (9) The co-operation of police forces with a view to preventing and combating terrorism, illegal drug trafficking and other forms of serious international crime." Articles K.1 and the following articles were rewritten in the *Amsterdam Treaty* (Articles 29 to 42), which was signed on 2 October 1997 and entered into force as of the first of May 1999.

Formally, Community law is extremely diversified. We can distinguish both primary and subordinate legislation.

The primary legislation consists of a collection of treaties which we have already mentioned: the three original treaties (*Treaty of Paris* of 1951 creating the ECSC; the *Treaties of Rome* of 1957 creating the EAEC and the EEC) and the amending treaties or acts (such as the *Single European Act* of 1986 and the *Maastricht Treaty* establishing the European Union of 1992).

The subordinate legislation consists of a collection of diverse instruments emanating from the Community bodies. The most important text here is Article 189 of the *Treaty of Rome* (249 *European Community Amsterdam*), establishing the European Community: "In order to accomplish their mission and under the conditions provided for in this treaty, the European Parliament, jointly with the Council, the Council and the Commission, shall issue regulations and directives, take decisions and formulate recommendations or opinions."

Regulations are the principal source of subordinate legislation and evoke domestic legislation. In accordance with Article 189-2 (249-2 *European Community Amsterdam*), "regulations have a general scope. All of their elements are obligatory and they are to be applied immediately in all Member States." Being of "general scope", regulations contain general and impersonal standards and in this respect differ from decisions which are instruments with a specific nature (see below). Furthermore, "all of the elements of regulations are obligatory", which means that States are prohibited from applying them incompletely and regulations can be distinguished from directives which only connect the States "in respect of the result" (see below). Finally, regulations are "to be applied immediately in all Member States".

In summary, regulations have legal effect on the domestic legal systems of the Member States automatically and on their own account without intervention of the States being required, which could "hinder the immediate effect of Community regulations and compromise their simultaneous and uniform application in all parts of the Community". Moreover, the text of Article 189 states that regulations are to be immediately applied *in* all Member States and not *by* all Member States, which clearly indicates that regulations are directly addressed to the citizens of the States and not to the States themselves.

In short, private individuals are bound by regulations which create rights and obligations for them, and as the Court of Justice reminds us, regulations, "because of their very nature and function in the system of sources of Community law, produce immediate effects and as such are suitable instruments for granting rights to private individuals which national courts have an obligation to protect".[6]

Directives are a type of framework law in that they must be supplemented by texts of application enacted by the States, allowing specific aspects of national legislation to be respected. In accordance with Article 189-3 (249-3 *European Community Amsterdam*), "directives connect each Member State to which they are addressed in respect of the result to be achieved, whilst leaving the decision on the form and means of incorporation with the national authorities." The result is that the States enjoy considerable freedom in choosing how to implement directives: they may opt for a statute, a decree, an order or even a circular. In practice, the States have increasingly limited room for manoeuvre with regard to the content of their text as the Community authorities are showing an increasing tendency towards drawing up extremely

---

[6] CJEC 14 1971, Politi, 43/71, Coll., p. 1030.

precise and detailed directives which reduce the number of options for the States and lead them to implement the content of directives faithfully into their own domestic law.

Community law is not strictly a branch of criminal law. Neither the *Treaty of Rome* of 1957 nor the *Single European Act* of 1986 grants criminal competence to the Community authorities and the *Maastricht Treaty* of 1992 in no way changes this situation. We must recognise that the opposite scenario would have dealt an extremely heavy blow to the principle of sovereignty. It would be difficult to allow criminal penalties to be instituted by a body which has not been elected by the people (the Council) and these penalties to be applied by a non-legal body (the Commission). This means that the States have the authority to determine the penalties (both in terms of their nature and amount) and the procedures. We could therefore be led to conclude that there is no Community criminal law and only domestic criminal laws. Such a claim, however, would be inaccurate, as Community law does comprise criminal aspects. Community criminal law does exist, as a Community component of European criminal law.

### The Negative Effect of Community Law on National Criminal Law

Community law has both a positive and a negative effect on national criminal law. The negative effect originates from the principle that Community law overrules domestic law: indeed, Community law can be applied immediately and directly within Member States' judiciaries.

The European Court of Justice, in its Costa ruling of 15 July 1964, clearly and for the first time established the principle of the rule of Community over domestic law: "The EEC Treaty introduced its own legal order, which was integrated into Member States' judicial systems when the treaty came into force, and which overrules their jurisdiction. This integration into each Member State's national law of provisions of community origin and more generally of the terms and essence of the treaty, have the corollary effect of making it impossible for the Member States to make any subsequent unilateral measure prevail against a legal order they have accepted, as it would not be capable of opposing the order successfully."[7]

In short, Community law must be applied directly and immediately. If it were not, it would remain a dead letter if a Member state were able to neutralise it via a subsequent law of its own. This European law therefore logically belongs to a higher order than domestic law.

What is more, Article 189 of the *Treaty of Rome* (249 *European Community Amsterdam*) does indeed state that the regulations have "mandatory" force, and are "directly applicable in each Member State". The

---

[7] JEC 15 1964, Costa, 6/64, Recueil CJEC, p. 1141; add. B. de Witte, 'Retour à "Costa"', *RTDE* 1984, 425.

Costa ruling adds an argument in favour of the rule of Community law: it is an argument derived from the unified nature of European law "the Community law's executive power could not vary from one Member State to another on the grounds of subsequent national legislation without endangering the realisation of the aims of the Treaty".

This rule of Community law over national law has two major effects: that of paralysing the opposing national norm, and that of obliging the national judge to give preference to the Community norm over any contradictory provision present in national law, even in subsequent legislation. Domestic jurisdiction also respects this principle. The result of this is a rapprochement of the various national criminal laws.

Furthermore, national criminal laws are influenced by Community standards (and in this way are harmonised). Although criminal law is in fact the competence of the States, the Court of Justice ensures that the penalties chosen do not represent indirect obstacles to realising the objectives contained in the treaties, which conveys their negative effect.

It is therefore decided that any penalty which is disproportionate to the nature of the offence constitutes a measure with the equivalent effect of a prohibited quantitative restriction.

Therefore the fact that a Community national has not declared his *or her* presence to the police within three days could not be punished with imprisonment, as this would represent a disproportionate penalty. Perhaps even more clearly, the Court of Justice reminds us that "a system of penalties must not compromise the freedoms provided for in the treaty" as "if a penalty was disproportionate to the seriousness of the offence it would become an obstacle to the freedom guaranteed by Community law".[8] By controlling proportionality in this way, the Court of Justice corrects the excesses of a particular State and allows domestic laws to be harmonised.

## The Positive Effect of Community Law on Criminal Law

European Community law has not only a negative but also a positive effect on national criminal law. Article 10 *EC* contains the principle that member states have the obligation to take all appropriate measures to ensure the effective application of Community law. According to the European Court of Justice, this means that violations of Community law are penalised under the same conditions as violations of a similar nature concerning national law norms, for in both cases it is essential that the penalty be effective, deterrent, and in proportion to the offence. This is the principle of assimilation. It does not follow that subordinate Community law may impose the obligation to penalise violations of directives or regulations, because criminal law is in fact the competence of the member states and not of the Community. This is the reason

---

[8] CJEC 25 February 1988, Rainer Drexl, *Rev. sc. crim.* 1988, 591 and obs. Bonichot.

why the *Convention of 26 July 1995 on the Protection of the European Communities' Financial Interests* has been set up. This Convention (The so-called *PFI Convention*) dictates that the Member States introduce the offence of "fraud interfering with the financial interest of the European Communities" into their national criminal legislation. This provision details precisely which element of the offence is substantive, and which element psychological. It is less precise when it comes to penalties; however, in cases of "serious fraud", the Convention makes provision for "custodial sentences with the possibility of extradition". It must be noted that this Convention has yet to be ratified.

This convention was necessary in view of the idea that penalising Euro-fraud is desired. This goal cannot be achieved by prescribing penalising in a directive or a regulation. Insofar as it deals with the sanctioning of subordinate Community law, member states are free in choosing the appropriate way of sanctioning the violation of subordinate Community law, provided that they obey the principle of assimilation. This freedom of the member states can lead to the penalising of community law at the national level. Primary Community law sometimes prescribes penalising of Community law.

There are two techniques which can lead to the penalising of Community law. The first one is the national method. This method is characterised by the fact that the Community only has formulated the substantive rule and has kept silence about the sanctioning, whilst the national authorities have chosen to prescribe, impose and execute a criminal sanction with regard to those who have violated the substantive Community norm.

The second one is the mixed method: Community law prescribes more or less precisely the way of sanctioning violations of the Community law, but imposing and executing sanctions are tasks of the member states. For instance Article 194 of the *Euratom Treaty* assimilates violations of Euratom-secrets to violations of comparable national secrets. So, the creation of offences under domestic law is based on a Community document; this illustrates the positive effect of the Community law here. Not only primary Community law, but also Community directives, once introduced into national law via a piece of national legislation, with penalties, can serve as a basis for sentencing should their provisions be infringed. The regulation 2988/95 on Euro-fraud can be considered an example of this mixed method, if one realises that the pecuniary sanctions which are prescribed in this regulation, accordingly on a Community level, can be considered punitive. Here we see that the idea of prohibiting the Community from acting in the field of criminal law is formally respected, but in fact overruled by means of labelling punitive sanctions as administrative sanctions that can be imposed in cases of minor fraud.

Primary Community law has gone farther and has introduced a third method of penalising, but not on the national level, violations of Community law. This third method, the so-called community method, consists of leaving the prescribing, imposing and executing of punitive sanctions to a Community institution. This is the case in the field of combating competition restrictions.

Article 87 of the *Treaty of Rome* (83-2a *European Community Amsterdam*) refers the administration of "fines and penalties" to a regulation of the Council of Ministers to ensure that the principle of free competition is respected. Even if these penalties do not have a criminal character, they are criminal *lato sensu*.

We have given the example of Community fraud to illustrate that Community law and criminal law get more and more intertwined. Let us conclude, then, that there is already a sort of Community criminal law in existence, in various different guises. And it would be highly surprising if this trend did not progress in the years to come.

# Changes in the Quantity, Quality and Significance of Pre-sentence Evidence in Criminal Trials in the US

*T.F. Courtless*

## Introduction

'Once-upon-a-time', the pre-sentence process in many American criminal courts was full of positivist penological influences. Convicted offenders' psyches, social and economic backgrounds, and criminal histories were analyzed with the goal of determining appropriate sentences. And these sentences were often of indeterminate length, release from prison or other sanctions depending on offenders' improvement or 'rehabilitation'.

In 1980, all this began to change. That year, the state of Minnesota implemented a guidelines system for setting presumptive sentences for convicted offenders.[1] These guidelines provide for a structured pre-sentence process that permitted only a small and specific number of evidentiary items to be considered in imposing sentences. The new system replaced the traditional pre-sentence process that relied upon a somewhat open-ended investigation by a probation officer. Judges were largely free to follow or deviate from the sentence recommendation of the investigating officer.

Following Minnesota's lead, many states and the federal government introduced sentencing guidelines. The following list includes the most commonly stated rationales for implementing guidelines:
- to establish rational and consistent sentencing standards;
- to reduce sentence disparities for similar offenses;
- to produce sentences that are neutral with respect to race, gender and the social and economic status of offenders.

Minnesota's stated explanation for its guidelines system probably best sums up the reasons for and expectations of those jurisdictions opting for a sentencing process utilizing guidelines: "[To set] rational and consistent sentencing standards [that] will reduce sentencing disparity [and result] in sentences that will be proportional to the severity of the offense (...) and the extent of the offender's criminal history."[2]

While obviously representing a very difficult challenge, the statement provides clues to certain underlying reasons for such a major shift in the pre-sentence process. One of these is the lack of patience with judicial discretion in imposing sentences. Studies in Minnesota and elsewhere had shown that judges were largely free to determine sentences that did not closely correspond

---

1 L.S. Branham & S. Krantz, *Cases and Materials on the Law of Sentencing, Corrections, and Prisoners' Rights*, St. Paul, MN: West Publishing Co., 5th ed. 1997, pp. 179-180.

[2] *Ibid.*, p. 180.

to statutory language. The result of what appeared to be unfettered judicial discretion was wide variation in sentences for offenders convicted for similar crimes.

Another reason for the shift to sentencing guidelines was the commitment of many to the then relatively new 'just deserts', retributive philosophy in American criminal justice. This philosophy argues that offenders deserve to be punished for the harm they have caused, and that their punishment needs to be 'commensurate' with the degree of that harm.[3] Such an approach does away with any pretense that the sentencing process should make use of a positivist examination of the individual offender in order to 'correct' or rehabilitate her or him.

Finally, sentencing guidelines, as we shall see, provide for plainly delimited periods of incarceration. Gone, in most guidelines jurisdictions, are indeterminate sentences. Clearly, many who supported the development of guidelines systems had become dissatisfied with the consequences (mainly with what was perceived as early release of prisoners) of sentences with open-ended terms. Along with a desire to eliminate indeterminate sentences, those advocating guidelines pushed for the abolition of parole. This, because early release on parole is another form of indeterminate sentence.

A national survey has found that even though many American states have retained indeterminate sentencing statutes, "these laws are becoming increasingly determinate by greater use of mandatory minimums, truth in sentencing provisions, and by reducing the amount of good time credits an inmate can earn (…)."[4]

As a general observation on the development of sentencing guidelines, we can say that they have come along at a time when a 'get tough on crime' movement was on the march. This movement includes abolition of parole and indeterminate sentences, truth-in-sentencing, limiting judicial discretion, and enthusiasm for a just deserts approach to sentencing.

## Pre-sentence Procedures in Non-guidelines Jurisdictions

Typically in American state and federal criminal courts, a period of time elapses between a finding of guilt and imposition of sentence. During this period, a pre-sentence investigation, which is mandatory in federal and most

---

[3] For a discussion of the concept of commensurate deserts, *see* M. Moore, 'The Moral Wrath of Retribution', in: A. von Hirsch *et al.* (eds.), *Principled Sentencing*, Boston: Northeastern University Press 1992, p. 188.

[4] *1996 National Survey of State Sentencing Structures*, Washington, DC: Bureau of Justice Assistance, March 1998, p. xi. States can regulate whether their inmates can earn time off their sentences by virtue of 'good behavior', or for other acceptable reasons. Each state having such regulations may have its own formula for awarding good time credits.

state courts, is conducted by a probation officer.[5] This officer reports the results of the investigation to the court (presiding judge). The report usually ends with a sentence recommendation which the judge may follow. These recommendations, as well as the sentence imposed must adhere to certain limitations set by statutes.

*Figure 1* shown below represents a composite pre-sentence report for a fictitious court that does not employ a sentencing guidelines system. As we can see, the data compiled by the probation officer include typical positivist factors that provide a social-psychological picture of the defendant. The reader of the report learns something of the social, economic and family background of the defendant, his feelings about the crime for which he stands convicted, and his criminal background. To complete the report the probation officer had to do 'field work' to interview relevant persons and dig into police, prosecutor, and court files. Her recommendation of intensive probation supervision may or may not be accepted by the judge. Typically, the sentence ordered by the judge may not be appealed by either the defendant or the prosecutor.

It is obvious that these pre-sentence investigation reports, while structured in terms of information categories, are quite subjective. The investigating officer must make a number of 'judgment calls' in recording and interpreting data. And, the final sentence recommendation is based on the officer's experience as well as the uniqueness of the defendant's background and offense.

To some extent this discussion of the process in non-guidelines jurisdictions provides only part of the picture because of the practice of plea-bargaining. This practice, which occurs in most criminal cases, results in a negotiated plea whereby the prosecutor and defendant (through an attorney) agree to plead guilty, usually to a reduced charge or a reduced number of charges.[6] Obviously, there is a *quid pro quo* operating here: reduced charges almost certainly result in a reduced sentence even before a pre-sentence investigation is conducted.

*Figure 1: Sample Pre-sentence Report*

**Pre-sentence Report for the Circuit Court of 'Tidewater' County**
*The People* v. *Andrew William Johnson*
Charge: Burglary
Date: September 16, 1999
Plea: Guilty
Judge: The Honorable Helen Ritchie Lukens

---

[5] For example, the *Federal Criminal Code* states in 18 *USC* §3552: "A United States probation officer shall make a presentence investigation of a defendant that is required pursuant to the provisions of Rule 32(c)of the *Federal Rules of Criminal Procedure*, and shall, before the imposition of sentence, report the results of the investigation to the court."
[6] For a discussion of negotiated pleas, *see* T.F. Courtless, *Corrections and the Criminal Justice System: Laws, Policies and Practices*, Belmont, CA: Wadsworth Publishing Co. 1998, pp. 54-55.

## Sources of Information
Defendant (interview)
Assistant State's Attorney John Wilkes Smith (interview)
Arthur R. Johnson, defendant's brother (interview)
Eunice B. Marvell, Tidewater High School Principal (interview)
State Police Bureau of Identification (records search)
State's Attorney's Office (records search)
Circuit Court (records search)

## Juvenile and Adult Record
No prior adult record. Two juvenile (B&E) – one at age 12 no disposition; one at age 14 resulting in 6-months probation.

## Official Version of the Offense
Defendant was arrested, charged, pled guilty and was convicted of one count of burglary. Offense took place at the private residence at 1234 Beach Rd. on May 2nd, 1999. Police were called at 2 AM by occupants who heard noises. Police arrived at scene at approximately 2:17 AM and saw defendant on foot, running from the scene. Upon apprehension (defendant did not resist) defendant was found to have possession of a wallet, jewelry, wrist watch, and cash ($125), all later identified as coming from the residence.
Defendant was charged initially with burglary, larceny, and destruction of property. Pleaded guilty to one count of burglary. Was convicted in Circuit Court on July 8th, 1999.

## Defendant's Version of the Offense
Defendant stated that he had been out of work for several months and needed money to move to Tempe, AZ with his girl friend to take a job he heard about. Claims he is sorry for the trouble he caused his victims. He rationalizes their loss by saying, "They got it all back".

## Social History
Defendant is a 20-year old white male, 5'10" tall, and weighs 158 lbs. He was born on January 15, 1976 in Taos, NM, the only child of Frank and Eleanor Johnson. Father was a non-commissioned Air Force officer. Mother was a housewife who accompanied her husband to various duty stations.
Mother died of ovarian cancer when defendant was four years old. Defendant lived with his father until age 17. Between mother's death and defendant left home, the family moved four times because of father's transfers to various bases. Father retired from the Air Force when defendant was 16-years old.
At the time of his offense defendant was living with his 20-year old girlfriend in an efficiency apartment. He has no children or other dependents. His assets consist of one pickup truck (a '72 GMC) which is 'up on blocks', and a few items of personal clothing.
Defendant claims no illegal substance abuse and only occasional alcohol use other than beer.

## Educational History
Defendant completed the 11th grade. He claims to have considered trying to earn a GED diploma. He regrets not completing high school. Interview with principal at his last school revealed that defendant was suspended on two occasions (once in 10th grade and once in 11th grade). The first was for fighting with another student in gym class. The second suspension was for threatening a teacher.
Defendant's grades were noted as ranging from fair to failing, although had he continued in school after the 11th grade, he probably would have graduated.

**Health History**
Other than the usual childhood illnesses, defendant has had no reported health problems. As far as can be determined, he has not experienced mental health problems significant enough to warrant intervention.

**Employment History**
Defendant's employment history is an unstable one. He has had odd jobs as a day laborer in construction. His last employment, which ended three months prior to the instant offense, was as a house painter, earning $5.00 per hour.

**Recommendation**
In view of the fact that this is defendant's first adult conviction, its non-violent nature, and his expression of regret, it is recommended that he be placed on intensive probation supervision for a period of three years. Defendant should be required to maintain regular employment and adhere to the following special conditions: (1) obtain a GED diploma; (2) vocational training; (3) random drug screening.

Respectfully submitted,
J.R. Hathaway, Senior Probation Officer

## Pre-sentence Procedures in Guidelines Jurisdictions

Before describing the procedures used to establish sentences in guidelines jurisdictions, we need to consider how sentencing guidelines were established, and what innovations they have brought to the sentencing process. First, in conformance with the rule of law, sentencing guidelines typically are crafted by commissions made up of legal and other appropriate professionals. These commissions are authorized by state legislators and the Congress of the US in the case of federal guidelines.[7] Guidelines thereby established are approved by the legislatures and then have the force of law.

According to a recent survey, 17 US states and the Federal courts have instituted sentencing guidelines, and of these ten have made the sentences presumptive.[8] Several other states are in the process of establishing sentencing commissions, and probably will develop sentencing guidelines.

Among the innovations guidelines have made to criminal justice in the US are the following:
- structured judicial discretion;
- appellate review of sentences;
- written record of reasons for sentences;
- determinate sentences;

---

[7] For example, the federal guidelines were developed by the US Sentencing Commission (hereinafter referred to as USSC). The commission was established pursuant to an act of Congress: The *Sentencing Reform Act* of 1984. The guidelines developed by USSC are issued under the authority of 28 *USC* §994(a).

[8] *1996 National Survey of State Sentencing Structures, supra,* note 4, at xii.

- abolition of parole.[9]

## Structured Judicial Discretion

As we said earlier, one of the goals of those advocating the use of sentencing guidelines was to limit judicial discretion in imposing sentences. As we shall see below, sentencing guidelines, where a judge is required to employ them,[10] severely restricts her or him to a quite narrow range of sentences.

## Appellate Review of Sentences

In both guideline and non-guideline jurisdictions, defendants are entitled to review pre-sentence reports, comment on them, and present evidence in court to support their arguments for sentences different than recommended in the reports.[11]

Unlike the case in non-guidelines jurisdictions, prosecutors as well as defendants can and do appeal guideline-generated sentences to an appellate court. While defendants have had the right to appeal sentences, the right of a prosecutor to appeal a sentence is rather unusual in American criminal procedure. The language in the US *Rules of Criminal Procedure* is quite specific in conferring this right to US Attorneys: "The Government may file a notice of appeal in the district court for review of an otherwise final sentence if the sentence:

1. was imposed in violation of law;
2. *was imposed as a result of an incorrect application of the sentencing guidelines* [emphasis added];
3. Is less than the sentence specified in the applicable guideline range (…);
4. was imposed for an offense for which there is no sentencing guideline and is plainly unreasonable."[12]

Minnesota's guidelines state that when "departing from the presumptive sentence a judge must provide written reasons which specify the substantial and compelling nature of the circumstances" justifying the departure.[13] Such justified departures are available in most states.

---

[9] R.P. Conaboy, 'The United States Sentencing Commission: A New Component in the Federal Criminal Justice System', in: *Federal Probation* 61 (1997), 59.
[10] Some jurisdictions do not require a judge to refer to sentencing guidelines when setting a sentence.
[11] The *Federal Rules of Criminal Procedure* spells out defendants' rights in Rule 32.
[12] 18 *USC* §3742(b).
[13] Krantz & Branham, *supra*, note 1, at 187.

## Written Record of Reasons for Sentences

Another innovation that serves as a brake on judicial discretion is the requirement that trial judges place on the record their reasons for deviating from the guideline sentence range. This not only puts judges on notice that their departures from the sentences derived from guidelines may be reviewed by a higher court, but also establishes a record which may be used by defendants and prosecutors should they appeal.

One of the most celebrated cases in which the prosecution appealed sentences that fell well below the guideline range occurred at the end of the trial of the police officers convicted of the beating of Rodney King.[14] Among the trial judge's written reasons for lenient sentencing: longer prison terms for police officers would subject them to violence in prison, and that their attack had been provoked by their victim. The trial judge was eventually ordered to re-sentence the defendants.

## Determinate Sentences

We cannot attribute the steady shift in the US toward determinate sentences solely to sentencing guidelines. That shift has been ongoing for some time prior to the implementation of Minnesota's guidelines. Probably beginning in the late 1960s, dissatisfaction with indeterminate sentencing was influencing many states to abandon sentences that once were the hallmark of the reformatory movement and the rehabilitative ideal in American penology.

The rapid spread of sentencing guidelines in the states and their adoption in the federal system has given added momentum to the movement away from indeterminate sentencing to fixed or determinate sentences. When a sentencing guideline sets a range of sentence for a judge to consider, typically the judge selects a term within the range. As we shall see below, these ranges are not very wide, and as we saw above, departures from a range (upward or downward) require written judicial justification.

## Abolition of Parole

The federal system and many states have abolished parole release for their prisoners. This, of course, fits in well with the distrust of indeterminate sentencing. Often seen as arbitrary, parole release decisions have the result of transferring length of sentence decisions away from judges and to independent parole boards.

For some time, critics of parole have joined forces with penal reformers under the banner of 'truth-in-sentencing'. They lobbied for and achieved

---

[14] Courtless, *supra*, note 6, at 62-63.

sentencing reforms that seemed to produce sentences that mean what judges pronounce at time of sentencing, not what, later, some administrative parole board might decide. There is some evidence that 'truth-in-sentencing', when it results in prison crowding, can and will be less 'truthful'.[15]

The pre-sentence investigation under a guidelines system is, or should be, a straightforward procedure. Looking at *Figure 2* we see a typical grid or matrix which incorporates the factors or variables which when examined and quantified determine the sentence range for a particular offender.

The grid we show is adapted from the USSC sentencing guidelines. In order to use the grid to determine the range of sentence, the investigating officer must examine a number of variables:
- base offense level;
- adjustments to the base offense level;
- defendant's acceptance of responsibility;
- defendant's criminal history category.

A brief examination of each of these will reveal how the guidelines follows.

Crimes are related to the offense level values shown in the far left column. Each crime is assigned a base value. For example, a burglary of a structure other than a residence is given a value of 12. This offense level may be adjusted upward or downward depending upon a number of factors as we see below.[16]

Adjustments to the offense level may be made depending on a number of variables:
- *the victim*: if a hate crime, the level increases by three; if a 'vulnerable' victim, the level is increased by two. If the victim is a government official, the level is increased by three. If the victim was physically restrained, the level increases by two. If the offense is related to international terrorism, the level increases by 12;
- *defendant's role in the crime*: if defendant played a major role in planning , organizing, or leading the criminal activity, the offense level is increased from two to four levels. If the offense involves a violation of a position of trust, add two levels. If defendant used a minor in the commission of the offense, add two levels;
- *obstruction of justice*: add two levels if defendant 'willfully obstructed or impeded' the administration of justice with respect to defendant's case;

---

[15] P. Griset, 'The Politics and Economics of Increased Correctional Discretion over Time: A New York Case Study', in: *Justice Quarterly* 12 (1995), pp. 307-323. T.B. Marvell & C.E. Moody, 'Determinate Sentencing and Abolishing Parole: The Long-term Impacts on Prisons and Crime', in: *Criminology* 34 (1996), pp. 107-128.

[16] Defendants who used a firearm in the commission of a crime will incur additional periods of incarceration accord to federal and state criminal statutes. These mandatory terms are added to whatever guideline ranges are calculated.

- *endangering another person while fleeing the administration of justice*: add
  two levels;
- *acceptance of responsibility*. Decrease offense by up to two levels if
  defendant indicates acceptance of intent to plead guilty.

Across the top of the guidelines grid, are the criminal history categories
which are to be applied to the defendant. In essence, these summarize the
defendant's prior criminal history from none or one prior offense (Category I)
to 13 or more (Category VI). A quick inspection of the grid shows that as the
number of prior offenses increases, a defendant's sentence range will increase.

Here is a summary of the data the sentencing grid requires:
- a detailed description of the offense for which defendant was convicted;
- an analysis of the role defendant played in the criminal activity;
- identification and classification of defendant's victim(s);
- defendant's acceptance/non-acceptance of responsibility for the offense;
- complete criminal background check.

If our non-residential burglar had a 'clean' record and his offense level
remained at 12, we see in *Figure 1* that his presumptive sentence would fall
between 10 and 16 months. An inspection of the sentence table also reveals
that, ordinarily, the defendant would not be eligible for probation.

We can see that the data to be obtained by the investigating officer in a
guidelines jurisdiction seem to be significantly different from those required in
non-guidelines jurisdictions. For one thing, it would appear that, except for the
acceptance of responsibility factor, the officer will rely mainly on official
police, prosecutor, and court records. The non-guidelines investigator, on the
other hand, must collect considerable qualitative data from a variety of
interview sources before making a recommendation to the court.

In reality, however, the guidelines-affected probation officer frequently
seeks information well beyond that required by sentencing guidelines grids.
One supervising US probation officer said that: "The applicable sentencing
guidelines and statutes determine the sentencing options that the probation
officer must recite in the pre-sentence report. Additionally, the probation
officer must study the case *to identify potential grounds for departure from the
guidelines* and then must analyze any potential departure to determine if it is
valid."[17]

According to this officer, a conscientious pre-sentence investigator needs
to examine nearly the whole range of offender background factors in order to
submit a meaningful report and recommendation to the court. In reality,
however, many pre-sentence reports contain little more than the information
required to compute a sentence range. Such reports make efficient use of time
which often is in short supply in a crowded urban court system. Denzlinger &
Miller, in writing about the probation officer's 'life after guidelines', report

---

[17] J.P. Storm, 'What United States Probation Officers Do', in: *Federal Probation* 61 (March
1997), 15.

that for many probation officers, there is no longer any 'behavioral science' in their reports to the court.[18]

A study of California pre-sentence procedures found that "individualized justice" based on behavioral science data was a "myth".[19] The researcher took a sample of pre-sentence reports and found a very high correlation between report sentence recommendations and sentences imposed. Among the reasons for this finding was the operation of plea-bargaining by defendants and prosecutors. If a plea agreement is reached in return for a sentence reduction, can one expect a probation officer to oppose the agreed to sentence? Another reason has to do with probation officers' understanding of what the judges to whom they report expect to get by way of sentence recommendations: "Judges expect probation officers to submit non-controversial reports that provide a facade of information, accompanied by bottom-line recommendations that do not deviate significantly from a consideration of offense and prior record."[20]

In fact, probation officers often feel that extensive investigations into matters beyond the formal elements that contribute to calculating sentence ranges constitute "dirty work" and that reports containing descriptions of offenders' social histories are "largely superfluous".[21] Some officers even report that their interviews of defendants are largely *pro forma* exercises designed to convey the idea that someone is paying attention to them. The social data collected from defendants and others is considered to be rarely relevant and can only "perpetuate the myth of individualized justice".[22]

We should point out here that some states have deliberately structured their sentencing guidelines so that 'extra-legal' or substantive factors can be taken into account. Pennsylvania, for example, provides for "standard, aggravated, and mitigated" ranges in its guideline grid.[23]

---

[18] J.D. Denzlinger & D.E. Miller, 'The Federal Probation Officer: Life Before and After Guideline Sentencing', in: *Federal Probation* 55 (1991), pp. 49-53.
[19] J. Rosecrance, 'Maintaining the Myth of Individualized Justice: Probation Pre-sentence Reports', in: *Justice Quarterly* 5 (1988), pp. 235-256.
[20] *Ibid.*, p. 237.
[21] *Ibid.*
[22] *Ibid.*, p. 253.
[23] J.T. Ulmer & J.H. Kramer, 'Court Communities Under Sentencing Guidelines: Dilemmas of Formal Rationality and Sentencing Disparity', in: *Criminology* 34 (1996), p. 386.

*Figure 2: Sentencing Table\**
*(in months of imprisonment)*

**Criminal History Category**

| OL | I<br>(0 or 1) | II<br>(2 or 3) | III<br>(4,5,6) | IV<br>(7,8,9) | V<br>(10,11,12) | VI<br>(13+) |
|----|------|------|------|------|------|------|
| 1 | 0-6 | 0-6 | 0-6 | 0-6 | 0-6 | 0-6 |
| 2 | 0-6 | 0-6 | 0-6 | 0-6 | 0-6 | 1-7 |
| 3 | 0-6 | 0-6 | 0-6 | 0-6 | 2-8 | 3-9 |
| 4 | 0-6 | 0-6 | 0-6 | 2-8 | 4-10 | 6-12 |
| 5 | 0-6 | 0-6 | 1-7 | 4-10 | 6-12 | 9-15 |
| 6 | 0-6 | 1-7 | 2-8 | 6-12 | 9-15 | 12-18 |
| 7 | 0-6 | 2-8 | 4-10 | 8-14 | 12-18 | 15-21 |
| 8 | 0-6 | 4-10 | 6-12 | 10-16 | 15-21 | 18-24 |
| 9 | 4-10 | 6-12 | 8-14 | 12-18 | 18-24 | 21-27 |
| 10 | 6-12 | 8-14 | 10-16 | 15-21 | 21-27 | 24-30 |
| 11 | 8-14 | 10-16 | 12-18 | 18-24 | 24-30 | 27-33 |
| 12 | 10-16 | 12-18 | 15-21 | 21-27 | 27-33 | 30-37 |
| ↓ | ↓ | ↓ | ↓ | ↓ | ↓ | ↓ |
| ↓ | ↓ | ↓ | ↓ | ↓ | ↓ | ↓ |
| 37 | 210-262 | 235-293 | 262-327 | 292-365 | 324-405 | 360-life |
| 38 | 235-293 | 262-327 | 292-365 | 324-405 | 360-life | 360-life |
| 39 | 262-327 | 292-365 | 324-405 | 360-life | 360-life | 360-life |
| 40 | 202-365 | 324-405 | 360-life | 360-life | 360-life | 360-life |
| 41 | 324-405 | 360-life | 360-life | 360-life | 360-life | 360-life |
| 42 | 360-life | 360-life | 360-life | 360-life | 360-life | 360-life |
| 43 | life | life | life | life | life | life |

OL = Offence Level

Shaded cells indicate sentence values for which probation may be granted. For many defendants whose sentences fall within shaded cells with high sentence values, probation is ordinarily coupled with intermittent incarceration.

\* This sentencing table is a composite or general model based on a number of state and federal guidelines.

## Research on the Impact of Sentencing Guidelines

Since 1980 when Minnesota adopted its guidelines-driven sentencing process, a number of studies have been undertaken aimed at evaluating the impact guidelines have had. This body of research has focused mainly on:
1. what evidence is actually being used by investigators in their reports to sentencing judges;
2. what, if any, impact guidelines systems have had on sentence disparities;
3. the effects guidelines have had on length of sentences; and
4. the consequences of guidelines sentencing for prison systems.

### Evidence Gathered for Pre-sentence Reports

It is difficult to determine whether sentencing guidelines have really altered the pre-sentence evidentiary landscape. Accounts by probation officers, those responsible for compiling and reporting pre-sentence information to the courts, offer contradictory conclusions as to guidelines' effects.

As we have seen earlier, some investigators believe that sentencing guidelines have had the effect of removing all 'behavioral' science evidence from the pre-sentence report. Gathering information beyond that required for calculating sentence ranges in guideline systems is considered to be 'dirty work', and of little if any value. Others suggest strongly that a good deal of the pre-guidelines evidence is still collected and reported to judges. The purpose seems to be to allow judges so inclined to justify departures from guideline sentence ranges.

### Guidelines and Sentence Disparities

Very little reliable data are available regarding whether the use of sentencing guidelines has had an impact on sentence disparities. We do know, as we have shown, that judges have used a variety of mechanisms to loosen the restrictions imposed by guidelines. These include the use of some subjective data collected by probation officers as well as systemic and organizational data such as size of prison and jail populations. Pervasive use of plea agreements must be counted on to perpetuate sentence disparities. Such agreements depend on such factors as defense attorney and prosecutor skills as well, certainly, the political context of specific crimes.

We do know that when judges depart from sentencing guidelines, disparities among sentences for similar offenses occur, and not all that infrequently. Women defendants, especially those who have dependent children or are pregnant tend to receive sentences that are more lenient than other women and men. Research also suggests strongly that employed whites who plead guilty and express 'remorse' are sentenced more leniently than others.[24]

### Effect of Guidelines on Length of Sentences

Closely related to the impact of guidelines on size of prison populations is the matter of length of sentence. Has the use of guidelines-generated presumptive sentences raised or lowered the average length of sentences served by prisoners? Since one of the goals of those advocating sentencing guidelines is

---

[24] *Ibid.*, p. 101.

to get tough on crime, it may well follow that getting tough means offenders spend more time in prison.

The only reliable data available to answer this question are those provided by the federal government's Bureau of Justice Statistics. According to a June 1999 report, "imposed prison terms [since the adoption of sentencing guidelines] increased from about 21 months, on average, (…) to about 47 months (…)."[25] Partly as a result of increases in sentence length and the federal prison population explosion, many offenders had their presumptive sentences reduced either at the time of sentencing or within one year of being sentenced.[26] Many of these reductions were granted for a defendant's 'substantial assistance' to the government. Obviously, basing sentence reductions on such a subjective term as 'substantial assistance' will lead to serious sentence disparities.

### Consequences for Prison Systems

A study of Minnesota's experience with its first-in-the-nation guidelines system, found that the size of the state's prison population had a good deal to do with whether judges followed guideline-determined sentences of incarceration.[27] In particular, the study found that judges used 'mitigated departures' from the guidelines to commit defendants to local jails when prison populations were deemed to be too high: "The only plausible explanation for this (…) is that the organizational imperative to maintain Minnesota's prison population within acceptable limits motivated judges to circumvent the guidelines by shifting the burden of incarceration from the state to the local level."[28]

In order to justify mitigated departures, judges needed pre-sentence evidence beyond that required to use the guidelines grid to fix a sentence range.

Interestingly, the Minnesota legislature responded to the increase in the prison population by permitting (and expanding) good-time credits to be used by inmates to obtain early release from their determinate sentences, and redefining the term, 'second or subsequent offense' so as to allow judges to order shorter sentences. Clearly, such measures violate one of the principle objectives in establishing a sentencing guidelines process: 'truth in sentencing'.

---

[25] *Ibid.*
[26] These reductions are available under §5K1 of the Federal guidelines and under Rule 35(b) of the *Federal Rules of Criminal Procedure*.
[27] L. Stolzenberg & S. J. D'Alessio, 'The Unintended Consequences of Linking Sentencing Guidelines to Prison Populations', in: *Criminology* 34 (1996), pp. 269-279.
[28] *Ibid.*, p. 277.

A study in three Pennsylvania counties found similar departures from guideline sentence ranges.[29] In these counties, and we may suspect in many others throughout the nation, one of the most significant factors influencing final sentencing decisions was plea bargaining. As one trial judge said: "Yes, people who go to trial and people who plead guilty get sentenced differently, but you've got to have some kind of reward to give people who plead. A guilty plea, the sooner the better, is an act of remorse, which we reward with leniency. In fact, I wish Pennsylvania had something like the Federal guidelines do, where they have a sentence reduction for pleading guilty."[30]

Another Pennsylvania judge put it even more bluntly: "If someone goes to trial [*i.e.*, pleads not guilty], they're likely to get a harsher sentence. It's the uncooperativeness of the defendant, the inability to admit he's done a criminal act. You have evidence to show that they did it. Admitting it is part of the therapy of getting better and if they're not ready to make that jump, I think they should be penalized."[31]

It is interesting to note this judge's positivist rationale for sentencing defendants in his court: some defendants are ready for therapeutic sentences, while others who demand their day in court, are to be penalized. What evidence, other than a guilty plea, do judges and their pre-sentence investigation officers have to examine in order to conclude that some defendants are ready for therapeutic intervention while others are not? This is a question we cannot answer.

This matter of pleading guilty in return for at least the expectation of lenient sentences has been troublesome for those lobbying for sentencing guidelines. How should the investigating officer proceed in applying the guidelines when the offense charged (to which a guilty plea is directed) is significantly different than the actual offense behavior? The USSC wrestled with this question when it developed the Federal sentencing guidelines. In the words of the Commission: "One of the most important questions for the Commission to decide was whether to base sentences upon the actual conduct in which the defendant engaged regardless of the charges for which he was indicted or convicted (...)."[32]

The Commission indicated that there really was little choice but to go with crimes actually charged against defendants. The fact that "nearly ninety percent of all federal criminal cases involve guilty pleas and many involve plea agreements [with prosecutors] (...)" convinced the Commission that it should not "make major changes in plea agreement practices (...)".[33]

---

[29] Ulmer & Kramer, *supra*, note 17.
[30] *Ibid.*, p. 395.
[31] *Ibid.*, pp. 395-396.
[32] USSC, *Federal Sentencing Guidelines Manual*, St. Paul, MN: West Publishing Co. 1995 ed., p. 4.
[33] *Ibid.*, p. 7.

Returning to the research of Ulmer & Kramer, a very real consequence of the widespread use of sentencing guidelines is to shift the responsibility for sentencing disparities to prosecutors. They conclude that: "this study highlights a fundamental dilemma of efforts to structure sentencing processes, and of sentencing in general. This dilemma involves (...) a key issue in the sociology of law – the tension between formal and substantive rationality in formal social control."[34]

It is not only in Minnesota and Pennsylvania that prison systems have been subjected to large increases in inmate populations. The US Federal prisons have experienced substantial increases in their populations since the initiation of federal sentencing guidelines. Between 1986 (the year guidelines were enacted into law) and 1996 (the last year for which census figures are available) the federal prison population jumped from 38,156 to 98,944. This represents a nearly 300% increase.[35] During the same time frame, the percentage of sentence time actually served increased from 58% to 87%.[36]

**Discussion**

Beginning in 1980 sentencing reform in the US has resulted in a number of changes in both sentencing statutes and procedures. Among these are the decline in the use of indeterminate sentences, mandatory minimum sentences, and the use of sentencing guidelines. The latter have carried much of the weight of the expectations of the reformers. These expectations include harsher punishments, truth-in-sentencing, fairness in the form of reduced sentence disparities and a restriction on the discretion exercised for so long by judges.

Looking at each one of these expectations we find mixed results. First, with regard to harsher punishments we can conclude that there is evidence to support a determination that sentences of imprisonment have lengthened since guidelines came into operation. We suspect that sentences have lengthened in most jurisdictions in the US, whether operating with or without guideline structures.

With respect to truth-in-sentencing, we can say that in some guidelines jurisdictions sentences imposed by judges are 'truthful' in that defendants will serve all or most of their sentences. However, we find that in a number of guidelines states, sentences have been less than truthful through the use of such devices as enhanced good-time credits. The major reason for this is that rigid adherence to truthful sentences (and longer sentences) has resulted in a

---

[34] J.T. Ulmer & J. Kramer, *supra*, note 17, at 403-404.

[35] W.J. Sobol & J. McGready, 'Time Served in Prison by Federal Offenders, 1986-97', in: *Special Report*, Washington, DC: U.S. Department of Justice, Bureau of Justice Statistics, June 1999, p. 2.

[36] *Ibid.*, p. 1.

number of states in a serious prison population problem. We will say more about this below.

It is significant to note at this point that, at least with respect to the Federal guidelines, the American public largely agrees with guideline sentences for most offenses. Peter Rossi and Richard Berk conducted a large-scale interview survey of 1,737 households, seeking to tap into the level of agreement between what people perceive as 'just' punishments and what the federal sentencing guidelines determine to be the sentences for a number of crime 'vignettes'.[37] In each vignette, respondents were given basic information regarding offense and offender background. In only two areas did respondents disagree significantly with the federal guidelines. For drug trafficking offenses, they selected more lenient sentences. For crimes against persons, they chose more severe sentences.

It is quite difficult to reach a conclusion regarding the issue of sentence disparities. This is especially so when prosecutorial discretion is so widely practiced in the US. Not only is the practice widespread, it is largely unregulated if not out of any realistic control. In theory, judges can refuse to accept plea agreements. However, this rarely happens. About the only oversight a judge exercises is to question defendants in open court regarding their pleas. That is, questioning them to ensure the voluntariness of their pleas and their understanding of the implications of a guilty plea.[38]

Finally, it is important to point out that sentence reformers must always take into account (but often do not in their zeal to reform) the systemic consequences of their proposals. Laws, policies, and practices with respect to penal sanctioning do not operate in a vacuum. As we have seen earlier, efforts to get tough on crime, bring about truth in sentencing, and achieve a just deserts emphasis in sentencing have resulted in substantial increases in prison populations, increases that many states simply cannot afford to allow to persist. A consequence of this is to corrupt sentencing guidelines in ways that will allow judges and prison systems to find ways to depart from presumptive sentence ranges.

This corruption has taken the form of including considerable subjective pre-sentencing data in reports to judges, giving them some basis for justifying departures from guideline ranges. Such departures not only take the form of more lenient sentences, but also have resulted in judges committing offenders to local jails rather than to overcrowded prisons. These departures can only

---

[37] P.H. Rossi & R.A. Berk, *Just Punishments: Federal Guidelines and the Public's Views Compared*, New York: Aldine De Gruyter 1997.

[38] Rule 11 (c) - (e) of the Federal Rule of Criminal Procedure reads in part: "Before accepting a plea of guilty (...), the court must address the defendant personally in open court and inform the defendant of, and determine that the defendant understands, the following: (...) the maximum possible penalty provided by law. (...) The court shall not accept a plea of guilty (...) without first determining that the plea is voluntary (...)."

perpetuate sentence disparities, a problem reformers sought to solve through the use of 'objective' pre-sentence data.

Sentence reformers who helped craft sentencing guidelines also failed fully to take into account another systemic stumbling block: prosecutorial discretion. While seeking to eliminate or severely reduce judicial discretion, the guidelines movement has been unable significantly to control the widespread use of plea agreements. These agreements can make a mockery of guideline sentence ranges. Plea bargaining effectively reduces the need for pre-sentence evidence gathering in many cases. Whether rightly or wrongly, entering a guilty plea is considered in most instances as an indication of remorse which becomes a piece of 'evidence' that produces a sentence that has been determined before any investigation by a probation officer.

**Addendum**

The discussion regarding the impact of sentencing guidelines on length of prison sentences should be updated with the latest information from the US Bureau of Justice Statistics.[39]

The Bureau reports that since the *Sentencing Reform Act* (the statute instituting the federal sentencing guidelines) the proportion of defendants sentenced to prison increased from 54% to 71% between 1988 and 1998. This increase is most pronounced for drug offenders sentenced under federal guidelines. Between 1988 and 1998, the proportion of drug offenders sentenced to incarceration rose from 79% to 92%.

Under guidelines, according to the Bureau, average prison sentence length increased from just over 55% to almost 59%. For drug offenders, average prison sentences increased from about 71 months to almost 79 months. However, the increase in sentences for those convictions of weapons offenses (primarily firearms-related crimes) was dramatic: from just over 52 months to more than 101 months!

These results clearly show that the impact of sentencing guidelines (at least on the federal level) are not across-the-board. Drug defendants and those convicted of offenses involving the use of weapons (firearms) may expect to face more severe punitive sanctions than others convicted in federal district courts.

---

[39] *Federal Criminal Case Processing, 1998* (Washington, DC, Department of Justice, September 1999). The findings reported here are found at p. 1 of the Bureau's report.

# Penal System, Penal Proceedings and Security in the Post-modern Era

*L.M. Desimoni*

## Introduction

It will perhaps seem strange that a man devoted to law may want to discuss a specific subject such as security by relating it to the changes and alterations in progress during this post-modern era, but I think that a purely technical approach to the matter would not be comprehensive enough, as will be explained below.

Thus, I shall first provide a philosophical and reflexive introduction to the subject before focusing on the lack or incapability of the norms *per se*, in order to find possible answers to such a complex question as Community Security.

## Philosophical and Reflexive Introduction to the Subject under Discussion, considering the World's Present State of Affairs

One of the main characteristics of the current change is the 'world dissemination' of the predominant trends. Although the term 'globalisation' has widely spread, it is still difficult to find an accurate definition. In that respect, Drucker states that internationalism and regionalism are creating a completely new, intricate and unprecedented political scheme.[1] These terms refer to the increasing direct interdependence among countries, societies, nations and individuals.

Furthermore, the idea that the economy model together with individual freedom would solve all the problems of societies marks the end of an era of highly controversial ideologies such as capitalism and 'statism'.

Thus, Fukuyama declares that, on the verge of the new millennium, the crisis of both authoritarianism and the socialist centralised system have left only one rival as a valid and potentially universal ideology: liberal democracy, the doctrine of individual freedom and political sovereignty.[2]

Consequently, we are now going through a transition stage, which some scholars have called the post-industrial era and others, the post-modern or post-capitalist era. The term 'globalisation' implies the recognition of the fact that there is not only a global capitalist market economy but also that supranational mechanisms should be devised in order to deal with problems affecting all humankind: famine, unemployment, security among political blocs, ecological disasters, etc.

---

[1] P. Drucker, *La Sociedad Poscapitalista*, Buenos Aires: Sudamericana 1987.
[2] F. Fukuyama, *El Fin de la Histotia y el último hombre*, Buenos Aires: Planeta 1992.

By now, I think everybody understands why a penal proceedings expert is interested in these subjects, alien as they may seem to law. But it is a conceptual mistake to think in such terms because law appears as a monumental cultural creation which is aimed to regulate men's harmonic living, the peaceful settlement of disputes and the equitable exchange of material assets.

Therefore, the economy, which was previously based on the use of land, labour, capital, force, nowadays depends on the differential use of knowledge, which Toffier calls "supersymbolic economy" and Drucker defines as "the society of knowledge".

There is no evidence that everybody will benefit to the same extent from these changes for, according to Toffler, "the world shall be divided in infopoors, and inforich, the differences shall deepen, the existence of inequalities, shall be considered a natural fact and new conflicts shall arise".[3]

Other scholars, as Forrester, consider that, though there may still be not sufficiently developed human and technical resources, a quarter of the world's population is in need of the basic welfare benefits. This is the great contradiction and shame that the current of thought has to face at the end of the century.[4]

This is the basis of the new hypothesis of conflict in the Third Millennium – The Crisis of Security – which replaces the war confrontations of the past. And this is so because the social inequalities that affect this important sector of the world population give rise to perverse effects: poverty, social rejection, violence generated by marginal activities, youth drug abuse and the astounding increase of criminal offences that involve extreme violence and total lack of concern for the life both of the criminal and the victim.

In that regard, a 1992 GATT report called *Human Development*, pointed out that it was necessary to develop world strategies in order to reassign resources directed to fight poverty, stop environmental damage, establish a true international co-operation and prevent the growth of crime, marginal activities, drug abuse, violence, vandalism and juvenile delinquency.

Furthermore, the report stated that poverty gives rise to general marginality and violence. According to the same report, the growth of coca and marijuana, and the abuse of such substances along with drug trafficking are consequences of the peasants' poverty and the marginal way of life in big cities.

In short, governments should focus on the fight against these problems because the constant advance of this post-modern world is not consistent with its counterpart: the systematic rejection of an important sector of society.

This is the most relevant paradox described by UNESCO: the rise of individual liberties and the consequent decline and detriment of human rights (human dignity), or in my opinion, of the rights inherent to humankind.

---

[3] Toffler, *Las guerras del futuro. La supervivencia en el alba del Siglo XXI,* Barcelona: Plaza y Janes 1994.
[4] V. Forrester, *El horror económico,* Buenos Aires 1997.

These antinomies have brought up evil results throughout the 20th century and, according to Fukuyama, they prove that the model of human society is not exhausted with liberalism and capitalism.

Concerning other periods, the Argentine philosopher Lindo declares that future observers will be surprised by the fact that human beings seemed unable to find answers to their problems, even though there existed enough resources to face the challenges of the time. We no longer depend exclusively on the benefits provided by nature or on the capacity of human labour to produce the necessary food. In addition, he states that the actual dilemma is either to subordinate economic development to human needs or to advance in the inexorable process of change towards new and permanent conflicts.[5]

Today, equity is a synonym of balance and survival, unless massive starvation of the poorest populations is accepted as a natural fact. Then, according to Forrester, humankind will be punished for this crime and will witness the elimination of social moral limits, reflected in urban violence, social disintegration, school violence, and all the terrible events described in police chronicles and everyday dramas.

In addition, he calls the attention of the readers to the fact that the crimes against humankind perpetrated in different historical periods were the sin of Humankind itself *(op. cit.)*.

After this brief reference to the historical and philosophical background of the current doctrines, we shall analyse the subject on proceedings and its influence on security.

## Normative Aspects – Penal and Proceedings – and their Influence on Security

To approach this subject, we must first ask whether the complex and multidisciplinary problem of urban security can be solved with only one tool: the substantial and formal penal norms. I must confess I doubt it.

In the case of Argentina and of other countries that, like us, follow a basic normative structure founded on Roman legislation and tradition, the evolution of which reached its highest level with French Revolution scholars, we enter the post-modern era and the third millennium with penal figures and proceeding techniques devised by 19th century scholars.

Should it not be necessary to implement a reengineering of the mentioned normative frame so as to satisfy the present political, sociological and technical needs? This is the situation and thus, it is necessary to relate law to economy, for the juridical frame has always rested on the economic structure of a given historical period or has appeared as a reaction.

---

[5] A. Perez Lindo, *Mutaciones, escenarios y filosofía del cambio del mundo.*

Given today's state of affairs, individual freedom is defined as a supreme asset, and the legal system is designed to prevent the abuses of the political power (or the system's establishment) against citizens.

This position also implies a certain impotence regarding the safeguard of the honest citizen against *marginal activities,* for offenders will always base their defence strategy on the old and famous protective shield *in dubio pro quilibet praesumitur bonus* (the alleged innocent party is presumed to tell the truth).

Some time ago, I thought that I had found the answer to this question. In my first book, I pointed out that such presumption of truth is entirely valid in the case of a person who has never committed a crime or has not been sentenced before, *his life style complies with the basic rules of social living and has legal means of support.*

On the other hand, their own personality and the lack of better opportunities derived from their personal background handicap other individuals.

This theory is rebutted by that sector of liberal philosophy that did not acknowledge the penal right of the offender, stating that he should be punished for his actions and not for his personal record.

However, there are not many alternatives: either to restrict individual liberties to ensure general security, or to grant them without limit, to the detriment of the latter.

This equation is difficult to solve with mathematical accuracy:

*Figure 1*

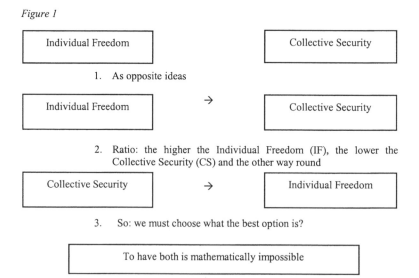

1. As opposite ideas

2. Ratio: the higher the Individual Freedom (IF), the lower the Collective Security (CS) and the other way round

3. So: we must choose what the best option is?

As can be noted, the subject should be analysed and discussed extensively, for it is not easy to find a definite solution in the short term. Therefore, we think it should be included in the normative reengineering proposed, and all the social actors involved should be summoned, the whole society through the participation of its representatives, members of the government, economists and law and security experts.

There is no doubt that human rights must always be in full force, but it does not follow that we should accept unlimited individual liberties to the detriment of other rights.

Another apparent contradiction is that, while more security and better legal proceedings are demanded, there is a tendency to strengthen individual rights, thus promoting the phenomenon of nullifies.

In the US, for example, Mayor Giuliani's administration has improved security levels, without changing the proceedings system and only based on a scheme called "Zero Tolerance" for marginal behaviour. Liberties were limited to a reasonable extent but, although the police was allowed to arrest suspects for several hours for identification purposes, this procedure was carried out within the frame of the constitutional guarantees. In spite of his decisions, nobody accused Giuliani of having violated human rights, fundamental but not absolute because they are limited by the rights of others.

Furthermore, Perez Lindo points out that today the only universal ethical reference source is the *International Code of Human Rights*, which should be called, in our opinion, Code of Human Dignity *(op. cit.)*. Perez Lindo also states that, following the same principles, each person and nation have the right to be different, diverse and to dissent. Therefore, although there is an ethical basis for world community life, at the same time, there is still an indefinite frame regarding personal values and beliefs. The lack of a clear definition in both levels (universal and existential) is responsible for many of the present dilemmas and conflicts. Has everybody the right to choose the moment of his own death, or is it an infringement to the principle of the respect for life? Has a group of people the right to decide its own annihilation, as was the case in Guyana? Up to what extent is violence in public areas admissible? What are the limits between public and private places?

In that sense, it should be noted that an over-inquisitive position is as harmful as the excessive safeguard of civil rights, which may pervert the essence of criminal proceedings and leave society defenceless before crime.

## Conclusion

As mentioned before, an extensive discussion involving all the social factors is unavoidable if we really want to solve the serious, complex and multidisciplinary matter of security.

All the factors involved present virtual aspects, so there should be a sort of system co-responsibility in the search for solutions to this difficult problem.

When full awareness of the problem is achieved, it will be possible to design a technical-juridical reengineering (substantial and formal) directed to update and simplify criminal proceedings, in order to attain the long desired goal: security.

# A Comparative Analysis of the Fault Requirements for Offences in the Netherlands and England & Wales

*A.M. Dingley*

## Introduction

This paper is the direct result of research I am doing at the Department of Criminal Law of the University of Groningen (the Netherlands). I aim to tell you something about this research and present some findings. I also hope to stimulate some discussion about my chosen topic of study.

As the title of this paper shows the topic is one of substantive criminal law. More specifically it deals with that part of the substantive criminal law that is called *mens rea*. *Mens rea* can be defined as the required mental element for criminal conduct. As the title of my paper shows this presentation is concerned with the working of *mens rea* in two different countries: the Netherlands and England & Wales. These two countries have been 'intentionally' selected. The different legal traditions make them ideally suited for comparison. The Netherlands is generally classified as a country belonging to the 'continental legal tradition' whereas the English law system qualifies as belonging to the common law. As continental and common law systems are typically considered to be at the opposite sides of each other it makes good sense to look at the differences and similarities of the *mens rea* in these countries.

I will start with an account of the way in which fault requirements work in Dutch law. I will do this by using the offence of *doodslag* as an example. After this I shall describe the *mens rea* in English law through the offence of *murder*.[1] In the conclusion I will advance some provisional findings.

### Fault Requirements according to Dutch Criminal Law – *Doodslag* as an Example

*Doodslag*
*He who intentionally takes the life of another is guilty of doodslag and liable to a term of imprisonment of not more than fifteen years or a fine of the fifth category.*

The offence of *doodslag* requires that the perpetrator took the other person's life with intent. Intent is the English translation of the Dutch fault requirement *opzet*. According to Dutch substantive criminal law each serious offence *(misdrijf)* requires the presence of *opzet*. For the few offences where no *opzet*

---

[1] I have chosen these two offences for a number of reasons. First of all, they are considered in both countries to be one of the most serious offences in the legal system. Secondly, they are relatively easy to compare as they have a number of similarities, as we will see later on.

is required, still a lesser degree of fault needs to be present. In these cases *culpa* is required. For instance, it is also an offence according to Dutch law to 'recklessly cause another persons death'. Recklessly here is the translation of *culpa*: *dood door schuld*.

I will only look at the concept of *opzet* as that is the fault element required for *doodslag* and is most suitable for comparison with the fault element required for murder.

The description of most individual offences includes a word that refers to the concept of *opzet*. This could be the word *opzet* itself or words like *oogmerk*[2] and *wetende dat*.[3] Sometimes there is not such a reference to *opzet* in the description of the offence at all. For example, the description of assault is: Assault is punished with a term of imprisonment of not more than two years or a penalty of the fourth category *(mishandeling*; Article 300 under 1 of the *Dutch Criminal Code (DCC))*. Although there is no reference to the word *opzet* the concept of *opzet* is still a requirement of the offence. The required *mens rea* for this offence is implied in the use of the word 'assault';[4] an unintentional assault is impossible.

The word *opzet* is in most cases used for offences that prohibit causing a certain result (like *doodslag*, it is forbidden *to intentionally cause* another person's death). *Oogmerk* is typically not used for offences that prohibit certain behaviour but normally refers to the perpetrator's purpose for committing the crime. And the fault element *wetende dat* refers to the perpetrator's knowledge at the time of committing the crime.

Although each offence has a reference to *opzet* there is no definition of the concept in the general part of the *DCC*. Some information about its meaning can be found in the notes of the parliamentary discussion preceding the enactment of the *DCC*. From these notes it is evident that the legislator at the end of the 19th century[5] centralised the will of the perpetrator.[6] However, the perpetrators knowledge was also deemed to be an important element of *mens rea*. How else can the use of the words *wetende dat* be explained? So, according to the legislator *opzet* means 'willingly and knowingly'. Sometimes the will-component is more prominent and at other times the knowledge component.

In Dutch criminal law dogmatics, the discussion about *opzet* has also focused on the difference between the will- and knowledge-component. Supporters of the will-side of *opzet* emphasised the perpetrators process of

---

[2] *Oogmerk* means aim, purpose. *Wetende dat* means knowingly.
[3] An example of an offence that requires *oogmerk* is theft (Article 310 *DCC*); an example of an offence that requires *wetende dat* is slander (Article 262 *DCC*).
[4] In Dutch this is called *ingeblikt opzet*.
[5] The *DCC* dates back to 1886.
[6] "*Opzet* is de wil om te doen of te laten die daden, welke bij de wet geboden of verboden zijn", in: Smidt I, p. 66 *et seq.*

forming a will. Opponents, however, saw the will as a necessary starting-point for a definition of *opzet* but thought that it required an element of knowledge to further give the concept its shape. Another important aspect of the discussion in dogmatics is that *opzet* was, and still is, considered to be a general concept that can apply to all serious offences. Notwithstanding that there is no such general definition in the *DCC*.

Although it has certain advantages to look at such an important concept from a general starting-point it is also necessary to pay some attention to the fact that *opzet* plays its most prominent part in the specific part of the *DCC*, namely in the definition of the specific offences. If we want to know the meaning of *opzet* as stated in the definition of a specific offence we need to look at how courts prove intention in an individual case. It is therefore necessary to also look at criminal procedure and look outside of the *DCC*.

When can it be said that behaviour is *opzettelijk* and when not? The legislator has not provided us with an answer to these questions. It was left to the courts to develop the meaning and boundaries of the concept. During the years the courts distinguished four degrees of *opzet*:

1. *opzet* defined as the perpetrators aim;
2. *opzet* defined as awareness of inevitability;
3. *opzet* defined as awareness of probability;
4. *opzet* defined as conditional *opzet*, awareness of possibility coupled with acceptance of this possibility.

For the offence of *doodslag* conditional *opzet* is the lowest degree of *opzet* which needs to be proven before a defendant can be convicted. How this works can be illustrated by looking at a well-known Dutch case where proof of *opzet* was at issue.

In the Dutch Supreme Court *(Hoge Raad)* case of January 3, 1978,[7] the defendant had been charged with taking the life of his girlfriend by smothering her with his hands. He admitted putting his hands on her throat until her lips turned blue and her tongue was sticking out of her mouth. Only he claimed to have stopped the minute she showed these signs. His testimony was meant to show that he did not have *opzet* with regard to taking her life. On appeal the Court of Appeal had convicted the defendant of *doodslag* against which conviction he appealed to the Supreme Court.

According to the Supreme Court the Court of Appeal was not wrong in holding that the defendant had the requisite *opzet* to take his girlfriend's life. The Supreme Court said that it was a generally known fact that keeping you hands on another person's throat in such away that this person's lips become blue and their tongue starts to hang out of their mouth, will not seldomly lead to that person's death. On the basis of this the Court could have held that the defendant should also have been aware of this reasonable possibility.

---

[7] *NJ* 1978, 627.

Furthermore, the Court was also not wrong in holding that the defendant must have consciously exposed himself to the risk of taking his girlfriends life by acting the way he did whilst aware of the possibility that she would be killed. The Supreme Court concluded that the Court of Appeal was not wrong in finding conditional *opzet* proven.

This decision shows that we need to look both at *opzet* as a general concept and *opzet* as a concept defined by case law. It shows that *opzet* is indeed willingly and knowingly. The terms 'generally known fact' and 'the defendant should have been aware' are both elements of knowing. 'Consciously exposed himself to the risk' is an element of will. Furthermore, it shows that as a starting point the general definition applies but that it is further shaped by its function in procedural law; the issue here was whether or not *opzet* could be found proven.

It is interesting to see if similar comments can be made about the way in which the *mens rea* of murder is shaped.

## Fault Requirements according to English Criminal Law – *Murder* as an Example

*Murder*
*It is murder for a person of sound memory and at the age of discretion, unlawfully to kill any human creature in being and under the Queens peace, with malice aforethought, either express or implied by law, provided the victim dies of the injury inflicted within a year and a day of the injury.*

The offence of murder requires that the perpetrator unlawfully killed another person with malice aforethought. Malice aforethought is the fault element that is required for murder.

According to English substantive criminal law all serious offences require *mens rea*. In English criminal law, the words used to denote these fault requirements are much more diverse than in its Dutch counterpart. As Professor Ashworth says it: "We will see that the fault requirements are diverse, not just terminologically but also in substance."[8] Numerous phrases are used to denote *mens rea* in specific offences, for instance dishonesty, intention, recklessness, gross negligence, knowingly and malice aforethought.

Unlike in Dutch substantive criminal law there is no general concept like the concept of *opzet*. *Mens rea* is presumed to be part of every offence (or at least each serious offence) but what this *mens rea* is remains rather vague. Part of this can be explained by the fact that there is no general English Criminal Code. This means that there has been no parliamentary discussion on fault requirements in general either.

---

[8] *Principles of Criminal Law*, 2nd ed., p. 151.

Traditionally, the English criminal law is unwritten law (common law). It has developed through court decisions and institutional writers from the 17th (Coke, Hale) and 18th century (Blackstone).

There is statutory law but these laws deal with a particular offence or a specific part of the criminal law. Over the years a vast number of statutes have come into force, like *The Offences against the Person Act 1861, Homicide Act 1957, Theft Act 1968, Road Traffic Act 1991*, but all attempts to enact a Criminal Code for England & Wales have failed.

The common law tradition of the English law means that we have to focus on court decisions if we want to find out more about fault requirements. Let us look at murder as an example. As mentioned above the required *mens rea* is malice aforethought. What is malice aforethought? Malice aforethought is a common law term. Originally, it was taken very literally. It meant that for behaviour to be murder the killing had to be done with premeditation, it had to be planned and thought out. A sudden homicide was not murder but manslaughter.[9] In practice, this interpretation of the term turned out to be too narrow. Other forms of homicide were thought to be just as reprehensible and deserving of the severest penalty.[10] The requirement of premeditation was therefore abandoned. From the second part of the 17th century there were three kinds of malice aforethought:

1. express malice;
2. implied malice;
3. constructive malice.

It is express malice where the accused has acted with an intent to kill. Implied malice is where the accused had an intent to cause grievous bodily harm and where the victim was killed because of this. Constructive malice existed in two forms. The first one is where the accused killed the victim in the course of committing a serious offence (felony-murder rule). Secondly, it was constructive malice when the accused killed the victim in the course of resisting, avoiding or preventing an arrest while trying to escape or helping someone else escape from custody (arrest-murder rule).

Constructive malice was abolished in 1957 by Section 1 of the *Homicide Act 1957* but express and implied malice were explicitly preserved. Since 1957 murder requires proof of an intent to kill or to cause grievous bodily harm. This requirement has led to much debate and judicial uncertainty ever since. Over a period of 29 years the courts have had to look at the *mens rea* of murder time and time again and had to shape the law on murder.

---

[9] This is similar to the distinction in Dutch law between *moord* and *doodslag. Doodslag* is intentionally taking another persons life whereas *moord* is intentionally and with premeditation taking another persons life.

[10] Until 1965 this was the death penalty. The *Murder (Abolition of Death Penalty) Act 1965* abolished this penalty and determined that a penalty of mandatory life imprisonment should come in its place.

In a number of decisions the Court of Appeal and the House of Lords have confirmed that it is enough for a murder conviction if it can be found proven that the defendant intended to cause grievous bodily harm. Intention or foresight as to endangering human life is not required.[11] However, most decisions have centred on the definition of the word intent in 'an intent to kill and an intent to cause grievous bodily harm'.

Between 1975 and 1986 the Court of Appeal and the House of Lords have tried to define the intent required for a conviction of murder. Various definitions have been given by the courts over the years. In *DPP* v. *Smith* the court said that it was malice aforethought if "the defendant as a reasonable man must have contemplated that grievous bodily harm was likely to result". In *R* v. *Hyam* the House of Lords equated foresight of consequences with intention. Some years later they formulated the following test to determine malice aforethought: "Firstly, was death or really serious injury in a murder case a natural consequence of the defendant's voluntary act. Secondly, did the defendant foresee that consequence as being a natural consequence of his act."[12]

In the case of *Hancock and Shankland*[13] the House of Lords altered the definition in *Moloney* to: "In a murder case where it is necessary to direct a jury on the issue of intent by reference to foresight of consequences of the probability of death or serious injury resulting from the act done may be critically important. Its importance will depend on the degree of probability: if the likelihood that death or serious injury will result is high, the probability of the result may be seen as overwhelming evidence of the existence of the intent to kill or injure." The last, and authoritative, decision was given in the case of *R* v. *Nedrick.*[14] There the Court of Appeal said: "Where the charge is murder and in the rare cases where the simple direction is not enough, the jury should be directed that they are not entitled to infer the necessary intention unless they feel sure that death or serious bodily harm was a virtual certainty (barring some unforeseen intervention) as a result of the defendant's actions and that the defendant appreciated that such was the case. Where a man realises that it is for all practical purposes inevitable that his actions will result in death or serious harm, the inference may be irresistible that he intended that result, however little he may have desired or wished it too happen. The decision is one to be reached for the jury on a consideration of all the evidence."

---

[11] *R* v. *Vickers*, 41 *Cr. App. Rep.* 189, *DPP* v. *Smith* (1961) *A.C.* 290, *R* v. *Hyam* (1975) *A.C.* 55, *R* v. *Cunningham* (1982) *A.C.* 566. In the recent case of *R* v. *Woollin* (1998) 3 *W.L.R.* 382, the House of Lords recognised the problematic nature of the grievous bodily harm rule, but stated that it should be the basic assumption upon which any analysis of the *mens rea* in murder should be carried out, unless Parliament determines otherwise.

[12] *R* v. *Moloney* (1985) 1 *All E.R.* 1025.

[13] (1986) 1 *All E.R.* 641.

[14] (1986) 3 *All E.R.* 1.

This case law shows that the courts have not really succeeded in defining 'intention' in the definition of murder; all they have done is formulate ways of proving intention. It also shows that a trial judge should preferably leave the question of intent to the jury without giving them any explanation of the meaning of this word. Only in exceptional cases should the judge give the jury a direction in terms of foresight. And then still, foresight is something from which the jury *can* infer that the defendant intended to kill or cause grievous bodily harm.

## Comparison/Concluding Remarks

In this paper I looked at the *mens rea* of two offences in two different countries. The required fault element for the Dutch offence of *doodslag* is *opzet*. The description of this fault requirement started with a disposition of the general concept of *opzet*. I then went on to explain how the concept had crystallised in case law in relation to the offence of *doodslag*.

The required *mens rea* for the English offence of murder is malice aforethought. Malice aforethought is one of the terms used to denote the presumption of *mens rea*. *Mens rea* as a concept is left undefined. The meaning of malice aforethought however has developed through the case law in relation to the offence of murder.

## General Comparative Remarks

The description of the fault elements required in Dutch and English law shows similarities insofar as both have developed in case law dealing with specific offences. The main difference however is the starting-point: according to Dutch substantive criminal law *opzet* is a general concept. This concept has developed in the criminal doctrine but also in the case law. It is not surprising that both doctrine and case law have influenced the concept of *opzet*. Dutch law has a long-standing tradition, influenced by German and French doctrine, of treating the substantive criminal law as containing general concepts.

Furthermore, in the case of *opzet* the concept plays its most prominent part in the description of specific offences. It is only natural then to look at how *opzet* works in relation to these offences.

The English criminal law has no such tradition of substantive criminal law being a matter of general concepts. Their common law has historically developed through court decisions and the works of writers of from the seventeenth and 18th century. Only later did the doctrine try to formulate principles that could be generally applicable.

## The *Doodslag* – Murder Comparison

*Doodslag* needs proof of conditional *opzet* as a minimum fault requirement. A defendant has conditional *opzet* in relation to *doodslag* where he should have been aware that his actions could cause another person to die (when this is a fact of general knowledge). By acting he also accepts these consequences (without necessary wanting them to happen). Murder requires proof of malice aforethought. Malice aforethought has been interpreted as meaning intent to kill or intent to cause grievous bodily harm. The lowest fault requirement for murder is therefore intent to cause grievous bodily harm. A defendant can be convicted of murder if a jury *infers* that serious bodily harm was a virtual certainty (barring some unforeseen intervention) and that the defendant appreciated that such was the case.

According to Dutch standards the fact that only an intent to cause grievous bodily harm needs to be proven for a murder conviction is strange, to say the least. For a *doodslag* conviction *opzet* of the victims death is required. However, the Dutch test has a more normative nature than the English one: the defendant should have been aware of the risk of his actions. According to English law the defendant's actual knowledge is somewhat more decisive although it is still the jury who can infer that the defendant had the requisite intent. Furthermore, in most cases the jury need not be give a direction on the mental element required for murder at all: in most cases it can be left to the common sense of the jury to decide whether or not the defendant intended to kill or cause grievous bodily harm.

This brings me to my last point and conclusion: many of the differences can be explained by the way in which these systems historically have operated. The dominance of the Dutch substantive criminal law can explain the emergence of an abstract notion of *opzet*. The traditional emphasis on case law and the way the jury-system works can explain why malice aforethought has developed in a more morally tinted way. But let us not forget that there are also similarities: most notably, the interdependence of substantive and procedural law in matters of *mens rea* in both countries.

# Victims of (Property) Crime on the Work of Police Officers and Criminal Investigators

*B. Dobovšek, G. Meško & P. Umek*[1]

## Back to Victims of Crime

After 1980 an enhanced interest in the victims of crime emerged within criminology, which influenced the development of victimology, *i.e.*, the science on victims. Before that period, the majority of criminological research was directed towards establishing victimisational risks, the characteristics of victims and the ways and kinds of the victim's contribution to the criminal act. Little attention was devoted to victims' responses and interventions aimed to assist victims.[2]

Recent victimological efforts demonstrate themselves especially in the care for victims, in the assistance of experts and an important role of victim aid organisations and associations. These proceed from an awareness of the sensitivity of the issues and the ways of dealing with it, which are too often neglected by the rather insensitive and formalistic judiciary and also the police.[3] The fact that the victim suffers several times, which is proved by experience and research results, is not taken into proper account. At first the victim experiences (in various forms) the actual criminal offence (primary victimisation), followed by a painful routine (in most cases) of investigative police procedures and the treatment during the criminal procedure, which in many respects gives priority to the perpetrators of criminal offences (secondary victimisation). We believe that in our country we have only reached the beginning in our efforts and knowledge of working with the victim in various fields, and that there are only some individuals who are aware of the importance of a professional approach to victims of various criminal offences, not only sexual abuse of children and rape.

The research into the responses of crime victims shows that almost all of them suffer at least temporary problems (of predominantly an emotional nature), whereas in some cases they last for a longer period of time and serious mental and physical problems may occur, most commonly linked to distress (negative consequences of a stressor, *i.e.*, in this case of a criminal offence).[4] The problems therefore do not fade away; they acquire a different form and studies have shown typical signs of post-traumatic stress disorder (anxiety, nervousness, depression, nightmares, disturbed sleep, sexual problems, problems in social activity, etc.). We must also take into account those persons

---

[1] The authors have agreed to be quoted according to alphabetical order.
[2] Sparks (1983).
[3] Meško (1998), p. 1076.
[4] Meško (1998), *ibid.*

who are in close personal relationship with the victim. Indirect victims are as a rule neglected in practice, and more often mentioned rather than seriously dealt with in literature. Indirect victims feel sadness, which can develop into real depression, they experience guilt and strong feelings of injustice as well. They are also hurt by being investigated for the suspicion that they might have committed the criminal offence. The partners of raped women have reported communication problems, sexual problems and a strong need to control emotions. Often one catastrophe (*e.g.* rape) is followed by another (the break-up of a relationship).

Mayhew (1984) studied victims of criminal offences in England and found that 40% of 3000 victims reported that victimisation did not have a special impact on them, while 12% stated that they had serious problems after the victimisation. Of 360 (12%) 24% were burglary victims, 20% were victims of vehicle theft, 30% were violence victims and 26% were victims of other criminal offences. The findings of this survey show that some people experience serious trauma, regardless of the fact whether the criminal offence was violent or not.

Psychological anguish of the victim, following criminal victimisation, is often severe. It depends partly on the nature of the incident, personal traits of the individual and also on the attitude of the police officers and criminal investigators investigating the criminal offence. How does experiencing a burglary affect the victim's state of mind?

Maguire (1980) interviewed 322 persons who had reported burglaries four to 10 weeks earlier. The first typical response of victims, upon noticing the burglary, was to look for a reasonable explanation (*e.g.* the children have had a party and therefore the flat is a mess) or to feel that something like that could not have happened. Agitation and unpleasant feelings accompanied the realisation that the flat had really been broken into. The author classified the victims according to their reactions to the burglary. Anger and agitation were the typical reactions of men (42%) and less typical of women (19%); 29% of women were shocked; only 13% of men experienced crying and bewilderment compared to 20% of women. 11% of men cited surprise as their reaction compared to 6% of women, and 4% of women and 13% of men reported fear. These responses ranged from mild to severe forms.

Four to ten weeks after the burglary, as many as 65% of victims stated that the experience of victimisation affected their lives. They still felt threatened and less safe, and often thought about the possibility of repeated victimisation. Their illusions about a humane society were shattered (8%), the feelings of fear were strengthened (15%) and difficulty in sleeping (8%) and various health problems (6%) appeared.

Women reported the strongest and most persistent psychological impact of victimisation. About 12% of all women used terms like pollution, intrusion or presence in the house. Many of them equated the act with sexual violence, the presence of a dirty stranger who violated their privacy and brought about the need to clean the house from top to bottom. Such effects persisted for several weeks and two victims even moved out from the flat which had been broken into, while five others burnt the furniture and clothes the burglar touched.

Other women changed their life habits. They increased their insurance, placed security locks and alarm devices or exaggerated with locking the door. An important finding of Maguire's survey is that victimisation has a strong impact on the sense of privacy and on the emotions of victims; that psychological damage is in most cases more important than material loss. Victimisation affects women more than men, especially divorced, widowed or single women.

Mawby carried out similar research in some towns in England, Germany, Poland and Hungary.[5] He interviewed burglary victims in order to acquire data on the impact of victimisation and their experience with different services (*e.g.* the police). As many as 90% of the victims said that they themselves or somebody in their family was affected emotionally, and 54% said that they were very affected.

Victims' satisfaction with the work of the police varied in different countries and it was found to be linked with the general opinion of the police, which is more positive in both western countries than in the two eastern ones. We were more interested in the criticism of police work rather than the comparison between different countries. The lack of feedback was the most common reproach in all four countries. The victims also said that police officers did not show enough interest during the investigative procedure and that they simply did not do enough and behaved indifferently towards them.[6]

In their book *Police Work,*[7] which is especially intended for policemen, English authors Ainsworth & Pease describe the characteristics of co-influence of the victim and police officer in investigating the criminal offence. Police officers are directed predominantly towards acquiring relevant data for the investigation of the reported criminal offence, whereas victims expect a more personal and holistic approach, for which police officers are poorly qualified. According to the authors, the victims may be very hurt and governed by fear that the burglar may come back. This fear is understandable but the victims conceal it and change their way of life because of it and thus prolong the unpleasant distressful effect. Police officers should be aware of that and should bring up this topic themselves, which would certainly contribute to psychological disburdening by the victim. He or she could find out during such talk that such a possibility is not very likely, and at the same time feel that his or her fears are common and that it is wise to express them.

---

[5] Mawby (1998), pp. 78-84.
[6] Mawby (1998), *ibid.*
[7] Ainsworth & Pease (1987), pp. 87-88.

An example:[8] John, a 42-year old bachelor, had been burgled. A policeman visited him and reported the following: "When I arrived, I found him busy fixing new locks to the doors and windows. He was clearly very disturbed by what on the face of it seemed like a relatively minor burglary. He said that, amongst other things, a few pieces of jewellery belonging to his late mother had been stolen. This had triggered sad memories of his parents' deaths and he was still depressed. I spent some time with him, reassuring him that his reactions to the burglary were far from unusual and that many victims go through the same. As I left, he said he felt much better and thanked me for coming."

Police officers are often the first to come into contact with victims, who may still be strongly affected by the criminal offence they have experienced. That is why the attitude towards the victim may have a decisive influence on what the victim decides to do, what impression he or she will get about the representatives of 'justice' and also how society as a whole regards crime. Recently it has also become important that the police should also offer other services to victims, such as advising them on how to reduce the possibility of further victimisation, provide information on the services which offer help to victims, and especially inform them on the progress of the investigation of the criminal offence. These are undoubtedly burning issues and they have made their way into various national and international documents. To improve the situation the Council of Europe in 1987 issued a recommendation on what the police should provide to the victims of criminal offences:[9]

1. police officers must be qualified to work with victims in a reassuring, understanding and constructive way;
2. police officers should inform victims on the possibilities of assistance, practical and legal advice;
3. the victim should also get the information on the progress and success of the police investigation.

Also the United Nations Resolution states that police officers should be qualified for the work with victims and for provision of immediate help. The International Association of Police Chiefs adopted a recommendation in which they call upon police officers to provide victims with information on social and financial services aimed at victims of criminal offences and to inform victims about the progress of the investigation. Despite all the adopted recommendations, victimological research still proves that victims are more or less dissatisfied with the work of the police.[10]

Let us try to identify some reasons for this less than sensitive attitude of police officers and criminal investigators towards crime victims, which persists despite the above- mentioned recommendations and resolutions:

---

[8] Mawby & Walklate (1994), p. 116.
[9] *Assistance to Victims and Prevention of Victimisation*, 1988.
[10] Adapted from Mawby & Walkgate (1994), pp. 95-128.

1. police officers did not enter the police force with a primary interest to help their fellow men and so we can assume that they do not have any real inclination for psycho-social work (this can be true of the whole group but not necessarily of individuals);
2. police training devotes little attention to the work with crime victims. Thus the work of the police officers and criminal investigators depends on their sensitivity rather than their expertise;
3. police officers and criminal investigators are oriented predominantly towards combating crime and detecting criminal offenders; victims and witnesses are only agents contributing to the detection of the criminal;
4. for police officers and criminal investigators, investigation of criminal offences is routine, everyday work, so they tend not to not think about the effect of a criminal act on an individual. The victim is in agony and expects compassionate and calming reactions from the policeman. In several surveys the victims described the police officers and criminal investigators as insensitive cynical doubters. Just as a bad doctor sees only illness in his or her patient, so a bad police officer or criminal investigator is interested only in the criminal offence and not the victim;
5. many criminal offences are misunderstood, in particular rape and rape victims, although also victims of other criminal offences (also burglaries) may be treated as accomplices.

How can this situation be overcome? The effects of education and training were studied and unfortunately it was proved that they are of rather short duration. It seems that the mentality and the inclination of both police officers and citizens – potential victims – would have to be changed, which is a long and complex process dependent especially on the adopted philosophy of policing and also of citizens' expectations.

There is no detailed research into the experience of crime victims. However, the public relations service of the Ministry of the Interior included in the Slovenian opinion poll for the year 1994 questions about how people perceive the police and safety and informed the public about the results of the poll. Work at border crossing got the highest marks and the prevention of violence and care for victims the lowest. No follow-up was undertaken and specific analyses done. Nor were special instructions issued for police officers and criminal investigators.[11]

In 1998 surveys were carried out in several Slovene towns. Their aim was to find out how the victims of property criminal offences (burglary, robbery, theft and fraud – Articles 211, 212, 217 and 218 of the *Penal Code*) appraise the attitude and work of police officers and criminal investigators who participated in the investigation of the criminal offence.

---

[11] Šetinc (1995).

## Research Results

### A Study on Police Crime Prevention[12]

*Characteristics of a studied sample:*
- *gender:* 253 female respondents, 199 male respondents;
- *age:* mean 39 years, mode 30 years;
- *educational level:* 45 primary school (10%), 73 vocational school (16.2%), 181 high school (40%), 103 higher education (22.8%) and 50 BA degree or higher (11.1%);
- *victims of crime:* 73 victims of crime (16.7%), 379 non-victims of crime (83.3%).

*Findings about fear of crime and a role of police:* the majority of respondents has not been scared of crime and did not perceive crime as a prevailing problem. Respondents thought that the most significant sources of danger in our society are the following:
- *traffic* – 251 (in 1995 410, in 1996 390, in 1997 360 and in 1998 310 persons died in traffic accidents on roads in Slovenia. The serious traffic accident rate in the years 1995-1998 compared to lethal consequences was 183,5/100,000 citizens);
- *crime* – 123 (the crime rate in Slovenia is around 2200 reported criminal offences/ 100,000 citizens);
- *aliens/migrants* – 78 (a preliminary study of the second generation of migrants living in the capital of Slovenia, Ljubljana, shows that re-offending rates have been much higher than that of native Slovenes. This can be the result of the stigmatising effect and the focusing of police activities on such groups).

The general attitude to the police force is quite positive and the efficiency of the police force regarding crime prevention, crime control and crime fighting has been regarded quite positively. Such a result shows a problem of drawing conclusions based on general attitudes. The measurement of attitudes demonstrates results which are quite positive but when specific and more accurate questions are asked the attitudes are less positive.

*Policing and crime prevention:* the visibility of police officers is assumed to be a problem. Respondents stated that police officers do not co-operate with people efficiently/substantially. Almost half of the respondents have needed help from the police. Respondents believed crime prevention to be an important police activity, especially in relation to giving advice for an individual's safety. Some of them would invite police officers into their homes but about the same number of respondents would not. The majority of respondents would provide police officers with information for crime detection and most would trust community police officers.

---

[12] Results of that research project were also introduced by G. Meško at the British Society of Criminology Conference in Liverpole, July 1999.

*Female – male*: female respondents saw crime in a more apocalyptic manner than male respondents. Men were more willing to invite police officers into their homes than female respondents. However, men met police officers more frequently and knew more in person (by name).

*Urban – Rural Areas*: people living in rural areas were more open with the police and willing to help in crime prevention. People from urban areas were more fearful of crime and perceived more of a threat of crime than people from rural areas. People from rural areas were more willing to provide information to the police than people in urban areas. It also seems that people from urban areas valued their privacy, more than people living in the rural areas.

*Victims of crime – non victims*: a comparison of those victimised and those who have not showed that victimised people's perception of threat and fear of crime is very much greater than non-victims. Victims of crime were disillusioned about police efficiency due to their past experience. They also assessed the police as ineffective and impersonal. The results imply that victims of crime wish to stress that the police should be more humane and sympathetic when dealing with them. In brief, police officers are expected to be more professional.

*Bivariate correlations*: analysis of the bivariate correlations allows the following speculations (selected correlations, $r = .40$ and higher):
- people who perceive more danger expect more help from the police;
- the level of perceived danger is related to the perception that crime is an omnipresent problem of society;
- their feelings about the police influence their belief about police efficiency;
- knowledge about police work influences belief about police efficiency;
- visibility of the police is enhanced by knowing police officers personally;
- community policing means an active role for the police in the local community;
- knowing police officers in person is closely related to trusting them;
- knowing police officers promotes a willingness to provide them with information.

The above mentioned findings are good indicators for developing education and training programmes for police officers and for subsequent studies.

### Victims of Property Crime and their Opinion about the Police

In Celje we sent to 50 property crime victims a questionnaire designed to establish how the victims experience the criminal investigators and the police, as well as criminal investigation as a whole. Thirty victims between the ages of 20 and 60 filled out the questionnaire (22 men and eight women). All the cases were dealt with by the criminal investigators of the Police Directorate Celje; some cases were successfully solved, the others not.

In Jesenice we sent 53 questionnaires to property crime victims who live in the area of the police station Jesenice. The criminal offences were also committed in this area. The police officers and criminal investigators of the police station Jesenice dealt with all the reported criminal offences. Thirty-six victims between the ages of 20 and 60 filled out the questionnaires (23 men and 13 women).

Both surveys included citizens who experienced a criminal offence in 1997. With the questionnaire we gathered some personal data on each victim (gender, age, education) and the anonymity of returned questionnaires was guaranteed.

The questionnaires used in Celje and Jesenice were not entirely the same, but they are comparable as they only differed in some questions. They both consisted of two parts. The first part comprised questions referring to gender, age and education. The second part inquired into the feelings and predominant reactions of victims when they realised a criminal offence had been committed. We were also interested to know what they experienced when they reported the offence and how they would assess the attitude and behaviour of the police officers in different phases of the investigation.

**Results and Discussion**

We are aware that the survey is somewhat deficient as the sample of victims is not representative of the Slovenian population and it is also very small. The findings are mostly of practical value and will affect the education and training process of police officers and criminal investigators. At the same time the publication of the results can serve to draw attention to the problematic relationship of police officers or criminal investigators and victims during crime investigations.

Of 66 property crime victims, the majority of them (59) experienced burglary and theft and their predominant behavioural and emotional reactions were surprise, anger, agitation and disappointment.

The reactions were predominantly emotional and similar to reactions ascertained by the authors of surveys in other countries. It is interesting though that the victims' reactions differ if we break the victims down by education. Those with the lowest level of education (completed primary school) more often react with anger than surprise. How should police officers and criminal investigators take these findings into account when they receive reports about criminal offences and when they begin collecting the first information? They should be aware that citizens, when reporting a criminal offence, are shocked and bewildered and therefore find it hard to answer even simple questions. Thus at the first contact police officers should act in a calming way and should help the person reporting a crime with providing the essential data for the beginning of the investigation, but should avoid suggestive questioning.

The victims' answers to the question of whom they first thought of when they noticed that a criminal offence had taken place also point to surprise and bewilderment. More than a half of the respondents did indeed think of the police officers and criminal investigator first, but as many as one third of them did not know what to do at the first moment. It is interesting that almost all women thought of the police and informed them about the offence. The reason why victims did not immediately inform the police is not only bewilderment but also ignorance, since many did not know that all they had to do was dial 113 to contact the police.

When reporting a criminal offence, victims usually inform the police officer on duty or the operation and communication centre by phone or in person. There they get the first instructions on what to do next. When asked to assess the police officers during this first contact, victims most often stated that police officers were friendly, that they asked after relevant data, gave them instructions and directions, whereas some found them very formal, and the answer "calming" was only the fifth most frequent. Some victims stated that the police officers made fun of them, were rude to them or even insulted them. Although such responses were rare, this way of reacting should not happen in practice regardless of the manner of reporting the offence, assessment of the incident or momentary mood of the officer. Police officers should be aware that further co-operation depends on the first impression and that personal contacts with police officers are the factor which determines one's opinion about the police and consequently the appraisal of police work.

We were interested in the attitude of police officers and criminal investigators towards the victims following the initial reporting of the offence. This second phase either takes place where the offence was committed, at the victim's home or at a police station. In this phase the police officer or criminal investigator talks to the victim for a longer time while collecting more detailed information. The victims assessed police officers and criminal investigators in a positive way and the answers were as follows (sorted by frequency):
- friendly;
- interested in the case;
- asked after relevant data;
- gave instructions and advice;
- acted calmingly;
- asked too few questions;
- was very formal.

The victims' experiences with the police officers and criminal investigators are predominantly favourable, for approximately 80% of all appraisals are positive and 20% negative. Men were more critical than women and so are young people as opposed to the elderly. The reasons for this could be found in personal characteristics of young people and men as well as in the attitude of police officers towards these groups. It seems that police officers and criminal investigators are not sufficiently aware of the interactions in interpersonal relations and therefore find it harder to control themselves, which affects their behaviour, making it less friendly. It is interesting that the police officers and criminal investigators dealing with these criminal offences generally thought that they did not pay enough attention to the victims, and blamed it on lack of time and inadequate qualification for the work with victims. They need further training and education in this field.

Over 80% of the victims thought that police officers and criminal investigators did take enough time to talk to them. The elderly were most satisfied and the youngest group (between 20 and 30) the least, with women being more critical than men.

We further asked the victims whether the police officers and criminal investigators informed them about their rights during the procedure and told them where they could obtain information about their case and whether they actually sought them and received them. When they reported the offence, 47 out of 66 victims were informed about the course of further procedure and their rights in the procedure, eight were partly informed and 11 said that they did not learn anything about it. During further procedure, police officers and criminal investigator advised 44 victims on where they could get the information on the progress of the case, and did not do the same in 22 cases. Twenty victims sought, and received, the information on the case, 11 did not get any information, and as many as 35 never even inquired about the course and the results of the investigation. Providing information must become permanent practice and can also be regulated systemically (printed brochures, cards, etc.), but represents a problem both in our countries and abroad as well. The question, though, is why so many people (over 50%) are not interested in the course and outcome of the criminal investigation? Is it because they are realistic and do not expect miracles from the police, or is it because they simply assume that it is the duty of the police to make contact with them? In literature on this topic it is recommended that the police officers should call victims and tell them about the progress of the investigation. In this way they fulfil the expectations and demands of the victim, who requires from them especially an interest in what has happened to them. What if the victims wish to forget or suppress the unpleasant and threatening event? In our opinion it is particularly such victims who need professional assistance and police officers should appropriately advise them to look for such help. Therefore it is very useful for the victim in all cases if the police officers call them and talk to them.

We also asked the victims if they were satisfied with the police officers and criminal investigators working on their case. As many as 46 victims were entirely satisfied with the attitude of police officers and criminal investigators, 20 were only partly satisfied and none were entirely dissatisfied. These answers yield the conclusion that police officers carry out their work with sufficient professionalism and with appropriate sensitivity; nevertheless the situation is not entirely satisfactory.

The questions in the survey were mostly of multiple-choice type, but victims were also asked to describe in their words how they experienced the investigation of the criminal offence and the majority obliged. The work of the police was assessed as being satisfactory, but it was criticised for being too bureaucratic, which probably prevents fieldwork. The victims stated that the police officers and criminal investigators were friendly, that they showed due interest for their case, but complained that until then they had not yet received an answer from the police telling them what had been achieved. Some said that the officers did not ask them enough questions and in their opinion did not look for all the traces in detail. They thought that their material damage was insufficient for criminal investigators to exercise their every effort in the criminal investigation. The victims were satisfied with the approach and attitude, but not so with the results of the investigation.

**Conclusion**

The results of the survey surprised us in a positive way and it was proved once again that we should not believe rumours or generalise individual cases. Surveys are an excellent way of getting objective data, which make planning and development possible.

The analysis of the questionnaire results showed that, while investigating property criminal offences, police officers and criminal investigators do not neglect victims and are increasingly more aware that an appropriate attitude towards the victim and care for them is an integral part of the investigation of criminal offences. Nevertheless, police officers and criminal investigators could do much more for the victims to ease their distress.

It seems that an especially problematic issue is provision of information to victims on the progress and results of the criminal investigation as well as types of available help. It might be worthwhile to think about having an officer who would be responsible for contact with victims of different criminal offences at bigger police stations and police directorates. This would be in line with the tendency of bringing the police closer to the public, which is one of the guidelines of our police force. In this way victims could get the information on their case and on how to obtain assistance (technical, legal, psychological, etc.). Of course, police officers and criminal investigators would need more knowledge on the needs of victims and how to work with them.

There is no simple solution to the problem of a good relationship with victims of criminal offences. This problem is not only connected with the knowledge of police officers and criminal investigators; it also involves some systemic issues. It has to do with the basic philosophy of policing, human resources, selection, education, training, motivation, nature of work, etc. Therefore isolated measures cannot bring about any considerable changes in working with crime victims.

B. Dobovšek, G. Meško & P. Umek

# References

**Ainsworth, P.B. & Pease, K.** (1987), *Police Work*, The British Psychological Society and Methuen, London.
*Assistance to Victims and Prevention of Victimisation* (1988). Recommendation No. R (87) 21 Adopted by the Committee of Ministers of the Council of Europe on 17 September 1987 and Explanatory Memorandum, Strasbourg.
**Davis, R.C., Lurigio, A.J. & Skogan, W.G.** (1997), *Victims of Crime*, Sage Publications, London.
**Maguire, M.** (1980), 'The Impact of Burglary Upon Victims', in: *British Journal of Criminology* 20, pp. 261-275.
**Mawby, R.** (1998), 'Primerjalna raziskava o policijskem delu v Angliji, Nemčiji, Poljski in Madžarski', in: M. Pagon & A. Anžič (eds.), *Proučevanje in primerjalni vidiki policijske dejavnosti v svetu*, Visoka policijsko-varnostna šola, Ljubljana, pp. 76-91[author query: please check reference].
**Mawby, R. & Walklate, S.** (1994), *Critical Victimology*, London: Sage.
**Meško, G.** (1998), 'Nekatere razsežnosti nasilne viktimizacije', in: *Teorija in praksa*, Ljubljana, let. 35, št. 6, str. 1076-1088.
**Sparks, R.F.** (1983), *Research on Victims of Crime: Accomplishments, Issues and New Directions*, Rockville.
**Šetinc, M.** (1995), *Javno mnenje 1994 – O policiji in varnosti*, interno gradivo MNZ, 12 s.

# Reliability of Personal Evidence – Islamic Law Perspective

*M.E. Elbushra*

## Introduction

Islamic law does not set forth any detailed system of criminal procedure, and there is no mandate in any source of Islamic law emphasising the existence of an investigative stage in the Islamic Criminal Justice system. The historical precedents do not indicate clearly that the stage of criminal investigation is acknowledged in solving the criminal cases. Ibn Al Qiyam Al-Jowaziya in his famous book titled *The Methods of Judgement (Al-Turug Al-Hukmiya)*[1] has stated that there is no provision in the *Shari'a*, which prescribes that all legal matters be assigned to one particular person or office. The arrangement and administration of criminal justice system and mechanisms are purely political issue and are left to the discretion of the authorities. It is acceptable to divide legal jurisdiction into several offices or aggregate them in one. The only condition for one who is appointed to practice law is that he should be competent and should possess the legal qualifications prescribed by the *Shari'a*.

Thus, methods of the criminal justice administration in Islamic law are considered to be a matter of policy and not of *Shari'a*. Consequently, the jurists *(Ulama)* and the legislative powers of the Islamic countries are authorised to organise and maintain criminal procedural systems congruent with the particular circumstances of time and place, within the spirit of the general principles of Islam. In the early Islamic era, the Administration of criminal justice was distributed among several offices such as the Head of the State *(Khalifa)*, the office of complaints *(Diwan Al-Mazalim)*, the Amir of the region, The Military Commander, the Chief of Police *(Sahib Al-Shurta)* and the inspector of markets. The Chief of the Police was concerned with the serious crimes, *Huddood* and *Quissas*, while other contraventions and simple crimes were in the jurisdiction of an official knows as market inspector. However, Islamic criminal justice system and procedure were not stagnant. The Islamic criminal procedural system has developed gradually to meet the requirements of the innumerable political, social and scientific changes which has occurred in the Islamic countries and the world.

Today, many Islamic countries have developed competent criminal justice systems consistent with many inevitable changes which has taken place in the field of the crime prevention and criminal justice. Globalisation of crime

---

[1] Abu Abdul Allah Shems Al-Deen M. Ibn Bakr (Ibn Al-Qiyam Al-Jowaziya) was a famous jurist in Islamic laws. He was born in 1271 in Damascus. His works are considered one of the most reliable references in *Shari'a*.

problems, concepts of the new world order, commitments in an international crime prevention and criminal justice programmes[2] were of great impact on the Islamic criminal justice system.

Islamic criminal law as well as the whole Islamic legal system is not codified or enacted by normal legislative bodies in a form of articles and sections. However the basic principles and legal rules were delineated and clarified by the following sources.

Firstly, original sources known as the Holy Book (Quran) and the Prophetic reports *(Sunna)*. Secondly, complementary sources including:

1. the consensus of opinion *(Ijma')*;
2. the analogy *(Quyass)*;
3. equity *(Istihsan)*;
4. textually unspecified interests of the people *(Maslaha Mursala)*;
5. avoidance of harm *(Sadd Al-Dharar)*;
6. compatibility of the means and the ends *(Istishab)*;
7. checking what is permissible and what is prohibited.[3]

Today, the new emergence of Islamic legal system in many parts of the world and escalation of transnational crime problems necessitate integration and reconciliation among various criminal justice systems prevailing in the world. This paper is intended to bridge the gap between basic principles of Islamic criminal procedure and evidence on one hand and basic rules and methods of the modern criminal procedure known in western countries on the other hand.

Whereas each type of crime in Islamic law required certain amount of proof, discussion of criminal investigation and evidence should not be dealt with in isolation from the objective criminal law. In Islamic law, crimes are defined and classified into three categories:

1. crimes punishable by fixed punishment, hereafter known as *Huddood*, including:
   - adultery *(Zina)*;
   - defamation or false accusation *(Qadhf)*;
   - drinking alcohol;
   - theft *(Sariga)*;
   - dacoity, highway robbery *(Qat Altariq)*;
   - apostasy *(Ridda)*;
2. crimes punishable by retaliation or blood money, hereafter known as *Quissas*, including all types of murder and injuries;

---

[2] *Report of the UN Commission on Crime Prevention and Criminal Justice on its second session,* E/CN.15/1993/9.
[3] The fundamental principle in Islam is that everything is permissible, unless it is obviously prohibited, condemned or frowned upon by one or more of the *Shari'a* sources.

3. crimes punishable by discretionary punishments, hereafter known as *Taazir*, including all forms of crimes, contravention, and negative social or religious behaviour.

With due respect to the various controversial views of Muslim jurists; this paper – relying on the opinion of the majority *(Rai al-jamhour)* – attempts to identify:

1. contemporary criminal investigation methods in the Islamic legal system;
2. personal evidence in the Islamic criminal law;
3. admissibility of scientific evidence before Islamic criminal law courts;
4. the role and powers of judges in Islamic law perspective.

## Contemporary Criminal Investigation in the Islamic Legal System

Influenced by the inherited basic principles and guidelines of the Islamic criminal law, many Islamic countries have adopted modern criminal justice systems following the models developed in the western countries. Tremendous efforts were made to upgrade standards of the criminal justice personnel and improve the legal processes as well as the operational methods. Scholars and governmental organisations from various Islamic countries have contributed in developing and formulating the UN standards, guidelines[4] and international instruments of the criminal justice. Although it may be noted that the UN standards and guidelines are not yet included in the legislation of the criminal justice in many Islamic countries, but, the positive impact of such standards and guidelines on the mechanism of the criminal justice system is remarkable.

Today, there are three distinct criminal procedural systems may be known throughout the world, namely:

1. the accusatorial system, which considers criminal action to be a common dispute between two equal parties, and their case is directly presented to the judge who should balance the claims of the litigants;
2. the inquisitorial system, where the criminal case proceeds through a pre-trail stage of investigation by judicial police bodies;
3. the mixed system which combines the aspects of both the accusatorial and the inquisitorial systems.

The criminal procedural systems known in Islamic countries are almost identified as a mixed system model. Unlike the accusatorial and inquisitorial systems the Islamic procedural system following the mixed model, has introduced the principle of the *Siyasat Al-Shari'a*. According to this principle, it is the duty of the political authorities to establish a criminal justice system

---

[4] UN guiding principles for crime prevention and criminal justice in the context of development and new economic order; basic principles on the independence of the judiciary; code of conduct for law enforcement official; standard minimum rules for the treatment of prisoners; standard minimum rules for the administration of juvenile justice; guidelines on the role of prosecutors; basic principles on the use of force and firearms by law enforcement officials.

which serve the public interest. Thus, although, the procedural system is not a matter of *Shari'a*, it is governed by the general principles of *Shari'a*.[5] Therefore, the criminal justice system of the Islamic countries consists of the following components:

1. police;
2. public prosecutors;
3. criminal courts;
4. corrections or penal institutions;
5. victim.

The police being most traditional organised forces in the Islamic countries conduct the main role in the criminal procedure. Usually, police officers detect crimes, gather evidence, make arrests and searches, conduct investigations and maintain forensic science laboratories and fingerprints bureaux. The police may make charges against the accused persons and conduct prosecution before criminal courts. Moreover, the police are in charge of the penal institutions and juvenile justice in many Islamic countries.

Although the responsibility of criminal investigation and gathering of evidence is vested by law upon police officers, many other public officials are involved in the pre-trial stage of criminal procedure in the Islamic countries. A recent study conducted by the Naif Arab Academy for Security Sciences has identified eight organisations involved in investigative activities, such organisations were classified according to the volume of their involvement as follows:

1. police officers;
2. public prosecutors;
3. security directors;
4. governors *(Muhafiz)*;
5. Regional directors;
6. chiefs of district police and guards;
7. chiefs and sheikhs of villages;
8. chiefs of air and sea transportation.

The above mentioned study, which was basically exploratory and descriptive in nature was verified by a field survey conducted in a forum composed of (1116) professionals to show the general trends towards such remarkable number of investigative organisations. The results of the survey has revealed that each of the organisations were supported or acceptable by the following rates:[6]

1. police officers: 66.8%;

---

[5] A.M. Awad, 'The rights of the accused in the Islamic criminal procedure', *Islamic Criminal Justice*, Bassioni M. Sherif, N.Y. Oclana Publications 1982.
[6] M.I. Zeid, *Criminal Justice Systems in the Arab Countries*, Naif Arab Academy for Security Sciences, Riyadh 1996.

2. public prosecutors: 77.9%;
3. security directors: 55.3%;
4. governors: 29%;
5. regional directors: 23.8%;
6. chiefs of district police and guards: 42.8%;
7. chiefs and sheikhs of villages: 14.5%;
8. chiefs of air and sea transportation: 28.8%.

Such results reflect that the criminal justice systems of the Arab countries are changing towards the inquisitorial systems and emphasising fair procedure. More involvement of public prosecutors at the state of the investigation is an indication of maintaining human rights, particularly, during collection of scientific evidence by the police or any other security organisation. In addition to the newly emerging role of the public prosecutor in the Islamic criminal justice systems, it is noteworthy to point out the role of the victim in Islamic criminal procedure as another considerable indication of justice and equity. The victim as a witness or as an individual claiming compensation and revenge is given due consideration throughout the investigation, trail and execution of judgements. Finally, there is no doubt that the role of the judge remains the most vital in the Islamic criminal procedure. Methods of collecting evidence, admissibility and scrutinisation of every related fact are left to the absolute satisfaction and certitude of the judge *(Yaggen Al-Ghadi)*.

**Procedures governing Investigations**

Islamic criminal procedure is initiated by a complaint from the injured person, his legal representative, relatives or any other person who believes that an offence has been committed. It is the duty of the public officials to lodge accusation in cases of crime committed within their jurisdictions.

Practically, such initiation of criminal procedure takes pace through a verbal or written report given to a police officer, public prosecutor, security officer or judge in charge of the jurisdiction where the crime has been committed. The above mentioned report, information or complaints should be registered by the police in a form of 'First Information Report' and entered into a judicial book kept at every police station known as 'Register of Crime Reports'. Following the registration of the information, the police commence the following investigative activities:
1. arrest of the accused person or persons if they are known;
2. visit the scene of the crime and collect evidence;
3. interrogate witnesses and accused persons;
4. conduct search of places and persons.

If in the course of such investigative activities, it appears to the police officer or the public prosecutor under whom the investigation is being made, that such investigation discloses reasonable grounds of suspicion against any person of having committed an offence, and that a trail should begin, he shall submit the case diary to the court or magistrate competent to take cognisance of the crime.

Compared with the western countries, stages of criminal procedure in the Islamic countries are very brief. In Islamic criminal procedure it is not essential to go through the elaborate stages of investigation, booking, formal complaint, initial appearance, preliminary hearing, arraignment etc. known in the western model of criminal procedure. It is a well-known fact that the arrest of the accused person should not take place, unless there is a reasonable ground or sufficient evidence to establish a criminal case against the accused. False or wrongful accusation of another person is considered a serious crime *(Quadhf)*. Arrest is one of the most critical issues in the developing countries, because the police are authorised to arrest without a judicial warrant in a large number of serious crimes. It is very common to commence investigative activities by arresting many persons or any one found at the scene of the alleged offence. Following the arrest investigators tend to utilise scientific methods to collect evidence against the persons under arrest. Due to such rapid and doubtful arrests and releases, official crime statistics of many countries reveal very high clearance rates and a very low conviction rates which is an indication of failure of the investigative methods and techniques. A comparative study carried out in Sudan, one of the countries applying Islamic criminal law, has revealed the following discrepancy:[7]

| Crimes | Years | 1994 | 1995 | 1996 |
|---|---|---|---|---|
| Total number of report crimes | | 503383 | 442105 | 459808 |
| Total number of arrested persons | | 370508 | 263011 | 298342 |
| Number of persons charged by the police and the public prosecutor | | 213419 (57.6%) | 205600 (78.1%) | 192640 (64.5%) |
| Number of convicted persons | | 16413 (4.4%) | 12800 (4.8%) | 15892 (5.3%) |

*Source: Annual crime report issued by the Central Criminal Investigation Department in Sudan, 1994-1996.*

It may be observed that there is a great need to reorganise the methods and procedures of criminal investigation in many developing Islamic countries to comply with the requirements and objectives of *Shari'a* law by minimising the discretionary powers of police in the domain of criminal justice.

---

[7] M.E. Elbushra, *Criminal Justice and Crime Problem in Sudan*, Khartoum University Press 1998.

## Reliability of Personal Evidence in the Islamic Criminal Law

Evidence in Islamic criminal law is distinguished by the following characteristics.

First, certain crimes known as *Huddood* require specific amount of evidence – well prescribed by Quran and *Sunna*. If such prescribed quality of evidence is not available *Huddood* penalty should not be inflicted upon the accused person. However, the judge may instead of the *Huddood* penalty, convict the accused person with a less serious offence and sentence him with any other penalty prescribe by the judge, according to his knowledge and discretionary powers.

Second, in Islamic criminal procedure, normally, burden of proof lies upon the plaintiff whether an individual or a public authority, but, when no substantial evidence is procurable from the side of the plaintiff or complainant, the defendant should be asked to take a solemn oath that he has not committed the alleged crime; and accordingly he may be acquitted.[8]

A person who gives evidence before a court should be mature adult, sane, objective in his testimony and not involved or interested in the criminal case in issue.

Third, Muslim jurists unanimously agree that the evidence given by a non-believer against a Muslim should not be accepted, unless the trail is taking place in a non-Muslim country.

Fourth, circumstantial evidence is well known in Islamic criminal law,[9] and it is left to the free discretion of the judge as well as his intellectual alertness and sense of observation and judgement.

Finally, there is no doubt that Quranic and prophetic parables as well as legislation and legal judgements of Muslim predecessors remain as principal paragons and guidelines for criminal courts and judges to determine procedures and methods of proof.

Being governed and guided by the above mentioned rules or evidence and procedures, Personal evidence in Islamic criminal law may be classified into seven types: testimony, confession, circumstantial evidence, oath by 50 persons, oath by the defendant, scientific evidence and the judge's personal observations.

---

[8] "If people are allowed their way of having their claims, they will claim the lives and properties of others, therefore, the defendant may take oath that he has not committed the crime for which he has been charged" (Prophetic report).

[9] If it be that his shirt / is rent from the front, then / is her tale true, and he is a liar, / but if it be that his shirt is torn from the back, / then is she the liar, / and he is telling truth (Chapter 12, verses 26-27).

## 1. Testimony *(Shahada)*

Islamic criminology emphasised the individual's inner characteristics which are related to the strength of his religious spirituality, belief and faith in God. If the individual's faith is weak he may normally become selfish, shameless, unjust and deviant. Islam strives by various means to preclude circumstances that may lead to crime, sinful acts and unfairness. Due to such deep rooted concepts it is prospective that individuals:
- are aware with the rights of the other individuals;
- are obligated to maintain peace, security and justice for others;
- have an inner feeling that God knows and sees every deed;
- have the spiritual obligation to give evidence or a testimony before a criminal court;[10]
- are mindful that concealing evidence, giving false testimony or confessing crime he has not committed is prohibited by God;[11]
- are aware that individuals are encouraged to give evidence and disclose facts for the sake of justice.

A testimony in Islamic criminal law is defined as a verbal report of what the witness has seen or heard about facts related to the alleged crime, provided that such report is made before a court of justice by a competent witness. Giving evidence by testimony is one of the principal Islamic obligations imposed upon the individuals, not only as a means of proof, but it is one of the religious objectives of Islam. Many Quranic verses have emphasised the necessity of testimony. In the light of such Quranic verses[12] basic features and rules of testimony may be outlined as follows:
- conditions related to the witness: jurists unanimously agree that admissible testimony should be given by an adult, male, sane, just *(Aadil)* and Muslim (in case of accused Muslim in Islamic country) witness, provided that he is not involved or interested in the alleged crime. However, jurists have controversial opinions on testimony given by a deaf, dump, blind, youth or a female witness. Even though, the majority of the jurists tend to consider testimony of such witnesses when ever they are capable to convey their

---

[10] Ye who believe! / Stand out firmly / For Allah, as witnesses / To fair dealing, and let not / The hatred of others / To you make you sware / To wrong and depart from justice, / Be just, that is / Next to piety, and fear Allah. / For Allah is well aquatinted with all that you do.

[11] We shall hide not / The evidence before Allah, if we do, / then behold! The sin be upon us (Chapter 6, Verses 44).

[12] Ye who believe! / When ye deal with each other, / In transactions involving future obligations / In a fixed period of time, / Reduce this to writing / Let a scribe write down / Faithfully as between / The parties; Let not the scribe / Refuse to write as Allah has taught him. / And get two witnesses out of your own men, / And if there are not two men. / Then a man and two women. / Such as ye choose. For witnesses, / So that if one of them errors, the other can remind her, / The witnesses should not refuse when they are called on (for evidence)(Chapter 3, verse 282).

knowledge to the satisfaction of the judge or the court, in several minor crimes *Taazir*;

- conditions related to the testimony: it is agreed that the testimony should be introduced formally by its specific verb 'I testify' *(Ashhadu)*, because of this verb, which is taken from the original Quranic source has great impact on the equitability of the individual who is spelling out his knowledge before a court of justice. Moreover, it is agreed that the contents of the testimony should be conformative to the facts surrounding the alleged crime. On the other hand, there are two conditions related to the contents of the testimony known as *Shart-Al-Asala* means that the testimony should be given directly by the original person who has the information and not as a hearsay or on behalf of another. *Shart Adem Al-Taqadum* means that the contents of the testimony should be given before the judge or court of justice without delay and within a reasonable period of time that does not amount to limitation. Majority of Muslim jurists necessitate *Shart Al-Asala* and *Shart Adem Al-Taqadum* for a testimony of the alleged crime is related to one of the rights of God, such as *Huddood* crimes. However, both conditions of *Asala* and *Adem Al-Taqadum* may not be on issue if the alleged crime is related to one of the rights of the people. That is to say, if the alleged crime is related to property or *Taazir*, hearsay evidence may be admissible and there may be no conditions of time limitation required;

- conditions related to female witnesses: *Shari'a* decrees that women's testimony is admissible on civil property cases, provided that there should be more than one female witness and supported by competent male testimony. In criminal cases testimony given by a female witness is admissible only to prove facts related to female affairs which are not accessible to the males, such as pregnancy and deliverance. However, only female testimony can never prove guilty in cases of *Huddood* or *Quissas*. Many jurists are of opinion that scientific evidence prepared by a female expert is admissible as well as that of a male expert.

## 2. Confession *(Iqurrar)*

Confessions made by accused person against himself is accepted in the Islamic criminal law to prove guilty in some crimes, provided that:
1. the accused person is held criminally responsible;
2. confession is not given under any sort of threat or inducement;
3. confession is given voluntarily by sane adult, and, under his own free will.

In addition to the above-mentioned provisions, confession is governed by further conditions in the following cases:
1. in crimes of *Huddood* or *Quissas* confession should be direct, obvious and explicit, and should be given before the court of justice;
2. in crimes of adultery confession should be given in detail showing the fact of the sexual intercourse known as penetration *(Ealaj)* The confession

should also be made four times repeatedly before different court sessions, and sexual intercourse was physically and practically possible by the two parties;

3. in case of theft the offender should make his confession twice before the court, and, provided that the victim is claiming restoration of his stolen property;

4. in case of drinking alcohol, the accused should confess twice before the court, while existence of an alcoholic smell around the accused.[13]

## 3. Circumstantial Evidence *(Quarina)*

Circumstantial evidence was illustrated in Quran by the story of Zulaikha who had attempted sexual assault on Prophet Joseph.[14] Scorning Zulaikha's love, Joseph tried to escape, but she tugged at his garment and toured a piece of the garment. Zulaikha accused Joseph as the one who attempted the sexual assault. However, Joseph's garment, which was torn at the backside, was considered as a circumstantial evidence to prove Joseph's acquittal. This example reveals the importance and legality of circumstantial evidence as a subsidiary means of proof, extricated by judges who have acute sense of observation, knowledge and experience.

## 4. Oath by 50 Persons *(Al-Qassama)*

*Al-Qassama* is a unique method of proof accepted only in *Quissas* (murder) cases, where no other evidence is available. In *Al-Qassama*, fifty solemn oaths are taken by the claimants or the defendants. The judge asks fifty of the defendants or the residents of the area where murder took place to swear that they did not commit the crime. If the defendants reject *Al-Qassama* the judge may ask the same from the claimants. If the number of those who taking oath is less than 50 some of them should repeat. Following *Al-Qassama Diya* blood money is paid to the claimants from the public funds.[15]

## 5. Oath of the Defendant *(Yameen)*

As a general principal, it is the responsibility of the claimant to produce substantial evidence to prove his allegation. However, if the defendant denies the allegation, he is obliged to take a solemn oath rejecting the claimant's

---

[13] I.A. Bek, *Methods of Proof in Shari'a*, Cairo: New Press 1985.

[14] If it be that his shirt is rent from the front, then is her tale true, and he is a liar. But if it be that his shirt, is torn from the back, then is she the liar, and he is telling the truth (Chapter 12, verses 26-27).

[15] B.F. Al-Suwayem, *The accused his rights and treatment*, Riyadh: Arab Security Studies and Training Centre 1987.

charge.[16] Oath in Islam as a broad concept has a great impact on judgements and decision making, because oath reflects the spiritual feelings of the individual as well as his faith and strength of belief. Therefore, Islam – unlike the modern laws – gives such privilege to both the claimant and the defendant as a matter of equity.

## 6. Scientific Evidence

Scientific evidence is the opinion and written reports produced by experts and scientists *(Ahal Al-Zikir)*. Scientific evidence is being utilised in many Islamic countries, particularly at the stage of the police investigations leading to substantial evidence. Tentatively, it should be noted that, whenever the conviction of any accused person is based upon scientific evidence, then, the punishment imposed should be *Taazir* punishment and not *Huddood*.[17] The majority of jurists consider the scientific evidence as a circumstantial evidence.

## 7. Judge's Personal Observations *(Illmu Al-Qadi)*

The judge may utilise his own observations and knowledge for inference of facts and conclusions leading to conviction of the accused in case of offences related with people's right *(Taazir)*.[18] However, the judge is not authorised to use his own testimony to convict an accused person in the crimes of *Huddood*.

## Admissibility of Scientific Evidence before Islamic Courts

Islam is known as a religion of sciences and knowledge. It recognises sciences and respects the scientists *(Ulama)* as leaders of their nations. Innumerable scientific facts which were manifested in Quran since the seventh century are now being identified and adopted by modern sciences and technologies as new innovations. Therefore, Muslims jurists agree upon the inevitable role of science and technology in all aspects of life to maintain interests of mankind, provided that it does not infringe the basic principles and objectives of *Shari'a*. Scientific and technological methods were most recommended in the field of criminal justice administration as one of the principal objectives of Islam.

In Islamic law judges are asked to examine and scrutinise all facts related to the crime or allegation pending trial. Doing such examinations judges are

---

[16] The Prophet is report to have said "If people were left free to make their own way of having their claims, they would have claimed the lives and properties of others; and it is right of the defendant to take the oath showing that he has not committed the crime for which he has been charged."

[17] S.B.M. A-Uteiby, *Use of scientific method of proof in Taazir cases*, Riyadh: Arab Security Studies and Training Centre, 1994.

[18] M. Al-Zuheily, *Wasail Al-Ithbath Fi Al-Sharia Al-Islamiya*, 2nd ed. 1988, p. 562.

authorised to look for scientific and technological means in order to reactivate and assess various views. In Islam, judges are urged to call competent experts and *Ulama* to give evidence related to their exclusive jurisdiction and professionals *(Ahal Al-Zikir)*.[19]

With growing awareness of the validity of scientific evidence in the Islamic countries, techniques of fingerprints, blood grouping, hair analysis, sound recording, polygraph and DNA, as well as the other physical crime prevention techniques, are being well considered in solving crime problems. However, it is still difficult to put forward the ambitious objectives in eliminating criminality and realising criminal justice. In fact the difficulties currently facing in implementing scientific methods of solving crimes is not much a unique problems of Islamic countries, it is more debatable even in the western nations. That may be due to either mistrusting the professionals who conduct detection and investigation by their communities, or misunderstanding the contemporary crime problem and seriousness of evading justice.

Police officers, public prosecutors and forensic science experts are part of the whole community: they have the same feelings, ethics and moralities of their communities. They do understand means of justice and respect the right of the accused as well as that of the victims. Unlike the other members of the society, professional investigators have the opportunity to interrogate hazardous murderers and terrorists. They have a chance to listen to crime victims telling harrowing stories about how they were robbed or raped. Such estimable experiences and many others should be considered in entrusting investigators and their scientific experts in the area of scientific evidence. In this respect, I am of the opinion that criminal courts in Islamic countries are rather lenient than those of the western countries in utilising scientific evidence. However, this conclusion is based on the assumption that there are certain shared factors, namely indisputable classification of crimes, systematic methods of proof and classification of the scientific evidence.

As mentioned earlier, Islamic law classifies crime into:

1. *Huddood* crimes,[20] which are punishable by fixed penalties provided in Quran. The amount and features of evidence required to prove guilty in such crimes and inflict the fixed penalties is well prescribed by Quran. Consequently, only scientific evidence is not enough to prove guilty in *Huddood* crime. On the contrary, scientific evidence may raise or disclose doubtful issues leading to acquittal of the accused persons;

2. *Quissas* crimes, including all types of culpable homicide and injuries are punishable with penalties fixed by Quran, but such penalties may be altered

---

[19] And before thee also / the apostles we sent / were but men, to whom / we granted inspiration: If ye / realise this not, as of those / who posses the message (Chapter 16, Verse 43).
[20] *Huddood* crimes are adultery, defamation or false accusation, drinking alcohol, theft, dacoity, Highway robbery and apostacy.

if the victim pardons the offender. Quran also prescribes the evidence required by *Shari'a* to prove guilty in *Quissas* crimes as testimony and confession. However, the scientific evidence here is indispensable to assess the volume of injury or identifying cause of death (*e.g.* scientific evidence may be essential to prove that the deceased person was or was not already dead, when the confessing accused attacked and stabbed him with the intention of murder);

3. *Taazir* crimes are not provided explicity in Quran or *Sunna*, but they cover all acts of disobedience to 'God's' commandment and social misconduct. *Taazir* crimes represent all crimes currently identified by western penal codes. Several *Taazir* crimes are now being identified by disciplines and regulations *(Anzima)* in a form of definitions, sections or articles providing penalties and methods of detection and proof. Therefore, the criminal courts as a direct or circumstantial evidence to prove guilty or acquittal in *Taazir* crimes without exemption accepts scientific evidence.

There are two methods of proof known as the *free* method of proof, where judges are left free to consider every type of evidence to prove the criminal case, and the *limited* method of proof, where the crime is proved only by the evidence prescribed by Quran or *Sunna*.

The distinction between free proof and limited proof becomes in issue only in the case of alleged offence is one of *Huddood* or *Quissas*. The majority of *Ulama* confine the legal methods of proof in testimony *(Shahada)* and confession *(Iqurrar)* as identified by Quran and *Sunna*. However, there are several jurists from Hanbaly sect advocate the method of free proof in *Huddood* and *Quissas* crimes to maintain the rights of the victims, achieve deterrence and realise justice in cases where the complainant fails to provide evidence as prescribed by the fixed method of proof.[21]

In the light of the above mentioned distinction between crimes of *Huddood*, *Quissas* and *Taazir*, and concerned with views of *Ulama* on the free and limited methods of proof, scientific evidence may be classified into the following categories showing the legality and admissibility of each category:

Firstly, evidence acquired secretly without the knowledge of the accused person, such as interception of communication. Here, there is no doubt that Islam gives due respect to the privacy of individuals. Several *Shari'a* sources has clearly restricted entry to premises of others or listening to their communication.[22] Therefore, collection of evidence secretly by any means of

---

[21] Ibn Al-Qiyam and Al-Jowaziya and Ibn Taimiya were among those who advocated free proof method.

[22] O ye who believe! / Avoid suspicion as much / (As possible); For suspicion / In some cases is a sin; / And spy not on each other, behind their backs. Would any / of you like to eat / The flesh of his dead brother? / Nay ye would Abbor it. / But fear God (Chapter 49, verse 12); O ye who believe! / Enter not houses other than your own. / Until ye have asked permission and saluted / Those in them; that is / Best for you, in order that / Ye may heed (what is seemly) / If you find no (to be continued)

illegal entry, bugging, electronic surveillance or any kind of interception are prohibited in Islamic law. Such detective or investigative activities are classified as acts of spreading mischief in the community, and, may amount to a criminal behaviour. However, if the people are facing serious crimes (organised crimes, terrorism, illegal trading in drugs, etc.) or any other eminent danger which may not be solved without utilising such secret scientific means, shall we still ignore scientific evidence?

Governed by *Shari'a* rules the answer may be one of the following options:

1. scientific evidence may be utilised if crime problems can be solved and interests of the people maintained as well as avoidance of spreading mischief;
2. if it is not possible to realise both objectives of solving crime problem and avoiding mischief, Muslim jurists agreed that:
   1. if the interests of people are greater than damages of mischief, the first should be taken and the later ignored;
   2. if the spread of mischief is greater than the interests of people, the first should be avoided sacrificing with people's interest;
   3. if both mischief spreading and maintenance of interests are equal, then it is recommended to ignore one of the activities or both.

Secondly, evidence obtained openly with the knowledge of the accused person, including *intimate* samples of blood, semens or any other tissue fluid, urine, saliva or pubic hair or swab taken from the person's body orifice, fingerprints and photographs, and *non-intimate* samples, such as hair other than pubic hair, samples taken from nail or under nail, teeth impression, part of person's body other than a body orifice.

Bearing in mind the public interests and considering the right of the accused person in the context of the general principles of *Shari'a*, Muslim jurists agree upon utilisation of scientific evidence acquired from the accused person to detect crimes and investigate all forms of crimes. Such evidence may be used to:

1. generate other admissible evidence (testimony or confession) in *Huddood* and *Quissas* cases;
2. create and strengthen judge's satisfaction in all criminal cases;
3. prove guilty in *Taazir* crimes in collaboration with other circumstantial evidence.

The above mentioned utilisation of the scientific evidence is recommended by Muslim jurists upon the following conditions:

---

one, enter not / Until permission is given to you; / If ye are asked to go back, go back (Chapter 24, Verses 27, 28); It is virtue if ye enter / Your houses from the back; / It is virtue if ye fear God. / Enter houses through the proper doors / And fear God: That ye may prosper (Chapter 2, verse 189).

1. the samples must not be taken without the consent or appropriate consent or judicial authorisation;
2. the accused should be informed with the fact of the sample taking;
3. samples should be taken by specialised expert or medical practitioner or medico legal experts;
4. taking of the samples should not be a probable cause of danger to the health or safety of the accused person;[23]
5. there must be a reasonable ground for suspecting the involvement of the person from whom the sample is to be taken;
6. there is need to solve the criminal case for the sake of general public interest.

Thirdly, evidence collected from the scene of the crime includes fingerprints, tool marks, paint flakes, forged documents and any other related physical evidence. Such materials may be examined by forensic science laboratory experts and compared with samples taken from the accused or previously registered information to cause identification and verification of facts related to crime. In this category, fingerprints are most reliable and authenticated because the fact that no two fingerprints are identical was revealed in Quran.[24] Scientific reports made by forensic science laboratory experts are accepted by *Shari'a* courts to prevent guilty in serious *Taazir* crimes.

Fourthly, evidence or statement taken from the accused person or a witness through scientific means such as Lie Detector (Polygraph), narco-analysis (truth-serum), suggestive hypnosis or auto-hypnosis are not admissible as evidence before Islamic Criminal Court. Because, such statement whether it is a testimony of a witness or a confession of an accused does not comply with requirements of either. Muslim jurists consider such evidence as a statement given involuntarily and without a free will of an insane person.

In fact, scientific evidence is being utilised in many Islamic countries, particularly at the stage of police investigations leading to substantial evidence. Almost, Islamic countries are continuously developing forensic science laboratories equipped with latest technologies including automised fingerprints processing, Gas chromatograph, Laser spectrometer and DNA analysis to improve the benefits of scientific evidence. Survey on *Shari'a* courts' judgement in Arab countries has revealed that scientific evidence had been notably accepted to prove guilty in *Taazir* crimes and penal law crimes. The Kingdom of Saudi Arabia as a leading Islamic country an example in this

---

[23] M.M. Al-Deen Awad, *Human Rights in the Criminal Procedure* (unpublished paper), Riyadh: Naif Arab Academy for Security Sciences 1989.
[24] Does man think we / cannot assemble his bones? / Nay, we are able to put / together in perfect order / The very tips of his fingers (Chapter 29, Verses 3).

case.[25] Tentatively, it should be noted that, whenever the conviction of any accused person is based upon scientific evidence, then, the punishment imposed should be *Taazir* punishment and not *Huddood*.[26]

It is most essential to emphasise here, the role of the judge in *Shari'a* criminal court. All types of evidence are left to the discretion of the judge and his absolute satisfaction. I believe Muslim jurists and judges in general tend to rely on well-established scientific methods of criminal investigation and evidence.

It is noteworthy that, Muslim scholars were profoundly aware that, if investigating crimes is urgent to realise justice, it should not be achieved abusively.[27] To abolish the devastating abuses of human dignity and all forms of criminality was one of the main principles and objectives of Islam as religion. Therefore, Islamic criminal law has provided the following safeguards guaranteeing protection of human rights during criminal investigation:[28]

1. every person is entitled to call upon the assistance of a lawyer *(Wakeel Al-Khusuma)*;
2. the right to speak freely or remain silent during interrogations;
3. right to privacy;
4. right to initial presumption of innocence;
5. right of interpreting any doubt in favour of the accused.

## The Role and Powers of Judges in Islamic Law Perspective

According to the Islamic law judges are completely free in defining the offences committed by the accused person, and they have an absolute power in the determination of sanctions on behalf of the head of the state, provided that the offence alleged to have been committed is not a *Hadd* or *Quissas*. Such sanctions are commonly known as *Ta'zir*. *Ta'zir* punishments range from a simple reprimand to any term of imprisonment, and from flogging to the capital punishment. *Ta'zir* punishment may include fines, seizure of property and confiscation of any substances related to any crime, contravention or

---

[25] Riyadh High Court, Judgement No. 69/1, 18/10/1403H "Theft"; Riyadh High Court, Judgement No. 151/10, 26/4/1409H "Adultery"; Riyadh High Court, Judgement No. 368/7/2, 2/9/1410H "Adultery"; Riyadh High Court, Judgement No. 59/4, 26/2/1413H "Drinking Alcohol"; Riyadh High Court, Judgement No. 114/2, 26/10/1413H "Theft".

[26] S.B.M.A.Uteiby, *Use of scientific method of proof in Taazir cases,* Riyadh: Arab Security Studies and Training Centre 1994.

[27] A. Awad Belal, *Procedural safeguards in Islamic Law and Islamic Criminal Justice*, Budapest: 11th International Congress in Criminology 1993.

[28] "Whoever listens to people's conversation without permission will have melted lead poured in his ears on the day of judgement" (Prophetic Report); Ye who believe! / Enter not houses other than / Your own, until ye have / Asked permission and saluted / Those in them: that is / Best for you, in order that / Ye may heed (what is seemly)(Chapter 24, Verses 28).

immoral act. *i* may be either the original punishment for crimes which have no fixed punishment or may be an additional punishment for crimes of *Huddood* and *Quissas*. In this context, there is no restriction on the judge's authority to choose the punishment of *Ta'zir* he considers suitable for the accused person. However, the judge must do his best to choose the proper punishment in each case by means of conscientious reasoning *(Ijtihad)* within what is expressed in the Quran and the *Sunna*, and guided by the other authenticated sources of Islamic criminal law legislation. The Quran and the Prophetic reports contain innumerable statements restricting or prohibiting several types of human activities classified as sins or transgressions against Islamic social system.

Examples of such statements may be helpful to clarify the judge's discretional powers:

1. usury *(Al-Riba)*: the Quran prohibits usury by the following verses:

> O ye who believe! / Fear Allah, and give up / What remains of your demand / For usury, if ye are / Indeed believers (Chapter 3, verse 278).

> If ye do it not, / Take notice of war / From Allah and His Messenger: / But if ye repent / Ye shall have / Your capital sums: / Deal not unjustly, / And ye shall not / Be dealt with unjustly (Chapter 3, Verse 275).

> But those who repeat / (The offence) are Companions / Of the Fire: they will / Abide therein (for ever) (Chapter 4, verse 275).

Therefore, usury is a prohibited activity and any one who engages in such an act deserves punishment which is not determined by Quran or *Sunna*. It is the duty of the judge to select a proper punishment he thinks fit the accused person as well as the prohibited behaviour, and in the light of the evidence provided and the circumstances of the case;

2. breach of trust: the Quran states:

> O ye that believe! / Betray not the trust / Of Allah and the Messenger, / Nor misappropriate knowingly / Things entrusted to you (Chapter 9, verse 27).

> All doth command you / To render back your Trusts / To those to whom they are due: / And when ye judge / Between people / That ye judge with justice: / Verily how excellent / Is the teaching which He giveth you! / For Allah is He Who heareth / And seeth all things (Chapter 5, verse 58).

The above mentioned two verses indicate that it is the command of the God to deliver back trusts, and disobedience of such a command by a Muslim is a serious sin. The judge should evaluate the volume of the seriousness of the sin by verse (b), which prohibits firstly, betray of the God and secondly, betray of the messenger and thirdly betray of trust;

3. bribery: as a dishonest means of gain, Quran has prohibited bribery by the following verse:

And do not eat up / Your property among yourselves / For vanities, not use it / As bait for the judges, / With intent that ye may / Eat up wrongfully and knlwingly / A little of (other) people's property (Chapter 2, Verse 188).

The above Quranic verse defines bribery as a sinful behaviour. Any person who offers bribe, accepts bribe or facilitates bribery causes illegal loss of property as well as causing illegal gain of property or right by another. The volume of illegal loss of property and damages caused by bribery are considered in determining the *Ta'zir* punishment by the judge.

From the above-mentioned examples, it is clear that there are extensive discretional powers at the judge's disposal, in all civil and criminal cases except *Huddood* crimes. Such discretionary powers are not only procedural, but wide enough to cover legislative fields where the judge is authorised to define the offences and acts of transgression as well as determination of punishment. Western scholars may deny the wide scope of discretionary powers given to the judge in Islamic law, due to its contradiction with the universally accepted constitutional principles of *Nulla poena sine lege*. The argument of Muslim scholars for this view is that Islam has also its universally accepted principles embodied in the Islamic constitution *(*Quran*).*[29] In fact, the discretionary powers of the judge are governed by the final end of Islamic law, which is the protection of religion, life, mind, lineage and property as well as realisation of justice and maintenance of the public interests. According to Ibn Al-Qayyim, all acts of judges and rulers are legitimate as far as those acts are to establish justice and prevent injustice.[30]

It is the duty of witnesses to bear testimony, and it is not lawful for them to conceal it when the party concerned demands it from them. In cases likely to result in corporal punishment, witnesses are at liberty either to give or withhold their testimony as they please: because in such cases they are distracted between two laudable actions, namely the establishment of the punishment, and the preservation of the criminal's character. Concealment of an offence of others is moreover, preferable because the Holy Prophet (peace and blessings of Allah be upon him) said to a person that had borne testimony: "Verily, it would have been better for you, if you have concealed it".

The evidence required in a case of adultery is that of four men, as has been ordained in the Quran, and the testimony of a woman in such a case is not admitted. Prophet Mohamed (peace and blessings of Allah be upon him), as the first judge in Islam, and with his judicial role in the first Islamic community is known as the best model of judges, during his time and his two immediate successors, it was an invariable rule to exclude the evidence of women in all cases inducing punishment or retaliation and also because the testimony of women involves a degree of doubt, as it is merely a substitute for

---

[29] *See* Al-Mughni, Vol. 10, pp. 340-351.
[30] *See* Ibn Al-Qayyim, *Al-Turuq Al-Hukmiya*, pp. 17-25.

evidence, being accepted only where the testimony of men cannot be had. It is, therefore, not admitted in any matter liable to drop from the evidence of doubt.

The evidence required in other criminal cases is the testimony of two men, according to the text of the Holy Quran; and the testimony of women is not admitted. In all other cases the evidence required is that of men, or of one man and two women, whether the case related to property or to other rights, such as marriage, divorce, pregnancy or the like. The Imam Al-Shafi has said that the evidence of one man and two women cannot be admitted, except in cases that relate to property or its dependencies, such as hire, bail and so forth; because the evidence of women is originally inadmissible on account of their weakness of understanding, their want of memory and incapacity of governing, whence it is that their evidence is not admitted in criminal cases.

In all rights whether of property or otherwise, the probity of the witness, and the use of word *'ashhadu'* (I bear witness) is absolutely requisite, even in the case of the evidence of women. If, therefore, a witness should say, "I know" or "know with certainty" without making use of the *'ashhadu'*, in that case his evidence cannot be admitted and with respect to the probity of the witness, it is indispensable.

If the defendant throws a reproach on the witnesses, it is in that case incumbent on the *Qadi* to institute an enquiry into their character, because, in the same manner as it is probable that a Muslim abstain from falsehood as being a thing prohibited in the religion he professes, so also it is probable that a Muslim will not unjustly reproach another.

It is not lawful for a person to give evidence on such matters as he has not actually seen personally. Consequently, the testimony of a person that has been punished for false accusation *(Qadhf)* is inadmissible.

If an infidel who has suffered punishment for *Qadhf* should afterwards become a Muslim, his evidence is then admissible; although, on account of the said punishment he had lost the qualification to give evidence, yet by his conversion to the Islamic faith he acquires a new competency in regard to evidence (namely, competency to give evidence relative to Muslims) and which is not affected by any matter that happened prior to the new circumstances.

Testimony in favour of a son or grandson, or in favour of a father or grandfather, is not admissible, because the Holy Prophet (peace and blessings of Allah be upon him) has so ordained. Besides, as there is kind of communion of benefits between these degrees of kindred, it follows that their testimony in matters relative to each other is in some degree a testimony in favour of themselves, and is, therefore, liable to suspicion. Also, the Holy Prophet (peace and blessings of Allah be upon him ) said: "We are not to credit (in civil cases) the evidence of a wife concerning her husband, or of a husband concerning his wife or of a hirer concerning his hireling."

The testimony of a convict or a person who has committed a serious crime, is not admissible, because in consequence of such crime he is unjust. The testimony of a person who receives usury is inadmissible and so, also, of one who plays for a stake at dice or chess.

The evidence of a person who openly inveighs against the Companions of the Holy Prophet (peace and blessings of Allah be upon him) and their disciples is not admissible, because of his apparent want of integrity. It is otherwise, however, where a person conceals his sentiments in regard to them, because in such case the want of integrity is not apparent

The Imam Abu Hanifa and Imam Al-Shafi' are of the opinion that a false witness must be stigmatised, but not chastised with blows. The two disciples are of the opinion that he must be scourged and confined.[31]

If the witnesses retract their testimony prior to the *Qadi* passing any decree, it becomes void; if, on the contrary, the *Qadi* passes a decree, and the witness afterwards retract their testimony, the decree is not thereby rendered void. The retraction of evidence is not valid, unless it be made in the presence of the *Qadi*.

As one of the methods of realising justice and fairness, Islam has condemned giving false, testimony. Muslims are commanded to bear witness to the truth, as shown by the following Quranic verses:

O ye who believe / stand out firmly! / For justice, as witness / To Allah, even as against / Yourselves, or your parents (Chapter 5, Verse 135).

Those witness no falsehood / And, if they pass by futility / They pass by it / With honourable (avoidance) (Chapter 18, verse 72).

## Conclusion

Realisation of justice, eradication of injustice and aggression, protection of life, property, lineage, mind and religion are principal objectives of Islam. Therefore, Islam has given the judiciary a leading role to maintain such objectives.

The emergence of Islamic legal system as a political and social issue in many parts of the world, escalation of national and transnational crime problems, need for co-operation to create and implement international instruments; are strong elements necessitating integration and reconciliation among various crime detection and investigation policies known throughout the world. Mutual understanding and exchange of knowledge and experiences among all professionals and scholars is one way of developing and promoting global methods and techniques of criminal investigation and evidence.

According to *Shari'a*, reorganising and developing methods of criminal procedure is a matter of politics left to the jurists *Ulama* and governments of the Islamic countries. Governors are authorised to maintain criminal

---

[31] M.I. Siddiqui, *The Penal Law of Islam*, Lahore: Kazi Publications 1985.

procedural systems suitable for particular circumstances of time and place, within the spirit of the general principles of Islamic justice.

To prove guilty in *Huddood* and *Quissas* crimes prescribed amount of personal evidence or testimony *(Shahada)* is required and scientific evidence may be accepted only for collaboration and clarification of particular facts according to the request of the judge. However, scientific evidence may be utilised to prove *Taazir* crimes including all forms of contemporary criminality, with due respect to the human rights and privacy.

Personal evidence *(Shahada)* in Islamic law perspective is a religious obligation, and individuals are encouraged to give evidence willingly. Therefore, personal evidence is reliable and available. Of, course the world is changing at a rapid pace both politically and socially, therefore, professions of criminal justice system require well educated personnel to meet the needs of solving global and multi-cultural crime problems. In this context I would like to submit the following recommendations:

Islamic criminal law and the Islamic criminal justice should be included in the educational syllabus of law faculties and school of criminal justice. Joint and comparative researches should be conducted by scholars from Islamic countries and western nations to bridge the gap between different legal systems known in the world.

International co-operation is urgent to develop global methods of investigation, techniques of evidence and realisation of criminal justice. International convention of exchange of evidence and criminal courts proceedings may be vital for treatment of transnational crime problems.

Individuals should be encouraged to give testimony willingly and faithfully, and they should be taught that giving evidence is a social and ethical obligation.

### References

**Al-Gassim, A.A.** (1993), *Criminal Evidence and Its Role in Proving Huddood and Quissas Crime*, Riyadh: Arab Security Studies and Training Center.
**Al-Semni, H.A.** (1983), *Legality of Evidence Through Scientific Methods*, Cairo University.
**Arab Security Studies and Training Center** (1976), 'The effect of Islamic Legislation on Crime Prevention', in: Saudi Arabia-Proceedings of the Symposium held in Riyadh.
**Awad, A.M.** (1982), 'The Rights of the Accused in the Islamic Criminal Procedure', S.M. Bassioni M, *Islamic Criminal Justice*, N.Y. Oclana Publications.
**Awad, M.M.** (1989), Human rights in the Criminal Procedure.
**Bander, F.A.** (1987), *The Accused, His Rights and Treatment*, Riyadh: Arab Security Studies and Training Center.
**Bek, I.A.** (1985), *Methods of Proof in Shari'a*, Cairo: Cairo New Press.
**Elbushra, M.E.** (1988), *The Role of the Police and Administration of Criminal Justice and Crime Prevention. Comparative Study of the Japanese and the Sudanese Experiences*, Doctoral Dissertation, Tokyo: Keio University.
**Ibrahim, H.M.I.** (1980), *The Modern Scientific Methods of Proof in Criminal Cases*, Doctoral Thesis, Cairo University.
**Kamly, M.H.** (1991), *Principle of Islamic Jurisprudence*, Cambridge.

**Levenson, H. & Fairweather, F.** (1990), *Police Powers*, London: Legal Action Group.

**Sadoon, B.M.A.** (1994), *Use of Scientific Method of Proof in Taazir Cases*, Riyadh: Arab Security Studies and Training Center.

**Siddiqi, M.I.** (1985), *The Penal Law of Islam*, Lahore: Kazi Publication.

**United Nations**, *Report of the Commission on Crime Prevention and Criminal Justice*, Second Session E/CN 15/1993/9.

**Zeid, M.I.** (1996), *The Criminal Justice System in the Arab Countries*, Riyadh: Naif Arab Academy for Security Sciences.

# Similarities and Differences: the Operation of the Exclusionary Rule in the US, Germany and the Netherlands

*M.C.D. Embregts*

## Introduction

The exclusionary rule is currently a hot item. Although it is not the only remedy against illegally obtained evidence, it is probably the most common one. The exclusionary rule is applied from Brazil to South Africa and from Australia to Canada. In this paper, I will concentrate on the following three countries: the US, Germany, and – my own country – the Netherlands.

In the three countries discussed, the exclusionary rule has the same foundation and purposes. It is therefore not surprising that, in many cases, the application of the exclusionary rule is the same in the US, Germany and the Netherlands. (See 'Similarities'.) However, it is striking that, although the foundation and purposes are the same, there are also differences in the application of the rule. One of these differences concerns the admissibility of evidence illegally obtained by third parties. (See 'Differences'.) These similarities and differences in application of the exclusionary rule can be explained in respect of which are considered to be its purposes. (See 'Similarities and Differences explained'.) I will end this article by formulating my view on the purposes of the exclusionary rule and how these purposes should be applied. (See 'Conclusion'.)

## Similarities

Let me start with an example. The alleged offender of a crime, let us call him Mr Jansen, has made a self-incriminating statement. In this statement, he admitted having committed a bank robbery. Mr Jansen was not informed about his right to remain silent. In the US, Germany and the Netherlands, his statement would not be admitted in evidence.[1]

Let us suppose that *after* the self-incriminating statement, Mr Jansen is informed about his right to remain silent. Mr Jansen gives a second statement with the same content as the first one. Is this statement excluded as well? No, not in the US, nor in Germany, nor in the Netherlands will this statement be suppressed.[2] The causal connection between the first statement and the second

---

[1] For the US, *Miranda* v. *Arizona*, 384 *U.S.* 436 (1966); for Germany, *BGHSt* 38, 214; for the Netherlands, HR (Dutch Supreme Court) 26 June 1979, *NJ* 1979, 567; HR 2 October 1979, *NJ* 1980, 243.

[2] For the US, *Wong Sun* v. *US*, 371 *U.S.* 471 (1963); for Germany, *BGHSt* 27, 355; *BGHSt* 35, 32; for the Netherlands, HR 22 September 1981, *NJ* 1981, 660; HR 25 March 1980, *NJ* 1980, 437.

one is attenuated.[3]

In this example, the exclusionary rule works the same in the US, Germany and the Netherlands. This is not surprising because in these three countries the exclusionary rule has the same foundation and the same purposes.[4]

Evidence is considered to be illegally obtained when human rights were violated in the gathering of the evidence.[5] This evidence is excluded because a conviction may not be based on such evidence.[6] The foundation of the exclusionary rule is found in the basic, legality principle: out of injustice, no justice can be born.

The exclusionary rule has three purposes. First of all, illegally obtained evidence is excluded in order to deter police misconduct. This purpose we could call prevention, because the exclusionary rule prevents misbehaviour by the police in this respect. The second purpose is demonstration, the imperative of judicial integrity. Excluding illegally obtained evidence assures people – all potential victims of unlawful government conduct – that the government would not benefit from its own lawless behaviour, thus minimising the risk of seriously undermining popular trust in the government. "Nothing can destroy a government more quickly than its failure to observe its own laws, or worse, its disregard of the charter of its own existence. (...) If the Government becomes a lawbreaker, it breeds contempt for law; it invites anarchy."[7] In this respect, the exclusionary rule is a device designed to enable the judiciary to avoid the taint of partnership in official lawlessness. Reparation is the third purpose. Victims of human rights violation are restored to the procedural position they would have been in if the irregularities had not occurred.

Although these three purposes may seem similar, each of them addresses different parties in society. Prevention addresses the police; demonstration concentrates on the judges; and reparation focuses primarily on the public. In the words of the US Supreme Court: "Our decision, founded on reason and truth, gives to the individual no more than that which the Constitution guarantees him, to the police officer no less than that to which honest law enforcement is entitled, and, to the courts, that judicial integrity so necessary

---

[3] *See* the case law listed in the previous note.
[4] W.R. Lafave, *Search and Seizure, A Treatise on the Fourth Amendment*, St. Paul, Minnesota: West Publishing Co., 3rd edition, 1996, Volume 1, pp. 19-20; H. Koriath, *Über Beweisverbote im Strafprozeß*, Schriften zum Strafrecht und Strafprozeßrecht Bd. 15, Frankfurt am Main: Peter Lang 1994, pp. 42-46; G.J.M. Corstens, *Het Nederlands strafprocesrecht*, Deventer: Gouda Quint, 3rd edition, 1999, pp. 656-657.
[5] Although it is beyond the scope of this paper, I would like to remark that *minor* violations of human rights should not necessarily lead to the inadmissibility of evidence obtained in this way. For example, police officers entering premises to be searched ten minutes before the search warrant becomes effective (HR 23 June 1987, *NJ* 1988, 354).
[6] Resolution IV-E-5 adopted by the International Association of Penal Law at its XVI[th] International Congress (Budapest, 11 September 1999) reads: "Conviction may not be based on evidence that has been obtained in violation of the human rights of the defendant".
[7] *Mapp* v. *Ohio*, 367 *U.S.* 643, 659 (1961).

in the true administration of justice."[8]

In addition to the foundation and purposes of the exclusionary rule, the way in which it is applied is also more or less the same in the US, Germany and the Netherlands.

For example, in the three countries discussed, the rule is extended to exclude the 'fruits of the poisonous tree'.[9] If illegally obtained evidence leads to other evidence, this evidence may be suppressed as well. Not only this extension to the exclusionary rule is similar. There are also two major restrictions to the application of the exclusionary rule in the US, Germany and the Netherlands. First, neither the evidence nor the fruit of the poisonous tree will be excluded if there is no or just an attenuated causal connection between the illegal act and this evidence.[10] Only the evidence, which would not have come to light *but for* the illegal actions of the police, is excluded.[11] Second, evidence is not excluded if it is not the *defendant*'s rights that were violated, but someone else's.[12]

## Differences

Although the exclusionary rule is implemented differently in the various criminal systems, its outcome is generally the same. Still there are differences between the three countries. One of these differences concerns evidence illegally obtained by third parties. In this paper, the concept of evidence illegally obtained by third parties does not include the situation in which the police are themselves involved in the illegal obtainment of evidence. When the police are in some way involved in the illegal gathering of evidence by third parties, there is no difference between the US, Germany and the Netherlands. In general, the evidence is then excluded.[13]

First another example. An ordinary citizen breaks into his boss's home and steals some personal papers he finds there. At home, he discovers that one of the letters is about the involvement of his boss in a drug deal a week earlier. He turns this letter over to the police, who start an investigation. After a while, the case lays before the court. The defendant's attorney asks for the exclusion

---

[8] *Mapp* v. *Ohio*, 367 *U.S.* 643, 660 (1961).
[9] For the US, *Silverthorne Lumber Co*. v. *US*, 251 *U.S.* 385 (1920); for Germany, *BGHSt* 29, 244; for the Netherlands, Hof Amsterdam (Court of Appeal of Amsterdam) 4 May 1979, *NJ* 1980, 48.
[10] *See* the case law mentioned in footnote 2.
[11] For the US (but for), *Wong Sun* v. *US*, 371 *U.S.* 471 (1963); for Germany *(unmittelbar auf)*, *BGHSt* 32, 68 (71); for the Netherlands *(uitsluitend door)*, HR 21 January 1997, *NJ* 1997, 309.
[12] For the US, *Rakas* v. *Illinois*, 439 *U.S.* 128 (1978); *US* v. *Salvucci*, 448 *U.S.* 83 (1980); *Rawlings* v. *Kentucky*, 448 *U.S.* 98 (1980); *US* v. *Payner*, 447 *U.S.* 727 (1980); for Germany, *BGHSt* 11, 213; for the Netherlands, HR 18 October 1988, *NJ* 1989, 306. This might be otherwise if the rights of the non-defendant were *grossly* violated (compare HR 12 January 1999, *NJ* 1999, 290).
[13] For the US, *Lustig* v. *US*, 338 *U.S.* 74 (1949); for Germany, *BGHSt* 34, 362; for the Netherlands, HR 18 February 1997, *NJ* 1997, 500.

of the letter, because it was obtained illegally by a third party (the employee).

In the US, the evidence will not be excluded.[14] Evidence illegally obtained by third parties is admissible. The main reason for this is that, according to the US Supreme Court, the major purpose of exclusion of evidence is to deter police misconduct.[15] If the police did not do anything wrong, there is no reason for excluding the evidence.[16]

In Germany, the defendant in this example could be lucky. In general, the rules laid down in the *German Code of Criminal Procedure (Strafprozeßordnung)* do not apply to third parties. However, evidence illegally obtained by third parties will be excluded if fundamental human rights were violated in gathering the evidence. For example, if a third party secretly recorded a conversation, the tape cannot be used as evidence. The use of the tape by a public prosecutor is seen as a new violation of the human right of privacy, which leads to the inadmissibility of the tape as evidence.[17] This shows that, in Germany, it is not that important *who* obtained the evidence. What matters is the way in which it was obtained.

In Dutch case law, there are only a few cases about evidence that was illegally obtained by third parties. The decisions in these cases differ so much that no general rule can be deduced from them.[18] The Dutch Supreme Court leaves open the possibility to exclude evidence illegally obtained by third parties, but it remains quite vague in which situations this would apply.[19] In Dutch literature, there is some agreement about whether evidence illegally obtained by third parties should or should not be admitted.[20] In the first place, authors agree that evidence illegally obtained by third parties should more often be admissible than evidence illegally obtained by the police. The second point of relative consensus is that there are definitely limits: not all evidence illegally obtained by third parties should be used. What these limits are is not clear. In general, it is agreed to that no human rights may be violated in the gathering of evidence by third parties.[21]

---

[14] *Burdeau* v. *McDowell*, 256 *U.S.* 465 (1921).

[15] In *US* v. *Janis*, 428 *U.S.* 433, 446 (1976) the Supreme Court states: "[T]he Court has established that the 'prime purpose' of the rule, if not the sole one, 'is to deter future unlawful police conduct'."

[16] Application of other remedies than the exclusion of the evidence is possible, but as the US Supreme Courts states in *Burdeau* v. *McDowell*, 256 *U.S.* 465, 475 (1921), with such remedies we are not now concerned.

[17] *BGHSt* 14, 358.

[18] HR 1 June 1999, *NJB* 1999, p. 1167, nr. 89; Hof Amsterdam 20 December 1984, *NJ* 1985, 321; HR 11 April 1995, *NJ* 1995, 537; HR 16 October 1990, *NJ* 1991, 175.

[19] HR 1 June 1999, *NJB* 1999, p. 1167, nr. 89.

[20] G.J.M. Corstens, *Het Nederlands strafprocesrecht*, Deventer: Gouda Quint 1999, p. 658; L.C.M. Meijers, *Politie, openbaar ministerie en bewijsverkrijging*, preadvies NJV, Zwolle: W.E.J. Tjeenk Willink 1982, p. 60.

[21] In his annotation to HR 11 April 1995, *NJ* 1995, 537, Corstens says that the answer to the question of which consequences are associated with evidence illegally obtained by third parties (to be continued)

## Similarities and Differences explained

The example of the employee who broke into his boss's home shows us a difference between the application of the exclusionary rule in Germany and its application in the US. The explanation for this different approach can be found in which of the purposes of the exclusionary rule is considered to be the leading one. In the US, the major purpose of exclusion of evidence is to prevent police misconduct. In Germany, the purpose of demonstration probably predominates.

It is striking that both the similarities and the differences in applicability of the exclusionary rule seem to ensue from the same thing, viz. its purposes. On the one hand, as we have seen in the example about self-incrimination, it seems that the three purposes lead, in general, to the same approach to admissibility of illegally obtained evidence. On the other hand, the purposes also lead to a different approach to admissibility of evidence when it is illegally obtained by third parties, because one purpose is considered more important than the others.

The similarities only *seem* to ensue from all three purposes. In the US, the purpose of prevention is not only the leading one in cases on the admissibility of evidence illegally obtained by third parties; it is so in all cases. In many cases, as we have seen, this does not lead to a different approach to the admissibility of illegally obtained evidence compared to Germany and the Netherlands. In cases on the admissibility of evidence illegally obtained by third parties differences break the surface.

## Conclusion

In my view, one purpose may not be emphasised at the expense of the others. All three purposes should be taken equally into account when answering questions on the admissibility of illegally obtained evidence. I am of the opinion that each one of the purposes is important. If one purpose is given more weight, the other important purposes may be undermined. Not taking the other purposes fully into account could lead to unwanted results, for example in the US where evidence illegally obtained by third parties is admissible because the *only* purpose proves to be prevention of police misconduct.

In answer to the question of admissibility of evidence illegally obtained by third parties, I therefore would opt for the German solution. In Germany, all three purposes are equally important, in the US the focus is on only one. Not only the police is obliged to follow the law but everyone is. If evidence obtained in violation of human rights is admitted because it was not obtained

---

depends on which purpose of exclusion is the leading one. I agree with him insofar as that, in general, one of the purposes is the decisive one, but in my opinion all three purposes must be considered.

by a police officer but by another citizen, the signal that is given, at least in my view, is that illegal gathering of evidence by third parties is actually approved. Perhaps there are more limits for evidence gathering by the police but, in my opinion, there should also be limits for the gathering of evidence by third parties. Instead of wondering who obtained the evidence, we should look at how it was obtained. If a third party violates human rights, the limit is exceeded. By excluding such evidence, the public is assured that the police do not only protect them from violation of human rights but also from violation of the same rights by third parties.[22] It enables the courts to dissociate themselves from all human rights violations (demonstration). In this way, the government will not profit from any (theirs and others people's) lawless behaviour, because the defendant is put in the same position he would have been in if his human rights had not been violated (reparation). In my view, even the purpose of prevention is served by excluding evidence illegally obtained by third parties because the police will not be tempted to encourage violation of human rights by third parties in any way because the evidence would also be excluded.

In the future, new questions on the admissibility of illegally obtained evidence will arise, or some 'old' questions may become more topical. In order to find answers to these questions, we should always look at all three purposes of exclusion of evidence. We should be careful in formulating such answers because the integrity of the criminal process is at stake.[23] This integrity is manifested in the evidence on which the conviction is based; therefore, the obtainment of the evidence itself should be fair.

---

[22] Neither the police nor third parties may violate human rights (for example, the right to privacy). Furthermore, there are specific human rights, which only operate between the defendant and the police (for example, the right to remain silent).

[23] P.A.M. Mevis, 'The Integrity of the Criminal Process Requires the Exclusion of Illegally Obtained Evidence', in: J.F. Nijboer & J.M. Reijntjes (eds.), *Proceedings of The First World Conference on New Trends in Criminal Investigation and Evidence*, Heerlen: Koninklijke Vermande bv/Open University of the Netherlands 1997, pp. 311-313.

# An Argumentative Analysis and Evaluation of Complex Cases in Dutch Criminal Law

*E.T. Feteris*

## Introduction

The famous Dutch *Ballpoint Case* is an example of a complex case in which there were various theories possible of how the death of Mrs de M., who had a BIC ballpoint behind the eyes, could be explained. Some experts argued that there was no other explanation for Mrs de M.'s death than that she accidentally fell on the ballpoint. Other experts argued that the theory that Mrs de M. was murdered was equally plausible as the explanation that she fell in the ballpoint by accident, and the therapist who acted as a witness stated that murder was the only possible explanation.

The courts were faced with the problem of choosing among the various explanations. In first instance, the district court 'believed' the murder theory, but finally, in appeal, the Court of Appeal decided that there was not enough proof for this theory so that the accused had to be acquitted.

Not only in the media, but also among lawyers, this so-called *Ballpoint Case* raised many questions with respect to the quality of the Dutch criminal system. A lot of mistakes were made by the courts during the trial.

In the reviews of this case, the main point of critique was that the decision of the district court was mainly based on the statement of the therapist, which turned out to be a very weak element. This amounts to the critique that the argumentation in the justification of the district court was unsatisfactory with respect to the central question whether J.T. had indeed killed his mother. According to the official rules and the official practice of district courts in criminal cases, the court has done nothing wrong. But considered from both the perspective of a fair trial and the perspective of a rational argumentative discussion, the argumentation of the district court with respect to the 'manner of death' can be criticised.

In my contribution I will go into the question of what went wrong in the *Ballpoint Case* from the perspective of argumentation theory. I will use the pragma-dialectical theory of Van Eemeren & Grootendorst developed in *Argumentation, communication, and fallacies* (1992) (also known as the theory of the 'Amsterdam School') as a magnifying glass for highlighting those aspects of the *Ballpoint Case* which can be criticised from the idealised perspective of a rational argumentative discussion. I will use this theory for analysing the *Ballpoint Case* as an argumentative discussion. I will demonstrate how implicit assumptions underlying the argumentation can be reconstructed in a rational way and how they can be criticised from the perspective of a rational discussion.

## The Reconstruction of the Argumentation Structure

In the *Ballpoint Case*, in May 1991, Mrs de M. is found dead in her house. Pathological investigation shows that she has a BIC ballpoint inside her head, behind her eye. An accident? A murder-case? The former husband and the son are under suspicion. Rumour has it that the son, during his school years, has referred to the perfect murder more than once. The police repress experts' reports in which the possibility of an accident is mentioned.

Finally, in 1994, J.T. (the son) is arrested. This is done after the police were given a statement by the therapist of the son, in which this therapist contended that the son confessed to her that he killed his mother. He would have shot a BIC ballpoint with a small crossbow. On the basis of this statement of the therapist, who wanted to remain an anonymous witness, in combination with the statement of the forensic pathologist and the statement of the police, the prosecutor starts a criminal procedure.

The district court sentences J.T. on September 29, 1995 for murder to 12 years imprisonment. J.T. appeals and after many procedural complications he is finally acquitted by the Court of Appeal in 1996. The Court of Appeal was not convinced that it would in any way be possible to kill someone this way, with a crossbow and a BIC ballpoint. Therefore the indicted fact could not be proven beyond reasonable doubt.

The justification of the decision of the judge in a criminal process in general consists of a complex argumentation, consisting of various 'levels' of subordinate argumentation. On the first level (level **I**) the argumentation consists of compound argumentation consisting of a description of the criminal offence. On the second level (level **II**) the argumentation consists of several single arguments, describing the facts which form instances of the components of the criminal offence. On the third level (level **III**) the argumentation consists of a number of single arguments, the evidence for these facts. The argumentation on level **III** is sometimes defended by further argumentation of the fourth level (level **IV**). In scheme:

*Figure 1: Justification of the Decision in Criminal Proceedings*

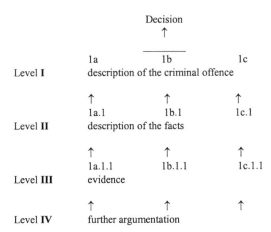

The point of view of the district court is that the accused must be sentenced with an imprisonment of 12 years. This standpoint is based on the argumentation (argumentation on level **I**) that, because certain facts can be considered as proven, ànd that these facts constitute an instance of the criminal offence of clause 289 of the *Criminal Code* and that the accused is guilty, the punishment which is connected to this criminal offence must be applied.[1]

The argumentation on level **II** in defence of the components of 1a, 1b and 1c consists of a description of the concrete facts. The concrete facts, in turn, are defended by arguments which imply that the court 'believes' the evidence as presented (argumentation level **III**). As a defence of the supportive force of the statements of the therapist (9) the court puts forward the argumentation on level **IV**). In the reconstruction this argument (13) is represented in the form of the two separate supporting the arguments 1a.1a.1 and 1a.1b.1, which have an identical content.

*Figure 2* describes the arguments on the various levels and *Figure 3* gives a schematic representation. The decimal numbers reflect the pragma-dialectical hierarchy. I have used the numbers 1-13 for reasons of efficiency: it is easier to refer to these numbers.

---

[1] In my analysis I reconstruct the various components of the criminal offence as separate arguments.

*Figure 2: Argumentation of the District Court*

*Decision*: the accused must be punished with an imprisonment of 12 years

**1a** intentionally and with forethought killed **(1)**

    **1a.1a** We are justified in believing that it is proven beyond reasonable doubt that J.T. acted intentionally and after clear thought and pre-meditated **(4)**

        **1a.1a.1** We are justified in 'believing' in the trustworthiness of the statements of the therapist that J.T. confessed to her that he, intentionally and after clear thought and premeditated, shot a ballpoint through one of her eyes into the head with a small crossbow **(9)**

            **1a.1a.1.1** The district court found her statement consistent and convincing **(13)**

    **1a.1b** We are justified in 'believing' that it is proven beyond reasonable doubt that he shot a ballpoint through one of her eyes into the head with a small crossbow **(5)**

        **1a.1b.1** We are justified in 'believing' in the trustworthiness of the statements of the therapist that J.T. confessed to her that he, intentionally and after clear thought and premeditated, shot a ballpoint through one of her eyes into the head with a small crossbow **(9)**

            **1a.1b.1.1** The district court found her statement consistent and convincing **(13)**

    **1a.1c** We are justified in 'believing' that it is proven beyond reasonable doubt that Mrs de M. died as a result of the fact that J.T. shot a ballpoint through one of her eyes with a small crossbow **(6)**

        **1a.1c.1** We are justified in 'believing' in the trustworthiness of the statements of the coroner's report **(10)**

**1b** On or about May 25, 1991 in Leiden **(2)**

    **1b.1** then and there **(7)**

        **1b.1.1** We are justified in 'believing' in the trustworthiness of the statements in the police report on the finding of the body **(11)**

**1c** A woman named Mrs de M. **(3)**

    **1c.1** A woman named Mrs de M. **(8)**

        **1c.1.1** We are justified in 'believing' in the trustworthiness of the statements in the police report on the investigation by the coroner **(12)**

*Figure 3: Schematic Representation of the Argumentation of the district court*

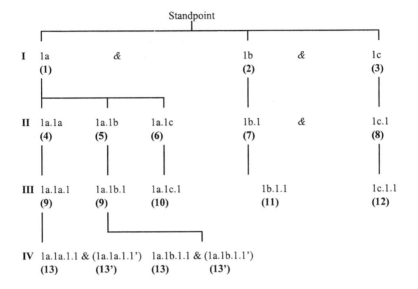

## The Reconstruction of Implicit Arguments

In the reconstruction of the argumentation, on various levels bridging arguments must be made explicit. Because our main concern is the argumentation with respect to the evidence, I concentrate on the argumentation on level **III** and **IV** of the argumentation where the various elements of the evidence are located and where the force of the evidence is justified. On these levels, various arguments must be made explicit.

A reconstruction of the arguments on which the discussion in the procedure before the district court centres is given in *Figure 4*. These are the bridging arguments for the argumentation consisting of 9 and 13.

*Figure 4: Reconstruction of Implicit Arguments*

A
5 We are justified in believing that it is proven beyond reasonable doubt that he shot a ballpoint through one of her eyes into the head with a small crossbow,

because

9 we are justified in 'believing' in the trustworthiness of the statements of the therapist that J.T. confessed to her that he, intentionally and after clear thought and premeditated, shot a ballpoint through one of her eyes into the head with a small crossbow,

and

(9')    if we are justified in 'believing' in the trustworthiness of the statements of the therapist that J.T. confessed to her that he, intentionally and after clear thought and premeditated, shot a ballpoint through one of her eyes into the head with a small crossbow, then we are justified in 'believing' that it is proven beyond reasonable doubt that he shot a ballpoint through one of her eyes into the head with a small crossbow.

B
9    We are justified in 'believing' in the trustworthiness of the statements of the therapist that J.T. confessed to her that he, intentionally and after clear thought and premeditated, shot a ballpoint through one of her eyes into the head with a small crossbow,

because

13    we find the statement of the therapist consistent and convincing.

(13')    If we find the statement of the therapist consistent and convincing, then we are justified in believing the trustworthiness s of the statements of the therapist that J.T. confessed to her that he, intentionally and after clear thought and premeditated, shot a ballpoint through one of her eyes into the head with a small crossbow

These arguments 9' and 13' form essential steps in the argumentation of the district court. In the evaluation it must be checked whether the explicit and implicit arguments can withstand rational critique.[2]

## The Evaluation of the Argumentation

In the evaluation we must check whether the arguments of the district court which have been called into question are acceptable. First I will focus on the acceptability of the line of argumentation defending (1a) with respect to the manner of death, which forms the central point of discussion. Then I will go into the question whether the district court has responded adequately to other attacks by the defence.

In the evaluation of the acceptability of the line of argumentation supporting 1a the relevant question to be answered is whether the *argumentation schemes* underlying the argumentation in defence of (1a) are applied correctly. This implies that it must be checked whether all relevant critical questions belonging to the argumentation scheme can be answered satisfactorily. Which argumentation schemes underlie the argumentation for the evidence in the decision of the district court?

---

[2] For a logical analysis of the contra-argumentation for the fact that J.T. cannot have killed his mother *see* Kaptein (1997), pp. 60-61.

As we have seen, the support for 1a (1) consists of the arguments reconstructed as the arguments 4, 5 and 6. The support for these arguments consists of 9, 10 and 13 (and 13').

Because the acceptability of the argumentation consisting of 9 is dependent on the argumentation consisting of 13 and 13', we must submit the latter to a critical test. The argumentation consisting of 13 and 13' is based on an argumentation scheme, which, in pragma-dialectical terms, expresses a *symptomatic* relation.[3] The court tries to defend its decision that $X$ has property $Z$ by pointing out that something, $Y$, is *characteristic* for $Z$:

- the statement of the therapist (X) is trustworthy (Z); because
- the statement of the therapist (X) is consistent and convinding (Y); and
- the fact that a statement is consistent and convincing (Y) is characteristic for the trustworthiness of a statement (Z).

The critical reactions that are relevant to this type of argumentation scheme are the following evaluative questions:

1. Is Y valid for X?
2. Is Y really characteristic for Z?
3. Are there any other characteristics (Y') which X must have in order to attach characteristic Z to X?

The relevant evaluative questions for the argumentation of the district court are:

1. Are we really justified in believing that the statement of the therapist was consistent and convincing (Y)?
2. Is being justified in believing that the statement of the therapist was consistent and convincing (Y) really a good reason for being justified in believing in the trustworthiness of the statements of the therapist that J.T. confessed to her that he shot a ballpoint through one of her eyes into the head with a small crossbow (Z)?
3. Can we not think of other relevant considerations (Y') for being justified in believing in the trustworthiness of the statements of the therapist that J.T. confessed to her that he shot a ballpoint through one of her eyes into the head with a small crossbow (Z)?

The acceptability of the argument depends on the question whether these questions can be answered satisfactorily.

With respect to the answer to the first question we could raise our doubts with respect to the fact that her statement was really *consistent* and *convincing*. The court does not explain in which respects the statement is consistent and why the statement of the therapist convinces it. What we miss here is an explanation of the considerations that made that the court felt convinced. So, from the perspective of a rational discussion we could say that the answer to

---

[3] *See* for a more extensive treatment of argumentation schemes Van Eemeren & Grootendorst (1992), pp. 94-102.

the first question is 'no', and the court would have to put forward supporting subordinate argumentation (apart from this, the argumentation seems circular: in order to be convinced of the truth of the statement the Court puts forward the argument that the statement is convincing).

With respect to the answer to the second question we could raise our doubts with respect to the fact that consistency is a sufficient reason for being justified in believing what the therapist has stated. In other words, are there any other considerations that are also relevant for the trustworthiness of her statement and can the earlier mentioned considerations form a sufficient ground in the absence of the later mentioned considerations? In this context, we could say that from empirical research we know that consistency of the statements of a witness is not always a guarantee for the truth of these statements.[4] So, to be able to show that the second question can be answered satisfactorily, the court would have to put forward supporting arguments.

With respect to the answer to the third question we could refer to the considerations given in the answer to the second question. Are there any other relevant considerations for believing in the statement and if these considerations are present, why are they not applied? Furthermore, we could say that such a 'double *de auditu*' statement must be submitted to more rigorous tests than the relatively weak criterion of consistency alone. So, to be able to show that the third question can be answered satisfactorily, the court would have to put forward compound argumentation.

So, what we miss in the argumentation of the court from the perspective or a rational discussion is a further elaboration on the grounds on which the court has decided that the statement of the therapist is convincing, and whether it meets other requirements of a trustworthy account of the behaviour of J.T and of his explanations for his behaviour. Further argumentation supporting 13 and 13' is required.

These further arguments which are needed as a support of 13 and 13' could be characterised as what Anderson calls the *background generalisations* upon which the relevance of the evidence rests. Wagenaar *et al.* (1993) call these considerations the *common-sense presumptions* which underlie the probative value of the evidence. These presumptions serve as the 'anchors', which constitute on various levels the 'sub-stories' on which the evidence is based. Twining calls them the *common sense generalisations* or *background*

---

[4] From empirical research by, among others, Loftus (1979) we know that witnesses often tell stories which are not only based on what they have observed, but also on inferences about what happened, and on transformations which make the recollection more consistent and more understandable. According to Crombag & Merckelbach (1997:314 ff) during the retention stage, memories change: (1) a witness can forget what he has observed, (2) he can add information from another source – *post hoc* information – to his memory, and (3) he can exchange parts of his own observation with information from another source. Therefore, recovered memories cannot be trusted completely for their truth.

*generalisations*, the generalisations that are left implicit in ordinary discourse. According to these authors, these common sense background generalisations must be made explicit in order to assess their acceptability. The acceptability depends on the question whether they correspond with certain starting points which are acceptable to the participants.

According to Twining, the problem with these generalisations is that they are at the same time necessary and dangerous. They are dangerous because, especially when unexpressed, they are often indeterminate in respect of frequency, level of abstraction, empirical reliability, defeasibility, identity (which generalisation). The danger is that these implicit value judgements are presented as if they were empirical facts or empirical rules of experience.[5]

In my analysis of the argumentation of the district court I have shown how the hierarchical relations between the various arguments can be reconstructed and which implicit arguments must be made explicit. On the basis of this analysis, in combination with the critical evaluation it becomes clear what the weak points of the argumentation of the district court are. In my opinion, such a rational reconstruction gives a clear answer to the question which 'anchors' or 'common-sense presumptions' or 'background generalisations' exactly underlie the decision from an argumentative perspective and how these hidden assumptions can be criticised.

Because, in the present form, the argumentation consisting of 13 and 13' is not acceptable, and these arguments form the final basis in a subordinate line of argumentation for argument (1)(1a), (1) is not acceptable from the perspective of a rational discussion. Because 13 and 13' form subordinate argumentation for (9), (9) is not acceptable, and because (9) forms subordinate argumentation for (4) and (5), these are not acceptable. And because (4) and (5) form together with (6) compound argumentation for (1), (1) is not acceptable.

So, according to pragma-dialectical rules standards the argumentation is not acceptable. This result is in line with the rules for anchoring the narrative supporting the decision developed by Wagenaar *et al.* (1993). According to

---

[5] In Dutch tax law, we can find various examples of decisions by the Supreme Court *(Hoge Raad)* criticising the use of 'individual knowledge' *(eigen wetenschap)* with respect to certain empirical facts as a basis for the decision that these facts can considered to be proven. The Supreme Court says that it is not allowed to use information, which is not derived from general accessible sources if these sources are not mentioned and if the parties did not have the opportunity to comment on this information. According to the Supreme Court, a decision based on this kind of individual knowledge is not justified according to the requirements of the Law *(see* HR, 3 April 1985, *BNB* 1986/74; HR 16 January 1985, *BNB* 1986/72; HR 26 November 1986, *BNB* 1987/32; HR 9 September 1987, *BNB* 1988/1). There are also situations in which the use of 'general rules of experience' can be criticised on the same grounds. If the knowledge about these rules is not generally known, a court cannot use them as a basis for its decision if it does not explain the sources of its knowledge.

their rules, essential components of the narrative must be anchored, the court must give reasons for the decision by specifying the narrative and the accompanying anchoring, and the court should explain the general beliefs used as anchors. As we have seen, this is not the case. Argument (13) needs support by anchors explaining why the court believes in the truth of the statement of the therapist.

Our final judgement about the argumentation line supporting argument (1)(1a) is therefore that it has not been justified beyond reasonable doubt that J.T. has killed his mother by shooting a ballpoint through one of her eyes into the head with a small crossbow. Because this argument forms part of compound argumentation, this implies that the decision has not been defended successfully.

Apart from this point of critique that the district court has not adequately justified its decision on the evidence, there is another weak point. As I have pointed out earlier, a 'double *de auditu*' statement is a very weak proof. The court does not say why the statements made by the police and the pathologist lend enough support to the relative weak evidence of only one witness.

### The Absence of a Refutation of the Critique of the Defence

Apart from this point of critique, there is a second reason why the argumentation of the district court with respect to argument (1a) does not meet the requirements of a rational legal discussion. One of the contra-arguments of the defence was that there was another plausible explanation for the presence of the BIC ballpoint in the head of Mrs de M. The defence puts forward the testimony of three experts: Worst, Van Rij and Visser. Worst and Van Rij are of the opinion that there is no other explanation for Mrs de M.'s death than that she accidentally fell on the ball-point, Visser thinks this explanation of the cause of death equally plausible as the murder theory.

On behalf of the defence, the ophthalmologists Worst and Van Rij contend that the fall theory is the most likely explanation of the death of Mrs de M. In his capacity as an expert witness, Worst contends that Mrs de M. most likely died because of a complicated, purely accidental, fall into the BIC ballpoint.[6] The ophthalmologist Van Rij confirms this opinion. He contends that the most probable cause of death of Mrs de M. is that she fell into the BIC ballpoint. According to him, murder by which the ballpoint has been shot into the eye by means of a shooting weapon is most unlikely.[7] The pathologist Visser (who has been present at the autopsy) contends in his capacity as expert witness that he does not agree with Worst's opinion that a fall into the ballpoint is the most

---

[6] *See* 'proces-verbaal van het verhoor van getuige/deskundige door de rechter-commissaris' of 25 August 1995, under point 17.
[7] *See* letter by Van Rij of June 17, 1995.

probable cause of death, but he does not say that it is an unlikely cause, and thus does not exclude the accident theory.[8] According to him there are three equally plausible causes of death: an accident, suicide and murder.

However, the district court does not reply to the contra-argument of the defence: it does not answer the question why the 'story' that the death of Mrs de M. is caused by a shot of the ballpoint with a small crossbow is more plausible than the 'story' that her death is caused by a fall into the ballpoint.

We could say that, because the district court does not refute the accident theory put forward by the two experts Worst and Van Rij (which is not denied by the third expert, the pathologist Visser) it does adequately answer the counter-arguments put forward by the defence, and therefore according to the pragma-dialectical rule 10 has not defended successfully argument (1) against attacks of the antagonist.[9]

With respect to this point, the evaluation is in tune with the rules developed by Wagenaar *et al.* According to their rule (7), there should be no competing story with equally good or better anchoring. Because the 'story' of Worst and van Rij has not been refuted by Visser, there is no reason to doubt the quality of its anchoring, and therefore the argumentation of the district court does not meet the requirement of rule 7.

So, according to our ideal norms for a rational discussion in criminal proceedings the justification of the district court is not acceptable on this second point.

## Conclusion

I have shown what went wrong in the *Ballpoint Case* from the perspective of an idealised critical discussion. What we saw was that, from the perspective of the rules of criminal procedure, the discussion in this case was correct with respect to the way in which the district court defended its decision. From the perspective of a fair trial and from the perspective of a rational discussion, however, several points of critique can be given.

The first point of critique concerns the quality of the argumentation of the district court with respect to the statements of the therapist. As we have seen, the argumentation with respect to these statements is based on a common-sense presumption which remains implicit and which can be criticised in various respects. Therefore, the anchor for the evidence, which supports the main part of the argumentation of the district court, turns out to be too weak to

---

[8] *See* 'proces-verbaal van het verhoor van getuige/deskundige Visser door de rechter commissaris' of 15 August 1995, under points 10 and 21.

[9] This critique is based on a pragma-dialectical perspective, which departs from a party model of the legal process. Of course, from another model in which the judge acts as an independent investigator, similar critique could be given.

consider these facts as proven beyond reasonable doubt. As a consequence, we are justified to have our doubts about the quality of the argumentation with respect to the 'manner of death' of the district court from the perspective of a rational discussion. From the perspective of a rational discussion which formulates norms which can be considered as a methodological maximum, a relevant ideal norm for a rational justification of a decision about the evidence in a criminal process could be that, if asked to do so, a judge is obliged to specify the grounds on which his belief in the testimony of an expert witness is based. Such an obligation would be required especially if, as in the *Ballpoint Case*, the decision rests for the main part on this testimony. In this way, the decision about the evidence could be criticised by the parties and other judges with respect to the quality of the evidence.

The second point of critique concerns the fact that the district court did not explicitly reject alternative explanations of the death of Mrs de M. From the perspective of a rational discussion, we could criticise the decision of the district court because of the fact that it did not give insight into the considerations for rejecting alternative explanations of the death of the mother. Because the district court did not react to adequately 'anchored' counter-arguments, the decision does not meet the requirements of a rational discussion. From the perspective of a rational discussion, a relevant ideal norm could be that, if the defence presents a relevant alternative view on the case which could be in favour of the accused, the judge has an obligation to explain why he thinks this alternative view less probable than the view presented by the prosecution.

An analysis and evaluation as I have given here makes clear how ideas taken from argumentation theory and legal theory can be used to show what the weak points are in decisions based on statements of experts. Because the rules of Dutch criminal procedure do not require more, a judge does not infringe the rules when he or she does not mention more than the content of the evidence material used for the decision. However, from the perspective of a rational discussion and a fair trial, such a justification is not adequate as an explanation of why the judge believes in the statements of witnesses or experts.

On the basis of a rational reconstruction of the argumentation in a concrete case, it can be clarified how implicit elements can be made explicit in an adequate way and in which respects these elements can be criticised. It can also be shown that often a judge does not account for his implicit preference for one story above another. From the perspective of a rational discussion it can be made clear in which respects the justification of a decision does not give enough insight into the assumptions underlying such a preference.

# Bibliography

**Anderson, T. & Twining, W.** (1991), *Analysis of evidence*, Boston and London: Butterworths.

**Cohen, L.J.** (1977), *The probable and the provable*, Oxford: Clarendon.

**Cohen, L.J.** (1989), *Memory in the real world*, Hove: Erlbaum.

**Eemeren, F.H. van, Feteris, E.T., Grootendorst, R., Haaften, T. van, Harder, W. den, Kloosterhuis, H., Kruiger, T. & Plug, J.** (1996), *Argumenteren voor juristen. Het analyseren en schrijven van juridische betogen en beleidsteksten (Argumentation for lawyers)*(3$^{rd}$ ed., 1$^{st}$ edition 1987), Groningen: Wolters-Noordhoff.

**Eemeren, F.H. van & Grootendorst, R.** (1992), *Argumentation, Communication, and Fallacies*, New York: Erlbaum.

**Eemeren, F.H. van & Grootendorst, R.** (1992), *Argumentation, communication, and fallacies. A pragma-dialectical perspective*, Hillsdale NJ: Erlbaum.

**Feteris, E.T.** (1987), 'The dialectical role of the judge in a Dutch legal process', in: Wenzel, J.W. (ed.), *Argument and critical practices. Proceedings of the fifth SCA/AFA conference on argumentation*, Annandale (VA): Speech Communication Association, pp. 335-339.

**Feteris, E.T.** (1989), *Discussieregels in het recht. Een pragma-dialectische analyse van het burgerlijk proces en het strafproces*, Dordrecht: Foris.

**Feteris, E.T.** (1990), 'Conditions and rules for rational discussion in a legal process: A pragma-dialectical perspective', in: *Argumentation and Advocacy. Journal of the American Forensic Association*, Vol. 26, No. 3, pp. 108-117.

**Feteris, E.T.** (1991), 'Normative reconstruction of legal discussions', in: *Proceedings of the Second International Conference on Argumentation, June 19-22 1990*, Amsterdam: SICSAT, pp. 768-775.

**Feteris, E.T.** (1993a), 'The judge as a critical antagonist in a legal process: a pragma-dialectical perspective', in: McKerrow, R.E. (ed.), *Argument and the Postmodern Challenge. Proceedings of the eighth SCA/AFA Conference on argumentation*, Annandale: Speech Communication Association, pp. 476-480.

**Feteris, E.T.** (1993b), 'Rationality in legal discussions: A pragma-dialectical perspective', in: *Informal Logic*, Vol. XV, No. 3, pp. 179-188.

**Feteris, E.T.** (1994a), 'Recent developments in legal argumentation theory: dialectical approaches to legal argumentation', in: *International Journal for the Semiotics of Law*, Vol. VII, no. 20, pp. 134-153.

**Feteris, E.T.** (1994b), *Redelijkheid in juridische argumentatie. Een overzicht van theorieën over het rechtvaardigen van juridische beslissingen*, Zwolle: Tjeenk Willink.

**Feteris, E.T.** (1995), 'The analysis and evaluation of legal argumentation from a pragma-dialectical perspective', in: Eemeren, F.H. van, Grootendorst, R., Blair, J.A. & Willard, Ch.A. (eds.), *Proceedings of the Third ISSA Conference on Argumentation*, Vol. IV, pp. 42-51.

**Feteris, E.T.** (1997a), 'The analysis and evaluation of argumentation in Dutch criminal proceedings from a pragma-dialectical perspective', in: J.F. Nijboer & J.M. Reijntjes (eds.), *Proceedings of the First World Conference on New Trends in Criminal Investigation and Evidence*, Lelystad: Koninklijke Vermande, pp. 57-62.

**Feteris, E.T.** (1997b), 'De deugdelijkheid van pragmatische argumentatie: heiligt het doel de middelen?', in: Feteris, E.T., Kloosterhuis, H., Plug, H.J. & Pontier, J.A. (eds.), *Op goede gronden. Bijdragen aan het Tweede Symposium Juridische Argumentatie*, Nijmegen: Ars Aequi, pp. 98-107.

**Henket, M.M.** (1997), 'Omgaan met de feiten. Opmerkingen naar aanleiding van de Leidse Balpenzaak', in: Feteris, E.T., Kloosterhuis, H., Plug, H.J. & Pontier, J.A. (eds.), *Op goede gronden. Bijdragen aan het Tweede Symposium Juridische Argumentatie*, Nijmegen: Ars Aequi, pp. 50-55.

**Jansen, H.** (1996), 'De beoordeling van a contrario-argumentatie in pragma-dialectisch perspectief', in: *Tijdschrift voor Taalbeheersing*, jrg. 18, nr. 3, pp. 240-255.

**Jansen, H.** (1997), 'Voorwaarden voor aanvaardbare a contrario-argumentatie', in: Feteris, E.T., Kloosterhuis, H., Plug, H.J. & Pontier, J.A. (eds.), *Op goede gronden. Bijdragen aan het Tweede Symposium Juridische Argumentatie*, Nijmegen: Ars Aequi, pp. 123-131.

**Kaptein, H.J.R.** (1997), 'Pennen als dodelijke wapens? Over criminele klok- en klepelkunde en een (logische?) kloof tussen feiten en recht', in: Feteris, E.T., Kloosterhuis, H., Plug, H.J. & Pontier, J.A. (eds.), *Op goede gronden. Bijdragen aan het Tweede Symposium Juridische Argumentatie*, Nijmegen: Ars Aequi, pp. 56-63.

**Kloosterhuis, H.** (1994), 'Analyzing analogy argumentation in judicial decisions', in: Eemeren, F.H. van & Grootendorst, R. (eds.), *Studies in pragma-dialectics*, Amsterdam: Sic Sat, pp. 238-246.

**Kloosterhuis, H.** (1995), 'The study of analogy argumentation in law: four pragma-dialectical starting points', in: Eemeren, F.H. van, Grootendorst, R., Blair, J.A. & Willard, Ch.A. (eds.), *Proceedings of the Third ISSA Conference on Argumentation. Special Fields and Cases*, Amsterdam: Sic Sat, pp. 138-145.

**Kloosterhuis, H.** (1996), 'The normative reconstruction of analogy argumentation in judicial decisions: a pragma-dialectical perspective', in: Gabbay, D.M. & Ohlbach, H.J. (eds.), *Proceedings of the International Conference on Formal and Applied Practical Reasoning*, Berlijn: Springer, pp. 375-383.

**Koppen, P.J. van, Hessing, D.J. & Crombag, H.F.M.** (1997), *Het hart van de zaak. Psychologie van het recht*, Deventer: Gouda Quint.

**Loftus, E.F.** (1979), *Eyewitness testimony*, Cambridge, M.A.: Harvard University Press.

**Merckelbach, H.L.G.J. & Crombag, H.F.M.** (1997), 'Hervonden herinneringen', in: Koppen, P.J. van, Hessing, D.J. & Crombag, H.F.M. (eds.), *Het hart van de zaak. Psychologie van het recht*, Deventer: Gouda Quint, pp. 334-352.

**Nijboer, J.F.** (1997), 'Over een balpen en een voorbeeldige voetballer', in: Feteris, E.T., Kloosterhuis, H., Plug, J. & Pontier, H. (eds.), *Op goede gronden, Bijdragen aan het tweede symposium juridische argumentatie*, Rotterdam June 14, 1996, pp. 64-70.

**MacCormick, N. & Summers, R.** (1991), *Interpreting statutes*, Aldershot etc.: Dartmouth.

**Plug, H.J.** (1994), 'Reconstructing complex argumentation in judicial decisions', in: Eemeren, F.H. van & Grootendorst, R. (eds.), *Studies in pragma-dialectics*, Amsterdam: Sic Sat, pp. 246-255.

**Plug, H.J.** (1995), 'The rational reconstruction of additional considerations in judicial decisions', in: Eemeren, F.H. van, Grootendorst, R., Blair, J.A. & Willard, Ch.A. (eds.), *Proceedings of the Third ISSA Conference on Argumentation. Special Fields and Cases*, Amsterdam: Sic Sat, pp. 61-72.

**Plug, H.J.** (1996), 'Complex argumentation in judicial decisions. Analyzing conflicting arguments', in: Gabbay, D.M. & Ohlbach, H.J. (eds.), *Proceedings of the International Conference on Formal and Applied Practical Reasoning*, Berlijn: Springer, pp. 464-479.

**Schum, D.A.** (1994), *The evidential foundations of probabilistic reasoning*, New York etc.: John Wiley & sons.

**Twining, W.** (1994), *Rethinking evidence* (first edition 1990), Oxford: Oxford University Press.

**Wagenaar, W.A., Koppen, P.J. van & Crombag, H.F.M.** (1993), *Anchored narratives. The psychology of criminal evidence*, London: Harvester Wheatsheaf.

# Expert Evidence Law Reform: an Australian Empirical Perspective

*I. Freckelton*

The role of expert witnesses in criminal litigation is fundamental to the achievement of just results for the prosecution and for the defense. However, in many countries within the adversarial tradition experts at the turn of the millennium remain mistrusted guests at the legal table. They are perceived as necessary but unwelcome invitees, possessed of an unethical propensity to tailor their views to the party which has brought them to the forensic banquet and using a vocabulary not readily able to be understood at table.

Experts, and in particular medical practitioners, scientists and accountants, for their part, for over a century have voiced their frustrations under the adversary system about the way that the guest list for the legal table has been drawn up. They have complained too about the pressures exerted upon them even prior to their arrival at the gathering. They have long remonstrated about the manners and ethics that they have found at table – so defective, they have said, that many worthies amongst their number do not to participate if given the choice.

Others from the professions have contended for upwards of one and a half centuries that, if professional mores and proprieties are to be the subject of fact-finding, they would prefer to be liberated from the shackles of the adversary-generated selection system. Many would have as those experts available to give opinion evidence practitioners from amongst an agreed panel of persons prepared to do forensic work. They would prefer too to have complex issues determined by a special jury of experts rather than by persons ignorant in the ways of their expertise. They argue that such changes would enhance the quality of the fact-finding process and promote respect within the professional communities, as well as the community generally, for the role of the law in adjudicating upon important interactions twixt professional and lay person.

Building upon the results of recent surveys of Australia's judges and magistrates about expert evidence, this paper reevaluates the debates about the role of experts as independent providers of opinion evidence within the adversary system.

## Expert Evidence within the Adversary System

Under the Anglo-Australian legal system, the quest is not for so elusive a concept as 'truth'. What is sought is a fair resolution of the differences between parties, be the litigation between the Crown and an accused in a criminal trial, between a plaintiff and a defendant in a civil dispute, or between a husband and wife in a matrimonial contest. The standard of proof is borne by the party initiating proceedings and may vary between criminal and non-criminal proceedings, but the role of the judge remains primarily to be at a remove from the interstices of party-party conflict and to ensure that the fight is fair and fought according to the rules. The judge is a ring-keeper[1] who traditionally has only intruded into the pugilism acted out at the bar table on behalf of the parties before him or her to prevent abuse of process and unfairness and to facilitate the decision-making process by a jury, if there is one. The question for the trier of fact, be it judge or jury, is whether the case for the Crown is proved beyond reasonable doubt or whether the case for the plaintiff or the applicant is proved on the balance of probabilities – on the evidence which is adduced.

The adducing of evidence is by and large under the version of the adversary system prevailing in Australia the province of the parties. They make their own decisions about the evidence that is called, affected by tactical considerations, the extent of their lawyers' competence, and their financial resources – the depth of their pockets. It occurs from time to time that key witnesses are not called by either side to the litigation. This happens less often in criminal matters because of the duty of the prosecution to call all relevant witnesses of truth, or at least to make them available, but it is by no means unknown for important potential witnesses to be secreted or taken out-of-play by being commissioned by one side in order to make them less accessible for the party to whose position their views are thought likely to incline. In such situations, there is some prerogative in the presiding judge to call a witness in criminal matters but it is scarcely ever done.[2] In civil matters, it has been held to be very dangerous for a judge to call a witness against the wishes of one of the parties.[3] Herein lies the fundamental difference between the adversarial and inquisitorial systems of justice. In the inquisitorial system, glimpsed in the Anglo-Australian tradition in the working of the coroners' courts, the trier of fact also carries the responsibility of having all pertinent evidence made available for the court's considerations; under the adversary system, the role of calling evidence is almost exclusively that of the parties, the decision to call witnesses dictated by an evaluation of the extent to which such evidence can be expected to advance the interests of the party contemplating calling them..

However, changes can be perceived in the absoluteness of these distinctions. Escalating costs, delays and concerns about the extent to which the criminal justice system is achieving just results are producing a legal environment in Australia which is conducive to change. The remainder of this paper examines some of the findings of a survey of judges conducted in the late 1990s within Australia to gauge judicial attitudes toward expert evidence

---

[1] *R* v. *Dora Harris* [1927] 2 *KB* 587, at 590.
[2] *R* v. *Damic* [1982] 2 *NSWLR* 750; *Titheradge* v. *The King* (1917) 24 *CLR* 107, at 116-7; *Whitehorn* v. *The Queen* (1983) 49 *ALR* 448; *R* v. *Apostilides* (1984) 53 *ALR* 445.
[3] *In re Enoch and Zaretzky* [1910] 1 *KB* 327, at 333.

and to analyze the *Directions* in which reform may head.

## The AIJA Survey Project

In 1997 and 1998 the first full survey of all Australian judges and magistrates took place. It was auspiced by the Australian Institute of Judicial Administration and by the National Institute of Forensic Science. The survey instrument had been developed from a 1996 draft which had been circulated for comment to trial and academic lawyers within Australia, the Netherlands, England, and the United States, as well as to sociologists and criminologists.[4] The aim of the survey project was to garner the views of trial judges[5] and magistrates[6] about expert evidence in order to procure data on the basis of which litigation reform could be undertaken, if necessary. The project took place subsequent to the Woolf Report in England,[7] after major expert evidence law reform at Federal level and in New South Wales, and in the context of ongoing controversy about the role of expert witnesses within the Australian criminal justice system.

The survey instruments received by the potential respondents were anonymous, thereby protecting judicial and magisterial independence, and encouraging frank provision of views. Both quantitative and qualitative data were obtained. The questions posed enabled respondents to select from various options and generally provided an 'other' category. The format of the questionnaire encouraged the recording of comments. Many respondents availed themselves liberally of this option.

Australia's population of just under 20,000,000 people has 478 judges, a small number of whom are exclusively appellate, and 401 magistrates. Two hundred and forty four judges provided responses to the questionnaire and 205 magistrates, resulting in a 51.05% response rate for judges and a 51.12% response rate for magistrates. However, given that the survey was only pertinent for trial judges, the actual response rate for this category was closer to 60%.

In the course of this paper reference will primarily be made to the views expressed by judges. This is for two reasons. First, it is judges who preside over criminal trials of consequence, magistrates dealing with the vast majority of criminal charges but the more serious, such as major assaults occasioning

---

[4] The results of the pilot study were written up in I. Freckelton, 'Judicial Attitudes Toward Scientific Evidence: the Antipodean Experience' (1997), 30(4) *University of California Davis Law Review* 1137.

[5] *See* I. Freckelton, P. Reddy & H. Selby, *Australian Judicial Perspectives on Expert Evidence*, Melbourne: AIJA 1999.

[6] *See* I. Freckelton, P. Reddy & H. Selby, *Australian Magistrates' Perspectives on Expert Evidence*, Melbourne: AIJA 2000 (forthcoming).

[7] Lord Woolf MR, *Access to Justice, Final Report to the Lord Chancellor on the Civil Justice System in England and Wales*, London: HMSO 1996.

injury, rape, large burglaries and thefts, substantial drug trafficking, manslaughter and murder are dealt with by intermediate and superior courts which are presided over by judges. In most jurisdictions in Australia such cases are heard with juries, although in some jurisdictions, such as in New South Wales, even serious cases can be determined by judges alone, at the election of the accused person. Secondly, the results of the judicial and magistrates' surveys are in most respects remarkably similar, and, for this purpose, little that is helpful would be achieved by presenting both sets of data.

**Bias**

The charge of 'bias' or 'partisanship' has been preferred against expert witnesses for the better part of two centuries. By the mid 19th century, the issue was one of considerable sensitivity. In the English trial of William Palmer for strychnine poisoning, for instance, Lord Campbell savagely criticized medical experts adduced for the defense, in particular singling out a Dr Herepath of Bristol: "[H]e has been prepared to come forward as a thoroughgoing partisan, advising the defence, suggesting question upon question on behalf of a man who he has again and again asserted he believed to be a poisoner. I abhor the traffic in testimony in which I regret to say men of science sometimes permit themselves to condescend."[8]

In a leading article in the 1897-98 *Harvard Law Review* Judge Foster noted that: "This 'bias', or inclination in favor of the party by whom the witness is employed, is probably the most frequent complaint of all against the expert witness; and the inclination of partiality is often characterized by terms indicating dishonesty and corruption."[9]

Ninety-nine years later, Lord Woolf's report into 'Access to Justice' stressed the potential that experts may espouse the views of those who commission their reports and call them as witnesses.[10] He classified impartiality on the part of expert witnesses as "of paramount importance".[11] Many of his proposals for reform were developed expressly to break down the

---

[8] D.H. Knott (ed.), *The Trial of William Palmer*, rev ER Watson, Notable British Trials Series, London: Hodges & Co 1856.

[9] W.L. Foster, 'Expert Testimony – Prevalent Complaints and Proposed Remedies' (1897-98), 11 *Harvard Law Review* 169, 171; *see also* Learned Hand, 'Historical and Practical Considerations Regarding Expert Testimony' (1901-2), 15 *Harvard Law Review* 40, 53.

[10] Lord Woolf MR, *Access to Justice, Final Report to the Lord Chancellor on the Civil Justice System in England and Wales*, London: HMSO 1996, p.143. He particularly noted the comment of the Court of Appeal in *Abbey National Mortgages Pty Ltd* v. *Key Surveyors Nationwide Ltd* [1996] EGCS 23: "For whatever reason, and whether consciously or unconsciously, the fact is that expert witnesses instructed on behalf of parties to litigation often tend (…) to espouse the cause of those instructing them to a greater or lesser extent, on occasions becoming more partisan than the parties."

[11] *Ibid.*, p. 142.

affiliation between experts and the commissioning parties with vested interests in the litigation.

In the US, the problem of expert bias is more remarked upon than in most other common law jurisdictions, Gross summing up the concerns unsubtly in 1991: "One of the most unfortunate consequences of our system of obtaining expert witnesses is that it breeds contempt all around. The contempt of lawyers and judges for experts is famous. They regularly describe expert witnesses as prostitutes, people who live by selling services that should not be for sale. They speak of maintaining 'stables' of experts, beasts to be chosen and harnessed at the will of their masters. No other category of witnesses, not even parties, is subject to such vilification."[12]

Judges were asked in the AIJA survey whether they had encountered a number of problems that could impact upon the utility of expert evidence. Two thirds of those who answered the question (68.10%, $n = 158$) reported that they 'occasionally encountered' bias on the part of experts, while just over a quarter (27.59%, $n = 64$) reported that they encountered this phenomenon 'often'. This latter statistic is in some ways the more significant. If bias is so prevalent that over a quarter of judges meet it often, this has ramifications for the functioning of criminal trial processes if it is not satisfactorily addressed. When asked about what quality they found most persuasive in an expert witness, judges also identified the absence of bias – 27.48% ($n = 194$) of responses identified 'clarity of explanation' as the most persuasive characteristic in an expert witness, while 25.64% ($n = 181$) identified 'impartiality'.

The questions about bias and partiality prompted a high incidence of commentary which particularly highlighted judges' views about the neutrality or lack of it on the part of expert witnesses. A number of judges caviled at the term 'bias', associating it with deliberate disingenuousness and locating the source of frequent disagreements amongst experts in other factors. One respondent commented that experts tend to favor the party calling them, but that to call this propensity 'bias' was too strong a use of the term. A similar view was expressed by another respondent: "I have never found an expert who has put forward a view which he/she does not genuinely hold, for the sake of merely supporting a case. Some views become untenable, but not because of 'bias' in the sense of a desire to further the case dishonestly." Another interpreted 'bias' as a "dishonest attempt to support the party calling the expert".

However, other judges appeared to take it as a given that a large proportion of expert witnesses were partisan. The comments which lamented the

---

[12] S.G. Gross, 'Expert Evidence' (1991), *Wisconsin Law Review* 1113, 1135; *see also* B.M. Epstein & M.S. Klein, 'The Use and Abuse of Expert Testimony in Product Liability Actions' (1987), 17 *Seton Hall Law Review* 656, 660; M.A. Hagen, *Whores of the Court*, New York: Regan Books 1997.

incidence of the abandonment of neutrality particularly singled out medical witnesses, and a number focussed upon the evidence given by psychiatrists. The comment of one judge seemed to sum up the views of many: "[Bias] is not unknown in other areas but is more entrenched in the medical profession." A number of cynical comments were notable: "I suspect that the expert says what she/he believes the party paying for the report/evidence wishes to read/hear"; "Bias is almost inevitable given that the expert is paid by one party and only called if his/her evidence helps the party's case"; "Experts seem to have a bias in favor of the party calling them. It may be an unconscious bias of course"; "The expert frequently slants his evidence in favor of the litigant on whose behalf his evidence is given."

A number of responses indicated that bias became apparent in the proclivity of some experts to function as advocates. Others identified as a category of particularly biased experts those who made their living or a substantial part of their living out of providing forensic advice. Again, medical witnesses were particularly identified in this regard. One judge summed up the views of several: "Experts very readily fall into categories when they develop an advising practice."

Some assumed that expert witnesses were not impartial but did not blame them: "Many experts are predictable in the sense of it is easy to know in advance what tack they will take. They are honest, but not necessarily objective."

The responses in relation to 'bias' were significant, particularly the considerable proportion of the Australian judiciary reporting a pattern of finding partisanship on the part of specialist witnesses called before them. The definition of bias, that is to say whether the connotation of the word necessarily involves deliberate or unwitting lack of objectivity, is less important. What appears to concern Australian judges is the product of the bias, namely reports and oral evidence that end up being partisan.

**Comprehensibility of Evidence**

If a decision-maker, be it a judge or a juror, is unable to comprehend expert evidence sufficiently to appreciate the distinctions in the terminology and opinions expressed by opposing witnesses, this too has the potential to lead to miscarriages of justice. The difficulty likely to be encountered by lay decision-makers in understanding the subtle differences of opinion amongst expert witnesses, especially where it is the subject of complex and conflicting testimony, has long been advanced as a ground for removing the calling and selection of experts from the responsibility of the parties and investing it in the hands of courts and tribunals – in other words, creating a system more akin to the continental systems of justice. It has also been argued to be a ground for removing decision-making in such matters from lay members of the public selected to be jurors.

The momentum to make such changes to the functioning of the adversary system can be identified in the mid-19th century when a series of initiatives was promoted as an improvement on the system obtaining at the time in England to remove decision-making in cases involving medical evidence from lay tribunals of fact to ones that were constituted by experts. The alternative mooted was the establishment of panels of experts from which court could draw when needing authoritative opinion from members of the learned colleges.[13]

The problem of wrong decision-making generated by misunderstanding or failure to understand expert medical evidence is generally said to relate to trials conducted before juries. Relatively little sound scholarship, though, has been devoted to assessing the limitations upon jurors' ability to understand and evaluate complex medical evidence. A range of impediments under the Anglo-Australian legal system stands in the way of approaching jurors to ask them about their impressions of their ability to cope with the intellectual rigors of criminal trials. Most of the research about levels of understanding and about the potential for prejudices and misunderstandings to infect the decision-making process in face of complex and conflicting expert evidence has been derived from North American mock juror studies, suggesting diversely that:

- jurors are more influenced by an expert's ability to convey technical information comprehensibly and to draw firm conclusions than by educational credentials;[14]
- jurors are impressed by an expert's reputation and educational credentials but clarity of presentation is the most important factor;[15]
- jurors want articulate experts, and to a lesser degree experts who draw firm conclusions;[16]
- jurors do not find experts who are very technical and complex very persuasive;[17]
- jurors with less management experience may be more suspicious of experts;[18]
- jurors are especially influenced by expert evidence given early in proceedings;[19]
- jurors may undervalue match probabilities in forensic science;[20]

---

[13] See C.A.G. Jones, Expert Witnesses, Clarendon Press, Oxford 1994.
[14] A. Champagne, D.W. Shuman & E. Whitaker, 'An Empirical Examination of the Use of Expert Witnesses in American Courts' (1991), 31 Jurimetrics Journal 375, 388.
[15] D.W. Shuman, A. Champagne & E. Whitaker, 'An Empirical Examination of the Use of Expert Witnesses in the Courts – Part II: A Three City Study' (1994), 34 Jurimetrics Journal 193.
[16] Ibid.
[17] Ibid.
[18] A.D. Austin, 'Jury Perceptions on Advocacy: A Case Study' (1982), 8 Litigation 15.
[19] N. Brekke & E. Borgida, 'Expert Psychological Testimony in Rape Trials: A Social-Cognitive Analysis' (1988), 55 Journal of Personality and Social Psychology 372.
[20] D.L. Faigman & A.J. Baglioni, 'Bayes' Theorem in the Trial process: Instructing Jurors on the (to be continued)

- jurors who are more educated may be less likely to accept the views of expert witnesses uncritically;[21]
- jurors who are more educated are more likely to participate actively in juror deliberations;[22]
- jurors who are younger find psychologists and psychiatrists more credible than do older jurors;[23]
- jurors who are older tend generally to believe expert witnesses more readily than do younger jurors;[24]
- while jurors are conscientious about their task, their enthusiasm and vigilance reduce in the course of the trial;[25]
- most jurors can understand and remember evidence from the trial where they were empanelled a short while before;[26]
- jurors rely on fluency, vocal inflection and appearance to evaluate witnesses generally;[27]
- jurors who find evidence unduly complex tend to turn to factors such as appearance and communication skills to evaluate its value;[28]
- jurors are suspicious of experts' impartiality if they learn that the experts have been paid by the lawyers representing the litigants;[29]
- male jurors tend to refer to abstract and rational concepts of fairness, whereas female jurors tend to refer to relationships and principles of affiliation and responsibility;[30]
- male jurors tend to approach decision-making in a more binary fashion (guilty/not guilty) than do female jurors;[31] and

---

Value of Statistical Evidence' (1988), 12 *Law and Human Behavior* 1.

[21] M.J. Saks & R.L. Wisler, 'Legal and Psychological Bases of Expert Testimony: Surveys of the Law and Jurors' (1984), 2 *Behavioral Sciences and the Law* 361, 435.

[22] R. Hastie, S.D. Penrod & N. Pennington, *Inside the Jury*, Cambridge: Harvard University Press 1983, pp. 137-8.

[23] R.J. Saks & R.L. Wisler, 'Legal and Psychological Bases of Expert Testimony: Surveys of the Law and Jurors' (1984), 2 *Behavioral Sciences and the Law* 361, 445.

[24] *Ibid.*

[25] G.M. Stephenson, *The Psychology of Criminal Justice*, Oxford: Blackwell 1992.

[26] M. Zander & P. Henderson, 'The Crown Court Study. Royal Commission on Criminal Justice, Study No 19, *Research Bulletin No 35*, Home Office, Research and Statistics Department, 1994. However, there are doubts about whether this is correct interpretation of the data: *see* A. Kapardis, *Psychology and Law*, Cambridge: Cambridge University Press 1997, p. 142.

[27] P. Rosenthal, 'Nature of Jury Response to the Expert Witness' (1983), 28 *Journal of Forensic Science* 528.

[28] *Ibid. See also* R.L. Tanton, 'Jury Preconceptions and their Effect on Expert Scientific Testimony' (1979), 24 *Journal of Forensic Science* 681. However, the Shuman *et al.* study and the Champagne *et al.* studies found that pleasant personality and attractive appearance were the least important factors to jurors in determining the credibility of an expert.

[29] *See* Shuman *et al.*, *op. cit.*; Champagne *et al.*, *op. cit.*

[30] A.B. Poulin, 'The Jury: the Criminal Justice System's Different Voice' (1994), 62 *University of Cincinatti Law Review* 1377.

[31] *Ibid.*, at 1396; *see also* L.G. Dooley, 'Sounds of Silence on the Civil Jury' (1991), 26 *Val U L Rev* 405.

- jurors who have previously functioned as jurors in previous criminal cases may be more prosecution-oriented[32] than first-time jurors.

Many of these research findings are open to criticism in terms of their methodology, their selection procedures, and their cultural matrix. Nonetheless they cannot be dismissed out of hand. Researchers Shuman, Champagne and Whitaker sum up the empirical state of knowledge disturbingly: "The typical juror forms impressions of experts stereotypically, based on the occupation of the experts, and superficially, based on the personal characteristics of the experts. (...) This image of jurors is troubling not only because it questions the capacity of the majority of the populace, but also because it flies in the face of 200 years of experience with the jury system. Our retention of the jury system with only minor tinkering over this time is an affirmation of our belief that the jury usually gets it right."[33]

In the AIJA survey judges were asked about whether they, as opposed to jurors, had encountered evidence which they had not been able to evaluate adequately because of its complexity. Just over half (53.19%, $n = 125$) said that they had not had such an experience, while just under a half (45.11%, $n = 106$) said that they had occasionally met such a problem. Only four judges said that they encountered such a problem "often" (1.70%). The numbers of judges sitting in the family and civil law jurisdictions who said that they had "never" been unable to understand expert evidence was higher than in the criminal law area.

A series of respondents made the point in comments that they had the power to rectify the situation by demanding clarification or obtaining explanations. How effective such measures had proved to be for the substantial percentage who had occasionally had problems in evaluating particularly complex expert evidence could not be evaluated from the answers provided.

Those judges who said that they had encountered such a problem were asked which discipline the expert witness had come from. Sixteen percent indicated psychiatry, thirteen percent said psychology and just over ten and a half percent said medicine and surgery. While the figures indicating difficulty with evidence given by mental health professionals are pronounced, the combined figures for medical evidence are even more so (26.5%), emphasizing both the amount of such evidence and the difficulty that is perceived to pose by many within Australia's judiciary. Whether these difficulties, as identified by the judges, and as speculated about by many commentators, will generate any serious momentum toward change in trial procedures remains to be seen. Early indications, though, suggest that they may.

---

[32] R. Hastie, S.D. Penrod & N. Pennington, *Inside the Jury*, Cambridge: Harvard University Press 1983, at p.143.
[33] D.W. Shuman, A. Champagne & E. Whitaker, 'Juror Assessments of the Believability of Expert Witnesses: A Literature Review' (1996), 36 *Jurimetrics Journal* 371, 382.

## Reforms

Many changes are afoot in Australia in relation to the admissibility of, and procedures regulating, expert evidence. Already disclosure of expert reports is mandated in all jurisdictions for civil litigation. Particularly onerous obligations to disclose material exist for defendants in some states in civil matters.[34]

In criminal matters throughout Australia the prosecution has to disclose reports of witnesses upon whom it intends to rely at trial in its depositions in criminal matters. The same kind of obligation now exists in a number of jurisdictions for the defense. For instance, in Victoria the "defence, must, if intending to call a person as an expert witness at the trial, at least 14 days before the day on which the trial is due to commence serve on the prosecution and file in court a copy of a statement of the expert witness."[35] The statement must contain the name and address of the witness; it must describe the qualifications of the witness to give evidence as an expert; and it must "set out the substance of the evidence it is proposed to adduce from the witness as an expert, including the opinion of the witness and the acts, facts, matters and circumstances on which the opinion is formed."[36]

Other proposals for reform of the use of expert evidence, however, have been advanced both in Australia and in other countries.

## Court-appointment of Expert Witnesses

One means of addressing the potential for unrepresentative, uninformed or difficult-to-comprehend expert evidence to lead decision-makers into error is for courts to call expert evidence where such a step is regarded as likely to advance the quality of fact-finding. However, this is a significant qualification upon the traditional functioning of the Anglo-Australian adversary process. Such court calling of expert witnesses has been little availed of under Australian, English and US law, especially in criminal matters, in spite of the fact that most judges technically have the power to initiate such a step. This said, it may be that changes to trial procedure (generated by intolerable delays and costs) at the start of the new millennium will bring back into favor the option of courts appointing their own experts where the trier of fact needs non-partisan expert evidence not otherwise made available by the prosecution or the defense.

---

[34] For instance, in Victoria, where a personal injury claim is made by a plaintiff, a defendant is obliged to serve upon the plaintiff any medical report (very widely defined) in their possession, custody or power, even if the defendant does not intend to rely upon it at trial: *Supreme Court Rules* (Vic), O33.07(3).

[35] *Crimes (Criminal Trials) Act 1999* (Vic), Section 9(1).

[36] *Crimes (Criminal Trials) Act 1999* (Vic), Section 9(2).

It may well be that the adherence of Australia's judiciary to the traditional demarcation of parties' and presiding judges' roles is starting to change. In the AIJA judicial survey a result comparable to results in a survey of US judges was notable. Many Australian judges stated that they had not themselves appointed expert witnesses but saw merit in the procedure. They thought that it might well be of advantage for the fact-finding process. The results from the survey bear further analysis as they are likely to add significantly to the lobby from a number of professional groups that they be relieved from formal allegiance to parties to litigation and identified as witnesses of the court.

Judges were asked about their powers to call expert witnesses to assist them in the evaluation of expert evidence. Just over half of those answering the question indicated that they had such a power (52.97%, $n = 116$), a slightly smaller number indicating to the contrary (47.03%, $n = 103$). Overwhelmingly, those possessed of such a power maintained that they had not exercised their power (81.88%, $n = 122$). Only a very small percentage of judges had appointed an expert witness themselves in the past five years. One in twenty answering the question (4.70%, $n = 7$) said that they had appointed an expert once in the last five years; 8.05% ($n = 12$) said that they had done so between once and five times, and 5.37% ($n = 8$) said that they had done so more than five times within that period. Judges were asked about why they had failed to appoint expert witnesses if they had the power to do so. The most common answer from those responding to the question ($n = 164$) was that it had not been "necessary" (41.46%, $n = 68$). Other answers included the response that no party had requested the judge to exercise the power (34.76%, $n = 57$). A smaller number of judges (10.66%, $n = 26$) maintained that they had declined to appoint an expert on the basis that such a measure would be contrary to the adversary process.

Significantly, of those who had appointed an expert, most judges found that the exercise had been "helpful" (69.23%, $n = 27$) or "very helpful" (28.21%, $n = 11$) to the fact-finding process. Only one judge, who apparently had had an adverse experience with the appointment of a court expert, indicated that the experience had been "unhelpful".

Judges were asked whether they were of the view that more use of court-appointed experts would be helpful to the fact-finding process. Nearly half of the judges answering the questionnaire expressed the opinion that it would be 'helpful' (48.77%, $n = 119$), with about a third expressing the contrary view (30.33%, $n = 74$). About one fifth of judges either did not have a view (10.66%, $n = 26$) or did not respond to the question (10.25%, $n = 25$).

The questions in relation to court-appointed experts prompted a high volume of comments. Some judges indicated that they had never even contemplated trespassing into the arena of litigation to such an extent as to appoint an expert. The extent to which such a measure is at odds with the traditional role of the judge as ring-keeper under the adversary system is captured by the response of one judge: "It has never occurred to me to do so and I have no idea how I would go about it". Other judges were troubled by the practicalities of such a course, one commenting that it was more trouble than it was worth and another identifying as "problems: (i) Who will pay the expert?; (ii) What opportunity do the parties have to influence the court expert's advice to the judge?" Other judges noted that the procedure of the court appointing experts could have ramifications for courts' budgets unless parties are prevailed upon to pay, an option that will not always be feasible. A number of judges noted that in certain compensation areas the court "has the benefit of Medical Panel certificates". By and large they indicated satisfaction with the process but in the same context one judge noted, "I believe I would have been assisted if I had exercised a power and called doctors in some instances."

Interestingly, the judicial comments were not characterized by a worry that court-appointed experts would exercise overmuch sway over the decision-making process, even if that task was the province of jurors. Such a concern has been expressed on occasions about involvement by judges in selecting and questioning witnesses but was rejected as a significant issue by researchers in 1991 who concluded that "fears that a court-appointed expert would overwhelm and unduly influence the jury are largely unsupported".[37]

The comments in relation to the utility of greater use of court-appointed experts provided something of a qualification upon the support otherwise given by the judges' answers. A series of respondents supported the more frequent appointment of experts by courts provided that the process was carefully case-managed. One judge indicated that: "The idea has a superficial appeal but: 1) The court-appointed expert acquires a status that is not warranted. 2) In cases of controversy between experts, it is usually because they come from different schools. Any court expert is likely also to come from one of the 2 'schools'. 3) A court expert is not needed usually to identify flaws in the opinions of the experts called. It would be of value and save costs if parties do not have an expert and can agree on one to be appointed by the court. They would also have to agree on the briefing given to the expert."[38]

The results of the survey of Australian judges have many features in common with the results obtained by Cecil and Willging in their survey of US

---

[37] N.J. Brekke, P.J. Enko, G. Clavet & E. Seelau, 'Of Juries and Court-Appointed Experts' (1991), 15 *Law and Human Behavior* 451, pp. 469-470.

[38] The comment is reminiscent of the equivocal support for such a procedure given by Lord Denning MR in *Re Saxton* [1962] 1 *WLR* 968 at 972: "It is said to be a rare thing for it to be done. I suppose that litigants realise that the court would attach great weight to the report of a court expert, and are reluctant thus to leave the decision of the case so much in his hands. If his report is against one side, that side will wish to call its own expert to contradict him, and then the other side will wish to call one too. So it would only mean that the parties would call their own experts as well. In the circumstances, the parties usually prefer to have the judge decide on the evidence of experts on either side, without resort to a court expert."

federal district court judges.[39] In that study, of the 86 judges who had availed themselves of the power to appoint experts (20% of the overall number), 255 appointments had been made. Fifty of the 86 judges who had made appointments replied that they perceived the appointment of court-appointed experts to be an extraordinary action: "The importance of reserving appointment of experts for cases involving special needs was especially apparent in the responses of the judges who had made only a single appointment. Thirty-two of the forty-five judges who had appointed an expert on a single occasion indicated that they had not used the procedure more often because the unique circumstances in which they employed the expert had not arisen again. They simply had not found another suitable occasion in which to appoint an expert."

Similarly, in the Cecil & Willging study, 87% of the judges indicated that court-appointed experts are likely to be helpful in at least some circumstances.[40] In other words, they manifested the same in-principle support for more extended use of court-appointed experts but shared with their Australian cousins a diffidence about exercising this aspect of their powers. Cecil & Willging concluded that this was attributable primarily to the difficulty of accommodating court-appointed experts in a legal system that values and generally anticipates adversarial presentation of evidence.[41]

However, it is apparent that pressures caused by the unavailability of legal aid, the high cost of litigation and the delays in cases being completed have generated an environment in Australia that is more amenable to fundamental change to litigation procedures than has previously existed. It may well be that the exclusive role of parties as the sole determiners of who will be called as expert witnesses will change in the foreseeable future.

**Enhanced Pre-trial Communication**

Another prominent feature of the qualitative data obtained by the AIJA judicial survey was the preparedness of many judges to contemplate procedures to bring experts together, generally pre-trial, to crystallize what matters they agreed about and those upon which there is disagreement. This approach appears to be born of frustration at the unnecessary canvassing within court of expert opinions not fundamentally in dispute and a perception

---

[39] J.S. Cecil & T.E. Willging, *Court-Appointed Experts: Defining the Role of Experts Appointed Under Federal Rule of Evidence, 706*, Washington DC: Federal Judicial Center 1993.

[40] *See also* the small and inconclusive study on the subject by A. Champagne, D.W. Shuman & E. Whitaker, 'The Problem with Empirical Examination of the Use of Court-Appointed Experts: A Report of Non-findings' (1996), 14 *Behavioral Sciences and the Law* 361.

[41] J.S. Cecil & T.E. Willging, *Court-Appointed Experts: Defining the Role of Experts Appointed Under Federal Rule of Evidence, 706*, Washington DC: Federal Judicial Center 1993, p. 5; *see also* J.M. Sink, 'The Unused Power of a Federal Judge to Call His Own Expert Witness' (1956), 29 *Southern California Law Review* 195.

that such processes are engendering unsatisfactory delays, expense and obfuscation within trials. Such an approach does not involve the imposition of arbitrary caps on the numbers of expert witnesses permitted to be called by parties but focuses upon enhancing the delineation of what is in dispute from what is not, and thereby factoring out sources of potential confusion and misunderstanding of the import of expert evidence.

## The Federal Court of Australia Initiative

In September 1998 the Federal Court of Australia released Practice Guidelines in relation to the use of expert evidence generally within its jurisdiction. They were the result of considerable consultation.[42] The Federal Court does not deal with first instance criminal matters, although it deals with them on appeal from the Australian Capital Territory and the Northern Territory. However, it is an increasingly influential court within the Australian legal system and its initiatives are frequently looked to by litigation reformers.[43]

The *1998 Practice Direction* prescribes that an expert has an over-riding duty to assist the Court on matters relevant to the expert's area of expertise. It stresses that an expert witness is not an advocate for a party. They state explicitly that an expert witness' paramount duty is to the Court and not to the person retaining the expert. Under the terms of the *Practice Direction*, legal practitioners are now required to provide any expert witnesses they intend retaining for a case, with a copy of the *Direction*.

Amongst other things, the *Practice Direction* requires expert witnesses to qualify findings in their reports (where they believe their report may be incomplete or inaccurate without some qualification), and to give reasons for their opinions. They must indicate what the material is upon which they rely for the purposes of their reports. This is but one aspect of the enhanced disclosure requirements under the *Direction*. Experts are also required to articulate any assumptions upon which they have acted in their expression of opinions. Expert witnesses are now also required to disclose all instructions given to them which define the scope of their reports, and to disclose the facts, matters and assumptions upon which their report proceeds. Expert witnesses must now also disclose if their opinions are not fully researched because they consider that insufficient data are available, and if a particular question or issue falls outside their field or expertise. In another major change, the *Practice Direction* provides that if expert witnesses retained by parties in a case meet at the *Direction* of the Court, it would be improper conduct for an

---

[42] *See* R.E. Cooper, 'Federal Court Expert Guidelines' (1998), 16(3) *Australian Bar Review* 203.
[43] Already the Professional Negligence List of the New South Wales Supreme Court has issued Practice Note No 104 to a similar effect: *see* (1999) 44 *NSWLR* 725; I. Freckelton, 'Forensic Experts' Codes of Ethics', in: I. Freckelton & H. Selby (eds.), *Expert Evidence*, 5 vols looseleaf service & CD Rom, Sydney: LBC 1993.

expert to be given or to accept instructions not to reach agreement in that meeting. The *Direction* instructs that if the expert witness cannot reach agreement on matters of expert opinion, they must provide reasons for this to the Court.

At the end of a report experts are expected to declare that "I [the expert] have made all the inquiries which the expert believes are desirable and appropriate and that no matters of significance which I [the expert] regard as relevant have, to my [the expert's] knowledge, been withheld from the Court." If, after exchange of reports or at any other stage, an expert witness changes his or her view on a material matter, having read another expert's report or for any other reason, the change of view should be communicated in writing (through legal representatives) without delay to each party to whom the expert witness's report has been provided and, when appropriate, to the Court. If an expert's opinion is not fully researched because the expert considers that insufficient data is available, or for any other reason, this must be stated with an indication that the opinion is no more than a provisional one. Where an expert witness who has prepared a report believes that it may be incomplete or inaccurate without some qualification, that qualification must be stated in the report. Experts are required, too, to indicate when they believe that a particular question or issue falls outside his or her field of expertise. Where an expert's report refers to photographs, plans, calculations, analyses, measurements, survey reports or other extrinsic matter, these must be provided to the opposite party at the same time as the exchange of reports. If, at a meeting directed by the Court, the experts cannot reach agreement on matters of expert opinion, they should specify reasons for being unable to do so.

The initiatives within the Federal Court's radical *Practice Direction* are aimed toward changing the culture that exists in some quarters of expert witness practice. They are aimed at crystallizing issues in dispute and enabling parties more effectively to evaluate the strength of not just expert reports but of individual opinions within them. They represent a significant intrusion into the style of expert reports as they have evolved in Australia. For instance, they require reference to assumptions, material upon which reliance is placed and disclosure of reasoning processes employed. Moreover, they state in unequivocal terms the obligation for expert witnesses not to function as, or regarded themselves as being, advocates for parties to the litigation. The *Direction* is likely to be emulated by many other superior courts in Australia and in due course to have a substantial impact upon the way in which expert evidence is presented in the criminal, as well as in the civil courts.

**The Future for Expert Witnesses in Australia**

The role of the forensic expert at the coalface of litigation is controversial and will remain so. The AIJA judicial survey has provided one point of view about the issue. It is not the only perspective but it is an informed one which merits close attention. It has highlighted the degree of judicial concern in Australia about partiality in expert reports and testimony and about the compromising of neutrality by expert witnesses. The preparedness of a substantial cross-section of judges to support in principle much more extensive calling of witnesses by the courts, even in criminal matters, bespeaks an inclination to look to the inquisitorial systems of justice for inspiration in terms of what is widely regarded as needed procedural reform.

The *1998 Federal Court Practice Direction* represents a major initiative generated by Australia's judiciary to change expert culture so as to orchestrate the provision of high quality, transparent information to the courts from professionals who are not suborned by the adversary processes. It represents a new preparedness to contemplate significant changes to the style of reports and giving of evidence by expert witnesses. Its effectiveness remains to be seen. Statements of requirement and of principle can readily enough be flouted in practice. The challenge for the Federal Court, and for courts which have gone some way toward emulating the Federal Court's reforms, such as the New South Wales Supreme Court, in its Professional Negligence List, is to enforce the requirements. If the results are positive, it is likely that the reforms will be imported into trial criminal courts.

The reforms initiated by Australia's Federal Court, however, will not meet all of the concerns of experts. Reformers will continue to articulate concerns about the subtle effects of the dynamics inherent in the functioning of the adversary system. They will worry too about the capacity of lay triers of fact to comprehend and evaluate the subtleties of experts' differences of opinion. Many will call for more involvement by the judiciary in reducing party-engineered obfuscation of expert evidence and the calling of witnesses unrepresentative of the community of informed opinion within areas of expert endeavor. Primary reliance for some time to come in Australia, though, will continue to be placed in the hands of counsel and the vagaries of the adversary system to make expert witnesses genuinely accountable – to expose frauds, fringe dwellers and practitioners of impoverished theories and methodologies.

# Monitoring Error in Forensic Science: Lessons to be learned from the Reviews of the FBI Laboratory

*I. Freckelton*

The known phenomenon of miscarriages of justice arising from erroneous science is undoubtedly only a small percentage of those cases that have reached the wrong result by reason of deficient science. Often the response to the issue from forensic science practitioners has been that the errors disclosed by those cases which can be identified relate to times well in the past and that it is unlikely that they would be repeated by reason of the remedial measures that have been subsequently implemented.

This paper considers the likelihood that such assertions are in fact grounded in reality by having regard to the 1997 and 1998 reports of the Office of the Inspector General into the FBI Laboratory. It argues that the thoroughgoing nature of the critique of the Laboratory's practices advanced by the Inspector General, as well as the follow-up report a year later, make it apparent that the gold standard of the forensic science world, the FBI Laboratory, was seriously methodologically defective in its procedures and averse to subscribing to sound scientific practice or to transparency and internal accountability. This carries with it many ramifications for comparable institutions in all jurisdictions and for courts in the continental and common law systems alike.

The time may have arrived when a new mechanism for monitoring the quality of forensic science and for promoting rigorous, impartial analysis of test data needs to be searched for. One option is the establishment of a standing body with significant powers to audit the activities, procedures and protocols of state-run forensic science laboratories.

**Sound Forensic Science**

Forensic science is distinctive within the discipline of science in that it relies for its integrity not just upon the quality of its knowledge and the means by which it is arrived at but upon the skills exhibited under the pressure of public scrutiny by its practitioners in the courts. However, regardless of the communication skills of forensic scientists, it is to the substance of their opinions and to the relationship between their opinions and the data upon which they are based that courts need to look if miscarriages of justice are to be avoided. The science must fundamentally be sound or in turn the courts' decisions in reliance upon the forensic science may miscarry. This involves the subscription of key scientists in prosecution laboratories to sound scientific and ethical practice.

As Melton usefully summarized it, scientific integrity incorporates the serious pursuit of a set of widely-recognized values in good scientific work:

univeralism, that is to say, the validity and truth of scientific statements should be separated from the personal characteristics of the scientist; communality, that is to say, scientific findings should be freely shared with others; disinterestedness, that is to say, the scientist's research should be guided by other than personal motives but by the wish to extend scientific knowledge; and organized skepticism, that is to say, scientists should examine openly, honestly and publicly each others' work critically.[1]

If forensic science were to operationalize such principles and if advocates were in fact to test their implementation effectively so as routinely to succeed in exposing departures from them, then miscarriages of justice ought not to occur.[2] In such a happy scenario, there would be no reason why forensic science should not govern itself and develop its own systems of accreditation, peer review and internal self-regulation, watched over always in individual cases by the courts. However, there has been a history of unsatisfactory compliance with self-governance in the forensic science area, as in many others. If the internal processes of self-regulation have latterly been shown to be seriously ineffective, then it would seem prudent for consideration to be given to external oversight of the performance of forensic science in the same way that ombudsmen and auditors have been given jurisdiction over many other occupations and professionals.

**Error in Forensic Science**

Much has been recorded about errors of forensic science which in turn have led to wrong results at law. The most prominent characteristic of such cases has proved to be not so much poor scientific practice but poor scientific practice amongst scientists called by the prosecution that has (not coincidentally) favored the case contended for by the prosecution. It has had its basis in the loss of neutrality by a proportion (often a small proportion) of state-employed forensic scientists – and then the failure by advocates to expose the problem effectively.

A few examples paint the picture. Dr Clift in England felt no ethical compunction about only presenting those aspects of his test results that assisted the prosecution.[3] In the IRA cases in England information that would

---

[1] R.K. Merton, *Social Theory and Social Structure*, New York: Free Press 1968, pp. 604-615. *See also* B. Barber, *Science and the Social Order*, New York: Free Press 1952.

[2] In the proceedings of the predecessor to this conference, I argued that the check and balance upon which both the adversarial and the inquisitorial systems depend, the informed and effective cross-examiner making forensic scientists accountable for their views, is often more rhetoric than reality: I. Freckelton, 'Wizards in the Crucible: Making the Boffins Accountable', in: J.F. Nijboer & J.M. Reijntjes (eds.), *Proceedings of the First World Conference on Criminal Investigation and Evidence*, The Hague: Koninklijke Vermande 1996.

[3] M. Hamer, 'How a Forensic Scientist Fell Foul of the Law' (1981), 91 *New Scientist* 575, at 576; *see further Preece* v. *HM Advocate* [1981] *Crim. L.R.* 783; J. Phillips, 'A Winter's Tale – (to be continued)

have assisted the defense was not communicated to the lawyers representing the accused men and women. Easy options assisting the prosecution case were taken by scientists when preliminary explosive analysis results corroborated the investigators' suspicions.[4] Barnes in Victoria, Australia, was content to provide to a court that information only which advanced the prosecution case.[5] So too was Sergeant Cocks in South Australia prepared to pursue only those theories of particle transference which were consistent with the criminal investigators' case theories.[6] In the *Chamberlain* case in the Northern Territory of Australia, the scientific investigation was embarked upon over-hastily and incompetently. Then it was terminated prematurely when what should have been regarded as preliminary results inculpated the popularly identified suspects of Baby Azaria's death, her parents.[7] In the *Ballpoint* Case in the Netherlands, too, a similar phenomenon can be discerned whereby precipitate assumptions favoring investigators' suspicions were too readily embraced by scientists.[8]

Another common theme is evident. Supervision of the inadequate practice of scientific practice was in each case deficient. The errors committed were fundamental in each instance but internal systems failed as badly as the external check and balance of cross-examination.

**The Report into the FBI Laboratory**

The FBI Laboratory in the US has long been the self-proclaimed leader of international state-run forensic science laboratories. It has been responsible for much of the cutting-edge research in world forensic science during the twentieth century. It has been generously funded and staffed by the US government and has been the preferred port of call for countless international scientists seeking to render themselves abreast of the latest developments in

---

"The Slings and Arrows of Expert Evidence'" (1983), 57(7) *Law Institute Journal* 710; A.R. Brownlie, 'Expert Evidence in the Light of *Preece* v. *HM Advocate*' (1982), 22 *Medicine, Science and the Law* 237; I. Freckelton, *The Trial of the Expert*, Melbourne: Oxford University Press 1987; J.H. Philips & J.K. Bowen, *Forensic Science and the Expert Witness*, Melbourne: LBC 1985, pp. 3-8.

[4] *R* v. *Maguire* [1992] *QB* 936; [1992] 2 *All E.R.* 433; *R* v. *McIlkenny* [1992] 2 *All E.R.* 417; *Ward* v. *The Queen* (1993) 96 *Cr. App. R.* 1, at 51. *See also* A. Samuels, 'Forensic Science and Miscarriages of Justice' (1994), 34(2) *Medicine, Science and the Law* 148; M. Mansfield & T. Wardle, *Presumed Guilty*, London: Mandarin 1993, p. 172.

[5] *See* I. Freckelton, 'Judicial Attitudes Toward Scientific Evidence: The Antipodean Experience' (1997), 30(4) *University of California Davis Law Review* 1137, pp. 1169-1176.

[6] *See* C. Shannon, *Report of the Royal Commission Concerning the Conviction of Edward Charles Splatt*, Adelaide: Govt Printer 1984.

[7] *See* T.R. Morling, *Report of the Royal Commission of Inquiry into the Convictions of Lindy and Michael Chamberlain*, Darwin: NT Govt Printer 1987.

[8] *See* M. Malsch & J.F. Nijboer (eds.), *Complex Cases: Perspectives on the Netherlands Criminal Justice System*, Amsterdam: Thela Thesis 1999.

forensic science and of current best practice.

Thus, an insight into the practices within the FBI Laboratory, into how it has dealt with internally generated concerns about its members' performance and into the quality of its work-product is of considerable international significance. This is so both at a symbolic level and as a matter of practical guidance to other laboratories, scientists and legal systems.

In September 1995 the Office of the Inspector General (OIG) from within the US Department of Justice commenced an 18 month investigation into the allegations of Frederic Whitehurst, a Supervisory Special Agent with a doctorate in chemistry, who had worked in the FBI Laboratory since 1986. The inquiry was conducted into the Explosives Unit (EU), the Materials Analysis Unit (MAU), and the Chemistry-Toxicology Unit (CTU), all of which were in the Scientific Analysis Section (SAS). The SAS was just one of five sections within the Laboratory.

A distinguished panel of forensic scientists from the US and overseas was convened to assist the investigation. The FBI provided more than 60,000 pages of documents in response to requests from the Office of the Inspector General, including case files, work notes, test results, policies and internal memoranda. More than 100 witnesses were interviewed. The OIG issued a 517-page report in April 1997 and a follow-up report in June 1998.

**The Major Findings of the OIG Report**

The investigation found most of Whitehurst's allegations to be unsubstantiated and in respect of some which it found made out noted that policies within the Laboratory had since changed to address a number of the difficulties identified by the OIG.

In terms of analyzing the potential for systemic flaws to enter into the practices of a Laboratory servicing the needs of prosecutors, the report of the Office of the Inspector General is without peer. This is so because of the extensiveness of the investigation and because of the co-operation with its inquiries ultimately secured from FBI scientists. The report provides a unique insight into how serious methodological deficiencies can infiltrate a scientific culture and how errors can thereby be generated, all of which were consistent with investigators' and prosecutors' hypotheses of suspect guilt.

The report identified scientifically flawed and inaccurate testimony in leading cases; testimony that went beyond the expert's areas on expertise; improper preparation of laboratory reports; insufficient documentation of test results; inadequate record management and retention systems; failures by management to resolve serious and credible allegations of incompetence, to resolve scientific disagreements, to establish and enforce validated procedures and protocols and to making a commitment to pursuing appropriate accreditation; and a flawed staffing structure within the Explosives Unit with examiners failing to possess requisite scientific qualifications.

The Office of the Inspector General recommended the 'reassignment' of a series of senior staff and proposed a series of procedural and methodological changes to practices within the Laboratory. The picture that emerges of the functioning of key components of the Laboratory over an extended period is grim.

### The FBI Laboratory Response to its Whistleblower

The institutional response of the FBI Laboratory to Whitehurst's allegations is illustrative of the systemic problems found by the OIG to have pervaded the administration of the Laboratory. Whitehurst raised concerns from his early days at the Laboratory about the quality of the work of his predecessor, Agent Terry Rudolph, who had been the Laboratory's senior examiner for the analysis of explosives residue. The OIG report identifies a grossly inadequate set of responses by the Laboratory to Whitehurst's legitimate concerns and to the complaints of an Assistant United States Attorney after the accused in the 1989 *Psinakis* case was acquitted.

Amongst the deficiencies were found to be the unsatisfactory responses was a report by Roger Martz, the chief of the Chemistry/Toxicology Unit, which upheld the analysis of Rudolph and reported that Rudolph had made no technical errors. This was subsequently found by the OIG to be "seriously deficient, that he failed to engage in the type of technical review that would actually have assessed the competence and sufficiency of the work purportedly performed by Rudolph."[9] This was followed by a further defective internal investigation and then after six years by an investigation by James Corby, the chief of the Material Analysis Unit. He found flaws so serious that he recommended that Rudolph be disciplined and removed from doing any further explosives work within the laboratory.

The response was to commission yet another review, this time by Corby's supervisor. Once again the review found serious deficiencies in Rudolph's work. It led to advice that Rudolph be seriously reprimanded. Instead the Laboratory Director merely orally admonished Rudolph and at the same time gave him a cheque for $500 which represented an incentive payment for recent work.[10]

### Specific Findings by the OIG

The series of reports into Rudolph's work tells a tale first of investigative incompetence and preparedness to whitewash and then of disinclination

---

[9] http://www.usdoj.gov/oig/fbilab1/00exesum.htm, p. 7.
[10] The OIG report makes the point that, "The monetary award meant that a decidedly mixed message was sent to Rudolph who reported to us that he was quite surprised by how leniently he had been handled." http://www.usdoj.gov/oig/fbilab1/00exesum.htm, p. 7.

amongst those at high levels within the Laboratory to take unequivocal and prompt measures to remove from within the Laboratory a scientist whose work was clearly of an unacceptable standard. A substantial portion of the investigations and of the response to them betrayed a culture that was conducive to scientific work of a defective standard and also of an institutional opposition to auditing itself rigorously and objectively.

The OIG report also identifies a series of occasions in high profile trials where scientific experts were prepared to tailor their investigations, their conclusions and their testimony to assist the prosecution. Significantly, not all of these were matters that formed the subject of grievances by the whistleblower, Whitehurst. For instance, the OIG concluded that the analytical work of Robert Webb, an examiner in the Materials Analysis Unit, who analyzed certain tape, paint, sealant and glue in relation to the charges arising out of the mail bomb assassination of Judge Vance stated "conclusions about his work more strongly than were warranted by the results of his examinations".[11]

The OIG also made other sinister findings about the performance of Williams. It determined that he had given inaccurate testimony about his role and about the formulas used in the FBI's manufacture of urea nitrate. In addition, it found that his testimony concerning his attempt to 'modify' one of Whitehurst's dictations was 'misleading'.

The OIG also investigated the testimony given in the midair explosion aboard Avianca Airlines Flight 203 shortly after its take-off from Bogota, Columbia, on 27 November 1989. Agent Hahn, an examiner in the Explosives Unit, testified at trials of those accused that a high velocity explosive had been used in the bombing. His opinion was based on his observation of indentations on the fuselage, known as 'pitting and cratering'. The OIG concluded that Hahn's correlation in favor of the prosecution of the pitting and cratering to a high velocity explosive within a narrow range of velocity of detonation was "scientifically unsound and not justified by his experience. Moreover, Hahn erred by not inquiring about the validity of the theory upon which he based his testimony concerning pitting and cratering."[12] The OIG also found that Hahn's evidence that certain of the passengers' injuries were indicative of a fuel-air explosion following the initial blast was flawed and exceeded the limits of his expertise.

In his statement of grievances, Whitehurst identified far-reaching methodological flaws in the testimony of David Williams, an examiner in the Explosives Unit, in the first of the *World Trade Center Bombing* cases – the Salameh trial. Williams testified in the trial as an explosives expert. He expressed the opinion that the defendants had the capacity to manufacture about 1200 pounds of urea nitrate, an explosive rarely used for criminal

---

[11] http://www.usdoj.gov/oig/fbilab1/00exesum.htm, p. 9.
[12] http://www.usdoj.gov/oig/fbilab1/00exesum.htm, p. 12.

purposes. He also testified that the main explosive in the World Trade Center bombing consisted of about 1200 pounds of urea nitrate. The difficulty correctly identified by Whitehurst arose from the fact that normally the way in which the main explosive of an exploded bomb is ascertained is by finding unconsumed particles or distinctive byproducts of the explosive amongst the debris, However, no such residue or debris had been found at the World Trade Center. Williams' testimony was not only guesswork, masquerading as scientific analysis, but was deliberately tailored to fill a deficit in the prosecution case – the difficulty in proving correspondence between the materials in the possession of the defendants and the substance that blew up the World Trade Center. As Williams conceded during the OIG investigation, "he had no basis from the crime scene for determining the type of explosive used, acknowledging that based on the crime scene the main charge could have been anything."[13]

The OIG report found similar flaws to apply to Williams' investigative work in relation to the *Oklahoma City Bombing* case. Williams' categorical identification of the main charge used in the bombing as ammonium nitrate fuel oil was found by the OIG to be "inappropriate based on the scientific evidence available to him". Williams did not draw a valid scientific conclusion but rather speculated from the fact that one of the defendants purchased components for ammonium nitrate fuel oil. "His estimate of the weight of the main charge was too specific, and again was based in part on the improper, non-scientific ground of what a defendant had allegedly purchased. In other respects as well, his work was flawed and lacked a scientific foundation. The errors he made were all tilted in such a way as to incriminate the defendants."[14] The defects in Williams' opinions did not emerge within the Laboratory or at trial because his supervisor did not properly review Williams' reports.

The OIG reported too on the scientific work that led to the conviction and imposition of a death sentence on the accused in *Florida* v. *George Trepal*, a case involving the adding of the poison thallium nitrate to bottles of Coca-Cola. The OIG found that the chief of the Chemical/Toxicology Unit offered opinions stronger for the prosecution than his analytical results could properly support. In addition to identifying his clear bias, the OIG found that he failed to conduct tests that he should have conducted, failed properly to document his work and testified inaccurately in key particulars.

The OIG made strong criticism too of the failure by the chief of the Chemistry-Toxicology Unit to keep proper records and take proper notes in relation to the OJ Simpson case. In addition, it commented that his testimony "ill served the FBI because it conveyed a lack of preparation, an inadequate level of training in toxicological issues, and deficient knowledge about other scientific matters that should be within the expertise of a chief of a unit

---

[13] http://www.usdoj.gov/oig/fbilab1/00exesum.htm, p. 11.
[14] http://www.usdoj.gov/oig/fbilab1/00exesum.htm, p. 14.

handling chemical and toxicological analyses within the Laboratory."[15]

In respect of a matter not raised by the whistleblower Whitehurst, but which came to light as a result of the concerns of a metallurgist working in the Materials Analysis Unit, the OIG concluded that a former head of the Hairs and Fibers Unit falsely testified in a hearing into the fitness for appointment of District Judge Hastings. The falsity was in relation to the conduct of a tensile test. The OIG also found that the witness testified beyond his area of expertise. It classified his testimony as "inexcusable" and also criticized the Laboratory's failure to deal properly with the colleague's complaint about it. This too was one of its criticisms of the Laboratory's response to the grievances of Whitehurst.

### The 1997 OIG Recommendations

The OIG found that the upper management of the FBI Laboratory had taken steps in the immediate past to implement change, upon recognizing the need for it. However, it noted that "[i]t is not clear from those policy changes that Laboratory top management has acknowledged that appropriate assessments of personnel are also required."[16] While the FBI concurred with nearly all of the OIG's systemic recommendations, it frequently disagreed with the application of the general principles that the OIG enunciated in assessing individual performances. This cannot but raise some doubts about the genuineness of the Laboratory's statements of preparedness to institute the reforms recommended by the OIG.

The OIG advanced some 40 recommendations, the most prominent of which were that:

- the laboratory pursue accreditation by the American Society of Crime Laboratory Directors/Accreditation Board (ASCLD/LAB);
- the Explosives Unit be restructured with its personnel being forensic scientists and that its mission be clarified;
- explosives examiners should advise and assist at crime scenes;
- the distinction between principal and auxiliary examiners in which auxiliary examiners' reports were fused into a single report by a principal examiner, be abolished;
- instead of there being one Laboratory report with analytical results reflected in the body of the report without attribution to individual examiners, each examiner who performed work should prepare and sign a separate report;
- analytical reports should be substantively reviewed by the unit chief or another examiner where necessary before being released in final reports;
- reports should be supported by adequate case files;

---

[15] http://www.usdoj.gov/oig/fbilab1/00exesum.htm, p. 14.
[16] http://www.usdoj.gov/oig/fbilab1/00exesum.htm, p. 23.

- reports should be clear, concise, objective and understandable, examiners' conclusions being limited to those that logically follow from the underlying data and analytical results;
- files should contain all relevant documentation of results and should be maintained so as to facilitate ready retrieval;
- the Scientific Analysis Section should develop and implement a co-ordinated training problem for examiners, this previously having been unit-conducted and developed *ad hoc*;
- a uniform program for training examiners in relation to giving evidence should be developed;
- testimony given by examiners should be monitored;
- the Laboratory should conduct retrospective case file reviews or "audits" to assure that reports are supported by appropriate analysis and documentation;
- written protocols should be developed for the scientific procedures which are utilized.

### The 1998 OIG Special Report

The OIG conducted a one-year follow-up review of the FBI Laboratory to assess the FBI's progress in implementing the OIG recommendations.[17] For obvious reasons, it did not attempt to cover the ground traversed by the ASCLD/LAB accreditation process. It noted that there had been substantial compliance with its recommendations but identified a series of ways in which the FBI Laboratory response fell short of the desirable mark.

At the time of reporting, the OIG noted that not only had the FBI Laboratory not replaced special agent bomb technicians with qualified scientists but the Materials Analysis Unit was of the view that it was inappropriate to employ scientists without bomb technician experience. One of them, for instance, had a background in 'soil science' rather than explosives, prompting the OIG to remark drily that this "may not be the type of 'pertinent discipline' our recommendation envisioned".[18]

The FBI rejected the recommendation that the chemical analysis of explosives be transferred from its traditional location. It also did not implement the OIG recommendation that previously qualified examiners periodically participate in moot-court exercises to sharpen their skills and provide training for trainees and less experienced examiners.

---

[17] The US Department of Justice / Office of the Inspector General, *The FBI Laboratory One year Later: A Follow-Up to the Inpsector-General's April 1997 Report on FBI Laboratory Practices and Alleged Misconduct in Explosives-Related and Other Cases*, OIG, June 1998: http://www.usdoj.gov/oig/fbil1yr.htm.

[18] http://www.usdoj.gov/oig/fbil1yr.htm, p. 3. The FBI wrote to the OIG distancing itself from the views of the unit chief and committing itself to implementation of the OIG recommendation.

An important aspect of the 1997 OIG report was that qualified examiners or unit chiefs monitor testimony by examiners at least once each year through direct observation of transcript review. Instead, the Laboratory implemented a system whereby examiner testimony was principally monitored by use of an evaluation form completed by the judge, prosecutor or defense counsel. In its 1998 follow-up, the OIG not surprisingly criticized this approach on the basis that it did not ensure substantive or technical monitoring of the examiner's testimony.[19]

## Lessons to be learned from the OIG Reports

The reports by the Office of the Inspector General into part of the FBI Laboratory provide a rare, informed perspective into the workings of a large government-run forensic science laboratory. The picture revealed is deeply disturbing both in relation to the incidence of scientifically unsound practices but also in relation to the culture of partiality existing within the institution. The extent to which the allegations preferred by the whistleblower Whitehurst were inadequately investigated and sanctioned over a period of six years speaks eloquently of the unreceptiveness of the institution to criticism, even internally generated.

More serious, though, is the profile of a significant number of senior staff within the Laboratory. It is one of scientists whose work methodology consistently unjustifiably favored investigative and prosecutorial hypotheses. Their methodology was then translated into defective reporting via written reports and by oral testimony.

The problems identified by the OIG in respect of the FBI Laboratory are consonant with the defects in the Home Office Laboratory in England and in a number of Australian forensic laboratories – a culture of partiality that it is difficult for laboratory managers, even if they have the will, to police effectively. The need for external overview is obvious. To an extent this is being addressed internationally by the implementation of quality assurance procedures and by many laboratories' voluntary submission to the stringencies of organizations such as ASCLD/LAB.

However, the institutionalization of bias is not easily broken down. Protocols and rhetoric can go some distance toward improved practice and toward creating expectations of objectivity, accountability and transparency of process amongst forensic scientists. The OIG reports into the FBI Laboratory are so disturbing however, when it is recognized how closely they adhere to fundamental critiques advanced of state-run scientific laboratories in England and Australia, that a more intrusive response is worth considering.

It is evident that the internal processes within the FBI Laboratory failed

---

[19] http://www.usdoj.gov/oig/fbil1yr.htm, p. 7.

lamentably to deal properly with the concerns of not just the whistleblower Whitehurst but also of others in the Laboratory who did not share his determination to pursue concerns about scientific practice. By contrast, though, the OIG, with whose investigation the FBI had no choice politically but to co-operate, was extremely successful in its inquiries. The OIG investigation was conducted by an elite team of scientists whose experience and competency commanded the confidence of scientists within the FBI Laboratory. It resulted in a fair-minded and fearless analysis of both individual and systemic performance within the Laboratory. The FBI, in spite of what were patently a number of reservations, in due course complied with almost all of the recommendations of the OIG.

Whether countries' legal systems are adversarial in which parties to litigation are responsible for locating and calling their own evidence, both lay and expert, or inquisitorial, in which it is the court which investigates and is responsible for ensuring that all pertinent information is placed before it and put on the public record, the problems of scientific partiality within state-run institutions are similar. This means that the solutions are likely also to be similar.

An ongoing equivalent to the OIG could usefully be set up in all countries in which forensic science evidence led by the prosecution in criminal cases emanates from a state-run institution. The role of such an institution should not be to function in any sense as an appellate trier of fact. Rather, its role should be to conduct independent audits of scientific and testamentary performance by forensic scientists. Its focus should be on systemic defects and upon unacceptable scientific and structural practices. One of its functions could be to facilitate the development of appropriate protocols, procedures, lines of supervisory authority and of peer review. It should have powers sufficient to enable it to conduct random, without-warning audits of scientific work in order to provide feedback to laboratories about the competency of their systems and of their employees. Naturally, where its investigations unearth serious scientific misdemeanors, such information could be made available to the representatives of convicted persons so as to enable them to make application for retrials where appropriate.

The creation of the standing equivalent to an OIG with jurisdiction to investigate and monitor the quality of the performance of state-run forensic science laboratories has the potential to play an important role in reducing the incidence of miscarriages of justice arising from defective scientific work. Such bodies need not proliferate in every country. Expertise and efficiency pooling could be achieved by the institutionalization of such bodies with jurisdiction to exercise their responsibilities in respect of associations of countries, such as the European Union, the Americas or Australasia. However, the OIG reports demand a response internationally that does more than acknowledge the need for improved accountability among forensic scientists. The time has arrived for a more intrusive and effective response to the risk of miscarriages of justice caused by pro-prosecution scientific bias and fraud.

# 'Not proven' as a Juridical Fact in Scotland, Norway and Italy

*G.C. Gebbie, S.E. Jebens & A. Mura*

## Introduction

At the present time, debate continues over the future shape of Europe and especially the European Union (EU). Questions of monetary and political union are discussed in an atmosphere where heat rather than light is often the result. At the same time as several countries from Eastern Europe are seeking membership of the EU, some countries outside of the Union are members of the European Economic Area. Each of these processes raises difficult questions and potential points of misunderstanding. If the 'New Europe' is to develop in a positive way then, its constituent peoples must learn more about each other and recognise that we share common problems but have diverse ways of addressing them. Our different legal systems may be the ideal place to start such a process. In comparing and contrasting them, we may discover whether or not these differences are more of form than of substance and that the threads of commonly applied concepts run through them. By such means, may come an understanding of the true nature of modern 'European' jurisprudence.

This study involves an examination of the legal systems of Scotland, Norway and Italy on a comparative basis and focussing on criminal procedure. Its aim is to discover to what extent, if any, each of these systems recognises the concept of 'Not proven' and what practical effects such recognition has for those involved in cases where it occurs. The section on Scotland is written by George Gebbie, who is a member of the Faculty of Advocates in Edinburgh. The section dealing with Norway is written by Sverre Erik Jebens, who is a Judge in the Court of Appeal in Trondheim. The section on Italy is written by Antonio Mura, who is an Assistant Attorney General in the Supreme Court of Cassation in Rome and President of a professional association of judges and prosecutors.

## Scotland

Scotland has no written *Constitution*. However it has a body of constitutional law which has developed through the centuries. In comparative law terms, the law of Scotland is a 'mixed system'. Its roots lie in the civil law and its philosophy of deductive reasoning (*i.e.*, individual cases decided upon the basis of general legal rules). However, almost 300 years of having all non-criminal cases subject to review by the House of Lords in England have inevitably led to some intrusion of the Anglo-American philosophy of inductive reasoning (*i.e.*, the existence and nature of general legal rules being inferred from decisions in individual cases). This is so even with the criminal law,[1] which has remained exclusively within the jurisdiction of the courts in Scotland. Since the provisions of the *Treaty of Union* were enacted by the Scots Parliament in 1707, all primary legislation for Scotland has to be enacted at Westminster in England. These two circumstances, the retention of jurisdiction in Scots criminal cases exclusively to the courts in Scotland and the lack of a legislature specifically dedicated to serving the needs of the Scottish legal system, have resulted in the criminal law of Scotland being predominantly judge made, or common law. The new Constitutional settlement in the UK has yet to impact on this. The basic rules governing the fairness of trials are substantially the same whether the procedure is solemn[2] or summary.[3] The common law nature of the three possible verdicts in Scots criminal law is maintained even in the latest statutory attempt at codifying its procedure. The *Criminal Procedure (Scotland) Act 1995 (1995 Act)* does not refer to the three available verdicts and refers, virtually throughout, only to verdicts of acquittal or conviction.

The *1995 Act* replaces the earlier *Criminal Procedure (Scotland) Act 1975*, which itself had replaced the *Criminal Procedure (Scotland) Act 1887*. Despite these Acts, the amendments to them and the passage of over 100 years of history, the current position of the statute law still makes no reference to the three possible verdicts. In dealing with both solemn and summary procedure the approach is virtually the same.

Sections 97 and 160 of the *1995 Act* deal with 'no case to answer' submissions under both solemn and summary procedure. For both sets of procedure, if the defence are successful in making such a submission at the end of the prosecution case, the *1995 Act* provides that it is the duty of the presiding judge (not the jury) to 'acquit' the accused of the particular offence in question. It does not specify which form the verdict should take. Since an accused is innocent until proven guilty, it may seem obvious that the verdict should be one of 'not guilty'. On the other hand, lack of a case to answer is a question which may be viewed as the *locus classicus* of 'not proven'. Experience shows that different judges have different ways of dealing with the situation. Some avoid the issue simply by saying that the accused is acquitted. There being two possible verdicts of acquittal, this seems to be the least satisfactory way of dealing with the matter.

Section 100 of the *1995 Act* deals with the 'Verdict of the Jury'. This of course is part of solemn and not summary procedure. This section provides

---

[1] Cf. the replacement of *jurisprudence constante* with the doctrine of *stare decisis*.

[2] The procedure relating to trials where a jury (numbering fifteen lay persons in Scotland) is the 'fact finder'.

[3] The procedure relating to trials where a judge (at the rank of a magistrate or a Sheriff) is the 'fact finder'.

that, unless otherwise directed, the verdict of the jury shall be pronounced orally by the foreman of the jury and how that should be done. It alludes to the jury being capable of returning a verdict which is not unanimous. It even provides that the jury may deliberate in the jury box in Court without having to retire from the courtroom to do so. Yet, nowhere does it specify the three possible verdicts open to the jury.

For summary procedure, where no jury is present, Section 162 of the *1995 Act* provides that, "[i]n a summary prosecution in a court consisting of more than one judge, if the judges are equally divided in opinion as to the guilt of the accused, the accused shall be found not guilty of the charge or part thereof on which such division of opinion exists."

This provision is, to say the least, unusual and not because, in common with the rest of the *1995 Act* it makes no mention of the three possible verdicts. Rather, if one considers its terms, one can see that a verdict may be required by law which does not reflect the view of any of the judges on a collegiate bench. For example, if the bench should comprise of two judges, one voting for 'guilty' and one for 'not proven', the section obliges them to bring in a verdict of 'not guilty' despite neither of them believing it to be appropriate.

If the two judges in the earlier example should turn to the 'Interpretation Section' of the *1995 Act* (Section 307), they will find no help there as regards the three verdicts. This is because, although this section runs to some four pages of the statute, it makes no mention of the word 'verdict'.

That the common law nature of the three possible verdicts in Scots criminal law is so strong, even today, is clear from the absence of reference to them in the statute law. This is emphasised by the difficulties which the statutory law has when touching on the subject, as can be seen from the *1995 Act*, Section 162 *(supra)*. In order to properly understand how the three verdicts operate in Scots Law today, it is important to understand how they developed.

Prior to the 17th century there were no standard verdicts brought in by juries in Scotland. Although there were a few occasions when a verdict of 'innocent' was returned, acquittals were usually expressed by the words 'cleanse' or 'acquit'; convictions by the words 'fylit' (fouled), 'culpable' or 'convict'. 'Guilty' and 'not guilty' did not arrive until some time after. They seem to have arrived, "during the period known as the Usurpation, when Cromwell imposed English Judges on Scotland".[4]

With the Restoration of the Monarchy came Charles II to the throne of both England and Scotland. With him too came an attempt to force Bishops upon the Church of Scotland by oppressive strong-arm tactics and by law. Such was the unpopularity of this policy that juries often refused to bring in convictions

---

[4] J.G. Wilson, *Not Proven*, Secker & Warburg, 10.

for crimes such as attending 'conventicles'.[5] To circumvent this difficulty the Lord Advocate[6] of the day, the Sir George MacKenzie (otherwise known as 'Bluidy[7] MacKenzie') introduced, "the doctrine that juries had no concern with anything except the evidence; their only function was to decide the facts and leave it to the Judges to determine the legal quality of these facts. They had to say, in other words, whether the Crown had proved the facts alleged or not so the verdicts of 'proven' and 'not proven' became standard forms in their turn." This division of the function of the jury from that of the Judge remains in force to this day.

'Proven' and 'not proven' remained the standard forms of verdict until 1728 and the case of Carnegie of Findhaven.[8] This case involved a charge of murdering the Earl of Strathmore. On the facts of the case Carnegie undoubtedly killed the Earl who accidentally got in the way of a sword thrust which Carnegie, who was drunk, was directing at another man called Lyon. The Earl told the doctors attending him on several occasions that he was sure that Carnegie had not meant to injure him. He died of his wounds two days later. At the trial, the Advocate representing Carnegie persuaded the jury to assert their rights and deliver a verdict of 'not guilty' (albeit that Carnegie had undoubtedly committed the culpable homicide of the Earl, even if not his murder). History does not record the Advocate's fee for working this forensic wonder. Whatever it was, it was not enough. Since 1728 it has become open to juries (or judges in summary procedure) to bring in one of three verdicts on a charge, namely 'not proven', 'not guilty' or 'guilty'.

The effect of a verdict of 'not proven' in a trial is exactly the same as verdict of 'not guilty'. It is a verdict of acquittal and the accused walks free on that charge and can never be brought to trial in respect of that alleged crime again. However that is not necessarily the end of the matter. Most criminal offences are also offences *in delict*. That is to say that they are also wrongs in civil law, for which the victim can seek redress from the perpetrator in the form of an award of damages made by the Civil Court. The difference is that the onus of proof on the prosecutor in the Criminal Court is to the standard of 'proof beyond a reasonable doubt', whereas in a civil action the onus on the pursuer is to the standard of 'proof upon a balance of probabilities'. There have recently been a couple of high profile cases, where persons acquitted by the 'not proven' verdict of a jury in criminal proceedings have later been found liable in damages by a Judge in civil proceedings arising from the same *species facti*. In theory, because of the difference in the standards of proof between criminal and civil cases, there is no reason why a person acquitted by a 'not

---

[5] 'Conventicles' were Calvinist Protestant religious services, which were conducted in the open air to avoid the detection, capture and torture of the faithful by the forces of the Crown.
[6] The Chief Law Officer of the Crown in Scotland and the Chief Prosecutor.
[7] Scots word meaning 'bloody' in English.
[8] Hume, 2 *Commentaries*, 440.

guilty' verdict should not suffer the same fate except that as a matter of practicality the pursuer in such cases is unlikely to win on the facts.

## Norway

Norway has a written *Constitution*, which contains several legal safeguards with respect to criminal cases as well as civil cases. Among the most important of these are para 96, which provides that no one can be punished unless according to a law applicable in the case, and para 97, which states that criminal and civil laws cannot be given retroactive effect. The Norwegian *Constitution* dates from 1814. It is greatly influenced by the ideas of personal freedom and individual rights, expressed in the French and American *Constitution*, which were passed some decades earlier.

When the Union with Denmark was dissolved in 1814, it had lasted for almost 500 years. Therefore, it should be of no surprise that, the Norwegian judiciary system is in many parts similar to the Danish system. In fact, the main differences within the Nordic countries in the fields of civil and criminal procedure law exist between Denmark and Norway on the one side, and Sweden and Finland on the other. In the latter countries there are, for instance, less use of juries in criminal cases than in Denmark and Norway.

The criminal justice system in Norway is mainly regulated by *the Penal Code of 1902* (as amended) and the *Criminal Procedure Act of 1981 (CPA 1981)*. The present Norwegian *CPA 1981* replaced the *Criminal Procedure Act of 1887*.[9] The latter one was known as *'The Jury Act'*, because it introduced the jury in criminal cases. Though the jury was retained in the *CPA 1981*, its importance has later declined, due to law reforms in 1989 and 1993.

There are no trials by jury in the city courts or the district courts, which, according to the law reform of 1993, handle all criminal cases in the first instance. At this stage, the criminal cases are handled by mixed courts, normally consisting of one judge and two lay assessors. Trial by jury is, due to the latest law reform, used only in the most serious appeal cases in the Courts of Appeal. In all other cases the Courts of Appeal are organised as mixed courts as well, normally with three judges and four lay assessors. The juries, therefore, play a relatively modest role in Norwegian criminal procedure.

It is an important principle in Norwegian criminal procedure law, as in most western countries, that the accused person is presumed to be innocent until he is eventually proven guilty in court. The burden of proof in a criminal case is placed upon the prosecution authorities. A person charged with a

---

[9] The *CPA 1981* is commented by H.Kr. Bjerke & E. Keiserud, *Straffeprosessloven med kommentarer (The Criminal Procedure Act commented)*, 1986.

criminal offence therefore has the benefit of the doubt, and can be convicted only if guilt beyond reasonable doubt is proved at the trial.[10]

In a criminal trial the main question for the court therefore is to decide whether the evidence produced is sufficient to demonstrate that the person charged is guilty of having committed the offence. If guilt beyond reasonable doubt is proved, the court will convict him, and if not, he will be acquitted. These are the only possible results in criminal cases in Norway, when it comes to the conclusion of the verdict on the question of guilt.

The *CPA 1981* contains several rules regarding the conclusion in a criminal case and the court's duty to give reasons for its decision on the question of guilt. This duty is applicable only in cases which are decided upon by mixed courts. However, the mixed courts handle the great majority of the cases. If the court finds the person charged guilty, it has to produce the reasons for this and express that guilt beyond reasonable doubt is proved.[11] If he is acquitted, the court has to express on what points the charge has not been proved.[12] Because of this, it is possible in many criminal cases to examine whether the court has found no proof at all or only insufficient proof for conviction.

In jury cases, the judges will ask the jury to answer specific questions on whether the person charged is guilty of having committed the actual offence. The jury can choose between two answers only, namely 'yes' or 'no'.[13] If the answer of the jury is 'no', it implies that guilt has not been proved beyond reasonable doubt. However, since the jury produces no reasons for its decisions, it is impossible to examine, on the basis of the verdict, on which points or to what extent the proof was regarded as insufficient. If the verdict is not quashed by the judges,[14] which happens rather seldom, the person charged will be either convicted or acquitted.

From this it follows that Norway, as different from Scotland, has no system of three possible verdicts in criminal cases. If guilt has not been proved beyond reasonable doubt, the person charged must be acquitted, even if the court has been in great doubt on the question of guilt. This is the situation both in cases decided upon by a mixed court and a jury. An acquittal in a criminal case therefore always implies that the person charged has been found not guilty.

The Norwegian *CPA 1981* contains several provisions on monetary compensation for damage caused by the prosecution, if the accused person is acquitted or the prosecution is discontinued.[15] One of the provisions brings

---

[10] This subject is dealt with in the main Norwegian work on criminal procedure law, which is Johs. Andenæs, *Norsk straffeprosess (The Norwegian Law on Criminal Procedure) Vol. I*, 126 ff., 1994.

[11] This follows from Article 40.2 of the *CPA 1981*.

[12] Article 40.4 of the *CPA 1981*.

[13] Article 365.1 of the *CPA 1981*.

[14] According to Article 376-'c' the court can quash a 'yes' verdict by the jury, if the court regards the proof as being insufficient for conviction. The court also has a more limited right to quash a 'no'-verdict, according to Article 376-'a' of the *CPA 1981*.

[15] The provisions are included in Chapter 31 of the *CPA 1981*.

forward the question of 'not proven' guilty, and therefore has some interest as far as the topic of this article is concerned.

As a main rule, the formerly charged person has to demonstrate the probability of not having committed the offence, in order to be entitled to compensation.[16] In this connection, the burden of proof is placed upon the formerly charged person. He has to prove that it is more likely that he has not committed the offence than the opposite. If the court finds that the acquitted person has failed in demonstrating this, compensation cannot be given according to the actual provision. This often implies, however, that the acquittal must be regarded as the consequence of guilt not being proved, rather than the person not being guilty. Therefore, the combination of the acquittal and the rejection of compensation could leave the formerly charged person in a somewhat similar situation as if he was only 'not proven' guilty in the criminal case.

These compensation cases bring forward another question of legal nature, related to the presumption of innocence. This principle is laid down in Article 6.2 of the *European Convention for the Protection of Human Rights and Fundamental Freedoms (ECHR)*, which expresses that "[e]veryone charged with a criminal offence shall be presumed innocent until proved guilty according to law". Therefore, if the court rejects the claim for compensation, it must avoid arguing in a way that questions the correctness of the acquittal in the criminal case. This follows from the decision by the European Court of Human Rights in the *Sekanina* case.[17] A group of legal experts has put forward a proposal to amend the rules on monetary compensation, in order to avoid the problems related to Article 6.2 of the *ECHR*. The government is expected to present the bill before parliament in the near future.

Summing up, 'not proven' is not a possible conclusion in a criminal case in Norway. As far as the question of guilt is concerned, the result can only be either a conviction or an acquittal. In the latter situation, the person charged is considered to be 'not guilty'.

The term 'not proven' is relevant only in the context of describing the conditions for a conviction verdict in a criminal case, in the sense that the prosecution has to prove the person charged is guilty beyond reasonable doubt. If the prosecution fails in proving this, however, the charged person is not only acquitted, but is also considered to be 'not guilty'.

Cases on compensation for damage caused by the prosecution bring forward the question on whether the acquittal in the criminal case must be the result of guilt not being proved, rather than guilt not existing. However, even if the acquitted person does not succeed in demonstrating the probability of not having committed the offence, he is still considered not guilty in the criminal

---

[16] Article 444.1 of the *CPA 1981*.
[17] *Sekanina* v. *Austria*; judgement passed on the 25th of August 1993 (21/1992/366/440).

case. When deciding upon the compensation claim, the court has to be very careful, and avoid questioning the correctness of the acquittal in the criminal case.

**Italy**

The Italian judicial system is a civil law system. The *Constitution of the Republic*, in force from 1948, devotes various rules to the provision of a Criminal Justice system and to its administration. It provides that:
- personal freedom is inviolable;[18]
- there is the right of defence against criminal prosecution[19] and it is inviolable;
- criminal liability is personal;[20]
- the accused cannot be considered guilty until his final conviction.[21]

At present, two codes regulate the Criminal Justice System: the *Penal Code* of 1930 (as amended) and the *Code of Criminal Procedure of 1988 (CCP 1988)*.

The latter replaced the *1930 Procedure Code* and caused the change from a fundamentally inquisitorial system to a basically (even though not completely) adversarial system. So, the *Giudice Istruttore* (investigating judge) has disappeared and many coercive powers of the public prosecutor have been removed. The new figure of the *Giudice per le indagini preliminari* (the judge competent during the preliminary investigations) does not investigate at all. He or she decides on the provisional measures through which the accused's freedom can be restricted and, at the end of the investigation carried out by the public prosecutor, decides if the accused must be committed for trial. A form of cross-examination has been introduced into the trial procedure, restricting the possibility of considering as evidence the statements issued by the witnesses to the prosecutor during the investigation.[22]

With regard to the requirements for any conviction, even though Italian law does not make use of the expression 'beyond a reasonable doubt', it is a general principle of the Italian tradition – both with the preceding and the

---

[18] Article 13 of the Italian *Constitution*. A restriction of the personal freedom can be ordered only by a judicial authority, through a justified act adopted in a case and with the formality that the law commands.

[19] The right of the defence is inviolable in every stage of the proceedings: Article 24.2 of the Italian *Constitution*.

[20] Article 27.1 of the Italian *Constitution*.

[21] Article 27.2 of the Italian *Constitution*.

[22] The Constitutional Court, moving from the assertion that, in the Italian constitutional system, the search for truth is the main aim of the penal trial, has assessed the unconstitutionality of some rules of the new *CCP 1988* and has repealed them. So, the constitutional sentences have reshaped the original lines of the Code written in 1988, setting up a system that only in part can be classified as adversary. The discussion on this topic is still heated.

present *CCP 1988* – that a judgement of conviction can be passed only if the judge has the necessary moral sureness.[23]

The constitutional 'presumption of innocence' (*rectius,* according to the Italian concept: 'presumption of not guilt') has primary importance for the subject matter. It has two distinct meanings:[24]

1. it rules the treatment of the accused during the trial, preventing from identifying him or her – at that stage – with the offender; and
2. it gives foundation to the basic decision rule *in dubio pro reo,*[25] that implies that the doubt is favourable to the accused and causes his or her acquittal.

Traditionally, in relation to the different probative results of the trial, the Italian codes of procedure have provided various kinds of acquittal and have indicated precise 'formulas' to express them. Every sentence must necessarily contain a written explanation of the reasons for the decision,[26] but, according to the general principle that regulates the matter, the judge[27] cannot use, in his or her sentences, conclusive formulas different from the ones listed by law. If more than one formula would suit the case, the judge must choose the formula that causes the smallest detriment to the defendant so discharged.[28]

According to Article 530 of the *CCP 1988,* the judge acquits the accused (specifying the reasons for the acquittal in the verdict) if the fact that the crime was actually committed was not established (formula: 'the fact does not obtain'), or the accused did not commit it, or it does not constitute a crime, or it was committed by someone who was not chargeable or not punishable. When there is no proof that the fact 'obtained', or that the accused committed the crime, or that the fact constitutes a crime, or there is no proof that the crime

---

[23] Court of Cassation, Section II, 2.7.1986, no. 12508. The necessity of a "tranquillising certainty" is stated by Section I, 23.5.1988, no. 8241.

[24] A. Ghiara, 'Presunzione di innocenza, presunzione di non-colpevolezza e formula dubitativa, anche alla luce degli interventi della Corte Costituzionale', in: *Rivista italiana di diritto e procedura penale,* 1, 72 (1974).

[25] The ancient Latin word *reus* means 'accused', or 'defendant', in the famous standard of judgement *in dubio pro reo* (*i.e.,* in case of doubt the decision must be in favour of the accused) and in the more general principle of *favor rei* (*i.e.,* preference for the accused. *See* G. Lozzi, 'Favor rei', in: *XVII Enciclopedia del diritto,* Giuffre' 1968, 15.

[26] Articles 125.3 and 546.1 of the *CCP 1988*; Articles 148 and 474 Code of 1930.

[27] In all respects taken into consideration in this paper, with regard to the Italian legal system, the same rules are also applied when a collegiate bench, instead of a single judge, is in charge of the trial.

[28] D. Siracusano, 'Assoluzione (diritto processuale penale)', in: *III Enciclopedia del diritto,* Giuffre', Varese 1958, 929: the full acquittal formula can be defined as 'fundamental'; if compared with it, the dubitative formula is definable as 'complementary', being not only a formula, but a kind of conviction, too. *See also* G. Sabatini, 'Classificazione e gerarchia delle formule di proscioglimento', in: *Giustizia penale III,* 459 (1953); E. Fortuna, 'Sentenza penale', in: *Enciclopedia giuridica, Istituto della enciclopedia italiana,* Roma 1992, 16. About the criterion of choice among various formulas: Court of Cassation, Section III, 23.6.1993, no. 9096.

was committed by someone who was chargeable, the accused is acquitted, too.[29]

The same judgement of 'not guilty' must be delivered when the evidence is insufficient or inconsistent with regard to any of these aspects.[30]

One provision of the *Code of Procedure of 1930*, which has not been re-enacted in the new Code, is the old Article 479.3. This provided that, if the evidence was 'not sufficient' for a conviction, then the accused had to be acquitted 'for lack of evidence'. This expression appeared for the first time in the Italian legal system in the *Code of Criminal Procedure of 1913*. A long evolution had led to that, moving from the earliest times of the ancient inquisitorial system, when ordinary punishments were inflicted in the presence of a *plena probatio* (*i.e.*, full proof) of guilt, whereas the *semiplenae probationes* (*i.e.*, half-proofs) implied reduced punishments: in this respect, scholars discuss the concept of 'punishment for the suspicion', which was inflicted upon the 'nearly-guilty', or 'probably guilty'.[31]

In its modern version the 'lack of evidence' did not imply a punishment any more; nevertheless it was a formula that ended up by casting an indelible shadow on the accused, in spite of his or her acquittal,[32] besides some negative consequences, like the registration of the sentence in the person's criminal record.[33]

When the *Code of Procedure of 1930* was in force, the acquittal with the dubitative formula had to be adopted 'whenever the evidence was not sufficient for a conviction'. This expression comprised two main hypotheses:

1. the case in which there were clashes and inconsistency between various pieces of evidence; and
2. the case in which there were some relevant pieces of evidence for the prosecution, but they were unclear, uncertain or inadequate to found a conviction.[34]

In the opinion of the Italian Supreme Court (the Court of Cassation) this system was not in conflict with the *ECHR*[35] and was founded on the

---

[29] In any of these cases, after the verdict has become final, the person acquitted cannot be charged again with the same crime (Article 649 *CCP 1988*), on the base of the principle of *ne bis in idem*. On the other hand, the fact that someone has been acquitted of a charge does not prevent the public prosecutor from charging someone else with the same crime.

[30] A similar sentence is also given if there is the proof for a justification or for an excuse, as well as if there are doubts about them.

[31] F. Cordero, *Procedura penale*, Giuffre', Milano 1993, 827.

[32] G.M. Anca, 'Insufficienza di prove', in: *VII Digesto – Discipline penalistiche*, Torino: Utet 1993, 148.

[33] Some scholars even spoke of 'semi-conviction', criticising that system and hoping for its reform: *see* M. Chiavaro, 'Ancora l'insufficienza di prove alla ribalta della Corte Costituzionale (nota a Corte Costituzionale n. 168/1973 e n. 171/1973)', in: *Giurisprudenza costituzionale*, 2640 (1973).

[34] G.M. Anca, *op. cit.*, p. 156.

[35] With reference to Article 6.2 of the *ECHR*: Court of Cassation, Section II, 18.11.1987, no. 3717.

'presumption of not guilt', provided by Article 27 of the Italian *Constitution*.[36] It follows from this that the burden of proof lies with the accuser (the public prosecutor), who had to demonstrate for certain not only that the crime was committed, but also that the accused was guilty of it.[37] The Court had also observed that, to found an acquittal for lack of evidence, the doubt had to be objective and insuperable. Before giving up to it, the judge had to make every possible effort to reach the truth.[38] However, mere suspicions, devoid of any support of evidence, should lead to a full acquittal, and not to a judgement of lack of evidence.[39]

The new *Code of Criminal Procedure* marks the victory of the critical opinions against the 'lack of evidence' formula, which was definitively revoked in 1988. Thus the judge is today compelled to apply the logic of 'yes or no'. This is presented as a triumph of progress and civilisation (although some have pointed out the risk that the judge, not having the old safety valve of the dubitative formula, could sometimes – in extreme cases – be led to convict in circumstances where the evidence is not entirely indisputable).

The innovation improves the burden of proof resting with the prosecutor, assuring that no negative or damaging consequence follows for the accused if the charge against him or her is not completely and perfectly proved.[40] Naturally, it is still possible that the judge, explaining the reasons for the judgement, expresses a state of uncertainty and doubt;[41] but the use of a conclusive formula different from the full acquittal is precluded. So, when the evidence for the prosecution is insufficient or inconsistent, when there is a full proof that the accused is not guilty and when there is no proof that he or she is guilty, the results are the same in every case. The accused is acquitted and he or she is considered as purely and simply not guilty, with respect to criminal as well as to civil liability. This bears upon issues such as legal expenses and to possible compensation for unjust detention.[42] As a rule, when the injured party has sued for damages in the criminal prosecution, or has been put in a position to do it, the final judgement of acquittal is decisive also on any claim for damages put in by that party, with regard (among other aspects) to the assessment that the accused did not commit the crime.[43] The acquittal is not

---

[36] Also the Italian Constitutional Court declared that the formula of 'lack of evidence' was in accordance with the constitutional principle: sentence no. 124/1972.

[37] Court of Cassation, Section I, 2.10.1989, no. 5370.

[38] Court of Cassation, Section IV, 5.5.1989, no. 10813; Section IV. 2.3.1988, no. 6343.

[39] Court of Cassation, Section VI, 26.11.1985, no. 2087.

[40] F. Ennio *et al.*, *Manuale pratico del nuovo processo penale*, Cedam: Padova 1993, p. 857.

[41] Court of Cassation, Section IV, 25.3.1992, no. 5356.

[42] Court of Cassation, Section IV, 18.12.1993, no. 1573. Nevertheless no compensation can be claimed if the uncertainty of the evidence is a consequence of (or has been increased by) the defendant's intentional or culpable behaviour: Court of Cassation, Section IV, 17.12.1992, no. 1529.

[43] Article 652 of the *CCP 1988*.

decisive only in some particular cases, *e.g.* when the action for compensation for damages is brought in a civil trial and the injured party decides not to 'transfer' it to the criminal trial.[44] In this case the lawsuit for damages is ruled by the *Code of Civil Procedure*.

## Conclusions and Points for Debate

The indispensability of the judicial function implies that the judge can never come to the conclusion that a case cannot be decided. He or she must pass a final judgement, in every case, being not allowed to declare *non liquet* (as it could be done in the ancient Roman law).

Moving from the obvious natural limits of any judicial verification, an intellectual presupposition must be assumed in the exercise of the judicial function. It is necessary to utilise a conventional conception of words like 'certainty' and 'truth'. Therefore – in the terms of a judicial decision – 'true' means "so highly probable as to allow the reasonable removal of any possible residual doubt"[45] or "guilt beyond a reasonable doubt being proved".[46]

Several situations are placed below this conventional threshold. When a full proof of guilt has not been reached, the (in historical terms) 'negative' judgement can assume various forms.[47] These fall (in the perspective here of interest) into two main categories. The first includes those situations in which there is no proof of a fact that the prosecutor had to demonstrate or there is full proof that it did not occur. The second category is quite different, from several points of view, and includes:
- those situations in which some circumstantial evidence for the prosecution has been collected but it turns out to be insufficient for reaching the standard required by full proofs;
- the situations in which there are conflicts and inconsistencies among various pieces of evidence; or, lastly,
- the situations in which the pieces of evidence are unclear, uncertain or inadequate as a basis for convicting.

A situation of doubt on the part of the judge can sometimes be psychologically natural on the basis of the evidence collected in the trial and surely it cannot be prevented in cases like the ones of the second category mentioned above. Even in jurisdictions (like Norway and Italy) where a 'not proven' conclusion of the trial is not allowed, the situation of 'lack of evidence' cannot be precluded in the logic-rational path of the judge's decision. The Italian Supreme Court has remarked: "Neither can the law

---

[44] Article 75.2 of the *CCP 1988*.
[45] F. Cordero, *op. cit.*, p. 828.
[46] J. Andenæs, *op. cit.*
[47] F. Cordero, *op. cit.*, p. 811.

prevent the judge from expressing reasons for perplexity, for uncertainty".[48] This is the situation in Norway as well, in cases decided upon by mixed courts. It follows from the obligation to indicate the points on which there was considered to be insufficient proof.[49]

It is a matter of choice by the law to provide or not to provide autonomous consideration and distinct juridical effects for the decisions based on a 'not proven' conclusion. A connection has been often noticed, historically, between the presence or the exclusion of 'not proven' formulas in a legal system and the basic nature of the procedural system itself. Formulas like 'not proven' or 'acquittal for lack of evidence' are typical of fundamentally inquisitorial systems, whereas generally they are not found in the adversary-oriented ones.[50] Having said that, it must be remembered in the context of this paper that Scots criminal law is essentially adversarial in its procedure.

Comparing and contrasting the three legal systems considered above, one is first of all struck by the very different historical and cultural backgrounds against which each has achieved its current state of development. Yet, when one comes to consider these three systems as they are today, it is clear that in certain fundamental respects the judicial process in each system displays a surprising level of similarity with the other two.

These similarities can be expressed as follows. All three systems take as their starting point a presumption of innocence compatible with that principle as it is laid down in Article 6.2 of the *ECHR*. In all three systems, failure by the prosecution to displace that presumption of innocence by means of adduced evidence amounting to proof of guilt will result in an acquittal.

As far as criminal responsibility is concerned, all acquittals under any of the three systems have exactly the same main effect, viz. that the presumption of innocence in favour of the person accused remains intact.

Taken as a whole, each of the three systems allows for acquittal in circumstances where uncertainty is the manifest ground for that judgement. Nevertheless, as regards their actual regulations, the three systems here considered are poles apart. Scotland, by established tradition, recognises the verdict of 'not proven'. In the opposite direction, Norway admits only two possible verdicts in criminal cases ('guilty' or 'not guilty'), so that the accused must be acquitted only with a verdict of 'not guilty'. This is so even in cases where the reason for the acquittal was doubt on the question of guilt. Only recently Italy has passed from the former to the latter model, characterised by two sole formulas of verdict. By now this new model can be considered firmly rooted in Italian procedure system, after a long debate and an historical

---

[48] Court of Cassation, Section IV, 25.3.1992, no. 5356.
[49] *See* footnote 12.
[50] G.M. Anca, *op. cit.*, p. 149.

progress which started from the existence of a formula of acquittal 'for lack of evidence' concerning the cases of evidence 'not sufficient' for a conviction.

Like for most of the comparisons among institutions, which have their roots in quite different lines of historical, juridical and social evolution, it would be inappropriate if not impossible to proclaim any of the legal systems here examined as being the best from every point of view.

The provision of verdicts that expressly indicate the 'not proven' result of a trial presents some clear advantages. The actual train of thought of the judge, the motivational path of his or her decision, can be known instantly. The decision is strictly adherent to the exact belief of the judge and that can sometimes make it psychologically easier for him or her to deliver the appropriate verdict, in the most difficult of cases.

On the other hand, permitting acquittal only by verdicts of 'not guilty', with their plain meaning of full acquittal and the exclusion of a statement of uncertainty by the judge, can be regarded as being quite positive in many other respects. The exclusion of the dubitative formulas finds a solid juridical base on the presumption of innocence, and is highly tenable from a logical point of view. In all the 'not proven' cases the conventional level of certainty has not been reached and that is correctly expressed by the formula of 'not guilty'. Accordingly, the burden of proof is completely (and justly) laid on the prosecutor.

Do the systems of this kind, which admit of full acquittals only, assure a higher standard of actual, substantial justice? For example, do they better comply with presumption of innocence as set out in Article 6.2 of the *ECHR* than 'not proven' verdicts. Alternatively are they indulging in legal fictions where the reality of a case being 'not proven' is already recognised elsewhere in the self-same systems. Should the formulas for conviction and acquittal be better expressed as 'proven' and 'not proven' in all cases. It seems certain that an international scientific debate on the subject might produce some interesting results, not least in the area of a developing Pan-European jurisprudence. To stimulate such a debate, building on information about such distant countries and disparate legal systems, this joint essay has been directed.

# *Trompe l'Oeuil*: the Admissibility of Expert Testimony on the Unreliability of Eyewitness Identifications

*M.W. Ghetti*

## Introduction

Usually DNA evidence is used to prove the guilt of a person – as it did recently in the sex-scandal case of the American president.[1] Increasingly, however, DNA evidence is being used to prove the innocence of convicted men.[2] With this irrefutable proof[3] of innocence comes the question, "Why and how was this person convicted of a crime they did not commit?" For, you see, the "cornerstone of the American justice system has long been that convicting the innocent is a bigger mistake than letting the guilty go free."[4] Blackstone said it well: "It is better that ten guilty persons go free than that one innocent person be convicted."[5] And, yet, estimates of wrongful convictions for serious crime in the US range from 7,500 to 150,000 persons per year.[6] And, what appears to be the major source of wrongful convictions? Erroneous eyewitness identifications.[7]

---

[1] *See* P.J. Sloyan, 'Specimen K39: For Clinton, Smoking Gun/Blood Sample May Be As Damaging As Nixon Tape', 9/24/98 *Newsday* A67, 1998 WL 2686558.

[2] *See* E. Connors, T. Lundregan, N. Miller & T. McEwen, *Convicted by Juries, Exonerated By Science: Case Studies in the Use of DNA Evidence to Establish Innocence After Trial* (Report No. NCJ161258), Washington, D.C.: US Department of Justice, Office of Justice Programs 1996 (hereinafter 'Case Studies'); C.R. Huff, A. Rattner & E. Sagarin, *Convicted but Innocent: Wrongful Conviction and Public Policy*, Thousand Oaks, CA: Sage 1996 (hereinafter 'Huff'); S.L. Sporer *et al.*, *Psychological Issues in Eyewitness Identification 3* (1996)(hereinafter 'Sporer').

[3] A few commentators would debate the 'irrefutability' of conclusions drawn from DNA evidence. *See e.g.* J.J. Koehler, 'DNA Matches and Statistics: Important Questions, Surprising Answers' (1993), 76 *Judicature* 222, and references cited therein.

[4] *See* Comment, 'The Unfortunate Faith: A Solution to the Unwarranted Reliance Upon Eyewitness Testimony' (1999), 5 *Tex. Wesleyan L. Rev.* 307, 329 (hereinafter 'Unfortunate').

[5] W. Blackstone, *Commentaries on the Law of England*, Bernard, C. Gavit ed., 1941, 909.

[6] *See* C. O'Hagan, 'When Seeing is Believing: The Case for Eyewitness Testimony' (1993), 81 *Geo. L. J.* 741 (hereinafter 'O'Hagan').

[7] *See* P.J. Cohen, 'How Shall They Be Known? *Daubert* v. *Merrell Dow Pharmaceuticals* and Eyewitness Identification' (1996), 16 *Pace L. Rev.* 237, 254 citing Tillman, 'Expert Testimony on Eyewitness Identification: The Constitution Says, "Let the Experts Speak"', 56 *Tenn. L. Rev.* 735, 736 (1989). *See also* Devenport, Penrod & Cutler, 'Eyewitness Identification Evidence' (1997), 3 *Psychol. Pub. Pol'y & L.* 338 (the publication of the American Psychological Association, Inc.)(hereinafter 'Devenport'); Unfortunate, *supra*, n. 4, at 313, citing Case Studies, *supra*, n. 2 (explaining the cause of 28 convictions of rapist-murders later vindicated by DNA evidence; 26 convictions were primarily by eyewitness testimony); A. Rattner, 'Convicted But Innocent' (1988), 12 *Law & Hum. Behav.* 283, 291 tbl 6 (hereinafter 'Rattner')(identifying nine major categories of errors; in 191 cases, eyewitness misidentification is the number one cause of error at 52.3%).

More then 300 studies have now been undertaken.[8] These studies indicate that the propensity for mistakes in eyewitness identifications is so great that it is nearly equal to all other forms of error combined.[9] A 1996 study indicated that more than 60% of over 500 erroneous convictions were based on eyewitness identifications.[10] Another 1988 study of 191 cases showed that over 52% were based on eyewitness identifications.[11]

Furthermore, treatises outlining the inherent unreliability of eyewitness identification date back to the turn of the century.[12] The problem has been recognized, studied and written about in Canada, continental Europe and Latin America.[13] Many of these countries have adopted special safeguards, some as long ago as 1882.[14]

However, despite this growing body of evidence of the unreliability of eyewitness identifications, juries (and often attorneys and judges) remain in the dark and continue to consider an eyewitness' identification as the strongest form of evidence.[15] Okay, you say. This is an easy problem to remedy. Educate the jury. However, in the vast majority of courts today, expert testimony on the unreliability of eyewitness identifications is excluded as being unnecessary or misleading.[16]

The purpose of this paper is twofold: to educate the reader as to the unreliability of eyewitness identifications and to persuade the reader of the necessity of expert testimony on the subject.

---

[8] *See* Devenport, *supra*, n. 7, at 338. *See also* Sporer, *supra*, n. 2, at 4, tbl. 1.1.

[9] *See* Sporer, *supra*, n. 2, at 4, tbl. 1.1.

[10] *See* Huff, *supra*, n. 2.

[11] *See* Rattner, *supra*, n. 7, at 291, tbl. 6.

[12] The problem of the potential unreliability of eyewitness identification has been with us for a long time. In 1908, C.C. Moore published *A Treatise of Facts on the Weight and Value of Evidence*. In sections 1221 through 1231, the author discusses in depth the inherent unreliability of eyewitness identification. In 1932, E.M. Borchard, Professor of Law of Yale University, published his book, *Convicting the Innocent, Errors of Criminal Justice*, where he discusses 65 cases where innocent people were convicted as a result of erroneous eyewitness identification. These cases occurred in 27 different states. In his treatise, *The Science of Judicial Proof*, p. 537 (3rd ed. 1937), J.H. Wigmore states that the whole process involved in testimony going to the identity of persons calls for caution and precaution. In 3 Wigmore, *Evidence in Trials at Common Law* (rev. ed. 1970), by Professor J.H. Chadbourn of Harvard University, it is stated on pp. 205-206, that some of the most tragic miscarriages of justice have been due to testimonial errors in the area of eyewitness identification and the whole process therefore calls for caution.

[13] *See State* v. *Warren*, 635 *P.2d* 1236, 1240 (Kan. 1981). *See also* Murray, 'The Criminal Lineup at Home and Abroad' (1966), *Utah L. Rev.* 610 (hereinafter 'Murray').

[14] *See* Murray, *supra*, n. 13, at 1236.

[15] *See* S. Penrod & B. Cutler, 'Witness Confidence and Witness Accuracy: Assessing their Forensic Relation' (1995), 1 *Psychol. Pub. Pol'y & L.* 817, 825 (hereinafter 'Penrod & Cutler'); Cohen, *supra*, n. 7, at 250, citing E.F. Loftus & J.M. Doyle, *Eyewitness Testimony: Civil and Criminal, 2* (1987)(hereinafter 'Loftus & Doyle').

[16] *See* discussion, *infra*, at n. 185, to 190.

## Why do Juries Erroneously convict based on Eyewitness Testimony?

### a. Generally

Why do juries erroneously convict based on eyewitness testimony? The many problems with eyewitness testimony have been extensively studied and discussed in legal and scientific literature.[17] I will attempt to briefly discuss these problems and give a few examples of the many that have been catalogued. Generally, the problems with eyewitness identifications revolve around its persuasiveness, its inherent unreliability, the ignorance of jurors, judges and lawyers and, the concept of primacy.

### b. Persuasiveness

Eyewitness testimony has a powerful impact on juries.[18] As has been noted, there is nothing more convincing than a live human being who takes the stand, points a finger at the defendant and says, "That's the one".[19] Consider the case of Robert Bailey.[20] According to the testimony of two eyewitnesses, Mr Bailey murdered an individual.[21] However, according to the testimony of two police officers, Mr Bailey was under arrest for drunken driving at the time of the murder and could not have committed the crime.[22] Nevertheless, the jury convicted Mr Bailey *and sentenced him to death!*[23] Only 48 hours before execution, Mr Bailey obtained a reprieve and he spent 16 years in prison before finally being released from prison.[24]

Additionally, there have been numerous controlled studies of the effect of eyewitness testimony on juries. Those studies have consistently shown that neither the existence nor non-existence of physical evidence nor the

---

[17] *See, e.g.,* B.L. Cutler & S.D. Penrod, *Mistaken Identification: The Eyewitness, Psychology and the Law* (1995)(hereinafter 'Cutler & Penrod'); Loftus & Doyle, *supra*, n. 17; Cohen, *supra*, n. 9; M.R. Leippe, 'The Case for Expert Testimony About Eyewitness Memory', 1 *Psychol. Pub. Pol'y & L.* 909 (1995)(hereinafter 'Leippe'); Penrod & Cutler, *supra*, n. 17. For a comprehensive bibliography on eyewitness identification issues *see* Cutler & Penrod at 269.

[18] *See Watkins* v. *Sowders*, 449 *U.S.* 341, 350-352 (1981)(Marshall, J., dissenting).

[19] *See* E.F. Loftus, 'Eyewitness Testimony', 19 *Harvard* (1979)(hereinafter 'Loftus, Eyewitness'); *Watkins* v. *Sowders*, *supra*, n. 20, 449 *U.S.*, at 352.

[20] *State ex rel Bailey* v. *Skeen*, 340 *U.S.* 949 (1951).

[21] *See* H.A. Bedau & M.L. Radelet, 'Miscarriages of Justice in Potentially Capital Cases', 40 *Stan. L. Rev.* 21, 93 (1987)(hereinafter 'Bedau') as set forth in Unfortunate, *supra*, n. 4, at 328, n. 191.

[22] *Id.*

[23] *Id.*

[24] 48 hours before his scheduled execution, Mr Bailey received a reprieve when the warden, who believed in his innocence, contacted Erle Stanley Gardner for help. *Id.* citing E. Gardner, *The Court of Last Resort* 232-45 (1952); Gardner, 'Helping the Innocent' (1970), 17 *UCLA L. Rev.* 535, 539. Mr. Gardner was the creator of the character Perry Mason and the author of over 100 books. He was also the driving force behind a group of sleuths called 'The Court of Last Resort'. Unfortunate, *supra*, n. 4, at 328, n. 191.

consistency of testimony significantly influenced verdicts. However, the number of eyewitnesses for each side did produce significant results.[25] For example, in one study,[26] where there were no eyewitnesses for the prosecution, the jury returned guilty verdicts only 10% of the time; where there was one eyewitness, the number jumped to 34% of the time and where there were two eyewitnesses, the number jumped to 45% of the time.[27] In another study involving a purported store robbery,[28] where there were no eyewitnesses, the jury returned a guilty verdict 18% of the time. Where there was only *one* eyewitness and the remaining evidence stayed the same, the conviction rate rose to 72%![29] Even when the eyewitness was clearly impeached with the fact that the eyewitness was not wearing glasses and could not see well, the conviction rate only declined to 68%.[30] In a third study involving the passing of a bad check,[31] when eyewitnesses testified, 78% of the time, the jury convicted. When a handwriting expert and no eyewitness testified, the conviction rate dropped to 34%.[32] Even the use of fingerprint and lie detector evidence scored lower than eyewitness testimony.[33]

Studies also show that jurors overestimate the accuracy of eyewitness identifications,[34] cannot tell the difference between accurate and inaccurate identifications,[35] and base their decisions on witness confidence,[36] which has been found to be the strongest factor influencing jurors[37] (and one of the weakest indicators of accuracy).[38] Take, for example, the case of an eighteen-year-old who had been sexually assaulted.[39] Shortly after the assault, she described her attacker as a white male with a full beard, a reddish blonde 'Afro' and a web-like cross-tattooed on his left hand. 15 months later, the victim viewed a photographic lineup in which the suspect alone had a beard.

---

[25] *See* Devenport, *supra*, n. 7, at 349-350.
[26] *Id.*
[27] *Id.*
[28] *See* Cohen, *supra*, n. 7, at 250, citing Loftus & Doyle, *supra*, n. 15, at 2.
[29] *Id.*
[30] *Id.*
[31] *See* Cohen, *supra*, n. 7, at 251, citing Loftus & Doyle, *supra*, n. 15, at 5.
[32] *Id.*
[33] *Id.*
[34] *See* Cohen, *supra*, n. 7, at 250, citing Loftus & Doyle, *supra*, n. 15, at 2; Penrod & Cutler, *supra*, n. 15, at 825.
[35] *Id.*
[36] *See* Penrod & Cutler, *supra*, n. 15, at 825; Cohen, *supra*, n. 7, at 250, citing Loftus & Doyle, *supra*, n. 15, at 2.
[37] *Id.*
[38] *See* Cohen, *supra*, n. 7, at 250, citing Loftus & Doyle, *supra*, n. 15, at 3; G.L. Wells & D.M. Murray, 'Eyewitness Confidence', in: *Eyewitness Testimony* 165 (Cambridge University Press 1984)(hereinafter 'Wells & Murray').
[39] *See* Cohen, *supra*, n. 7, at 255, citing C. Mayer, 'Due Process Challenges to Eyewitness Identification Based on Pretrial Photographic Arrays' (1994), 13 *Pace L. Rev.* 815, 816-817 (hereinafter 'Mayer').

victim viewed a photographic lineup in which the suspect alone had a beard. She pointed to the suspect saying, "That's him". Two months later, he was arrested. After his arrest, the victim again identified him in a live lineup after being told that the person she had identified in the photo lineup was also in the live lineup. Again, the suspect was the only one in the lineup with a beard. The prosecution was based almost entirely on the visual identification. At the trial, two years after the attack, the victim was *absolutely certain* of her identification and, in less than 90 minutes, the defendant was found guilty. The jurors stated that it was the victims' absolute confidence that convinced them to convict for six years the defendant insisted he was innocent. This was finally proven true by indisputable DNA evidence.[40]

### c. Unreliability

Despite its persuasive effect, eyewitness testimony is "notoriously unreliable"[41] and "proverbially untrustworthy".[42] Consider the results of the following studies. In one study,[43] students were sent into various convenience stores and told to engage the store clerk for several minutes. About two hours later, the clerks were asked to identify the student in a lineup. Seventy-three clerks participated and identified a person as the student 146 times. The student was in the lineup only 50 times; thus, the clerks identified *the wrong person* 66%![44] In another study of clerks in convenience stores,[45] when the student was in the lineup, the clerks correctly identified him only 41% of the time. When the student was not in the lineup at all, the clerks identified the wrong person 34% of the time.[46] And, in a third study of convenience store clerks,[47] the clerks were wrong 56% of the time.[48] Yet another study was done in a bank setting where the student was directed to engage the teller for about

---

[40] *Id.*

[41] *Watkins* v. *Sowders, supra*, n. 18, 449 *U.S.*, at 350-52.

[42] *US* v. *Wade*, 388 *U.S.* 218, 228 (1967)(Felix Frankfurter, J.).

[43] *See* J.C. Brigham, A. Maass, L.D. Snyder & K. Spaulding, 'Accuracy of Eyewitness Identifications in a Field Setting' (1982), 42 *Journal of Personality and Social Psychology* 673-680 (hereinafter 'Brigham'). *See also* C. Krafka & S. Penrod, 'Reinstatement of Context in a Field Experiment on Eyewitness Identification' (1985), 49 *Journal of Personality and Social Psychology* 58-69 (hereinafter 'Krafka'); M.A. Pigott, J.C. Brigham & R.K. Bothwell, 'A Field Study of the Relationship Between Quality of Eyewitnesses' Descriptions and Identification Accuracy' (1990), 17 *Journal of Police Science and Administration* 84-88 (hereinafter 'Pigott'); S.J. Platz & H.M. Hosch, 'Cross-racial/ethnic Eyewitness Identification: A Field Study' (1988)(bank setting), 18 *Journal of Applied Social Psychology* 972-984 (hereinafter 'Platz'); Devenport, *supra*, n. 7, at 339.

[44] *Id.*

[45] *Id.*; Devenport, *supra*, n. 7, at 338-339.

[46] *Id.*

[47] *Id.*; Devenport, *supra*, n. 7, at 339.

[48] *Id.*

questioned four to five hours later. When the student was present in the lineup, the tellers were only correct 48% of the time; when the student was not in the lineup, the tellers incorrectly identified someone else 38% of the time.[50]

Eyewitness identification is based on one psychological component: memory. And, although we joke about having 'photographic' memories, a number of researchers have shown that when a person experiences an important event, he does not simply "record it in memory like a videotape".[51] Rather, most analysts divide the memory process into three major stages. First, a witness perceives the event, and the information is entered into the memory system. This is called the *acquisition stage*. Next, some time passes before a witness attempts to remember the event, and this is called the *retention stage*. Finally, the witness tries to recall the stored information, and this is called the *retrieval stage*.[52]

The acquisition stage is affected by event factors and witness factors. Event factors include such things as lighting, length of event, distance involved, and the presence or absence of violence.[53] Witness factors include such things as event stress, fear (*e.g.* 'weapon focus'), life stress (recent negative life changes cause small memory deficits),[54] witness expectations, age (the very young and very old have unique problems) and gender.[55] The retention stage is affected by the length of retention intervals and post-event information.[56] Finally, the retrieval stage is influenced by the method of questioning and the confidence level of the witness.[57]

## The Acquisition Stage

When a person witnesses a crime, "a great deal of sensory input is acquired in an emotionally disturbing environment."[58] There is a considerable amount of experimental data that perceptual accuracy is greatest at moderate levels of stress but decreases significantly as stress increases[59] and, although it is commonly believed that witnesses remember better when under stress,[60] the

---

[50] *Id.*
[51] *See* Loftus & Doyle, *supra*, n. 15, at 10.
[52] *Id.*
[53] *See* E.F. Loftus *et al.*, 'The Psychology of Eyewitness Testimony', in: *Psychological Methods in Criminal Investigation and Evidence* 6-13 (D.C. Raskin (ed.) 1989)(hereinafter 'Loftus, Psychology').
[54] *See* Loftus & Doyle, *supra*, n. 15, at 31.
[55] *See* Loftus & Doyle, *supra*, n. 15, at 38-41; Loftus, Psychology, *supra*, n. 53, at 13-25.
[56] *See* Loftus & Doyle, *supra*, n. 15, at 59.
[57] *See* Loftus & Doyle, *supra*, n. 15, at 64.
[58] *See* Cohen, *supra*, n. 7, at 243, citing Loftus, Psychology, *supra*, n. 53, at 19 and Loftus & Doyle, *supra*, n. 15, at 11.
[59] *See* Cohen, *supra*, n. 7, at 243, citing Loftus, Psychology, *supra*, n. 53, at 33.
[60] *See* Cohen, *supra*, n. 7, at 243, citing Loftus & Doyle, *supra*, n. 15, at 27. *See also US* v. *Sebetich*, 776 *F.2d* 412, 419 (5ᵗʰ Cir. 1997).

opposite is actually true.[61] Consider, for example, a recent mice experiment at the University of Southern Florida. In 1998, psychology professor David Diamond placed mice in a controlled environment. In the environment was a pool of water and, just below the surface of the waterline, a 'secret' exit to another chamber of the environment. The mice learned the location of the exit and perfected their method of escape through the hidden chamber. Then a cat – an element of stress – entered the environment. Not one of the mice could remember the location of the secret exit, proving that stress affects memory.[62]

Studies have also shown that eyewitness identifications are even *less* accurate when a weapon is present than when no weapon is used.[63] This is true because crime victims spend far more time concentrating on the weapon than in processing other aspects of the crime.[64] This is commonly known as 'weapon focus'.[65] Studies have shown that subjecting a person to a holdup or murder diminishes their ability to perceive, remember and recall.[66] And, yet, a juror would be more inclined to believe the victim than an uninvolved witness.

How we see an event depends on what we believe and what we expect.[67] Consider the story of five men who went on a deer-hunting trip, during which their car broke down.[68] Two of the men went for help while the other three stayed behind with the car. Unknown to those who stayed behind, one of the men who went for help doubled back and continued to look for deer in the forest. When those remaining with the car saw a movement in the forest, they perceived it as a deer and shot it. At their trial for negligent homicide, one of the defendants exclaimed, "In my thoughts and my eyes, it was a deer".[69] In another study,[70] participants looked at a picture of a New York subway car in which a neatly dressed African-American man wore a tie while a white man held a razor blade. The two men were in a heated discussion. When recalling the drawing, over half the witnesses mistakenly recalled that the razor was in the hand of the black man.[71]

---

[61] *See* Cohen, *supra*, n. 7, at 243, citing Loftus, Psychology, *supra*, n. 53, at 33. *See also US* v. *Norwood*, 939 *F. Supp.* 1132, 1137 (D.N.J. 1996).

[62] *See* D.M. Diamond *et al.*, *New Frontiers in Stress Research Modulation of Brain Function* 117 (Aharon Levy *et al.* (eds.) 1998)(hereinafter 'Diamond') as told in Unfortunate, *supra*, n. 4, at 316-317.

[63] *See US* v. *Norwood*, *supra*, n. 61, at 1137; Unfortunate, *supra*, n. 4, at 121, 314.

[64] *See* Loftus & Doyle, *supra*, n. 15, at 30.

[65] *Id.*

[66] *See* Leippe, *supra*, n. 17, at 917.

[67] *See* Unfortunate, *supra*, n. 4, at 315; Loftus, Eyewitness, *supra*, n. 19, at 37.

[68] *See* Cohen, *supra*, n. 7, at 245, citing Loftus, Eyewitness, *supra*, n. 19, at 36-37.

[69] *Id.*

[70] *See* G.W. Allport & L. Postman, *The Psychology of Rumor* 71 (1947)(hereinafter 'Allport'); Cohen, *supra*, n. 7, at 245, citing Loftus, Eyewitness, *supra*, n. 19, at 38.

[71] *See* Cohen, *supra*, n. 97 at 245, citing Loftus, Eyewitness, *supra*, n. 19, at 38.

Although the interaction of expectations and race are important due to cultural expectations that represent classic stereotyping,[72] there is yet a more serious problem at the acquisition stage that relates to race: cross-racial misidentification.[73] Substantial scientific proof exists that *all* people have difficulty in identifying persons of another race.[74] Although often derided as racial stereotyping, studies show that people are simply better at recognizing faces of persons of their own race than of a different race.[75] Unfortunately, whether pejorative or not, cross-racial misidentifications are disproportionately responsible for wrongful convictions.[76] And, contrary to widely held assumptions, racial attitudes and amount of interracial experience cannot be related systematically to recognition accuracy for any race since it is unrelated to prejudice and inexperience.[77] However, "some jurors may deny the existence of cross-racial misidentification in the misguided belief that it is merely a racist myth exemplified by the derogatory remark, 'They all look alike to me', while others may believe in the reality of this effect but be reluctant to discuss it in jury deliberations for fear of being perceived as bigots themselves."[78] And, to further complicate the problem, judges have also developed a reluctance to even admit the existence of the problem, let alone provide the jury with the information necessary to evaluate its impact.[79]

**The Retention Stage**

Mental processes continue between the time an event is perceived and when it might be recalled. This is known as the retention stage.[80] We all joke about our memories. However, it is scientific fact that most forgetting takes place within the first hours following an event or, in any event, within the first few days.[81] Furthermore, as that memory data bank loses information, it also tends to fill those voids with post-event information. It is not uncommon for a witness to discuss an exciting event during the months that follow it.[82] This post-event exposure to new information can dramatically effect memory of the original event.[83] Called "transference",[84] post-event information cannot only *enhance*

---

[72] *See* Loftus, Eyewitness, *supra*, n. 19, at 37; *see US* v. *Telfaire*, 469 F.2d 552 (D.C. Cir. 1972).
[73] For a discussion of cross-racial studies, *see* S.L. Johnson, 'Cross-Racial Identification Errors in Criminal Cases', 69 *Cornell L. Rev.* 934 (1984)(hereinafter 'Johnson').
[74] *See* Johnson, *supra*, n. 73, at 938.
[75] *See* Loftus, Eyewitness, *supra*, n. 19, at 136.
[76] *See* Johnson, *supra*, n. 73, at 938.
[77] *See* Loftus, Eyewitness, *supra*, n. 19, at 137-138.
[78] *People* v. *McDonald*, 690 P.2d 709, 721(Cal. 1984)(en banc).
[79] *See US* v. *Telfaire*, *supra*, n. 72, 469 F.2d at 559; *US* v. *Downing*, 753 F.2d 1224, 1231 (3d Cir. 1985): "studies demonstrate the inherent unreliability of cross racial identifications".
[80] *See* Loftus & Doyle, *supra*, n. 15, at 11.
[81] *See US* v. *Norwood*, *supra*, n. 61, at 1138.
[82] *See* Cohen, *supra*, n. 7, at 246.
[83] *See* Loftus, Eyewitness, *supra*, n. 19, at 64.

existing memories but can *change* a witness' memory and even cause nonexistent details to become incorporated into a previously acquired memory.[85] When a witness later learns new information that conflicts with the original input, many will compromise between what they saw and what they were later told.[86] The changes to the witness' recollection result because "memory is not a static imprint but is effected by events occurring after the initial perception."[87] Memory is constantly changing and with each flux, reliability is diminished.[88]

Consider the case of Walter Snyder, Jr.[89] After the rape of a woman in his neighborhood, the police photographed Mr Snyder and placed his picture in a photographic lineup. However, after viewing the lineup, the victim, who did not know Mr Snyder, failed to identify him as the perpetrator. Seeing Mr Snyder washing his car a few days later, though, she became convinced that he was the rapist and he was later convicted. Six and one-half years later, Mr Snyder was proven innocent through DNA tests.[90]

Another not uncommon situation is where a picture of a familiar person the eyewitness might see in an everyday situation (*e.g.* as a customer in a neighborhood store or restaurant or another student at school or co-worker at a business) shows up in a lineup. The eyewitness may relate their familiarity with the person to the crime rather than to the other circumstance.[91]

**The Retrieval Stage**

Finally, in a criminal setting, the eyewitness must get the information from his or her memory and give it to another person, usually the police, then a judge and/or jury. At this stage of retrieval, the presentation and form of the retrieval inquiry can significantly affect an eyewitness' memory.[92]

In a lineup situation, three things can affect the eyewitness' recall: foil bias (how much the others in the lineup, the 'foils', resemble the suspect), instruction bias (how much the instructions given to the eyewitness influence

---

[84] *See* Cohen, *supra*, n. 7, at 249, citing Loftus, Eyewitness, *supra*, n. 19, at 142. *See also US* v. *Norwood*, *supra*, n. 61, 939 F. Supp. at 1137.

[85] *See* Loftus, Eyewitness, *supra*, n. 19, at 55. *See also Arizona* v. *Chapple*, 660 P.2d 1208, 1221 (Ariz. 1983).

[86] *See* Cohen, *supra*, n. 7, at 247, citing Loftus, Eyewitness, *supra*, n. 19, at 56.

[87] Unfortunate, *supra*, n.4, at 316

[88] P.J. Neusfeld, 'Have You No Sense of Decency?' (1993), 84 *J. Crim. L. & Criminology* 189, 197 (hereinafter 'Neusfeld').

[89] Neusfeld, at 197-98.

[90] *Id.* Under Virginia law, Mr Snyder was ineligible for a new trial. On April 23, 1993, Governor Douglas Wilder pardoned Mr Snyder. Mr Snyder served seven years of a 45-year sentence for rape.

[91] *See* Cohen, *supra*, n. 7, at 249, citing Loftus, Eyewitness, *supra*, n. 19, at 142.

[92] *See* Cohen, *supra*, n. 7, at 247, citing Loftus, Eyewitness, *supra*, n. 19, at 77.

his choice), and presentation bias (whether persons are presented sequentially, one at a time or in a group).[93]

*Foil and instruction bias*: obviously, the less the other members of a lineup look like the suspect, the more probable it is that the eyewitness will pick the only one who looks like the person she thought she saw (foil bias). Further complicating the process, the mere knowledge that the suspect has been included in the lineup can affect the witness' response.[94] If an eyewitness is told to point out the person he saw commit the crime, he is more likely to choose someone – anyone – than if he is told that the lineup may or may not contain the person he saw commit the crime and to tell the questioner whether or not he sees him.[95] For example, in one study where the offender was *not* in the lineup,[96] when the eyewitness was told to point out the person he saw commit the crime, 78% of the time he pointed to someone whereas when the eyewitness was told the offender may or may not be in the lineup, he only pointed out an offender 33% of the time.[97]

*Presentation bias*: it has also proven to make a significant difference if the eyewitness is shown the suspects one by one and instructed to tell the questioner whether or not the person is the one who committed the crime on each person without the ability to go back and reconsider rather than if he is shown five people all together at one time.[98] Consider, would you rather a short-answer test or a multiple choice? A simultaneous presentation allows the witness to compare the persons in the lineup, therefore performing a discrimination task whereas a sequential presentation requires the witness to

---

[93] *See* R.C.L. Lindsay & G.L. Wells, 'What Price Justice? Exploring the Relationship of Lineup Fairness to Identification Accuracy' (1980), 4 *Law & Human Behavior* 303-314 (hereinafter 'Lindsay & Wells'). *See also* G.L. Wells & R.C.L. Lindsay, 'On Estimating the Diagnosticity of Eyewitness Nonidentifications' (1980), 88 *Psychological Bulletin* 776-784 (hereinafter 'Wells & Lindsay').

[94] *See* Loftus & Doyle, *supra*, n. 15, at 82.

[95] It also reduces the chances of an improper identification if these instructions are read rather than stated without prompting. *See* Loftus & Doyle, *supra*, n. 15, at 82, 83; B.L. Cutler, S.D. Penrod & T.K. Martens, 'The Reliability of Eyewitness Identifications: The Role of System and Estimator Variables' (1987), 11 *Law and Human Behavior* 233-258 (hereinafter 'Martens'); R.S. Malpass & P.G. Devine, 'Eyewitness Identification: Lineup Instructions and the Absence of the Offender' (1981), 66 *Journal of Applied Psychology* 482-489 (hereinafter 'Malpass'); B. Paley & R.E. Geiselman, 'The Effects of Alternative Photospread Instructions on Suspect Identification Performance' (1989), 7 *American Journal of Forensic Psychology* 3-13 (hereinafter 'Paley'); Devenport, *supra*, n. 7, at 342-343.

[96] *See* Loftus & Doyle, *supra*, n. 15, at 82.

[97] *Id.*

[98] *See* L. Lindsay & Fulford, 'Sequential Lineup Presentation: Technique Matters' (1991), 76 *Journal of Applied Psychology* 741-745 (hereinafter 'Lindsay, Lea'); R.C. Lindsay, J.A. Lea, G.J. Nosworthy, J.A. Fulford, J. Hector, V. LeVan & C. Seabrook, 'Biased Lineups: Sequential Presentation Reduces the Problem' (1991), 76 *Journal of Applied Psychology* 796-802 (hereinafter 'Nosworthy'); Lindsay & Wells, 'Improving Eyewitness Identifications From Lineups: Simultaneous versus Sequential Lineup Presentations' (1985), 70 *Journal of Applied Psychology* 556-564 (hereinafter 'Lindsey, Improving').

perform a more recall-oriented task when he compares each suspect with his memory bank rather than with each other.[99]

How a witness is questioned, whether pretrial or during the trial, is of great importance and easily subject to bias.[100] Forming questions so as to affect answers is a classic trial advocacy technique. Why? Well, for one thing, simply mentioning an object in a question has been shown to significantly increase the chances that the witness will 'remember' it.[101] At the same time, not mentioning the object in the question can result in its being forgotten.[102] Consider the following studies.

In study number one,[103] volunteers became 'eyewitnesses' of sorts when they observed a movie of an intersection collision caused by a failure of one car to obey a stop sign that was clearly visible in the film. When asked "How fast was the car going when it ran the stop sign?", 53% of the 'eyewitnesses' later said they saw the stop sign. When asked "How fast was the car going when it turned right?," only 35% of the 'eyewitnesses' later said they saw a stop sign.[104]

In study number two,[105] the two groups of volunteers/eyewitnesses were either asked "How fast were the cars going when they *crashed* into each other?" or "How fast were the cars going when they *hit* each other?" The first group estimated a faster speed and 32% of them later said they saw glass at the collision site. The second group estimated the cars were going slower and only 14% saw glass at the collision site. *There was NO glass at the collision site!*[106]

In a third study, in a textbook trial advocacy outcome, when eyewitnesses were asked how *tall* a suspect was, they estimated 79 inches average. When asked how *short* a suspect was, they estimated 69 inches![107]

Finally, although intuitively it is inconceivable that a very confident eyewitness could be dead wrong, the confidence a witness has in her identification has little to no correlation to accuracy.[108] Consider the case of

---

[99] *See* G.L. Wells, 'How Adequate is Human Intuition for Judging Eyewitness Testimony?', in: G.L. Wells & E.F. Loftus (eds.), *Eyewitness Testimony: Psychological Perspectives*, New York: Cambridge University Press, 1984, pp. 256-272 (hereinafter 'Wells & Loftus'). Despite this finding, one survey found that out of 220 police departments, less then 10% use the sequential lineup. *See* M.S. Wogalter, R.S. Malpass & M.A. Burger, 'How Police Officers Conduct Lineups: A National Survey' (1993), 37 *Proceedings of the Human Factors and Ergonomics Society* 640-644 (hereinafter 'Wogalter').

[100] *See* Cohen, *supra*, n. 7, at 247, citing Loftus, Eyewitness, *supra*, n. 19, at 77.

[101] *See* Loftus, Eyewitness, *supra*, n. 19, at 56.

[102] *Id.*

[103] *See* Loftus, Eyewitness, *supra*, n. 19, at 55-56.

[104] *Id.*

[105] *See* Loftus, Eyewitness, *supra*, n. 19, at 77-78.

[106] *Id.*

[107] *See* Loftus, Eyewitness, *supra*, n. 19, at 94.

[108] *See* Cohen, *supra*, n. 7, at 250, citing Loftus & Doyle, *supra*, n. 15, at 2; Wells & Murray, *supra*, n. 38, at 165.

Catherine Secor, on which the movie 'Sommersby' was loosely based.[109] On Christmas Day in 1800, Catherine Secor married Thomas Hoag. By March of 1801, Hoag had left and never returned. The abandoned wife pressed a bigamy suit arising from this marriage against a resident of New York, one Joseph Parker. Both sides of the controversy offered direct eyewitness testimony. Secor and an array of witnesses swore that Hoag and Parker was the same person. Secor and her witnesses had known this man for several months, convinced that he was Mr Hoag. Parker's witnesses stated that Parker was in New York at the time of the short marriage and did not leave the city, making it an impossibility that Parker was Hoag. The court held against Secor and her witnesses. The decision hinged upon the fact that Thomas Hoag had a scar on the bottom of his foot and Parker did not. Incredibly, Catherine Secor had testified mistakenly concerning the identity of her own husband and, despite the final verdict, continued to maintain the Parker was her husband![110]

A 1987 study[111] of 35 eyewitnesses indicated that confident eyewitnesses were only slightly more accurate than those who were not confident.[112] Other studies have indicated that witnesses can be *more* confident when incorrect than when correct.[113] Furthermore, a number of other studies have shown that eyewitnesses who have publicly stated their choice will stick with that choice even when incorrect 78% of the time![114]

**Jurors do not know**

Did you believe at some time in your life that eyewitness testimony was the most reliable evidence? You would not be alone if you did. Numerous studies have shown that *most* people believe this to be so[115] and that the general public also believes that eyewitness identification is simple.[116] The average juror is unaware of the unreliability of eyewitness identifications and that the issues surrounding memory processing are complex and counterintuitive.[117] And, if the juror thinks memory is simple, it will be unlikely to consider the internal

---

[109] See J.K. Riley, 'A Remarkable Case of Disputed Identity' (1998), 70 Feb. *N.Y.St.B.J.* 8 (hereinafter 'Riley').

[110] *Id.*

[111] See R.K. Bothwell, K.A. Deffenbacher & J.C. Brigham, 'Correlation of Eyewitness Accuracy and Confidence: Optimality Hypothesis Revisited' (1987), 72 *Journal of Applied Psychology* 691-695 (hereinafter 'Bothwell').

[112] *Id.*

[113] See Cohen, *supra*, n. 7, at 250, citing Loftus, Eyewitness, *supra*, n. 19, at 101.

[114] See Loftus & Doyle, *supra*, n. 15, at 82.

[115] See Cohen, *supra*, n. 7, at 272.

[116] See Cohen, *supra*, n. 7, at 241, citing Loftus & Doyle, *supra*, n. 15, at 6.

[117] See Unfortunate, *supra*, n. 4, at 309; R.L. Valladares & F. Forsman, 'Attacking Reliability of Eyewitness Testimony After Daubert' (1997), 21 Jun. *Champion* 60, 61 (NACDL)(hereinafter 'Valladares') citing Cutler & Penrod, *supra*, n. 19, at 207-209; Cohen, *supra*, n. 7, at 268-269 citing *People* v. *McDonald*, 690 *P.2d* 709, 720 (Cal. 1984)*(en banc)*.

and external factors that might affect it.[118] You see, counterintuitive evidence –
evidence that runs counter to common sense – deludes a jury.[119] Studies show
that jurors overbelieve eyewitnesses, that they have great difficulty
distinguishing between accurate and inaccurate eyewitness testimony and that
they give much too much weight to witness confidence.[120]

Numerous experiments have been conducted where simulated crimes have
been committed in front of mock eyewitnesses and then the eyewitness is
asked to identify the perpetrator. Mock jurors are then asked to 'postdict'[121]
how correct the eyewitness was in his identification. Research conducted using
this methodology has found that laypersons often predict higher witness
identification accuracy rates than are generally found. In one study,[122] a theft
was staged. Where the witnesses were told that the value of the object stolen
was low, they only correctly identified the perpetrator 19% of the time.[123] The
mock jurors postdicted that they would accurately identify the perpetrator 66%
of the time.[124] Where the mock jurors were not told that the value of the object
stolen was high until after they witnessed the crime, they only correctly
identified the perpetrator 13% of the time.[125] The mock jurors postdicted the
witnesses accuracy to be 60%.[126]

Another study involved a staged vandalism where the eyewitnesses read
about a perpetrator absent lineup.[127] When the witnesses were given biased
instructions, they incorrectly identified a suspect 78% of the time.[128] The mock
jurors postdicted that they would be wrong only 16% of the time.[129] Even
when given unbiased instructions, the witnesses were wrong 33% of the
time.[130] The mock jurors postdicted inaccuracy at an even higher rate: 18%.[131]

---

[118] *See* Cohen, *supra*, n. 7, at 273.

[119] *See* Valladares, *supra*, n. 117, at 61.

[120] *See* Penrod & Cutler, *supra*, n. 15, at 825.

[121] Postdiction is having laypersons 'predict' the outcome of previously conducted eyewitness
identification experiments before knowing the actual results. During postdiction studies, students
and laypersons read written summaries of an eyewitness identification experiment and then
postdict the identification accuracy rates of the participants in the original experiment. By
comparing the postdicted identification accuracy rates with the experimental results, researchers
are able to assess the sensitivity of prospective jurors to the specific factors manipulated in the
experiment. Devenport, *supra*, n. 7, at 346.

[122] *Id.*

[123] *See* M.R. Leippe, G.L. Wells & T.M. Ostrum, 'Crime Seriousness as a Determinant of
Accuracy in Eyewitness Identification' (1978), 63 *Journal of Applied Psychology* 345-351
(hereinafter 'Leippe & Wells'). *See also* Devenport, *supra*, n. 7, at 347.

[124] *See* Devenport, *supra*, n. 7, at 346-347.

[125] *Id.*

[126] *Id.*

[127] *Id.*

[128] *See* Wells & Loftus, *supra*, n. 99, at 256-272.

[129] *See* Devenport, *supra*, n. 7, at 347

[130] *Id.*

[131] *Id.*

Obviously, the participants were clearly unaware of a factor that clearly contributes to misidentification – instruction bias.

In a cross-racial misidentification study,[132] only 32% of white clerks correctly identified black perpetrators.[133] The mock jurors estimated that the eyewitnesses would be correct 51% of the time.[134] Only 31% of the black clerks correctly identified white perpetrators.[135] Mock jurors estimated accuracy at 70%,[136] obviously indicating a misperception about the ability of blacks to correctly identify whites.

In yet another study of the effect of using leading versus non-leading questions,[137] jurors were only able to identify inaccurate witnesses 14% of the time when non-leading questions were used and 27% of the time when leading questions were used.[138] That means that over 70% of the time, the mock jurors believed the witness who was wrong... three out of four times, the jurors could have rendered the wrong verdict!

In a number of other studies of factors which effect verdicts,[139] although jurors might have been sensitive to some of the following, they were *not* found to significantly effect verdicts: presence or lack of physical evidence, inconsistent testimony, level of detail in testimony, foil bias and instruction bias, presentation bias, disguise, presence of weapon, violence, retention interval, and relative alibi.[140] On the other hand, the number of eyewitnesses had a high correlation to the verdict and the existence of a non-relative alibi was significant but the most significant, most relied on factor in a trial still proved to be eyewitness confidence.[141]

Why is this so? Perhaps because jurors naturally empathize with the personal account of a person who has endured horrendous hardship and are slow to believe him to be mistaken or guilty of perjury.[142] You see, as between any two stories, jurors are likely to choose the one that most closely comports with

---

[132] J.C. Brigham & R.K. Bothwell, 'The Ability of Prospective Jurors to Estimate the Accuracy of Eyewitness Identifications', 7 *Law and Human Behavior* 19-30 (1983)(hereinafter 'Brigham & Bothwell'). Brigham and Bothwell gave their participants descriptions of Brigham's 1982 cross-race recognition studies set forth in Brigham, *supra*, n. 43.

[133] *See* Devenport, *supra*, n. 7, at 347.

[134] *Id.*

[135] *Id.*

[136] *Id.*

[137] G.L. Wells, R.C.L. Lindsay & T.J. Ferguson, 'Accuracy, Confidence, and Juror Perceptions in Eyewitness Identification' (1979), 64 *Journal of Applied Psychology* 440-448 (hereinafter 'Ferguson'). *See also* Devenport, *supra*, n. 7, at 348, 349.

[138] *Id.*

[139] *See* Cutler *et al.* (1988); Lindsay *et al.* (1986); Devenport, *supra*, n. 7, at 350, 353; B.E. Bell & E.F. Loftus, 'Trivial Persuasion in the Courtroom: The Power of (a Few) Minor Details' (1989), 56 *Journal of Personality and Social Psychology* 669-679 (hereinafter 'Bell').

[140] *Id.*

[141] *Id.*

[142] *See* R.H. Underwood, 'The Limits of Cross-Examination' (1997), 21 *Am. J. Trial Advoc.* 113, 122 (hereinafter 'Underwood').

their own experience and appeals to common sense.[143] And, as stated before, the inaccuracy and unreliability of eyewitness identifications is counterintuitive and does not 'appeal to common sense'.

**Solutions**

So, here we are with numerous studies showing that the average juror does not understand the science behind memory and eyewitness identification, cannot tell the difference between an accurate and inaccurate witness and is, therefore, too often sending innocent person to jail. What can be done?

"An important theme in American criminal jurisprudence is that a jury can sift through conflicting claims to arrive at a correct verdict, and that vigorous direct and cross-examination combined with the court's instruction of how to apply law to fact will suffice to achieve justice."[144] Thus, traditionally, five devices have been used to 'correct' the problem of erroneous eyewitness identifications: presence of counsel at post-indictment lineups, motions to suppress identifications, cross-examination, jury instructions, and closing arguments.[145] These safeguards, however, are a based on assumptions regarding attorney, judge and juror commonsense knowledge of the factors influencing eyewitness identification accuracy.[146] As will be seen below, although these devices help to a degree, they are not sufficient to solve the problem.

*Counsel:* in the US, a defendant has only had a right to have an attorney available at a post-indictment lineup since 1967[147] and has no right to counsel at photographic lineups[148] or at lineups conducted prior to being charged with a crime.[149] Needless to say, law enforcement agencies now hold live lineups *prior to* indictment whenever possible or using photographic lineups.[150] Thus, the right to counsel to protect a suspect in a lineup identification situation is fairly empty.

Furthermore, many studies[151] have shown that although lawyers have some commonsense knowledge about the effects of race, stress/violence,[152] lighting,

---

[143] *See* S. Lubet, *Modern Trial Advocacy: Analysis and Practice* 389 (NITA 1993)(hereinafter 'Lubet').

[144] Cohen, *supra*, n. 7, at 258.

[145] *See US* v. *Wade, supra*, n. 44, 388 *U.S.* 218, *Kirby* v. *Illinois*, 406 *U.S.* 682 (1971), *US* v. *Ash*, 413 *U.S.* 300 (U.S.D.Col. 1973).

[146] *See* Devenport, *supra*, n. 7, at 338, 339.

[147] *US* v. *Wade, supra*, n. 42, 388 *U.S.*, at 220.

[148] *US* v. *Ash, supra*, n. 145, 413 *U.S.* 300.

[149] *Kirby* v. *Illinois, supra*, n. 145, 406 *U.S.* 682.

[150] *See* Loftus, Eyewitness, *supra*, n. 19, at 185. *See also* S.E. Holtshouser, 'Eyewitness Identification Testimony and the Need for Cautionary Jury Instructions in Criminal Cases' (1983), 60 *Wash.U.L.Q.* 1387, 1388-89 (hereinafter 'Holtshouser').

[151] *See* J.C. Brigham & M.P. Wolfskiel, 'Opinions of Attorneys and Law Enforcement Personnel on the Accuracy of Eyewitness Identifications' (1983), 42 *Journal of Personality and Social* (to be continued)

viewing conditions and foil bias,[153] they have less knowledge/sensitivity to instruction bias and they lack knowledge regarding eyewitness confidence and presentation bias.[154] Without this key knowledge or sensitivity, counsel cannot be very effective protection.[155]

*Suppression:* motions to suppress evidence are used to exclude evidence which has been unconstitutionally obtained or which might be admitted in violation of a person's constitutional rights, generally their right to due process. Decisions on motions to suppress are made by judges. One of the severe problems with our system is that many judges believe that an eyewitness is the most reliable of witnesses[156] and that jurors are fully capable of determining credibility through perceiving cross-examination.[157] Judges, generally, are sensitive to foil and instruction bias, but, even where they exist, tend to be concerned about entering the jury's 'province' of assessing credibility.[158] Studies show, however, that judges are generally unaware of presentation bias and, in fact, view sequential lineups as more suggestive than simultaneous lineups.[159] Unfortunately, most judges tend not to suppress unless there is a constitutional right to counsel issue present, which, as we have seen above, is rare.

*Cross-examination:* under the American adversary system of justice, cross-examination has always been considered the most effective way to ascertain the truth.[160] However, cross-examination is based on the jury having a base of knowledge from which to draw inferences from counsel's questions and the witness' answer[161] – no witness *admits* they are wrong, mistaken or lying! The problem is that many of the problems inherent in eyewitness testimony, as we have seen, are counterintuitive and contradict common beliefs.[162] Consequently, cross-examination may not be effective. For example, unless a juror understands the effect the form of a question has on memory, a question

---

*Psychology*, 673-680 (hereinafter 'Brigham & Wolfskiel'); G.L. Rahaim & S.L. Brodsky, 'Empirical Evidence versus Common Sense: Juror and Lawyer Knowledge of Eyewitness Accuracy' (1982), 7 *Law and Psychology Review*, 1-15 (hereinafter 'Rahaim'); V. Stinson, J.L. Devenport, B.L. Cutler & D.A. Kravitz, 'How Effective is the Presence-of-Counsel Safeguard? Attorney Perceptions of Suggestiveness, Fairness, and Correctability of Biased Lineup Procedures' (1996), 81 *Journal of Applied Psychology*, 64-75 (hereinafter 'Stinson'); Penrod & Cutler, *supra*, n. 15, at 817-845.

[152] *See* Devenport, *supra*, n. 7, at 340-341, citing Penrod & Cutler, *id.*
[153] *See* Devenport, *supra*, n. 7, at 343.
[154] *Id.*, citing Penrod & Cutler, *id.*
[155] *Id.*
[156] *See State* v. *Warren*, *supra*, n. 13, 635 *P.2d*, at 1241.
[157] *Id.*
[158] *See* Devenport, *supra*, n. 7, at 345.
[159] *Id.*
[160] *See Watkins* v. *Sowders*, *supra*, n. 18, 449 *U.S.*, at 349.
[161] *See* Devenport, *supra*, n. 7, at 346.
[162] *See* Valladares, *supra*, n. 117, at 61.

to the eyewitness about whether he was asked by the police if the suspect was tall or short, will not only go over a juror's head, it may serve to mislead and confuse him. As another example, rather than helping, cross-examination can exacerbate the problem of witness confidence.[163] If a witness honestly believes his or her testimony is accurate and his response to cross-examination exudes confidence, then the jury will accept that identification and the 'badgering' attorney will be disliked.[164]

*Jury instructions:* in the US, some courts give instructions on eyewitness identifications while others do not.[165] However, except for California,[166] even where instructions are given, they do not go far enough and basically point out problems that jurors have commonsense knowledge of, such as physical problems, but do not instruct the jury on the physiology and psychology of the memory process.[167] Furthermore, it is universally known that jury instruction

---

[163] *See* Cohen, *supra*, n. 7, at 273.

[164] *Id.*

[165] *See* V.M. Gulbis, 'Necessity of, and Prejudicial Effect of Omitting, Cautionary Instruction to Jury as to Reliability of, or Factors to be Considered in Evaluating, Eyewitness Identification Testimony – State Cases', 23 *A.LR.* 4th 1089.

[166] California's instruction on eyewitnesses goes the farthest of any state instructions. *See* CALJIC, as set forth in *People* v. *Gaglione*, 26 Cal. App. 4th 1291, 1302, 32 Cal. Rptr. 2d 169, 175 (CA, 1st Distr. 1994). *Gaglione* is a good example of the 'Catch 22' situation relevant to expert testimony and/or instructions on eyewitness identifications. The judge would not give more explicit instructions for fear of endorsing a particular theory relating to eyewitness identifications. And, yet, he would not allow experts to testify on such theories. Thus, the jury received no education on the pitfalls of eyewitness identifications. *Id.* at 1302-1304.

[167] The District of Columbia circuit set forth some 'model jury instructions' on eyewitness identification that have been followed by many state and federal courts. They are: "[Y]ou, the jury, must be satisfied beyond a reasonable doubt of the accuracy of the identification of the defendant before you may convict him. If you are not convinced beyond a reasonable doubt that the defendant was the person who committed the crime, you must find the defendant not guilty. Identification testimony is an expression of belief or impression by the witness. Its value depends on the opportunity the witness had to observe the offender at the time of the offense and to make a reliable identification later. In appraising the identification testimony of a witness, you should consider the following: (1) Are you convinced that the witness had the capacity and an adequate opportunity to observe the offender? (...) [This] will be affected by such matters as how long or short a time was available, how far or close the witness was, how good were lighting conditions, whether the witness had occasion to see or know the person in the past. (...) (2) Are you satisfied that the identification made by the witness subsequent to the offense was the product of his recollection? You may take into account both the strength of the identification and the circumstances under which the identification was made. If the identification by the witness may have been influenced by the circumstances under which the defendant was presented to him for identification, you should scrutinize the identification with great care. You may also consider the length of time that lapsed between the occurrence of the crime and the next opportunity of the witness to see the defendant as a factor bearing on the reliability of the identification. [You may *[sic]* take into account any occasions in which the witness failed to make an identification of defendant, or made an identification that was inconsistent with his identification at trial.]* (3) Finally, you must consider the credibility of each identification witness in the same way as any other witness, consider whether he is truthful, and consider whether he had the capacity and opportunity to make a reliable observation on the matter covered in this testimony.
(to be continued)

is one of the most boring parts of the trial[168] and comes too late in the process to undo a powerful eyewitness' testimony which may be firmly embedded, by the end of the trial, in the juror's minds.[169] Finally, although it is possible that an improved instruction including directions on the psychology of memory and identification, if even possible,[170] might educate and guide the jurors to more accurate verdicts, there is no scientific evidence that cautionary jury instructions, coming at the end of the trial, are effective.[171] On the whole, such instructions do not serve as an effective safeguard against erroneous convictions based on mistaken identifications.[172]

*Closing Argument:* final argument is the moment when all of the lawyer's organizational, analytical, interpretative and forensic skills are brought to bear on the task of persuading the jury.[173] The attorney in final argument is free to draw and urge inferences and conclusions[174] and can, at this point, comment on the credibility of witnesses.[175] However, closing argument cannot paint a picture unsupported by the evidence[176] – it must reflect and encompass *only* the evidence presented at trial.[177]

If there has been no evidence at trial about factors related to erroneous eyewitness identification, an attorney cannot comment on these factors in closing. Furthermore, the jury will only accept inferences if they are well grounded in common understanding.[178] When key events or occurrences are in dispute, an effective closing argument will first make use of common sense.[179] Remember, as between any two stories, a jury is likely to choose one that most closely comports with its own experience.[180] No matter how great a closing argument is, it will not be accepted by a jury unless it makes sense to them.[181] But, as we have seen, knowledge of the unreliability of eyewitness testimony is *not* within a juror's common experience. Nor, in most cases, has it been presented as evidence at trial. Thus, without expert testimony on eyewitness

---

*Sentence in brackets [ ] to be used only if appropriate. Instructions to be inserted or modified as appropriate to the proof and contentions." See US v. *Telfaire*, *supra*, n. 72, 469 *F.2d* 552, 555-556.

[168] See Lubet, *supra*, n. 143, at 426.

[169] See Cohen, *supra*, n. 7, at 272, 273.

[170] See Gulbis, *supra*, n. 165, 23 *A.LR.* 4th 1089 for a listing of state cases relating to this issue.

[171] See Cohen, *supra*, n. 7, at 272.

[172] See Penrod & Cutler, *supra*, n. 15, at 835; E. Greene, 'Judge's Instruction on Eyewitness Testimony: Evaluation and Revision' (1996), 81 *Journal of Applied Psychology* 757, 768 (hereinafter 'Greene').

[173] See Lubet, *supra*, n. 143, at 385.

[174] See Lubet, *supra*, n. 143, at 393.

[175] See Lubet, *supra*, n. 143, at 399, 420.

[176] See Lubet, *supra*, n. 143, at 385.

[177] See Lubet, *supra*, n. 143, at 386.

[178] See Lubet, *supra*, n. 143, at 394.

[179] See Lubet, *supra*, n. 143, at 389.

[180] *Id.*

[181] See Lubet, *supra*, n. 143, at 421.

identification, an attorney enters closing argument with her hands are tied behind her back.

### Primacy and Opening Statements

There is another way that the unreliability of eyewitness identifications heavily impacts a defense attorney's ability to argue her client's case. The principle of primacy states that in all aspects of a trial, a jury will remember best what they hear first.[182] Furthermore, studies show that once a jury has been given a reason to trust a witness, it will be more difficult for the other side to damage him.[183] Unfortunately, the defendant's evidence, whether in the form of cross-examination or extrinsic impeachment, is always delayed until after the witness has made a positive impression on the jury.[184] Opening statements, however, give the defendant a chance to make an early impression and often make the difference in the outcome of a case.[185] Studies have shown that jury verdicts are, in the substantial majority of cases, consistent with the initial impressions made by the jury during opening statements.[186] "The jurors are more receptive to information during the opening statement than at any other stage of the process."[187] Opening statement is crucial, since the mental image that the jurors hold while hearing the evidence will directly influence the way that they interpret it.[188] The jury will tend to filter all of the evidence through a lens that the attorney has created in opening statement.[189] This can substantially affect the conclusions a juror makes about the credibility of a witness.

Opening statements assist the jury in understanding the evidence to be presented at trial.[190] Jurors are presented with an overview of the case so that they will be better equipped to make sense of the evidence as it is actually presented. The institutional purpose of the opening statement, then, is to ease the jury's burden by making the trial more understandable.[191] As noted above and shown in various studies, jurors need to know the factors that affect accuracy in eyewitness identifications *before* they hear the testimony in order to properly judge that testimony. Attorneys should be allowed to prepare the jurors to judge the witness' testimony during opening statement by premiering for them what an expert will testify to during the trial.

---

[182] *See* Lubet, *supra*, n. 143, at 348.
[183] *See* Lubet, *supra*, n. 143, at 358.
[184] *See* Lubet, *supra*, n. 143, at 336.
[185] *See* T.A. Mauet, *Trial Techniques*, Aspen Publishers, Inc. 1996, 43.
[186] *Id.*
[187] *See* Mauet, *supra*, n. 185, at 44.
[188] *See* Lubet, *supra*, n. 143, at 335.
[189] *Id.*
[190] *See* Lubet, *supra*, n. 143, at 336.
[191] *See* Lubet, *supra*, n. 143, at 337.

However, during opening statements, attorneys can only state facts that will be proven during the trial. Courts and commentators alike are almost unanimously in argument that opening statements may only be used to inform the jury of "what the evidence will show".[192] Counsel may not argue the case during opening, may not assert personal knowledge of facts, may not urge the jury to draw inferences from the facts or to reach certain conclusions, may not explain the importance of certain items of evidence, suggest how evidence should be weighed or comment directly on the credibility of a witness.[193] In opening statement, counsel is restricted to offering a preview of the anticipated testimony, exhibits and other evidence. You can, however, provide the jury with facts that detract from the opposition's case[194]... if the facts will be entered into evidence at trial.

Thus, if you cannot admit expert testimony on the unreliability of eyewitness testimony during trial, then you cannot mention it in opening. Therefore, when the jury later hears the eyewitness testimony, it will filter it through the foggy commonsense lens of reliability rather than through the clear lens of truth as to reliability. And, once the jury has heard the testimony of the eyewitness, it will be very difficult to get the jury to distrust his testimony through the 'traditional safeguards' of cross-examination, jury instructions, or closing argument.

## Experts

Enter the expert. Expert witnesses have been utilized in the search for truth since ancient Egyptian days.[195] However, historically, the courts of the US have not warmly embraced expert witnesses on eyewitness testimony.[196] Generally, courts have been concerned about six things:

---

[192] *Id.*

[193] *Id. See also* Lubet, *supra*, n. 143, at 339, 432, citing Rule 4.3(e), 'Model Rules of Professional Conduct'; Mauet, *supra*, n. 185, at 49.

[194] *See* Lubet, *supra*, n. 143, at 346.

[195] The ancient Egyptians utilized expert witnesses in the search for the truth. *See* R.F. Taylor, 'A Comparative Study of Expert Testimony in France and the US: Philosophical Underpinnings, History, Practice, and Procedure' (1996), 31 *Tex. Int'l L. J.* 181, 184 (hereinafter 'Taylor'). Experts served an advisory role in early English courts. S. Landsman, 'One Hundred Years of Rectitude: Medical Witnesses at the Old Bailey, 1717-1817' (1998), 16 *Law & Hist. Rev.* 445, 446 (hereinafter 'Landsman').

[196] Expert testimony on eyewitness identifications is at the discretion of the court in specific jurisdictions and inadmissible *per se* in others. H.J. Hallisey, 'Experts on Eyewitness Testimony in Court – A Short Historical Perspective' (1995), 39 *How. L. J.* 237 (hereinafter 'Hallisey'). *See also* Unfortunate, *supra*, n. 4, at 308. Compare *US* v. *Fosher*, 590 *F.2d* 381 (1st Cir. 1979); *US* v. *Thevis*, 665 *F.2d* 616 (5th Cir. 1982); *US* v. *Green*, 548 *F.2d* 1261 (6th Cir. 1977); *US* v. *Watson*, 587 *F.2d* 365 (7th Cir. 1978) and *US* v. *Brown*, 540 *F.2d* 1048 (10th Cir. 1976), with *US* v. *Holloway*, 971 *F.2d* 675 (11th Cir. 1992).

1. such testimony is not generally accepted or scientifically valid;[197]
2. such testimony is presented as an opinion on credibility and, therefore, "invades the province" of the jury to determine credibility and weight;[198]
3. such testimony is *not* presented as an opinion but only in general terms and, therefore, does not help the jury because jurors can use their common sense to determine reliability;[199]
4. because of its aura of reliability and trustworthiness, such testimony would be given too much weight and would mislead the jury;[200]
5. such testimony over-emphasizes the unreliability of eyewitness testimony and may make an already doubtful jury too skeptical of an otherwise reliable witness;[201] and
6. such testimony will confuse jurors where identification is not a central issue in the case.

There is an answer, though, to each of these concerns.

*Scientific Validity:* in 1993, the law in the US concerning the admission of scientific evidence and expert testimony changed.[202] Prior to 1993, the law was governed by a court decision known as *Frye* v. *US*.[203] The rule developed in *Frye* stated that scientific evidence was admissible only if the technique had gained general acceptance in the particular field in which it belonged.[204] This was a rigidly applied test and kept much developing scientific evidence out of court. In 1993, the US Supreme Court decided the case of *Daubert* v. *Merrell Dow Pharmaceuticals*.[205] In the opinion, the Court determined that the *Federal Rules of Evidence (FRE)*, enacted after the *Frye* decision, governed the admissibility of scientific evidence and that the *Frye* rule was at odds with the liberal thrust of the *FRE* and their general approach of relaxing the traditional barriers to opinion testimony.[206]

The federal rules of evidence which govern admission of scientific and expert evidence in the US are *FREs* 702, 401, 402 and 403. *FRE* 702 allows expert testimony if it will assist the trier of fact to understand the evidence or

---

[197] *See US* v. *Garcia*, 40 *M.J.* 533, 536 (1994), *aff'd*, 44 *M.J.* 27, *cert. denied*, 519 *U.S.* 865, 117 *S.Ct.* 174 (1996).

[198] *US* v. *Amaral*, 488 *F.2d* 1148, 1153 (9th Cir. 1973); *US* v. *Rincon (Rincon I)*, 984 *F.2d* 1003, 1005 (9th Cir.), *vacated*, 510 *U.S.* 801 (1993); *US* v. *Garcia, supra*, n. 199, 40 *M.J.* at 536.

[199] O'Hagan, *supra*, n. 6, at 759-60; *US* v. *Gambino*, 818 *F. Supp.* 536, 538 (E.D.N.Y. 1993); *US* v. *Garcia, supra*, n. 199, 40 *M.J.*, at 536.

[200] *US* v. *Rincon (Rincon I), supra*, n. 198, 984 *F.2d*, at 1006; *US* v. *Rahm*, 993 *F.2d* 1405, 1415 (9th Cir. 1993).

[201] *US* v. *Rahm, supra* n. 200, 993 *F.2d* at 1415; *US* v. *Rincon (Rincon I), supra*, n. 198, 984 *F.2d*, at 1006.

[202] *See Daubert* v. *Merrell Dow Pharmaceuticals, Inc.*, 509 *U.S.* 579, 113 *S.Ct.* 2786, 125 *L. Ed. 2d* 469 (1993).

[203] 293 *F.* 1012 (D.C. Cir. 1923)(concerning admissibility of lie detector results).

[204] 293 *F.*, at 1013-1014.

[205] 509 *U.S.* 579, 113 *S.Ct.* 2786, 125 *L. Ed. 2d* 469 (1993).

[206] 509 *U.S.* at 588, 113 *S.Ct.*, at 2794. *See also* Valladares, *supra*, n. 117, at 64.

to determine a fact in issue.[207] *FRE* 402 provides that all relevant evidence is admissible unless excluded by some other provision.[208] *FRE* 401 provides that relevant evidence is any evidence which has *any* tendency to make the existence of any fact that is of consequence to the action more or less probable than it would be without the evidence.[209] *FRE* 403 excludes evidence if the dangers of unfair prejudice, waste of time, or needless presentation of cumulative evidence substantially outweigh its probative value.[210] Most, if not all, states in the union have adopted some form of these rules of evidence.

The Supreme Court, in its opinion in *Daubert*, in a sense combined aspects of these rules to create six factors for trial courts to consider when ruling on the admissibility of scientific evidence through expert testimony. These six factors are:
1. whether the technology is testable;
2. what the known or potential rate of error is;
3. the amount and type of publication of research on the topic;
4. peer review of the expert's ideas;
5. the qualifications of the expert and the nature of his testimony; and
6. the level of acceptance of the technique/technology in a relevant scientific community.[211]

Generally, the admissibility of expert testimony is left to the wide discretion of the trial judge who is said to play the role of 'gatekeeper' under the *Daubert* decision.[212] His or her decision will stand unless an appellate court views it as an abuse of discretion – which is *very* rare.[213]

Expert testimony on factors affecting eyewitness identification is scientifically valid[214] and generally accepted by the psychological community – it meets the *Daubert* test. The large amount of information developed by psychologists who have studied the phenomenon of memory is testable and has been tested.[215] The data has been subjected to peer review and publication, the mainstay of the scientific community.[216] These experts who would testify on the various intricacies of the memory processes and the theories relating thereto have gained general acceptance within their "relevant scientific

---

[207] *FRE* 702.
[208] *FRE* 402.
[209] *FRE* 401.
[210] *FRE* 403.
[211] *See*, generally, *Daubert, supra,* n. 202 509 *U.S.* at 593-595, 113 *S.Ct.*, at 2796-2798. *See also* R.B. Handberg, 'Expert Testimony on Eyewitness Identification: A New Pair of Glasses for the Jury' (1995), 32 *Am. Crim. L. Rev.* 1013, 1029 (hereinafter 'Handberg').
[212] *See* Handberg, *supra*, n. 211, at 1029.
[213] *Id.*
[214] *See US* v. *Moore*, 786 *F.2d* 1308, 1312 (5th Cir. 1986).
[215] *See* references to studies and experiments throughout this article.
[216] *See* references to publications throughout this article.

communities".[217] Thus, courts today should no longer be concerned that expert testimony on eyewitness identifications is not generally accepted or scientifically valid. As the federal Fifth Circuit Court of Appeal has stated, "[s]cientific validity of the studies confirming the many weaknesses of eyewitness identification cannot be seriously questioned at this point."[218]

*Province of Jury:* as to invading the province of the jury, most expert testimony is not presented as an opinion but as educational information in an attempt to bolster the jury's ability to assess the evidence.[219] "[A]lthough jurors may not be totally unaware of the (...) psychological factors bearing on eyewitness identification, the body of information now available on these matters is 'sufficiently beyond common experience' that in appropriate cases expert opinion thereon could at least 'assist the trier of fact'."[220] Thus, testimony by noted experts such as Loftus, Wall & Doyle should be admitted to educate the jurors.[221] The testimony should "summarize the results of studies, the methodologies involved, and, perhaps, provide some general comments on how the psychological studies may be applied to the 'real world'."[222]

Furthermore, even if it were an opinion, the *Federal Rules of Evidence* now allow an expert to give an opinion on the ultimate issues in a case other than the guilt/innocence of a defendant.[223] Nowhere do the rules exclude expert opinions on credibility.

*Helpfulness:* as to not being helpful to the jury, the courts have ruled that an expert can be used if testimony would help the jury understand evidence that is simply difficult although not beyond ordinary understanding.[224] Experts on eyewitness identifications typically focus on how the process of perception, memory, and retrieval of information work in generally and how specific circumstances surrounding an identification at issue may have affected accuracy.[225] Numerous experiments have shown that expert testimony increased jurors' sensitivity to the effects of weapon focus, eyewitness confidence and to the witnessing and identifying conditions and that jurors were more likely to use this information in rendering a verdict.[226] For example,

---

[217] *See* S.M. Kassin *et al.*, 'The General Acceptance of Psychological Research on Eyewitness Testimony: A Survey of the Experts' (1989), 77 *Am. Psychologist* 1089 (hereinafter 'Kassin').

[218] *US* v. *Moore*, 786 *F.2d* 1308, 1312 (5th Cir. 1986).

[219] *See* Cohen, *supra*, n. 7, at 278.

[220] *People* v. *McDonald*, *supra*, n. 117, 690 *P.2d*, at 721.

[221] *See* Cohen, *supra*, n. 7, at 277-278.

[222] *See* Cohen, *supra*, n. 7, at 278.

[223] *FRE* 704.

[224] *See US* v. *Downing*, *supra*, n. 79, 753 *F.2d* 1224.

[225] *See* C..M. Walters, 'Admission of Expert Testimony on Eyewitness Identification' (1985), 73 *Cal. L. Rev.* 1402, 1407 (hereinafter 'Walters').

[226] *See* Devenport, *supra*, n. 7, at 356.

in one study,[227] where jurors were exposed to expert testimony, 39% voted to convict whereas where jurors were not exposed to expert testimony, 58% voted to convict. In another study, where the jurors were exposed to the expert testimony prior to the eyewitness testimony, 41% voted to convict whereas if the jury was exposed to the expert testimony after the eyewitness testimony, 62% voted to convict.[228] Furthermore, as seen above, determinations of eyewitness reliability run counterintuitive to common sense and, therefore, experts are needed to counter what a juror's common sense will lead them to believe.

Juror skepticism refers to a tendency to doubt or disbelieve an eyewitness' testimony.[229] "Although juror skepticism is increased when a jury is exposed to expert testimony, [t]here is no data to substantiate the contention that expert testimony will inevitably produce a jury that is 'too skeptical' of the witness. There is simply no objective evidence that to allow expert testimony would yield injustice."[230] "[E]xpert testimony appears to improve [juror] sensitivity to the factors that influence memory without enhancing skepticism toward the accuracy of eyewitness identifications."[231]

Finally, there is little to no empirical evidence that juries are confused by expert testimony on factors concerning eyewitness identifications.[232]

## Trends

Unfortunately, the courts in the US continue to be slow to allow expert testimony regarding the unreliability of eyewitness identifications. As of today, it continues to be inadmissible per se in one circuit of the federal appellate courts.[233]

Slowly but surely, though, it appears things are changing. Recently, several circuits have suggested that this evidence warrants a more hospitable reception.[234] The courts recognize that there is more expert literature on the subject, more experts testifying and more skepticism about the reliability of such testimony based on the DNA studies being done which have exculpated

---

[227] *See* Devenport, *supra*, n. 7, at 355, citing Loftus (1980).
[228] *Id.*, citing Wells *et al.* (1980).
[229] *See* Devenport, *supra*, n. 7, at 354.
[230] Cohen, *supra*, n. 7, at 274-275.
[231] Penrod & Cutler, *supra*, n. 15, at 842.
[232] *See* Cutler & Penrod, *supra*, n. 17, at 250.
[233] *See US* v. *Holloway*, 971 *F.2d* 675, 679 (11ᵗʰ Cir. 1992); Unfortunate, *supra*, n. 6, at 308.
[234] *See, e.g. US* v. *Norwood*, 939 *F.* Supp. 1132, 1135-1137 (D.N.J. 1996); *US* v. *Garcia*, *supra*, n. 197, 40 *M.J.* 533; *US* v. *Brien*, 59 *F.3d* 274, 277 (1ˢᵗ Cir.), *cert. denied*, 516 *U.S.* 953, 116 *S.Ct.* 401 (1995); *US* v. *Rincon I*, *supra*, n. 198, 984 *F.2d*, at 1006; *US* v. *Stevens*, 935 *F.2d* 1380, 1384 (3ʳᵈ Cir. 1991); *US* v. *Moore*, *supra*, n. 214, 786 *F.2d*, at 1312; *US* v. *Downing*, *supra*, n. 79, 753 *F.2d* 1224.

convicted men and women.[235] To quote the First Circuit Court of Appeals: "It
may be that a door once largely shut is now somewhat ajar."[236] The modern
trend is to admit expert testimony on the impact psychological factors such as
stress, suggestibility, feedback and confidence have on the reliability of an
eyewitness identification when the identification is a critical issue in the
case.[237]

**What to do**

So, how do you get it in? Numerous suggestions have been and can be made.
First, choose your expert carefully.[238] Next, learn everything you can on
methodology and results. Read all the research in the field.[239] Be sure the
expert is thoroughly familiar with *Daubert*.[240] Be prepared to show the judge
that the average juror cannot appraise the effect of certain factors on
reliability.[241] File a motion in limine to have the judge rule prior to trial on the
admissibility of the testimony.

At the hearing on the motion in limine, make a detailed proffer on the
record.[242] This proffer should show how the expert's testimony relates to the
facts and issues in the case (eyewitness weaknesses). It should show that there
is a special need for the expert; that the eyewitness' testimony is crucial to the
prosecution's case and, therefore, attacking said witness' credibility is crucial
to your defense. It is particularly important that you proffer detailed testimony
of the expert's methodology;[243] that you proffer the substance of what the
expert's testimony will be;[244] that you show that the expert will discuss the
studies and experiments conducted in the area, how they were performed, the
rates of error and the results and that you give this substantive information to
the judge; and that you proffer all of the data and literature in the field which

---

[235] *See US* v. *Brien*, *supra*, n. 234, 59 *F.3d*, at 277.

[236] *Id.*

[237] *See US* v. *Garcia*, *supra*, n. 197, 40 *M.J.*, at 536. *See also US* v. *Brown*, 45 *M.J.* 514, 517
(1996)(current trend is to admit expert testimony on the impact psychological factors have on the
reliability of eyewitness identifications).

[238] In order to promote fairness and justice, the court has the prerogative of calling its own expert,
and, if necessary, of examining such an expert. *See FRE* 706, which provides: "The court may on
its own motion or on the motion of any party enter an order to show cause why expert witnesses
should not be appointed, and may request the parties to submit nominations. The court may
appoint any expert witness agreed upon by the parties, and may appoint expert witnesses of its
own selection (...). The witness shall be subject to cross-examination by each party, including a
party calling the witness." *See also* Cohen, *supra*, n. 7, at 281.

[239] *See* Valladares, *supra*, n. 117, at 64.

[240] *Id.*

[241] *See* Cohen, *supra*, n. 7, at 268, citing *People* v. *McDonald*, *supra*, n. 117, 690 *P.2d*, at 722.

[242] *See* Valladares, *supra*, n. 117, at 65; *US* v. *Downing*, *supra*, n. 81, 753 *F.2d*, at 1242.

[243] *See US* v. *Jordan*, 924 *F. Supp.* 443, 448 (W.D.N.Y. 1996). *See also* Valladares, *supra*, n. 117,
at 65.

[244] *See US* v. *Jordan, supra*, n. 243, 924 *F. Supp.*, at 447.

underlies the expert's assumptions and conclusions.[245] You should also make it clear that the expert will not offer an opinion on any particular witness.[246] You should be aware that the court may not be persuaded by a written proffer but may require the testimony of the expert pretrial.[247] Furthermore, it may be helpful to conduct a demonstration of the methodology underlying the research so as to convince the judge that the principles relating to eyewitness identification are counterintuitive and not within the ordinary experiences of an average juror.[248]

If the court rules against admissibility of your expert's testimony pretrial, you can still request a ruling during trial. At that point, you may have additional information with which to persuade a judge obtained during *voir dire*. *Voir dire* is the process of questioning venire members, in order to select those who will serve on the jury. It is usually done by the attorneys, although sometimes can be done by the court.[249] Jury questionnaires may be used to direct questions to the entire venire panel. The questions on the questionnaires are usually fashioned by the attorneys, subject to court approval.[250] Most courts allow attorneys to ask prospective jurors about their attitudes and possible preconceptions or prejudices concerning legal and factual issues in the case.[251] There are numerous sources of *voir dire* questions relating to eyewitness testimony.[252] Examples of a few such questions would include, "Would the way a witness is questioned affect their answer?", "If a witness is absolutely confident they saw a suspect commit a crime, is it likely that they are wrong?", "Who is more likely to make an accurate identification of a suspect, the victim or an uninvolved witness?"[253] Armed with answers from your jury indicating a lack of knowledge or misunderstanding of the factors affecting the reliability of eyewitness identifications, you should be able to get your expert's testimony admitted. If not, you certainly have ammunition for appeal.

Finally, if you get to trial with your expert, the expert should describe the tests and experiments to the jury rather than testifying to a bunch of numbers.[254]

---

[245] *Id. See also US* v. *Brien, supra,* n. 234, 59 *F.3d,* at 277.

[246] *See People* v. *McDonald, supra,* n. 117, 690 *P.2d,* at 716.

[247] *See US* v. *Jordan, supra,* n. 243, 924 *F. Supp.,* at 448.

[248] *See* Valladares, *supra,* n. 117, at 65.

[249] *See* Lubet, *supra,* n. 143, at 442.

[250] *See* Lubet, *supra,* n. 143, at 444.

[251] *See* Lubet, *supra,* n. 143, at 447.

[252] *See* C.E. Bennett & R.B. Hirschhorn, *Bennett's Guide to Jury Selection and Trial Dynamics in Civil and Criminal Litigation,* Bennett Jury Selection Sec. 5N (West 1995)(hereinafter 'Bennett's'). *See also* Sec. 12Z and Sec. 12EE.

[253] *See id.* for additional questions.

[254] *See* Devenport, *supra,* n. 7, at 356, citing Cutler *et al.* (1989).

## Conclusion

By focusing on the *expert* testimony, the courts have failed to consider the underlying lay *eyewitness* testimony, which is the real issue.[255] Eyewitness testimony is inherently unreliable and misleading. Is it not ironic that eyewitness testimony is 'generally accepted' by the legal community but testimony regarding its *un*reliability is considered novel?[256]

The true resolution of the problems associated with eyewitness testimony would be to ban most eyewitness testimony, particularly if there is only one eyewitness. Ancient Jewish law banned testimony by an uncorroborated single witness: the Bible tells us that "on the testimony of two or three witnesses a man shall be put to death, but no one shall be put to death on the testimony of only one witness."[257] And the courts in Ancient Rome required more than one witness: a Roman rule of law and ancient proverb states *unus testis nullus testis* (one witness is no witness).[258] Nevertheless, in the US a majority of the jurisdictions adhere to the rule that *uncorroborated* identification testimony of a single witness can convict.[259]

Although perhaps logical to some, banning eyewitness testimony is unworkable because "[i]t is fundamental that the testimony of witnesses, both in civil and criminal cases, is admissible if predicated upon concrete facts within their own observation."[260] Thus, if it must be allowed, it is only reasonable that to counterbalance such inherently unreliable evidence and make it less misleading and prejudicial, expert testimony on the factors affecting reliability must be allowed.

---

[255] *See* Cohen, *supra*, n. 7, at 277.

[256] *See* Cohen, *supra*, n. 9, at 267.

[257] Deuteronomy 17:6 (NIV): "On the testimony of two or three witnesses a man shall be put to death, but no one shall be put to death on the testimony of only one witness."

[258] *Cassell's Latin Dictionary* 624, 601, 398 (5th ed. 1968). *See* F.R. Herrmann & B.M. Speer, 'Facing the Accuser: Ancient and Medieval Precursors of the Confrontation Clause' (1994), 34 *Va. J. Int'l L.* 481, 546 (hereinafter 'Herrmann').

[259] *See* Holtshouser, *supra*, n. 152, at 1391-92.

[260] *US* v. *Brown*, 540 *F.2d* 1048, 1053 (10th Cir. 1976).

# Deception Detection: examining the Consistency Heuristic

*P.A. Granhag & L.A. Strömwall*

One of the most delicate tasks to be faced within the psycho-legal domain is to assess the credibility of a testimony. Maybe a child's story about sexual abuse, an alibi presented by someone who is accused of murder, or a witness' statement about a shooting. Importantly, both police officers and those working within the judicial arena have to take a stand with respect to questions like these on a daily basis.

Ideas about how we should go about assessing credibility are not lacking. Some suggest that we should employ the physiological-change approach, using the polygraph as a lie detector,[1] others advocate the behavioural-clue approach, represented by, for example, the work done on facial micro-expressions[2] and facial and bodily cues.[3] Finally, there is the verbal-content approach, which heads for a statement's stylistic and semantic characteristics.[4]

One of the most commonly used verbal criteria when assessing credibility on the basis of consecutive statements is *consistency*. For example, Greuel (1992) interviewed 51 police officers on their beliefs about cues associated with deception in rape cases. By far the most frequently reported cue, indicative of deception, was inconsistency of statements (mentioned by almost nine out of ten officers).

A catalogue containing all cases where consistency has played a key role would be extensive. For example, at the time of writing the judicial centre of attention in Sweden is a trial where three persons are accused of having murdered two police officers in a very cold blooded way. The trial has had extensive media coverage and daily fragments from the proceedings are played in the news. Both the experts in the courtroom and the laity in front of the TV sets are very much engaged in the same puzzle. That is, to try to sort out who did what by comparing the different statements. Obviously, the puzzle is complicated as one must keep track both on what each suspect has said during the course of repeated interrogations, and to what extent each suspect's statements matches the statements given by the others.

Although suspects commonly have to go through repeated interrogations, the major part of the research done on deception has focused on situations where each suspect is questioned about a particular event just once.[5] To remedy this shortcoming we have conducted a series of experiments addressing questions such as:

---

[1] *See e.g.* Raskin (1982).
[2] *See e.g.* Ekman (1985).
[3] *See e.g.* Vrij (1998).
[4] *See e.g.* Undeutsch (1989).
[5] Cf. Burgoon, Buller, Ebesu & Rockwell (1994).

1. How frequently is the consistency heuristic used as one has access to (1) consecutive statements from one and the same suspect or (2) several suspects' statements about one and the same event?
2. To what extent do people agree as to whether or not a specific series of consecutive statements is consistent?
3. Which factors affect how people perceive and rate the degree of consistency?
4. Do statements produced by truth tellers differ, in terms of consistency, from statements produced by liars?

Below, we will deal with each of these four forensically important questions.

## Usage of the Consistency Heuristic

Granhag & Strömwall (1999) staged a robbery and knife stabbing for 24 witnesses. Each witness was then interrogated on three different occasions (after three hours, four days and 11 days). Half of the witnesses were instructed to tell the truth and half to distort the event in such a way that the actual victim was made to be the perpetrator. The video-recorded interrogations were then shown to 144 observers. Each observer was asked to try to detect deception on the basis of one witness' set of interrogations. Finally, each observer was asked to justify the veracity judgement made. It was found that 40% of all verbal cues mentioned dealt with consistency. Computed over verbal and non-verbal cues collapsed, more than one third of all cues mentioned related to the consistency of the statements. This compared to a condition where the observers had to base their veracity judgements on one single statement only and no one used the consistency category. In short, up to the present time we have conducted three studies in which we have mapped the subjective cues used as judges base their veracity judgements on consecutive statements. In each of these studies, consistency has been the by far most frequently used cue.[6] Importantly, our experimental findings are supported by studies from applied psycho-legal contexts.[7]

Furthermore, in a recent study we traced the frequency of the consistency heuristic for contexts where the observers had access to consecutive statements given by one single suspect, as well as for contexts where the observers had access to statements given by two persons who were suspected of being in collusion.[8] Interestingly, we found that the consistency heuristic was used twice as often for the context were the observers based their veracity judgements on statements produced by two suspects, compared to the situation

---

[6] Granhag & Strömwall (in press), Granhag & Strömwall (1999); Granhag, Strömwall, & Reiman (2000a).
[7] *See e.g.* Gregow (1996); Greuel (1992).
[8] Granhag, Strömwall & Reiman (2000a).

where they based their judgements on consecutive statements produced by one single suspect.

Our research also shows that people very much agree as to how the consistency heuristic should be used.[9] In short, the assumption is that consistency is diagnostic for truth and inconsistency is diagnostic for deception. Preliminary results from an ongoing study where we have asked 75 experienced police officers about their beliefs on a number of forensically relevant matters gives further support to this finding. Our data show that eight of 10 police officers believe that consecutive statements given by truth tellers will be more consistent than consecutive statements given by liars.[10] Furthermore, our data show that this 'rule' seems to hold irrespective of whether one matches consecutive statements given by one single suspect or statements given by different suspects who might be in collusion.[11] In addition, our research shows that the consistency heuristic is equally frequent for justifying truth-judgements, *i.e.*, 'the statements are consistent, therefore true', as it is for justifying lie-judgements, *i.e.*, 'the statements are inconsistent, therefore not true'.[12]

In sum, both the mapping of cues used in applied[13] and experimental[14] settings shows that the consistency heuristic is very frequently used. In addition, both professional lie-catchers, such as police officers,[15] and less professional ones, such as students,[16] seem to agree as to how the consistency heuristic should be used. That is, the assumption is that consistency implies truth and inconsistency implies deception.

**Consistent or Inconsistent – to what Extent do People agree?**

We now know that people tend to be in agreement as to how the consistency heuristic should be used. What we do not know is to what extent people agree as to whether a specific series of consecutive statements is consistent or not. Obviously, such a question deals with interrater reliability. This type of reliability refers to the level of agreement found among multiple persons who have been engaged in the very same task with the very same information at hand.

Granhag & Strömwall (in press) showed one particular suspect – who had been interrogated on three different occasions – to 125 observers. Critically, all observers watched the same suspect. Mapping the subjective cues given to

---

[9] *See e.g.* Granhag & Strömwall (in press).
[10] Granhag & Strömwall (2000).
[11] Granhag, Strömwall & Reiman (2000a).
[12] Granhag & Strömwall (1999, in press); Granhag, Strömwall, & Reiman (2000a).
[13] Cf. Greuel (1992).
[14] Cf. Granhag & Strömwall (in press).
[15] Granhag & Strömwall (2000).
[16] Cf. Granhag & Strömwall (in press).

justify the veracity-judgements, it was found that the most frequently used cue was the consistency heuristic. Interestingly, out of those 78 observers who stated that they had used the consistency heuristic, 38 perceived the three statements to be consistent over time, whereas 40 observers perceived the same three statements to be inconsistent over time. Differently put, this finding lends strong evidence to the idea that what is judged as consistent by one person might very well be judged as inconsistent by another. This particular result was foreshadowed by findings presented by Jackson Granhag (1997).

Furthermore, Granhag & Strömwall (in press) suggest that the finding that there are high levels of inter-observer disagreement as to how the degree of consistency (and, for that matter, other cues to deception) is *perceived* might work as a complementary explanation of the poor performance generally found in experiments on deception detection.[17] That is, suppose for a moment that the degree of consistency actually is a sound index of veracity (whether or not this assumption is true will be discussed below). Then suppose that this particular heuristic is taught during a workshop on deception detection, *i.e.*, the trainees are told that "consistent statements are often true and inconsistent statements are often lies". At the end of the day the trainees are faced with a test where they are to decide whether a suspect, who has been interrogated on numerous occasions, is lying or telling the truth. Based on what we know from previous research, we have reason to expect that:

1. consistency will be the most frequently used heuristic;[18] and
2. the level of inter-observer disagreement for this particular heuristic will be high.[19]

That is, some trainees will say "the statements are consistent over time – therefore I believe he is telling the truth", while others will say "the statements are not consistent over time – therefore I believe he is lying". Hence, we have good reason to believe that the percentage of accurate decisions, across the whole group of trainees, will be moderate.

In sum, in the above section we have presented data showing that one and the same series of consecutive statements may be characterised as consistent by one judge and inconsistent by another. In other words, whether or not a series of consecutive statements is to be perceived as consistent, is largely moderated by *individual factors*. As will be evidenced below, individual factors are not the only type of factors that affect how people perceive and rate consistency.

---

[17] Cf. Kalbfleisch (1994); Vrij (2000).
[18] *See e.g.* Granhag & Strömwall (1999).
[19] Granhag & Strömwall (in press).

## The Malleable Nature of Consistency

A large corpus of psychological research shows that people's perceptions and judgements are moderated by a host of different factors. For example, a plethora of studies shows that *social factors* can influence both people's perceptions,[20] memory[21] and meta-memory.[22] Furthermore, led by authorities such as Tversky & Kahneman, the 'heuristics and biases' program has produced ample evidence that people's judgements can be affected by a large number of different *cognitive factors.*[23]

Our current examination would be far from complete without any information about factors, other than individual ones, that might moderate how people perceive and rate consistency. Below we will therefore give a brief review of three experiments, all focusing on to what extent consistency is inherently malleable. All experiments reviewed are taken from a forthcoming study conducted by Strömwall & Granhag (2000).

*Experiment 1.* In this experiment we investigated the extent to which the perception of consistency is moderated by the mode in which the to-be-rated-statements are presented. In short, we used a design where the participants in the first condition listened to audiotapes from three interrogations held with one single suspect (sound only); the participants in the second condition read the transcribed protocols stemming from the same three interrogations (text only), and finally, in the third condition the participants watched the three interrogations on video (vision and sound). Statistical analyses showed a main effect bordering on significance, and *post hoc* tests showed that the participants who had read the transcribed protocols judged the statements to be less consistent over time than did the participants in the two other conditions. In a follow up experiment we investigated differences, in terms of consistency ratings, between a group who had seen the interrogations on video and a group who had read the transcripts from the same three interrogations. Again, we found a strong, but non-significant, trend indicating that reading the transcripts lead to lower consistency ratings. In sum, these two experiments indicate that there is probably more to consistency than what is actually said during the interrogations.

*Experiment 2.* Research shows that people who are repeatedly exposed to one and the same stimulus often tend to like this stimulus more and more. This finding is the same whether the stimulus be tone sequences, random shapes or photographs of unfamiliar faces.[24] This phenomenon has been referred to as the *mere exposure effect.* A related effect, with relevance for psycho-legal

---

[20] *See e.g.* Asch (1951).
[21] *See e.g.* Hoffman, Granhag, Kwong See & Loftus (1999).
[22] *See e.g.* Luus & Wells (1994).
[23] *See e.g.* Tversky & Kahneman (1974).
[24] *See e.g.* Brooks & Watkins (1989).

contexts, is the so called *reiteration effect*.[25] The reiteration effect tells us that by repeating an assertion (*e.g.*, "he held the knife in his left hand") one's confidence in its truth will increase.[26] In *Experiment 2* our question was: to what extent, if any, will consistency be affected by the mere exposure effect?

To answer this question we used the following design: participants in the experimental condition first watched three interrogations with one and the same suspect and then rated consistency. Next, they watched the same three interrogations twice more, and finally they rated consistency again. Participants in the control condition watched the same three interrogations three times in a row and then made a consistency rating. Note that all participants were shown the three interrogations the same number of times (three), but that the participants in the experimental condition rated consistency twice, while the participants in the control condition only rated consistency once. We found that within the experimental condition the second set of consistency ratings was significantly lower than the first set. Further, we found that the second set of consistency ratings made in the experimental condition was significantly lower than the (one and only) set of consistency ratings made in the control condition. In short, this experiment shows that the perception of consistency is indeed affected by the mere exposure effect. Specifically, if judges are asked to take a stand regarding consistency both after watching the interrogations for the first time, and again after watching the same interrogations for the third time, repeated exposure will lead to lower consistency ratings.

*Experiment 3.* In a third experiment we, again, employed a between-subject design and showed the same three interrogations (with one single suspect) to participants in three different conditions. For the first condition the participants were instructed to seek and note inconsistencies, for the second condition the participants were to seek and note consistencies, and for the third condition (a control condition) the participants were not given any instructions in terms of consistency. We hypothesised that the mean degree of consistency would be lower for the condition in which the participants had sought inconsistencies, compared to the conditions in which they had sought consistencies. In short, we found no effect of our manipulation. That is, the three conditions did not differ in terms of consistency. Differently put, our 'seek and thou shall find' instruction did not seem to affect the overall consistency rating.

In addition, in several experiments we have measured the correlation between the type of veracity judgement made (truth or lie) and the stated degree of consistency. We have found that this correlation is higher in situations where the participants first make a veracity judgement and then

---

[25] *See e.g.* Hertwig, Gigerenzer & Hoffrage (1997).
[26] For a discussion of the reiteration effect in eyewitness contexts, *see* Granhag, Strömwall & Allwood (in press).

make a consistency rating,[27] compared to situations where they first rate consistency and then make a veracity judgement.[28] A reasonable interpretation of this finding is that the type of veracity judgement made tends to bleed into the consistency rating to a rather large extent, with higher consistency ratings if one believe that a person is telling the truth, and lower consistency ratings if one believe he is lying. This, while the type of veracity judgement made seems less affected by a preceding rating of consistency. Importantly, for all three experiments reviewed above the participants made ratings of consistency before they made judgements of veracity.

In sum, so far we have investigated a very limited set of all factors that might moderate consistency. Still, we believe that it is rather safe to conclude that people's perceptions and judgements of consistency are affected by both *individual* and *situational factors*.

## Are Truthful Statements more Consistent than Deceptive?

Research on deception has, to a very large extent, neglected the question of whether truthful statements are more consistent than deceptive. This is noteworthy, given that the consistency heuristic is so frequently used.

In two studies we have collected three different sets of consistency ratings.[29] First, we have asked those who were interrogated how they perceived their own statements in terms of consistency over time. Second, we have collected consistency ratings from those who were appointed to try to detect deception. Third, we have collected so-called base-line consistency ratings from a separate group of participants, who were instructed to focus on the consistency (instead of the veracity) of the statements.

In the study outlined above by Granhag & Strömwall (1999), 24 witnesses watched a staged robbery and were then interrogated on three different occasions. Half of the witnesses were told to lie about the event and the other half was told to tell the truth. We found that the consistency ratings given by the liars did not differ from the consistency ratings given by the truth tellers. That is, liars and truth tellers perceived themselves to have produced equally consistent statements. Furthermore, each suspect was assessed, both in terms of veracity and consistency, by six observers who had seen the interrogations on video (in all we used 144 observers). No difference, in terms of consistency, was found between those observers who rated truth tellers and those who rated liars. Finally, we collected base-line consistency ratings from 48 observers, who were specifically asked to focus on the consistency of the particular testimony they were shown. Again, it was found that liars were rated as being equally consistent as truth tellers.

---

[27] *E.g.*, $r = .47, p < .0001$, in Granhag & Strömwall (in press).
[28] *E.g.*, $r = .28, p > .05$, in Granhag & Strömwall (1999).
[29] Granhag & Strömwall (1999); Granhag, Strömwall & Reiman (2000b).

Granhag, Strömwall & Reiman (2000b) used a design where 20 pairs of friends of undergraduate students volunteered to participate in a study on 'decision making'. Unaware that they – at a later point – would face in-depth questions about the event, half of the pairs started off by having lunch (they were lured into believing that this was a pre-payment for the experiment they were to take part in). After returning from lunch, the pairs were separated and each pair member was instructed that he/she was now to be interrogated about what happened during the lunch. The other half of the pairs did not get any free lunch. Instead, they were told to jointly invent that they had had lunch together on a certain day. In short, they were instructed to fabricate an alibi that would withstand later interrogation. In sum, we ended up with ten lying and ten truth telling pairs, where each pair member had been interrogated separately on two different occasions with an interval of seven days. Hence, by using such a design, we made it possible to study both issues related to consistency within single suspects, as well as issues related to consistency within pairs of suspects.

Again, we found that the consistency ratings given by the liars did not differ from the consistency ratings given by the truth tellers; lying and truth telling suspects saw themselves as being equally consistent over time. Nor did we find any differences in terms of consistency between those observers who had watched liars and those who had watched truth tellers. This finding was irrespective of whether we compared ratings pertaining to consistency within single suspects over time (single liars v. single truth tellers), or ratings pertaining to consistency within pairs of suspects (lying pairs v. truth telling pairs). Turning to the ratings adopted from the participants in the base-line condition (those explicitly told to focus on the consistency of the statements), we found some interesting results. First, liars – compared to truth tellers – were on average rated as being more consistent over time. Secondly, statements produced by lying pairs were on average given significantly higher consistency ratings, compared to statements produced by truth telling pairs. In other words: liars were perceived as being more consistent than truth tellers, both in terms of consistency within single suspects and consistency within pairs.

In the section above we have discussed results stemming from consistency ratings performed by three different groups (viz. the suspects themselves, observers with main focus on veracity, and observers with main focus on consistency). However, we have not yet touched upon the important question of whether more textual oriented measures will indicate any differences in terms of consistency between truthful and deceptive statements.

In an ingenious attempt to address this question Wagenaar & Dalderop (1994) sent six pairs to the zoo. Six other pairs were instructed to invent a story about a joint visit to the same zoo. Later, all participants answered both a free-recall question and seven specific questions. The questions were answered individually and in writing. Consistency within pairs was scored both in terms of explicitly stated facts (*e.g.*, both members in the pair said "it rained in the morning") and facts that were mentioned in a more implicit manner (*e.g.*, one pair member said "it rained in the morning and in the afternoon" and the other said "in the afternoon it started to rain again"). Irrespective of the type of scoring procedure used, the result showed that the lying pairs were significantly more consistent than the truth telling pairs.

Here it should be noted that there is no principled way for measuring consistency. Furthermore, in the work of developing a measure capturing 'pure consistency' one would not only face problems of an exegetic nature. That is, judging from the findings reviewed above, we have reason to believe that peoples' consistency ratings are affected by additional factors than what is actually said in the to-be-compared-statements.[30] In short, consistency is probably to be found both in the ear and the eye of the beholder.

In sum, it seems that there are larger differences for the consistency ratings pertaining to within pair comparisons, with higher consistency between lying pair members than between truth telling pair members,[31] as opposed to the consistency ratings pertaining to within single suspects comparisons, where liars and truth tellers seem to be equally consistent over time.[32]

One way to understand the above findings might be to place the consistency heuristic in the light of an essay written by the French philosopher Montaigne, *A liar should have good memory*. As the title indicates, Montaigne points out that a sound memory is an absolute prerequisite if one really wants to master the art of deception. Indeed, successful liars know to appreciate the value of remembering their initial story, and are well aware that inconsistent accounts can lead to their unmasking.[33]

However, the memory factor also plays a key role for those who choose to tell the truth. Turning to what we know about human memory, there are at least two crucial findings we need to acknowledge. First, there is an overwhelming corpus of research showing the malleable nature of memory. For example, studies from the eyewitness paradigm show that a witness, asked to recall repeatedly a particular event, tends to both gain, lose and change details over time.[34] Second, there is an equally impressive body of research showing that people who have witnessed the same event do not only tend to remember different things, but they also tend to remember the same things differently.[35] In sum, the finding that deceptive statements – compared to truthful – are equally (or more) consistent might be explained by liars trying to

---

[30] Cf. Strömwall & Granhag (2000), *Experiment 1*.
[31] Wagenaar & Dalderop (1994); Granhag, Strömwall & Reiman (2000b).
[32] Granhag & Strömwall (1999); Granhag, Strömwall & Reiman (2000b).
[33] *See e.g.* Ekman (1985).
[34] *See* Turtle & Yuille (1994).
[35] *See e.g.* Loftus (1979); Loftus & Ketcham (1991).

remember what they have said in previous interrogations, while truth tellers often try to remember what they actually experienced.

One way to map the predictive accuracy of the cues used in deception detection contexts is to calculate *diagnostic values*. The higher the diagnostic value, the better the predictive accuracy. For example, a cue with a diagnostic value of 10 says that it is 10 times more likely that a judgement based on that particular cue is correct than incorrect. According to Wagenaar, Van Koppen & Crombag (1993) the diagnostic values found in forensic contexts typically vary between 1 and 2, and rarely exceed 5.

In two studies we have made attempts to arrest the predictive accuracy of the consistency heuristic. In Granhag & Strömwall (1999) we found low diagnostic values both when the heuristic was used as "consistent over time – therefore true" ($dv = 1.34$) and when the heuristic was used as "inconsistent over time – therefore deceptive" ($dv = 1.50$). In addition, Granhag, Strömwall & Reiman (2000a) found low diagnostic values both when the consistency heuristic was used in reference to single suspects, and when it was used in reference to pairs of suspects. Obviously, these findings are not surprising given that we know that liars are perceived as equally (or more) consistent than truth tellers.[36]

## Conclusions

Our inventory of the psychological research conducted on deception shows that questions focusing on the link between repeated interrogations and deception detection performance has been neglected.[37] Consequently, questions concerning consistency have been given very little attention. Given the high likelihood that a suspect will be interrogated on numerous occasions, and that the consistency heuristic is frequently used when assessing credibility, we believe that this is alarming. The goal of the present paper was to examine the consistency heuristic as it is used in deception detection contexts. In short, we believe that such an investigation is of paramount psycho-legal importance.

Epitomised, our examination of the consistency heuristic showed the following:

1. as the basis for detecting deception changes from only one statement to consecutive statements, the distribution of the cues used to justify the veracity judgements changes dramatically. That is, the consistency heuristic becomes by far the most frequently used cue. Further, the consistency heuristic is very common in situations where observers base their judgements on consecutive statements given by one single suspect,

---

[36] *See e.g.* Granhag, Strömwall & Reiman (2000b).
[37] Cf. Vrij (1999).

and even more common when they base their veracity judgements on statements produced by two suspects (who might be in collusion);

2. people do not seem to agree as to whether a specific set of consecutive statements is consistent or not. In other words, the degree of consistency seems to be coupled to a low degree of inter-observer agreement. Speculative as it is, it might be that many testimonies – comprising consecutive statements from the same suspect – carry a disposition to be perceived as *both* consistent and inconsistent;

3. how people perceive and rate consistency is – in addition to individual factors – also affected by situational factors. Examples of two such factors are type of presentation mode and the mere exposure effect. In short, consistency seems to be malleable in its nature. Our data also indicate that it might very well be that people's perceptions and ratings of consistency are, to a larger extent, affected by *unobtrusive* means, such as presentation mode and mere exposure, than *obtrusive* means, such as instructions to seek inconsistencies;[38]

4. statements produced by liars seem to be equally (or more) consistent than statements produced by truth tellers. More specifically, this seems to hold both for within single suspects and within pairs of suspects.

Turning to the psycho-legal implications of our examination, the question remains as to how the findings reviewed above should be condensed and translated into applied recommendations. A tempting answer would be: lie-catchers – ignore consistency and you would be better off! However, we believe that such a recommendation would be both ineffective and naive. Instead, the important aim must be to further pursue research on the consistency heuristic. For example, investigate whether or not consecutive statements produced by truth tellers are characterised by an idiosyncratic type of inconsistency (*e.g.* relatively more omission errors and relatively few commission and contradiction errors). Similarly, we need to know whether or not consecutive statements produced by liars are characterised by a idiosyncratic type of consistency.[39] At this very moment we are taxing our resources trying to answer both these and related questions.[40]

Finally, we believe that our findings combined questions whether any single credibility assessment based on consistency should be labelled and treated as an 'expert opinion'. Further, we need to acknowledge the danger hidden in the possibility that judges will find a liar's consistent statements crediting, and a truth teller's inconsistent statements incriminating. In sum, with reference to the converging evidence resulting from our examination, we strongly suggest that the consistency heuristic should be exercised with great caution.

---

[38] Cf. Allwood & Granhag (1996).
[39] *E.g.* a relatively rehearsed type of story, cf. Ekman (1989).
[40] *See e.g.* Granhag, Strömwall & Reiman (2000b).

# References

**Allwood, C.M. & Granhag, P.A.** (1996), 'Considering the knowledge you have: Effects on realism in confidence judgements', in: *European Journal of Cognitive Psychology*, 8, pp. 235-256.

**Asch, S.** (1951), 'Effects of group pressure upon the modification and distortion of judgements', in: Guetzkow, H. (Ed.), *Groups, Leadership and Men*, Pittsburgh: Carnegie.

**Brooks III, J.O. & Watkins, M.J.** (1989), 'Recognition memory and the mere exposure effect', in: *Journal of Experimental Psychology: Learning, Memory, and Cognition*, 15, pp. 968-976.

**Burgoon, J.K., Buller, D.B., Ebesu, A.S. & Rockwell, P.** (1994), 'Interpersonal deception: V. Accuracy in deception detection', in: *Communication Monographs*, 61, pp. 303-325.

**Ekman, P.** (1985), *Telling Lies – Clues to deceit in the marketplace, politics, and marriage*, New York: W.W. Norton & Co.

**Ekman, P.** (1989), 'Why lies fail and what behaviors betray a lie', in: Yuille, J.C. (ed.), *Credibility Assessment*, Dordrecht, the Netherlands: Kluwer Academic Press, pp. 71-81.

**Granhag, P.A. & Strömwall, L.A.** (1999), *Repeated interrogations: Objective and subjective cues to deception*. Manuscript submitted for publication.

**Granhag, P.A. & Strömwall, L.A.** (2000), *Psychologists, police officers and judges - An inventory of beliefs about eyewitness memory and deception*, Manuscript under preparation. Department of Psychology, Göteborg University.

**Granhag, P.A. & Strömwall, L.A.** (in press), 'The effects of preconceptions on deception detection and new answers to why lie-catchers often fail', in: *Psychology, Crime & Law*.

**Granhag, P.A., Strömwall, L.A. & Allwood, C.M.** (in press), 'Effects of reiteration, memory, and feedback on eyewitnesses' confidence', in: *Applied Cognitive Psychology*.

**Granhag, P.A., Strömwall, L.A. & Reiman, A.-C.** (2000a), *Deception among pairs: "We said we had lunch together – hopefully they swallowed it!"*, Manuscript under preparation. Department of Psychology, Göteborg University.

**Granhag, P.A., Strömwall, L.A. & Reiman, A.-C.** (2000b), *True and false alibies: Differences and similarities*, Manuscript under preparation. Department of Psychology, Göteborg University.

**Gregow, T.** (1996), 'Några synpunkter på frågan om bevisprövning och bevisvärdering i mål om sexuella övergrepp mot barn', in: *Svensk Juristtidning*, 7, pp. 509-523.

**Greuel, L.** (1992), 'Police officers' beliefs about cues associated with deception in rape cases', in: Lösel, F., Bender, D. & Bliesener, T. (eds.), *Psychology and Law – International Perspectives*, Berlin: Walter de Gruyter, pp. 234-239.

**Hertwig, R., Gigerenzer, G. & Hoffrage, U.** (1997), 'The reiteration effect in hindsight bias', in: *Psychological Review*, 104, pp. 194-202.

**Hoffman, H.G., Granhag, P.A., Kwong See, S.T. & Loftus, E.F.** (1999), *Social influences on reality monitoring decisions*, manuscript submitted for publication.

**Jackson, J.L. & Granhag, P.A.** (1997), 'The truth or fantasy: The ability of barristers and laypersons to detect deception in children's testimony', in: Nijboer, J.F. & Reijntjes, J.M. (eds.), *New Trends in Criminal Investigation and Evidence – Proceedings of the First World Conference on New Trends in Criminal Investigation and Evidence*, Lelystad, the Netherlands: Koninklijke Vermande B.V., pp. 213-220.

**Kalbfleisch, P.J.** (1994), 'The language of detecting deceit', in: *Journal of Language and Social Psychology*, 13, pp. 469-497.

**Loftus, E.F.** (1979), *Eyewitness testimony*, Cambridge, MA: Harvard University Press.

**Loftus, E.F. & Ketcham, K.** (1991), *Witness for the defence: The accused, the eyewitness, and the expert who puts memory on trial*, New York: St. Martin's Press.

**Luus, C.A.E. & Wells, G.L.** (1994), 'The malleability of eyewitness confidence: Co-witness and perseverance effects', in: *Journal of Applied Psychology*, 79, pp. 714-723.

**Raskin, D.C.** (1982), 'The scientific basis of polygraph techniques and their use in the judicial process', in: Trankell, A. (ed.), *Reconstructing the past*, Deventer, the Netherlands: Kluwer Academic Press, pp. 319-371.

**Strömwall, L.A. & Granhag, P.A.** (2000), *Deception detection: The malleability of Consistency*, manuscript under preparation. Department of Psychology, Göteborg University.

**Turtle, J.W. & Yuille, J.C.** (1994), 'Lost but not forgotten details: Repeated eyewitness recall leads to reminiscence but not hypermnesia', in: *Journal of Applied Psychology*, 79, pp. 260-271.

**Tversky, A. & Kahneman, D.** (1974), 'Judgement under uncertainty: Heuristics and biases', in: *Science*, 185, pp. 1124-1131.

**Undeutsch, U.** (1989), 'The development of Statement Reality Analysis', in: Yuille, J.C. (ed.), *Credibility Assessment*, Dordrecht, the Netherlands: Kluwer Academic Press, pp. 101-119.

**Vrij, A.** (1998), 'Non-verbal communication and credibility', in: Memon, A., Vrij, A. & Bull, R. (eds.), *Psychology and Law. Truthfulness, Accuracy and Credibility*, Cambridge, UK: McGraw-Hill, pp. 32-58.

**Vrij, A.** (1999), 'Interviewing to detect deception', in: Memon, A. & Bull, R. (eds.), *Handbook of the Psychology of Interviewing*, Chicester: John Wiley & Sons.

**Vrij, A.** (2000), *Detecting lies and deceit: Psychology of lying and its implications of professional practice*, Chicester: John Wiley & Sons.

**Wagenaar, W.A. & Dalderop, A.** (1994), *Remembering the zoo: A comparison of true and false stories told by pairs of witnesses*, manuscript. Department of Experimental Psychology, Leiden University, the Netherlands.

**Wagenaar, W.A., Koppen, P.J. van & Crombag, H.F.M.** (1993), *Anchored narratives. The psychology of criminal evidence*, New York: St. Martin's Press.

# Hearsay Evidence in Criminal Proceedings – Proposals for Hearsay Reform: the Admissibility Wheel

*L.A.O. McGrath*

## Introduction: the Hearsay Rule at Common Law

The rule against hearsay at common law prohibits[1] the use of secondary evidence being relayed by a witness who has not perceived the evidence through his or her own senses. The rule forbids the use of evidence that is not given first-hand by the actual declarant in a court of law. The current paper will not scrutinise all the arguments for and against reform of the rule, but one can assume, that I am a proponent of reform but not of abolition.

Some common arguments for the rule's retention are that it serves to preserve the process of cross-examination of evidence given under oath. There are also fears that such secondary evidence may suffer in terms of reliability, be open to the risk of concoction and have the effect of confusing or swaying a jury. However, there also exists a number of arguments in favour of modifying the rule which I shall present to you in a coherent form that compliments the operation of the rule, by taking into account evidence that, while being hearsay in nature, can warrant a further opportunity to be tested for possible admissibility in criminal trials.

"Any legal system has to decide how to assess evidence. In many systems, the process of finding facts and justifying conclusions based on them is hidden. The judge reads the file and draws conclusions from it. Because in the common law system, material is presented in open court and in view of the other party, the judge has to make an explicit and transparently justified decision to include material. This provides an opportunity to examine the reasoning process which any judge must go through. This text offers a model of how we might conceptualise the decisions the judge has to take and how that decision-making process might be improved."[2]

## The Admissibility Wheel

At common law, the rule against hearsay evidence as applied in criminal proceedings has been the subject of widespread criticism. The strict application of this exclusionary rule has been associated with all too many decisions connected with the possible and actual miscarriage of justice. The admissibility wheel is offered as a compliment to the existing state of law on

---

[1] Subject to a number of common law and statutory exceptions.
[2] As depicted by Professor John Bell of the University of Leeds, in a recent discussion concerning the admissibility wheel and the transparency of the common law.

hearsay. It takes account of a number of pertinent questions when assessing the admissibility of secondary evidence, gleaned from the experience of both common law and civil law systems. Offering a distinct conceptual structure, the wheel could serve as an operative tool in the assessment of secondary evidence which, while *relevant, necessary or probative,* fails to attain admissibility on the mandate of a historical and harsh exclusionary rule with a narrowly prescribed list of exceptions.

The wheel operates by suggesting that a number of questions be asked in relation to probative hearsay. The questions posed by the wheel interrelate, drawing upon the likelihood or otherwise, of the evidence to assist in explaining the existing facts of a case. The wheel operates as a spinning device somewhat like a roulette wheel, at which the ball (the hearsay evidence) may be launched. I use this analogy simply to indicate that the questions posed on the wheel may be addressed in any order. The object of the wheel is to apply these questions in order to re-examine cogent hearsay that is excluded from trial under the existing rules of evidence. It promotes a common-sense approach to the pre-trial assessment of evidence, supplementing the operation of the hearsay rule and its exceptions. When we refer to 'common sense', we are embarking upon the territory of the jury, whose function at common law is to assess the weight of evidence and to decide upon the truth likelihood of the facts presented at trial. Rules of exclusion such as the hearsay rule, can prevent a jury from exposure to certain classes of evidence of a secondary nature, despite how cogent this evidence might be. This practice can deprive fact finders (the jury) of their function to relatively assess the weight of evidence. The justification for depriving a jury of access to certain evidence is based on a rule utilitarian approach which has been judicially developed to protect jurors from hearing tainted evidence. Yet, in systems of law where the judges are the fact finders, similar assessments of evidential material have to be made. The purpose of the wheel is to ensure that probative hearsay is given an opportunity to qualify as admissible and be examined by juries at common law.[3]

In order that hearsay evidence be given this opportunity to attain admissibility, it must be shown either that;
1. the hearsay evidence is the best evidence available to a party's case and corroborates other existing evidence. (Especially where this relates to evidence for the defence in a criminal trial.); or
2. the hearsay evidence bears such an impression on the facts in the case, that its exclusion would have the result of perverting rectitude of decision.

These are the criteria that ought to be satisfied by a piece of hearsay seeking to be considered in the light of the admissibility wheel. One additional factor that will allow a piece of evidence to be considered in the light of the

---

[3] Subject to a judicial warning concerning the trustworthiness of evidence coming from a secondary source.

wheel, is what I call the *right to assessment*, which occurs when the hearsay evidence contains pertinent information falling within no established exception. Evidence fitting into this category is justifiably placed as a mandatory factor on the admissibility wheel on the grounds that it may contain cogent evidence that has no place in law where its admissibility can be argued. Of course, it will be necessary to establish what is meant in this context by *pertinence*. A piece of evidence might be said to be pertinent when it satisfies the requirements of (1) or (2) above. It may be stressed then, that the admissibility wheel intervenes where the existing exceptions to the hearsay rule afford no opportunity for probative hearsay to be included at trial. It allows for a scope, not provided by the existing rule on hearsay, to admit cogent evidence that the judiciary have had no discretion to admit, despite the logic in many noted cases, of including such evidence.

Once the disputed hearsay has satisfied the above standard of pertinence, the evidence may then be subjected to the following questions on the admissibility wheel:

- is the hearsay reliable and necessary to a party's case?
- is the hearsay relevant to a fact in issue?
- does the hearsay have weight and probative value warranting the jury's consideration?
- does the hearsay indicate third party knowledge of facts suggesting the accused's possible innocence?
- does the hearsay indicate some fear or state of mind relevant to a fact in issue?
- was there an intention to create a belief in the hearsay assertion?

Most of the questions on the wheel refer to the nature of the disputed evidence and its relevance or necessity to a party's case. However, the question concerning the intention to create a belief in the hearsay assertion, stands apart from the rest as it focuses on the intention of the hearsay declarant at the time the statement was made. This particular approach to hearsay evidence comes directly from the US *Federal Rules of Evidence*[4] where the test of admissibility is based on the maker's intention when uttering the statement or making the gesture. This distinction is not yet recognised in English Law.

**The Need for Coherence**

"The inadmissibility of hearsay evidence can lead to anomalous results." Such was the opinion of the British Law Commission[5] in its *Report on Hearsay and Related Topics* in June of 1997. In England as in many other common law

---

[4] Rule 801(a).
[5] *Evidence in Criminal Proceedings: Hearsay and Related Topics*, Law Com No 245, London, p. 36, para 4.4.

systems, a number of criminal cases have been tried in the absence of cogent hearsay and the perverse results arising from such ill-informed decisions, has led to a strong wave of criticism.[6] The decisions in many of these cases have been scrutinised by academics and mourned by a number of judges and practitioners who advocate reform. When constructing the admissibility wheel, it was necessary to address these decisions in an attempt to formulate an approach to cogent hearsay that dispenses with the automatic exclusion that can give rise to a miscarriage of justice.[7]

## The Merits of the Wheel

"There is no one coherent law of hearsay, but many laws reflecting different concerns."[8] The trouble with the application of the rule in criminal proceedings, is that it gives the advocate such narrow scope for admitting relevant, reliable or necessary hearsay, as he is confined to admission within a limited number of exceptions. Furthermore, these exceptions have been judicially altered over time such that it has become difficult to assess what evidence is hearsay and what is hearsay but admissible under the exceptions. However, despite such alterations, little attention has been given to addressing that hearsay which fails to satisfy the requirements set down by the existing exceptions. It is at this point that the admissibility wheel can take effect. To its merit, the wheel advances the concept of the pre-trial assessment of evidence where information can be examined by advocates and judges, thus lowering the risk of hearsay arguments arising at trial. In addition, the wheel may act as an aid to judicial discretion by providing a form by which such discretion may be exercised. A further merit of the wheel is that it is designed to include a cross-reference safeguard. This may require some explanation. At the parameter of the wheel, the questions which I have mentioned above may indicate a tendency to interrelate. This relationship was intentional, in order to offer a continuos examination of cogent hearsay by assessing the evidence in a resolved manner. For example, it might be suggested that information that is relevant amounts to the same thing as information that is necessary. In some cases and under some circumstances, this might be the case. However, when it comes to assessing the admissibility of inadmissible evidence, information that is relevant to a party's case may not always be necessary to the argument of that case, but merely incidental to it. In other circumstances, the disputed hearsay may be both relevant to the case and necessary to a party's argument

---

[6] *Blastland* [1986] AC 41; *Harry* [1988] 86 *Cr App* 105; *Kearley* [1992] *AC* 228.
[7] "The existing law leads to injustices which only the Court of Appeal can remedy, and then only after the defendant may have been deprived of his or her liberty and much public money wasted" (Law Com No 245, p. 39, para 4.13).
[8] A.A.S Zuckerman, *Law Commission Consultation Paper No 138 on Hearsay. (1) The Futility of Hearsay CLR 1996*, Sweet & Maxwell, p. 6.

of it, being perhaps the only evidence that advances a defendant's innocence,[9] or the necessary evidence that holds a strong prosecution case together.[10] I understand that there are many arguments that hearsay ought be admitted only to assist the defence, but the admissibility wheel has a distinct conceptual structure that takes account of the admissibility of both prosecution and defence evidence. As the wheel is proposed to operate in conjunction with judicial discretion and the existing hearsay rule, this point may be a subject of practice.

## Hearsay and Jury Decision making

A possible argument against the use of the wheel is that it does nothing to prevent the breed of fears that are commonly associated with offering hearsay evidence to a jury. Despite these many arguments, empirical studies have shown that there is little to suggest that jurors might not be adequately able to assess the weight of most hearsay given with or without a judicial warning.[11] Assessing the weight that ought to be attributed to evidence is a function of the jury once admissibility has been judicially established. It is an affront to justice to usurp this jury function and the arguments that suggest juror incompetence regarding hearsay have no direct validity or proof. Such arguments stem from a historical suspicion about the ability of lay persons to assess the truth value of secondary evidence in relation to original evidence. The British Law Commission in conducting its research, maintained that so long as juries are used to following complex directions regarding the use that might be made of various types of evidence in common law courts, there is no reason to suggest that they will be incapable of following a judicial directing concerning the weight that may be attributed to hearsay.[12]

## Admissibility Tests

As mentioned above, the questions posed by the wheel may, in some circumstances overlap. For example, issues that in one set of circumstances tend toward admissibility under the fear or state of mind justification may also fall within the third party knowledge justification, since knowledge may in some cases be construed as a state of mind. An example cited earlier was the relevance-necessity overlap. It is not suggested that, if either or all of these questions are answered in the affirmative, that the evidence should be

---

[9] *Blastland* [1986] *AC* 41.
[10] *Kearley* [1992] *AC* 228.
[11] Meine, Park, Borgida & Anderson, 'The Evaluation of Hearsay Evidence', in: *Research of the American Psychological Association*, Boston, Mass. Aug. 1990. Rakos & Landsman, 'Researching the Hearsay Rule', *Minn LR* 76 1991-92, p. 664.
[12] Law Com No 245, p. 31, para 3.26.

admitted. Rather, if the questions on the wheel are put to the disputed evidence and answered affirmatively, perhaps this should be taken into account judicially before such evidence is abandoned. All but one of the wheel's considerations require a 'yes' answer to favour admissibility. The consideration that deals with 'an intention to assert', gleaned from the *Federal Rules of Evidence*, requires that a 'no' answer be given if the evidence is to favour admissibility. This is because it is argued that a statement or action that is not expressly asserted with the intention of creating a belief in the assertion will not pose the usual risks of concoction commonly feared of hearsay. This consideration on the wheel draws a line between express and implied assertions in the context of reliability, inferring that implied assertions make less suspicious evidence. Wherever one stands on this argument, it should be conceded that any merit in it should not lead to admissibility directly, but should fall at least to be considered.

The method of the admissibility wheel then, is that cogent but disputed hearsay is run through the wheel, given an opportunity to be caught by one of the considerations of admissibility located on the cogs. As the wheel spins, the disputed information is filtered by the process and evidence that fails to satisfy these extra tests of admissibility, will spin out to the outer area of inadmissible evidence.

It is not proposed that the common law system should abandon this rule utilitarian approach to evidence and go as far as the continental practice of leaving all to the discretion of the judge. Many of the legal rules that act as constraints on the decision making processes of common law judges have evolved to create a procedural block on fairness at trial that they had originally aimed to prevent. The admissibility wheel is offered as way of making complex rules of evidence, such as the hearsay rule, more transparent. Conversely, civil law judges who are not under the microscope of a transparent system of law, and who do not operate a rule against hearsay evidence, may find use for the wheel as a method which can act as a constraint on an opaque discretion-based decision making process.

# The Accused's Right to Silence with Specific Reference to Tanzania

*E.G. Hoseah*

### The Right to Remain Silent

The right to remain silent is an implicit right under the Tanzania *Constitution*. Article 13(6)(d) of the *Constitution* provides: "For the purposes of preserving the right or equality of human being, human dignity shall be protected in all activities pertaining to criminal investigations and process, and in any other matters, for which a person is restrained, or in the execution of a sentence."[1]

The presumption of innocence is recognised in the major international human rights documents. Article 11(1) of the *Universal Declaration of Human Rights*, adopted in December 10, 1948 by the General Assembly of the United Nations, provides: "Everyone charged with a criminal offence shall have the right to be presumed innocent until proved guilty according to law".

Article 13(6) of the Tanzania *Constitution* states: "No person charged with a criminal offence shall be treated as guilty of the offence until guilty of that offence."

The *International Covenant on Civil and Political Rights 1996*, Article 14(2) provides: "Every one charged with a criminal offence shall have right to be presumed innocent until proved guilty according to law."

The right to remain silent is an important principle against self-incrimination because a fair balance has to be struck and maintained. The state's primary responsibility of maintaining law and order has to be counter balanced by the inviolability of the human personality as Chief Justice Earl Warren of the US Supreme Court in the celebrated decision of *Miranda* v. *Arizona*[2] expressing the views of five members of the Court, laid down the governing principles, the most important of which is that, as a constitutional pre-requisite to the admissibility of such statements the suspect must, in the absence of a clear, intelligent waiver of the constitutional rights involved, be warned prior to questioning that he has a right to remain silent, that any statement he does make may be used as evidence against him, and that he has a right to the presence of an attorney, either retained or appointed.

The Chief Justice further wrote: "Our accusatory system of criminal justice demands that the government seeking to punish an individual produce the evidence against him by its own independent labours, rather than by the cruel, simple expedient of compelling it from his own mouth. (…) The privilege it fulfilled only when the person is guaranteed the right to remain silent unless he

---

[1] The *Constitution of the United Republic of Tanzania of 1977* as amended from time to time.
[2] 384 *U.S.* 436 (1966).

chooses to speak in the unlettered exercise of his own will." (emphasis supplied).

In Tanzania, under Section 52(1), (2) and (3) of the *Criminal Procedure Act*,[3] a police officer,[4] when questioning a suspect on reasonable suspicion that an offence has been committed, has a statutory duty to first inform the suspect that he may refuse to answer any questions put to him. Once the suspect has been so informed of his right to remain silent or refuse to answer any questions put to him, he shall sign or thumb print an acknowledgement, in accordance with a prescribed form, of the fact that he has been so informed and of the date on which, and the time at which, he is so informed.

However, the difficulty in ensuring that this right to remain silent is observed, depends on the suspect/defendant's knowledge that he is aware of the existence of such a statutory duty imposed to police officers when interviewing or interrogating the suspects.

The number of practising lawyers in the country is about 390. The entire population of the country is above 30 million people. Out of these 30 million people, 85% is unaware of the existence of such statutory right of the suspect charged with an offence to remain silent.

It is rather of grave concern within the law enforcement agencies that this right to remain silent is not effectively applied in all cases at all times.

The Police Manuals[5] as analysed in the *Miranda* case suggest that the police officers are told that it is encouraged that: "Interrogation should take place in the investigator's office or at least in a room of his on choice. The subject should be deprived of even psychological advantage. In his own home, he may be confident, indignant, or recalcitrant. He is more keenly aware of his rights and more reluctant to tell of his indiscretions or criminal behaviour within the walls of his home. Moreover, his family and other friends are nearby, their presence lending moral support. In his own office, the investigator possesses all the advantages. The atmosphere suggests the invincibility of the forces of the law."[6]

In the US, the *Fifth Amendment* privilege is so fundamental and the expedient of giving an adequate warning to the suspect as to the availability of the privilege will not pause to inquire in individual cases whether the

---

[3] Act no. 9 of 1985.

[4] The word 'police officer' includes any member of the police force and, includes any member of the people's militia when exercising police functions in accordance with the laws for the time being in force.

[5] Kidd, *Police Interrogation* (1940), Mulbar, *Interrogation* (1951); Dienstein, *Ethics for the Crime Investigator* (1952); La Fave, *Arrest: The Decision to take a Suspect into Custody* (1965); La Fave, 'Detention for Investigation by the Police: An Analysis of Current Practices' (1962), *Wash. Univ. L.Q.* 331; Barret, *Police Practices and the Law is the Principal Psychological Factor contributing to a Successful Interrogation*; '...From Arrest to Release or Charge', 50 *Calif. L. Rev.* 11(1962); Inbau & Reid, *Criminal Interrogation and confessions* (1962).

[6] *Miranda* v. *Arizona, supra*.

defendant was aware of his rights without a warning being given. A warning at the time of the interrogation is important to overcome its pressures and to ensure that the individual's free will to exercise the privilege to remain silent at the time in point is observed.

In analysing the evidence in the *Miranda* case, the Supreme Court found that the petitioner, Ernesto Miranda, while undergoing police interrogation, was questioned by two police officers. The officers admitted at trial that Miranda was not advised that he had a right to have an attorney present. Two hours later, the officers emerged from the interrogation room with a written confession signed by Miranda. At the top of the statement was a typed paragraph stating that the confession was made voluntarily, without threats or promises or immunity and "with full knowledge of my rights, understanding any statement I make may be used against me".[7]

The US Supreme Court reversed the decision of the Supreme Court of Arizona which held that Miranda's constitutional rights were not violated in obtaining the confession and which had affirmed the conviction. Dissenting opinions (Clark in part, Harlan, White and Stewart) in the *Miranda* case were of the view that the majority decision of the Court represents poor constitutional law and entails harmful consequences.

In summary, the reasons that they advanced are that the thrust of new rules is to negate all pressures, to reinforce the nervous or ignorant suspect, and ultimately to discourage any confession at all. Viewed as a choice based on pure policy, these new rules prove to be a highly debatable, if not one-sided, appraisal of the competing interests, imposed on widespread objection, at the very time when judicial restraint is not called for by the circumstances.

The dissenting justices further contend that the unspoken assumption, that any pressure violates the privilege, was not supported by the precedents and that it was not shown why the *Fifth Amendment* prohibits that relatively mild pressure the 'Due Process Clause' permits. They also said that while the majority found no pertinent difference between judicial proceedings and police interrogation, to them, the difference was so vast as to disqualify wholly the *Sixth Amendment* precedents as suitable analogies in the *Miranda* case.

The Court's new code would markedly decrease the number of confessions and to suggest or provide counsel for the suspect simply invites the end of the interrogation. The Court was taking a real risk with society's welfare in imposing its new regime on the country. The social costs of crime would be too great to call the new rules anything but a hazardous experimentation.

In conclusion, the dissenting justices were of the firm view that there was nothing wrong or immoral and certainly nothing unconstitutional, in the police's asking a suspect whom they had reasonable cause to arrest whether or

---

[7] *Ibid.*

not he killed his wife or in confronting him with the evidence on which the arrest was based.

Moreover, it is by no means certain that the process of confessing is injurious to the accused. To the contrary it may provide psychological relief and enhance the prospects for rehabilitation.

In Tanzania, during criminal proceedings (trial), if the prosecution does not produce the accused's/defendant's statement as required above, then the court shall assume, unless the contrary is proved, that the person was not so informed.

*A proviso* is inserted under sub-section (4) of Section 52 of the above law that, "[n]otwithstanding the preceding provisions of this section, where a police officer in the course of interrogating any person under this section, believes that there is sufficient evidence to warrant that person being charged with an offence, he shall proceed to charge him accordingly and to caution in writing and if practicable orally in the prescribed manner, and to inform him that an inference adverse to him may be drawn from his failure or refusal to answer any question or from his failure or refusal to disclose at that stage any matter which may be material to the charge."

The law recognises the accused's/defendant's rights[8] where a person is under restraint, a police officer is duty bound not to ask him any question, or ask him to do anything in relation to investigation concerned, unless:

1. the police officer has told him his name and rank;
2. the person has been informed by a police officer, in a language in which he is fluent, in writing and, if practicable orally, of the fact that he is under restraint and of the offence in respect of which he is under restraint; and
3. the person has been cautioned by a police officer in the following manner, namely, by informing him, or causing him to be informed, in a language in which he is fluent, in writing in accordance with prescribed form and, if practicable orally:
    1. that he is not obliged to answer any question asked of him by a police officer, other than a question seeking particulars of his name and address; and
    2. that, subject to this Act, he may communicate with a relative or friend.

The law also provides that, "[a] police officer shall, upon request by a person who is under restraint, cause reasonable facilities to be provided to enable the person to communicate with a lawyer, a relative or friend of his choice."[9]

However, the same law imposes certain conditions to the right of the suspect in the following manner: if the police officer believes on reasonable grounds that it is necessary to prevent the person under restraint from

---

[8] Section 53 of Act no. 9 of 1985.
[9] *Ibid.*, Section 54(1).

communicating with the person for purpose of preventing: the escape of an accomplice of the person under restraint; or the loss, destruction or fabrication of evidence relating to the offence.[10]

It is clear from the above provisions of law that, although he is entitled to obtain information with respect to a suspected offence, a police officer has no lawful power to compel the person questioned to answer.

The right to remain silent becomes engaged in the event that the person who wishes to assert it has been either arrested or detained. Conduct falling short of arrest or detention will not suffice to invoke the guarantee, respect to any statements he might give to the police.

Cory, J.A. on behalf of other Justices of the Ontario Court of Appeal, wrote that: "It would appear that Sections 11(c) and 13 of the *Charter* deal only with the testimonial right not to testify and are not applicable to the facts of this case. That is to say, a person charged with an offence cannot be compelled to be a witness in those same proceedings. Further, there is the right of a witness not to have incriminating evidence used against him or her in subsequent proceedings."

However, the right against self-incrimination cannot be limited to Sections 11(c) and 13 of the *Charter*. Consideration must still be given to the extent to which that same right, at least to the extent that it is encompassed within the principle of the right to remain silent, is protected by Section 7 of the *Charter*.[11]

The right to remain silent is a well-settled principle in almost all democratic Commonwealth countries. This right is operative from the investigative stage of the criminal process, that is, arrest, interrogation and confession. An accused/defendant is under no legal obligation to speak to the police authorities and there is no legal power vested in the police to compel the accused/defendant to speak.

## The Right to Legal Counsel

In Tanzania, the case of *Thomas Mjengi* v. *R.*[12] dealt with the right to legal counsel. The two appellants Thomas s/o Mjengi and Ramadhani s/o Mussa were charged and convicted of robbery with violence c/s 285 and 286 of the penal code; cap. 16. They were each sentenced to the prescribed minimum sentence of 30 years imprisonment and ten strokes of corporal punishment *(sic)*. They appealed to the High Court against conviction and sentence.

Under Section 3 of the *Legal Aid (Criminal Proceedings) Act*[13] the Court appointed an advocate to represent the appellants.

---

[10] *Ibid.*, Section 54(2).
[11] *Ibid.*
[12] (1992) *TLR* 157 (HC).
[13] Act no. 21 of 1969.

On appeal, counsel for the defendant raised three matters of constitutional importance and public interests as well. The first issue was that the trial was a nullity because the indigent appellants were denied their right to free legal aid payable by the state nor were they informed of their right to engage counsel at their own expense. Secondly, that the mandatory minimum sentence of 30 years imprisonment is an inhuman and degrading punishment and so unconstitutional. Thirdly, that corporal punishment is inhuman and degrading punishment and so unconstitutional.

Mwalusanya, J. deciding the appeal, began by addressing the first issue of the right to legal representation. He wrote: "The constitutional right to legal representation stands on two legs – first under Article 13(6)(a) of our constitution which provides for the right to be heard. There are two persuasive authorities which interpret the phrase 'fair hearing' in their constitutions to include the right to legal representation paid for by the state for an indigent person whose constitutional rights are at stake. First we have the case of *Powell* v. *Alabama* (1932) 287 *U.S.* 45 decided by the US Supreme Court. Then from Zimbabwe the Supreme Court there in the case of *Dube & Another* v. *The State*: Supreme Court Judgement No. 212/1988. The third persuasive authority is the decision of the Supreme Court of the Republic of Ireland in the case of *The State (Healy)* v. *Donoghue* (1976) *IR* 325.

The second leg on which the constitutional right rests is on the right to personal freedom under Article 15(2) of our constitution. That Article stipulates that no one shall be deprived of his personal liberty except by procedure established by law. In India in the case of *Maneka Gandhi* v. *Union of India* (1978) 2 *S.C.R.* 248, interpreting a similar provision, it was held by the Supreme Court there, that no procedure can be regarded as a reasonable, fair and just which does not afford legal representation to an accused person who is placed in jeopardy of his life or personal liberty in a criminal proceedings. The above decision was in principle adopted by the Tanzania Court of Appeal in the case of *DPP* v. *Daudi Pete*: Criminal Appeal no 28/1990 (unreported)."

The judge further found that the right to legal representation is contained in Section 310 of the *Criminal Procedure Act*[15] which provides that: "Any person accused before any criminal court, other than a primary court may of right be defended by an advocate of the High Court, subject always to the provisions of any rules of court made by the High Court under powers conferred by Article 26 of the *Tanganyika Order in Council, 1920* from time to time in force."

---

[14] *See* footnote 1.
[15] Act no. 9 of 1985, *See also Laurent s/o Joseph* v. *R.* (1981) TLR 351, which held that in either case whether the offence is triable by the High Court or Subordinate Court, the trial is a nullity if the indigent accused person was not provided with counsel, at least for a serious offences. *See also Mohamed s/o Salim* v. *R.* (1958) *E.A.* 202.

On the second issue, the Judge stated that the mandatory minimum sentence of 30 years imprisonment under the minimum sentences Act no. 1 of 1972 as amended by Act no. 10 of 1989 is unconstitutional and void because it is inhuman and degrading punishment. On the third issue of corporal punishment, the judge held that the mandatory minimum sentence of 122 strokes of corporal punishment is unconstitutional and void as it is an inhuman and degrading punishment prohibited by Article 13(b)(e) of the *Constitution*.

The proper test whether a punishment is inhuman and degrading is the disproportionate test. The judge concluded that a derogation clause should not be interpreted as entitling the government to impose vague or arbitrary limitations on basic human rights, but that limitation should be reasonable and only be invoked when there exists adequate safeguards and effective remedies against abuse.

### Can the Court draw an Adverse Inference when an Accused remains Silent?

On adverse inference drawn by the court on the accused's silence, the case of *Boniface Mboje & Another* v. *R.*[16] is significant. The facts of the case are that the two appellants were charged with the offence of stealing contrary to Section 265 of the penal code. It was alleged that they jointly and together stole an assortment of carpentry tools belonging to one Doto Shija.

The stolen goods were later identified by the owner and after close of the prosecution's case at trial, the first appellant changed his plea from that of not guilty to that of guilty to the charge. The court found him guilty and convicted after trial. Both appellants were sentenced to six years imprisonment. They appealed to the High Court against this sentence.

The second appellant was convicted because he was implicated by the co-accused's statement. The trial court appeared to have convicted him simply because he chose to say nothing in his defence, when the options that were open to him were pointed and explained at the close of the prosecution's case.

Sekule, J. held that it is true that a court can draw an adverse inference on an accused's choice of silence. But this alone cannot be a basis of a conviction in the absence of evidence establishing an accused's guilt. The appeal was allowed. The second appellant's conviction was quashed and sentence set aside. The sentence of six years imprisonment meted to the first appellant, was found to be manifestly excessive and for that reason it was reduced to one of three years imprisonment.

In another case of *Mrisho Salum* v. *R.*,[17] the trial court ruled that since the appellant absconded from lawful custody after hearing the first prosecution

---

[16] (1991) *TLR* 156 (HC).
[17] (1991) *TLR* 158 (HC).

witness, it was reasonable to draw an adverse inference against the accused and that a prima facie case was established against him. The court went on to convict him in absentia as charged and sentenced him to 13 years imprisonment for house breaking and stealing and one year imprisonment for unlawful possession of bhang. He appealed to the High Court.

Sekule, J. held that the appellant's action of running away was not sufficient, in itself, to show that he was a party to the commission of the offences of housebreaking and stealing. As the first prosecution witness did not mention anything on bhang, the court was not justified in holding that a prima facie case had been established in respect of it. The provisions of Section 227 of the *Criminal Procedure Act* are applicable where the accused fails to appear on a date fixed for continuation of hearing after the close of the prosecution case or on the date fixed for passing the sentence. On the basis of Section 226 of the *Criminal Procedure Act* the trial court had a duty to hear the prosecution case to the end and if it was satisfied that the evidence adduced warranted a conviction it could have proceeded to convict the appellant in absentia. The appeal succeeded, conviction quashed and the sentence set aside and the appellant released.

The statutory foundation for the Court to draw an adverse inference is provided for under Section 231(1) and (3) of the *Criminal Procedure Act*[18] that: "231(1) At the close of the evidence in support of the charge, it is appears to the court that a case is made against the accused person sufficiently to require him to make a defence either in relation to the offence with which he is charged or in relation to any other offence of which the provisions of Section 312-321 inclusive of this Act he is liable to be convicted, the court shall again explain inclusive substance of the charge to the accused and inform him of his right:

1. to give evidence whether or not on oath or affirmation, on his own behalf;
2. to call witnesses in his defence; and shall then ask the accused person, or his advocate, if it is intended to exercise any of the above rights and shall record the answer. The Court shall then call on the accused person to enter on his defence save where the accused person does not wish to exercise either of the above rights;
3. if the accused, after he has been informed in terms of subsection (1) elects to remain silent the court shall be entitled to draw an adverse inference against him and the court as well as the prosecution shall be permitted to comment on the failure by the accused to give evidence."[19]

As we have noted in the *Mrisho Salum* case,[20] the adverse inference against the accused is not an automatic condition. The Court has to consider all factors

---

[18] *See* footnote 3.
[19] *Ibid.*
[20] *See* footnote 6.

in relation to the charge and draw a fair assessment of the evidence adduced before it.

### The International Criminal Tribunal Experience

The right of suspects to be informed before questioning of their rights is an important safeguard of the right to a fair trail. The Yugoslavia and Rwanda Tribunals' Rules require that the suspect shall be informed of the rights to legal counsel or free legal assistance, to free interpretation and to remain silent, in a language the suspect understands before being questioned by the prosecutor.[21]

Article 26(6) of the International Law Commission draft statute, which applies to a suspect whether at liberty or under restraint requires that: "A person suspected of a crime under this statute shall: a) prior to being questioned, be informed that the person is a suspect and of four rights: *to silence*, to legal counsel or free legal assistance, no to be compelled to testify or confess and to have translation and interpretation."[22] (Emphasis added.)

The right to silence is clearly an important element in criminal justice systems as it augments the cardinal principle of the presumption of innocence and the right of the defendant or accused person not to be compelled to testify or confess guilt.

Access of the defendant to the outside world-families and friends, lawyers and independent medical attention are important factors for the lawfulness of the defendant's detention. Such access is an important safeguard against torture and ill treatment. The right to silent and access to the outside world are safeguards, which are necessary in the criminal justice system to guarantee fairness and preservation of the integrity of the Rule of law.

### Conclusion

The right to silence is a human rights requirement in the discharge of criminal investigation and compilation of evidence in the criminal justice system. It is therefore, a necessary safeguard against the powerful state apparatuses that might infringe on individual liberty and freedoms as protected by the constitutions. The poor, the weak and the rich alike, must be equally and similarly protected by the due process of the Rule of law which requires fairness, justice and equality before the law. The major challenge ahead is how and to what extent; the unsophisticated, the uneducated and the poor, particularly in the south, are most hard hit by the brutality of non-adherence to

---

[21] *Yugoslavia Rules*, Rule 42(A), *Rwanda Rules*, Rule 42(A).
[22] *See* United Nations, *Human Rights and Pre-Trial Detention: A Handbook of International Standards Relating to Pre-Trial Detention*, 1994.

the Rule of law and the abuse of pre-trial safeguards available to the suspect or defendant.

The Canadian Law Reform Commission proposes here: "You have a right to remain silent, and you are free to exercise that right at anytime. If you wish to make a statement or answer questions, anything you say may be introduced as evidence in court. Before you make a statement or answer any questions you may contact a lawyer. This warning shall be given orally and may also be given in writing."[23]

The above discussion has shown that if an individual is held by the police for interrogation and indicates in any manner, at any time prior to or during questioning, that he wishes to remain silent, the interrogation must cease. The rules of procedure and practice are that the suspect must be accorded the privilege against self-incrimination unless he decides to waive that privilege.

The need for counsel as discussed above, is an important protection and privilege against self-incrimination. Counsel may be present prior to questioning by a police officer and also during the actual interrogation, if the accused/suspect so wishes.

In Tanzania, the court taking into account the circumstances of the case before it, may draw an adverse inference where the accused decides to remain silent while knowing that the court had ruled that the prosecution side had advanced sufficient evidence in support of the charge; then that would require any reasonable person to advance evidence that would cast doubt to the evidence submitted by the prosecution.

What we should expect as another challenge ahead is what Cardozo, J. stated in *Synder* v. *Massachusetts*[24] that "Justice, though due to the accused, is due to the accuser also. The concept of fairness must not be strained till it is narrowed to a filament. We are to keep the balance true."[25]

The right to silence is an important safeguard against self-incrimination by the suspect/accused and perhaps, in case of Tanzania, this right to remain silent does not extend beyond trial at the stage where the accused is required by law to make his/her defence as required by Section 231(3) of the *Criminal Procedure Act (supra)*.

---

[23] Report no. 23 Questioning Suspects (1985) 12-13.
[24] 291 *U.S.* 97, 122.
[25] *Ibid.*

# The Paradox of Privilege Law

*E.J. Imwinkelried*

American privilege law is entering a paradoxical stage – a development which has important implications for other liberal democracies. The paradox revolves around Dean Wigmore's instrumental theory for privilege doctrine.[1] For a good part of the 20th century, that theory has dominated American legal reasoning about privileges. Moreover, the theory has influenced the development of privilege in other countries, including Canada.

According to the instrumental theory, the end objective of privilege law is encouraging certain types of desirable consultations and revelations such as disclosures between spouses and between clients and their attorneys. The theory conceives privileges as an essential means to attaining that end. The underlying behavioral assumption is that but for the assurance of confidentiality provided by the privilege, these parties would be unwilling to consult or make necessary revelations. On this assumption, the recognition of evidentiary privileges not only serves a legitimate social function. Further, given that assumption, the recognition of privileges comes virtually cost free. The US Supreme Court has said as much in its two most recent privilege decisions, *Jaffee*[2] dealing with the psychotherapist privilege and *Swidler & Berlin*[3] concerning the attorney-client privilege. In both decisions, the Court asserted that the judicial enforcement of privileges entails little or no cost to the judicial system. The Court declared that but for the existence of the privilege, the patient or client would probably not make the statement to begin with. The theory posits that without the privilege, the potential evidence – the statement – would not come into existence.

If one accepts that behavioral assumption, the instrumental theory is a comforting one. The theory is comforting because it eliminates any theoretical tension between promoting the privileged relations and promoting rectitude of decision by the courts.[4] The application of the privileges does not deprive the courts of any relevant evidence that would otherwise have come into existence. The courts may consistently and simultaneously pursue the goals of promoting the privileged relationships and accurately applying the substantive law to the facts of the pending case. The rub, though, is that this consistency is illusory. There is mounting evidence that in reality, there is tension between these two goals. The purpose of this paper is to identify the tension and sketch the ramifications of the tension.

---

[1] 8 J. Wigmore, Evidence { 2285 (McNaughton (ed.), 1961).

[2] *Jaffee* v. *Redmond*, 518 *U.S.* 1 (1996).

[3] *Swidler & Berlin* v. *US*, 524 *U.S.* 399 (1998).

[4] E.J. Imwinkelried, 'The Rivalry Between Truth and Privilege: The Weakness of the Supreme Court's Instrumental Reasoning in Jaffee v. Redmond, 518 *U.S.* 1 (1996)', 49 *Hastings L.J.* 969 (1998).

### One Term of the Paradox: the US Supreme Court's Steadfast Adherence to the Instrumental Theory

On the one hand, at the very highest levels the American judiciary seems more committed to Dean Wigmore's instrumental theory than ever before. That certainly holds true in the case of the US Supreme Court. The two recent cases in point are *Jaffee*[5] and *Swidler & Berlin*.[6] Both decisions fit the same mold: the Court expressly cites Dean Wigmore, relies exclusively on his instrumental theory, and classifies the privilege in issue as absolute. Although in each opinion the Court acknowledges that the privilege might be subject to exceptions defined in advance, the Court insists that the privilege is not subject to ad hoc, case-specific balancing. No matter how compelling the litigant's need for the allegedly privileged information, the showing of need cannot override the privilege.

The Court rendered its decision in *Jaffee v. Redmond*[7] in 1996. There the party objecting to discovery claimed a psychotherapist privilege. The lower court decision had been handed down by the Court of Appeals for the Seventh Circuit.[8] The intermediate appellate court recognized a psychotherapist privilege. However, in doing so, the court relied on humanistic as well as instrumental rationales. In addition to citing Dean Wigmore's theory, the court argued that the recognition of a privilege would safeguard a zone of privacy fostering personal autonomy.[9] Moreover, the court concluded that the new privilege should be classified as conditional or qualified.[10] The court appreciated that the recognition of a privilege could obstruct the search for truth. The court stated that in an extreme case, a litigant's acute need for the privileged information might surmount the privilege. Yet, on the facts of the case, the court ruled that the privilege claim ought to have been sustained.[11]

Although the Supreme Court affirmed the judgement of the Seventh Circuit,[12] the Supreme Court parted company with the Seventh Circuit in two respects. First, the Court relied exclusively on instrumental reasoning. The Court completely disregarded the alternative, humanistic rationale advanced by the Seventh Circuit. Second, the Court ruled emphatically that any psychotherapist privilege had to be absolute in character. Writing for the majority, Mr. Justice Stevens asserted: "We reject the balancing component of the privilege implemented by [the Court of Appeals]. (...) Making the promise of confidentiality contingent upon a trial judge's later evaluation of the relative importance of the patient's interest in privacy and the evidentiary need for

---

[5] *Jaffee v. Redmond*, 518 *U.S.* 1 (1996).
[6] *Swidler & Berlin v. US*, 524 *U.S.* 399 (1998).
[7] 518 *U.S.* 1 (1996).
[8] *Jaffee v. Redmond*, 51 *F.3d* 1346 (7th Cir. 1995), *aff'd*, 518 *U.S.* 1 (1996).
[9] *Id.*, at 1356.
[10] *Id.*, at 1357.
[11] *Id.*, at 1358.
[12] *Jaffee v. Redmond*, 518 *U.S.* 1 (1996).

disclosure would eviscerate the effectiveness of the privilege. [I]f the purpose of the privilege is to be served, the participants 'must be able to predict with some degree of certainty whether particular discussions will be protected. An uncertain privilege, or one which purports to be certain but results in widely varying applications by the courts, is little better than no privilege at all.'"[13]

Like Dean Wigmore, Justice Stevens viewed the absolute nature of privileges as a corollary of the instrumental theory. A privilege can furnish the requisite assurance of confidentiality only if any exceptions are specified both clearly and in advance. Allowing the privilege to be defeated by a later case-specific balancing supposedly erodes the assurance. To decide whether to consult and reveal, the person must be able to forecast whether a privilege will protect his or her revelation. Classifying the privilege as qualified would deny the person that ability. The Supreme Court's 1998 decision in *Swidler & Berlin* v. *US*[14] is strikingly similar to its opinion in *Jaffee*. There the Court held that an absolute attorney-client privilege survives the client's death. The client in question was himself a lawyer, Deputy White House Counsel Vincent W. Foster, Jr. In 1993 various officers of the White House Travel Office had been dismissed. There had been an investigation of the dismissals. Later the Office of the Independent Counsel investigated to determine whether false statements had been made or obstruction of justice had occurred during the 1993 investigation.[15] Foster had participated in the 1993 investigation. After the Independent Counsel began his investigation, Foster consulted a private attorney, James Hamilton, at the firm of Swidler & Berlin. Foster met with Hamilton for two hours. Hamilton took three pages of handwritten notes of the meeting. One of the initial entries in the notes was the word "Privileged".[16] Foster committed suicide nine days later. The Independent Counsel later learned that Foster had consulted Hamilton. At the Independent Counsel's request, a federal grand jury issued subpoenas to Hamilton and Swidler & Berlin for the handwritten notes. In response, they moved to quash on the ground that the attorney-client privilege protected the notes.

In *Swidler & Berlin*, the lower court was the Court of Appeals for the District of Columbia Circuit.[17] The District of Columbia Circuit's opinion was kindred to the Seventh Circuit's opinion in *Jaffee*. Just as the Seventh Circuit had recognized a psychotherapist privilege, the District of Columbia Circuit ruled that there was an applicable attorney-client privilege. The parallel to the Seventh Circuit decision continued; like the Seventh Circuit, the District of Columbia Circuit cited humanistic privacy concerns as well as Dean Wigmore's instrumental theory. Finally, the District of Columbia Circuit concluded that in fact situations

---

[13] *Id.*, at 17-18.
[14] 524 *U.S.* 399 (1998).
[15] *Id.*, at 401.
[16] *Id.*, at 402.
[17] *In re Sealed Case*, 124 *F.3d* 230 (D.C.Cir. 1997), *rev'd*, 524 *U.S.* 399 (1998).

such as *Swidler & Berlin*, the privilege should be deemed qualified rather than absolute.[18] In the court's mind, the key parameters of the fact situation were that the client was now deceased and that the client's revelations were logically relevant in a federal criminal investigation. The court reasoned that compelling posthumous disclosure represented less of an intrusion on the client's privacy. The court added that there is a heightened public interest in disclosure when the information is sought in a criminal proceeding rather than a civil action.

As in *Jaffee*, the Supreme Court voiced its disagreement with the lower court. Once again the Court eschewed any reliance on the humanistic theory suggested by the lower court. Chief Justice Rehnquist's majority opinion is based squarely and exclusively on Wigmore's instrumental theory. Further, the Court again avowed that any privilege must be absolute. The Chief Justice wrote: "Balancing ex post the importance of the information against client interests, even limited to criminal cases, introduces substantial uncertainty, into the privilege's application. For just that reason, we have rejected use of a balancing test in defining the contours of the privilege. See (…) *Jaffee* (…)."[19]

The upshot is that in both cases, the Supreme Court's opinions would have pleased Dean Wigmore. The Court not only wholeheartedly embraced the dean's instrumental theory. Moreover, the Court adopted the theory to the exclusion of humanistic theories advanced by the lower courts and accepted the most important implication of the theory, namely, the conclusion that privileges must be categorized as absolute rather than conditional.

### The Second Term of the Paradox: the Mounting Evidence of the Weakness of the Instrumental Theory

The crux of the paradox is that at the same time the US Supreme Court is affirming, if not intensifying, its commitment to the instrumental theory, there is mounting evidence of the theory's weakness.

Interestingly enough, in footnote in both *Jaffee*[20] and *Swidler*,[21] the Court felt obliged to cite "[e]mpirical evidence"[22] of the validity of the instrumental theory. That sense of obligation is understandable. It is certainly not evident *a priori* that but for the existence of evidentiary privileges, spouses would not freely converse or clients would withhold vital information from attorneys. The problem is that the studies cited by the Court fall short of establishing the proposition that in the typical case, the patient or client would refuse to either confer or make necessary disclosures.

For example, a close examination of the studies cited by the Court in *Jaffee*,

---

[18] *Id.*, at 231-35.
[19] *Swidler & Berlin* v. *US*, 524 *U.S.* 399, 409 (1998).
[20] *Jaffee* v. *Redmond*, 518 *U.S.* 1, 10 n. 9 (1996).
[21] *Swidler & Berlin* v. *US*, 524 *U.S.* 399, 409-10, n. 4 (1998).
[22] *Id.*

the psychotherapy case, tends to support the following findings: the average patient is far more concerned about out-of-court disclosure to third parties such as employers than judicially supervised disclosure in court;[23] and in deciding whether to make a revelation to a psychotherapist, the typical patient relies more on his or her sense of the psychotherapist's professional ethics than any assumption about the existence of an evidentiary privilege.[24] In short, there is "little [empirical] evidence that the lack of a privilege would deter patients from consulting (...) psychiatrists (...)."[25] Likewise, on scrutiny, the empirical studies of the attorney-client privilege point to the same conclusions.[26] One of the leading studies of that privilege found that the typical client was willing to confide in his or her attorney even though the client erroneously assumed that the exceptions to the scope of the privilege are far more extensive than they in fact are.[27]

To be sure, the data is quite limited, and further research is warranted. However, there is good reason to doubt whether empirical research will ever validate the behavioral assumption underlying the instrumental theory. In many, perhaps most, cases, these consultations occur "prelitigation".[28] The conversants meet "before a law suit was ever dreamed of".[29] In addition, even when there is a prospect of litigation on the horizon, the person may be "caught up in the urgency of their immediate problem".[30] The layperson's focus is "on the 'here and now' rather than on disclosure [in court] at some indefinite future time".[31] The concrete, immediate problem probably looms first and foremost in the layperson's mind. As Professor Edward Cleary, the Reporter for the *Federal Rules of Evidence* Advisory Committee, remarked during the Congressional hearings on the then draft Federal Rules, it is fanciful to assume that the patient needs the incentive of an evidentiary privilege to respond to the physician's questions when the patient believes that "life itself may be in jeopardy".[32] Similarly, the instrumental case for a spousal communications privilege rests on "highly suspect" "assumptions concerning the (...) psychology of married

---

[23] E.J. Imwinkelried, 'The Rivalry Between Truth and Privilege: The Weakness of the Supreme Court's Instrumental Reasoning in Jaffee v. Redmond, 518 *U.S.* 1 (1996)', 49 *Hastings L.J.* 969 (1998), 976-78.

[24] *Id.*, at 979.

[25] S.B. McNicol, *The Law of Privilege* (1992), 341-49.

[26] R.C. Wydick, 'The Attorney-Client Privilege: Does It Really Have Life Everlasting?', 87 *Ky.L.J.* 1165 (1998-99), 1171-73.

[27] F. Zacharias, 'Rethinking Confidentiality', 74 *Iowa L.Rev.* 351 (1989), 394-95.

[28] *Federal Rules of Evidence*, Com.Jud., US Senate, 93d Cong., 2d Sess. 88 (1974)(the statement of Professor J. Francis Paschal of Duke University Law School).

[29] *Id.*

[30] E.J. Imwinkelried, 'Court Ducks Larger Privilege Issues Yet Again', *Nat'l L.J.*, July 20, 1998, p. A22.

[31] *Id.*

[32] Rules of Evidence, Special Subcomm. Reform Fed. Crim. Laws, Comm.Jud., H.Rep., 93d Cong., 1st Sess. 557 (1973)(statement of Professor Edward Cleary).

persons".[33] If a spouse fears that a problem poses a severe, imminent threat to either the marriage or the welfare of a family member, it is questionable to presume that the spouse would refrain from discussing the problem with his or her marriage partner but for the existence of an evidentiary privilege.

It is to be expected that as lawyers and judges, we almost constantly have litigation on our mind. However, it is a mistake to project the same mindset to the laypersons who confer with their spouses and consult professionals, even attorneys. Further, if there are doubts about the validity of the instrumental theory in the US, there is all the more reason to question exclusive reliance on the theory in other liberal democracies. It is a commonplace observation that the US is the most litigious society in the world – perhaps in world history.[34] Given the litigious nature of American society, one would think that the case for reliance on the instrumental theory would be stronger in the US than anywhere else. If there are flaws in the case in the US, the case would presumably be even weaker elsewhere.

This is not to say that the instrumental theory is utterly devoid of merit. The theory has greater utility and validity in such contexts as governmental privilege. A private citizen contemplating reporting a crime to the police might well be reluctant to come forward if he or she feared that anyone subsequently charged with the crime could routinely learn the informant's identity. That fear could be a significant deterrent to informants in prosecutions involving gangs and organized crime. In addition, in a given case, the behavioral assumption underlying the instrumental theory might hold true. In *Jaffee*, the person who consulted the psychotherapist was a police officer with legal training. The officer consulted the therapist for a substantial period of time; and while the opinion is unclear on this point, the consultations might well have continued after the lawsuit was threatened or even filed. On these facts, the patient could certainly have been more guarded in her revelations to the therapist if she had not been confident that a privilege shielded their consultations. The point is not that the instrumental theory should be altogether abandoned. Rather, the point is that the Supreme Court has erred in relying solely on the instrumental theory to the complete exclusion of other considerations in shaping American privilege doctrine.

### The Possible Resolutions of the Paradox

In light of the foregoing analysis, what are the possible resolutions of the paradox? There are at least three candidates: the maintenance of the status quo–continued, exclusive reliance on the instrumental theory; a radical abolition of all or most privileges; or the development of an alternative, non-instrumental theory

---

[33] 1 McCormick, *Evidence* (86, at 309 (4ᵗʰ ed. 1992).
[34] *See* Note, 'The Privilege of Self-Critical Analysis: Encouraging Recognition of the Misunderstood Privilege', 8 *Kan.J.L. & Pub.Pol.* 221, 236 (1999).

to supplement the now dominant instrumental model.

One possibility is to maintain the status quo. The American courts could simply continue to place exclusive reliance on the instrumental theory for privilege law. In effect, they could adopt an attitude of denial toward the seeming weaknesses in the instrumental theory.

At one time, this option might have been a lively option. However, it will become increasingly unacceptable. In 1993, in *Daubert* v. *Merrell Dow Pharmaceuticals Inc.*[35], the Supreme Court adopted a new empirical validation standard for determining the admissibility of purportedly scientific evidence.[36] In 1999, the Court indicated that to an extent, the new test applies across the board to all species of expert testimony.[37] Taking their cue from the Supreme Court, the lower courts have applied the test to soft as well as hard science.[38] Thanks in part to the *Daubert* standard, the courts are becoming more adept at identifying empirical issues and evaluating empirical showings. As time passes, unless the studies of the real world impact of evidentiary privileges yield markedly different findings than in the past, it will be less and less tenable to blind ourselves to the deficiencies in the instrumental theory. Intellectual dishonesty will demand that the courts confront those deficiencies.

Another option would be abolishing all or most privileges. As radical as that step might appear, logic suggests that if the only justification for privileges is the instrumental theory and that theory is flawed, the option deserves consideration.

Yet, in the final analysis, that option will prove unacceptable. An abolitionist trend has swept through American evidence law.[39] The standards in many areas of evidence doctrine have been lowered and relaxed.[40] In particular, the *Federal Rules of Evidence* have eased admissibility criteria in such doctrinal areas as expert testimony,[41] hearsay,[42] authentication[43] and best evidence.[44] Only one doctrinal area – privilege – has largely resisted this trend.[45]

The Supreme Court decisions mentioned above are illustrative. In *Swidler*,[46] the Court declined the Independent Counsel's invitation to narrow the scope of the attorney-client privilege. Thus, the Court held the line on a recognized

---

[35] 509 *U.S.* 579 (1993).
[36] *See* generally B. Black, F.J. Ayala & C. Saffran-Brinks, 'Science and the Law in the Wake of *Daubert*: A New Search for Scientific Knowledge', 72 *Tex.L.Rev.* 715 (1994).
[37] *Kumho Tire Co., Ltd.* v. *Carmichael*, 119 *S.Ct.* 1167 (1999).
[38] Comment, 'Admissibility of Expert Psychological Evidence in the Federal Courts', 27 *Ariz.St.L.J.* 1315 (1995).
[39] A. Stein, 'The Refoundation of Evidence Law, 9 *Canad.J.Law & Jurisprud.* 279 (1996).
[40] F. Rossi, 'The Silent Revolution', 9 *Litigation* 13 (Wint. 1983).
[41] Article VII, *Fed.R.Evid.*, 28 U.S.C.A..
[42] *Id.*, at Article VIII.
[43] *Id.*, at Article IX.
[44] *Id.*, at Article X.
[45] R.C. Park, 'An Outsider's View of Common Law Evidence', 96 *Mich.L.Rev.* (1998), 1486, 1500 (1998); A. Stein, 'The Foundation of Evidence Law', 9 *Canad.J. Law & Jurisprud.* 279 (1996).
[46] *Swidler & Berlin* v. *US*, 524 *U.S.* 399 (1998).

privilege. In *Jaffee*,[47] the Court went farther and added a new privilege to the list of those previously recognized in federal practice. Nor is this trend confined to jurisprudence; the state legislatures are in step with the trend. By way of example, in recent years roughly half the state legislatures have codified a privilege for environmental audits.[48] This trend reflects a widespread social consensus that privacy needs additional protection.[49] Many businesses engaged in e-commerce now advertise their privacy policies because they believe that a strong, announced policy gives them a competitive advantage in the market.[50] Nor is this felt need for privacy confined to the US. In part as a backlash against the anti-privacy policies of the totalitarian Nazi regime,[51] many European countries have taken a more proactive approach to formalizing legal protection for privacy rights. For instance, in the mid-1990s, the Council of Ministers adopted a new directive restricting the transmission of personally identifiable information.[52] The European Union has gone to the length of threatening to ban information transfers to the US unless the US adopts more stringent practices to protect the privacy of personal information.[53] In all likelihood, the future holds greater legal protection in store for privacy rights both in the US and abroad. The solid consensus favoring firmer legal protection for privacy makes it highly improbable that the abolition of all or most privileges would be politically palatable.

The third option holds the greatest promise – developing a humanistic theory to supplement, rather than completely supplant, the instrumental theory. Forty years ago Professor David Louisell outlined a non-instrumental theory resting primarily on privacy.[54] The theory has gained some judicial adherents in the US.[55] As Professor Archibald has pointed out, there are also Canadian cases lending support to the privacy theory.

However, resting a humanistic theory squarely on privacy is problematic: privacy is simply not an ultimate value in liberal democratic theory. Nor is it an

---

[47] *Jaffee* v. *Redmond*, 518 *U.S.* 1 (1996).

[48] Comment, 'The Self-Critical Analysis Privilege for Products Liability: What Is It, and How Can It Be Achieved in Wisconsin?', 1999 *Wis.L.Rev.* 119, 120.

[49] R.B. Lillich, *International Human Rights: Problems of Law, Policy and Practice* 12 (2d ed. 1991); R. Dixon, 'Needed: A Bold New Privacy Law', *Nat'l L.J.*, Apr. 19, 1999, at p. A29; M. Horn, 'Shifting Lines of Privacy', *U.S. News & World Rep.*, Oct. 26, 1998, at p. 57; J. Lang, 'Privacy: Video Surveillance of Public Is Massive, Unchecked', *The Sacramento Bee*, Feb. 7, 1999, at pp. H1, H6; G.T. Marx, 'Privacy Lost', *Cal.Lawyer* 48 (Jan. 1999); J. Quittner, 'Invasion of Privacy', *Time*, Aug. 25, 1997, at p. 28.

[50] N. Aswad, 'Consumer Protection – Internet Privacy', 68 *U.S.L.W. (BNA)* 2115 (Aug. 31, 1999).

[51] W.L. Fishman, 'Closing the Privacy Gap', *Legal Times*, Sep. 15, 1997, at p. 29.

[52] Directive 94/96/EC of the European Parliament and of the Council, Official Journal of the European Communities No. L. 281, 31-50 (Nov. 23, 1995).

[53] A. Gregorits, 'EU Privacy Directive Will Take Effect Even Without Implementing Legislation', 67 *U.S.L.W. (BNA)* 2179 (Oct. 6, 1998).

[54] D.W. Louisell, 'Confidentiality, Conformity and Confusion: Privileges in Federal Court Today', 31 *Tul.L.Rev.* 101 (1956).

[55] *State* v. *Sugar*, 417 *A.2d* 474 (N.J. 1980)(the attorney-client privilege); 1 McCormick, *Evidence* {98 (5th ed. 1999)(discussing cases suggesting a privacy rationale for the medical privileges).

intrinsic moral good. It is true that persons seeking spiritual counseling value the privacy of their consultations with religious functionaries such as priests. However, it is equally true that criminal conspirators value privacy. Revolutionaries planning the violent overthrow of the state are especially jealous of the privacy of their discussions.[56]

Moreover, privacy can be a dangerously nebulous concept. In American tort law alone, privacy has taken the form of four distinct civil wrongs.[57]

It seems sounder to link privilege doctrine directly to the democratic value of autonomy. I am attempting to develop that linkage in the volume of *The New Wigmore* devoted to evidentiary privileges.[58] Unlike privacy, autonomy is an ultimate value in liberal democratic theory. The basic premise of the autonomy theory is that a liberal democracy should assist its citizens in making intelligent, independent choices as to fundamental life preferences.[59] As cognitive beings, citizens partially realize themselves by making intelligent life preference choices. The difficulty is that in some cases, they lack the information or expertise needed to make a truly informed choice. In these cases, they must consult a third party, usually a professional such as a clergy person or attorney, about both the range of choice and the ramifications of individual choices. However, as volitional beings, citizens also fulfill themselves by making independent life preference choices. A dilemma arises because, in the process of consulting a third party in order to make an intelligent choice, the citizen exposes himself or herself to the risks of manipulation and coercion – which can undermine the independence of the ultimate choice.

In his influential work, *The Morality of Freedom,*[60] Joseph Raz contends that in a liberal democratic state, government should not only refrain from violating citizens' autonomy; more importantly, he argues for the normative proposition that when circumstances create a significant threat to citizens' autonomy, government ought to intervene to protect autonomy. This argument is explicitly normative; unlike Dean Wigmore's instrumental theory, the argument does not turn on suspect empirical assumptions about human behavior. When a citizen consults an expert about a life preference choice, there is a threat to the citizen's autonomy; in these consultative relationships the citizen is less likely to be on his or her guard, and the citizen is vulnerable to manipulations precisely because he or she lacks expertise in the subject-matter of the consultation. Under the positive

---

[56] E.J. Imwinkelried, 'The Rivalry Between Truth and Privilege: The Weakness of the Supreme Court's Instrumental Reasoning in Jaffee v. Redmond, 518 U.S. 1 (1996)', 49 *Hastings L.J.* 969, 984-85 (1998).

[57] Prosser & Keeton on the Law of Torts { 117 (5ᵗʰ ed. 1984).

[58] One volume of the treatise has already been released. D.P. Leonard, *Selected Rules of Limited Admissibility, the New Wigmore* (1996).

[59] There is an initial sketch of this theory in E.J. Imwinkelried, 'The Rivalry Between Truth and Privilege: The Weakness of the Supreme Court's Instrumental Reasoning in Jaffee v. Redmond, 518 U.S. 1 (1996)', 49 *Hastings L.J.* 969, 985-88 (1998).

[60] J. Raz, *The Morality of Freedom* (1986).

theory of freedom, society should take steps to reduce the risk to the consulting citizen's autonomy. Society can do so by shielding the consultative relationship with an evidentiary privilege. Knowing of the privilege, the citizen will feel freer to reveal any relevant information to the expert; that freedom enhances the intelligence of the ultimate life preference choice. Further, knowing of the privilege, the consultant can feel freer to give advice that promotes the citizen's interest in a single-minded fashion; the consultant need not fear that his or her advice will be exposed to public opprobrium. Hence, the recognition of an evidentiary privilege is an appropriate means of safeguarding the individual citizen's right to make life preference choices which are at once intelligent and independent. In this theory, privacy is not a primary right; rather, it is conceived of as a condition for promoting personal autonomy.

However, this partial statement of the humanistic theory of evidentiary privileges leaves an important question unanswered. A key question in privilege doctrine is which relations deserve the protection of an evidentiary privilege. It seems clear from his paper that he has doubts whether the evolving privacy rationale in Canadian jurisprudence satisfactorily answers that question. He distinguishes the traditional 'class' privileges in Canadian law from the new privileges emerging in a case-by-case manner under the umbrella of privacy. As previously stated, privacy can be a vague, nebulous concept. The Canadian experience seems to confirm that statement. However, the problem is not peculiar to the privacy rationale. For that matter, the expression, consultations about 'fundamental' life preferences, is hardly self-defining.

For that reason, I propose that the American courts and legislatures turn to their domestic constitutional law to identify those fundamental life preference choices. Simply stated, a consultative relationship deserves an evidentiary privilege only if the consultations relate to an area of life in which there is a full-fledged constitutional right to independent decision-making. There are a number of areas of choice in which the American courts have fashioned such a right under the *First, Fifth* or *Sixth Amendment*. For example, the Supreme Court has recognized a constitutional right for choices related to a person's health.[61] Whatever the content of the citizen's life plan, physical and mental health are important means to the end of achieving the plan objectives. In addition, the Court has indicated that the citizen has a constitutional right to make independent decisions about the legal system. The Court has recognized that the defendant needs the guiding hand of counsel to make intelligent legal decisions;[62] charges against an accused can be dismissed if the state imperils that independence by unduly interfering with the attorney-client relationship.[63] Again, whatever the content of a citizen's life plan, his or her preferences may collide with those of

---

[61] *Whalen* v. *Roe*, 429 *U.S.* 589 (1977); *Griswold* v. *Connecticut*, 381 *U.S.* 479 (1965).

[62] *Gideon* v. *Wainwright*, 372 *U.S.* 335 (1963); 1 McCormick, *Evidence* { 87, at 314 (2ᵈ ed. 1992).

[63] *US* v. *Blasco*, 702 *F.2d* 1315, 1329 (11ᵗʰ Cir. 1983), *cert.denied*, 464 *U.S.* 914 (1983); *Bishop* v. *Rose*, 701 *F.2d* 1150, 1157 (6ᵗʰ Cir. 1983); *State* v. *Sugar*, 84 *N.J.* 1, 417 *A.2d* 474 (1980).

other citizens; and in the event of such conflicts, the citizen must resort to the justice system in order to uphold his or her preferences. Like physical and mental health, resort to the legal system can become a vital means of achieving the citizen's life plan. The courts have also found a constitutional right to independent decision-making in matters of religion and ethics.[64] These decisions are at the very heart of a person's life plan; these are the choices which enable the citizen to construct the meaning of his or her life.[65] Finally, under the substantive due process doctrine the Supreme Court has conferred a measure of constitutional protection on the citizen's independent decision-making with respect to his or her family.[66] The vast majority of the citizens of liberal democracies possess some family ties; and like the citizen's religious beliefs, those ties can have a profound influence on the individual citizen's life preference choices. These four strands of case law can guide the courts' identification of the areas in which citizens make truly 'fundamental' life preference choices. This body of case law should aid the courts to identify privileged relationships in a principled, predictable[67] manner.

## Conclusion

Placing greater stress on a humanistic rationale in American privilege doctrine would have a major impact on both domestic American law and its relationship to privilege law in other liberal democracies.

Accentuating a humanistic rationale would likely have two notable effects on domestic American privilege doctrine. First, it would probably lead to extending evidentiary privileges to a wider range of social relations. For example, as a question from the audience by Dean James Klebba suggested, shifting toward an autonomy-based theory would strengthen the case for a broad family privilege rather than the narrow spousal privilege currently recognized in most American jurisdictions. A second, likely impact would be reclassifying many, if not most, privileges as conditional or qualified – the result reached by the Canadian courts in their case-by-case decisions. As previously stated, as conceived by Dean Wigmore, as a practical matter the instrumental rationale required that most privileges be treated as absolute. Allowing a judge to later surmount the privilege

---

[64] Note, 'Forgive Us Our Sins: The Inadequacies of the Clergy-Penitent Privilege', 73 *N.Y.U.L.Rev.* 225 (1998), 235-36.

[65] G. Dworkin, *The theory and practice of autonomy 110* (1988).

[66] *Flowers* v. *Seki*, 45 *F.Supp.2d* 794, 799 (D.Haw. 1998).

[67] As the Supreme Court indicated in both *Jaffee* and *Swidler*, the instrumental theory demands that the courts and legislatures formulate bright line standards for privilege doctrine. Without clear standards, the person cannot confidently forecast whether a privilege will protect his or her revelation. It is true that bright line standards would be less critical under a humanistic theory. However, it would still be inefficient and wasteful of judicial resources to rely on vaguely phrased standards. The extant bodies of constitutional law should make the identification of privileged relations substantially more predictable.

on the basis of a case-specific showing of need supposedly undermined the high degree of predictability mandated by the instrumental theory. A humanistic theory would not require the same degree of predictability and is hence more compatible with a regime of conditional privileges which can be defeated by a showing of need. Ultimately, a humanistic theory is rights-based. Even the constitutionally-based privileges recognized by American courts are qualified in nature.[68] In that light, it is anomalous to treat statutory and common-law privileges as absolute. Reclassifying those privileges under a humanistic theory would end that anomaly. The adoption of the humanistic theory would also affect the relationship between American privilege doctrine and the privilege law in other liberal democracies. Currently, the democracies differ markedly over the question of which social relationships deserve the protection of an evidentiary privilege. At one extreme, the UK recognizes less than a handful of true evidentiary privileges. At the other end of the spectrum, many European legal systems such as Germany tend to extend privileges to a very wide range of social relations with expansive protection for family and even financial relations.[69] The legal systems in the US and Australia fall in the middle of the spectrum; they recognize more privileges than the UK but fewer than most European democracies. At least in the case of the US, the limited range of privilege protection is partially explicable in terms of our heavy reliance on the instrumental theory. There are so few relationships in which it can be plausibly claimed that but for the existence of an evidentiary privilege, the parties would not consult and communicate. De-emphasizing the instrumental theory would push American privilege doctrine toward greater convergence with European privilege doctrine. That result should not come as any surprise; the proposed humanistic theory rests on the value of personal autonomy, and that it is a value not only shared but prized by every democratic system. Autonomy is at the heart of the humanistic theory, and the same value plays a central role in democratic political theory.

---

[68] *US* v. *Nixon*, 418 *U.S.* 683 (1974)(the privilege for confidential Presidential communications); Comment, 'Piercing the Shield: Reporter Privilege in Minnesota Following State v. Turner', 82 *Minn.L.Rev.* 1563, 1574-75 (1998)("nine out of the ten [federal] circuits that have addressed the issue have (...) recognize[d] a qualified *First Amendment* privilege for journalists to resist compelled disclosure").

[69] R.J. Allen, S. Kock, K. Riechenberg & D.T. Rosen, 'The German Advantage in Civil Procedure: A Plea for More Details and Fewer Generalities in Comparative Scholarship', 82 *Nw.U.L.Rev.* 705, 731-32 (1988); J. Langbein, 'The German Advantage in Civil Procedure', 52 *U.Chi.L.Rev.* 823, 829 (1985); R.C. Park, 'An Outsider's View of Common Law of Evidence', 96 *Mich.L.Rev.* 1486, 1500 (1998).

# Criminal Evidence Obtained Abroad – how to assess the Legality of obtaining it

*J.I.M.G. Jahae, P.A.M. Mevis, J.M. Reijntjes & J.Y. Taekema.*

Traditionally criminal evidence is obtained in the territory of the state where the trial will be held. In many countries this situation is changing fundamentally. In a rapidly increasing number of criminal cases, and especially in the more important ones (*e.g.* nearly all main drug trafficking cases) evidence has to be found in the territory and/or with the assistance of the authorities of other states. This is creating several rather specific problems, which are not easily resolved. They are caused in part by peculiarities of the (domestic) law of evidence, and are partly embedded in the so-called 'international criminal law'. Here we will consider one of those problems, viz. whether (alleged) irregularities in obtaining evidence abroad should have any effect in the criminal procedure and, if so, what effect.

In discussing this problem, we should keep in mind that it is influenced by a variety of rules, originating at different levels and in different categories of law. They may be simplified in a the following diagram:

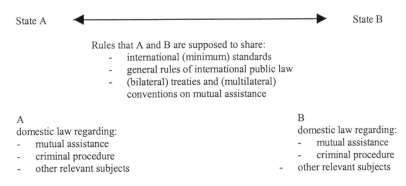

State A ← → State B

Rules that A and B are supposed to share:
- international (minimum) standards
- general rules of international public law
- (bilateral) treaties and (multilateral) conventions on mutual assistance

A
domestic law regarding:
- mutual assistance
- criminal procedure
- other relevant subjects

B
domestic law regarding:
- mutual assistance
- criminal procedure
- other relevant subjects

For the courts it would be most convenient to decide cases with international implications the same way as domestic ones. But is it still acceptable to circumvent difficulties by 'nationalising' procedures with international aspects? Acceptance of transnational gathering of criminal evidence during the investigative and prosecution phases without establishing a proper judicial control during the trial will cause a lack of balance, which inevitably creates grave risks for the integrity and fairness of the proceedings.

When the decision is made to honour a request for mutual assistance in criminal matters, the relevant treaty pertaining to the subject and/or domestic law usually prescribe the application of the laws and regulations of the requested state, according to the principle of *locus regit actum*. See *e.g.* Article 3(1) of the *European Convention on mutual assistance in criminal matters*

*(ECMA)*: "The requested Party shall execute *in the manner provided for by its law* any letters rogatory relating to a criminal matter and addressed to it by the judicial authorities of the requesting Party for the purpose of procuring evidence (...)."

This same principle is followed in most treaties on mutual assistance in criminal matters; thus Article 24(1) of the *Agreement on extradition and mutual assistance in criminal matters between the Kingdom of Belgium, the Grand Duchy of Luxembourg and the Kingdom of the Netherlands* reads: "Commissions rogatory will be executed by the competent judicial authorities of the requested party in the same way as commissions rogatory from a domestic judicial authority".

We will focus on the effects of infringements on these rules of statute law, for example a search and seizure without a warrant. In doing so, we cannot avoid a closely related question, viz. what effect should be given to irregularities in *transmitting* evidence obtained abroad: transfer when this is not allowed by either the applicable treaty or by the domestic law of the state where the evidence has been obtained; and transfer by ways and means other than those provided for by law.[1]

We will not deal with the opposite problem, whether in obtaining evidence abroad prescriptions of the domestic law of the requesting state should be followed (cautioning of suspects, interrogation of witnesses under oath, the manner of taking such an oath, the assistance of defence attorney's, etc.)[2] and, if so, how this should be guaranteed. Nevertheless this is an interesting question, because we see a tendency to emphasise the role of the domestic law of the requesting state, in order to guarantee that the evidence obtained can actually be used in court.[3] By reducing the role of the domestic law of the requested state, part of the problems occupying us here could be resolved, as well. However, they will never be eliminated in this way.

It is even possible that evidence has been obtained abroad without any support and/or knowledge of the competent foreign authorities. Does the same rule apply in these circumstances as often is maintained in extradition law: *male captus, bene detentus*? When evidence has been gathered in the territory of another state, without any involvement of the local authorities, the first and main issue will be the infringement made upon the sovereignty of the state where the material has been 'found'. This question is outside the scope of our consideration. However, it is closely related to our problem: as soon as the injured state shows itself to be satisfied, without having requested the return of

---

[1] Compare the simple solution given in a decision of the Dutch Supreme Court of 25 June 1996, *NJ* 1996, 716: Dutch courts do not have to assess whether evidence obtained abroad has been transferred in the way prescribed by the domestic law of the requested state.

[2] *See* on this subject *e.g.* S.A. Saltzburg, 'The Reach of the Bill of Rights Beyond the Terra Firma of the US', 20 *Virginia Journal of International Law* (1980), pp. 742-76.

[3] Compare the 1999 draft agreement on mutual assistance in criminal matters between the member states of the European Union, published in *Pb EC* 1999 C 251/2.

the materials that were illegally obtained, the question arises whether the non-compliance with the rules of mutual assistance should have any procedural effect, as well. The same applies in cases where consent was given, although not by a competent authority.

Our problem can be approached from (at least) two different angles. It may be seen as a problem of *international* law. This is the traditional point of view, emphasising the *international* aspects of 'international criminal law'. It may lead to the position that the criminal justice authorities do not need – or even are not allowed – to take into account illegalities in obtaining evidence committed abroad:

- because "one nation must recognise the act of the sovereign power of another, so long as it has jurisdiction under international law, even if it is improper according to the internal law of the latter state".[4] The rationale given for this 'silver platter'-rule is not always convincing. The American Supreme Court has stated this rationale to be "that it would be exceedingly difficult to determine the validity of an act of a foreign state and that it would be highly offensive to the foreign state if the question were wrongly decided."[5] The first part of this statement strikes at the core of the problem; the second part, however, seems too general to be acceptable;

- because the accused should not benefit from the protection offered by the domestic law of the requested state. For this reason he is denied the right to *invoke* the protection of the statutes that have been infringed. This should not be confused with the reverse position that the law of the *requesting* state is not applicable to activities against citizens in the requested state. Compare the American decision that the *Constitution* of the US (and especially its *Fourth Amendment*) is not applicable to search and seizure in Mexican territory against a Mexican citizen, although effected by American agents,[6] contrary to the older approach that "the government of the US only has the powers entrusted to it by the *Constitution*. Whenever and wherever it acts it relies on the *Constitution* as the source of its powers. Whenever it acts, it must, therefore, accept the limits on its powers imposed by the same *Constitution* that provides the affirmative grant of power";[7]

- because the subject matter is seen as a question between sovereign states only, governed exclusively by international law; in this respect citizens are

---

[4] W.J.A., 'The new international "silver platter" doctrine: admissibility in federal courts of evidence illegally obtained by foreign officers in a foreign country', 2 *International Law and Politics* (1969) pp. 280/313, cited from p. 303.

[5] W.J.A., l.c.

[6] *US* v. *Verdugo-Urquidez*, 494 *U.S.* 259 (1990), *International Legal Materials* 1990, p. 441. This decision seems to have overruled *Gambino* v. *US*, 275 *U.S.* 310 (1927), holding that evidence should be excluded, when obtained by an illegal search and seizure made solely on behalf of the US.

[7] As defended by Saltzburg, *op. cit.*, cited from p. 745.

not regarded as subjects of law, possessing individual rights, with the result that again they do not have a *locus standi*. In this approach obtaining evidence contrary to the domestic law of the requested state or contrary to the rules specified in the applicable treaty seems to have no effect at all – at least not for the citizens concerned. However, an approach from international law does not *need* to lead to such a negative conclusion. A more moderate version of this approach, for example, could imply that there will be no effect, *unless* the national judicial authorities themselves were at fault and have to take (at least co-)responsibility for the illegality which has been committed.

This category also includes the much less far-reaching restriction implying that evidence, although found by foreign officials in completely foreign operations, should be excluded if it is shown that it was obtained in a manner that 'shocked the conscience' (read: by torture). This position has been taken by US courts.[8]

But we already see how the emphasis is shifting from truly international aspects (the relations between States A and B) to the criminal law aspects: the *use* of the evidence concerned. In any case this approach does not prevent the exclusion of evidence which – due to infringement of certain rules – has lost its reliability.

If our problem could be reduced to a debate between governments, there is no procedural issue. The authorities concerned just have to settle their differences in one way or another, without the admissibility of the evidence being directly at stake. In itself this is a tempting solution, of course, not only for the prosecuting authorities, but also for the community as a whole, as debates in court will be prevented and in most cases no new barriers will be created for the rightful punishment of criminals. But on further consideration, one could think that it is no solution at all.

International law owes its existence to the rise of national states, in a century in which the people or the nation were identified with the state (and vice versa). The state was an abstraction, personified by its government, which however at the same time did represent a tangible reality: the citizens. Gradually, international law developed into the law applicable between two or more of those abstractions, now designated as *sovereign* states. This led to the actual paradox: states in fact do not create law. This is, after all, always and only done by their citizens. But then it would be a rather strange situation if those citizens themselves would not be parties to the international law created, or could only participate through the mediation of the state.

Criminal investigation, and more generally obtaining evidence, is governed everywhere by prescriptions of formal law, although this differs considerably

---

[8] S.M. Kaplan, 'The applicability of the exclusionary rule in federal court to evidence seized and confessions obtained in foreign countries', 16 *Columbia Journal of Transnational Law* (1977), pp. 495/520.

from place to place. In many countries, although not in all, infringements on those prescriptions will have (procedural) consequences; if so, the consequences will not always be the same everywhere. In relation to our subject, the most important is the difference between countries which use exclusionary rules and those that do not.

The number of countries excluding evidence that has been irregularly obtained seems to be growing. The dividing line between excluding and non-excluding countries is independent of that between common law and continental law. In addition to the US, excluding countries are *e.g.* Canada, South Africa, England and Wales, Belgium and the Netherlands.

In the US and in Belgium the exclusionary rules are based on case law, in South Africa on the Constitution. In Canada Section 24.2 of the *Charter of Rights and Freedoms* reads, "Where (...) a court concludes that evidence was obtained in a manner that infringed or denied any rights or freedoms guaranteed in this *Charter*, the evidence shall be excluded if it is established that, having regard to all the circumstances, the admission of it in the proceedings would bring the administration of justice into disrepute." In England & Wales Article 78(1) of the *Police and Criminal Evidence Act 1984* states: "In any proceedings the court may refuse to allow evidence on which the prosecution proposes to rely to be given if it appears to the court that, having regard to all the circumstances, including the circumstances in which the evidence was obtained, the admission of the evidence would have such an adverse effect on the fairness of the proceedings that the court ought not to admit it." In the Netherlands exclusion, originally based on case law, has found its legitimacy in Article 359a of the *Code of Criminal Procedure*, saying: "1. If it appears to the court that (in obtaining evidence) formal obligations have not been complied with and this omission cannot be remedied, it may decide that: a. (...), b. the evidence which has been obtained as a result of the omission will not be accepted. 2. (In doing so) the court has to take into account the interests promoted by the violated rule, the seriousness of the omission and the harm caused by the omission." In practice this leads to a much stricter application of exclusion than *e.g.* in England & Wales.[9]

In countries which exclude illegally obtained evidence, it is hard to explain why evidence that should be excluded if obtained within the own borders, will not be excluded if obtained elsewhere. But one could also wonder why materials, which – due to irregularities – may not be used in the country where they have been found, will be accepted as evidence in another, viz. the requesting country.

---

[9] The opinions of the *international* courts on the use of illegally obtained evidence have been described by W.M. Reisman & E.E. Freedman, 'The plaintiff's dilemma: illegally obtained evidence and admissibility in international adjudication', 76 *The American Journal of International Law* (1982), pp. 737-753.

Nevertheless some countries stick to such approaches. This has a lot to do with the ratio of the exclusion of illegally obtained evidence.[10] Sometimes exclusionary rules are only regarded as intending to compel respect for the *domestic* law of the prosecuting state. In the US, for instance, the rationales given for the exclusion of illegally obtained evidence are: "nothing can destroy a government more quickly than its failure to observe its own laws"[11] and "the prime purpose is to deter future unlawful police conduct".[12] Accordingly, only infringements of the US *Constitution* will have effect.[13] In our opinion, however, the exclusion of evidence which has been illegally obtained abroad should have quite another rationale: the prevention of inequality!

The development of cross-border criminality forces the countries of Western Europe to intensify and – for this purpose – to facilitate their mutual assistance in criminal matters. In the countries that comprise the European Union this coincides with their aspiration to enhance co-operation in general. On 5 December 1977 the French president Valéry Giscard d'Estaing asked for the creation of *one* "espace judiciare"; although his proposals were rejected, the completion of what he meant is quickly approaching. Should the benefits be for the prosecuting authorities only? Is it not a general rule which requires that where the position of the prosecution is strengthened, the defence should be reinforced too? Should there not be 'equality of arms' in the broadest sense? All the countries concerned ratified the *European Convention for the Protection of Human Rights and Fundamental Freedoms (ECHR)* – but this does not mean anything, as far as our problem is concerned. The European Court at Strasbourg always took the position that it cannot take into consideration the admissibility of evidence, which has to be assessed exclusively by the national courts.[14] Its role is restricted to guaranteeing certain procedural rights, such as that of adversarial argument in court.

This leads to the conclusion that, the more successful the 'internationalisation' of criminal law and, especially, criminal procedure is, the more the 'criminal' aspects of 'international criminal law' need to be emphasised. After all, mutual assistance only covers the international law aspects of investigating crime abroad; in addition, this kind of investigation has to be regarded as being an integral part of the criminal process. The more intensive the assistance from abroad, the less reason there is to approach it only from its international-law-aspects! A position, that international criminal law is just the criminal part of international law, becomes untenable.

---

[10] Compare R. Tullis & L. Ludlow, 'Admissibility of Evidence Seized in Another Jurisdiction: Choice of Law and the Exclusionary Rule', 10 *University of San Francisco Law Review* (1975), pp. 67-91.

[11] *Mapp* v. *Ohio*, 367 *U.S.* 643 (1961).

[12] *US* v. *Calandra*, 414 *U.S.* 338 (1974).

[13] On the other hand WJA *(op. cit.)* defended a much broader application of the exclusionary rule.

[14] *See e.g. Schenk* v. *Switzerland*, judgement of 12 July 1988, Series A No. 140, paras 45 and 46, recently confirmed in *García Ruiz* v. *Spain*, judgement of 21 January 1999.

One could leave it to every separate country to decide for itself which sanctions should be applicable, if evidence has been obtained illegally (albeit abroad). Often no one in the requested state will dispute the legality of the activities of the local authorities, simply because no one is interested in doing so. Usually the legality of those activities does not come into the picture until the evidence obtained is being introduced in a criminal trial in the requesting country. In many cases the court will rely, and may rely, upon the (international law) rule of mutual trust: the court may take as a premise that the requested state respected the applicable prescriptions of treaty and domestic law, unless certain contradictory indications exist.

As a general rule, this seems to be justified. This compels the defence to become informed about the relevant law of the requested state. Nowadays this is not very difficult, if the defence really *wants* to be informed. The contacts and relations between law firms in different countries are intensifying quickly; the ties are becoming stronger and stronger. Nevertheless our impression is that the existing opportunities could be used much more effectively.

However, the defence may not be expected to offer some kind of prima facie evidence of irregularities. Such evidence would be hard to obtain in a domestic context – to gather it abroad will in most cases be impossible –, however a close co-operation with local law firms has been established. It should be sufficient to cast a reasonable degree of doubt; if a well-grounded attack has been launched on the legality of the activities in the requested state, then the courts should not be permitted to hide behind the rule of mutual trust. However, the main problem is again, how can the courts in the adjudicating state *know* whether the alleged irregularities really occurred and what effects they would have on the admissibility of the evidence in the requested state. Can they investigate this issue and make a decision without the help of a court in the requested country? In our opinion, this is practically impossible – and that is exactly why in most countries the courts do not (and are even not allowed to) apply foreign law. The *Additional Protocol to the European Convention on Information on Foreign Law* (Strasbourg, 15 March 1978) can offer some help, but it is seldom used.

See Article 1: "The Contracting Parties undertake to supply one another (...) with information on their substantive and procedural law (...) in the criminal field (...)." Usually, in the cases interesting us not only is simple information by the judicial authorities needed, but an explicit and impartial court decision.

Our problems may be illustrated by the following three cases. The first is an atypical one, because in fact, it is too simple. It concerns one of the rare cases in which the irregularity of what was undertaken in the requested state cannot be doubted.

*Case 1.* The island of Aruba is a more or less autonomous part of the Kingdom of the Netherlands. It has its own *Code of Criminal Procedure*. The treaty on mutual assistance in criminal matters, concluded between the

Kingdom and the US, is applicable in the whole Kingdom, thus including Aruba (since 15 September 1983). For a long time the problem has existed that this treaty was not implemented by enabling legislation in Aruban domestic law. This meant for instance that, although the treaty contains the well-known formula that "requests for search and seizure (shall be executed) in accordance with (the) laws and practices" of the requested state, Aruban statute law did not provide for search and seizure at the request of a foreign authority. It was not clear how such search and seizure should be effected on Aruba, and whether citizens could later invoke the protection of the courts – in sharp contrast to the situation in the Netherlands, where this matter has been regulated in the *Code of Criminal Procedure*. As a consequence there was an obligation for the Aruban authorities to give judicial assistance, if requested, without statute law regulating how this should be done. On the other hand, according to Dutch (and so also Aruban) case law, the authorities may not infringe on the rights of citizens unless statute law expressly permits them to do so.

It is highly improbable that the Aruban *or* the American authorities were not aware of this situation for some time: some literature[15] on the subject was published, and the impossibility of applying the treaty was invoked in court, when judicial assistance was requested by the American authorities. However, primarily due to inadequate defence strategies, the Dutch Supreme Court, which is also the highest court of justice for Aruba, never had to address this point.[16] The judicial authorities on Aruba took the only point of view which made it possible for them to apply the treaty without it being implemented by enabling domestic law. They said: for infringements of the rights of citizens we do need a basis in law, but this law may also be treaty law; the relevant treaty itself is sufficient to legitimise search and seizure. Searches and seizures should simply be conducted as if ordered by the competent authorities in a domestic case. So the treaty was applied directly, as if it were self-executing.[17]

Then, in 1992, the American authorities requested search and seizure on Aruba in a major money laundering case. The local authorities duly complied, found some evidence and delivered it to the Americans. One of the persons whose offices had been searched started a civil procedure against the Aruban authorities, claiming that the search and seizure had been illegal. He won his

---

[15] J.M. Reijntjes, note under Court of First Instance Curaçao 19.01.1984, in: *Journal for Antillian Law/Justicia* 1984, p. 297, *id.*, 'Het ontworpen Wetboek van Strafvordering', *Journal for Antillian Law/Justicia* 1989, pp. 209/216, the same, note under Court of First Instance Aruba 24 December 1991, *Journal for Antillian Law/Justicia* 1993, p. 230, and the same, note under Joint Court of Justice (*i.e.*, the Court of Appeal) for the Netherlands Antilles and Aruba 17.03.1992, *Journal for Antillian Law/Justicia* 1993, p. 236.

[16] Compare HR 4 March 1994, *NJ* 1994, 475, with a note by Th.W. van Veen; HR 11 November 1994, *NJ* 1995, 99; HR 9 February 1996, *NJ* 1996, 379 and HR 9 February 1996, *NJ* 1996, 380.

[17] Others to the contrary thought that treaties on judicial assistance in criminal matters can *never* be directly applicable; see R.C.P. Haentjens, *Schets van het Nederlandse kleine rechtshulprecht*, Arnhem: Gouda Quint 1992, 2$^d$ ed., p. 83.

case: in 1998 the Supreme Court decided that the treaty could have been directly applicable, but only if it expressly said so and/or did not leave any doubt as to how it should be implemented in practice. Because the treaty was silent regarding its direct applicability and did leave doubts as to the way it should be implemented, according to the Supreme Court, the search of the premises of the complainant and the seizure of his properties had been illegal.[18]

In the meantime Aruba enacted a new *Code of Criminal Procedure*, which *does* regulate mutual judicial assistance. Thus, the basic problem has been resolved, but not the problem of the Aruban whose premises had been raided. The US requested his extradition, partly on the evidence which had been obtained illegally. The Attorney General of Aruba, at the request of the Court, asked the American authorities to assure that this evidence would be excluded, but they refused to do so. Then the Court found that under the US-Dutch Extradition Treaty, it did not have any authority to exclude or restrict the use of evidence by the US itself. The extradition was declared to be admissible,[19] and the subject duly transferred to Miami. He is now awaiting trial there. May the American authorities use the evidence which they obtained as a result of the illegal search and seizure? The case is relatively simple: the highest local court – the Supreme Court of the Netherlands – decided that without any doubt the evidence was obtained illegally.[20] It did not specify what consequences this should have; but no doubt in an *Aruban* criminal trial such material would be excluded. Shall it make any difference, that it is intended to be used in the US?

*Case 2.* In 1993, an English jury was directed to acquit a man we will call Jones, on a major drug trafficking charge. After his release, Jones allegedly told the arresting officers: "I'm just off to spend my £ 87 million and you can't reach me". However this may be, he was declared 'target number one', the investigation into his activities became a top priority and a special task group of police and customs and excise officers was formed. In the summer of 1995, this team established that Jones was spending more and more time in the Netherlands, until in late autumn 1995 they became aware that he had actually moved there to stay.

The English tried to interest the Dutch police authorities and urged them to take action. The Dutch authorities agreed to take on the case, although reluctantly. The English provided them with two formal reports containing information on Jones being in touch with several Colombian people, preparing a huge cocaine import into the Netherlands, using a certain telephone number.

---

[18] HR 9 January 1998, *NJ* 1998, 724 with a note by T.M. Schalken; *see also* Court of First Instance Aruba 05.06.1992, *Journal for Antillian Law/Justicia* 1993, p. 113, with a note by J.M. Reijntjes.

[19] Joint Court 15 April 1998 nr. AR 148/97, not published.

[20] In this aspect the case is comparable to *Stonehill* v. *US*, 405 *F.2d* 738 (9th Cir. 1968), although that was not a criminal, but a tax case; the illegality of a search and seizure was determined by the Philippine Supreme Court. *See* W.J.A., *op. cit.*

This information had been gathered in May 1996, while Jones was actually living in the Netherlands.

The Dutch police was granted an order to tap several telephones in the Netherlands. After several hours of tapping the policemen realised that they were not able to understand the back-slang several of the people on the phone were using. They eventually asked some Liverpuddlian officers to help them out. These were all too happy to comply. They came to the Netherlands and were so to speak seated in the front-row of the theatre when they caught discussions on the phone concerning a possibly corrupted senior Merseyside police officer. They passed this information on via an English liaison officer who was located in the Netherlands. This information ultimately led to a separate English investigation into several of Jones' co-defendants and this senior police officer, later charged with a conspiracy to obstruct the course of justice. The English authorities requested the Dutch to extradite Jones.

In the meantime, the Dutch operation had come to its end. Several people were arrested, among them Jones. He was charged with serious drug offences and brought to trial.

So the investigation resulted in three separate trials in two different countries,

1. the Dutch drug trial against Jones;
2. the English trial with charges of conspiracy to obstruct the course of justice;
3. the extradition procedure.

In the Dutch drug trial, the defence argued that the evidence on which the investigation was initiated had been obtained illegally and should therefore be excluded; it was alleged that the English had gathered information by tapping Jones' mobile phone in the Netherlands and/or bugging his Dutch house. The defence wanted to examine a number of witnesses in order to assess the way in which the information was gathered. The Dutch prosecutor stated that before he permitted the (Dutch) investigation to be initiated, the competent British authorities assured him explicitly that their information was obtained in a legal manner. Now one may ask oneself: was the defence entitled to investigate the way the initial information was obtained, or was that irrelevant because the Dutch could (or even had to) rely on the English authorities when these stated that all information had been lawfully obtained? And should the material obtained abroad be assessed differently depending on the intended use; in other words: will there be a difference if the information is going to be used as starting information for an investigation or if it is going to be offered as evidence in court?

The defence furthermore claimed that the transfer of the information the Merseyside officers overheard while translating the phone conversations had been illegal. The use of a tapping order as given by the Dutch examining magistrate is restricted to investigative and evidential purposes in a *Dutch* investigation. In other words: the infringement of the privacy rights is limited to the specifics of the warrant.

The defence in the English trial argued exactly the same point, viz. that the evidence transferred from the Netherlands had to be excluded since this transfer was illegal because it constituted a breach of Dutch law by English police officers. Those officers were instructed to operate solely as interpreters; they were strictly instructed not to pass on any information they overheard since that was illegal under Dutch law. Does it make a difference for the judgement in the receiving state if the information in the requested state is obtained solely on request or if it was already obtained regardless of any request and independently in a separate domestic investigation? If, for instance infiltration rules in the Netherlands are much more strict than in the UK, two possibilities arise:

1. in a pending English infiltration which is perfectly legal according to British standards but clearly unlawful according to Dutch standards, evidence is gathered that turns out to be useful in a Dutch investigation;
2. the Dutch ask the English to instigate an infiltration operation in order to gather evidence for a Dutch investigation, which it is clear the Dutch themselves would never be allowed to conduct.

*Case 3.* A Turkish national, living in the Netherlands, was convicted of importing 170 kg of heroine from Turkey into the Netherlands. Part of the evidence had been obtained in Turkey, under the *European Convention on Mutual Judicial Assistance*. The defence brought the case before the Supreme Court and took the following position:

1. some evidence has been obtained by police infiltration into allegedly criminal circles in Turkey; there is a substantial chance that this operation has been contrary to Turkish domestic law, because it lacked the consent of the competent Turkish authorities;
2. under Turkish domestic law the person whose telephone has been tapped (here: the defendant) should receive official notice of this police activity as soon as it ended. This rule has been neglected, so the evidence obtained by tapping should be excluded.

Here we will only give the decision of the Supreme Court[21] regarding the first complaint. It decided that the lower courts had sufficient reason to accept that the required consent had been given and that the position of the defence had been insufficiently substantiated to require further investigation. In other words: it is up to the defence to clear up such a question.

When we accept that irregularities could have effects, six different approaches could be envisioned:

1. the irregularity will have the same effect in the requesting state as it would have had in the requested state.[22] This approach is closely connected to the

---

[21] HR 18 May 1999 nr. 109.075 (to be published).
[22] Accepted by the International Association of Penal Law, XVI[th] International Congress, Budapest, September 1999, Section IV, resolution C 3 (Newsletter 1992/2 p. 69); rejected by the HR 18 May 1999 nr. 109.075.

old principle, also accepted in international law, that no one (not even a state) can transfer to another more power (or rights) than he himself possesses.[23] It guarantees equality towards the requested state. Compare, in relation to the transfer of criminal prosecutions, Article 552gg(1) of the *Dutch Code of Criminal Procedure*: "Documents relating activities of public functionaries in investigating and prosecuting offences, which have been produced by the competent authorities of the requesting state, will have the same probatory value in the requested state as comparable documents drawn up by the competent authorities of that state, on the understanding that *their probatory value never may exceed the probatory value which they would have had in the requesting state*";

2. the irregularity will have the same effect in the requesting state as it would have had if it had been committed there. "This rule will place all nations on notice of the high regard of our courts for individual's rights, and will relieve the courts of the problem of applying different standards according to the place where (the irregularity) occurred", an American wrote.[24] Such an approach seems to be especially attractive when the requesting state practices exclusion of illegally obtained evidence and the requested state does not: it guarantees equality within the requesting state.

3. the law of the state will be applied which leads to the highest level of exclusion. This would mean that 'double admissibility' of evidence is required.[25] Although it is the most promising for the defendant, this solution has to be rejected in advance, because it lacks a proper ratio and is incompatible with the European aspirations to dismantle as many barriers to mutual assistance in criminal matters as possible.

4. irregularities will only have effect when they infringe upon fundamental rights of the defendant which have been guaranteed in treaties like the *ECHR*.[26] Compare Article 15 of the *(UN) Convention against torture and other cruel, inhuman or degrading treatment or punishment*, excluding statements obtained by torture, even when thought reliable: "Each State party shall ensure that any statement which is established to have been made as a result of torture shall not be invoked as evidence in any proceedings, except against a person accused of torture as evidence that the statement was made." The Dutch Supreme Court decided on the second complaint in case 3: although there is no obligation for the courts to apply

---

[23] Ulpianus (D. 50.17.54); J. Locke, *Two Treatises of Government* II.135.
[24] H.S. Chandler, 'Searches south of the border: admission of evidence seized by foreign officials', 54 *Cornell Law Review* (1968), 886-898, p. 898.
[25] Defended in C. Gane & M. Mackarel, 'The Admissibility of Evidence Obtained from Abroad into Criminal Proceedings – The Interpretation of Mutual Legal Assistance Treaties and Use of Evidence Irregularly Obtained', *European Journal of Crime, Criminal Law and Criminal Justice* 1996, pp. 98-119.
[26] Seen as a minimum standard by the International Association of Penal Law, XVI[th] Int. Congress, section IV resolution E 5 (*Newsletter* 1999/2, p. 73); accepted by the Belgian Supreme Court 12 October 1993 nr. 6420, *Revue de droit pénal* 1994 p. 792.

Turkish law, the Dutch examining magistrate did inform the defendant that in Turkey his telephone had been tapped; if there had been an illegality under Turkish law, in any case the fundamental rights of the defendant (especially his right to a fair trial) have not been violated, for which reason the evidence obtained did not have to be excluded.[27] Compare exclusion in the case of "conduct so shocking that it not only violates (the) notions of due process (in the requesting state), but also violates fundamental international norms for decency."[28] Admission of evidence affected by such irregularities would – in the terms of the US Supreme Court – "serve to defeat the state's efforts to employ the exclusionary rule as a means to assure obedience to the treaty concerned."[29] This approach has the advantage, that the courts in the adjudicating state will be able to decide without being dependent on assistance from the requested state, as soon as an irregularity has been established. However, in many cases properly establishing an irregularity is the main difficulty. And will what in State A is seen as an infringement of a fundamental right, be seen in the same light in State B? If not, the problem is only half resolved; and, last and least there are the minimal approaches:

5.   the illegality only has effect when using the evidence obtained would bring the administration of justice into disrepute, or affect the judicial integrity of the forum court; and

6.   the illegality only has effect when it makes the evidence unreliable and the use of such evidence would distort the fact-finding process.[30]

The fifth and sixth approach have the same advantage as the one mentioned under number four: the courts in the adjudicating state will not find any special difficulty in assessing the reliability of the evidence presented to them – as soon as they properly established how it was obtained.

Could the problem also be resolved between the EU member states by introducing a special procedure before the European Court of Justice? This could be especially interesting because it is precisely these states that are eliminating all barriers against judicial assistance one by one. But could the ECJ (already) be trusted to answer such sensitive questions regarding the law of the requested state (illegalities, consequences) and the law of the requesting state (consequence)? We doubt it.

Some authors required reciprocity:[31] State A would only have to exclude evidence from State B, when State B would exclude evidence from State A. In our opinion, this again is an example of an improper invasion of international

---

[27] HR 18 May 1999 nr. 109.075.

[28] Saltzburg, *op. cit.*, p. 775.

[29] *Elkins* v. *US*, 364 *U.S.* 206 (1960).

[30] Saltzburg, *op. cit.*, p. 775.

[31] *See* W.H. Theis, 'Choice of law and the administration of the exclusionary rule in criminal cases', 44 *Tennessee Law Review* (1977), p. 1943/1083 (concentrating on the relations between US state jurisdictions and between US state and federal jurisdictions).

law concepts into criminal procedure. What does a defendant have to do with reciprocity, or, more generally, with the relations between A and B?

The second and third cases in particular illustrate a fundamental change in the practice of mutual assistance in criminal matters in the last one or two decades. For a long time, this kind of co-operation had a rather static character. Usually the requesting authorities needed the assistance of the requested state on a very specific point, such as the seizure of certain documents. Nowadays, the character of the international co-operation in criminal matters is becoming more dynamic, especially within the European Union. A form of co-operation has been created establishing a *closed network* of (criminal) law enforcement in which the circumstance that a crime is committed in the territory of more than one state, in itself does not reduce the chances for effective law enforcement.

Our first case demonstrated how extremely difficult it will be to solve the problem when *no* authoritative decision by a competent authority in the requested state is available regarding the legality of the activities of the local judicial authorities. We conclude that the problem cannot be resolved exclusively by domestic law. Emphasising the 'criminal' aspects of international criminal law can only bear fruit when the international aspects are not eliminated or ignored. Only treaties may provide a solution for our problem.[32]

Our second and third case also illustrates the difficult position of the defence. The decision of the Dutch Supreme Court in *case 2* is illuminating: the prosecuting authorities had no reason to doubt the legality of the activities, resulting in the information received from the English authorities. Even if it had been revealed at a later stage that the information had been obtained illegally, this *in itself* would not lead to the rejection of the prosecution; and, because the information was not used as evidence in court, no exclusionary rules were applicable in any case.[33]

Although several solutions can be imagined, all seem to have their disadvantages. A treaty could, *e.g.*, provide for a procedure of *ex officio* assessment by a court in the requested state. It would be feasible to require an initiative from the defendant, but this probably would create too many practical difficulties. Often in this phase there is no defendant, or he does not yet know about the case because he has not yet been indicted; will an ex officio assessment, without any defence contribution, be effective? The court should not only assess whether all applicable prescriptions have been complied with, but also – if an irregularity is found – what effect it should have under its domestic law, and why. Should this be conclusive for the effect in the

---

[32] In the same sense *Individu en internationale rechtshulp in strafzaken*, Report on the position of defendants and other involved persons in relation to international mutual assistance in criminal matters, the Hague 1993, pp. 31-32 and 52-53.
[33] HR 16 November 1999 nr. 111.161, yet to be published.

requesting state? Although this position actually has been defended,[34] we do not believe it to be quite rational. Suppose, *e.g.*, that the requested state never applies exclusionary rules, and the requesting state does – should the evidence not then be excluded? That would hardly be acceptable. But the opposite situation would also meet resistance.

The effect which a concrete irregularity should have can only be assessed by an authority knowing the ins and outs of the criminal case concerned; moreover, exclusion of evidence may only be based on domestic law. So the court called upon to give the verdict will also be the only acceptable authority to decide whether and to what extent irregularities in the requested state need to have a procedural effect. The general opinion about the subject in the requested state will have to be taken into account, but only that in the requesting state may be conclusive. This illustrates, by the way, the importance of a certain common body of procedural prescriptions!

Another option could be to again amend the *European Convention on Information on Foreign Law*, by providing for a court decision, explicitly answering questions posed under Article 1 of the *Additional Protocol*.

We are aware that we have not offered a ready-made solution; we clearly are not able to do so yet. More extensive research and reflection is needed, and some inspiration would be helpful, as well. What we intended to do was no more than to outline the problem, highlighting its procedural features (in contrast to the international law aspects), emphasising the resulting inequality if no proper solution can be found, and showing the direction future research on the subject should take. We hope we have made it clear how important and how urgent such research is.

---

[34] Thus A.M.M. Orie, *Internationale opsporing*, in *Internationalisering van het strafrecht*, series Strafrecht en Criminologie Vol. 6, Nijmegen: AA Libri 1986, pp. 165-179, p. 179; a similar proposal – but restricted to the specific category of offences against the financial interests of the EU – has been made in M. Delmas-Marty, *Corpus Juris*, Antwerpen: Intersentia 1999, pp. 182-187.

# The DNA Database in the Netherlands

*H.J.T. Janssen*

## Introduction

The Netherlands Forensic Institute (NFI) is part of the Dutch Ministry of Justice and is the only institute of this kind in the Netherlands. In 1994, the Dutch law was supplemented with regulations which enlarged the use of DNA investigation in criminal cases, including the development of a DNA database. Since then, the NFI has been appointed as the administrator of the Dutch DNA database. In this paper an overview of the Dutch situation at present on the DNA database will be given and the expectation for the future when the law will be changed.

## Elements of the Dutch DNA Legislation in Relation to the Database

Some key elements of the existing DNA legislation in relation to the database were very important for the development of the Dutch DNA database:
- the compulsory sampling of bodily material;
- the sampling by a surgeon, not by a police officer;
- the role of the investigating judge;
- the role of the prosecutor.

### a. The Compulsory sampling of Bodily Material

A difference in regard to other countries is the fact that a blood sample, a buccal cell sample or plucked hairs are intimate samples. Therefore the legal regulations are very strict.

According to the law only the investigating judge can require the suspect to give bodily material when he refuses to give a sample voluntarily. However, the compulsory sampling is restricted to crimes liable to a penalty of eight years or more of imprisonment. The warrant can also be given if it concerns specific offences with a maximum punishment of at least six years of imprisonment, such as serious kinds of maltreatment and public violence. It is necessary that facts and circumstances indicate serious charges against the suspect and DNA investigation is necessary in the pursuit of truth.

In the new legislation which will be discussed in parliament in the year 2000 the condition that DNA investigation is necessary in the pursuit of truth will no longer be a criterium. A point of discussion in parliament will also be the reduction of the maximum penalty from eight years to four years. As it seems now the minister of justice and the members of parliament are in favour of a reduction. So then it will become much easier to force a suspect to give bodily material when he is refusing to do so.

## b. The Role of the Investigating Judge in Relation to the Database

At present the investigating judge is involved in cases with a suspect and he is the only person to order a compulsory sample. In practice a legal problem arises sometimes when a suspect confesses to a crime. In this case the investigating judge finds it no longer necessary to demand a DNA investigation, because it is no longer necessary in the pursuit of truth. As a result no DNA profile of the suspect is produced and put into the database. This situation would give for instance a serial rapist the possibility of confessing to one crime to prevent that a DNA investigation is started and also that other unsolved crimes could be solved by a search with his DNA profile in the database. Therefore this criterium can prevent a future possibility to trace a repeated offender by the DNA database. Of course this can give a conflict with a prosecutor: he wants to have a DNA investigation, but the judge refuses.

Another problem which is limiting the use of the DNA database is the fact that the judge has an examining task only in the case he is working on. He finds himself not competent to demand a search in the database if there is no suspicion in relation to possible other crimes commited by the suspect. Because of this reason it is true that DNA profiles are put into the database, but an order from a investigating judge for search against other profiles is not given. Having said it must be emphasized that the employees of the DNA laboratory are not police officers. Therefore they do not have the competence to perform a search automatically in the DNA database without a request of the judge or prosecutor, at this moment.

## c. The Role of the Prosecutor

Today the competence to order a DNA investigation in a crime without a suspect is given to the prosecutor and is not limited to the kind of crime. The prosecutor can independently demand the laboratory to start a DNA investigation of the biological evidence sample in order to determine its origin. He can also order to compare the DNA profile of the biological evidence sample with DNA profiles of suspects in prior criminal cases and DNA profiles of biological crime scene samples in the DNA database. A match has then to be reported to the prosecutor.

In the future, if the parliament agrees, the prosecutor can give an order to take a compulsory sample and ask for a DNA investigation in case of a suspect is known. Then there will be the possibility to get a DNA profile of that offender and to put it into the database.

Another improvement will be the fact that a DNA investigation will automatically include a search in the DNA database. An order of a judge or prosecutor is no longer needed.

These changes as mentioned before will overcome a lot of todays problems and this will enlarge the possibilities of the use of the DNA database.

## Content of the DNA Database

The DNA database consists of information on the following categories:
- suspects;
- biological stains in cases without a suspect;
- not identified mortal remains.

Please take note that until now no DNA profiles from victims or other persons than suspects are stored in the database.

The increasing possibilities of the DNA profiling however have created the wish to expand the possible use of the DNA database. There is a request from the minister of justice to develop a database for missing persons. A number of legal questions, especially in the field of privacy, have to be solved. When having a DNA database from missing persons and their relatives, the number of categories in the database has to be expanded. However, it will not be allowed to involve missing persons or their relatives in a search in the criminal database.

Also it will be possible to put into the database DNA profiles of deceased victims of a violent crime. A future search in the database can reveal the identity of the suspect. In a search in the database a DNA profile is compared with all other profiles in the database. A shortcoming in the present database is the fact that there is no possibility to distinguish searches between the different categories of DNA profiles. To have more possibilities the Netherlands Forensic Institute is going to change to the CODIS system, which looks very promising at this point.

DNA profiles of suspects will be deleted after a period of thirty years and those of samples detected at the scene of crime after a period of eighteen years. By order of the prosecutor the DNA profile of a suspect has to be deleted immediately when the registered person was suspected wrongly or when he is aquitted or discharged.

A big problem in the Netherlands is the feedback from the prosecutors office. Hardly ever an order is given to remove DNA profiles. A problem can arise when as a result of a search in the database a hit is produced with a suspect in a previous case. When it becomes clear that this DNA profile should have been removed in an earlier stage, then there is unlawful evidence which a judge cannot use.

Acknowledging this problem, the proposal for new legislation includes the obligation for the prosecutors' office to keep the Netherlands Forensic Institute informed.

Unfortunately the laboratory cannot perform another analysis on the reference sample of a suspect if he is pointed out by a search in the DNA database as a suspect in another case. The Dutch law at this moment obliges the laboratory to destroy all cellmaterial from a suspect when it is not necessary anymore for the investigation. According to the law the investigating judge has to give an order to destroy the cell material. In practice

369

however, it is very rare to receive an order to destroy the material. But this still means that re-use of the material is not allowed.

Another disadvantage of the lack of the possibility to re-analyse the cellmaterial of the suspect in relation to the DNA database, is that when DNA markers will change in the future. Then it will not be possible to analyse those new DNA markers in cellmaterial of the suspects in the database. The database will become obsolete in the future. This argument has also been used to convince the legislator and the members of parliament to create the possibility of re-analysing cellmaterial from suspects which has been kept in the laboratory.

Hopefully the new legislation will create possibilities to store reference samples for future use.

### Foreign Requests for Information

By opening the European borders crime is becoming more and more international. Cross border criminality therefore is expected to increase in the years to come.

A point of concern is what to do with foreign requests to perform a search in the database. Until now this is still a tedious procedure. A request from a foreign authority has to be sent to the office of international legal assistance in criminal matters of the Ministry of Justice.They send the request to the laboratory. The result of the search in the database has to be sent to the foreign authority via the same office at the ministry of justice. If there exists a treaty between two countries, for example Schengen countries, the foreign request can be sent from a prosecuter abroad to a prosecuter in the Netherlands. He will judge the request and send it to the laboratory. The result of the search has to take the same way back. Due to this time-consuming procedure, it does not contribute to a quick investigation.

In connection to this a few words have to be spend on the development of international cooperation on the judicial level. The European countries still have their own national legislation on DNA or no legislation at all. A lot of effort has been put in standardisation of the DNA technique in the last few years. Now it is very important to put a lot of energy into developing legislation and harmonisation of the different DNA legislations. Only then will it be possible to come to a quick exchange of DNA profiles in criminal investigations, in Europe and worldwide.

Having described some legal points in relation to the development of the DNA database in the Netherlands now more about the actual database itself.

## The DNA Database

Although the legislation created the possibility to build a DNA database, it took until 1997 before the Dutch database came into practice. The decision was made to start the DNA database when STRs were introduced into casework. To give an idea of the estimated size of the database, it was expected that on a yearly basis about 500 samples of suspects would be analysed for a DNA profile and put into the database next to 1,000 scene of crime samples.

The Netherlands Forensic Institute is using STR multimix reactions in casework. The resulting DNA-STR profiles form the basis of the DNA intelligence database.

## Two Pilotstudies

Recognising the limitations of the DNA legislation and the limited use of the DNA database it was the right moment to stress the potential of the DNA database in order to convince the politicians to enlarge the DNA legislation.

In 1998 a pilotstudy called *DNA and burglary* was started by two police forces in the Netherlands in co-operation with the Netherlands Forensic Institute and the proscecutors offices in Utrecht en Breda. The Utrecht police covers a municipal area, the police force of Brabant a more rural region.

In the pilot study stains recovered at the scene of a burglary were send to the laboratory. Because of the capacity of our laboratory only a limited number of cases could be sent in. At the end of the pilot in December 1998 the investigations in 562 cases resulted in 391 DNA profiles.

The results of the success rate in this project are shown in the next table:

| Type of evidence | Number of traces | Number of profiles | Percentage |
|---|---|---|---|
| Blood | 247 | 226 | 92 |
| Cigarette butts | 197 | 127 | 65 |
| Saliva | 84 | 31 | 37 |
| Hairs | 21 | 4 | 20 |
| Other cell material | 13 | 3 | 23 |
| **Total** | **562** | **391** | **70** |

When looking at the results per districts the following remarks can be made:

| Police Force | Number of cases | Number of matched cases | | | | |
|---|---|---|---|---|---|---|
| | | 2 | 3 | 4 | 10 | 16 |
| Brabant | 224 | 16 | 7 | 2 | 1 | 1 |
| Utrecht | 205 | 19 | 4 | 2 | | |

In 23 cases a suspect could be indicated. However, it concerned only five suspects in total from whom bodily cell material had been received. In one

371

police-region one suspect could be indicated as the offender of 16 burglaries. Another suspect was indicated as offender in four of those 16 cases. They belonged to a group of four persons suspected for more than 100 burglaries.

Another big investigation is of great importance to the database. It concerns the search for a serial rapist, also in the region of Utrecht, the fourth biggest city in the Netherlands.

In the years 1995 and 1996 a number of 18 rapes and attempts of rapes took place in the Utrecht area. From semen stains found in two cases we were able to determine a DNA profile. The rapes caused quite a lot of anxiety in the Utrecht area.

Testimonies of victims indicated that the offender was a white Dutch speaking man who was between 20 and 40 years old. He was supposed to be between 1.65 and 1.85 m tall. The offender must have known the area.

In an early investigation in 1998 already 25 cases were examined in order to look for the DNA profile of the rapist, without the required result. Public opinion and the attention of the press forced the police to continue the investigation on a large scale. This resulted in a request of the prosecutor to start an extensive investigation, concerning all rape cases dated from 1987 with a description of the rapist as being a white man with a sturdy figure.

First the unsolved cases from the Utrecht area were investigated. Then the circle around Utrecht became wider and wider. At the end the cases from all over the Netherlands were investigated.

The investigation was divided in three portions:
1. the search of 570 cases with known suspects;
2. the search of 735 cases without a suspect;
3. the search of known people mass screening.

It was decided to start with the cases with a suspect. In these investigations a problem arised. When a suspect was known in a case we were not allowed to use the reference sample of the suspect. Therefore it was necessary to analyse the remained semen stains in those cases.

The second group consisted of 735 cases without a suspect.

The third part of the investigation was the screening of a group of 104 individuals. 86 Individuals cooperated, nine refused to cooperate and another nine persons could not be found. None of the individuals matched with the DNA profile of the semenstains of the serial rapist. This investigation was the first mass screening in the Netherlands and gave very interesting results on the basis of the comparison of the DNA profiles of the semenstains in the cases which were involved in this project.

| | Number of matched cases | | | |
|---|---|---|---|---|
| | 2 | 3 | 4 | 5 |
| Number of times | 35 | 8 | 1 | 1 |

A striking point is that until now the prosecutor has not given his permission for a comparison with other profiles in the database.

## Other Results of the DNA Database

The total content of the database on November 1, 1999 is shown in the table below.

| Number of cases | Number of suspects | Number of stains |
|---|---|---|
| 2241 | 618 | 2649 |

The content of the database until now has resulted in several hits in different categories of cases, such as sexual assaults, robberies, burglaries, murder.

Because of the legal limitations, the Dutch DNA database has not the dimension as expected to have when the DNA legislation became effective. By developing the DNA database, several shortcomings of the existing DNA legislation became clear. Hopefully the new legislation will enlarge the possibilities of the DNA database.

## Conclusion

As a conclusion it can be stated that even with the relative small number of data the database has been proved to be successful. The results have made quite an impression on the politicians and it has helped to convince them to enlarge the legal possibilities of DNA investigation.

If the legal situation in the Netherlands is changed the use of the DNA database will become more prominent. The proposed change of the law will result in more profiles of offenders in our database and an increase of the number of solved crimes in the Netherlands. Also the impact on the organisation of the DNA department of the NFI will be important. DNA investigation in a for example burglary case will become usual. This means that the number of burglary cases can grow to 10,000 a year in a few years time. Also in many other cases a DNA investigation will be performed

Then DNA database will have a big influence in the future fight against criminality. A lot of things have to be done in the next years. A passionate time is ahead of us.

# Improperly Obtained Evidence and the End(s) of Punishment

*H.J.R. Kaptein*

### The Exclusionary Rule: the Legal Community v. the People?

In many contemporary legal orders, the standard sanction against improperly obtained criminal evidence is exclusion of such evidence, or even a bar to the public prosecution. Vigorously defended by criminal lawyers and other legal scholars and practitioners, the exclusionary rule and related sanctioning of improper procedure by letting suspects and criminal defendants go free have time and again met with equally vigorous criticism by other legal scholars and practitioners and predominantly by non-legal people. Such criticism may not always be silenced by the sobering fact that improper procedure in collecting evidence is the exception rather than the rule, at least in *civilised* legal orders.

A core criticism may be: "How may it be that law designed to punish offenders lets them go free when they have been unfairly treated in the administration of criminal justice? What about victims of crime and other citizens? Are they not entitled to punishment against offenders? Putting crime and punishment on the same scales as improper officials' conduct is comparing the incomparable."

Against this, criminal lawyers and others stress the paramount importance of fair treatment of all citizens by criminal authorities. They may say: "And what if it happened to you?! What if police burglars break through your front door at night without any warrant, in order to get hold of an old bike stolen by you years ago, when you were still studying law? Would you say ok let's get me punished, I deserve it?"

Criminal lawyers and others are no doubt right in stressing the importance of prohibiting and sanctioning improper methods in obtaining evidence. However, a distinction must be made between the importance of such prohibition by itself on the one hand and different ways of sanctioning breaches of such prohibition on the other. Or: prohibition of improperly obtaining evidence does not by itself imply exclusionary rule sanctioning, as there may be other ways to sanction authorities' trespassing in collecting evidence and other ways to compensate for such conduct.

Here an attempt will be made to discuss exclusionary versus inclusionary solutions from the perspective of different conceptions of justification of material criminal law and punishment. This may be thought to come down to a category error in confusing matters of material and formal criminal law. Criminal procedure concerns citizens, suspects and criminal defendants who may or may not be deserving punishment, in contrast to material criminal law having to do with degrees of punishment for offenders in the first place. Still, different solutions of the procedural problem of improperly obtained evidence appear to be deeply related to different conceptions of justification of material criminal law and punishment.

By way of introduction, the exclusionary rule and a few of its strong and weak points will be discussed in some detail. It may appear that commonly conceived considerations for and against may not tip the scales, leading to one more reason to discuss the problem of improperly obtained evidence from perspectives of material criminal law.

Thus exclusion of improperly obtained evidence appears to be compatible with conceptions of punishment in terms of serving general interests, for example in terms of prevention of crime as a public good, to be weighed against other public goods like sanctioning and compensating citizens' rights against unfair treatment by criminal authorities.

On the other hand, criticism against the exclusionary rule appears to be, however implicitly, partly determined by retributivist conceptions of material criminal law, related to rights to punishment not easily outweighed by other factors, like claims stemming from improper treatment in the collection of evidence.

Discussion on these different conceptions of punishment and their manifold varieties seems not to have led to reasoned consensus yet. However, it is widely agreed upon that victims of crime are to gain more predominant roles in the administration of criminal justice. Developments in such directions have to do with rights to retribution in their original meaning of rights to compensation or reparation for victims. Such rights are incompatible with exclusionary sanctioning.

Respecting victims of crime may foster the search for inclusionary solutions, like disciplinary and/or criminal procedure against officials, and/or damages. Such inclusionary solutions are not unproblematic either. On the other hand, such solutions may be rational even in a purely general interest conception of criminal law.

Still, in less then perfect legal practice exclusionary solutions may be more effective. Discussion of exclusionary rule problems and alternatives may show the general importance of discussing problems of criminal procedure in connection with different conceptions of the justification of punishment and the importance of attention to victims' rights and interests.

### Standard Arguments for and against Exclusion: an Undecided Issue

The factual content of improperly obtained evidence may or may not be contaminated by improper methods. Two examples: an illegal blood test may still lead to factually indubitable proof of physiological conditions for drunkenness. On the other hand, something resembling a confession extorted by physical force may be completely contrary to the facts of the matter. It goes without saying that the last kind of evidence is to be excluded by all means. There may be more or less complex borderline cases, for example having to do with suspects' statements towards criminal officials not preceded by cautioning.

The question remains whether both kinds of evidence ought to be treated the same way. Or: ought factually reliable but improperly obtained evidence to be excluded like unreliable or even false improperly obtained evidence ought to be excluded? Even if this may imply that persons deserving punishment on the basis of factually reliable evidence go free that way?

More than a few related considerations favour exclusion. Fundamental is the overriding importance of integrity in criminal procedure. Improperly obtained evidence and in fact whatever improper conduct and its products are to have no place in the administration of criminal justice. Of course, one reason for this is the basic fact that criminal procedure is effected by the (more or less) almighty state against (more or less) powerless individuals.

Also, products of improper officials' conduct may be regarded as 'forbidden fruits', to be excluded from any *civilised* criminal procedure. In terms of a counterfactual conditional it might be argued that if criminal officials had conducted inquiries in proper ways, then the evidence at hand would not have been obtained. No possibly intractable problems of distinguishing between improperly obtained evidence not factually contaminated and evidence factually contaminated by improper methods rise under the exclusionary rule, as both kinds of evidence are ruled out.

The state ought to be sanctioned for improper conduct toward citizens and/or suspects in criminal matters. Mistreated citizens, suspects and criminal defendants may be compensated by freedom from punishment. Also, criminal courts generally have no other means of sanctioning the state and compensating criminal defendants than by letting such defendants go free, by exclusion of improperly obtained evidence (that is, if such evidence is decisive) or by barring the public prosecution. Indeed, a major advantage of the exclusionary rule is its immediate applicability, leading to direct sanctioning and compensation. No separate, time-consuming and expensive extra procedures with possibly uncertain outcomes are needed.

On the other hand, exclusion of improperly obtained evidence faces more or less serious objections. First and foremost, a distinction must be made between the question whether somebody deserves punishment and the question whether that person has been the subject of unfair treatment in the administration of criminal justice. Such questions seem to belong to rather different categories. Excluding improperly obtained evidence seems to come down to a kind of conjuring away what made somebody deserving punishment in the first place.

Also, distinctions between contexts of discovery and contexts of justification may be brought to bear against exclusion of improperly obtained evidence. In principle, it makes no sense to confuse ways of obtaining evidence with the quality of evidence itself.[1]

Special prevention may be of such paramount importance that the exclusionary rule may lead to dangerous consequences, by letting possibly deadly recidivists go free. That is, if no other measures are available to ward off clear and present danger.

Even if letting persons possibly deserving punishment go free may be the right kind of sanction against the state and the right kind of compensation for improperly treated criminal defendants, then still there may still be gross disproportion between relatively harmless improper treatment on the one hand and the 'loss' of severe punishment for serious crime on the other. Or between grossly unfair treatment in collecting evidence concerning petty crime sanctioned by petty fines.

Such disproportional relationships, apart from other disadvantages of the exclusionary rule, may lead courts and legislatures to limit exclusion. Thus exclusion may be applied only in cases of evidence unobtainable by proper methods and/or only in cases of intentional misconduct, etc. Only limited reduction of punishment may be prescribed by way of sanctioning of compensation. Such limitation may undo protection and compensation for subjects of possibly improper administration of criminal justice.

However gross mistreatment may have been, if a case does not reach a court, there will be no exclusion. Against this it may be stated that there will be no punishment in such cases anyway. But mistreated citizens and suspects may well be completely innocent. Also, acquittal for other reasons than exclusion and innocence precludes any exclusionary sanctioning and compensation.

Improperly obtained evidence may be no legal and/or factual presupposition for conviction, given sufficient alternative evidence. Thus improperly obtained evidence may not stand in the way of conviction, that is, if improper conduct is not sufficiently unfair or illegal to warrant a bar to the public prosecution. There will be no sanctioning and compensation at all, then, notwithstanding possibly serious infraction of rights to proper treatment.

Though improperly obtained evidence is to play no role under the exclusionary rule, exclusion of evidence by courts deciding upon criminal cases implies that such courts do know about such evidence. Which implies that such evidence may play informal but nonetheless decisive roles in court decisions. Also, unwanted consequences of exclusion of improperly obtained evidence may be done away with by courts liberally interpreting or even misinterpreting rules and principles protecting against improper collection of criminal evidence.

Effectiveness of the exclusionary rule may well be undermined by police and public prosecution officials' attitudes like: possibly improper collection of

---

[1] *See* for example Golding (1984), ch. 1.

evidence may just be given a try, if courts judge things to have gone wrong, there is still nothing lost, as things are back to the original situation, then.

Even if improper officials' conduct may be relatively rare in *civilised* legal orders, public trust in criminal courts may be seriously undermined by exclusion of improperly obtained evidence (and by related sanctioning of misconduct leading to persons possibly deserving punishment going free).[2] Irrational as such mistrust may seem, it still is a factor of major importance.

Such advantages and disadvantages do not seem to outweigh each other.[3] Probably the core objection comes down to the possibly guilty going free. But how unjust is this? Conceptions of justification of material criminal law and punishment are important here.

### Public Interest Conceptions Compatible with Exclusion

Exclusionary rule consequences seem to do public interests no good. Surely public interests are not served by letting possible offenders go free? Plausible as this may seem, things may well be the other way round. If justification of criminal law and punishment is to be found in some or other service to public interests, among other things in terms of special and/or general prevention, then positive consequences of excluding improperly obtained evidence may be weighed against negative consequences of freedom from punishment for possible offenders.

It may even be put that citizens have rights against improper criminal procedure in collecting evidence or otherwise and that clear and direct sanctioning and compensation for violation of such rights have priority over public interests in sufficient punishment.[4] That is, unless general levels of punishment are so low as to seriously endanger public interests. However, given the relative rarity of cases of improperly obtained evidence in *civilised* legal orders it is rather unlikely that application of the exclusionary rule will by itself lead to dangerously lower levels of punishment.

So the main point here is the possibility of weighing. This may be further clarified by an important difference. Punishing even a single innocent person not only violates basic rights against undeserved punishment, but also leads to public unrest and to fear to undergo the same ill-deserved treatment. On the other hand, given generally sufficient levels of punishment, relatively few offenders going free may do no great harm to public interests. In public interest conceptions it certainly does not violate any rights. This asymmetric relationship is all the more important in legal orders in which improper officials' conduct in collecting evidence is the exception rather than the rule.

---

[2] *See also* Perrin *et al.* (1998).
[3] *See also* Zuckerman (1989), ch. 16, and Galligan (ed.)(1992) for other strong and weak points of exclusion.
[4] *See* Dworkin (1986) about priority of rights over public interests in general.

So the conclusion is clear, as far as public interest conceptions of criminal law and punishment are concerned. Such conceptions not only accommodate exclusion of improperly obtained evidence. Such conceptions may also offer arguments in favour of exclusion, in terms of weighing public interests in punishment against public interests in proper administration of criminal justice.

It is to be kept in mind that public interest conceptions of material criminal law and punishment do not assume rights to punishment against individual offenders. Such offenders going free in certain or possibly even in many cases may be detrimental to public interests, but does not violate any rights. It is sufficient levels of punishment that count. But however rational exclusion of improper evidence may seem in public interest conceptions, in at least one kind of case such exclusion may still lead to infringement of rights indubitable even in whatever public interest conception. As noted before, special prevention may be necessary to save life and/or other matters of overriding importance. Everybody has a right to be protected from such dangers in the first place and indeed in such cases it may be difficult if not impossible to accommodate the exclusionary rule in whatever public interest conception of criminal law and punishment. That is, again, if no other effective measures against dangerous recidivists are available.

### Retribution and Exclusion: less Easy Relationships

Exclusion of improperly obtained evidence is still less easily compatible with retributivist conceptions of criminal law and punishment. In such conceptions the state is regarded as having a duty to punish the guilty whenever possible, whether such punishment serves public interests like prevention of crime or not. Freedom from punishment for offenders by exclusion of improperly obtained evidence seems to be violation of the essence of punishment as being the necessary answer to crime, then.

Much more so than in public interest conceptions, application of the exclusionary rule leads to conflicts of rights in retributivist conceptions. Is the state to be punished for improper conduct and is the offender to be compensated, or is the offender to receive due punishment? Not much room for weighing and compensation here: rights to punishment against offenders come first.

Still, retributivist conceptions may accommodate some or other weighing in terms of sufficient punishment. Such retributivism may leave room for non-retributive considerations in determining degrees of punishment, for example in terms of general and special prevention. Or it may be put that sufficient retribution is the goal, instead of retribution against all crime. Then, like in non-retributivist public interest conceptions, a slightly lower general level of punishment may be outweighed by positive consequences of the exclusionary rule.

However, popular resistance against the exclusionary rule may well be explained by implicitly absolutist retributive conceptions. The Kantian *fiat justitia pereat mundus* is indeed incompatible with exclusionary rule consequences. But it is deeply implausible and rather impracticable, however deep-seated and widespread such absolutist retributivism may be. The exclusionary rule is not really excluded by material criminal law considerations yet.

**Victims' Rights against Exclusion?**

Discussion of justification of criminal law and punishment in terms of public interests and/or retribution seems not to lead to reasoned consensus either. It will probably go without saying that exclusion of improperly obtained evidence is highly rational if punishment must be regarded as essentially unjustified, as in more radical versions of abolitionism. Then anything leading to lesser punishment or no punishment at all is preferable to punishment for no good reason.

However, at least some justification for criminal law and punishment may be found in respect for victims of crime. More than a few contemporary criminal legal orders display victim friendly tendencies in legislation, prosecution and adjudication. Retribution in criminal law may be at least partly be plausibly reinterpreted as material and symbolical compensation and reparation by offenders.[5] Originally, *retribuere* means, of course, to repay, etc.

Excluding improperly obtained evidence is at odds with rights of crime victims to compensation and satisfaction through punishment and possibly complementary compensatory measures against offenders. Also, victims of crime may put it that they have nothing to do with improper officials' conduct possibly leading to forfeiture of state rights to punishment. Or: the exclusionary rule belongs to conceptions of criminal law limited to relationships between (possible) offenders and the state, representing public interests.

Respect for victims may well be on more driving force behind popular resistance against the exclusionary rule. However difficult the issue of respect for victims in criminal law may be, such popular resistance may be rather less irrational than its *fiat justitia pereat mundus* counterpart. So the question remains whether there may be inclusionary answers to improperly obtained evidence, compatible with respect for victims.

**Inclusionary Answers**

The core idea of inclusionary solutions is decoupling punishment for offences committed by subjects of officials' misconduct from punishment and

---

[5] *See* Barnett (1998); Wright (1999); Kaptein (forthcoming).

compensation for such officials' misconduct. In principle, full punishment is to be meted out for both kinds of offence. Officials' misconduct may be countered by disciplinary or even criminal sanctions. Also, damages may be awarded to victims of improperly obtained evidence.[6] Only in cases of fines, monetary compensation may come to resemble exclusionary rule consequences, as offenders may pay less in cases in which they are entitled to damages to be paid for by the state. Or even by individual officials, in cases of intentionally serious misconduct.

Such alternative sanctions may not only be compatible with retribution and respect for victims in not letting offenders go free, but may also be superior in other respects. It may even be argued that public interest justifications of punishment, indeed compatible with but not presupposing exclusion of improperly obtained evidence, may be better served by punishment against officials and damages for victims of officials' misconduct. Anyway, public trust in the administration of criminal justice may be fostered by inclusive solutions more than by exclusion of improperly obtained evidence.

In more than a few legal orders, changes in legislation may not be necessary to reinstate inclusionary protection against and compensation by the state for officials' misconduct. For example: tort law may offer more opportunities than are normally realised, though it may need reform in these respects too.

Inclusionary answers may have one more advantage. It is said that recent developments in criminal procedure in more than a few legal orders drift away from citizens', suspects' and defendants' protection, in emphasising 'fighting crime', motivated by respect for victims among other reasons. This may lead to watering down exclusionary rule protection. Inclusionary solutions do not force to weighing such factors, as sanctioning and compensating for improper officials' conduct is fully compatible with punishing the guilty.

Such 'having the cake and eat it' solutions have an air of the ideal, seemingly catering for all possible rights and interests at stake. In that sense too, such solutions may be called inclusive. However, there may be a less attractive air of idealism here. For example: will public prosecution offices be willing to go after offending officials, 'their own people'? For bad or sometimes even for good reasons, it may be argued that more important things are to be done.

It may be thought that such problems are less serious concerning disciplinary punishment, as disciplinary procedures do not necessarily depend upon public prosecution offices. But then again experience with disciplinary procedure against criminal law officials and officials in general for that matter has not always been encouraging either. Vexing *entre nous* problems of disciplinary law have to be solved here too.

---

[6] *See also* Schlesinger (1977); Perrin *et al.* (1998).

## Cautionary Concluding Remarks

Indeed, inclusionary solutions will function properly only in legal orders realised by honest (and professionally capable) officials in proceeding against improper conduct of other officials. This leads to a paradox, as it goes without saying that in such circumstances improper officials' conduct in collecting evidence will be rare exceptions. This may be illustrated by Scandinavian legal orders, relying as they do on exclusively inclusionary solutions.

In more difficult situations, notwithstanding its disadvantages for victims of crime, rough and ready exclusionary solutions may still be preferable, at least in the sense of being more effective. Which surely does not mean that different kinds of curtailing the exclusionary rule in many legal orders are to be welcomed. Thus improperly obtained evidence may indeed not be excluded as such, but may lead to less punishment. This is not even curtailing, but is at odds with basic ideas behind the exclusionary rule, like removal of all factors threatening the integrity of the administration of criminal justice.[7] This is no respect for persons mistreated by criminal law officials nor is it real respect for victims of crime.

In practice, such watering down may only be accepted, at least from the standpoint of victims of improperly obtained evidence, if supplementary inclusionary countermeasures are strongly promoted. And of course it must be stressed again that criticism against exclusion of improperly obtained evidence does not at all amount to criticism of rules and principles of citizens' protection against the administration of criminal justice.

Clarifying problems of improperly obtained evidence may lead to more general rethinking relationships between criminal procedure and material criminal law. Not only in such relationships rights and interests of crime victims are of paramount importance.

## References

**Barnett, R.E.** (1998), *The Structure of Liberty: Justice and The Rule of Law*, Oxford: Clarendon Press.

**Dworkin, R.M.** (1986), *Law's Empire*, Harvard University Press, Cambridge, Mass.

**Galligan, D.J.** (ed.)(1992), *Procedure*, Aldershot.

**Golding, M.P.** (1984), *Legal Reasoning*, Alfred A. Knopf, Inc., New York.

**Kaptein, H.J.R.**, 'Reconciliation of retribution and reparation: integrating victims' perspectives in principles of criminal law and punishment', in: *Rechtstheorie* (forthcoming).

**Mevis, P.A.M.** (1997), 'The integrity of the criminal process requires the exclusion of illegally obtained evidence', in: *Proceedings of The First World Conference on New Trends in Criminal Investigation and Evidence*, Vermande, Lelystad.

**Perrin, L.T., Caldwell, H.M., Chase, C.A. & Fagan, R.W.** (1998), 'If it's broken, fix it: moving beyond the exclusionary rule – A new and extensive empirical study of the exclusionary rule and a call for a civil administrative remedy to partially replace the rule', in: *Iowa law review* (83/4), pp. 669-766

---

[7] *See* Mevis (1997).

383

H.J.R. Kaptein

**Schlesinger, S.R.** (1977), *Exclusionary Injustice: The Problem Of Illegally Obtained Evidence*, Marcel Dekker, New York & Basel.
**Wright, M.** (1999), *Restoring Respect for Justice: A Symposium*, Waterside Press, Winchester.
**Zuckerman, A.A.S.** (1989), *The Principles of Criminal Evidence*, Clarendon Press, Oxford.

# Child and Adolescent as a Victim of Adult Crime

*S. Katalinic, I. Katalinic, R. Dobi-Babic & D. Cuculic*

## Introduction

On December 16, 1998 the Croatian House of Parliament has brought the resolution about the proclamation of the *Croatian Family Code (CFC)* based on Article 89 of the *Constitution* of the Republic of Croatia. On the base of Article 86 *CFC*, a child has the right to life and healthcare, safety and family education regarding its physical, mental and emotional needs. In consideration of Article 91 *CFC*, parents are obligated to care for their child's life and health. regarding the regulation of health jurisdiction and medical science demands parents have to enable all measures for health promotion and health caring and recovery of their children. They have to protect the child from humiliation and physical abuse from other persons (Article 91 *CFC*).[1]

The principal forms of child and adolescent abuse are physical, psychical sexual and incest, as well as the combination of previous forms.

A child that has been abused and neglected for a long period of time could show the following symptoms: distrust, low self-esteem, depression, suicidal behaviour, aggression, multiple personal disorders, disturbed relations with a group of children of the same age, unsuccessful school results, eating disorders, drug and/or alcohol abuse, revictimisation, hypersexual behaviour and somatic disorders.

To resolve this phenomenon, it is necessary to promptly stop any further abuse. Croatian judicature is protecting children and adolescents from any kind of abuse by the *Croatian Penal Code (CPC)*. The laws can only be applied if the criminal act is denounced, with a note that not denouncing is also a criminal act (Article 300 *CPC*).[2]

The new *CPC* was proclaimed on January 1, 1998. Chapter 16 of this Code regulates the criminal acts against marriage, family and minors, bigamy, making not permitted marriage possible, violating the family duties, violating the duties of supporting, child or adolescent kidnapping, change of marital status, illegitimate life with a minor and obstructing and unperforming of measures for child and adolescent protection.[3]

It is not necessary that the signs and behaviour disorders are visible to confirm the existence of the crime of child or adolescent neglecting and abuse (Article 213 *CPC*). Subsection1 of this Article says that the parent, adopter, tutor or any other person who 'roughly' neglects his or her duties, *i.e.*, taking

---

[1] *Kazneni zakon Republike Hrvatske*, NN 110/97.
[2] *Ibid.*
[3] Articles 206-215 *CPC*.

care of a child or a adolescent or its education, will be punished by a fine or an imprisonment up to three years. Whether or not the neglecting is roughly should be judged objectively by the intensity, frequency, consequences and circumstances of the neglecting.

A parent, adopter, tutor or any other person that is abusing a child or n adolescent, forcing a child or adolescent to labour inappropriate to its age, or forcing a child or adolescent to excessive labour, begging or force a child or adolescent to harmful behaviour for their development because of self-interest, will be punished by a fine or imprisonment up to three years. If a crime with severe body injuries was committed on a child or adolescent, or if its health was heavily disturbed, or when the victim had exposed himself to begging, prostitution or other forms of asocial behaviour and delinquency, the perpetrator will be punished with imprisonment from three to five years (Article 213 Subsections 1 and 2 *CPC*).

In a case of heavy health disorder (physical or psychical) of a child or an adolescent and also when the victim was exposed to crime acts, prostitution or an other form of asocial behaviour, the crime will be qualified as a hard qualified form of crime. The factors responsible for developing deviation behaviour of a minor could be determined by using adequate diagnostic methods by the local, authorised centres for social care.

**Methods of Work**

We have evaluated penal reports of child and adolescent neglect and abuse during the past 10 years at the County Police Direction in Rijeka. The results of this evaluation are as follows.

During the past 10 years, 89 cases of neglect and abuse of children and adolescents were reported. The total number of perpetrators is 118, of which 63 (53%) are women and 55 (47%) are men. A total of 92% of the perpetrators are the parents of the victimised children and adolescents. The other 8% are tutors, relatives, friends or teachers.

The reports show that every second male perpetrator is not only abusing his children, but also his intimate partner.

Male perpetrators are between 20 and 65 years old, with an average of 43 years. Female perpetrators are between 20 and 60 years old, with an average of 38 years. Considering the marital status of the perpetrators, 85% of the male perpetrators are married, 9.5% are divorced and 5.5% are living in illegitimate relation with a female partner. Female perpetrators are in 49% of the cases married, while 19% are living alone, 16% are divorced, 11% are living in illegitimate relation with a male partner and 5% are widow.

A total of 55% of the perpetrators have a low economical status and the rest a good one. The nationalities of the perpetrators are as follows:

| Nationality | Male | Female |
|-------------|------|--------|
| Albanian | 7% | 1.5% |
| Croatian | 58% | 57% |
| Gypsy | 5% | 16% |
| Muslim | 13% | 11% |
| Serb | 13% | 14% |
| Other | 2% | 1.5% |

Thirty-eight percent of the male perpetrators have not had a formal education (*i.e.*, have not finished elementary school), 25% have finished primary school and 36% have finished high school. Thirty-two percent of the female perpetrators have no formal education, 41% have finished primary school, 25% have finished high school and one person has a university degree.

The following organisations and persons started all penal denunciation for child and adolescent neglect and abuse in the last 10 years:
- police: 42%;
- health services: 13%;
- Centre for Social Care: 11%;
- district state attorney: 10%;
- a victim's close relative: 9%;
- school: 7%;
- neighbour: 2%;
- victim itself: 2%;
- second non-abusive parent: 2%;
- kindergarten: 1%.

The records show that 64% of the male perpetrators, as well as 22% of the female perpetrators, are alcohol abusers, with the remark that in 89 penal denunciations 8% of them both parents are alcohol abusers. Form our records 10% out of the 118 perpetrators have grown with an alcohol abusive father, 4% with an alcohol abusive mother and 4% with both parents as alcohol abusers.

Regarding the total number of perpetrator's born children, we see that 27% of them have one child, 41% two, 15% three, 13% four and 5% five and more children.

The 89 penal denunciations also show that 144 children and adolescents were neglected and abused, from which 99 (69%) are boys and 45 (31%) girls. Seventy-two boys are older than seven years, of which 58% are in elementary school and 42% in high school, while 27 girls are older than seven years, of which 59% are in elementary school and 41% in high school.

Analysing criminal records, medical documentation on existing of physical injuries of abused victims can be founds. We had 20 cases of light body injuries, of which 13 were boys and seven girls, which gives incidence of a total of 14% of neglected and abused children and adolescents. We also had six cases of heavy body injuries of a child or an adolescent, of which four were boys and two girls. Some parents do not even hesitate from injuring their own mentally or physically disabled children: seven victims were boys and two were girls. The physically injured children are mostly at school age.

The types of physical injuries are:
- haemathomas: 44%;
- scratches: 21%;
- stripes: 21%;
- article luxations: 4%;
- brain contusions: 3%;
- bone fractures: 2%.

The locations of the body injury are:
- head/neck injuries: 37%;
- leg injuries: 21%;
- hand injuries: 17%;
- back injuries: 16%;
- chest injuries: 10%.

Except body evidence of children and adolescent abuse, it can also be found in different somatic disorders like intestinal disturbances (six cases), *enuresis nocturna* (five cases), malnutrition (four cases), epilepsy (two cases), *dysmenorhea* (two cases), *hypothyreosis* and *anaemia*.

Analysing the material, the following psychical disorders in neglected and abused children and adolescents were found: asocial behaviour, leak of communication, disorders of visual-motor co-ordination, suppression or accentuated aggression, hyperactivity, psychomotor anxiety, depression, neurotic disturbances, insomnia, psychopathological personality disorder and different fears (like *pavor nocturna*).

A common consequence of continual childhood neglect and abuse is delinquency and other forms of asocial behaviour, especially by the boys. It is visible that 44% of the boys have police records of different criminal acts, usually burglaries, with an average of 14 criminal acts for a person.

A total of eight children were sexually abused, which makes an indicence of 6%, with two cases of rape and seven cases of lechery. Mental retarded girls were also sexually abused. The average duration of molestation is 10 years before accuse is started. The consequences for the children are mostly psychological such as lack of concentration, aggression, psychomotor restless, bad school results and psychopathological personality disorders.

**Discussion**

During the last three decades psychologists have found out that emotional competencies are declining world wide. Because of that, among the young people are rising problems such as despair, alienation, drug abuse, crime and violence, depression or eating disorder, unwanted pregnancies, bullying and dropping out of school.[4] Children are often growing in a very difficult atmosphere. Violence has penetrated human thoughts. We have forgotten that the problems could be resolved using the words, good will and understanding.

A child never lies when something bad happens to him. A neglected and abused child is looking for help. The problem of child and adolescent tyranny by the adults is rising around the world and also in Croatia in spite of the fact that the children are legally and morally protected. Dates from the US show billions of minors who were victimised by adults.[5]

This paper includes penal acts from Croatian County with approximately 300,000 inhabitants. A total of 464 criminal acts against children and adolescents were reported during the last 10 years at the County Police Direction. About 36% of all these cases are sexual crimes against children and adolescents, 31% violation of parenthood duties, 24% of child and adolescent abuse and 9% of other crimes.

As we can see from the evidence of this Police Direction, every fourth crime against childrens and adolescents is neglect and abuse by an adult. During a 10-year period, we had 89 penal reports for criminal acts, Article 213 *CPC* and adolescent neglect and abuse. Just to mention that in the former *CPC* the number of the penal act 'child and adolescent neglect and abuse was Article 97.

The number of penal reports are progressively rising in Croatia because of the fact that public opinion about child and/or adolescent neglect and abuse is more sensible. We have 118 persons who committed this crime, and in the 89 penal reports 58 cases were denounced one perpetrator, 29 two perpetrators and in 2 reports three perpetrators. The most surprising is that 53% of all perpetrators are women, not men what is world wide fact. Women who neglect and abuse the children and adolescents are mostly self-supporting parent, low educated, without any source of her own money, without adequate place to live not only for her but also for her children. Women are responsible for neglecting children and adolescents and men for abuse: 70% of the children and adolescents body injuries are caused by men.

Alcohol abuse is the most predicting factor for development of a violent mentality toward the other person and also toward itself and to aggressive behaviour.[6] We can confirm this because 64% of our male perpetrators are abusing alcohol as well as the 22% female perpetrators. Psychiatric diseases are also a common consequence of chronic alcohol abuse, based on the penal records 50% of the women and 44% of the men who maltreat minors.

---

[4] D. Goleman, 'A coming crisis: rising IQ, dropping EQ', in: *Working with emotional intelligence*, Bantam Books 1998, 1:13.

[5] G. Obradović-Dragišić, D. Babić, *Za nasilje nema opravdanja*, Zagreb: CESI 1999, V:32-37, VI: 38-40.

[6] D. Kozarić-Kovačić, M. Grubišić-Ilić & V. Grozdanić, 'Akutno opito stanje', in: D. Kozarić-Kovačić, *Forenzička psihijatrija*, Zagreb 1998, II: 3: 108-116.

Najavits *et al.* have proved that 39% to 59% of the women substance abusers show high rates of PTSD, most commonly deriving from a history of repetitive childhood physical and/or sexual assault. Rates for men are two to three times lower and typically stem from combat or crime trauma.[7]

Bremner *et al.* have proved that PTSP patients had a 12% smaller left hypocampal volume relative to the sane control group.[8]

We have records that 15% of the male perpetrators were actively involved in the Croatian army at the battlefield. This analyse includes the years of war from 1992 till 1995 at the territory of Croatia against the Serbian army. We have also found that 63% of the war veterans have threatened their own children with the firearms they got during the war.

Wright *et al.* have confirmed that child abuse and wife abuse is linked with incidence of 30% to 59%.[9] Coohey *et al.* showed after estimating their results that exposure to aggression or domestic violence in childhood is the most potent predictor for a mother physical abused of her child.[10]

Our incidence is 50% what correlates with similar studies.

Data from the US from one cross-sectional chart review from paediatric hospitalisation during 1988-1990 show incidence of 2.5% abused children, 3,1% of neglected children from total sample. Their results confirm the associations among neglect, poverty and single-parent families.[11]

We do not have such precise dates, but the penal act from Article 213 *CPC* is represent with 0.2% of all penal crimes Police Direction in Rijeka during the past 10 years. This small incidence does not reflect the present situation. As through the centuries before, most of the violence remains strictly within families. The fact that the first time that child and adolescent neglect and abuse was proclaimed as a penal crime was in 1889 in France is the best example for this.[12]

Sporadically reaction of social services, educational institutions, police forces and legal services has too many reasons. The social services do not co-operate with services of penal persecution probably because of fear loose credibility of territory they supervise. Services of penal persecution are

---

[7] L.M. Najavits, R.D. Weiss & S.R. Shaw, 'The link between substance abuse and posttraumatic stress disorder in women. A research review', *A.J.Addict* 1997 (Fall), 6, 4, 273-283.

[8] J.D. Bremner, P. Randall, E. Vermetten & L. Staib, 'Magnetic resonance imaging-based measurement of hippocampal volume in posttraumatic stress disorder related to childhood physical and sexual abuse – a preliminary report, *Biol.Psychiatry* 1997 (January), 41(1): 23-32.

[9] R.J. Wright, R.O. Wright & N.E. Isaac, 'Response to battered mother in the paediatric emergency direction: a call for an interdisciplinary approach to family violence', *Paediatrics* 1997 (February) 99(2): 186-192.

[10] C. Coohey & N. Braun, 'Toward an integrated framework for understanding child physical abuse', *Child Abuse Neg.* 1998 (November) 21: 11, 1081-1094.

[11] U. Thyen, J.M. Leventhal, S.R. Yazdgerdi & J.M. Perrin, 'Concerns about child maltreatment in hospitalised children', *Child Abuse Negl.* 1997 (February) 21(2):187-198.

[12] F. Hirjan & M. Singer, *Maloljentici u krivičnom pravu*, Zagreb: Globus 1987, 2:258-282.

senseless because of prejudice that neglect and punishment are parents' educational measures.[13] Maybe the judges consider a child not reliable as a witness of a penal crime. A statement made by an abused child is powerful and absolutely reliable source as the evidence in court.[14] The present possibility to influence and suggest on a child, a hearing of child witness needs careful preparation. Sometimes it is necessary to conduct the hearing in presence of parent and psychologist. Questions must be simple and without any trace of suggestibility.[15]

Growing and living in a violent environment is corroding stability of society. Continuous neglect and abuse can create a new abuser, delinquent, asocial person who is incapable to contribute in modern development. Around 90 families have created 144 abused children. These children will create more or less 250 human beings. What is going to happen to them?

Child abuse must be suspected in any case where there is no clear injury mechanism or when a discrepancy exists between the severity of the injury and alleged mechanism.[16]

Statistics have shown that more than half of the child abuse victims have fractures, intraretinal haemorrhages, somatic symptoms, functional disability and irritable bowel syndrome.[17]

Quantitative EEG of abused children shows the abnormality and besides that, scientists have found deficits in executive functioning and working memory.[18]

Consequences of neglect and abuse are reflecting on personal life and health and can be visible immediately or/and after a while. From our records more than 85% of maltreatment lasted from two to 10 years.

---

[13] Ibid.

[14] B. Pavisic, D. Modly et al., Kriminalstika, Rijeka: University in Rijeka 1995, 15: 175.

[15] M. Monk, 'Interviewing suspected victims of child maltreatment in the emergency direction', J.Emerg.Nurs. 1998 (February), 24(1): 31-34.

[16] J.H. Beaty, 'Orthopaedic aspects of child abuse', Curr.Opin.Pediatr. 1997 (February) 9(1):100-102; O. Paut, T. Jouglet & J. Camboulives, 'Severe trauma in children', Arch.Pediatr. 1997 (May) 4(5): 443-459.

[17] S. Sinal & C.D. Stewart, 'Physical abuse of children: a review for orthopaedic surgeons', J.South Orthop.Assoc. 1998 (Winter), 7(4): 264-276; J.N. Rohrbach, D. Benz, W. Friedrichs et al., 'Ocular pathology of child abuse', Klin.Monatsbl.Augenheilkd. 1997 (February), 210(3): 133-138; J. Leserman, Z. Li, D.A. Drossman & Y.J. Hu, 'Selected symptoms associated with sexual and physical abuse history among female patients with gastrointestinal disorders: the compact on subsequent health care visits', Psychol.Med. 1998 (March), 28(2): 417-425; N.J. Talley, P.M. Boyce & M. Jones, 'Is the association between irritable bowel syndrome and abuse explained by neuroticism? A population based study', Gut 1998 (January), 42(1): 47-53.

[18] Y. Ito, M.H. Teicher, C.A. Glod & E. Ackerman, 'Preliminary evidence for aberrant cortical development in abused children: a quantitative EEG study', J. Neuropsychiatry Clin.Neurosci. 1998 (Summer), 10(3): 298-307; S. Raskin, 'The relationship between sexual abuse and mild traumatic brain injury', Brain Inj. 1997 (August), 11(8): 587-603.

All over the world people are more sensitive on physical evidence. But psychological sequels are more sophisticate and socially undesirable. Almost 90 years ago, congressman Silovic has concluded that alcoholism and child neglect and abuse are the most important causes of criminal behaviour.

Delinquency develops in the age of puberty. If we look at our male victims, 72 of the boys are in school age and 61% of them have a criminal record and all of them are criminal recidivists in performing the burglaries, sex offences, organised crime, etc.

Child neglect and abuse is often found in records of the worst violent crimes.[19] Child abuse requires a multidisciplinary approach.[20] The social service system needs to rediscover its roots in supporting families under stress, including cases of moderate maltreatment. A decisive legal intervention is needed in cases of serious family violence.[21]

## Conclusion

During the past 10 years, 89 criminal investigations for 'child and adolescent neglect and abuse' were started, 89 penal acts for crime mentioned previously were committed. In 89 penal crimes 118 perpetrators are reported, 53% female and 47% male, of which 92% are parents of neglected and abused children, mostly Croatian, without adequate economical establishment, low educated.

The most of the male perpetrators are married, have a job, every second male perpetrator is abusing the entire family, they are alcohol abusers, responsible for child or adolescent physical, psychological and sexual abuse.

The most of the female perpetrators are self-supporting parent, without secure source of income, and are responsible for neglecting their own children and adolescents.

---

[19] K.M. Heide, 'Juvenile homicide in America: how can we stop the killing?', *Behav.Sci.Law* 1997, 15: 2, 203-220; K.S. Miller & J.F. Knutson, 'Reports of severe physical punishmentand exposure to animal cruelty by inmates convicted of felonies and university students', *Child Abuse Negl.* 1997 (January), 21(1): 59-82.

[20] N. Kini & S. Lazoritz, 'Evaluation for possible physical or sexual abuse', *Pediatr.Clin.North.Am.* 1998 (February), 45: 1, 105-219.

[21] R.E. Emery & B.L. Laumann, 'An overview of the nature, causes and consequences of abusive family relationships. Toward differentiating maltreatment and violence', *Am.Psychol.* 1998 (February), 53: 2, 121-135.

# The Expanding Right to Silence in Europe and America: is it a Good Thing and where should it end?

*G. Van Kessel*

## Introduction

There is little value in discussing the right to silence[1] as an independent concept. As when evaluating any guarantee of fairness for criminal defendants, meaningful analysis requires identifying the particular aspect of the right and the stage of the criminal process in which it operates. But most important, and often overlooked, is the need to measure the right in the context of the characteristics of the procedural system involved. Placing defense rights in proper procedural perspective is becoming increasingly significant in light of the growing acceptance of decisions of international tribunals based on human rights principles arising from international treaties and the resulting trend toward unification of procedural systems.

Evaluating the right to silence in light of the procedural context in which it operates is particularly challenging when one considers the rapid changes in justice systems throughout the world, especially the movements toward adversary procedures in Continental Europe. Nevertheless, it is of the utmost importance when inquiring as to the meaning of the various aspects of the right to silence to recognize how they change and take on different forms in different procedural contexts. The significance of a particular aspect of the right cannot be judged independently, but only as it operates within a specific

---

[1] In this article the terms 'right to silence' and 'privilege against self-incrimination' will refer to identical protections and will be used interchangeably. But the two guarantees often are viewed differently. For example, the European Court of Human Rights (ECrtHR) seems to regard the right to silence and the privilege against self-incrimination as closely related, but not identical. The Court tends to emphasize the right to silence in the context of police interrogation, while relying on the privilege when considering judicial or other formal means of compulsion. *See Funke* v. *France* (Feb. 1993) Series A, Vol. 256-A; *Murray (John)* v. *UK* (Jan. 1994) No. 18731/91; *Saunders* v. *United Kingdom* (Dec. 1996) 43/1994/490/572. The Court's language in *Funke* connecting the right to silence with police interrogation and its later reliance on the privilege when dealing with official compulsion under oath in *Saunders* suggests the Court perceives different roles for the silence right and the privilege. In the US, however, the privilege applies in both contexts. *See Murphy* v. *Waterfront Comm.*, 378 *U.S.* 52 (1964) and *Kastigar* v. *US*, 406 *U.S.* 441 (1972)(applying the privilege to formal, quasi-judicial inquiries); *Miranda* v. *Arizona*, 384 *U.S.* 436, 458, 461 (1966) and *Pennsylvania* v. *Muniz*, 496 *U.S.* 582, note 10 (1990)(stating that "all the principles embodied in the privilege apply to informal compulsion exerted by law-enforcement officers during in-custody questioning.") Furthermore, while *Miranda* applied the privilege to custodial questioning, it crafted the warnings in terms of "the right to remain silent".

procedural system.

I first will review global trends toward adversary procedures and toward recognition of a right to silence. I will then describe the approaches of contemporary Continental, English and American systems toward the right to silence. I will point out how the right to silence is intimately connected to the procedural system in which it operates. The silence right generally is much stronger in adversary than in inquiry style systems, particularly when the adversary system operates in conjunction with a bifurcated court as in the context of Anglo-American jury trials. Global trends toward adversary procedures have been, and likely will continue to be, accompanied by growing recognition of a right to silence. Furthermore, I will contend that the right to silence and adversary procedures reinforce the other. Adversary procedures naturally lead to a more expansive right to silence and an expanding right to silence naturally leads away from inquiry and toward more adversary style procedures.

I will conclude with thoughts on the appropriate role of international tribunals in fixing the parameters of the right to silence as an essential aspect of fair criminal procedure. In brief, courts should recognize that the faces of the right to silence change according to the procedural context in which they operate and should allow for different forms of right according to a country's particular legal culture and procedural system.

An important challenge going into the next millennium will concern whether modern systems of justice can incorporate the beneficial elements of adversary procedures, such as increased opportunities to confront adverse witnesses, without excessively expanding the right to silence and sacrificing evidence from those most likely to have it.

The silence right has many faces, and their importance varies with the values one believes is served by the right.[2] That aspect of the right which prohibits adverse inferences from silence differs significantly from a rule prohibiting enforcement of a subpoena which demands production of incriminating documents or a rule forbidding continued questioning once a person expresses a desire to remain silent or to speak with an attorney. Also, the character of a particular silence right differs according to the stage of the criminal process in which it comes into play. For example, the prohibition on adverse inferences from silence takes on a different character when it is applied at the trial, as opposed to during pretrial interrogation. There are three main contexts in which the right to silence operates as a limit on the government using a criminal suspect or defendant as a source of testimonial evidence: (1) Pretrial judicial orders seeking production of physical evidence

---

[2] Identifying the fundamental values served by the right to silence and associated protections is beyond the scope of this paper.

or documents (pre-existing materials); (2) Pretrial questioning of suspects by police, prosecutors, magistrates, or grand juries; and (3) Speaking or testifying at trial. Usually, the right to silence gains strength as the criminal process progresses. In the US, for example, the right to silence is narrowest at the first stage where it does not protect the contents of documents, even those prepared by an accused, but only protects the act of production and then only in some contexts. The right is broader in the second context where suspects faced with custodial questioning must be informed of their right to silence and right to counsel. The right is most protective at the trial where neither the prosecutor nor the judge may so much as even call upon the defendant to speak at all and where the fact finder is prohibited from drawing any adverse inferences from defendant's silence.

## Global Perspectives on Adversary Trends and the Right to Silence

A global review of procedural trends and the right to silence will provide a helpful perspective with which to evaluate the right to silence in relation to the character of different procedural systems. Thus, before analyzing the relationship between procedural systems and the right to silence, I will briefly review global trends toward adversary procedures, increased recognition of a right to silence, and contemporary Continental, English and American approaches toward the right to silence.

Criminal justice systems on the Continent and in many other parts of the world are rapidly moving toward more adversary forms of investigation and adjudication. Witness, for example, the increasing prominence of the parties and their lawyers, along with diminishing judicial authority and the fact that both prosecutors and defense lawyers becoming somewhat more active and more partisan. During the pretrial phase, for example, prosecutorial power has been enhanced with the decline, and in some countries the elimination, of the investigating magistrate. At the trial, there has been a trend toward allowing lawyers to question witnesses directly rather than through the presiding judge. Furthermore, the importance and complexity of the rules of procedure and evidence are on the increase. In most Continental countries there has been a shift in emphasis from the pretrial to the trial phase, and a decrease in the use of written and increase in the use of oral evidence which has resulted in more examination of witnesses at the trial and a rehabilitation of the trial stage. Finally, there is a growing reliance on plea bargaining analogues and other alternatives to the traditional trial.

England, however, provides a contrast in its movement away from some adversary procedures. This trend can be seen from the 1988 expansion of statutory hearsay exceptions which allow first-hand documentary hearsay and thereby diminish confrontation rights, adoption to mutual pretrial discovery rules, attacks on the right to jury trial and reduced use of the jury in practice. Furthermore, the new limits on the right to silence tend to reflect a more traditional inquiry-style system of justice.[3]

Until rather recently, the right to silence as we know it did not exist in either Continental or Anglo-American systems of justice.[4] Following the decline of ancient modes of proof such as the ordeal, Continental inquisitory systems adopted strict proof rules and came to depend on judicially authorized torture to extract confessions. The English, while not using judicially sanctioned torture in ordinary criminal cases, still depended greatly on testimonial evidence from defendants, both during pretrial questioning of justices of the peace and at trial. Until the presence of lawyers and adoption of adversary procedures in the late 18th and early 19th centuries, virtually no one refused to speak either during pretrial interrogation or at trial.[5] In America, while the right to silence was recognized in the form of the *Fifth Amendment* privilege, it had little practical significance throughout the 19th century since virtually all defendants talked both pretrial and at trial.[6] Thus, until the modern era, as a practical matter, the right to silence was either weak or non-existent both on the Continent and in English and American justice systems.

The last half of the 19th century has witnessed a significant expansion of the right to silence. The trend across Europe during the last half of the 20th century has been toward greater protections for criminal defendants, including widespread recognition of a right to silence and a privilege against self-incrimination. In the early 1990s, decisions of the European Court of Human Rights (ECrtHR) held that although the Convention contains no explicit guarantee of a right to silence, "there could be no doubt that the right to remain silent and the privilege are generally recognized international standards which lay at the heart of fair procedure under Article 6 [which guarantees the right to a fair and public hearing]."[7] Rules of some international tribunals go

---

[3] The new *Human Rights Bill* incorporating Convention law likely will put a break on some of these trends.

[4] *See* R.H. Helmholz, 'Origins of the Privilege Against Self-incrimination: The Role of the European IUS Commune', 65 *N.Y.U.L. Rev.* 962, 982 (1990); M.R.T. MacNair, 'The Early Development of the Privilege Against Self-Incrimination', 10 *Oxford J. Legal Stud.* 66 (1990).

[5] J.H. Langbein, 'The Historical Origins of the Privilege Against Self-incrimination at Common Law', 92 *Mich. L. Rev.* 1047, 1061-63 (1994)(hereinafter 'Langbein, *Origins*'). In Langbein's study of London trials from 1670s through mid-1730s, he did not come across a single case in which defendant refused to speak or even made the least allusion to the privilege. His later review of trial reports into the 1770s also found no claim of the privilege. Another study by Beattie for the years between 1660 and 1800 found "no thought that a prisoner had a right to remain silent". Langbein, *Origins*, at 1066.

[6] E. Moglen, 'Taking the Fifth: Reconsidering the Origins of the Constitutional Privilege Against Self-incrimination', 92 *Mich. L. Rev.* 1086, 1098, 1121-24 (1994).

[7] *Funke* v. *France* (Feb. 1993) Series A, Vol. 256-A; *Murray (John)* v. *UK* (Jan. 1994) No. (to be continued)

further and specifically incorporate a right not to be compelled to testify against oneself or to confess guilt.[8]

In terms of specific protections, virtually all countries of Europe now (1) prohibit the use or threat of force or violence and require exclusion of coerced confessions, (2) recognize the rule against official or legal compulsion, that is, forbid forcing one by legal mandate to give incriminating testimony under oath that could be used in a criminal prosecution, (3) provide for some form of caution requiring notice of the right to remain silent both at pretrial questioning and at trial, and accept rules which, at least technically, prohibit courts from considering defendant's silence as evidence of guilt.

However, there is no Continental consensus concerning a right to counsel during initial interrogation.[9] In many countries the right does not exist or is severely limited during initial periods of police interrogation. The ECrtHR found a qualified right to counsel at the investigation stage, but noted that such right "is not explicitly set out in the Convention and might be subject to restrictions for good cause". England is the exception. The *Police and Criminal Evidence Act 1984 (PACE)* guarantees suspects a legally enforceable right to the presence of a solicitor during police station interviews.

In summary, the right to silence, traditionally very weak or non-existent in civil law countries, is gaining strength as countries move toward adversary forms of investigation and adjudication. This trend is evident around the globe. Even in Japan, where change comes slowly and the legal culture expects suspects to speak, there is now a '*Miranda* society' which advocates greater rights for criminal defendants.

Despite Continental trends toward recognition of right to silence, vast differences remain between common law and civil law countries with respect to the nature and scope of these rights. Modern Continental systems still strongly encourage suspects to actively participate as a testimonial resource. During the pretrial phase, most countries have a permissive approach to assertion of rights which allows continued questioning of one who wishes to remain silent and many countries deny or severely limit the right to counsel during initial questioning by police.[10] At trial, Continental systems limit the

---

18731/91; *Saunders* v. *United Kingdom* (Dec. 1996) 43/1994/490/572.

[8] The statutes of both the International Criminal Tribunal for the Former Yugoslavia (ICTY) and the International Criminal Tribunal for Rwanda (ICTR) provide that the accused shall be entitled "to a fair and public hearing" (ICTY Article 21(2) and ICTR Article 20(2)), to the presumption of innocence (ICTY Article 21(3) and ICTR Article 20(3)), and "not to be compelled to testify against himself or herself or to confess guilt" (ICTY Article 21(4)(g) and ICTR Article 20(4)(g)).

[9] *See* G. Van Kessel, 'European Perspectives on the Accused as a Source of Testimonial Evidence', 100 *W. Virg. L. Rev.* 799, 810-813 (1998).

[10] A suspect's refuse to answer police questions does not prevent police from continuing to question and seeking to persuade the suspect to answer. As long as an English suspect is properly (to be continued)

harm from speaking by avoiding the American practice of conditioning the use of defendant's prior convictions on whether he speaks at trial and increase the cost of refusing to speak by procedural devices and expectations such as the unitary court in which professional fact finders are aware of defendant's pretrial silence, the unitary trial which induces defendant to answer questions as to guilt if wishes to speak on sentencing, and a courtroom procedure in which the presiding judge as one of the fact finders calls upon defendant to answer questions.

Throughout the criminal process, the Continental legal and social culture places great importance on accurate fact finding, expects the accused to participate actively in the criminal process, and assumes that the right to silence should not present substantial barriers to testimonial evidence from defendants. Furthermore, Continental lawyers are less contentious and combative and are more accepting of accommodation and compromise. Equally important, usually there are clear advantages in early co-operation due to (1) dominance of the case file, (2) the episodic nature of the proceedings, and (3) the general expectation that the guilty should confess and the innocent should present their alibis or other defenses at an early point in the process. As a result, the vast majority of Continental defendants confess[11] and virtually all defendants talk to the police and speak at trial. Continentals, it seems, can afford a right to silence since the right is weakly enforced and rarely claimed.

The English experience provides an example of a counter-trend in silence rights. England has narrowed the right to silence by allowing adverse inferences from defendant's refusal to give testimonial evidence.

Formerly, the *Judges Rules* provided for cautioning suspects concerning their right to silence, but was weakly enforced and failed to afford an effective right to counsel during police interviews. Miscarriages of justice in such cases as the Guilford Four and the Birmingham Six led to adoption of *PACE* (1984) which reinforced the right to silence by providing for more effective access to solicitors, supervision of the interrogation process by quasi-independent custodial officers, recording requirements, and wider judicial exclusionary rules. English judges soon began to use their enhanced exclusionary powers to effectuate the new rights. As a result of expansion and more vigorous enforcement of the right to silence, British confession rates began to decline

---

cautioned, interrogation can continue in the face of protestations and objections, subject only to the probation against such pressures as would amount to oppression or coercion. *PACE* did not change this principle. *See* authorities cited in Van Kessel, *supra*, note 9, at 49-50. *See also* Pizzi, *supra*, note 67, at 66-67 (explaining that when an English suspect refuses to answer a question, police often will proceed to the next question).

[11] For example, in the Netherlands 80% of suspects confess at some point during the police investigation. *See* P.T.C. van Kampen, *Expert Evidence Compared: Rules and Practices in the Dutch and American Criminal Justice Systems*, at 58 (1998).

towards American levels.

Reacting to these trends, Parliament enacted *The Criminal Justice and Public Order Act 1994*, which substantially altered the right to silence by permitting the trier of fact to draw adverse inferences from both silence during police interrogation and at trial. The new caution stated, "You do not have to say anything. But it may harm your defense if you do not mention when questioned something which you later rely on in court. Anything you do say may be given in evidence." Two general provisions regarding adverse inferences.[12] Section 34 permits inferences to be drawn from an accused's failure to mention facts when questioned or charged that are later relied on in his defense when he could reasonably have been expected to mention such facts. Section 35 permits adverse inferences to be drawn from failure of accused "without good cause" to testify or to answer any question at trial. The Act states that an accused is "not compellable to give evidence on his own behalf, and he shall accordingly not be guilty of contempt of court by reason of a failure to do so."

Cases interpreting the new Act have assumed that generally it is appropriate to look for an explanation from the accused where such an explanation could reasonably be expected. Solicitors usually advise suspects to answer questions, and in the unusual case where solicitors do not, it is clear that solicitor advice to remain silent usually will not prevent the jury from drawing of adverse inferences.

Europeans have adopted a right to silence, but with accommodations which reduce its cost to society. European systems encourage suspects to speak at trial by limiting the dangers of testifying and by increasing the cost of silence. Both Continental and English systems limit the harm from speaking by not conditioning use of prior convictions on whether the accused agrees to speak.[13] Both systems increase the cost of refusing to speak, but by different methods. Continental systems do it by procedural devices, professional practices and expectations. England seeks to achieve similar results by explicitly authorizing the fact finder to draw adverse inferences from silence.

In this way, the right to silence in Europe is unlike other rights such as right to notice of charges, discovery, and appointment of counsel – the exercise of which generally is viewed as essential to a fair process. It is somewhat like the right to jury trial in America which is universally acknowledged as fundamental to fairness, but is rarely exercised in view of

---

[12] The act also contains two specific provisions, one permitting adverse inferences to be drawn from an accused's failure or refusal to account for objects, substances, or marks (Section 36) and another permitting adverse inferences to be drawn from an accused's failure or refusal to account for his presence at a particular place (Section 37).

[13] In addition, Continental rules do not threaten the accused with perjury for false testimony.

more efficient alternatives such as plea bargaining and diversion. Its existence, rather than its exercise, is regarded as essential to fair procedure. The right to silence is valued while silence itself is discouraged.

In America today, the legal community places great importance on defendant's right to silence both during pre-trial custodial questioning and at trial. Americans seem to have accepted the proposition that the more one is suspected of criminal activity, the less we should look to that person for an explanation of his conduct.

As a result, while most suspects in America speak at some point, they tend to speak to police less frequently and to testify at trial less often than they did in the past, and certainly much less than their Continental or English counterparts. In brief, at the pretrial stage, while most suspects waive their rights and made talk, a significant or substantial percentage of those questioned. Damaging (incriminating) statements are found in slightly less than 50% of criminal cases.[14]

Why do suspects in America speak to police and confess less frequently than in Continental countries? The right to silence caution likely is not alone of great significance. The real bite comes from associated rules and practices such as the strict cut-off rules which require terminating interrogation whenever a suspect declines to speak or requests a lawyer. While *Miranda* and its progeny do not require the presence of station-house lawyers[15] or even give defendants the right on request to see a lawyer unless interrogated,[16] the *Miranda-Edwards* rules require terminating interrogation whenever a suspect

---

[14] For a review of the relevant studies, *see* P.G. Cassell & B.S. Hayman, 'Police Interrogation in the 1990s: An Empirical Study of the Effects of Miranda', 43 *UCLA L. Rev.* 839 (1996)(hereinafter 'Cassell, *Empirical Study*'); P.G. Cassell, 'Miranda's Social Cost: An Empirical Reassessment', 90 *Northwestern U.L. Rev.* 387 (1996)(hereinafter 'Cassell, *Empirical Reassessment*'); P.G. Cassell, 'All Benefits, No Costs: The Grand Illusion of Miranda's Defenders', 90 *Northwestern U.L. Rev.* 1084 (1996)(hereinafter 'Cassell, *Grand Illusion*'). *See also* G. Van Kessel, 'The Suspect as a Source of Testimonial Evidence: A Comparison of the English and American Approaches', 38 *Hist. L.J.* 1 (1986)(hereinafter 'Van Kessel, *Testimonial Evidence*'). For a contrary view on the significance interrogation studies, *see* S.J. Schulhofer, 'Miranda's Practical Effect: Substantial Benefits and Vanishingly Small Social Costs', 90 *Northwestern U.L. Rev.* 500 (1996)(hereinafter 'Schulhofer, *Substantial Benefits*').

[15] *See Davis* v. *US*, 384 *U.S.* 436, 474 (1994)(noting that *Miranda* rejected the notion "that each police station must have a 'station house lawyer' present at all times to advise prisoners").

[16] *See Moran* v. *Burbine*, 475 *U.S.* 412 (1986)(finding that *Miranda* had been waived despite fact that defendant had not been informed that counsel purporting to represent him had called police and requested that no questioning take place and that police had assured counsel that defendant would not be questioned); *Duckworth* v. *Eagan*, 492 *U.S.* 195 (1989) (holding that *Miranda* does not require that lawyers be producible on call, but only that a suspect be informed that he has the right to counsel before and during questioning and that counsel would be appointed for him if he could not afford one). Thus, "[i]f police cannot provide appointed counsel, *Miranda* requires only that police not question a suspect (…)." *Id.*, at 204.

declines to speak or requests a lawyer.[17] Such rules contrast sharply with the Continental and English approaches which allow continued questioning in the face of a suspect's refusal to speak.[18]

Most significant is the American professional culture in which defense lawyers virtually always strongly advise suspects not to talk to police.[19] For example, O.J. Simpson had gone to police headquarters voluntarily, submitted to questioning for 32 minutes, gave a blood sample and returned home.[20] But at a bail hearing where Simpson attempted to explain why he had fled in the Bronco, his lawyer Shapiro advised him to remain silent. He kept talking, and

---

[17] *Miranda* v. *Arizona*, 384 *U.S.* 436 (1966). *See Michigan* v. *Mosley*, 423 *U.S.* 96 (1975) (describing a person's "right to cut off questioning" as a "critical safeguard" and stating that *Miranda* requires a "fully effective means (...) to notify the person of his right of silence and to assure that the exercise of the right will be scrupulously honored"); *Edwards* v. *Arizona*, 451 *U.S.* 477 (1981)(announcing a stricter rule when defendant requests a lawyer – that once a suspect has asserted his right to counsel under *Miranda*, there can be no further interrogation until counsel has been made available to him unless defendant himself initiates further conversations with the police); *Smith* v. *Illinois*, 469 *U.S.* 91 (1984)(characterizing *Edwards* as a "ridged prophylactic rule" which embodies two distinct inquiries: (1) Whether defendant actually invoked his right to counsel and (2) if he did, the court may admit responses to further questioning only if defendant both (a) initiated further discussions with the police and (b) knowingly and intelligently waived the right he had invoked); *Arizona* v. *Roberson*, 486 *U.S.* 675 (1988)(holding that once a suspect cuts off custodial interrogation by invoking his right to counsel, he may not, as long as he remains in custody, be questioned by the original interrogators or others about an offense wholly unrelated to the crime as to which he has already requested counsel, unless counsel has been provided him or the suspect himself initiates further communications with officials); *Minnick* v. *Mississippi*, 498 *U.S.* 146 (1990)(holding that *Edwards'* protection does not cease once suspect has consulted with his attorney, such that once defendant has requested an attorney, interrogation must cease and police may not reinitiate questioning without an attorney present even though defendant has consulted with his attorney).

[18] Although voluntary statements obtained in violation of these rules can be used to impeach, courts are beginning to permit civil actions against police for 'going beyond *Miranda*' and continuing to ask questions after a suspect has asked for a lawyer. *See Cooper B. Dupnick*, 963 *F.2d* 1220 (9th Cir. 1992)(Cooper II); *CACJ* v. *Butts*, F.3d (9th Cir 1999)(establishing clear rule that continued interrogation after defendant's invocation of the right to counsel constituted a clear violation of the *Fifth Amendment* giving rise to civil liability in which qualified immunity is unavailable.

[19] Justice Jackson's well known observation over forty years ago still states the accepted wisdom of criminal defense lawyers in this country: "[A]ny lawyer worth his salt will tell the suspect in no uncertain terms to make no statement to police under any circumstances." *Watts* v. *Indiana*, 338 *U.S.* 49, 59 (1949)(Jackson, J., concurring and dissenting).

[20] P. Arenella, 'Forward: O.J. Lessons', 69 *So. Cal. L. Rev.* 1233, 1237 (1996). Arenella characterized the police questioning as "polite" and asks why the detectives did not engage in more prolonged and tougher interrogation since he had waived his right to silence and to counsel. While regarding this as "one of the mysteries of the case", Arenella asks whether detectives would have adopted the same polite and deferential style of questioning if they were dealing "with a more typical suspect". Arenella, 'O.J. Lessons', at 1237, note 8.

finally Shapiro warned Simpson, "I will not allow you to speak and I will resign as your lawyer if you continue to do so".

At trial, the trend since the 1960s has been toward fewer defendants taking the stand at trial. In Colonial America, virtually all defendants testified at trial, and this situation persisted throughout the first half of this century.[21] However, following *Griffin* and decisions of the 1960s and 1970s strengthening the right to silence, it appears that fewer and fewer defendants are testifying. A study of Philadelphia felony trials in the 1980s revealed that nearly one-half of felony defendants and 57% of misdemeanor defendants did not testify at trial.[22] A study of 37 capital jury trials in California from 1988 to 1992 found that "with a few notable exceptions, most defendants did not testify".[23] Only 27% testified at the guilt phase and only 22% testified at the penalty trial (four who had not testified at the guilt trial and four who had) such that overall, only 38% took the stand either at the guilt or the penalty trial.

There are several reasons for this trend. First, America's super-adversary trial procedure shields defendant from inquiry by focusing the trial on the lawyers rather than on the accused. American trials often seem to disregard the most important individual in the trial. At times, the accused may appear set apart or even isolated from the trial process and with increasing frequency, defendants are not taking the stand at trial.

Second, rules of procedure and evidence tend to dissuade defendants from testifying. America's evidence rules say to the defendant, "If you testify, the jury will become aware of your felonious history and you will be cross-examined by an aggressive prosecutor,[24] but if you remain silent, neither your

---

[21] Even studies of trials in the 1920s and the 1950s reveal that very few defendants refused to testify at trial and that few were helped by such refusals. *See* A. Train, *The Prisoner at the Bar*, 209-212 (1923)(referring to an empirical study revealing that only 23 out of 300 defendants choose to remain silent at trial [21 of these were convicted anyway]). In their study of the American jury, Kalven & Zeisel describe an empirical Chicago Jury Study of trials conducted during the middle and late 1950s showing that 91 percent of defendants without prior records and 74 percent of those with prior records, choose to testify at trial. H. Kalven & H. Zeisel, *The American Jury*, 146 (1966).

[22] Schulhofer, 'Some Kind Words for the Privilege Against Self-incrimination', 26 *Val. L. Rev.* 311, 329-30 (1991)(hereinafter 'Schulhofer, *Kind Words*').

[23] S.E. Sundby, 'The Capital Jury and Absolution: The Intersection of Trial Strategy, Remorse, and the Death Penalty', 83 *Cornell L. Rev.* 1557 (1998)(hereinafter 'Sundby, *Capital Jury*'). The aim of the study was to assess the effect of remorse on a jury's decision to impose a sentence of death or life without parole. Figures were drawn from the California segment of The Capital Jury Project (CJP) which involved a study of 37 capital cases which were tried to jury during the years 1988 to 1992. Sundby, *Capital Jury*, at 83.

[24] The threat of felony conviction impeachment can be a powerful deterrent to taking the witness stand. A study of American jury trials found that a defendant was almost three times more likely to refuse to testify if he had a criminal record than if not. *See* H. Kalven & H. Zeisel, *The American Jury*, 146 (1966).

past nor your present silence will be mentioned by the judge or prosecutor, and if you wish, the jury will be cautioned against drawing adverse inferences."[25] Testifying defendants also may be impeached by some forms of illegally obtained evidence.[26]

Procedural rules such as the rule prohibiting adverse inferences from refusal to testify provide the defendant with a more secure refuge from factual inquiries than in Continental trials. With the elimination of testimonial disqualification and the eventual requirement that if an accused wished to speak, he or she must do so under oath, most states and the federal government adopted rules preventing adverse comment or inference on defendant's silence. By the time of *Griffin* v. *California*,[27] only six states allowed adverse comment,[28] and in 1981, the Supreme Court held that the trial judge must on request admonish the jury to disregard the fact that defendant claimed the privilege and did not testify.[29] The recent expansion of the rule against adverse inferences to the sentencing stage expands defendant's refuge from fact finding inquiries. The prohibition on holding silence against the accused at sentencing provides an incentive for the defendant to claim the privilege and, with respect to aggravating factors, and to sit back and tell the prosecutor to 'prove it'.[30]

The courtroom arrangement and choreography also greatly reduces the exposure of the accused. American defense lawyers generally sit beside the accused, often between him and the jury, whereas in Continental trials, lawyers usually sit in back of the accused and are restricted in prompting his responses. In England, the accused (who is placed in a dock at the center-rear of the courtroom) is even more separated from his barrister who sits in the front benches some distance away.

Finally, there appears to be a trend toward greater acceptance of the right to silence by both the courts and the American public, which suggests that juries may be taking it more seriously. The common perception has been that the right to silence at trial is rather anemic and generally of little consequence. Jurors, and even professional judges, ordinarily expect the defendant to give evidence and will hold it against defendant if he does not take the stand. However, due to extensive media coverage of high profile trials, the public is

---

[25] *See Griffin* v. *California*, 380 *U.S.* 609 (1965); *Carter* v. *Kentucky*, 450 *U.S.* 288 (1981)(holding that the defendant can require the court to instruct the jury that silence must be disregarded).

[26] *See Harris* v. *New York*, 401 *U.S.* 222 (1971) and *US* v. *Havens*, 446 *U.S.* 620 (1980).

[27] 380 *U.S.* 609 (1965).

[28] The states were California, Connecticut, Iowa, New Jersey, New Mexico and Ohio. *See Griffin*, 380 *U.S.*, at 611-12, note 3.

[29] *Carter* v. *Kentucky*, 450 *U.S.* 288 (1981).

[30] *Mitchell* v. *US*, 526 *U.S.* 314 (1999).

being exposed to situations in which the defendant does not make pre-trial statements or testify at trial. When neither the judge nor the lawyers ask why the accused fails to talk, the public slowly becomes accustomed to a system in which the accused is a silent and passive observer of the courtroom action. In recent years, both the legal profession and the public have become more accustomed to criminal trials in which the defendant remains silent while his lawyers attack the prosecution's case, and have become more comfortable with the notion that the accused is not expected to personally provide his version of the events.

This changing perception was recognized recently by the Supreme Court. Holding that in federal court, a guilty plea does not waive the *Fifth Amendment* privilege at the sentencing phase, and that the sentencing judge may not draw an adverse inference from defendant's silence in determining the facts about the crime which bear upon the severity of the sentence,[31] the Court described the rule against adverse inferences from silence as "of proven utility". Noting the suggestion in prior cases that the public expects the defendant to testify, the Court believed that times have changed: "It is far from clear that citizens and jurors today remain so skeptical of the principle or are often willing to ignore the prohibition against adverse inferences from silence. (…) Principles once unsettled can find general and wide acceptance in the legal culture, and there can be little doubt that the rule prohibiting an inference of guilt from a D's rightful silence has become an essential feature of our legal tradition."[32]

While the dissenters disagreed with majority's description of the no-adverse-inference rule as "an essential feature of our legal tradition", they acknowledged that it "may be true" that the rule has found "wide acceptance in our legal culture" which they found an "adequate reason not to overrule" it.[33]

With the Supreme Court recently reaffirming, and to some extent expanding the *Miranda* rules, and with the Court extending *Griffin* to the sentencing stage, when only one justice was willing to reconsider the case, it appears that today the right to remain silent and the privilege against self-incrimination are gaining strength in the US and that the prospect of America following the English approach is rather remote.

---

[31] *Mitchell* v. *US*, 526 *U.S.* 314 (1999).
[32] *Mitchell* v. *US*, 526 *U.S.* 314 (1999).
[33] Only Justice Thomas advocated a reexamination of *Griffin*.

## Evaluating the Right to Silence in Relation to Different Procedural Systems

What can we learn from the forgoing trends and from the fact that we find different forms of the right to silence in inquiry and adversary systems?

First, the right to silence is intimately related to the procedural system in which it operates. Although technically, the silence right is not essential to a system that replaces an active judge with a contest between two opponents before a passive fact finder,[34] there appears to be a natural connection between the right to silence and adversary procedures. Existence of the jury also is significant, since it assumes a bifurcated court which can more easily enforce exclusionary rules, such as those baring consideration of pretrial refusals to speak.[35]

Second, the silence right generally is much stronger in adversary than in inquiry style systems, particularly when the adversary system operates in conjunction with a bifurcated court as in the context of Anglo-American jury trials. For example, that aspect of the right to silence which limits adverse inferences from silence usually is (1) weakest in Continental inquiry systems where the fact finder is aware of D's pretrial silence and lawyers almost invariably advise D to speak at trial, (2) stronger in moderately adversary systems where the bifurcated court better enforces the pretrial right to silence by hiding its exercise from the fact finder and lawyers are more aggressive in asserting defendants' rights, and (3) strongest in super-adversary systems such as in America, where lawyers invariably will counsel suspects to refuse to speak to the police and where judges and juries have become more accepting of refusals of suspects to speak to police or to testify in court.

Third, the right to silence and adversary procedures appear to reinforce each other. Not only do adversary procedures naturally lead to a more expansive right to silence, an expanding right to silence naturally leads away from inquiry and toward adversary style procedures. The primary reason for this tendency is that the most effective method of strengthening the silence right is to enhance the power of lawyers to shield the accused from an inquiry into the events surrounding the charges. A secondary reason is that a bifurcates trial system such as in common law jury trials is more effective in shielding the fact finder from defendant's exercise of the right in the context of police

---

[34] For example, adversary systems with very limited silence rights are found in Japan and Israel.

[35] However, the jury and the bifurcated court is much less connected to the silence right than are adversary procedures. Existence of the jury alone does not necessarily mean a strong right to silence. For example, a jury system may provide few silence rights. Belgium's assize court provides a jury trial in a traditional inquiry format, but gives little protection to defendant's right to silence.

questioning.

First, since the right to silence tends to gain strength in direct proportion to the degree of a system's adversariness, global shifts toward adversary procedures likely will be accompanied by a more vigorous right to silence. With current strong movements toward adversary procedures, activist national courts and international tribunals may greatly expand the right to silence, possibly to the point of holding invalid the new English provisions regarding adverse inferences. The ECrtHR may well invigorate the right to silence as it has expanded the right to examine witnesses under Article 6 of the Convention. If so, Europe may be on the road toward a super-broad, American-style right to silence. However, there comes a point when more of a good thing is not always best. There are as many dangers from an extremely broad right to silence, as from uncontrolled police interrogation. The American experience provides an example of the downside of an expansive and operational right to silence. In America truth-discovery is subsidiary to disposal of cases. Tremendous pressures are permitted, but at the plea bargaining stage where the emphasis is on disposing of cases rather than finding out what happened and why.

Second, in view of the fact that an expanding right to silence naturally leads away from inquiry and toward adversary style procedures, what would be the consequences of an ever-expanding right to silence? If Continental countries were to enforce the right to silence so that it enjoys the same effectiveness as in America, modern inquiry systems would look quite different. Picture on the Continent an American-style right to silence together with an English-style stationhouse lawyer. During the pretrial phase, rules would prohibit continued questioning of suspects who indicate that they wish not to speak and would provide a right to counsel at police questioning which would include (1) advise of the right to the presence of counsel during questioning, (2) availability of free stationhouse counsel for those who request assistance of a lawyer, (3) a rule against questioning, even regarding unrelated offenses, once a suspect indicates a desire for a lawyer unless and until a lawyer is present, and (4) a legal culture in which lawyers believe it best to advise suspects to refuse to speak with law authorities and where presence of an attorney means the end of questioning. Finally, statements taken in violation of the foregoing rules would automatically be excluded. The trial would take place before a bifurcated court in which the fact finders are unaware of evidence such as defendant's silence which technically cannot be used to support a judgment. Also, there would be a bifurcated trial procedure which avoids pressuring the defendant to answer questions relating to guilt if he wishes to speak only on sentencing and a courtroom procedure in which presiding judge avoids ever calling on the accused to answer any questions. Finally, the adjudication process would operate within a legal culture that does not expect the accused to participate actively in the criminal process.

The forgoing requirements essentially would amount to a widespread adoption of adversary rules of procedure and evidence which likely would alter the practices of criminal defense lawyers such that they would become more like American lawyers – contentiousness and determined to marginalize the accused from the investigation and adjudication process by counseling suspects to refuse to answer police questions or to testify in court. Obviously, such procedures would be incompatible with contemporary Continental limits on enforcement of the right, as well as the very foundations of Continental inquiry systems.

First, the silence right should be evaluated in light of the overall procedural and professional environment. What seem to be mere collateral protections, such as the right to assistance of counsel and to recording of interrogations, may be even more significant than rules that appear more directly related to the silence right, such as the right to silence caution and the ban on adverse inferences from defendant's exercise of the right. For example, by affording prosecutions in addition to right to silence cautions, such as the presence of free stationhouse counsel, supervision by an independent custody officer, and mandatory recording of interrogations, England may offer a broader right to silence than countries that prohibit adverse inferences from its exercise but limit silence protections to a simple caution. Silence rights developed by international courts should be flexible enough to take into account such the presence of such collateral protections.

Most important, law-making bodies, especially international tribunals, should take into account the context in which silence rights operate and allow different forms of right to silence protections according to a country's particular legal culture and procedural system. Tribunals defining and enforcing silence rights across diverse justice systems should be cognizant of the fact that guarantees associated with the right to silence generally are much more potent in common law adversary systems with juries than in civil law inquiry systems with unitary courts. Such tribunals should recognize these differences and allow different forms of right to silence protections according to a country's particular legal culture and procedural system. A simple 'one size fits all' approach to the character of the right to silence in diverse legal systems would be the worst answer to a very complex problem.

## Conclusion

Returning to the question whether the expanding right to silence in Europe and America is a good thing and where should it end, I believe that to a point, the current global trends toward adversary procedures and silence rights are beneficial. But in my view, America has gone too far already, while many countries of Europe have more appropriately accommodated defendant's right to silence and society's interest in truth-discovery in criminal cases. England, for example, has attempted such accommodation in the context of an adversary system with a bifurcated court, a bifurcated trial, and moderately partisan lawyers – a procedural context which provides fertile soil for the silence right and threatens to cut off an important source of evidence. While reducing the attraction of refusals to speak, England has provided other protections, such as the presence of a stationhouse lawyer and tape recording. We should recognize the need to balance the suspect's right to silence against society's need for highly relevant and important evidence and should view such accommodations in light of the particular country's procedural system of justice.

Going into the next millennium, Europe will face the question whether it is possible to control expansion of the right to silence as justice systems become increasingly adversarial. Specifically, will it be possible for national systems of justice to incorporate beneficial adversary elements, such as increased opportunities to confront adverse witnesses, without sacrificing important evidence from those most likely to have it?

Some would welcome an expansive right to silence imposed by national courts or international tribunals. But we should consider whether an extremely strong right to silence is desirable. In the traditional inquiry trial, the most active participants are the presiding judge and the defendant. A strong adversary system replaces the active judge with powerful lawyer-contestants. A strong right to silence allows the lawyers to replace the defendant as well. Is this what we want our justice systems to look like in the 21$^{st}$ century?

# Differences in Evidence Rules as between Civil and Criminal Cases under the *Federal Rules of Evidence*

*J.M. Klebba*

This paper is a part of a larger comparative approach to the differences in evidentiary rules in civil and criminal trials. However, the emphasis in this paper is on the rules of evidence in the US and specifically in the *Federal Rules of Evidence (FRE)* and state evidentiary codes which are based on the *Federal Rules*. Detailed evidentiary rules of *admissibility* seem to be unique to the Anglo-American system. This emphasis on rules of admissibility in turn seems to be related to the role of the lay jury in Anglo-American law. The great American evidence scholar, J.B. Thayer, went so far as to refer to the law of evidence as "the child of the jury system".[1] Assuming this centrality of the jury system to the system of detailed rules of evidence, we might expect that in systems where there are no civil jury trials or few civil jury trials but many criminal jury trials, then the rules of evidence would be more detailed in systems of criminal procedure than in systems of civil procedure and perhaps the rules of admissibility would be significantly different, with some types of evidence being more freely admissible in civil cases than in criminal cases. But is this in fact true in US jurisdictions? Before the trend toward codification of evidence rules became dominant, most state courts as well as the US Federal Courts followed the common law rules of evidence. In these 'common law' states, it was often difficult to say that courts followed different evidence rules in civil cases than in criminal cases because unless there was a *reported appellate* decision on a particular point of evidence law one could not say definitively what the 'law' of the jurisdiction was on this point of evidence law.

However, Louisiana, a mixed common/civil law jurisdiction, provides an interesting case study. In contrast to those areas of private law governed by the *Louisiana Civil Code*, the procedural law of Louisiana was much less influenced by the civilian tradition. In evidence law, there is little that could be explicitly traced to civilian concepts. But, perhaps, it was due to the civilian tradition that on the criminal side a large number of the common law precepts of evidence are contained in either the *Code of Criminal Procedure* or the *Louisiana Revised Statutes*. On the other hand, there were many fewer codal or statutory provisions governing the admissibility of evidence in civil cases. This was the state of affairs prior to Louisiana's adoption of a *Code of Evidence* modeled largely on the *Federal Rules* in 1990.[2]

---

[1] Thayer, *A Preliminary Treatise on Evidence at Common Law*, 266, 509 (1898).
[2] For the most comprehensive compilation of Louisiana evidence law prior to the *Code of Evidence*, see G. Pugh, *Louisiana Evidence Law – Selected Commentary From the Louisiana Law Review and Pertinent Legislation*, the Bobbs/Merrill Company, Inc. 1974. Professor Pugh's book dramatically illustrates a large number of areas of evidence law where there is explicit legislation on the criminal (to be continued)

For a number of years, there were few civil jury trials in Louisiana even though, as in most states and in the *Federal Constitution*, there is a guarantee of a right to a civil jury trial to a party who requests it. This was generally attributed to the fact that there was extensive appellate review of facts found by jury which tended to undermine the 'populist' appeal of civil jury trials. For a number of reasons, jury trials have become more often requested in civil cases in recent years. This trend was well established by the time the present *Code of Evidence* was adopted in 1990. Perhaps this increase in the number of civil jury trials provided a portion of the impetus for a unified evidence code which applies generally to both civil and criminal cases with a few scattered exceptions.

It is the few 'scattered exceptions' between rules of evidence in civil cases and criminal cases that is the focus of this paper. What follows in the remainder of this paper is a rule-by-rule analysis of the relatively few differences between the evidence rules applicable to civil cases and those applicable to criminal cases in the *FREs*. In some cases, the different rules are dictated by US Constitutional protections afforded to criminal defendants but not to civil litigants. In other cases the variations may be due to substantive and procedural differences between the civil and criminal law, including the relative importance and frequency of jury trials. But, in other situations the differences between civil and criminal evidence rules may not be sufficiently justified by any of the above factors. On the other hand, there may be other situations where the present *FREs* (or state variations thereof) should go further in distinguishing between criminal and civil trials.

### Judicial Notice of Adjudicative Facts

Judicial notice has a different and more narrow effect in criminal cases than in civil cases. Rule 201(g) provides: "Instructing Jury: in a civil action or proceeding, the court shall instruct the jury to accept as conclusive any fact judicially noticed. In a criminal case, the court shall instruct the jury that it may, but is not required to accept as conclusive any fact judicially noticed."[3]

In explaining this difference in the instructions given to a jury in civil case and criminal cases, the Advisory Committee's Notes say: "Within its relatively narrow area of adjudicative facts, the rule contemplates there is to be no evidence before the jury in disproof in civil cases. The judge instructs the jury to take judicially noticed facts as conclusive. This position is justified by the undesirable effects of the opposite rule in limiting the rebutting party, though not his opponent, to admissible evidence, in defeating the reasons for judicial notice, and in affecting the substantive law to an extent and in ways largely unforeseeable. Ample protection and flexibility are afforded by the broad provision for opportunity to be heard on request, set forth in subdivision (e)."

---

side and only silence on the civil side.

[3] *FRE* 201(g).

Criminal cases are treated somewhat differently in the rule. While matters falling within the common fund of information supposed to be possessed by jurors need not be proved,[4] these are not, properly speaking, adjudicative facts but an aspect of legal reasoning. The considerations which underlie the general rule that a verdict cannot be directed against the accused in a criminal case seem to foreclose the judge's directing the jury on the basis of judicial notice to accept as conclusive any adjudicative facts in the case.[5] However, this view presents no obstacle to the judge's advising the jury as to a matter judicially noticed, if he instructs them that it need not be taken as conclusive.[6]

While not explicitly stated by the Advisory Committee, the rule against instructing a jury that is required to accept judicially notice facts as conclusive seem to be clearly based upon Federal constitutional provisions as interpreted the US Supreme Court. The Supreme Court held in the case of *In re Winship*,[7] that according to the Due Process clause, a criminal defendant can be convicted only "upon proof beyond a reasonable doubt of every fact necessary to constitute the crime with which he is charged".[8] In two cases decided subsequently in 1979, the Court made clear that this interpretation of the Due Process clause did not permit of mandatory presumptions in criminal cases.[9]

### Circumstantial Use of Character Evidence

Rule 404 generally prohibits the circumstantial use of character evidence in either civil or criminal cases.[10] However, there are two important exceptions to this rule which permit character evidence to be used in criminal cases but not in analogous civil cases. These two exceptions are:

1. *character of the accused:* evidence of a pertinent trait of character of the accused, or by the prosecution to rebut the same;[11]
2. *character of the victim:* evidence of a pertinent trait of character of the victim of the crime offered by an accused or by the prosecution to rebut the same, are evidence of a character trait of peacefulness of the victim offered by the prosecution in a homicide case to rebut evidence that the victim was the first aggressor.[12]

---

[4] *See State* v. *Dunn,* 221 *Mo.* 530, 120 *S.W.* 1179 (1909).
[5] *State* v. *Main,* 91 *R.I.* 338, 180 *A.2d* 814 (1962); *State* v. *Lawrence,* 120 *Utah* 323, 234 *P.2d* 600 (1951). Cf. *People* v. *Mayes,* 113 *Cal.* 618, 45 *P.* 860 (1896); *Ross* v. *US,* 374 *F.2d* 97 (8th Cir. 1967).
[6] Advisory Committee Notes to *FRE* 201(g), 56 *F.R.D.* 183,201.
[7] 397 *U.S.* 358 (1970).
[8] *Id.,* at 364.
[9] *Ulster County* v. *Allen,* 442 *U.S.* 140 (1979); *Sandstrom* v. *Montana* 442 *U.S.* 510 (1979).
[10] "Evidence of a person's character or a trait of character is not admissible for the purpose of proving action in conformity therewith on a particular occasion, except (...)." *FRE* 404(a).
[11] *FRE* 404(a)(1).
[12] *FRE* 404(a)(2).

It should be noted that it is the accused in the criminal case who holds the key to the admissibility of this type of character evidence. Where the character of the accused is concerned, this evidence can come in to the case only where the accused first puts on a 'good character' witness on his or her own behalf. Only then may the prosecution respond with 'bad character' witnesses. The situation is similar with the use of circumstantial evidence concerning the character of the victim. Except in homicide cases where the accused pleads self-defense, the prosecution may not introduce 'good character' evidence about the alleged victim unless the accused has first introduced 'bad character' evidence about the victim. In homicide cases where the accused pleads self defense, the accused has, in effect, accused the victim of being a violent person and the prosecution is permitted to rebut this with 'good', *i.e.*, peaceable character evidence about the victim.

A few American jurisdictions permit some use of character evidence in civil cases where a civil offense charged against the defendant could also be the basis of a criminal prosecution or conduct involving 'moral turpitude'. The use of the character evidence can only be initiated by the civil defendant. This variation of the character evidence rule is sometimes called the 'crime-tort' doctrine.[13] Sometimes the argument has been made even more broadly: why should not the defendant in an accident case be permitted to introduce evidence that he or she possesses the general traits of being a careful driver as a means of arguing circumstantially against the charge that the defendant was driving negligently at the time of the occurrence of the accident which precipitated the law suit? The Advisory Committee Notes address this issue, though perhaps not convincingly: "The argument is made that circumstantial use of character ought to be allowed in civil cases to the same extent as in criminal cases, *i.e.*, evidence of good (non-prejudicial) character would be admissible in the first instance, subject to rebuttal by evidence of bad character.[14] *Uniform Rule* 47 goes farther, in that it assumes that character evidence in general satisfies the conditions of relevancy, except as provided in *Uniform Rule* 48. The difficulty with expanding the use of character evidence in civil cases is set forth by the California Law Revision Commission in its ultimate rejection of *Uniform Rule 47, id.*, 615: character evidence is of slight probative value and may be very prejudicial. It tends to distract the trier of fact from the main question of what actually happened on the particular occasion. It subtly permits the trier of fact to reward the good man and to punish the bad man because of their respective characters despite what the evidence in the case

---

[13] *See* R.C. Park, D.P. Leonard & S.H. Goldberg, *Evidence Law: A Student's Guide to the Law of Evidence as Applied in American Trials*, West 1998, §5.14; *See also* generally 1A J.H. Wigmore, 'Evidence in Trials at Common Law', §65, 67 *Peter Tillers. Rev.* 1983.

[14] Falknor, 'Extrinsic Policies Affecting Admissibility', 10 *Rutgers L.Rev.* 574, 581-583 (1956); 'Tentative Recommendation and a Study Relating to the Uniform Rules of Evidence(Art. VI. Extrinsic Policies Affecting Admissibility)', *Cal. Law Revision Comm'n, Rep., Rec. & Studies*, 657-658 (1964).

shows actually happened."[15]

A problem with the quotation cited from the California Law Revision Commission is that it is an argument not only against the use of character evidence in civil cases but also in criminal cases. How can this discrepancy be explained? Most frequently, this inconsistency between civil evidence rules and criminal evidence rules is explained by the 'presumption of innocence' in criminal cases, a preference for freeing the guilty rather than convicting the innocent or simply as a 'rule of mercy' for the accused in a criminal trial.[16]

### Comparison of Rule 408 on Compromise and Offers to compromise and Rule 410 on Inadmissibility of Pleas, Plea Discussions and Related Statements

These two rules are among several rules in Article IV of the *Federal Rules* which exclude evidence that is arguably relevant in a logical sense in order to effectuate public policy norms which are considered to be more important than the relevance of the evidence in question. In this, the Article IV exclusionary rules are similar to evidentiary privileges.

Rule 408 and Rule 410 share a common purpose, namely to encourage parties to voluntarily settle cases before trial. Rule 408 is designed to encourage settlement of civil cases, while Rule 410 is designed to encourage the equivalent of settlement, *i.e.*, plea-bargaining, of criminal cases. The orderly functioning of both civil and criminal courts within existing fiscal restraints *requires* that the vast majority of both civil and criminal cases be disposed of without going to trial. Thus, these two rules exclude evidence of statements which may point toward the civil or criminal liability of a party if those statements are made in the process of attempting to settle a case before trial.

However, there are some important differences between the two rules. The exclusionary principle works in some cases in civil cases where it does not in criminal cases. These differences can probably be explained by the fact that a civil litigant is in most respects the master of his or her own law suit and that there is a larger sphere of party controlled negotiations in civil cases than in criminal cases. Rule 408[17] contemplates that compromise negotiations will often

---

[15] Advisory Committee Notes: *FRE* 404, 56 *F.R.D.* 183,219.

[16] *See* H.R. Uviller, 'Evidence of Character to Prove Conduct: Illusion, Illogic, and Injustice in the Courtroom', 130 *U. Pa. L. Rev.* 845 (1982); R.C. Wydick, 'Character Evidence: A Guided Tour of the Grotesque Structure', 21 *U.C. Davis L. Rev.* 123 (1987).

[17] "Evidence of (1) furnishing or offering or promising to furnish, or (2) accepting or offering or promising to accept, a valuable consideration in compromising or attempting to compromise a claim which was disputed as to either validity or amount, is not admissible to prove liability for or invalidity of the claim or its amount. Evidence of conduct or statements made in compromise negotiations is likewise not admissible. This rule does not require the exclusion of any evidence otherwise discoverable merely because it is presented in the course of compromise negotiations. This rule also does not require exclusion when the evidence is offered for another purpose, such as proving bias or prejudice of a witness, negativing a contention of undue delay, or proving an effort to obstruct a criminal investigation or prosecution" (*FRE* 408).

be carried on by the parties themselves before lawyers are brought into the dispute. A typical scenario might be one where two drivers involved in a minor traffic accident settle their dispute on the spot with one driver agreeing to make a flat sum payment to the other or to pay the repair bills. The Advisory Committee Notes following Rule 408, in fact, illustrate that the drafters of the rule expanded the scope of statements which are inadmissible in order to make it easier for lay parties to carry on compromise negotiations without the intervention of lawyers.[18]

In contrast, under the present text of Rule 410[19] it is clear that only the prosecuting authority can engage in compromise negotiations on behalf of the government. Thus, any admission of guilt or factual statements which might indicate guilt, even though made in the hope of obtaining leniency or a lesser charge, are potentially admissible in evidence and not within the exclusionary language of the rule if made to *agents of the government other than an attorney for the prosecuting authority*. This includes statements made to police, FBI agents, postal inspectors, customs officials, etc. The wording of Rule 410 prior to amendments which became effective in 1980 were susceptible of an interpretation that statements to non-attorney agents of the government could be protected under Rule 410. However, the Advisory Committee's Note to the 1980 amendments make it clear that the change made by those amendments was designed to close this potential "loop hole".[20]

There is yet one more aspect of the 'compromise exclusionary rule' which points up the policy differences between civil and criminal procedure. One of the

---

[18] Under the common law rule, an offer of compromise was not admissible but related statements of fact which could constitute admission of liability were admissible unless stated in a 'hypothetical' manner using lawyerly words such as 'without prejudice' in conjunction with the offer of compromise. In order to eliminate such potential snares, the exclusionary rule was broadened to include "evidence of conduct or statements made in compromise negotiations". *See* Advisory Committee's notes following Rule 408, 56 *F.R.D.* 183,226.

[19] Rule 410. Inadmissibility of Pleas, Plea Discussions, and Related Statements. Except as otherwise provided in this rule, evidence of the following is not, in any civil or criminal proceeding, admissible against the defendant who made the plea or was a participant in the plea discussions:
-   a plea of guilty which was later withdrawn;
-   a plea of *nolo contendere*;
-   any statement made in the course of any proceedings under Rule 11 of the *Federal Rules of Criminal Procedure* or comparable state procedure regarding either of the foregoing pleas; or
-   any statement made in the course of plea discussions with an attorney for the prosecuting authority which do not result in a plea of guilty or which result in a plea of guilty later withdrawn. However, such a statement is admissible (1) in any proceeding wherein another statement made in the course of the same plea or plea discussions has been introduced and the statement ought in fairness be considered contemporaneously with it, or (2) in a criminal proceeding for perjury or false statement if the statement was made by the defendant under oath, on the record and in the presence of counsel.

[20] *See* Advisory Committee's Note at 77 *F.R.D.* 507, 533. The Advisory's Committee's Note cautions, however, that such statements made by a defendant to a law enforcement agent are not "inevitably admissible" and may be inadmissible by virtue of "that body of law dealing with police interrogation" (*e.g.*, the *Miranda* doctrine, *Miranda* v. *Arizona*, 384 *U.S.* 436 (1966).

exceptions to Rule 408 is where evidence of an offer of compromise is introduced for the purpose of "proving an effort to obstruct a criminal investigation or prosecution". In explaining this exception, the Advisory Committee's Notes state: "An effort to 'buy off' the prosecution or a prosecution witness in a criminal case is not within the policy of the Rule of Exclusion."[21] Again, we see the same theme as implicit in Rule 410, namely that where a criminal case is concerned only the prosecuting authority shall make a decision that involves the dismissal of the case.

### Exclusion of Evidence about the Alleged Victim's Past Sexual Behavior or Predisposition in Sex Offense Cases

This exclusionary rule was enacted in a number of states before it became a part of the *FRE* in 1978. Sometimes referred to as the 'Rape Shield Law' it is designed to protect a rape victim against demeaning and either irrelevant or marginally relevant inquiry into her past sex life. As originally enacted, the rule only applied to criminal cases. As amended in 1994, the present rule[22] applies to both criminal and civil cases. However, the exceptions to the rule applicable to a criminal case which are set forth in Rule 412(b)(1) are more specific than the exceptions for civil cases which are set forth in 412(b)(2). The Advisory Committee's comments explain this difference because of "the difficulty of foreseeing future developments in the law". The comments also state that "greater flexibility is needed to accommodate evolving causes of action such as claims for

---

[21] Advisory Committee's Note to *FRE* 408 at 56 *F.R.D.* 183, 226.

[22] Rule 412. Sex Offense Cases; Relevance of Alleged Victim's Past Sexual Behavior or Alleged Sexual Predisposition. *(a) Evidence generally inadmissible.* The following evidence is not admissible in any civil or criminal proceeding involving alleged sexual misconduct except as provided in subdivisions (b) and (c): Evidence offered to prove that any alleged victim engaged in other sexual behavior. Evidence offered to prove any alleged victim's sexual predisposition. *(b) Exceptions.* In a criminal case, the following evidence is admissible, if otherwise admissible under these rules: (A) evidence of specific instances of sexual behavior by the alleged victim offered to prove that a person other than the accused was the source of semen, injury, or physical evidence; (B) evidence of specific instances of sexual behavior by the alleged victim with respect to the person accused of the sexual misconduct offered by the accused to prove consent or by the prosecution; and (C) evidence the exclusion of which would violate the constitutional rights of the defendant. In a civil case, evidence offered to prove the sexual behavior or sexual predisposition of any alleged victim is admissible if it is otherwise admissible under these rules and its probative value substantially outweighs the danger of harm to any victim and of unfair prejudice to any party. Evidence of an alleged victim's reputation is admissible only if it has been placed in controversy by the alleged victim. *(c) Procedure to determine admissibility.* A party intending to offer evidence under subdivision (b) must – file a written motion at least 14 days before trial specifically describing the evidence and stating the purpose for which it is offered unless the court, for good cause requires a different time for filing or permits filing during trial; and serve the motion on all parties and notify the alleged victim or, when appropriate, the alleged victim's guardian or representative. Before admitting evidence under this rule the court must conduct a hearing in camera and afford the victim and parties a right to attend and be heard. The motion, related papers, and the record of the hearing must be sealed and remain under seal unless the court orders otherwise.

sexual harassment."[23]

It is difficult to say whether the exceptions with regard to criminal cases are, on the whole, more or less stringent than those applicable to civil cases. On the one hand, it might be said that it is easier to introduce evidence about the past sexual behavior of the victim in criminal cases because if any of the three subdivisions of (b)(1) are satisfied it appears that the evidence *must* come in whereas, at least with regard to (b)(1)(A) or (b)(1)(B), the evidence could still be excluded in civil cases if the judge makes a discretionary determination that the probative value does not "substantially outweigh the danger of harm to any victim and of unfair prejudice to any party". But, on the other hand, the argument could be made that this type of evidence is more freely admissible in civil cases since the judge in civil cases can make a discretionary balancing decision to admit evidence of past sexual behavior of the victim in situations that would not fit under any of the three specific categories of 412(b)(1).

If evidence of past sexual behavior is indeed more freely admitted in civil cases than in criminal cases under Rule 412, then this seems to run counter to the principle implicit in other *FRE* noted in this paper that a criminal defendant is entitled to greater protection than a civil defendant based on such factors as the higher burden of proof in criminal cases, the 'presumption of innocence' and constitutional guarantees that are applicable to criminal defendants but not civil litigants. Perhaps, a stricter standard for admitting evidence of the victim's past sexual conduct and thus the greater degree of protection afforded to a victim in a criminal rape case might be justified by arguing that the interest of society in prosecuting a defendant in a criminal case is stronger than the interest of an individual victim in pursuing a civil case for damages. One could cite the fact that Rule 412 did not initially apply at all in civil cases to support this proposition. However, it is not all clear that the drafters had this kind of distinction in mind and it is not supported by the Advisory Committee's Notes. Until there has been further development of the case law, all that can be said at this point is that the standards for admissibility of prior sexual behavior is different and more discretionary in civil cases than in criminal cases, but not that the standard for admissibility is inherently more stringent in one type of case than the other.

### Rules 413, 414 and 415: Evidence of Similar Crimes and Similar Acts in Sexual Assault and Child Molestation Cases

These three rules were enacted by Congress without the benefit of the normal process of drafting by the Advisory Committee and promulgation by the Supreme Court. They were heavily criticized by many if not most evidence experts.[24] Like

---

[23] Notes of Advisory Committee, 1994 Amendment to *FRE* 412.

[24] *See, e.g.,* K.K. Baker, 'Once a Rapist? Motivational Evidence and Relevancy in Rape Law', 110 *Harv. L. Rev.* 563 (1977); C.R. Callen, 'Proving the Case: Simpson, *Fuhrman, Grice and Character Evidence*', 67 *U. of Colo. L. Rev.* 777 (1966); E.J. Imwinkelried, 'Some Comments About Mr. Karp's (to be continued)

Rule 412 these three rules substantially changed the preexisting common law and *FRE* doctrine on character evidence. But, while Rule 412 *excludes* some character evidence that was previously admissible in favor of a criminal or civil defendant against the victim, these three rules *make admissible* against the criminal or civil defendant, circumstantial uses of character evidence that were previously inadmissible. Rule 413[25] makes admissible evidence of other crimes by the defendant in criminal prosecutions for rape or other sexual assault cases. Rule 414[26] applies to evidence of similar crimes in criminal prosecutions for child molestation.

Rule 415[27] basically incorporates the same admissibility standard of 413 and 414 to make admissible evidence of similar offenses *in a civil case* concerning either sexual assault or child molestation. The standard for admissibility in Rule 415 is the same as in Rules 413 and 414. There is no apparent reason why a different rule was drafted to deal with the civil cases as contrasted with the structure Rule 412 which had separate sections dealing with criminal and civil cases where there actually is a difference in the admissibility standards for criminal and civil cases. It seems the only reason for this difference of approach is that Rules 413 and 414 and 415 went through a different, and many would say less careful, drafting process.

### Differences Attributable to the Rules of Decision Act and Erie Doctrine: Rules of Privilege and Competency

Article V of the *FRE* dealing with privileges, as originally submitted to Congress, contained a detailed restatement of the common law of privileges but with some significant innovations. But, Congress rejected this approach and enacted but a single rule dealing with privileges. This rule provides that "except as otherwise required by the *Constitution* of the US or provided by Act of Congress in rules prescribed by the Supreme Court pursuant to statutory authority" privileges shall be "governed by the principles of the Common Law as they may be interpreted by the courts of the US in the light of reason and experience".[28] Thus, with respect to criminal cases and civil cases based on federal law, courts are directed

---

Remarks on Propensity Evidence', 70 *Chi-Kent L. Rev.* 37 (1994).

[25] In a criminal case in which the defendant is accused of an offense of sexual assault, evidence of the defendant's commission of another offense or offenses of sexual assault is admissible, and may be considered for its bearing on any matter to which it is relevant (*FRE* 413(a)).

[26] In a criminal case in which the defendant is accused of an offense of child molestation, evidence of the defendant's commission of another offense or offenses of child molestation is admissible, and may be considered for its bearing on any matter to which it is relevant (*FRE* 414(a)).

[27] In a civil case in which a claim for damages or other relief is predicated on a party's alleged commission of conduct constituting an offense of sexual assault or child molestation, evidence of that party's commission of another offense or offenses of sexual assault or child molestation is admissible and may be considered as provided in Rule 413 and Rule 414 of these rules (*FRE* 415(a)).

[28] *FRE* 501.

to continue the case-by-case common law development of privilege as it existed prior to the enactment of the *FRE*. But, Rule 501 goes on to say that "in civil actions and proceedings with respect to an element of a claim or defense as to which state law supplies the rule of decision, the privilege of a witness, person, government, state, or a political subdivision shall be determined in accordance with state law." The only criminal cases that would be brought in a federal court are cases based on federal criminal law. Civil cases may either be based upon federal law or based on diversity of citizenship in which case state law governs as provided by the *Rules of Decision Act*[29] and the Erie Doctrine.[30] Congress made the judgment that the rules of privilege, unlike other of the common law rules of evidence, are based in part on policies which are not strictly procedural but on substantive considerations of privacy which go beyond the efficiency of the fact finding process.

Congress made a similar judgment with regard to competency of witnesses.[31] Thus, in all criminal cases, the first sentence of Rule 601 applies whereas in civil cases in Federal Court on the basis of diversity of citizenship are where otherwise state law supplies Rule of Decision, the federal judge must look to the rules of competency which are in effect in the relevant state court.

## Impeachment by Evidence of Conviction of Crime

Rule 609[32] has been one of the most controversial of the *FRE* and has been much litigated. The theory of this rule, which for the most part codifies common law doctrine, is that any witness who has been convicted of a serious crime or a crime involving dishonesty, is by that reason, less worthy of belief as a *witness*. The greatest controversy in the application of this rule has been in situations where the *witness* is also the *defendant* in a criminal case. When an accused takes the stand in his or her own defense, evidence of prior crimes may be introduced on an 'impeachment' theory in spite of the fact that the prosecution would be prohibited from using this same evidence as circumstantial character evidence, *i.e.*, on a theory that since the defendant committed crimes previously he or she is likely

---

[29] 28 *USC*, §2072.

[30] *See Erie R. Co.* v. *Thomkins*, 304 *U.S.* 64 (1938).

[31] Every person is competent to be a witness except as otherwise provided in these rules. However, in civil actions and proceedings, with respect to an element of a claim or defense as to which State law supplies the rule of decision, the competency of a witness shall be determined in accordance with State law (*FRE* 601).

[32] *(a) General rule.* For the purpose of attacking the credibility of a witness, (1) evidence that a witness other than an accused has been convicted of a crime shall be admitted, subject to Rule 403, if the crime was punishable by death or imprisonment in excess of one year under the law which the witness was convicted, and evidence that an accused has been convicted of such a crime shall be admitted if the court determines that the probative value of admitting this evidence outweighs its prejudicial effect to the accused; and (2) evidence that any witness has been convicted of a crime shall be admitted if it involved dishonesty or false statement, regardless of the punishment (*FRE* 609).

to have committed the crime currently charged. As noted previously in this paper, this type of character evidence is generally prohibited by Rule 404 unless the defendant first introduces good character evidence, and even then is limited to reputation and opinion, and is not provable by direct evidence of the commission of prior crimes. This could be particularly prejudicial and damaging to an accused who has been previously convicted of crimes similar to the one now charged. Because of this potential for prejudice, the rule gives special protections to criminal defendant/witnesses which are not given to any other witnesses.

As originally drafted, the rule contained some troublesome ambiguities. One problem was that the original rule used the word "defendant" rather than "accused" which is used elsewhere in the *FRE* to refer to a *criminal* defendant, thus raising the possibility that special protections were to be also afforded to a civil defendant and not to a civil plaintiff or other witnesses. Also, the original language raised questions as to whether the accused could invoke the special balancing test when defense witnesses other than the defendant were called to testify. An amendment made in 1990 clarified these questions. Under the present wording of the Rule, an accused who is a witness and has been convicted of a felony (a crime punishable by death or imprisonment in excess of one year) is to be admissible only if the court determines that the probative value of this evidence outweighs the prejudicial effect to the accused. Thus, there is a slight presumption *against* the admissibility of such prior crimes evidence relating to the accused. On the other hand, evidence that any other witness than the accused has been convicted of such a crime shall be admitted unless, as provided in Rule 403, the probative value of the prior crimes evidence is "substantially outweighed by the danger of unfair prejudice, confusion of the issues, or misleading the jury, or by considerations of undue delay, waste of time, or needless presentation of cumulative evidence."[33] Thus, using the Rule 403 standard establishes a fairly strong presumption *in favor* of the admissibility of the prior crimes evidence to impeach the witness other than the accused. It should be noted as before the 1990 amendment, evidence that *any* witness including the accused has committed a crime, whether or not a felony, involving 'dishonesty or false statement' is admissible without regard to any balancing test, *i.e.*, in spite of the possible prejudicial effect on the accused.

### Writing used to Refresh Memory: Order to produce

Rule 612 provides that in certain cases where one party uses a writing to refresh memory for the purpose of testifying either before or during trial, the adverse party is entitled to have the writing produced, to inspect it, to cross examine the witness and to introduce portions in evidence.[34] This rule provides for sanctions

---

[33] *FRE* 403.
[34] *FRE* 612.

if after being ordered to produce the writing a party does not do so. The sanction is stricter and more specific if the party failing to comply with a production order is the prosecution in a criminal case: "If a writing is not produced or delivered pursuant to order under this rule, the court shall make any order justice requires, except that in criminal cases when the prosecution elects not to comply, the order shall be one striking the testimony or, if the court in its discretion determines that the interests of justice so require, declaring a mistrial."

In this rule, the more specific sanction in favor of a criminal defendant is imposed because of the Confrontation Clause of the *Sixth Amendment* of the US *Constitution*. The Confrontation Clause looms as an even more important factor with regard to the next topic, namely the hearsay rules and exceptions thereto.

### Hearsay Exceptions and the Confrontation Clause

Given the fact that there is a substantial overlap between the purposes of the Confrontation Clause and that of the Hearsay Rule, there is only one situation identified in the hearsay provisions of the *FRE* where evidence is specifically admissible in a civil case but not in a criminal case. This is in Rule 803(8) regarding the admissibility of public records and reports. The Rule provides that the following public records reports are not excluded by the Hearsay Rule even thought the declarant is available as a witness: "Records, reports, statements, or data compilations, in any form, of public offices or agencies, setting forth (A) the activities of the office or agency or (B) matters observed pursuant to duty imposed by law as to which matters there was a duty to report, excluding, however, in criminal cases matters observed by police officers and other law enforcement personnel, or (C) in civil actions and proceedings and against the Government in criminal cases, factual findings resulting from an investigation made pursuant to authority granted by law, unless the sources of information or other circumstances indicate lack of trustworthiness."[35]

There was some debate over the adoption of this provision in the report of the House Committee on the Judiciary on the floor of the House of Representatives and in the Senate Committee on the Judiciary.[36] Both the debate in the House and the Advisory Committee Notes identified the reason for having a different rule in criminal cases as being the Confrontation Clause but also, running through the House debate is the notion that the normal presumption of reliability of regularly kept records, inherent in both public and business records, is not necessarily present in the inherently adversarial relationship between police and investigative

---

[35] *FRE* 803(8).
[36] Report of House Committee on the Judiciary, *House Comm. On Judiciary, Fed. Rules of Evidence*, H.r. Rep. No. 650, 93d Cong., 1ˢᵗ Sess., p. 14 (1973); 1974 *US Code Cong. & Ad. News* 7075, 7088; House of Representatives: February 6, 1974, 120 *Cong. Rec.* 2387 (1974); Report of Senate Committee on the Judiciary, *Senate Comm. On Judiciary, Fed. Rules of Evidence*, S. Rep. No. 1277, 93d Cong., 2d Sess., p. 17 (1974); 1974 *US Code Cong. & Ad. News* 7051, 7064.

officers and a criminal defendant.

The hearsay exceptions under *FRE* 804 apply only in situations where the out of court declarant is considered "unavailable as a witness". There is a detailed definition of the definition "unavailability" in Rule 804(a).[37] Most of the cases in which the Supreme Court has made hearsay exceptions against the requirements of the Confrontation Clause have been in the context of the 804 exceptions.[38]

The 804(b) exceptions contain a few minor variations between civil and criminal cases. The rule providing exception for former testimony provides as follows: "(1) Former testimony. Testimony given as a witness at another hearing of the same or a different proceeding, or in a deposition taken in compliance with law in the course of the same or another proceeding, if the party against whom the testimony is now offered, or, in a civil action or proceeding, a predecessor in interest, had an opportunity and similar motive to develop the testimony by direct, cross, or redirect examination."[39]

This rule does not really entail a substantial difference between civil and criminal cases inasmuch as the concept of a 'predecessor in interest' is a property or contract law concept which has no application in a criminal case.

The *FRE* liberalized the usual common law approach to 'dying declarations' which at common law applied only to homicide actions. Present Federal Rule extends this to civil actions for wrongful death.[40] There is a curious gap in the rule as presently enacted. It is theoretically possible that in a civil case for personal injury not resulting in death an injured plaintiff may genuinely believe death to be imminent, not actually die, but be unavailable at trial for some other reason such as illness or infirmity. Under the new definition contained in Rule 804(b)(2), the declarant's statement could nevertheless quality as a 'dying declaration'. However, if the victim in an assault and battery case makes a statement regarding the identity of his attacker, genuinely believes himself to be dying, but does not

---

[37] *(a) Definition of unavailability.* "Unavailability as a witness" includes situations in which the declarant – is exempted by ruling of the court on the ground of privilege from testifying concerning the subject matter of the declarant's statement; or persists in refusing to testify concerning the subject matter of the declarant's statement despite an order of the court to do so; or testifies to a lack of memory of the subject matter of the declarant's statement; or is unable to be present or to testify at the hearing because of death or then existing physical or mental illness or infirmity; or is absent from the hearing and the proponent of his statement has been unable to procure the declarant's attendance (or in the case of a hearsay exception under subdivision (b)(2), (3), or (4), the declarant's attendance or testimony) by process or other reasonable means. A declarant is not available as a witness if his exemption, refusal, claim of lack of memory, inability, or absence is due to the procurement or wrongdoing of the proponent of a statement for the purpose of preventing the witness from attending or testifying.

[38] *See, e.g., California* v. *Green*, 399 *U.S.* 149, (1970); *Douglas* v. *Alabama*, 380 *U.S.* 415 (1965); *Bruton* v. *US*, 389 *U.S.* 818 (1968); *Lee* v. *Illinois*, 476 *U.S.* 530 (1986); *Ohio* v. *Roberts*, 448 *U.S.* 56 (1980); *Dutton* v. *Evans*, 400 *U.S.* 74 (1970).

[39] *FRE* 804(b)(1).

[40] *Statement under belief of impending death.* In a prosecution for homicide or in a civil action or proceeding, a statement made by a declarant while believing that the declarant's death was imminent, concerning the cause or circumstances of what the declarant believed to be his impending death.

die, this does not qualify under the 'dying declaration' exception to the *FRE*. This is because the only type of a criminal case in which a 'dying declaration' or statement of an impending death is admissible is in a homicide case. It is not clear whether the drafters thought through the implications of this distinction. Perhaps, they made the assumption that any civil action in which a dying declaration statement was offered would be a wrongful death action. On the other hand, if they did consider the possibility that 'a dying declaration' could be introduced in a civil action for personal injury short of death, perhaps, they were unwilling to extend this rule to the analogous situation involving a criminal proceeding for assault and battery because of fears of running afoul of the Confrontation Clause by extending this exception to a situation not sanctioned by long historical usage.

At common law the hearsay exception for statements against interest applied only to declarations against 'pecuniary or proprietary interest'. The drafters of the *FRE* took the controversial step of extending the corresponding Federal Rule[41] to statements which "so far tended to subject the declarant to civil or criminal liability, or to render invalid a claim by the declarant against another, that a reasonable person in the declarant's position would not have made the statement unless believing it to be true." However, with regard to statement tending to expose the declarant to *criminal liability* and introduced to exculpate the accused (*e.g.*, statements by a third person confessing to the very crime which the accused is charged), the drafters inserted a unique requirement not found in any of the other exceptions to the hearsay rule, namely a corroboration requirement: "A statement tending to expose the declarant to criminal liability and offered to exculpate the accused is not admissible unless corroborating circumstances clearly indicate the trustworthiness of the statement." The Advisory's Committee Note indicates that the reason for this unique requirement is "a distrust of evidence of confessions by third persons offered to exculpate the accused arising from suspicions of fabrication either of the fact of the making of the confession or in its contents enhanced in either instance by the required unavailability of the declarant."[42] A classic example of a statement against penal interest which would be viewed with suspicion would be an alleged statement by a prisoner, now deceased or whose whereabouts are unknown, confessing to the crime with which the current defendant is charged, when this statement was allegedly made to another prisoner who now wishes to testify to this effect on behalf of the accused.

## Conclusion

There are relatively few differences between the rules of evidence applied in civil cases and those applied in criminal cases. Some rules, by the nature of the subject matter, are going to be applicable either exclusively or largely in one or the other

---

[41] *FRE* 804(b)(3).
[42] Advisory's Committee Note to *FRE* 804(b)(3) at 46 *F.R.D.* 183, 327.

type of case. Where there are differences between civil and criminal cases with regard to a type of evidence that could theoretically be introduced in either a civil or a criminal case, the reasons for the differences are not always apparent. But, a rationale can often be found in US Constitutional provisions protecting the accused, the higher burden of proof ('beyond a reasonable doubt') in criminal cases than in civil cases ('preponderance of the evidence') and in differences in the aims of the criminal and civil law. In some cases perhaps the *FRE* should go further in making civil/criminal distinctions. A closer examination of some of the 803 exceptions which provide for the admissibility of hearsay evidence even when the declarant is available to testify might suggest that some of these rules should incorporate at least a preference for live testimony in criminal cases.

# DNA Tests and Individual Identification

*L. Levine & L. Kobilinsky*

Forensic genetics is that branch of science which enables one to link a suspect to a victim by establishing the identity and source of biological evidence (blood, semen, hair, etc.) found at the crime scene, on the victim, or one the suspect. The procedure in this type of investigation is to first determine whether the suspect can be excluded from consideration as the possible perpetrator of the crime. If, after testing for a number of traits, one cannot exclude the suspect, the task is to determine how many other people in the relevant geographical population have the same combination (profile) of characteristics. It is clear that the larger the number of genetically-determined traits which are examined, the greater the probability not only of excluding an innocent individual but also of identifying a guilty person.

In selecting traits for analysis, the rule has been to choose those which exhibit a considerable amount of *polymorphism* (variability) in different populations. The reasoning, quite correctly, has been that with increased polymorphism, the population frequency of each variant of the trait will be reduced, so that the achievement of a given level of probability for the occurrence of a particular profile will require the analysis of fewer traits. This is especially important when sample size is limited or sample quality has been compromised due to environmental insult.

Genetic testing can take one of two forms. One type consists of various biochemical tests (serological, electrophoretic, complementarity, etc.) that examine either the project formed by genes or some characteristic of a section of the DNA of the individual. Any differences observed are taken as indicators of differences in the nucleotide-base sequences of the respective DNA sources.

The second type of genetic testing is an actual analysis and subsequent comparison of the nucleotide-base sequence of the DNAs obtained from various sources.

Most of the forensic testing done at present involves biochemical tests. Unfortunately, there are a number of problems involved in the interpretation of the test results. As an example, we can consider the blood types. Each of the A-B-O-AB blood types can be distinguished from the others through the use of tests that involve antigen-antibody reactions. The use of this type of test-procedure which categorizes the variability exhibited by the blood groups is an example of *serological polymorphism*. The test is excellent for distinguishing among the various blood types, thereby excluding any suspect who has a blood type different from the source of the evidence. However, a study of the A-B-O genes in a large population found there were actually four different DNA nucleotide-base sequences (alleles) for the 'A' gene, three alleles for the

'B' gene, and six alleles for the 'O' gene.[1] Serological tests cannot distinguish among the various alleles of each of the blood group genes. As a result, a situation can arise in which individuals (source of the evidence and the suspect) with different nucleotide-base sequences (genotypes) are categorized as having the same form of the trait (phenotype). This would lead to the false inclusion of an individual as a suspect in a crime as a result of a serological test when a DNA nucleotide-base sequence analysis would lead to the exclusion of the person.

In the above example, we have an ambiguous situation in which serological polymorphism can provide for the identification of genetic differences among blood types but not for genetic differences within individual blood group genes. It follows that if for the sake of speed and economy, serological testing is performed on blood samples and two specimens show the same phenotype, a DNA nucleotide-base analysis must be performed in order to provide proof of a genetic match between suspect and source of the evidence.

Another genetically determined trait that is used in criminal investigations is the Group-Specific Component (Gc) of blood serum. Gc is a protein that binds to and acts as a carrier of vitamin-D while the vitamin is transported by the blood stream. The carrier protein is also referred to as the Vitamin-D-Binding protein (DBP).

Through the use of conventional electrophoresis, it was found that a Gc protein could have one of three forms (1S, IF, 2). Based on the laboratory method utilized to detect DBP variants, the variability is categorized as an example of *electrophoretic polymorphism*. In the conventional, electrophoretic process used, the separation of proteins took place in a slab-gel (supporting medium) which as been prepared with chemical designed to give the medium a constant pH (acidity or alkalinity). A newer technique, called isoelectric-focusing (IEF), is a form of electrophoresis in which the gel medium is prepared with reagents that establish a pH gradient across the length of the gel. This type of gradient allows for the separation of proteins based not only on size but also on net charge. Thus, this technique is far more sensitive to slight genetically determined differences in protein structure and provides a much higher degree of resolution of proteins present in the specimen. In fact, IEF has led to the discovery of more than 120 Gc variants.[2]

Similar to the situation previously discussed, any technique that determines Gc protein variation should be used solely to exclude individuals as suspects if their DBP is found to differ from that of the evidence. If, however, the two samples are found to have the same electrophoretic phenotype, DNA nucleotide-base analysis is required to avoid a possible false inclusion.

A more complex situation is found in the HLA (Human Leukocyte Antigens) immune system. A large number of major units have been identified

---

[1] Ogasawara *et al.* (1996).
[2] Cleve & Constans (1988).

within this system including HLA DQA1, which has found wide usage in forensic genetics. The detection of variability in this gene involves a two step process. First, approximately one-third of the 768 nucleotides of the gene is amplified through the use of the Polymerase Chain Reaction (PCR) process.[3] This is followed by exposure of the amplified PCR product to a number of previously synthesized sections of DNA, called probes, which have sequences of nucleotides that are complementary to various portions of the amplified region of the DQAI gene. A generally available commercial kit provides seven probes which have an overlapping pattern of nucleotide sequences, covering an 84-nucleotide portion of the gene. The kit is able to distinguish seven variants in nucleotide sequence of the gene, constituting an example of complementarity (*DNA-probe) polymorphism.*

As a result of DNA base sequencing, it was found that the amount of genetic variability of HLA DQA1 is far greater than revealed by the probes. The World Health Organization Nomenclature Committee for Factors of the HLA system has reported the existence of 20 alleles,[4] each of which is identified by the kit as belonging to one of its seven groups. Here, too, any samples which are categorized by the kit as having the same phenotype, be analyzed further to determine whether the genotypes of the samples are the same.

In addition to those DNA nucleotides that function as the elemental units of genes, there are DNA nucleotides which do not have any known role in producing the traits of an individual. These nonfunctional nucleotides are often present in large numbers, forming substantial segments of a person's total DNA. The segments usually consist of a number of repetitions of a given sequence (core) of nucleotides. Even human population has been found to contain variants for the number of cores contained in these nonfunctional nucleotide assemblages. However, each DNA segment is inherited as a unit, much like an allele of a gene. The variability found in these segments is an example of *core-repeat polymorphism.*

Based on the characteristic number of nucleotides in their cores, a distinction has been made between what are called Short Tandem Repeats (STRs) and Variable Number of Tandem Repeats (VNTRs). A STR will have between three and seven nucleotides in each of its cores, whereas a VNTR will have between nine and 45 nucleotides. In both cases, a core may be repeated up to 100 times.

A STR that is frequently used in forensic cases is called HUMTHO1. It is located on human chromosome pair #11, and typically has from six to 14 repeats of a core sequence consisting of the four nucleotides AATG. In a laboratory analysis, HUMTHO1 from a given source is amplified by PCR. The subsequently formed PCR product is then subjected to electrophoresis. Depending on whether both #11 chromosomes do or do not contain the same

---

[3] Mullis & Faloona (1987).
[4] March (1998); Luo *et al.* (1999).

number of cores, there will be one or two bands on the electrophoretic gel. A so-called 'ladder', each 'rung' consisting of a known number of cores, is compared with the band or bands of the source. A match of a 'band' with a 'rung' indicates how many cores are contained in the band. The bands are then assigned identifying numbers that correspond to the number of cores in the segment (5,6,7…14). Unfortunately, variations in nucleotide sequence have been found in one or more of the cores of like-sized repeats. In one such case, it was discovered that core #7 of a ten core-repeat segment was a trimer (ATG) rather than the expected tetramere (AATG).[5] In another case, involving a 14 core-repeat segment, it was found that core #4 consisted of an ATG trimer and, in addition, core #7 contained a different nucleotide sequence (AACG) than that usually found in the tetramers of HUMTHO1.[6] Similar situations have been discovered in another STR[7] and in a VNTR.[8] This uncertainty as to whether a 'band match' is to be considered as proof of a 'genetic match' can only be resolved by DNA nucleotide-base sequence analysis.

In the foregoing situations and in many others which were not discussed, the existence of phenotypic (serological, etc.) polymorphism can be used only to exclude a suspect as the possible perpetrator of a crime. The fact that different genotypes can produce the same phenotype leads to the realization that only DNA nucleotide-base sequencing can establish genetic identification, thereby allowing a suspect to be included.

If an individual cannot be excluded as a suspect in a crime, the task remains to calculate the probability of the occurrence of that particular genetic profile in the relevant geographic population. This requires that we establish, through an examination of published databases, what the frequency of each ascertained genotype is in the population to which the suspect belongs. Once this is done, we can multiply the individual genotype population frequencies together to obtain an estimate of the occurrence of the genetic profile of the suspect. This procedure is called the 'product rule'. It may be used only when the genotypes involved are distributed in the population independently of each other (*i.e.*, located on different chromosomes) and, in addition, if they do not affect the survival of the individual (*i.e.*, selectively neutral).

An important problem may arise in establishing a database of genotype frequencies, especially as related to large-sized populations. It is possible that there may be a genetic-substructuring of the population. Surveys of well studied traits show that in most cases, large populations are not genetically homogeneous but are mosaics of a number of diverse genetic groups. This requires that the frequencies of the various genotypes be ascertained for each subgroup so that the calculation of the occurrence of the suspect's genetic profile will reflect his or her subgroup. The need for this approach can be seen

---

[5] Puers *et al.* (1993).
[6] Gene *et al.* (1996).
[7] Brinkmann *et al.* (1996).
[8] Harashima *et al.* (1997).

in a study of the genotypic variation in the VNTR, D1S80, in three ethnic groups living in Brussels. Significant differences in allele frequencies were found between the native Belgium population and both the Turkish and Moroccan migrant groups living in the city.[9]

An important consideration in all cases is to decide how rare must the profile be in the population in order to be able to declare with scientific confidence that the evidence links the suspect to the victim. The truth is that no absolute standard exists. Quite clearly, the less frequent a particular pattern of genotypes in the population, the greater chance that the evidence came from the suspect. For nations which have small to moderate-sized populations, as those found in Europe (Denmark = 5 million; the Netherlands = 16 million; Germany = 82 million; Russia = 147 million), a probability of 1 per million would, in all likelihood, prove convincing in a trial. For nations which have large-sized populations (Indonesia = 207 million; US = 270 million; India = 989 million; China = 1.2 billion), a probability of 1 per 100 million would most likely be accepted as establishing the source of the evidence. If, as discussed above, population subgroups are taken into account, a frequency of 1 per million will probably be found adequate for most cases. Another factor adds support for a 1 per million criterion. Those under the age of 10 and those over the age of 70 totaling about 20% of a population, can usually be eliminated as suspects in a violent crime, such as murder or manslaughter, thereby reducing the size of the relevant population to about 80% of the total. For rape cases, in addition to the age-related group, we would eliminate all females, thereby reducing the potential suspect group to about 40% of the population.

As an epilogue, it should be pointed out that if out of a series of five or more genetic systems analyzed, the suspect is excluded by only one genetic marker, there may be the possibility that the source of the evidence is a close relative of the suspect, namely, a parent, a sibling or a child. Although this situation is not central to our consideration, the value of this type of information is worth noting.

## Bibliography

**Brinkmann, B., Sajantila, A., Goedde, H.W., Matsumoto, H., Nishi, K. & Wiegand, J.P.** (1996), 'Population genetic comparisons among eight populations using allele frequency and sequence data from three microsatellite loci', in: *Eur. J. Hum. Genet* 4: 175-182.

**Cleve, H. & Constans, J.** (1988), 'The mutants of the Vitamin-D-Binding protein: more than 120 variants of the GC/DBP system', in: *Vox Sang* 54: 215-225.

**Gene, M., Huguet, E., Moreno, P., Sanchez, C., Carracedo, A. & Corbella, J.** (1996), 'Population study of the STRs HUMTHO1 (including a new variant) and HUMVWA31A in Catalonia (northeast Spain)', in: *Int. J. Legal Med.* 108: 318-320.

**Harashima, N., Liu, C., Katsuyama, Y., Ota, M. & Fukushima, H.** (1997), 'Sequence variation of allele 27 at the D1S80 locus', in: *Int. J. Legal Med.* 110: 22-26.

---

[9] Sepulchre *et al.* (1995).

**Luo, M., Blanchard, J. Maclean, I. & Brunham, R.** (1999), 'Identification of a novel HLA-DQA1 allele (DQA1*0106) by sequence-based DQA1 typing', in: *Tissue Antigens* 53: 595-596.

**Marsh, S.G.E.** (1998), 'HLA class II region sequences', in: *Tissue Antigens* 51: 467-507.

Mullis, K.B. & Faloona, F.A. (1987), 'Specific synthesis of DNA *in vitro* via a polymerase-catalyzed chain reaction', in: *Methods in Enzymology* 155 (Part F), pp. 335-350.

**Ogasawara, K., Bannai, M., Saitou, N., Yabe, R., Nakata, K., Takenaka, M., Fujisawa, K., Uchikawa, M., Ishikawa, Y., Juji, T. & Tokunaga, K.** (1996), 'Extensive polymorphism of ABO blood group gene: three major lineages of the alleles for the common ABO phenotypes', in: *Hum. Genet.* 87: 777-783.

**Puers, C., Hammond, H.A., Jin, L., Caskey, C.T. & Schumm, J.W.** (1993), 'Identification of repeat sequence heterogeneity at the polymorphic short tandem repeat locus HUMTHO1 $(AATG)_n$ and reassignment of alleles in population analysis by using a locus-specific allele ladder', in: *Am. J. Hum. Genet.* 53: 953-958.

**Sepulchre, M.A., Wiegand, P. & Brinkmann, B.** (1995), 'D1S80 (pMCT118): Analysis of 3 ethnic subpopulations living in Brussels', in: *Int. J. Legal Med.* 108:45-47.

# Commanding Decryption and the Privilege against Self-incrimination

*B.J. Koops*

## Introduction[1]

Suppose you are a police officer on the brink of finding out who committed the murder you are investigating. You have probable cause to suspect someone, and you have his phone wiretapped. Unfortunately, when you listen to the taped conversations, you only hear gibberish. Did you intercept a fax message? No, it turns out that the suspect regularly scrambles his wire communications: he uses encryption to keep his conversations and computer messages secret. This, then, does not lead you any further.

Therefore, you decide to do a search at the suspect's place. There is no incriminating evidence readily at hand, but you have reason to believe that in the computer, incriminating messages may be stored, and perhaps also a diary. You browse eagerly in his computer, but when you click on the file *diary.doc*, the computer asks for your password for decryption. The file turns out to be encrypted – it looks like this:

```
qANQR1DBwU4DoFOjvEqaYQoQCADuZoWNo9hpUCugPFABqjbmsQwElkYgRxH5Dm5
Yh7seCQ1CG31AWkacOl/DVpmxpL7Og9nMiBmmucNg5BZn9kkrqT3qJhw7gbzPtwsJ4W
gP3KHx3A/Ep7+4BnZFCVc1sNlN4CpE7UiELWliee/R450+E+2y32lC/nKdgHbzDw/HGL2l
Y88TV/+R4xQxr65/ECSCVGWtzZpAkkCaQwVdMQi2S7QZQNf3SLOIc1RPWFftNH9xzI
OGloyfOYWI/wwZmxHQeNIMuYt
```

So, what do you do? The only way to get that last bit of information you need to finalise the evidence, is to command the suspect to decrypt the scrambled files or to give you his password. But would this not force him to provide evidence against himself?

It is likely that a power to demand decryption is an infringement of the privilege against self-incrimination. Since this privilege is not absolute, the legislature could, in principle, decide to enact such a power. Is this justified? To what extent does the privilege against self-incrimination stretch? In this paper, I will deal with these questions, and suggest a way for legislatures to answer them. I will base my analysis on the situation in the Netherlands, and indicate the discussion in the UK, where these questions have been discussed

---

[1] This paper is based on research I conducted with a grant from the National Programme Information Technology and Law (ITeR). The text of this paper was finished on 1 January 2000. A more extensive study in Dutch has appeared in B.J. Koops, *Verdachte en ontsleutelplicht: hoe ver reikt nemo tenetur?*, ITeR series Volume 31, Deventer: Kluwer 2000.

on the basis of legislative proposals.[2]

## The Crypto Controversy

Cryptography (secret writing), or crypto for short, is a means to hide data from unauthorised people. Since the 1970s, robust and reliable automated crypto systems provide efficient and generally uncrackable protection of communications and stored data. Since the mid-1990s, crypto programs have become user-friendlier and more widespread, and you can download several good programs from the Internet, such as Pretty Good Privacy.

To encrypt data, you need a crypto program and a key. For *de*crypting the data, you need the decryption key, which is the same as the *en*cryption key in 'symmetric' cryptography (such as DES), or a *different* one in 'asymmetric' or 'public-key' cryptography (such as PGP). The decryption key (which is indeed key to keeping the data secret) must be kept secret, and is generally stored safely on a diskette or a hard disk, protected by a password.

More and more people are starting to use cryptography, and it is being built in in programs and the information infrastructure, because it is one of the best ways to provide information security – a requisite for electronic commerce. Since the middle of the 1990s, cryptography has proved itself an essential tool in the information society.

However, cryptography is not only used to safeguard e-commerce. Criminals are increasingly becoming aware of its potential to shield their incriminating information traffic from eavesdropping and computer-searching police. This has caused governments to think of ways to promote the good uses of cryptography and at the same time of preventing criminals from using it to thwart the police. This has turned out to be impossible. Whatever governments have come up with, such as requirements to store keys with third parties, has proved ineffective and unacceptable to the large majority of information citizens. My research into this issue has led me to the conclusion that the only way to really do something about the crypto problems for law enforcement, is to enact a power for the police to require suspects to decrypt.[3] Whether that is acceptable, in the light of the privilege against self-incrimination, is a complex issue, which requires careful study of the background of the privilege and of the pros and cons of such a power. So far, governments have been wary with infringing the privilege against self-incrimination for this purpose.

---

[2] For an analysis of the situation in US law, *see* Reitinger (1996) and Sergienko (1996).
[3] *See* my thesis, Koops (1998), in particular Chapter 8.

## Current Legal Status of the Decryption Command in the Netherlands

During the Dutch parliamentary discussions over the *Computer Crime Act (CCA)* in 1992, the legislature became aware of the potential problems cryptography poses to law enforcement. They decided to introduce a power for the police to command someone to decrypt during a search. They respected, however, the privilege against self-incrimination, and so this command cannot be given to suspects (Article 125m of the *Dutch Code of Criminal Procedure (DCCP)*). Then, in January 1998, a follow-up to the *CCA* was proposed, the *Computer Crime Act II*. This contained the power to demand people to decrypt data collected during a search or in a wiretap, and this time, the act proposed to also give this command to suspects, if there is grave evidence *(ernstige bezwaren)* against the suspect and if this is urgently necessary for finding the truth. Several protests from the legal community were raised, and the Minister decided to withdraw the provision in the draft law that was submitted to Parliament in July 1999,[4] thus – again – respecting the privilege against self-incrimination.

## Current Legal Status of the Decryption Command in the UK

In the UK, the government has been developing a crypto policy since 1996, with numerous consultation documents and proposals to regulate cryptography. Earlier versions of the policy were based on the idea that the crypto problem for law enforcement could be addressed by requiring people to deposit their keys with third parties. Given the much protest from UK citizens, and the intrinsic problems of such an approach, the government gradually moved to a position of voluntary key deposits and a requirement for people to decrypt when commanded by the police. This approach culminated in the consultation document *Building Confidence in Electronic Commerce* of 5 March 1999 and the subsequent *E-Communications Bill*. The consultation document proposed a power to require any person, upon service of a written notice, to produce plaintext or a decryption key (or password protecting a key). The ability to serve a written notice will be ancillary to powers for wiretapping or searching and seizing. According to the government, this power would not infringe the privilege against self-incrimination. To ensure compliance, the government would make it an offence not to comply with the terms of a written notice without reasonable excuse.

Then, on 23 July 1999, the government published a draft *Electronic Communications Bill*, together with a new consultation document *Promoting Electronic Commerce. Consultation on Draft Legislation and the Government's Response to the Trade and Industry Committee's Report*, which

---

[4] Kamerstukken II 1998-1999, 26 671, nrs. 1-3.

also contains the Explanatory Notes to the draft Bill.

Article 10 of the draft bill contained a power to require disclosure of a crypto key. For encrypted material lawfully obtained, a written notice can be given to a person who appears to be in the possession of the key, to provide the encrypted information in intelligible form (that is, in the condition in which it was before any encryption or similar process was applied to it), or, if the notice explicitly orders so, to disclose the key. The notice needs to be authorised by the appropriate authority (depending on the powers under which the encrypted material was obtained), such as the Secretary of State, a judge, or a senior police officer.

Failing to comply with such a notice is an offence punishable with up to two years' imprisonment. It is a defence to show that you do not have the key, if you give sufficient information to enable possession of the key; likewise, it is a defence to show that it is not reasonably practicable to disclose the key, if you show that you provided it as soon as this was reasonably practicable.

This section of the *EC Bill* in particular caused a storm of protests, both from the ICT and the legal communities in the UK. The power was generally thought to breach the right to a fair trial as enshrined in Article 6 of the *European Convention of Human Rights (ECHR)*.[5] The law-enforcement problems caused by cryptography were considered by far not serious enough to warrant the burden-of-proof reversal and the high punishment for not co-operating. The objections were illustrated by a letter sent by the organisation Stand to Jack Straw, Home Secretary, containing an 'confession to a crime' encrypted with a key pair generated on Straw's name. The Metropolitan Police was informed that Straw was in possession of this information, and the keys were then destroyed by Stand. This way, Straw would be liable for two years in prison, unless he could prove that he did not know the key – which he could not, because Stand might have sent him a copy.[6]

After much protest, the government withdrew the contentious provision from the *E-Communications Bill*, in order to re-insert it in a *Regulation of Investigatory Powers Bill*. The government was, however, still of the opinion that the power to demand decryption from suspects does not infringe art. 6 of the *ECHR*. As of January 2000, the discussions on the issue continue in the UK, and it is unclear what the outcome will be.

### The Privilege against Self-incrimination

To be able to judge whether and to what extent a decryption command infringes the privilege against self-incrimination, and whether such an infringement is acceptable given the interests at stake, one must study the way the privilege has been interpreted and what infringements have been allowed

---

[5] *See, e.g.*, Beatson & Eicke (1999).
[6] Stand (1999).

to date. I will therefore first analyse the privilege, and subsequently give an overview of infringements that have been allowed in Dutch law.

The privilege against self-incrimination is a fundamental legal principle that is part of the right to a fair trial. It says that a suspect cannot be forced to incriminate himself or to yield evidence against himself. The privilege is recognised in most countries, either explicitly in the constitution or implicitly through case law. It is included explicitly in several international treaties, such as the *International Covenant on Civil and Political Rights* (Article 14 para 3 sub g: everyone charged with a criminal offence has the right not to be compelled to testify against himself or to confess guilt) and the *Statute for the International Criminal Court* (Article 55 para 1 sub a: a person shall not be compelled to incriminate himself or herself or to confess guilt).

Moreover, the privilege is enshrined in Article 6 of the *ECHR*, as interpreted by the European Court. The right to a fair trial incorporates "the right of anyone 'charged with a criminal offence', within the autonomous meaning of this expression in Article 6,[7] to remain silent and not to contribute to incriminating himself."[8] In three cases,[9] the European Court has laid down the basis for determining the meaning of the privilege against self-incrimination, but at the same time, it has caused considerable confusion over this meaning. The *Saunders* case seems to give the most definitive statement about the privilege. The privilege is primarily concerned, however, with respecting the will of an accused person to remain silent. It does not extend to the use in criminal proceedings of material which may be obtained from the accused through the use of compulsory powers but which has an existence independent of the will of the suspect such as, *inter alia*, documents acquired pursuant to a warrant, breath, blood and urine samples and bodily tissue for the purpose of DNA testing.

There is not a general definition of the privilege against self-incrimination in Dutch law. The *Constitution* and the *DCCP* do not mention it. The *DCCP* does contain several Articles that reflect the privilege; for instance, a command to hand over goods or a command to provide access to a protected computer cannot be given to a suspect (Article 107 and Article 125m para 1 *DCCP*).

The Dutch Supreme Court has initially said that "it would ill be in keeping with the spirit of the *DCCP*" if "the suspect would be compelled to contribute to his own conviction under threat of punishment",[10] but since 1977, it has often repeated the magic formula: "there is no unconditional right or principle

---

[7] The 'autonomous meaning' of the term "criminal charge" means that the European Court does not only look at the classification of the alleged offence in a nation's law (criminal or otherwise), but also at the nature of the offence and the nature of the penalty threatened.

[8] ECrtHR 25 February 1993 (*Funke* v. *France*).

[9] ECrtHR 25 February 1993 (*Funke* v. *France*), ECrtHR 17 December 1996 (*Saunders* v. *UK*) and ECrtHR 8 February 1996 (*Murray* v. *UK*).

[10] HR 16 January 1928, *NJ* 1928, p. 233.

that a suspect can not in any way be obliged to co-operate in the obtaining of possibly incriminating evidence".[11] The system of Dutch law indicates that, in general, suspects cannot be required to actively co-operate, but they do have to suffer acts that can incriminate them, such as the taking of blood samples. In special laws, dealing, *e.g.*, with environment and tax crime, there are more compulsory powers for the police to require active co-operation from people, including suspects, such as handing over documents. An important reason for the difference between general and special criminal law is that, in the latter, co-operation requirements are considered necessary to find evidence at all that a crime as such has been committed. If people would be able to refuse to give tax documents to tax officials, tax crimes would not be discovered anymore, let alone prosecuted – so the argument goes.

From the European and Dutch interpretations of the privilege, one can conclude that although the privilege against self-incrimination is usually defined quite broadly ("not contribute to incriminating one-self"), the scope of the privilege is rather limited. It is a strong barrier to the compelled rendering of *testimonial* evidence, implying a suspect's act or statement which somehow or other involves the use of his mind, but it is only a weak barrier to other means of compelled co-operation, such as suffering blood samples or handing over tax documents. In my understanding, the privilege does stretch to these kinds of 'co-operation' as well (contrary to what the European Court in *Saunders* suggested) because the suspect co-operates in incriminating himself, but the privilege has a weaker impact on this kind of co-operation.

To understand why this is so, one should try to distil the rationale of the privilege from its history. People have suggested various reasons for the privilege:

1. humanity: it is not humane to force someone to contribute to his own misfortune;
2. autonomy: a suspect is free to choose an attitude in criminal proceedings, he can decide whether he wants to co-operate or not;
3. reliability: evidence must be reliable;
4. prohibition of pressure: the privilege is a safeguard against the police using (too much) pressure to force a suspect to co-operate.

The third option has great explicative value. The disclosure of things which exist 'outside of the will of the suspect' provides reliable evidence, whereas testimonial statements generally do not (you do not know whether the suspect tells the truth). Thus, the privilege contributes to truth finding and shields the judiciary from "miscarriages of justice", as the European Court stated in *Murray*. However, I think it is impossible (and unnecessary) to pinpoint a single rationale: all of the above grounds have something to say for them and explain different aspects of the privilege.

---

[11] HR 15 February 1977, *NJ* 1977, 557, m.nt. GEM.

One must realise that the privilege works on different levels. First, it is a principle the legislature has to take into account when introducing investigation powers. They cannot enact a power that unduly forces a suspect to incriminate himself. Here, the reliability rationale plays an important part: the more reliable evidence a power yields (such as breathalyser tests for drunk driving), the less strongly does the privilege work. And conversely, the less reliable a power is (such as requiring a suspect to make a statement on his involvement with the crime), the more strongly the privilege works.[12]

Second, the privilege has influence on the implementation of investigation powers. Here, it prevents the police from putting too much pressure on a suspect to co-operate when they use compulsory powers; this is the rationale of prohibition of pressure.

Third, the privilege plays a part in court. The court must decide whether information obtained through pressure on a suspect to co-operate is admissible as evidence. This is not a simple deduction from the wording of the law that allows investigation powers. Even if the police have the power to compel co-operation, such as handing over documents in a tax investigation, it does not follow automatically that the resulting data can be used as evidence. This can be illustrated by the *Saunders* case. The law that compels people to make statements is acceptable in light of the privilege – it targets people not charged with a criminal offence. However, in Saunders' case, the statements could not be used as evidence, because they had been used in the criminal proceedings in a way incompatible with the privilege. The privilege-infringing use of the statements was mainly caused by the influence the use of the documents had had on Saunders' attitude in court, particularly given the negative impression it created with the jury. Thus, the autonomy of the suspect and the prohibition of pressure are paramount in colouring the privilege as used in court, besides the reliability of the evidence.

### Does a Decryption Command infringe the Privilege?

From the definition of the privilege, it is clear that a decryption command is an infringement. Whether the suspect decrypts himself or whether he hands over a key and tells the password, in all cases, he actively co-operates in an activity that results directly in possibly incriminating evidence. Moreover, in most cases, the suspect will have to show or use the contents of his mind, because the password protecting the key is stored there. If the password is written down somewhere, the police can seize the paper or copy the password themselves; the decryption command is targeted precisely at cases in which the password is not readily available to the police.

One can argue over the question to what extent telling a password is

---

[12] *See* Schalken's annotation of HR 29 October 1996, *NJ* 1997, 232.

testimonial (in Dutch, a *verklaring*). On the one hand, it is not a statement concerning facts or circumstances – it is more like a physical key in that it either works or does not work. In that respect, the password is independent of the will of the suspect, because he cannot alter it with his will power. On the other hand, since the password exists in the mind (assuming the password is not written down somewhere), the suspect must operate his mind to reveal it. In that respect, the password has an existence which does depend upon his will, because if he refuses to give it (*e.g.*, because he has forgotten it), the password, to all practical purposes, does not exist anymore. This means that, even if the password itself is not testimonial, the act of giving it will usually be testimonial: it reveals knowledge of the suspect. Only if it is a foregone conclusion that the suspect knows the password, can one hold that revealing the password is not testimonial.

This seems exactly the criterion that was pivotal to the *Funke* case, which the European Court decided in 1993. Funke was forced by French custom officials to hand over bank account documents "which they believed must exist, although they were not certain of the fact". Although the court decision is an obscure one, which has triggered divergent interpretations, I believe that this question whether the government knew or not that Funke had the power to comply was a crucial factor in deciding there had been an infringement of the privilege against self-incrimination. Because the officials were *not* sure that Funke had the documents, their forcing him to hand them over was incompatible with the privilege. After all, his refusal to comply could not lead to any conclusion: it may have been caused by unwillingness, but also by inability.[13]

In consequence, a decryption command is in all cases an infringement of the privilege against self-incrimination that prevents incriminating oneself, and it is also an infringement of the strong privilege that prevents providing testimonial evidence, if it is not a foregone conclusion that the suspect knows the password.

### Precedents for infringing the Privilege in Dutch Law

Now, we are to decide whether a power to require suspects to decrypt is acceptable given the privilege and the other interests at stake. This primarily concerns the first level on which the privilege operates: that of the legislature. In balancing the interests at stake, the legislature must bear in mind the system of the law and the arguments one can use to infringe fundamental rights.

---

[13] For this interpretation of *Funke* and the related case of *Fisher* v. *US, see* Koops (1998), p. 175. The same interpretation is given by Rozemond (1998), p. 316. *See also* the recent certiorari granted by the Supreme Court in *US* v. *Hubbell* (D.C. Cir., 167 *F.3d* 552): the *Fifth Amendment* protects the production of business and financial records, unless the government can show its prior knowledge of the information.

Therefore, one must analyse what laws the legislature has passed until now to allow infringements. For brevity's sake, I restrict myself to the Dutch situation.

First, several laws require people to make testimonial statements. There are reporting requirements: *e.g.*, doctors carrying out euthanasia, farmers dealing with manure, and financial institutions accepting unusual amounts of money all have to file reports. These can lead the Public Prosecutor to start an investigation, if the report suggests that rules have not been complied with. Generally, the information contained in the reports can be used as evidence in a criminal trial, because the reporting law addresses non-suspects in regulatory, not criminal, affairs. In certain laws, however, an exception has been made: the law requiring the reporting of unusual financial transactions stipulates that the information cannot be used in a prosecution of financial institutions for receiving (in Dutch *heling*). This is because the law is targeted at catching money-laundering criminals, not the reporting financial institutions.

Then, in several special laws, there are requirements to provide information, *e.g.*, in supervisory activities concerning taxes, drugs, or weapons. Usually, the supervisory officials can require people to provide information, but if the addressee is a suspect, he can refuse to testify. This is not so in the *Law on Weapons and Munitions*: if a suspect does not comply with an order to provide information, he can be fined. This exception may be explained by the importance of controlling the risk of weapons, the restricted scope of the law, and the low punishment, leading to the infringement of the privilege against self-incrimination to be acceptable to the legislature.

Then, witnesses usually are obliged to speak. In criminal cases, however, they can refuse to answer a question if in answering they would incriminate themselves. In parliamentary inquests, they cannot refuse to speak, but a special provision forbids using their answers as evidence in criminal cases. Thus, there are different levels of self-incrimination protection: suspects never have to answer, witnesses in criminal cases can only refuse to answer certain questions, and witnesses in parliamentary inquests always have to answer, but resulting evidence is inadmissible.

A special case is car registration-number liability. The holder of a registration number is liable for certain offences committed with the car, unless he tells the police who was the driver. If he fails to indicate the driver, the registration-number holder can be sentenced to the same punishment as can be given for the offence at issue. Thus, in fact, people are forced to give information, and a refusal is penalised. This infringement of the privilege against self-incrimination should be explained by the special circumstances of the *Road Traffic Act*, where car owners are considered to have a responsibility to prevent others to use their cars to endanger road safety with impunity. Still, it is the only case in Dutch law where suspects can be forced to make a statement (the name and full address of the driver) while a refusal to comply is punishable with a prison sentence. As such, it hardly fits in with the way Dutch law has incorporated the privilege against self-incrimination.

The general conclusion must be that suspects can, in principle, never be forced to make statements. People who are not a suspect, however, can be forced to give testimonial evidence, although they can usually refuse to comply if they would incriminate themselves. Generally, resulting evidence may not be used against them in court. It is only in very few, restricted areas (weapons, traffic) that compelled statements may be admissible as evidence.

Second, there are requirements to force suspects to actively co-operate with the police – a broader class of co-operation and less contentious than providing testimonial evidence because the right to silence need not be at stake. One can think of the many requirements in special laws to hand over documents or things that may be helpful for uncovering the truth. Also, in traffic law, people suspected of drunk driving have to actively co-operate with a blood or breath test. If suspects refuse to co-operate, they can be punished with a prison sentence (in tax law), or with the same punishment as can be given for drunk driving (in traffic law). Here, therefore, we see that the privilege is infringed, but that the legislature has allowed this infringement after a balancing of the interests at stake. In these cases, the privilege against self-incrimination has less weight because it concerns material independent of the will of the accused. Thus, the necessities of enforcing special laws (regulating specific kinds of economic activities) can be considered to outweigh the privilege. Further arguments for this balance are the relatively low punishments (in the special laws) and the subsidiarity principle, which holds that a compulsory power which breaches fundamental rights is more acceptable if there are no other powers available to achieve the goals of the legislation (which is a particularly valid argument in the traffic law, because drunk driving can hardly be proved otherwise).

This overview leads to the conclusion that, in general criminal law, suspects do not have to co-operate. In special laws, they often have to actively co-operate, but they usually cannot be forced to give testimonial evidence. Infringements of the privilege against self-incrimination are allowed more easily in special laws, largely because of the principle of subsidiarity (it is harder to prosecute crime in economic-activity regulating areas, because the crime is usually more covert) and because of the principle of proportionality (the more restricted the scope of the law, the less an infringement forced co-operation is).

Furthermore, the laws show different ways of incorporating the privilege against self-incrimination: sometimes, people cannot be forced to co-operate; sometimes, they can be addressed with a co-operation command but they can refuse to comply; sometimes, they are obliged to comply, but resulting data cannot be used as evidence against them at all; and sometimes, people are obliged to co-operate, but resulting evidence is inadmissible in court under certain circumstances. Only laws of the last category concern true infringements of the privilege against self-incrimination.

## Options for commanding Decryption

Now, if we look at the issue at hand, the analysis of precedents suggests various ways of enacting a decryption command within – and outside of – the limits of the privilege against self-incrimination. I present these in order of increasing infringement of the privilege against self-incrimination:

1. a decryption command that cannot be given to suspects;
2. a decryption command to all persons. People can refuse if by complying they would incriminate themselves;
3. a decryption command to all persons. Suspects have to comply. Resulting data cannot be used for investigation;
4. a decryption command to all persons. Suspects have to comply. Resulting data cannot be used as evidence;
5. a decryption command to all persons. Suspects have to comply. Resulting data *can* be used as evidence only if certain conditions apply or *cannot* be used as evidence only if certain conditions apply;
6. a decryption command to all persons. Suspects have to comply. Resulting data can be used as evidence.

Moreover, these options can be chosen for

A. criminal law in general (the *Code of Criminal Procedure*); or
B. only specific laws (such as tax law, environment law, or drugs law).

To ensure effectiveness, one can choose various enforcement options. A refusal to comply with a decryption command:

i. is punishable as not complying with a legal order (like Article 184 *DCCP*, maximum three months' imprisonment);
ii. is punishable in its own right, with a specific maximum punishment that
   - is the same for all crimes;
   - is somehow tied to the crime being investigated; or
iii. can be used as evidence by drawing an adverse inference in the case against the addressee.

In all options, variables can be added to limit the scope of the power (and the consequent infringement), such as restricting the power to serious crimes, a requirement of probable cause (in Dutch *redelijke verdenking*) or of grave evidence (in Dutch *ernstige bezwaren*), and requirements of urgency and necessity.

As Dutch law currently stands, A1i is the case.[14] The issue in the Netherlands, then, is to what extent a 'heavier' law can and should be

---

[14] In various special laws, requirements to co-operate can be interpreted as including a command to decrypt, like the requirement in tax law to show books, which must be presented in an understandable format; these could be seen as decryption commands of the type B2ii and B3ii (and B6ii in the case of the munitions law requirement to co-operate).

established, where A6 is the most far-reaching.

## Enforcement and Ability to decrypt

One of the major factors in the decision to introduce a decryption-order law targeted at suspects is enforcement. After all, if the order is to be effective, there must be a threat of punishment for not complying. Such a punishment can only be given to people who *wilfully* do not comply. Otherwise, a risk liability would be introduced for encryption use: if you ever find yourself in front of the police asking you to decrypt, you have to comply, whether or not you are able to. That is unacceptable, given the importance of cryptography in the information society and the fact that using encryption is in no way of itself a dangerous activity. Therefore, if someone is to be punished for not decrypting, the police will have to show that he was able to decrypt.

Here, problems emerge. Addressees can generally easily hide unwillingness to co-operate under retorts of "I forgot my password", "These random data must have been copied to my computer when I downloaded something from the Internet – I have no idea what they are" and "I have not used that decryption key for over a year".[15] Especially the retort that the addressee forgot his password is difficult to refute. The police can give arguments why someone should be able to remember his password (*e.g.*, because he is a professional crypto user who has never forgotten his password at the office), but there are too many arguments the suspect can give to make this unlikely (*e.g.*, "I used a particularly difficult password, as my crypto consultant advised me, which I was not allowed to write down – and I have not used it that often").

Moreover, calculating criminals have plenty of opportunities to anticipate a decryption order. For instance, they can remove all header information so that one cannot see whether the file is encrypted or just consists of random data, they can often change key pairs, and they can antedate files in their computers so that they can argue that they no longer remember the key with which it was encrypted long ago. Also, the crypto community will devise robust schemes for 'perfect forward secrecy', in which it is not possible for the user to decrypt the data after a certain period.

As a result, a decryption order will be particularly powerless against calculating criminals, while less-calculating criminals can benefit from an I-forgot-my-password retort. Therefore, it will hardly be useful to put a significant punishment on not complying with a decryption order – the prosecution will have too hard a task to show that someone wilfully did not comply.

---

[15] *See* Koops (1999), section 4, for an overview of these technical issues.

## Choosing an Option

In the scope of this article, I cannot provide a definitive answer to the question what kind of decryption command the Dutch or UK legislatures should choose. This, after all, is a question which requires thorough analysis of several issues, as well as a political balancing of interests. Rather, I shall indicate the procedure legislatures have to follow to be able to make a justified and reasonable choice.

To introduce a decryption command that balances the interests of crime fighting and the right to a fair trial, the legislature must analyse the following: what is the *scope of the privilege* against self-incrimination in their law system? I have indicated this for the Dutch situation above.

What *kind of crimes* is at stake in which the investigation is hampered by encryption? Are these numerous, more general crimes, or mainly certain specific crimes? How serious are these crimes? This analysis should be based on empirical studies of investigation practice.[16] My current impression is that cryptography has truly obstructed investigation in only very few cases to date, although this may change significantly if cryptography is built in in mass-market software, such as operating systems and mail programs.

*How* does cryptography hamper investigation? Does it mainly hamper the (initial stages of) investigation (notably in wiretaps), making it more difficult to find out who may be involved in the crime, or does it obstruct the stage of prosecution, making it difficult to finalise the evidence (notably in computer searches)?

What *alternatives* are there to investigate and gather sufficient evidence? Does this depend on the kind of crime and investigation involved? *E.g.*, it may be the case that in general investigation, there are sufficient other alternatives (such as infiltration, or using directional microphones and bugs), whereas in specific supervision procedures and investigations (such as tax and environment law), there are far less viable alternatives. Here, one must also assess the extent to which the alternatives infringe fundamental rights, such as the right to privacy and the right to a fair trial, in order to assess what is the least burdensome power.

If a power to demand decryption is found necessary, what *safeguards* should be in place to make it as little infringing as possible within the limits of effectiveness? Here, one must choose conditions of the seriousness of the crimes for which the power can be exerted, the amount of suspicion against the addressee, the likelihood of the encrypted data at issue to be useful or necessary for the investigation, and the like. The legislature should look at

---

[16] Denning & Baugh (1997), have initiated such an empirical study, but this was rather preliminary and *ad hoc*. No data avail for the Netherlands. Governments should stimulate studies of the extent to which investigation is hampered by cryptography, rather than roughly indicate the theoretical problems.

comparable investigation powers to make the decryption command neatly fit in with the system of the law. Moreover, a safeguard should be built-in to prevent keys used for digital signatures to be handed over.

What kind of *enforcement* is required? Here, the legislature must choose between the general penalisation of not complying with a legal order, a specific penalisation for not complying with this order – with an appropriate and just maximum punishment, and a provision that allows the judge to draw an adverse inference from a refusal to comply (effectively reversing the burden of proof for the incriminating nature of the encrypted data). Generally, the enforcement will not be effective given the ease with which addressees can claim not to be able to comply. This is a strong argument against a severe infringement of the privilege against self-incrimination.

## Conclusion

Cryptography is a potential problem for law enforcement, hampering wiretaps and computer searches. The only way to really solve this problem would be to force suspects to decrypt, but this infringes the privilege against self-incrimination. Governments can decide to introduce a power to command suspects to decrypt, if a full analysis of the problems in practice and the system of the law lead them to account more weight to the necessity of fighting crime than to the privilege against self-incrimination in this particular respect. It is likely, however, that such a power will not be effective if targeted at suspects. As a result, there should be the most serious and compelling arguments to introduce a decryption power to suspects nonetheless – such as the fact that cryptography is definitively blocking a large number of prosecutions of serious crimes, in which there is no alternative but to get the key to decrypt possibly incriminating evidence. At present, this is far from the case, and it is unlikely that such will ever be the case.

Therefore, an infringement of the privilege against self-incrimination is not warranted. The current Dutch provision that a decryption order can not be given to suspects is a sound one.

## References

**Beatson, J. & Eicke, T.** (1999), 'In the matter of the draft Electronic Communications Bill and in the matter of a human rights audit for Justice and FIPR', 7 October 1999, http://www.fipr.org/ecomm99/ecommaud.html.

**Denning, D. & Baugh, W.** (1997), *Cases involving encryption in crime and terrorism*, version 10 Oct. 1997, http://www.cs.georgetown.edu/~denning/crypto/cases.html.

**Koops, B.J.** (1998), *The Crypto Controversy. A Key Conflict in the Information Society*, The Hague: Kluwer Law International.

**Koops, B.J.** (1999), *Crypto and Self-Incrimination FAQ*, version 1.1, 13 August 1999, http://cwis.kub.nl/~frw/people/koops/casi-faq.htm.

**Reitinger, P.R.** (1996), 'Compelled Production of Plaintext and Keys', in: *University of Chicago Legal Forum* 1996, pp. 171-206.

**Rozemond, K.** (1998), *Strafvorderlijke rechtsvinding*, Deventer: Gouda Quint.

**Schalken, T.** (1996), annotation of HR 29 October 1996, NJ 1997, 232.

**Sergienko, G.** (1996), 'Self Incrimination and Cryptographic Keys', in: *Richmond Journal of Law & Technology*, No. 1 (1996), http://www.urich.edu/~jolt/v2i1/sergienko.html.

**Stand** (1999), Hutty, M., Stand.org.uk, 'Letter to Jack Straw, Home Secretary', http://www.stand.org.uk/dearjack/, no date (accessed 24 November 1999).

# The Process of Interrogating Criminal Suspects in the United States

*P. Marcus*

The criminal investigation process is a difficult and complex one, emphasizing heavily the questioning of accused suspects. Numerous constitutional provisions are considered by US courts in reviewing interrogation and resulting confessions offered at trial against defendants. Three of the most important are analyzed in this essay.

## The Due Process Approach to Reviewing Confessions

The most traditional review in the US arises under the Due Process Clause of the *Fourteenth Amendment* to the US *Constitution*. The earliest due process opinions centered on efforts at ensuring the reliability of confessions. Here inquiries were made chiefly into whether a statement was voluntarily given.[1] The key consideration with voluntariness is whether the defendant was freely speaking when he confessed. A 'totality of the circumstances' analysis of voluntariness is a case-specific approach in which courts inquire into the character and nature of the person who gave the confession, and the conduct of the officers who obtained it.[2] Courts have looked to such factors as the officers' personal knowledge of the suspect, that person's age and relative experience, the location of the person at the time of confession, and the length of the interrogation period.[3]

This 'totality of the circumstances' analysis can create severe problems. By its nature, a test that considers all the important factual considerations is case specific. Therefore, there will be many prosecutions where judges will not find much in the way of useful precedent upon which to ground their decisions. For the lawyer, the task is a difficult one as all parties inquire into quite specific – and often contradicting – circumstances.

One useful tool for courts struggling with the voluntariness test was the Supreme Court's decision, in a series of opinions, to exclude confessions obtained from witnesses who were brought before a judicial magistrate only after a significant delay. The length of time that an interrogation proceeded before a statement was obtained is one factor taken into consideration in assessing the voluntariness of a confession. Officers might hold a suspect for days before bringing that person before a magistrate. In order to resolve this problem, the Supreme Court adopted a special exclusionary rule for incriminating statements

---

[1] The US Supreme Court adopted the English common law notion of voluntariness in its first decisions regarding confessions and other incriminating statements. *See Hopt* v. *Utah*, 110 *U.S.* 574 (1884).

[2] *See Henry* v. *Kernan*, 177 *F.3d* 1152 (9th Cir. 1999).

[3] *See, e.g., Brooks* v. *Florida*, 389 *U.S.* 413 (1967); *Beecher* v. *Alabama*, 389 *U.S.* 35 (1967).

obtained after a major delay in bringing the accused to a hearing. Named the *McNabb-Mallory Rule*,[4] delayed confessions were suppressed, but not on Constitutional grounds. Instead, the Court used its supervisory power over the administration of criminal justice to exclude the confessions because the suspects had not been brought before a judicial officer in a timely fashion. This approach was solidified by *Federal Rule of Criminal Procedure* 5(a) which requires that a person be taken before a judicial officer without unnecessary delay.[5]

The *McNabb-Mallory Rule* was never treated as an absolute prohibition upon interrogations conducted before an initial appearance. Even a delay in questioning would be allowed in investigatory situations if necessary. Later, however, Congress seemingly eliminated the force of the *McNabb-Mallory Rule* by legislating that a confession "shall not be inadmissible solely because of delay in bringing such person before a magistrate (...)".[6] The rule is not, though, completely dead, and it continues to be applied in cases involving unusual circumstances.[7]

Reversing earlier precedent, the Supreme Court has ruled that a harmless error test is to be applied to determine whether the erroneous admission of a coerced confession should result in the conviction being overturned. Still, it is exceedingly difficult for the government to show, beyond a reasonable doubt, that the confession did not contribute to the verdict. Indeed, in the very opinion establishing the harmless error test with involuntarily confessions the Court found prejudice. There, an informer cellmate offered to protect the defendant from other prisoners in exchange for 'the truth'; the resulting confession was shown to be central to the conviction.[8]

---

[4] *McNabb* v. *US*, 318 *U.S.* 332 (1943); *Mallory* v. *US*, 354 *U.S.* 449 (1957).

[5] Rule 5. Initial Appearance Before the Magistrate (a) In general. An officer making an arrest under a warrant issued upon a compliant or any person making an arrest without a warrant shall take the arrested person without unnecessary delay before the nearest available federal magistrate or, in the event that a federal magistrate is not reasonably available, before a state or local judicial officer authorized by 18 *U.S.C.* § 3041. If a person arrested without a warrant is brought before a magistrate, a complaint shall be filed forthwith which shall comply with the requirements of Rule 4(a) with respect to the showing of probable cause. When a person, arrested with or without a warrant or given a summons, appears initially before the magistrate, the magistrate shall proceed in accordance with the applicable subdivisions of this rule.

[6] 18 *U.S.C.* § 3501(c).

[7] *See, e.g., US* v. *Superville*, 40 *F. Supp. 2d* 672 (D. Virgin Is. 1999) where the confession was given eight days after arrest and before a judicial appearance.

[8] *Arizona* v. *Fulminante*, 499 *U.S.* 279 (1991). Justice Kennedy, concurring, emphasized the point that the government's burden is heavy. The court conducting a harmless-error inquiry must appreciate the indelible impact a full confession may have on the trier of fact, as distinguished, for instance, from the impact of an isolated statement that incriminates the defendant only when connected with other evidence. If the jury believes that a defendant has admitted the crime, it doubtless will be tempted to rest its decision on that evidence alone, without careful consideration of the other evidence in the case. Apart, perhaps, from a videotape of the crime, one would have difficulty finding evidence more damaging to a criminal defendant's plea of innocence. *See also Henry* v. *Kernan*, *supra*, where the confession was called "critical evidence".

As noted earlier, courts are directed to use a totality of the circumstances approach to determine whether the confession of a defendant has been compelled by government action.[9] A variety of such circumstances may be significant in particular cases. The most obvious question at the outset is whether the police used force to elicit the confession. Confessions obtained through use of actual physical force are inadmissible. "[O]ne truncheon blow on the head" will result in the inadmissibility of any confession.[10] But officers do not need to go that far. Threats or warnings of violence made in the hope of eliciting an incriminating statement will also result in exclusion of any confessions obtained.[11]

Lies by officers also raise serious questions. Deception alone will not often render a confession invalid. Overstatement of the strength of the case against the defendant is not itself usually seen as coercion. The confession will not be considered inadmissible against the defendant unless the deception is extreme and relates to the prosecution process itself. All sorts of lies concerning the investigator's case are permitted. As one court put the matter, "A defendant's will is not overborne simply because he is led to believe that the government's knowledge of his guilt is greater than it actually is."[12] These false statements have been allowed: fingerprints found at the scene of the crime,[13] confessions by co-defendant,[14] impact of laboratory tests.[15]

Where, however, officers have misled the defendant concerning the manner in which she is to be prosecuted, the courts have been far more inclined to find a resulting confession involuntary.[16] These false statements have not been allowed: defendant would not go to jail if she confessed,[17] promise that defendant would not be charged with murder,[18] remark that defendant was not the focus of investigation,[19] statement that if defendant did not talk she would be convicted and might not ever see her children again.[20]

Another troubling techniques involves the use of police officers, both uniformed and undercover, to elicit incriminating statements by having the officers befriend defendants. Such actions do not often render a confession inadmissible. But in the extreme case, when the officer actually is a friend of the suspect, and relies heavily on that friendship, a resulting confession may be found

---

[9] *Haynes* v. *Washington*, 373 *U.S.* 503 (1963).

[10] *Fikes* v. *Alabama*, 352 *U.S.* 191 (1957).

[11] *See, e.g., Beecher* v. *Alabama*, 389 *U.S.* 35 (1967).

[12] *Ledbetter* v. *Edwards*, 35 *F.3d* 1062, 1070 (6th Cir. 1994), *cert. denied*, 515 *U.S.* 1145.

[13] *Id.* But *see People* v. *Randle*, 366 *S.E.2d* 750 (W.Va. 1988).

[14] *Sandifer* v. *Alabama*, 517 *So.2d* 646 (1987).

[15] *State* v. *C.J.M.*, 409 *N.W.2d* 857 (Minn. 1987).

[16] Such statements by the police, one court wrote, "will be regarded as coercive per se, thus obviating the need for a 'totality of circumstances' analysis of voluntariness." *People* v. *Kelekolio*, 849 *P.2d* 58, 73 (Haw. 1993).

[17] *US* v. *Pinto*, 671 *F. Supp.* 41 (D. Me. 1987).

[18] *State* v. *Ritter*, 485 *S.E.2d* 492 (Ga. 1997).

[19] *US* v. *Salisbury*, 966 *F. Supp.* 1082 (N.D.Ala. 1997).

[20] *Lynumn* v. *Illinois*, 372 *U.S.* 528 (1963).

to be involuntary. In the leading Supreme Court decision, the investigators directed another officer, an old friend of the defendant, to urge the defendant to confess by telling him that the officer would be punished by his superiors. The Court determined that the officer's conversations with the defendant amounted to official interrogation and that the defendant's statement was involuntary, for his "will was overborne by official pressure, fatigue, and sympathy falsely aroused (…)."[21]

### Application of the Right to Counsel, Pre-trial Statements

The *Sixth Amendment* to the US Constitution provides that "in all criminal prosecutions, the accused shall enjoy the right to (…) the Assistance of Counsel for his defense." *Gideon* v. *Wainright*[22] dramatically changed the entire criminal justice process by requiring counsel, even for indigent defendants, in all serious cases. The holding had a great impact on the interrogation process in several ways.

The *Sixth Amendment* right to counsel attaches when a person's status changes from "suspect" to "accused". This distinction is critical, for a suspect is not accused when she has been seized or even arrested. The right only begins to apply when the individual has been charged with a crime.[23] In stark contrast, the *Fifth Amendment* right to counsel under *Miranda* attaches whenever a suspect is subjected to a custodial interrogation, regardless of whether that suspect has been charged with a crime.[24]

Even if it satisfies the voluntariness test, a confession may still be inadmissible if it is found to have been obtained by officers in violation of the defendant's *Sixth Amendment* right to counsel. In the leading case, an indicted defendant had retained counsel.[25] Though he was not in custody, he made incriminating statements to a co-conspirator, acting for the government and carrying a radio transmitter. Because the defendant had been formally charged, he was entitled to have his lawyer present during any interrogation, even by an undercover agent. While the charge could still be pursued, the incriminating statements had to be excluded from trial.[26]

---

[21] *Spano* v. *New York*, 360 *U.S.* 315, 323 (1959).

[22] 372 *U.S.* 335 (1963).

[23] Therefore, the *Sixth Amendment* applies after the defendant has been indicted or arraigned, or when she is at a preliminary examination. *Moore* v. *Illinois*, 434 *U.S.* 220 (1977). The individual does not, however, have *Sixth Amendment* rights when testifying before a grand jury, for that process is deemed investigatory rather than accusatory. *US* v. *Mandujano*, 425 *U.S.* 564 (1976). The courts are split as to whether the judicial issuance of an arrest warrant marks the beginning of the right to counsel.

[24] *See* text accompanying notes 32-59, *infra*.

[25] *Massiah* v. *US*, 377 *U.S.* 201 (1964).

[26] The *Sixth Amendment* violation was serious, particularly "because he did not even know that he was under interrogation by a government agent." 377 *U.S.* at 206.

The government is not prohibited from continuing to investigate or place under surveillance a defendant once the adversarial process has begun, but any questioning conducted must be in compliance with the *Sixth Amendment*. As soon as adversary proceedings have commenced against an individual, he has a right to legal representation when the government interrogates him, even if he is not in custody.

Once the right to counsel has attached, a criminal defendant's waiver of the *Sixth Amendment* benefits must be explicit. Courts will carefully examine any circumstances in which a statement is made by a defendant who has retained counsel but did not have the assistance of the attorney during interrogation. The statement of law is concrete, its application can be extremely difficult. In one especially complicated case,[27] the defendant was arrested and was transported hundreds of miles. During that lengthy trip the officers engaged in actions found to be interrogation, they were designed to elicit a response from the defendant. Even though the defendant had been warned several times of his rights to a lawyer and silence, no waiver was found. The key was that the police made no serious effort "at all to ascertain whether [he] wished to relinquish that right [to a lawyer]."[28]

A defendant may agree – without notice to his lawyer – to be questioned by police without an attorney present.[29] But in order for the waiver to be upheld it must be clear and unambiguous. The prosecutor has a heavy burden to demonstrate that the defendant "voluntarily, knowingly and intelligently"[30] waived the right.

Finally, it must be noted that the *Sixth Amendment* is offense specific. The right to a lawyer applies if the defendant has been charged with an offense. The right does not apply to any crimes for which she has not been charged.[31] *Miranda*, in contrast, applies to any crime so long as the defendant is in custody during interrogation.

## *Miranda* v. *Arizona*[32]

When a law enforcement officer interrogates a person in custody, the officer must advise the suspect of certain rights. Absent this advice and an effective waiver, any resulting statement by the suspect is inadmissible to prove that person's guilt at trial. The core of the *Miranda* decision is the Court's conclusion that custodial interrogation, under the *Fifth Amendment* privilege against self-incrimination, is inherently coercive. The warnings required by *Miranda* are an attempt to

---

[27] *Brewer* v. *Williams*, 430 *U.S.* 387 (1977).
[28] *Id.*, at 405.
[29] *Id.*
[30] *Johnson* v. *Zerbst*, 304 *U.S.* 458 (1938).
[31] *Illinois* v. *Perkins*, 496 *U.S.* 292 (1990).
[32] 384 *U.S.* 436 (1966).

compensate for this coercion and make it more likely that any statements given during such interrogation are voluntary.[33]

The decision in *Miranda* came at a time when the law surrounding the voluntariness of statements seemed particularly hazy due to its required fact specific determinations.[34] The mandate of verbal warnings, and satisfaction of the rights they contained, provided a bright line rule for officers, prosecutors, and defendants. It was the Supreme Court's strongest effort to ensure compliance with, and awareness of, the rights of the accused.[35]

Statements stemming from custodial interrogation of the defendant may not be used unless the prosecution demonstrates the use of procedural safeguards effective to secure the privilege against self-incrimination. The Court described custodial interrogation as questioning initiated by law enforcement officers after a person has been taken into custody or otherwise deprived of the freedom of action in any significant way. As for the required procedural safeguards, the Supreme Court instructed: "[U]nless other fully effective means are devised to inform accused persons of their right of silence and to assure a continuous opportunity to exercise it, the following measures are required. Prior to any questioning, the person must be warned that he has a right to remain silent, that any statement he does make may be used as evidence against him, and that he has a right to the presence of an attorney, either retained or appointed. The defendant may waive effectuation of these rights, provided the waiver is made voluntarily, knowingly and intelligently. If, however, he indicates in any manner and at any stage of the process that he wishes to consult with an attorney before speaking there can be no questioning."[36]

The Court further instructed that "if the individual is alone and indicates in any manner that he does not wish to be interrogated, the police may not question him."[37]

*Miranda* warnings are only required when a suspect is interrogated while *in custody*. A defendant is in custody if her freedom of movement has been substantially limited by the police.[38] Even if the investigation of a crime has focused on the defendant, the custody requirement has only been met if the defendant is truly unable to leave during questioning.[39] The test for custody is objective, would a reasonable person have felt free to leave. The determination

---

[33] "Unless adequate protective devices are employed to dispel the compulsion inherent in custodial surroundings, no statement obtained from the defendant can truly be the product of his free choice." *Id.*, at 458.

[34] *See* text accompanying notes 1-21, *supra.*

[35] For a wide ranging discussion of the perceived strengths and weaknesses of the *Miranda* approach, *see* the various essays in Leo and Thomas, *The Miranda Debate*, Northeastern U. Press, 1998.

[36] 384 *U.S.* at 444.

[37] *Id.*

[38] *Oregon* v. *Mathiason*, 429 *U.S.* 492 (1977).

[39] *Beckwith* v. *US*, 425 *U.S.* 341 (1976). An ordinary traffic stop does not constitute 'custody' for the purposes of *Miranda. Berkemeier* v. *McCarty*, 468 *U.S.* 420 (1984).

of custody depends on the particular circumstances of the interrogation, not on the subjective views of either the officers or the person being interrogated.[40] Custody is shown when there is restraint on freedom of movement of the degree associated with a formal arrest.

A defendant's statement is subject to *Miranda* only if it is given in response to police interrogation. Volunteered statements, spontaneous remarks not made in response to questioning, are not covered.[41] The Supreme Court has, however, gone well beyond the notion of direct questioning by the police in finding interrogation present. Interrogation is not limited to any particular law enforcement type of activity; rather, the inquiry is whether the officers should know that their actions are reasonably likely to elicit an incriminating response from the suspect. As a consequence, officers speaking to one another about the severity of the crime is not interrogation,[42] while officers having a similar conversation with the suspect is interrogation.[43] Many state and lower court opinions have looked to the particular police actions in deciding if the suspect, under the Supreme Court's test, was interrogated.[44]

The Supreme Court required in its holding that a person in custody must be adequately and effectively apprised of these rights before interrogation will be allowed:

- the suspect has the right to remain silent;
- anything he says can and will be used against him at trial;
- the suspect has the right to the assistance of a lawyer;
- if the suspect cannot afford a lawyer, the government will provide one for him.[45]

While most police departments now direct officers to follow the warnings almost precisely as given above, the Supreme Court does not require a specific 'script' for the warnings. Warnings that are not exactly as set out above may still comply with *Miranda* if the defendant is given adequate information with respect to the right to have an attorney present and the right to remain silent.[46]

---

[40] *Stansbury* v. *California*, 511 *U.S.* 318 (1994).

[41] *See Stanley* v. *Wainwright*, 604 *F.2d* 379 (5th Cir. 1979), *cert. denied*, 447 *U.S.* 925 (1980); *People* v. *Leffew*, 228 *N.W.2d* 449 (Mich. 1975).

[42] *Rhode Island* v. *Innis*, 446 *U.S.* 291 (1980).

[43] Though the decision was rendered in the *Sixth Amendment* setting. *Brewer* v. *Williams*, *supra*.

[44] *See, e.g.*, *Lewis* v. *State*, 486 *U.S.* 1036 (1988) [denial of writ of certiorari in case in which defendant was shown videotape of crime]; *People* v. *Ferro*, 472 *N.E.2d* 13 (N.Y. 1984), *cert. denied*, 472 *U.S.* 1007 (1985) [stolen goods placed directly in front of defendant's cell]; *US* v. *Mesa*, 638 *F.2d* 582 (3rd Cir. 1980) [hostage negotiations].

[45] 384 *U.S.* at 445.

[46] In *California* v. *Prysock*, 453 *U.S.* 355 (1981) the defendant was not specifically told of "his right to the services of a free attorney before and during interrogation". The Court rejected the defense challenge emphasizing that no rigid adherence to the language of *Miranda* is mandated. It was sufficient that the defendant in more general terms "was told of his right to have a lawyer present prior to and during interrogation, and his right to have a lawyer appointed at no cost if he could not afford one."

As with most constitutional protections, rights grounded in *Miranda* may be waived.[47] While the waiver need not be express or explicit,[48] waiver will not be found simply because the suspect later spoke.[49] The government has "a heavy burden (...) to demonstrate that the defendant knowingly and intelligently waived [the rights]."[50] The prosecution must show that the defendant both understood the rights and voluntarily relinquished them. The issue is often raised. Judges must look to a variety of factual circumstances to determine if the waiver was both knowing and voluntary. The problem is particularly acute with defendants whose native language is not English,[51] who have mental problems,[52] or are minors.[53]

Where the defendant has indicated a desire to remain silent, all questioning must stop.[54] Questioning may resume after a significant period of time has passed and *Miranda* warnings have been repeated.[55] It is still not settled whether the subject of the later inquiry must be restricted to a crime that was not the subject of the first interrogation.[56] In contrast, where the defendant asks to see a lawyer,

---

[47] The seminal waiver case is *Johnson* v. *Zerbst*, 304 *U.S.* 458, 464 (1938):
It has been pointed out that "courts indulge every reasonable presumption against waiver" of fundamental constitutional rights and that we "do not presume acquiescence in the loss of fundamental rights." A waiver is ordinarily an intentional relinquishment or abandonment of a known right or privilege. The determination of whether there has been an intelligent waiver of right to counsel must depend, in each case, upon the particular facts and circumstances surrounding that case, including the background, experience, and conduct of the accused.

[48] *North Carolina* v. *Butler*, 441 *U.S.* 369 (1979).

[49] A striking set of facts was before the Supreme Court in *Tague* v. *Louisiana*, 444 *U.S.* 469 (1980). There the arresting officer at the suppression hearing testified that he read petitioner his *Miranda* rights from a card, that he could not presently remember what those rights were, that he could not recall whether he asked petitioner whether he understood the rights as read to him, and that he could not say yes or no whether he rendered any tests to determine whether petitioner was literate or otherwise capable of understanding his rights. The state supreme court held that the officer was not compelled to give an intelligence test to a person who has been advised of his rights to determine if he understands them. Absent a clear and readily apparent lack thereof, it can be presumed that a person has capacity to understand, and the burden is on the one claiming a lack of capacity to show that lack. The US Supreme Court summarily reversed, for "the courts must presume that a defendant did not waive his rights; the prosecution's burden is great."

[50] *Miranda, supra*, 384 *U.S.* at 475.

[51] *See, e.g.*, *US* v. *Garibay*, 143 *F.3d* 534 (9th Cir. 1998).

[52] *See, e.g.*, *US* v. *Aikens*, 13 *F.Supp.2d* 28 (D.D.C. 1998).

[53] The leading case is *Fare* v. *Michael C.*, 442 *U.S.* 707 (1979). *See also*, *In re B.M.B.*, 955 *P.2d* 1302 (Kan. 1998); *People* v. *Jones*, 566 *N.W.2d* 317 (Minn. 1997).

[54] As stated in *Miranda, supra*, 384 *U.S.* at 473: once warnings have been given, the subsequent procedure is clear. If the individual indicates in any manner, at any time prior to or during questioning, that he wishes to remain silent, the interrogation must cease. At this point he has shown that he intends to exercise his *Fifth Amendment* privilege; any statement taken after the person invokes his privilege cannot be other than the product of compulsion, subtle or otherwise. Without the right to cut off questioning, the setting of in-custody interrogation operates on the individual to overcome free choice in producing a statement after the privilege has been once invoked.

[55] *Michigan* v. *Mosely*, 423 *U.S.* 96 (1975).

[56] Compare *US* v. *Cody*, 114 *F.3d* 772, 775 (8th Cir. 1997), with, *Weeks* v. *Angelone*, 176 *F.3d* 249, 269 (4th Cir. 1999), *cert. granted* (on other grounds), 120 *S.Ct.* 30 (1999).

questioning may not be resumed.[57] The request for counsel must, though, be clear.[58] Moreover, the defendant herself may choose to reinitiate the interrogation process.[59]

The impact of *Miranda* can be striking. Still, it is limited in scope. While it is error for jurors to hear an involuntary confession, even for impeachment purposes,[60] that is not true with *Miranda*. A confession obtained in violation of *Miranda* may be used to impeach a defendant's testimony if the defendant takes the stand and testifies at trial in contradiction of the earlier confession.[61]

The US Congress was not enthusiastic about the holding in *Miranda*. In an effort "to offset the 'harmful' effects" of the Court's decision,[62] Congress enacted legislation which required federal judges to consider the giving of warnings as only one factor in determining whether the confession was voluntary and admissible.[63] For almost thirty years the courts, and the Justice Department, have generally avoided reliance on the statute which seemingly conflicted with the holding in *Miranda*.[64]

---

[57] *Edwards* v. *Arizona*, 451 *U.S.* 477 (1981). This is true even if the second interrogation is conducted by an officer who did not participate in the first. *Arizona* v. *Roberson*, 486 *U.S.* 675 (1988).

[58] Such clarity was not found in *Davis* v. *US*, 512 *U.S.* 452 (1994) where the defendant at the start of interrogation said, "Maybe I should talk to a lawyer". The Supreme Court explained: a suspect must articulate his desire to have counsel present sufficiently clearly that a reasonable police officer in the circumstance would understand the statement to be a request for an attorney [or the result would be to] transform the *Miranda* safeguards into wholly irrational obstacles to legitimate police investigative activity.

[59] As in *Oregon* v. *Bradshaw*, 462 *U.S.* 1039 (1983) where the suspect said to the officer, "Well, what is going to happen to me now?"

[60] *Mincey* v. *Arizona*, 437 *U.S.* 385 (1978).

[61] *Harris* v. *New York*, 401 *U.S.* 222 (1971). It must be the defendant herself who testifies for impeachment to be allowed. *James* v. *Illinois*, 493 *U.S.* 307 (1990).

[62] *US* v. *Crocker*, 510 *F.2d* 1129, 1136 (10th Cir. 1975).

[63] 18 *U.S.C.* § 3501 provides: (a) In any criminal prosecution brought by the US or by the District of Columbia, a confession shall be admissible in evidence if it is voluntarily given. (b) The trial judge in determining the issue of voluntariness shall take into consideration all the circumstances surrounding the giving of the confession, including (1) the time elapsing between arrest and arraignment of the defendant making the confessions, if it was made after arrest and before arraignment, (2) whether such defendant knew the nature of the offense with which he was charged or of which he was suspected at the time of making the confession, (3) whether or not such defendant was advised or knew that he was not required to make any statement and that any such statement could be used against him, (4) whether or not such defendant had been advised prior to questioning of his right to the assistance of counsel; and (5) whether or not such defendant was without the assistance of counsel when questioned and when giving such confession. The presence or absence of any of the above-mentioned factors to be taken into consideration by the judge need not be conclusive on the issue of voluntariness of the confession.

[64] Recently, however, one court – over a vigorous dissent – applied the statute in finding a confession voluntary and therefore admissible, even though in violation of *Miranda*. *US* v. *Dickerson*, 166 *F.3d* 667 (4th Cir. 1999).

## Conclusion

The judicial review of the interrogation process in the US demonstrates clearly the combination of legal bases which must be considered with even the most routine investigative procedures. Defendants may properly raise issues concerning due process, the right to counsel and also the privilege against self-incrimination. These rights are not mutually exclusive. In many cases, no serious challenge can be brought under any of the three. In some cases, however, all three may be implicated and result in the exclusion of resulting confessions.

# Proof-taking before International Tribunals

*R. May*

## Introduction

This paper will focus on proof-taking before the Tribunals, particularly on the International Criminal Tribunal for the former Yugoslavia (ICTY). Occasional reference will be made for purposes of comparison to the post-World War II Tribunals and to the *Statute* of the permanent International Criminal Court *(ICC Statute)*.

The purpose of this paper is to discuss:
- the general approach taken by the ICTY towards the evidence put before it;
- the exclusion of evidence by the Tribunal;
- recent developments aimed at expediting the trials.

Before embarking on this discussion some general matters should be borne in mind. First, three matters which *inter alia* distinguish the ICTY from national jurisdictions:

1. the Tribunal has a limited mandate, *i.e.* to try serious violations of international humanitarian law committed in the former Yugoslavia since 1991;
2. its procedure is governed by a short *Statute* (34 Articles) and the *Rules of Procedure and Evidence*. These Rules were drafted by the Judges of the Tribunal and are amended by them;
3. while the procedure is generally adversarial in nature it does have some features of the civil law system. This has led to comments to the effect that the Tribunal's practice is a mixture of both systems. However, it may be better to regard it as a unique system, adapted to its own purposes and, therefore, it is not necessarily helpful to think of its rules merely as transplants from the civil or common law systems. What is relevant is to see how they fit into the Tribunal's own system.

Secondly, three matters, common to various national jurisdictions, which must be borne in mind when considering the Tribunal's approach to evidence:

1. the trials before the Tribunal take the form of bench trials by a Chamber of three Judges who are the Judges both of fact and law;
2. the burden of proof throughout the trial is on the prosecution and the standard to which it must prove its case is this: a Trial Chamber must be satisfied beyond reasonable doubt of the guilt of an accused before convicting him;
3. judgement and sentence are combined. If an accused is convicted there is no separate sentencing procedure: it follows that evidence relating to sentence, *e.g.* mitigation must be called during the trial.

## The Tribunal's Approach to Evidence

### Types of Evidence

Reliance is placed, first, on live evidence. Rule 90(A) provides that "witnesses shall, in principle, be heard directly by the Chambers". This rule is subject to exception, to be discussed below. However, it sets out the general rule for the reception of evidence. The Tribunal thus places emphasis on the witnesses being heard by the Court: this means that the witness is subject to cross-examination and the Court can observe the witness's demeanour. However, the result has been the calling of a large number of witnesses in many of the trials as the following table of cases shows:

| Case | No. of Witnesses | Exhibits |
| --- | --- | --- |
| Tadic | 126 | 461 |
| Blaskic | 161 | 1423 |
| Kupreskic | 157 | 700 |

These figures may be compared with the Nuremberg Trial where 113 witnesses, including 19 accused, gave evidence but thousands of documents and affidavits were admitted; and the Tokyo trial where 419 witnesses gave evidence but about 5000 exhibits were admitted.

As the above figures show, a large number of documentary and other exhibits are produced in the trials before the Tribunal. Documents are generally admissible because of the relaxed approach to hearsay evidence (discussed below). A document may be excluded because of doubts about its authenticity, but such issues are often more relevant to the weight to be given to an exhibit than to its admissibility into evidence. The other types of evidence include video-recordings of events, newscasts and television film. Such evidence is freely admissible. For instance, in one case, an accused based his alibi in part on a video recording, filmed on the day when the alleged crimes occurred.

### Presentation of Evidence

The presentation of evidence essentially follows the adversarial model. It is governed by Rule 85 which provides for the following order of evidence. The prosecution calls its evidence followed by the defence. The prosecution may then call evidence in rebuttal and the defence call evidence in rejoinder. (This order must be followed: in one case the prosecution's request to reopen its case with the evidence of further rebuttal witnesses was denied.[1] The Trial Chamber said "there should be a point where accusation ends and answering the

---

[1] *Delalic*, Decision, 19 August 1998.

allegations begins".) The Trial Chamber may then call evidence: a power which Chambers are prepared to exercise. In *Blaskic* the Trial Chamber called nine witnesses to give evidence after the parties had closed their cases. Finally, the Rule provides that any relevant information which may assist the Trial Chamber in determining an appropriate sentence may be presented.[2] However, in practice, such information is usually produced during the cases of the various parties.

## The Examination of Witnesses

Rule 85 provides for examination-in-chief, cross-examination and re-examination; and for the party calling a witness to examine the witness in chief.[3] All this will be familiar to common lawyers. However, the right to cross-examine is not unlimited. Cross-examination is restricted to matters arising from examination in chief, to matters affecting credibility and such additional matters as the Court may, in its discretion, allow.[4] The purpose in restricting the scope of cross-examination is to keep it within bounds and to avoid unnecessary expenditure of time. Following a recent rule change, a party cross-examining a witness is required to put to the witness the party's case on matters about which the witness can give relevant evidence.[5] The purpose of this amendment is to:
- ensure that a witness may deal with all matters when giving evidence rather than having to return at a later stage of the trial; and
- to clarify the issues in the case.

## Admissibility of Evidence

In their search for truth war crimes tribunals have generally refused to be bound by a technical approach to the admission of evidence. This reflects the potential difficulties in obtaining probative evidence in these unusual circumstances. Thus, the Chief Prosecutor of the post-World War II trials under *Control Council Law No. 10*, Brigadier-General Telford Taylor, commented: "Both the [Nuremberg] Charter and the Ordinance [governing the trials] recognise the necessity for liberal rules of evidence concerning the events transpiring in the Third Reich where the lips of many potential witnesses were sealed by violence and many records have disappeared either by intention or by the fortunes of war."[6]

---

[2] Rule 85(A)(vi).
[3] Rule 85(B).
[4] Rule 90(H).
[5] *Ibid.*
[6] Telford Taylor, Vol. 15, *Trials of War Criminals Before the Nurernberg Military Tribunals Under Control Council Law No. 10 (1946-1949)*, at 894 (hereinafter "NMT").

This view has been reflected by a Judge of the ICTY who has referred to the "peculiarities and difficulties of unearthing and assembling materials for war crimes prosecutions conducted in relation to the territory of the former Yugoslavia".[7] As a result the ICTY has taken a flexible approach to the admissibility of evidence. The Rules relating to evidence follow this approach. Their purpose is to promote fair and expeditious trials, leaving the Trial Chambers flexibility in achieving this goal.[8] Four examples may be given:

Rule 89(C) provides that a Trial Chamber may admit "any relevant evidence which it deems to have probative value". Therefore, since there is no jury to be shielded from prejudicial material, the general tendency is to admit relevant evidence.

The Chambers are not bound by national rules of evidence.[9] In cases not provided for in the *Rules of Procedure and Evidence*, a Chamber must apply rules of evidence "which best favour a fair determination of matters before it and which are consonant with the spirit of the *Statute* and the general principles of law".[10]

There is no requirement that evidence be corroborated: a conviction may be founded on the evidence of a single credible, reliable witness.[11] The same principle applies in the ICTR[12] and has been suggested for the ICC.[13] The Tribunal has taken a robust approach to the admission of hearsay evidence. In *Tadic*, the first case before the Tribunal, the Trial Chamber admitted hearsay evidence, provided that it was relevant, probative and reliable; having regard to whether it was truthful, voluntary and trustworthy.[14] It may be noted that this decision by a Trial Chamber composed of Judges from a common law background was followed by a Trial Chamber, mainly composed of Judges with a civil law background. The latter Trial Chamber said that the Tribunal was a *sui generis* institution with its own Rules of Procedure which do not constitute a transposition of national legal systems.[15] More recently, the Appeals Chamber has referred to the practice of the Tribunal to admit hearsay evidence as well settled and said that Trial Chambers have a broad discretion under Rule 89(C) to admit relevant hearsay evidence.[16] The *ICC Statute*

---

[7] Separate Opinion of Judge Shahabuddeen, *Kovacevic*, Appeals Chamber Decision, 2 July 1998.

[8] *Aleksovski*, Appeals Chamber Decision, 16 February 1999 at para. 19.

[9] Rule 89(A).

[10] Rule 89(B).

[11] *Tadic*, Opinion and Judgement, 7 May 1997, at paras. 535-539.

[12] *Akayesu* Judgement, 2 Sept. 1998, paras. 132-135.

[13] *See* the ICC Prepcom *Draft Rules of Procedure and Evidence* (PCNICC/1999/L.4/Rev.1) at *Rule 6.2(C)*: Without prejudice to Article 66, paragraph 3 (which provides for a standard of proof of guilt beyond reasonable doubt) a Chamber of the Court shall not impose a legal requirement that corroboration is required in order to prove any crime within the jurisdiction of the Court, in particular crimes of sexual violence.

[14] *Tadic*, Decision, 5 August 1996.

[15] *Blaskic*, Decision, 21 January 1998.

[16] *Aleksovski*, Appeals Chamber Decision, 16 February 1999, at para. 15.

indicates that it may take a broadly similar approach. *Article* 69 of the *Statute* provides that "[t]he Court may rule on the relevance or admissibility of any evidence, taking into account, *inter alia*, the probative value of the evidence and any prejudice that such evidence may cause to a fair trial or to a fair evaluation of the testimony of a witness, in accordance with the *Rules of Procedure and Evidence*."

### The Exclusion of Evidence by the Tribunal

The ICTY has not followed the post-World War II tribunals in the exclusion of entire categories of evidence. For instance, the Nuremberg Tribunal refused the accused permission to produce documents implicating the Allies in war crimes,[17] and the Tokyo Tribunal excluded evidence relating to the decision to use the atom bomb.[18] However, these decisions were connected with the irrelevance of the evidence to the issues in the trial.[19] Similar considerations led one Trial Chamber of the ICTY, in a case involving alleged crimes arising from the armed conflict between Bosnian Croats and Bosnian Muslims, to exclude evidence of crimes committed by the 'other side' (characterised by the Trial Chamber as *'tu quoque'* evidence). The Trial Chamber also excluded evidence relating to the issue of which side was responsible for starting the conflict unless calling the evidence had a particular purpose relevant to the trial.[20]

It may also be noted that in the same Decision the Trial Chamber commented on the relevance of character evidence to trials before the Tribunal. The Trial Chamber said: "Evidence of the accused's character prior to the events for which he is indicted before the International Tribunal is not a relevant issue in as much as (...) war crimes and crimes against humanity may be committed by persons with no prior convictions or history of violence (...) consequently evidence of prior good, or bad, conduct on the part of the accused before the armed conflict began is rarely of any probative value before the International Tribunal."[21] (Evidence of good character may, however, be relevant to issues concerning an appropriate sentence.)

---

[17] *See,* for instance, K.R. Chaney, 'Pitfalls and Imperatives: Applying the Lessons of Nuremberg to the Yugoslav War Crimes Trials', 14 *Dick. J. Int'l L.* 76 (1995).

[18] *See,* for instance, Dissenting Opinion of Justice Pal (25 July 1946), reprinted in B.V.A. Röling & C.F. Ruters (eds.), 2 *The Tokyo Judgment: The International Military Tribunal for the Far East (IMFTE)*, 29 April 1946-12 November 1948 (1977), at 641.

[19] "Of all the rules of evidence, the most universal and the most obvious is that the evidence adduced should be alike directed and confined to the matters which are in dispute or which form the subject of investigation. Anything which is neither directly nor indirectly relevant to these matters ought, at once, to be put aside", Justice Pal, *supra.*

[20] *Kupreskic et al,* Decision, 17 February 1999.

[21] *Ibid.*

## The Rules

The most important rule in connection with the exclusion of evidence is Rule 89(D) which provides that a Chamber may exclude evidence "if its probative value is substantially outweighed by the need to ensure a fair trial". The Trial Chambers are, accordingly, provided with a broad discretion to exclude prejudicial evidence of little probative value. It is not possible to lay down general rules for the exercise of such a discretion since each case will turn on its own facts. However, the Rule must contemplate that Trial Chambers will ask themselves whether the probative value of the evidence is outweighed by its prejudicial effect on the fairness of the trial; and, if so, is it substantially outweighed? Only if the answer to both questions is 'yes' will the evidence be excluded.

Rule 95 provides Trial Chambers with a power to exclude evidence "if obtained by methods which cast substantial doubt on its reliability or if its admission is antithetical to, and would seriously damage, the integrity of the proceedings."[22] (A similar provision is to be found in the *ICC Statute*.) Two examples of the exercise of the Court's powers under Rule 95 may be given.

In the case of *Delalic et al.* one of the accused was arrested in Austria and questioned by the Austrian police. The Austrian rules of procedure prevented counsel from being present during the interview. The evidence of the interview was excluded by the Trial Chamber. It was held that statements obtained by oppressive conduct and which were not voluntary could not pass the test under Rule 95. The burden of proof was on the prosecution to prove 'beyond reasonable doubt' that the statement was voluntary. It may, therefore, be difficult for statements, taken in violation of the rights of the accused, to fall within Rule 95.[23]

In *Kordic* the defence sought to exclude materials obtained by the prosecution during the execution of a warrant to search offices in a municipal building in Bosnia. The defence submitted that the evidence should be excluded under Rule 95 since the prosecution did not have the power to search for and seize evidence in a sovereign State without the consent of the State or its participation: the prosecution should have resorted to customary international rules of judicial assistance in its attempt to obtain this evidence. Accordingly, the defence submitted that its admission would be antithetical to the integrity of the proceedings. The prosecution submitted that the accused had no standing to challenge the admissibility of the evidence since only a State could challenge any violation of its sovereignty. Secondly, the prosecution had the power, under the *Statute* and *Rules*, to conduct on-site

---

[22] Article 69(7): "Evidence obtained by means of a violation of this Statute or internationally recognised human rights shall not be admissible if: (a) The violation casts substantial doubt on the reliability of the evidence; or (b) The admission of the evidence would be antithetical to and would seriously damage the integrity of the proceedings."

[23] *Delalic et al.*, Decision, 2 September 1997.

investigations and there was no need to resort to the rules of judicial assistance. The Trial Chamber held that:

- the accused was entitled to challenge the admissibility of the evidence; but
- the submission under Rule 95 failed since the prosecution was within its powers in searching for and seizing the material: all States having an obligation to lend co-operation and assistance to the Tribunal under Article 29 of the *Statute*, stemming from the *Charter* of the United Nations (in particular Article 25 and Chapter VII). There was no need to resort to customary international rules of judicial assistance.[24]

## National Security Interests and Confidentiality

Evidence may be excluded and access to materials denied on the grounds that disclosure would be harmful to the national security interests of a State or for other reasons of confidentiality. The war in the former Yugoslavia involved the security interests of various States and there was an international presence in its territory during much of the conflict. More importantly, the States formerly a part of Yugoslavia may have access to materials which could be relevant to proceedings before the Tribunal. These States have on occasion been requested and ordered to provide materials under Article 29, which obliges them to co-operate with the Tribunal. On occasion they have responded by arguing that States have a blanket right to withhold documents because to disclose them would prejudice the State's national security interests. In *Blaskic* the Appeals Chamber considered whether the Tribunal could be prevented from examining documents which raise national security concerns. The Chamber said: "The International Tribunal was established for the prosecution of persons responsible for war crimes, crimes against humanity and genocide; these are crimes related to armed conflict and military operations. It is, therefore, evident that military documents or other evidentiary material connected with military operations may be of crucial importance, either for the prosecution or the defence, to prove or disprove the alleged culpability of an indictee, particularly when command responsibility is involved.[25] (...) [T]o allow national security considerations to prevent the International Tribunal from obtaining documents that might prove of decisive importance to the conduct of trials would be tantamount to undermining the very essence of the International Tribunal's functions."[26]

Thus, documents may be disclosable, despite national security concerns. However, procedures have been established to ensure confidentiality. These procedures have recently been codified in Rule 54*bis*. They allow for the

---

[24] *Kordic*, Decision, 25 June 1999.
[25] *Blaskic*, Judgement on the Request of the Republic of Croatia for Review of the Decision of Trial Chamber II of 18 July 1997, 29 October 1997, at para 65.
[26] *Ibid.*, para. 64.

designation of one Judge by the Trial Chamber to scrutinise the materials; closed and *ex parte* proceedings; and allowing the documents to be submitted in their redacted form with an attached affidavit by a senior State official explaining the reasons for the redaction. It may also be noted that the *ICC Statute* treats these matters extensively and provides for an elaborate procedure to meet the national security concerns of States which may deny a request for assistance only if the request concerns the production of documents or disclosure of evidence which relates to its national security.[27]

A claim of confidentiality may also be made by non-governmental organisations which, in the course of their work, have access to materials which may be of significance to cases before the Tribunal. Recently a question arose whether a former employee of the International Committee of the Red Cross could be compelled to testify. The Trial Chamber (by a majority) decided that the organisation in question had a right under customary international law to non-disclosure of the information at its disposal, since States party to the Geneva Conventions and its Protocols must be taken to have accepted the fundamental principles on which the ICRC operates, *i.e.* impartiality, neutrality and confidentiality. The majority said that although the Tribunal and the ICRC share common goals, their functions and tasks are different: the ICRC's activities have been described as 'preventive' while the International Tribunal is empowered to prosecute breaches of international humanitarian law once they have occurred.[28] On the other hand, the dissenting judge held that a balancing exercise had to be carried out and the interests of the ICRC had to be weighed against the importance of the evidence: however, the judge held that in the instant case the balance favoured the ICRC.[29]

It may be noted that similar protection is proposed for the ICRC in relation to the ICC. A draft rule would grant the organisation a privilege: however, if the Court determines that the evidence is of great importance to a particular case, efforts must be made to resolve the matter by co-operative means.[30]

## Other Methods of presenting Evidence

The ICTY has introduced a number of measures in order to provide for other methods of presenting evidence in order to expedite trials. Some of these measures are considered here:

Affidavit evidence played an extensive part in the post-World War II trials. They were introduced by both prosecution and defence in large numbers: more by the defence than the prosecution. However, if all the available witnesses had been called to give their evidence live, rather than by affidavit, the trials

---

[27] Article 90(4), *ICC Statute*.
[28] *Simic et al.*, Decision, 1 October 1999.
[29] Separate Opinion of Judge Hunt.
[30] Draft Rule 6.4(C) of the Prep Com's Draft Rules, *supra*.

would have lasted much longer than they did and fewer trials would have been held.[31] At Nuremberg affidavits were first introduced where witnesses were unavailable to give evidence: however, the practice soon became common in the interests of saving time. The opposing party would put interrogatories to the witness or would be allowed to cross-examine. In the case of the International Military Tribunal at Tokyo, affidavits were expressly admissible under the Charter, although one Judge stated that the first decision to admit affidavit evidence was debated at length and then accepted "with a certain amount of misgivings". The Tribunal recognised that by allowing affidavit evidence, the rule against leading questions lost all its importance and the effect of the interrogatory on which the affidavit was based "increases the range but decreases the accuracy of the narration".[32]

Affidavits are admissible in the ICTY under Rule 94*ter*. This rule was introduced earlier this year. It provides that a party may submit affidavits in corroboration of testimony; *i.e.*, it is contemplated that they should be used to support evidence already given before the Trial Chamber and thus avoid repetition of live testimony. The other party then has five days in which to object: if no objection is received the affidavits are admissible. If there is objection and the Trial Chamber so rules, or if the Trial Chamber so orders, the witness must be called for cross-examination. Thus, affidavits may play a part in providing supporting evidence while the court retains the discretion to order a witness to be cross-examined where the interests of justice so require. However, there is little evidence of this rule being much used to date.

Deposition evidence also played an extensive part in the post-World War II trials. The Charter permitted the appointment of officers for tasks designated by the Tribunal, including the power to have evidence taken on commission.[33] At Nuremberg, Commissioners heard 101 defence witnesses and were presented with over 1800 affidavits and reports containing summaries of nearly 200,000 affidavits, relating to the case against the accused organisations.[34]

Evidence was also taken on commission in five of the 12 subsequent trials. For example, in the *Ministries* case, the Tribunal ordered that both documentary evidence and the evidence of witnesses be taken by Commissioners during the presentation of the prosecution case. Commissioners were even given the power to rule on motions in the first instance. This procedure was extended to the defence case "because of the undue amount of time which has been used and is being consumed in the

---

[31] Vol. 15 Trials of War Criminals Before the Nuremberg Military Tribunals under Control Council Law No. 10 (1946-1949) at 746.
[32] Separate Opinion of Judge Pal, *supra*, at p. 36.
[33] Article 17(e).
[34] 15 NMT, *supra*, at p. 587.

presentation of evidence on behalf of the defence and the necessity for greater expedition of trial".[35]

The Rules of the ICTY have always provided for evidence to be given by way of deposition. As originally drafted Rule 71 provided that depositions could only be taken in exceptional circumstances and in the interests of justice. This led the Appeals Chamber to state that the Rule must be construed strictly and in accordance with its original purpose of providing an exception to the general rule that witnesses be heard directly by the Trial Chamber.[36] This restriction has not prevented the use of the rule to allow for the taking of deposition evidence in other cases where both parties have given their consent to this course. For instance, in one case a Trial Chamber ordered depositions to be taken from 70 witnesses by a Presiding Officer, noting that "exceptional circumstances exist to warrant the use of deposition evidence under Rule 71 (...) namely, the length of pre-trial detention of the accused and the complexity of the cases currently assigned to this Trial Chamber, which precludes it from setting a date for the commencement of this trial."[37]

Meanwhile, the rule has been amended to make it more flexible and to serve the purpose of expediting trials. The need to demonstrate exceptional circumstances has been removed, but it must still be in the interests of justice to order the taking of depositions. This requirement will cover such issues as the importance of the evidence and whether it is in dispute. Depositions may now be taken either at the seat of, or away from, the Tribunal and may be initiated by a party or by the Trial Chamber acting *proprio motu*. The witness is subject to examination and cross-examination by the parties under a Presiding Officer who must ensure that the deposition is taken in accordance with the rules. Objections to the admissibility of evidence are reserved for the Trial Chamber.[38]

A similar change has been made in the rule relating to evidence by video-conference link. Rule 90(A) permitted a Trial Chamber "in exceptional circumstances and in the interests of justice" to authorise the receipt of testimony via videoconference link. Evidence was received in this way in the *Tadic* case. However, the Trial Chamber noted that "the evidentiary value of testimony of a witness who is physically present is weightier than testimony given by video-link" and said that the "hearing of witnesses by video-link should therefore be avoided as much as possible".[39] The Trial Chamber therefore attached two conditions to the use of such evidence: (1) that the testimony of a witness is shown to be sufficiently important to make it unfair

---

[35] *Ibid.,* at pp. 590-591.
[36] *Kupreskic,* Appeals Chamber Decision, 15 July 1999.
[37] *Kvocka et al.,* Decision to Proceed by Way of Deposition Pursuant to Rule 71, 15 November 1999.
[38] Rule 71(E).
[39] *Tadic,* Decision on the Defence Motions to Summon and Protect Defence Witnesses and on the Giving of Evidence by Video-Link, paras 11, 19.

to proceed without it; and (2) that the witness is unable or unwilling to come to the International Tribunal.[40] Following this ruling, a Trial Chamber in another case allowed the evidence of about ten defence witnesses who were unwilling, or unable, to come to the Tribunal to be heard via video-conference link.[41]

A new rule now provides that at the request of either party a Trial Chamber may, in the interests of justice, order that testimony be received via videoconference link.[42] This follows the rule change in relation to depositions, and for the same reasons, *i.e.* to provide for flexibility and to expedite trials.

### Transcripts from Related Cases

In some of the cases before the ICTY there is a large amount of overlap in the evidence presented. As a result the same witnesses may be called to give similar evidence in a number of trials. The question then arises as to whether the transcript of a witness's evidence in one trial should be admissible in a later trial involving similar circumstances.

This question also arose in the Control Council Law No. 10 trials held at Nuremberg. Under Article VII of its *Governing Ordinance*, 'records' of other military tribunals were admissible. It was argued that 'records' should be interpreted to include extracts from a witness's evidence in one of the other trials; the purpose being to save time and to avoid the difficulties in calling witnesses. These extracts usually covered a single point or relatively minor matters and were generally admitted. In the *Farben* case, the Tribunal admitted such an extract on the same basis as affidavit evidence, provided that the prosecution produced the witness for cross-examination upon request of the defence.[43]

A similar question arose before the Appeals Chamber of the ICTY in *Aleksovski*.[44] The Appeals Chamber held that transcripts of evidence given by a witness in one trial are admissible as hearsay evidence in another trial and that the Trial Chamber's discretion to admit such evidence is not fettered by Rule 90(A) (which provides that witnesses shall, in principle, be heard directly by Trial Chambers). The Appeals Chamber recognised that the accused would thereby be denied the opportunity of cross-examining the witness, but pointed out that this is the case with any hearsay evidence. This disadvantage was mitigated in two ways: (1) the witness had previously been cross-examined by the defence in a case based on the same factual allegations; (2) the residual disadvantage to the accused was outweighed by the disadvantage which would be occasioned to the prosecution by the exclusion of this evidence.

---

[40] *Idem*, para 21.
[41] *Dokmanovic*, Decision on the Defence Motion for Videoconference Link, 29 April 1998.
[42] Rule 71*bis*.
[43] 15 NMT, *supra*, at p. 901.
[44] *Aleksovski*, Appeals Chamber Decision, *supra*, 16 February 1999.

The use of transcripts has significant timesaving potential in future trials. However, the rights of the accused must be protected. In another case, therefore, the Trial Chamber held admissible transcripts from a related case, but in doing so did not preclude the defence from making application to cross-examine the witnesses if there were significant relevant matters not raised in the related case which should be raised in the instant case.[45]

It may be noted that the *ICC Statute* makes provision for most of the above options. Article 69(2) states that the testimony of a witness at trial shall be given in person, except to the extent provided by the Article of the *ICC Statute* governing protective measures. The Court may permit the giving of oral or recorded testimony by means of video or audio technology, the introduction of documents or written transcripts, in so far as these measures are not prejudicial to or inconsistent with the rights of the accused. The draft rules proposed by the Preparatory Committee stress that the parties, any victims or their representatives, and the Trial Chamber retain the right to examine the witness if these procedures are used.[46]

**Pre-trial Management**

The rules of the ICTY relating to pre-trial management are set to play an increasingly important part in the expediting of cases. The purpose is to clarify the issues in the case as early as possible and to get the case ready so that the trial itself may proceed expeditiously.

At first this was a matter of practice.[47] Later, amendments to the *Rules* provided for the designation of a pre-trial Judge and for 'Pre-trial' and 'Pre-defence' Conferences respectively to be held before the prosecution and defence cases.[48] Under these Rules the Trial Chamber could order the parties to file (1) pre-trial briefs; (2) statements of what was admitted and what was in dispute in the law or in fact; and (3) lists of witnesses and exhibits on which they intend to rely at trial.

Under the most recent amendments to the Rules the pre-trial Judge will be in the driving seat and will oversee the filing of these documents.[49] The timetable contemplates, first, that the Prosecutor should file the documents (as above). The pre-trial Judge will then require the parties to meet and discuss the issues relevant to the preparation of the case.

After all filings and full disclosure by the prosecutor the pre-trial Judge will set time limits for the defence to file a pre-trial brief setting out: (1) in general terms the nature of the defence; (2) the matters on which the accused takes issue with the prosecution; and (3) the reasons for so doing. Thus, the

---

[45] *Kordic*, Decision, 29 July 1999.
[46] Draft Rules 6.26-6.27, ICC Prep Com Draft Rules, *supra*.
[47] *Dokmanovic*, Order, 28 Nov. 1997.
[48] Rules 65*bis*, 73*bis* and 73*ter*.
[49] IT/32/Rev. 17, Rule 65*ter*.

defence will be required to make these disclosures *before* the case begins rather than at the close of the prosecution case (as the Rules previously required). The object is to clarify the issues so that it is clear what is in dispute and what is not, thus saving the calling of unnecessary witnesses to deal with matters not in dispute. The approach to both sides is one of 'cards on the table'. The aim is to assist in the resolution of preliminary issues before the trial. The trial itself can then focus on the essential issues in dispute.

The Trial Chamber retains the power to call on the parties to shorten the estimated length of examination-in-chief of some witnesses, or to reduce the number of witnesses being called to prove the same facts.[50]

The roles of the pre-trial Judges or Trial Chambers in pre-trial management are not to be confused with that of the Pre-trial Chamber in the future ICC: the latter will also have powers of investigation.[51]

**Conclusion**

The Tribunal is gathering experience in international criminal evidence and procedure and constructing its own system. It has generally taken a flexible approach to evidence, in keeping with the tradition of the post-World War II trials. It seems the ICC will also follow this approach. But the International Tribunal has an advantage: its Judges have been able to amend its Rules relatively easily in order to meet new challenges and to find new ways to expedite trials within the boundaries established by the *ICC Statute*. Rules of evidence in the case of the ICC are already provided for in the *Statute* and since the *ICC Statute* is a Treaty it will be both difficult and slow to amend it. The Judges of the ICC will have only a limited role in this process.

---

[50] Rules 73*bis* and 73*ter*.
[51] *See* for example, Article 57(3) of the *ICC Statute*.

# Playing by the Rules: a Comparative Perspective of Exclusionary Rules of Expert Evidence in South Africa

*L. Meintjes-Van der Walt*

## Introduction

The trial proceedings in South Africa, the Netherlands and England & Wales are subject to certain rules which govern the nature of the trial in terms of both the order of events and to a greater or lesser extent (depending on the jurisdiction) questions of admissibility of, presentation and justification of expert evidence.

English law of evidence is characterised by exclusionary rules of evidence, which prevents certain evidence from being brought before the trier of fact.[1] The origin of these rules has traditionally been associated with jury trials.[2] Even though trial by jury has been abolished in South Africa, the exclusionary rules of evidence have been retained. This fact supports the view of some commentators that suggests that a second factor responsible for the origin and continuance of the exclusionary rules is the adversarial procedure itself.[3]

The Dutch criminal justice system by contrast is not characterised by an intricate system of admissibility rules. The differences in approach between the common law and continental law is succinctly stated by Mannheim:[4] "English law of evidence is mainly concerned with the question of *admissibility*, continental law more with the question of *value*. English law eliminates a great deal of evidence at the very beginning, because it may mislead the jury. Continental law comparatively seldom prohibits the admission of evidence. That was originally a consequence of trial without jury."[5] (My emphasis.)

---

[1] *Phipson on Evidence* (1928) para 1.02; Twining *Theories of Evidence: Bentham and Wigmore* (1989).

[2] Love, 'The Applicability of Rules of Evidence in Non-Jury Trials', 1951-1952 (24) *Rocky ML Review* 480: "It is no secret that the Anglo-American system of evidence is a product of the jury system. The theory of the rules is bottomed on a deep-rooted distrust of the lay mind, based in turn on the supposition that a jury is unable to hear doubtful evidence without giving to it the same weight as the direct evidence of a truthful witness. Even today the jurymen are considered children who cannot be trusted. The system has been likened to a sieve and is premised on the principle of exclusion, consisting as it does of a body of rules of admissibility. As such, the system is distinctly a thing apart from an approach to the problem of discovering truth by reference to a pure science of logical proof".

[3] Tapper & Cross, *Evidence*, 6th ed. (1985) 1. A third factor is said to be the importance attached to the oath.

[4] Mannheim, 'Trial by Jury in Modern Continental Criminal Law', 1937 53 *LQR* 388.

[5] *Ibid.*, 388-389.

This does not mean that rules of evidence are not present in continental law. In civil law jurisdictions, as Nijboer explains, these rules are modelled as decision and argumentation rules.[6] These rules determine the bases on which courts may decide whether or not to hear experts and other witnesses presented by the prosecution or defence, as well as the grounds for determining the means of proof that a court may utilise in coming to a decision.[7] Although the Dutch system is inherently a system of free proof, those rules of evidence that do exist, have as their purpose the same objectives as the exclusionary rules of evidence in common law jurisdictions.[8] Those objectives are to vouchsafe that evidence used by the trier of fact is not only relevant, but also reliable.[9]

Given that relevance and reliability are the respective purposes of the rules of evidence and procedure, this paper investigates the development of certain rules of evidence pertaining specifically to the realm of expert evidence. Section 2 by way of introduction, briefly looks at the concepts relevance and reliability. The paper also discusses the extent to which it can be said that these rules exist in all three comparator countries, either in the guise of admissibility rules or as decision and argumentation rules. The primary focus in this paper is on the rules which in common law jurisdictions can be described as 'admissibility rules of expert evidence'. The extent to which the objectives of reliability and relevance is realised within the comparator jurisdictions is thus investigated under the convenience headings of 'The Field of Expertise Rule', 'The Common Knowledge Rule', 'The Ultimate Issue Rule' and 'The Basis Rule'.[10]

This paper also sets out to analyse and critically evaluate the *rationes* for the different rules of evidence pertaining to the evidence of expert witnesses in South Africa, the Netherlands and England & Wales. Finally, the paper gives consideration to whether these so-called rules of expert evidence should, in the South African context, continue to function as rules of admissibility.

## Relevance and Reliability

No matter how qualified an expert is or how incontrovertible the proofs of the field of expertise to which he attests, such evidence is meaningless to the criminal justice process, unless the evidence is relevant to the issues

---

[6] Nijboer, 'Common Law Tradition in Evidence Scholarship Observed from a Continental Perspective', 1993 41 *Am. J. Comp. Law* 299 314.

[7] According to Article 338 of the *Dutch Code of Criminal Procedure* only the following categories of evidence may serve as a 'legal means of proof': (1) the judge's own observations (2) statements made by the accused (3) statements made by a witness (4) statements made by an expert (5) written documents.

[8] Nijboer, *supra*, 318-319.

[9] *Ibid. See also* the *United States Federal Rules of Evidence (FRE)*, FRE 702 that requires admissible expert evidence to be reliable and relevant.

[10] Freckelton, *The Trial of the Expert* (1987).

concerned.[11]

Experts testifying to their opinions are customarily regarded as an exception to the opinion rule in English and South African law.[12] The general rule of evidence is that evidence of opinion is excluded, and that witnesses may only testify as to what they themselves have perceived with one of their five senses. The opinion of an expert is, however, admissible if it is relevant. It is relevant if the expert by reason of his special knowledge or skill is better qualified to draw an inference than the trier of fact.[13] An expert witness is therefore not deemed to be of assistance to the court where the area of his testimony falls within the common knowledge of the trier of fact. This test for relevance contains within it two of the rules of evidence customarily applied to expert evidence viz. the so-called 'Field of Expertise Rule' and the 'Common Knowledge Rule'. In *Holtzhauzen* v. *Roodt*[14] the admissibility of the opinion evidence of two witnesses whom the defendant in a defamation action proposed to call, was challenged. The one witness, a psychologist, social worker and counsellor, would testify that women who have been raped would not often reveal the incident to third parties immediately after it has occurred and that it was common for such victims to exhibit radical changes in behaviour. The evidence of this witness was received because it was helpful and of assistance to the court since the witness was better qualified than the judicial officer to draw the inferences in question.

The other witness, a clinical psychologist, would testify that the defendant had consulted him on a number of occasions and had told him that she had been raped by the plaintiff, that she had said so twice whilst under hypnosis during therapy sessions, and that it was his opinion that she was telling the truth. This challenge was, however, successful, the court holding that evidence of that kind was irrelevant since it would lead to the balancing of opinion between witnesses which would "tend to shift responsibility from the Bench to the witness-box" and to a procedure which would resemble a "gladiatorial pit between witnesses rather than a cool and hopefully calm assessment of the evidence in its entirety as received from all witnesses, not just experts".[15] This successful challenge of the expert opinion of the clinical psychologist in *Holtzhauzen* v. *Roodt* can be seen as the court's application of what has become to be known as the 'Ultimate Issue Rule'. Historically the courts have always striven to prevent any witness from expressing his opinion on an issue

---

[11] *S* v. *Shivute* 1991 1 *SACR* 656 (NM) 662e; *S* v. *Loubscher* 1979 3 *SA* 47 (A) 57 F-G; 60 B-C.

[12] Zeffertt, 'Opinion Evidence', 1976 *SALJ* 275. It should be noted that the opinion rule assumes that there is a clear distinction between fact and opinion which does not accord with reality, as observed by Thayer: "In a sense all testimony as to matters of fact is opinion evidence: *i.e* it is a conclusion from phenomena and mental impressions." Thayer, *A Preliminary Treatise on the Law of Evidence*, (1898).

[13] Hoffmann & Zeffertt, *The South African Law of Evidence*, 4th ed. (1988) 97.

[14] 1997 4 *SA* 766 (W).

[15] *Ibid.*, 774 I-J.

which the court has to decide.

As has been indicated above, the primary requirement which any piece of evidence tendered in common law courts must satisfy, is that it must be relevant.[16] Relevance usually relates to the probative potential of an item of information to support or negate the existence of a fact of consequence *(factum probandum)*. Any item of evidence must therefore, have the potential rationally to affect the decision.[17]

'Relevance' is, however, as Damaška[18] indicates, not an issue that determines admissibility in the Continental legal tradition. On the continent the probative potential of an item of evidence is seldom considered apart from the reliability of source. Where this is done, it would be to determine whether an item is 'material'. 'Materiality' in turn deals with the issue whether an item of information is capable of establishing a fact that would make a difference in terms of the case's legal theory.[19]

Although logically relevant, evidence at common law may be excluded if its probative value is substantially outweighed by the danger of unfair prejudice, confusion of the issues or by considerations of undue delay.[20] The reliability of the evidence could thus influence its juridical relevance and hence its admissibility. This is illustrated in *R* v. *Trupedo*[21] where evidence as

---

[16] *See* Section 210 of the *Criminal Procedure Act*: irrelevant evidence inadmissible. No evidence as to any fact, matter or thing shall be admissible which is irrelevant or immaterial and which cannot conduce to prove or disprove any point or fact at issue in criminal proceedings. The following definition of 'relevant' by Stephen, *Digest of the Law of Evidence*, 11th ed. (1930) Article 1 was approved by Watermeyer CJ in *R* v. *Katz* 1946 *AD* 781. "The word relevant means that any two facts to which it is applied are so related to each other that according to the common course of events one, either taken by itself, or in connection with other facts, proves or renders probable the past, present or future existence or non-existence of the other."

[17] Thayer, *Preliminary Treatise on Evidence at Common Law*, (1969) states: "The law furnishes no test of relevancy. For this, it tacitly refers to logic and experience", 265. *See also* Thayer, 'Law and Logic', 1900 14 *Harv LR* 139.

[18] Damaška, *Evidence Law Adrift*, (1997) 55.

[19] *Ibid.*

[20] *Makin* v. *AG for New South Wales* [1894] *AC* 57; *R* v. *Katz* 1946 *AD* 71; *Gosschalk* v. *Rossouw* 1966 2 *SA* 485 (A). The weighing up of the prejudicial effect against the probative value of the evidence as exclusionary standard, is clearly distinguished by Sopinka J in the Canadian case of *R* v. *Mohad* 1994 114 *DLR* (4th 419 (SCC) from the relevance enquiry: "Although *prima facie* admissible if so related to a fact in issue that it tends to establish it, that does not end the inquiry. This merely determines the logical relevance of the evidence. Other considerations enter into the decision as to admissibility. This further inquiry may be described as a cost benefit analysis. (…) Cost in this context is not used in its traditional economic sense but rather in terms of its impact on the trial process. Evidence that is otherwise logically relevant may be excluded on this basis, if its probative value is overborne by its prejudicial effect, if it involves an inordinate amount of time which is not commensurate with its value or if it is misleading in the sense that its effect on the trier of fact, particularly a jury, is out of proportion to its reliability. While frequently considered as an aspect of legal relevance, the exclusion of logically relevant evidence on these grounds is more properly regarded as a general exclusionary rule." (427-8)

[21] 1920 *AD* 58 62.

to the behaviour of a police dog in identifying an intruder was rejected on the grounds of irrelevance.[22] Chief Justice Innes stated: "We have no scientific or accurate knowledge as to the faculty by which dogs of certain breeds are said to be able to follow the scent of one human being, rejecting the scent of all others." It was further held that even if the evidence is not regarded as hearsay "there is too much uncertainty as to the constancy of [the dog's] behaviour and as to the extent of the factor of error involved to justify us in drawing legal inferences therefrom."[23] He concluded that the evidence was not relevant, but that relevance is a question of fact.[24] In *S* v. *Shabalala*[25] it was shown that expert testimony if shown to be reliable of tracking by dogs, may very well be admissible. One way in which an expert can convince the court of the reliability of his evidence, could be by clearly showing the bases for his opinions. This requirement has developed into what has become known as the 'Basis Rule'.

The following sections discuss the significance of evidential rules for expert evidence under the headings of 'The Field of Expertise Rule', 'The Common Knowledge Rule', 'The Ultimate Issue Rule' and 'The Basis Rule' in turn.

### The Field of Expertise Rule

Although expert witnesses have been permitted to give evidence on an indefinite number of subjects, it has always been based on the principle that they should be properly designated experts. In South Africa and England & Wales, the testimony of experts who do not possess the required expertise is inadmissible.

In English and South African law the requirement of expertise does not mean that the witness needs to be professionally trained in the particular area, neither does it mean that the fact that the witness is a professional, necessarily qualifies him as an expert.[26] The latter instance is concisely stated by Addleson

---

[22] *Ibid.*, 63.

[23] *Id.*

[24] *Trupedo's* case, for instance, is not authority for the broad proposition that evidence of tracking by dogs is in all circumstances or in any situation irrelevant, but merely that the evidence on the facts of that particular case was irrelevant. *See* Hoffmann 1974 *SALJ* 237 238. As Nestadt AJA pointed out in *S* v. *Shabalala* 1986 4 *SA* 734 (A) 742. *Trupedo's* case, did not decide that evidence of tracking by dogs may never, in any situation be relevant, but rather that it was irrelevant given (1) the proven body of scientific knowledge and (2) the system of trial by jury. Of these two variables, only the first was treated in *Shabalala's* case as being significant. If, for example, acceptable expert testimony had been adduced in that case which established the reliability of tracking by dogs, the court would be free to consider whether a proper foundation had been laid for the reception of the evidence.

[25] 1986 4 *SA* 734 (A).

[26] *See Wigmore on Evidence* (1988) Vol 2 750: "The object is to be sure that the question to the witness will be answered by a person who is fitted to answer it. His fitness, then, is a fitness to
(to be continued)

J in *Menday* v. *Protea Assurance Co (Pty) Ltd*:[27] "However eminent an expert may be in a general field, he does not constitute an expert in a particular sphere unless by special study or experience he is qualified to express an opinion on that topic. The danger of holding otherwise – of being overawed by a recital of degrees and diplomas – are obvious; the Court has then no way of being satisfied that it is not being blinded by pure 'theory' untested by knowledge or practice. The expert must either himself have knowledge or experience in the special field on which he testifies (whatever general knowledge he may also have in pure theory) or he must rely on knowledge or experience of experts other than themselves who are shown to be acceptable experts in that field."

The *Dutch Code of Criminal Procedure* does not set out any specific criteria for expertise and Article 299, that deals with the involvement of the expert in the criminal process, merely states that a person submitting a written report should be an expert and should furnish reasons. The issue of what constitutes expertise in terms of Article 343[28] of the *Dutch Criminal Code* was decided by the *Hoge Raad* (the Supreme Court of the Netherlands) in 1928.[29] The term *'wetenschap'* (knowledge) in that provision was said to include: "all special knowledge one possesses or is assumed to possess, even though such knowledge does not qualify as 'science' in the more limited sense of the word, corresponding to the fact that since long, experts have been heard in criminal processes whose special knowledge did not make them practitioners of science."[30]

Whether Dutch courts consider whether experts are sufficiently qualified to act as such is often not apparent from decisions of the courts. Therefore, as in South Africa and England & Wales, experts need not be professionals or academically qualified, as long as they have relevant experience and knowledge in the particular field.[31]

---

answer on that point. He may be fitted to answer about countless other matters, but that does not justify accepting his views on the matter in hand. Since experiential capacity is always relative to the matter in hand, the witness may, from question to question, enter or leave the class of persons fitted to answer, and the distinction depends on the kind of subject primarily, not on the kind of person." In *Mohamed* v. *Shaik* 1978 4 *SA* 523 (N) the court held that a general medical practitioner, even though he held the degrees MB ChB and had four years' experience, was not qualified to speak authoritatively on the significance of findings in a pathologist's report concerning the fertility of semen.

[27] 1976 1 *SA* 565 (ECD).

[28] Article 343 *Dutch Code of Criminal Procedure*: "A statement by an expert is understood to be his opinion, made in the course of the investigation of the trial, as to what his knowledge teaches him about that which is the subject of his opinion."

[29] HR 24 July 1928, *NJ* 1929.

[30] *Ibid.*, 150. Cf. Borst, *De Bewijsmiddelen in Strafzaken*, who argues for a more restricted meaning of *'wetenschap'* to only mean 'an ordered system of knowledge' (262-264).

[31] Hielkema, 'Experts in Dutch Criminal Procedure', in: Malsch & Nijboer (eds.), *Complex Cases Perspectives on the Netherlands Criminal Justice System* (1999), p. 28.

In practice experts are seldom called to testify in open court and judges
therefore limit themselves to documented expert evidence contained in the
*dossier*. In the absence of *viva voce* evidence, the court in consequence,
seldom has the opportunity to elicit information from expert witnesses
regarding their expertise. Van Kampen[32] offers a further reason for Dutch
courts not querying expert expertise, namely that the majority of Dutch expert
reports are compiled by permanent forensic experts or specially trained police
officers, who are under permanent oath[33] and are deemed to testify only within
the bounds of their professional expertise. Potential problems can arise in the
case of documented expert evidence emanating from other experts, who do not
fall within these categories and who therefore not endowed with the same
credentials. This has led to a growing concern among academics in the
Netherlands who suggest that the Dutch courts and prosecutors should
scrutinise the qualifications of persons reporting to them more closely.[34]
Extreme care and scrutiny are therefore required, particularly in the areas of
new and sometimes ill defined areas of so-called expertise.

*Hoge Raad* decisions indicate that the decision whether someone is an
expert or not, falls within the province of the trial court, a discretion with
which the *Hoge Raad* will not interfere.[35] Traditionally trial courts were under
no obligation to justify their determination whether a person was an expert or
not.[36] This practice exhibits similarities to the common law admissibility rules
where as a general rule, reasons for holding expert evidence admissible need
not be given by trial courts. If on face value the expert has the qualifications
and competence to perform the necessary procedures to come to a conclusion,
there is no requirement that reasons should be given for admitting such
evidence.[37] Reasons are only required to substantiate a decision that accords
weight to such admitted expertise.[38] Recently in the Netherlands, as a result of
the "Anatomically Correct Dolls" decision[39] as well as the so-called
"Shoeprint" case[41] where the defence explicitly[42] challenged the reliability of

---

[32] Van Kampen, *Expert Evidence Compared Rules and Practices in the Dutch and American
Criminal Justice System* (1998).
[33] Articles 228.2, 152 and 229.4 *Dutch Code of Criminal Procedure. See also Deskundigen in
Nederlandse Strafzaken* (1996).
[34] Nijboer, *Forensische Expertise* (1990), p. 65; Hielkema, pp. 43-134; Crombag, Van Koppen &
Wagenaar, *Dubieuze Zaken De Psychologie van Strafrechtelijk Bewijs* (1992), pp. 314-315.
[35] HR 27 March 1933 *NJ* 1933 907; HR 18 October 1977 *NJ* 1978 534; HR 13 January 1981 *NJ*
1981 79 m.nt. ThWvV; HR 12 January 1993 *DD* 93.239.
[36] HR 18 October 1977 *NJ* 1989 534; HR 18 September 1978 *NJ* 1979 120; HR 12 January 1993
*DD* 93 239. *See* further Knigge 'Het Wettelijk Bewijsstelsel', in: Knigge (ed.), *Leerstukken van
Strafprocesrecht* (1991), p. 115.
[37] *S* v. *Williams* 1985 1 *SA* 750 (k) 753 G-I; *S* v. *Nyathe* 1988 2 *SA* 211 (0) 215 I; *S* v. *Adams*
1983 2 *SA* 577 (A); *S* v. *Januarie* 1980 2 *SA* 598 (c) 600 B-C; *S* v. *Ramgobin* 1986 4 *SA* 117 (N).
[38] *S* v. *Nyathe* 1988 2 *SA* 211 (OPA) 216.
[39] HR 28 February 1989, *NJ* 1989, 748, m.nt. 'tH; *see also* HR 14 March 1989, *NJ* 1989, 747.
[40] HR 27 January 1998, *NJ* 1998, 404, m.nt. JR (this case concerned an orthopaedic shoemaker as
(to be continued)

experts and their reports, trial courts relying on the evidence of experts now are required to explain why the experts' methods are considered reliable and to what extent the experts are deemed to be adequately qualified.[43] These *Hoge Raad* decisions seem to imply that if a trial court cannot justify why a person should be considered an expert, such person will not be deemed an expert and no reliance can be placed on his opinion.[44] Where trial courts have not motivated why an expert is considered such and his statement is preferred on a crucial aspect despite a challenge, the *Hoge Raad* can reverse the decision.[45]

From the above analysis one could, therefore, infer that the degree and nature of the expert's specialised knowledge is an issue which needs to be determined by the trial court in all three comparator countries. Where expertise of the expert is contested, the courts in all three comparator countries will have to give reasons why reliance is placed on that evidence. These court practices prompt one to ask whether the differences between South Africa and England & Wales on the one hand and the Netherlands on the other hand, are not in fact more apparent than real. Whether the 'expertise rule' is formulated as an admissibility rule or as a decision rule, the effect in practice is really the same. The evidence of experts who do not possess sufficient skill will be held to be inadmissible in South Africa as well as in England & Wales. By contrast, in the Netherlands such evidence will be admissible. However, although admissible, evidence by experts who are not adequately qualified, cannot be used by judges as a basis for their findings. Thus, even though couched as a decision-making rule, the effect in practice would be the same as if the evidence had been excluded at the outset.

The application of the common law 'Field of Expertise' rule in South Africa and England & Wales has focused on the skill, experience and training of the particular expert. Court experts are required therefore to indicate to the court, that they have been trained in a particular discipline or have gained experience in a particular field. Court *dicta* are usually silent on which particular fields or areas of expertise and skill would qualify a witness as an

---

a shoeprint expert).

[41] HR 27 January 1998, *NJ* 1998, 404, m.nt. JR (this case concerned an orthopaedic shoemaker as a shoeprint expert).

[42] It is not necessary for the court to respond to general or implicit challenges regarding whether or not the expert is sufficiently qualified to testify to a particular field of expertise. *See* HR 3 March 1998 *NJB* 1998 No 52.

[43] *See* HR 30 March 1999, *NJ* 1999, 415, where the judge of Appeal held that the court had not given sufficient consideration to the controversial nature of the methods applied by the psychologist *in casu*.

[44] In the Dutch criminal justice system it is the court and not the prosecutor who bears the burden of proving the case beyond a reasonable doubt. Langemeier, 'Beweringslast en Bewijsrisico in het Strafproces', 1931 *TVS* 73. *See also* Nijboer & Sennef for a critical commentary on the approach in Dutch courts to the justification of their decisions: *motivering van de bewezenverklaring*. 'Justification', in: Malsch & Nijboer, *Complex Cases* (1999), pp. 11-26.

[45] Reijntjes' note HR 27 January 1998, *NJ* 1998, 404.

expert.

In the past, when court experts came from widely accepted fields of knowledge, such an enquiry as indicated above would have been superfluous. However, in the rapidly developing world of science and technology, new and novel theories and techniques are constantly emerging. This area between the acknowledged accepted fields of expertise and cutting-edge experimentation has been aptly referred to as the 'twilight zone' of expertise.[46] These novel techniques could be potentially powerful tools of inculpability[47] as well as exculpability.[48] The issue of how the legal system should deal with expert evidence that has not fully "emerged from the experimental to the demonstrable" confronted the United Court of Appeals for the District of Columbia as early as 1923.[49] In *Frye*, the court was confronted with the admissibility of a primitive precursor to the polygraph. The criterion for admissibility was held to be whether the basis of the theory or technique had gained 'general acceptance' within the relevant field: "While the courts will go a long way in admitting expert testimony deduced from a well recognised scientific principle of discovery, the thing from which the detection is made must be sufficiently established to have gained general acceptance in the particular field in which it belongs."[50]

In 1993 the "general acceptance in the scientific community" test as propounded by the *Frye*[51] case, was substituted in Federal courts by the so-called "reliability" test propounded in the *Daubert*[52] matter. The majority in *Daubert* v. *Merrell Dow Pharmaceuticals* noted the distinction between scientific 'validity' (does the principle support what it purports to show?) and 'reliability' (does application of the principle produce consistent results?). The court further maintained that in a case involving scientific evidence, evidentiary reliability (which they defined as "trustworthiness") was necessary as a precondition to admissibility. This would be "based upon scientific validity". It held that the requirement that the evidence "assist" the trier of fact necessitates a valid scientific connection to the pertinent inquiry as a condition of admissibility. The court held that the following series of *indicia* would generally be relevant to the inquiry whether particular scientific evidence would assist the trier of fact:

1. whether it can be or has been tested;
2. whether the theory or technique has been subjected to peer review and publication as a means of increasing the likelihood that substantive flaws in methodology will be detected;

---

[46] *Frye* v. *United States* 293 F1013 (1923).
[47] For example DNA fingerprinting, voice identification, polygraph, offender profiling.
[48] For example DNA fingerprinting, battered woman syndrome, post traumatic stress syndrome.
[49] *Frye* v. *United States* 293 F1013 (1923).
[50] *Ibid.*
[51] 293 F1013 (1923).
[52] *Daubert* v. *Merrell Dow Pharmaceuticals* 113 *S.Ct.* 2786 (1993).

3. whether the known or potential rate of error and the existence and maintenance of standards controlling the technique's operation have been established; and finally

4. whether a technique has gained general acceptance within the scientific community.

In England & Wales and South Africa there are no reported cases where courts had to decide on the admissibility of novel forms of scientific[53] expertise.

In contrast to the American approach, it seems that in these two countries the reliability of scientific evidence is usually a factor to be considered in the determination of the weight which should be accorded to the evidence, rather than a factor determining its admissibility.[54] Novel scientific techniques have also not been the subject of jurisprudential analysis in the Netherlands. In the Netherlands it is practice, rather than admissibility rules, that dictates that certain novel methods of expert evidence such as bite mark evidence, the results of lie detectors, hypnosis and the use of truth serum, will not be used by trial courts.[55]

It can be expected that with the rapid development of new scientific, technical and social scientific techniques and procedures, part of an on-going debate would be consideration by all three comparator countries of ways and means to develop criteria and standards by which to determine whether certain types of evidence should be admitted by courts. However, as the American experience has indicated, such criteria are often difficult to define, giving weight to the existing practice in South Africa, England & Wales as well as in the Netherlands, to admit such evidence and leaving it to the parties and the trier of fact to determine the degree of reliance that should be placed on the evidence. In the determination of the *value* that should attach to such evidence, courts may, I suggest, borrow profitably from the guidelines set out in *Daubert*.[56]

### The Common Knowledge Rule

Courts in the common law legal system have traditionally refused to hear expert evidence on matters they have classified as areas of common knowledge, declaring that in such circumstances no assistance is required from experts.[57] Evidence would usually be deemed to be of assistance or 'helpful' if it has the capacity to add to the knowledge of the triers of facts and to assist in

---

[53] *See*, however, *R* v. *Trupedo* 1920 *AD* 58 and *S* v. *Shabalala* 1986 4 *SA* 734 (A) dealing with admissibility of evidence of the behaviour of tracking dogs and how the reliability of the procedure could influence the admissibility of the evidence.
[54] Unless it can be shown that it is so unreliable that it is irrelevant.
[55] Van Kampen, *Expert Evidence Compared* (1998), p. 269.
[56] This is, however, a topic that does not fall within the parameters of this paper.
[57] *R* v. *Turner* [1975] 1 *QB* 834 841.

their deliberations.[58] In the leading English decision on the common
knowledge rule, *R* v. *Turner*,[59] it was held that: "An expert's opinion is
admissible to furnish the court with scientific information which is likely to be
outside the experience and knowledge of a judge or jury. If on the proven facts
a judge or jury can form their own conclusions without help, then the opinion
of an expert is unnecessary. In such a case if it is given dressed up in scientific
jargon it may make judgement more difficult. The fact that an expert witness
has impressive scientific qualifications does not by that fact alone make his
opinion on matters of human nature and behaviour within the limit of
normality any more helpful than that of jurors themselves; but there is a danger
that they may think it does."[60]

In *S* v. *Nel*[61] the Cape Provincial Division approved and applied the rule set
out in *Turner* on the basis that post 30 May 1961 English decisions have
persuasive authority in South Africa.[62]

In the Netherlands, the helpfulness or otherwise of expert evidence is not a
criterion that determines the admissibility of the evidence. However, in
practice when an investigating or trial judge calls upon experts, it would be
because their assistance and advice are considered to be helpful and necessary.
Article 339 of the *Dutch Criminal Code of Procedure* specifically states that
no proof is required of facts or circumstances that belong to the realm of
common knowledge. The defence may on the basis of article 263 of the *Dutch
Code of Criminal Procedure* request the prosecutor to summons a particular
expert for the court hearing. Where this request is refused, and the accused
appeals to the court to accede to the request, it can be refused on the basis that
it is not necessary. In my view, the potential of being of assistance to the trier
of fact would also in this context be a factor that would inform the court in
reaching its decision.

Where "assistance to the trier of fact" is, therefore, a touchstone that can
prevent expert evidence from being introduced, the rationale for the exclusion
needs to be closely scrutinised. Whereas both common law and continental
judges are likely to consider evidence in the field of physical and medical
sciences as likely to be beyond the realm of common knowledge, evidence
relating to human behaviour has the potential to present difficulties.

Judges in England & Wales seem to have an ambivalent attitude towards
evidence from experts on mental conditions. To some extent, they recognise
that a psychiatrist or psychologist may be able to provide useful testimony

---

[58] Raitt, 'A New Criterion for the Admissibility of Scientific Evidence – The Metamorphosis of
Helpfulness', in: Reece (ed.), *Law & Science Current Legal Issues* (1998), vol 1 153. *See also S*
v. *Van As* 1991 (2) *SA SV* (W) 86e; *Colgate Palmolive (Pty) Ltd* v. *Elida-Gibbs (Pty) Ltd* 1989 3
*SA* 759 (W).
[59] [1975] 1 *QB* 834.
[60] *Ibid* 841.
[61] 1990 2 *SACR* 136 (C).
[62] *See also* Section 252 of Act 51 of 1970.

about matters that are outside the experience of judges or jurors. At the same time, it is feared that mental experts will usurp the role of the jury or other trier of fact,[63] unless a clear line is drawn between abnormal and normal mental states. The latter has been held to include lust, anger and other undesirable emotions which, judges believe are perfectly capable of being understood by ordinary people without expert assistance.[64] In practice this has meant that experts can only testify on the 'abnormal'.[65] It has even been suggested[66] that for expert testimony to be admissible, not only must there be a degree of abnormality in the accused's mental state, but there should also be a degree of abnormality sufficient to take his condition "beyond the experience of non-medical people".[67]

Therefore, where an accused, puts forward a defence, such as provocation or duress, which depends on subjective criteria, expert evidence will be inadmissible. In R v. Turner[68] in which the appellant relied upon a defence of provocation at his trial for the murder of his girlfriend, whom he had killed with a hammer, upon hearing of her infidelity, the trial judge, Bridge J refused to admit psychiatric evidence. His decision was upheld by the Court of Appeal.[69] This decision confirmed the Court of Appeal's earlier judgement in R v. Chard[70] and has subsequently been followed in Weightman v. The Queen[71] but distinguished the Privy Council's decision in Lowery v. R[72] on its

---

[63] See the Ultimate Issue Rule infra.

[64] See R v. Turner [1975] 1 QB 834 at 841: "Jurors do not need psychiatrists to tell them how ordinary folk who are not suffering from any mental illness are likely to react to the stresses and strains of life."

[65] R v. Reynolds [1989] Crim L.R. 220; Weightman v. The Queen [1991] Crim L.R. 204.

[66] Experts have been permitted to give evidence on the following issues: R v. Holmes (1953) 1 WLR 686 (whether an accused was suffering from a disease of the mind within the Mc'Naghten rules); R v. Bailey (1977) 66 Cr.App.R. 31 (whether an accused is suffering from diminished responsibility, but note the distinction drawn between diminished responsibility and other forms of incapacity, e.g. drunkenness in R v. Tandy [1989] 1 All E.R. 267); R v. Smith (1979) 1 WLR 1445 (whether the accused who had put forward a defence of sane automatism, was sleep-walking); Toohey v. Metropolitan Police Commissioner [1965] AC 595 HL (whether a witness is suffering from a mental disability such as to render him incapable of giving reliable evidence – but expert evidence will not be admitted on the question whether a witness who has a normal capacity for reliability is actually giving reliable evidence, see R v. Mackenney (1983) 76 Cr.App.R. 27); R v. Toner (1991) 93 Cr.App.R. 382 (as to the possible effects of a medical condition on a person's mental processes and ability to form an intent); R v. Silcott, Braithwaite and Raghip The Times 9 December 1991 (as to the reliability of a confession made by a person who was abnormally susceptible to suggestion).

[67] Weightman v The Queen [1991] Crim L.R. 204.

[68] Supra, footnote 59.

[69] [1975] QB 834 840.

[70] (1971) Cr.App.R. 268.

[71] [1991] Crim L.R. 204. In Weightman the Court of Appeal upheld the trial court's refusal to admit psychiatric evidence, about the existence of a personality disorder known as 'la belle indifference', characterised by emotional superficiality, impulsive behaviour when under stress and a reduced capacity to develop enduring relationships with others. This case is discussed by Mackay & Colman 'Excluded Expert Evidence: A Tale of Ordinary Folk and Common
(to be continued)

own special facts.[73]

Some recent decisions of the Court of Appeal such as *R* v. *Humphreys*[74]
and *R* v. *Thornton (no 2)*,[75] seem to suggest that expert evidence might in the
context of 'battered woman syndrome' be relevant in provocation cases.[76] In
the case of defences of duress, expert evidence is as a general rule
inadmissible to show whether an accused suffered from a predisposition that
would likely make him vulnerable to duress.[77] An exception has, however
been recognised in *R* v. *Emery*[78] where the appellant relied on duress as a
defence to a charge of child cruelty. Expert evidence was allowed to show that
a woman in the position of the appellant, though being initially of reasonable
firmness might if exposed to long term violence and abuse, come to suffer
from a condition of 'dependent helplessness' that would prevent her from
defending her child from similar abuse.[79] It has been accepted that "in a proper
case",[80] psychiatric evidence can be given to indicate that a person is incapable
of giving reliable evidence because of a "psychiatric disability", which
"substantially affects the witness's capacity to give reliable evidence".[81]

Expert psychiatric or psychological evidence relating to the *mens rea* of an
accused person is, however, inadmissible,[82] so too is expert evidence with
regard to the reliability of witnesses in general. More recently in *R* v.
*Robinson*[83] it was held that evidence of a psychiatrist or psychologist may be
admissible to show that a witness or a confession is unreliable, where the
mental condition of the witness or accused is such that it is outside the
ordinary experience of the jury, including where the person is suffering from a
personality disorder so severe that, although not a mental illness, it may be

---

Experience', [1991] *Crim L.R.* 800.

[72] [1974] *AC* 85.

[73] The Court distinguished the case of *Lowery* v. *The Queen*, saying that the issues in that case
were "unusual" and that therefore it was not considered "an authority for the proposition that in
all cases psychologists and psychiatrists can be called to prove the probability of the accused's
veracity".

[74] [1995] 4 *All E.R.* 1008.

[75] [1996] *Crim L.R.* 597.

[76] It is, however, difficult to reconcile these cases with the House of Lords' decision in *R* v.
*Morhall* [1996] 1 *AC* 90 or that of the Privy Council in *Luc Thiet-thuan v R* [1996] 3 *WLR* 45.

[77] *R* v. *Hegarty* [1994] *Crim L.R.* 353; *R* v. *Horne* [1994] *Crim L.R.* 584 and *R* v. *Hurst* [1995] 1
*Cr.App.R.* 82.

[78] (1993) 14 *Cr.App.R.* 394.

[79] *Ibid.*, 398.

[80] *R* v. *Mackenney* (1983) 76 *Cr.App.R.* 271.

[81] *Idem.*

[82] *R* v. *Reynolds* [1989] *Crim L.R.* 220. Cf. Zuckerman, *Principles of Criminal Evidence* (1989),
p. 67, who indicates that although it has been supposed at times that expert opinion on the
existence or non-existence of a constitutive fact such as *mens rea* is inadmissible, he is, doubtful
whether such a rule has ever been in operation as cases purportedly supporting it are often
explicable on different grounds.

[83] (1994) 98 *Cr.App.R.* 370.

categorised as a mental disorder. A psychiatrist or psychologist cannot, however, give reasons why a witness should be regarded as reliable.

Although the *Turner* rule has been held to form part of South African law,[84] an overview of criminal cases does not manifest a strict adherence with the normal/abnormal test as a criterion for exclusion. This development in South African law may be the result of the fact that adjudication lies within the province of professional judges. South African courts have held that where an accused relies on the defence of sane automatism or non-pathological criminal incapacity,[85] it is necessary for the defence to lay a proper basis to upset the inference[86] that sane persons who engage in conduct which would ordinarily give rise to criminal liability, do so consciously and voluntarily.[87] This could in certain circumstances require the defence to call psychiatric expertise. In South Africa the emphasis in the application of the *Turner* rule seems to be different. The test is far less concerned with the question whether the evidence falls within the common knowledge of the trier of fact; it is rather an enquiry as to whether the expert evidence proffered can assist or be helpful to the trier of fact.[88] In such a system there is far lesser reason for trial judges to act in a gate-keeping capacity, as they, like their continental brethren, are also the ultimate triers of fact.

This does not, however, mean that South African courts do not subscribe to the normal/abnormal distinction of the Turner rule. In *S* v. *Nel*[89] the court held that there is no real analogy between cases of physical affliction which adversely affect the capacity of a witness to testify accurately and reliably (in which instances expert evidence to establish such affliction would be admissible), and intellectual and psychological disabilities of a relatively normal kind.[90] The appellant *in casu* sought to lead psychiatric evidence of the fact that one of the witnesses who had been called to testify on her behalf was 'mildly to moderately retarded' and likely to become uncommunicative when subjected to the strain of testifying in a court. Such evidence was held inadmissible. The reason was that such disabilities, where they affect personality, powers of exposition and articulation are capable of being assessed by the court reasonably adequately while the witness is giving evidence.[91] While the court acknowledged that expert evidence may contribute

---

[84] *S* v. *Nel, supra.*
[85] *S* v. *Campher* 1987 1 *SA* 94 (A); *S* v. *Laubscher* 1988 1 *SA* 163 (A); *S* v. *Smith* 1990 1 *SACR* 130 (A); *S* v. *Potgieter* 1994 1 *SACR* 61 (A); *S* v. *Kensley* 1995 1 *SACR* 646 (A); *S* v. *Cunningham* 1996 1 *SACR* 631 (A); *S v Di Blasi* 1996 1 *SACR* 1 (A); *S v Wiid* 1990 1 *SACR* 561 (A); *S* v. *Nursingh* 1995 2 *SACR* 331 (D); *S* v. *Gesualdo* 1997 2 *SACR* 68 (W).
[86] *S* v. *Kok* 1998 1 *SACR* 532 (NPD) 346 e-f. *See also S* v. *Cunningham, supra.*
[87] *S* v. *Kok, supra,* 346f.
[88] Magistrate or in the High Court a judge sitting with assessors.
[89] 1990 (2) *SACR* 136 (C).
[90] *Ibid.,* 143 c-d.
[91] *Ibid.,* 143 d-e.

to a more reliable and accurate assessment, it held that the cost of expert evidence far outweighed the marginal benefit of a more accurate assessment of the witness.[92] Where the courts are concerned with defective intelligence not within the realm of the normal, expert evidence will be admissible. In the English case *R* v. *Masin*,[93] the accused who had an IQ of 72, was extremely immature and had limited understanding of the ways of the world, was charged with rape. Expert evidence was sought to be adduced to the effect that he would have been unable to comprehend adequately the nuances of sexual interplay and may have misconstrued the girl's willingness or unwillingness to engage in sexual intercourse.[94] Lord Lane held that in cases where an accused is formally classified as "mentally defective" (where the IQ level is 69 or below), then subject to its relevance to the particular case, psychiatric evidence will be admissible.[95] This would enlighten the jury on a matter of abnormality which would *ex hypothesi* not be common knowledge. However, where an accused is within the scale of normality, expert evidence will not be necessary and therefore would be excluded.[96] This approach manifests similarities with the decision in *S* v. *J*[97] in South Africa. *In casu* a paediatric registrar was permitted to give evidence to the effect that the rape complainant's IQ level was 34.9, to lay the foundation for other non-expert testimony of how she would have come across to the accused and thus whether the accused subjectively could have appreciated her incapacity to consent. The assumption that lay people, are competent to evaluate human behaviour, in certain circumstances as Colman & Mackay[98] indicate, may rest on the false premise that "[t]he behaviour of normal human beings is essentially transparent". This notion is likely to be challenged by most psychologists on the basis of research that has established that many areas of human behaviour, although occurring on a daily basis, may be so complex as to defy simple comprehension.[99] Colman & Mackay indicate that there is a considerable body of research in support of the argument that much common sense is "demonstratively counter intuitive in the sense that 'ordinary men and women' generally misunderstand [it]".[100]

---

[92] *Ibid.*, 143 e-f.

[93] [1986] *Crim L.R.* 395.

[94] *Ibid.*

[95] *Ibid.*

[96] *Id. See also* Beaumont, 'Psychiatric Evidence: Over-rationalising the Abnormal', [1988] *Criminal Law Review* 290.

[97] 1989 (1) SA 525 (A).

[98] Colman & Mackay, 'Legal Issues Surrounding the Admissibility of Expert Psychological and Psychiatric Testimony', 1993 20 *Issues in Criminology and Legal Psychology* 46.

[99] Mackay & Colman, 'Equivocal Rulings on Expert Psychological and Psychiatric Evidence: Turning a Muddle into a Nonsense', 1996 *Crim L.R.* 88.

[100] Colman & Mackay (1993), 20 *Issues in Criminology and Legal Psychology* 46. In their article they describe five examples of situations including obedience to authority and bystander apathy where the outcome of experiments was contrary to what the average person predicted. (48-49).

In the above discussion it was shown that judges in the Netherlands have the power to call for the introduction of expertise when they deem it necessary. It has also been argued that such evidence will be deemed necessary where it is considered helpful to the trier of fact. There is, therefore, no likelihood of the Dutch criminal justice system being inundated with expert evidence that is unnecessary and irrelevant. Likewise the 'common knowledge' rule applied in South Africa, England & Wales serve the same purpose in preventing courts from being overwhelmed by expert evidence that is irrelevant on the basis that it is unlikely to be helpful to the trier of fact or that it pertains to areas which can be understood by ordinary people without expert assistance. It has also been indicated that proof with regard to facts and circumstances that belong to the realm of common knowledge is not required in the Netherlands.[101] Consequently judges in all three comparator countries need to grapple with the question regarding the scope of common knowledge. The analysis above, however, indicates that the application of the normal/abnormal dichotomy as enunciated in *Turner* with regard to human behaviour may result in arbitrary distinctions with regard to the normal/abnormal distinction. These concerns were articulated by the High Court of Australia in *Murphy* v. *Queen*.[102]

The court its comment on the remark by Lawton LJ in *Turner* that "[j]urors do not need psychiatrists to tell them how ordinary folk who are not suffering from any mental illness are likely to react to the stresses and strains of life": there are difficulties with such a statement. To begin with, it assumes that 'ordinary' or 'normal' has some clearly understood meaning and, as a corollary, that the distinction between normal and abnormal is well recognised. Further, it assumes that the common sense of jurors is an adequate guide to the conduct of people who are 'normal' even though they may suffer from some relevant disability. And it assumes that the expertise of psychiatrists (or, in the present case, psychologists) extends only to those who are 'abnormal'. None of these assumptions will stand close scrutiny."

I submit that the *Turner* rule needs to be reconsidered, as the uncritical application of this rule, could result in expert evidence being excluded that has the potential to contribute to the understanding of the issue before the court.

### The Ultimate Issue Rule

As indicated in the discussion above expert psychiatric or psychological evidence relating to the *mens rea* of an accused is inadmissable. Recently the classical approach expounded in *S* v. *Harris*[103] was once again followed by the

---

[101] Article 339 of the *Dutch Code of Criminal Procedure*.
[102] (1988-89) 167 *CLR* 94 110.
[103] 1965 2 *SA* 340 (A).

South African Supreme Court of Appeal in *S* v. *September*.[104] "[I]n the
ultimate analysis, the crucial issue of appellant's criminal responsibility for his
actions at the relevant time is a matter to be determined, not by the
psychiatrists, but by the Court itself. In determining that issue the Court (...)
must of necessity have regard not only to the expert medical evidence but also
to all the other facts of the case, including the reliability of appellant as witness
and the nature of his proved action throughout the relevant period."

Although it does not say so expressly, this *dictum* reflects the sentiment
that expert witnesses may not express an opinion on the question which the
court has to decide – the so-called ultimate issue rule.[105] Jackson[106] defines
ultimate issues in criminal trials as: "material facts which must be proved by
the prosecution beyond reasonable doubt before a defendant can be found
guilty of a particular offence (...)". The ultimate issue rule is said to be based
upon the fear that the function of the tribunal of fact may be 'usurped' by the
expert's provision of expert evidence which touches upon issues integral to the
determination of the case. Therefore traditionally common law courts have
been loathe to admit an expert witness to give evidence which involves
interpreting and/or applying a legal concepts[107] or on any issue that the trier of
fact must decide on for the ultimate resolution of the case. The problem with
the ultimate issue rule is that it does not recognise the fact that in some cases
an expert witness will have difficulty expressing a relevant opinion without
answering the ultimate issue itself.

Hodgkinson[108] however indicates that the rule, as an exclusionary measure,
is not strictly applied in England & Wales and has assumed a narrow
application.[109] This has led commentators to regard the rule as obsolescent,[110]
redundant[111] or considered to force experts into "expressing their opinions on
crucial aspects of the proceedings in indirect and elusive terms, rather than
using the terminology that they customarily employ."[112] In *R* v. *Stockwell*[113]
Lord Taylor LCJ, acknowledging that the issue whether an expert can give an

---

[104] 1996 1 *SACR* 325 (A).

[105] Wigmore, *A Treatise on the Anglo-Amercian System of Evidence in Trials at Common Law*,
3rd ed. (1940) described the rule as "simply one of those impossible and misconceived utterances
which lack any justification in principle" (2557) and its justification as avoiding usurpation of
the function of the jury as a "mere bit of empty rhetoric" (2556).

[106] Jackson, 'The Ultimate Issue Rule: One Rule Too Many', 1984 *Crim L.R.* 75.

[107] Robertson & Vignaux, *Interpreting Evidence: Evaluating Forensic Science in the Courtroom*
(1995), p. 62. *See also IBM S.A.* v. *CIR* 1985 4 *SA* 852 (A) 874 A-B; *Metro Transport* v.
*National Transport Commission* 1981 3 *SA* 114 (W) 120A; *S* v. *H* 1981 2 *SA* 586 (SWA) 589A.

[108] Hodgkinson, *Expert Evidence: Law and Practice* (1990), p. 150.

[109] *See DPP* v. *A & BC Chewing Gum Ltd* [1968] 1 *QB* 159. *See also S* v. *Haasbroek* 1969 2 *SA*
624 (A) 631 A-C.

[110] *Ibid*.

[111] Jackson, 'The Ultimate Issue Rule: One Rule Too Many', 1984 *Crim L.R.* 75.

[112] Freckelton, *The Trial of the Expert* (1987), p. 75.

[113] (1993) 97 *CAR* 260.

opinion on what has been called the ultimate issue has long been a vexed question, continued by saying: "The rationale behind the supposed prohibition is that the expert should not usurp the functions of the jury. But since counsel can bring the witness so close to opinions on the ultimate issue that the inference as to his view is obvious, the rule can only be (...) a matter of form rather than substance. In our view an expert is called to give his opinion and he should be allowed to do so. It is, however, important that the judge should make clear to the jury that they are not bound by the expert's opinion, and that the issue is for them to decide."

Robertson & Vignaux, however, argue that the rule should remain as it is based on logic.[114] According to their argument, an analysis of cases in which expert evidence has been challenged on the basis of the ultimate issue rule are instances where the experts have expressed an opinion on the ultimate issue assuming certain prior odds.[115] This could occur where an expert testifies to the probability of a match found to exist, for example, between a blood stain found at the scene of the crime and the accused's blood, by expressing his opinion as a likelihood of the accused being guilty where expert evidence is based on probabilities, Robertson & Vignaux point out that the value of all probabilities depends on the assumptions and information used in assessing them. By using Bayes' Theorem they illustrate that knowledge about a hypothesis starts with odds in favour of it. In a murder case it could be the testimony of an eyewitness observing the accused in the vicinity of the place where the body of the victim was found. These are known as "prior odds".[116] According to the theorem the prior odds must be multiplied by the likelihood ratio of every new piece of evidence to give the "posterior odds".[117] If an expert, therefore, gives an opinion on the likelihood of the accused being guilty (the ultimate issue) such an expert, is not only testifying as to the strength of the scientific evidence, but basing his opinion on an assumption of prior odds. Robertson & Vignaux suggest that forensic scientific evidence which has a likelihood ratio (R), is best presented in the following form: "This evidence is R times more probable if the accused left the mark than if someone else did. This evidence therefore supports the proposition that the accused left the mark", or: "whatever odds you assess that the accused was present on the basis of other evidence, my evidence multiplies those odds by R".[118]

For this reason, the Court of Appeal held in *R v. Doheny*[119] that an expert giving evidence which has a quantifiable likelihood ratio should confine himself to explaining or quantifying that ratio.

---

[114] *Supra*, 64.
[115] Robertson & Vignaux, p. 65.
[116] *Ibid.*, 17.
[117] *Ibid.*
[118] *Ibid.*, 65.
[119] [1996] *TLR* 504.

The concerns highlighted by Robertson & Vignaux need not be addressed by retaining the ultimate issue rule as an exclusionary measure. I suggest that their fears can be assuaged in two ways: on the one hand the evidence of experts who base their conclusions on prior odds (the cogency and weight of which still need to be assessed in coming to their conclusion) can be surmounted by excluding such evidence as going beyond the scope of the expert's expertise. On the other hand, it can be argued that even where expert evidence is admitted on the ultimate issue, it remains as any other issues testified to, mere evidence, that must be weighed by the ultimate trier of fact. Once such evidence is admitted it does not mean that fact finders necessarily need to rely on such evidence. Acknowledgement of this reality explains why the ultimate issue rule seen in the Netherlands as a decision-making rule. While in the Netherlands experts are also not allowed to draw conclusions because it is the task of the legal decision-maker, awareness of these problems can inform decision-makers of the pitfalls of relying on such evidence.[120]

In the South African context where there is no need for protecting the jury from powerful expert opinions and where professional judges are free to decide what weight they will attach to an expert's opinion, there is particularly no need for the perpetuation of the ultimate issue rule as an exclusionary rule. The problem surrounding experts expressing probabilities in such a way that they trespass on the ultimate issue, is however, an issue that decision-makers should give careful consideration to when evaluating such evidence.

**The Basis Rule**

An expert opinion given in the absence of reasons for reaching such a conclusion can have negligible probative value. Experts in all three comparator jurisdictions are expected to state the facts or data upon which their opinions are based.[121] In *Coopers (South Africa) (Pty) Ltd* v. *Deutsche Gesellschaft für Schädlingsbekämpfung Mbh*[122] it was said: "[A]n expert's opinion represents his reasoned conclusion based on certain facts or data, which are either common cause, or established by his own evidence or that of some other witness. Except possibly where it is not controverted, an expert's bold statement of his opinion is not of any real assistance. Proper evaluation of the opinion can only be undertaken if the process of reasoning which led to the conclusion, including the premises from which the reasoning proceeds, are disclosed by the expert."[123]

---

[120] Sjerps, 'Pros and Cons of Bayesian Reasoning in Forensic Science', in: Nijboer & Sprangers *Harmonisation in Forensic Expertise* (2000).

[121] *Coopers (South Africa) (Pty) Ltd* v. *Deutsche Gesellschaft für Schädlingsbekämfung Mbh* 1976 3 SA 352 (A); *R* v. *Jacobs* 1940 *TPD* 142, at 146. See also *R* v. *Morela* 1947 3 *SA* 147 (A); *S* v. *Mthize and Others* 1999 1 *SACR* 256 (WLD).

[122] 1976 3 *SA* 352 (A).

[123] *Ibid.*, 371.

The so-called basis rule is usually not seen as an admissibility rule of expert evidence, but rather refers to factors that could impact on the evaluation of expert evidence.[124] At common law admissibility does, however, become an issue as a result of the practice that experts often give opinion evidence on information provided by others.[125] The common law rule against hearsay, if strictly applied, would often prevent the expert from giving his opinion because his reasoning and conclusions will be governed by matters which he has come to know in the course of his training and profession, from what he has read or from what he has heard from others who have the specialisation. The logistical difficulties posed where every original source is to be called as a witness, have prompted a practice of circumvention of the hearsay rule. Where expert opinion evidence is given when not all its bases have been proved to the court, the rule is that such basis material must be proved by admissible evidence.[126] An expert testifying on information which has been supplied to him could however, be the thin end of the wedge by which certain inadmissible material (which would not otherwise have been introduced) is brought to the attention of the tribunal of fact. Schuller[127] raises the additional danger that hearsay transmitted by an expert, as opposed to a lay witness, may carry convincing weight: "The oft-expressed concern that expert testimony will be over-valued by the jurors because of its aura of scientific reliability and trustworthiness"[128] suggests that hearsay conveyed via an expert, as opposed to a non-expert witness, may carry greater weight. The 'paramessage' elements, such as prestige and expertise, that accompany the expert's 'message'[129] may lend greater credibility to the hearsay information."

Common law courts are faced with the dilemma of reaching an appropriate balance between the admission of such hearsay and the ability of the tribunal to adequately evaluate the quality and reliability of such expert evidence. Too much hearsay will not only make evaluation of the evidence difficult, but could impinge on the other party's right to cross-examine in circumstances

---

[124] S v. Baleka (3) 1986 4 SA 1005 (T) 1021 C-D; S v. Ramgobin 1986 4 SA 117 (N) 146 D-G; S v. Adams 1983 2 SA 577 (A) 586 A-B.

[125] Hodgkinson supra remarks that "The use of hearsay by experts occur both at an explicit level, at which particular hearsay sources are specifically referred to or produced in evidence, and at an implicit level, at which it is assumed that many of the expert's views will be informed by knowledge gained externally to the case, and in particular from the books, articles, papers and statistics through which the learning of a specialist discipline is disseminated to its members." (181)

[126] In R v. Turner [1975] 1 QB 834 Lawton LJ succinctly explained the English law position to be the following: "It is not for this court to instruct psychiatrists how to draft their reports, but those who call psychiatrists as witnesses should remember that the facts upon which they base their opinions must be proved by admissible evidence. This elementary principle is frequently overlooked."

[127] Schuller, 'Expert Evidence and Hearsay', 1995 19 Law and Human Behaviour 345.

[128] See Vidmar & Schuller (1989).

[129] Rosental (1993).

where the witness is a mere conduit pipe of another who cannot be confronted. This dilemma had to be confronted by the English Court of Appeal in *R* v. *Abodom*.[130] Scientists from the Home Office gave evidence of the similarity of glass samples taken from the Appellant's shoes and the composition of a window found to be broken at the scene of the crime. One of the experts testified that the refractive index of the particles found embedded in the appellant's shoes was identical to that of the window glass and gave evidence that according to statistics compiled by the Home Office, only 4% of glass samples tested possessed that specific refractive index.[131]

On appeal it was argued that the expert evidence was based upon what was at that time[132] inadmissible hearsay and so should not have been admitted as the experts have no personal knowledge of the tests from which the statistics had been assembled. In dismissing the appeal, the Court made an important distinction between "primary facts" as bases of expert evidence, which have to be strictly proved and "secondary facts", as *in casu*, which the Court held were exempt from the operation of the hearsay rule.[133] The Court in the course of its *ratio decidendi* acknowledged: "[that] the process of taking account of information stemming from the work of others in the same field is an essential ingredient of the nature of expert evidence."[134]

The expert will still be at an advantage over the tribunal of fact when analysing and drawing information from specialised sources within his field.[135] As Hodgkinson[136] indicates, this exception to the hearsay rule is allowed, as the expert cannot be prevented from relying on these sources, when giving his opinion. The proper approach according to the *Abadom* case is "where [experts have drawn on the work of others in arriving at their conclusion], they should refer to this material in their evidence so that the cogency and probative value of their conclusion can be tested and evaluated by reference to it (...)."[137] The *Abadom* decision extended the rule that experts may express their views based on secondary sources that are standard in their discipline to include "knowledge of unpublished material and (...) their evaluation of it".[138]

The various sources that an expert can rely on were commented on in *S* v. *Kimimbi*[139] and *Menday* v. *Protea Assurance Co Ltd*.[140] In the latter case

---

[130] [1983] 1 *WLR* 126; 1 *All E.R.* 364, at 369; 76 *Crim App R* 48, at 53.
[131] *Ibid.*
[132] The published statistics would now be admissible under Section 24 of the *Criminal Justice Act 1988*.
[133] *Ibid.*, 129-130.
[134] *Ibid.*, 131.
[135] Hodgkinson, *supra*, 116.
[136] *Ibid.*
[137] [1983] 1 *WLR* 126 131.
[138] *Ibid.*
[139] 1963 3 *SA* 250 (ECD).
[140] 1976 1 *SA* 565 (ECD).

Addleson J set out the approach to be followed where an expert relies on passages in a text book: "[The expert] must [show] firstly, that he (or, by reason of his own training, affirm at least in principle) the correctness of the statements in that book, and, secondly, that the work to which he refers to is reliable in the sense that it has been written by a person of established repute or proved experience in the field. In other words, an expert with purely theoretical knowledge cannot in my view support his opinion in a special field (of which he has no personal experience or knowledge) by referring to passages in a work which has itself not been shown to be authoritative. Again the dangers of holding the contrary are obvious."[141]

One way for a trial judge to decide whether to admit evidence by an expert who relies on unadmitted data is to determine whether this data is of a type reasonable relied upon by experts in that field.[142] In the Netherlands the use by an expert of sources that constitute hearsay is unlikely to pose problems in view of the general practice of courts to use hearsay statements as evidence.[143]

There is also no 'basis rule' that determines the admissibility of evidence, an expert is required at least to base his opinion upon that which "his knowledge teaches him" regarding the specific field.[144] In addition, Article 299.2 of the *Dutch Code of Criminal Procedure* states that not only should a person submitting a written report to the court be an expert, but he should also substantiate his opinion by including reasons for that opinion. Despite the fact that Article 299.2 *Dutch Code of Criminal Procedure* requires that experts should support their conclusions with reasons, the *Hoge Raad*[145] is hesitant to hold that failure to supply "reasons for knowing" constitutes reversible error. The *Hoge Raad*[146] had to consider an appeal from the Court of Appeal of 's-Hertogenbosch, which had relied on a medical report finding an accused guilty of sexual abuse. The report did not explain what investigation was performed by the medical expert, nor stated the basis or method on which the expert had made a diagnosis of sexual abuse. Defence counsel argued on appeal that the expert's opinion of sexual abuse was unacceptable as means of proof, on the grounds of the expert's failure to substantiate it with reasons. The *Hoge Raad* held that the appellate Court could consider the expert's documentary

---

[141] *Ibid.*, 569 H.

[142] Carlson, 'Experts, Judges and Commentators: The Underlying Debate about an Expert's Underlying Data', 1996 47 *Mercer Law Review* 481 491.

[143] HR 20 December 1926, 1929 85ff.

[144] Article 343 *Dutch Code of Criminal Procedure*: "A statement by an expert is understood to be his opinion, made in the course of the investigation at the trial, as to *what his knowledge teaches him about* that which is *the subject of his opinion*." (My emphasis.)
Article 344 *Dutch Code of Criminal Procedure*: "1 Written documents are understood to be: (...) (4) reports of experts entailing their opinion as to *what their knowledge teaches* them about that which is the *subject of their opinion*." (My emphasis.)

[145] HR 23 June 1930, *NJ* 1930, 1477; HR 18 October 1977, *NJ* 1978, 534; HR 26 September 1995, *NJ* 1996, 41.

[146] HR 26 September 1995, *NJ* 1996, 41.

statement as expressing his expert opinion on the issue and hence no reversible error had been committed.

In view of decisions in the "Anatomically Correct Dolls" and "Shoeprint" cases[147] it can be said that Dutch trial courts need not justify their decisions, unless the defence has made a specific and detailed challenge as to the reliability of the method that the expert used to draw his conclusions. If, however, the expert is not required by practice to state his reasons and methodology used, such a challenge will be difficult for the defence to launch. According to the "Anatomically Correct Dolls" case and the "Shoeprint" case, where the reliability of expert reports are contested by the defence, trial courts relying on such expert evidence, would need to explain why they consider the expert's method to be reliable. If the expert report does not state the reasons and the methodology used by the expert the court will be without the means to justify its decision. The line of reasoning in the "Anatomically Correct Dolls" case and the "Shoeprint" case seems difficult to reconcile with the decision in the 's-Hertogenbosch sexual abuse case. Surely, good science and good law would require that an expert should state his "reasons for knowing" when submitting a written report to court, especially as this is required by the *Code of Criminal Procedure*.

The basis rule as applied in South Africa and England & Wales appears to function as in the Netherlands, more as a decision-making rule than an exclusionary rule. Stating the basis for experts' conclusions is essential to the judicial decision-making process, as without stating the facts or data upon which such opinions are based, their bold statements provide no means of accountability. The requirement that an expert should state the reasons for his opinion serves as an important touchstone of reliability.

**Conclusion**

In all three comparator countries rules which either determine admissibility and/or the probative value of expert evidence are apparent. Whether the 'Expertise', 'Common Knowledge' or 'Basis' Rules are seen as admissibility or as decision-making rules, is immaterial. Their ultimate objectives are the same. Most of the rules of evidence followed in England & Wales and South Africa were designed to withhold evidence from the jury that may unduly bias them against the accused that is potentially too unreliable to be of any use. The South African Criminal Justice process however, no longer functions with a judge and jury. Damaška[148] remarks that it is the environment of the Bifurcated court that facilitates the effective enforcement of the exclusionary rules. South African criminal tribunals can be seen as unitary courts, where the judge

---

[147] Discussed *supra*.
[148] Damaška, 'Evidence Legal Perspective', in: Carson & Bull (eds.), *Handbook of Psychology in Legal Contexts* (1995), p. 170.

determines not only the admissibility of evidence, but is also the ultimate trier of fact. In this respect, South Africa is closer to the Dutch System. It is also for this reason that it is argued here that the debate with regard to threshold tests[149] for expert evidence need not, as in the US, concern South African courts as a vexable admissibility issue. John Jackson[150] observes that there has, in recent years, generally been an increasing move away from rules of evidence in favour of the principle of free proof. In terms of this principle, triers of fact are permitted to evaluate all evidence that is sufficiently relevant without the need for stringent exclusionary rules. Likewise, I should like to argue here, that as South Africa has unitary courts staffed by professional judges a strict application of the so-called rules of expert evidence is no longer essential. Where expert evidence is likely to assist the trier of fact and therefore logically relevant, it should be admitted. If during the course of the trial it appears to be unreliable, the trier of fact is free to elect not to rely on such evidence as in the Netherlands. Problems associated with experts testifying to the ultimate issue, such as the guilt of an accused, can usually be excluded on the grounds that such evidence goes beyond the field of expertise of the particular expert, making the independent existence of the ultimate issue rule superfluous. Abolishing the 'Ultimate Issue Rule' in South Africa would be in line with law reform[151] in many other countries. Where experts do give evidence on the ultimate issue that the court has to decide it should, however, be balanced by an appropriate system of testing the quality, reliability and accountability of their evidence.[152] This does not mean, however, that the criteria traditionally contained in the exclusionary rules cannot be used as decision-making rules by triers of fact. The unitary system as applied in South Africa is an additional reason why the ultimate issue rule has no justification for its continued existence.

---

[149] *Frye* v. *United States* 293 F1013 1014 (1923); *Daubert* v. *Merrell Dow Pharmaceuticals* 125 *L Ed (2d)* 469; 113 *S.Ct.* 2786 (1973). *See also Kumho Tire Co Ltd* v. *Carmichael* 23 March 1999 131 *F.3d* 1433 (1998).

[150] Jackson, 'Evidence: Legal Perspective', in: Carson & Bull (eds.), *Handbook of Psychology in Legal Contexts* (1995), p. 170.

[151] *See* the recommendations of Law Commissions from other Commonwealth Countries. Australian Law Reform Commission *Evidence* Report No 36 AGPS Canberra 1988; Ontario Law Reform Commission *Report on the Law Reform Commission* Govt Printer Ontario 1976, Scottish Law Commission *Law of Evidence* Memo No 46 Edinburgh 1983; Federal Provincial Task Force on Uniform Rules of Evidence *Report* 1982; New Zealand Law Commission *Evidence Law: Expert Evidence and Opinion Evidence* Preliminary Paper No 13 New Zealand Law Commission Wellington 1991

[152] Carson, 'Beyond the Ultimate Issue', in: Lösel, Bender & Bliesener (eds.), *Psychology and Law: International Perspectives* (1992), p. 447.

# Artificial Intelligence and Criminal Evidence: a Few Topics

*E. Nissan*

## What can AI offer Research on Criminal Evidence

An important part of the programme of the conference in Amsterdam was about current achievements or efforts, and, especially, the prospects of attempts to apply artificial intelligence (AI) – a quite various repertoire of techniques and endeavours from within computer science – to the domain of criminal evidence. Back from chairing a session at the conference, I trust the general readership of the proceedings would benefit from considerations (however selective) more general than the specialists' special issue of papers from the conference, edited by Peter Tillers and scheduled to appear in the *Cardozo Law Review*, or, for that matter, the papers in my own forthcoming collection.[1]

In the present paper I intend to provide a broad, if selective overview, and especially an opinion, in the first part, the rest being devoted to a brief description of some of my own work. The project in the domain in which I take especial pride is ALIBI, an automated planning prototype which impersonates a suspect trying to exculpate himself (though on a common-sense rather than sound legal ground, and though – as implemented – without taking into account the need to reason about complicity); the early yet significant stage of that project dates back from the late 1980s, so ALIBI is arguably one of the precursors of the current upsurge of interest in the meet of artificial intelligence and criminal evidence.

Of the computer programmes described by the speakers at the conference in Amsterdam, two stand apart by how neatly representative they are of entirely different ways to approach the task of applying AI to criminal evidence, and moreover, of different ways to conceive of AI itself:

1. Josephson in his lecture at the conference described the application – to the facts, hypotheses, or anyway predicates of an actual criminal case from the US (as reported in the media) – of an AI programme which embodies a neat theory of 'abduction' (or 'best explanation') from theories of automated reasoning;

2. Asaro, an investigating magistrate and prosecutor from an Italian magistrate court, demonstrated DAEDALUS, a programme he developed single-handedly for assisting, documenting, and validating every single step that an investigating magistrate or prosecutor takes in his routine work; *e.g.*, the interrogation of the plaintiff, suspect, and witnesses. The tool has spurred such enthusiasm with the judiciary in Italy, that almost all

---

[1] Martino & Nissan (to appear).

judiciary offices now want it to be adopted experimentally, and Asaro himself was seconded to assist in that role the Minister of Justice.

These developments concerning DAEDALUS were the latest, in the span of the few weeks right before, during, and following the conference in Amsterdam. Why is DAEDALUS an AI tool? On close scrutiny, the design of the tool features no flamboyant, hallmark AI technique that has not become commonplace in this decade. Yet, DAEDALUS is a tool in which AI can take pride, because of how closely and 'intelligently' this tool fits the judiciary task in its ergonomic, practical context.

DAEDALUS checks for the integrity of the procedure and data, and advises the user about how to proceed; it even 'becomes upset' on learning that action was taken by the magistrate or the police without DAEDALUS being informed and kept abreast... And for good reason for that matter, especially if one is to consider the effects of the Napoleonic wars on continental law.

Tracing the impact of the French *Code d'Instruction Criminelle* on Dutch courtroom practice, Nijboer & Sennef[2] point out that "the dossier was the central file to which 'internal' control of higher authorities was applied. Law enforcement officials performed their checks using the dossier as the exclusive source of information about what happened in a case. In the dossier they could check whether all necessary, formal controls had been met and whether or not all relevant formalities had been carried out. The importance of the dossier is reflected in the Latin [maxim]: *quod non est in actis, non est in mundo* (what cannot be found in the acts of the dossier, does not exist in reality)."[3]

Now, turning to Josephson's application of abduction: what is special about abduction, as being a neat AI formalism? Deduction is using standard valid inference to derive a fact from background knowledge. Abduction, on the other hand, is deriving an explanation for observed facts. Specifically, we make some observations (evidence), and select a set of assumptions from which, together with the background knowledge about the world, the evidence can be proved. Charniak & Shimony (1990) point out that whereas an abductive theory for generating explanations is known to be in certain philosophical respects problematic,[4] it is also problematic in practical respects from an AI viewpoint, as "there are many possible sets of assumptions, which together with our knowledge of the world would serve to explain (prove) the desired fact. Somehow, a choice between the sets must be made."[5] The technique "is nevertheless an attractive one for people in AI, since it ties something we know little about (explanation) to something we as a community know quite a bit more about (theorem proving)",[6] so various solutions have been proposed,

---

[2] In Malsch & Nijboer (1999).
[3] *Ibid.*, pp. 14-15.
[4] McDermott (1987).
[5] Charniak & Shimony, *ibid.*
[6] *Ibid.*

that involve limiting simplifications. "Cost-based abduction is [a] generalisation of these theorem proving techniques. It allows any formula to be assumed, and assigns all assumed formulas a non-negative real number cost. The best explanation is then the proof with the minimum cost."[7] For example, in their paper I have been quoting from, Charniak & Shimony "provide a probabilistic semantics for cost-based abduction", *i.e.*, the problem is shown to be amenable to probabilistic evidential reasoning on belief networks: a cost-based proof, *i.e.*, explanation, of some facts is transformed into a graph, and this in turn is used, with the costs, to define a probability distribution. It was shown *(ibid.)* "that the maximum a-posteriori (MAP) assignment of truth-values to the network corresponds to the minimal cost proof", where "a MAP assignment is the way to set the values of all random variables such that their joint probability is highest".[8]

Do not take this concise explanation of abduction to reflect on what Josephson does, but the way I formulated the above, you have to beware: there is a landmine there, unfortunately of a metaphorical kind that (unlike in the military) could never be outlawed from scholarship. What is more is, if you have read thus far, you have surely either passed over it, whether you skipped it or forcefully threaded upon it. Scholars who have followed the debate (war?) between the Bayesian enthusiasts and the Bayesio-skeptics in recent years could see why. Abduction requires quantification; which kind of metrics are you going to use? are you going to reason about it by relying on Bayes theorem?[9] In the range of opinions, the most extreme authors in the Bayesian camp, Robertson & Vignaux, are the authors of a readable book (1995).

My concern in this paper is not just with what computing – whether or not resorting to such methods that traditionally fall within AI in particular – may do for narrow specialties of the forensic sciences.[10] As to discovering evidence involved in computer crime, this being another forensic specialty, it goes without saying that it requires expertise in computing, falling as it does within the domain of computer security. Forensic accountancy has to deal with computer records.[11] Or then consider the context of paternity claims: Egeland *et al.* (1997) describes PATER, a software system for probabilistic computations for paternity and identification cases, in cases where DNA profiles of some people are known, but their family relationship is in doubt. PATER is claimed to be able to handle complex cases where potential mutations are accounted for. Or then again, take forensic odontology: whereas

---

[7] *Ibid.*

[8] *Ibid.*

[9] On this controversy, *see* for example Allen & Redmayne (1997), Tillers & Green (1988). *See* my long review of the former in Martino & Nissan (to appear).

[10] *See*, *e.g.*, Bohan (1991) on the role, in court, of computer-aided accident reconstruction.

[11] *See* Bologna & Lindquist (1995) on fraud auditing and forensic accounting, especially in the US context.

the dentist who used to have a person in care may help in identification by means of stored X-ray items, there is, as well, a different kind of application: "Bite marks left on human tissue and bitten material have become an important aspect of scientific evidence used for the conviction or acquittal of a suspect," to say it with the abstract of Nambiar *et al.* (1995), which among the other things describes the use of a computer program for shape analysis. Moreover – and this is of interest here because some of the material in this paper is concerned with the linguistic and pragmatic interpretation of narratives or other linguistic communication – we are not specifically concerned here with forensic linguistics the way it has been practised thus far; forensic linguistics as a discipline has a specialised forum, the *Routledge Journal Forensic Linguistics.*[12]

## A Foray into Cognition and into the Common-sense of Narratives

In the span of a symposium or session – all the more so at the meet of AI and Law or in particular AI and Criminal Evidence – we cannot expect to see all areas represented, as there is multitude of subjects indeed. Even though the application of AI to Criminal Evidence is a relatively new area, disparate techniques from AI and disparate aspects of Criminal Evidence can conceivably be matched (or combined in more complex ways). You may visualise this as a table (a computer scientist or mathematician would say: "a Cartesian product") of items from AI and items from Criminal Evidence. Next, imagine ticking those cases in the table which configurate a given piece of research. Much of this is still merely potential, and the multiplicity of topics is daunting, yet presenting the prospects the way I just did may give you an indication of the magnitude of that potential. In my comment on one of the talks at the conference, I actually showed transparencies on the so-called 'blackboard' technique from AI, which is particularly suited for combining the contribution of several sources of knowledge to problem-solving in such context where we cannot even start to imagine any given, preordained sequence for the dynamics of the process; the intended benefit of that mini-lesson was for those in the audience who came from a background in law, and I hope they forgave me the technicality of the subject, as there were cartoons in the transparencies to enliven the presentation. If I was able to convey an idea of merely the potential, that should suffice.

Having said that about subjects that were per force absent from the AI sessions: take, for example, jury psychology research. That area of research is thriving in North America.[13] "One development in traditional jurisprudential

---

[12] Cf. Gibbons (1994), Shuy (1993).

[13] *See*, e.g., Hastie (1993), *Inside the Juror*, a book I reviewed for Martino & Nissan (to appear). For the domain covered by *Inside the Juror*, the present reader is referred to Hastie's overview in his long, articulate, usefully detailed introduction.

scholarship is a candidate for the role of a general theory of juror decision making; namely the utilitarian model of rational decision making that has been imported into jurisprudence from economics."[14] Optimal decision making has been modelled, in the literature, not just for the role of the juror, but for the judge, attorney, police, and perpetrators of criminal behaviour as well; yet, optimality, or rationality, for decision making is too strong an assumption.[15] The research in Hastie's volume "focuses on the manner in which jurors behave before they enter the social context of deliberation in criminal felony cases",[16] with "at least four competing approaches represented" among behavioural scientists' descriptive models of decision making,[17] namely, such that are "based on probability theory, 'cognitive' algebra, stochastic processes, and information processing theory". Bayes' theorem is involved, in the former, for descriptive purposes in contributions to Hastie's volume, being applied to the psychological processes in which a juror is engaged, rather than in prescribing how to evaluate evidence to reach a verdict, "or to evaluate and improve jurors' performance".[18]

Pennington & Hastie present a cognitive theory of story construction on the part of the juror.[19] I propose that models of narrative understanding from natural-language processing within AI are in order, if one is to apply, next, AI to the legal narrative. To start with, legal researchers, presumably aware of the debate on legal "anchored narratives",[20] but with little knowledge of research on narratives within AI, may wish to read such a classic in automated understanding of and question-answering about multiparagraph narratives as Dyer (1983), possibly along with the discussion of five earlier programmes in Schank & Riesbeck (1981). By now, such analyses even resort to models neural computations, the latter's application in computational linguistics being the subject of Sharkey (1992), whose Chapter 11 – by Lee, Flowers & Dyer – describes DYNASTY, "a symbolic/connectionist hybrid script-based story processing system (...) which incorporates DSR [i.e., distributed semantic representation] learning and 6 script related processing modules. Each module communicates through a global dictionary where DSRs are stored."[21] Let us suffice to note here that what originally used to be the Yale school of natural-language processing, i.e., the one adopting representation in terms of 'conceptual dependencies', offers this advantage for reasoning on legal narratives, namely that inference is based on cues (even emotionally

---

[14] *Ibid.*, p. 4.
[15] *Ibid.*, p. 5.
[16] *Ibid.*
[17] *Ibid.*, p. 10.
[18] *Ibid.*, p. 12.
[19] Hastie (1999).
[20] Wagenaar *et al.* (1993), Jackson (1996). *See also* pp. 95-98 in Twining (1999).
[21] Lee *et al.* in Sharkey, p. 215.

interpreted displays on the part of the involved characters) of which the artificial tool tries to make sense based on a network of goals and plans. Goal-driven inference is essential to such common sense as on *mens rea*; moreover, standard situational patterns are also resorted to. The alternative for analysing narratives (in literary or, especially, folklore studies, but also in computational linguistics) is by resorting to so-called 'story grammars',[22] which have disadvantages for the requirements of open-minded reasoning on legal narratives, while arguably being of some use in models of how jurors or the lay public may reason on a sensational case, where the risk is high that stereotypes of characters and situations be involved in such reasoning.

I would also like to bring to the readers' attention the fact that research on natural-language processing within AI has been producing, for a fairly long time, rather sophisticated models of characters' or relaters' perspectives at variance on a given event or sequence of events. Different accounts of a political demonstration at Yale University are generated by Eduard Hovy's (1990) PAULINE system; it impersonates, in turn, characters with different leanings, and generates stylistically appropriate texts, to convey their viewpoint. Rhetorical goals (of either opinions or style) and associated strategies are employed, that are intermediaries between the speaker's interpersonal goals, and syntactic decisions to be taken according to the rhetorical strategies. Stylistic rhetorical goals in PAULINE include: formality, simplicity, timidity, partiality, detail, haste, force, floridity (with unusual words), color, personal reference, open-mindedness and respect.

That AI may achieve something of the like must be viewed as quite appealing for legal professionals who are well aware of the role of persuasion techniques in legal communication, or what quite befittingly goes by the name 'forensic rhetoric'.[23] That is, unless you agree with the opinion of a magistrate who in quite recent times told another magistrate: "You've got so much to do; stop toying with computers!"

In his approach to legal narratives, semiotician of law Bernard Jackson is right to distinguish between the semantics and the pragmatics of a legal narrative, where by its pragmatics he means what is made of that narrative by presentations in court. Conveying an impression, manipulating an image, is of course also something we would expect of the defendant, among others. Ron Allen's critique of the Bayesian approach is based, among the other things, on the vulnerability to lying, lying on the part of the witnesses. What has AI to say about the relation between truth and manipulative presentation?

A program, IMP, from the early 1980s[24] was devised for the latter task. IMP may try to mislead on purpose, without actually lying. A dialog system, it

---

[22] Frisch & Perlis (1981), Garnham (1983).
[23] *See, e.g.,* Lucas & McCoy (1993).
[24] Jameson (1983).

impersonates a realtor, trying to rent moderately priced furnished rooms on the Hamburg market. Well-informed about the market, IMP assumes that the customer possesses the same general information, against which the customer assesses the qualities of the room considered. The program tries to convey a good impression about the goods, and about itself as well. It would not volunteer damaging information, unless a direct, specific relevant question is made. IMP has a goal of maintaining a neutral image of itself and an impression of completeness for its own answers; on occasion, it reportedly simulated insulted surprise if an intervening question by the customer seems to imply (by detailed questioning) that IMP is concealing information. This kind of research does not directly address legal issues, but given that all of this (and much more) already exists in the repertoire of AI achievements, legitimately raises expectations among legal researchers.

Needless to say, AI models will eventually have to incorporate some common sense about much more than the above, to be able to deal with human narratives 'sensibly'. Interdisciplinary awareness is the name of the game. Self-narrations – as known from psychology but also as relevant to Law, or, for that matter, literary studies (which, in turn, have a lot to say about narrated time vs. the time of the narration) – are accounts of a narrator about oneself. An account is conceptualised and proposed possibly of long spans out of one's biography. Like in defence in law, such a task also requires coherent reorganisation of events and mental states. Even when no liability is involved, there is no way self-narration may fit a rigid schema ('emptying the sack', as though, where discrete, fixed objects are to be supposedly found). On top of the task of re-storying one's experiences, there is also the aspect of story-connecting, which introduces sharing experiences or agency with other agents; connecting to each other's stories occurs, *e.g.*, when individual stories of spouses continue as a couple's story.

**The Impact of the Historical Background**

I had mentioned, above, Josephson's recent work on abduction as applied to predicates which constitute legal narratives, Asaro's practical framework for capturing the routine work of enquiries for a country with investigating magistrates, as well as the work by Schum on marshalling the evidence by means of formalisms manipulating Wigmorean diagrams, and the work by Gaines et al. On juror models by means of neural models of computation. It must be recognised however that whereas the two historically mainstream research communities of AI research as applied to law (first a predominantly Latin group of logicists who mainly researched deontic logics,[25] and thereafter the predominantly Anglo-Saxon, considerably broader group of scholars who

---

[25] On these, *see* Nissan (1998a).

publish in a Boston-based journal) have been slow in turning their efforts specifically to criminal evidence. Evidence would turn up on occasion when a different theme was principal. A very large corpus of research literature, and the respective repertoire of techniques, of specific concern with AI & Law now exist,[26] but then the emphasis often is on the inference logic, or, then, on models of argumentation. Argumentation research applied to the expert witnesses in court, as carried out by Ghita Holmstrom-Hintikka (1995), is also quite relevant to AI & Law.[27]

Inference logics and argumentation are, of course, crucial areas, and Law in general is such a rich-textures area of application that it is a real challenge for AI to exercise there its 'muscles' (Ron Allen at the conference raised for a moment, in a rhetorical context, the perspective of law colonising AI, whether it could do it or not, yet I would more easily visualise an AI enthusiast from computing enraptured in a fantasy about the opposite taking place: neither extreme option is going to materialise, I suppose, to almost everybody's satisfaction or relief).

The fact remains that Evidence and Proof as an area of law had to subject to a long march into visibility within AI & Law. In turn, we are now experiencing a situation where legal evidence scholars with a special interest in formalism (Wigmorean diagrams, Bayesianism, lashing at the latter, and so on) appear to be in a broad agreement to give AI its chance inasmuch a flexible, malleable toolbox or discipline that appears nowadays to be more promising than what came about to be – in terms of general acceptability – of the promises of older, narrower classes of formalisms.[28] The general benefit, I would say, is in that there apparently is now more interest in the narrative per se than in the outcome of judicial decision-making, and this because AI provides tools for representing narrative elements, not just the truth-values of inference. Moreover, tools like DAEDALUS show the sophistication attained by what has a considerably paler precedent in administrative tools which belonged in legal computing, but from which the AI Gotha (or even the AI & Law Gotha) used to be punctilious about taking one's distances. Nowadays it is for everybody to see that there is no reason for that to be the case. AI has yet to show it is practical for the judiciary; DAEDALUS did it, *ergo* DAEDALUS is a pride for AI & Law.

The enterprise of AI for legal evidence will eventually have to meet high standards, whatever the task or sets of tasks it will settle upon as being appropriate. On the spur of the good will it has been meeting on the part of legal evidence scholars, it will be essential that AI as being applied to the domain will not only pursue the development of building blocks or either

---

[26] Hunter & Zeleznikow (1994).
[27] *See* her essay in Martino & Nissan (to appear).
[28] *See, e.g.*, Allen's paper in Martino & Nissan (to appear).

integrated or disparate tasks, but also keep in touch with specific concerns of the users it ultimately seeks for itself. Applications such as Asaro's in DAEDALUS have such a delimited scope and niche of use as to make them uncontroversial, unlike Bayesianism. Not that Asaro's architecture precludes the addition of a complementary quantitative model, yet it would at most apply to prosecutorial discretion: the costs of whether to proceed. Not so, in AI & Law, anything that will have to do with assessing probatory strength for the purposes of fact finding: this could not but be controversial, with claims of oracular trans-rational value being bestowed upon a pet formalism. The fact remains that a tool for the prosecutor is not the same as a tool for affecting and orienting the outcome of the fact finders' decision making in court. This is why even Bayesian enthusiasts concede that one thing is using Bayesianism in court, another thing is studying a case in other circumstances, *e.g.*, in retrospect as in Kadane & Schum's (1996) generally acclaimed analysis of Sacco & Vanzetti.[29]

Voltaire was, in his times, what the Bayesioskeptics are in the present state of the art (so it is the case to acknowledge that *la faute est à Voltaire*, if you want to blame somebody). Lying on the part of either the plaintiff or the defendant is what, Voltaire argued, probabilistic reasoning cannot defeat.[30] In her history of theories of circumstantial evidence, Isabella Rosoni (1995), whose Italian volume I reviewed at length in Martino & Nissan (to appear), devotes much attention to the meet of probability theory and theories of judicial proof. This meet is the subject of Lorraine Daston's own acclaimed book (1988). In Rosoni's words (in my translation): "A dissonant voice in so compact a chorus was Voltaire's. Yet, the French philosopher deals with the problem critically, and without claiming to solve it. His Essai *sur les probabilites en fait de justice* [1772] is less than enthusiastic about the analysis of probabilities as applied to criminal law";[31] Voltaire's argument against the technique is that 'half-certitude' leads to 'half-proofs', *i.e.*, to doubts and then to 'half-truths'. Voltaire advocated confining application to civil cases (without acknowledging Voltaire, something like that is in line with what some have been advocating in our days). Moreover, discussing one such case that took place in Brussels, and in which an old widow sued her confessor to have an alleged debt returned, Voltaire develops a probabilistic analysis, states that the parties' claims are equiprobable, and concludes: "*Mais si les témoins vrais ou faux persistent, si l'une des deux parties s'obstine à dire: 'J'ai preté cent*

---

[29] *See* in particular Vern Walker's review essay in Martino & Nissan (to appear).
[30] A sophisticated contrary stance is represented by Kadane & Schum's analysis of Sacco & Vanzetti.
[31] Rosoni, p. 277.

*mille ecus', et l'autre à nier qu'elle ait recu cet argent; si les preuves manquent, à quoi serviront les probabilités?*"[32]

We know that the courts function nevertheless, and moreover it is no news that the principle of the intimate conviction of the fact finders has carried the day; on the Continent, this is indeed the Romanist sense of 'free proof', as the latter "has different connotations in Romanist and common law systems. Historically, in Continental Europe free proof (especially, *frei Beweiswurdigung, l'intime conviction*) was contrasted with legal proof *(probatio legalis, preuve légale, gesetzliche Beweistheorie)*. These terms referred primarily to the evaluation of evidence",[33] emancipating judicial evaluation of the evidence from the older law of proof (a process that Rosoni analyses, and which among the other things led to the demise of torture), and anyway, "replac[ing] a body of rules of quantum and weight which were never of significance in England",[34] as "throughout history Anglo-American triers of fact have been almost entirely free from rules of quantum and weight",[35] and in 1908 in the US, John Henry Wigmore (1863-1943) "went so far as to say that to talk of rules of weight or credibility in the common law system is 'moral treason'".[36] Anyway, clearly the very need that invited attempts at solution by calculating the probabilities, attempts that Voltaire was criticising, is rooted in the transition (still earlier than the one mentioned by Twining) from a system based on oaths (at least in civil law), to a system where fact finding is not contented with the device.

When it comes to quantum and weight – let us avoid confusion. It is not that nowadays home affairs and justice are not resorting to assessing the credibility of depositions by some kind of informal or even formal measures, of which the specialists are the forensic psychologists (as they claim with some good reason).

Here is a caveat for AI researchers. Writing as I do from the coign of vantage of AI & Law, I feel that researchers who set to investigate in the domain of legal evidence in terms of narrative structure, agents, epistemic states, perception, and emotion, will derive important benefits from studying, for example, reference texts on testimony and psychological evaluation thereof, not just (at least) the standard texts on criminal procedure and of legal evidence scholarship. More thorough acquaintance should go some way toward avoiding some naive approaches to knowledge representation, as well as avoiding too exclusive a focus on law or on logic. AI has a wealth of

---

[32] "But if the truthful or false witnesses insist, if one of the parties still claims: 'I lent 100,000 ecus', whereas the other party still denies having received that money; if the evidence is missing, what are probabilities good for?" Rosoni, p. 278.

[33] Twining 1997, pp. 446-447.

[34] *Ibid.*, footnote 23.

[35] *Ibid.*, p. 448.

[36] footnote 26.

formalisms that variously suit legal computing; it is in applications to evidence that it is more poignantly evident (to me at the very least) that the AI side cannot be legitimately divorced from its concerns with the human mind. Focusing on a disembodied, flawless logic would not do. Not when we are concerned with how humans make sense of human stories.

## The Classicist Lure for Neatness vs. Baroque Architecture

A point made by Barnden at the conference in Amsterdam is that there are too many things to represent for preferring a neat theory from AI in alternative to trying to capture as much as possible by AI techniques regardless of how nicely this fits in any given theory. The divide between the 'neaties' and the 'messies' in AI is a major one, and in my view, for all of AI & Law having much to offer by way of neat logic theories in its published literature, ongoing research into AI for criminal evidence must refrain from disdaining 'messy', pragmatic, miscellaneous representations. Take multi-agent modelling within AI, an area quite relevant to robotics, but that arguably may eventually enter into the picture of our present field of interest; Agre & Rosenschein (1996) is a bulky special issue on *Computational Theories of Interaction and Agency*, and there is no dearth of logic-based research going around in that domain. Yet, Agre in his introduction[37] was rather quick to point out that inefficiency "has cast shadows on formal logic as a research tool in AI", an evidently abhorrent proposition to, perhaps, the majority of established AI researchers: being a 'neaty' is glamorous, especially if you are mainly interested in proving theorems. Legal scholars from the present audience will certainly agree that what they would much prefer in AI is some valid help in going toward better legal evidence and proof. We need an architectural framework, and this one is acceptable even if 'messy' in the above technical sense, whereas the benefits of logic may nevertheless accrue within such a framework. As Agre[38] conceded, to logic-oriented authors "the basic point of logic is not architectural but semantic", for the purpose of "sorting out the meanings of representational elements, with no inherent commitments about" actual implementation.[39]

Some authors use logic as a syntax, uncoupled from concern with truth values; see for example Martino & Alchourron's essay 'Logic Without Truth' (1990): "G.H. von Wright has said on more than one occasion that logic goes beyond truth and falsity; F. Miro' Quesada maintains that the subject of logic is not immediately concerned with truth and falsity but, rather, the inheritability of any value transmitted through the notion of consequence. Tarski, Jaskowski, Gentzen, Wittgenstein and Belnap, even though they do not

---

[37] *Ibid.*, p. 39.
[38] *Ibid.*
[39] *Ibid.*

express themselves in the same terms as us, created all the conditions and criteria for upholding the main thesis of this article."[40]

When it comes to legal evidence scholarship, fine points have been made about adopting a correspondence theory of truth or, instead, a coherence theory of truth.[41] Twining maintains "that the Rationalist Model does not involve a necessary commitment to a correspondence theory of truth (if, indeed, this is a meaningful term) and that it is useful for some purposes to distinguish between logic (normative), analysis of discourse (empirical), and appraisal of discourse by seeing how far actual practice falls short of logical standards and heuristic precepts, including advice on good practice."[42]

Much could be said on the role of logic within the framework of AI & Law (or of AI in general). Yet, this paper of mine is intended to be an informal introductory, deliberately impressionistic presentation of AI's role, actual or potential, and therefore I am leaving out leads that would carry out far away into an in-depth discussion: to reuse Twining's metaphor,[43] "[t]his is not the place to pursue these hares", but rather a place where to light up foci of curiosity.

**On some Elusive Desiderata**

Let us go back to the remark, made earlier on, about the affective side of criminal interrogations, and the assumptions made concerning the suspects. The topic of Steinross & Kleinman (1989) is how investigative detectives cope with emotional labour. "Those called upon to make clients feel good (*e.g.*, flight attendants) must suppress their own feelings of anger; those called upon to make others feel bad (*e.g.*, bill collectors) must suppress their own feelings of compassion."[44] As Steinross and Kleinman summarise their own findings in the abstract of their article, "[t]he detectives we studied disliked their encounters with victims, but enjoyed their encounters with criminals". Whereas "[t]hey could not (…) transform their uncomfortable encounters with victims into a positive experience", "[t]he detectives discounted criminals' emotional displays as inauthentic, redefined their emotional labor as relevant to catching criminals, and turned the encounters into a game."[45] Empathy is, therefore, the key to their dislike of encounters with victims, whereas the absence of empathy enables their 'game' with their quarry.

---

[40] *Ibid.*, p. 56, footnote 10.
[41] Twining, in Malsch & Nijboer (1999).
[42] *Ibid.*, p. 71, footnote 9.
[43] *Ibid.*, p. 72.
[44] *Ibid.*, p. 435.
[45] *Ibid.*, p. 435.

Philosophers of action have discussed emotion,[46] and logicians concerned with action (such as Belnap) have been attentive to what the former had to say about that. As to artificial intelligence research (many of whose practitioners are logicians indeed), some reasoning about emotions can be found in Michael Dyer's already mentioned book – and his work is not in logic theories – or then in other, even considerably earlier publications on automated dialogue systems from AI. The simulation of emotions is now an emerging area within AI,[47] not just for such recreational contexts as the case is of the dog-robot developed and recently launched on the market by Sony Corp.

Going back specifically to the emotions of investigative detectives, it should be noted that professional psychology – within social psychology research – is not deprived of interest for AI.

These things are unlikely to be represented in such future AI tools that are specifically concerned with legal matters, which in turn may include the need to interpret mannerisms in human communication; yet, once AI research in general becomes more knowledgeable, in its formal representations, of phenomena such as the ones described above (it is merely a desideratum right now), then even that may in the long term come within the grasp of some of the tools you may conceive of. This is far away, but just as you can entertain hopes for the short and medium term (for the short term, you have got Asaro's DAEDALUS), nurturing expectation for the longer run is also in order, and, still better, giving specifications for future research to be carried out.

Some such research, whether appropriate or not for our general theme of AI for Criminal Evidence, is starting way, way out of what would ostensibly qualify. Take the already mentioned dog-robot, developed and recently launched by Sony. It simulates a pet (the politically correct replacement for 'pet' is 'companion animal'); the robotic pet will, according to the advertisements, learn and respond according to the efforts the owner will invest in it. Sony was also developing a robotic talking head. In 1998, Kim Binsted of Sony, then organising a symposium on AI models of humour, referred me to a different robotic simulation; judge by yourself how relevant it appears to be to a judiciary context: "similar work going on at ETL: I remember they had three talking heads, supposedly representing two lawyers and a judge, arguing a case (...)". ETL is the Electrotechnical Laboratory, in Tsukuba, of the Agency of Industrial Science and Technology (AIST) of Japan's Ministry of International Trade and Industry. Binsted's reference was to a paper published in 1997 by Katsumi Nitta, Osamu Hasegawa & Tomoyoshi Akiba in one of the satellite workshops of IJCAI, the leading AI conference world wide.[48]

---

[46] Kenny (1963).
[47] Nissan (1999a).
[48] Nitta *et al.* 1997.

Even in such situations where it would look like the artificial agent should have some model of emotion, it may nevertheless be the case that something more abstract could do without but the shallowest reference to affect. Let us consider an example, from social psychology. Gender and emotion in a professional culture is the subject of Pierce (1996). A book in workplace ethnography, it "examines the gendered nature of today's large corporate law firms". Jennifer Pierce "portrays the dilemma that female attorneys face: a woman using tough, aggressive tactics – the ideal combative litigator – is often regarded as brash or even obnoxious by her male colleagues. Yet any lack of toughness would mark her as ineffective."

Well, not only AI could potentially have something to say about this, but it actually does say something quite relevant (which, what is more, does not explicitly touch upon emotion): the dilemma of contrary imperatives is well known from research into deontic logic. Conflicts and obligations, or contrary-to-duty obligations are interesting for deontic logics, as these are modal logics whose modal operators concern obligation and permission (obligation being deontic necessity, this in turn being different from ontological necessity).

Philosophers, logicians, and AI & Law researchers have been concerned with how to deal with conflicts of obligations. The *locus classicus* of contrary-to-duty obligations is Sophocles' tragedy *Antigone* where the protagonist buries her brother in defiance of the Theban king Creon. Yet you do not necessarily have to get the baddies into the picture to have a conflict of obligations. I will say it in the words of the late Hector-Neri Castañeda: "Conflicts of duties or obligations are an essential part of life. Some conflicts of duties arise from contradictions in a system of norms. In such cases we simply have to revise the system and restore consistency. However, most conflicts arise from collisions between systems of rules converging at the same circumstances. Then we confront sets of deontic truths in tension; clearly a tension among truths does not yield a contradiction. For instance you have two debts having payments due on the same day, but you cannot make both payments. Here typically there is no question of revising a system of rules. The rules remain in place, and you must find a solution that acknowledges both obligations to pay. The obligation you leave unfulfilled remains operative: later on you can truly assert that you ought to (should) have paid it, even though you didn't and couldn't."[49]

Are the logicists among the AI people eager to work on complex narratives from the human social realm? In my experience – this is what I typed at first – that is the exception (and barely that) rather than the rule. Having typed 'and barely that', I was to discover on re-reading this, I had subliminally excluded beforehand from the 'rule' one given individual plus two categories of researchers:

---

[49] Castañeda (1992), p. 116.

- Antonio Martino, one of the founding fathers of computing for the Law (and of AI & Law within it), the scholar to whom I owe my coming to this discipline from AI. A logician in the tradition of the philosophy of Law, yet he has been telling colleagues in recent years: "For thirty years, we have been amusing ourselves [with theoretical models]; now is the time to show we come forth with practical systems". Hence, the development of an international Master certification in New Technologies for the Legal Professions, achieving the goal with which the establishment was undertaken of the CHASQUI network of universities, of which Martino is the co-ordinator and which I represent in the UK (several institutions from both sides of the Atlantic signed the documents of the new phase of this collaboration, during a ceremony in March 1999 in the new office of the Vice Chancellor, *i.e.*, rector, of the University of Greenwich in London, in front of the City on the River Thames; it used to be the official residence of an Admiral, at the campus of the Royal Naval College we have recently acquired;[50]
- the practitioners or critics of forensic statistics, whose initiative it was to have the symposium on AI & Law at this conference, and who formed the bulk of the audience at the respective sessions (whatever happened to cross-fertilisation? Hence the importance of having as general a paper as this one in the general proceedings of the conference: *verba volant*, even if they were not heard or heeded, whereas *scripta manent*, what is in an archival forum made accessible to the entire body of researchers who attended and to others yet – will hopefully be read, and if it is not too much hoping, arise more definite interest);
- last but by no way the least, the shortcomings of the theorist's characterisations delineated above cannot conceivably apply to the two luminaries – Zadeh and Pawlak – who graced the conference with their presence. For those among the readers who don't know that, Pawlak's and Zadeh's greatest gift (next to establishing the mathematics of the imprecise, *i.e.*, of vagueness) as made to both AI and a variety of application domains alike, arguably consists in this:
  - their willingness to combine their having initiated and established their respective, sound and flourishing streams of theoretical work, namely, Zadeh's (1964) fuzzy set theory;[51]
  - with their own personal remarkable degree of attentiveness to applications. Zadeh himself has published in the context of criminology and rehabilitation over 25 years ago,[52] whereas Kokawa *et al.* (1975), an

---

[50] *See* http://www.gre.ac.uk/~E.Nissan/Chasqui/signature_ceremony.html.
[51] *See* Pawlak's rough set theory (Pawlak (1991)).
[52] Zadeh (1973).

example from cognitive studies, was an early application of his formalism to memory and recall,

This attentiveness on the part of Zadeh and Pawlak is made quite effective by the large following they have among researchers, but also by each of them being 'a very great expositor' (as Zadeh described Pawlak in his talk at the conference). Those who listened to them will agree. In his talk at the Amsterdam confereence, Zadeh showed how expressions in natural English can be precised, *i.e.*, filtered (by means of given functions to be unobtrusively inserted into the English text) into a precise formulation of the particular sense (out of several classes) in which the linguistic variables as in the original text are fuzzy approximations. There is a huge literature on fuzzy formalisms and applications, as well as a specialised journal, *Fuzzy Sets and Systems*; there are several branches of theory, let alone domains of applications in the literature. In Zadeh's own web page at Berkeley, a section titled 'Statistics on the impact of fuzzy logic' states: "A measure of the wide-ranging impact of Lotfi Zadeh's work on fuzzy logic is the number of papers in the literature which contain the word 'fuzzy' in the title. The data drawn from the INSPEC and Mathematical Reviews databases are summarized below". Let it suffice to quote here the grand total, being 15,631 titles in INSPEC for 1981-1996 (of which 10,733 in 1993-1996) and 5,660 titles from 1981-1992 in the Math Reviews database.

I find myself in agreement with John Barnden when, at the conference, he argued for the need to combine approaches from the repertoire of AI, in line with the 'messy' tradition within AI. The 'neaties' enamoured of one theory are less amenable to be willing to soil it with applications, especially in such rich-textured a domain as Criminal Evidence within law, but then it is up to the 'messies' within AI & Law to recycle and adapt either the native luggage of the 'messy' tradition, or the theories from 'neaty' streams of research, in the service of application to the domain a forum of which is now playing host to the present paper.

## AI's Neaties, AI's Messies and who will yake on Organised Crime

Let us start this section from the 'neaty' camp within AI. So much so indeed, that we will even start from the logicians *tout court*, neater-than-thou logicists among the AIers follow suit. Our goal here will be to assess the repertoire of techniques from AI or some more mathematically oriented fold when it comes to pick out who will go, conquer the reasoning about complicity, and bring the gangs within the grasp of future AI tools for Criminal Evidence.

Representative works in the logic of agency include Belnap's and Segerberg's. In contrast to Belnap's modal logic of agency, there is also an ontological approach to agency, an approach which avoids expressing agency by means of modal operators. Logics of agency have been the topic of a special issue of *Studia Logica*, 51(3/4), in 1992. The main thrust in such research is within logic, even though Perloff's paper in Martino & Nissan (to appear) shows how an approach to the logic of agency such as developed by Belnap (Perloff's colleague and sometime co-author) can be applied to the discussion and representation of concrete legal cases.

Permissibility (deontic possibility) in relation to ability (ontological possibility for an agent to perform an action) is, of course, the *raison d'être* of legal norms.[53] Modal logics of action – and in these, *stit* is the model operator of 'seeing to it that' – have been studied in relation to deontic modals, as well as to ability and decision-making in accordance with these,[54] with either single or multiple agents.

Quite afar from such logic-centred approaches to action or to ability, *ad hoc* works in AI have also been reasoning on deliberating to act based on available abilities: later on, I am going to discuss briefly my own BASKETBALL expert system.[55] Note also that ability and social perception of it vis-à-vis status is the subject of SKILL, which is discussed along with my ALIBI model in Fakhel-Eldeen *et al.* (1993). More formal approaches to representation (though less logic-obsessed than, obviously, the logicians' output) have attempted to provide general frameworks for dealing with agents' negotiation and planning, and, making considerations relevant to augmenting the ALIBI model (on which, see in the next section). In Nissan & Rousseau (1997) I have discussed how to make use of such formalisms.

Multi-agent models have been booming in AI, typical applications being in robotics.[56] Anyway, a major problem with both theories of action from logic or AI, and models of multi-agent interaction from AI and robotics, or even AI or economic formal models of negotiation, is the limitative assumptions about the universe. It suits robotics, it suits much less well attempts at modelling the behaviour of human agents (as opposed to tools for helping human negotiations, such as, in AI & Law, John Zeleznikow's remarkable projects). In general, refer to research on autonomous agents within distributed AI.

About 50 years ago, a relative of mine who – a teenager at the time, but with the looks of a young man having attained his majority – was visiting the Topkapi museum in Istanbul as a tourist. He stumbled and, reaching out with his hand, he accidentally tore a unique piece of tapestry that had been made by the prominent favourite of a sultan. Understandably embarrassed, the young man, eager to own up to the damage he had made, reached out into his pocket and offered to the staff of the museum who had rushed in some small change. They declined, did not blame him, and concentrated on assessing the damage to the tapestry instead of paying further attention to him. Very kind on their

---

[53] On ability as dealt with in philosophical logic, *see, e.g.*, Brown (1990).
[54] Horty & Belnap (1995).
[55] Nissan *et al.* (1992).
[56] Agre & Rosenschein (1996).

part, you will agree, especially if you are used to a litigation-happy culture. This is a good illustration of whether the 'stit' operator from modal logics of action (agent A sees to it that Q) should or should not apply. The harmful action was, after all, unintended. Yet, there *were* goals involved. What is the goal of a person who is stumbling while reaching out with a hand? How would you explain a hasty attempt on the part of the embarrassed youth to repay the damage with the small change he took out of his pocket? It was all the money he was carrying there and then) on the part of the embarrassed youth?

This network of goals and plans is served wonderfully by Dyer's approach in his BORIS programme.[57] This is paragraph 4 from a story that Dyer discusses as having been analysed by BORIS.[58] The next day, as Richard was driving to the restaurant, he barely avoided hitting an old man on the street. He felt extremely upset by the incident, and had three drinks at the restaurant. When Paul [an old friend, now a lawyer, with whom Richard had not been in contact for years until the time of the story] arrived Richard was fairly drunk. After the food came, Richard spilled a cup of coffee on Paul. Paul seemed very annoyed by this so Richard offered to drive him home for a change of clothes.

BORIS was able to answer questions on this story sensibly, making inferences not only based on what is explicitly stated, but also based on general patterns from common-sense about the worlds and about social interaction; *e.g.*:
-   How did Richard feel when the coffee spilled?
    BORIS: RICHARD WAS UNHAPPY.
-   Why did Richard spill the coffee?
    BORIS: RICHARD WAS DRUNK.

The next paragraph in the story is as follows:[59] when Paul walked into the bedroom and found Sarah with another man he nearly had a heart attack. Then he realised what a blessing it was. With Richard there as a witness, Sarah's divorce case was shot. Richard congratulated Paul and suggested that they celebrate at dinner. Paul was eager to comply.

When answering questions on this, BORIS was able to reason about the outcome of the divorce case, or, for that matter, that what Paul felt on coming home was surprise. "[W]hen people read about a husband who catches his wife being unfaithful, they do not immediately think of lawyers. However, if a lawyer is mentioned next: after George caught his wife committing adultery George decided that he needed a lawyer. They are not surprised. In contrast, consider the following fragment: after George caught his wife committing adultery George decided that he needed a basketball player. In this case people

---

[57] Dyer (1983).
[58] *Ibid.*, p. 4.
[59] *Ibid.*, p. 5.

become very confused because they can not find any relationship between adultery and basketball players."[60]

In BORIS, the situational pattern 'hidden blessing' corresponds to the following, in terms of goals and plans:[61] $x$ experiences a goal failure, caused by an event E. $x$ has a realisation (*i.e.*, an MBUILD in Conceptual Dependency notation) that E also enables (or causes) another goal to succeed.

Realising the hierarchy of goals, or their relative importance, is essential, as shown by Jaime Carbonell (1981) in his POLITICS system. Carbonell related about a bug who earlier on in his project had caused the programme – when reasoning about the perception of the imminent threat of the Soviet Union invading Czechoslovakia requiring the American president to intervene at a time when the relations between the US and the Soviet Union had recently soured (because of spy allegations) so that the influence of the President on Brezhnev could be expected to be less effective concerning the Czechoslovak crisis – to wrongly infer that the President should congratulate Brezhnev, as this is what people are supposed to do when they need to improve their relations. The achievement of a lesser goal was being suggested, with a plan that would harm a more important goal. Other AI tools known from the research literature have been reasoning about international politics. ABDUL/ILANA was an AI programme that used to simulate the generation of adversary arguments on an international conflict.[62] Schrodt *et al.* (1994) reported about KEDS, a programme which processes event data from a Reuters data source. Yet another programme, CYRUS, used to reason on the travels and meetings of Cyrus Vance from his tenure as US Secretary of State under the Carter administration. While applying Roger Schank's Dynamic memory model, Janet Kolodner's CYRUS is particularly significant in the history of case-based reasoning (CBR) from AI, as it applies difference-based automated dynamic indexing and reorganising; with difference-based indexing, similar cases are stored and distinguished according to automatically identified differentiating features of the given case.[63] The kind of CBR model from CYRUS was to inspire, *e.g.*, PERSUADER,[64] a tool for negotiation in adversarial conflicts.

Earlier on, we had discussed complicity among perpetrators of a crime or a conspiracy to commit a crime. Yet, other kinds of accomplices exist. Quite importantly for application to Law BORIS has a general pattern about legal disputes, and, more in particular, in BORIS "the WITNESS rule states that a

---

[60] *Ibid.*, pp. 10-11.
[61] *Ibid.*, p. 43.
[62] Flowers *et al.* (1982).
[63] *See* Kolodner (1984).
[64] Sycara (1987).

witness provides evidence for a violation. However, the BIAS rule qualifies the WITNESS rule by rejecting a biased evidence."[65]

Take the case of George and Ann's divorce: "It is important to realise the status of the outcome supported by the reasoning since one can reason about events which have not yet occurred. When David reassures George that George will win, BORIS must not mistakenly think that George has actually won the house and the children. However, once we are in court, BORIS must realise that the outcome DECISION-FOR-WIFE in the judge's reasoning has actually caused the outcome of Ann winning the house and children."[66]

I promised to come back to case-based reasoning as being a class of techniques within AI.[67] The concern of enhancing uniformity of sentencing in criminal cases for given categories of offences, in a country with a bench-trial tradition, is the motive behind the AI tool whose name is the same as the title of their essay. Kerner's doctoral project consisted of developing a CBR tool which would suggest a sentence to the judge, based on precedents in Israeli Law (which is, in the main, like the Anglo-American system, except in that there is no jury, and the fact-finders are only the judges who are judging the given case). The precedents are identified by the tool among former trials judged at Israeli courts, and such that the narrative of the criminal event is similar, though possibly (and quite likely) differing by significant details, which may be aggravating or attenuating circumstances. The tool provides an explanation to justify its advice to the judge in the case at hand. The tool has been praised by members of the judiciary and related professions, and also resulted in an IPA Award for Kerner from the Information Processing Association of Israel. In the US, where trials for such offences would be by jury, Ron Allen (p.c.) is against case-based reasoning as could be understood for fact-finding in Law, and where criminal procedure envisages lay fact-finders I can see his point indeed.

**My own Work: a Rapid Fragmentary View**

Readers of this proceedings volume who are willing to invest in AI applications to its general theme – Criminal Evidence – more reading efforts (needless to say, I strongly recommend that), will have to turn to the special issue of the *Cardozo Law Review*, and I also hope they are going to read my edited works with Martino,[68] on AI or a field therein as applied to either Evidence or other areas within Law.

---

[65] *Ibid.*, p. 249.
[66] *Ibid.*, p. 250.
[67] Watson & Marir (1994), Kolodner (1993a, b); *see* an array of applications (also) in, *e.g.*, Knight & Nissan (1999b), Liang & Turban (1993). 'The Judge's Apprentice', by Y. Hacohen-Kerner & U. Schild, is an article from Knight & Nissan's collection.
[68] Martino & Nissan (1998).

In the rest of this paper, I am going to mention works of mine, especially such that are concerned with Law. For example, I have been dealing with temporal reasoning, in Law or otherwise,[69] and, again in Law, with spatial reasoning of various kinds.[70] Not that the techniques or tasks developed within some of my other projects for different applications are necessarily deprived of potential interest.

For example, the resource-allocation, planning and counterplanning reasoning in the BASKETBALL expert system[71] is applied to evaluating one's team's resources as it is pitted against another team, and suggesting a playing strategy according to the way it is expected that the other team would play given their resources. *Mutatis mutandis*, it would not be utterly inconceivable that the pool of resources be elements of evidence, or financial resources and so on, being assessed by the parties, possibly prosecution where prosecutorial discretion is an option, when considering whether to go to court, of opt fo plea bargaining, or letting a case drop. It would most certainly require an entire reconception of the relatively modest design of BASKETBALL, yet the latter may provide matter for thought. Note that BASKETBALL is both a planner which gives advice about action to be undertaken, and a resource allocator, which provides advice on how to allocate resources (these being the team players to the various roles, and the strategic and tactic repertoire of how to play). Other allocation tools I have co-developed are FUELCON and FUELGEN.[72]

TAMBALACOQUE,[73] so named after a tree at risk from the island of Mauritius, the topic of a short paper in biology that was TAMBALACOQUE's first application, is a mark-up language (like HTML, in whose format most Web pages are coded); it is intended for inserting argumentation structure into a scientific text. Well, a mark-up language, per se, let you do the analysis, instead of having the computer do it for you, and this is definitely less ambitious than what AI & Law research into legal argumentation has been doing in recent years. Yet, it is an option.

SEPPHORIS, a knowledge-representation formalism,[74] is more ambitious than TAMBALACOQUE, and moreover, it is applied to events and legal conditions and stipulations. Its syntax is open, in the sense that it can be supplemented with other syntactic features.

In contrast, Nissan (1992) introduced a kind of representation and coding,[75] that takes into account the parallel nature of some legal textual corpora, such

---

[69] Martino & Nissan (1998), Knight & Nissan (1999a), Nissan (1998b).

[70] Nissan (1997b).

[71] Nissan, Simhon & Zigdon (1992).

[72] *See, e.g.*, Nissan (1998c) and Nissan *et al.* (2000).

[73] Nissan & Shimony (1996).

[74] Nissan (1995a).

[75] Based on a syntax I had originally introduced for a different domain.

as Italy's regional constitutions. This is a specialistic concern for representation, and is closer to the text than to the narrative or stipulative structure you would handle with SEPPHORIS at a level where the original text is not involved. Representing the shared core and the differences of the conceptual content of Italy's regional constitutions is something different from how discrepancies are treated in prototype theory as known from cognitive linguistics, even as extended to more generally allowing such rules that are not defeated by exceptions. As to when it is legitimate for exceptions to be admitted in knowledge representation within AI, a classic essay is Ronald Brachman's *I Lied About the Trees* (1985).

My talk at the conference comprised a short description of ALIBI, plus the topics of a paper in two parts about identification (or doing without it) that is currently in preparation. Two cases were discussed:

- the lawsuit against Barnum concerning the Cardiff Giant. He claimed that that supposed 'archaeological find' was a fake, and that he was the one exhibiting the real one. The investors involved in the other exhibition sued him, but lost the case when the 'discoverer' acknowledged that the find was a fake. The court found for Barnum, as he could not be condemned for calling a fake what it actually was – a fake;
- an Early Modern case of proving widowhood, from the Levant. The husband had travelled through the Ottoman empire and then to India, in one of whose port-cities he was mortally wounded. Testimony partly overlaps and is anyway chained in a nice way that was found to be acceptable by a court of three. The case provides me with an opportunity to discuss aspects of spatial and temporal reasoning.

No doubt, the project in which I take more pride in this forum is ALIBI, a prototype with several versions that, from the late 1980s, has been a precursor of the concerns of AI with criminal evidence and exculpation therefrom. For sure, it was tested on a few simple sample narratives,[76] some later stage is still rather speculative,[77] and in some instances the explanation or excuse the felon caught red-handed would make is hilariously meagre in probatory terms. The latter, however, happened because the given situation was desperate, and ALIBI, while impersonating the suspect, was trying too hard to explain out the ascertained narrative elements by denying *mens rea*, that the emplotment, however sensibly contrived, is unconvincing.[78]

The task of an agent trying to prove his innocence is self-exculpation, whether this is defence in court, or denying one's guilt during criminal investigation by the police. A toddler denying wrongdoing to his parents is engaging in the same sort of activity.[79] To my knowledge, ALIBI, developed

---

[76] Kuflik *et al.* (1991) and Fakher-Eldeen *et al.* (1993).
[77] Nissan & Rousseau (1997).
[78] Nissan (1996).
[79] *See* the essay *Avoiders vs. Amenders* by Barrett *et al.* (1993).

by a team I supervised, was the first programme ever whose task was the generation of statements denying wrongdoing (or, in ALIBI3, avowing to a lesser liability). Short of space, I will not be discussing here the architecture of the programme, so let me just recapitulate some features of the input and output. Basically, ALIBI, ALIBI2, and ALIBI3 are versions of a planner trying to detect alternative courses of action, with different conditions or weights applying. The input fed into ALIBI (I am not particular now about which version I am referring to) is a charge against the defendant, who is impersonated by the programme. The charge – a rudimentary 'police report' – is composed of a list of actions. It is a short list of predicates, not free texts (even though in ALIBI2 some progress was made in that direction), or a statement of a freely composed, coherent narrative. Even though the programme itself does not have a strong model of episodes, to humans faced with ALIBI's input and output, reasoning is definitely concerned with a coherent episode. The optimisation side of ALIBI more clearly entered the picture with the version named ALIBI3. Like ALIBI1 and ALIBI2 (the latter enhanced with a simple natural-language processing interface), ALIBI3 proposes several alternative accounts of the actions appearing in the charge, with an effort being made to exclude from the explanation such admissions that involve liability. ALIBI3 is also able, short of finding a totally innocent explanation, to propose such exculpations that admit to some lesser offence than as emerging from the input 'police report'.

Processing has the program recursively decompose the actions in the input, into a tree of actions, down to elementary, atomic actions. Moreover, actions are stripped of their deontic connotation. For example, 'stealing' is stripped down to 'taking', and it is up to the system to concoct such a plan where that act of taking fits in a way that is legitimate for the defendant. Generating the justification corresponds to a reconstitution of actions into a different tree. Then the terminal actions in the decomposition tree are differently reconstituted into alternative explanations that eliminate or minimise liability.

In one of the stories, a man is accused of having shot and wounded a jeweller, while robbing him. One effect of 'wounding' is that the wounded jeweller was unable to take care of his property. This is exploited by an excuse ALIBI makes (if an excuse it is, rather than the factual truth). It states that, having shot the jeweller incidentally, the defendant did take away property, but it was in order to look after it and then return it. Another effect of 'wounding' is that the wounded jeweller needed medical aid. The defendant may supplement his excuse by claiming he *ran* away, in order to get such help for the jeweller. 'Armed threat' is an interpretation involving the effect of holding a weapon and possibly pointing it (which happens to be at somebody who then feels threatened), but ALIBI may try to admit to physically holding the object (which happens to be a weapon), while denying the intentions ascribed (of threatening an interlocutor who is therefore a victim), possibly implying an inadequacy of the defendant at realising the interlocutor's interpretation of the situation. Actually, one excuse ALIBI tries, is that the defendant was carrying the weapon for an innocent purpose, and, possibly forgetting about its presence, was innocently talking to the victim, and was unaware the latter acted by feeling threatened.

In Nissan (1996), an attempt is made at explaining why, whereas some of the excuses made by ALIBI sound sensible, some other explanations produced sound ludicrous. To the extent that it has been possible to reasonably track down the evolution of such examples, to which an audience got exposure at a lecture given in Italy, into jokes and cartoons anonymously published afterwards in an Italian crossword magazine, with no mention of computing.[80] For example, the following caption (here in my translation) looks like it is an adaptation of one of the pretexts made up by ALIBI: "It's all a mistake, Your Honour! My client had no intention whatsoever to rob the bank: he just wanted to get a loan, and showed his submachine gun to pawn it (...)". Nissan[81] is concerned not with ALIBI's uneven proficiency at making up good pretexts, but rather with ALIBI's failure at producing such excuses that are invariably humorous: "In respect of humour research, the 'career' some ALIBI stories had (unacknowledged) in the joke circuit does not detract from ALIBI being deeply problematic in respect of humour research. No explicit model of humour is embodied in this automated inventor of pretexts. 'Look: no hands!' is no legitimate boast. The very fact some items are humorous, and some are not, testifies to the fact that ALIBI is not actually capturing a category in humour. It's an intersection that occurs. Is it by mere chance? Let us get a closer look. Some of the output pretexts may seem to be reasonable. A few are rather insipient. And some again, sound funny instead: funny, but not insulse. (...) It's the very *alacrity* that attracts amused appreciation. It may be that this is a subclass of the *exaggeration* class in the perspective of humour. Indeed, when the input has ALIBI face damning evidence, the simulated (very rudimentary) agent trying nevertheless to exculpate 'himself' makes a display of an exaggerated effort at concocting an explanation. Exaggerated, in face of the likelihood of achieving persuasion. (...) Why did 'he' run away with the jewels? Don't worry: the incapacitated owner could not guard his property, so the indicted man took it in order not to leave it unguarded. Another favour 'he' was doing the jeweller. You're not convinced? Try something better than that yourself. It's an extremely damning charge. If you recognise it was you, and still are trying to exculpate yourself, you may be clever, but we are unlikely to be fooled. We may even recognise you are making the best in a bad fix, we cannot empathise but can be appreciative. We are not gloating: we are just amused."

---

[80] *Ibid.*, Sec. 3.
[81] *Ibid.*, Sec. 4.

# A Bibliography of Cited References

**Agre, P.E. & Rosenschein, J.** (eds.) (1996), *Computational Theories of Interaction and Agency*, Cambridge, MA: The MIT Press, 1996.

**Allen, R. & Redmayne, M.** (eds.) (1997), 'Bayesianism and Juridical Proof' (special issue), *The International Journal of Evidence and Proof*, 1. London: Blackstone.

**Barrett, K.C., Zahn-Waxler, C. & Cole, P.M.** (1993), 'Avoiders vs. Amenders: Implications for the Investigation of Guilt and Shame During Toddlerhood?', in: *Cognition & Emotion*, 7(6): pp. 481-506.

**Bohan, T.L.** (1991), *Computer-aided Accident Reconstruction, Its Role in Court*, SAE Technical Papers Series, 12 p.

**Bologna, J. & Lindquist, R.J.** (1995), *Fraud Auditing and Forensic Accounting: New Tools and Techniques* (2nd ed.), New York: Wiley.

**Brachman, R.J.** (1985), 'I Lied About the Trees. Or, Defaults and Definitions in Knowledge Representation', in: *AI Magazine*, 6(3): pp. 80-93.

**Brown, M.** (1990), 'Action and Ability', in: *Journal of Philosophical Logic*, 19: pp. 95-114.

**Carbonell, J.** (1981), 'POLITICS' & 'MicroPOLITICS', Chs. 11 & 12 in Schank & Riesbeck (1981), pp. 259-307 & 308-317.

**Castañeda, H.-N.** (1992), 'The Content of Legal Speech Acts and Deontic Logic', in: A.A. Martino (ed.), *Expert Systems in Law*, Amsterdam: North-Holland (Elsevier), pp. 107-131.

**Charniak, E. & Shimony, S.E.** (1990), 'Probabilistic Semantics for Cost-based Abduction', in: *Proceedings of the 11th Annual National Conference on Artificial Intelligence (AAAI'90)*, AAAI Press, Menlo Park, California, pp. 106-111.

**Craig, I.** (1995), *Blackboard Systems*, Norwood, NY: Ablex.

**Daston, L.** (1998), *Classical Probability in the Enlightenment*, Princeton, NJ: Princeton University Press.

**Dyer, M.G.** (1983), *In-Depth Understanding: A Computer Model of Integrated Processing of Narrative Comprehension*, Cambridge, MA: The MIT Press.

**Fakher-Eldeen, F., Kuflik, T., Nissan, E., Puni, G., Salfati, R., Shaul, Y. & Spanioli, A.** (1993) 'Interpretation of Imputed Behavior in ALIBI (1 to 3) and SKILL', in: *Informatica e Diritto*, Year XIX, 2nd Series, Vol. II, No. 1/2, pp. 213-242.

**Flowers, M., McGuire, R. & Birnbaum, L.** (1982), 'Adversary Arguments and the Logic of Personal Attacks', in: W. Lehnert & M. Ringle (eds.), *Strategies for Natural Language Processing*, Hillsdale, NJ: Lawrence Erlbaum Associates, pp. 275-294.

**Frisch, A.M. & Perlis, D.** (1981), 'A Re-evaluation of Story Grammars', in: *Cognitive Science*, 5(1): pp. 79-86.

**Garnham, A.** (1983), 'What's Wrong with Story Grammars?', in: *Cognition*, 15: pp. 145-154.

**Hastie, R.** (ed.) (1993), *Inside the Juror: The Psychology of Juror Decision Making* (Cambridge Series on Judgment and Decision Making), Cambridge, U.K.: Cambridge University Press, 1993 (hc), 1994 (pb).

**Horty, J.F. & Belnap, N.** (1995), 'The Deliberative Stit: A Study of Action, Omission, Ability and Obligation', in: *The Journal of Philosophical Logic*, 24: pp. 583-644.

**Hovy, E.H.** (1990), 'Pragmatics and Natural Language Generation', in: *Artificial Intelligence*, 43(2): pp. 153-198.

**Hunter, D. & Zeleznikow, J.** (1994), 'An Overview of Some Reasoning Formalisms as Applied to Law', in: *Think*, 3: pp. 24-40.

**Jackson, B.S.** (1996), '"Anchored Narratives" and the Interface of Law, Psychology and Semiotics', in: *Legal and Criminological Psychology*, 1(1): pp. 17-45.

**Jameson, A.** (1983), 'Impression Monitoring in Evaluation-oriented Dialog: The Role of the Listener's Assumed Expectations and Values in the Generation of Informative Statements', in *Proceedings of the Eighth International Joint Conference on Artificial Intelligence (IJCAI'83)*, Karlsruhe, Germany, Vol. 2, pp. 616-620.

**Kenny, A.** (1963), Action, *Emotion and Will*, London: Routledge and Kegan Paul.

**Knight, B. & Nissan, E.** (eds.)(1999a), *Temporal Logic in Engineering. Special issue of: Artificial Intelligence for Engineering Design, Analysis and Manufacturing (AIEDAM)*, 13(2).

**Knight, B. & Nissan, E.** (eds.)(1999b), 'Forum on Case-Based Reasoning', thematic section in: *New Review of Applied Expert Systems*, 5: pp. 141-212 & 226-231.

**Kokawa, M., Nakamura, K. & Oda, M.** (1975), 'Experimental Approach to Fuzzy Simulation of Memorizing, Forgetting, and Inference Process', in: L. Zadeh, K.S. Fu, K. Tanaka & M. Shimura (eds.), *Fuzzy Sets and Their Application to Cognitive and Decision Processes*, Orlando, FL: Academic Press, pp. 409-428.

**Kuflik, T., Nissan, E. & Puni, G.** (1991), 'Finding Excuses With ALIBI: Alternative Plans That Are Deontically More Defensible', in: *Computers and Artificial Intelligence*, 10(4), pp. 297-325, 1991.

**Lucas, R.H. & McCoy, K.B.** (1993), *The Winning Edge: Effective Communication and Persuasion Techniques for Lawyers*, (Trial Practice Library, Wiley Law Publications), New York: Wiley.

**Malsch, M. & Nijboer, J.F.** (1999), *Complex Cases: Perspectives on the Netherlands Criminal Justice System*, Amsterdam: Thela Thesis.

**Martino, A.A. & Nissan, E.** (eds.)(1998), 'Formal Models of Legal Time. Law, Computers and Artificial Intelligence', special issue of: *Information and Communications Technology Law*, 7(3).

**Martino, A.A. & Nissan, E.** (eds.)(to appear), *Formal Approaches to Legal Evidence*. Thematic volume (divided, in two journals).

**McDermott, D.V.** (1987), 'Critique of pure reason', in: *Computational Intelligence*, 3, pp. 151-160.

**Meyer, J.-J.Ch. & Wieringa, R.J.** (1993), 'Deontic Logic: A Concise Overview', in: J.-J.Ch. Meyer & R.J. Wieringa (eds.), *Deontic Logic in Computer Science: Normative System Specification*, New York: John Wiley & Sons, pp. 3-19.

**Nambiar, P., Bridges, T.E. & Brown, K.A.** (1995), 'Quantitative Forensic Evaluation of Bite Marks with the Aid of a Shape Analysis Computer Program. I: The Development of SCIP and the Similarity Index', in: *Journal of Forensic Odontostomatology* 13(2), pp. 18-25.

**Nii, H.P.** (1986b), 'Blackboard Systems: Blackboard Application Systems from a Knowledge Based Perspective', in: *AI Magazine* 7(3).

**Nissan, E.** (1992), 'Deviation Models of Regulation: A Knowledge-Based Approach', in: *Informatica e Diritto*, Year XVIII, 2nd Series, Vol. I, No. 1/2, pp. 181-212.

**Nissan, E.** (1995a), 'SEPPHORIS: An Augmented Hypergraph-Grammar Representation for Events, Stipulations, and Legal Prescriptions', in: *Law, Computers, and Artificial Intelligence*, 4(1), pp. 33-77.

**Nissan, E.** (1995b), 'Meanings, Expression, and Prototypes', in: *Pragmatics and Cognition*, 3(2): pp. 317-364.

**Nissan, E.** (1996), 'From ALIBI to COLUMBUS', in: J. Hulstijn & A. Nijholt (eds.), *Proceedings of the 12th Twente Workshop on Language Technology (TWLT 12)*, University of Twente, Netherlands, Sept. 1996, pp. 69-85.

**Nissan, E.** (1997b), 'Notions of Place' (2 parts), in: A.A. Martino (ed.), *Logica delle norme*, Pisa: SEU, pp. 256-302 & 303-361.

**Nissan, E.** (1998a), 'Advances in Deontic Logic' (review), in: *Computers and Artificial Intelligence*, 17(4), pp. 392-400.

**Nissan, E.** (1998b), 'Review of: A.G.B. ter Meulen, Representing Time in Natural Language: The Dynamic Interpretation of Tense and Aspect, The MIT Press, 1997', in: *Computers and Artificial Intelligence*, 17(1), pp. 98-100.

**Nissan, E.** (ed.)(1998c), 'Forum on Refuelling Techniques for Nuclear Power Plants' (5 papers on the FUELCON and FUELGEN projects), thematic section in: *New Review of Applied Expert Systems*, 4: pp. 139-194.

**Nissan, E.** (1999a), 'Review of: R.W. Picard, Affective (sic) Computing, Cambridge, MA: MIT Press, 1997', in: *Pragmatics and Cognition*, 7(1): pp. 226-239.

**Nissan, E. & Rousseau, D.** (1997), 'Towards AI Formalisms for Legal Evidence', in: Z.W. Ras & A. Skowron (eds.), *Foundations of Intelligent Systems: Proceedings of the 10th International Symposium (ISMIS'97)*, Heidelberg: Springer-Verlag, pp. 328-337.

**Nissan, E. & Shimony, S.E.** (1996), 'TAMBALACOQUE: For a Formal Account of the Gist of a Scholarly Argument', in: *Knowledge Organization*, 23(3), pp. 135-146.

**Nissan, E., Simhon, D. & Zigdon, N.** (1992), 'Resource Evaluation and Counterplanning With Multiple-Layer Rulesets in the BASKETBALL Expert System', in: *Proceedings of the International Conference on Computer Applications in Sport and Physical Education*, Wingate Institute, Israel, pp. 60-80.

**Nissan, E., Galperin, A., Zhao, J., Knight, B. & Soper, A.** (2000), 'From FUELCON to FUELGEN: Tools for Fuel Reload Pattern Design', Ch. 20 in: D. Ruan (ed.), *Fuzzy Systems and Soft Computing in Nuclear Engineering* ('Studies in Fuzziness and Soft Computing' series, 38). Heidelberg: Physica-Verlag (Springer-Verlag), pp. 432-448.

**Nitta, K., Hasegawa, O. & Akiba, T.** (1997), 'An Experimental Multimodal Disputation System', in: *The Proceedings of the ICJAI Workshop on Intelligent Multimodal Systems*, IJCAI'97, pp. 23-28. The web page of ETL, with which the authors were affiliated, is http://www.etl.go.jp/welcome.html

**Pawlak, Z.** (1991), *Rough Sets: Theoretical Aspects of Reasoning About Data*, Dordrecht: Kluwer.

**Pierce, J.L.** (1996), *Gender Trials: Emotional Lives in Contemporary Law Firms*, Berkeley: University of California Press. [On the workplace pragmatics of women at legal firms.]

**Robertson, B. & Vignaux, G.A.** (1995), *Interpreting Evidence: Evaluating Forensic Science in the Courtroom*, Chichester: Wiley, 1995.

**Schank, R.C. & Riesbeck, C.K.** (eds.)(1981), *Inside Computer Understanding: Five Programs Plus Miniatures*, Hillsdale, NJ: Lawrence Erlbaum Associates.

**Schrodt, P.A., Davis, S.G. & Weddle, J.L.** (1994), 'Political Science: KEDS – A Program for the Machine Coding of Event Data', in: *Social Science Computer Review* [Duke UP], 12(4), pp. 561-587.

**Sharkey, N.** (ed.) (1992), *Connectionist Natural Language Processing: Readings from 'Connection Science'* [1989-1991], Dordrecht: Kluwer (hc) & Oxford: Intellect (pb).

**Shuy, R.W.** (1993), *Language Crimes: The Use and Abuse of Language Evidence in the Courtroom*, Oxford: Blackwell.

**Steinross, B. & Kleinman, S.** (1989), 'The Highs and Lows of Emotional Labor: Detectives' Encounters With Criminals and Victims', in: *Journal of Contemporary Ethnography*, 17(4): pp. 435-452.

**Sycara, E.P.** (1987), 'Resolving Adversarial Conflicts: An Approach to Integrating Case-Based and Analytic Methods', in: *Technical Report GIT-ICS-87/26*, School of Information and Computer Science, Georgia Institute of Technology, Atlanta, GA.

**Tillers, P. & Green, E.** (eds.) (1988), *Probability and Inference in the Law of Evidence: The Uses and Limits of Bayesianism* (Boston Studies in the Philosophy of Science, 109), Boston & Dordrecht: Kluwer.

**Twining, W.L.** (1997), 'Freedom of Proof and the Reform of Criminal Evidence', in: E. Harnon & A. Stein (eds.), *Rights of the Accused, Crime Control and Protection of Victims*, Special volume, *Israel Law Review*, 31(1-3).

**Wagenaar, W.A., van Koppen, P.J. & Crombag, H.F.M.** (1993), *Anchored Narratives: The Psychology of Criminal Evidence*, Hemel Hampstead: Harvester Wheatsheaf.

**Yager, R.R. & Filev, D.P.** (1994), *Essentials of Fuzzy Modeling and control*, New York: Wiley.

**Zadeh, L.A.** (1964), 'Fuzzy Sets', in: *Memo*. ERL, No. 64-44, University of California, Berkeley. Then in: Information Control, 8 (1965): pp. 338-353.

**Zadeh, L.A.** (1973), 'A System-theoretic View of Behaviour Modification', in: H. Wheeler (ed.), *Beyond the Punitive Society*, San Francisco, CA: Freeman, pp. 160-169.

**Zadeh, L.A.** (1995), 'Probability Theory and Fuzzy Logic Are Complementary Rather Than Competitive', in: *Technometrics* (37), pp. 271-276.

# Doing International Justice: the International Criminal Tribunal for the Former Yugoslavia – the Role of the Judge

*F.J. Pakes*

### Introduction[1]

The International Criminal Tribunal for the former Yugoslavia (ICTY) was established in 1993 by the UN's Security Council. Its specific assignment is to prosecute and sentence persons responsible for the violations since 1991 of international humanitarian law in the Former Yugoslavia. Sentencing those responsible would contribute to ensuring that these atrocities are halted, and that justice would be done. In this fashion, the Tribunal would contribute to the restoration and maintenance of peace.

The Tribunal has been in existence for six years and is in full swing. Three courtrooms are in use in its building in The Hague, the Netherlands. In its 1997 annual report, the Tribunal regrets to say that it remains a partial failure (ICTY, 1997). The majority of indictees continue to remain free, seemingly enjoying absolute immunity. The main obstacles the Tribunal is facing are lack international co-operation in investigation and prosecution on the one hand, and lack of funding on the other.[2] Therefore it has not been able to achieve what it set out to do.

The actual achievements of the Tribunal, although covered world wide by the mass media, do not seem to have been the focus of much scientific research. This paper describes research that focuses on the actual administration of justice by the Tribunal. It will examine courtroom interactions at trials conducted by the trial chambers of the Tribunal. More specifically, the role of the Judge in proceedings will be examined. Before that, we will describe the ICTY's procedure in general and courtroom procedure in particular.

### Characteristics of the Tribunal

The Tribunal and its 'sister court' the International Criminal Tribunal for Rwanda (ICTR) are the first International Criminal Courts that have been founded by the UN's security counsel. This sets them apart from tribunals that have been in operation in the past, most notably the tribunals in Nuremberg and Tokyo after World War II.[3] The ICTY is responsible for trying those suspected of being responsible for the violations of international humanitarian law in the Former

---

[1] Thanks to Mr Glyn Morgan, Intelligence Officer, Office of the Prosecutor, for helpful comments and advice.
[2] Joyner (1995), Akhavan (1993) and O'Brien (1993).
[3] *See* on the latter Röling & Cassese (1993).

Yugoslavia since 1991. The part of its *Statute* that constitutes the *Criminal Code* consists of four clusters of crimes. These are 'Grave Breaches' of the *Geneva Convention 1949* (Article 2 of the *Statute*), 'Violations of the Laws and Customs of War' (Article 3), 'Genocide' (Article 4) and 'Crimes against Humanity' (Article 5). Two comments about these crimes are worth making. The first comment is that rape can be classified as a 'Crime against Humanity' for the first time. In order to qualify as such, an individual found guilty of a 'Crime against Humanity' by means of rape, must be proven to have committed rape as part of a systematic and wide spread campaign.

Secondly, the *Statute* does not mention 'ethnic cleansing' as such. The practise of ethnic cleansing, however, may constitute a 'Crime against Humanity' when it involves the deportation of large groups of citizens, or 'Genocide' when it involves murder of a systematic and widespread nature.

**ICTY's Criminal Justice Procedure**

From a global perspective, the criminal justice procedure adopted by the Tribunal follows the following lines. Further to investigations conducted or information received, the prosecution can be said to start when a person is indicted. The indictment is subsequently reviewed by judicial chambers. When indictees are in their national territory UN member states have an obligation to arrest these indictees and deliver them to the Tribunal in The Hague. Several indictees have surrendered themselves or have been arrested by the authorities in the country they are in, or by other organisations. Shortly after arrival in The Hague where the accused normally will be detained (although provisional release is a possibility), an initial hearing will take place in which a plea can be entered. Not guilty pleas are followed by a full-blown trial, whereas guilty pleas when accepted are followed by a procedure primarily focused on sentencing. Trials at the Tribunal tend to be lengthy. They usually involve dozens of witnesses and go on for several months. Following a guilty verdict an accused can go on appeal where the case will be tried *de novo*. The prosecution has a right to appeal as well. The Tribunal's statute also allows for the possibility of review, when at a later stage information comes to light that may have led to an acquittal had this information been available when the trial was conducted.

**Courtroom Procedures**

The courtroom procedures have been said to be of a rather adversarial nature.[4] The principle of immediacy is, unlike in some 'inquisitorial' countries, such as the Netherlands[5] strictly adhered to. Judges do not receive a case file beforehand[6]

---

[4] Tochilovski (1997).
[5] Corstens (1996).
[6] Although recently the practice of providing Judges with case files has been introduced.

and have to rely on courtroom witness testimony for acquiring information about the case. Witnesses are examined by the party that called them, and subsequently cross-examined by the opposing party. Following this, the party that called the defendant can examine the witness again in a rebuttal, and finally the opposing party has another chance to ask questions in a rejoinder. Judges are also allowed to ask questions themselves.

One consequence of this arrangement is that many vulnerable witnesses are to testify in court where they in more inquisitorial trial systems often do not need to. The Tribunal has the full modern range of technological options available to accommodate the needs of vulnerable witnesses, such as video links, masking devices for appearance as well as for voice distortion, while on occasion a satellite link with a witness in the former Yugoslavia has been used as well.

An obvious departure from the adversarial tradition is the absence of juries anywhere in the proceedings. A panel of three Judges decides on guilt as well as on sentencing. A majority finding of two against one is in principle sufficient for a guilty verdict, as state of affairs that has not remained without criticism.[7] Another difference is that prosecutors at the Tribunal have extensive rights to appeal against acquittals.

Judges are appointed after a vote by the UN's General Assembly. States can nominate a maximum of two Judges, only one of which can be a national of that country. In order to be nominated, Judges have to be eligible for the highest judicial offices in their home countries, and of high moral character, integrity and impartiality. The UN Security Council processes this list of nominates and produces a 'short list' of candidates, "taking due account of the adequate representation of the principal legal systems of the world" (*Statute*, Article 13.2.c). Judges are appointed for four years with the possibility of re-election. Not more than one Judge per state can be appointed by the Tribunal.[8] President of the Tribunal is Judge Gabrielle Kirk McDonald from the US. She is to be succeeded by Judge Jorda from France.

## ICTY's Output

Thus far the Tribunal has indicted close to 100 people. These include Serbs, Bosnians, as well as Croats. Thus far, only about 30 indictees have been arrested or have surrendered themselves and transferred to the Tribunal. Although UN member states have an obligation to arrest these indictees, some states in the former Yugoslavia have been said to be not particularly forthcoming in doing so.[9] This has led to the step taken by the President of the Tribunal to officially notify the UN of the non-compliance of the republic of Croatia, in August 1999.

---

[7] Pruitt (1997).
[8] In July 1999, a number of 14 Judges were in office. They are from Australia, China, Colombia, Egypt, France, Guyana, Italy, Jamaica, Malaysia, Morocco, Portugal, UK, US and Zambia.
[9] ICTY (1997, 1998).

Partly because of the lack of co-operation of some of the states in the former Yugoslavia, the number of cases that have been tried is small. One case has been administered following a guilty plea. Erdemovic[10] has been sentenced to five years imprisonment, and is serving his sentence in Norway. Contested trials have resulted in convictions for Tadic,[11] Alexovski[12] and three of the four defendants who were tried together in the so-called *Celebici*[13] case. Of these four, only Delalic has been found not guilty on all counts. He regained his freedom after having spent two and half years in pre-trial detention. Furthermore, Jelisic[14] pleaded guilty to all but one counts, the one being the sole count of genocide brought against him. He was acquitted on that charge and sentenced for the remaining counts that he did not contest. Alexovski was tried on two counts of 'Grave Breaches' of the *1949 Geneva Conventions* and found guilty. Also, Furundzija[15] was found guilty of 'Violations of the Laws and Customs of War' and sentenced to 10 years imprisonment. He has lodged an appeal. The case of Tadic is the only case thus far on which the ICTY's appeals court have rendered a verdict. Initially, he was found guilty and sentenced to 20 years imprisonment. The decision to acquit him on some of the charges was reversed for some but not all of these, and he was sentenced to 25 years of imprisonment on this occasion.

Given the fact that the Judges who conduct the trial are the actual decision makers on guilt or innocence and on sentencing, their role is crucial with regard to how justice is actually administered. The procedural rules give them considerable leeway in deciding how to run a trial. Judges could decide to be large reactive. They could choose to let prosecution and defence do the witness examinations and only rule on objections and other issues, such as the admission of items of evidence. On the other hand, Judges could decide to adopt a more active position. They are allowed to ask questions themselves and it is up to them to decide to what extent they wish to exercise that right. In addition, Judges can call witnesses themselves. Again, it is a matter of choice or preference to what extent Judges regard this as the proper interpretation of their role, as they are, in a way, both Judge and jury at trial.

Since Judges work at the Tribunal for a limited period of time after having been on the bench in their home countries for probably many years, it is not unreasonable to assume that Judges might 'bring their domestic legal culture with them' when they sit as a Judge at the tribunal. Although we have to resort to crude generalisations, we would expect Judges accustomed to an adversarial manner of trial proceedings to be more reactive whereas Judges from an inquisitorial tradition might be expected to conduct their trials in a more proactive

---

[10] *The Prosecutor* v. *Erdemovic* (IT-96-22).
[11] *The Prosecutor* v. *Tadic* (IT-94-01).
[12] *The Prosecutor* v. *Alexovski* (IT-95-14/1).
[13] *The Prosecutor* v. *Delalic and others* (IT-96-21), 'Celebici'.
[14] *The Prosecutor* v. *Jelisic* (IT-95-10).
[15] *The Prosecutor* v. *Furundzija* (IT-95-17/1-A).

manner.

This paper examines to what extent we can actually observe these different styles of courtroom interactions between Judges and witnesses in the ICTY's courtrooms.

**The Present Research**

This research reported in this paper has used transcripts of trials conducted at the ICTY as the raw data. In two cases, witness examinations, cross examinations, rebuttals and rejoinders have been analysed.[16] The defendants involved were Tadic and Blaskic.[17]

In the case of Blaskic it was alleged that from May 1992 to January 1994 members of the armed forces of the Croatian Defence Council ('HVO') committed serious violations of international humanitarian law against Bosnian Muslims in Bosnia and Herzegovina. It is alleged that Blaskic held the rank of Colonel and later of General and Commander in the HVO. The indictment charges the accused with various instances of 'Grave Breaches' of the *1949 Geneva Conventions*, 'Violations of the Laws or Customs of War' and 'Crimes against Humanity'. The case of Blaskic is, at the time of writing, awaiting the verdict.

The indictment involving Tadic alleges that between late May 1992 and 31 December 1992, Dusko Tadic participated in attacks on and the seizure, murder and maltreatment of Bosnian Muslims and Croats in the Prijedor municipality in Bosnia, both within and outside prison camps. The indictment charged him with several instances of 'Crimes against Humanity', 'Grave Breaches' of the *1949 Geneva Conventions* and 'Violations of the Laws or Customs of War'.

Both cases were selected because of the composition of the courts conducting these trials. As we assume that the identity and background of the Presiding Judge might have a strong impact on how the court would conduct the trial, we decided to examine one case involving a French Presiding Judge, and one case with an American Presiding Judge. Our rationale was that a Judge coming from the French inquisitorial tradition would be more inclined to take an active stance at trial, as is common in France, whereas an American Presiding Judge would probably more inclined to be more like a passive referee, as is more common in the US. The Blaskic case is presided over by Judge Jorda, from France. Both other Judges are Judge Shahabuddeen from Guyana and Judge Rodrigues from Portugal. The Tadic case was presided over by President Judge MacDonald from the US. The other two Judges on the bench were Judge Stephen from Australia and Judge Vohrah from Malaysia.

In analysing these witness appearances, we primarily examined the Judges'

---

[16] Trial transcripts are available on the Tribunal's Internet page: http://www.un.org/icty.
[17] *The Prosecutor* v. *Blaskic* (IT-95-14-T).

behaviour. We examined the nature of interruptions, either prompted by one of the parties, or not; questions asked by one of the Judges; the introduction of witnesses; and other interactions with either party or the witness whilst the witness was on the witness stand.

### Questions posed by a Judge to the Witness

Just by examining the number of questions asked, we can see that Judge Jorda's style of conducting a trial was more active than that of Judge McDonald. The French Judge asked more factual questions himself after both parties have finished their questioning, as do both other Judges on the panel. Based on a sample, we estimate that Judges asked almost twice as many questions directly to the witness in the Blaskic case as compared to the case of Tadic. In at least two witness appearances in the Tadic case, the Presiding Judge did not even ask her colleagues whether there were any questions they would like to ask. In one of these instances, one of both other Judges actually took the initiative and asked two questions himself.

Generally, the impression is that in the Tadic case, the Judges were aware of their right to ask questions, but exercised this right rather sparingly. In the Blaskic case, however, Judges did seem to regard their own questioning session as a more integral part of a witness examination, even if they often restricted themselves to a rather small number of questions.

### Interruptions by a Judge during Examinations

Unprompted interruptions in the Tadic case were quite rare. Most often, they did not relate to the behaviour of the parties, but to either the technical apparatus assisting the court or the translation. Only in a few cases did a Judge, usually Presiding Judge MacDonald, intervene during examinations. These were invariably minor interruptions, relating to points of clarification, or a request to one of the parties to repeat a certain question.

Usually, when a Judge in the Tadic case interrupted, it is addressed towards one of both parties. The witness was not often addressed directly. Additionally, interruptions in the form of objections of either party were rather a rarity as well. In most examinations, only one, two or none at all were observed.

In the case of Blaskic, interruptions by the court during examinations were slightly more frequent. The French Presiding Judge clearly sees it as his task to be more active, and steer the behaviour of both parties to a larger extent. An example occurred in the examination of witness Ahmic. The Presiding Judge showed clear impatience with the prosecution, because of their objection to the defence's summarisation of what the witness had said just before. Prosecutor Mr Kehoe argued that this summarisation was inconsistent with what the witness had actually said himself. The Presiding Judge was clearly not impressed with this objection:

"Mr Prosecutor, this is the last objection, otherwise I am going to ask the questions myself of the witness."[18]

A point of note is that this witness was 18 years of age at the time of the examination. He testified about events in a prison camp that he witnessed when he was only 14 years old. The Judge showed great awareness with regard to the distress that the court appearance may cause this witness. It is therefore probably fair to say that this relates to the reason why the Judge was rather strict with regard to how both parties examine this particular witness. The quotation also, obviously, shows that for this Presiding Judge, examining a witness directly is a distinct possibility, although Judge Jorda did not carry out this threat.

When Judge Jorda felt that a line of questioning was not relevant, or when he was dissatisfied with an answer given by a witness, Judge Jorda regularly interrupted and addressed either the party of the witness directly. When Professor Bilandzic testified about historical aspects to the situation in the former Yugoslavia, the Presiding Judge was keen to step in when the answers seemed to lose their relevance to the case: "Mr Professor, it's a legal discussion, this is not a historic conference. I understand you have a great number of things to say, but we need to cut back to the subject at hand."[19]

When subsequently the prosecutor again asked the witness to cover similar ground another dismissal from the Presiding Judge was received. These examples illustrate the active manner in which this Presiding Judge conducted the trial.

### Witness Introductions by the Presiding Judge

The differences in approach to conducting a trial at ICTY become most apparent when we compare the fashion in which witnesses are introduced to courtroom procedures in both cases. In the trial of Tadic, the American Judge hardly played a role in this respect. Apart from having each witness take the oath, she left it to the parties to get on with their examination. In the Blaskic case, however, Judge Jorda addressed the witness rather elaborately and in doing so, appeared to be instructing both parties at the same time. Consider the following quotation, which contains the introduction of the witness, British politician Mr Paddy Ashdown.

"Mr Ashdown, you have agreed to testify at the request of the Prosecution as part of the trial before the International Criminal Tribunal for the Former Yugoslavia against General Blaskic, who is in this courtroom. The Prosecutor has given us a summary of the main points of your testimony. You are very well familiar with the type of procedures that are in effect at this Tribunal, which to a large extent come from proceedings which you are familiar with, so you will not be surprised that you will be asked to answer the Prosecutor's questions. However, the Tribunal would very much like this testimony to be as spontaneous

---

[18] Witness Ahmic, 2 October 1997, transcript page 7393.
[19] Witness Bilandzic, 9 September 1998, transcript page 11383.

as possible, and that of course the Prosecutor can ask you for clarifications about this or that point."[20]

Similarly, anonymous witness, with alias JJ, was introduced to the proceedings as follows: "You agreed to come to testify in the trial, which is here at the International Tribunal, of General Blaskic who is in this courtroom. Speak without fear. You are being protected by international justice. The Prosecutor told us what the main lines of your statement will be, which will make the proceedings go more smoothly. You will speak freely, and you will be guided by the Prosecutor's questions."[21]

Both quotations are typical for the fashion in which Judge Jorda introduced witnesses to the courtroom procedure. Notable is the fact that the Judge encouraged witnesses to speak freely, saying in one instance that the testimony should be 'as spontaneous as possible'. In the other instance, the Judge emphasised that the prosecutor's questions should be taken as 'guidance'. The aim of this introduction seems to be to invite the parties to ask broad ranging open questions that the witness can answer without interruption. In the Tadic case, we simply did not observe such interactions. The Presiding Judge usually instructed prosecution or defence counsel to proceed without any form of instruction.

Additionally, Judge Jorda required both parties to introduce each witness to him before they were called. In this introduction, the identity of the witness was divulged, or their alias if they testify anonymously. It also included an overview of the issues on which the witness will testify, why the testimony will be relevant and what counts of the indictment the testimony will pertain to. These introductions could be quite elaborate. One might speculate whether they served a function similar to reading the case file before trail, which is common practice in many inquisitorial systems whereas it was, until very recently, not common practice at the ICTY.

Such introductions were absent in the case of Tadic. The Judges in this case simply assume a referee-like role and leave it to the parties to elicit the information from witnesses in the fashion they regard as most appropriate.

Finally, it must be noted that in the case of Blaskic, nine witnesses were called on initiative of the bench. This did not occur at all in the case of Tadic, which is further evidence for that fact that the judges in Blaskic are simply more active when conducting their trial than the bench in Tadic.

---

[20] Witness Ashdown, 19 March 1998, trial transcript, page 7325.
[21] Witness JJ, 19 March 1998, trial transcript, page 7393.

## Concluding Remarks

In the number and content of the questions they ask, the way in which they interrupt proceedings, and the way in which they decide to introduce witnesses and have witnesses introduced to them, we can clearly distinguish two styles of conducting an ICTY trial. One is more reminiscent of a continental inquisitorial tradition. In this tradition, Judges tend to be important fact finders at trial. The other style, adopted by Judge MacDonald in the trial of Tadic involves a judge as a referee who does very little in terms of actual fact finding. In this style, decision makers leave that up to the parties. It more closely resembles the traditional role of a Judge in adversarial proceedings.

So which approach is most appropriate? ICTY 'inquisitorial style' or 'adversarial style'? This is arguably a question of comparative criminal justice within one and the same criminal court. Damaška (1986) argues that the difference between adversarial and inquisitorial systems is in its core a difference between values. The highest value in adversarial systems is assigned to *equality* between both parties. Trials are seen as a platform for conflict resolution. If both parties have the opportunity to present their evidence in front of an impartial decision maker, justice will emerge, provided that both parties have equal opportunities of putting their views forward. Such an approach would require for a decision maker to be passive, and to leave it to the parties to produce the goods in terms of evidence.

In inquisitorial systems, *truth* is said to be most important. In order to find the truth, more responsibilities with regard to information gathering are put on the shoulders of the actual decision maker. When finding the truth, rather than resolution of conflict is the objective, it makes sense to have the decision maker more involved in eliciting information that neither party (for whatever reason) has brought forward.

Finding the truth relates to a further aim of the Tribunal which is to keep a record concerning the atrocities committed in the former Yugoslavia. As it was mentioned in their 1998 annual report: "Ensuring that history listens is a most important function of the Tribunal. Through our proceedings we strive to establish as judicial fact the full details of the madness that transpired in the former Yugoslavia. In the years and decades to come, no one will be able to deny the depths to which their brother and sister human beings sank. And by recording the capacity for evil in all of us, it is hoped to recognise warning signs in the future and to act with sufficient speed and determination to prevent such bloodshed."[22]

This objective goes well beyond the 'conflict resolution' objective commonly associated with adversarial systems. When the full details of what happened have to be laid bare, an active position for a Judge who will examine witnesses if

---

[22] ICTY, 1998, para 294.

dissatisfied with the parties' examinations, in order for all the information to be elicited, appears to be the most appropriate position.

Tochilovski (1998) argues accordingly that the passivity of the bench can go too far. The following quote from the Tadic judgment illustrates his argument: "The prosecution failed to elicit clear and definitive evidence from witnesses about the condition of the four prisoners after they had been assaulted. (...) The witness was not asked whether or not [the victim] was dead, and no further details regarding his condition were elicited. For these reasons the Trial Chamber finds that the Prosecution has failed to establish beyond reasonable doubt that any of these four prisoners died."[23]

Tochilovski objects here to the courts passivity. When the prosecution fails to elicit a certain fact in a witness testimony, there is nothing to prevent a court to ask the witness those questions themselves in order to obtain that information. To acquit a defendant on certain counts, only on the grounds that the prosecution did not ask certain questions to a witness is taking the position of passivity too far.

On the other hand, an over-involved Judge is traditionally warned against, because it might lead to a loss of impartiality or perceived impartiality of the Judge or court. This argument obviously carries weight, not only because of the general notion of impartial courts within any formulation of the rule of law, but also because the ICTY's impartiality has been questioned, especially in some of the states in the former Yugoslavia. However, impartiality would hardly be jeopardised by Judges adopting a slightly more active stance at trial, and it will prevent acquittals on the basis of what the courts perceives are insufficient witness examinations. It also fits better with ICTY's ambition of leaving a record for future generations relating to what actually happened in the former Yugoslavia. The importance of the latter aim can hardly be overestimated. It would be wise if the importance of this aim would be reflected in the way in which ICTY trials were conducted.

## References

**Akvahan, P.** (1993), 'Punishing war crimes in the former Yugoslavia: A critical juncture for the new world order', in: *Human rights quarterly* 15, pp. 262-289.
**Cassese, A. & Röling, B.V.A.** (1993), *The Tokyo trial and beyond*, Cambridge, UK: Polity Press.
**Corstens, G.J.M.** (1996), *Het Nederlandse strafprocesrecht*, Arnhem: Gouda Quint.
**Damaška, M.R.** (1986), *The faces of justice and state authority: a comparative approach to the legal process*, New Haven: Yale University Press.
**ICTY** (1997), *Fourth annual report of the international tribunal for the prosecution of persons responsible for serious violations of international humanitarian law committed in the territory of the former Yugoslavia since 1991*, The Hague, the Netherlands: ICTY.
**ICTY** (1998), *Fifth annual report of the international tribunal for the prosecution of persons responsible for serious violations of international humanitarian law committed in the territory of the former Yugoslavia since 1991*, The Hague, the Netherlands: ICTY.

---

[23] Opinion and Judgement, *The Prosecutor* v. *Tadic* (IT-94-1-T), 7 May 1997, paras 238 and 241.

**ICTY** (1993), *Statute*, The Hague, the Netherlands: ICTY.

**Joyner, C.C.** (1995), 'Strengthening enforcement of humanitarian law: Reflections on the international criminal tribunal for the former Yugoslavia', in: *Duke journal of comparative and international law* 6, pp. 79-101.

**O'Brien, J.C.** (1993), 'The international tribunal for violations of international humanitarian law in the former Yugoslavia', in: *The American journal of international law* 87, pp. 639-659.

**Pruitt, R.C.** (1997), 'Guilt by majority in the International Criminal Tribunal for the Former Yugoslavia: does this meet the standard of proof 'Beyond Reasonable Doubt'?', in: *Leiden journal for international law* 10, pp. 557-578.

**Tochilovski, V.** (1998), 'Trial in international criminal jurisdictions: battle or scrutiny?', in: *European journal of crime, criminal law and criminal justice* 6, pp. 55-60.

# ICC – Opportunities for the Defence

*Th.A. de Roos*

## Introduction

My subject concerns the facilities and opportunities for the defence and defence lawyers in the criminal procedures before the International Criminal Tribunal and – in the future – the International Criminal Court (ICC). We dispose by now of some interesting case law of the International criminal Tribunal for the former Yugoslavia (ICTY), and this experience of course is very important for the course to be followed by the ICC in the future. The ICTY had to develop its procedural principles mainly on untrodden field, for its *Statute* and other UN documents did not give very much guidance. It adopted *Rules of Procedure and Evidence*, which already soon have been repeatedly amended. This took place against the legal background of a kind of mixture of common law and civil law traditions, the common law element being dominant but far from monopolistic, if only because there is no jury system but a body of professional judges.

Striking examples of the difficulties and setbacks for the defence are given by Mr Wladimirow, who led the defence team for Tadic during the first instance proceedings (as you may know the case against Tadic was the first one to be heard by the ICTY). Because the war in Bosnia was ongoing during the trial, the defence, which had to go after witnesses itself in that region to support the alibi claim of the defendant, was comparatively in a backward position. It has to be noted that for continental lawyers this style of operating – going after evidence yourself instead of leaving that job to the prosecution and the judges – is highly unusual. On the other hand, for instance American lawyers must be very puzzled by what they undoubtedly perceive as a rather passive attitude of Dutch or German defence lawyers in criminal cases. The very challenging feature of the ICTY proceedings for continental European lawyers has to do with this common law element.

The Wladimirow team obviously obtained no co-operation from local authorities whatsoever, and as the defence did not enjoy the opportunity to participate in or at least accompany the investigations of the prosecution team, it was highly dependent from the court for producing witnesses on behalf of Mr Tadic.

As we know very well from our national criminal law systems, the opportunity to examine witnesses against the accused is a rather crucial right. It is laid down in national legislation, but also in al human rights treaties such as the *European Convention for the Protection of Human Rights and Fundamental Freedoms (ECHR)* and the *International Covenant on Civil and Political Rights (ICCPR)*, and it is also to be found in the statutes of the International Criminal Court (*Treaty of Rome, 17 July 1998*) and the *Statute* of the ICTY. But on the other hand, in those latter documents regulations regarding witness protection have also been inserted. These provide for protection measures which are fit to hamper very much the right for the defence to examine witnesses. This conflict is not unknown in the national legal systems, nor is it absent in the case law of – for instance – the Strasbourg Court on Human Rights. This Court repeatedly had to address problems regarding a fair trial and the acceptability of restrictions of defence rights, originating from the need to protect witnesses whose testimony could not easily be missed by the prosecution The first question I would like to go into this afternoon concerns the way the ICTY did approach this dilemma.

The second problem I want address has to do with the equally crucial right for the defence to produce testimony on behalf of the accused by bringing witnesses to trial. In this field, some important decisions have been taken by the ICTY, which probably will furnish guidance to the practice of the ICC as soon as it will start its activity. A considerable complication here is of course, that not only the witnesses for the prosecution, but also those for the defence often may have valid grounds for fear, as they are living in dangerous areas and quite possibly face retaliation. A more specific problem concerning the defence witnesses is perhaps, that these are themselves sometimes on the list of the prosecutor to be brought to the Tribunal. In that case, they will not be very eager to come to the courtroom from their own free will, unless they are granted safe conduct.

**No Defence Unit**

Before going into these two issues I have to draw your attention to the in my opinion unlucky fact that by the *Treaty of Rome* that provided the legal foundation for the ICC, a Victim and Witness Unit has been instituted, but an analogous institution in behalf of the defence is lacking. The very young International Criminal Defence Attorneys Association (ICDAA) undertook efforts in Rome to have such a Defence Unit incorporated in the Treaty, but it did not succeed. As Strijards, one of the Dutch representatives during the negotiations in Rome, has pointed out, the ICC will not be a very wealthy institution and it will (as an independent organisation, separate from the UN) be dependent from its sponsors (not only the UN but also the participating states). That means inevitably that there will rise problems in providing sufficient financial support for defence activities, especially research on the *locus delicti* and questioning witnesses abroad. In order to gather those funds, one needs an official institute, based on the *ICC Treaty*. Such a defence unit also could provide for professional standards, ethical codes and disciplinary law for the lawyers involved. It could promote know how and professional abilities (such as speaking English fluently and knowledge of common law concepts). Most importantly, this unit could negotiate with the prosecution about accompanying his research team in investigations on site, which is now not foreseen at all. According to Strijards,[1] if the *Rules of Procedure* of the ICC will not create a defence unit simply by stipulating that it exists and is linked to the ICC, there is no legal basis for defence lawyers tot get admission to the research sites if they are not travelling in the company of the prosecutor. As Antoine Buchet, member of the French delegation at the ICC PrepCom in New York 1999 put it: "Procedures should be provided for organized precisely to enable the judges to play their roles as impartial referees, which has been entrusted to them by the Statute. Jurisdictional controls should be installed to enable defence counsel to exercise a type of appeal every time the Registrar makes a decision bearing consequences for the way the judicial procedure should be conducted. However necessary these judiciary controls may be, they will not be sufficient. It is imperative that defence counsel can count on the Registrar, on the one hand, who would not only be given powers but also responsibilities in matters regarding the respect of defence rights, and, on the other hand, on a professional organization, outside the Court, which would help them exercise their profession under the best conditions."[2] Here, many difficulties will have to be surmounted and many problems solved; not in the last place the financial one. International justice is expensive, and the subject is controversial "since may people tend to think that it is only wasting money and time on war criminals".[3] For the credibility of the Court, however, this financial effort is indispensable. The issue has been discussed once again, and not for the last time, during a conference in The Hague on 3 and 4 November 2000 under the title: The Position of the Defence at the International Criminal Court and the Role of the Netherlands as Host-State. There, also the issue of the Code of Conduct and the organisation and control of the defence was addressed.

### Anonymous and Threatened Witnesses and the Rights of the Accused

In the *Tadic* case the ICTY ruled that the interest in the ability of the defendant to establish facts must be weighed against the interest of the anonymity of the witness. It continued as follows: "The balancing of these interests is inherent in the notion of 'fair trial'. A fair trial means not only fair treatment to the defendant but also to the prosecution and to the witness."

Now, this is a remarkable citation. Not because of the fact that the Court takes into account the interests of the witness/victim. In the case law of the Strasbourg Court this is a well-known element. Although the *ECHR* is written exclusively as a document, protecting the rights of the accused in a criminal

---

[1] G. Strijards, 'The need for an Independent Defence Unit', in: H. Bevers & Ch. Joubert (eds.), *An Independent Defence before the International Criminal Court*, Amsterdam: Thela Thesis 2000, pp. 55-69.

[2] A. Buchet, 'Effectiveness and Independence in the Implementation of the Rights of the Defence before the ICC', in: Bevers/Joubert (eds.), p. 76.

[3] H. Bevers, 'Discussion', in: Bevers/Joubert (eds.), p. 83.

procedure, the Court expressly recognised, for instance in the *Doorson* case against the Netherlands, the interests of the victim/witness under Article 6. But there is a difference between the interest of the witness and the interest of the prosecution. From a dogmatic point of view, I think it is misleading to place the prosecution and its interests and rights in a human rights context.

According to the Trial Chamber in the *Tadic* case, the limitation on the accused's right to examine, or have examined, the witnesses against him, which is implicit in allowing anonymous testimony, does not standing alone, violate his right to a fair trial.

Now, we have to keep in mind that the *Rules of Evidence* do not contain the principle *unus testis nullus testis*, and that there is no written restriction to the use of anonymous testimony whatsoever. Furthermore, the *Rules of Evidence* do not exclude hearsay testimony, although this kind of evidence will be handled with due care. Only Rule 95 sets some – rather wide – boundary lines: "No evidence shall be admissible if obtained by methods which cast substantial doubt on its reliability or if its admission is anti-ethical to and would seriously damage the integrity of the proceedings." This is a remarkable formulation. Which level of damage to the integrity of the proceedings should be acceptable?

It has to be noted then, that the Tribunal has a wide discretion in admitting evidence. The essential requirement here is that the evidence should be relevant and of probative value (Rule 89(D)).

In creating its own criteria, the Trial Chamber drew its inspiration from courts throughout the world, including the European Human Rights Court, but it carefully avoided to commit itself to the standards laid down in any other treaty, national legislation or court decision. So, it expressly did not follow the suggestion of the defence that the *Kostowski* decision of the Strasbourg Court has to be seen as the 'bottom line' for the acceptance of anonymous testimony. This attitude was justified by taking into consideration the specific context of the ICTY (war situation, atrocious crimes, particularly vulnerable and harassed witnesses, etc.). Accordingly, it stressed that the right of the accused to examine the witnesses against him may only be restricted in exceptional circumstances, but it added that the situation of armed conflict in the former Yugoslavia, where the alleged atrocities were committed, was an exceptional circumstance *'par excellence'*.

In this vein, the Trial Chamber developed some criteria for the use of anonymous testimony:
- there always has to be an objective basis for the fear for safety; the subjective emotional feeling is not sufficient;
- the testimony has to be important for the prosecution's case;
- the prosecution has to establish that the witness is impartial, and the report made up on that issue has to be disclosed to the defence insofar as is consistent with the protection sought;

- no anonymity will be granted for witnesses with an extensive criminal background or to an accomplice to the alleged crimes;
- the fact that a witness protection program is lacking in the case that national states do not provide for them, and the fact that the witnesses may have still living relatives in the region must be taken into account;
- the subsidiarity principle: if any lesser measure will do, that measure should be applied in stead of the use of anonymous testimony.

In the *Blaskic* case, the Trial Chamber I ruled that it would be prepared to consider granting anonymity for certain witnesses if the prosecution could meet the standards laid down by Trial Chamber II in the *Tadic* case, provided that the prosecution supported its accusation with relevant proof, especially with regard to the importance of the testimony of these witnesses and a positive showing as to their credibility.

In my opinion, this set of criteria gives the court a wider discretion than the *Kostowski* decision and also than (for instance) Dutch legislation. According to the *Dutch Code of Criminal Procedure (DCCP)*, the court may not consider the accusation proven solely on the ground of anonymous testimony. (Statements of threatened witnesses, recognised by the *Rechter-Commissaris*, or written documents containing statements of persons whose identity remains unknown; Article 344a *DCCP*.) Furthermore, the *DCCP* contains the *unus testis nullus testis* principle (Article 342, Section 3 *DCCP*). The practice of the ICTY seems to fall short of both European and Dutch legal standards in this respect. There is no guarantee that a witness will not give false evidence against an accused who perhaps did commit crimes, but not the crimes he is indicted for. According to the *Rules of Evidence* (Rule 96), the accused may be convicted on the basis of just the victim's statements. When the victim/witness also remains anonymous it is not exaggerated to speak of a Kafkaesque situation.

My view is in accordance with the separate opinion of Judge Stephen, who put forward that allowing anonymity for prosecution witnesses where it is likely to substantially disadvantage the accused cannot validly be ordered by the Tribunal, and that the *Rules of Procedure* give no support for anonymity of witnesses at the expense of fairness of trial and the rights of the accused spelt out in Article 21.

While preserving a broad margin of discretion as to anonymous testimony, the Trial Chamber decidedly was not blind for the legitimate interests of the defence. I stressed the point of anonymity mainly to address the fundamental question which role exceptional circumstances may play in restricting the procedural position and interests of the accused. I take it, that these rights, although they may not be absolute, have to be considered as *'Notstandsfest'* to a high degree. This seems to be also the opinion of such an authoritative expert as Manfred Novak in his commentary on the *ICCPR*, and the Human Rights Committee in its General Comments.

But let us consider now which methods are developed and applied by the ICTY (often invited by the defence) to mobilise (so to speak) testimony that is hard to get for the truth finding, also on behalf of the defendant. There are less farstretching possibilities disposable to protect witnesses which have been applied by the ICTY.

First, confidentiality. Sometimes, it is also in the interest of the defence to ask for confidentiality, that is, non disclosure of the identity of the witness to the press and the public. The Court may rule that no pictures are to be taken, that the use of a pseudonym is accepted, etc. Then, the Trial Chamber might order a closed session, but only "when other measures will not provide the degree of protection required". Also, a so-called 'private session' has been applied, *i.e.*, preventing the sound being released from the courtroom to the public gallery. By the use of the technical facilities of the ICTY, it is possible to provide for an electronic disguise of the face and the voice of the witness. When this method is used, the courtroom blinds are partially closed and the witness stand is shielded.

Secondly, videoconferencing. Very interesting is the application of videoconferencing in the courtroom, It makes it possible, also for the defence, to hear witnesses who are not able or willing to come over to the court session. It is for the party making the application for video link testimony to make adequate arrangements for an appropriate location, conducive to truthful statements. A Presiding Officer has to control the identity, to make sure that the testimony is given freely and voluntarily, and to administer the oath. The step to allow video-link testimony should be welcomed in all its aspects. It could present a sufficient alternative option, be it second best, for of course hearing the witness directly in the courtroom is better. In the *Tadic* case, the Trial Chamber granted the hearing of witnesses by video link, thus deviating from the general rule that witnesses have to be physically present in the courtroom. It ruled: "(...) Because of the extraordinary circumstances attendant upon conducing a trial while a conflict is ongoing or recently ended, it is in the interest of justice for the Trial Chamber to be flexible and endeavour to provide the parties with the opportunity to give evidence by video link."

Finally, there is the practice of safe conduct for witnesses who have reason to fear that they will be arrested. Safe conduct is not expressly provided for in the Statute or in the Rules of procedure. The Trial Chamber ruled that a safe conduct order may be made on the basis of its general power of Rule 54, referring to the mutual legal aid treaties which know that kind of provision since a long time. In the *Tadic* case, the Trial Chamber granted safe conduct for four witnesses.

## Conclusion

All taken together, it is fair to say that the ICTY up to now has done a pretty good job in protecting not only witnesses, but also those of the accused, namely the opportunity to introduce testimony into the trial. The anonymous testimony however says a matter of concern, as it is in for instance the Dutch criminal law practice. But the ICTY has been creative and innovative and therefore it could very well be a source of inspiration for national criminal law systems. The role of the defence lawyers in this respect has been an essential one. If the defence lawyers in he future for the ICC would not be of the same level of professionality, that would be a very bad thing for the quality and fairness, and consequently also for the legitimacy of that court.

This leaves for me one thing to consider. In his lecture on the investigation of war crimes in Slovenia for the First World Conference on New Trends in Criminal Investigation and Evidence, which was held in The Hague in 1995, Mr Maver said: "Another problem is that defence lawyers can cause psychological harm to victims in the hope of discrediting their testimony. As Wiesenthal has stated, witnesses suffered not only because they had to meet their former torturers but also because of 'the unbelievable provocations' of he defence attorneys (quotation from Wiesenthal). This kind of problem can be expected during trials against war criminals from the former Yugoslavia."

Obviously, nothing of the kind did happen so far. In fact, it is a matter of professionality to operate effectively as a defence attorney on behalf of your client, without traumatising the victim/witness, let alone provocating it. However emotion-ridden the trial may be, it is up to the tribunal and the professional parties to lead the struggle for truth in a fair and careful way. We have to be careful not to come into a situation in which (in the words of James Sloan) rights of the accused will be "argued away" – "rights, which have been hard fought for in the national setting (...). If the rights of the accused, as defined in an international setting, are a step back from those same rights in the national setting, then the ICTY (and I may add: also the ICC, de R.) will be wavering from its course".

# Participant Monitoring: no Confidence in Confidants?

*S. Sharpe*

## Introduction

Participant monitoring is a term used to describe the process of recording and intercepting private conversations with the consent of one of the parties to the exchanges. There may be a bugging of premises, a wiring of persons or an interception of a public telephone system, but in all cases the consent of one party is deemed to take the process outside of constitutional and statutory constraints and to free law enforcers to act without legal limitation and neutral authorisation, not only as to the cause for the monitoring, but also as to the period of the monitoring and the tactics used during the operation.[1]

In this paper, I propose to examine the issues that have arisen in certain common law jurisdictions from the reception of criminal evidence obtained in this way. I suggest that in respect of England & Wales, current jurisprudence may be in conflict with Articles 6, 8 and 10 of the *European Convention on Human Rights and Fundamental Freedoms (ECHR)*, now incorporated into domestic law by the *Human Rights Act 1998*. The conclusion reached is that electronic monitoring should be adduced at trial only where, irrespective of one party's co-operation, the criteria for the issuance of a judicial warrant are proved to have been met.

## Consensual eavesdropping as an Evasion of Legal Requirements

Listening into private conversations conducted between citizens is an effective tool of crime control, essentially because it *is* covert. The target of the eavesdropping is unaware that law enforcement officers, or agents acting on their behalf, are monitoring and recording conversation for potential use in establishing a criminal charge. It is this false sense of privacy that leads the target to reveal matters that would not be disclosed to the police or government interrogator. Whether the situation is set up merely to create a false sense of security, or whether it goes further and there is an attempt to induce admissions from a suspect, some degree of deception is involved. In England & Wales there is a rather confused picture as to the legality of these operations. This is because each type of surveillance is regarded as a distinct

---

[1] NCIS (together with the NCS and HMC&E) has published a series of voluntary Codes on covert investigations (1999). However, these, although aspiring to incorporate the equivalent statutory requirements into some forms of participant monitoring, are not legally compelling and authorisations remain the responsibility of investigators.

form of criminal investigation,[2] rather than as a specific example of the search powers possessed by law enforcers. There are piecemeal legislative provisions that partially govern surveillance activities, but no cohesive statutory scheme. Whilst this lack of cohesion is being addressed by the government, although only in respect of telephone interception,[3] 'consensual' eavesdropping, in all its forms, remains unaffected by any proposals for reform.

The use of persons as electronically equipped decoys was probably the earliest form of participant monitoring to receive judicial attention in the US,[4] but despite its established usage in this jurisdiction, it was not until the case of *R v. Smurthwaite and Gill*[5] that recognition was expressly given to the enhanced reliability of such evidence. If there is an 'unassailable record', then this will be a factor in favour of the admission of covertly obtained evidence.[6] There is no statutory regulation of the practice of wiring individuals and it is, of course, inconceivable that such an activity could take place without the consent of the party who is being used to monitor the conversation. No argument has as yet been taken that the obtaining of this evidence is a form of search. Instead, the focus has been on its use as confession evidence and arguments have turned upon issues of alleged entrapment and upon the evasion by the police of Code C of the *Police and Criminal Evidence Act 1984 (PACE)*, the statutory Code governing the questioning of suspects by the police and other law enforcement officers.[7] There is a serious issue as to how far the substantially increased procedural safeguards vouchsafed to suspects by the *PACE* provisions have led to an increase in participant monitoring. If law enforcers feel unduly constrained by due process safeguards in the context of formal interviewing, the obvious escape route is to utilise other unregulated

---

[2] The decision in *Katz v. US* (1967) 398 *U.S.* 347 allowed for the development of principled criteria for all forms of surveillance activity (*see U.S.C.* Title 18 Sections 2510-2520). Traditionally, English courts have not treated surveillance as an aspect of search, but until the *Human Rights Act 1998*, no right to privacy and hence no right to be protected from unreasonable searches, existed.

[3] Home Office Consultation Paper Cm. 4368 (1999), *Interception of Communications in the United Kingdom*. It is likely that a more unified system of authorisation in respect of telephone interception will be adopted. However, this will not affect the bugging of premises or of persons.

[4] *On Lee v. US* (1951) 343 *U.S.* 747; an undercover agent was wired and the conversation transmitted via a microphone to a police receiver.

[5] [1994] 1 *All E.R.* 898; *see also R v. Bryce*, [1992] 4 *All E.R.* 567, where the absence of a "neutral reliable record" was a factor in the decision to exclude evidence of an undercover police officer. Both *Smurthwaite* and *Bryce* were argued on the basis of entrapment.

[6] Above, at p. 903. Note that the reverse argument has been made in the US, *i.e.*, that the fact of *transmission* of a private conversation breaches the *Fourth Amendment*. *See* the dissenting judgments in *US v. White* (1971) 401 *U.S.* 745 and below.

[7] Police thereby evade the need to caution a suspect, or to question him at a police station where immediate access to a solicitor must be provided in all but exceptional circumstances.

techniques to gather evidence. The courts are being used as testing grounds of these techniques and, at present, appear to be largely condoning their exercise.[8]

The bugging of premises does not only raise questions as to the admissibility of incriminating statements. The practice has also resulted in arguments as to trespass and the relevance, even prior to the *Human Rights Act*, of Article 8 of the *ECHR*. In *R* v. *Khan*[9] it was submitted that the installation of a listening device to the wall of a flat was both a civil trespass and a breach of the right to respect for private and family life and home.[10] These arguments did not persuade the court to exclude the evidence resulting from the bugging. However, although appeal to the House of Lords was ultimately unsuccessful, Lord Nolan expressed the view that the absence of any statutory system governing the bugging of premises was 'astonishing'.[11] The resultant concern that such activity would indeed not be 'in accordance with the law' under Article 8(2),[12] led to the enactment of Part Three of the *Police Act 1997*. This statute now governs 'entry onto or interference with property',[13] but the Act will not bite where an occupier consents. Authorisation is not required where there is no trespassory entry. It would seem that consent should be a first rather than last resort, since authorisation will only be granted when the authorising officer believes that the action 'cannot reasonably be achieved by other means'.[14] In this respect, the *Police Act* echoes the thematic basis of *PACE*, which requires searches to be conducted by consent whenever possible and treats the issuance of orders or warrants as a last resort.[15] However, this philosophy, whilst premised on an historically justified dislike of the issuance of warrants and a belief that they are an inherently oppressive tool of crime control,[16] allows police to evade statutory requirements by seeking the consent of an occupant of premises to the installation of a listening device. Consent relieves the police from having to satisfy an authorising officer

---

[8] *See* S. Sharpe, *Judicial Discretion and Criminal Investigation* (1998), for the nexus between judicial decision making and the legitimisation of police methodology.

[9] [1996] 3 *All E.R.* 289.

[10] The right to respect for correspondence is also protected. Article 8 does not specifically protect against unreasonable searches, but this must be implicit in the wider right to privacy.

[11] Above, at p.302. *Home Office Administrative Guidelines, Guidelines on the Use of Equipment in Police Operations* (1984) governed such activity until 22nd February 1999 when Part Three of the *Police Act 1997* came into force.

[12] Article 8(2) gives a public authority a margin of appreciation where intrusion is in accordance with the law and is necessary in a democratic society *(inter alia)* "for the prevention of disorder or crime". The European Court of Human Rights (ECrtHR) has declared the case of *Khan* v. *United Kingdom*, App. no. 35394/97, admissible without prejudgement as to the merits. This case was heard under *Protocol 11* arrangements.

[13] Section 92.

[14] Section 93(2)(b).

[15] *See* Section 8 and Schedule 1 paras 2(b) and 14. *See also* the Royal Commission on Criminal Procedure Cmnd. 8092 (1981), para 3.42.

[16] *See* S. Sharpe, 'Search warrants: process protection or process validation?, (1999) *International Journal of Evidence and Proof.*

that the eavesdropping is "necessary – on the ground that it is likely to be of substantial value in the prevention or detection of serious crime".[17] Under the applicable voluntary *NCIS Code* of 1999, there is only an obligation to satisfy the authorising officer that the exercise is "likely to be of value" in "the prevention or detection of crime", "the maintenance of public order or community safety", or "the assessment or imposition of any tax or duty".[18] It also relieves officers from prospective or retrospective scrutiny by a Commissioner.[19] Thus even in those especially sensitive situations protected under Section 97 by a requirement for prospective authorisation, because bugging is to take place in a dwelling, hotel bedroom, or office,[20] an occupier may give consent and avoid the necessity for prior approval by a Commissioner. Even where confidential or privileged material may be acquired, consent will avoid the need to comply with that section.[21]

In England & Wales, statute law governing the tapping of public telephone systems has given rise to considerable difficulty of interpretation when determining the admissibility of such intercepts in criminal trials. The *Interception Of Communications Act 1985* was enacted in the wake of the application to the European Court of Human Rights in *Malone* v. *United Kingdom*.[22] The object was to provide certainty and clarity and thereby to ensure that the procedure was 'in accordance with the law' for the purposes of Article 8. However, the drafting of certain crucial sections was far from clear. In the seminal case of *R* v. *Preston*,[23] the House of Lords confirmed that the prosecution should not disclose the fact that interception had taken place, nor adduce any conversations intercepted pursuant to the Act in evidence. The purpose of authorisation under Section 2 of the Act is "the purpose of preventing or detecting serious crime".[24] There is no basis for extending that purpose to the prosecution of offences. This limitation makes sense of 'the otherwise impenetrable'[25] Section 9 which prohibits any cross-examination directed to establish whether an offence of 'intentional interception' has been committed. In other words, no questions can be raised as to whether a warrant was validly granted by the Secretary of State under Section 2 of the Act,[26] nor whether there are reasonable grounds to believe that one party has consented to

---

[17] *Police Act 1997*, Section 93(2)(a).

[18] *NCIS Surveillance Code of Practice*, Section 2.

[19] Sections 96, 97 and 107.

[20] Section 97(2)(b). These situations mirror the pre-*Katz* concept of "constitutionally protected areas"; *see Gouled* v. *US* (1921) 255 *U.S.* 289; *Lustig* v. *US* (1949) 338 *U.S.* 74.

[21] In such circumstances the *NCIS Code* requires a Chief Constable or equivalent to authorise the surveillance on the basis that it relates to 'serious crime'.

[22] (1984) 7 *E.H.R.R.* 14.

[23] [1994] *AC* 130, [1993] 4 *All E.R.* 638. *See also Preston* v. *UK* (1997) 6 *EHLRR* 695.

[24] *ICA 1985*, Section 1(2)(a).

[25] Per Lord Mustill in *Preston* [1993] 4 *All E.R.* 667.

[26] *ICA 1985*, Section 1(2)(a).

the interception.[27] Consensual intercepts do not fall within Section 2 and may be adduced in evidence. However, Section 9 applies notwithstanding that they can be relied upon as part of the Crown's case against an accused.[28] This leads to the bizarre consequence that the prosecution cannot be examined as to whether or not there is a valid basis for belief in the consent to interception on the part of the instigator or of the receiver of the telephone conversation. Covertly gathered evidence may be admitted, but not challenged. This provides an attractive prospect for law enforcers and may frequently render statutory regulation meaningless.

Having briefly mentioned the main aspects of the relevant statutory provisions and the advantages to the police in bypassing them through a consensual procedure, I shall now examine some of the evidential and rights issues that flow from the use of participant monitoring. There are three general areas of concern. The first of these is that the consent obtained may not be consent given by a neutral party in the criminal proceedings. Secondly, the monitoring may involve obtaining an admission by deception and trickery. Thirdly, there may be no adherence to any probable cause/reasonable grounds requirement and thus an invasion of privacy unprotected by the judicial scrutiny afforded to a warrant.

In some jurisdictions, challenge to participant monitoring may be made on either the second or the third basis. In Canada, for instance, the *Charter of Rights* entrenches both the right to remain silent[29] and the right to be secure against an unreasonable search.[30] Which one of these two rights is the more seriously infringed by participant monitoring is a moot point, but both have been in issue before the Supreme Court. However, where no right to privacy exists, the only argument that can be raised is that there is an improperly obtained confession. This has been the situation hitherto in England & Wales. It is therefore possible for different legal perspectives to be adopted in relation to virtually identical facts. For instance, in *R* v. *A*,[31] the Wellington Court of Appeal considered the legality of a microphone attached to an undercover officer on the basis that the recorded evidence obtained was a search that was governed by the New Zealand *Bill of Rights Act 1990*. However, in *R* v. *Swaffield* and *R* v. *Pavic*,[32] the secret recording of conversations between the appellants and, in the first case, an undercover officer and, in second, a friend of the suspect working on behalf of the police, was considered by the

---

[27] *Ibid.*, Section 1(2)(b).

[28] *R* v. *Rasool* [1997] 1 *WLR* 1092; *R* v. *Owen, R* v. *Stephen* [1999] 2 *Cr.App.R.* 59 Cp. *Morgans* v. *DPP* [1999] 2 *Cr.App.R.* 99.

[29] Section 7 gives a general right not to be deprived of life, liberty or security of person except in accordance with the principles of fundamental justice.

[30] Section 8.

[31] [1994] 1 *NZLR* 429. It was held that the recording was not unreasonable despite the absence of a warrant. *R* v. *Duarte* (above) was not followed.

[32] (1998) 151 *ALR* 98.

Australian High Court on the basis that this was confession evidence and that the matter turned upon the discretion to exclude evidence for reasons of fairness or public policy. Whilst the tendency may be for telephone interception to be regarded as a search and for conversation recorded face to face to be regarded as a confession/ admission, I would suggest that there is no real logic to this evidential classification when, in both cases, the privacy of the conversation is violated.

## Consent to Monitoring granted by a State Agent

The first, and least debated, issue that I shall deal with is consent. Consent is necessarily, in the context of criminal investigation, given by one party and not by both participants to the conversation that is recorded or intercepted. This one-sided consent does not seem to affect the lawfulness of the activity in the eyes of the vast majority of courts receiving such evidence. Even in jurisdictions that purport to have a written Constitution, it is occasionally unclear whether the consent of both parties is necessary to prevent a violation of the right to privacy. In *Commonwealth* v. *Blood*,[33] the Massachusetts Supreme Court did state that without the consent of 'all the partakers of the conversation,' a warrantless recording would be 'unreasonably intrusive' and in *R* v. *Duarte*,[34] La Forest J. expressed the view that "'consent surveillance' is an unhappy term to describe a practice where only one party to a conversation has agreed to have it recorded". Such sentiments notwithstanding, it would seem that in common law jurisdictions there is a conceit of a presumed assumption of risk by the suspect. He is deemed to be aware that his words may be used against him, even when spoken to apparent friends. The question of assumed risk is considered further (below) in the context of deception and trickery. But there must surely be wider implications for society as a whole in respect of the preservation of rights to free speech when there is no security in respect of words spoken in private.

In respect of the *identity* of the consenting party, there is a particular problem where a law enforcement agency is the occupier of the premises that are being bugged, or the subscriber to the telephone line being tapped. In such a situation, consent is an inevitability and any suspect who enters such premises and unwittingly incriminates himself is 'fair game'. One example of this scenario is the case of *R* v. *Christou and Wright*[35] where, in a sting operation set up to combat high incidents of burglary and robbery in the area, police took over business premises and purported to run a second hand jewellery shop. Those who entered and tendered stolen goods for sale were

---

[33] (1987) 507 *NE.2d* 1029; *see also State of Alaska* v. *Glass* (1978) Alaska 583 *P.2d* 872.
[34] (1990) 65 *D.L.R.* (4th) 240.
[35] [1992] 4 *All E.R.* 559.

secretly recorded by means of visual and aural recording devices. The occupiers of the premises who were giving consent to the bugging were therefore the police themselves. However, this was a bugging of premises to which the public had access. It could therefore be argued that a reduced 'expectation of privacy'[36] attached to acts or conversations taking place on the premises and, irrespective of the absence, at that time, of a right to privacy in English law, it is hardly surprising that argument was centred on the implicit deception taking place.

In other circumstances, a suspect is incarcerated in a police or prison cell and, since the individual has no choice as to his or her location, it can be argued that bugging the cell offends against the privacy principle that 'every man has the right to keep his own sentiments' and the 'right to judge whether he will make them public or commit them only to the sight of his friends'.[37] In *R* v. *Bailey* and *R* v. *Smith*[38] for instance, the police bugged a cell in which suspects were detained after charge. The police had already interrogated the accused at length, but they had relied upon their right to silence. The listening equipment was installed whilst the accused attended court on an application by the prosecution for further remand in custody. On return from court, the police made 'sure' that there would be no suspicion of bugging by acing out a charade that they were unhappy about placing the two men in the same cell, when in actuality this is exactly what they wanted to do. The Court of Appeal upheld the convictions for robbery that were based, in part, on damaging admissions recorded in the police cell. The defendants could not seek a right "to be protected from any opportunity to speak incriminatingly to each other if they chose to do so".[39] The Court did not address the fact that the defendants had no other available venue in which to talk confidentially.

Consent may be given by police officers acting undercover, or by informers, or criminal associates working on behalf of the police to incriminate a suspect. In the latter case, the motives of the individual giving consent are highly suspect. There may be much to gain from implicating another in a crime, either in terms of 'deals' with officers over prosecution and sentence, or in respect of payments made for information given. In England & Wales, this means of evidence gathering coincides with an increased use of targeting and pro-active policing. The practice has now been endorsed, even where both parties conversing have already been charged and there is at least the possibility that a deal may have been done partially to exonerate one defendant

---

[36] *See Katz* v. *US* 398 *U.S.* 347(1967).
[37] *Miller* v. *Taylor* (1769) 4 *Burr.* 2303, 98 *E.R.* 201. *See also Warden* v. *Hayden* (1967) 387 *U.S.* 294 per Douglas J.: "The individual should have the freedom to select for himself the time and circumstances when he will share his secrets with others and decide the extent of that sharing."
[38] (1993) 97 *Cr.App.R.* 365; *see also R* v. *Roberts* [1997] 1 *Cr.App.R.* 217 .
[39] *Ibid.*, at 374.

at the expense of the other.[40] In the US, the wiring of an acquaintance, who may himself have criminal connections, is condoned.[41] The practice would appear to have survived *Katz* v. *US* in respect of the rationale that a misplaced confidence in the listener to the conversation involves no violation of privacy rights.[42] As in England & Wales, the very reliability of the evidence militates against its suppression.

In Canada, whilst there has been acknowledgement that a friend of the suspect, who has made an arrangement with the police and who agrees to be used to tape record conversations is an 'agent of the state',[43] any resulting statements will, none the less, be admitted unless, the informer elicited the information in breach of the privilege against self-incrimination.[44] However, in *R* v. *Duarte*,[45] a case of telephone tapping with the consent of a police informer, the Canadian Supreme Court held that the interception was an unreasonable *search* and that it did violate section 8 of the *Charter of Rights*. It was said by La Forest J. "where persons have reasonable grounds to believe their communications are private communications – the unauthorised surreptitious electronic recording of those communications cannot fail to be perceived as an intrusion on a reasonable expectation of privacy."[46]

### Admissions, Deception and Trickery

A second and, arguably, more substantial problem surrounding the practice of participant monitoring is that, at least on some level, a deception is being applied to the suspect. In some cases, this deception may be an implied one and involves creating the false impression that the targeted individual is not at risk of self-incrimination. The suspect is unaware that his words and/or actions are being intercepted or recorded, but there is no pressure on him to make admissions.[47] In such circumstances, English courts do not view sympathetically claims by a defendant that there has been improper incrimination and that any resultant confession should be excluded. Even the fact that statutory protections are evaded does not normally result in the

---

[40] *R* v. *Stephen Paul Roberts* [1997] 1 *Cr.App.R.* 217. There was at least a possibility that one of two co-accused may have been induced by police to reduce his own liability by extracting admissions from the other, even though the court did not accept that this had occurred. *See also R* v. *Hallsworth*, C.A. (Crim.Div.) 3rd April 1998.

[41] *On Lee* v. *US* (1951) 343 *U.S.* 747 and *US* v. *Franks* (1976) *F.2d* 25 where the government dropped criminal charges against the informant.

[42] The judgement in *US* v. *White* (1971) 401 *U.S.* 745 is nor a unanimous one. *See also Hoffa* v. *US* (1966) 385 *U.S.* 293, *US* v. *Caceres* (1979) 440 *U.S.* 741 and *Khulman* v. *Wilson* (1986) 477 *U.S.* 436, discussed below.

[43] *R* v. *Broyles* (1991) 68 *C.C.C.* (3rd) 308.

[44] *Broyles* (above), *R* v. *Herbert* (1990) 57 *C.C.C.* (3rd) 1, and *see* below.

[45] (1990) 65 *D.L.R.* (4th) 240.

[46] The evidence was not, finally, suppressed under Section 24.

[47] *See R* v. *Christou* (above) and *R* v. *Bailey* (above).

exclusion of the evidence. Section 78 of *PACE* gives the judiciary a discretionary power to exclude prosecution evidence before it is adduced at trial. Section 78(1) reads: "In any proceedings the court may refuse to allow evidence on which the prosecution proposes to rely to be given if it appears to the court that, having regard to all the circumstances, including the circumstances in which the evidence was obtained, the admission of the evidence would have such an adverse effect on the fairness of the proceedings that the court ought not to admit it."

This section is concerned with trial fairness and not, primarily, investigative fairness. It has been interpreted so as to permit the exclusion of evidence where the police have behaved flagrantly in breach of *PACE* and the Codes made thereunder,[48] but it has also been interpreted as justifying the admission of evidence on the basis that, despite any 'irregularity' in the way it has been obtained, the evidence is reliable and that it is therefore safe to permit it to form part of the Crown's case.[49] Where evidence is incontrovertibly reliable because it is electronically recorded, the English courts are likely to seek arguments minimise the effect of any police impropriety. Thus, the often quoted aphorism in such situations is that no trick or deception has been 'applied' to the defendant; rather the defendant has 'voluntarily' applied himself to the trick.[50] The fact that the 'trick' may encourage or even provoke criminal activity because, as in *Christou and Wright,* it facilitates the disposal of stolen goods is apparently irrelevant. Further, any 'unfairness' to the accused in admitting the evidence is said to be diminished by the fact that there has been no oppressive conduct in obtaining the evidence.[51] However, it is undeniable that the suspect has not been cautioned that his words may be used against him. Had he been asked to provide answers by a person disclosing his status of police officer, then the full panoply of *PACE* protections would have kicked into operation. In addition to cautioning requirements, *Code C11.1* would have prohibited questioning regarding 'involvement or 'suspected involvement' in a criminal offence other than at a police station.[52] Once at the police station, the suspect would be informed of his *PACE* protections by the custody officer and asked if he wished to speak privately with a solicitor, whose advice would be free.[53] Small wonder then, that state investigators

[48] *R* v. *Canale* [1990] 2 *All E.R.* 187; *R* v. *Quinn* [1995] 1 *Cr.App.R.* 480.
[49] *R* v. *Smurthwaite and Gill* [1994] 1 *All E.R.* 898; *R* v. *Chalkley and Jeffries* [1998] 2 *All E.R.* 155; *see*, generally, S. Sharpe, *Judicial Discretion and Criminal Investigation.*
[50] *Christou* (above).
[51] *Bailey* (above).
[52] Other than in exceptional circumstances, where the delay involved in taking the suspect to a police station might lead to interference with or harm to evidence, or harm to people, or to the alerting of suspects, or hinder the recovery of property.
[53] *PACE Code C3.1* and 3.2. Section 58 of *PACE* provides for presumptive immediate access to legal advice on arrest and custodial detention.

would prefer to catch their targets 'off-guard' and avoid the complications of a formal interview!

In other common law jurisdictions, statutory provisions concerning detention and questioning may not be as detailed or, in a federal system, as uniform as in England & Wales. However, whilst this might seem to leave suspects at a theoretical disadvantage when arguing that participant monitoring is an improper activity, there has been a judicial response that is substantially similar to that achieved under *PACE*. The question is not whether a confession[54] should be admitted, but, conversely, the extent to which the questioning offends against the common law right of silence. In the US, the English analysis of applying oneself to the deception is transmuted into the concept of a voluntary assumption of 'risk' that conversations may be repeated to others, even in the form of prosecution testimony. In *Kuhlman* v. *Wilson*,[55] the Supreme Court Considered an argument that the accused's *Sixth Amendment* right to counsel had been infringed by the admission in evidence of conversations between himself and a cell mate. The fellow prisoner was, in fact, a police informant. The accused had been arraigned and, thus, could not be *interrogated* in the absence of counsel unless there had been waiver. However, it was held that 'spontaneous' and 'unsolicited' remarks did not infringe the *Sixth Amendment*. Distinguishing *US* v. *Henry*[56] and *Massiah* v. *US*,[57] the Court considered that there had been no deliberate elicitation of material by the informant. There was therefore no 'functional equivalent of interrogation'. Mr Justice Burger expressed this by stating that there was a "vast difference" between placing an ear within the cell and placing "a voice in the cell to encourage conversation for the 'ear' to record". Pressure or inducement to speak turns the conversation into an interrogation or interview. Creating an environment where a suspect or accused is likely to reveal incriminating evidence to an eavesdropper does not.

In Canada, the right of silence and the right to counsel[58] are also in issue whenever implicitly deceptive eavesdropping takes place. The first question is whether the accused is being exposed to 'the unequal power of the prosecution' by the existence of an adversary relationship between the state and that individual.[59] Prior to charge, there is no infringement of the right to silence as a consequence of wiring an informer. Even after charge, when that adversary relationship exists, 'passive surveillance' will not infringe the right

---

[54] Under Section 82 of *PACE* a confession is 'any statement wholly or partly adverse to the person who made it'. It may be by words 'or otherwise' and need not be to a 'person in authority'.
[55] (1986) 477 *U.S.* 436.
[56] (1980) 447 *U.S.* 264.
[57] (1964) 377 *U.S.* 201.
[58] Section 10(b) of the *Charter*.
[59] *R* v. *Herbert* (1990) 57 *C.C.C.* (3rd) 1.

of silence.[60] A "distinction must be made between the use of undercover agents to observe the suspect, and the use of undercover officers to actively elicit information in violation of the suspect's right to remain silent."[61]

An objection to this approach is that it tends to categorise participant monitoring as black or white, as either interrogation or eavesdropping. It does not take account of the many shades of grey in between. Ruses, such as using a trusted friend to speak to the suspect,[62] or allowing an informant to give the impression that he is himself a suspect when he is not,[63] are subtle psychological tactics used by the police to obtain evidence when straightforward and open interrogation has failed. Such tactics need not involve questioning by the informant, but they may elicit incriminatory statements none the less. Perhaps, more usually, a combination of 'tendentious observations and expressions of solicitude' may combine with questioning to incriminate the detainee.[64] A second objection is that a link between the right to silence and the right to counsel leads to a confinement of protection to post charge, custodial conversations. There is an argument that the use of these tactics pre-charge, when the police may have failed even to obtain enough evidence to arrest the suspect, is just as much an invasion of the privilege against self-incrimination. I accept that in England & Wales, it is most unlikely that such conversations would be suppressed, but the potential for doing so does exist under Section 78, even though it is rarely applied.

**Unreasonable Searches**

The other main basis of challenge to participant monitoring is that an unreasonable search has taken place. Unreasonableness is said to arise from the fact that there is no statutory or judicial control over electronic monitoring that is taking place. In the US, the covert electronic recording of face to face conversations has given rise to argument that there has been a warrantless search in breach of the *Fourth Amendment*.[65] The same argument would have been thought to have arisen in Canada under Section 8 of the *Charter*. However, in *Broyles*[66] and *Brown*[67] electronic recording was used, but the

---

[60] Though in *Herbert* Sopinka J. conceded that 'electronic' participant surveillance raised different constitutional issues under Section 8, *see* below.
[61] *Ibid.*, per MacLachlin J.
[62] *Broyles* v. *The Queen* (1991) 68 *C.C.C.* (3rd) 308 where the conversation *did* violate Section 7. Important factors were the friendship between the informer and the accused and the deliberate denigration of the accused's lawyer by the informant.
[63] *R* v. *Pavic* (1998) 151 *A.L.R.* 98.
[64] *R* v. *Pfenig (No.1)* (1992) 57 *SASR* 507.
[65] *See US* v. *White* (1971) 401 *U.S.* 745; *US* v. *Caceres* (1979) 440 *U.S.* 741. In *Kuhlman* v. *Wilson* (above) the conversation was noted manually after it had taken place.
[66] Above. Tapes were adduced in evidence.
[67] (1993) 83 *C.C.C.* (3rd) 129. A body-back recorder was used.

challenge to the evidence was none the less confined to Sections 7 and 10(b) of the *Charter*. This is perhaps surprising in view of dicta in *Herbert*[68] that the electronic gathering of statements would bring in the further question of whether there had been an unreasonable search. Whilst there is no doubt that those jurisdictions that have a constitutional right to privacy treat telephone tapping and electronic tagging as aspects of search, surveillance recordings of the words or actions of a suspect may be as challenged as unreasonable searches only when there is no consenting participant involved in the conversation.[69] For some reason, the fact that a conversation takes place in the *presence* of an agent can result in lawyers considering issues of self-incrimination alone.

However, even where search is raised as an issue, the courts have been unwilling to suppress evidence obtained through participant monitoring. In *US v. White*[70] government agents had testified as to the content of a conversation that had been contemporaneously overheard by them and transmitted with the consent of a participating informer. The informer could not be traced at the time of trial. The Supreme Court, although divided as to the reasoning, held that no *Fourth Amendment* violation had taken place. *Katz v. US*[71] established that the *Fourth Amendment* protects "people not places". The issue is not whether a physical trespass has occurred in respect of the monitoring, but whether a reasonable expectation of privacy has been violated. Much of the debate in *US v. White* was concerned with whether *Katz* had retrospective effect. However, from our point of view the interesting dicta are those concerning the general applicability of *Katz* to consensual monitoring. A rationalisation, that is very similar to that used to defeat the 'admissions by trickery argument', discussed above, is employed to validate such investigatory practices. The Supreme Court in *White* stated: "[H]owever strongly a defendant may trust an apparent colleague, his expectations in this respect are not protected by the *Fourth Amendment* when it turns out that the colleague is a government agent regularly communicating with the authorities."[72]

The fact that the conversation had then been transmitted directly to third parties made no difference to this analysis. A 'risk' is assumed by a suspect whenever he confides in another and that assumption of risk includes both that the conversation might be electronically recorded and that it might be

---

[68] Above.
[69] *See Wong* v. *The Queen* (1990) 3 *S.C.R.* 36, a surreptitious surveillance video of gaming activities in a hotel bedroom was challenged under Section 8 of the *Charter*. The accused had been recorded without judicial authorisation, but with the knowledge and co-operation of the hotel management.
[70] (1971) 401 *U.S.* 745.
[71] (1967) 398 *U.S.* 347.
[72] Affirming *Hoffa* v. *US* (1966) 385 *U.S.* 293.

contemporaneously transmitted. As in England & Wales, there was a clear policy to admit 'relevant and probative' evidence which was also 'accurate and reliable'. Mr Justice Harlan (dissenting) considered that "a rule of law that permits official monitoring of private discourse limited only to the need to locate a willing assistant" would restrict spontaneous and, in some cases, frivolous or defiant discourse "that liberates daily life". The link between freedom of speech and privacy is not one that finds much jurisprudential support, but I would argue that these rights form two sides of a triangle, the third being the right of silence.[73]

A finding that no reasonable expectation of privacy has been violated relieves investigators from the need to apply for a search warrant. No judicial scrutiny is interposed on the situation. There is no need to convince a neutral third party that probable cause exists. There is no need to be specific about the location or individuals to be targeted.[74] There is no need to restrict surveillance to a prescribed period of time.[75] The concept of 'proportionality' (in European terminology) or 'minimisation' (in American terminology) does not necessarily intrude to limit investigation. In *R* v. *Duarte*,[76] the Canadian Supreme Court has accepted that the interception and recording of conversations on the basis of the consent of *one* party only is an unreasonable search within Section 8 of the *Charter*. Expressly rejecting the American authorities on this point, La Forest J. considered that "the constitutionality of 'participant surveillance' should fall to be determined by the application of the same standard as that employed in third party surveillance" and that, following the seminal case of *Hunter* v. *Southam*,[77] all such warrantless searches are presumptively unreasonable. A difficulty remains that the admission of the evidence obtained in *Duarte* was not considered to bring the administration of justice into disrepute.[78] However, in that case, the investigators had acted in

---

[73] *See also* La Forest J. in *R* v. *Duarte* (1990) 65 *D.L.R.* (4th) 240 at 250. Professor Amsterdam in 'Perspectives On The Fourth Amendment', (1974) 58 *Minnesota LR* 349, at 407, states that "it is too late in the game to dispute that privacy includes the privacy of communicative relationships with others; Mr Katz was in a telephone booth, not a water closet." He also rejects distinctions based on the use of electronic technologies stating that the "only difference is that under electronic surveillance you are afraid to talk to anybody in your office over the phone, whilst under a spy system you are afraid to talk to anybody at all." In Germany, where Article 10 of the *Basic Law* protects the right to secrecy of correspondence, post and telecommunications as a discrete entitlement, the theoretical basis is though to have originated in the concept of freedom of expression (secrecy of letters) and only later became an aspect of the right to privacy recognised in Article 2 (B. Ruiz (1997), *Privacy in Telecommunications*, Kluwer Int.).

[74] But the *NCIS Codes on Interception of Communications and Surveillance* do require internal police authorisation to be given only where the premises and the target are specified.

[75] The *Codes* (above) limit consensual surveillance and interception to the same period as that authorised by statute.

[76] Above.

[77] (1984) 97 *D.L.R.* (4th) 641.

[78] Section 24(2) of the *Charter*.

good faith in accordance with the law as it had been for many years before the *Charter*. The decision itself has provided a basis for exclusion because it will no longer be possible for officers to argue that they acted on an "entirely reasonable misunderstanding of the law".

In England & Wales, no issue of whether a search, in such circumstances, is a 'reasonable' one has yet arisen. However, once the *Human Rights Act 1998* is in force, Article 8 of the *ECHR* will become a natural part of legal discourse and the question of reasonableness must be addressed. A major difficulty is that even non consensual electronic searches usually require no *judicial* authorisation.[79] In a nutshell, the wiring of individuals requires no statutory authorisation at all, the trespassory bugging of premises normally requires only the authorisation of a senior police officer and the intercepting of telephones, but only those within the public telecommunications system, is authorised by warrant granted by a Secretary of State. There is a debate about how far this situation will be compatible with Article 8, but that discussion is not within the remit of this paper. There is, further, an argument that the consensual wiring of individuals or the consensual bugging of premises may amount to an unreasonable search in line with *Duarte*, above. However, there is, in addition, a problem that is *specific* to English law on the interception of communications. This is the use of consent to make admissible against a suspect electronically intercepted evidence that would otherwise be inadmissible. The situation has arisen through a combination of convoluted statutory drafting and a literal judicial interpretation of the law. As stated above, Section 9 of the *Interception of Communications Act 1985* prevents any evidence being adduced, or any cross-examination taking place to establish whether any illegal interception has occurred within Section 1 of the Act, or whether a warrant has been issued under Section 2. Whilst in *Preston*,[80] the House of Lords concluded that the statute made even the existence of an intercept, and thus its contents, non disclosable and inadmissible, subsequent case law has confined this proposition to *warranted* intercepts.

In *R* v. *Rasool*,[81] the Court of Appeal revisited the earlier case of *R* v. *Effik*.[82] In *Effik* intercepted conversation taking place via a cordless phone had been admitted in evidence. In *Rasool*, Stuart-Smith L.J., relying on comments made during the Court of Appeal hearing in *Effik*, stated that the dicta in

---

[79] An exception arises under the *Police Act 1997* Section 97 when a private house, office or hotel bedroom is to be bugged, or where the operation could result in the obtaining of knowledge relating to confidential information or matters subject to legal privilege; *see* above.

[80] [1994] *AC* 130 and above.

[81] [1997] 1 *W.L.R.* 1092.

[82] (1992) 95 *Cr.App.R.* 427 CA; [1994] 3 *All E.R.* 458 HL. A cordless telephone was considered *not* to be part of the public telecommunications system and hence outside the Act. The same result is reached by a different route in Germany where a portable telephone is not protected under Article 10 of the *Basic Law*, since the use of radio waves or microwaves is deemed to take the communication outside the protection of secrecy.

*Preston* were confined to "the context of the case" and had "no application to a consensual interception". The fact that Section 9 prevented challenge to the lawfulness of the interception was "not sufficient by itself to prevent the admissibility of the substance of a consensual interception". The analysis in this case may be incorrect, but it has had an enormous impact upon the practice of participant monitoring. If the police can persuade an individual to agree to an interception, any recorded statements that incriminate the suspect may be used against him. If, on the other hand, the Secretary of State grants a warrant authorising interception, they may not.

Legal illogicality does not stop there. In *Rasool*, it was assumed that the fact that the evidence may have been obtained unlawfully was 'irrelevant' to the question of admissibility. However, Section 78 of *PACE*, discussed above, would be applicable to an illegal intercept and it would be a matter for the trial judge to determine whether the fairness of the proceedings had been affected by the illegality. Admittedly, the reliability of the evidence will mean that it is strongly probative of guilt and this was held to justify the admission of incriminating evidence in the case of *R* v. *Hallsworth*,[83] a rare example of Section 78 being argued in respect of consensual telephone tapping. In *Hallsworth*, however, there was no issue about the genuine consent of the participant. The objection, on the contrary, was that the participant was a close criminal associate of the appellant and had every motive to drag the appellant down by conducting an 'interview' with him. The kernel of the illogicality that flows from *Rasool* is that recordings from 'consensual' interceptions may be received in evidence, but in seeking to challenge their admissibility under Section 78, no question may be asked to establish whether, under Section 1(2)(b) of the *Interception of Communications Act 1985*, the interceptor had reasonable grounds for believing that a party to the conversation consented to the interception. Thus it is not possible to allege or establish that the interception is in breach of the Act. Such an unfortunate conclusion will, hopefully, not survive the implementation of the *Human Rights Act*. It, arguably, offends against both Article 6 and Article 8 of the *ECHR*.

The situation becomes even more untenable from a human rights perspective when the judgement in *Rasool* is applied to a situation where the law enforcement agency is the subscriber to the telephone line that is being intercepted.[84] In *R* v. *Owen and Stephen*[85] prison authorities listened to and recorded the telephone conversations of those in custody. Prison officers had placed warning notices on the telephones, but these were frequently removed by prisoners. The fact that the prison authorities may well not have had any reasonable belief that the appellant consented to the interception was irrelevant

---

[83] C.A. 3rd April 1998.
[84] *See* above.
[85] [1999] 2 *Cr.App.R.* 59.

and uncontestable. The *reductio ad absurdum* of all of this is that prosecution evidence is "excluded when a warrant has been obtained, even if the defence wanted to see it admitted, but not when the material has been obtained illegally."[86]

## The Human Rights Dimension under the European Convention Jurisprudence

Surprisingly, the recent European Court decision concerning the use of participant monitoring in *Rasool*, does not. in fact, support the argument that Articles 10, 8 and 6 of the *ECHR* may be infringed by the provisions of *IOCA 1985*. The decision is analysed at length because it encapsulates many of the matters debated above. In *Choudhary* v. *United Kingdom*[87] the Court had to consider the admissibility of an application by an individual whose telephone conversations with a police informant had been intercepted and recorded. Damaging statements made to this informant were relied on by the Crown and admitted by the trial judge. A subsequent appeal to the Court of Appeal against conviction was dismissed. Before the *ECHR*, the applicant had two complaints in respect of the interception and these reflect the two major issues raised in this paper. The first was that there had been an unreasonable search since the interception was not in accordance with the law under Article 8(2). The Court found minimal significance in the fact that it was impermissible for the applicant (under Section 9 of *IOCA*) to cross-examine as to whether the authorities had reasonable grounds to believe that the informant had consented to the interception. This prohibition, it was argued, infringed Article 6(1) and 6(3)(d) of the *ECHR*. The Court disagreed and came to the extremely facile conclusion that since the interception had emanated from the telephone line of a house that was, on occasion, occupied by the informant and, since the trial judge had found that this provided the police officer with reasonable grounds to believe in consent to the interception, no further enquiry was necessary. In fact, the recording equipment had had been installed in the absence of the informant. The informant was a hostile Crown witness and the telephone line was not held in the name of the informant. This assessment by the *ECHR* betrays the lack of criticism of national procedures that bedevils its decision making and illustrates a reluctance to interfere with factual findings even when those findings have substantial human rights implications. It also may possibly reveal a lack of empathy with adversarial systems resulting in an overly simplistic faith in the judiciary as guarantors of the integrity of the system and a failure to appreciate the value-laden decision making taking place within the

---

[86] *Morgans* v. *DPP* [1999] 2 *Cr.App.R.* 99.
[87] App. no. 40084/98.

system, leading to the securing of convictions, especially in the case of serious crime.[88]

The second argument that was raised by the applicant was the issue of self-incrimination. He claimed that he had been tricked into making certain admissions and that this trickery breached Article 6(1) and 6(2). The European Court adopted an extremely narrow view of self-incrimination, confining it to compulsion and coercion and thus to evidence obtained 'in defiance of the will of the accused' and by State authorities. This narrow interpretation, limiting the protection of the privilege to 'involuntary' confessions, does not accord with the English *PACE* provisions, nor does it accord with the right of silence cases in Canada and the US.[89] The Court stated that it 'would have "been open to the applicant to put this argument [the alleged trickery] to the jury", but this is to overlook the inherent reliability of electronically recorded evidence. Once legally admitted, it *has* to weigh with the jury (arbiters of fact) because it is extremely probative evidence. It is to be hoped that that this decision is an aberrant one, but I fear that it may not be. It would appear that the *ECHR* is far more concerned with the formality of the monitoring process (whether the procedure is set out in clear and accessible legislation) than with whether the substance of the formal procedures adversely affects the due process rights of citizens.[90] This assertion is exemplified in an analogous case heard against France, where the dominant feature of criminal process is, of course, an inquisitorial system. The *ECHR* found that consensual interception violated the Convention. In *A* v. *France*[91] a police officer had been approached by a man who had been contacted by the applicant with a view to hiring him as a potential contract killer. The option to record incriminating conversations was taken up by the police prior to any official investigation being commenced under the supervision of an investigating judge. It was thus inconsistent with national law.[92] The breach of Article 8 that resulted does not seem to be any more morally culpable than the events which occurred in *Choudhary* and, indeed, there was no doubt as to the consent of at least one of the parties to the

---

[88] *See* S. Kadish & M. Kadish (1973), *Discretion to Disobey*, Stanford; J. Bell (1983), *Policy Arguments in Judicial Decisions*, Clarendon; S. Sharpe (1998), *Judicial Discretion and Criminal Investigation*, Sweets.

[89] *See US* v. *Henry* (1980) 447 *U.S.* 264 and *Broyles* v. *The Queen* (1991) 68 *C.C.C.* (3rd) 308.

[90] *See Christie* v. *United Kingdom* App. no. 21482/93 and *Preston* v. *United Kingdom* App. no. 24193/94 concerning IOCA and cp. *Khan* v. *United Kingdom* (note 12) concerning the absence of statutory provision in respect of bugging premises.

[91] (1993) 17 *E.H.R.R.* 462.

[92] Articles 100-1000.7 of the *Code of Criminal Procedure* (effective July 1991) only allow authorisation by an investigating judge in cases of 'serious crime' (a crime attracting at least two years imprisonment). There are detailed provisions concerning the duration and monitoring of such interceptions.

interception, for it was at his *request*.[93] However, because the *substance* of the law had been broken, the complaint was upheld.

A ray of hope resides in dicta contained in the case of *Kopp* v. *Switzerland*.[94] Here the tapping of a lawyer's telephone lines raised the question of the common law equivalent of legal professional privilege. This was not a case involving consensual monitoring, but the case is, I feel, significant as giving an indication that the Court might look at the *reality* of national privacy protections rather than confining itself to considering whether the letter of the law has been broken. It was said that the 'quality of the legal rules' contained in the Swiss *Federal Criminal Procedure Act* should be examined by the *ECHR*. This examination involved making an assessment of the 'foreseeability of the law'. The law must be sufficiently clear "to give citizens adequate indication as to the circumstances and conditions on which public authorities are empowered to resort to any such secret measures." Such foreseeability does not exist within a system which allows the authorities to by pass the statutory limitations and conditions that attach to powers to obtain confession evidence and to obtain evidence by means of search. However, in England & Wales, law enforcers may do so by relying on the co-operation of a participant in the investigation. A further point made in *Kopp* was that there must not be a divergence between the substantive law and the actual day to day practice of investigating officials. Such a divergence could be said to be positively encouraged when 'consensual' practices are judicially endorsed despite the fact that the reality of police belief in consent cannot be challenged in any judicial proceedings. To this extent, *Kopp* is not entirely consistent with the admissibility decision in *Choudhary*, but *Kopp* concerned a legal professional and *Choudhary* a drugs dealer. Further, subjectivity apart, the search in *Kopp* was far more wide ranging and involved the lawyer as a channel of communication rather than as the suspect. But perhaps most importantly, *Kopp* was a decision based on a review of an inquisitorial procedure where, under the *Federal Criminal Procedure Act*, telephone interception is authorised by an investigating judge and confirmed by the President of the Indictment Division. The interception and processing of calls by members of the executive thus offended against *both* the substance and the quality of the law.

---

[93] Under the *Post Office and Telecommunications Code*, the consent of one party is sufficient to prevent a breach of confidentiality arising and therefore to prevent an offence taking place. However, there was held to be an interference with the applicant's right to respect for her correspondence and also with her private life. The government tried unsuccessfully to argue that a conversation concerning potential offending did not interfere with 'the intimate side' of her private life under Article 368 of the *Criminal Code*.

[94] (1998) 27 *E.H.R.R.* 91.

## Conclusion

In my, necessarily brief, overview of the problems associated with participant monitoring, I have attempted to draw attention to how this practice extinguishes procedural protections and due process rights that usually apply to those suspected of crime. The courts in England & Wales, through the exercise of judicial discretion, endorse deceptive practices by law enforcers even when this evades statutory controls. I would suggest that the courts in the US and Canada, whilst measuring investigative behaviour against a constitutional yardstick, still do not always go as far as might be hoped in protecting suspects from trickery. Whilst accepting that the 'war against crime' requires law enforcers to use subtler and more covert tactics, it would, I suggest, be unfortunate if the principle of integrity of the criminal process were to be displaced by a principle of criminal investigation based on optimum expediency.

Participant monitoring raises questions about self-incrimination, about privacy and about freedom of speech. These rights are protected by Articles 6, 8 and 10 of the *ECHR* and they will have greater impact on the criminal process of England & Wales once the *Human Rights Act* is implemented. One stance that English judges might take in the future is to suppress all recorded evidence of conversations unless satisfied that the requirements for issuing a warrant or authorisation were present when the recording took place. This would ensure that probable cause existed in relation to a suspect *before* the recording took place, thereby avoiding 'fishing expeditions' or incitement by the police. It would ensure that there had been a strictly agreed limit to the length of time for which and place at which the recording occurred. It should also limit the use of participant monitoring to serious crime.[95] Finally, and perhaps most importantly, it would ensure that evidence obtained by means of participant monitoring would only be admitted where the 'last resort' principle applied.[96] In other words, the evidence would only be admitted when it could be shown that it could not reasonably have been obtained by other methods.[97] This last condition is, of course, of particular significance in cases of

---

[95] I concede that this definition is not a precisely consistent one. The *PACE* definition does not coincide with that in the *ICA 1985* and the *Police Act 1997*.

[96] *PACE* Section 8(3) and Schedule 1 para 2(b); *ICA* Section 2(2); *Police Act 1997* Section 93(2). The orthodox view of physical search is that it should, where possible, take place with the consent, or at least the co-operation of the *target* of the search.

[97] Although the *NCIS Codes* purport to embrace the necessity principle, it is clear that this principle is not considered to be limited to the situation where all other measures have failed, but includes the rather more subjective test that the police do not consider that it is practicable to achieve the evidence by other means 'within a reasonable time' or to the 'necessary evidential standard'. Even the *Home Office Guidelines* that predated the *NCIS Codes* required in paragraph 4(d) that "normal methods of investigation must have been tried and failed, or must, from the nature of things, be unlikely to succeed if tried".

conversations between participants and the suspected or accused person. Police officers should not be able to avoid overt questioning in other than exceptional circumstances.[98]

There would be no advantage to law enforcers in gaining covert evidence by consent rather than applying for appropriate authorisation, in those situations where a such procedure exists. Further, the approach would lead to increased judicial scrutiny of police methodologies, which would be no bad thing. Deception, even implied deception, on the part of agents of the law should not be seen as desirable, or even as normative conduct, but as an exceptional investigatory tactic that must be justified to the court of trial. I would suggest that a proper application of the proportionality principle and Article 8(2) of the *ECHR* should demand no less.

---

[98] One situation might be where there were reasonable grounds to believe that the life or bodily security of individuals would be at serious risk unless evidence of proposed criminal conduct was obtained.

# Whistleblowers, Witness Protection and Open Justice

*M. Spencer*

> "(...) [N]o private obligations can dispense with the universal one which lies on every member of the Society to discover every design which may be formed, contrary to the laws of the Society, to destroy the public welfare."[1]

> "While witness intimidation occurs frequently in the organised crime context, it is by no means limited to that situation."[2]

## Introduction

This paper examines the protection English law affords to a specific group of witnesses, namely those giving evidence against their employers in proceedings arising from disclosures of wrongdoing at work ('whistleblowing'). It is suggested that there is a contradiction in government policy in this area. Both whistleblowers and witnesses are performing a public service. However the official treatment of these two practices differs somewhat. Encouragement is given to public spirited individuals to speak out about workplace malpractices which may be detrimental to society while, in contrast, recent policy decisions are giving more scope for witnesses to avoid appearing publicly in court. In examining these two developments the paper leads to some more general observations on the extent which the growing emphasis on 'witness protection' may disadvantage defendants and have undesirable consequences for the integrity of the trial process.

## Responsible Citizenship

In the past decade the major political parties have sought to encourage responsible citizenship. For example in 1990 the House of Commons Commission on Citizenship proclaimed that: "(...) the challenge to our society in the late twentieth century is to create conditions where all who wish can become actively involved, can understand and participate, can influence, persuade, campaign and whistleblow and in the making of decisions can work together for the mutual good."[3] In the last decade or so a number of major accidents, financial scandals and breaches of safety have illustrated that employees are often in a better position to discern potential and actual wrongdoing at their place of work than official regulatory agencies. Such employees if they 'blew the whistle' before a crisis came to a head would in

---

[1] *Annesley* v. *The Earl of Anglesea* [1743] *State Tr.* 1139.
[2] M.H. Graham, 'Witness Intimidation', (1984) *Florida State University Law Review*, pp. 240-243.
[3] *Encouraging Citizenship*, London: HMSO 1990.

many cases be doing a public service.[4] In some cases such precautionary activity might be welcomed by employers who might be thus enabled to change internal procedures but in other cases employees might face victimisation. Increased employment protection is now afforded to them by the *Public Interest Disclosure Act 1998 (PIDA)* whose objective is "to protect individuals who make certain disclosures of information in the public interest". This defines a 'qualifying disclosure' as one made in 'good faith' and which a worker reasonably believes tends to show one or more of the following: a criminal offence, failure to comply with any legal obligation, a miscarriage of justice, a danger to the health and safety of any individual, damage to the environment or deliberate concealment of information tending to show any of these. Disclosure of these should be made internally or to 'prescribed persons'. Such 'prescribed persons' include the Financial Services Authority, the Audit Commission, the Environment Agency and the Health and Safety Executive. In other limited circumstances disclosures may be made to outside bodies such as the Press and the police if they are made in good faith, the worker reasonably believes her allegations to be substantially true, she is not acting for personal gain, and has either already informed her employer or prescribed person or has not done so because she reasonably believes they would act to her detriment or destroy evidence. The PIDA gives employment protection if the worker makes a 'qualifying disclosure' and is victimised as a result but in the case of a dismissed employee the outcome of any proceedings may be compensation rather than reinstatement. The main function of the Act is thus to extend the scope of the provisions on unfair dismissal and action short of dismissal.

The PIDA originated as a *Private Members' Bill* but it obtained government support.[5] In a parallel but unrelated development the Government has shown its commitment to protecting witnesses as well as whistleblowers. The Labour Party Manifesto 1997 declared that "greater protection will be provided for victims in rape and serious sexual offence trials and those subject to intimidation including witnesses." Shortly after taking office in 1997 the Blair government appointed a Home Office sponsored committee on the subject. Its report, *Speaking up for Justice*,[6] put such witnesses into two categories namely those who are vulnerable because of personal characteristics and those whose vulnerabilities depend on circumstances, such as relationship to the defendant. Many of its proposals have been incorporated into the Youth

---

[4] *See* D. Lewis, 'Whistleblowers and Job Security', (1995) 58 *Modern Law Review*, 208-221.
[5] For an account of the history of the legislation *see* D. Lewis, 'The Public Interest Disclosure Act 1998', (1998) 27 *Industrial Law Journal*, 325-329.
[6] *Speaking up for Justice. Report of the Interdepartmental Working Group on the Treatment of Vulnerable or Intimidated Witnesses in the Criminal Justice System*, Home Office, June 1998.

Justice and *Criminal Evidence Act 1999* (henceforth referred to as the *1999 Act*).[7] Another policy development which has implications for witness protection is the proposal to reform the law against the admissibility of hearsay evidence.[8] Though none of these measures are specifically designed to protect employees who make disclosures in the public interest this paper will demonstrate that they are sufficiently broad based to cover those whose disclosures lead to subsequent civil or criminal proceedings and who might fear retaliation from their employers. Such employees are obviously in a subordinate and thus vulnerable position vis-à-vis their employers.

**Existing Sanctions against Witness Victimisation**

The history of employment legislation has shown that complainants might indeed suffer retaliation. There have been attempts to deal with this by statute. For example Section 4(1) of the *Sex Discrimination Act 1975* and Section 2(1) of the *Race Relations Act 1976* allow a complaint to be brought where the discrimination takes place by reason that the person victimised has "given evidence or information in connection with proceedings brought by any person against the discriminator or any other person" under the Act, or "has alleged that the discriminator or any other person has committed an act which (…) would amount to a contravention of" the Act. This protection is unavailable if the allegation made by the victim is false and not made in good faith.

These sections have been very restrictively interpreted particularly in relation to the establishing of causation.[9] Some additional protection against victimisation is afforded to those who bring proceedings against an employer to enforce a relevant statutory right, such as health and safety legislation, or allege that the employer had infringed a relevant statutory right.[10]

Employer victimisation of witnesses is a long-standing phenomenon. More than a century ago the House of Commons was outraged by a particularly blatant example. John Hood an employee of Cambrian Railway Company for over 20 years gave devastating evidence to a select committee about the hours of work endured by railway workers. As a result he was dismissed. The directors of the company were summoned to the Bar of the House and told: "A great principle has been infringed, the principle that evidence given before this House should be free and unrestrained."[11] The outcome was the enactment of the *Witnesses (Public Inquiries) Protection Act 1892* which is still in force.

---

[7] Most of the provisions of the *1999 Act* will be brought into force during 2000.

[8] *See Evidence in Criminal Proceedings: Hearsay and Related Topics*, Law Com. No. 245. Cm 3670, Law Commission 1997.

[9] *See* for example *Aziz* v. *Trinity Street Taxis*, [1988] 3 *W.L.R.* 79

[10] *See Employment Rights Act 1996*, Sections 104 and 104A.

[11] For an account of this incident and the subsequent legislation *see* Y. Cripps, *The Legal Implications of Disclosure in the Public Interest* (2nd ed.), Sweet and Maxwell 1994, Chapter 10.

Section 2 provides that: "Every person who commits any of the following acts, that is to say who threatens or in any way punishes, damnifies or injures or attempts to punish, damnify or injure any person for having given evidence upon any inquiry or on account of the evidence which he has given upon any such inquiry shall, unless such evidence was given in bad faith, be guilty of a misdemeanour and be liable on conviction thereof to a maximum penalty of one hundred pounds, or to a maximum imprisonment of three months."

Section 4 provides that: "(…) any sum of money which [the court] may think reasonable, having regard to all the circumstances of the cases, by way of satisfaction or compensation for any loss of situation, wages, status, or other damnification or injury suffered by the complainant through or by means of the offence."

The Act did not cover traditional courts because there the common law of contempt was deemed adequate. Contempt in relation to court proceedings, most commonly examined in the context of publications, also has wide ranging application to the sort of private threats faced by witnesses particularly those made in an employment context. The scope of contempt in this connection is given by Smith & Hogan: "It is common law misdemeanour to attempt to dissuade or prevent a witness from appearing or giving evidence, or to alter evidence previously given in a preliminary enquiry."[12]

It appears that threats to take retaliatory action are covered. Thus for example in *R* v. *Kellett* the defendant was held to be in contempt for making a threat to a neighbour that she would be sued for slander if she gave evidence against him in divorce suit proceedings.[13] Some threats of course may amount to taking action which an employer is lawfully entitled to do, such as a threat to dismiss, refuse to promote or transfer to another site. A finding of contempt may still be made in these circumstances. In *Re Martin (Peter)* the Divisional Court held that it was contempt for a solicitor to make a lawful but "wholly improper, unfair and immoderate" threat to report a barrister to the Inner Temple if he did not desist from a private prosecution.[14] In *R* v. *Kellett* Stephenson LJ said: "The exercise of a legal right to dismiss or to evict a person who has given evidence does not excuse interfering with the administration of justice by deterring persons who might wish to give evidence in other cases, or prevent such interference from being a contempt."[15] If the retaliation is taken after the proceedings are over contempt may still apply.

In *Attorney-General* v. *Butterworth* the Court of Appeal held that victimising a witness after he had given evidence amounts to contempt of court.[16] Here a union official was removed as delegate after he had given

---

[12] Smith & Hogan, *Criminal Law* (38th ed., 1973), p. 1234, para 3463.
[13] [1975] 3 *All E.R.* 468
[14] (1986) *Times Law Report*, April 23.
[15] *Sup. cit.*
[16] [1962] 3 *W.L.R.* 819.

evidence at the Restrictive Practices Court. Donovan LJ pointed out that the trial judge had rightly sounded a warning to any large employer of labour who might announce that any employee who gave evidence against him in any case would suffer for it. He agreed that such a case might need special consideration and justify an extension of the principles which the court extracted from existing authorities limiting the offence of contempt of court to interference in pending cases. Further indication of the scope of contempt proceedings is given by *Peach Grey* v. *Sommers.*[17] This established that industrial tribunals were courts for the purposes of a finding of contempt by the Divisional Court.

Despite these indications of the broad application of the law of contempt to cases of witness intimidation there are some limitations and uncertainties in this area of law. These include the question of how close the act of contempt has to be to court proceedings,[18] uncertainty over the nature of the *mens rea,*[19] and the limited penalties available.[20] One particular weakness is that the law of contempt does not allow for compensation to be made to victims. In view of this the Report of the Committee on Contempt of Court recommended stronger sanctions and that "to take or threaten reprisals against a witness after the proceedings are concluded should no longer be a contempt but that it should instead be made an indictable offence. (...) We see no reason why the victim should not be entitled to compensation, and we recommend that it should be open to the court to award it as it can do under section 4 of the *1892 Act.*"[21] Twenty years later action was taken by the passing of the Criminal Justice and *Public Order Act 1994.* Section 51 created two new offences, namely intimidating a witness and harming or threatening to harm a witness but did not provide for compensation for the victim. The offences could apply to intimidation in employment because the range of activities covered includes financial harm to the person or property. The act or threat must be intended to intimidate. Witness intimidation applies to current investigations and harming or threatening to harm a witness applies after the trial has ended. The perpetrator must know or believe that the other person is helping or has helped an investigation, is a witness or potential witness juror or potential juror. The perpetrator must have acted or threatened the person because they believed this and with the intention of obstructing the course of justice. Because of the difficulty of proof the Act specifies that it is presumed that the perpetrator intended to pervert the course of justice unless the contrary is proven. No time

---

[17] [1995] *I.R.L.R.* 363.
[18] *See Attorney-General* v. *Sport Newspapers Ltd*, [1991] 1 *W.L.R.* 1194, where there was disagreement on this issue between Bingham LJ and Hodgson J.
[19] *See* Section 6(c) *Contempt of Court Act 1981* and *Attorney-General* v. *Times Group Newspapers*, [1989] *QB* 110.
[20] *See Morris* v. *Crown Office*, [1970] 2 *QB* 114 and *R* v. *Palmer*, [1992] 1 *W.L.R.* 568.
[21] Cmnd 5794, 1974.

limits are set for the prosecution to bring such a case. However there is no presumption of intent where the alleged harm or threat came more than a year after the conclusion of proceedings. In 1998 there were 411 convictions under Section 51.[22] There are no figures as to whether any of these were acts taken by employers against employees. Speaking up for Justice recommended that the offence of witness intimidation be extended to cover civil proceeding and the *Home Office Policy Document Action for Justice* has it stated that "this will be considered as part of the Lord Chancellor's further civil justice reforms".[23]

### Evidential Protection – Anonymity and Hearsay

The intent of the PIDA is obviously that employee whistleblowers should not be anonymous since they will only get employment protection if they can establish a causal connection between their loss of job etc. and the giving of information. It may be that they prefer to remain anonymous and not risk reprisals at all although there is a commonly held revulsion against unnamed informants.[24] There is however a public policy consideration in providing informants with anonymity. As John Niblett points out: "The term informant embraces a number of individuals from the 'supergrass' and paid informant who are providing information for some form of personal advantage to someone who provides information that comes to light as part of their employment. (...) [A]ll deserve anonymity unless disclosure is essential to prove innocence."[25]

Mindful of the real risk of retaliation against informants the Report of the Royal Commission on Standards of Conduct in Public Life concluded: "We have already discussed the problem of an employee fearing victimisation if he makes a complaint against his colleagues or employers. (...) It is impossible for the police to give a prospective complainant a guarantee of permanent confidentiality since his evidence might be essential to enable a prosecution to be mounted. We are however assured that the police will always do their best to protect the anonymity of those who complain to them and will make arrangements to hear a complaint in ways that are least likely to bring him to the attention of his colleagues."[26]

---

[22] Information supplied to author by Crime and Criminal Justice Unit of the Home Office, December 1999.

[23] *Action for Justice. Implementing the 'Speaking up for Justice' Report on Vulnerable or Intimidated Witnesses in the Criminal Justice System in England and Wales*, Home Office, November 1999, p. 6.

[24] *See* for example letter to the Editor from Lady Wheldon, *The Times* 12 November 1980: "Unnamed disclosures leave a whiff of self-righteousness or mischief or cowardice about them, sometimes all three. Those who purvey them never entirely escape the stain."

[25] J. Niblett, *Disclosure in Criminal Proceedings*, Blackstone Press 1997, p. 144.

[26] *Report of the Royal Commission on Standards of Conduct in Public Life*, Cmnd 6524, (1976) para 287.

The courts may provide protection to informants. Thus a species of confidence was identified in *Alfred Crompton Amusement Machines Ltd* v. *Customs and Excise Commissioners (No 2)* and it was held that the sources of information obtained in confidence for tax valuation purposes was not disclosable.[27] However by contrast the 'interests of justice' required an order for discovery in *Norwich Pharmacal* v. *Customs and Excise Commissioners.*[28] In this case the appellant, the holder of a patent on a chemical compound, wanted to inspect certain documents in the possession of the Commissioners of Customs and Excise which contained the names and addressers of importers of the same compound. The House of Lords ordered the Commissioners to disclose the names and addresses of the importers. Lord Reid said: "(…) [I]f through no fault of his own a person gets mixed up in the tortious acts of others so as to facilitate their wrongdoing he may incur no personal liability but comes under a duty to assist the person who has been wronged by giving him full information and disclosing the identity of the wrongdoers."[29]

This principle was applied to a whistleblower in the more recent case of *P* v. *T.*[30] The plaintiff had been employed by the defendant company. He was dismissed and the managing director told him that someone had made serious allegations about his conduct with outside contractors. The informant wanted to remain anonymous. The plaintiff's employment prospects were so blighted that he began proceedings in the High Court for breach of contract and conspiracy against the company. In addition he asked the court to order disclosure of the documents and information provided by the informant so he could initiate defamation proceedings. Sir Richard Scott V-C held that discovery should be ordered to enable the plaintiff to consider an action for defamation and/or malicious falsehood.

Informants who are called as witnesses at trial cannot generally expect anonymity. One of the ingredients of a fair trial is the right to confront one's accuser in open court. This is an aspect of natural justice and is enshrined in Article 6(3)(d) of the *European Convention on Human Rights (ECHR)*. This Article asserts that "everyone charged with a criminal offence" has "minimum rights" which include to the "right to examine and have examined witnesses called against him". The Convention is now part of English law by virtue of the *Human Rights Act 1998*. There are difficulties in drawing on the existing *ECHR* case law to attempt to anticipate how the principle will be applied in English courts. In the first place civil law procedures draw more heavily on pre-trial hearings than is common in English law for example by allowing witnesses to be cross examined by counsel in the absence of the defendant.

---

[27] [1974] *AC* 405.
[28] [1974] *AC* 133.
[29] *Ibid.*, p. 175.
[30] [1997] 1 *W.L.R.* 1309.

Also the *ECHR* cases do not set out exact procedures to be followed.[31] There is continual stress in the Strasbourg jurisprudence on the importance of taking account of all the circumstances of each specific case. Nonetheless it is instructive to examine the general thrust of the case law which has does not insist as an absolute principle that witnesses must always be available in open court to be cross examined.

For example in *Doorson* v. *Netherlands* the European Court of Human Rights (ECrtHR) was prepared to balance the interests of intimidated witnesses with those of the defendant.[32] It stated: "It is true that Article 6 does not explicitly require the interests of witnesses in general and those of victims called upon to testify in particular to be taken into consideration. However, their life, liberty or security of person may be at stake as may interests coming generally within the ambit of Article 8 of the Convention. Such interests of witnesses and victims are in principle protected by other, substantive provisions of the Convention which imply that Contracting States should organise their criminal proceedings in such a way that those interests are not unjustifiably imperilled. Against this background the interests of the defence are balanced against those of witnesses or victims called upon to testify."[33]

Here witnesses who knew the accused, an alleged drug dealer, were permitted to testify anonymously out of the presence of the defence. Counsel were able to cross examine them at an earlier hearing. The ECrtHR was prepared to accept this procedure, swayed in part by the consideration that the conviction was not based wholly on the evidence of these witnesses. It noted that the witnesses anticipated rather than actually experienced intimidation but observed: "Although there has been no suggestion that they were ever threatened by the applicant himself, the decision to maintain their anonymity cannot be regarded as unreasonable per se. Regard must be had to the fact, as established by the domestic courts and not contested by the applicant that drug dealers frequently resorted to threats or actual violence against persons who gave evidence against them."[34] The Court concluded: "On balance, while it would clearly have been preferable for the applicant to have attended the questioning of the witnesses, the Court of Appeal was entitled to consider that the applicant's interests were outweighed by the need to ensure the safety of the witnesses. More generally the Convention does not preclude identification – for the purposes of Article 6(3)(d) – of an accused with his Counsel."[35]

The earlier case of *Kostovski* v. *Netherlands* involved police informants who were allowed by the national court to give evidence anonymously. Here however the ECrtHR was not convinced of the efficacy of this procedure. It

---

[31] *See* A. Ashworth, 'Article 6 and the Fairness of Trials', (1999) *Crim.L.R.* 261-272.
[32] (1996) 23 *E.H.R.R.* 330.
[33] *Ibid.*, para 70.
[34] *Ibid.*, para 71.
[35] *Ibid.*, para 74.

stated that "[i]n principle all the evidence must be produced in the presence of the accused at a public hearing with a view to adversarial argument. However, to use statements obtained at the pre-trial stage as evidence is not in itself inconsistent with Article 6(3)(a) and (1), provided the rights of the defendant have been respected. This does not mean however that in order to be used as evidence statement of witnesses should always be made at a public hearing in court."[36] Thus though the Court found a violation of Article 6 in this instance it was clearly not disposed to see the right to confrontation as an absolute. Sharpe sees in this case a "crime control versus due process audit".[37] This is certainly implicit Kostovski in the following observation on the importance of balancing the interests concerned: "While the Court recognised the force of the Government's reference to an increase in the intimidation of witnesses and to the need to balance the various interests involved, it observed that the right to a fair administration of justice cannot be sacrificed to expediency. The Convention did not prelude reliance on anonymous sources at the investigation stage of criminal proceedings. Yet the use of anonymous statements as sufficient evidence to found a conviction was a different matter. It involved limitations on the rights of the defence which were irreconcilable with the guarantees in Article 6."[38]

Again in *Van Mechelen* v. *Netherlands*, the Court, while finding a violation when police officers were allowed to testify anonymously by sound link, accepted that "the use of anonymous witnesses to found a conviction is not under all circumstances incompatible with the Convention".[39] It saw also the need for the interests of the defence to be balanced with those of witnesses or victims called to testify.[40] In this particular instance not enough effort had been made to assess the extent of the threat to the witnesses.

Thus there is a clear indication in the Strasbourg cases that the interests of the defendants and those of the witnesses should be balanced in deciding what are appropriate trial ures. Admittedly overall the Court is quite robust about the importance of allowing the defendant's right to cross-examine witnesses[41] although this is waived in some, albeit rare, occasions. There is evidence also in the context of English law that the need for a balancing process is acknowledged. For example the Law Commission's Report refers to victims' rights: "(…) [V]ictims of crimes have human rights as well, and if a country's rules of criminal law, procedure or evidence are ineffective to protect such

---

[36] (1990) 12 *E.H.R.R.* 434, para 41.
[37] S. Sharpe, 'Article 6 and the Disclosure of Evidence in Criminal Trials', (1999) *Crim.L.R.* 276, p. 282.
[38] *Sup. cit.*, paras 44-45.
[39] (1998) 25 *E.H.H.R.* 657, para 52.
[40] *Ibid.*, para 53.
[41] *See* for example *Unterpinger* v. *Austria* (1986), 13 *E.H.R.R.*, *Ludi* v. *Switzerland* (1992), 15 *E.H.R.R.* and *Said* v. *France* (1994), 17 *E.H.R.R.* 251.

victims, this deficiency sometimes enables them to complain that their rights under the Convention have been infringed." It did not specify what cases it had in mind.[42]

In practice there are a number of mechanisms available in English law to protect witnesses facing court appearances who feel intimidated. On very rare occasions witnesses may be able to remain anonymous. One such was the case of *R* v. *Taylor (Gary)*.[43] Here a frightened schoolgirl who had witnessed the burying of a body was allowed to testify behind a screen anonymously. The Appeal Court observed however: "A defendant in a criminal trial had a fundamental right to see and to know the identity of his accusers, including witnesses for the prosecution. That right should only be denied in rare and exceptional circumstances; whether such circumstances existed was pre-eminently a matter for the exercise of the trial judge's discretion."[44] Commenting on this case May writes: "It is submitted that (with these considerations in mind) courts should be prepared to take a robust attitude and allow witnesses protection in appropriate cases in order to counter what appears to be a growing trend towards intimidation of witnesses."[45]

A more frequently available route for the intimidated witness to avoid the ordeal of testifying in person is the submission of evidence by written statement. Of course this will not generally be done anonymously and so an employer who wanted to take reprisals would be likely to be able to discover the identity of her accuser.[46] Nonetheless recent developments in creating new statutory exceptions to the law against hearsay give additional opportunities for witnesses to avoid the experience of being cross examined by defendants. The *Criminal Justice Act 1988 inter alia* allowed the admission of first hand documentary hearsay and of multiple documentary hearsay produced in the course of business or trade if the witnesses had made or endorsed a written statement or supplied information as part of a criminal investigation and did not give evidence "through fear or because he is kept out of the way".[47] There is no requirement for the fear to be caused by the defendant directly and in *R* v. *Acton Justices ex parte McMullen* the Divisional Court rejected the view that the fear should based on reasonable grounds. Watkins LJ said: "It is not helpful in this context to speak of the objective or subjective approach and wholly inappropriate in my view to introduce the concept of reasonable grounds." He also implied that the court should inquire into the basis of the fear by saying that, "[i]t will be sufficient that the court on the evidence is sure

---

[42] *Sup. cit.*, para 5.22.

[43] *The Times*, August 17 1994.

[44] *Ibid.*

[45] R. May, *Criminal Evidence* (4th ed.), Sweet & Maxwell 1999, p. 486.

[46] "It has recently become the practice for the address of a witness to be removed from his or her statement(s) prior to prosecution disclosure to the defence," *Speaking up for Justice*, p. 52.

[47] *See* Sections 23, 24.

that the witness is in fear as a consequence of the commission of the material offence or of something said or done subsequently in relation to that offence and the possibility of the witness testifying as to it."[48] However in Martin the Court of Appeal held that there was no need to inquire into the cause of the fear, the fact of the fear was enough.[49]

Although these cases indicate that hearsay evidence is acceptable under these conditions it should be stressed that the court has a discretion to refuse to admit such statement. Also by virtue of Section 26 there is a presumption of non-admissibility unless the 'interests of justice' require otherwise. In fact English courts have shown some reluctance to take an overly liberal stance on admissibility and for example in R v. Radak the Court of Appeal held it would be unfair to admit a written statement from a witness who was in the US.[50] The evidence could have been obtained on commission in the US when there would have been an opportunity to cross examine the witness. It was stressed that the defendant's right to equality with the prosecution as to the summoning and examining of witnesses had to be safeguarded in accordance with Article 6(3)(a).

It has been suggested that the existing statutory provisions on hearsay are not compatible with the ECHR.[51] However this is by no means self evident. In Gokal the Court of Appeal held there was no breach of Article 6(3)(d) in admitting documentary hearsay because whole basis of Section 26 is to assess interests of justice by reference to risk of unfairness to the accused; and the Commission refused to admit an application in Trivedi v. UK.[52] It considered in the latter case that the admission of written statements from patients of the defendant doctor who were medically unfit was fair in all the circumstances of the case. The trial judge had properly directed the jury to give less weight to this evidence and there was other evidence in the case.

Interestingly the Law Commission considers that current hearsay provisions are not protective enough of witnesses. It clearly links its proposals for reform to the issue of witness intimidation arguing that changes are needed "bearing in mind the magnitude and significance of the problem of frightened witnesses".[53] In a parallel comment the Home Office refers to the Law Commission's proposals as part of its witness protection programme.[54] The Law Commission recommends a more general exception for documentary and first hand oral hearsay for those who do not give evidence through fear

---

[48] (1991) 92 Cr.App.R. 98, pp. 105-106.
[49] [1996] Crim.L.R. 589
[50] The Times Law Reports, October 2 1988.
[51] See Ashworth, sup. cit., p. 269.
[52] [1997] 2 Cr.App.R. 266; [1997] E.H.R.L.R. 520.
[53] Sup. cit., para 8.55.
[54] See Action for Justice, p. 11.

including that of 'financial loss'.[55] This exception will not be limited as at present to situations where the statement is made as part of evidence gathering. Fear of loss of employment for example would clearly fit in this category of exception.

Thus statutory changes and proposed changes have introduced a new category of hearsay exception based on the fear a witness has of appearing in court. That fear need not be a fear of physical attack. This is in marked contrast to the meaning attached to fear as a defence in cases of contempt. For example in *R* v. *Lewis* the Court of Appeal accepted the defence of duress to a charge of contempt of court.[56] A victim of a serious assault in prison refused to give evidence against his attacker. The Court accepted that there was "evidence which satisfies a court that he knew or was aware that he was exposing himself to the risks of threat of death or serious bodily harm if he failed to participate in or conform to the wishes of his criminal associates." It is significant that even where statements are admitted under Section 23 because of the fear of the witness this does not preclude a subsequent finding of contempt. In *R* v. *Montgomery* the trial judge said to the accused who had refused to act as a witness in a trial where the victim had been severely injured: "You have shown yourself to be a coward. You do not want to be seen to be letting the side down at this stage. I do accept that you are afraid of what may happen to either you or even other members of your family from persons you do not name but the way to deal with that is to make a statement to the police and to have those persons arrested and locked up and kept away."[57]

The increasing official attention given to protecting witnesses is not surprising. There have indeed been instances of severe intimidation. Rape victims in particular have been subject to traumatic cross examination by their alleged attacker in person. Such cases may undermine public confidence in the criminal justice system and make potential witnesses hesitant about giving information to the police or other investigative agencies. However it is arguable that in dealing with these serious cases Parliament has drawn too wide a net. Witness intimidation clearly can cover a very wide range of actions or threats to take action. Witnesses who give evidence against their employer or fellow employees are certainly vulnerable to reprisals such as dismissal. Such witnesses could benefit from the proposed changes to the law on hearsay and the other measures which enable the witness to be shielded from the defendant. It is submitted however that extending these forms of witness protection to adult witnesses who are put in financial rather than physical fear would be an undesirable development since it would further erode an important ingredient of a fair trial. As Friedman put it "(...) lurking within the

---

[55] *Sup. cit.*, para 8.65.
[56] (1992) 96 *Cr.App.R.* 412.
[57] [1995] 2 *All E.R.* 28.

rule against hearsay and often shrouded by its many excesses and oddities is a principle of magnificent importance, a principle first enunciated long before the development of the common law system but one that achieved its full development within that system. This is the principle that a person may not offer testimony against a criminal defendant unless it is given under oath face to face with the accused and subject to cross examination."[58]

He finds the proposals of the Law Commission on hearsay "disquieting" and says that they are moves in the wrong direction. Friedman accepts that there might be occasions when the right to confrontation is forfeited. He writes that the "(...) accused forfeits any objection to a testimonial statement if his own wrongdoing accounts for the inability to take the testimony under satisfactory conditions."[59] It appears he considers that forfeiture should apply to only the most extreme examples of witness intimidation by the defendant. He gives the following examples: "The defendant might have murdered, kidnapped or intimidated her or persuaded her by improper means not to testify". He seems to imply that allowing evidence to be given by written statement is not appropriate in cases of less extreme intimidation for he concludes, "the witness's legitimate interests should be guarded not be denying a longstanding right of the defendant but by preparing the witness, supporting her, protecting her against violence, intimidation and abusive examination and if need be to provide representation for her."[60] He stresses that court proceedings cannot always be trouble free zones: "(...) we cannot eliminate the trauma from the process without gutting the system."[61]

There is much force in this argument. Irrespective of the practical issue of whether cross examination is an effective engine for the discovery of truth the integrity of the trial process and the appearance of fairness demand that defendants must not be denied the right to confront their accusers. If they take action or make threats against a witness then there is scope through the law of contempt or by specific criminal sanctions to exact sanctions. The danger is that the most serious cases of extreme intimidation which demand a high level of witness protection will lead to a more general erosion of the right to confrontation.

There is, it is submitted, a dangerous current tendency to privatise criminal proceedings in the sense that an emphasis is put on the contest as being that between defendant and witness, specifically the victim as witness. The most significant motor for change has been apparently unfair defence methods in rape cases. Victims have been on occasion humiliated and frightened during

---

[58] R. Friedman, 'Thoughts from Across the Water on Hearsay and Confrontation', (1988) *Crim.L.R.* 697.

[59] *Ibid.*, p. 707.

[60] *Ibid.*, p. 709. The Home Office is implementing an extensive programme of police support for witnesses. *See Speaking up for Justice.*

[61] *Ibid.*, p. 709.

cross-examination. Evidential changes designed primarily to deal with this admittedly troubling if rare problem have wider repercussions. For example Sections 34-40 of the *1999 Act* prohibit unrepresented defendants from cross examining adult witnesses and child witnesses in trial for rape and certain other sexual offences. They also give the court power to prohibit cross examination of witnesses by unrepresented defendants in other circumstances. Speaking up for Justice does not however give any instances where such cross examination has presented difficulties in trials other than those for rape. Intimidated witnesses may be also protected by various procedural mechanisms, most of them introduced initially to protect child witnesses, including screens, video recorded evidence and television links. The *1999 Act* will allow the extension of these to adult witnesses at the discretion of the court.

## Conclusion

The principle behind the witness protection measures outlined above is the understandable one of ensuring that the witness is not unduly intimidated. Her needs are therefore considered along with those of the defendant. But the increasing tendency to balance the interests of witnesses and defendants is misguided. The two are not commensurate. As a general rule the defendant is in greater jeopardy than the witness if the trial process is flawed. The two protagonists in a criminal trial are the defendant and the state. The defendant is confronted with the might of the state in facing prosecution and measures which undermine her capacity to meet that must be deprecated.

The blurring of the principle of a fair trial in the interests of 'balancing' the needs of witness and defendant is theoretically untenable. Witnesses, even victim witnesses, are not parties in the trial although political considerations may require that the mounting public concern over protecting witnesses is satisfied. Aleinikoff has made a comprehensive study of judicial emphasis on 'balance' in the context of US constitutional issues. He concludes his review of the case law with a comment which is relevant also to this discussion of the danger of allowing principles to be submerged in the balancing of competing interests: "Balancing has turned us away from the *Constitution* supplying 'reasonable' policy making in lieu of a theoretical investigation of rights, principles and structures." He argues that political considerations mean that all too frequently rights are no longer trumps but simply cards of higher value in the same suit.[62]

A willingness to give evidence in open court is a crucially important social act, not a one which should be dominated by individual risk assessment. Just

---

[62] T.A. Aleinikoff, 'Constitutional Law in the Age of Balancing', (1987) *Yale Law Journal* 943, at 1004 and 992.

as whistleblowing is to be encouraged in the interests of the public good so, it is submitted, should witnesses be encouraged to see their role as one prompted by a sense of social responsibility. Those measures outlined above which would allow witnesses to avoid court confrontations are cause for concern. It would be anomalous if whistleblowers were encouraged to act openly in initially alerting responsible bodies about damaging or potentially damaging workplace activities but then had the opportunity to be shielded from the public eye, and in particular the eyes of the accused, in any subsequent criminal proceedings. The charity Public Concern at Work reports that it had 1,315 requests for legal advice in the years between 1993 to 1998. These included numerous employees concerned about serious malpractice in their workplace involving a risk to the wider public.[63] The enactment of the *PIDA* and the accompanying publicity is likely to encourage more such activity and possibly lead to reprisals or threats by resentful employers. This may amount to what the Home Office calls "low-level intimidation".[64] For those who are so intimidated but not covered by the *PIDA* because they are not making what is defined as a "protected disclosure" consideration should be given to strengthening existing criminal sanctions with compensation or reinstatement orders along the lines of the *Witness (Public Inquiries) Protection Act 1892*. The rights of defendants and those of witnesses, including victims, are not commensurate and occasions when the right to confrontation is denied because witnesses are frightened should be very rare. In short there is a need to reassert, in relation both to those acting as witnesses and to those acting as whistleblowers, what one distinguished commentator has identified as a "community ethic".[65]

---

[63] *Public Interest Whistleblowing: A Report on the Activities of Public Concern at Work 1993-1998.*
[64] *See Action for Justice*, p. 6.
[65] Sir G. Borrie (chairman of the Commission on Social Justice 1997-1992), 'Four Windows on Whistleblowing', (1996) *Public Concern at Work*, p. 18.

# Disclosure in the Criminal Trial

*J. Sprack*

The system of disclosure in England & Wales was subjected to a seismic shift by the *Criminal Procedure and Investigations Act 1996*. This replaced the common law duty of prosecution disclosure with a statutory scheme consisting of four main elements:[1]

1. the police duty to record and retain material gathered or generated in the course of an investigation;
2. the prosecution duty to make primary disclosure of material which might undermine its case;
3. the defence duty to make disclosure of the case which it intends to present at trial;
4. the prosecution duty (once the defence has complied with step three above) to make disclosure of material which might reasonably be expected to assist the defence.

The changes have proved highly controversial. Many practitioners allege that material which could prove useful to the defence is routinely not disclosed by the police. From the prosecution's point of view, there sometimes appears to be a conflict between the demands of ethics and the bare requirements of the statutory scheme. There is also a widespread perception that defence disclosure is just not working in practice.

Two developments which are in progress may shed some light on the way in which the duty is now interpreted and carried out. First, the Crown Prosecution Service Inspectorate has conducted a thematic review within the Crown Prosecution Service (CPS).[2] Second, the Home Office is in the process of commissioning independent research into the operation of the disclosure scheme, involving scrutiny of the police, the CPS, defence lawyers and the courts. This research should take place during the course of 2000, with a report available early in 2001.

In the meanwhile, a survey conducted by the Criminal Bar Association, the British Academy of Forensic Sciences and the Law Society was released in November 1999 with a commentary by Anthony Heaton-Armstrong. Its contents make disturbing reading. The centre-piece of the report consists of an analysis of some 200 responses to a questionnaire sent to barristers with a

---

[1] For a summary of the changes, *see* Sprack, 'The CPIA 1996: (1) The Duty of Disclosure', [1997] *Crim.L.R.* 308; for more detail, *see* Leng & Taylor, *The CPIA 1996*, London: Blackstone 1996, Chapters 1 and 2.
[2] Crown Prosecution Service, *Report on the Thematic Review of the Disclosure of Unused Material*, March 2000.

criminal practice, most of whom appear for both prosecution and defence. The following statistics paint a gloomy picture:

- 83% of these practitioners said that the schedules of unused material (which are compiled by the police and form the basis on which disclosure can be requested) were unlikely to be comprehensive and reliable;
- 85% said that the items on these schedules were insufficiently described;
- over 90% said that there was no reliable means of independent scrutiny;
- 87% said that decisions by police officers as to whether material undermined the prosecution case (*i.e.*, fulfilled the test for primary prosecution disclosure) were unreliable;
- 75% said that the prosecution played an inactive role in scrutinising secondary disclosure;
- 80% said that decisions on secondary disclosure were unreliable;
- 84% said that the statutory disclosure provisions were not working well.

These defects were seen as endemic to a system where the police have been charged with ensuring that the defence gets access to the material which will help it to secure an acquittal. One practitioner summed up the general tone of the responses with the words: "The fox is in charge of the hen house".

The implementation of the *Human Rights Act 1998* in October 2000 will mean that the *European Convention on Human Rights (ECHR)* is incorporated into English law. What is at present a feeling of unease about the operation of the statutory system for disclosure will be translated into a series of challenges to the way in which it operates in practice. The relationship between disclosure in the criminal trial in England & Wales and the fairness of the trial itself will inevitably come under closer scrutiny.

In the light of all these developments, it seems timely to examine the rationale for a meaningful duty of disclosure by the prosecution, and the reservations which are sometimes expressed about the way in which full-blooded disclosure may operate in practice.

## Arguments for Full Disclosure

The following are perhaps the main arguments of principle which may be put forward in favour of full disclosure by the prosecution.

First, *it is necessary in order to ensure that the accused has a fair trial.* There is a massive disparity of resources between the defendant and the State. The police have the fruits of the investigation, to which the defence has only limited access. The police inevitably focus at an early stage upon obtaining evidence which fits their theory of the case, with the suspect at the centre of it. As it was put in the case of *R* v. *Winston Brown*,[3] "(...) the right of every accused to a fair trial is a basic or fundamental right. That means that under

---

[3] (1995) 1 *Cr.App.R.* 191, at 198 per Steyn LJ.

our unwritten constitution those rights are regarded as deserving of special protection by the courts. However, in our adversarial system, in which the police and prosecution control the investigatory process, an accused's right to fair disclosure is an inseparable part of his right to a fair trial. That is the framework in which the development of common law rules about disclosure by the Crown must be seen."

Second, *it is required by the United Kingdom's treaty obligations.* There is a duty to disclose which flows from international treaty obligations, and particularly from the *ECHR*. The principle of equality of arms is crucial in respect of Article 6 of the Convention. Of particular relevance are

- Article 6(3)(b), since adequate facilities for the preparation of a defence must be taken to include the necessary information to undertake that preparation; and
- Article 6(3)(d) since in order to be able to obtain the attendance of witnesses to assist its case, the defence needs to know of their existence and the evidence which they can give.

In *Edwards* v. *United Kingdom*,[4] the European Court of Human Rights (ECrtHR) stated that prosecution disclosure of all "material evidence for and against the accused" was a requirement of a fair trial under Article 6. In *Kostovski* v. *Netherlands*,[5] the ECrtHR indicated the "obvious inherent dangers" if the defence "lacks the information permitting it to test the author's reliability or cast doubt upon his credibility".

Third, *disclosure assists in the search for truth.* In the adversarial system, the prosecution puts forward an hypothesis at trial which involves as its central feature the guilt of the accused. The defence has the role of testing that hypothesis, and of putting forward any alternative hypothesis. It needs knowledge in order to carry out that testing function. The central role of prosecution disclosure is not, of course, confined to the adversarial system. In some ways, it is even more obvious in the inquisitorial system, as an integral part of the search for truth. Brants & Field describe the process in this way:[6] "(...) [W]here structures entrench the active truth finder, as in the inquisitorial criminal process, the central imperative is the prompting of doubt and reflective re-analysis. In part this requires a cultural ethos of reflexivity and a strong continuing commitment to dialogue and dialectic as a means of verifying truth. But the process is certainly strengthened where others have the ability to propose alternative hypotheses and suggest alternative testing methods. *If that role were to be played by the defence – and it is the defence that has the obvious self-interest in doing this with vigour – it would require, if*

---

[4] (1993) 96 *Cr.App.R.* 1.
[5] (1989) 12 *E.H.R.R.* 434.
[6] Nederlandse Vereniging voor Rechtsvergelijking, *Participation Rights and Proactive Policing* (No 51), Utrecht: Kluwer 1995, pp. 11-12.

*not complete equality of arms, at least the information base on which to propose alternative hypotheses and to challenge existing theory.*"(Emphasis added.)

Fourth, *the absence of disclosure is likely to lead to miscarriages of justice.* As it was put in the case of Judith Ward, the most famous of the high-profile miscarriage of justice cases which shook the English criminal justice system in the 1990s: "Non-disclosure is a potent source of injustice".[7]

It was largely as a result of a series of notorious miscarriage of justice cases, many of them involving shortcomings on the part of the prosecution apparatus in the process of disclosure, that the Royal Commission on Criminal Justice was set up. Some commentators regard it as ironic that, in defiance of its origins, the Royal Commission came up with proposals to relax the prosecution duty of disclosure, and fix the defence with its own duty of disclosure. It was these proposals, of course, which formed the foundations of the statutory scheme introduced in the *Criminal Procedure and Investigations Act 1996* which are the subject of this paper.[8]

Fifth, *disclosure is in accordance with the general ideal of the relationship of the citizen to the state.* As Gerry Maher put it, "Citizens should be seen as active participating subjects in criminal process rather than passive objects in proceedings controlled by and belonging to the state."[9] He argues that the ideals of participatory citizenship demand that dialogue should be central to the notion of procedural fairness in the criminal justice system, and sees the criminal process as a communicative enterprise which involves directly speaking to someone about their conduct and justifying blame.

Put into a procedural framework, this means that the duty of disclosure is not just about a fair trial and the search for truth, but is also about the relationship between the protagonists and the system. The right to disclosure is owned not only by the defence lawyers but by the defendant. An illustration of the distinction appears in the way in which the argument on the procedure for claiming public interest immunity was treated in the Court of Appeal in *Davis Johnson and Rowe.*[10] Lord Taylor CJ said, in dealing with the question whether disclosure of 'sensitive' material can be restricted to counsel alone: "Before us, Mr Mansfield [counsel for the appellant] submitted first that, where the court has to consider disclosure, it cannot be right to require counsel for the defence to give an undertaking not to reveal what passes in court to his instructing solicitors and client. (...) We agree. It would wholly undermine

---

[7] *Ward* [1993] 2 *All E.R.* 577, at 599.

[8] For a striking example of the potency of non-disclosure as a source of injustice, *see Taylor and Taylor* (1994) 98 *Cr.App.R.* 361, at 366.

[9] 'Dialogue and the Criminal Process', in: E. Attwooll & D. Goldberg (eds.), *Criminal Justice,* Stuttgart: Franz Steiner Verlag 1995, p. 46.

[10] (1993) 97 *Cr.App.R.* 110.

counsel's relationship with his client if he were privy to issues in court but could reveal neither the discussion nor even the issues to his client."

Sixth, *disclosure involves a healthy scrutiny of the investigatory process.* Procedural errors, failure to follow up evidential leads, inefficiency and wrongdoing are liable to exposure in court. In certain cases they may result in acquittal, this removing the incentive to bend the rules. The light which this process throws on the criminal justice system is necessary so that remedial action can be taken. The case for this sort of scrutiny was put (in the context of the justification of the doctrine of abuse of process) by Lord Griffiths:[11] "If the court is to have the power to interfere with the prosecution in the present circumstances it must be because the judiciary accept a responsibility for the maintenance of the rule of law that embraces a willingness to oversee executive action and to refuse to countenance behaviour that threatens either basic human rights or the rule of law. My Lords, I have no doubt that the judiciary should accept this responsibility in the field of criminal law."

And seventh, *the prosecution is the trustee of the information which is acquired in the course of investigation, and not its owner.* The concept was articulated clearly by the Supreme Court of Canada in their leading judgement on the subject of disclosure:[12] "(...) [T]he fruits of the investigation (...) are not the property of the Crown for use in securing conviction, but the property of the public to be used to ensure that justice is done."

## Some Qualifications

Of course, the argument is hardly ever conducted in terms of support or opposition to disclosure in principle. There is general acceptance that a measure of disclosure is necessary and desirable. The controversy arises when one attempts to determine how much disclosure there should be, and looks at the related questions of who should be responsible for it, and whether any element of prosecution disclosure should be subject to a requirement that the defence should meet certain obligations. That brings us to the reservations which are frequently expressed about extensive disclosure, of which the most important are perhaps these.

*Excessive disclosure is inefficient.* The Royal Commission on Criminal Justice was impressed with the extent of the practical difficulties faced by the police in meeting the duty of disclosure as it was defined after *Ward*,[13] and before the introduction of the statutory scheme. As they put it: "The police set up large data bases in the course of their investigations, some of which involve

---

[11] *Horseferry Road Magistrates' Court ex parte Bennett (No 1)* (1994) 98 *Cr.App.R.* 114, at 125.
[12] *Stinchcombe* (1992) 68 *C.C.C.* (3d) 1, at p. 7; [1991] 3 *S.C.R.* 326. *See also* O'Connor, *Justice in Error*, London: Blackstone 1993, p. 117, and Pollard, 'A Case for Disclosure', [1994] *Crim.L.R.* 42.
[13] [1993] 2 *All E.R.* 577

a series of linked cases, especially where serial murderers or rapists are concerned, or where professional criminals are responsible for organised crime on a national or international scale. Even in some straightforward cases the amount of material collected during the course of the investigation can be voluminous."[14]

To what extent is the argument about the waste of resources well-founded? In the great majority of cases the prosecution will either make use of all the relevant material (so that none of it needs to be disclosed as 'unused'), or will find the task of photocopying a few additional pages undemanding. In those cases where the unused material is bulky, then the concept of relevance comes into play. If the unused material is irrelevant, then the argument about inefficiency would indeed be compelling. If it is relevant, then it seems right that it should be disclosed, and the time spent in discovering it (whether by prosecution or defence) is time well spent in securing the ends of justice.

*Encouraging invented defences.* Defendants (or unethical defence lawyers) may use material discovered, or the procedure, to invent defences. As it was put in the Consultation Document which preceded the passage through Parliament of the *Criminal Procedure and Investigations Act 1996*:[15] "[T]he Government does not believe that it is in the public interest to require the prosecution to provide access to large quantities of material which is not relevant to the prosecution case or to any defence advanced. This simply makes the trial more burdensome, and encourages defendants to delve into such material to seek to obscure the real issues or even on occasions to come forward with a plausible but fictitious defence.

While there are no doubt some instances where the defendant does invent a defence on the basis of disclosed material, the trial process ought to be sufficiently rigorous to minimise the danger of its succeeding. In so far as this reservation is really about so-called ambush defences which are raised late and take the prosecution by surprise, it needs to be approached with a great deal of caution, Research on the topic has suggested that such ambush defences are both rarely raised, and usually unsuccessful.[16]

*Exposing sensitive material.* Unused material may be 'sensitive' (*e.g.* providing clues to the identity of an informer) leading the prosecution to avoid disclosure by abandoning the case. This was put forward as an argument for limiting the extent of disclosure in *The Report of the Royal Commission on Criminal Justice*[17] and the Home Office consultation document which followed it.[18] Whilst the reduction of the extent of disclosure is one way of

---

[14] *Report of the Royal Commission on Criminal Justice*, Cm 2263, HMSO 1993, para 41.

[15] Home Office, *Disclosure: A consultation paper*, London: HMSO Cm2864 1995, para 16.

[16] Leng, *The Right to Silence in Police Interrogation*, 1993, Royal Commission on Criminal Justice, Study No 10.

[17] *Op. cit.*, n. 13.

[18] *Op. cit.*, n. 14.

avoiding this problem, it is a rather blunt instrument, since it will also involve non-disclosure of material which is not in the least sensitive. It is difficult to see why the well-established doctrine of public interest immunity is not better fitted to protect sensitive material.

*Errors in the investigatory process can be dealt with by police disciplinary processes and separate legal remedies.* They should not result in a windfall for the accused (contrast the sixth point above). Again in the context of the doctrine of abuse of process, the dissenting opinion of Lord Oliver in *Horseferry Road Magistrates' Court Ex parte Bennett*[19] sets out the argument: "The question raised by this appeal is whether, in addition to such remedies as may be available in civil proceedings, the court should assume the duty of overseeing, controlling and punishing an abuse of executive power leading up to properly instituted criminal proceedings not by means of the conventional remedies invoked at the instance of the person claiming to have been injured by such abuse but by restraining the further prosecution of those proceedings. The results of the assumption of such a jurisdiction are threefold; and they are surprising. First, the trial put in train by a charge which has been properly laid will not take place and the person charged (if guilty) will escape a just punishment; secondly, the civil remedies available to that person will remain enforceable; and thirdly, the public interest in the prosecution and punishment of crime will have been defeated not by a necessary process of penalising those responsible for executive abuse but simply for the purpose of manifesting judicial disapproval..."

But the problem which this argument poses is: how else will the errors and wrongdoing of the investigators be dealt with? Obviously, the hope is that the internal disciplinary machinery, in combination with civil remedies, will provide the necessary solution. In practice, however, those who suffer from the abuse of power are in a poor position to pursue their civil remedies, and likely to get little sympathy if they do. If the wrongdoing is not subject to disclosure, it will never attract attention in the courtroom context, and hence it may not come to the attention of those charged with supervising the investigators. In any event, if the malpractice does not result in an acquittal, then there is no incentive for supervisors within the police force to take action. There is an all-too-human temptation for senior management to turn a blind eye to behaviour which, whilst reprehensible in theory, does seem to achieve results in practice.

---

[19] *Op. cit.*, n. 12, at p 130.

### The *CPIA 1996* and the *European Convention on Human Rights*

The implementation of the *Human Rights Act 1998*, and the incorporation of the relevant Articles of the Convention into English law pose questions about the extent to which the duty of disclosure measures up to *ECHR* jurisprudence.[20] For example:

1. is the dependence of secondary disclosure upon defence disclosure compatible with fairness under Article 6? In *Edwards* v. *United Kingdom*,[21] which was decided before the *CPIA 1996*, the court said: "It is a requirement of fairness under Article 6, indeed one which is recognised under English law, that the prosecution must disclose to the defence all material evidence for or against the accused". The statutory scheme lays down that some of that disclosure is subject to compliance by the defence with the duty to provide a defence statement;

2. does the requirement of defence disclosure ("(...) the accused must give a defence statement to the court and the prosecutor," Section 5(5) *CPIA 1996*) violate Article 6(2) of the *ECHR*: "Everyone charged with a criminal offence shall be presumed innocent until proved guilty according to law". The potential violation lies in the use which the prosecution may make of the defence statement in discharging the burden of proof which is placed upon it;

3. what about disclosure of material which may undermine the credibility of a *defence* witness? Such material does not fit the test for primary disclosure, since it does not undermine the prosecution case. Nor does it easily satisfy the test for secondary disclosure – it is not material which might reasonably be expected to assist the *defence*. It is actually material which might assist the *prosecution* if the defence does decide to call that particular witness. It is therefore routinely withheld from the defence, and in this respect the statutory position is no different from that under the common law which preceded it.[22] In *Jespers* v. *Belgium*,[23] the Commission stated that "(...) everyone charged with a criminal offence should enjoy the opportunity to acquaint himself, for the purpose of preparing his defence, with the results of investigations carried out throughout the proceedings (...) a right to access to the prosecution file (...) can be inferred from Art. 6(3)(b).";

---

[20] Sharpe, 'Article 6 and the Disclosure of Evidence in Criminal Trials', [1999] *Crim.L.R.* 273, takes the view that the *CPIA 1996* is unlikely to be impugned by the *ECHR*. But it is suggested that the question will be whether a particular trial was fair in the light of the defects in disclosure on the facts of the case in question, rather than whether the statute in principle violates the Convention.

[21] *Op. cit.*, n. 3.

[22] *See R* v. *Winston Brown, op. cit.*, n. 2. The rationale seems to be that the prosecution may be able to use such material in cross-examination to expose an untruthful defence witness.

[23] (1981) 27 *D.R.* 61.

4. is the *ex parte* procedure for the hearing of public interest immunity applications in breach of the *ECHR*? In *Davis and Rowe*[24] the applicants alleged that this procedure violated their rights under Article 6 of the *ECHR*. Such a procedure allows the prosecution to put the case for the grant of public interest immunity, so as to avoid disclosure, and does not allow for any countervailing argument on behalf of the defence. In October 1998, the Commission held that the application was admissible, and should be heard by the Court. The problem perceived by the Commission was that none of the judges who heard the case had the benefit of arguments from both sides on the balance to be struck between the need for secrecy and the defendants' right to a fair trial. It is not altogether surprising that the Commission saw this as potentially infringing the right to a fair trial entrenched in Article 6(1). The decision of the full Court in due course as to whether there was a violation is awaited at the time of writing, and is likely to be a most important one for the practice adopted in relation to disclosure in public interest immunity cases;

5. should there be full disclosure where the defendant intends to plead guilty? The criminal justice system in England & Wales is heavily reliant upon the guilty plea. Whatever the arguments about the necessity for that reliance, it is surely right that defendants should only make their decision as to plea in full knowledge of the strength of the prosecution case (including any material which might undermine it). Yet the duty of primary disclosure in relation to offences is effectively confined to those where the accused pleads not guilty.

Some, if not all of the questions posed above are likely to be argued, both in the domestic courts and in Strasbourg over the next few years. When they are considered, it is crucial that the principled basis for disclosure is kept clearly in focus. It is also important that the courts should keep in mind the practical effects of defective disclosure. The integrity of the criminal justice system is too dependent upon equal access to information for administrative convenience and cost cutting to dominate the development of the law on disclosure.

---

[24] [1999] *Crim.L.R.* 410.

# Non-trial Settlement in the European *Corpus Iuris*

*E.F. Stamhuis*

## Introduction

In the European Union's combat against frauds that damage the financial interests of the Union the role of the *Corpus Iuris* has not at all finished, although for example the Dutch government wants to let us believe the opposite.[1] Not only is the process of debating and amending this *Corpus* still going on, the debate on this subject in the European Parliament received new incentives with the Draft Report of the Committee on Budgetary Control, putting forward a motion for a resolution to further develop the ideas and principles laid down in the *Corpus Iuris* so far.[2] The discussion moves in particular on an institutional level: will there be a European Public Prosecutor, yes or no, comprising the Eurolegal questions of where to find the legal basis for further initiatives in the relevant Treaties. Since this is not a workshop on European law and since I am not an expert in that field, I will leave all these issues aside, however interesting they may be, and ask your attention for another aspect of the development towards a European *Corpus Iuris*, which is the thrust towards comparing and uniforming the criminal law and criminal procedure that it entails.

The regulation of out-of-court settlement in the *Corpus Iuris* shows a preference for a transaction model and is to be found in Article 22, carrying conditions that are of a substantive and procedural nature respectively. It is therefore a good example to clarify what is going on in the development towards a more uniform European system in criminal law and procedure and to discuss the possible benefits or disadvantages of the proposals so far. In this paper I will first describe the conditions for a settlement under Article 22 and while doing so introduce the comparative perspective by referring to various forms of settlements from the practice of some member states. Besides giving a comparative analysis I will evaluate the settlement with the basic rules formulated by the Council of Europe in 1987 in its Recommendation on the simplification of criminal justice.[3] Although the non-trial disposal in the *Corpus* has obvious advantages, there remain some matters to attend to in the further development. But first of all I would like to pose the more general and fundamental question, that will be addressed in my paper only indirectly: what makes the out-of-court settlement in this field so special that the model of the administrative fining practice developed by the European Commission could not be adopted and a transaction model had

---

[1] *See* the discussion note, offered to the Senate Chamber of Parliament by Letter of July 2,1999; Eerste Kamer, 1998-1999, 25922 (R1613), nr. 62f.
[2] Draft Report on introducing protection under criminal law of the Union's financial interests, part the planned revision of the TEU, rapp. Diemut R. Theato, September 22, 1999, PE 231.653.
[3] Recommendation No. R (87) 18, adopted on September 17, 1987.

to be introduced? There is some evidence from member states that it will end there anyway, so why not make the giant step now?

**Conditions for Transaction**

Article 22 of the *Corpus* deals with the bringing and termination of a prosecution for the offences listed in the Articles 1 to 8 of the *Corpus*, such as fraud to the detriment of the European Communities, market-rigging, money laundering and certain forms of malpractice by officials. Paragraph 2 carries the provision for the termination:[4]

> For the same offences, the prosecution is extinguished on the death of the defendant (or if it concerns a group, the dissolution of the group), or by expiry of the limitation period or by settlement:
> a) ......
> b) settlement is ruled out in the case of repeated offences, where arms or forgery were used, or if the sum involved is 50.000 Euros or more. In other cases, it may be proposed by the national authorities to the European Public Prosecutor (EPP), both for cases under national jurisdiction (cf. Article 19(4a), and cases under European jurisdiction, according to the following conditions: the defendant freely admits his guilt, the authorities have sufficient evidence of guilt to justify committal to trial, the decision to come to a settlement is made publicly, and the agreement concluded respects the principle of proportionality. In the case of refusal, the EPP must, if there are grounds, call in the case. The settlement agreement is subject to the control of the judge of freedoms.

The substantive conditions first of all aim at the strict limitation of the scope of this transaction. They are to be understood as an expression of the low seriousness of the crime. Other features are:
- it can only deal with a first offence, assuming that reoffending contributes to the seriousness of the second offence;
- offences involving the use of arms or forgery are not to be settled by transaction, presupposing that the use of these instruments make an offence too serious for settlement, irrespective of other features such as the damage done;
- offences involving a sum of 50.000 Euros or more are excluded from settlement.

The limitation to cases of low seriousness is widespread in Europe. It is related to the general idea, that a non-trial settlement is a minus compared to a regular trial on the following grounds. Firstly, it is considered to be the prerogative of a court to impose imprisonment (which is laid down in Article 5 *ECHR* as well), so for that reason offences that merit a custodial sanction, regularly the more serious, have to go to court. Secondly, dealing with offences by way of non-trial settlements is considered to be low level in terms of

---

[4] I use the text of the original proposal of the *Corpus Iuris*, in a Dutch-French bilingual edition from Intersentia Rechtswetenschappen, Antwerpen-Groningen 1998, as amended in the Florence proposals.

procedural rights and guarantees. Therefore a defendant can only be asked to accept one when there is not too much at stake. The agreement of the defendant is required, because of the principle, laid down in written constitutions all over continental Europe, that no one can be withheld from the court designated to him by law, unless with his consent. In conclusion, a limited scope of Article 22(2) is fully acceptable from a comparative perspective.[5] There is a lot to be said in particular about the specific wordings, interpretative questions that may arise and the validity of the indicators as such. I will leave that to another opportunity. It is in relation to the expression of this limitation in terms of factual circumstances that I have some criticism. I think it gives a false feeling of security, always reflects a high degree of arbitrariness and is very susceptible to the changing moods of day to day politics. The seriousness indicators of the offence involved are never immune to manipulation in a concrete case. It is the investigating authority at first and the prosecuting authority thereafter that can decide whether or not certain aspects will be included in the investigation, will be laid down in written evidence and will be taken into account when deciding on the use of the power to prosecute. Especially when out of court settlement is very attractive in terms of time and preparatory effort there will be a risk of downgrading the case, from the outset or later on. These three indicators can therefore function in accordance with their ratio as criteria for the decision to settle. But to the same extent they can be used as criteria to be met afterwards when the decision to settle has been made on other policy grounds and so become the masks at a *bal masqué*.

In a modern criminal justice system the use of these discretionary powers inevitably becomes a subject of criminal policy. The indicators now used, all relating to specific features of the individual offence, will only hamper this and force the policy to go under ground, so to speak. In my opinion it would have been better to express the limited scope of the transaction under Article 22(2) in terms of the limited penalties, that can be agreed upon.[6] In public policy guidelines the EPP can express its intention when to use Article 22(2) and when not. Not only can these guidelines easily be adapted to changing demands, the introduction will keep the responsibilities for the choices for the transaction clear and the relation between instruments and the policy goals more transparent and therefore more open to debate and control. The specific level of the penalty-maximum will have a certain arbitrariness as well, but at least the debate will be concentrated on the question: to what level of penalty do we accept a non-trial disposal? That I would consider to be an asset to the development of European criminal procedures.

---

[5] Compare among others the limitations to the German *Strafbefehl* (only for the less serious *Vergehen*), the Scottish fiscal fine (only for district court offences), the English fixed penalty notice (only for the less serious road traffic offences) and the Italian *decreto* (only for offences for which a fine is appropriate).

[6] The exclusion of custodial sanctions seems obvious to me. Apart from that a range of financial sanctions seem acceptable and appropriate: fines, if felt necessary limited to a certain percentage of the maximum fine, returning the illegally received funds or making amends for the damage caused.

The principle of proportionality is the second substantive quality indicator in Article 22(2). It is one of the fundamental principles in the *Corpus Iuris* and is laid down a/o in Article 15. The punishment must fit the crime and the offender. In determining the proper sanction the following aspects must be taken into account: the fault of the offender, the seriousness of the offence and the extent of his participation in it. Furthermore, the following circumstances may be considered as well: the accused's previous conduct, including previous convictions and other sanctions, his general character (good or bad), his motives, his economic and social situation and any efforts to repair damages. Other favourable factors, accepted by national law, may also be treated as relevant. The reference *expressis verbis* to this principle in Article 22(2) renders the whole range of factors relevant to the sanction that will result from a settlement under this provision. This is not as hollow a statement as it seems to be, because the proportionality check is a very important instrument for judicial control in the hands of the judge of freedoms to whom the settlement is submitted for approval. It can be used as a safeguard against penalties that are too severe as well as against double downgrading for efficiency purposes alone. With that I mean downgrading the offences to be disposed of by way of the settlement, accumulating with a sanction, too lenient in comparison with what the courts impose on a comparable factual basis. This proportionality principle is the instrument with which the judge can guard over equality and by doing so he can offer a balance against powers of the EPP that are too extended. Proportionality is an accepted principle in most member states, also for their out of court settlements, and has been used some times to correct authorities, who did not show enough respect for the strong relation between facts and punishment.[7] I will address judicial control as a topic separately later in my paper.

I now come to the procedural provisions for the settlement under Article 22(2). I list them here before I make some remarks about them that are inspired by the comparative perspective:
1. the EPP is the competent authority;
2. the defendant must have given a free and clear admission of guilt;
3. there is sufficient evidence of guilt to justify committal to trial;
4. the decision to enter into an agreement must be made public;
5. the agreement is subject to the control of the judge of freedoms.

As was already stressed above, the power to prosecute is a discretionary one in the *Corpus Iuris*. By giving the power to settle to the EPP this becomes an instrument in the implementation of this discretion. Apart from what already has been said about guidelines I want to mention here the parties that are ruled out. Obviously the courts are no partner to the agreement. In the decision to prosecute the judge of freedoms holds a corrective power. It is not his own decision, but in the *Corpus* he has been given a role comparable to a committal for trial. We will

---

[7] Compare the influence of the Italian court on the outcome of the *pattegiamento*; A. den Hartog & E.F. Stamhuis, *Onderhandelen in strafzaken*, Deventer: Gouda Quint 1996, p. 224.

attend the role of this judge in a moment and continue with the conclusion that other parties, such as the EU Commission, do not take part in the agreement. It is therefore a matter of policy of the EPP how much room is given to the view of the communitarian institutions. The national authorities have a better position in this respect. They can propose a case to the EPP for a settlement under Article 22(2).[8]

The settlement must have a double basis. It must be accepted by the defendant and it must rely on evidential ground, solid enough to justify the committal. Because the national systems in member states differ considerably in this matter it is of paramount importance to give a clear regulation of the position of the defendant and his declaration. In one member state the official declaration is considered to render any further evidence to the facts superfluous,[9] in another it is a statement of facts that needs support from other evidence before it can justify a committal.[10,11] How the accumulation of conditions (2) and (3) must be understood is therefore to be clarified here. Condition (2) cannot be considered as an equivalent of a guilty plea, because that would be incompatible with condition (3). The defendant does not waive his right to the evidence backup that the third condition requires, he only accepts a lower level of proof as a factual basis for his penalty than would be applied when he would have gone to court. Now that a separate admission of guilt is required its main essence is a party declaration to the acceptance of the disposal by way of settlement. In as far as the admission may add to the evidence of the case, it contributes to the meeting of condition (3). How many additional evidence is required under condition (3) remains unclear. As soon as the defendant has admitted his guilt, the standard of proof for committal is almost accomplished. For this unclarity to be avoided I would suggest two questions to be put to the defendant:

1. do you accept your case to be disposed of by the settlement as is proposed by the EPP?; and
2. do you admit that you have committed the offence of which you have been accused?

Now particularly the first question must be inserted in the words of condition (2) by way of interpretation. Moreover my proposal would prevent condition (3) from dissolution in a one-sided interpretation of condition (2) as a full waiver of further factual support for the penalty to be agreed upon. For that the condition

---

[8] The application of supplementary national provisions to the benefit of the victimised communitarian institution is a different and complicated matter, related to the interpretation and application of Article 35 of the *Corpus*. *E.g.* in the Netherlands the victim has a statutory right to put a transaction settlement before a court.

[9] Compare the states that accept a guilty plea, such as England and Scotland.

[10] In the Netherlands the defendant can prevent the trial if he can convince the court in chambers, that the only evidence will be the statement of the defendant himself.

[11] In the *Corpus* the level of proof for committal is expressed as serious grounds to believe that the accused person has committed the offence; *see* Article 25b(2).

of sufficient evidence is too much an asset in comparison with many out-of-court settlements now in practice.[12]

With condition (4), the decision is made public, the *Corpus* responds to an often expressed objection to agreements between prosecution and defence. These agreements are the result of secret negotiations between both parties, to which the public eye has no access, as it is said. In this way public control of the criminal justice administration is frustrated. And indeed, the publicity principle, also laid down in Article 6 *ECHR*, is better served when the occurrence and scope of the settlement disposals are made public. Whether or not this would be best done in the way now proposed in Article 22(2) seems to be open to debate. Individual announcements may exert reactions from the public that may not amount to a well balanced evaluation of the decision. Apart from that, publicity can work as a disincentive to accept a settlement. Let us not forget, that publicity is considered to serve punitive goals by the *Corpus* itself. Publication of the conviction is listed as an additional penalty. An annual report on the settlement practice may well serve the interests at stake here. As soon as there are guidelines issued they should be made public as well.

The final topic to which I want to pay attention to is the involvement of the judge of freedoms. With the condition of approval from the judge of freedoms (added in a later stage) the settlement under Article 22(2) is no longer an out-of-court settlement in pure form. But since the judge of freedoms has only a limited role, the settlement remains a non-trial disposal, which was the aim here in the first place. The task of the judge of freedoms is, according to an explanatory text, only to check whether the conditions of Article 22(2) have been fulfilled in a particular case. The arguments in favour of involvement of the judge of freedoms are obvious.

First of all, it is the same judge as the one who has to decide on committal for trial after closing the investigation. In safeguarding the standard of proof for the settlement (which is the same as it is for committal) he will guarantee, that the factual basis for the intervention is the same for the agreement as for the start of a trial.

Secondly, while checking the voluntariness of the defendant's co-operation, the judge of freedoms offers a general safeguard against abuse of power on the side of the EPP as well as a concrete check of the informed consent that is necessary for the waiver of procedural rights that is the consequence of the agreement. This check includes whether the defendant has had a proper opportunity to consult with his attorney before giving his consent, with proper access to the relevant documents.

Finally, the upholding of equality in sanctioning practice, to which the condition of proportionality enables, is a benefit that I already mentioned above. The proportionality check can move on different levels: depending on what the EPP is obliged to present to the judge, the judge will or will not be able to correct

---

[12] All agreements that are shaped as a guilty plea; transaction in the Netherlands.

the factual basis of the settlement. If he is provided with the complete file, he may even construct other offences than the EPP had in mind for the settlement. If he has no access to all the facts of the case, he can still compare the settlement's outcome with what the court imposes in cases with the same factual basis.[13] Before implementing this judicial control, it has to be made clear whether or not it is within the power of this judge to seek a higher penalty. Must he consider the EPP's proposal as a maximum, or can he reject the proposal on the ground that it is too lenient. From the current text of Article 22 one can derive arguments for both a limited and a broader view on the proportionality check. There are various other matters that are unattended yet, such as the procedural requirements for the judicial control. Will he or will he not arrange for a hearing to find out the defendant's position? Can he rely on papers only? We will have to await further developments on this and other topics.

It may be helpful to stress, that the judicial control under Article 22(2) is not the access to court, which a defendant must be granted if he denies the EPP proposal. It is an extra check, that cannot be waived by the defendant and will only be superfluous as soon as the defendant appears non-co-operative. When that happens, the proposal should be withdrawn and the case can go to court, still via the judge of freedoms in a committal hearing.

The involvement of the judge of freedoms is all the more remarkable in the institutional perspective. I promised not to deal with this, so I make only one brief remark: here we would have a number of individual judges, appointed in national courts, who have to counterbalance the powers of the communitarian EPP. How will they gain enough weight to do that, and how will they arrange for a certain level of equality, that the EPP may expect? From this point of view, the national proliferation of the judge of freedoms was a weak spot in the original concept of the *Corpus*, and is duly amended in the Draft Report of the European Parliamentary Commission, mentioned above. That proposes to appoint a judge of freedoms in the European Court of Justice.

## Evaluation

As evaluation criteria I propose the rules and principles that the Council of Europe adopted in 1987 (No. R (87) 18), because they are to the point, accepted on an international level and show enough distance towards the various national varieties and idiosyncracies. In this recommendation a division is made between out-of-court settlements and other simplified procedures, especially the penal order. One can challenge this division, because usually penal orders are also out-of-court settlements, but the principles are practically the same. They have to be understood as an attempt to serve the proper administration of justice in a more uniform way, in the growing awareness of the problems caused by case-overload and delays in court disposals. First of all it is stressed that out-of-court settlements

---

[13] Compare the role of the court after a negotiated guilty plea in England and Scotland.

are appropriate and to be promoted for minor offences only. However, it is not clarified how the relative seriousness of the offence is to be determined. The *Corpus* is in full harmony with this idea. After this principal idea various other principles are set out.

The first principle for these disposals is that the law should prescribe the conditions that can be proposed, in particular: payment of a sum of money, restitution of the illegally obtained advantages and victim compensation. Article 22(2) does not clearly state which proposals are acceptable in a settlement. The explanation to the original version of the *Corpus* more or less assumes that financial penalties are the first to be thought of, but a list of options is not available. Therefore we remain in the dark as to whether sanctions can be enforced under a settlement that cannot be imposed by the court. Article 15 lists the penalties that can be imposed and for example future behaviour is not among them, although that may well serve punitive goals such as prevention. Can the EPP under Article 22(2) agree with the defendant that he or his enterprise withdraws from economic activity for a certain period?

The next principle in the Council of Europe resolution requires an indication in the law of the competent authority, which is done in Article 22(2)(see above). Connected hereto the recommendation pleads for the settlement proposal to be open to review if the defendant has objections. That aspect is not mentioned in Article 22(2), leading to the conclusion that it is left to the policy of the EPP. Will the EPP be prepared to a certain exchange of views before a proposal is considered to be final or will it make only one offer and will it be: take it or leave it for the defendant. Someone may call this a negotiation stage, which is not wholly unjustified. The *Corpus* in its current form does not prevent or prohibit bargaining over the agreement, but I do not consider this to be negative, taking into account the other conditions and safeguards.

The text of the *Corpus* does not include the obligation of issuing guidelines and tables of amounts payable, which the resolution prefers. I already argued that it is to be expected that the EPP will issue such guidelines. The EPP will be organised as a body of officials, with national delegates and a central communitarian office, and in seeking uniformity and transparency it cannot do without guidelines or instructions on how to use the discretionary powers. As soon as they are issued, the guidelines, etc. will be published according to normal practice.

Two final requirements in the resolution are aimed at the protection of the defendant, before and after the agreement has been accomplished. The defendant must have the freedom to ignore the offer. To most of us this may not come as a surprise, but this requirement will make us at least critical towards the practice, addressed in the explanatory text,[14] of automatically arising the level of the penalty when the defendant is convicted in court after his denial of a settlement.

---

[14] *Corpus Iuris* 1998, p. 144: a limitation of power of the court in this respect is rejected for practical reasons.

However practical this may be I would consider it incompatible with the rights of a defendant, when a court should punish him for going to court and using his rights. We touch here upon an argument in favour of the punitive order model. In that model the penalty's enforceability does not depend on the acceptance by the defendant. He can go to court but does not run the risk of coming out worse as long as the facts appear to be the same before the court as they were before the authority that gave the order. In the agreement model the authorities have to ascertain agreement before the penalty is enforceable. Every persuasive action may evolve into a threat to voluntariness.

Once an agreement is reached and approved by the judge of freedoms the right to prosecute is renounced definitively. That conclusion is based on the use of the term extinction of prosecution in Article 22(2) and renders this settlement in accordance with the last requirement in the resolution. It is yet to be established what happens when the defendant changes his attitude after his initial co-operation and refuses to complete the fulfilment of his obligations under the penalty. Different disposals in member states have different answers to this question. Does the right to prosecute revive or does the settlement result in an enforceable penalty, for example after the judge's approval? The current text of Article 22(2) tends to go in the first direction, but a more expressed opinion is necessary.

I already paid attention to the publication of the settlement practice. Remarkably the resolution of the Council of Europe does not go further than an annual report and explicitly recommends secrecy on the identity of the offenders who have settled with the authorities. It is a referral to an attractive feature in some member states of the non-trial disposals, namely that a public hearing is avoided and in that way damage to the reputation of the offender prevented. That is considered to be justified by the fact that a settlement is not a formal conviction and the unconvicted are entitled to special protection. The option of secrecy is obviously ignored in the *Corpus*. I would have considered secrecy somewhat overdone, bearing in mind that the huge penalties that communitarian institutions impose nowadays do not prevent disclosure of the identity of the person or enterprise. Before, I have already dealt with the advantages of the publicity.

### Epilogue

In this paper I have given an analysis of some aspects of the non-trial disposal that is included in the *Corpus Iuris*. I have made some remarks from a comparative perspective that resulted in issues to be clarified before implementation of this disposal as well as in suggestions for minor changes or a certain policy line in the practical use of this disposal. In the evaluation I have given consideration to the compatibility of this settlement disposal with an internationally accepted standard. At the end of the day I would like to put forward the view that this part of the *Corpus Iuris* deserves to be developed further, although some amendments are deemed necessary.

# Pre-trial Detention: Justiciability of the Right to Liberty under the South African *Constitution*

*E. Steyn*

## Introduction

The detention of criminal suspects raises the issue of the right to human liberty in any criminal process. On 27 April 1994[1] South Africa moved into a new legal and constitutional dispensation. The new democratic order in South Africa, in which individual liberty is specifically protected by a justiciable *Bill of Rights*,[2] has brought bail as a way of granting a suspect such liberty to the fore. This question has been made more urgent by increased in crime and particularly a public fear of crime. The guarantees of liberty and other provisions governing bail have been attacked as 'unnecessary' constraints on crime control.

This paper considers the right of an accused person to his or her liberty[3] whilst awaiting trial and the constitutionally recognised limitations on this right. It outlines legislative attempts to introduce procedures for deciding on the release of suspects. It then critically analyses the recent decision of the South African Constitutional Court in *S* v. *Dlamini*; *S* v. *Dladla and Others*; *S* v. *Joubert*; *S* v. *Schietekat*[4] in some detail on the constitutionality of this legislation. This analysis finally pays attention to the Court's ruling that

---

[1] It is on this day that the *interim Constitution* of the Republic of South Africa with its *Bill of Rights Act 200* of 1993 came into operation. Through the *interim Constitution* South Africa moved from a constitutional framework of parliamentary sovereignty, to the present situation where the *Constitution* with its bill of rights, is the supreme law of the land. The final *Constitution of the Republic of South Africa Act 108* of 1996 came into operation on the 4th February 1997.

[2] Under a justiciable bill of rights a court has the power to test not only executive acts but also legislation against the norms laid down in the bill of rights and to annul any such acts and legislation which are contrary to the said norms. *See* generally M. Cappeletti, 'Judicial review of constitutionality of state action: Its expansion and legitimacy', 1992 *TSAR* 256; H.F.E. Ruppel, 'A bill of rights: Practical implications for legal practice – a Namibian perspective', 1992 *SAPL* 51.

[3] The right to liberty and to be released on bail is recognised in Article 9(3) And article 14 of the *International Covenant on Civil and Political Rights (ICCPR)*, Article 11 of the *United Nations Universal Declaration of Human Rights* and Article 6(2) of the *European Convention for the Protection of Human Rights and Fundamental Freedoms (ECHR)*. Article 14 of the *ICCPR* is the perhaps the most important international provision in this context as it is widely seen as a statement of the international law rules governing a fair trial. Article 14(2) provides: "Everyone charged with a criminal offence shall have the right to be presumed innocent until proved guilty according to law." The right to bail before trial is rooted ultimately in Chapter 39 of the *Magna Carta*, which states: "No free man shall be taken, imprisoned, disseised, outlawed, banished, or in any way destroyed, nor will We proceed against or prosecute him, except by the lawful judgment of his peers and by the law of the land." *See* A.E. Dick Howard, *Magna Carta: Text and Commentary* (1964), at 43.

[4] 1999 (2) *SACR* 51 (CC); 1999 (4) *SA* 623 (CC).

evidence presented at the bail hearing may be used in the subsequent trial and the effect that this may have on applicants exercising their right to liberty in future.

## Freedom and Liberty

It can be said that the South African *Constitution*, both in its 1993-interim[5] and 1996-final versions,[6] with their justiciable bills of rights has re-affirmed the fundamental common law principle of freedom by requiring that an accused person be released from detention if the 'interests of justice' permit such release. Such personal freedom is acknowledged internationally,[7] together with the fact that every person is presumed innocent until proven guilty. The 1994 and 1996 *Constitutions* that led the South African criminal justice system in a new direction by establishing a new constitutional democracy, also provided for the *Constitution* to become the supreme law of the land,[8] binding all executive and judicial organs of the State. More significantly, in the context of this discussion, the *Constitution* granted comprehensive protection of the right to freedom in terms of Section 12 and Section 35(1)(f) of the *Constitution* (as did the equivalent provisions of the *interim Constitution*).[9,10]

Since a constitutional rights analysis requires that the content of a right be determined in order to examine the scope to be given to it, an evaluation of the

---

[5] The *interim Constitution of the Republic of South Africa Act 200* of 1993, provided in terms of Section 25(2)(d) as follows: "Every person arrested for the alleged commission of an offence shall, in addition to the rights which he or she has as a detained person, have the right – (d) to be released from detention with or without bail, unless the interests of justice require otherwise."

[6] The *Constitution of the Republic of South Africa Act 108* of 1996, provides in terms of Section 35(1)(f) as follows: "Everyone who is arrested for allegedly committing an offence has the right – (f) to be released from detention if the interests of justice permit, subject to reasonable conditions."

[7] Cf. Article 11 of the *United Nations Universal Declaration of Human Rights*, Article 6(2) of the *ECHR* and Article 14 of the *ICCPR*. Article 14 of the *ICCPR* is widely seen as the most important international rule governing a fair trial. For this reason its provisions have been adopted by the international tribunals established to try persons for human rights violations in the former Yugoslavia and Rwanda and by the International Law Commission in its proposals for a permanent International Criminal Court.

[8] Section 2 of the final *Constitution* provides for its supremacy.

[9] *See* Section 11 of the *interim Constitution* that provided: "(1) Every person shall have the right to freedom and security of the person, which shall include the right not to be detained without trial. (2) No person shall be subject to torture of any kind, whether physical, emotional or emotional, nor shall any person be subject to cruel, inhuman or degrading treatment or punishment."

[10] *See* Section 12 of the *Constitution* that provides: "Freedom and security of the person – (1) Everyone has the right to freedom and security of the person, which includes the right – (a) not to be deprived of freedom arbitrarily or without just cause; (b) not to be detained without trial; (c) to be free from all forms of violence from either public or private sources; (d) not to be tortured in any way; and (e) not to be treated or punished in a cruel, inhuman or degrading way. (2) Everyone has the right to bodily and psychological integrity, which includes the right – (a) to make decisions concerning reproduction; (b) to security in and control over their body; and (c) not to be subjected to medical or scientific experiments without their informed consent.

right to liberty will be considered as part of this analysis. It forms an essential precursor to an evaluation of the Constitutional Court's *Dlamini*[11] judgement, in which the right to liberty was restrictively interpreted.

When one considers the primary purpose of the right to freedom and security, which is protected in terms Section 12(1) of the *Constitution*, it appears that it is aimed at outlawing or at the very least, attempting to minimise restrictions on liberty which may result from arbitrary pre-trial incarcerations or restrictive bail conditions.[12]

However, in the *Dlamini* case the Constitutional Court restricted the right to liberty so severely by the application of the general limitation clause[13] of the *Constitution* that pre-trial detention when accused persons are charged with having allegedly committed serious offences, may very likely become the norm, in the South African criminal justice system rather than the exception. This interpretation adopted by the Court is in stark contrast with its interpretations of the right to freedom and liberty in the past. In fact, not so long ago the Constitutional Court considered personal freedom as such an important right in the protection of human dignity that it held that the right had an intrinsic constitutional value of its own.[14] Viewed, therefore, against the background of the Court's earlier decisions it seemed reasonable to expect that the Court would give a broad interpretation to the right to liberty in order to give true recognition to the right.[15] However, in *Dlamini* the Court failed to do so.

---

[11] It is submitted that the scope of a right should always be determined in order to qualify its essential content. *See* Van Wyk *et al.*, *Rights and Constitutionalism* (1994), at 650.

[12] De Waal *et al.* in *The Bill of Rights Handbook* (1999) at 233 maintain that the provision should be taken to protect an individual's physical integrity against invasion from public and private sources. It therefore also protects the individual against invasions of physical integrity by way of arbitrary arrest, violence, torture of cruel treatment or punishment.

[13] *See* Section 36 of the *Constitution* as discussed *infra*.

[14] *See Ferreira* v. *Levin NO and Others* 1996 (1) *BCLR* 1 (CC) at para 49, wherein Ackermann J interpreted the meaning of freedom as follows: "Although freedom is indispensable for the protection of dignity, it has an intrinsic constitutional value of its own. It is likewise the foundation of the other rights that are specifically entrenched. Viewed form this perspective, the starting point must be that an individual's right to freedom must be defined as widely as possible, consonant with a similar breath of freedom of others."

[15] In the matter of *Bernstein and Others* v. *Bester NO and Others* 1996 (4) *BCLR* 449 (CC) para 145; O'Regan J interpreted freedom as having two inter-related constitutional aspects: the first is a procedural aspect which requires that *no-one be deprived of physical freedom unless fair* and lawful procedures have been followed. Requiring deprivation of freedom to be in accordance with procedural fairness is a substantive commitment in the Constitution. The other constitutional aspect of freedom lies in a recognition that, in certain circumstances, even when fair and *lawful procedures have been followed*, the deprivation of freedom will not be constitutional, because the *grounds upon which freedom has been curtailed are unacceptable*." (Emphasis added.)

## Bail

Bail can be defined in South African law as the practice of releasing an accused person before a trial on the accused's promise to return.[16] Such promise is then secured by some form of collateral, usually money, that the accused pays to the court and which the court can retain if he does not appear for trial. Our bail process has also been consistent with the presumption of innocence.[17] Because of this presumption courts traditionally grant bail whenever possible and try to lean in favour of the liberty of the accused, provided that it is in the 'interests of justice' to do so.[18] Bail is statutorily defined in our system in terms of Section 58 of the *Criminal Procedure Act*,[19] and is regulated by Sections 58 to 71 of that Act and Section 35 of the *Constitution*.[20] The most important provision to consider for purposes of this discussion is Section 60 of the *CPA*.

---

[16] *See R* v. *Wilson alias Gannon* 1914 *TPD* 5, at 6.

[17] It is important to note that this presumption has been recognised since 1789. Article 9 of the French Declaration *des droits de l'homme et du citoyen* for example began with the words: "Every man being counted innocent until he has been pronounced guilty, if it is thought indispensable to arrest him, all severity that may not be necessary to secure his person ought to be strictly suppressed by law." Scholars, like H.J. Berman, maintain that this French doctrine was originally intended to operate, primarily, at the stage of investigation. *See* H.J. Berman, 'The Presumption of Innocence: Another Reply', (1980) 28 *American Journal of Comp. Law* 615, 622. *See Krause* v. *Switzerland* (7986/77) *DR* 13, 73. In this matter the European Commission of Human Rights stated in similar vein that the principle of the presumption of innocence is in the first instance a procedural guarantee applying in any kind of criminal procedure; its application reaches therefore much further than just the trial. *See Stack* v. *Boyle* 342 *U.S.* 1 (1951), where Vinson CJ stated with reference to the right to bail, "this traditional right to freedom before conviction permits the unhampered preparation of a defence, and serves to prevent the infliction of punishment prior to conviction. Unless this right to bail before the trial is preserved, the presumption of innocence, secured only after centuries of struggle, would loose its meaning"(at 6).

[18] *S* v. *Smith* 1969 (4) *SA* 175 (N), at 177E-F.

[19] *Act 51* of 1977, hereinafter referred to as *CPA*.

[20] Section 35 of the *Constitution* provides for the rights of arrested, detained, and accused persons: (1) Everyone who is arrested for allegedly committing an offence has the right – (d) to be brought before a court as soon as reasonably possible, but not later than 48 hours after the arrest; or the end of the first court day after the expiry of the 48 hours, if the 48 hours expire outside ordinary court hours or a day which is not an ordinary court day; (e) at the first court appearance after being arrested, to be charged or to be informed of the reason for the detention to continue, or to be released; and (f) to be released from detention if the interests of justice permit, subject to reasonable conditions. (3) Every accused has a right to a fair trial, which includes the right – (h) to be presumed innocent.

## Impact of the *Constitution* and the 1995[21] and 1997[22] Legislative Amendments on Bail in South Africa

Under South African common law bail applications were regarded as *sui generis* applications and the *onus* was on the accused to show on a balance of probabilities that they should be released.[23] When the *interim Constitution* came into operation in 1994, it spelt out detainees' rights and, as a result, the situation changed. The interpretation and application of these rights initially caused much confusion amongst members of the judiciary. This was particularly true with respect to how they should interpret the concept, 'interests of justice', and how they should determine who should bear the *onus* in a bail application. A host of decisions followed, all considering the *onus* of the parties in bail applications. Most important was the decision in *Ellish en Andere* v. *Prokureur-Generaal, Witwatersrandse Plaaslike Afdeling*,[24] where the court attempted to move away from the question of *onus* by deciding that there could be no question of an *onus* of proof in a bail application. The state had the duty to commence with the leading of evidence in the application. Van Schalkwyk J stated that if, at the end of the enquiry, there was still a balance between the interests of the accused and those of justice, then the accused had to get the benefit of the doubt and be released on bail.

Fortunately, the confusion that reigned was clarified by the legislature which amended Section 60 of the *CPA* to fit with the constitutional norm expressed in Section 25(2)(d) of the *interim Constitution*.[25] In the amended section the legislature did not set a *numerus clausus*[26] of instances defining 'interests of justice' but left the list open-ended to allow room for judicial interpretation. The 1995 amendments emphasised that presiding officers should acknowledge their new roles and functions in dealing with bail applications,[27] and that every presiding officer should consider what effect the release of the detainee would have on the 'interests of justice'. Significant from the perspective of crime control, was the fact that it was no longer required of presiding officers that they act as neutral umpires in bail hearings,

---

[21] Section 60, as amended by Section 3 of the *Second Criminal Procedure Amendment Act 75* of 1995.

[22] *Second Criminal Procedure Amendment Act 85* of 1997.

[23] *See S* v. *Hlongwa* 1979 (4) *SA* 112 (D).

[24] 1994 (2) *SACR* 579 (W).

[25] Section 25(2)(d) of the *interim Constitution* provided as follows: "(2) Every person arrested for the alleged commission of an offence shall, in addition to the rights which he or she has as a detained person, have the right – (d) to be released from detention with or without bail, unless the interests of justice require otherwise."

[26] P.M. Bekker, 'Interpretation of the right to bail and the limitation clause of the Constitution of the Republic of South Africa', (1994) 57 *THRHR* 490.

[27] *See Ellish en Andere* v. *Prokureur-Generaal, Witwatersrandse Provinsiale Afdeling* 1994 (2) *SACR* 579 (W). This approach is confirmed by Section 60(3) as introduced by the *Second Criminal Procedure Amendment Act 75* of 1995.

but that they were obliged to act inquisitorially and to investigate each matter.[28]

The 1995 legislation also introduced Subsection 60(11) into the principle Act. This new subsection caused some controversy because it created a reverse *onus* whereby the accused was required to satisfy the court, in matters where specified very serious offences[29] had been committed or where specified serious offences[30] had been re-committed, whilst the accused person was out on bail, to convince the court that the 'interests of justice' did not require his detention. The wording of the legislation was clear to the effect that in all other instances the state bore the *onus* to prove that the accused should not be released from detention. The 1995 amendments were considered to be good law. In a positive sense the law now offered sufficient protection to all, including victims and witnesses, that had been lacking after the inception of the *interim Constitution*. Moreover, it was widely believed that the law as amended was restrictive but constitutionally sound.

Despite the fact that adequate legislation was in place to protect the rights of the community, the South African public remained convinced that the right to bail was to be blamed for the increase in crime. This belief was strengthened by one case in particular, concerning a victim called Mamokgethi Malebane.[31] This case sparked an outcry from the community that courts were failing to protect innocent victims, by granting bail too readily to hardened criminals.[32] Suggestions were made that the bail law should be tightened further. The government's response to these calls for vengeance was to amend the bail law by enacting the *1997 Criminal Procedure Second Amendment Act*.[33] In an attempt to make it more difficult for accused persons to apply for bail, however, government overstepped the boundaries of constitutional criminal

---

[28] This approach is confirmed by Section 60(3) as introduced by the *Second Criminal Procedure Amendment Act 75* of 1995.

[29] These offences which are listed in terms of Schedule 5 of the *CPA* and are: Treason; Murder, involving the use of a dangerous weapon or firearm as defined in the *Dangerous Weapons Act*, Act 71 of 1968; Rape; Robbery with aggravating circumstances and robbery of a motor vehicle; Any offence referred to in Sections 13(f) and 14(b) of the *Drugs and Drug Trafficking Act* 140 of 1992; Any statutory offence relating to the trafficking of, dealing in or smuggling of firearms, explosives or armament, or the possession of an automatic or semi-automatic firearm, explosives or armament; Any offence relating to exchange control, corruption, fraud, forgery, uttering or theft involving amounts in excess of R500 000,00.

[30] These offences are listed in terms of another schedule to the *CPA*, namely Schedule 1. Offences listed in terms of Schedule 1 are serious offences like treason, murder, sedition, rape, indecent assault and robbery, to name a few.

[31] The victim in this case, Mamogethi Malebane, was killed by the accused, Dan Mabote, shortly before she had to testify against him. The accused was released by the court on bail of R2000 despite the fact that the police were investigating two other matters of rape against him and that the police had opposed the bail application in the matter.

[32] *See* 'Justice betrayal of innocence', *The Weekly Mail and Guardian* 9 May 1997, at 9; 'Selmaats slaan man na moord op kind', *Die Burger* 2 August 1997, at 4.

[33] Act 85 of 1997.

justice. The controversial provisions that were adopted were Subsections 60(8A), 60(11), 60(11A) and 60(11B)(c) of the *CPA* as amended. Particularly controversial were those provisions that in essence require that an accused adduce evidence that 'exceptional circumstances'[34] exist which in the 'interests of justice' permit his release, or require that an accused adduce evidence which will satisfy the court that the 'interests of justice' permit his release.[35]

As the term 'exceptional circumstances' was not defined in any way it has created considerable uncertainty and caused interpretation problems for the courts. The new legislation requires that courts not only consider the conventional factors of whether the accused will stand trial and/or interfere with witnesses but, in terms of the legislation, courts are also duty bound to consider whether the release of an accused person will undermine the public's sense of peace and security or its confidence in the criminal justice system.[36]

### Reflections on *Dlamini*

The decision of the Constitutional Court should be considered against the background of the South African bail process that has always recognised the presumption of innocence as a substantive principle of fundamental justice, which has protected the fundamental rights of liberty and human dignity of any person accused by the state of committing a crime.[37] Such recognition is given in the judgement of Mohamed AJ (as he then was) in the decision of *S* v. *Acheson*:[38] "An accused person cannot be kept in detention pending his trial as a form of anticipatory punishment. The presumption of the law is that he is innocent until his guilt has been established in Court. The Court will therefore

---

[34] *See* Section 60(11)(a) of the *CPA* that provides: "(11) Notwithstanding any provision of this Act, where an accused is charged with an offence referred to – (a) In Schedule 6, the court shall order that the accused be detained in custody until he or she is dealt with in accordance with the law, unless the accused, having been given a reasonable opportunity to do so, adduces evidence which satisfies the court that exceptional circumstances exist which in the interests of justice permit his or her release."

[35] *See* Section 60(11)(b) of the *CPA* that provides: "(11) Notwithstanding any provision of this Act, where an accused is charged with an offence referred to – (b) In Schedule 5, but not Schedule 6, the court shall order that the accused be detained in custody until he or she is dealt with in accordance with the law, unless the accused, having been given a reasonable opportunity to do so, adduces evidence which satisfies the court that the interests of justice permit his or her release.

[36] *See* Section 60(4)(e) of the *CPA* that reads as follows: "(4) The refusal to grant bail and the detention of an accused in custody shall be in the interests of justice where one or where one or more of the following grounds are established: (e) where in exceptional circumstances there is the likelihood that the release of the accused will disturb the public order or undermine the public peace or security; or *[sic]*."

[37] *See S* v. *Fourie* 1973 (1) *SA* 100 (D).

[38] 1991 (2) *SA* 805 (Nm). Although this is a Namibian High Court decision, it has relevance for the South African courts, since the law is essentially the same in both countries. In addition, it should be noted that Mahomed J was a South African judge that was seconded to the Namibian Court. He is now appointed as Chief Justice in South Africa.

ordinarily grant bail to an accused person unless this is likely to prejudice the ends of justice."[39]

Despite the recognition given internationally to the right to be presumed innocent,[40] the Constitutional Court in *Dlamini* preferred to define the right so narrowly, as not to have a function in the interpretation of rules relating to liberty. As a result of the Court's interpretation the right will never operate at the pre-trial stage of the criminal process at all. In view of this interpretation it is feared that the right to liberty will soon become meaningless if an accused can no longer rely on the presumption of innocence in order to claim his or her personal freedom. It is acknowledged that the right to bail is not an absolute right and that accused persons should be incarcerated in instances where the state has strong countervailing considerations that call for their incarceration; but this should not translate into pre-trial detention whenever it is alleged that an accused has committed a serious offence.

The sad reality is that the time that it takes to bring accused persons to trial has increased dramatically in South Africa. South Africa's criminal justice system is in a crisis, which in turn causes systemic delays. These delays do not only affect the quality of state witnesses' testimony in the long run, but if an accused is detained, also affect the fairness of their trial. So the effect of the 1997 amendments will be particularly harsh for people accused of committing a crime.

## Limitation Analysis

Unlike the *Constitution* of the US that has no limitation clause, the South African *Constitution*, like the Canadian *Charter*[41] and the German *Grundgesetz*,[42] sets out explicitly how limitations on fundamental rights are to be justified.[43] The South African *Constitution* contains a general limitation clause that specifies the criteria for the restriction of the rights contained in the *Bill of Rights*.[44] A law that infringes upon a specific right of the *Constitution*

---

[39] *Acheson, supra*, at 822A-B.

[40] Cf. statement by Dickson CJC in *R v. Oakes* 26 *D.L.R.* (4th) 200, at 212-213: "The presumption of innocence protects the fundamental liberty and human dignity of any and every person accused by the State of criminal conduct. An individual charged with a criminal offence faces grave social and personal consequences, including potential loss of physical liberty, subjection to social stigma and ostracism from the community, as well as other social, psychological and economic harms. In light of the gravity of these consequences, the presumption of innocence is crucial."

[41] *See* Section 1 of the Canadian *Charter of Rights and Freedoms*.

[42] *See* Section 19 of the German *Grundgesetz*.

[43] A. Cachalia *et al., Fundamental Rights In The New Constitution*, at 109.

[44] Section 36 of the *Constitution* provides: "(1) The rights in the Bill of Rights may be limited only in terms of law of general application to the extent that the limitation is reasonable and justifiable in an open and democratic society based on human dignity, equality and freedom, taking into account all relevant factors, including – (a) the nature of the right; (b) the importance of the purpose of the limitation; (c) the nature and extent of the limitation; (d) the relation between the (to be continued)

may be saved, and therefore be regarded as constitutional, because of the application of the limitation clause. The reasons for limiting a right need to be special, exceptionally cogent and within the criteria spelled out in terms of Section 36(1) of the *Constitution*.

The South African courts have adopted what can be described as a 'two-stage' approach in determining the constitutionality of an Act. As Kentridge AJ pointed out in the Constitutional Court decision *S* v. *Zuma and Others*:[45] "The single stage approach (as in the US *Constitution* or the Hong Kong *Bill of Rights*) may call for a more flexible approach to the construction of the fundamental right, whereas the two-stage approach may call for a broader interpretation of the fundamental right, qualified only at the second stage."[46]

The limitation clause fulfils a particularly important function at the second stage of the constitutional enquiry, since it will determine whether a provision that is in conflict with the *Constitution* can be justified in terms of the limitation clause.[47]

In *S* v. *Makwanyane and Another*[48] Chaskalson P stated that any enquiry that considered whether the limitations criteria of Section 33[49] were met involved the weighing up of competing values and ultimately an assessment based on proportionality. He stated: "In the balancing process the relevant considerations will include the nature of the right that is limited and its importance to an open and democratic society based on freedom and equality; the purpose for which the right is limited and the importance of that purpose to such a society; the extent of the limitation, its efficacy and, particularly where the limitation has to be necessary, whether the desired ends could reasonably be achieved through other means less damaging to the right in question."[50]

Considering the way that the Court went about applying the limitation clause in *Dlamini*, it appears that much has changed since *Makwanyane* was decided. One of the main justification grounds used by the Court in *Dlamini* was the high level of crime. This is evident from the following finding by the Court: "There can be no quibble with Mr D'Oliveira's submission that over the last few years our society has experienced a deplorable level of violent crime. (…) Mr D'Oliveira was correct when he argued that it is against this background that we should assess the provisions of Section 60(11)(a)."[51]

---

limitation and its purpose; and (e) less restrictive means to achieve the purpose. (2) Except as provided in subsection (1) or in any other provision of the Constitution, no law may limit any right entrenched in the Bill of Rights."

[45] 1995 (2) *SA* 642 (CC).

[46] *Zuma, supra*, at 654G-H.

[47] Kentridge AJ in *S* v. *Zuma and Others*, gives a clear exposition of the approach to be adopted in determining the constitutionality of a statutory provision.

[48] 1995 (3) *SA* 391 (CC).

[49] The limitation provision under the *interim Constitution*.

[50] *Makwanyane, supra*, para 104.

[51] *Dlamini, supra*, para 67.

It is astonishing that Kriegler J who wrote the unanimous decision of the Court could accept the argument on behalf of the government on such a crucial issue. It was also Justice Kriegler who in *Makwayane* virtually required an empirical study to gauge the deterrent effect of the death penalty, when the state sought to argue that it had served as a sufficient deterrent in combating crime.[52] The change in the approach to constitutional interpretation from *Makwanyane* to *Dlamini* is also evident from Mohamed DP's reasons for not accepting deterrence as a valid factor limiting the rights of the accused in the former case.[53]

The Constitutional Court in its consideration of the constitutionality of Subsections 60(4)(e) and (8A) of the *CPA* held that the provisions do infringe upon an accused's right to be released on reasonable conditions, but that the provisions passed constitutional muster through the application of the limitation clause.[54] Most disturbing is the fact that the Court considers the prevalence of crime in South Africa, and the public's response, to be convincing enough to limit an accused's right to be released before trial. Having made the finding that the provisions infringe upon the right set out in terms of Section 35(1)(f) of the *Constitution*, it is baffling how the Court could give so much weight to public opinion in light of its own pronouncements on that factor.

The Constitutional Court had held in *Makwanyane* that public opinion should not be used as a constitutional yardstick in a democratic society. With reference to public opinion Chaskalson P commented as follows: "Public opinion may have some relevance to the enquiry, but, in itself, it is no substitute for the duty vested in the Courts to interpret the *Constitution* and to uphold its provisions without fear or favour. If public opinion were to be decisive, there would be no need for constitutional adjudication. The protection of rights could then be left to Parliament, which has a mandate from

---

[52] Kriegler J in *Makwanyane, supra,* stated: "no empirical study, no statistical exercise and no theoretical analysis has been able to demonstrate that capital punishment has any deterrent force greater than that of a really heavy sentence of imprisonment" (para 212).

[53] See *Makwanyane, supra,* para 290: "We were not furnished with any reliable research dealing with the relationship between the rate of serious offences and the proportion of successful apprehensions and convictions following on the commission of serious offences. This would have been a significant enquiry. It appears to me to be an inherent probability that the more successful the police are in solving serious crimes and the more successful they are in apprehending the criminals concerned and securing their convictions, the greater will be the perception of risk for those contemplating such offences. That increase in the perception of risk, contemplated by the offender, would bear a relationship to the rate at which serious offences are committed. Successful arrest and conviction must operate as a deterrent and the State should, within the limits of its undoubtedly constrained resources, seek to deter serious crime by adequate remuneration for the police force; by incentives to improve their training and skill; by augmenting their numbers in key areas; and by facilitating their legitimacy in the perception of the communities in which they work."

[54] See *Dlamini, supra,* para 55.

the public, and is answerable to the public for the way its mandate is exercised, but this would be a return to parliamentary sovereignty, and a retreat from the new legal order established by the 1993 *Constitution*. By the same token the issue of the constitutionality of capital punishment cannot be referred to a referendum, in which a majority view would prevail over the wishes of any minority. The very reason for establishing the new legal order, and for vesting the power of judicial review of all legislation in the courts, was to protect the rights of minorities and others who cannot protect their rights adequately through the democratic process. Those who are entitled to claim this protection include the social outcasts and marginalised people of our society. It is only if there is a willingness to protect the worst and the weakest amongst us that all of us can be secure that our own rights will be protected."[55]

Chaskalson had also held that the *Constitution* exists so as to protect minorities from the whims of public opinion.[56] In support of this view he had cited the reasons of Justice Powell in *Furman* v. *Georgia*:[57] "(...) [T]he weight of the evidence indicates that the public generally has not accepted either the morality or the social merit of the views so passionately advocated by the articulate spokesmen for abolition. But however one may assess amorphous ebb and flow of public opinion generally on this volatile issue, this type of inquiry lies at the periphery – not the core – of the judicial process in constitutional cases. The assessment of popular opinion is essentially a legislative, and not a judicial, function."[58]

Yet in *Dlamini* the Court held "public response" to the prevalence of crime in South Africa was a sufficient ground for limiting the accused's right to liberty.[59]

---

[55] *Makwanyane, supra*, para 88.

[56] *Id.*

[57] 408 *U.S.* 238 (1972).

[58] Cited in *Makwanyane, supra*, para 89, at 432A-B.

[59] *See* reasons in *Dlamini, supra*, para 55 wherein he stated as follows: "There is force in the argument. Ordinarily, the factors identified in section 60(4)(e) and (8A) would not be relevant in establishing whether the interests of justice permit the release of the accused. It would be disturbing that an individual's legitimate interests should so invasively be subjected to societal interests. It is indeed even more disturbing where the two provisions do not postulate that the likelihood of public disorder should in any way be laid at the door of the accused. The mere likelihood of such disorder independently of any influence on the part of the accused, would suffice. Nevertheless, albeit reluctantly and subject to express qualifications to be mentioned shortly, I believe the provisions pass constitutional muster. I do so on the basis that although they do infringe the section 35(1)(f) right to be released on reasonable conditions, they are saved by section 36 of the Constitution. It would be irresponsible to ignore the harsh reality of the society in which the Constitution is to operate. *Crime is a serious national concern, and a worrying feature for some time has been public eruptions of violence related to court proceedings. In the present context we are not so much concerned with violent public reaction to unpopular verdicts or sentences, but with such reactions to unpopular grants of bail.* There is widespread misunderstanding regarding the purpose and effect of bail. Manifestly, much must still be done to instil in the community a proper understanding of the presumption of innocence and the qualified (to be continued)

### The Admissibility of the Evidence at Bail Proceedings in the Subsequent Trial

The common law has always played a very special role in both the law of evidence and criminal procedure. This is evident in the statutory recognition that it receives in terms of the *Criminal Procedure Act.*[60] The state has always been able tender such testimony as proof by applying Section 235 of the *CPA*. The question, however, in the context of bail applications is whether such proof, as prescribed in Section 60(11B)(c)[61] of the *CPA*, does not infringe upon an accused's right to a fair trial.

One of the very first cases that decided upon the constitutionality of admitting the record of such a bail proceeding was *S* v. *Botha and Others.*[62] Myburgh J stated the dilemma faced by an accused applying for bail in the following terms: "If the evidence given by an accused at a bail application is admissible later at trial, the accused faces a dilemma: if he fails to give evidence or refuses to answer incriminating questions, he may be refused bail, yet, if he does give evidence and answers incriminating questions in order to get bail, he foregoes his right to remain silent and the privilege against self-incrimination. In the interest of a fair trial, the accused should not have to choose."[63]

In *Botha* it was argued that the proceedings of a bail application should be excluded from the subsequent trial on the following grounds: first, that it infringed upon an accused's right against self-incrimination; and secondly, that

---

right to freedom pending trial under section 35(1)(f). The ugly fact remains, however, that public peace and security are at times endangered by the release of persons charged with offences that incite public outrage. *Schietekat* is a good example. *Dladla* again exemplifies a different type of situation where continued detention is in the interests of the public peace. Experience has shown that organised community violence, be it instigated by quasi-political motives or by territorial battles for control of communities for commercial purposes, does subside while ringleaders are in custody. Their arrest and detention on serious charges does instil confidence in the criminal justice system and does tend to settle disquiet, whether the arrestees are warlords or drug-lords. In my view, open and democratic societies based on human dignity, equality and freedom, after weighing the factors enumerated in paragraphs (a) to (e) of section 36(1) of the Constitution, would find subsections 60(4)(e) and (8A) reasonable and justifiable in the prevailing climate in our country."(Emphasis added.)

[60] This Section 225 of the *CPA* provides as follows: "The law as to the admissibility of evidence which was in force in respect of criminal proceedings on the thirtieth day of May, 1961, shall apply in any case not expressly provided for by this Act or any other law."

[61] This section reads: "(11B)(c) The record of the bail proceedings, excluding the information in paragraph (a), shall form part of the record of the trial of the accused following such bail proceedings: Provided that if the accused elects to testify during the course of the bail proceedings the court must inform him or her of the fact that anything he or she says, may be used against him or her at his or her trial and such evidence becomes admissible in any subsequent proceedings."

[62] 1995 (2) *SACR* 605 (W).

[63] *Botha, supra,* 611i-j.

it was in violation of an accused's fair trial rights in terms of Section 25[64] of the *interim Constitution*. In regard to the protection afforded by the *Constitution* against self-incrimination, Myburgh J said: "It is clear that accused I cannot have a fair trial if he is cross-examined on the incriminating evidence he gave at the bail application if he did so in ignorance of the right to refuse to answer incriminating questions. The question is whether accused I was unaware of the rule against self-incrimination. When accused I was told by one of the arresting officers that he had a 'swygreg' he was informed of no more than that he had a right to remain silent. He was not told that he had a right to refuse to answer incriminating questions. The magistrate did not inform him of that right. (...) The record of the bail application does not give any indication that accused I was aware of the right against self-incrimination. Secondly, the mere fact that he was represented by lawyers does not justify the inference that they advised him of the right. They themselves may not have appreciated that their client enjoyed two distinct rights: the right to remain silent and the right against self-incrimination."[65]

It was held by the court in *Botha* that the evidence given at a bail hearing should be held distinct from the trial in the same way that evidence adduced in a trail-within-a-trial is excluded as testimony. Shortly after *Botha* the legislature considered it necessary to intervene and specify by statute that bail proceedings would be admissible as evidence at the trial. The result was that the *Criminal Procedure Act* was accordingly amended in 1997, and Subsection 60(11B)(c) was adopted.[66] This provision was not positively accepted by human rights lawyers. The Cape High Court expressed its disapproval of the provision in *S* v. *Schietekat.*[67] Slomowitz AJ held in *S* v. *Schietekat* that Subsection (11B)(c) of the *CPA* was invalid in that it was inconsistent with the *Constitution*. He reasoned as follows: "A bail proceeding is not a Star Chamber. Whatever the purpose of Parliament may have been in enacting it [the *Second Criminal Procedure Amendment Act*], its effect is malevolent. An accused may only elect to exercise his right to apply for bail on pain of being interrogated on the merits of the case against him, thus to have his own testimony used against him as part of the State's case when he eventually comes to be tried. It is by fashioning this weapon that those who would seek their liberty are to be discouraged from asking for it? (...) Upon testifying an accused might well incriminate himself, whether of the crime charged or, what

---

[64] More specifically Section 25(3)(c) and (d) of the *interim Constitution*.

[65] *Botha, supra*, 610f-j.

[66] Section 60(11B)(c) now provides as follows: "The record of the bail proceedings, excluding the information in para (a), shall form part of the record of the trial of the accused following upon such bail proceedings: provided that if the accused elects to testify during the course of the bail proceedings the court must inform him or her of the fact that anything he or she says, may be used against him or her at his or her trial and such evidence becomes admissible in any subsequent proceedings."

[67] 1998 (2) *SACR* 707 (C). Cf. *S* v. *C* 1998 (2) *SACR* 71 (C).

is more serious, of other offences unknown and uncharged. I am bound to hold, as I do, that the Subsection violates the Constitution."[68]

This approach can be contrasted with the Constitutional Court's view on the constitutionality of the provision. In *Dlamini* Kriegler J made it clear that the facts of that case and *Botha* should be distinguished: in *Botha* it was held that the accused testified without being informed of his right against self-incrimination, whereas in *Dlamini* the accused was properly informed of his right to remain silent and the right not to incriminate himself. He reflected on the tension that exists between the right of an accused to make an effective application for bail by adducing evidence and the list of rights under Section 35(1) and (3) of the *Constitution*. However, he did not consider the tension as exceptional or unusual or uniquely applicable to bail applicants. Rather, he observed, that what was required of an accused under the circumstances was to exercise an informed choice.[69] The Court went further and criticised the *Botha* judgement on the basis that effectively it had given the accused the right to lie in a bail application and not to be confronted with the lies in the later trial. Kriegler J in *Dlamini* interpreted the right of an accused not to incriminate himself as meaning that he may not be compelled to testify. Based on the Court's interpretation, an accused had to exercise a discretion whether or not to testify in his bail application, and if he did so, he could not claim that the proceedings should not be not be quoted in the trial.[70]

It is submitted that in its interpretation of the right not to incriminate oneself and the right to remain silent, the Court lost sight of the fact that an accused is not exercising a choice when he decides to testify in his own bail application. He has no choice. Without his testimony to support his application he would be denied his freedom. Section 60(11)(a) creates an *onus,* which should be discharged, and the only way in which it can be discharged is to tender testimony. In my mind there is no choice under such circumstances. Kriegler J justified the infringement upon the right to remain silent by making

---

[68] *Schietekat, supra,* 715g-i.

[69] *Dlamini, supra,* para 93.

[70] See *Dlamini, supra,* para 95: In effect the reasoning in *Botha* wishes to give the accused the best of both alternatives or, as it was put bluntly in *Dlamini,* the right to lie: one can advance any version of the facts without any risk of a come-back at the trial; and there one can choose another version with impunity. However, the protection of an arrestee provided under the right to remain silent in the *Constitution* – or the right not to be compelled to confess or make admissions – offers no blanket protection against having to make a choice. It is true, the principal objective of the *Bill of Rights* is to protect the individual against abuse of state power; and it does so, among others, by shielding the individual faced with a criminal charge against having to help prove that charge. That shield against compulsion does not mean, however, that an applicant for bail can choose to speak but not to be quoted. As a matter of policy the prosecution must prove its case without the accused being compelled to furnish supporting evidence. But if the accused, actin freely and in the exercise of an informed choice, elects to testify in support of a bail application, the right to silence is in no way impaired. Nor is it impaired, retrospectively as it were, if the testimony voluntarily given is subsequently held against the accused."

comparisons with other stages of the trial process. I am not convinced that the choice exercised by an accused whether to volunteer to give a statement to the police or respond to their questions can be made analogous with the choice exercised to apply for bail. Should an accused exercise his right to remain silent when asked to give a statement to the police; he will not be punished by being detained but should he wish to exercise this right when applying for bail, it is more than likely that he will be detained. The other examples used by Kriegler J are by no means more persuasive.[71]

The Court relied on an earlier judgement of the Supreme Court of Appeal in *S* v. *Nomzaza*[72] to demonstrate that an accused could never, not even under common law, succeed with a claim that incriminating evidential material given by himself could be excluded.[73] What the Court failed to recognise, however, is the difference between the element of implied compulsion to testify under the 1997 legislation and incriminating statements made freely and voluntarily by an accused in the course of a ordinary criminal trial under common law. The decision of *Nomzaza* is to be distinguished from what Subsection 60(B)(c) is regulating and cannot be used in support of saving the provision.

**Conclusion**

The Constitutional Court should act as the primary protector of fundamental human rights, such as the right to liberty that is enshrined in the *Constitution*. It has failed to act in accordance with its duty to grant such protection. It is a sad fact that the Court which began by interpreting rights liberally has finally succumbed to public pressure by upholding draconian bail legislation. *Dlamini* afforded the Court an opportunity to educate the South African public to accept that a fair trial means a constitutional trial for all people, even those accused of having committed offences.

---

[71] *See Dlamini, supra*, para 94.
[72] 1996 (2) *SACR* 14 (A).
[73] *Dlamini, supra*, para 96.

# The Application of Polygraph in Police Inquests in the Republic of Croatia

*M. Šuperina & Ž. Bagić*

### History of Polygraph in the Republic of Croatia

The first polygraph experimental tests in Croatia took place in Zagreb, at the Institute for Criminal Forensics, in April 1959. The institute was part of the Ministry of Internal Affairs of the Republic of Croatia (formerly Yugoslavia). Ivan Babić, the then Head of the forensic laboratory, conducted the experiments. The Keeler polygraph was acquired in the US.

At first, polygraph tests were administered secretly because the orthodox socialist doctrine had a negative or at least ambivalent attitude towards the procedure, *e.g.*, as was the case in the Soviet Union. It was well known that polygraphic testings were efficient in crime fighting from the experiences of the US police forces, but ideologically they were considered "capitalistic inquisitorial means for obtaining confessions" (as stated by Mr Babić during an interview). Only a small number of police executives were familiar with the experiments.

At the time, the results of the experiments performed on the criminal population were not published in either internal police publications nor in the press. Apart from stated reasons, police officials also exhibited a certain aversion towards writing about polygraphs "for security reasons", *i.e.* "that criminals do not learn tricks of the trade". There were also qualms about judicial bodies raising questions of legal justifiability.

The situation described did not last long. Soon the experimental phase was over and the operative phase of utilising the polygraph in crime fighting began.

The first significant case solved with the aid of polygraph was spectacular and paved the way to polygraph use. In November 1969 a man was reported missing in a village near Zagreb and every attempt to find him failed. Some clues indicated that his own son had murdered him and hidden the body. A polygraph examiner, D. Papes, questioned the suspect using the POT method based on police notions of where the body might have been hidden. The examiner was using a sketch of the terrain made for that purpose. After 14 days of daily questioning and on the basis of the suspect's reactions, a place in a meadow was located where the body of the murdered victim was buried. The murderer was sentenced to 11 years of imprisonment.

The case was published in an official police journal, as well as in newspapers. This provoked the interest of police officials for the use of polygraph in their operational work. Doubts about the efficiency of polygraph were removed and its use spread throughout the Republic of Croatia (and former Yugoslavia) and ever since it has been used in any complicated and serious criminal investigation.

Nevertheless, back then, neither expert literature on polygraph nor polygraph seminars existed. In addition, for ideological and security reasons, polygraph experts were not allowed to specialise abroad.

A significant step forward was made when, for police purposes, the following books were translated into Croatian:
- C. D. Lee, *Instrumental Lie Detection* (ed. 1953);
- Inbau-Reid, *Lie Detection and Criminal Interrogation* (ed. 1953);
- Inbau-Reid, *Truth and Deception* (ed. 1966);
- Burkett-Feldmonn, *Manual for the Use of Lie Detector*;
- Inbau-Reid-Lee, *Truth and Deception* (ed. 1977).

In the period between 1959 and 1967, polygraph was used by the City of Zagreb Police Department only; other police headquarters had neither polygraphs nor polygraph examiners. Therefore, polygraph examiners from Zagreb had to work hard investigating all serious criminal cases in Croatia (and in the former Federation of Yugoslavia). During this period several polygraph examiners operated the polygraph. They all contributed to the implementation of polygraph in police work. Unfortunately, however, only a negligible number of professional articles on polygraph were published during this period, while the education of beginners was restricted to mere oral teaching and application-oriented approach. Theoretical approach or research did not exist. The first examiners who worked with polygraph were lawyers and investigators. Poligraph testings were carried out from time to time – there was no continuity because examiners had other responsibilities in their police work.

The year of 1967 was, in a way, a breaking point in the development of polygraphic technique in Croatia. At the time, the City of Zagreb Police Department polygraph examiner was Zvonimir Roso, who, in addition to being a criminal investigator, was studying psychology. Already during his first year of office he achieved great success using polygraph in determining perpetrators of offences.

In 1967, the Croatian judiciary gave its opinion regarding the legal status of polygraph for the first time. An attempted murder case provided the opportunity. Z. Roso, the polygraph examiner, who acted as a witness, explained that material evidence had been gathered by polygraphic testings. Using the POT polygraphic method, he had discovered the place where the suspect had hidden the rifle used, according to expert opinion, by him in the shooting. The offender was sentenced, and the Zagreb district court verdict mentions, among other evidence, the results of the polygraphic tests. The Croatian Supreme Court declined the appeal and confirmed the original verdict. To our best knowledge, this was the first case a Supreme Court of any European country accepted polygraph results as equal evidence. However, legal regulations soon changed so that polygraphic testing results were once again not admissible as evidence in legal proceedings in Croatia. Today they are only one of the means used by police in the investigation of criminal acts.

Roso introduced standards for polygraph examiners based on the American model. His work and recommendations helped polygraph operations achieve professional status, resulting in examiners working continually, not from case to case any longer.

The polygraph lab was now fully equipped, new instruments were purchased, new conditions and standards set, and professional literature was regularly read. The education of police officials was expanded to include the possibilities of polygraphic testings in their work. The Zagreb Polygraph School was established, being the only one in former Yugoslavia. Roso wrote some 30 professional papers and studies on the use of polygraph in police investigations and two books: *Polygraph in Criminology* (1987) and *Police Investigation* (1988, 1995). He did not disregard education either; he unselfishly imparted his theoretical and practical knowledge to colleagues and students at the Police Academy. In the period between 1967 to 1979, he trained all polygraph examiners in Croatia (and former Yugoslavia). His work resulted in the establishment of polygraph labs in all important police centres.

He also developed official and personal contacts with the leading polygraph experts in the world, thus enabling the exchange of experiences.

He classified polygraphic documentation and established polygraphic files, as well as created polygraphic forms and records. A statement in writing indicating consent is a standard part of polygraphic documentation. Earlier, merely oral consent was required. He produced photo-studies of polygraphic testings and reports for court hearings, which was a novelty back then. He requested polygraph examiners to be present at interrogations concerning serious offences in order to be able to get first-hand information of the events and create testing plans. His request was accepted. After more than 13 years of working on the development of polygraphic procedure in the City of Zagreb Police Department, he then, in 1979, started lecturing at the Police Academy in Zagreb. He retired in 1990 and has since been doing theoretical work in criminology and truth verification. He died in Zagreb in 1996.

In 1997 a board of experts was set up at the Higher Police School that produced the curriculum for the Polygraph Seminar. The seminar started in 1998 and lasted for as long as 11 months. The first 12 trainees successfully completed this seminar in February 1999 and received Certificates recognising them as official Polygraph Examiners. Amongst the trainees there were two from the Republic of Slovenia.

The following are the results of the seminar as well as of the continuing study of expert literature by the lecturers of the Higher Police School:
- a research project entitled *Ascertaining the Validity of Polygraphic Testings*, conducted by Z. Dujmović, PhD, T. Ljubin, MSc, and M. Šuperina, MSc;

- the regulation of polygraph application in criminal investigations by the *Police Authorities Act*;
- the *Polygraphic Testings Statute* of the Ministry of Internal Affairs of the Republic of Croatia – Head of the Committee M. Šuperina, MSc;
- annual Conferences of Polygraph Examiners of the Ministry of Internal Affairs of the Republic of Croatia in Pula, Valbandon.

## The Legal Regulation of the Use of Polygraph in Criminal Investigations

The use of polygraph and the experiments conducted raise certain questions with respect to the theory and practice of procedural criminal law. These relate specifically to the possibility of utilising the results of polygraphic testings during the course of criminal proceedings. The use of polygraph and the procedure of polygraphic testing, when viewed from the standpoint of basic principles of procedural criminal law, encounter several objections. The arguments listed against the use of polygraph mostly refer to the limitation of the freedom of choice where voluntary consent to polygraphic testing of the person involved is concerned (in most cases a suspect, sometimes even a defendant).

The essence of this objection is not the voluntary consent to polygraphic testing, *i.e.*, the act of expression of free will, in hope of some informal or formal procedure confirming or confuting a certain fact, but the presumption of guilt in case of declining this mode of interrogation (even if the person is merely a suspect).

Therefore adherents of the objection claim the discussion of voluntary consent is futile because testings are carried out on police premises, thereby creating fear and a psychological conflict within the testee regarding 'voluntary consent'.

This objection is countered with the argument of the principles of legality and presumption of innocence. Observance of these and other basic principles (both of criminal law and criminology), are part of all measures and activities (be they operative-tactical or investigatory) performed by police officials according to Articles 177 and 184 of the *Criminal Proceedings Act*.

Other objections concentrate mostly on the technique of polygraphic testings and the instrument that registers examinee's psycho-physiological reactions to questions asked. Closely related to these are other difficulties pertaining to non-legal scholarship and science which are still disputable.

Especially interesting problems or questions still unresolved include relationships between the examiner and the examinee, the former's possible influence on the latter and the results obtained by the questioning. These issues led some legal theoreticians to raise the question of the credibility of the results in determining facts important for criminal proceedings. There is no doubt that the qualification and the expertise of the examiner are amongst the most important factors that influence the testings, and the interpretation of the obtained results.

Such general opinions and viewpoints about the use of polygraph are present in almost all countries, so this paper focuses on legal regulations of the use of polygraph and its practical criminological application, as seen through the perspective of questions posed most often, *i.e.*, problems associated with polygraphic testings and the potential application of gained results in criminal proceedings (either in their formal or informal part). The question whether or not to use the polygraph is not discussed; *emphasis is laid on how to use it and how to regulate its use legally*.

Closely related is the problem of police authority during the course of criminological investigations and the use of polygraph with respect to the protection of basic human rights and liberties and the regard for fundamental principles of fact and evidence determination (the principles of formality, legality, material truth establishment and immediate judicial evidence deliberation).

Successful crime fighting entails full detection and explication, which in turn demand such conditions that would realise the basic postulate of Croatian criminal legislation in practice: "that no innocent person be convicted, while the offender be sanctioned according to criminal laws on the basis of legally administered proceedings".[1]

One of the most difficult tasks that police officials face is information, evidence and lead gathering – and their analytic synthesis in order to verify whether the suspect is telling the truth or not.

The path to material truth is very difficult and delicate and demands a lot of assiduousness and self-abnegation. Throughout history, man has utilised various methods to expose falsehood and reach material truth. These methods were conditioned by the development of society and science at any given time. Hand in hand with the development of science, especially criminology, the techniques of identification and detection of offence perpetrators have been improved.

Polygraph and polygraphic technique are far from offering the full solution to the problem of detection of offence perpetrators. Nevertheless, practice has proven that a skilled and experienced polygraph examiner can contribute to the solution of very complex criminal cases, and that many offences would have remained unsolved without the application of polygraph.

*Polygraphic criminological technique* is one of the relatively new means that the police use in crime fighting during the stages leading to criminal proceedings. The scope of application in that field is vast indeed: from detection of offence perpetrators, collection of material evidence and information important for criminal proceedings, to the elimination of wrongly

---

[1] Article 1 of the *Criminal Proceedings Act*.

accused persons during the course of criminological investigation. Polygraphic test is a painless and relatively fast procedure, which in practice excludes lengthy, unpleasant and tiring informative interrogations performed in order to gather information about offences and their perpetrators. Criminologists that utilise this technique properly, given the right conditions and the respect for the personality of the testee and his or her rights, will save a lot of time, energy and resources. Of course, the Constitutional and legal principles concerning the citizens' rights and liberties are to be disregarded at no time.

Polygraphic testing of suspects, as seen from the standpoint of criminology, is part of the important operative-tactical and technical activities carried out with the intent to detect unknown perpetrators and explicate offences, gather evidence (material and personal) for successful commencement and conduct of criminal proceedings, and eliminate innocent persons. Therefore, the general, global, aim of this activity, that can be undertaken by police officials during the stages leading to criminal proceedings, is to execute their basic duties as outlined in the Article 1 of the *Internal Affairs Act (IAA)* and Article 177, Sections 1 and 2 of the *Criminal Proceedings Act (CPA)*.

According to the *CPA* the results of polygraphic testings *cannot serve as evidence in criminal proceedings*, which means that judicial decisions cannot be based on them in the legal sense. However, results of polygraphic testings can gain the importance of indications, the so-called *orientational-eliminational indications*, which can serve as the criminological basis for undertaking other operative-tactical, technical and investigational measures and activities that will secure evidence, of personal or material nature (ambush, surveillance, investigation, premises and location searches, expert analysis, temporary impoundment of objects).

Legally, the use of polygraph in criminal proceedings is regulated by stipulations stated in Article 177, Section 2 of the *CPA*, with other operative-tactical measures and activities that are undertaken by police officials with the intention of the realisation of their basic duties (Article 177, Section 1 of the *CPA*). Therefore, in the situations that furnish reasonable doubt that an offence that is mandatorily investigated has been committed, police officials *are required to undertake the necessary measures and activities* with the aim of detecting the perpetrator of the offence, preventing hiding or escape of the perpetrator or accomplices, detecting or securing the vestiges of the offence and objects that can serve as evidence, as well as gathering all information that might be useful for the successful conduct of criminal proceedings.

Measures and activities that police officials can undertake to accomplish these aims are partially regulated by Article 177, Section 2 of the *CPA*, where only some are listed, as for example: obtaining needed information from citizens, inspection of vehicles, persons and baggage, restriction of movement in a certain area for the necessary period, undertaking measures to identify persons and objects, ordering search for persons and things. At the end of this list, the legislators, bearing in mind numerous measures and activities that are available to police officials, provide a general clause: "(...) and undertake other necessary measures and activities". The essence of this provision is not to hinder police officials with procedural limitations in detection of offences and their perpetrators, i.e. to enable them to apply up-to-date criminological methods, the use of polygraph during the course of criminological investigation in the stages leading to criminal proceedings being implied.

The *Temporary Regulations of the Ministry of Internal Affairs of the Republic of Croatia (MIA Regulations)* elaborate on the use of polygraph, *i.e.* polygraphic testings conducted by police officials in Articles 193, 194 and 195. Section 1 of Article 193 of the *MIA Regulations* determines the main reasons that render polygraphic testing of a person admissible, in cases when elimination (narrowing down) of suspects, determination of the perpetrator of the offence, and tracing of leads, objects or other evidence concerning the perpetrator and offence, are needed. This section is useful for determining the importance of polygraphic testings in the course of the criminological process.

Judging by the main reasons of polygraph use in criminological investigations, despite some restrictions stated in the *CPA* and the *MIA Regulations*, polygraph testings perform two important roles during the course of criminological process:

1. the direct role, direction of the work of police officials in offence explication; and
2. the indirect role, by no means less important, gaining insights about facts relevant for conduct of subsequent criminal proceedings.

*The direct role of polygraph* has been confirmed by numerous cases, which proved that the use of polygraph in this stage of procedure significantly helped criminologists. Based on specific reactions, they reinforced their convictions with the certainty of "heading in the right direction," and the certainty that the same train of inquest needed to be pursued, respecting the criminological *prescript of plurality of assumed versions* and their *logical elimination and supplementation*. In the case of reverse assumption, eliminating the examinees, on one hand, they simplified the conduct of the operative plan of criminological process in progress, thus avoiding a waste of precious time. Therefore, the direct use of polygraph, in the course of the criminological process conducted by operative officials, shows that gained results by means of polygraph employment can be used as a serious foundation for offence explication, perpetrator detection and suspect elimination, as well as trails, objects and other evidence concerning the offence and perpetrator detection or as a new orientation for further inquests.

*The indirect role* of polygraph use and thus gained results, which is not negligible, is performed "with the object of gathering all information that could be of use for successful conduct of criminal proceedings".[2] This method of finding out essential information is especially relevant in those investigations where, without this information, it would be impossible to find leads or indications that could be put to use by criminology, principally by criminological technology. Moreover, the method also appears in those investigations which reveal no witnesses, so the only avenue of approach that remains is the interrogation of suspects.

Article 230 of the *CPA* stipulates that the body conducting an investigation is to, despite defendant's (or suspect's) confession, gather other evidence as well. In case of clear and complete confession and if substantiated by other evidence, it is to be undertaken at the State Attorney's suggestion only. Contemporary theory considers the need for ascertaining a defendant's confession to be a principle of material truth establishment. The principles demand the highest degree of elimination of the possibility of an innocent person's conviction, that would exist if the procedural authorities, in the interest of procedural economy, would be exonerated from the duty of case investigation in the event of defendant's confession of the offence that he or she is charged with. With that in mind, Croatian *CPA*, in heretofore mentioned ordinances, orders the criminal proceedings authorities to investigate facts further even in the case of a defendant's confession, namely if a confession is not clear or complete during investigation, and unconditionally during court hearings.

Section 2 of Article 193 of the *MIA Regulations* stipulates that a police official and polygraph examiner are to forewarn persons to be tested *that they are not obliged to consent to polygraphic testing*.

Based on the constitutional principle and stipulation of Article 29, Sections 2 and 3, of the *Constitution* of the Republic of Croatia, Article 4 of the *CPA* prohibits the coercion of confession or any other statement from the defendant (and analogously from the suspect), or any other person involved in the proceedings. Article 225 of the *CPA* stipulates respect of suspect's personality during interrogation. The same article prohibits the use of force, threats or similar means in obtaining statements or confessions. It is also prohibited to obtain such statements using suggestive or capricious questions or deception. With the aim of comprehensive protection and respect for the suspect's personality, Croatian *CPA* guarantees the suspect the right to silence, because according to Article 225, Section 2, the suspect (defendant) is to be informed of his right to silence; "(...) he will be informed that he is neither required to state his defence, nor to answer questions asked".

In addition to this warning that polygraphic testing is to be performed *with his or her voluntary consent only*, during the introductory conversation a polygraph examiner, or a police official, is to explain the procedure which the

---

[2] Article 177, Section 1 of the *CPA*.

polygraphic testing will follow, and the principle of the operation of the polygraphic instrument as well to the prospective testee, prior to requested consent. In this way, the person that polygraphic testing is suggested to is capable of conscious and free decision of whether or not he or she wishes to consent to polygraphic testing.

Even so, the *CPA* also provides other provisions referring to determination of facts relevant for criminal proceedings not connected to procedural activities of defendant interrogation stated in Article 208, and other stipulations of the *CPA, i.e.* determination of certain facts by obtaining them from the defendant, but not through interrogation, but physical examination. The legal stipulation stated in Article 265 of the *CPA* clarifies that the legislators differentiate between undertaking of that procedural activity *with and without defendant's consent* ("(...) it will also be undertaken without his or her consent if necessary in order to determine facts relevant to criminal proceedings"). In addition, Section 2 of the same article authorises blood tests and other medical activities, conducted according to the principles of medicine, for analysis and determination of other important facts for criminal proceedings *without the examined person's consent*, if such activities do not jeopardise his or her health.

With regard to prohibition of certain procedures for fact determination relevant for criminal proceedings, the *CPA* explicitly prohibits the use of medical interventions on the defendant (suspect) or witness, or administration of such means that would influence their volition during statement rendering. The use of medical interventions or means that would influence defendant's or witness's volition is prohibited, with no exceptions, and violates basic principles of Croatian criminal proceedings. Medical interventions comprise procedures such as lobotomy or hypnosis, while means that influence defendant's or witness's volition refer mostly to narcoanalysis (the administration of scopolamine, morphine, pontatole, eripane, muscarine and other alcaloids). With regard to this prohibition, it is plain that polygraph as a specific psychometrics method does not belong either under the term 'medical intervention' or under the term 'means that influence volition for statement rendering', which is completely understandable, for at no price, even not determining the truth, is suspect's human dignity and integrity to be put at risk.

Polygraphic testing is conducted on the basis of suspect's complete voluntariness. The use of force in any form is excluded, for a certain amount of co-operation is necessary, which an expert examiner always accomplishes. It is not possible to imagine coerced polygraphic testings because the testee himself would practically make them impossible by refusing to co-operate and not abiding by the rules of conduct during the examination. Besides, recorded polygrams would not be valid, *i.e.* it would not be possible to interpret them correctly. Recorded coerced polygrams would display aberrations, particularly of fear and uncontrolled movements.

In addition, Article 194, Section 1 of the *Temporary Statute of the MIA* requires that the Register of conducted polygraphic testings includes the warning that the person was informed of not being obliged to consent to the testing, and his or her written consent. Polygraphic testings administered without the testee's consent would violate Article 9 of the *CPA*.

Therefore, the assertion that polygraphic examination restricts individuals' volition is denied because they express their will by their consent and signature, *i.e.* they assent to polygraphic testing, previously being acquainted with the procedure of testing and the principles of polygraph operation. This is especially prominent in cases when the suspect himself demands polygraphic testing, thereby expressly waiving his right to silence, moreover, and expressing desire for polygraphic testing. It is hence assumed that, in regulated cases like these, the suspect is fully aware of his actions and the purpose of polygraphic testing during the course of criminological process, when any information may prove to be of exceptional value.

## The *Polygraphic Testings Statute* of the MIA of the Republic of Croatia

The Criminology Police Sector of the MIA of the RC originated the idea of a polygraphic testings statute as the result of endeavours to legally regulate certain important issues concerning the application of polygraphic testings. In 1998, a committee was set up with the purpose of producing an outline of such a statute. Members were M. Šuperina (Higher Police School), A. Vrdoljak (Centre for Criminal Forensics Ivan Vučetić) and R. Vrečko (a polygraph examiner of the City of Zagreb Police Department). All theoretical and practical experiences that could have been gathered within the nine months of extensive literature research and actual problems exploration were used in production of the regulations. The final version of the Statute was completed in September 1999, and submitted to the Minister of the MIA of the RC for authorisation.

The contents of the *Polygraphic Testings Statute* regulate:
- conditions and procedure of polygraphic testings;
- categories of individuals that can be subjected to polygraphic testing;
- obligations of polygraph examiners and police officials during the procedure of polygraphic testings;
- rights and obligations of and the conditions for polygraph examiners;
- necessary equipment and minimal standards that must be met;
- forms and modes of polygraphic testings record keeping and Register filling;

The contents of the regulations comprised in the Statute delineate the rights and obligations of:
- individuals that polygraphic testing is suggested to;
- arrested individuals that polygraphic testing is suggested to;
- the police official in charge of the particular criminal investigation;

- the polygraph examiner that conducts the polygraphic testing;
- all polygraph examiners of the MIA of the RC.

The basic elements of the analysed regulations are hereby presented. Assumptions presumed in the creation of the text were the principles of criminal proceedings, criminology and internationally accepted standards, amongst which the following are emphasised:

- the principle of legality;
- the principle of legal conduct of police officials;
- the principle of protection of human personality and dignity;
- the principle of protection of individual liberties;
- the principle of assumption of defendant's (suspect's) innocence;
- the principle of legal evidence;
- the principle of confidentiality of suspect's personal information in criminal investigation;
- the principle of economical procedure of criminal proceedings;
- the principle of legal aid.

The application of primary principles that refer to *individuals that polygraphic testing has been proposed to* come to the fore in particular with subsequent issues:

- polygraphic testing, as part of criminal investigations conducted by police officials, is allowed only for the purpose of:
  1. exclusion of innocent persons from suspects;
  2. detection of offences, perpetrators and their accomplices;
  3. finding leads and objects related to offences and perpetrators;
  4. determination of facts and circumstances of offence commitment;
  5. ascertaining suspicious statements of suspects or witnesses;
- the following individuals must not be tested:
  1. individuals under the influence of alcohol, narcotics or other psychoactive substances;
  2. individuals with serious heart failures;
  3. individuals in the state of shock;
  4. individuals taking tranquillisers;
  5. individuals that exhibit visible signs of mental illness or disturbances;
  6. individuals in the sate of intensive physical pain;
  7. pregnant women;
- individuals can be subjected to polygraphic testing when conditions that prohibit such testing are no longer present;
- no person under the age of 16 is to be polygraphically tested;
- the individual that is to be polygraphically tested *must be forewarned: that he or she is under no obligation to consent to such testing*; of restrictions of polygraphic testing; and that a voluntary consent is needed for polygraphic testing and that the consent is affirmed by signing the written consent form in the polygraphic testing Register;

- the consent must be accompanied by a statement of alcoholic beverages, narcotics or other psychoactive substances consummation;
- the individual that has consented to polygraphic testing must be acquainted with the testing method, the principles of polygraphic instrument operation, and questions that will be posed during polygraphic testing;
- the individual that has consented to polygraphic testing or that is being polygraphically tested has the right to withdraw his consent at any time.
- polygraphic testing may be recorded by technical audio-visual devices for the purposes of education of future polygraph trainees of the Polygraph Seminar. The recording made must not contain data refering to the identity of the individual tested. Polygraphic testing is not to be recorded if reasons stated in Article 293 of the *CPA* are violated. Recording of polygraphic testing is permitted only with the consent of the individual polygraphically tested. The consent of the individual polygraphically tested is to be acquired before the testing. The consent is entered into the polygraphic testing Register and must be signed by the consenting individual.

The application of primary principles that refer to *arrested individuals that polygraphic testing has been proposed to* come to the fore in particular with subsequent issues:

- during polygraphic testing of an arrested individual the police official and the polygraph examiner are required to observe the prescripts that generally apply for any individual that polygraphic testing has been proposed to;
- the criminal investigator must inform the polygraph examiner that the arrested individual has been treated in accordance with Article 6 of the *CPA* (the individual must be informed of the basis for arrest, that he need not make any statements, that he has the right to a counsellor of his own choice, that on his request the individual he determines will be notified of the arrest), and that stipulations of Article 177, Sections 4 and 5 of the *CPA* have been met (if the arrested individual wishes so, his attorney may monitor the polygraphic testing);
- the polygraph examiner is obliged to enable the arrested individual's counsellor to monitor the polygraphic testing. The counsellor confirms monitoring in the polygraphic testing Register.

The application of primary principles that refer to *the police official in charge of particular criminal investigation* come to the fore in particular with subsequent issues:

- the police official that proposes polygraphic testing to an individual, must proceed in accordance with the procedures for interrogation (he must not use force, threats, deceit, or suggestive questions);
- the criminal investigator must state the exact reasons for proposing polygraphic testing to the polygraph examiner. Likewise, the criminal investigator is required to enumerate all the questions he wishes to process by means of polygraphic testing;

- the polygraph examiner has to be acquainted with the criminal investigation up to the point of polygraphic testing, especially with the treatment of the individual to be polygraphically tested (among other things, time of arrival on police premises, duration and content of the interview with the investigator, interval elapsed during transfer to polygraph lab, food and beverages consumed by the testee on police premises or before coming there, personal relationships with the individuals encompassed by criminal investigation, individual's earlier statements, statements of other persons gathered during the criminal investigation);
- the police official is not present during polygraphic examination in polygraph lab.

The application of primary principles that refer to *the polygraph examiner who administers the polygraphic testing* come to the fore in particular with subsequent issues:

- the polygraph examiner is required to abide by all heretofore mentioned regulations;
- polygraphic testings can only be conducted in polygraph labs with equipment that meets minimal prescribed standards;
- polygraphic testings can only be administered by polygraph examiners who meet minimal prescribed criteria and who successfully completed the Polygraph Seminar;
- polygraph examiners are required to further educate themselves continuously and attend the Conference of Polygraph Examiners at least once every year;
- during the course of polygraphic testing, the polygraph examiner is required to complete the prescribed Register and collect prescribed statements signed by the testee;
- the polygraph examiner cannot conduct polygraphic testings if:
  1. he has suffered damage by the offence related to the polygraphic testing;
  2. the polygraphic testee, his counsellor, injured party, its legal representative or delegate, are his spouse, relative in the vertical line to any degree, relative in the horizontal line to the fourth degree, or in-laws to the second degree;
  3. he is related to the suspect, his counsellor, prosecutor or injured party as a guardian, ward, adoptive parent, adoptive child, fosterer or foster-child;
  4. he is employed in the same police institution as the suspect or any other polygraph testee;
  5. it is the opinion of the polygraph examiner that there are other circumstances not mentioned in the Statute which can raise doubts as to his impartiality.

- the polygraph examiner is required to inform the immediate authority in the police institution where he is employed of the reasons for his exemption;
- the polygraph examiner must avoid contact with persons related to the offence or event that requires polygraphic testing, except the individual he is to test, on account of gathering information necessary for polygraphic testing.

It is our strong belief that this regulation of polygraphic testing prescripts will raise the standards of polygraphic testings. The Croatian general public will be acquainted with these prescripts when published.

## Police Polygraph Labs in the Republic of Croatia (Examiners and Equipment)

### City of Zagreb Police Department
- Polygraph lab established in 1960.
- Polygraph examiners since the establishment of the lab: Ivan Babić, Dragutin Papeš, Josip Lohna, Stjepan Rajki, Stojan Kolevski, Vjekoslav Špehar, Milan Turkalj and Petar Smolčić.
- Polygraph examiners currently working at the lab: Romeo Vrečko, Rudolf Perković and Goran Les.
- Equipment: Polygraph 'Lafayette', model 'Diplomat', ink printout, 2 pieces, and Polygraph 'Lafayette', LX2000-305.

### County of Primorsko-goranska Police Department
- Polygraph lab established in 1970.
- Polygraph examiners since the establishment of the lab: Branko Vamas, Radoslav Banić, and Momčilo Danilović.
- Polygraph examiners currently working at the lab: Sonja Klarić and Tomislav Versic.
- Equipment: Polygraph 'Lafayette', model 'Diplomat', ink printout and model 'Ambassador', thermal printout.

### County of Splitsko-dalmatinska Police Department
- Polygraph lab established in 1977.
- Polygraph examiners since the establishment of the lab: Željko Gulisija, Jovo Njegovan and Morislav Skorput.
- Polygraph examiners currently working at the lab: Mile Adžić.
- Equipment: Polygraph 'Lafayette', model 'Ambassador', thermal printout.

### County of Osječko-baranjska Police Department
- Polygraph lab established in 1986.
- Polygraph examiners since the establishment of the lab: Zvonko Jurman and Danko Vojnović.
- Polygraph examiner currently working at the lab: Stjepan Međugorac.

- Equipment: Polygraph 'Lafayette', model 'Diplomat', thermal printout.

### County of Istra Police Department
- Polygraph lab established in 1994.
- Polygraph examiner: Danko Vojnović and Alen Peruško.
- Equipment: Polygraph 'Lafayette', model 'Ambassador', thermal printout.

### Varaždin Police Department
- Polygraph lab established in 1995.
- Polygraph examiner: Krešo Bosak.
- Equipment: Polygraph 'Lafayette', model 'Diplomat', ink printout.

### County of Dubrovačko-neretvanska Police Department
- Polygraph lab established in 1995.
- Polygraph examiner: Vladimir Cica.
- Equipment: Polygraph 'Lafayette', LX2000-305.

### County of Slavonski Brod Police Department
- Polygraph lab established in December 1999.
- Polygraph examiner: Ratković Mladen.
- Equipment: Polygraph 'Lafayette', LX2000-305.

# L'évolution de la notion de blanchiment d'argent en France: de l'infraction spécifique à l'infraction autonome

*A. Teissier*

Les premières opérations de blanchissage de l'argent sale se firent, aux USA, à l'époque de la prohibition américaine, par l'achat de chaînes de blanchisseries pour dégager des bénéfices taxables et officiels.[1] Il semble que la première utilisation, dans un cadre judiciaire ou juridique, de l'expression 'blanchiment de l'argent', date de 1982 aux USA.[2] L'utilisation de ce terme a été contestée par les banquiers genevois qui lui préfèrent celui de "recyclage".[3] Cependant, l'Article 305*bis* du *Code Pénal* suisse traite du blanchissage, tout comme la Recommandation R(80)10 et le projet de convention de Vienne.[4] Les trois termes (blanchiment, blanchissement et blanchissage) recouvrent la même réalité (celle de recycler l'argent sale), mais actuellement, celui de blanchiment est préféré.[5] Cette expression n'a été consacrée législativement en France que par la loi du 13 mai 1996.[6]

On ne peut nier l'utilité du blanchiment pour l'économie d'un pays, les trafiquants réinvestissant une partie, au moins, de leurs bénéfices dans leur pays.[7] Néanmoins, globalement, le blanchiment est largement négatif.[8] C'est pourquoi le champ d'application de l'infraction de blanchiment ne cesse de s'élargir, on le voit dans le cadre des dispositions nationales comme internationales.

A l'origine par blanchiment de capitaux on envisageait le blanchiment des fonds provenant exclusivement du trafic de stupéfiants.[9] Mais, devant "la

---

[1] E. Chambost, *Guide de la banque de la banque suisse et de ses secrets*, ed. Balland 1987, p. 34; G. Picca, 'Le "blanchiment" des produits du crime: vers de nouvelles stratégies internationales ?', *RIPCT* 1992, p. 483 ; E/CN.15/1992/4/Add.5, p. 5 ; C.R., 'Blanchissage ou blanchiment ?', *Journal de Genève*, 2 mars 1995.

[2] E./CN 15/1992/4/Add 5, n° 13, p. 5 ; C.R., 'Blanchissage ou blanchiment ?', *op. cit.*

[3] J. Ziegler, *La Suisse lave plus blanc*, ed. Seuil 1990, p. 92 ; Laservoisier emploi également le terme de recyclage ainsi que C. Charmes dans *Le recyclage de l'or noir*, Promovere, n° 31, septembre 1982, pp. 95 à 102.

[4] Article 1er j).

[5] E. Schaeffer, 'Le blanchiment et l'argent', *RJPIC* 1993, p. 245.

[6] M. Hunault, *Rapport*, Assemblée Nationale, n° 2518, 1996, p. 6.

[7] A. Proenza, 'Blanche Colombie', *Le Monde*, 7 mars 1996 ; B. Morel & F. Rychen, *Le marché des drogues*, Monde en cours, ed. De l'Aube 1994, p. 110.

[8] E. Inciyan, 'Un système financier gangrené par les narcodollars', *Le Monde*, 23 novembre 1995, p. 11 ; S. Didier, *Rapport*, Assemblée Nationale, n° 1167, 1994, p. 7 ; B. Morel & F. Rychen, *op. cit.*, p. 9; G. Kellens, 'Les rapports entre criminalité organisée et ordre culturel', Criminalité organisé et ordre dans la société, Colloque organisé par l'ISPEC, Aix en Provence, 5 au 7 juin 1996.

[9] La *Convention de Vienne* contre le trafic illicite de stupéfiants et de substances psychotropes en son Article 3-1. Le règlement type concernant les délits de blanchiment des avoirs provenant du trafic illicite des drogues et les délits connexes adopté par l'Assemblée générale de l'OEA (à suivre)

difficulté d'apporter la preuve que ce blanchiment porte de façon spécifique sur des fonds issus du trafic de stupéfiants", le GAFI, dès 1989, a recommandé d'incriminer le blanchiment de capitaux se rapportant à toutes les infractions graves, et/ou à toutes les infractions qui génèrent un montant important de produits.[10] La *Convention du Conseil de l'Europe*, de septembre 1990, étend également l'infraction de blanchiment aux produits de toute infraction pénale.[11] De plus, la directive européenne du 10 juin 1991 donne une définition identique[12] du blanchiment, eu égard au fait que "le phénomène du blanchiment de capitaux concerne non seulement le produit d'infractions liées au trafic de stupéfiants, mais aussi le produit d'autres activités criminelles (telles que le crime organisé et le terrorisme)." Sa rédaction laisse aux Etats le choix d'élargir ou non le blanchiment de l'argent au profit d'activités terroristes,[13] mais la Commission européenne envisage d'étendre uniformément la directive à d'autres activités criminelles.[14] Enfin, en 1992, le Secrétaire Général de l'ONU[15] prônait la même solution et indiquait qu'en adoptant la Convention de 1988, la collectivité internationale avait exprimé la réprobation universelle provoquée par le blanchiment de l'argent lié à la drogue mais qu'il n'y avait pas "de justification de principe pour proscrire le blanchiment de l'argent découlant de telle ou telle activité criminelle génératrice de profit et non d'autres activités criminelles".

Un tel élargissement des cas d'infractions de blanchiment est souhaité par certains afin de lutter contre l'économie souterraine[16] et la délinquance financière.[17] Un récent colloque a démontré "un consensus quant à l'intérêt d'élargir la liste des infractions à retenir dans le cadre de la répression du blanchiment de l'argent sale,"[18] ce qui permettrait de poursuivre aussi bien le

---

(Organisation des Etats Américains) en mai 1992 définit le blanchiment de l'argent. (Jimenez, *Inter Américan Measures to Combat Money Laundering: the OAS Model Regulations Concerning Laundering Offenses Connected to Illicit Drug Trafficking and Related Offenses. International Enforcement Law Reporter*, p. 168, cité par W.C. Gilmore, 'Les réactions internationales au blanchiment de capitaux: exposé sommaire', Conférence sur le blanchiment de capitaux, Strasbourg, 28 au 30 septembre 1992, ML 92 (10), Conseil de l'Europe, pp. 10-11.

[10] GAFI, Recommandation n° 5 (Rapport) et Rapport, 1991/92, n° 71.

[11] Convention Conseil de l'Europe, septembre 1990, Articles 1e et 6 ; W.C. Gilmore, *op. cit.*, p. 7.

[12] Ainsi, est défini comme blanchiment de capitaux le blanchiment d'argent provenant d'une activité criminelle c'est-à-dire d'une infraction définie par la *Convention de Vienne* (Article 3 §1(a)) ainsi que toute autre activité criminelle définie comme telle pour les besoins de la présente directive par chaque Etat membre (Directive 10 juin 1991 Article 1).

[13] J. Pardon, 'Le blanchiment de l'argent et la lutte contre la criminalité axée sur le profit', *RDPC* 1992, pp. 755-756.

[14] Europolitique, n° 1639.

[15] E/CN 15/1992/4/Add 5, n° 83, p. 28.

[16] P. Masson & G. Larcher, *Rapport*, Sénat, n° 72, 1992/93, TI, p. 53; F. d'Aubert & B. Gallet, *Rapport*, Assemblée Nationale, n° 3251, 1993, p. 112.

[17] T. Jean Pierre & P. de Meritens, *op. cit.*, pp. 40-41.

[18] E. Schaeffer, 'Le blanchiment de l'argent', *RJPIC* 1993, p. 245.

blanchiment de l'argent sale ou 'noir' mais aussi le blanchiment de l'argent 'gris', produit de l'évasion fiscale et des détournements frauduleux.[19]

Désormais, presque tous les membres ont adopté des lois incriminant le blanchiment de l'argent de la drogue[20] et le nombre de pays où le blanchiment du produit d'activités criminelles est incriminé a très nettement progressé.[21]

En France, s'est dessinée une évolution: dans un premier temps, le blanchiment ne s'est appliqué qu'au produit des infractions très spécifiques. Alors qu'aujourd'hui, dans un but répressif, l'infraction de blanchiment a été érigée en infraction autonome.

### Le blanchiment, infraction à portée limitée

Dans une première période, le blanchiment n'a visé que le trafic de stupéfiants, il n'a pas été étendu aux profits réalisés par le crime organisé, seule l'obligation de déclaration des soupçons, introduite par une loi de 1990, devant notamment être effectuée par les banques (en violation du secret bancaire), y faisait référence alors, parallèlement, que le blanchiment des produits du proxénétisme était réprimé.

### Les deux infractions particulières

Le blanchiment des produits du trafic de stupéfiants et du proxénétisme sont depuis longtemps incriminés.

Après avoir longtemps cherché à infléchir, de diverses manières, sur l'offre et la demande de produits stupéfiants,[22] la majorité des pays industrialisés tente désormais de contrôler ou d'entraver les flux financiers générés par le trafic de stupéfiants, c'est-à-dire de contrôler le 'blanchiment' de capitaux.[23] Certes, la

---

[19] J. Ziegler, *op. cit.*

[20] Rapport GAFI, 1993/1994, *op. cit.*, p. 22.

[21] Rapport GAFI, 1993/1994, *op. cit.*, p. 27 ; M. Hunault, *op. cit.*, p.5.

[22] J. Pardon, *op. cit.*, p. 740.

[23] G. Falcone & M. Padovani, *Cosa Nostra, le juge et les hommes d'honneur*, ed. N°1, Austral 1991, p. 146; E. Inciyan, 'Les Douze se préparent à changer de stratégie dans leur lutte contre la drogue', *Le Monde*, 14 décembre 1993; P. Beregovoy, 'La lutte contre le blanchiment des capitaux', *RJC*, 1990, pp. 377 à 384 ; Conseil économique et social, ONU, Commission pour la prévention du crime et la justice pénale, 23 mars 1992, Renforcement de la coopération internationale en matière de prévention de la criminalité et de justice pénale, y compris la coopération technique dans les pays en développement, l'accent étant mis en particulier sur la lutte contre les activités criminelles organisées, Note du Secrétaire général, Additif: Blanchiment de l'argent et questions connexes: nécessité d'une coopération internationale E/CN 15/1992/4/ Add. 5 (n° 5, p. 3 et n° 8, p. 4); O. Brout, *Drogues et relations internationales*, ed. Complexes 1991, p. 34 ; J.L. Debre in Rapport F. Colcombet, Assemblée Nationale, n° 1401, 1989/90, p. 9 ; E. Inciyan, 'Le blanchiment de l'argent de la drogue gangrène l'économie mondiale', *Le Monde*, 29 juin 1994; Rapport P. Cooney au Parlement européen, 23/4/1992, n° A3 O358/91, p. 12; Association belge des banques, Aspects et documents, n° 117, pp. 5-6 ; M. Matthey, 'Les mesures suisses contre le blanchiment de fonds', p. 216 ; E/CN 15/1992/4/Add 5, p. 8, n° 18. (à suivre)

lutte contre le blanchiment ne permettra pas de résoudre totalement le problème de la drogue mais cela fait partie d'un ensemble qui contribuera à son éviction.[24]

Une étude récente fait état de 500 milliards de dollars blanchis par an soit 2% du PIB mondial.[25] Cette masse d'argent[26] est réinvestie par les trafiquants de drogue dans un but de respectabilité,[27] de sécurité[28] et de profit :[29] les intérêts rapportés par les sommes blanchies ont été évalués par le Parlement Européen à 820 milliards de dollars pour dix ans,[30] c'est-à-dire $ 232,115 par minute.

L'incrimination du blanchiment de l'argent de la drogue remonte en France à une loi du 31 décembre 1987 qui a introduit un alinéa 3 dans l'Article L627 au *Code de la Santé Publique (CSP)*. Incrimination reprise dans le nouveau *Code Pénal* à l'Article 222-38 sous réserve d'une légère modification de son champ d'application: le blanchiment pouvant porter sur le produit des infractions réprimées par l'Article 222-37 alinéa 2 (facilitation de l'usage de stupéfiants, utilisation ou acceptation d'ordonnances fictives) ce que ne prévoyait pas l'Article L627 *CSP*.

Si l'Académie française définit le blanchiment comme le fait de "réintroduire dans le circuit financier des fonds provenant d'actions ou de trafics délictueux afin d'en dissimuler leur véritable origine,"[31] l'infraction de blanchiment[32] est longtemps restée circonscrite au placement, à la dissimulation ou à la conversion de ressources ou de biens issus du seul trafic de stupéfiants.[33] Ainsi, pour que puisse être appliquée l'infraction spéciale de blanchiment prévue à l'Article 222-38 du *Code Pénal*, l'infraction principale doit consister en une des infractions prévues aux Articles 222-34 à 222-37 du *Code Pénal* c'est-à-dire, soit dans un crime de direction ou d'organisation d'un groupement destiné au trafic de production ou de fabrication illicites, soit dans un délit d'importation illicite, d'exportation illicite, de transport, détention,

---

D'autres doutent que la suppression des officines de blanchissage fasse cesser le trafic de drogue mais soulignent que la poursuite du blanchiment est plus efficace: I. Walter, *L'argent secret*, ed. J.C. Lattes 1985, pp. 234-235.

[24] J.F. Thony, 'Blanchiment de l'argent de la drogue: les instruments internationaux de la lutte', *RJPIC* 1993, pp. 153 et 154.

[25] Étude d'experts du FMI (V. Tanzi & P. Quick), AFP, 'Le blanchiment financier atteindrait 2% du PIB mondial', *Le Monde*, 31 juillet 1996, p. 16.

[26] J.C. Grimal, *L'économie mondiale de la drogue*, Le Monde Poche 1993, p.116; Rapport GAFI (1er), pp. 15-16, "La nature des fonds résultant du trafic de drogue doit être transformée, afin de réduire les énormes volumes de liquidités qu'il engendre (…)."

[27] T. Jean Pierre & P. de Meritens, *op. cit.*, 17.

[28] Recommandation R(80) 10, p. 8, n° 33: "et pour mettre à l'abri ces fonds".

[29] E/CN 15/1992/4/ Add. 5, n° 20, p. 8.

[30] F. d'Aubert & B. Gallet, *Rapport*, Assemblée Nationale, n° 3251, 1993, p. 53.

[31] M. Hunault, *Rapport*, Assemblée Nationale, n° 2518, 1996, p. 5.

[32] Article L627 al 3 *Code de la Santé Publique* introduit par la loi du 31 décembre 1987, Article 415c. douanes (loi 23 décembre 1988), Article 222-38 du *Code Pénal*.

[33] F. d'Aubert & B. Gallet, *Rapport*, Assemblée Nationale, n° 3251, p. 103.

offre, cession, de facilitation d'usage illicite, d'ordonnances fictives ou de complaisance.

Il est pourtant difficile, voire impossible, lorsqu'on effectue une enquête, de déterminer l'origine de l'argent sale, celui-ci pouvant par exemple provenir d'une fraude fiscale, motif bien souvent invoquée par les blanchisseurs pour tenter de minimiser leur responsabilité.[34]

Le *Code Pénal*, entré en vigueur en 1994, a repris, dans son Article 225-6 2è, l'incrimination du blanchiment des produits du proxénétisme qui avait été créée en 1960 et qui figurait à l'Article 335-5 de l'ancien *Code Pénal*. Est ainsi incriminé le fait de faciliter, de quelque manière que ce soit, à un proxénète, la justification de ressources fictives. On précisera que le proxénétisme est "notamment le fait, par quiconque, de quelque manière que ce soit, de tirer profit de la prostitution d'autrui, d'en partager les produits ou de recevoir des subsides d'une personne se livrant habituellement à la prostitution" (Article 225-5) et qu'est assimilé au proxénétisme, le fait, par quiconque, de quelque manière que ce soit, de ne pouvoir justifier de ressources correspondant à son train de vie, tout en vivant avec une personne qui se livre habituellement à la prostitution ou tout en étant en relations habituelles avec une ou plusieurs personnes se livrant à la prostitution (Article 225-6, 3è).

Cette incrimination du seul blanchiment des profits issus du trafic de stupéfiants et du proxénétisme dissimulait le refus d'une incrimination générale.

### Le refus d'une incrimination générale

La conception adoptée par la France a été critiquée lors de la réunion du GAFI III qui s'est tenue à Lugano en 1992. C'est dans ce cadre qu'est intervenue la loi du 29 janvier 1993 qui a étendu aux cas d'organisations criminelles, l'obligation, pour les banques, de déclarer leurs soupçons.[35] Par contre, l'infraction de blanchiment n'a pas été étendue à ce cas, ce qui n'était pas très cohérent, d'autant que l'activité des organisations criminelles a pris, au cours des dernières années, une ampleur internationale.[36] Néanmoins la France ne se sentait que très peu concernée par le crime organisé, n'étant qu'un lieu de transit ou de refuge pour des mafiosi ou yakusa.[37] Alors que selon de nombreuses sources, la France serait utilisée à toutes les étapes du blanchiment

---

[34] F. d'Aubert & B. Gallet, *op. cit.*, n° 32.

[35] Notes bleues, 16 au 30 juin 1993, n° 17, pp. 1 et 2.

[36] J. Borricand, *Rapport introductif Criminalité et ordre dans la société*, E/CONF 88/2, p. 5, n° 17.

[37] M. Cusson, 'La notion de crime organisé', *Criminalité organisée et ordre dans la société, op. cit.*

(placement, empilage et intégration) en raison de la richesse de ce pays et de la stabilité de sa monnaie.

Les termes 'organisations criminelles' n'ont pas fait l'objet d'une définition législative.[38] Les établissements de crédit disposent donc d'une grande liberté d'appréciation en la matière.[39] Du fait de cet élargissement du champ de l'obligation de dénonciation, les établissements de crédit ne se heurtent plus à la difficulté qu'ils rencontraient, jusque là, pour opérer la distinction entre le blanchiment de l'argent de la drogue et le blanchiment provenant d'autres activités illicites. Par ailleurs, on a pu grâce à la nouvelle formule utilisée par le législateur, s'aligner sur les définitions adoptées par les autres pays avec lesquels une coopération peut être établie.[40]

Devant le silence de la loi, la doctrine a suggéré de se référer à quelques critères permettant de déterminer ce qu'il faut entendre par 'organisations criminelles'.[41] Le Ministère des finances et du budget a également tenté d'en faire autant lors des travaux parlementaires qui ont conduit à la loi du 13 mai 1996. Dans le cadre d'un colloque portant sur la Criminalité organisée et l'Ordre dans la société[42] plusieurs définitions ont été proposées.[43] Enfin, au niveau de l'ONU, un consensus s'est formé à propos de la notion de 'criminalité organisée': on estime que "les participants à des organisations criminelles sont des personnes qui s'associent en vue d'entreprendre une activité criminelle sur une base plus au moins durable. Généralement, ils s'adonnent à la criminalité d'entreprise, à savoir la fourniture de biens et de services illicites, ou de biens licites acquis par des moyens illicites comme le vol ou l'escroquerie."[44]

L'une des sources les plus importantes des bénéfices réalisés par les organisations criminelles transnationales provient du trafic de stupéfiants, les bénéfices[45] font l'objet d'un recyclage dans le système financier mondial.[46] C'est pourquoi criminalité organisée et trafic de stupéfiants ont des liens étroits. On observe, cependant, dans la plupart des Etats membres une tendance allant dans le sens d'une couverture du blanchiment du produit de

---

[38] Contrairement à ce qui a été fait en Grèce et en Italie : J. Borricand, *op. cit.*, 35, p. 5.

[39] M. Kistler, *La vigilance requise en matière d'opérations financières, Etude de l'article 305 ter du code pénal suisse,* Thèse, Lausanne, ed. Schultess, Zurich 1994, p. 1.

[40] M. Sapin, JO, Sénat, séance 19 décembre 1992, p. 4424 et Ministre de l'Economie et des finances, JO, Assemblée Nationale, 2ème séance du 17 décembre 1992, p. 7462 et 1ère séance du 15 décembre 1992, p. 7202 ; C. Guettier, *La loi anti-corruption, loi n° 93-122 du 29 janvier 1993,* ed. Dalloz 1993, p. 174.

[41] M. Arnould, *op. cit.*, 1, n° 9.

[42] Colloque ISPEC, Aix en Provence, 5 au 7 juin 1996.

[43] M. Cusson, 'La notion de crime organisé'; Mme Zhang; M. Quille citait une définition d'Interpol de 1988; L. Palmieri.

[44] "Problèmes et dangers causé par la criminalité transnationale organisée dans les diverses régions du monde", *ONU*, Conférence de Naples, E/CONF 88/2, p. 5, n° 9.

[45] E/CONF 88/2, p. 27, n° 91.

[46] E/CONF 88/2, p. 27, n° 89.

tout délit grave ou toute activité criminelle, tant dans la législation relative au blanchiment de capitaux que dans le droit pénal. Cette couverture est de nature à contribuer à l'élimination des disparités existant dans les régimes de prévention et de répression des Etats membres et à faciliter la coopération interétatique dans ce domaine.[47]

### Le blanchiment, infraction à portée générale

Les produits d'un certain nombre d'infractions très lucratives, ont besoin d'être blanchis. Force est de constater, qu'aujourd'hui, il y a un développement considérable du blanchiment de produits de délits autres que ceux liés aux stupéfiants.[48]

Cela justifie la création d'une infraction générique sans pour autant entraîner la disparition des infractions spéciales.

En 1994, un projet de loi a été déposé au Conseil d'Etat. Il visait à élargir le délit de blanchiment à tous les capitaux illicites, quelqu'ils soient,[49] afin de mettre un terme aux difficultés rencontrées jusque là à propos de l'origine des fonds.[50] Cette extension de l'incrimination était destinée, selon M. Falletti, directeur des Affaires criminelles, "à favoriser l'entraide internationale pour la confiscation des produits en provenance de ces trafics".[51]

En raison de sa généralité, le Ministre de la Justice, M. Toubon, fut amené à apporter quelques précisions: "Le délit de blanchiment demeure un délit intentionnel (…). Il sera donc nécessaire, pour l'établir en matière fiscale, de prouver que le prévenu savait que l'argent blanchi provenait d'une fraude fiscale. Or le délit de fraude fiscale n'est pas, comme un vol ou un meurtre, un délit d'évidence: c'est un délit occulte et complexe pour lequel la justice exige un système de preuve si lourd qu'aucun amalgame ne saurait s'établir entre le fraudeur et la personne qui lui aurait involontairement prêté son concours."[52]

Le projet de 1994 a donné naissance à la loi n° 96-392 du 13 mai 1996.[53] Cette loi, comme cela avait été le cas pour le projet de loi, a soulevé des critiques notamment de la part des banques.[54]

---

[47] Rapport COM 95 (54), p. 6.

[48] Rapport GAFI, 1993/1994, p. 42.

[49] "Le gouvernement prévoit de poursuivre plus largement le blanchiment de capitaux", *La vie judiciaire*, n° 2524, 22 au 28 août 1994; 'Le blanchiment et la lutte contre le trafic des stupéfiants', *Le courrier de la Chancellerie*, 1994, n° 29.

[50] J.C. Marin (interview), 'La sécurité juridique est aujourd'hui un élément déterminant de la qualité d'une place financière', *Rapport moral sur l'argent dans le monde* 1994, p. 78 ; circulaire du 10 juin 1996, n° 96-11/G.

[51] *La vie judiciaire*, n° 2514, 13 au 19 juin 1994.

[52] Dans J.B. de Montvalon, 'M. Toubon dissipe les inquiétudes des banques sur le délit de blanchiment', *Le Monde*, 19 octobre 1995.

[53] *JO*, 14 mai 1996.

[54] C. Dupuy & X. de Roux, dans M. Hunault, *op. cit.*, 6, p. 9 ; J. Pannier, 'Du contrôle des changes au contrôle des capitaux', *RDB*, n° 28, p. 206.

Cette loi a introduit les Articles 324-1 à 324-9 dans le Livre III, Titre II du *Code Pénal*, relatif aux atteintes aux biens autres que les appropriations frauduleuses, dans un Chapitre IV intitulé 'Du blanchiment'.

Depuis la promulgation de ce texte, le délit de blanchiment ne s'applique plus seulement à des infractions particulières comme le trafic de stupéfiants ou le proxénétisme, mais constitue une infraction générique ou générale[55] puisqu'est qualifié de blanchiment celui des produits de tout crime ou délit, sans qu'aucune distinction ne soit effectuée, qu'ils soient punis par le Code pénal, d'autres codes ou des lois extérieures.

Il n'en reste pas moins, qu'en pratique, le blanchiment concernera surtout "des infractions susceptibles d'apporter un profit financier, comme le trafic de véhicules volés, le trafic d'armes, le trafic d'oeuvres d'art, le trafic de fausse monnaie, les extorsions, le proxénétisme, les actes de terrorisme ou la corruption et, plus généralement toutes les formes de délinquance ou de criminalité organisées,"[56] mais, avant tout et surtout, le trafic de drogues.

Il n'est fait référence au crime organisé que comme circonstance aggravante de l'infraction de blanchiment, lorsque celui-ci est commis en bande organisée. Dans ce cas les peines sont doublées.[57]

Les dispositions spécifiques relatives à l'argent de la drogue ou du proxénétisme n'ont pas été supprimées par la loi du 13 mai 1996. Bien au contraire, ce texte a renforcé les dispositions spéciales qui existaient auparavant puisqu'il a modifié l'Article 415 du *Code des Douanes*[58] et a créé une nouvelle infraction particulière: le blanchiment des profits issus d'un délit prévu par le *Code des Douanes*, "afin que l'Administration des douanes puisse intervenir en matière de blanchiment de fonds provenant de tout délit douanier, dès lors que les faits revêtent un caractère international".[59] Cela s'étend donc non seulement au trafic de stupéfiants mais aussi d'armes, d'explosifs, de matériel de guerre, de contrefaçon, ou de fraude au budget communautaire.[60]

Par conséquent, en France, le blanchiment d'argent peut constituer des infractions spéciales suivant les activités qui ont permis la constitution de profits devant être blanchis ou une infraction autonome.

---

[55] P. Mehaignerie, *Document*, Sénat, 1993/94, p. 3.

[56] F. le Gunehec, 'Premier aperçu des dispositions pénales de la loi n° 96-392 du 13 mai relative à la lutte contre le blanchiment et le trafic de stupéfiants', *JCP* 1996, n° 27, *Actualités*, n° 5; T. Afschrift & A. Rombouts, 'La loi sur le blanchiment est elle applicable aux infractions fiscales?', *JT* 1992, n° 5643, n° 3.

[57] Ce délit aggravé est puni de 10 ans d'emprisonnement.

[58] Opérations financières entre la France et l'étranger.

[59] M. Culioli, *JCl, Pénal*, Articles 324-1 à 324-9, fasc. 10, 1997, n° 7.

[60] M. Culioli, *JCl, Pénal*, Articles 324-1 à 324-9, fasc. 20, 1997, n° 25.

# Epistemic and Non-epistemic Language in the Law of Evidence

*F. Toepel*

## Introduction

It has become usual in recent German writings on evidence to correct traditional conceptions by emphasising that the truth is not looked for or found, but only constructed.[1] And not just German professors cherish such an opinion, but also, for example, judges of the *Bundesgerichtshof*,[2] the highest criminal court in Germany, and of the German Constitutional Court.[3] Though the paper presented by Professor Allen at this conference has shown that American judges seem to be different and mainly orient themselves by applying common sense, voices worried by scepticism are not lacking in American literature. Damaška in his book *Evidence Law Adrift* mentions that philosophers proposing classical views of truth and reality are intellectually on the defensive in the twilight of the 20th century,[4] and he objects against scepticist tendencies only on account of pragmatic considerations for the field of evidence, while leaving it open whether such a standpoint could be correct in principle: "unless some view that truth is a matter of correspondence is accepted, our present evidentiary arrangements are deprived of meaning. Where 'the covenant between word and world' is broken, it makes no sense to worry about accuracy in fact finding or about judgements that fail to reflect the truth."[5] Therefore I would consider it quite useful to find a compelling argument that shows once and for ever the irrelevance of scepticist theories not only for our present evidentiary arrangements, but for any contriveable system of evidence.

A common feature of all theories denying that truth could be given a sensible interpretation apart from a mere construction by a mind, is the demand for a new language. According to these theories truth and reality ought to be reformulated in epistemic – that is to say mind-dependent – terms. Consequently, in the following section I shall deal with the question whether

---

[1] Cf. Calliess, *Theorie der Strafe im demokratischen und sozialen Rechtsstaat*, Frankfurt/Main 1984, p. 46; Grasnick, *140 Jahre Goltdammer's Archiv FS Pötz*, Berlin etc. 1992, p. 55(69); Lesch, *Strafprozeßrecht*, Neuwied 1999, pp. 3, 99; Egon Müller, *Strafverteidiger* 1996, 358(359); Paulus, *FS Spendel*, Heidelberg 1993, p. 687(697); Ransiek, *Die Rechte des Beschuldigten in der Polizeivernehmung*, Bielefeld 1990, S. 94; Volk, *FS Salger*, Köln 1995, pp. 411 ff.

[2] Cf. the statement of the (former) Judge Herdegen, JZ 1998, 54.

[3] Cf. Judge Hassemer, *Einführung in die Grundlagen des Strafrechts*, München 1990, pp. 131 ff. A follower of Luhmann, Di Fabio, has just been voted into a senate of the German Constitutional Court.

[4] Damaška, *Evidence Law Adrift*, New Haven etc. 1997, p. 94.

[5] *Ibid.*, p. 95.

such a reformulation of truth in mind-dependent terms is at all possible. The answer shall be in the affirmative. Then, in the last section of the paper, I want to ask whether the result in the preceding section can be generalised, *i.e.* whether the examples of a possible reformulation of truth and reality in mind-dependent terms within some contexts are a token for the fact that language can be totally reduced to mind-dependent terms. The answer to this question shall be in the negative.

## The Possibility to reinterpret Language in Epistemic Terms

For the sake of clarity, to see how it is possible to reinterpret language in mind-dependent – epistemic – terms, I first want to make clear what is meant precisely by the distinction between epistemic and non-epistemic language. Epistemic language is language relating to a person's internal states that are directly accessible to her without having to draw inferences and by which she may strive to acquire knowledge. The most obvious candidates for epistemic language are situations where persons talk about their own epistemic states: "I have seen that there is a dark spot on y's white shirt." "I have believed that x caused y's injury." Such sentences can be split up into two parts. The *kind* of a person's epistemic state is specified, whether something is believed, felt, heard or seen, for example; and the *content* of the epistemic state is spoken about, *'that which'* is believed, felt, heard or seen. Philosophers use the term proposition for such that-clauses. The proposition "that x caused y's injury" or "that there is a dark stain on y's white shirt" can be true or false. The man in the street applies the terms true or false to express whether the propositional content of a person's epistemic states corresponds to a mind-independent reality or not. This also is the account of the correspondence theory of truth[6]. According to such a view talk about epistemic states includes necessarily the use of non-epistemic language. The truth or falsity of propositions relates not to the person's internal states, but is dependent on an assumed *world*.

This model does well fit the 'optimistic tendency of Anglo-American Evidence Scholarship'.[7] Wigmore, for example, defines evidence as a relative term, a relation that invokes appeal to two kinds of fact as part of the reality: appeal to the *factum probans* or evidentiary fact has the function to support the belief in another fact, the *factum probandum*.[8] Ideally, in a successful proof the statements about *factum probans* and *factum probandum* both correspond to chunks of reality independent of the mind of the reasoner. The *factum probans* and the *factum probandum* therefore are non-epistemic – *i.e.*, mind-independent – elements of proof. The statements stating the facts must be true,

---

[6] Austin, *Philosophical Papers*, 3rd ed., Oxford 1979, pp. 117 ff.; Searle, *The Construction of Social Reality*, Harmondsworth 1995, pp. 213 ff.

[7] Twining, *Rethinking Evidence*, Oxford 1990, p. 75.

[8] Wigmore, *The Science of Judicial Proof as Given by Logic, Psychology and General Experience, and Illustrated in Judicial Trials*, Boston 1937, §§ 3 f.; reprinted also in Anderson & Twining, *Analysis of Evidence*, London 1991, pp. 54 ff.

and truth is found by discovering that the propositional content of the statements matches the reality.[9]

Scepticist philosophers typically attack this picture by criticising the possibility of inductive reasoning as an instrument to bridge the gap between the epistemic states and the world. An inductive inference starts with premises stating the observation of a finite number of instances and ends with drawing general conclusions from these observations. The particular premises do not entail the general conclusion. So the truth of the premises does not logically guarantee the truth of the conclusion. So nothing guarantees the truth of the conclusion. Since all our general beliefs about the world are held on account of inductive reasoning and even observation presupposes general beliefs, no belief about the world is guaranteed by anything. Therefore scepticists recommend to drop reference to a mind-independent world.

In this paper I shall confine myself to the description, how the two modern thinkers that are highly respected by German legal scholars try to bring about such a reduction of traditional non-epistemic to epistemic terms, because my point of departure was scepticism in modern German writings on evidence. The two modern thinkers are Habermas and Luhmann, both being originally sociologists. Habermas and Luhmann enjoy such an amount of popularity in Germany, because their theories are seen as new stages in the development of older philosophical concepts. Roughly, it could be said that Habermas tries to continue a Kantian tradition, while Luhmann preferred to be associated with Hegel.

## Habermas and Kant

Only the *early* Habermas can be seen as a (pragmatist) variant of scepticism. Therefore only his former theory is of interest here.[10] Habermas himself now describes his earlier consensus criterion of truth as resulting from "an overgeneralization of the special case of the validity concerning moral judgements and norms".[11]

The idea that the criteria for truth and validity are at least parallel notions can already be noticed in Kant's philosophy. Kant's scepticist tendency is wellknown. Kant thinks knowledge of objects – of things in themselves – is only possible, if the totality of all conditions for those objects would be known to a person.[12] Since it is impossible to be sure at a certain time to have recognised all characteristics of an object that will ever be detected in the future, objects in themselves can never be known. That does not mean nothing

---

[9] Cf. Searle, *op. cit.*, p. 217.

[10] At present, Habermas acknowledges that reasonable human beings always appeal to a mind-independent reality and that truth is a non-epistemic notion Habermas, *Wahrheit und Rechtfertigung*, Frankfurt/Main 1999, pp. 46, 249, 259.

[11] *Ibid.*, pp. 15 f.

[12] Kant, *Kritik der reinen Vernunft*, Vorrede zur 2. Aufl. (Akademie-Ausgabe), reprinted, Berlin 1968, vol. 3, pp. 17 ff.

can be known about the real world. Kant accepts the possibility of knowledge concerning the objects as 'appearances'.[13] Kantian appearances are features ultimately caused by the things in themselves that 'affect' the observer's senses. Yet the part of the appearances originating in the observer's own characteristics cannot be separated from the part caused by the things in themselves. One can only be certain that the whole mixture has been brought about by the observer's activity of constructing the world. The appearances are something belonging to the observer, not to a mind-independent world.

Before such a background the need to avoid errors seems to be the more pressing. Kant thinks that the same method which he proposed in his political writings,[14] namely the use of reason in public, could be effective in finding out the truth, too.[15] Reason must be "authorised to speak in public, because otherwise truth would not be brought to daylight."[16]

Thus it becomes plausible that for the Kantian Habermas discourses are the cement of the universe as well and agreements reached in an ideal discourse situation take over the role formerly occupied by reality.[17] The early Habermas does not recognise a reality independent of the (reasoner's or – in an ideal discourse – the participants') justified statements.[18] But the term discourse is a bit confusing, because Habermas adds only in a footnote that a discourse presupposes not necessarily the participation of more than one person: Hypothetical reasoning can be viewed as an 'inner discourse'.[19] Also, the qualification that a consensus must be reached in an *ideal* discourse is a misleading expression: this ideal situation merely consists of what is presupposed by a reasonable person in every communication[20] (or in every piece of reasoning in case of an 'inner discourse').

An obvious objection against this theory would be that the question whether there is an agreement reached in an ideal discourse concerning some statement can be considered not less difficult to answer than the question whether the statement corresponds to a mind-independent reality. But Habermas could easily defend himself by pointing out that the discourse need not be a 'real' discourse, it can take place within the mind of the reasoner. So, the reasoner is able to judge for himself whether he has observed the

---

[13] *Erscheinungen*, Kant, *ibid.*, 1. *Transzendentale Elementarlehre*, 1. Teil, Einleitung, §8 Allgemeine Anmerkungen, p. 71. Kant distinguishes appearances which are ultimately caused by the things in themselves from mere illusions – 'bloßer Schein'.

[14] Kant, *Was ist Aufklärung?* (Akademie-Ausgabe), reprinted, Berlin 1968, vol. 8, pp. 33 (34, 36 f.); cf. also Habermas, in: *Materialien zu Kants Rechtsphilosophie* (Batscha ed.), pp. 175 ff.

[15] Kant, *Der Streit der Fakultäten, Introduction* (Akademie-Ausgabe), reprinted, Berlin 1968, vol. 7, p. 20.

[16] *Ibid.*

[17] Cf. Habermas, *Vorstudien und Ergänzungen zur Theorie des kommunikativen Handelns*, Frankfurt/Main 1984, pp. 159 ff.

[18] Habermas, in: Habermas/Luhmann, *Theorie der Gesellschaft oder Sozialtechnologie – Was leistet die Systemforschung?*, Frankfurt/Main 1971, p. 124.

[19] Habermas, *Vorstudien*, p. 134.

[20] *Ibid.*, p. 181.

conditions of an ideal discourse. He is not dependent on 'the intrusion of experience from outside into his argumentation'.[21]

"It is true that x caused y's injury" for such a reasoner would mean that "[g]iven the conditions for an ideal discourse, the participants of such a discourse would come to the conclusion that x caused y's injury". The proposition "that x caused y's injury" here is no longer a statement about a mind-independent world, but merely about words used by participants after coming to a conclusion in an ideal discourse situation. The words are dependent only on the consensus of the participants, on their minds. Truth and reality become epistemic notions.

## Luhmann and Hegel

The starting-point for Luhmann could have been Hegel's picture of science: Hegel speaks about science as a "subjective process of cognition. Its purpose is freedom, and cognition is the way to create this freedom for itself."[22] Hegel meant by these 'clear' statements that science is not only learning by doing, but also creating itself by doing.

Perhaps, inspired by this picture Luhmann contrived his system theory, the version of German scepticism most thoroughly worked out. Luhmann's interest focuses on so-called autopoietic systems. Autopoietic systems are self-producing systems. These systems create themselves by differentiating between themselves and their environment[23] just like Hegel's process of learning to know creates its own history. The differentiation is twofold:[24] The autopoietic systems produce the difference between the system and the environment by their operations.[25] But they also reproduce this difference within the system.[26] Autopoietic systems are psychological or social. Statements made by a human being about the world can be seen as constructions by a psychological system, insofar as a human being is a psychological system. These statements are constructions of the autopoietic system's environment. A 'real' environment can never be known, because the systems do not have any cognitive contact with it at all. Therefore reference to the environment by an autopoietic system is always only reference to a construction. Reference to a 'real' environment does not make any sense

---

[21] *Ibid.*, p. 181.

[22] Hegel, *Enzyclopädie der philosophischen Wissenschaften*, Berlin 1830, §576: "(...) die Wissenschaft erscheint als subjektives Erkennen, dessen Zweck die Freiheit und es selbst der Weg ist, sich dieselbe hervorzubringen"; cf. also Habermas, in: Habermas/Luhmann, *Theorie*, pp. 230 f.

[23] Luhmann, *Die Gesellschaft der Gesellschaft*, Frankfurt/Main 1997, pp. 60 ff.

[24] *Ibid.*, p. 45: "The difference system/environment is twofold, a difference produced *by* the system and a difference observed *within* the system." (All translations, also in the following footnotes, by me, F.T.)

[25] Observe the oval lines in the figure on p. 654.

[26] Observe the vertical lines in the figure on p. 654.

insofar.[27] Talking about the environment as such a construction corresponds to using exclusively epistemic language.

If a human being, *i.e.*, at least partly a psychological system, utters the statement "I have believed that x caused y's injury," then this would mean according to Luhmann "I have constructed within me the belief that x caused y's injury". At least, this is how the system should observe itself, after having been enlightened by Luhmann.

So far, there is no place for truth in the classical sense of the correspondence theory in such a concept, for if reference to the environment can only be reference to a construction by the speaker there is no reality left with which to compare it. But that does not seem to be important, because it only matters whether the system can integrate the belief "that x caused y's injury," for example, in itself and survive.[28]

## The Parallel Structure of Traditional and Scepticist Theories

It thus has been shown that non-epistemic language about reality can indeed be replaced by epistemic terms. The question still remaining to be answered is whether a total reduction of language to such mind-dependent terms is possible.

I think the negative answer is easy to find, if we return to Hegel's and Luhmann's constructions for a moment. Hegel had already accepted a distinction of thought and being,[29] though he emphasised that both are intimately connected.[30] For Luhmann a corresponding difference can be noticed in the way how systems 'observe'[31] the environment of a system. He calls a first-order observer the system that observes its own environment. The psychological systems of people engaging in normal social communication are first-order observers, for example. Higher-order observers are systems that observe the first-order observers. For the first-order observer the world is something ontically given.[32] He cannot at the same time reflect himself as a

---

[27] Luhmann, *op. cit.*, p. 92: "All observation of the environment must be carried out within the system as an internal activity with the help of the system's own distinctions." *Ibid.*, p. 98: "The difference between system and environment appears within the system in the form of differences concerning the direction of references – and only thus. (...) The system reproduces itself in the imaginary space of its references." Reproduction here must be understood in the sense of Luhmann's definition, *ibid.*, p. 97: "Reproduction is in the old sense of the word: production out of products, determination of the system's state as a starting-point for every further determination of the system's state."

[28] Cf. Luhmann, *Soziologische Aufklärung* Bd. 6, Opladen 1995, p. 12: "The basic question is: Does it [*i.e.* the system] continue or cease to be?"

[29] Hegel, *Enzyklopädie*, § 70.

[30] *Ibid.*, § 51, additional remark.

[31] Note that for Luhmann 'observing' is itself higher order language and can only mean 'distinguishing from the system' within the system, because there is no possibility of contact with a 'real' environment.

[32] Luhmann, *op. cit.*, pp. 1120 f.; cf. also the figure on p. 654.

system that creates this environment. Otherwise he could not refer to the environment in the way he does. Only the second-order observer, for example the sociologist, is able to observe the first-order observer, but again, he may not reflect that his observations are only constructions of his own system. No observer can observe himself during his operation of observing. Luhmann calls this the blind spot.[33] As the activity of the lawyers is always – at least partly – a first-order observation in the sense of Luhmann, they are compelled to view the world as something 'ontically given'. Therefore, to be able to create a useful theory even the hardened scepticist Luhmann has to take account of the fact that an observer – from the observer's own perspective – is referring to an environment independent of the observer. The difference between system and environment made by a first-order observer is exactly parallel with the use of epistemic and non-epistemic language in proof.

This enables us to evaluate the conclusion of the preceding section with greater precision: The reduction to epistemic language is consistent only from the perspective of a higher-order observer. A system can view the environment of other systems as mind-dependent constructions. It can also observe its own former self in this way.

This is the reason why I formulated my examples in the previous section in the perfect tense. Nobody can say simultaneously "I believe that x caused y's injury, and I believe that this is an illusion." A system may not take part in normal communication and observe itself from a higher level simultaneously without paralysing the same communication. If I believe that my belief that x caused y's injury is an illusion I do not believe that x caused y's injury any more. I am not any more observing myself from a higher-order level, because there remains no first-order level to observe.[34]

This resurrection of the distinction between epistemic and non-epistemic language can be detected also in the theories of Kant and Habermas. Kant merely substitutes the difference between epistemic state and reality by the difference between intellect and appearances within the mind. Hegel pointed out, too, that Kant did not influence the sciences. When there were quotations of Kant in scientific works they could always be seen as a superfluous ornament.[35]

The early Habermas also conceded that truth claims are only viewed as problematic constructions within discourses. In connection with actions these claims are just assumed by the actor 'in a naive way'.[36] So, reference to a discourse or to the process of reasoning is superfluous in this context. The explanation for such an exception can be found in Luhmann's account: it is impossible to act on the condition that a statement is true and to think of its

---

[33] *Ibid.*
[34] Luhmann, *op. cit.*, p. 93.
[35] Hegel, *Enzyklopädie*, § 60, at the end of the paragraph.
[36] Habermas, *Vorstudien*, p. 135.

content as a mere construction at the same time.[37] In the moment where a person crosses the borderline from theoretical to practical reasoning she necessarily presupposes that it matters what she is deciding to do. This involves a correspondence notion of truth.[38]

Insofar as the law of evidence is concerned, the possible reduction of non-epistemic language to epistemic terms is thus irrelevant. Damaška's intuition mentioned at the beginning was right, but not only for pragmatic reasons. The use of non-epistemic language must rather be regarded as a necessary presupposition for *all* serious communication. So, even German legal scholars following the scepticist tradition can remain practising lawyers in the morning and armchair philosophers in the evening without having to get a headache. Only insofar, as they claim substantive changes would have to be made in the law of evidence because of their criticism are they simply wrong.

One legal scholar who accepts Luhmann's theory, for example, reached the conclusion that the presumption of innocence can only be viewed as a 'bad metaphor'.[39] I suspect he could have reached this result by looking at the process of proving from the second-order level in the following way: as a second-order observer he sees before him the psychological systems of the judge, the proponent and the opponent of evidence. But he is not only able to observe psychological systems. For Luhmann, there exist social systems, too. The system of law is such a system. Every system constructs its own environment. What is more plausible, therefore, than the assumption that in legal contexts the relevant environment should be that of the system of law? This system creates its environment concerning the crime by passing the final verdict of 'guilty of manslaughter'. From that moment on the social system accepts 'guilty of manslaughter' as its environment, not before. If the system of law's observation is the relevant construction of the environment, then the accused was not only presumed innocent before the verdict, but he *was* innocent until his guilt was constructed in the verdict.

Yet the traditional concept of the presumption of innocence can also be explained by Luhmann's theory, if the viewpoint is changed to first-order observation by the psychological systems of the participants in a legal process,

---

[37] Accepting Habermas's recent change of mind, cf. footnote 10 above, therefore was not necessary for the survival of traditional models of proof employed by the practising lawyer.

[38] Either a proposition matters, because it is true, or it does not matter, because we are not justified to say the proposition is true. There is no third possibility. We cannot rely on something as being 'preliminarily true' as some pragmatist theories of truth have suggested, for example the early Habermas, in: Habermas/Luhmann, *Theorie der Gesellschaft oder Sozialtechnologie – Was leistet die Systemforschung?*, Frankfurt/Main 1971, p. 225. At least, we cannot reflect it as being only 'preliminarily' true while acting. This remains valid even, if we conceive a legal trial as a 'Punch-and-Judy show' invented in the brain of the 'participant'. As soon as the reasoner begins to notice that he cannot change his perceptions of the trial by wishful thinking, he encounters something 'given'. It does not matter whether this something is located inside or outside the brain. His brain, in that respect, belongs to his environment, cf. also Searle, *op. cit.*, pp. 171 f., who makes a similar point concerning brains in a vat.

[39] Lesch, *Strafprozeßrecht*, p. 99.

the court, the proponent or the opponent of evidence. These persons view the world necessarily as something 'ontically given'. From such a perspective at the beginning of the trial it is contingent whether the accused has committed the crime or not. No jury would be epistemologically justified in such a situation to say the accused would definitely not have committed the crime. It rather has to be accepted on account of a *norm* that everyone charged with a criminal offence shall be presumed innocent until proved guilty according to the law.[40] If the rule is addressed to the participants in the legal process it has to be seen from a first-order perspective. If it is just a standard for evaluating the situation with no intention to influence the first-order observer, for example the practising lawyer, a higher-order observation may be possible, too. Yet no legal authority could adopt such a perspective. Even the court of appeal in case of a possible violation of the presumption of innocence usually does not ask whether the accused *was* innocent before the verdict, but only whether members of the court perceivably made up their mind that the accused was guilty without having proved it according to the standards of the law. Besides, what would this author who criticised the presumption of innocence as a bad metaphor say, if I would tell him that to me from a third-order level his observation on the second-order level does not seem to be plausible at all, but only his totally unwarranted construction of what is going on in the law of evidence?[41]

---

[40] Article 6 (2) of the *European Convention of Human Rights*.

[41] In the discussion at the conference Professor Alex Stein argued that Luhmann would have to face the same question concerning his system theory. Yet there is one way out: Luhmann could say that he is not interested in how the situation could be seen from another perspective. Either you accept his standpoint, or the communication has to stop, because it makes no sense any more. In fact, I have witnessed scholars convinced by Luhmann argue along these lines. But only prophets or unquestioned authorities can afford such a standpoint. Legal scholars, for example, have to provide for the possibility to criticize their assumptions on the same terms as they criticize others. Therefore they cannot rely on a scepticist premiss in their argumentation which could be applied to assess their own standpoint.

**Luhmann's Autopoietic System**

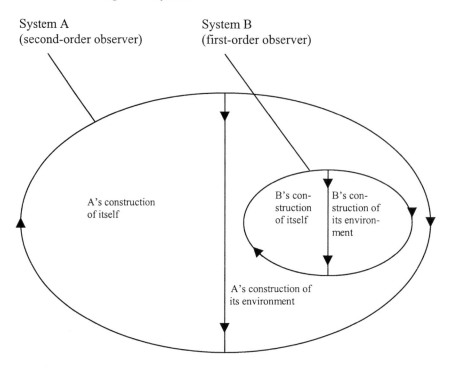

System A                                    System B
(second-order observer)          (first-order observer)

A's construction
of itself

B's con-        B's con-
struction       struction of
of itself       its environ-
                ment

A's construction of
its environment

→        = creative operations of the autopoietic system (oval lines are a
         production of the difference system/environment *by* the system;
         vertical lines are an observation of the difference system/environment
         *within* the system).

# The Putting into Perspective of the Exclusionary Rule: some General Remarks and the Belgian Experience

*P. Traest*

## Introduction

The exclusionary rule concerns one of the most interesting and important issues of the law of criminal procedure. Moreover, the discussions about the possible justifications of this exclusionary rule are dealing with the fundamental values of our criminal procedure system. The decision of the judge about illegally obtained evidence is a very delicate one because this trial judge has to take into account the obligation for the judicial authorities to respect the rule of law as well as the protection of that same rule of law by punishing the author of a criminal offence. It is clear that this is a very difficult task with a 'political' dimension.

In this text, some possible justifications of the exclusionary rule will shortly be remembered. In a second part, we will look at the Belgian jurisprudence and more specifically the putting into perspective of the exclusionary rule since 1990. The Belgian Court of Cassation has indeed put into perspective the exclusionary rule in some decisions and in cases where the investigating magistrate and the police authorities could not be blamed for any illegal act in gathering the evidence. In these cases, the evidence had been gathered partially by a private citizen who had committed an offence or at least an illegal act in doing so.

## Some Possible Justifications of the Exclusionary Rule

Most of the arguments cited in legal doctrine concerning the exclusion of illegally or improperly obtained evidence are deduced in one way or another from the respect for the rule of law in a democratic state and the idea of the necessity of a due process in the context of a bill of rights. The exclusionary rule is concerned with legality in the criminal process. This legality ranges from search, seizure and arrest through to trial proceedings and final appeal or review.[1] In this view, the state authorities and the investigating magistrates and police officers are obliged to respect the legal principles governing the gathering of evidence. If they fail to do so, a sanction is required. After all, if there should be no reaction on the ignoring of legal and constitutional principles by criminal investigators, this might affect in the long run the rules that the government in a constitutional state must respect.

However, the idea of respect for the constitutional state and the necessity for sanctions in case of violations of the applicable legal rules by the investigating magistrates and police alone do not explain why such sanctions should take place

---

[1] P. Schwikkard, A. St Q Skeen & S. van der Merwe, *Principles of evidence*, Juta 1997, pp. 144-145.

in the criminal trial itself by excluding evidence and why the sanctioning of the person in question that committed the illegal act is not sufficient.

Corstens, councillor in the Dutch Court of Cassation *(Hoge Raad)*, gives three reasons why the exclusion of evidence is defendable in such cases.[2] First, he mentions the argument of reparation. Every injustice demands as much as possible reparation, which can be obtained by dropping the illegally gained advantages. This explanation is linked to the principle of vindication (also known as remedial theory), which implies that the object of the exclusionary rule is to vindicate the accused for the infringement of his rights.[3] This theory could run up against the difficulty of maintaining a satisfactory balance between illegality and its remedy.

Secondly, he mentions the demonstration-argument. The public has to see clearly that the authorities have to respect the rules themselves. The most explicit demonstration of this principle is the exclusion of the illegally obtained evidence. It is obvious that a disciplinary sanction against the police officer does not have the same demonstrative effect as the exclusion of the illegally obtained evidence.

The third reason concerns the efficiency. Next time, police officers will hopefully prevent obtaining the evidence in an illegal way. However, it should be clear that this argument is secondary and therefore should not be overstressed. If the exclusionary rule provides an incentive for compliance, this must merely be considered an additional advantage. Zuckerman points out that there are from a practical point of view a number of reasons for doubting whether a general exclusionary rule would have significant deterrent effects. One of these reasons is that the violation of search rules would involve exclusion at some distant date and is therefore unlikely to constitute a serious brake on illegal searches.[4]

The exclusion of illegally obtained evidence on the basis of the ratio of the due process of law can not be seen as a sanction but is far more a legal consequence that can be invoked before a criminal court.

Some authors refer to the principle of judicial integrity or the principle of legitimacy.[5] However, this principle is not very clear as a justification of the exclusionary rule. Where this principle is being used by Zuckerman to justify a balanced application of the exclusion of evidence, the same principle appears to be used in the jurisprudence of the US Supreme Court as an reason for a radical exclusion of all irregularly obtained evidence.[6]

The social need to balance two conflicting constitutional requirements is in itself a powerful consideration. According to Zuckerman, it is important that the courts should be seen to exercise a balancing jurisdiction, because this will inform the public of the difficulty of choosing between admissibility and inadmissibility

---

[2] G.J.M. Corstens, *Het Nederlands strafprocesrecht*, Arnhem: Gouda Quint 1995, p. 636.
[3] A. Zuckerman, *The principles of criminal evidence*, Oxford: Clarendon Press 1989, p. 346.
[4] *Id.*, pp. 349-350.
[5] *Id.*, p. 350.
[6] *E.g.* P. Schwikkard, A. St Q Skeen & S. van der Merwe, *Principles of evidence*, Juta 1997, p. 146.

and might lead to the support even from those who might have preferred a different result in an individual case. The principle of judicial integrity seems to be too vague to serve as a basis for an exclusion of irregularly obtained evidence. Therefore, it is obvious that the integrity of the judicial authorities does not necessarily have to lead in all cases to an absolute exclusion of all illegally or improperly obtained evidence. After all, the integrity of the judicial authorities is not necessarily violated when the judge, in deciding which consequence should be given to illegally obtained evidence, takes other acceptable and with the constitutional state compatible interests (*e.g.* the protection of the rule of law against criminal offences) into account.

### The Belgian Jurisprudence

The exclusionary rule can be considered as a fundamental and traditional principle in Belgian law of criminal procedure. In a decision of 12 March 1923, the Court of Cassation ruled that illegally obtained evidence may not be used as an element of proof against a person in a criminal case. It can be said that the exclusionary rule was born in Belgium a long time before the existence of this principle in many other countries.

Since this decision, the exclusionary rule is being used constantly, and this especially in the case of information obtained via an irregular house search. In an important decision of 13 May 1986, the Court of Cassation extended the above-mentioned rule. In the meantime, the scope of the exclusionary rule itself was given in a very clear way.[7] Based on this decision, it can be stated that the exclusionary rule as seen in Belgian jurisprudence is related to evidence gathered on three different manners:
- by an unlawful act;
- by an act in violation of formal procedural rules;
- by an act that is incompatible with the general principles of law.

Within the first group, one can situate violations of professional secrecy, confidentiality of mail and illegal monitoring operations.

The third group of evidence that must be excluded concerns evidence obtained with violation of the right to remain silent, the loyalty of criminal proceedings, the privacy of citizens and the physical and psychical integrity of individuals. The Court of Cassation has always applied very strictly this jurisprudence. For instance, in the above mentioned decision of 13 May 1986 the Court ruled – in a case of tax fraud – that the confession of the person involved could not be used as an element of proof because this confession had been obtained by a violation of the right to silence of the person concerned. In fact, the inspectors had promised the person that he would not be brought to justice if he collaborated with the inspectors and told them the whole truth. This 'trick' was considered as a

---

[7] Cass., 13 May 1986, *Arresten van het Hof van Cassatie*, 1985-86, nr. 558.

violation of the right to silence of the accused and had to lead to the exclusion of his confession.

This situation has to be distinguished from that where evidence is not obtained in an illegal manner, but where the finding of a criminal offence is accompanied by an offence. In this case, the legality of evidence is not necessarily affected, *e.g.* when the violation of a speed limit was determined by a civilian who, driving at the same speed, committed necessarily the same offence.[8]

## The Exclusionary Rule in Belgium since 1990

Since 1990, there is a clear tendency in the jurisprudence of the Court of Cassation to limit in a number of situations the effect and the strict application of the exclusionary rule. This putting into perspective of the exclusionary rule was applied specifically in cases where the evidence had been obtained as a result of an unlawful act by another person than the investigating police officers or magistrates.

In two cases the Court of Cassation was confronted with an element of evidence that was originally obtained in an illegal way by a third party but came – independent of the gathering of the evidence by this third person – in the hands of the judicial authorities. In the first case, someone had stolen the 'black' (unofficial) accounting from the accused with the intention of blackmailing him. Later on, the thief changed his plan and gave the documents to a third party who handed them over to the police. The owner of the accounting, who had in the meantime pressed charges for theft, was however convicted on the base of these documents. The Court of Cassation rejected his appeal and decided that the stolen accounting could be used as evidence. The Court stated that "the single fact that a document was stolen from the owner, not necessarily implies that its use in court is irregular." Moreover the court, as well as the first judge, determined that "nor the persons charged with the investigation, nor the informant had committed an unlawful act in order to get in possession of the documents" and "that there is no connection between the theft of the accounting and the delivering of these documents to the prosecuting officers".[9]

In a second similar case, a woman stole a briefcase with charging documents concerning tax-fraud from her husband, with the intention to use these documents in a divorce proceeding. The briefcase was found during a house search, which led to the seizure of the documents. The Court of Cassation decided in a judgement of 17 April 1991 that these documents could be used against the owner because the investigating officers obtained the information while conducting a legal house search, and no connection could be made between the theft of the briefcase and the delivering of the documents to the judicial authorities. The

---

[8] Cass., 6 September 1977, *Pasicrisie*, 1978, I, 13.
[9] Cass., 17 January 1990, *Pas*, 1990, I, nr. 310, *Rechtskundig Weekblad*, 1990-91, pp. 463-464, comments by Huybrechts.

Court also stipulates that the theft of the briefcase not necessarily implies that the documents cannot be used in court.[10]

Two remarks can be made. First, these two decisions seem to be inspired by the idea that the exclusionary rule is meant to sanction investigating police officers or magistrates that have acted improperly in the course of their investigation. The argumentation of the Court of Cassation can only be correct when the exclusion of evidence is seen as a sanction for improper acting investigating officers. However, if the fairness of the trial is regarded as basic assumption, it makes no difference whether the unlawful act is committed by the investigating officers or a third party. After all, the use of proof gathered via illegal conduct can not lead to conviction. This also goes for unlawful acts from third parties, even when they did not intend to obtain evidence. A distinction according to the quality of the person who obtained the evidence irregularly, cannot be linked to the ratio of the exclusion of evidence itself.

Secondly, the connection between the criminal offence committed by a third party and the delivering of the evidence to investigating officers will be mostly very difficult to prove for the accused.

In a judgement of 4 January 1994, the Court of Cassation had to decide once more on the putting into perspective of the exclusionary rule. A night watchman in a hotel copied during his employment information from the unofficial accounting of the owner of the hotel and sent it anonymously to the judicial authorities. The owner of the hotel was prosecuted for fraud. However, the Court of Appeal decided to discharge the accused because the furnishing of proof was founded on irregular obtained evidence, i.e., the information from the anonymous report. The trial judge (Court of Appeal) believed that the night watchman could only have obtained the information irregularly by misusing the relationship with his employer. It should be remarked that the behaviour of the night watchman could be considered as an 'urgent reason' to fire him, but that he did not commit a criminal offence. This remark is rather important.

In its judgement of 4 January 1994, the Court of Cassation confirms the principle of exclusion of irregularly obtained evidence and states that the judge cannot convict a person for a criminal offence when the evidence presented was obtained irregularly or illegally by the official authorities charged with the investigation or prosecution of such act, or by the reporter of the offence.

However, the court decided that the information obtained by the night watchman could be used as evidence, since he had access to the information because of his employment and did not have to commit a criminal offence to do so.[11] After all, the circumstance that the employee had undoubtedly misused his right to access the information does not necessarily imply that he committed a criminal offence. Because in this case there was indeed a connection with the

---

[10] Cass., 17 April 1991, *Revue de droit pénal et de criminologie*, 1992, pp. 94-107, comments by De Valkeneer.

[11] Cass., 4 January 1994, *Arresten van het Hof van Cassatie*, 1994, nr. 1.

delivery of the information to the judicial authorities, it can be assumed that the evidence, when obtained by committing a criminal offence, should have been refused.

Although not directly in relationship with the exclusion of irregularly obtained evidence, a judgement of 30 May 1995[12] can be mentioned as well. In this judgement, a distinction was made between a report of a criminal offence and the evidence itself. The Belgian judicial authorities received information the French police regarding the involvement of a Belgian citizen in a case of drug trafficking. However, the French police obtained the information via an illegal telephone tapping operation executed in France. Based on this information, the Belgian judicial authorities started an investigation and the drug trafficker was convicted. The Court of Appeal discharged the accused because the Belgian investigation could not be seen independently from the French – illegal – investigation. The Court of Cassation did not share this point of view. The Court stated that a distinction should be made between the proof of a criminal offence and the report of such offence, which can not be ignored. The circumstance that the reporter knew about the offence because of an illegal act does not imply that no evidence could be used that was later gathered regularly. In case of denunciation, the public prosecutor has to verify whether it is possible to collect regular evidence.

At first sight, the distinction between the denunciation of an offence and the evidence is logical and attractive. However, it is difficult to handle because it implies that the furnishing of proof has nothing to do with the reporting of the criminal offence and the information delivered by the reporter. Just like a possible collusion between judicial authorities and private parties, this is very hard to proof for the accused. This reasoning can definitely not be supported when, as in the above mentioned case, public officers deliver illegally obtained information to their colleagues. If the report of the criminal offence would have been done by a private person, the distinction between denunciation and evidence that was obtained afterwards is more understandable. However, the danger of such reasoning is obvious: in the end, this could lead to the depreciation of the subtle and balanced rule itself of the legality of furnishing of proof.

In a judgement of 9 December 1997, the rule of the above mentioned judgement of 4 January 1994 was confirmed. The reporter of a fiscal fraud accidentally obtained charging documents that were, so he stated, dropped in his letterbox. However, the documents were not immediately handed over to the judicial authorities but were hidden for a while. Later they were given to a third person. Subsequently the public prosecutor obtained the documents. The Court of Appeal did not allow the use of the documents because the reporter had used the documents in an irregular way, *i.e.*, with a purpose for which he was not authorised. The Court of Cassation recalls the rule of the judgement of 4 January 1994, according to which the acquiring of proof via a criminal offence committed by investigating officers or the reporter of an offence leads to the exclusion of

---

[12] Cass., 30 May 1995, *Arresten van het Hof van Cassatie*, 1995, nr. 267.

evidence. However, the court considers the furnishing of proof to be regular when the reporter of a criminal offence obtained the evidence by coincidence without committing an offence or an irregularity, even if he hid the documents deceptively. The court also considers the furnishing of proof to be correct, although the documents were used without any permission to do so. The judgement of the Court of Appeal was therefore quashed.[13]

This judgement is clearly compatible with the previous jurisprudence that was developed since 1990. Indeed, the reporter of a criminal offence has not committed an offence himself. However, it must be remarked that the highest court pays little attention to the question what the original source of the evidence was. This judgement gives the impression that the accidental acquisition of the documents by the reporter of the criminal offence automatically implies that no longer has to be evaluated whether there was no previous offence when distributing the documents. It is *e.g.* definitely possible that the documents were given to the reporter of the offence by a person who was bound by professional secrecy. Obviously, if this would be the case, this jurisprudence implies that an accidental acquisition by the reporter of an offence can neutralise and erase previous irregularities. This is not acceptable.

In the recent judgement of 23 December 1998 (*Agusta-Dassault* case), the Court of Cassation confirms once more the above-mentioned rule regarding the regular acquisition of charging evidence. A Swiss judge was reproached to have broken the Swiss law by revealing the identity of the persons who protested the blocking of and the investigation of a banking account in Switzerland. The Court of Cassation restates the rule according to which no investigating officer or reporter of a criminal offence can obtain evidence by committing an offence. However, in this particular case, the Court believed that the announcement can not be regarded as an act of investigation, but as an act of the Swiss judge which could only have affected the temporary detention of the two accused persons. The evidence was therefore not excluded.

In addition, the latter judgement seems to use the previous jurisprudence developed since 1990 as a starting point.

**Evaluation**

The image given by the jurisprudence since then is very balanced. The exclusionary rule remains applicable to elements of proof obtained by individuals charged with the investigation of criminal offences and who can be blamed for an offence or irregularity. Concerning illegal behaviour of a third person, we find that this can only lead to the exclusion of evidence when this behaviour can be blamed on the reporter of the criminal offence. If the illegal act is performed by a private person, evidence should not be excluded unless there is a connection

---

[13] Cass., 9 December 1997, *Algemeen Juridisch Tijdschrift*, 1998-99, 297.

between this act and the delivery of the evidence to the officers charged with the investigation and prosecution.

The putting into perspective of the exclusionary rule can be evaluated in a positive and a negative way.

As an advantage of this tendency of putting into perspective the exclusionary rule, it can be mentioned that this jurisprudence is compatible with the opinion shared by the majority of the citizens concerning this issue. Without the intention to consider this element to be decisive, one can not neglect the fact that many citizens do not understand that trustworthy evidence should be excluded because of the way it was obtained. This incomprehension tends to increase in a social context that is characterised by an increasing attention for safety and an increasing repressive attitude of policymakers.

Another advantage of this option is the fact that the exclusion of evidence is linked to the incorrect attitude of the government and its investigating officers. Because the sanction on the irregularity of the furnishing of proof is limited to cases wherein government officials can be blamed with unlawful behaviour, one could argue that the government is forced to take full responsibility and protect investigations for unlawful acts.

Nevertheless, there are also arguments against the putting into perspective of the exclusionary rule. First, this implies that an unlawful act can be used to convict a person prosecuted for a criminal offence. Even if the investigating officer cannot be blamed for an incorrect attitude, the public prosecutor takes advantage of an illegality committed by a third party. This is very peculiar in a constitutional state, where the integrity of criminal proceedings should be given full attention.

Besides, this jurisprudence makes abuses possible. As mentioned above, it will be very difficult for the accused, if not impossible, to prove the connection between the illegality committed by a third person and the acquisition of the evidence by the public prosecutor. Possible collusion from investigating officers with private persons (*e.g.* private detectives) should be taken into account. Also, there has lately being given many attention to an increase of the role of the private sector in the judicial field, for example concerning safety-assignments. Involving private persons in the administration of justice is definitely a very dangerous option when possible illegalities committed by these persons can not be sanctioned within the context of the criminal trial itself. This way, the threat exist that zones are created wherein the legality of the furnishing of proof will be less guaranteed than normally would be the case. Obviously, this evolution cannot be supported.

It should rather be stressed that law in general and the rules regarding the evidence in particular can be seen as the mirror of our society. The need to eliminate some formalities in the law of criminal procedure cannot be denied, but one should be aware of the danger of accepting the negation of some essential rules and principles. This is what could happen if the exclusionary rule would be strongly put into perspective.

# Teaching Scientific Evidence and Forensics at a Small Law School (with Emphasis on Evaluating Evidence: Prosecutors, Experts and Professional Ethics)

*R.H. Underwood*

## Introduction

While American law schools have been doing a better job of late bringing basic advocacy training into the curriculum, they have not done a very good job of equipping their students for the tasks of evaluating, presenting and attacking expert testimony. In this short paper I would like to comment on some of the challenges presented by the flood of expert testimony in our courts, and how I have attempted to address the educational needs of the students at our relatively small law school.

I have taught a basic course on evidence law for twenty years, written a handbook on the law of evidence,[1] and taught trial advocacy courses to students and practicing lawyers.[2] Still, I must admit that the introduction of new techniques and even entire new disciplines has left me in the position of playing catch-up. There is also the matter of resources. A law school with only 25 or so faculty to teach 425 to 450 students the basics – the 'blue plate special'[3] – can only offer so many courses. There is little room or time for advanced courses in evidence and trial procedure. I am afraid that we have given science and scientific evidence rather short shrift.[4]

I should also admit, 'up front', that like many lawyers, I am more or less pre-Copernican in my education, training, and experience. I have no formal training in the forensic sciences, and no experience as a prosecutor. My somewhat limited practice had been in civil litigation and, oddly enough, most

---

[1] R.H. Underwood & G. Weissenberger, *Kentucky Evidence Law Courtroom Manual* (Anderson, updated yearly).

[2] For many years the University of Kentucky CLE program offered a *9-Day Intensive Course on Trial Advocacy*. The course was offered to practicing lawyers in the early Summer, before the start of our regular Summer school session. Unfortunately, the program became too costly for a self-supporting CLE program. Fortunately, with some funding and assistance from Kentucky's Attorney General, the Law School plans to update its courtroom facilities and offer a new Prosecutor's 'training school' during our fall semester.

[3] I would say that our teaching philosophy has been to provide excellent teaching of the basics – the bar courses – at the expense of the exotic and trendy, although we are beginning to expand our offering of seminars to satisfy our 'Substantial Writing Requirement'.

[4] Other law schools are way ahead of us on this front. Cardozo Law School sponsored two symposia, the first in 1991 styled 'Decision And Inference In Litigation', in 13 *Cardozo L. Rev.* (1991), and the more recent styled 'Scientific Evidence After The Death Of Frye: Criminal Forensics and DNA Evidence', in 15 *Cardozo L. Rev.* (1994). The University Of California at Davis sponsored a *Scientific Evidence Symposium* that was inspired by the first INREP conference. Papers presented can be found at 30 *U.C. Davis L. Rev.* 941 *et seq.* (1997).

of my research and writing has been in the area of professional ethics.[5] I came by my new found interest in scientific evidence and forensics, not because of any scientific or prosecutorial bent, but because I have spent a lot of time rubbing elbows with a number of local physicians and scientists who have been kind enough to assist me in teaching a survey course in Legal Medicine.[6] Suddenly I had to become conversant with such esoteric topics as genetic testing and DNA – a 'Brave New World' for me.[7] I became aware of the need to prepare young lawyers to be *skeptical of* and *challenge* scientific evidence and professed expertise when I was writing a series of articles on the law of perjury.[8] In those articles I addressed the problems of false expert testimony, police perjury, and prosecutorial misconduct.

**Some of the Challenges**

I am going to group the challenges of 'evaluation' of scientific evidence under four headings – *system or control* problems, *accuracy* problems, *honesty* problems and *lawyer skills* problems. These are merely convenient, descriptive labels. Needless to say, these broad categories overlap.

There is also nothing original about my selection of these categories.[9] As Professor Imwinkelried notes, "at the same time the use of scientific testimony is accelerating, we are gaining alarming insights into the level of scientific misanalysis. (...) [Sometimes] the source of error is reliance on inadequately validated theory. [*system or control* problems] (...) In other cases, the error is sloppy test procedure [*accuracy* problems]."[10] Other commentators have

---

[5] R.H. Underwood & W. Fortune, *Trial Ethics*, Little Brown 1988; W. Fortune, R.H. Underwood & E.J. Imwinkelried, *Modern Litigation and Professional Responsibility*, Aspen 1996; R.H. Underwood (ed.), *Kentucky Legal Ethics and Professional Responsibility Desk Book*, UK/CLE 1993. I served as the Chairman of the Kentucky Bar Association Ethics and Ethics Hotline Committees for 14 years.

[6] I am particularly indebted to the many fine physicians and scientists from the College of Medicine, University of Kentucky, and from the University of Kentucky Chandler Medical Center, as well as the scientists and technicians working at the Kentucky State Police Crime Laboratory, and investigators in the Lexington-Fayette County, Kentucky, Police Department, all of whom have volunteered their time. *Qui docet discit.*

[7] *See* R.H. Underwood & R. Cadle, 'Genetics, Genetic Testing, and the Specter of Discrimination: A Discussion Using Hypothetical Cases', 85 *KY. L.J.* 665 (1996-97).

[8] *See, e.g.*, R.H. Underwood, 'The Professional and the Liar', 87 *KY. L.J.* 919 (1999); 'Perjury! The Charges & Defenses', 36 *Duquesne L.Rev.* 715 (1998); 'Perjury: An Anthology', 13 *Ariz. J. Int'l & Comp. L.* 307; 'Truth Verifiers: From The Hot Iron to the Lie Detector', 84 *KY. L.J.* 597 (1995-96); '"X-Spurt" Witnesses', 19 *Am. J. Trial Advoc.* 343 (1995); 'False Witness: A Lawyer's History of the Law of Perjury', 10 13 *Ariz. J. Int'l & Comp. L.* 215 (1993-94).

[9] In 'Novel Scientific Evidence In Criminal cases: Some Words of Caution', 84 *J. Crim. L. & Criminology* 1 (1993), Professor Moenssens provides a longer list of reasons to be cautious in accepting medical and other scientific evidence in criminal cases, all of which could be gathered under my headings.

[10] E.J. Imwinkelried, 'Foreword [to Scientific Evidence Symposium]', 30 *U.C. Davis L. Rev.* 941 (to be continued)

pointed out the obvious but often overlooked fact that the science may be valid but the witness may be biased, conflicted, or dishonest (*honesty* problems).[11] My *lawyer skills* category recognizes that many times lawyers default[12] on their professional obligation to challenge the evidence.

Although this short sketch suggests the possibilities that test results may be inaccurate, that some forensic scientists may be over-zealous or manipulated by their prosecutorial 'customers', and that some 'experts' may be down-right dishonest, I need to add a word of caution. Most of the time the test results will be accurate and the forensic scientists will be honest and professional. Counsel must, as a professional, be skeptical of the opposition and do his or her homework and 'discovery'. But in many cases the decision not to confront the forensic evidence and the forensic scientist directly will be the 'correct' decision.

### System or Control Problems

The 'control' problems are that we want useful testimony from the expert witness, but we also want the witness to avoid 'advocacy'. And we do not want the witness to exert too great an influence – we do not want the expert to usurp the function of the trier of fact.[13] As philosopher C.A.J. Coady puts it, "[one] can concede the important, even essential, role of the expert witness (...) [and yet worry about] whether the vastly increased role of experts in the law poses a threat to the proper exercise of the court's arbitral role."[14]

One suspects that the control problems are perceived to be more worrying where the law operates through an adversary system.[15] Coady describes the

---

(1997).

[11] *See, e.g.*, R.H. Underwood, "'X-Spurt' Witness', 19 *Am. J. Trial Advoc.* 343 (1995); P. Giannelli, 'The Abuse Of Scientific Evidence In Criminal Cases: The Need For Independent Crime Laboratories', 4 *Va. J. Soc. Pol'y & L.* 439 (1997).

[12] Sometimes lawyers do not challenge the evidence for a reason, even when it is challengeable. A lawyer's judgment on a tactical point may be the 'right' judgment, and yet leave scientist and layman alike disappointed. Compare C. Wecht, 'Legal Medicine And Forensic Science: Parameters Of Utilization In Criminal Cases', 34 *Duquesne L. Rev.* 797 (1996).

[13] C.A.J. Coady, *Testimony: A Philosophical Study* 289 (1992). The control problems were described and lamented by Learned Hand in his famous article 'Historical And Practical Considerations Regarding Expert Testimony', 15 *Harvard. L. Rev.* 40 (1901-02).

[14] *Id.* at 300.

[15] M. Ladd, 'Expert Testimony', 5 *Vand. L. Rev.* 414 (1952): "With the rise of the adversary system in which witnesses were looked upon as being called by the parties and expected to represent their position in the case, it was not surprising that the use of scientific proof developed into a testimonial battle of experts. (...) [M]uch might be gained from the inquisitorial practice by having the experts exchange the information which they had with each other and then determine the conclusions to be drawn." *See also*, I. Freckelton, *The Trial Of The Expert: A Study Of Expert Evidence And Forensic Experts*, 'Foreword' by Hon. Justice M.D. Kirby, C.M.G., pp. ix, xii (Melbourne: Oxford University Press 1987); M. Redmayne, 'Expert Evidence And Scientific Disagreement', 30 *U.C. Davis* 1027, 1072 (1997); Hand, *supra*, note 15, at 56: "[The jury] will do (to be continued)

relationship between the law and expert testimony in English law as a 'shotgun marriage' in which the men of law have attempted to keep the expert in a 'subordinate role'. He suggests that the tensions may be more aggravated in America, where "the relationship [between the law and expert testimony] seems more like open concubinage, with all the shifting complexities of power and dominance that image suggests."[16]

The adversary system, adversary politics and adversary rhetoric complicate things. At the risk of sounding like an enemy of the adversary system (I am not), and at the risk of sounding overly simplistic (I may be) I think there is something to the following. In America lawyers can be grouped into sociological and political camps.[17] One camp is made up of plaintiffs' lawyers in civil cases. This is a large and increasingly well-organized group that knows how to get its points across. Conservative politicians refer to this group as 'The Trial Lawyers'.[18] The second is made up of defense lawyers in civil cases. This group is less well organized than the first, and probably smaller in number. But it supports and is supported by corporations and insurance companies.[19] Then

---

no better with the so-called testimony of experts than without, except where it is unanimous. If the jury must decide between [conflicting experts] they are as badly off as if they had none to help them." Compare P.T.C. van Kampen & J.F. Nijboer, 'Daubert In The Lowlands', 30 U.C. Davis L. Rev. 951, 985 (1997): "(...) [U]nder Dutch law, both culturally and institutionally (...), [t]he expert is primarily an assistant to the court (...) [and] (...) expertise and experts have been regarded in terms of neutrality and impartiality. (...) In the Dutch legal system, experts are expected to solve disagreements among themselves and not bring them into the open. The joint report that follows their negotiation catches two flies at once; it legitimizes reliance on experts in light of the perceived impartiality and neutrality of their arguments, and it prevents potential conflicts from disrupting the proceedings." These Dutch authorities suggest that "the American legal system's involvement with these cases and its struggle to stop the flood of unreliable scientific expert evidence, a struggle of which [Daubert v. Merrell Dow Pharmaceuticals, Inc., 509 U.S. 579 (1993)] is representative, seems to have few parallels in the western world." Id at 9. See also J. Langbein, 'The German Advantage in Civil Procedure', 52 U. Chi. L. Rev. 823, 835 (1985)(in Germany the experts are thought of as 'judge's aides'). For evidence that the 'Junk Science' problem is real in the US and in Commonwealth countries see P. Giannelli, "Junk Science': The Criminal Cases', 84 J. Crim. L. & Criminology 105 (1993); D. Bernstein, 'Junk Science In The United States And The Commonwealth', Yale J. Int'l L. 123 (1996).

[16] Coady, supra, note 14, at 277.

[17] See, e.g., the hostility expressed by a spokesman for the plaintiff's bar in the 'Preface' to the American Lawyer's Code Of Conduct (1982): "[The draft Model Rules of Professional Conduct are the product of] (...) the sort of thinking you get from a commission made up of lawyers who work for institutional clients, in institutional firms, and who have lost site of the lawyer's basic function. Lawyers are not licensed to write prospectuses for giant corporations, or to haggle with federal agencies over regulations and operating rights. We are licensed to represent people in court, which often means people in trouble with the law, and with the government. We are the citizens' champions against official tyranny."

[18] Lawyer-bashers associate the group with hot-button code words like 'contingent fee' and 'entrepreneurial' litigation. For their part, 'The Trial Lawyers' are virtually of a mind that critics of 'junk science' like P. Huber (Galileo's Revenge [1991]), are purveyors of 'junk scholarship'. See 'Galileo's Retort: Peter Huber's Junk Scholarship', 42 Am. U. L. Rev.1637 (1993).

[19] Lawyer-bashers like to think this group consists of corporate lackeys who specialize in delay (to be continued)

there are the prosecutors (and other government lawyers – lawyers in enforcement agencies who use scientific evidence, such as the FDA and EPA)[20] at the state and federal level, and their opposites, the criminal defense lawyers. Again, I think that we can safely assume that there are more criminal defense lawyers in the private bar than there are prosecutors.[21] The numbers favor the plaintiffs' bar on the civil side and the defense bar on the criminal side. Still, judges do not exactly let lawyers vote on what the rules should be, and where the actual power of persuasion lies is not clear – and the locus of power changes over time, just as the judicial attitude changes over time. My point is that in America we have a free and independent bar, but lawyers of these particular feather do flock together, philosophically and politically (with a small 'p').

The forces on opposite sides of the 'v.' have different ideas about the desirability of limits on the introduction of scientific evidence. The civil plaintiffs' bar wants a loose standard for the admission of scientific evidence – the plaintiffs' lawyers would prefer that the question be one of evidentiary weight or sufficiency. Presumably they would like the *Daubert* problem be treated as a *FRE* 104 (b) problem.[22] The civil defense lawyers want a strict, *Frye*-type standard, and want the court to treat the problem as a *FRE* 104 (a) problem. Now I am going to go even further out on the limb, and suggest that on the criminal side of the house, the prosecutors want a liberal standard of admissibility, or at least a standard that will apply in the same way[23] to both the prosecution and the defense. On the other hand, the criminal defense lawyers want a strict, *Frye*-type standard to be applied to the prosecution, but want a more liberal standard or no standard at all, to be applied to the defense.[24] All of these contending groups advance plausible arguments in support of their positions; and the language of *Daubert* is sufficiently cryptic to give all of these groups some comfort.[25] So the fight over the meaning of

---

and feed from the 'billable hour machine'.

[20] On the alleged abuse of 'junk' or 'regulatory' science by government lawyers *see* E. Efron, *The Apocalyptics* (1984).

[21] Although if you watch much American TV, you know that every lawyer claims to have been a 'former federal prosecutor'. My own view is that the term 'former federal prosecutor' is virtually devoid of meaning.

[22] For a thoughtful discussion of the difference between a *FRE* 104 (a) and a *FRE* 104 (b) approach *see* E. Scallen & W. Wiethoff, 'The Ethos Of Expert Witness: Confusing The Admissibility,Sufficiency And Credibility Of Expert Testimony', 49 *Hastings L.J.* 1143 (1998).

[23] They like the 'sauce rule'. "What's sauce for the goose is sauce for the gander."

[24] *See, e.g.,* E. Margolin, '*Daubert*: Comments On The Scientific Evidence Symposium', 30 *U.C. Davis L. Rev.* 1249 (1997). Cf., C. Slobogin, 'Psychiatric Evidence In Criminal Trials: To Junk Or Not To Junk?', 40 *Wm. & Mary L. Rev.* 1, 54-56 (1998).

[25] For a recent offering on this point *see* G.M. Fenner, 'The *Daubert* Handbook: The Case, Its Essential Dilemma, And It's Progeny', 29 *Creighton L. Rev.* 939 (1996): "This is the dilemma of *Daubert*: *Daubert* is at the same time *both more restrictive* of expert evidence *and less restrictive* of expert evidence."(emphasis added)

*Daubert* rages on. I would invite anyone who questions my admittedly stereotyped observations about the politics of the situation to read the contentious literature that appeared following the publication of the Federal Judicial Center's *Daubert Handbook.*[26]

This choosing up of sides was exhibited before and after the decision of the *Kumho Tire* case.[27] I call *Kumho Tire* a 'My Cousin Vinnie'[28] type case. The plaintiff in *Kumho Tire* was trying to make a case against a tire manufacturer by offering the testimony of a 'tire failure expert', who would have testified that a defect in a tire's manufacture or design caused a blow-out and a fatal accident. After holding a '*Daubert* hearing', the trial judge refused to admit the testimony, finding that it was not reliable, and alluding to some of the *Daubert* guidelines. I think the testimony was weak by anyone's standards – except, of course, the standards of the plaintiff and his lawyer.[29] The policy question is whether we want to let this kind of evidence 'come in for what it is worth' (and trust the jurors?) or have a 'judicial gatekeeper' screen it out (because our view of the abilities of jurors is, well, somewhat elitist?). The trial judge's nostrils and *Daubert* told him that he did not have to let the jury hear the expert's testimony. The plaintiff insisted that this was not scientific testimony, but instead technical or skills testimony, and that the *Daubert* criteria should not have been used to judge its reliability. The appellate court agreed with the plaintiff and reversed. The case then went up to the US Supreme Court.

Before *Kuhmo Tire* was decided, proponents of forensic evidence in criminal cases, and the plaintiffs' lawyers in civil cases, were arguing that the *Daubert* criteria are actually more liberal than *Frye* (a plausible argument), and that in any event their application should be limited to cases involving pure science, or at least some kind of science, as opposed to practical or technical skill (a less plausible argument).[30] The Supreme Court surprised the

---

[26] *See, e.g.,* M. Curridan, 'Plaintiffs' Lawyers Rap Evidence Manual', 81-MAR *A.B.A.J.* 20 (1995). *See also* Underwood, *supra*, note 12, at 351-352.

[27] 143 *L.Ed.2d* 238 (1999).

[28] In the movie by the same name a novice defense lawyer was representing his cousin, who had been charged with murdering a 'convenience store' clerk. The defendant was saved when the lawyer's girlfriend, the daughter of an auto mechanic, took the stand and provided convincing technical evidence that 'incriminating' skid marks left at the scene could not have been left by the defendant's car.

[29] Nothing fosters belief like self-interest. The expert conceded that the allegedly defective tire had been in use so long that some of the tread was bald; the tire should have been taken out of service; the tire had been inadequately repaired for punctures, and it bore marks indicative of abuse rather than defect. The expert sidestepped all of this by advancing a theory shared by no one else in the industry, and unsupported in the literature, that there needed to be at least two signs of abuse. I think that it is not too extreme a suggestion to characterize the opinion as self-sealing advocacy rather than helpful testimony. The expert sees only what he needs to support his argument, and responds to embarrassing or inconvenient facts by thinking up some new, untested theory.

[30] Cf., *United States* v. *Starzecpyzel*, 880 *F.Supp.* 1027 (S.D.N.Y. 1995). *See also* M. Saks, 'Merlin And Solomon: Lessons From The Law's Formative Encounters With Forensic Identification Science, 49 *Hastings L.J.* 1069, 1133-1134 (1998).

commentators by rejecting any 'scientific v. technical' dichotomy. I did not find the Court's decision the least bit surprising or reactionary; but perhaps that is because I did not read all that much into *Daubert* in the first place. While Justice Blackmun may have been more comfortable than most judges and lawyers when it came to rubbing elbows with scientists[31] and reasoning in terms that *seemed* scientific,[32] his judicial opinions did not 'do' science. He did not provide, and could not have provided, a (dare I say it?) litmus test. Although he used a great number of words to get his point across,[33] arguably all he was saying in *Daubert* was that in some circumstances the judge has discretion, and should exercise that discretion, to prevent the jury from even hearing the expert's testimony because the expert is just too 'far out'. And although *Daubert* offered criteria or considerations rooted in Justice Blackmun's notion of what *science* is, these criteria may not be that special.[34] Science may not be that *heretical*[35] after all.

In any event, I think that it was predictable that the *Daubert* Court would express time-honored judicial views about the control problems, and pick the *FRE* 104(a) route as one[36] means of maintaining judicial control over the expert (and the jury?); but also say that resort to *Frye* alone would result in the exclusion of too much expert evidence. Still, *Frye* had the virtue of allowing the trial judge to base his 104(a) decision on what the scientists think about a science. After *Daubert* the judge may have to make his or her own judgment about the reliability of the expert's science. "By a preponderance of the evidence, the proponent of the expert evidence has to demonstrate to the judge that it is good evidence, perhaps in spite of what other experts think about it."[37] This sounds good, but it may be a rather daunting task in particular cases. The judge must decide "at least three questions: (1) whether the witness is indeed expert in the field; (2) whether the field is a genuine area of science; (3)

---

[31] Justice Blackmun had been counsel to the Mayo Clinic.

[32] I agree with those commentators who argue that in the real world, falsifiability may not be of that much use as a judicial tool for distinguishing good science from bad. *See, e.g.*, Redmayne, *supra*, note 16, at 1078-79.

[33] *See* J. McElhaney, 'Trial Notebook: Fixing The Expert Mess', *Litig.*, Fall 1993, at 53.

[34] Rational or "Critical Man (...) does not stand or fall by his theories because in a sense he has none, merely working hypotheses. (...) The correct methodology of science is the correct methodology of civilization too." P. Johnson, *Enemies of Society* 145 (1977).

[35] But *see* A. Cromer, *Uncommon Sense: The Heretical Nature Of Science* (1993).

[36] The 'ultimate issue' rule was another control device, but it has largely been abandoned in American jurisdictions, except insofar as psychiatric and psychological experts are concerned. *See FRE* 704 (b). *See also* Scallen & Wiethoff, 'The Ethos Of Expert Witnesses: Confusing The Admissibility, Sufficiency And Credibility Of Expert Testimony', 48 *Hastings L.J.* 1143, 1166 (1998), discussing the *John Hinkley* case (attempted assassination of Ronald Reagan) and the amendment of *FRE* 704, which otherwise abolished the 'ultimate issue' rule, and the *Dan White* murder case (the so-called 'Twinkie' defense case) and subsequent amendment of the California Penal Code; Freckelton, *supra*, note 16, at 68-81.

[37] Fenner, *supra*, note 26, at 948.

whether, given a positive answer to (1) and (2), his particular depositions are credible. (...) All three of these questions pose difficulty for a legal tribunal since they seem to be questions that only an expert can answer. Hence the specter of a vicious logical regress arises."[38] This "logical regress" might be avoided if we opted for some procedural 'reform' based on the European model, or referred the matter to some certifying body or institution.[39] Of course, such reforms might present their own problems,[40] and most elements of the bar would oppose such 'reforms'.

In cases involving nascent, novel, or neo-science,[41] or involving the 'soft' social[42] or psychological sciences,[43] or involving 'non-science' technical or skills experts, the judge may have to hold a *'Daubert* hearing'.[44] So the *Daubert* case perpetuates the problem of "logical regress", sets up the need for a new form of mini-trial, and offers yet another stage for the adversary rhetoricians. My prediction is that in civil cases, *Daubert* hearings will result in additional delay and litigation cost. At least for the time being, the defense bar will over-litigate *Daubert* issues.[45] Will the *Daubert* hearing eliminate 'Junk Science' or will it turn out to be yet another negative development in civil litigation?

On the criminal side of the house, the defense bar may see *Daubert* as an invitation to challenge previously accepted types of forensic evidence.[46] My prediction here is that most everything successfully offered in the past by prosecutors will survive *Daubert* scrutiny.[47] But at least defendants will have

---

[38] Coady, *supra*, note 14, at 291.

[39] *See* Coady's proposal at 282-83. *See also* G. McAbee, 'Improper Expert Medical Testimony: Existing and Proposed Mechanisms of Oversight', 19 *J. Legal Med.* 257 (1998).

[40] *See* A. Kozinski, 'Brave New World', 30 *U.C. Davis L. Rev.* 997, 1010 (1997)(questioning whether in the Dutch system, the experts do not, in effect, become the judges, and judges who operate in secret).

[41] These terms are used in Coady, *supra*, note 14.

[42] For an interesting article on the injection of so-called 'junk social science' into appellate briefs *see* M. Rustad & T. Koenig, 'The Supreme Court And Junk Social Science: Selective Distortion In Amicus Briefs', 72 *N.C. L. Rev.* 91 (1993).

[43] Coady offers cogent criticisms of the appearance of the witnesses of psychology, sociology, and anthropology. *See* Coady, *supra*, note 14, Chapters 15 and 16. *See also* C. Ewing, 'Expert Witnesses: Can Psychiatrists Give Reliable Testimony In Criminal Trials?', 83-APR *A.B.A.J.* 76 (1997)(short article alluding to J. Grisham's novel *A Time To Kill*, in which both the prosecution and the defense present fraudulent expert testimony).

[44] But *see* Greenwell v. *Boatwright*, 199 *W.L.R.* 548023 (6th Cir. 1999)(trial court not required to hold an actual hearing to comply with *Daubert*). *See also* Fugate v. *Commonwealth*, 993 *S.W.2d* 931 (Ky. 1999)(RFLP and PCR DNA testing admissible in future without *Daubert* hearing).

[45] The wheels of the 'billable hour machine' will clatter merrily.

[46] *See, e.g.*, Margolin, *supra*, note 25; R. Jonakait, 'The Meaning Of *Daubert* And What It Means For Forensic Science', 15 *Cardozo L. Rev.* 2103 (1994).

[47] *See* Margolin, *supra*, note 25, at 1255 ("When the Supreme Court decided *Daubert*, a paroxysm of creative inventiveness seized the criminal defense bar (...). Hope seemed luxuriously victorious over experience.") One of my operating assumptions as an American lawyer is that the judge (in state court) is probably a former prosecutor. In contrast, in federal court, the judge is probably a (to be continued)

another weapon to use against their own lawyers when litigating post-conviction (*alleging* that counsel did not raise the issue or pursue it with enough competence and zeal).[48] Obviously, we are going to have to give our students more skills training so that they can participate successfully in the *Daubert* dance.

## Accuracy Problems

Lawyers and judges, and critics of expert evidence, assume that the public in general, and jurors in particular, accord an 'honorific' status to the expert.[49] Indeed, the time-honored catechism in which the proponent 'tenders the expert to the court' and receives an acknowledgment from the judge that the witness may now testify to the jury as an 'expert' has been condemned in a number of American jurisdictions, including my own, on the theory that jurors can be swept away by any hint of judicial certification of a witness's authority![50] "To the degree that an expert can parade as (...) a scientist (...) his opinion [may] have a weight and authority that it may not deserve, not only because he may not be a particularly good specimen of *'homo scientificus'* but also because *what he testifies to may be much more contestable than the deferential lay*

---

former Senatorial campaign manager.

[48] Some plaintiffs' lawyers on the civil side argue that *Daubert* puts them at risk *unfairly*. They worry about taking a novel or cutting edge case, investing huge sums of money on expert witness fees and other litigation expenses, having the case thrown out by the judge on *Daubert* grounds (unfairly? -By surprise?), and then being sued by their disappointed client for malpractice. Of course, the counterarguments are that the 'entrepreneur' lawyer takes his or her chances along with the client. The disappointed client would have to show that but for negligence in the selection of the expert, or in the preparation or presentation of the expert's testimony, the client would have won the cutting edge case.

[49] Are our assumptions about juror attitudes justified, or are they simply elitist? Perhaps not all of them are justified, according to D. Shuman *et al.*, 'Assessing The Believability Of Expert Witnesses: Science In The Jurybox', 37 *Jurimetrics J.* 23 (1996). The major findings discussed in this piece were that jurors do not give more credence to experts from hard sciences than those in soft fields, and that jurors decide not on the basis of their own characteristics but on the experts qualifications, use of good reasoning, familiarity with the facts of the case, and the experts appearance of impartiality. These findings contradict those of prior 'studies'. Even more interesting is the fact that this recent study found that jurors are influenced by who retained the expert, and that jurors tend to believe the defense experts in civil cases. Should we reevaluate some of our assumptions about the inability of jurors to evaluate and discount 'junk science'. *See also* J. Doyle, 'Scientific Evidence Symposium: Applying Lawyer's Expertise To Scientific Experts: Some Thoughts About Trial Court Analysis Of The Prejudicial Effects Of Admitting And Excluding Expert Scientific Testimony', 25 *Wm. & Mary L. Rev.* 619 (1984).

[50] *See Luttrell* v. *Commonwealth*, 952 *S.W.2d* 216 (Ky. 1997) and *Berry* v. *City of Detroit*, 25 *F.3d* 1342 (6th Cir. 1994). I feel like these opinions make much ado about nothing. But compare C. Richey, 'Proposals To Eliminate The Prejudicial Effect Of The Use Of The Word "Expert" Under The Federal Rules Of Evidence In Civil And Criminal Jury Trials', 154 *F.R.D.* 537, at 554-555 (1994).

*person is inclined to believe."*[51] (Emphasis added.)

We have already noted that a lot of forensic science procedures could be challenged if the *Daubert* criteria were applied rigorously. Professor Jonakait[52] and others[53] have argued that some procedures have been subjected to little or no testing, and that "most of the forensic sciences operate outside of [any] peer review system". Publication is limited. Many techniques are not used 'outside' and may not be generally accepted, at least by the larger scientific community.

Then there is the problem of 'error rate'.[54] *Daubert* invites the opponent of the scientific testimony to make much ado about 'error rates'. Jonakait claims that "little is (...) known about the true error rates for almost all forensic science techniques (...) [and that] [t]he few disclosed error rates (...) are shockingly high."[55] It is no wonder that "the argument that the testing laboratory *might* have made an error appears to be the most fruitful line of attack in DNA cases."[56] Indeed, the National Research Council's report *DNA In Forensic Science* (NRC I, 1992) actually encouraged such attacks when it initially suggested that the results of laboratory proficiency testing be used in

---

[51] Coady, *supra*, note 14, at 280.

[52] R. Jonakait, 'Forensic Science: The Need For Regulation', 4 *Harv. J.L. & Tech.* 109 (1991); R. Jonakait, 'The Meaning Of *Daubert* And What That Means For Forensic Science', 15 *Cardozo L. Rev.* 2103 (1994).

[53] *See, e.g.*, A. Moenssens, 'Novel Scientific Evidence In Criminal Cases: Some Words Of Caution', 84 *J. Crim. L. & Criminology* 1 (1993); P. Giannelli, 'Book Review – The DNA Story: An Alternative View', 88 *J. Crim. L. & Criminology* (1997). *See also* M. Saks & J. Koehler, 'What DNA "Fingerprinting" Can Teach The Law About The Rest Of Forensic Science', 13 *Cardozo L. Rev.* 361 (1991)("Most forensic sciences, including DNA typing, rely on assumptions that have not been verified by empirical testing.") For an interesting if somewhat overheated point-counterpoint *see* D.M. Risinger & M. Saks, 'Science And Nonscience In The Courts; *Daubert* Meets Handwriting Identification Expertise', 82 *Iowa L. Rev.* 21 (1996) vs. A. Moenssens, 'Handwriting Identification Evidence In The Post-*Daubert* World', 66 *U.M.K.C. L. Rev.* 251 (1997), with a reply in D.M. Risinger, M. Denbeaux & M. Saks, 'Brave New "Post-*Daubert* World" – A Reply To Professor Moenssens', 29 *Seton Hall L. Rev.* 405 (1998).

[54] Here I refer to the need to assess real error rates based on the actual use of techniques and procedures. For discussion of the importance of the distinction between actual and theoretical error rates *see* Jonakait, 15 *Cardozo L. Rev.* 2103, at 2115-116; M. Burger, 'Laboratory Error Seen Through The Lens Of Science And Policy', 30 *U.C. Davis L. Rev. 1081* (1997).

[55] Jonakait, 15 *Cardozo L. Rev.* 2103, at 2117. *See also* R. Jonakait, 'Stories, Forensic Science, And Improved Verdicts', 13 *Cardozo L. Rev.* 343, 350-351 (1991)(arguing that information regarding error rates should be presented to the jury); R. Lempert, 'Some Caveats Concerning DNA As Criminal Identification Evidence: With Thanks To The Reverend Bayes', 13 *Cardozo L. Rev.* 303, 324 (1991)(discussing evidence of high error rates in forensic laboratories – "Forensic experts often present their findings with great confidence, but infallibility is unfortunately not a characteristic of forensic laboratories.") *See also* R. McDonald, 'Juries And Crime Labs: Correcting The Weak Links In The DNA Chain', 24 *Am. J.L. & Med.* 345 (1998)("The problem with DNA evidence is no longer one of validity, but one of proficiency.")

[56] Redmayne, *supra*, note 16, at 38 (emphasis added). At this point I should note that I tend to agree that overall error rates may not be all that relevant. *See, e.g.*, D. Balding, 'Errors And Misunderstandings In The Second NRC Report', 37 *Jurimetrics J.* 469 (1997); Berger, *supra*, note 61.

deciding whether testimony should be admitted.[57]

Actually 'error rate' may refer to more than one thing and suggest multiple avenues of attack. What was Justice Blackmun talking about when he alluded to the importance of 'error rate'? Are we to consider the degree of error inherent in a test or technique even when it is properly conducted (theoretical accuracy)? Or are we talking about performance rates on a particular lab's or a particular individual's proficiency tests? Should an expert be required to combine the probability of a match due to lab error with the random-match probabilities (RMP)?[58] Should the jury be told anything about 'error rates'?[59] Or should we demand some evidence of actual human error *in the particular case* before we inject 'possibilities' into the trial? If we are primarily concerned with the possibility of actual error in the particular case, can the risks be minimized by providing opportunities for reciprocal discovery and testing? Now that the courts have accepted PCR testing, there should be material around for the defense to test if they really want to.[60]

I get my students thinking about the problem of human error (not to mention dishonesty) by assigning the case of *In the Matter of an Investigation of the West Virginia State Police Crime Laboratory, Serology Division*.[61] Reports of investigations of other crime laboratories are also available on several forensic web pages on the Internet.[62]

In the case of the West Virginia lab, the operating procedures of the serology department were found to be deficient in the following particulars: "[There was][1] no written documentation of testing methodology; [2] no

---

[57] *Committee On DNA Technology In Forensic Science, National Research Council, DNA Technology In Forensic Science* (1992), or *NRC 1*. The report had something for everyone, at least after its contents was subjected to a little spin. Accordingly, it is cited by both 'sides of the v.'. *See* D. DeBenedicts, 'DNA Report Raises Concerns', 78-JUL *A.B.A.J.* 20 (1992).

[58] *Committee On DNA Forensic Science: An Update, National research Council, The Evaluation Of Forensic DNA Evidence* (1996), the *NRC 2*, says NO. For a useful discussion of *NRC 2 see* 'DNA, NAS, NRC, DAB, RFLP, PCR, And More: An Introduction To The Symposium On The 1996 NRC Report On Forensic DNA Evidence', 37 *Jurimetrics J.* 395 (1997).

[59] According to *NRC 2*, prosecutors should not be required to inform the jury of laboratory proficiency-testing rates.

[60] Of course, there is the problem of paying for a defense expert. *See* J. Devlin, 'Comment: Genetics And Justice: An Indigent Defendant's Right To DNA Expert Assistance', 1998 *U. Chi. Legal F.* 395, 397 (1998): "(…) [A] DNA expert can help a criminal defendant in four ways. First, a defense expert can search for possible error by the prosecution's testing laboratory. Second, a defense expert can conduct independent tests on any unused DNA samples. Third, a defense expert can testify at trial about the problems with DNA statistics and potentially offer the jury a lower probability estimate. Fourth, a defense expert can point out the shortcomings of the newer DNA testing method, if the prosecutor uses it. A defendant who cannot afford his own expert will lose these benefits unless the government provides one for him."

[61] 190 *W.Va.* 321, 438 *S.E.2d* 501 (1993).

[62] There are a number of interesting and useful forensic web sites. I refer my students to the *Depaul University Center for Law and Science, Scientific Testimony: An Online Journal, Kim Kruglick's Forensic Resource and Criminal Law Search Site* and *The Evidence Site*. The Kentucky State Police Crime Laboratory can be visited at firearmsID.com.

written quality assurance program; [3] no written internal or external auditing procedures [4] no routine proficiency testing of laboratory technicians; [5] no technical review of work product; [6] no written documentation of instrument maintenance and calibration; [7] no written testing procedures manual; [there was] [8] [a] failure to follow generally accepted scientific testing standards with respect to certain tests; [9] inadequate record-keeping; and [10] [a] failure to conduct collateral testing."[63]

I also added to the required reading some common sense articles on the ways in which error can be injected into evidence collection, testing, and the documentation of same.[64] Forensic scientists may view such 'checklists' as defense lawyers propaganda, and complain that such laundry lists invite wasteful discovery and harassment. But there are bad labs as well as good labs. Pointless discovery and harassment are to be avoided; but counsel cannot afford to take evidence at face value either.

A related problem is the 'gee whiz factor'. Assuming that we have an 'accurate' result, and that the expert is not trying to mislead the jury (which I will discuss as an *honesty* problem), what is the result going to mean to the lay jurors? Given their lack of scientific sophistication and 'innumeracy',[65] jurors are likely to overestimate the significance of the result.[66] Professor Jonakait provides us with one of his own experiences with possible juror confusion: "The split verdicts could only be explained by the serological evidence. The two defendants linked by the forensic scientist to the victim were convicted. (...) Such evidence has an important impact on jury verdicts (...) [but does] one in a hundred mean a 99% certainty that Jose was guilty (...)."[67]

Professor Moenssens is of the view that jurors often confuse issues, assuming that statistical percentages reported by forensic experts are statements about the probability of guilt. He contends that jurors do this

---

[63] 438 *S.E.2d* at 504.

[64] *See, e.g.*, M. Valley, California, lawyer Kim Kruglick's 'A Beginner's Primer on the Investigation of Forensic Evidence. This is available at Scientific Testimony: An Online Journal', www.scientific.org/tutorials/articles/kruglick. Kruglick provides the novice with a useful "Discoverable Materials Checklist" (laboratory specific, technician specific, and case specific documentation that should be available to the defense – for example, did you get all of the laboratory bench notes?) as well as a "Forensic Case Issue Checklist" that suggests many avenues of attack. *See also* P. Giannelli, 'Criminal Discovery, Scientific Evidence, And DNA', 44 *Vand. L. Rev.* 791 (1991).

[65] Juror 'innumeracy' is referred to in mathematician J. Allen Paulos' book *A Mathematician Reads The Newspaper* (1995). *See also* D.H. Kaye & J. Koehler, 'Can Jurors Understand Probabilistic Evidence?', *J. Royal Sts. Soc'y*, Series A 75, 77 (1991).

[66] *See* W. Thompson & E. Schumann, 'Interpretation of Statistical Evidence In Criminal Trials: The Prosecutor's Fallacy and the Defense Attorney's Fallacy', 11 *Law & Human Behavior* 167 (1987). *See also* sources collected in Underwood, '"X-Spurt" Witnesses', *supra*, note 9, at 387-88. *See also* J. Koehler, 'Error And Exaggeration In The Presentation Of DNA Evidence At Trial', 34 *Jurimetrics J.* 21 (1994).

[67] *See* R. Jonakait, 'Stories, Forensic Science, And Improved Verdicts', 13 *Cardozo L. Rev.* 343, 345 (1991).

despite cautionary instructions; and that jurors are sometimes urged to do this by the fallacious arguments of prosecutors.[68]

## Honesty Problems

It is no secret that expert witnesses can be co-opted by the prosecution – they may be little more than 'hired guns of the state'.[69] And even honest witnesses who are trying to be objective may not be asked the right questions and may have their testimony filtered or contorted by the advocate.[70]

"Untoward results follow when expert evidence in complex cases is presented in adversarial fashion: expert witnesses are manipulated for partisan purposes, some relevant scientific findings are never introduced, and unwarranted conclusions are not distinguished from valid research. (...) Forensic scientists have special grievances over the adversary system."[71]

Professor Coady agrees, noting that: "The adversary system is probably the best tool we have for detecting (...) [overconfidence, self-deception and dishonesty] (...) though, ironically, it is itself responsible for one common defect, namely, the expert's temptation to identify overmuch with the cause of his 'side'."[72]

Good detectives follow the evidence. They do not manipulate the evidence

---

[68] A. Moenssens *et al.*, *Scientific Evidence In Civil And Criminal Cases*, 4th ed., 583-585 (1995). For a case of similar confusion on the civil side, *see* K. Browne, 'The Strangely Persistent "Transposition Fallacy": Why "Statistically Significant" Evidence Of Discrimination May Not Be Significant', 14 *Lab. Law.* 437 (1998)(discussing the transposition fallacy of equating "the probability of A given B" with "the probability of B given A", which the author contends American courts commit in discrimination cases). On the role of fallacy in forensic proof and argument *see* R.H. Underwood, 'Logic And The Common Law Trial', 18 *Am. J. Trial Advoc.* 151 (1994).

[69] *See, e.g.*, W. Thompson, 'A Sociological Perspective On The Science Of Forensic DNA Testing', 30 *U.C. Davis L. Rev.* 1113 (1997); M. Ketchum, 'Comment: Expert Witnesses For The Persecution? Establishing An Expert Witness's Bias Through The Discovery And Admission Of Financial Records', 63 *UMKC L. Rev.* 133 (1994). I have not found this to be true of good labs and good forensic scientists. For example, the Associate Medical Examiners in Kentucky pride themselves on being equally available to the defense as well as the prosecution. Indeed, they are more than happy to give lectures on forensic science to defense oriented organizations.

[70] Of course, this is also true on the defense 'side of the v.', and true of expert witnesses in civil cases. For convincing commentary *see* C. Jones, *Expert Witnesses; Science, Medicine, and the Practice of Law* (1994); I. Freckelton, *The Trial Of The Expert: A Study Of Expert Evidence And Forensic Experts* (1987).

[71] F. Strier, 'Making Jury Trials More Truthful', *U.C. Davis L. Rev.* 95, 113-115 (1996). *See also* P. Sperlich, 'Scientific Evidence in the Courts: The Disutility of Adversary Proceedings', 66 *Judicature* 472, 474-75 (1982).

[72] C.A.J. Coady, *Testimony: A Philosophical Study* (1992), at p. 295. Coady proposes, not the abandonment of the adversary system, but rather some reforms. He proposes the foundation of independent institutes of forensic science. Of course, the trick is to insure that the independence is not illusory. *See also* P. Giannelli, 'The Abuse Of Scientific Evidence In Criminal Cases: The Need For Independent Crime Laboratories', 4 *Va. J. Soc. Pol'y & L.* 439 (1997).

to fit their pre-conceived notions or theories. But we all know that there are bad detectives as well as over-zealous prosecutors.[73] Forensic scientist D. H. Garrison, Jr. puts it this way: "Bad science is what forensic science becomes when an attorney or prosecutor, who often display[s] all the ethics of a full-grown hamster, get[s] a forensic scientist to play ball, to get with [the advocate's] program and see [the advocate's] big picture."[74]

Sometimes prosecutors will 'shop around' until they find an expert who will tell them what they want to hear. This happened in the infamous *Rolando Cruz* case.[75] "The first lab guy says it's not the boot. (...) We don't like that answer, so there's no paper [report]. We go to a second guy who used to do our lab. He says yes. So we write a report on Mr Yes. Then Louise Robbins arrives. This is the boot, she says. That'll be $10,000. So now we have evidence."[76] This also happened in several cases involving police serologist Fred Zain.[77] Under suspicion of faking test results, Zain left his job as head of a serology lab in West Virginia, to take a position in a Texas crime lab. When the remaining West Virginia lab technicians were unable to give the prosecutors the results they wanted, they shipped the work off to Texas, to the accommodating Officer Zain.[78] Garrison reports a variation of 'shopping' he calls 'Jeopardy' [after a game show], in which the lab manager or prosecutor "gives (...) subordinates [the] desired answer and demand[s] that they come up with the appropriate research questions to support it."

Lawyer and Criminology Professor Thompson tells a troubling tale about DNA. "(...)[T]he laboratory report indicated that the DNA test had produced powerful evidence against both suspects [Thompson's client suspect 1 and suspect 2 who was not his client] – a five locus match between each suspect and the DNA found in semen extracted from the victim. The report has no indication that the evidence against suspect 1 was weaker than that against suspect 2. (...) Examination of the underlying autorads confirmed a clear, unambiguous match with suspect 2, but indicated the evidence against suspect 1 was ambiguous and equivocal. (...) My initial suspicion was examiner bias. (...) When I raised concerns about examiner bias (...) the prosecution took the position that the autorads had been scored objectively by a computer-assisted

---

[73] *See* Underwood, 'The Professional and the Liar', *supra*, note 9.

[74] D. H. Garrison, Jr., 'Bad Science', www.chem.vt.edu/ethics/garrison/bad science.htm.

[75] For a general discussion of the case *see* Underwood, 'The Professional and the Liar', *supra*, note 9.

[76] P. Giannelli, 'Expert Qualifications & Testimony', Conference on Science and Law, San Diego, April 15, 1999, available on 'Scientific Testimony: An Online Journal', quoting a former detective who was interviewed by Barry Siegel of the L.A. Times. *See also Buckley* v. *Fitzsimmons*, 509 U.S. 259 (1993).

[77] *See* discussion below in text at note 101.

[78] *In re Investigation of West Virginia State Police Crime Lab, Serology Division*, 438 S.E.2d 501, 512 (1993). For other discussions *see* Freckelton, *supra*, note 16, at 123-150; A. Moenssens, *Scientific Evidence In Civil And Criminal Cases*, 4th ed. (1995) pp. 618-620.

imaging device. The prosecution claimed a scanner was used to create a digital image of each autorad (...) making the process entirely objective. (...) I obtained a court order that required the forensic laboratory to re-score the autorads with the computer imaging device while an independent expert and I watched. (...) During this rescoring, the claim that the process was objective evaporated. (...) In order to detect bands in the male vaginal extract lane that corresponded to those of suspect 1, the analyst had to increase the sensitivity of the computer to the point that it detected many additional 'bands' that matched neither suspect. The analyst then performed a 'manual override' of the computer's scoring, instructing the computer to 'delete' (*i.e.*, ignore) all of the bands that matched neither suspect. (...) When asked to state the basis for 'deleting' some bands while leaving others, the analyst responded that he could tell by looking at the undeleted bands, which happened to match my client, were 'true' bands while the others were not. A number of the bands he deleted had higher optical densities than the bands scored matching my client. So much for objectivity."[79]

There are lots of ways of getting people to play ball. Some who cannot be bought can be persuaded. There are reported cases involving experts who were pressured to change their results or delete potentially exculpatory results from their reports.[80] And experts can be steered, or have their testimony 'structured' by prosecutors and police who withhold information or feed only selected information to the expert witness.[81]

Sometimes forensic scientists and bench operators are coached to give opinions outside of their expertise (or anyone else's for that matter). Garrison alludes to a case in which a bartender, who had been the victim of a robbery, testified that the defendant had had a glass of beer in his tavern earlier in the evening. Three unwashed glasses found at the scene of the robbery were tested. Two had prints, but they were not the defendants. The prosecutor attempted to get the print examiner to testify that the defendant must have used the third glass and then wiped it clean.[82] While Garrison reports that the print examiner refused to so testify, there are reported cases in which similar testimony appears to have been given.[83]

Sometimes it is the questions that are asked, *or not asked*, which result in

---

[79] W. Thompson, 'A Sociological Perspective On The Science Of Forensic DNA Testing', 30 *U.C. Davis L. Rev.* 1113, 1127-1128 (1997).
[80] Giannelli, *supra*, notes 12, 16 and 77 collects a number of cases, including *Jones* v. *City of Chicago*, 856 *F.2d* 985 (7th Cir. 1988).
[81] *See* Jones, *supra*, note 71, at 217-218. *See also* J. Thornton, 'Uses And Abuses Of Forensic Science', 69 *A.B.A.J.* 288, 292 (1983); M. Saks, 'Accuracy v. Advocacy: Expert Testimony Before The Bench', *Technology Review*, Aug.-Sept. 1987, at 43, 44-45, noting that the information submitted to the forensic scientist may be selected and screened, and that such manipulation may result in a skewed opinion.
[82] Garrison, *supra*, note 75.
[83] Compare *United States* v. *Booth*, 669 *F.2d* 1231 (9th Cir. 1981).

misleading opinion testimony. According to Garrison, prosecutors and defense lawyers alike try to get experts to provide improper opinions about 'intent' or 'absence of intent' – questions the expert cannot answer, and which must be answered by the jury – by "disguising a question to [the] expert as something vaguely science-like in nature".[84] For example, a firearms expert has no way of knowing the 'intent behind the bullet'. But the prosecutor may invite a helpful and prejudicial comment or two, and some witnesses will accept the invitation. One might profitably compare this sort of thing to some of the defendant sponsored psychiatric testimony in Dan White trial (which involved, among other things, the 'Twinkie Defense'), in which the defense experts frequently "usurped the juror's prerogative to decide matters of guilt and innocence".[85] The defendant's suspicious reloading of the gun was an 'automatic action', and the defendant 'was literally not focusing' when he shot George Moscone two times in the head.[86]

Pathologist Michael Baden admits that "'consistent with' is one of those catch-all phrases that means [little more than] something could be possible. It is used a lot (...) especially on the witness stand when evidence can be interpreted in more than one way."[87] In the famous *Sacco & Vanzetti* case[88] Captain William Proctor, the ballistics expert, testified:

"Q: Have you an opinion as to whether bullet 3 was fired from the Colt automatic which is in evidence [Sacco's pistol]?

A: I have.

Q: And what is your opinion?

A: My opinion is that it is *consistent with* being fired by that pistol."[89]

The presiding judge accepted this as if it were a statement that "it was (...) [Sacco's] pistol that fired the bullet that caused the death of Berardelli".[90] Later Captain Proctor would give an affidavit that he was never able to find any convincing evidence to support another expert's testimony that the bullet was marked with scratches to prove that it went through Sacco's pistol. He also said that he had told the district attorney that he would answer 'no' if he were asked if he had found any such 'affirmative' evidence, but that *he had not been asked* that question at the trial.[91] A similar abdication of responsibility occurred in the notorious and perplexing *Dotson-Webb* rape case. Forensic

---

[84] D.H. Garrison, Jr., 'Intent Behind the Bullet', www.chem.vt.edu/ethics/garrison/intent.htm.
[85] E.A. Scallen & W. Wiethoff, 'The Ethos Of Expert Witnesses: Confusing The Admissibility, Sufficiency And Credibility Of Expert Testimony', 48 *Hastings L.J.* 1143, 1163 (1998).
[86] *Id.* at 1164.
[87] M. Baden & J. Hennessee, *Unnatural Death: Confessions Of A Medical Examiner* 22 (1989). *See* discussion in Underwood, "'X-Spurt" Witnesses', *supra*, note 9, at 394-396.
[88] *See Commonwealth* v. *Sacco*, 261 *Mass.* 12, 158 *N.E.* 167, cert. denied, 275 *U.S.* 574 (1927).
[89] H. Ehrman, *The Case that Will Not Die: Commonwealth v. Sacco & Vanzetti* 266 (1969).
[90] The quotation is from the judge's instructions to the jury. *Id.*, at 268.
[91] B. Jackson, *The Black Flag: A Look Back At The Strange case Of Nicola Sacco and Bartolomeo Vanzetti*, 22-23, 54, 107 (1981).

scientist Timothy Dixon had testified that seminal material in victim Webb's panties matched Dotson's blood type; but he did not disclose that Webb's own vaginal discharges could have yielded the same results. When he was asked later why he had not so testified his excuse was that he was not asked![92]

Outright lying seems to occur more frequently than one would suspect. There are at least a few bad apples who have told outright lies about everything from their academic credentials to the tests they performed and the results they obtained.[93]

Professor Coady alludes to an excerpt from an American cartoon version of Robin Hood in criticizing the way we lawyers meekly accept the qualifications of the expert:

"MOUSE:   Who are you?
FOX:      I'm Robin Hood.
MOUSE:    You don't look like Robin Hood, but if you say you are then it must be true, because Robin Hood wouldn't tell a lie."[94]

Nevertheless, several commentators have offered up collections of cases involving experts who lied about their credentials. For example, one firearms expert apparently went so far as to take credit for some aspect of the development of penicillin and the atomic bomb.[95] Lab technicians have been prosecuted for lying about their academic credentials.[96] On the *civil* side of the house, a Dr. Jeffrey Goltz was recently convicted of perjury for lying about his credentials in a civil case.[97]

Perhaps the most spectacular cases of lying involved Fred Zain, the former Chief of Serology at the West Virginia State Police Crime Laboratory, Dr. Ralph Erdmann, a pathologist for 42 Texas counties, and the late Dr. Louise Robbins, an anthropologist for hire who is remembered for her bogus shoeprint

---

[92] *See* Giannelli, *supra*, note 77, citing B. Fleetwood, 'From The People Who Brought You The Twinkie Defense; The Rise Of The Expert Witness Industry', 19 *Washington Monthly* 33 (June 1987).

[93] *State* v. *Ruybal*, 408 A.2d 1284 (Me. 1979); *State* v. *DeFronzo*, 394 N.E.2d 1027 (Ohio Common Pleas 1978). *See also Skaggs* v. *Commonwealth*, 803 S.W.2d 573 (Ky. 1990).

[94] Coady, *supra*, note 14, at 277.

[95] *See* P. Giannelli, *supra*, note 77, citing Starrs, 'Mountebanks Among Forensic Scientists', in: R. Saferstein (ed.), 2 *Forensic Science Handbook* 1, 7, 20-29 (1988).

[96] *Id.*, citing as examples *State* v. *Elder*, 199 Kan. 607, 433 P.2d 462 (1967); *State* v. *DeFronzo*, 394 N.E.2d 1027. 1030 (Ohio Common Pleas 1978). For more cases *see* P. Giannelli, 'The Abuse Of Scientific Evidence In Criminal Cases: The Need For Independent Crime Laboratories', 4 *Va. J. Soc. Pol'y & L.* 439, 468, note 175 (1997); A. Moenssens, 'Novel Scientific Evidence In Criminal Cases: Some Words of Caution', 84 *J. Crim. L & Criminology* 1 (1993).

[97] R. Marcus, 'Prosecution Happens Over Civil Perjury', *Seattle Times*, Tuesday March 3, 1998, reports the perjury conviction and 18 month prison sentence of orthopedic surgeon Jeffrey Goltz. Goltz had clearly lied about his education and training while testifying as an expert witness in a personal injury case. For discussions of his fibs *see Richardson* v. *National Railroad Passenger Corporation*, 150 F.R.D. 1 (D.D.C. 1993), aff'd 49 F.3d 760 (D.C. App. 1995). For other misconduct by Dr. Goltz *see National Capital Orthopedic Associates, P.C.* v. *Jeffrey Goltz, M.D.*, 1997 WL 625117 (D.Md. 1997).

and 'Cinderella' testimony[98] in a number of criminal cases, including *Buckley* v. *Fitzsimmons*.[99]

The specific acts of misconduct by the pro-prosecution Officer Zain were enumerated as follows: "[1] overstating the strength of results; [2] overstating the frequency of genetic matches on individual pieces of evidence; [3] misreporting the frequency of genetic matches on multiple pieces of evidence; [4] reporting that multiple items had been tested, when only a single item had been tested; [5] reporting inconclusive results as conclusive; [6] repeatedly altering laboratory records; [7] grouping results to create the erroneous impression that genetic markers had been obtained from all samples tested; [8] failing to report conflicting results; [10] implying a match with a suspect when testing supported only a match with the victim; and [11] reporting scientifically impossible or improbable results."[100]

For his part, Erdmann became infamous for faking autopsy results – indeed, generating entire fake autopsies![101] In one case a defendant attempted to prove that his robbery victim was not harmed, and that she must have died of a heart attack rather than strangulation. The prosecution responded with Erdmann's testimony that her coronary arteries were like those of a 30-year-old. To prove his point he swore that certain microscopic slides were those of the 80-year-old victim. He did not reveal that he had made the slides from the arteries taken from the autopsy of a 30-year-old![102] In another case Erdmann amended one of his 'findings' after his initial testimony conflicted with the prosecutor's theory. He had testified originally that a bullet hole had definitely not been made by a small .22 caliber weapon, but the prosecution had built its case around a .22 caliber – so Erdman went back on the stand after a short recess to say that the bullet hole had been a .22 caliber that had been enlarged (the hole was in the skull!) by maggots. The defense sat passively. When the testimony was ultimately challenged later at trial the court would not allow the jurors to hear the evidence of blatant contradiction![103]

We have already discussed how Dr. Robbins was 'for hire' by prosecutors who were willing to shop for an expert. Still, her most fantastic performance

---

[98] The 'Cinderella cases' involved Robbins' claimed ability to match footprints with the insoles of shoes belonging to suspects.

[99] 509 *U.S.* 259, 113 *S.Ct.* 2606, 125 *L.Ed.2d* 209 (1993). The case resurfaced and continues to generate controversy because of alleged prosecutorial misconduct in the prosecution(s) of Rolando Cruz, another suspect in the same crime. For discussions *see* Underwood, '"X-Spurt" Witnesses', 19 *Am. J. Trial Advoc.* 343 (1995; R.H. Underwood, 'The Professional And The Liar', 87 *Ky. L. J.* 919 (1999).

[100] 438 *S.E.2d* at 516.

[101] P. Giannelli, 'The Abuse Of Scientific Evidence In Criminal Cases: The Need For Independent Crime Laboratories', 4 *Va. J. Soc. Pol'y & L.* 439, 449 (1997).

[102] C. Wecht, 'Legal Medicine And Forensic Science: Parameters Of Utilization In Criminal Cases', 34 *Duquesne L. Rev.* 797, 809 (1996).

[103] R. Fricker, 'Reasonable Doubts', 79-DEC. *A.B.A.J.* 39 (1993).

came when she gave an opinion that, based on her examination of a human footprint, the print had been made by a prehistoric woman who was five and a half months pregnant at the time she made the impression![104]

Despite the fact that forensic scientists may join, and tout their memberships in a variety of professional organizations, many of which have adopted codes of ethics, there is virtually no risk of sanctions from professional organizations. [105]

Perhaps the most distressing aspect of the honesty problem is the complicity of lawyers – particularly prosecutors. If we cannot expect[106] decency from our prosecutors, what can we expect to get from the other 'side of the v.'? Yet the literature is full of cases in which prosecutors went along with, and in a few cases even solicited, bogus evidence, while at the same time withholding exculpatory evidence.[107] This has been done in spite of prosecutors' constitutional duty to disclose when asked, and despite prosecutors' affirmative[108] ethical responsibility to disclose even in the absence of a triggering request.[109]

When I was looking for articles for my students to read I came across a piece by former Attorney General Dick Thornburgh. Thornburgh is a respected politician – a former governor of Pennsylvania. I would not have counted him as an ethics expert, although I would not have counted him out either. When I saw that he had written an article styled 'Junk Science – The Lawyer's Ethical Responsibilities',[110] I hoped that he had written, *ex cathedra*, on the subjects of 'junk science' in criminal cases and prosecutorial misconduct. Alas, my hopes were dashed. He held forth on the subject of the breast implant cases, and hammered the civil plaintiffs' bar![111]

---

[104] M. Hanson, 'Believe It Or Not', 79 *A.B.A.J.* 64 (June 1993).

[105] *See* P. Giannelli, 'The Abuse Of Scientific Evidence In Criminal Cases: The Need For Independent Crime Laboratories', 4 *Va. J. Soc. Pol'y & L.* 439, 454 (1997); L.T. Perrin, 'Expert Witness Testimony: Back To The Future', 29 *U. Rich. L. Rev.* 1389, 1390 (1995).

[106] Compare *Berger* v. *United States*, 295 *U.S.* 78, 88 (1935): "It is as much [the prosecutor's] duty to refrain from improper methods calculated to produce a wrongful conviction as it is to use every legitimate means to bring about a just one."

[107] *See* P. Giannelli, 'The Abuse Of Scientific Evidence In Criminal Cases: The Need For Independent Crime Laboratories', 4 *Va. J. Soc. Pol'y & L.* 439 (1997); R.H. Underwood, '"X-Spurt" Witnesses', 19 *Am. J. Trial Advoc.* 343 (1995); R.H. Underwood, 'The Professional And The Liar', 87 *Ky. L.J.* 919 (1999). *See also* K. Rosenthal, 'Prosecutor Misconduct, Convictions, and Double Jeopardy: Case Studies In An Emerging Jurisprudence', 71 *Temp. L. Rev.* 887 (1998)(collecting cases).

[108] A.B.A. Model Rule of Professional Conduct 3.8(d).

[109] *See also* J. Weeks, 'No Wrong Without A Remedy: The Effective Enforcement Of The Duty Of Prosecutors To Disclose Exculpatory Evidence', 22 *Okla. City L. Rev.* 833, 898 (1997)("(…)[T]he disciplinary process has been almost totally ineffective in sanctioning even egregious *Brady* violations.")

[110] 25 *Fordham Urb. L.J.* 449 (1998).

[111] Mr. Thornburgh is now in 'private practice' in a large law firm. Of course, in the US prosecutors enjoy absolute immunity for malicious prosecution, so most of the theorizing about (to be continued)

## Lawyer Skills Problems

One of the common complaints of the 'critics' is that lawyers do not challenge questionable forensic testimony. The testimony may be 'too good to be true' or even suggest the impossible. But in too many a case the defense lawyer sits by as silent as the proverbial 'potted palm'.[112] This is hardly a new phenomenon. It has been reported that in the infamous *Dreyfus* case, the expert testimony of the great criminalist Alphonse Bertillon incorrectly concluded that the incriminating document passing French military information to the Germans was written by the innocent Dreyfus. But Bertillon's testimony (by deposition) was "in fact so incomprehensible that it escaped cross examination at trial."[113] There is nothing new under the sun.

Law schools skills training cannot solve this problem; but we can at least give our students a little head start. At the very least, we can give our students some limited experience with real experts in a variety of fields. Students can be given an opportunity to work with experts on a one-on-one basis in the 'legal clinic' or in a seminar. Students can tour the crime lab. The more adventurous can attend an autopsy. Students can study the codes of ethics promulgated by the various professional associations,[114] and can learn effective techniques for cross-examination in trial advocacy courses.[115]

The University of Kentucky College of Law offers a new seminar on Scientific Evidence and Forensics. When I developed the materials[116] for this

---

discipline and tort liability for harm caused by 'junk science' tends to focus on plaintiffs' lawyers. *See, e.g.*, C. Bowman & E. Mertz, 'Attorneys As gatekeepers To The Court: The Potential Liability Of Attorneys Bringing Suits Based On Recovered Memories Of Childhood Sexual Abuse', 27 *Hofstra L. Rev.* 223 (1998).

[112] *See* Giannelli, *supra*, note 77 citing cases involving claims of "ineffective assistance of counsel". In one case in which a prosecution was dropped because of conflicting an inconclusive expert testimony, Giannelli reports that one of the defense lawyers admitted, "I suppose I was like the average citizen. They said it was a match, I thought it was like a fingerprint". Giannelli's source was Baker & Lieberman, 'Faulty Ballistics in Deputy's Arrest', *L.A. Times*, May 22, 1989. *See also* J. Doyle, 'Applying Lawyer's Expertise To Scientific Experts: Some thoughts About Trial Court Analysis Of The Prejudicial Effects Of Admitting And Excluding Expert Scientific Testimony', 25 *Wm. & Mary L. Rev.* 619 (1984), quoting Professor Saltzburg: "(…)[T]he adversary system is largely based on exposure of weaknesses in witnesses, testimony, and physical evidence through cross-examination, impeachment, and counter-evidence. Evidence not attacked is evidence readily accepted."

[113] F. Taroni, C. Champod & P. Margot, 'Forerunners Of Bayesianism In Early Forensic Science', 38 *Jurimetrics J.* 183, 189 (1997).

[114] *See* discussion in A. Moenssens *et al.*, *supra*, note 69, at 91-92. Many of these codes can be found on the forensic web sites.

[115] For a pre-*Daubert* article that is still extremely useful *see* L. Miller, 'Cross-Examination Of Expert Witnesses: Dispelling The Aura Of Reliability', 42 *U. Miami L. Rev.* 1073 (1988).

[116] Professor Imwinkelried of the University of California at Davis generously provided me with ideas, his syllabus and his course materials. He is way ahead of me. He emphasized the importance of giving each student the opportunity to talk to and work closely with an expert witness in some technical or scientific field.

seminar I had a number of modest goals that I wanted to achieve. First of all, I wanted to build up a library of books and articles for my students and for local practitioners. While you may not view this as a library for the scientist or technician, I think it provides a good basic library for lawyers and law students *(Appendix A)*. I also wanted to build up a 'bank' of helpful experts. I made, at best, a modest start. In the words of Professor Moenssens, "myopic presentation [of expert testimony] can be avoided only by maintaining an intelligible dialogue with the expert."[117] These volunteer experts agreed to help the students prepare their class presentations and research papers.

I also wanted to give the students an introduction to the forensic sciences, and some basic instruction on the role of the medical examiner, DNA evidence, the polygraph, etc. With that end in mind I sought assistance from our State Medical Examiners, our Forensic Anthropologist and others. In the end we were able to present seven two-hour 'Modules' of instruction by guest lecturers *(Appendix B)*. In the weeks that followed, the students completed their papers and did their class presentations on a variety of topics *(Appendix C)*.

I will be happy to send a copy of my syllabus to anyone who is interested in offering a similar seminar.

## Appendixes

*Appendix A: Readings and Videos on Reserve*

**Books**

**Anderson, W.** (1998), *Forensic Sciences In Clinical Medicine: A Case Study Approach.*
**Baden, M.** *et al.* (1992), *Unnatural Death: Confessions of a Medical Examiner.*
**Browning, M. & Maples, W.** (1995), *Dead Men Do Tell Tales: The Strange And Fascinating Cases of a Forensic Anthropologist.*
**Coady, C.A.J.** (1992), *Testimony: A Philosophical Study.*
**Dimaio, V. & Dana, S.** (1998), *Handbook of Forensic Pathology.*
**Dix, J. & Ernst, M.** (1999*), Handbook For Death Scene Investigators.*
**Faigman, D.** *et al.* (1997*), Modern Scientific Evidence: The Law and Science of Expert Testimony* (2 vol.).
**Foster, K. & Huber, P.** (1997), *Judging Science: Scientific Knowledge and the Federal Courts.*
**Freckelton, I.** (1987), *The Trial Of The Expert: A Study Of Expert Evidence And Forensic Experts.*
**Gerberth, V.** (1996), *Practical Homicide Investigation Tactics, procedures and Forensic Techniques.*
**Gianelli, P. & Imwinkelried, E.J.** (1993), *Scientific Evidence* (2d ed., 2 vol.).
**Graham & Hanzlick** (1997), *Forensic Pathology in Criminal Cases.*
**Haskell, N.** (1990), *Entomology And Death, A Procedural Guide.*
**Imwinkelried, E.J.** (1997), *The Methods of Attacking Scientific Evidence.*
**Imwinkelried, E.J.** (1998), *Evidentiary Foundations* (4th ed.).

---

[117] A. Moenssens *et al.*, *Scientific Evidence in Civil and Criminal Cases*, 4th ed., iii (Foundation Press, 1995).

**Jackson, D.** (1996), *The Bone Detectives: How Forensic Anthropologists Solve Crimes And uncover Mysteries Of The Dead.*
**Jones, C.A.G.** (1994), *Expert Witnesses: Science. Medicine, and the Practice of Law.*
**Kaye, D.H.** (1997), *Science In Evidence.*
**Kurland, M.** (1995), *How To Solve A Murder: The Forensic Handbook.*
**Lykken, D.** (1981), *A Tremor In The Blood: Uses And Abuses Of The Lie Detector.*
**Matte, J.** (1996), *Forensic Psychophysiology Using The Polygraph: Scientific Truth Verification – Lie Detection.*
**Moenssens, A.** *et al.* (1995), *Scientific Evidence In Civil and Criminal Cases*, 4th ed.
**Mueller, C. & Kirkpatrick, L.** (1999), *Evidence*, 2d ed.
**Nickell, J. & Fischer, J.** (1999), *Crime Science: Methods of Forensic Detection.*
**Patterson (ed.),** *Lawyers' Medical Cyclopedia* (multi-volume). See Vol 4B, Ch.32A on Autopsies by Drs. Hunsaker and Davis.
**Saferstein, R.** (1997), *Criminalistics*, 6th ed.
**Stevens. S. & Klarner, A.** (1990), *Deadly Doses: A Writer's Guide To Poisons.*
**Tiger, M.** (1993), *Examining Witnesses.*
**Wecht, C.** (1997), *Forensic Sciences* (5 vols.).
**Wecht, C.** (1994), *Legal Medicine.*
**Wecht, C.** (1994), *Cause of Death.*
**Wilson, K.** (1992), *Cause of Death: A Writer's Guide To Death, Murder and Forensic Medicine.*
**Wingate, A.** (1992), *Scene of the Crime: A Writer's Guide to Crime scene Investigations.*

### Articles

**Apfel, D.,** 'Clinical Markers Establishing A Causal Relationship Between Birth Asphyxia And Cerebral Palsy: A Primer For Trial Lawyers', 21 *Am. J. Trial Advoc.* 1 (1997).
**Balding, D.** (in Symposium: The Evaluation Of Forensic DNA Evidence), 'Errors And Misunderstandings In The Second NRC Report', 37 *Jurimetrics J.* 469 (1997).
**Berger, M.,** 'Laboratory Error Seen Through The Lens Of Science And Policy', *30 U.C. Davis L.Rev.* 1081 (1997).
**Bernstein, D.,** 'Junk Science In The United States And The Commonwealth', 21 *Yale J. Int'l L.* 123 (1996).
**Biffl, E.,** 'Psychological Autopsies: Do They Belong In The Courtroom', 24 *Am. J. Crim. L.* 123 (1996).
**Boeschen, L.** *et al.,* 'Rape Trauma Experts In The Courtroom', 4 *Psychol. Pub. Pol'y & L.* 414 (1998).
**Browne, K.,** 'The Strangely Persistent "Transposition Fallacy": Why "Statistically Significant" Evidence Of Discrimination May Not Be Significant', 14 *Lab. Law* 437 (1998)
**Busloff, S.,** 'Can Your Eyes Be Used Against You? The Use Of The Horizontal Gaze Nystagmus Test In The Courtroom', 84 *J. Crim. L. & Criminology* 203 (1993).
**Daniels, Ch.,** 'New Frontiers In Polygraph Evidence: Law and Tactics', 21 *Jul Champion* 16 (1997).
'Developments In The Law – Confronting The New Challenges Of Scientific Evidence', 108 *Harv. L. Rev.* 1482 (1995).
**Donnelly, P. & Friedman, R.,** 'DNA Database Searches And The Legal Consumption Of Scientific Evidence', 97 *Mich. L. Rev.* 931 (1999).
**Duncan, K.,** '"Lies, Damn Lies, And Statistics"? Psychological Syndrome Evidence In The Courtroom After Daubert', 71 *Ind. L.J.* 753 (1996).
**Faigman, D.,** 'Mapping The Labyrinth Of Scientific Evidence', 46 *Hastings L.J.* 555 (1995).
**Fenner, G.M.,** 'The Daubert Handbook: The Case, Its Essential Dilemma, And Its Progeny', 29 *Creighton L. Rev.* 939 (1996).
**Feinberg, S., Krislov, S. & Straf, M.,** 'Understanding And Evaluating Statistical Evidence In Litigation', 36 *Jurimetrics J.* 1 (1995).
**Gallai, D.,** 'Polygraph Evidence In Federal Courts: Should It Be Admissible?', *36 Am. Crim. L.*

*Rev.* 87 (1999).

**Giannelli, P.,** Polygraph Evidence Post-Daubert, 49 *Hastings L.J.* 895 (1998).

**Giannelli, P.,** 'The Abuse Of Scientific Evidence In Criminal Cases: The Need For Independent Crime Laboratories', 4 *Va. J. Soc. Pol'y & L.* 439 (1997).

**Giannelli, P.,** 'The DNA Story: An Alternative View', 88 *J. Crim. L. & Criminology* 380 (1997).

**Giannelli, P.,** '"Junk Science": The Criminal Cases', 84 *J. Crim. L. & Criminology* 105 (1993).

**Giannelli, P.,** 'Criminal Discovery, Scientific Evidence and DNA', 44 *Vand. L. Rev.* 791 (1991).

**Giannelli, P.,** 'The Admissibility Of Laboratory Reports In Criminal Trials: The Reliability Of Scientific Proof', 49 *Ohio St. L.J.* 671 (1988).

**Giuliana, A.,** 'Between A Rock And A Hurd Place: Protecting The Criminal Defendant's Right To Testify After Her Testimony Has Been Hypnotically Refreshed', 65 *Fordham L. Rev.* 2151 (1997).

**Hamilton, B.,** 'Expert Testimony On The Reliability Of Eyewitness Identifications: A Critical Analysis Of Its Admissibility', 54 *Mo. L. Rev.* 734 (1989).

**Hallisey, R.,** 'Experts On Eyewitness Testimony In Court – A Short Historical Perspective', 39 *How. L.J.* 237 (1995).

**Henseler, T.,** 'A Critical Look At The Admissibility Of Polygraph Evidence In The Wake Of Daubert: The Lie Detector Fails The Test', 46 *Cath. U.L.Rev.* 1247 (1997).

**Imwinkelried, E.J. & McCall, J.,** 'Issues Once Moot: The Other Evidentiary Objections To The Admission Of Exculpatory Polygraph Examinations', 32 *Wake Forest L. Rev.* 1045 (1997).

**Imwinkelried, E.J.,** 'The Debate In The DNA Cases Over The Foundation For The Admission Of Scientific Evidence: The Importance Of Human Error As A Cause Of Forensic Misanalysis', 69 *Wash. U. L.Q.* 19 (1991).

**Imwinkelried, E.J.,** 'The Standard For Admitting Scientific Evidence: A Critique From The Perspective Of Juror Psychology', 28 *Villanova L. Rev.* 554 (1982-83).

**Jonakait, R.,** 'The Meaning Of Daubert And What That Means For Forensic Science', 15 *Cardozo L. Rev.* 2103 (1994).

**Kampen, P.T.C. van & Nijboer, J.F.,** 'Daubert In The Lowlands', 30 *U.C. Davis L. Rev.* 951 (1997).

**Kaye, D.H.,** 'DNA, NAS, NRC, RFLP, PCR, And More: An Introduction To The Symposium On The 1996 NRC Report On Forensic DNA Evidence', 37 *Jurimetrics J.* 395 (1997).

**Kaye, D.H.,** 'The Admissibility Of DNA Testing', 13 *Cardozo L. Rev.* 353 (1991).

**Kesan, J.,** 'An Autopsy Of Scientific Evidence In A Post-Daubert World', 84 *Geo. L.J.* 1985 (1996).

**Kesan, J.,** 'A Critical Examination Of The Post-Daubert Scientific Evidence Landscape', 52 *Food & Drug L.J.* 225 (1997).

**Ketchum, M.,** 'Experts: Witnesses For The Persecution? Establishing An Expert Witness's Bias Through The Discovery And Admission Of Financial Records', 63 *U.M.K.C. L. Rev.* 133 (1994).

**Klein, M.,** 'Daubert Worldwide Judicial Management Of Humanity's Specialized Knowledge', 30 *U.C. Davis L. Rev.* 1229 (1997).

**Kobayashi, J.,** 'Killing Them Softly With Your Song: Problems With Proof Of Causal relationship By Statistical Methods And Probability Theory And Expert Opinions With Suggested Methods For Analysis And Cross-Examination, And Notes About Epidemiological Studies And Animal Data As Causation Evidence', 363 *Pli/Lit* 37 (1988).

**Koehler, J.,** 'Error And Exaggeration In The Presentation Of DNA Evidence At Trial', 34 *Jurimetrics J.* 21 (1993).

**Kulynych, J.,** 'Brain, Mind, And Criminal Behavior: Neuroimages As Scientific Evidence', 36 *Jurimetrics J.* 235 (1996).

**Leiter, B.,** 'The Epistemology Of Admissibility: Why Even Good Philosophy Of Science Would Not Make For Good Philosophy Of Evidence', 1997 *B.Y.U.L.Rev.* 803 (1997).

**Lempert, R.,** 'Some Caveats Concerning DNA As Criminal Identification Evidence: With Thanks To The Reverand Bayes', 13 *Cardozo L. Rev.* 303 (1991).

**Lynch, D.,** 'Post-Daubert Admissibility Of Repressed Memories', 20 *Nov Champion* 14 (1996).

**Lubet, S.,** 'Expert Testimony', 17 *Am. J. Trial Advoc.* 399 (1993).

**McAbee, G.**, 'Improper Expert Medical Testimony: Existing Mechanisms Of Oversight', 19 *J. Legal Med.* 257 (1998).

**McCall, J.**, 'The Personhood Argument Against Polygraph Evidence, Or "Even If The Polygraph Really Works, Will Courts Admit The Results?"', 49 *Hastings L.J.* 925 (1998).

**McDonald, R.**, 'Juries And Crime Labs; Correcting The Weak Links In The DNA Chain', 24 *Am. J.L. & Med.* 345 (1998).

**Margolin, E.**, 'Daubert: Comments On The Scientific Evidence Symposium', 30 *U.C. Davis L. Rev.* 1249 (1997).

**Mello, M.**, 'Outlaw Executive: "Crazy Joe", The Hypnotized Witness, And The Mirage Of Clemency In Florida', 23 *J. Contemp. L.* 1 (1997).

**Miller, L.**, 'Cross-Examination Of Expert Witnesses: Dispelling The Aura Of Reliability', 42 *U. Miami L. Rev.* 1073 (1988).

**Moenssens, A.**, 'Handwriting Evidence In The Post-Daubert World', 66 *U.M.K.C. L. Rev.* 251 (1997).

**Moenssens, A.**, 'Novel Scientific Evidence In Criminal Cases: Some Words Of Caution', 84 *J. Crim. L. & Criminology* 1 (1993).

**Nesson, Ch. & Demers, J.**, 'Gatekeeping: An Enhanced Foundational Approach To Determining The Admissibility Of Scientific Evidence', 49 *Hastings L.J.* 335 (1998).

**Monahan, E. & Clark, J.**, 'Funds For Defense Expertise: What A National Benchmarks Require', 21 *May Champion* 12 (1997).

**Parker, B. & Vittoria, A.**, 'Debunking Junk Science: Techniques For Effective Use Of Biostatistics', 66 *Def. Couns. J.* 33 (1999).

**Parker, B. & Vittoria, A.**, 'Effective Strategies For Closing The Door On Junk Science', 65 *Def. Couns. J.* 338 (19__).

**Parker, J.**, 'Daubert's Debut: The Supreme Court, The Economics Of Scientific Evidence, And The Adversarial System', 4 *Sup. Ct. Econ. Rev.* 1 (1995).

**Price, J. & Kelly, G.**, 'Junk Science In The Courtroom: Causes, Effects and Controls', 19 *Hamline L. Rev.* 395 (1996).

**Redmayne, M.**, 'Expert Evidence And Scientific Disagreement', 30 *U.C. Davis L. Rev.* 1027 (1997).

**Richey, Ch.**, 'Proposals To Eliminate The Prejudicial Effect Of The Use Of The Word "Expert" Under The Federal Rules Of Evidence In Civil And Criminal Jury Trials', 154 *F.R.D.* 537 (1994).

**Richmond, D.**, 'Regulating Expert Testimony', 62 *Mo. L. Rev.* 485 (1997).

**Risinger, D.M. & Saks, M.**, 'Science And Nonscience In The Courts: Daubert Meets Handwriting Identification Expertise', 82 *Iowa L. Rev.* 21 (1996).

**Risinger, D.M. & Saks, M.**, 'Exorcism As A Proxy For Rational Knowledge: The Lessons Of Handwriting Identification "Expertise"', 137 *U. Pa. L. Rev.* 732 (1989).

**Rosenthal, K.**, 'Prosecutor Misconduct, Convictions, And Double Jeopardy: Case Studies In An Emerging Jurisprudence', 71 *Temp. L. Rev.* 887 (1998).

**Rozzano, L.**, 'The Use Of Hypnosis In Criminal Trials: The Black Letter Of The Black Art', 21 *Loy. L.A. L. Rev.* 635 (1988).

**Rustad, M. & Koenig, Th.**, 'The Supreme Court and Junk Social Science: Selective Distortion In Amicus Briefs', 72 *N.C.L. Rev.* 91 (1993).

**Sabot, J.**, 'Expert Testimony On Organized Crime Under The Federal Rules of Evidence: United States v. Frank Locasio and John Gotti', 22 *Hofstra L. Rev.* 177

**Saks, M.**, 'Merlin And Solomon: Lessons From The Law's Formative Encounters With Forensic Identification Science', 49 *Hastings L.J.* 1069 (1998).

**Saks, M. & Koehler, J.**, 'What DNA "Fingerprinting" Can Teach The Law About The Rest Of Forensic Science', 1 *Cardozo L. Rev.* 361 (1991).

**Scallen, E.A. & Wiethoff, W.**, 'The Ethos Of Expert Witnesses: Confusing The Admissibility, Sufficiency And Credibility Of Expert Testimony', 49 *Hastings L.J.* 1143 (198).

**Schuman, D.**, 'Juror Assessments Of The Believability Of Expert Witnesses: A Literature Review', 36 *Jurimetrics J.* 371 (1996).

**Sensbaugh, G. & Kaye D.H.**, 'Non-Human DNA Evidence', 39 *Jurimetrics J.* 1 (1998).

**Slobogin, Chr.**, 'Psychiatric Evidence In Criminal Trials: To Junk Or Not To Junk?', 40 *Wm. &*

*Mary L. Rev.* 1 (1998).

**Spadaro, J.,** 'An Elusive Search For The truth: The Admissibility Of Repressed And Recovered Memories In Light Of Daubert v. Merrel Dow Pharmaceuticals, Inc.', 30 *Conn. L. Rev.* 1147 (1998).

**Strier, F.,** 'Making Jury Trials More Truthful', 30 *U.C. Davis L. Rev.* 95 (1996).

**Taroni, F., Champod, C. & Margot, P.,** 'Forerunners Of Bayesianism In Early Forensic Science', 38 *Jurimetrics J.* 183 (1998).

**Taylor, G.,** 'Fake Evidence Becomes Real Problem', *The Nat'l L.J.*, Monday, October 9, 1995.

**Taylor, M. & Spangler, R.,** 'Capital Culpability: Daubert Necessitates Re-Evaluation Of Condemned Persons With Borderline Intelligence As Measured By The Weschler Adult Intelligence Scale – Revised (WAIS-R)', 21 *The Advocate*, No. 3, 40 (May 1999).

**Thames, J.,** It's Not Bad Law – It's Bad Science: Problems With Expert Testimony In Trial Proceedings', 18 *Am. J. Trial Advoc.* 545 (1995).

**Thompson, W.,** 'A Sociological Perspective On The Science Of Forensic DNA Testing', 30 *U.C. Davis L. Rev.* 1113 (1997).

**Thompson, W. & Schuman, E.,** 'Interpretation Of Statistical Evidence In Criminal Trials: The Prosecutor's Fallacy and the Defense Lawyer's Fallacy', 11 *Law & Human Behavior* 167 (1987).

**Thornburgh, D.,** 'Junk Science – The Lawyer's Ethical Responsibilities', 25 *Fordham Urb. L.J.* 449 (1998).

**Underwood, R.H.,** 'The Professional And The Liar', 87 *Ky. L. J.* 919 (1999).

**Underwood, R.H.,** 'Truth Verifiers: From The Hot Iron To The Lie Detector', 84 *Ky. L.J.* 597 (1995-96).

**Underwood, R.H.,** '"X-Spurt" Witnesses', 19 *Am. J. Trial Advoc.* 343 (1995).

**Underwood, R.H.,** 'Logic And The Common Law Trial', 18 *Am. J. Trial Advoc.* 151 (1994).

**Tol, J. Van,** 'Detecting, Deterring And Punishing The Use Of Fraudulent Academic Credentials: A Play In Two Acts', 30 *Santa Clara L. Rev.* 791 (1990).

**Wecht, C.,** 'Legal Medicine And Forensic Science: Parameters Of Utilization In Criminal Cases', 34 DUQ. L. REV. 797 (1996).

**Videos**

L20 Liar - Deception In Society
M16 The Wilson Murder; Forensic Experts At Odds
M17 The Magic Bullet; Ballistics
M18 Postal Mortem ; Explosives and Document Forensics
M19 Southside Strangler: DNA Science
O5 Detectives Of Death: 20th Century - O.J. Simpson

**Appendix B – Revised – Modules**

1. Aug. 25 Forensic Pathology, Dr. Greg Davis and Dr. John Hunsaker (Read Moenssens 680-756).
2. Sept. 1 Forensic Anthropology, Dr. Emily Craig (Read Moenssens 990-1063).
3. Sept. 8 Fingerprints and Trace Evidence, Sgt. Mark Barnard (Read Moenssens 495-554; 555-629).
4. Sept. 15 DNA, Lucy Davis (Read Moenssens 870-963).
5. Sept. 22 Firearms, Ronnie Freels (Read Moenssens 307-396).
6. Sept. 29 Detection of Deception, Dr. Michael Nietzel (Read Moenssens 1195-1230).
7. Oct. 6 Begin student presentations - two per class period.
8. Oct. 13 Student presentations.
9. Oct. 20 Student presentations.
10. Oct. 27 Student presentations.
11. Nov. 3 Student presentations.
12. Nov. 10 Student presentations.
13. Nov. 17 Student presentations.

14.  Nov. 24  Student presentations.
15.  Dec. 1    Civil Cases: Practitioner's Views / Cutting Edge, by Sam Davies.

**Appendix C – Topics**

accident reconstruction
accounting
arson analysis
ballistics
bitemark identification
bloodspatter and stain
chromatographic analysis
drug testing
entomology
explosives analysis
eyewitness identification
fingerprints
firearms
flammability analysis
footprints and tiremarks
genetic markers – RFLP and PCR DNA tying
handwriting
hypnosis
intoxification testing
mass spectrometry
molecular biology
memory – recovered memory
neuroscience
NMR spectroscopy
pathology
pharmacology
polygraph
psychiatry
psychology
questioned documents
radar
serology
sound spectrometry
statistics
toolmark identification
toxicology
trace evidence – hair, glass, paint, and soil
valuation

# New Trends in International Co-operation in Criminal Matters in the European Union

*G. Vermeulen*

## Introduction

Mutual (legal) assistance in criminal matters is not just one of the traditional forms of international co-operation in criminal matters. In daily practice, its importance for international criminal law enforcement and in particular for combating international organised crime, is much more significant than that of any other form of judicial co-operation, be it extradition, transfer of proceedings, or transfer of the execution of sentences.

Traditionally, the co-operation levels relevant to mutual assistance in criminal matters between European states have been the Council of Europe, the Benelux Economic Union, the Nordic Union and the bilateral level. As for the Council of Europe, reference must be made to the *1959 European Convention on Mutual Assistance in Criminal Matters (ECMA)*[1] – ratified by all EU Member States – and the *1978 Additional Protocol to this Convention*[2] – ratified by all Member States but Belgium and Luxembourg. In the relations between the Benelux countries, the *ECMA* does not apply; mutual assistance is governed by chapter II of the *1962 Benelux Treaty on Extradition and Mutual Assistance in Criminal Matters*.[3] Further, a number of European states decided to supplement the provisions of the *ECMA* or to facilitate its application by concluding additional bilateral[4] or – in the case of the Nordic countries –

---

[1] Strasbourg, 20 April 1959, *European Treaty Series*, No 30.
[2] Strasbourg, 17 March 1978, *European Treaty Series*, No 99.
[3] *Traité d'extradition et d'entraide judiciaire en matière pénale entre le Royaume de Belgique, le Grand-Duché de Luxembourg et le Royaume des Pays-Bas*, Brussels, 27 June 1962, Union Economique Bénélux, Textes de Base.
[4] *See*, as regards the mutual relations between the EU Member States: *Vertrag vom 31. Jänner 1972 zwischen der Republik Österreich und der Bundesrepublik Deutschland über die Ergänzung des Europäischen Übereinkommens über die Rechtshilfe in Strafsachen vom 20. April 1959 und die Erleichterung seiner Anwendung*, Bonn, *Bundesgesetzblatt für die Republik Österreich*, 31 January 1977, No 36; *Vertrag vom 20. Februar 1973 zwischen der Republik Österreich und der Italienischen Republik über die Ergänzung des Europäischen Übereinkommens über die Rechtshilfe in Strafsachen vom 20. April 1959 und die Erleichterung seiner Anwendung*, Vienna, *Bundesgesetzblatt für die Republik Österreich*, 29 November 1977, No 558; *Convention du 24 octobre 1974 entre la République française et la République d'Allemagne additionnelle à la Convention européenne d'entraide judiciaire en matière pénale du 20 avril 1959*, *Journal officiel de la République française*, 13 January 1981; *Aanvullend Akkoord van 6 maart en 18 juli 1975 gesloten bij wisseling van brieven, tussen de Regering van het Koninkrijk België en de Regering van de Bondsrepubliek Duitsland, bij het Europees Verdrag voor onderlinge gerechtelijke hulp in strafbare zaken, ondertekend te Straatsburg op 20 april 1959*, Brussels, *Belgisch Staatsblad*, 20 August 1978; *Overeenkomst van 30 augustus 1979 tussen het Koninkrijk der Nederlanden en de Bondsrepubliek Duitsland betreffende de* (to be continued)

multilateral[5] treaties and conventions.[6]

In the mid-80s, new co-operation levels – Schengen and the EC/EU level – were established. Next to it, the Council of Europe continued drawing up new legal instruments relating to or having relevance for mutual legal assistance. Special attention must be given here to the *1990 European Convention on Laundering, Search, Seizure and Confiscation of the Proceeds of Crime.*[7] Further, it should be mentioned that since 1995, the Council of Europe's Committee of Experts on the Operation of European Conventions in the Penal Field (PC-OC) has worked on a Preliminary Draft Second Additional Protocol to the *ECMA.*[8] Negotiations on the Draft Protocol, which is intended to adapt the 1959 mutual assistance mechanisms to the needs of (organised) crime fighting in the 21st century, are still ongoing.

## Schengen

In 1985, Germany, France and the Benelux countries concluded the so-called *Schengen Agreement.* It was followed by the so-called *Schengen Implementing Convention (SIC)*[9] in 1990, containing provisions on mutual assistance in criminal matters (Articles 48-53) and intended to supplement and facilitate the implementation of the *ECMA* and of chapter II of the *1962 Benelux Treaty.* The *SIC* entered into force on 26 March 1995 for the 5 initial Schengen countries plus Spain and Portugal. Since, it has entered into force in 10 Member States[10] and was on 1 May 1999[11] even integrated in the European Union structure. In the meantime, the UK has also officially applied for participation in the Schengen *acquis.*[12] Entry into force for the Nordic countries has been scheduled for 1 October 2000.

---

aanvulling en het vergemakkelijken van de toepassing van het Europees Verdrag aangaande de wederzijdse rechtshulp in strafzaken van 20 april 1959, Wittem, *Tractatenblad van het Koninkrijk der Nederlanden,* 1979, No 143; *Vertrag vom 18. November 1983 zwischen der Republik Österreich und der Französischen Republik zu dem Europäischen Übereinkommen über die Rechtshilfe in Strafsachen vom 20. April 1959,* Paris, *Bundesgesetzblatt für die Republik Österreich,* 9 August 1985, No 331.

[5] *See* the 1974 *Nordic Convention on mutual assistance in criminal matters (Nordisk overenskomst av 26. april 1974 om gjensidig rettshjelp),* Kopenhagen, *justisdepartementets rundskriv* G-140/75 (Norway).

[6] In accordance with Article 26.3 of the *ECMA.*

[7] Strasbourg, 8 November 1990, *European Treaty Series,* No 141.

[8] *See e.g.* Council of Europe, PC-OC (98) 6, Strasbourg, 19 February 1998.

[9] *Convention d'application de l'Accord de Schengen du 14 juin 1985 entre les Gouvernements des Etats de l'Union Economique Bénélux, de la République fédérale d'Allemagne et de la République française, relatif à la suppression graduelle des contrôles aux frontières communes,* Schengen, 19 June 1990, Moniteur Belge, 15 October 1993.

[10] Not yet for the Nordic Member States (Denmark, Finland, Sweden), Ireland and the United Kingdom.

[11] Date of the entry into force of the *Amsterdam Treaty.*

[12] With the exception of border controls.

For almost five years now, the provisions of the *SIC* on mutual assistance have been applied by – and to the satisfaction of – many practitioners throughout Europe. For the sake of completeness, the changes prompted by the *SIC*, are briefly recalled hereafter. In Article 49, the scope of the traditional multilateral European mutual legal assistance treaties (the *ECMA* and the *1962 Benelux Treaty*) has been widened substantially.[13] Article 50 contains an undertaking for the Schengen countries to give each other, in accordance with the *ECMA* and the *1962 Benelux Treaty*, mutual assistance as regards infringements of their rules of law with respect to excise duty, VAT and customs duties. Article 51 *SIC* facilitated the conditions for the admissibility of letters rogatory for search or seizure. The execution of such letters rogatory may not (any more) be made dependent on the condition that the offences giving rise to the letters rogatory are extraditable offences. Article 52 has introduced the possibility to transmit procedural documents directly by post to persons who are in the territory of another Schengen country, simultaneously providing guarantees for translation of the documents concerned into a language the addressee understands. Article 53, finally, allows for the direct transmission and return of requests for assistance between the judicial authorities being locally competent for their sending and answering.

**European Union**

Since the mid-80s on, the (then) 12 Member States of the European Communities (EC) have also concluded, in the framework of the so-called European Political Co-operation (EPC), a series of five agreements/conventions with relevance for judicial co-operation in criminal matters.[14] None of them, however, pertained to mutual legal assistance. Only with the entry into force of the *Maastricht Treaty on European Union (TEU)*

---

[13] Mutual assistance is now also being afforded in proceedings brought by the administrative authorities, in proceedings for compensation in respect of unjustified prosecution or conviction, in proceedings in non-contentious matters, to communicate legal statements relating to the execution of an sentence or measure, the imposition of a fine or the payment of costs of proceedings, and in respect of measures relating to the suspension of delivery of a sentence or measure, conditional release or the postponement or suspension of execution of a sentence or measure.

[14] *Agreement on the application among the Member States of the European Communities of the Council of Europe Convention on the transfer of sentenced persons*, Brussels, 25 May 1987; *Convention between the Member States of the European Communities on double jeopardy*, Brussels, 25 May 1987; *Agreement between the Member States of the European Communities on the simplification and modernisation of methods of transmitting extradition requests*, San Sebastian, 26 May 1989; *Agreement between the Member States of the European Communities on the transfer of proceedings in criminal matters*, Rome, 6 November 1990; *Convention between the Member States of the European Communities on the enforcement of foreign criminal sentences*, Brussels, 13 November 1991. For the full text in English, *see* the web site of the European Judicial Network (http://ue.eu.int/ejn/index.htm), 4, sub a).

on 1 November 1993, judicial co-operation in criminal matters formally became a matter of common interest for the EU Member States.[15] Within the framework of the 'Third Pillar' of the EU, negotiations[16] were then started with a view to drawing up an EU convention on mutual assistance in criminal matters, additional to the *ECMA*, its *1978 Protocol*, Chapter II of the *1962 Benelux Convention* and Articles 48-53 of the *SIC*. The draft Convention[17] is expected to be adopted under the Portuguese Presidency of the EU Council, in March 2000.

Discussion on the provisions to be inserted in the convention regarding the interception of satellite telecommunications, have been a continuous stumbling-block in the negotiations of the past two years, and forms the main reason why it has been impossible to reach a final agreement on the draft convention. The Third Pillar negotiations on mutual legal assistance, however, have not only focused on the drafting of a new EU convention. They have resulted in the adoption by the JHA Council, on the basis of Article K.3.2, under b) *TEU*, of a number of joint actions, which are only binding upon the governments of the Member States but have no direct effect for the citizens. Nonetheless, they do and will continue to have an impact on the practical and logistic organisation of judicial co-operation between the Member States, in particular in the field of mutual assistance in criminal matters. The joint actions pertaining to or having relevance for mutual legal assistance are: the *1996 Joint Action concerning a framework for the exchange of liaison magistrates to improve judicial co-operation between the Member States of the EU*,[18] the *1998 Joint Actions on the creation of a European Judicial Network*[19]

---

[15] *See* Article K.1.7 *TEU*.

[16] For a profound analysis and critical evaluation of the negotiations on the new convention, since the entry into force of the Maastricht Treaty, *see* G. Vermeulen, *Wederzijdse rechtshulp in strafzaken in de Europese Unie: naar een volwaardige eigen rechtshulpruimte voor de Lid-Staten?*, Antwerpen – Apeldoorn, Maklu 1999, XXX + 632 p. Concerning the recent developments in the field of mutual assistance in criminal matters at the EU level, *see also* G. Vermeulen, 'Een verhoogde slagkracht voor de kleine rechtshulp? Over nieuwe middelen in de strijd tegen de internationale drughandel en de georganiseerde criminaliteit', in: B. de Ruyver, P. de Somere, G. Vermeulen, A. Noirfalise & Ch. Figiel (eds.), *Het Drugbeleid in België: actuele ontwikkelingen. La politique en matière de drogues en Belgique: développements actuels*, Antwerp – Apeldoorn, Maklu 1998, 119-125; G. Vermeulen, 'Nieuwe ontwikkelingen inzake internationale justitiële samenwerking in strafzaken in Europa', in: G. Vermeulen, T. Vanderbeken & B. De Ruyver (eds.), *Internationaal strafrecht. Actuele ontwikkelingen in België en Europa – Droit pénal international. Développements actuels en Belgique et en Europe*, Bruges: Vanden Broele 1998, pp. 7-36.

[17] *See Draft Council Act establishing the Convention on Mutual Assistance in Criminal Matters between the Member States of the European Union, Official Journal*, 2 September 1999, C 251, 1-11 For a more recent version of the draft, *see e.g.* Council of the European Union, 13451/99 COPEN 60, Brussels, 29 November 1999.

[18] Brussels, 22 April 1996, *Official Journal*, L 105/1-2, 27 April 1996.

[19] Brussels, 29 June 1998, *Official Journal*, L 191/4-7, 7 July 1998.

and *on good practice in mutual legal assistance in criminal matters*[20] and the *1998 Joint Action on the laundering of money, the identification, tracing, freezing, seizing and confiscation of instrumentalities and the proceeds from crime.*[21] Also of particular importance with regard to mutual legal assistance, is the *1997 Convention on Mutual Assistance and Co-operation between Customs Administrations* (the so-called *Naples II Convention*),[22] a legal instrument with the potential strength of a convention adopted on the basis of Article K.3.2, under c) *TEU*.

Below, the focus is on the draft EU convention which is still under negotiation. First, attention is given to the relationship between the future EU convention and respectively the *SIC*, the Preliminary Draft Second Additional Protocol to the *ECMA* and the *Naples II Convention*. Next, a brief overview of the major new trends and co-operation mechanisms contained in the draft is given. Finally, brief reference is made to the special meeting of the European Council for JHA, held in a Tampere (Finland) on 15-16 October 1999, and its importance for the future of mutual assistance and co-operation in criminal matters between the Member States.

## Relationship with other (Draft) 'Convention-type' Legal Instruments

The future EU convention on mutual assistance is intended to supplement the *SIC*. In that respect, it is regrettable that the draft convention does not take over the entire Schengen *acquis* with regard to mutual assistance. The scope of the *SIC* remains wider (Article 49) and the *SIC* remains more flexible as regards the execution of letters rogatory for search or seizure and assistance in fiscal matters. Moreover, the option to leave part of the *acquis* of the Articles 49-53 *SIC* on one side, is inconsistent with the integration of the full Schengen *acquis* in the European Union as from the entry into force of the *Amsterdam Treaty*. In fact, the post-Amsterdam situation is ambiguous: both the new EU convention and the *SIC* – having also acquired the status of a EU convention – supplement the traditional Council of Europe and Benelux instruments, whereas the only logical option would have been to make sure that the new EU convention would cover the entire *acquis* of the Articles 49-53 *SIC*, as such making the *SIC* superfluous in the relations between the EU Member States.[23]

The previous years have been characterised by a total absence of co-ordination between the activities of the Third Pillar Working Group on Mutual

---

[20] Brussels, 29 June 1998, *Official Journal*, L 191/1-3, 7 July 1998.

[21] Brussels, 9 December 1998, *Official Journal*, L 333/1-3, 9 December 1998.

[22] Brussels, 18 December 1997, *Official Journal*, C 24/1-22, 23 January 1998.

[23] Moreover, this is exactly the scenario behind Article 142.1 *SIC*, providing for the possibility for the Schengen countries to decide on the substitution of certain provisions of the *SIC* when these have been covered by conventions concluded between EC Member States.

Assistance, responsible for drafting the new EU convention, and the PC-OC, working on a Preliminary Draft Second Additional Protocol to the *ECMA*.

Not in the slightest way has the drafting process in the EU been influenced by the Council of Europe negotiations in the field of mutual assistance in criminal matters. For the same problems/questions (*forum regit actum*,[24] controlled deliveries, infiltration, etc.) different legal solutions and options have been adopted at EU and Council of Europe level. Moreover, the differences between the EU and the Council of Europe (draft) instruments do not reflect existing differences in the intensity of inter-state co-operation on EU or Council of Europe level. The items that the new EU convention will cover, have been decided *ad hoc*.

As such, the only hope for a consistent European legal framework is that the EU acts as an experimental garden for the Council of Europe, the PC-OC taking over the options decided upon at EU level.

It must be recalled that, according to the *Naples II Convention* the judicial authorities in charge of the criminal investigation of customs offences, may either make use of the *Naples II Convention* or revert to the regular channels of mutual legal assistance (such as the *ECMA*, the *1962 Benelux Treaty*, the *SIC* or even the new EU convention on mutual assistance in criminal matters) as a basis for requesting assistance or co-operation. Following from the fact that on some issues (controlled deliveries, infiltration, etc.), the options selected in the Naples II and the new EU convention differ, the judicial authorities are invited (incited?) in a number of cases to perform 'convention shopping': they may choose in favour of the rules/the convention that best suit(s) them. The better solution would surely have been to avoid adopting different solutions or options for the same problems/questions in two third pillar conventions.

### New Trends

Below, a brief overview is given of the major new trends and co-operation mechanisms contained in the future EU mutual legal assistance convention. The following questions pass in review: compliance with formalities and procedures indicated and deadlines set by the requesting Member State (1), interception of telecommunications (2), cross-border use of technical equipment (for observation purposes) (3), controlled deliveries (4), covert investigations (infiltration) (5), joint (multi-national) investigation teams (6), sending and service of procedural documents (7) hearing by video or telephone conference (8), temporary transfer of persons held in custody for purposes of investigation (9) and direct transmission of requests for mutual

---

[24] Principle according to which the formalities and procedures of the requesting state have to be complied with in carrying out mutual legal assistance requests, the requesting state being the forum state, *i.e.* the state where the investigations or the trial take place.

assistance (10).

## 1. Compliance with Formalities and Procedures indicated by and Deadlines set by the Requesting Member State

Compliance with *formalities and procedures* indicated by the requesting Member State is a new concept. It is the reverse of the traditional *locus regit actum* rule,[25] as contained in Article 3 of the *ECMA* and Article 24 of the *1962 Benelux Treaty*. Until now, the *locus regit actum* principle has never really been challenged, not even in more recent conventions such as the *1988 UN Convention against Illicit Traffic in Narcotic Drugs and Psychotropic Substances* or the *1990 European Convention on Laundering, Search, Seizure and Confiscation of the Proceeds of Crime*. Both conventions stick to the traditional *locus regit actum* concept; only to the extent that it does not conflict with their domestic law, there is an obligation on the requested state to execute requests in accordance with the procedures specified in the request, by the requesting state.[26]

The new EU mutual assistance convention introduces the *forum regit actum*[27] concept, thus causing a revolution in the European practice of the past 40 years. According to the new rule, the requested Member State will have to comply with formalities and procedures expressly indicated by the requesting Member State, provided that these are not contrary to the *fundamental principles of law* of the requested Member State. In other words, compatibility with the own legal system will only be marginally tested in future. In addition, the requested Member State is under duty to inform the requesting Member State when the request cannot (fully) be executed in accordance with the procedural requirements set by the requesting Member State.

The rationale of the new concept is clear. The requested procedural and investigative actions should to the maximum extent be regarded as an extra-territorial extension of the criminal investigations or procedures conducted in the *forum* state. International compatibility of evidence gathering is of growing importance, particularly in view of the control of organised crime.

The new rule is especially important to the extent that the presence of the defence counsel at the execution of letters rogatory is requested for. However, the scope of the rule is broader, not limited even to the execution of letters rogatory. The sole two forms of co-operation to which the *forum regit actum* principle will not apply, are controlled deliveries and covert investigations.

---

[25] Rule according to which the formalities and procedures of the requested state have to be complied with in carrying out mutual legal assistance requests, the requesting state being the state where the request is carried out, *i.e.* the state being the locus of the action requested for.

[26] *See* Articles 5.4, under d) and 7.12 of the 1988 *UN Convention* and Articles 9 and 12 of the *1990 European Convention*.

[27] *See* footnote 25.

Compliance by the requested Member State with *deadlines* indicated by the requesting Member State is also revolutionary.

The new EU convention does not only introduce an obligation to execute requests for assistance as soon as possible, it also urges the requested Member State to take maximal account of deadlines set by the requesting Member State. The possibility for the requesting Member State to set deadlines is counterbalanced by an obligation for the latter to explain the reason for setting a deadline. In addition, the requesting Member State has the duty to inform the requesting Member State if it is foreseeable that the deadline set for execution cannot be complied with.

The *1998 Joint Action on good practice in mutual legal assistance in criminal matters*, mentioned above, is also relevant in this context. It contains an obligation for the Member States to deposit with the General Secretariat of the Council of the EU a statement of good practice in executing requests for legal assistance. This statement must among other things include an undertaking to acknowledge, where requested to do so by the requesting Member State (*i.e.* in case of urgency or if necessary in the light of the circumstances of the case), all requests and written enquiries concerning the execution of requests, unless a substantive reply is sent quickly. Acknowledgements must provide the requesting authority with the name and contact details of the authority/person responsible for executing the request. Such a mechanism may be of great practical value. In the meantime, most of the Member States have made the required statement.[28]

## 2. Interception of (GSM and Satellite) Telecommunications

Neither the *ECMA*, nor the *1962 Benelux Treaty* nor the *SIC* provides for an explicit, adequate legal basis for co-operation in the interception of telecommunications. The only – non-binding – international legal instrument dealing with the matter is Recommendation No R(85)10 of the Committee of Ministers of the Council of Europe concerning the practical application of the *ECMA* in respect of letters rogatory for the interception of telecommunications.

Moreover, new, mobile – GSM and satellite – telecommunication systems have been developed.[29] Further, future international co-operation also needs to take account of the concept of real-time interception,[30] where the intercepted signal is directly transmitted to a law enforcement monitoring facility (in

---

[28] The text of the statements is on the web site of the European Judicial Network (http://ue.eu.int/ejn /index.htm).

[29] Both GSM and satellite systems are characterised by the fact that the sole identification datum is the SIM card (Subscriber Identity Module).

[30] Introduced for the first time in the EU context by the Council resolution of 17 January 1995 on the lawful interception of telecommunications.

another Member State).

As already mentioned above, discussions on the provisions to be inserted in the new EU convention on the interception of satellite telecommunications have been the main stumbling-block in the negotiations during the past year.

For the sake of clarity, it should be noted that networks for personal satellite communications make use of new types of satellites, *i.e.* satellites in a low or medium earth orbit[31] (so-called LEO or MEO satellites), which can be reached directly with a portable handset. Next to satellites, the systems concerned consist of a network of ground stations, acting as a gateway between the satellite constellation and the regular earth infrastructure for (mobile or fixed) telecommunication. Ground stations are the places where the signal transferred via the satellite (network) re-enters the earth infrastructure. *Iridium, e.g.*, the satellite-based system which the first became operational, on 1 November 1998,[32] has *one* ground station (in Italy) for an area covering over 40 countries (among which all EU Member States). Most likely, the situation will not be much different for other systems[33] that will become operational (in future). As signals routed via satellite systems cannot be intercepted while being transferred from the portable handset to the satellite and the best place therefore to intercept them is the local ground station, the relevant ground station will be an important intermediary in all interception scenarios.

During the EU negotiations of the past years, the leading principle has been that the Member State hosting the relevant ground station, must be asked for its technical assistance in the interception of the telecommunication of any target person on the EU territory (and that the Member State where the target can be found, must be asked for its permission or is given the right to impose conditions to the interception or to prohibit the use of data gathered via interception while the target was on its territory). In July 1998 however, *Iridium* has proposed an alternative approach, allowing for the judicial authorities in the Member States to ask the *local* service provider for help in the interception of a target's telecommunication, the service providers having remote control over the (in the case of *Iridium*: Italian) ground station and thus capable of carrying out interception themselves.

General agreement was reached within the JHA Council that the remote approach is a convenient option. However, as the remote or service provider approach would only apply in the scenario where the target whose communication is to be intercepted, can be found in the territory of the investigating Member State, it does not offer a complete solution for the

---

[31] This is contrary to geostationary satellites (so-called GEO satellites), which are in a high earth orbit and thus require high capacity transmitting equipment. GEOs are traditionally being used for military, meteo or broadcasting activities and for certain telecommunication applications, such as telecommunication from boats or plains or global positioning systems.

[32] The pre-launch of the system was already on 23 September 1998.

[33] Other (future) systems using LEO satellites, are Globalstar, Orbcomm, TeledeSIC, M-Star, Celestri and Skybridge. Systems that (will) use MEO satellites, are *e.g.* Odyssey and ICO.

interception needs in a European context. Other scenarios, which apparently could not be covered by the remote approach, include those where the target is located in another Member State and the relevant ground station is also in that or still in another Member State, or in the investigating Member State itself. Also the scenario where the target is in another Member State and the relevant ground station is hosted by a non-Member State would not be covered by the remote approach. A complete solution would moreover need to take account of even more complex scenarios, where the target moves/has moved from the intercepting (Member) state to a(nother) Member State, which is neither the requesting, nor the intercepting Member State.

The main obstacle in reaching a final agreement on provisions concerning the interception of telecommunications in the new EU convention on mutual assistance, has been the UK's unwillingness to accept that the Member State on whose territory a target is intercepted should be informed thereof, in the case where the the interceptions concerned has been *authorised by secret services*. At this stage of the negotiations however, it seems that the (other) Member States will accept that the new rules on interception will only apply to interception orders authorised in the course of criminal investigations which present the following characteristics: "an investigation *following* the commission of a specific criminal offence, including attempts in so far as they are criminalised under national law, in order to identify and arrest, charge, prosecute or deliver judgement on those responsible". Thus, proactive or administrative interceptions authorised by secret services would indeed not be subject to the obligation to inform the Member State on whose territory the target is or has been intercepted about the interception concerned.[34]

### 3. Cross-border Use of Technical Equipment (for Observation Purposes)

Further it has been stated that in a Protocol to the new EU convention on mutual assistance provision would probably be made for the cross-border use of electronic equipment on the territory of another Member State. If this were to be the case indeed, the existing juridical vacuum/vagueness with regard to cross-border electronic surveillance would come to an end. Also, it would be clear that co-operation in this field is actually a prerogative of the authorities in charge of criminal investigations – in most Member States: the judicial authorities – and that electronic surveillance on the territory of another

---

[34] However, it would be stated in the explanatory report to the convention – as a compromise – that the obligation contained to inform another Member State in certain situations of interceptions relates to "what in most Member States would fall under the concept of criminal investigations and that this cannot be interpreted *a contrario* so as to permit interception in other situations which are not covered [read: interceptions ordered by secret services], and that those situations are covered by the general principles of international law, which remain unaffected by the convention" (Council of the European Union, 13451/99 COPEN 60, Brussels, 29 November 1999, 5).

Member State cannot be decided at police level.

## 4. Controlled Deliveries

The new EU convention contains an undertaking for the Member States to ensure that, at the request of another Member State, controlled deliveries may be permitted on their territory.

Unlike in the *1988 UN Convention* (Article 11) and the *SIC* (Article 73), the technique may also be applied in combating other forms of crime than illicit traffic in narcotic drugs and psychotropic substances. It may be applied in the framework of criminal investigations into any extraditable offences.[35]

The decision to carry out controlled deliveries is taken by the competent authorities of the requested Member State. Also the competence to act and to direct the operations lies with these authorities. By way of exception to the new *forum regit actum* rule *(supra)*, the law and procedures of the requested Member State are applicable.

## 5. Covert Investigations (Infiltration)

Until now, international co-operation in the field of covert investigations has usually been performed at police level, in a juridical vacuum, facilitated by *e.g.* the International Working Group on Undercover Policing (IWG). The IWG, in which police or secret services of 13 European states take part,[36] facilitates the continuation of covert investigations on the territory of other states, as well as the placing of undercover agents at each other's disposal.[37]

The new EU convention creates an international legal basis in the context of judicial co-operation in criminal matters for the operation of investigations into crime by officers acting under covert or false identity. Implicitly, the convention allows for three different co-operation scenarios: the continuation of an infiltration operation on the territory of another Member State, the 'lending' of a foreign undercover agent for the purpose of an infiltration operation on its own territory, and the operation of an infiltration operation in the requested Member State by (an) undercover agent(s) of that Member State,

---

[35] Note that it is unclear which is the point of reference for deciding whether an offence is extraditable (the *1996 EU convention* relating to extradition, the multilateral treaty applying in the bilateral relation between the Member States concerned, the national law of the requested Member State).

[36] *See also* G. Vermeulen, 'A European Judicial Network linked to Europol? In Search of a Model for Structuring Trans-National Criminal Investigations in the EU', *Maastricht Journal of European and Comparative Law* 1997, nr. 4, 348-349; G. Vermeulen, 'A Judicial Counterpart for Europol: Should the European Union Establish a Network of Prosecuting and Investigating Officials?', *UCLA Journal of International Law and Foreign Affairs* 1997-98, nr. 2, 228-229.

[37] The IWG maintains a directory listing the special skills of the undercover agents of its member agencies.

on the request of the requesting Member State.

A decision on the request is taken by the competent authorities of the requested Member State with due regard to its national law and procedures. As in the case of controlled deliveries, the new *forum regit actum* rule *(supra)* does not apply: the relevant law and procedures of the Member State where the action takes place must be observed. The duration, the detailed conditions, the preparation, the supervision and the security of the infiltration operations are agreed between both Member States concerned.

## 6. Joint (Multi-national) Investigation Teams

The new EU convention will also allow for the setting up of joint (multi-national) investigation teams, composed of judicial, police and/or customs officers or even of officials of international organisations/bodies (*e.g.* Europol). Such teams may be set up for a specific purpose and for a limited period, where difficult and demanding investigations having links with other Member States are required or where co-ordinated, concerted action between the Member States concerned is necessary. The teams will be headed and led by an official from the Member State where the team is operating and seconded team members operating in another Member State will be bound by the law of that Member State. In other words: the traditional *locus regit actum* rule would still apply. Apart from being allowed to be present when investigative measures are taken, seconded team members may moreover be entrusted with the task of certain investigative measures, and team members may request their own authorities to take the necessary investigative measures in their own Member States as if they would be taken in a domestic investigation. Also, information lawfully obtained by seconded team members may be used in their own Member State.

## 7. Sending and Service of Procedural Documents

Further, the new EU convention also reinforces and refines the *acquis* of Article 52 *SIC*. It introduces an *obligation* – instead of a *possibility* – to send procedural documents intended for persons on the territory of another Member State directly by post. Only in a limited number of cases, documents may still be sent via the traditional channels (*i.e.* between judicial authorities, according to Article 7 of the *ECMA*).

A clear step forward is also that the *Schengen Agreement* guarantees as regards translation of (the important passages of) procedural documents are extended to the sending and service of documents *via* the traditional channels. Moreover, all procedural documents (either sent directly by post or *via* the traditional channels) must be accompanied by a report stating that the addressee may obtain information from the Member State where the document was issued regarding his/her rights and obligations concerning the document he/she received (*e.g.* if there is an obligation to appear).

Finally, the Articles 8, 9 and 12 of the *ECMA* and the Articles 32, 34 and 35 of the *1962 Benelux Treaty* are applicable (by analogy).

## 8. Hearing by Video or Telephone Conference

The *1962 Benelux Treaty* is the only multilateral legal assistance treaty in Europe containing an obligation for persons to appear in the requesting state, with a view to being heard there as a witness or expert. In many cases therefore, hearing by video or telephone conference could be an alternative solution. As the technique of video conferencing allows for hearing persons on a distance, hearing by videoconference is also important with a view to protecting crown witnesses or so-called *pentiti*.

The new EU convention contains a consistent set of rules on hearing by means of video or telephone conference. According to the convention, hearing by video or telephone conference is a combination of a regular request for assistance (by the requested Member State) and a direct exercise of jurisdiction (by the requesting Member State). On the one hand, the *requested* Member State is responsible for summoning the person to be heard, for realising the real time link technically, for making sure that its fundamental procedural guarantees are observed and for exercising a number of controls at the place of the hearing. On the other hand, the hearing is conducted by or under the direction of a judicial authority of the *requesting* Member State.

The convention primarily allows for the hearing of witnesses and experts, either in the investigation or the trial stage. As for hearing by videoconference, the technique could also apply to accused persons – *i.e.* in the trial stage. On this point, however, the Member States have been given an opting out possibility. In any case, the consent of the accused is necessary. Worth mentioning also is that the necessary technical means for videoconferencing may be made available by the requesting Member State.

In the course of either types of hearing, the person to be heard may claim the right not to testify which would accrue to him/her under the law of either the requested or the requesting Member State, so that there a loss of rights can be avoided. Measures extending to the protection of the person heard (*e.g.* voice or image deformation) may be agreed. Finally, the requested Member State must make sure that perjury and unlawful refusal to testify can be punished according to its national law.

## 9. Temporary Transfer of Persons held in Custody to the Requested Member State

The *ECMA* (Article 11) and the *1962 Benelux Treaty* (Article 33) already provide for a possible temporary transfer of detained persons to the *requesting* state. In imitation of a number of bilateral mutual legal assistance treaties,[38] additional to the *ECMA*, the new EU convention allows for the temporary transfer of persons held in custody to the *requested* Member State also.

Transfer will be possible in the framework of an investigation requested for, for which the presence of a person held in custody on the territory of the requesting Member State is required (*e.g.* confrontation, reconstruction, recognition of places). However, the Member States may declare that the transfer of a detained person to their territory will be dependent on the consent of the person concerned.

## 10. Direct Transmission of Requests for Mutual Assistance

Finally, the new EU convention reinforces the *acquis* of Article 53 *SIC*. Instead of a mere *possibility*, it introduces an *obligation* to make requests for mutual assistance as well as spontaneous communications directly between the judicial authorities with territorial competence for their service and execution, and to return them through the same channels. It also extends the possibility contained in Article 53.5 *SIC* to directly transmit information laid with a view to proceedings in respect of infringements of the legislation on driving and rest time, to *any* offences.

The convention also allows for direct transmission where the competent authority is a judicial or central authority in one Member State and (in respect of requests concerning controlled deliveries or covert investigations) a *police or customs* authority, or (in respect of administrative offences) an *administrative* authority in the other Member State. Clearly, the goal has been to maximise flexibility in the transmission of requests.

There is one important possible restriction though. Member States may declare that its judicial authorities do not (in general) have authority to execute requests received directly. In the absence of such a declaration, however, the local judicial authorities will have the autonomy to *execute* requests received directly, and not only to *receive* them.[39] Further, the obligation of direct transmission is also without prejudice to the possibility of requests being sent or returned *in specific cases* between central authorities or between a central authority in one Member State and a judicial authority in another Member State. In a limited number of cases, finally, documents will have to be sent *via* the central authorities (a/o requests for temporary transfer of persons held in

---

[38] The *acquis* of Article 25*bis* of the *1962 Benelux Treaty* has (unfortunately) been overlooked.

[39] A number of Schengen countries interpret Article 53.1 *SIC* in this way.

custody).

## Tampere European Council: even Newer Trends!

Two decisions taken by the heads of state and government of the EU at the special meeting of the European Council, held in Tampere (Finland) on 15-16 October 1999, will potentially have an important impact on future mutual assistance and co-operation in criminal matters between the Member States of the EU.

Among other things, the European leaders recognised the need for enhanced *mutual recognition*, not only of judgements – in the trial stage – but also of *judicial decisions taken in the investigation stage*. It can be assumed that this principle will quite radically change traditional co-operation in the field of mutual assistance, as this would mean that judicial decisions or orders (*e.g.* to hear witnesses abroad, to carry out a house serach or to seize evidence abroad, to intercept the telecommunication of a target in the territory of another Member State) would sort of have a direct effect in the Member State where they need to be carried out, the latter not being allowed to invoke traditional grounds for refusal or to check whether the actions concerned would be allowed according to its own law, in a domestic case.

According to the decision of the Tampere European Council, an action plan for implementation of the mutual recognition principle is to be adopted in December 2000 already.

At the Tampere European Council, it was also decided that a new international body – Eurojust – should be set up, composed of national prosecutors, magistrates or police officers of equivalent competence, detached from each Member State according to its legal system. Eurojust will have to work closely together with the European Judicial Network, on the basis of crime analyses carried out at Europol level. The formal recognition of the heads of state and government that there is a need to establish a judicial counterpart for Europol, is to be seen as once another step[40] in the establishment of a 'genuine European legal area' in which the judicial authorities – in most Member States traditionally in charge of criminal investigations – will be enabled to control and guide European police co-operation with a view to combating (organised) crime.

According to the Tampere conclusions, a legal instrument on Eurojust must be adopted by the end of 2001, under Belgian Presidency of the EU Council.

---

[40] Also for co-operation with regard to controlled deliveries, covert investigations and the cross-border use of technical equipment (for observation purposes) the traditional – national – prerogatives of the judicial authorities were formally recognised *(supra)*.

# Telling and Detecting Lies as a Function of Raising the Stakes[1]

*A. Vrij*

A meta-analysis including more than 40 deception studies has provided evidence that deceiving others is correlated with more speech disturbances, a higher pitched voice, slower speech, longer pauses, and a decrease in illustrators, and hand/finger, foot and leg movements.[2]

By way of explaining these findings, three main theoretical frameworks are usually offered: The emotional framework, the cognitive framework, and the attempted control framework.[3] Whilst all three frameworks emphasise different aspects of deception, they are not mutually exclusive and all three can occur simultaneously in one lie.

The increase in pitch of voice and speech disturbances can be explained by the emotional framework. This framework proposes that deception causes physiological reactions, such as high blood pressure, increased heart rate, and an increased respiration rate. The physiological reaction is the consequence of arousal that is associated with deception. The arousal is the result of emotions experienced during deception. Deception may result in three different types of emotion: guilt, fear or excitement.[4] Liars may feel guilty, as a result of being aware of doing things which they are not allowed to do; or they may be afraid of getting caught. Finally, they may feel excited by having the opportunity of fooling someone.

An increase in speech disturbances can also be explained by the cognitive framework. This framework further provides an explanation for an increase in pauses, a slower speech and a decrease in hand, leg and foot movements. The cognitive framework emphasises that deception may be a cognitively complex task. It is sometimes more difficult to fabricate a plausible and convincing lie that is consistent with everything the observer knows or might find out than it is to tell the truth. Evidence has demonstrated that people engaging in cognitively complex tasks make more speech disturbances, speak more slowly and wait longer before giving an answer.[5] They also make fewer hand and arm movements.[6] It is suggested that the decrease in hand and arm movements is

---

[1] This study was sponsored by the Leverhulme Trust.
[2] Vrij (2000).
[3] Burgoon, Kelly, Newton & Keely-Dyreson (1989); DePaulo (1988, 1992); DePaulo & Kirkendol (1989); DePaulo, Stone & Lassiter (1985a); Ekman (1989, 1992); Ekman & Friesen (1972); Goldman-Eisler (1968); Knapp, Hart & Dennis (1974); Köhnken (1989, 1990); Riggio & Friedman (1983); Vrij (1998); Zuckerman, DePaulo & Rosenthal (1981).
[4] Ekman (1992).
[5] Goldman-Eisler (1968).
[6] Ekman & Friesen (1972).

based on the fact that a greater cognitive load results in a neglect of body language, reducing overall animation.[7]

A decrease in movements can also be explained by the attempted control framework. This framework emphasises that liars tend to control their behaviour, both in order to avoid giving possible nonverbal indicators of their deception and to enhance the credibility of the impression they make on others. Paradoxically, deceivers' very attempts to control their behaviour serve as cues to deception. The controlled behaviour will appear as planned, rehearsed, and lacking in spontaneity. Therefore, by believing that unnecessary non-functional movements will make them appear suspicious,[8] liars will move very deliberately and tend to avoid movements which are not strictly essential. This results in an unusual degree of rigidity and inhibition. Although both the attempted control and the cognitive load framework predict a decrease in movements during deception, the explanations are different. According to the attempted control framework a decrease in movements is caused by an overcontrol of movements. The cognitive load framework on the other hand, does not contend that liars try to control their behaviour, rather the decrease in movements is held to be the result of a neglect of body language.

Perhaps the most striking finding in previous research is that liars don't seem to show behavioural cues of nervousness such as gaze aversion and fidgeting. This is striking, because there is a strong and widespread belief amongst people that liars do show these behaviours.[9] These beliefs are not only held by lay people, but also by professional lie catchers, such as police detectives.[10]

One possible reason why liars in experimental studies don't show clear patterns of nervous behaviour[11] is that they are simply not nervous enough during these experiments. In order to raise the stakes, lying is often introduced as an important skill, and successful liars are promised money or other rewards. Although this results in raising the stakes to some extent, probably comparable to the stakes in most real-life situations,[12] such studies do not tell us much about lying in high-stake situations, such as police interviews.[13] It may be the case that behavioural cues to deceit differ in low- and high-stake situations, that is, it may be the case that liars will show the nervous behaviours

---

[7] Ekman & Friesen (1972).

[8] Vrij & Semin (1996).

[9] *See* DePaulo (1992), DePaulo *et al.* (1985a); Vrij (1991, 2000); Zuckerman & Driver (1985) and Zuckerman *et al.* (1981) for reviews concerning people's beliefs about behavioural cues to deception.

[10] Vrij & Semin (1996).

[11] When we mention nervous behavior we refer to behavior such as gaze aversion, fidgeting, stuttering and so on, and not to micro facial expressions of emotions (Ekman, 1992). We will refer to this in the discussion.

[12] DePaulo, Kashy, Kirkendol, Wyer & Epstein (1996).

[13] Ekman (1992); Frank & Ekman (1997); Vrij, Akehurst & Morris (1997); Vrij & Semin (1996); Vrij, Semin & Bull (1996).

which observers expect them to show when the stakes are high, but not when the stakes are low. In order to investigate this, observation of liars in realistic high-stake situations is necessary. Vrij & Mann (in press) conducted such a study. They analysed the behaviour of a man while he was interviewed by the police about a murder (the interviews were videotaped which enabled us to analyse the man's behaviour afterwards). Because of the nature of his crime, the murderer was aware that his conviction would most likely result in a sentence of life imprisonment. Although the man initially denied knowing and killing the victim, substantial evidence (for instance, a hair of the victim was found in the man's car) obtained by the police showed that he was lying. On the basis of this substantial evidence, the man confessed to killing the victim and was later convicted of murder.

Perhaps surprisingly, the behaviour shown by the murderer during his high stake lie corresponds with the behaviour of liars in laboratory experiments. That is, his deception was associated with an increase in speech disturbances, a slower speech, more pauses, and a decrease in illustrators and hand/finger movements. This case study suggests that increased stakes in deception situations do not necessarily result in an increase in nervous behaviours such as gaze aversion and fidgeting. However, in Vrij & Mann's (in press) study the behaviour of just one man was analysed. We cannot rule out that he was exceptional and that many people, as police officers believe, do show gaze aversion and an increase in movements – such as fidgeting – in high stake lies. *Study 1* was carried out to investigate this. Nursing students were interviewed while lying or telling the truth in 'low stake' and 'high stake' situations (see the Method for further details). The interviews were videotaped and the nurses' behaviour was scored afterwards. Of particular interest was whether the students would show more gaze aversion and more fidgeting in the high stake lie situation compared to the low stake lie situation.

In a series of experiments in which the stakes were manipulated, DePaulo and her colleagues found that high stake lies were easier to detect than low stake lies.[14] These findings suggest that there is a difference in liars' demeanour in low and high stake situations, although not necessarily differences in gaze aversion or fidgeting. In *Study 2*, college students were shown a sample of the videotaped interviews with the nursing students (derived from *Study 1*) and were asked after each interview whether the nurse was lying or not. Based upon previous research we did not expect clear behavioural differences between the liars involved in low and high stake lies in *Study 1*, but we did expect the observers in *Study 2* to be better at detecting high stake lies than low stake lies.

---

[14] DePaulo, Kirkendol, Tang & O'Brien (1988); DePaulo, Lanier & Davis (1983); DePaulo, LeMay & Epstein (1991); DePaulo, Stone & Lassiter (1985b); Lane & DePaulo (1999).

## *Study 1* – Method

A total of 58 nursing students participated, 8 males and 50 females. Their average age was $M = 24.57$ years ($SD = 6.2$ years).

Nursing students were recruited at the University of Portsmouth nursing school. They were asked to participate in a study about 'telling lies'. Each student participated individually and received £5 for their participation. The participants were told that they would see a video and that they would be interviewed twice about this video. In one interview they had to recall what they had seen and in the other interview they had to lie. The order in which the truthful and deceptive interviews took place was counterbalanced. Only the first interviews (deceptive for some participants and truthful for others) were analysed, creating a between-subjects design. We introduced the study to the participants as a within-subjects design because we wanted all participants to lie in one condition. We did this for motivation purposes: In this case nobody could think that they were allocated to a 'control condition'. The nurses were shown a video of 118 seconds in length. This videotaped event featured a colour presentation of the theft of a bag from a patient by a visitor. In the video, a woman enters a hospital and walks to the first floor. While walking down the corridor, she notices a patient lying in bed with a handbag next to her. The visitor enters her room, looks at the patient's name plate and pretends that she knows the patient. She then takes the bag and starts to walk out of the room. The patient notices the theft and asks the visitor to return the handbag. A nurse comes in and asks what is going on. The patient tells the nurse that she does not know the visitor and that the visitor is trying to steal her bag. The visitor tells the nurse that she is the patient's neighbour and that the patient is confused. The visitor then leaves the room. The video finishes with the visitor smiling as she opens the patient's purse and notices money in it.

After watching the video, participants in the *truthful condition* ($N = 28$) were asked the following three general and open-ended questions: What did the nurse do? What did the patient do? And what did the visitor do? They were asked to answer all questions truthfully. Participants in the *deception condition* ($N = 30$) were asked to lie while answering the same three questions. In order to make the task not too difficult for the participants they were informed about two of the three questions that would be asked before the interview started and they were given time to think about their answers. The questions about which the participants were prewarned were counterbalanced. Analyses showed that this manipulation had no effect on either the verbal or nonverbal behaviour displayed by the participants and will therefore be disregarded in this article. Participants in the *low stakes situation* ($N = 28$) were given the following information prior to the interview: "Before you start, I should assure you that this is a very easy task, because it is very difficult for other people to tell when you are lying, so relax." Participants in the *high stakes situation* ($N = 30$) were told prior to the interview that "this study is examining your ability to lie.

Research has shown that nursing ability is related to ability to lie effectively. So try to be as convincing as possible."[15] "The videocamera in this room is focused on you and is linked with a TV-screen which is located in the room next to us. In that room, four raters will be watching your interview on a TV screen and will be coding you as to how well you lie." The participants were then brought to the adjacent room where the four raters were sitting opposite the TV screen on which the empty chair in the interview room was visible. The interviewer brought the participants back to the interview room and started the interview. All interviews were videotaped and audiotaped and were transcribed verbatim from the audiotapes (the transcripts included the stutters made by the participants).

Two observers coded the behaviour of the participants independently, and Pearson's correlations were conducted between the two sets of data from the two coders to detect any differences in judgement. The observers were not informed as to whether the participants were lying or telling the truth and had not seen the stimulus video. They employed a coding system used by us in previous studies.[16] The following ten behaviours were coded (the 'ah' and 'non-ah' speech disturbances were scored on the basis of a typed verbatim text):

-   gaze aversion: number of seconds in which the participant looked away from the interviewer (two coders, $r = .96, p < .01$);
-   smiling: frequency of smiles and laughs (two coders, $r = .98, p < .01$);
-   illustrators: frequency of arm and hand movements which were designed to modify and/or supplement what was being said verbally[17] (two coders, $r = .97, p < .01$);
-   adaptors: frequency of scratching the head, wrists, etc. (rubbing one's hands together was not coded as adaptors but as hand and finger movements)(two coders, $r = .98, p < .01$);
-   frequency of hand and finger movements: movements of the hands or fingers without moving the arms (two coders, $r = .98, p < .01$);
-   frequency of foot and leg movements: movements of feet or legs. Simultaneous movements of feet and legs were scored as one movement (two coders, $r = .94, p < .01$);
-   ah disturbances: frequency of saying 'ah' or 'mm' between words (one coder);
-   non-ah disturbances: frequency of word and/or sentence repetition, sentence change, sentence incompletion, and slips of the tongue (two coders, $r = .91, p < .01$);

---

[15] Previous research has indicated that this information does increase participants' motivation to perform well. DePaulo, Kirkendol, Tang & O'Brien (1988); DePaulo, Lanier & Davis (1983).
[16] Akehurst & Vrij (1999); Vrij (1991, 1995); Vrij, Semin & Bull (1996); Vrij, Akehurst & Morris (1997).
[17] Ekman & Friesen (1969).

- latency period: period of time between the question being asked and the answer being given (one coder);
- speech rate: length of interview divided by the number of words (counted with a software computer package)(one coder).

The Pearson's correlations show evidence of a strong consistency between the two coders. Thus, the behavioural scores were based on the average scores of the two coders and are presented in *Table 1*. The reported duration and frequencies of all categories of nonverbal behaviour were corrected for the length of the interviews or for the number of spoken words. Patterns listed from gaze aversion down to foot and leg movements were calculated on a per minute basis. Patterns for ah and non-ah disturbances were calculated per 100 words. Latency period scores represent the average latency period per question.

### *Study 1* – Results

Data were analysed with a MANOVA following a 2 (Deception: yes or no) X 2 (Stakes: high or low) X 2 (Gender) factorial design.[18] The analysis revealed a marginal significant effect for Deception, $F(10, 42) = 1.84$, $p = .08$. Of particular interest is the 'Stakes by Deception' interaction effect which was not significant, $F(10, 42) = 1.11$, *ns*. Neither of the other three interaction effects nor the 'Stakes' main effect were significant. Mean scores and univariate tests regarding the 'Deception' main effect are provided in *Table 1*. The table shows that compared to truth tellers liars showed more gaze aversion, fewer illustrators, and fewer hand and finger movements.

---

[18] Sex of participant was included as a factor in the design to increase the precision of the error term. The results of this factor are not of actual relevance for this article and will therefore not be reported in the main text. The MANOVA showed a main effect for Gender. Univariate tests showed that males showed more gaze aversion and made more hand and finger movements than females.

*Table 1: Nonverbal Behaviour as a Function of Deception*

| Behaviour | Condition | | | | |
|---|---|---|---|---|---|
| | truth | | lie | | $F(1, 55)$ |
| | m | (sd) | m | (sd) | |
| gaze aversion | 2.78 | (5.2) | 3.30 | (6.4) | 6.15** |
| smiles | .62 | (1.0) | .84 | (1.8) | .13 |
| illustrators | 5.01 | (6.8) | 2.50 | (4.2) | 3.15* |
| adaptors | 2.27 | (5.9) | .83 | (3.0) | .29 |
| hand/finger movements | 11.99 | (14.5) | 7.34 | (8.3) | 3.37* |
| foot/leg movements | 11.60 | (9.5) | 11.90 | (17.3) | 1.36 |
| ah speech disturbances | 4.00 | (4.2) | 4.20 | (3.2) | .27 |
| non-ah speech disturbances | 1.20 | (1.4) | 1.25 | (1.6) | .47 |
| latency period | 1.98 | (1.3) | 2.91 | (2.4) | .65 |
| speech rate | 79.51 | (18.2) | 88.50 | (21.5) | 2.99 |

** $p < .01$    * $p < .05$    ' $p < .10$

## Study 2 – Method

A total of 61 university students participated in this experiment, 36 males and 25 females. Their average age was 21 years ($SD = 2.1$ years).

For the present study, a videotape was compiled with fragments of 30 different interviews randomly selected from *Study 1* and consisted of ten truths, ten low stake lies and ten high stake lies. The truths, low stake lies and high stake lies were put onto the videotape in a random order. A MANOVA was carried out in which the behaviours shown in the 30 selected interviews were compared with the behaviours shown in the 28 not selected interviews. This MANOVA did not reveal a significant effect, indicating that the 30 interviews selected for *Study 2* were a representative sample of *Study 1*.

Students visiting the Students' Union at the University of Portsmouth were asked to participate in a short study testing the ability to detect lies. Only a small minority of students who were approached (less than 10%) refused to participate. Participants were brought to a room in the Students' Union and exposed to the videotape of 30 fragments. They were given the following instructions: "You will see 30 videoclips of 30 different people who are either lying or telling the truth about a film they just saw. Please indicate after each clip whether or not the person is lying." In order to do this the participants were given a questionnaire which clearly showed headings (fragment 1, fragment 2, fragment 3, etc.) and under each heading the question: "Is this person lying? (yes or no)". Accuracy rates (the percentage of correct answers) for truths, low stake lies and high stake lies were calculated.

## *Study 2* – Results

The accuracy rates for truths, low stake lies and high stake lies are depicted in *Table 2*.

*Table 2: Accuracy and Confidence Scores as a Function of Stakes*

|  | Condition | | | |
|---|---|---|---|---|
|  | truth | low | high | $F(2,120)$ |
| accuracy | $.57^b$ | $.48^a$ | $.58^b$ | $3.25*$ |

*Note*: Only means with a different superscript differ significantly from each other (p < .05)
* p < .05          ** p < .01

*Table 2* reveals that the observers were better at detecting high stake lies (58%) than low stake lies (48%), $F(1, 60) = 4.24$, $p < .05$, which supports the hypothesis. Comparing the accuracy rates for detecting lies with the accuracy rate for detecting truths (57%), it can be seen that observers were relatively poor at detecting low stake lies (rather than particularly good at detecting high stake lies).

## Discussion

*Study 1* investigated differences between truth telling and lying in low and high stake situations. Several differences between liars and truth tellers emerged. However, of particular interest for the present study was that the Stakes manipulation did not yield any significant effect. The combination of presence of a Deception main effect and absence of a 'Stakes' X 'Deception' interaction effect implies that similar differences emerged between liars and truth tellers in the low stake situation as in the high stake situation. This is perhaps surprising given the clear difference between the low and high stake situation. In the low stake situation the participants were assured that they would face an easy task and that they could relax. In the high stake situation they were told that being a good liar might be a predictor for their future career. Additionally, they were observed by four other people and they were aware of this. These clearly different circumstances, however, did not result in any noticeable differences in behaviour. In other words, the study does not support the widespread belief that an increase in stakes is associated with an increase in gaze aversion and fidgeting. However, the results of *Study 2* indicate that there *were* differences between the liars in high and low stake situations, as the high stake lies were easier to detect than the low stake lies. The question arises as to which differences did emerge between low and high stake liars which were apparently spotted by the observers. We have to speculate about this as our data do not provide an answer.

First, it might be that the high stake liars showed micro facial expressions of emotions, which Ekman (1992) has found to correlate with high stake lies. We do not believe this is a plausible option. Spotting micro facial expressions would have required very high quality close-up video footage of the face (as they usually last only a fraction of a second), which was not available to the observers. Apart from the quality of the videotape, our observers were untrained lie detectors (college students) which makes it doubtful whether they would have paid attention to these cues and would have spotted these cues if the quality of the videotape would have enable them to do so.

A second option is that the liars engaged in high stake lies in *Study 1* were prone to the so-called motivational impairment effect: the tendency of highly motivated liars to show behaviour which appears rigid, rehearsed and planned.[19] It might have been that the high stake liars sat more still than the low lie stakes liars (moved their heads and trunks less) and that observers have noticed this. Unfortunately, our data do not allow us to check this assumption as we did not score trunk and head movements. However, we did score limb movements, and the motivational impairment effect predicts that high motivated liars would show fewer limb movements than low motivated liars. We found no support for this assumption.

A third option is that the speech content of the high and low stake liars differed from each other. We doubt whether this was the case. First, there is no theoretical reason why speech content would differ in both conditions. Second, although not reported here, the speech content of the participants has been analysed utilising Criteria-Based Content Analysis, a sophisticated and detailed method to assess the veracity of statements.[20] CBCA scores between high and low stake liars did not differ significantly from each other, neither did any of the individual CBCA-criteria.

In summary, we found support for the widespread belief that high stake lies are easier to detect than low stake lies, however, this is not the result of liars in high stake situations showing more gaze aversion or more fidgeting.

### References

**Akehurst, L. & Vrij, A.** (1999), 'Creating suspects during police interviews', in: *Journal of Applied Social Psychology* 29, 192-210.
**Burgoon, J.K., Kelly, D.L., Newton, D.A. & Keely-Dyreson, M.P.** (1989), 'The nature of arousal and nonverbal indices', in: *Human Communication Research* 16, 217-255.
**DePaulo, B.M.** (1988), 'Nonverbal aspects of deception', in: *Journal of Nonverbal Behaviour* 12, 153-162.
**DePaulo, B.M.** (1992), 'Nonverbal behaviour and self-presentation', in: *Psychological Bulletin* 111, 233-243.

---

[19] DePaulo & Kirkendol (1989); DePaulo, Kirkendol, Tang & O'Brien (1988); DePaulo, Lanier & Davis (1983).
[20] *See* Vrij (2000) and Vrij & Akehurst (1998) for an overview of the CBCA method and CBCA research.

**DePaulo, B.M., Kashy, D.A., Kirkendol, S.E., Wyer, M.M. & Epstein, J.A.** (1996), 'Lying in everyday life', in: *Journal of Personality and Social Psychology* 70, 979-995.

**DePaulo, B.M. & Kirkendol, S.E.** (1989), 'The motivational impairment effect in the communication of deception', in: J.C. Yuille (ed.), *Credibility assessment*, Dordrecht: Kluwer Academic Press, pp. 51-70.

**DePaulo, B.M., Kirkendol, S.E., Tang, J. & O'Brien, T.P.** (1988), 'The motivational impairment effect in the communication of deception: Replications and extensions', in: *Journal of Nonverbal Behaviour* 12, 177-201.

**DePaulo, B.M., Lanier, K. & Davis, T.** (1983), 'Detecting the deceit of the motivated liar', in: *Journal of Personality and Social Psychology* 45, 1096-1103.

**DePaulo, B.M., LeMay, C.S. & Epstein, J.A.** (1991), 'Effects of importance of success and expectations for success on effectiveness at deceiving', in: *Personality and Social Psychology Bulletin* 17, 14-24.

**DePaulo, B.M., Stone, J.L. & Lassiter, G.D.** (1985a), 'Deceiving and detecting deceit', in: B.R. Schenkler (ed.), *The self and social life*, New York: McGraw-Hill, pp. 323-370.

**DePaulo, B.M., Stone, J.I. & Lassiter, G.D.** (1985b), 'Telling ingratiating lies: Effects of target sex and target attractiveness on verbal and nonverbal deceptive success', in: *Journal of Personality and Social Psychology* 48, 1191-2103.

**Ekman, P.** (1989), 'Why lies fall and what behaviours betray a lie', in: J.C. Yuille (ed.), *Credibility Assessment*, Dordrecht: Kluwer Academic Publishers, pp. 71-82.

**Ekman, P.** (1992), *Telling lies*, New York: W.W. Norton.

**Ekman, P. & Friesen, W.V.** (1969), 'The repertoire of nonverbal behaviour: Categories, origins, usage, and coding', in: *Semiotica* 1, 49-98.

**Ekman, P. & Friesen, W.V.** (1972), 'Hand movements', in: *Journal of Communication* 22, 353-374.

**Frank, M.G. & Ekman, P.** (1997), 'The ability to detect deceit generalizes across different types of high-stake lies', in: *Journal of Personality and Social Psychology* 72, 1429-1439.

**Goldman-Eisler, F.** (1968). *Psycholinguistics: experiments in spontaneous speech*, New York: Doubleday.

**Knapp, M.L., Hart, R.P. & Dennis, H.S.** (1974), 'An exploration of deception as a communication construct', in: *Human Communication Research* 1, 15-29.

**Köhnken, G.** (1989), 'Behavioral correlates of statement credibility: theories, paradigms and results', in: H. Wegener, F. Lösel, & J. Haisch (eds.), *Criminal behaviour and the justice system: psychological perspectives*, New York: Springer-Verlag, pp. 271-289.

**Köhnken, G.** (1990), *Glaubwürdigkeit: Untersuchungen zu einem psychologischen konstrukt*, München: Psychologie Verlags Union.

**Lane, J.D., & DePaulo, B.M.** (1999), 'Completing Coyne's cycle: Dysphorics' ability to detect deception', in: *Journal of Research in Personality* 33, 311-329.

**Riggio, R.E. & Friedman, H.S.** (1983), 'Individual differences and cues to deception', in: *Journal of Personality and Social Psychology* 45, 899-915.

**Vrij, A.** (1991), *Misverstanden tussen politie en allochtonen: sociaal-psychologische aspecten van verdacht zijn*, Amsterdam: VU Uitgeverij.

**Vrij, A.** (1995), 'Behavioral correlates of deception in a simulated police interview', in: *Journal of Psychology* 129, 15-29.

**Vrij, A.** (1998), 'Nonverbal communication and credibility', in: A. Memon, A. Vrij & R. Bull, *Accuracy and perceived credibility of victims, witnesses, and suspects*, Maidenhead: McGraw-Hill, pp. 32-53.

**Vrij, A.** (2000), *Detecting lies and deceit: Psychology of lying and its implications for professional practice*, Chichester: John Wiley and Sons.

**Vrij, A. & Akehurst, L.** (1998), 'Verbal communication and credibility: Statement Validity Assessment', in: A. Memon, A. Vrij & R. Bull, *Psychology and Law: Truthfulness, accuracy, and credibility*, New York: McGraw-Hill, pp. 3-26.

**Vrij, A., Akehurst, L. & Morris, P.** (1997), 'Individual differences in hand movements during deception', in: *Journal of Nonverbal Behavior* 21, 87-102.

**Vrij, A. & Mann, S.** (in press), 'Telling and detecting lies in a high-stake situation: The case of a convicted murderer', in: *Applied Cognitive Psychology*.

**Vrij, & Semin, G.R.** (1996), 'Lie experts' beliefs about nonverbal indicators of deception', in: *Journal of Nonverbal Behaviour* 20, 65-81.

**Vrij, A., Semin, G.R. & Bull, R.** (1996), 'Insight into behaviour displayed during deception', in: *Human Communication Research* 22, 544-562.

**Zuckerman, M., DePaulo, B.M. & Rosenthal, R.** (1981), 'Verbal and nonverbal communication of deception', in: L. Berkowitz (ed.), *Advances in experimental social psychology, vol. 14*, New York: Academic Press, pp. 1-59.

**Zuckerman, M., & Driver, R.E.** (1985), 'Telling lies: Verbal and nonverbal correlates of deception', in: A.W. Siegman & S. Feldstein (eds.), *Multichannel integrations of nonverbal behaviour*, Hillsdale NJ: Erlbaum, pp. 129-147.

# Argumentation and Theory of Evidence

*D.N. Walton*

The purpose of this paper is to present some new methods widely in use in argumentation theory and informal logic that have applications to the theory of evidence in law. In recent years, a new pragma-dialectical approach[1] to argumentation, along with developments in the analysis of logical fallacies[2] and dialogue logic,[3] has forged these methods together into a single new approach to the evaluation of arguments. This new approach expands the traditional focus of logic on deductive and inductive arguments. It enables a critic to evaluate an argument with respect to how it was used for some communicative purpose in a given case. Research efforts by legal scholars have already been made to applying this new approach to legal argumentation and evidence.[4] In this paper, a general overview is given to show how the new methods are applicable to evidence theory in law. In addition to being a survey, the article also presents a new view of some key notions vital to the legal logic of evidence.

The two key notions that are most central are those of relevance and probative weight. The notions can be modeled in a new way (or in a way that seems new to many) by introducing a dialogue-based theory of argumentation in which inferences of different kinds are chained together to aim at proving an ultimate conclusion of the dialogue. These notions were already prominent in Wigmore's theory of evidence,[5] and the roots of them trace back though Locke and Bentham[6] to the ancient notion of plausibility in Greek philosophy.[7] But they seem new because they have been ignored for a long time in mainstream logic, and because only now have they been put together in such a way that they can be modeled in a formal structure. Many of Wigmore's ideas, like 'evidence charts' and 'probative weight', that formerly seemed obscure, form a logical point of view, are shown to have a precise logical structure. They show the way to developing new methods for the analysis and evaluation of legal argumentation. Prominent in the new approach is the technique of argument diagramming. Wigmore is shown to have been an important precursor of modern informal logic through his pioneering use of argument diagramming as applied to case studies of legal evidence.

---

[1] Van Eemeren & Grootendorst (1984; 1992).
[2] Hamblin (1970).
[3] Hamblin (1971); Rescher (1977); Barth & Krabbe (1982); Walton & Krabbe (1995).
[4] Alexy (1989); Feteris (1999); Lodder (1999).
[5] Wigmore (1940; 1983).
[6] Twining (1985).
[7] Gagarin (1984).

D.N. Walton

## Main Concepts of Argumentation Theory

In this section, a simplified account of the framework of argument evaluation is presented.[8] According to this account, an argument, or other move in argumentation, should be evaluated in light of how that argument was supposedly used for some communicative purpose in a given case. An argument that is supposed to be part of a persuasion dialogue might be evaluated quite differently, in some cases, is used in a negotiation type of dialogue. The reason is that persuasion dialogue and negotiation dialogue have a different purpose. The purpose of persuasion dialogue is for the one party to use rational argumentation to try to prove a particular proposition that is doubted by the other party. The purpose of negotiation is not to prove a particular proposition is true or false, but to 'make a deal' by agreeing to divide up some disputed interests. Using a threat as an argument is often quite legitimate in a negotiation. But using a threat is quite inappropriate in a persuasion dialogue. It has no place as 'evidence' or as a rational argument that is useful to contribute properly to the goal of this type of dialogue.

The six basic types of dialogue are outlined in figure 1.[9]

*Figure 1:* *Types of Dialogue*

| Type of dialogue | Initial situation | Participant's goal | Goal of dialogue |
|---|---|---|---|
| Persuasion | Conflict of opinions | Persuade other party | Resolve or clarify issue |
| Inquiry | Need to have proof | Find and verify evidence | (Dis)prove hypothesis |
| Negotiation | Conflict of interests | Get what you most want | Reasonable settlement that both can live with |
| Information-seeking | Need information | Acquire or give information | Exchange information |
| Deliberation | Dilemma or practical choice | Co-ordinate goals and actions | Decide best available course of action |
| Eristic | Personal conflict | Verbally hit out at opponent | Reveal deeper basis of conflict |

All these types of dialogue can be used as normative models for evaluating arguments in different kinds of cases of legal argumentation. But probably the most central kind of case you are wondering about is the use of argumentation in a trial, like a criminal trial, for example. In the model of the new dialectic, this type of argumentation is best viewed as a kind of persuasion dialogue, although a very special kind surrounded with many special procedural rules

---

[8] Walton & Krabbe (1995); Walton (1998).
[9] Described in Walton & Krabbe (1995) and Walton (1998).

depending on the court, the jurisdiction, etc. But there is also information-seeking dialogue involved, for example in the use of expert testimony.

Relevance of an argument, in the logical sense, according to the new dialectic[10] is dependent on the type of dialogue the argument is supposedly part of. As noted above, for example, an argument expressing a threat may be relevant in a negotiation dialogue but irrelevant in a persuasion dialogue. Wigmore was aware of this conversational relativity of relevance. He cited a case of an ordinary conversation to show how there can be a shift from one type of dialogue to another.[11] Two gentlemen in a train are discussing the issue of whether a certain type of rose can be grown from cuttings in their climate. Just then the waiter puts menus before them and asks what they will have for dinner. The conversation shifts from the discussion about the persuasion dialogue about rose growing to a deliberation on what to choose for dinner.

In a persuasion dialogue, there is a central thesis or proposition to be proved by one party. In a legal trial it is called the *factum probandum*. The one side tries to prove this thesis by putting forward arguments while the other side tries to cast doubt on the worth of these arguments. The side who has the burden of proof, called the proponent, uses a series of small steps that are connected to each other. Each single step is an inference, and represents an argument of a distinctive type. Some arguments are deductive, and some are inductive, but many of them tend to fall into a third category. This third category, as shown in *Figure 2*, is often called 'abductive'.[12]

This third category is especially important in legal argumentation, of the kind used for example in a trial, because so much of the evidence in a trial tends to be defeasible. Testimonial and circumstantial, by their very nature, belong in the third category. Testimonial evidence depends on the credibility of a witness, and circumstantial evidence is drawn by an inference in which the conclusion is an extrapolation from the premise. Most of the evidence introduced in a trial comes though the examination of witnesses. The arguments used by both sides in a case cite the statements drawn from the witnesses as 'evidence'. This legal usage always seems to me a bit peculiar, because a witness could be mistaken, or could be lying. What one witness says can even contradict, or appear to contradict, what another says. It appears from this usage that legal evidence is taken to be a fallible or defeasible notion. Something a witness said is 'evidence' for now, even though it may later be refuted, or shown to be false testimony. At any rate, the inferential structure of evidence takes various forms as species of arguments. Argument from testimony is classified as a species of argument from position to know.[13] According to this form of argument, if someone who is in a position to know

---

[10] Walton (1998).
[11] Wigmore (1935), p. 8.
[12] Josephson & Josephson (1994).
[13] In Walton (1996), pp. 61-67.

whether a statement is true or false asserts it is true (or false) then that is a reason for tentatively accepting the conclusion that it is true (or false). But these kinds of inferences are inherently presumptive in nature. Forms of argument representing many different kinds of presumptive arguments have now been studied and classified in recent work in argumentation theory.

*Figure 2:*   *Types of Arguments*

**Deductively Valid Arguments**

All birds fly
Tweety is a bird
_____

Tweety flies

**Inductively Strong Arguments**

Most birds fly
Tweety is a bird
_____

Tweety flies

**Abductively Plausible Arguments**

Birds (typically) fly
Tweety is a bird
_____

Tweety flies

## Argumentation Schemes

Logic may be no help when it comes to judging whether an individual statement is plausible or not. A statement has probative weight if it appears to be plausible. But that may just be a matter of how things appear. Where logic is valuable is in judging how probative weight is transferred over inferences. In particular, such inferences typically have the form of one of the kinds of arguments we know as argumentation schemes. Each argumentation scheme has an attached set of appropriate critical questions. The critical questions are those a rational respondent in a dialogue should ask when confronted with this type of argument, as used by the other party in the dialogue.

The argument from position to know is a common form of argument in which one party asks a second party for information that the second party is presumed to possess. For example, suppose a stranger to a city asks a passerby where the Central Station is located. The stranger presumes that the passerby may have this information, if the passerby looks like a person who is familiar with the area. Argument from position to know has the following general form.

*Argument from Position to know*

**Major Premise**: Source *a* is in a position to know about things in a certain subject domain *S* containing proposition *A*.
**Minor Premise**: *a* asserts that *A* (in Domain *S*) is true (false).
**Conclusion**: *A* is true (false).

Matching the argument from position to know are the following three critical questions:

**CQ1**: Is *a* in a position to know whether *A* is true (false)?
**CQ2**: Is *a* an honest (trustworthy, reliable) source?
**CQ3**: Did *a* assert that *A* is true (false)?

The argument from position to know is taken shifts a weight of presumption in a dialogue towards one side. If an appropriate critical question is posed by the respondent, the weight to restore presumption shifts to the other side. Only if the question is answered satisfactorily is the original weight of presumption restored.

Argument from expert opinion, often called the appeal to expert opinion in logic textbooks, is a special subtype of argument from position to know. Argument from expert opinion has the following form (argumentation scheme):[14]

*Argument from Expert Opinion*

**Major Premise**: Source *E* is an expert in subject domain *S* containing proposition *A*.
**Minor Premise**: *E* asserts that proposition *A* (in domain *S*) is true (false).
**Conclusion**: *A* may plausibly be taken to be true (false).

Appeal to expert opinion is subject to defeat, because experts are fallible. Appeal to expert opinion, as a species of argument from position to know, brings forward a weight of presumption subject to retraction depending on the asking of appropriate critical questions by the respondent in a dialogue. The following six basic critical questions for the appeal to expert opinion are:[15]

1. *Expertise Question:* How credible is *E* as an expert source?
2. *Field Question:* Is *E* an expert in the field that *A* is in?
3. *Opinion Question:* What did *E* assert that implies *A*?
4. *Trustworthiness Question:* Is *E* personally reliable as a source?
5. *Consistency Question:* Is *A* consistent with what other experts assert?
6. *Backup Evidence Question:* Is *A*'s assertion based on evidence?

Each of these critical questions is very important to evaluating an appeal to expert opinion used in a given case. In many legal cases, there are expert witnesses on both sides, and so asking the consistency question may trigger

---

[14] As given in Walton (1997), p. 210.
[15] Cited in Walton (1997), p. 223.

other questions. Thus uncertainty raised by the asking of a basic critical question can lead to various subquestions extending the dialogue.

It may not be clear how question 1, concerning credibility, is different from question 4, concerning personal reliability. According to previous analyses[16] the two questions should be seen as different. The trustworthiness question is a matter of the honesty of a source. It is a question of the ethical character of a source. The expertise question is a matter of the competence of the expert. An expert has credibility because she has knowledge and good judgment skills in applying that knowledge to a problem. The expert's competence is perhaps the more obvious factor on which an appeal to expert opinion rests as a good argument. But as Waller has shown,[17] the testimony of a lying expert can be just as misleading and devoid of value as the testimony of a sincere incompetent.

Position to know argumentation is based on the assumption that if someone is a source regarding some proposition that is in question, then she is in a position to know whether that proposition is true or not. This kind of argumentation is useful is because the user does not have direct access to the evidence in a way that the source does. An assumption is that the source is reliable – meaning that it is reasonable to presume that the source will give an accurate, true, or at least reliable account of what happened, as the situation appears to her.[18] Thus one common aspect of both schemes presented above is that the worth of the argument is based on the credibility of the proponent as a reliable source who has ethical character for honesty. Thus critical questions addressed to the character of the proponent are, in principle, relevant.

The schemes outlined above are only some of the many argumentation schemes that are vitally important in legal argumentation and evidence. The presumptive argumentation schemes presented in Walton (1996) comprise many of the most important kinds of inference that are used in legal argumentation. Perelman & Olbrechts-Tyteca (1969) identified many other distinctive kinds of arguments that can be used to carry probative weight in relation to a disputed issue on a provisional basis. Arthur Hastings' Ph.D. thesis (1963) presented the first systematic modern taxonomy describing many of these argumentation schemes, along with examples of their use in everyday conversational argumentation. Recently Kienpointner (1992) has produced quite a comprehensive listing of many argumentation schemes, stressing particularly the deductive and inductive forms not included in the treatment of Walton (1996). Among the presumptive argumentation schemes presented and analyzed in Walton (1996) are argument from sign, argument from example, argument from commitment, argument from position to know, argument from expert opinion, argument from analogy, argument from precedent, argument

---

[16] Waller (1988), p. 126; Walton (1997), pp. 213-217.
[17] 1988, p. 126.
[18] Wagenaar, van Koppen & Crombag (1993).

from gradualism, and the slippery slope argument. In other recent writings on argumentation, like Van Eemeren & Grootendorst (1992), there is a good deal of stress laid on how important argumentation schemes are in any attempt to evaluate common arguments in everyday reasoning as correct or fallacious, acceptable or questionable.

### Chaining of Inferences in a Typical Case

To grasp the elements of evidence, and how they work together in a case to make something evidence, we need to illustrate how reasoning is used in a typical case. But if that typical case is too complex, as it would be in any realistic case, how these elements work together will be lost in a sea of details. For in any real case, a body of evidence is a mass of small details making up a large picture. So let us take a very sketchy kind of case that is too hypothetical and incomplete to be real, but that is specific enough to suggest how the logically essential components of evidence in a real case typically function together to support a conclusion. Let us take a case of fact-finding reasoning used in a criminal case. Let us say that Pek is a murder suspect in a stabbing, and the knife, supposedly the murder weapon, is found at the crime scene. Then a forensic investigation reveals that Pek's fingerprint is found on the knife. In comparable cases using the same kind of reasoning, the evidence could be fingerprints, blood samples, or any other empirical finding of these kinds. But just to choose an example, let us consider a case where the evidence is a fingerprint. Why, in such a case, is the fingerprint correctly taken to be evidence? This simple question will seem trivial to some, but from a logical point of view, it is a lot harder to answer than you might initially think. Of course it is easy to say that it is just common sense that the fingerprint is evidence. But from a point of view of logic and evidence theory, the aim is to try to grasp how reasoning can correctly be used in such common sense judgments, and what sort of reasoning it is. The reasoning needs to have some kind of identifiable logical structure so that any given case can be examined to judge whether it fits this structure or not. The structure is a chain of reasoning. But what are the links in the chain? Does each link have a form of inference? How are the links connected together to move towards the ultimate conclusion in a case? How can we judge the strength or weakness of each individual link? And how can these judgments be summed up within a mass of evidence in a given case? The typical case outlined below is a purely hypothetical case used to illustrate some main features of the argument diagramming technique as applied to reasoning about legal evidence. Please note that it is not an actual case, or meant to represent any real case.

Turning to our hypothetical case, the best beginning point to answering all these questions begins with a consideration of how argument from expert opinion is used within the chain of reasoning. It is known scientifically that each person's fingerprint has characteristics that make it special to that person.

717

It is known from a lot of experience with the technique of fingerprinting that the chances of two different persons having the very same (or an indistinguishable) fingerprint are statistically remote. Experts can use technology to judge whether the fingerprint can be identified as Pek's. So from such a determination, that Pek's fingerprint is on the knife, an inference can be drawn that Pek touched the knife. In a given case, this inference could be wrong. Bob's fingerprint could have been 'planted' on the knife. Or the forensic fingerprint analysis could have been tampered with somehow. Such alternative explanations of how Pek's fingerprint got on the knife are logically possible. There could be all sorts of alternative explanations why Pek's fingerprint was on the knife. But unless there is a reason to assume that one of these other explanations is applicable, the conclusion that Pek touched the knife can reasonably be drawn by a plausible inference.

But even though the conclusion can be plausibly be drawn that Pek touched the knife, in the absence of evidence to the contrary in the case, how can the process of reasoning get from there to the conclusion that Pek killed the victim? That process is based on a cluster of plausible inferences that lead to the ultimate conclusion that Bob killed the victim. The first premise is that the knife was found at the crime scene. Another premise is the proposition that the cause of death was by stabbing with a knife, as would be established by the expert analysis of the medical examiner. Putting these two premises together generates the conclusion that the knife was the murder weapon. Now we have two important conclusions that have tentatively been supported by plausible reasoning. One is that Pek touched the knife. The other is that the knife is the murder weapon. Now the problem is to reconstruct the chain of reasoning that would, in the normal kind of case we are considering, lead to the ultimate conclusion that Pek killed the victim.

The key link is the following inference. Since Pek touched the knife (or so we presume from the reasoning above), it can be assumed that Pek used the knife to stab the victim. The connection here is a plausibilistic one, based on an abductive inference about the normal and expected ways of doing things in everyday life. To stab someone with a knife, you normally grasp the knife. A normal way of carrying out that action is to grasp the knife with your hand, without any glove, or other barrier between your hand and the knife. This normal way of doing things is familiar from common experience. And so if a person's fingerprint is on the knife, and the conclusion can be drawn that he touched the knife, leaving the fingerprint as evidence, then that evidence generates more evidence. In this case the inference plausibly drawn form the evidence is that Pek used the knife to stab the victim. So as soon as Pek's fingerprint is found on the knife, the plausible conclusion drawn, in light of the prior chain of reasoning outlined above, that Pek is that pek used the knife to stab the victim. This factual finding is mainly what is needed to prove the ultimate conclusion that Pek killed the victim.

You might think this foregoing analysis of the chain of reasoning in such a typical case is trivial. It seems trivial, because it is based on many common sense assumptions that we normally take for granted in everyday reasoning. But is just this kind of everyday plausibilistic reasoning that is characteristic of the argumentation in legal evidence. So for any theory of evidence, the question of how the inference from the fingerprint to the ultimate conclusion is, or should be drawn in a case like this one, is absolutely vital. From a viewpoint of a theory of evidence, the problem is to find the structure that holds the body of evidence together in a case, by connecting all the logical inferences together in some kind of coherent structure. Four possible answers to the question are the following:

1. the conclusion is drawn by inference to the best explanation;
2. the conclusion is drawn by argument from sign;
3. the conclusion is drawn by an abductive or plausible inference, based on a hypothesis;
4. the conclusion is drawn by a chaining together of a sequence of inferences represented by an argument diagram.

These answers are all correct, and each of them is part of grasping how argumentation works in legal evidence. Each single step of inference tends to be abductive, and is an instance of inference to the best explanation. Many of the steps have the form of argument from sign. But the most important aspect of evidence, and the best place to begin any account of how argumentation works in cases of legal evidence, is with item 4.

**Argument Diagramming**

The technique of argument diagramming models premises and conclusions in an extended sequence of arguments as points (vertices) in a directed graph (digraph). It tends to be assumed that argument digraphs are a recent innovation of informal logic. But, although it is not widely known in informal logic circles, the legal evidence theorist John H. Wigmore worked out the practical foundations of the technique in the 19th century, and applied it to extensive case studies of legal evidence. A Wigmore evidence chart is what now is called an argument diagram. It is a directed graph structure made up of points that represent propositions and arrows that represent steps of inference. The best simple illustration is Wigmore's own diagram representing a typical mass of evidence.[19]

---

[19] Wigmore (1983), p. 956.

*Wigmore's Diagram Representing A Typical Mass of Evidence*

Wigmore uses P to represent the proposition to be proved *(factum probandum)*. T represents a 'testimonial assertion', and C represents a 'circumstance'. Describing the diagram below, Wigmore wrote, "the following chart will illustrate the analysis of a typical mass of evidence for any proposition whatever."

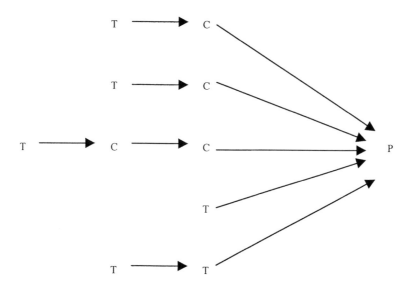

John Henry Wigmore, *Evidence in Trials at Common Law*, vol. 1a, ed. Peter Tillers, Boston, Little, Brown and Company, 1983, p. 956.

Wigmore worked out many highly detailed cases using his advanced, but often though to be eccentric, system of notation. But advances in artificial intelligence and argumentation theory are more and more vindicating the worth of Wigmore's technique.

The best way to simply illustrate how argument diagramming applies to cases of legal evidence is to work up an elementary diagram to represent the chain of reasoning in the hypothetical case of Pek and Vik. The argument diagram worked up below will show how the inferences in the case of Pek and Vik need to be fitted in with additional inferences to make up a chain of reasoning. First, some context of the argumentation used in the case needs to be stated, as follows.

Case: Pek is a murder suspect in a case in which Vik died, apparently of multiple stab wounds. A knife, supposedly the murder weapon, was found at the crime scene. The police investigated the crime scene and collected all the evidence they could find.

The diagram needs to begin with the contextual statement of the case, above, and then reconstruct what conclusions can be drawn. In any real case, there would be many details that would be important. If the argumentation were to be considered in a trial, for example, there would be examination of witnesses, and what inferences could be drawn would depend on details of the examination process. Ignoring many of these details that would be vital in any actual case, the object here is to show in a typical kind of case the general pattern of how the most important kinds of inferences can be chained together so that some ultimate conclusion can be inferred. The first inference to consider is the following:

1. a fingerprint was found on the knife;
2. the fingerprint on the knife is Pek's fingerprint;
3. therefore, Pek's fingerprint is on the knife.

Both premises of this argument would need to be supported by further arguments in the typical kind of case considered here. But especially the second premise needs support. It is based on an appeal to expert opinion. The form of the argument required to support this premise can be expressed by the following inference:

4. source *E* is an expert in forensic science containing knowledge of fingerprinting;
5. source *E* says that the fingerprint on the knife is Pek's fingerprint;
2. therefore, the fingerprint on the knife is Pek's fingerprint.

Then there is a third inference that is an important part of the chain of reasoning:

6. the knife was found at the crime scene;
7. the cause of death was stabbing with a knife;
8. therefore, the knife found at the scene was (plausibly) used to kill Vik.

This inference is plausibilistic. Further evidence could show it to be wrong. But it has a weight of presumption if it can be supported. The second premise needs to be supported by an appeal to expert opinion, something like the following one:

9. the medical examiner is an expert on cause of death;
10. the medical examiner says that the case of death was stabbing with a knife;
7. therefore, the cause of death was stabbing with a knife.

Finally there is another key inference that links the fingerprint to the stabbing. This inference can be reconstructed as follows:

11. if Pek's fingerprint is on the knife, and the knife found at the scene was (plausibly) used to kill Vic, then it is plausible to hypothesize that Pek used the knife to stab Vik;
3. Pek's fingerprint is on the knife;
7. the knife found at the scene was (plausibly) used to kill Vik;
8. Pek used the knife to stab Vik.

Finally, one last inference is required:

12. If Pek used the knife to stab Vik, and the cause of death was stabbing with a knife, then Pek killed Vic;

8. Pek used the knife to stab Vik;

7. The cause of death was stabbing with a knife;

13. Pek killed Vik.

Proposition 13 would represent an important factual finding in a criminal case of the kind being discussed. It would be an important finding in relation to the ultimate issue in a murder trial. The chain of reasoning in the argumentation leading to proposition 13 can be represented by the argument diagram in Digraph Pek, below.

Why is it that as soon as Pek's fingerprint is found on the knife, the conclusion that Pek killed Vik can be inferred by the chain of plausible reasoning represented in Digraph Pek? The reason is contextual. Pek is a murder suspect in a stabbing. This fact places the above chain of inferences in a context. That context can be sketched out as follows. Vik was found dead by the police. He had apparently been stabbed to death with the knife found at the scene. Legally, there is an issue raised by such a finding. Whoever did the stabbing, or was responsible for it, could be guilty of the crime of murder. The officials responsible for investigating such crimes need to find the stabber, along with whatever else they can find that is relevant to the issue of murder, or that might throw light on what happened. Hence the proposition that some person, say Pek, is the stabber, is relevant. It is a proposition that is very worthy of being proved or disproved. Therefore, any reasoning based on findings in the case that is useful to prove or disprove this proposition is relevant. So suppose then that Pek's fingerprint is found on the knife. Suppose also that Pek is a suspect, because, he was somehow closely related to the victim or known to the victim. In such a context, the proposition that Pek's fingerprint was found on the knife is relevant.

To sum up this section, it was shown by examining a typical case that the relationship between the evidence (the fingerprint) and the *factum probandum* is more complex than it looks. A series of interlocked inferences are involved. The whole structure of the reasoning used in the case can be represented by an argument diagram. A path running through the diagram shows the connection between the fingerprint finding and the *factum probandum*. It is this connection that can be used to shows why the one proposition is relevant to the other, in the sense of 'relevant' appropriate for evidence.

**Digraph of the Chain of reasoning in the Hypothetical Case of Pek and Vik**

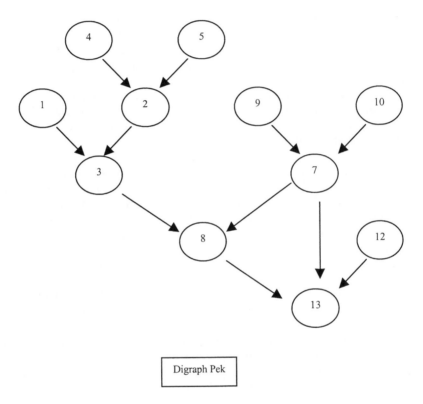

Digraph Pek

## What is Relevance?

What do we mean by 'relevant' in relation to evidence? The term 'relevant' is very vague, and could mean anything at all. But for purposes of argumentation theory, what it should mean can be very briefly explained as follows. One proposition is dialectically relevant to another proposition if and only if there is a chain of reasoning that leads from the one proposition to the other. What this means is that by a process of reasoning, you can get from the one proposition as starting point to the other proposition as end point. Hence potentially, the one proposition can be used to prove or disprove the other. The Wigmorite way to express relevance in legal argumentation to say the one proposition has potential 'probative weight' as part of a chain of argumentation that could lead to the other proposition as conclusion. In the present case then, the problem is – how do we get from what has been found or presumed to be found in the case to the highly relevant conclusion (in the context) that Pek killed Vik. This conclusion is relevant in the context of the case generally, because if the proposition 'Pek killed Vik' is true, then there is a potentially plausible line of inference from there in the case to the ultimate conclusion that Bob is guilty of the crime murdering the victim. It may not work out that way in the end. But there is a pretty good expectation, as far as we may be able to tell at the beginning stages of the investigation or trial, that things will or may go that way.

The inferences shown in the argument diagram above function together in a chain of reasoning that leads to the conclusion that Pek killed Vik. The conclusions of each of the subarguments function as premises in other arguments that exclude persons other than Pek who are linked to the knife and the crime scene. The chain of argumentation narrows down the range of possible perpetrators, strongly indicating Pek. The chain of reasoning ties Pek directly to the use of the murder weapon, suggesting he actually carried out the stabbing personally. All propositions in the argument diagram are significant as evidence in the case for two reasons. First, they can be used, as in the chain of reasoning sketched out above, to infer the conclusion that Pek killed Vik. Second, that conclusion is relevant, along with other evidence, as leading towards the ultimate conclusion that Pek is guilty of murder. The argument diagram displays the chain of reasoning used to get from the various findings in the case, that function as premises, to the conclusion that Pek Killed Vik. The conclusion is, of course, only a plausible hypothesis that is a best explanation of the findings in the case. So the argument diagram displays the network of inferences that makes up the mass of evidence in the case. The 'evidence' so-called is represented not only by the presumed facts reported by police investigators. It is also represented by the inferences that can be logically inferred from these presumed facts by plausible reasoning. The whole package of evidence for the contention that Pek killed Vik represented by the argument diagram, is based on an argument reconstruction of the case. In this reconstruction, implicit premises are filled in, based on the argumentation schemes that reveal the form of each step of inference. Typically, in a case of evidence in a criminal trial, for example, much of the evidence will be based on arguments that have the form of appeal to expert opinion. Knowing the structure of this argumentation schemes is vital to reconstructing the argument diagram for a given case.

Finally, the primary question can be answered. Why is the fingerprint rightly thought to be dialectically relevant as evidence? The answer comes in two parts. First, we need to ask an additional question for reasons of specification. What is the fingerprint supposedly evidence of? The answer to this question in a legal context is supplied by citing some ultimate conclusion (*factum probandum*) that is supposedly at issue. Supposedly, the fingerprint is a finding that can be potentially used to bear as an argument on some crime or wrongdoing that is of concern, or legal interest. In the hypothetical case considered above, the crime is murder. So then the fingerprint is potentially evidence in a murder case. Why then is the fingerprint considered to be relevant evidence? The answer is that the finding of the fingerprint can be used as a premise in both of the basic inferences above, and these two inferences lead by a chain of reasoning to the ultimate conclusion to be proved or disproved in the case.

It has been shown that relevance is determined by several factors in a given case. One factor is the type of dialogue. A second factor is the goal of the dialogue, or what is to proved, disproved, or otherwise settled by the argumentation in the dialogue. A third factor is the argumentation scheme, and the critical questions matching the scheme. A fourth factor is how the given proposition, or bit of evidence, can be chained forward so that the *factum probandum* is the end point in an argument diagram representing a chaining forward from that given proposition. What shows the connection is an argument diagram, a directed graph that leads from the one proposition to the other. The problem is that in the middle of an argument – for example, in a trial – it may be difficult or even impossible to judge in advance what direction a line of argumentation may take. For practical purposes, relevance will be judged according to the purpose of the dialogue and the practical constraints on it. Relevance is often a practical matter of avoiding undue delay and costs so that a meeting, trial, or other type of speech event, can fairly give a hearing to the arguments with significant probative value on both sides.

A brief comment must be made here on the distinction between logical relevance and legal relevance. This distinction was fundamental to the great controversies among the leading evidence theorists cited in the footnotes to Tillers' edition of Wigmore's *Treatise*.[20] These controversies show that there are great differences of opinion about the relationship between logical evidence and legal evidence. All that can be said here is that legal relevance is determined by legal rules like the *FRE* (1997), and by the application of these rules to cases. But underlying legal relevance thee should be a coherent notion of logical relevance. Above, it has been argued that logical relevance is best seen as dialectical. In other words, it should be seen not only as a matter of logical reasoning, but as a matter of how that reasoning has been used for some purpose in a dialogue in a given case.

### What is Probative Weight?

The view of how relevance works in the simple case briefly sketched out above is inferential and contextual. It is inferential in the sense that it implies that relevant evidence is always evidence for something – some conclusion that can be drawn or inferred. It is contextual in the sense that it implies that something is relevant evidence only to the extent that it can be used to help settle some claim that is in dispute, or subject to doubt. These claims often

---

[20] Wigmore (1983), vol.1a.

seem to defy ordinary usage. We sometimes say that an object, like a freezer chest, for example, is relevant evidence. But on the view of relevance defended here, an object like a freezer chest would only be relevant evidence to the extent that inferences can be drawn from presenting it or seeing it. It is relevant if these inferences can be used to help settle some claim that is subject to doubt or disputation. For example, if the freezer chest was alleged to have held a body cut up by a murderer, then it could function as evidence. But Wigmore would have said that presenting such a freezer chest in court could be classified as 'autoptic proference', even though, in ordinary discourse, the freezer chest itself would be called evidence.

On the view presented here, evidence always involves an inference, from a set of statements called premises to a statement called a conclusion of the inference. As noted above, such an inference can meet three types of standards of structural correctness – a deductive standard, an inductive standard, and a presumptive (abductive) standard. But structural correctness is not enough to make an inference qualify as evidence. There is another requirement. The premises must have probative weight, and the probative weight of the premises must be transferred forward to, or 'thrown onto' the conclusion. This 'throwing forward' is called the probative function. The probative function of an inference is the using of the probative weight of the premises, along with the structural correctness of the inference, to increase the probative weight of the conclusion.

But such a throwing of probative weight forward in a single inference may be of no significance in seeing the inference as evidence. For it to represent evidence, there must be some ultimate proposition that is in doubt, or is unsettled, and the single inference must have some place in a chain of inferences that has this ultimate proposition as its ultimate conclusion. As shown by the simple example above, this factor is the chaining forward of a sequence of inferences in evidence. In any given case, of the kind of interest in legal argumentation, evidence is judged in relation to a whole body of evidence in a case. A single inference by itself generally means very little. What is important is how it fits into the body of evidence in the case. Such a body of evidence is made up of a large network of sequences of inference, each inference chained to others.

A key question is – what is probative weight? Probative weight is something that contributes to making a proposition seem to be true. Probative weight gives a rational agent a reason to think or judge that the proposition is true, even though, once further facts are known, the proposition could turn out to be shown false. Other than making these rather cryptic remarks, the notion of probative weight cannot be fully and exactly defined. Probative weight can be equated with plausibility, or what seems to be true. But what is it to seem to be true or to appear to be plausible? The plausible is connected with the normal or expectable flow of events so that a report is plausible if it appears that it could well have happened.[21] For example, suppose Helen visited her grandmother who was being cared for in a senior citizen's home, and she noticed cuts on her grandmother's arm. Her grandmother could not remember how she got the cuts. Helen was worried because she began to suspect that her grandmother was being mistreated. She asked the nurse for an explanation. The nurse showed Helen a handrail on the stairway bolted to the wall with metal plates. She showed Helen how her grandmother has stumbled on the stairs, grasped the handrail, and then moved to the wall where she cut her arm on the metal plate. This explanation appeared quite plausible to Helen, after she thought about it. Her grandmother was often forgetful about daily events in the recent past. Even though she said she could not recall falling on the stairs, it was quite possible that she forgot the incident. So what does 'plausible' mean in a case like this. It means that Helen found the story of the falling on the stairs incident believable enough that it resolved the doubts or worries she had about mistreatment. The story or account given by the nurse seemed enough like it could be true. Why? Because it seemed 'in place' in the setting. It seemed like a fairly normal, expectable or typical kind of event that might easily have happened in the setting. We have an old, frail, forgetful person. We have steep stairs that the old person was always walking down to get to the common room. An dos forth. When you look at the total situation and all the elements in it, it adds up, as we say. The story of the falling against the metal plate is plausible. And if the nurse appears to be truthful, and there is no reason to discount or disbelieve what she says, its plausibility is reason to accept it.

## Wigmore on Probative Weight

Wigmore's theory of evidence is based on the concept of probative weight, and how probative weights of single propositions in a case are distributed in a total body of evidence. According to his theory, the total body of evidence on either side of a legal case can be represented as a network of connected inferences. The whole network is connected to and leads towards a single proposition – the ultimate conclusion at issue. A strong point in Wigmore's theory is that it treats legal evidence as based on plausible inferences of a kind that can carry probative weight, but are potentially subject to defeat by the introduction of further evidence as a case evolves.

Twining (1985) has shown how Wigmore's theory of evidence was based on Bentham's notion of probative weight. Bentham called probative weight 'probability', but it strongly appears that when used he used this term, he had something in mind like the ancient notion of 'probability' or plausibility. In Bentham's theory,[22] there are two parts to establishing the probability of a

---

[21] Rescher (1977).
[22] Bentham (1962).

proposition, as shown, for example, by cases of witness testimony. One is the probability of the proposition itself, which might be indicated by the confidence of the witness. The other is the adjustment of the original probability value carried out as a result of the process of examining the testimony.[23] Other factors mentioned by Bentham are the internal consistency of the testimony, and the usual or unusual nature of the event itself. For example, if a witness claimed that damage to a garden was caused by a falling balloon, the unusual nature of this event would tend to detract from its probability.[24] Judging from this example, probability in Bentham's sense is contextual, and is highly reminiscent of the ancient notion of plausibility.

One of the central ideas in Bentham's theory of evidence is the so-called 'chain of reasoning', defined as a sequence of inferences,[25] such that each premise or conclusion has a given probative weight, or degree of probability, and this weight is redistributed as new evidence comes in. Wigmore, like Bentham, built the theory of evidence around the notion of a chain of plausible inference forming the body of evidence in a case. As an example of such a plausible inference Wigmore[26] of a man who came into possession of a large sum of money after a robbery. Once established, this fact leads by plausible inference to the conclusion (hypothesis) that he got the money from a robbery. But the inference is only one explanation among other hypotheses that could also explain the given fact. There could be several other explanations – the man could have received a legacy, or made some winnings in a gambling game. So the conclusion drawn is best seen as an 'inference to the best explanation' – a plausible but defeasible inference.

Does the root of this Benthamite idea of probative weight or plausible inference go even farther back? For starters we could note that it is expressed in Locke's *Essay Concerning Human Understanding*, in Book 4, Chapter 15. Locke's example[27] is the story of the Dutch ambassador who told the king of Siam that the water in Holland would sometimes freeze so hard that people could walk on it. The king, because of his lack of experience of cold conditions, found the story implausible. At any rate, it is clear that Locke was familiar with plausible reasoning as an epistemological concept. But it is not hard to see that the roots of plausible reasoning go back much further. As Jonsen & Toulmin (1988) showed, the medieval tradition of casuistry deriving from Cicero's method of weighing 'probable reasons' on both sides of a legal or ethical case, had plausibility ('probability' it was called) as its central tool of reasoning. The casuists would weigh up the probable arguments on both

---

[23] Twining (1985), p. 28.
[24] Twining (1985), p. 54.
[25] P. 65.
[26] 1940, p. 420.
[27] Locke (1726), p. 276.

sides of a case, and then decide which opinion, in the case of a conflict of opinions, was the more probable.

So although the concept of plausible reasoning has not been in the mainstream of logic, it has a history of use, both in ethics and in philosophy of law. Wigmore's theory of evidence was based on the notion of probative weight in Bentham and Locke. But this notion had ancient roots even older than the time of Cicero. It was an ides that was highly familiar to the ancient Greek philosophers.

## Revival of the Ancient Notion of Plausibility

One of these is the ancient concept of plausibility or seeming-to-be-true, often translated from the Greek as 'probability'. But to modern ears, the term 'probability' means numerical probability in the statistical sense. In the ancient sense, it refers to something that is generally accepted as true, or seems to be true, based on appearances. In this ancient sense, probability is a fallible guide to acceptance. While it is often a reasonable basis for acceptance, it can be wrong. In some cases it can even be contradictory, because the appearances are conflicting. In some cases, it can also be misleading. Nevertheless, in many cases, plausibility is all we have to go by, and if harder evidence is not available, it is best to reason with plausibility-based evidence, and even to tentatively accept it, and act on it. new dialectic.

The most famous illustration of plausible reasoning in the ancient world was a matched pair of arguments called the eikotic argument and the reverse eikotic argument. A description of this pair of arguments can be found in Plato, but Plato cited two sophists, Corax and Tisias, who lived around the middle of the fifth century BC,[28] as the inventors. The eikotic argument was also described by Aristotle in the *Rhetoric* (1402a17-1402a28), where it was attributed to Corax.

## The Eikotic Argument

In a trial concerning a fight reported to have taken place between two men, one man was visibly bigger and stronger than the other. The weaker man, appealing to the jury, asked whether it appears likely to them he, the smaller and weaker man, would likely have assaulted a much bigger and stronger man. Would this hypothesis be plausible? Putting themselves into the position of the smaller man in the given situation, the people in the jury could each individually appreciate that it would be unlikely they would attack the larger man. The conclusion: it is improbable that the smaller man attacked the larger.

The probative function of the eikotic argument as used in such a case depends on a balance of considerations. Suppose that it is just one man's word

---

[28] Gagarin (1994), p. 50.

against the other's, and that no so-called 'hard evidence' is available. The case hangs on a balance. A small weight of plausible evidence on one the side or the other could tilt the balance one way or the other. The weight of plausibility yielded by the eikotic argument would have probative weight against the proposition that the smaller man attacked the larger.

It is interesting to note that it is possible to have a reverse eikotic argument, of a kind that is opposed to the original eikotic argument.

## The Reverse Eikotic Argument

The stronger man asks the jury whether it is plausible that he, an obviously much stronger and larger man, would assault the visibly smaller and weaker man. His reasoning runs as follows: he knows how guilty such an assault would appear if the case came before a court. Givent this awareness, is it plausible to think that he would attack the weaker man? The conclusion to be drawn is that such a hypothesis is improbable.

The reverse eikotic argument tilts the probative weight back to the other side. According to Gagarin,[29] the reverse eikotic argument was a typical 'turning-of the-tables' argument favored by the sophists of the second half of the fifth century BC.

This notion of plausible inference is very interesting, and one can easily see why is of importance in the kind of argumentation typically used in legal reasoning. But how could such reasoning, subjective as it appears to be, ever be evaluated systematically? In the modern (as opposed to postmodern) view, plausibility is 'subjective', and therefore is of no value as evidence, because all evidence should be based either on deductive reasoning to probabilistic reasoning, in the inductive or statistical sense. But the old idea of plausibility postulates a third kind of reasoning other than deductive and inductive. This third form of plausibilistic reasoning is now often called abductive inference, or inference to the best explanation, and is central to new work on artificial intelligence in computer science. But interestingly, this third form of reasoning was recognized and described by Wigmore very clearly, and used in his theory of evidence. From a logical point of view, Wigmore was a man well ahead of his time, and was a strong exponent of plausible reasoning.

## Concluding Remark

Above have been sketched out a number of methods and concepts that are currently being developed in applied logic and argumentation theory, including dialogue theory with its classification of types of dialogue, dialectical relevance, argumentation schemes, argument diagrams and plausible reasoning. Wigmore, in developing his theory of evidence, was already relying

---

[29] 1994, p. 51.

heavily on these concepts and methods. He was much hampered by their lack of development at the time. He did rely on authors like Alfred Sidgwick, an early precursor of informal logic, but Sidgwick's work was unfashionable, and nothing was done in logic to develop it.[30] The tools and techniques needed to support Wigmore's theory were just not there. Wigmore's poineering attempt to develop the argument diagramming technique, his method of evidence charts, for example, was not a success. He took the central notion of probative weight from Locke and Bentham, but mainstream logic did not have the resources to analyze these ideas at the time, or for some time after Wigmore's death. Some aspects of Wigmore's theory have been very influential in law, but other aspects it, for a long time, just looked obscure and quaint to both logicians and legal evidence scholars. Once Wigmore's theory of evidence is supplemented by these new methods however, it looks much more like a theory that does have an underlying logical structure. It is now possible to see how Wigmore was actually an important precursor of the informal logic movement.

Perhaps part of the problem is that the argument diagramming technique did not have any immediately obvious and attractive applications for lawyers. It did not seem to be obviously useful to help an advocate in court, for example, to help improve her argumentation in a case before a finder of fact. It did not obviously seem to be helpful to a judge in summing up the evidence and the line of argumentation on both sides of case. Where the new argumentation-based approach to evidence does seem to be most useful is for the purely theoretical purpose of grasping the structure of logical reasoning in the argumentation in legal evidence. Of course, the case of Pek and Vik outlined above is purely hypothetical, and is highly simplistic in representing the complex mass of evidence that would be characteristic of any real court case. But the structure of the evidence in the case is certainly realistic enough to show the promise of the new approach. From a viewpoint of evidence theory, the new dialectical approach to argumentation outlined above is a promising advance. It shows how sequential logical reasoning represented by argument diagrams, as well as argumentation schemes and dialectical relevance, are clearly identifiable structural components of the argumentation used in legal evidence. Could these techniques have any practical use apart from their purely theoretical use in legal logic? One application that could be suggested is that of the analysis of trial records to reconstruct a precis of the evidence in a given case that could be helpful to lawyers in new trials. The argument diagram could be used to abstract out the key steps of argumentation in the network of reasoning central to the main line of argument in a case. Argument diagrams possibly also helpful to teaching skills of logical reasoning in evidence courses in law schools, once the applicability of these new techniques to legal cases has been more fully worked out. Wigmore used rather

---

[30] Hamblin (1970).

complicated looking evidence charts to represent the argumentation on both sides of a case, showing how all the small steps of not very persuasive arguments make up a mass of evidence that is persuasive. New techniques of informal logic could simplify these evidence charts, and work them up in a form that could be attractive and useful in summarizing the core structure of the evidence in a case.

## Bibliography

**Alexy, R.** (1989), *A Theory of Legal Argumentation*, Oxford: Clarendon Press.
**Barth, E.M. & Krabbe, E.C.W.** (1982) *From Axiom to Dialogue*, de Gruyter.
**Bentham, J.** (1962), *Rationale of Judicial Evidence*, vol. 7 of *The Works of Jeremy Bentham*, ed. John Bowring, New York: Russell and Russell.
**Eemeren, F.H. van & Grootendorst, R.** (1984), *Speech Acts in Communicative Discussions*, Dordrecht: Foris.
**Eemeren, F.H. van & Grootendorst, R.** (1992), *Argumentation, Communication and Fallacies*, Hillsdale: N.J., Erlbaum.
***Federal Rules of Evidence (FRE), A Hypertext Publication, Legal Information Institute*,** 1997, http:www.law.cornell.edu/rules/fre.
**Feteris, E.T.** (1999), *Fundamentals of Legal Argumentation*, Dordrecht: Kluwer.
**Gagarin, M.** (1994), 'Probability and Persuasion: Plato and Early Greek Rhetoric', in: *Persuasion: Greek Rhetoric in Action*, Worthington, I. (ed.), London: Routledge 1994, pp. 46-68.
**Hamblin, Ch.** (1970), *Fallacies*, London: Methuen.
**Hastings, A.C.** (1963), *A Reformulation of the Modes of Reasoning in Argumentation*, Evanston, Illinois, Ph.D. Dissertation.
**Jonsen, A.R. & Toulmin, S.** (1988), *The Abuse of Casuistry : A History of Moral Reasoning*, Berkeley: University of California Press.
**Josephson, J.R. & Josephson, S.G.** (1994), *Abductive Inference : Computation, Philosophy, Technology*, New York: Cambridge University Press.
**Kienpointner, M.** (1992), *Alltagslogik: Struktur und Funktion von Argumentationsmustern*, Stuttgart: Fromman-Holzboog.
**Locke, J.** (1726), *An Essay Concerning Human Understanding*, 9th ed., London: A. Churchill.
**Lodder, A.R.** (1999), *Dialaw: On Legal Justification and Dialogical Models of Argumentation*, Dordrecht, Kluwer.
**Rescher, N.** (1976), *Plausible Reasoning*, Assen: Van Gorcum.
**Rescher, N.** (1977), *Dialectics*, Albany: State University of New York Press.
**Twining, W.** (1985), *Theories of Evidence : Bentham and Wigmore*, London: Weidenfeld and Nicolson.
**Wagenaar, W.A., Koppen, P.J. van & Crombag, H.F.M.** (1993) *Anchored Narratives: The Psychology of Criminal Evidence*, Hertfordshire: Harvester Wheatsheaf.
**Waller, B.N.** (1988), *Critical Thinking: Consider the Verdict*, Englewood Cliffs: Prentice Hall.
**Walton, D.N.** (1996), *Argumentation Schemes for Presumptive Reasoning*, Mahwah: N.J., Erlbaum.
**Walton, D.N.** (1997), *Appeal to Expert Opinion*, University Park: Penn Sate Press.
**Walton, D.N.** (1998), *The New Dialectic: Conversational Contexts of Argument*, Toronto: University of Toronto press.
**Walton, D.N. & Krabbe, E.C.W.** (1995), *Commitment in Dialogue*, Albany, New York.
**Wigmore, J.H.** (1935), *A Student's Textbook of the Law of Evidence*, Brooklyn: The Foundation Press.
**Wigmore, J.H.** (1940), *A Treatise on the Anglo-American System of Evidence*, vol. 1 (of 10 volumes), 3rd ed., Boston: Little, Brown and Company 1940.
**Wigmore, J.H.** (1983), *Evidence in Trials at Common Law*, vol.1a (of ten volumes), Tillers, P. (ed.), Boston: Little, Brown and Company.

# The American Version of the Rules of Evidence – can they be improved?

*L.H. Whinery*

## A. The Historical Background[1]

### Introduction

In this century, now coming to a close, pleading and evidence have both been subjects of concern to lawyers, judges and scholars in their endeavors to throw off the bonds of the pre-20th century formalistic procedural era when pleading and evidence rules were applied with rigid adherence to precedent. During that era little, if any, concern was given to the critical study of the merits of the rules for their effectiveness in the fair and expeditious trial of issues of fact. This has now changed with pleading and evidence having been the object of frequent study, revision and reform proposals by qualified professionals endeavoring to translate the workable and unworkable of experience into acceptable criteria for the future.[2] However, the modernization of pleading has proceeded at a much faster pace than that of evidence. The *Field Code,* the *Federal Rules of Civil and Criminal Procedure* and the adoption of modern rules of pleading and practice among the several states represented reform efforts in pleading and practice advancing at a faster pace than in the law of evidence. Prior to 1975, there were a few isolated instances of piecemeal revision in the law of evidence. But, on the whole, progress was slow.

One of the first to advocate modernization in the law of evidence was the English reformer, Jeremy Bentham.[3] James Bradley Thayer,[4] Roscoe Pound,[5] John H. Wigmore[6] and many others followed Bentham in speaking out against

---

[1] 'The Historical Background' of this paper is derived in part from L.H. Whinery, *Oklahoma Evidence*, pp. 16-23 (1994).
[2] For an earlier historical treatment of attempts at evidence law reform, *see* L.H. Whinery, 'The Uniform Rules of Evidence and the North Dakota Law of Evidence', 32 *N.D.L.Rev.* 205-208 (1956).
[3] J. Bentham, *A Treatise On Judicial Evidence*, Dumont 1825. *See further*, L.C. Kirkpatrick, 'Scholarly and Institutional Challenges to the Law of Evidence: From Bentham to the ADR Movement', 25 *Loy. of L.A.L Rev.* 837 (1992), for a thoughtful analysis of Bentham's views on the exclusionary rules of evidence.
[4] J.B. Thayer, *A Preliminary Treatise on Evidence at the Common Law* (1898).
[5] R. Pound, 'The Causes of Popular Dissatisfaction with the Administration of Justice', 29 *A.B.A.Rep.* 305 (Pt. I 1906), reprinted, 20 *J.Am.Jud.Soc.* 178 (1937), with an introduction by J.H. Wigmore, Roscoe Pound's St. Paul Address of 1906 – The Spark That Kindled the White Flame of Progress. *Id.*, at 176.
[6] J.H. Wigmore, *Evidence*, xiv (3[d] ed. 1940).

the illogic and inconsistency inherent in the rigid application of the traditional exclusionary rules of evidence.

## The Commonwealth Fund Proposals

One of the early efforts in this country to secure revision in the common law of evidence was the work of a committee headed by Professor Edmund M. Morgan under the auspices of the Commonwealth Fund of New York.[7] The Committee dismissed as impractical the early suggestion of a single reform either by abolishing the rules of evidence generally or by preparing a model code of evidence. Instead it dealt with specific reforms and finally recommended the passage of five uniform statutes.[8] They were:

1. rules of evidence should apply only to matters actually in dispute;[9]
2. trial judges should be given the power to comment on the weight of the evidence;[10]
3. the rule disqualifying an interested person as a witness in an action against the representative of a deceased or an incompetent should be abolished;[11]
4. declarations of deceased or insane persons should be admitted if made in good faith before the commencement of the action and if within the personal knowledge of the declarant;[12] and
5. entries made in the regular course of business should be admitted to prove the transaction recorded in the entry.[13]

However, after nine years few states had adopted even these modest recommendations of the Committee,[14] though at least one of the proposals has had a significant impact on the development of a major area of the law of evidence. This is the regular course of business entry exception to the hearsay rule which has been incorporated into most modern statutory reforms. It is now a well-recognized exception to the hearsay rule in a majority of the jurisdictions in the US.[15] Others, such as the proposal giving the trial judge the power to comment on the weight of the evidence, have had much less influence. For example, Congress later deleted Rule 105 of the *Proposed Federal Rules of Evidence* authorizing the trial court to sum up and comment

---

[7] E.M. Morgan, *The Law of Evidence: Some Proposals For Its Reform* (1927).

[8] *Id.*, at xix-xx.

[9] *Id.*, at 1.

[10] *Id.*, at 9.

[11] *Id.*, at 23.

[12] *Id.*, at 37.

[13] *Id.*, at 51.

[14] J.E. Tracy, 'What Progress in Reform of Evidence Rules?', 20 *J.Am.Jud.Soc.* 80, 81 (1936). *See also* E.M. Morgan & J.M. Maguire, 'Looking Backward and Forward at Evidence', 50 *Harv.L.Rev.* 909 (1937).

[15] J.H. Wigmore, *Evidence*, § 1561a. *See also*, Rules 803(6) of the *Federal* and *Uniform Rules of Evidence*, respectively, embodying the business record exception to the hearsay rule.

on the weight of the evidence to the jury because it was an authority not granted to most state trial courts due to its highly controversial nature. At the same time, the House and Senate Judiciary Committees acknowledged that the common law giving federal courts the power to summarize and comment on the weight of the evidence was left undisturbed by the deletion of Proposed Rule 105.[16]

## The 1937 American Bar Association Study

In 1937 a committee of the Section of Judicial Administration of the American Bar Association conducted a study directed toward revision of the law of evidence.[17] In its report submitted a year later the Committee recognized the value of the rules of evidence in their skeletal framework, but criticized the petty elaboration and distinction that had crept into the law.[18] The report dealt with recommendations as to both general features of procedure in the administration of rules of evidence and changes in specific rules governing the admissibility of evidence which it deemed most necessary, feasible and simple.[19] The 1937 committee recommended 18 changes in specific rules, including all of the recommendations made in the report of the Commonwealth Fund Committee. However, there are no specific changes in the law which resulted directly from the Committee's work even though the American Bar Association approved its recommendations. [20]

## The *Model Code of Evidence*

The first major evidence reform project began in 1939 when the Director of the American Law Institute announced the appropriation of funds by the Carnegie Corporation for the drafting of a model code of evidence.[21] The original intention of the Institute had been to restate the law of evidence. However, the ultimate conclusion was that the existing defects and confusions could be remedied only by legislative action. Professor Morgan was named reporter with Professor John M. Maguire as his Chief Assistant and Professor Wigmore as Chief Consultant.[22] The *Model Code of Evidence* was completed and approved by the Institute in 1942.[23]

---

[16] Report, Committee on the Judiciary, House of Representatives, 93rd Congress, 1st Session, Report No. 93650, November 15, 1973, p. 5.
[17] 62 *A.B.A.Rep.* 58 (1937).
[18] 63 *A.B.A.Rep.* 570, 576 (1938).
[19] *Id.*, at 571 *et seq.*
[20] *Id.*, at 154.
[21] 16 *A.L.I.Proc.* 469 (1939).
[22] *Id.*
[23] 19 *A.L.I.Proc.* 257 (1942).

During the three-year period of drafting, the Reporter and his assistants had the benefit of debate by the members of the Institute and suggestions and criticisms of judges and lawyers composing the evidence editorial group of the Institute, as well as those of various lawyers throughout the country at bar association meetings where the proposed *Model Code* was discussed.[24] However, soon after the *Model Code's* approval it became apparent that it would not be accepted generally by the profession. The principal criticism centered around the liberal modification of the exclusionary rules and the resultant discretion given to the trial judge.[25] The Reporter and Committee did not expect universal and immediate acceptance, although the ultimate hope was that the *Model Code* would find more general acceptance than it did.[26]

## The *Uniform Rules of Evidence of 1953*

During the period 1920-1949, the Conference of Commissioners on Uniform State Laws also devoted considerable attention to the law of evidence. A number of uniform and model acts designed to remedy specific evidentiary problems were promulgated by the Conference.[27]

The Conference's efforts received a measure of success by the adoption of these acts in the various states.[28] However, in view of the unfavorable reception given to the *Model Code* and the still recognized need for general legislative revision, the Executive Committee recommended in 1948 that the Conference cooperate with the American Law Institute in adopting or revising the *Model Code* or otherwise establishing uniform rules of evidence.[29] This proposal was referred to the Civil Procedure Acts Section of the Conference.[30] A special study committee was then appointed to study and prepare the drafts.[31] The drafting committee included Judge Spencer A. Gard of Iola, Kansas, as Chairman, three practitioners and three law teachers.[32] Later a

---

[24] *Model Code of Evidence*, ix-xii (1942). For transcripts of the debates by the Institute, *see* 17 *A.L.I.Proc.* 66-148 (1940)(Tentative Draft No. 1); 18 *A.L.I.Proc.* 84-252 (1941)(Tentative Draft No.2 ); 19 *A.L.I.Proc.* 74-257 (1942)(Proposed Final Draft).

[25] 20 *A.L.I.Proc.* 49-52 (1943). *See also* J.H. Wigmore, 'The American Law Institute Code of Evidence Rules: A Dissent', 28 *A.B.A.J.* 23 (1942); Panel Discussion, Spotlight on Evidence, 27 *J.Am.Jud.Soc.* 113, 114 (1943).

[26] 20 *A.L.I.Proc.* 49-52 (1943).

[27] For a list of these model and uniform acts with the adopting states, *see Handbook, Nat'l Conf. of Comm. on Uniform State Laws*, 303-304 (1955).

[28] *Id.*

[29] *Handbook, Nat'l Conf. of Comm. on Uniform State Laws*, 92 (1948).

[30] *Handbook, Nat'l Conf. of Comm. on Uniform State Laws*, 46 (1949).

[31] *Id.*, at 190.

[32] J.E. Estes, Dallas, Texas; J.C. Pryor, Burlington, Iowa; R.E. Woodside, Attorney General, Harrisburg, Pennsylvania; Dean M. Ladd, University of Iowa Law School; C.T. McCormick, Professor of Law, University of Texas; and M.E. Pirsig, Professor of Law, University of Minnesota.

committee under the chairmanship of Professor Morgan was appointed to represent the American Law Institute to advise the Conference committee so that any uniform rules promulgated might receive the approval of the Institute.[33]

Initially, the Conference committee recognized the value of the thorough and candid work of those responsible for the drafting of the *Model Code* and based its preparation of uniform rules on this proposal. However, experience had shown that the far-reaching changes manifested in the *Model Code* were not acceptable to the profession generally. It was then determined that each of the *Model Code* rules should be tested by the criteria of acceptability and uniformity. The rules meeting these tests were retained; those that did not were either modified, revised, or rejected.[34] The final draft of the *Uniform Rules of Evidence of 1953* was submitted to and approved by the Conference on August 22, 1953.[35] They were then approved by the American Bar Association.[36] The American Law Institute gave its approval in 1954.[37] These rules attracted considerable attention throughout the country and, generally speaking, were less controversial than the *Model Code*, although only a few jurisdictions adopted them in substance or with modifications. These are California, Kansas, New Jersey, The Panama Canal Zone and the Virgin Islands.[38]

### The *Uniform Rules of Evidence of 1974*

The 1953 *Uniform Rules* remained the recommended rules of the Conference of Commissioners on Uniform State Laws until 1974. At this time, the Conference promulgated the *Uniform Rules of Evidence of 1974*.[39] These rules were essentially the same as the *Federal Rules of Evidence* adopted by Congress in 1975 with the important addition of a comprehensive Article V dealing with privileged communications. Article V of the *1974 Uniform Rules* was taken from Article V of the Supreme Court's *Proposed Federal Rules* which was deleted by Congress in the enactment of the *Federal Rules* to incorporate in a single Rule 501 the federal common law relating to privileged communications.[40]

---

[33] *Handbook, Nat'l Conf. of Comm. on Uniform State Laws*, 162 (1953).
[34] *Id.*, at 161-163 for a complete summary of the Conference committee approach and its work.
[35] *Id.*, at 102-103. For interim reports of the Conference committee *see Handbook, Nat'l Conf. of Comm. on Uniform State Laws* for 1951 and 1952.
[36] 78 *A.B.A.Rep.* 134 (1953).
[37] 31 *A.L.I.Proc.* 44 (1954).
[38] *Handbook, Nat'l Conf. of Comm. on Uniform State Laws*, 367 (1976).
[39] *Handbook Nat'l Conf. of Comm. on State Laws*, 916 *et seq.* (1974). *See also, Uniform Rules of Evidence* (U.L.A.) Rules 101 *et seq.* (WESTLAW: U.L.A. database, ci('rev' & 101).
[40] Rule 501 of the *Federal Rules* provides: "Except as otherwise required by the Constitution of the US or provided by Act of Congress or in rules prescribed by the Supreme Court pursuant to statutory authority, the privilege of a witness, person, government, State, or political subdivision (to be continued)

Later, at its 95th Annual Conference in Boston, Massachusetts, on August 1-8, 1986, the Conference approved and recommended the enactment of amendments to the *1974 Uniform Rules*. These included a new rule relating to the inadmissibility of the prior sexual behavior of the victim in prosecutions for sexual offenses;[41] amendments to the lawyer-client[42] and husband-wife[43] privileges to bring them into conformity with recent decisions of the Supreme Court of the US; a new rule codifying the holding in a recent decision of the Supreme Court of the US relating to impeachment for bias;[44] amendments relating to the definition and meaning of hearsay,[45] including a new rule permitting the admission of statements of children relating to sexual abuse or physical violence;[46] and a new rule designed to simplify the authentication of foreign and business documents.[47]

Finally, in July of this year meeting in its 108th Year in Denver, Colorado, the Conference adopted additional amendments to the *Uniform Rules of Evidence* following a comprehensive review of the *Uniform Rules* by a Study Committee appointed February 6, 1993 and later a Drafting Committee appointed August 1, 1995 to implement the recommendations of the Study Committee. However, unlike the promulgation of the 1974 *Uniform Rules* or their subsequent amendment in 1986, the 1999 amendments constitute a comprehensive review and revision of the *Uniform Rules* without necessarily following the work product of the *Federal Rules of Evidence* or their subsequent amendments.

There are two principal reasons for this divergent approach. First, there is some question whether uniformity between federal and state rules of evidence is practical or feasible. The earlier Drafting Committees were charged, where reasonably possible, with bringing the language of the *Uniform Rules of Evidence of 1974* and their subsequent amendment in 1986 into line with the comparable provisions in the *Federal Rules*. The underlying theory was, apparently, that a trial practitioner need master only one set of rules to comfortably practice in both federal and state forums located in the various district, circuit and state courts. However, this theory does not often work as well as expected due to differing interpretations of the black letter of the rules

---

thereof shall be governed by the principles of the common law as they may be interpreted by the courts of the US in the light of reason and experience. However, in civil actions and proceedings, with respect to an element of a claim or defense as to which state law supplies the rule of decision, the privilege of a witness, person, government, state, or political subdivision thereof shall be determined in accordance with State law."

[41] *Uniform Rules of Evidence* (U.L.A.) Rule 412 (WESTLAW: U.L.A. database, ci('rev' & 412).

[42] *Id.*, at Rule 502.

[43] *Id.*, at Rule 504.

[44] *Id.*, at Rule 616. *See US* v. *Abel*, 469 *U.S.* 45, 105 *S.Ct.* 465, 83 *L.Ed.2d* 450 (1984).

[45] *Id.*, at Rule 801.

[46] *Id.*, at Rule 807.

[47] *Id.*, at Rule 902(11).

of evidence by different courts, even sister, federal and state jurisdictions. As a result, familiarity with the rules must often be resolved on a case by case and jurisdiction by jurisdiction basis.

Second, societal changes, advances in both the hard and soft sciences and improvements in information technology have exposed many problematic evidentiary situations routinely faced by lawyers and judges. With increasing frequency, the rules fail to fit into a new environment, or alternatively, if they do fit, they may produce measurable inequity. These may, or may not, be seen as significant issues in the drafting of evidentiary rules applicable in other jurisdictional settings.

Accordingly, the amendments to the *Uniform Rules of Evidence (1999)* recommended by the Drafting Committee and adopted by the Conference do not necessarily reflect precise regard to other existing work product. Notable in this respect, to accommodate the admissibility of electronic evidence, is substituting the word "record" for such terms as "writing", "recordings", "photographs" and "data compilations" throughout the *Uniform Rules* and then defining "record" in a definitions rule as "information that is inscribed on a tangible medium or that is stored in an electronic or other medium and is retrievable in perceivable form".[48]

Additional amendments to the *Uniform Rules* were also adopted by the Conference, including amendments to the rules in Article I, General Provisions,[49] in Article III, Presumptions,[50] in Article IV, Relevancy,[51] in Article V, Privileges,[52] in Article VI, Witnesses,[53] in Article VII, Opinions and

---

[48] *Uniform Rules of Evidence (1999)*, Rule 101(3).

[49] Rule 103 was amended by creating a new subdivision (c) to provide that a definitive pretrial ruling on the admissibility of evidence need not be renewed at trial to preserve the question for consideration on appeal. Rule 104 was amended by creating a new subdivision (b) to establish a procedural rule for determining the existence of a privileged communication.

[50] Article III was revised to include a definitions rule and clarify the meaning, establishment and rebuttal of presumptions.

[51] Rule 404(b) was amended to provide procedural rules for determining the admissibility in criminal cases of other crimes, wrongs, or acts when offered for a purpose other than to prove action in conformity therewith on a particular occasion. Rule 407 was amended to provide that the exclusion of subsequent remedial measures to prove negligence or culpable conduct is also applicable in products liability cases and to make the rule applicable to remedial measures taken after the sale of a product to a user or consumer. Rule 410 providing for the exclusion of pleas and offers to plead in criminal cases was amended to conform the *Uniform Rule* to Rule 410 of the *Federal Rules of Evidence*. Rule 412 was revised to clarify the circumstances under which the prior sexual behavior of an alleged victim is subject to exclusion in sexual offense cases.

[52] Rule 503 was amended to incorporate a mental health provider privilege in the physician and psychotherapist-patient privilege.

[53] Rule 609(a)(2) was amended to provide that convictions, regardless of punishment, offered to impeach a witness are admissible only if the crime forming the basis for the conviction embraces an element of truthfulness or untruthfulness and to incorporate procedural rules governing the admissibility of convictions for impeachment purposes.

Expert Testimony,[54] in Article VIII, Hearsay,[55] and in Article IX, Authentication and Identification.[56] Article X, Contents and Writings, Recordings, and Photographs, was also revised to make the Article consistent with the other amendments to the *Uniform Rules* to accommodate the admissibility of electronic records.

Finally, structural revisions were made in the *Uniform Rules*, including revising Rules 101 and 102 to create a definitions rule as Rule 101 and deleting Rule 101 to combine it in a new Rule 102 dealing with the scope of the *Uniform Rules*.

## The *Federal Rules of Evidence* of 1975

In 1943 the Committee on Jurisprudence and Law Reform of the American Bar Association was charged with the duty of studying the need for improving the law of evidence in the federal courts. Among other proposals for reform, the Committee was to consider the *Model Code* as a basis.[57] The Committee reported back in 1944 and the House of Delegates approved its proposal that the American Bar Association recommend a study of the *Model Code* by the Advisory Committee on the Rules of Civil and Criminal Procedure of the Supreme Court to determine the extent to which its provisions should be

---

[54] Rule 701 was amended to clarify that an expert may not render an expert opinion under the guise of testifying as a non-expert without qualifying as an expert under Rule 702 governing the admissibility of expert testimony. Rule 702 was amended to convert the Frye standard of admissibility into a presumption of reliability or unreliability depending upon whether the science, technology, or specialized knowledge has substantial acceptance within the concerned scientific community and to provide for the rebuttal of the presumption through resort to reliability criteria, including the criteria established in *Daubert* v. *Merrell Dow Pharmaceuticals, Inc.*, 509 *U.S.* 579, 113 *S.Ct.* 2786, 125 *L.Ed.2d* 469 (1993) and *Kumho Tire Co.* v. *Carmichael, U.S.*, 119 *S.Ct.* 1167, *L.Ed.2d* (1999).

[55] Rule 801(b)(1)(B) was amended to incorporate a pre-motive requirement for the admissibility of a prior consistent statement offered to rebut an express or implied charge against the declarant of recent fabrication or improper influence or motive. Rule 803(6), the business records exception to the hearsay rule, was amended to provide that the foundational requirements of the exception can be satisfied through certification without requiring the production of a foundation witness. Rules 803(24) and 804(b)(5), the residual exceptions to the hearsay rule, were combined into a single Rule 808 and revised to prohibit the admissibility of a statement under this exception which simply fails to meet all of the foundational requirements for admissibility under one of the more specific exceptions of Rules 803(1) through (23) or 804(b)(1) through (5). Rule 804(b)(6), a new rule, was adopted to permit the admission of a hearsay declarant's statement when offered against a party who engaged or acquiesced in procuring the unavailability of the declarant to testify as a witness. Rule 807 was revised to provide greater restrictions on the admissibility of statements of children relating to acts of neglect, physical or sexual abuse.

[56] Rule 902, Self-Authentication, was revised in subdivisions (11) and (12) to establish a procedure for the authentication of domestic and foreign records of regularly conducted activity to complement the amendment of Rule 803(6) eliminating the necessity for the calling of foundation witnesses.

[57] 68 *A.B.A.Rep.* 146 (1943).

adopted as rules of procedure.[58] This proposal did not result in any elaboration on the then existing Rule 43 of the *Federal Rules of Civil Procedure* governing the admissibility of evidence in the federal courts.[59] It was not until 20 years later that a movement began anew for the promulgation of comprehensive rules of evidence for the federal courts.

In March 1965, Chief Justice Earl Warren appointed an advisory committee to formulate rules of evidence for the federal courts. It was a distinguished committee of lawyers and judges from throughout the US. It was under the Chairmanship of Albert E. Jenner, Jr., of Chicago, with Professor Edward W. Cleary serving as Reporter. The Committee worked for more than six years preparing both a Preliminary Draft and Revised Draft. The Revised draft was circulated in 1971[60] and, by an order entered on November 20, 1972, with Mr Justice Douglas dissenting, the Supreme Court promulgated the *Federal Rules of Evidence* to become effective July 1, 1973.[61] On February 5, 1973 the rules were sent to Congress by Chief Justice Warren Burger, but the effective date of the rules was deferred until they had been approved expressly by Congress.[62] After Congressional review and amendment of the rules in various respects, Congress enacted the rules into law to become effective on July 1, 1975.[63]

Interestingly, as was somewhat the case with the adoption of the *Federal Rules of Civil Procedure,* the enactment of the *Federal Rules of Evidence* spearheaded new reform efforts throughout the country. Nevada, New Mexico and Wisconsin were early state leaders in adopting the *Federal Rules.*[64] Some version of the *Federal Rules*, or their counterpart in the *1974 Uniform Rules*, has now been enacted in 38 states,[65] the US Military[66] and Puerto Rico.[67] They

---

[58] 69 *A.B.A.Rep.* 185 (1944).
[59] C.E. Clark, 'Foreword to A Symposium on the *Uniform Rules of Evidence*', 10 *Rutgers L.Rev.* 479, 482 (1956); E.M. Morgan, 'The Future of the Law of Evidence', 29 *Tex.L.Rev.* 587 (1951); W.P. Armstrong, 'Proposed Amendments to *Federal Rules of Civil Procedure*', 4 *F.R.D.* 124, 137-138 (1946).
[60] 51 *F.R.D.* 315.
[61] 56 *F.R.D.* 183.
[62] *Pub.L.No.* 93-12.
[63] *H.R.* 5463, *Pub.L.No.* 93-595, approved January 2, 1975. For an exhaustive history of the promulgation of the *Federal Rules of Evidence*, see Ch.A. Wright & K.W. Graham, Jr., *Federal Practice and Procedure: Evidence*, §§ 5001-5007.
[64] See *Nev.Rev.Stat.*, Title 4, § 47.020 *et seq.*, effective July 1, 1971; *N.M.Stat.Ann.* § 20-4-101 *et seq.*, effective July 1, 1973; and *Wis.Stat.Ann.* § 901.01 *et seq.*, effective January 1, 1974.
[65] *Alaska R.Evid.* 101-1101; *Ariz.R.Evid.* 101-1103; *Ark.R.Evid.* 101-1102; *Colo.R.Evid.* 101-1103; *Del.R.Evid.* 101-1103; *West's Fla.Stat.Ann.* §§ 909.101-909.958 (1979); *Hawaii R.Evid.* 101-1102; *Idaho R.Evid.* 101-2203; *Ind.R.Evid.* 101-1101; *Iowa R.Evid.* 101-1103; *Ky.R.Evid.* 101-1104; *La.R.Evid.* 101-1103; *Maine R.Evid.* 101-1102; *Mich.R.Evid.* 101-1102; *Minn.R.Evid.* 101-1101; *Miss.R.Evid.* 101-1103; *Mont.R.Evid.* 100-1008; *Neb.R.Evid.* 101-1103; *Nev.Rev.Stat.* §§ 47/2020-55.030 (1987); *N.H.R.Evid.* 101-1103; *N.J.R.Evid.* 101-1103; *N.M.R.Evid.* 101-1102; *N.C.R.Evid.* 101-1102; *N.D.R.Evid.* 101-1103; *Ohio R.Evid.* 101-1103; 12 *Okla.Stat.* §§2101-3103 (1981 & Supp. 1989); *Ore.R.Evid.* 100-1008; *R.I.R.Evid.* 100-1108; *S.C.R.Evid.* 101-1103; (to be continued)

have also influenced the development of the law of evidence in States which have yet to adopt them.

Except for technical amendments and clarifying changes, there were only five substantive changes in the *Federal Rules* during the period 1975 to 1991. In 1978 Rule 412 was added to exclude evidence of prior sexual behavior of alleged victims to prove consent in prosecutions of defendants for sexual misconduct. In 1994 Rule 412 was revised to clarify some of the confusion in the 1978 Rule and expand its protection by making it applicable in both criminal and civil cases and in all cases without regard to whether the alleged victim or person accused is a party to the litigation. In 1980 the 1985 version of Rule 410 dealing with the exclusion of compromises in criminal cases was revised to conform the rule to Rule 11(e)(6) of the *Federal Rules of Criminal Procedure*. In 1984 Rule 704 permitting opinions on an ultimate issue in a case within limitations was amended to add a subdivision (b) prohibiting an expert witness from rendering an opinion in a criminal case regarding the requisite mental state of a defendant constituting an element of the crime charged. In 1990 Rule 609(a) was amended to remove the limitation that a conviction for impeachment purposes could only be elicited on cross-examination and to permit its admissibility on the direct examination of an accused to 'remove the sting' of the potential admission of the impeaching evidence on cross-examination. The rule was also amended to subject the admissibility of a conviction of a witness other than a criminal defendant to the balancing process of Rule 403. Finally, in 1991 Rule 404(b) was amended by adding a pretrial notice requirement in criminal cases on the issue of the admissibility of other crimes, wrongs, or acts evidence when offered for a purpose other than to prove action in conformity therewith on a particular occasion.

Other than these foregoing amendments, the *Federal Rules* remained essentially the same until 1994 when Congress enacted the controversial Rules 413, 414 and 415 and a newly appointed Advisory Committee initiated a review of the *Federal Rules* to determine whether additional substantive amendments should be made. Rule 413 authorizes the admission of other offenses of sexual assault in the prosecution of an accused for sexual assault. Rule 414 permits the admission of other offenses of child molestation in the prosecution of an accused for an offense of child molestation. Rule 415 permits the admission of other offenses of sexual assault or child molestation in a civil action for damages against a person alleged to have committed a sexual assault or act child molestation.

---

*S.D.R.Evid.* 19-9-1 *et seq.*; *Tenn.R.Evid.* 101 *et seq.*; *Tex.R.Evid.* 100-1008; *Utah R.Evid.* 101-1103; *Vt.R.Evid.* 101-1103; *Wash.R.Evid.* 101-1103; *W.Va.R.Evid.* 101-1102; *Wis.Stat.Ann.* 901.01-911.02; *Wyo.R.Evid.* 101-1104.
[66] *Military R.Evid.* 101-1103.
[67] *P.R.R.Evid.* 1-84.

The initial review of the *Federal Rules* by the Advisory Committee resulted in four additional amendments in 1994. First, Rule 407, excluding evidence of subsequent remedial measures was amended to add the words "an injury or harm allegedly caused by" to clarify that the Rule applies only to changes made after the occurrence that produced the damages giving rise to the cause of action. In addition, the Rule was amended to provide that evidence of subsequent remedial measures is inadmissible in products liability cases as well as cases involving negligence and culpable conduct.

Second, Rule 801(d)(2)(E) was amended, first, to codify the holding in *Bourjaily* v. *US*,[68] by providing that a court shall consider the contents of a coconspirator's statement in determining "the existence of the conspiracy and the participation therein of the declarant and the party against whom the statement is offered". Second, the amendment resolved an issue on which the Supreme Court reserved decision by providing that the contents of the statement alone are not sufficient to establish a conspiracy in which the declarant and the defendant participated. Third, the reasoning of *Bourjaily* was extended to treat analogously preliminary questions relating to the declarant's authority under subdivision (C) and the agency or employment relationship and its scope under subdivision (D) of Rule 801(d)(2).

Third, Rules 803(24) and 804(b)(5), the identical residual exceptions, were combined into one exception as Rule 807.

Fourth, a new Rule 804(b)(5) was added as a prophylactic rule to provide that a party forfeits the right to object to the admission of a declarant's prior statement on hearsay grounds when the party's deliberate wrongdoing or acquiescence in that wrongdoing has procured the unavailability of the declarant.

There are now additional amendments proposed which have been approved by the Judicial Conference of the US and submitted to the Supreme Court of the US for its approval. These are proposed amendments to Rules 103,[69] 404(a),[70] 701,[71] 702,[72] 703,[73] 803(6)[74] and 902.[75]

---

[68] 483 *U.S.* 171 (1987), 107 *S.Ct.* 2775, 97 *L.Ed.2d* 144 (1987).

[69] Rule 103(a), as in the case of amended *Uniform Rule* 103, would provide that a party need not renew an objection or offer of proof at trial to preserve a claim of error on appeal if the court makes a definitive pretrial ruling on the record either admitting or excluding the evidence.

[70] Rule 404(a)(1) would be amended to provide that when an accused attacks the character of an alleged victim of a crime under subdivision (a)(2) of Rule 404(a), the door is opened to an attack on the same character trait of the accused.

[71] Rule 701, as in the case of amended *Uniform Rule* 701, would be amended to eliminate the risk of an expert testifying on scientific, technical, or other specialized knowledge as a lay witness under Rule 701 without complying with the foundational requirements for the admissibility of expert testimony under proposed Rule 702.

[72] Rule 702 would be amended to include a standard of reliability for the admissibility of expert testimony in response to *Daubert* v. *Merrell Dow Pharmaceuticals, Inc.*, 509 *U.S.* 579, 113 *S.Ct.* 2786, 125 *L.Ed.2d* 469 (1993) and *Kumho Tire Co.* v. *Carmichael, U.S.*, 119 *S.Ct.* 1167, *L.Ed.2d* (1999).

**Evidence Reform – Summary**

The foregoing highlights efforts for evidence reform in the US. Viewed from one perspective, there are few areas of law in which there has been more agitation, more scholarly effort, and more money expended for reform efforts than in the law of evidence. Yet change and modernization has been slow. The influence of precedent, the natural inclination to cling to the familiar, the adversary system, the jury system, limiting judicial discretion and the burden of learning 'new rules and procedures' reflect the reluctance of lawyers to accept change. The fact that judges and lawyers may have used the existing evidentiary rules with a considerable amount of common sense may also partly explain the often expressed satisfaction with the *status quo*.[76]

At the same time, incompleteness in the rules, ambiguity in the black letter of the rules and related interpretive problems and developments in the decisional law, together with societal changes, advances in the hard and soft sciences and improvements in information technology, may all lead to difficulties in ruling on the admissibility of evidence with probable injustice to the parties which is not easily overcome by the 'common sense' approach.

Viewed from another perspective, we inevitably build upon the work and studies of countless generations of lawyers, judges and scholars. The work of Thayer, Wigmore, Morgan, McCormick, Cleary, Jenner and Gard, to mention only a few, and the scores of other draftsmen who worked on the *1942 Model Code of Evidence*, the *1953, 1974* and *1999 Uniform Rules of Evidence* and the *Federal Rules of Evidence,* as amended, together with the drafts and notes for these reform efforts, have all had a significant impact upon the enactment of improved rules of evidence. Without these earlier efforts the modernization of the law of evidence might never have been initiated. Moreover, the countless hours of effort which have been devoted to the examination and re-examination of the law of evidence at both the federal and state level in the last

---

[73] Rule 703 would be amended to emphasize that an expert's reasonable reliance on facts or data that are otherwise admissible to form an opinion or inference may not be disclosed to the jury by the proponent of the opinion or inference unless the court determines that the probative value of the facts or data outweigh their prejudicial effect.

[74] Rule 803(6), the business records exception to the hearsay rule, would be amended to provide that the foundation requirements of Rule 803(6) can be satisfied through certification without requiring the production and testimony of a foundation witness.

[75] Rule 902 would be amended in subdivisions (11) and (12) to set forth a procedure by which the parties can authenticate domestic and foreign records of regularly conducted activity through certification in lieu of the testimony of a foundation witness. The amendment would thereby complement the proposed amendment to Rule 803(6) eliminating the necessity for the calling of a foundation witness.

[76] C.E. Clark, 'Foreword to A Symposium on the *Uniform Rules of Evidence*', 10 *Rutgers L.Rev.* 479, 480 (1956).

75 years may have culminated, beginning in the 1970s at least, in products worthy of the effort upon which future reforms can be based.

## B. The Criteria for Developing, Evaluating the Effectiveness and Improving the Rules of Evidence

There are at least six criteria through which to promulgate, revise and evaluate rules of evidence. These are:

1. the promulgation of the rules through a deliberative process involving the development of rational hypotheses, reasoned debate and thoughtful drafting;
2. anticipating evidentiary issues that may arise under the rules;
3. evaluating the efficacy of the rules through empirical studies;
4. formulating the rules to be rigid enough to promote accuracy in fact finding, yet flexible enough to insure individuality in application;
5. responding to the appellate interpretation of the rules; and
6. assessing the degree of congruence between the rules and their efficiency in producing desired results.

These analytical tools can be of great value in the further development and improvement of the American law of evidence.

At the same time, these criteria have to be evaluated in the context of the four most pervasive features of American fact finding. These are: first, the influence of precedent; second, the more recent view that the common law of evidence, as with its codified successors, is the child of the adversary system of adjudication;[77] third, the older view, as expressed by Thayer, that our system is "the child of the jury system";[78] and fourth, the perceived need for restricting judicial discretion. As has already been ably noted, the more pervasive of these four features of fact finding depends upon the type of fact finding that is identified for examination. It is precedent if the focus is on the admission of evidence under a well-established and recognized exception to the hearsay rule. It is the adversary system if the focus is on the presentation of evidence. It is the jury system if the focus is on the exclusion of evidence.[79] It is limiting judicial discretion if the focus is on the abolishment of an exclusionary rule. In any event, these four features of American fact finding must be reckoned with in assessing the utility of the foregoing criteria in the pursuit of improvements in the American law of evidence.

In this effort to develop and analyze these criteria in relation to the American system of fact finding to improve the rules of evidence, my concern is not directed toward evidentiary issues of American constitutional dimension,

---

[77] E.M. Morgan, 'The Jury and the Exclusionary Rules of Evidence', 4 *U.Chi.L.Rev.* 247 (1937).
[78] J.B. Thayer, *A Preliminary Treatise on the Law of Evidence* 266 (1898).
[79] *See* M.R. Damaška, *Evidence Law Adrift* 2 (1997).

notably the right of confrontation, the exclusion of confessions and unlawfully obtained evidence and the privilege against self-incrimination. The value impregnated aspects of these areas of evidentiary inquiry do not lend themselves to black letter analysis. As observed in the Advisory Committee Note to Proposed Rule 501 of the *Federal Rules of Evidence*: "No attempt is made in these rules to incorporate the constitutional provisions which relate to the admission and exclusion of evidence, whether denominated as privileges or not. The grand design of these provisions does not readily lend itself to codification. The final reference must be the provisions themselves and the decisions construing them. Nor is formulating a rule an appropriate means of settling unresolved constitutional questions."[80]

## C. The Criteria explained and illustrated

### The Promulgation of Rules of Evidence

As evidenced by the historical development of the *Model Code of Evidence* and the *Federal* and *Uniform Rules of Evidence*, the promulgation of rules of evidence should involve a deliberative process through the development of rational hypotheses, reasoned debate and thoughtful drafting. The antithesis of this is the promulgation of rules of evidence through political expediency or simple adversarial advantage.

As to crafting rules of evidence through political expediency, I refer to the enactment by the Congress of the US of Rules 413 through 415 of the *Federal Rules of Evidence* that took effect on July 9, 1995.[81] The President, anxious to secure passage of the *Violent Crime Control and Enforcement Act* of 1994, yielded to political pressure from Congress and agreed to the inclusion of the three rules in the Act to make evidence of a defendant's past similar acts admissible in civil and criminal proceedings for sexual assault and child molestation cases.[82]

The overwhelming majority of judges, lawyers, law professors and legal organizations who responded to the *Federal Rules of Evidence* Advisory Committee's call for public response opposed the enactment of Rules 413 through 415 without equivocation. The principal objections were two fold. First, the rules would permit the admission of unfairly prejudicial evidence by focusing on convicting or imposing liability on a criminal or civil defendant for what the defendant *is* rather than what the defendant *has done*.

---

[80] 56 *F.R.D.* 183, 230-231 (1973).

[81] *Pub.L.* 103-222, § 320935(a), 108 *Stat.* 2135.

[82] *See* C. Zehran, '2 NY Reps Turned Tide', *Newsday*, August 23, 1994, at A 19 and K.Q. Seelye, 'House Approves Crimes Bill After Days of Bargaining, Giving Victory to Clinton', *N.Y. Times*, August 22, 1994, A1, at B6.

Second, the rules contained numerous drafting problems apparently not intended by their authors, including mandating the admissibility of the evidence without regard to other rules of evidence, such as Rule 403 of the *Federal Rules of Evidence* requiring the balancing of the relevancy of evidence against its potential for unfair prejudice and Rule 801 of the Rules proscribing the admission of hearsay evidence. This, in turn, it was argued, would raise serious constitutional questions, such as the right of confrontation in criminal proceedings where Rules 413 and 414 might be invoked.[83]

However, in spite of these expressed concerns, they have been given surprising vitality among the Federal Circuit Courts where the validity of the Rules has been challenged. In spite of some expressed judicial concern[84] and a lack of state acceptance of the rules,[85] all of the federal courts which have considered the issue have concluded that the rules do not violate the Due Process Clause of the US *Constitution* subject to balancing the relevancy of the evidence against its potential for unfair prejudice within Rule 403 of the *Federal Rules of Evidence*.[86] A similar result has been reached in California

---

[83] Alternatively, the Standing Committee and the Judicial Conference of the US recommended the adoption of an amendment to Rules 404 and 405 of the *Federal Rules of Evidence* where admissibility of such evidence could be appropriately circumscribed. However, Congress elected not to accept the recommendation.

[84] *See* the dissenting opinion from an order denying a petition for rehearing *en banc* in *US* v. *Mound*, 157 *F.3d* 1153 (8th Cir. 1998).

[85] There is no state which has adopted these rules to date. In Arizona, their adoption was considered by the Supreme Court of Arizona, but rejected largely for the same reasons they were rejected by the Judicial Conference of the US. *See* R.L. Gottsfield, 'We Just Don't Get It: Improper Admission of Other Acts Under Evidence Rules 404 (b) as Needless Cause of Reversal in Civil and Criminal Cases', *Ariz.Att'y*, April 1997, at 24. Connecticut has reprinted *Federal Rules* 413 through 415 in its *Trial Lawyers Guide to Evidence*, but they are inapplicable in state court proceedings. Indiana has a rule similar to *Federal Rule* 414, but it is more carefully drawn with procedural safeguards. *See Ind.Code Ann.* § 35-37-4-15 (West 1997). California also has statutes authorizing the introduction of prior sexual offenses or acts of domestic violence subject to balancing relevancy against unfair prejudice. *See Cal.Evid.Code* §§ 1108, 1109 (West 1997), respectively. Missouri also had a blanket rule admitting evidence of prior acts of child molestation similar to *Federal Rule* 414. *See Mo.Ann.Stat.* § 566.025 (West 1978). However, it has now been held unconstitutional by the Supreme Court of Missouri under Article I, Sections 17 and 18 the Missouri Constitution providing, respectively, "[t]hat no person shall be prosecuted criminally for felony or misdemeanor otherwise than by indictment or information" and "[t]hat in criminal prosecutions that accused shall have the right (…) to demand the nature and cause of the accusation; (…)." Otherwise, the Court reasoned, a jury could "improperly convict the defendant because of his propensity to commit such crimes without regard to whether he is actually guilty of the charged crime. As a result, the defendant is forced to defend against the uncharged conduct in addition to the charged crime. It was also contended in this case that the statute violated the *Fifth, Sixth* and *Fourteenth Amendments* to the US *Constitution*. However, the Court did not reach these issues by concluding that the challenge under the Missouri Constitution was dispositive. *See State* v. *Burns*, 978 *S.W.2d* 759 (Mo. 1998).

[86] *See United State* v. *Mound*, 149 *F.3d* 799 (8th Cir. 1998); *US* v. *Summer*, 119 *F.3d* 658 (8th Cir. 1997); *US* v. *Castillo*, 140 *F.3d* 874 (10th Cir. 1998); *US* v. *Guardia*, 135 *F.3d* 1326 (10th Cir. (to be continued)

with the Court of Appeal holding that Section 1108 of its *Evidence Code* authorizing another sexual offense by the defendant admissible in the defendant's prosecution for a sexual offense is valid against constitutional claims of a denial of due process and equal protection of the laws and a dilution of the standard of proof beyond a reasonable doubt since Section 1108 expressly mandates the balancing of the probative value of the evidence against the danger of unfair prejudice under Section 352.[87] However, interestingly, and in juxtaposition to these decisions, the Supreme Court of Missouri has held a statute similar to Rule 414 unconstitutional under Missouri constitutional provisions similar to those contained in the US *Constitution*.[88]

Reasoned differences of opinion may exist with respect to the relevancy of past acts of sexual assault or child molestation in the commission of a charged crime of sexual assault or child molestation, to the potential of such evidence to unfairly prejudice the defendant, or to the constitutionality of rules authorizing the admission of such evidence.[89] However, the point is that Rules 413 through 415 were not developed through the formulation of a rational hypothesis, reasoned debate and thoughtful drafting. Otherwise, a better work product might have resulted and judicial intervention to interpret the meaning of the Rules 413 and 414 might have been avoided.

I have also alluded to drafting rules of evidence to secure an adversarial advantage which is counter productive in the development of a rational body of evidentiary law. Here, I would call your attention to a personal experience involving the adaptation of the *Federal Rules of Evidence* in the enactment of the *Oklahoma Evidence Code*. Rule 801(d)(2) exempts from the hearsay rule admissions by party-opponents on the theory that their admissibility in evidence is the result of the adversary system in which no guarantee of trustworthiness is required. Included within the categories of admissions in Rule 801(d)(2) are admissions offered against a party that are made by an agent of a party while acting within the scope of employment. *Federal Rule* 801(d)(2)(D) expressly provides: "The statement is offered against a party and is (D) a statement by a party's agent or servant concerning a matter within the scope of the agency or employment, made during the existence of the relationship (...)."[90]

In the drafting of the *Oklahoma Evidence Code*, plaintiff oriented members of the drafting committee prevailed in altering the language of Oklahoma's parallel rule, Section 2801 (4)(b)(5) as follows: "(b) the statement is offered

---

1998); *US* v. *Enjady*, 134 *F.3d* 1427 (10th Cir. 1998); and *US* v. *Larson*, 112 *F.3d* 600 (2nd Cir. 1997).

[87] *See People* v. *Fitch*, (App. 3 Dist. 1997) 63 *Cal.Rptr.* 753, 55 *Cal.App. 4th* 172.

[88] *See* note 85, *supra*.

[89] *See* M.A. Mendez, 'Character Evidence Reconsidered: "People Do Not Seem to be Predictable Characters"', 49 *Hast.L.J.* 871 (1998).

[90] *Federal Rules of Evidence*, Rule 801(d)(2)(D).

against a party and is (4) a statement by (...) [a party's] agent or servant concerning a matter within the scope of (...) [the agent's] agency or employment (...)."[91]

By eliminating the language "made during the existence of the employment" the vicarious admission rule was broadened to admit statements against an employer by an agent after the employment relationship was terminated. This version of the rule was initially adopted by the Oklahoma Legislature.[92] Was it a wise decision?

The *Federal Rule* ensures the reliability of the statement by requiring that the statement be made during the existence of the employment relationship when it would be unlikely that an employee would jeopardize the employment by making statements which would impact unfavorably on the employer.

In contrast, the *Oklahoma Rule*, as originally enacted, would pose a great risk to the employer because the employer would have difficulty refuting a statement made by the employee after the termination of the employment relationship, especially if the employee was not available at trial and subject to cross-examination. In short, the rule not only removed the reliability factor inherent in requiring the statement to be made during the existence of the relationship, it favored plaintiff-oriented litigants and disfavored defense oriented litigants. The rule was the product of adversarial advantage. The rule stopped short of being the product of a rational hypothesis, reasoned debate and thoughtful drafting.

The footnote to this scenario is that I prevailed upon the Legislature in 1991 to insert the limiting language into the *Oklahoma Rule* so it is now in accord with the *Federal Rule*.[93]

**Anticipating Evidentiary Issues in the Drafting of Rules of Evidence**

An evidentiary system should not be a closed system. As observed in the Prefatory Note to the *Uniform Rules of Evidence (1999)*, "Societal change, advances in both the hard and soft science and improvements in information technology have exposed many problematic evidentiary situations routinely faced by lawyers and judges. With increasing frequency, the rules fail to fit into a new environment, or alternatively, if they fit they produce measurable inequity."

With this in mind the Drafting Committee undertook to depart significantly in the Revision of the *Uniform Rules of Evidence of 1974, As Amended*, to accommodate the admissibility of evidence kept in electronic form. Although

---

[91] Laws 1978, c. 285, § 801, effective October 1, 1978.
[92] *Ibid.*
[93] Laws 1991, c. 62 § 6, effective September 1, 1991. *See also* L.H. Whinery, 'The Oklahoma Evidence Code: Ten Years of Judicial Review', 43 *Okla.L.Rev.* 193, 203-204 (1990), for an elaboration on the background and amendment of Section 2801(4)(b)(4) of the Code.

the *Uniform Rules* prior to their amendment this year included specific reference to 'data compilations' to accommodate the admissibility of records stored electronically, many business and governmental records do not now consist solely of data compilations. Rather, in today's technological environment, records are kept in a variety of mediums other than in just data compilations. "Records" may include items created, or originated, on a computer, such as through word processing or spreadsheet programs; records sent and received, such as electronic mail; data stored through scanning or image processing of paper originals; and information compiled into data bases. One, or all, of these processes may be involved in ordinary and customary business and record keeping. In consequence, modern technology suggests that any of the foregoing types of records should be admissible when they are relevant if reasonable evidentiary thresholds of admissibility are satisfied.

Relying on the previous work and recommendations of the Task Force on Electronic Evidence, Subcommittee on Law of Commerce in Cyberspace, Section on Business Law of the American Bar Association, the Drafting Committee recommended amendments that were adopted by the National Conference of Commissioners on Uniform State Laws to accommodate these developments. The amendments substitute the word "record" for the terms "writing", "recorded statement", "memorandum", "report", "document" and "data compilation" where they appear throughout the *Uniform Rules*, specifically in Rules 106, 612, 801(a), 803(5) through 803(17), 901 through 903 and 1001 through 1007. At the same time the use of the word "record" accommodates the evidentiary use of these more traditional forms of record keeping.

"Record" is then separately defined in a newly created definitions Rule 101 to mean "information that is inscribed on a tangible medium or that is stored in an electronic or other medium and is retrievable in perceivable form".[94] This definition is derived from § 5-201(a)(14) of the *Uniform Commercial Code* and carries forward consistently the established policy of the Conference to accommodate the use of electronic evidence in business and governmental transactions. This anticipation of potential evidentiary issues is sound in both theory and practice.

The Advisory Committee on the *Federal Rules of Evidence* has yet to decide whether similar amendments to the *Federal Rules* should be undertaken. In a working memorandum to the Committee, the Reporter has made the following observations: "The goal of the Advisory Committee on Evidence Rules is, by general consensus, far more limited – to respond to specific instances where the Rules are not working. With respect to computerization, the *Federal Rules* (...) seem to be working quite well, at least at this point. Moreover, since the *Uniform Rules* are not widely adopted,

---

[94] Rule 101(3), *Uniform Rules of Evidence* (1999).

amendments to those rules can be promulgated without the concern that settled practices and substantial case law will be disrupted. The concern over upsetting settled expectations must obviously be taken into account in any attempt to amend the *Federal Rules*."

Finally, the *Uniform Rules* proposals on computerized evidence must be considered in the context of other *Uniform Rules* ventures, particularly in the area of Uniform Commercial Code and electronic contracting. The *Uniform Rules* project is, quite understandably, integrating language pertinent to computerization throughout the *Uniform Rules*. There is no such need for integration, at this time with respect to the *Federal Rules of Evidence*.

Ultimately it is for the Committee to decide whether it is worth the effort to amend so many rules. If the decision is in the affirmative, the *Uniform Rules* proposal should provide an excellent model.[95]

**Evaluation of Rules of Evidence through Empirical Studies**

Resort to social science methodology in the study of the American Legal System is by no means unknown. It has its origins in the emergence of the American Legal Realist Movement in the 1920s.[96] In particular, since 1950 increasing attention has been given to the value of empirical research in testing underlying assumptions concerning various aspects of the law and its administration, but with particular emphasis on the study of court systems and procedure. The University of Chicago Jury Project pioneered by Professors Kalven and Zeisel was perhaps the first significant effort to employ social science methodology in assessing the effectiveness of the jury system in the trial of issues of fact.[97] Later, the work of Professor Maurice Rosenberg of Columbia University added efficacy to the value of empirical research in his study of New Jersey pretrial procedures.[98] In the intervening years down to the present time this early work has inspired an increased interest in empirical

---

[95] Memorandum, Progress Report on Accommodating Technological Advances in the Presentation of Evidence, March 1, 1998.

[96] D.M. Trubek, *The Handmaiden's Revenge: On Reading and Using the Mewer Sociology of Civil Procedure*, 111, 116 (1988). *See also* J. Monahan & L. Walker, 'Empirical Questions Without Empirical Answers', 1991 *Wis.L.Rev.* 569, and P.D. Carrington, 'Foreword: The Scientific Study of Legal Institutions', 51 *Law and Contemp.Probs.* 1 (1988).

[97] *See* H. Kalven & H. Zeisel, *The American Jury* (1966).

[98] *See* M. Rosenberg, *The Pretrial Conference and Effective Justice: A Controlled Test in Personal Injury Litigation* (1964), and M. Rosenberg, 'The Impact of Procedure Impact Studies on the Administration of Justice', 51 *Law & Contemp.Probs.* 13, 17-20 (1988). *See also* M. Stevenson *et al.*, 'The Impact of Pretrial Conferences: An Interim Report on the Ontario Pretrial Conference Experiment', 15 *Osgoode Hall L.J.* 591 (1977).

research, but most of which has centered on adjudication, civil procedure and court management.[99]

There is certainly an impressive list of empirical studies that have been carried out over the last 45 years since the pioneering work of Kalven and Zeisel and others. However, it is also noteworthy to observe that these studies represent only a small fraction of the legal academy's preoccupation with doctrinal scholarship. Although doctrinal scholarship is of value and has made significant contributions to the development of the substantive and procedural law,[100] it still has its critics. As has been argued elsewhere, doctrinal scholarship first, almost always engages "in normative argument rather than to better account for what now exists". Second, it "derives its premises from postulates that are essentially normative." Third, it often "ignores the positive behavioral side of relevant disciplines, such as economics, political science, and sociology" or derives its theory "from other academic fields that do not seem to take facts seriously". Fourth, it is often "free standing, self-referential, self-justifying, even solipsistic" which "neither looks backward to a tradition of theory building nor forward to a tradition of theory testing".[101]

Among the reasons cited for this neglect of empirical research among law professors are inconvenience,[102] lack of control,[103] tedium,[104] uncertainty,[105] ideology,[106] monetary resources,[107] time,[108] tenure[109] and training[110] and viable

---

[99] *See*, in this connection, M. Chiorazzi *et al.*, 'Empirical Studies in Civil Procedure: A Selected Annotated Bibliography', 51 *Law & Contemp.Probs.* 87 (1988), annotating extensive studies relating to court management, trial, alternate dispute resolution, small court claims and appeals. *See also* 'Empirical Studies of Civil Procedure, Parts I & II', 51 *Law & Contempt.Probs.* 1 (1988).

[100] *See*, in this connection, R.C. Park, 'Evidence Scholarship, Old and New', 75 *Minn.L.Rev.* 849, 859-871 (1991), for an exposition of the value of doctrinal scholarship in the law of evidence.

[101] P.H. Schuck, 'Why Don't Law Professors Do More Empirical Research?', 39 *J.Legal Ed.* 323, 327-328 (1989).

[102] It is inconvenient because it cannot be carried on within the confines of law school offices and libraries. *See* P.H. Shuck, *supra*, note 101, at 331.

[103] There is a lack of control over research hypotheses because informants may not be candid, data may be incomplete, irrelevant, or miscoded, computers may not work, or research assistants may fail to perform assigned tasks. *See* P.H. Schuck, *supra*, note 101, at 331.

[104] The research is tedious because the accumulation, management and analysis of data require resources that are often not readily available within the legal community. *See* P.H. Schuck, *supra*, note 101, at 331.

[105] There is uncertainty in the conclusions to be drawn from empirical studies as compared to traditional legal scholarship that is often designed to arrive at a predestined conclusion. *See* P.H. Schuck, *supra*, note 101, at 332. *See also* J.G. Getman, 'Contributions of Empirical Data to Legal Research', 35 *J.Legal Ed.* 489, 493 (1985).

[106] Ideologically the legal academy is oriented toward the pursuit of desired policy outcomes which may, or may not, be consistent with the results obtained through empirical research. *See* P.H. Schuck, *supra*, note 101, at 332.

[107] Empirical research is expensive and a deterrent to investment, particularly where the eventual return is contingent. *See* P.H. Schuck, *supra*, note 101, at 332. *See also* J.G. Getman, *supra*, note 105 at 493.

issues to explore.[111] All of these impediments to empirical research within the legal community are realistic as demonstrated by the seven-year-long Predictive Sentencing Project at The University of Oklahoma.[112] At the same time, the Project's successful conclusion, though not in the hoped for outcome, proved that these negative factors are not insurmountable.[113] In any event, empirical research deserves encouragement and greater attention across the broad spectrum of the law than it has been given in the past when it is measured against the value to be derived by sophisticated investigation into the underpinning for our assumptions about how well the law works. As expressed elsewhere, "[e]mpirical study has the potential to illuminate the workings of the legal system, to reveal its shortcomings, problems, successes, and illusions, in a way that no amount of library research or subtle thinking can match."[114]

This is no less true of evidence than it is with respect to substantive and other procedurally oriented areas of the law. There has already been some impressive empirical research that focuses on evidence. This includes research relating to eyewitness identification testimony,[115] the science of proof,[116] and forensic evidence.[117] These important and useful studies are about evidence, but they are not about the rules of evidence themselves. However, there have been some thought provoking studies on the rules of evidence. These include a study on admonishments to the jury,[118] the exclusionary rule in search and

---

[108] The research is time consuming which often requires collaboration with other disciplines. *See* P.H. Schuck, *supra*, note 101, at 332. *See also* J.G. Getman, *supra*, note 105, at 493.

[109] The tenure decision may inhibit interest in empirical research by junior faculty where that decision may be affected by incomplete or inconclusive results, or success that may be attributed to a collaborator. *See* P.H. Schuck, *supra*, note 101, at 332.

[110] The requisite training for empirical research often goes well beyond the analytical skills that are important in the legal community by requiring, in addition to legal skills, an understanding of methodology and recourse to paradigms outside of the law which legal scholars do not have the energy or time to acquire. *See* P.H. Schuck, *supra*, note 101, at 333.

[111] It has been suggested that it is often difficult to find appropriate empirical issues in the law to investigate. *See* P.H. Schuck, *supra*, note 101, at 333. *See also* J.G. Getman, *supra*, note 105, at 493.

[112] L.H. Whinery *et al.*, *Predictive Sentencing: An Empirical Evaluation* (1976).

[113] *Ibid.*

[114] J.G. Getman, 'Contributions of Empirical Data to Legal Research', 35 *J.Legal Ed.* 489, 489 (1985). *See also* J.B. Dworkin & A. DeNisi, 'Empirical Research on Labor Relations Law: A Review, Some Problems, and Some Directions for Future Research', 28 *Lab.L.J.* 563 (1977).

[115] *See*, for example, B. Cutler & S. Penrod, 'Forensically Relevant Moderators of the Relation Between Eyewitness Identification and Accuracy and Confidence', 74 *J.Applied Psychology* 650, 652 (1989).

[116] *See* P. Tillers & E. Green (eds.), *Probability and Inference in the Law of Evidence: The Limits and Use of Bayesianism* (1988).

[117] *See*, for example, D.M. Risinger, M.P. Denbeaux & M.J. Saks, 'Exorcism of Ignorance as a Proxy For Rational Knowledge: The Lessons of Handwriting Identification "Expertise"', 137 *U.Pa.L.R.* 731 (1989).

[118] A.V. Tanford, 'Thinking About Elephants: Admonitions, Empirical Research and Legal Policy', 60 *UMKC L.Rev.* 645 (1992).

seizure,[119] the confidentiality rules,[120] discretion under the *Federal Rules of Evidence*[121] and the evaluation of the judicial ability of judges to evaluate the prejudicial effect of evidence on juries.[122] As these studies indicate, I believe that empirical studies to test the efficacy of the rules of evidence are useful components in improving our evidentiary system.

Consider, for example, Rule 407 of the *Federal Rules of Evidence*. It provides as follows: "When, after an injury or harm allegedly caused by an event, measures are taken that, if taken previously, would have made the injury or harm less likely to occur, evidence of the subsequent measures is not admissible to prove negligence, culpable conduct, a defect in a product, a defect in a product's design, or a need for a warning or instruction. This rule does not require the exclusion of evidence of subsequent measures when offered for another purpose, such as proving ownership, control, or feasibility of precautionary measures, if controverted, or impeachment."

Rule 407 of the *Uniform Rules of Evidence (1999)*, approved by the National Conference of Commissioners on Uniform State Laws in July, 1999, is the same as Rule 407 of the *Federal Rules* with the exception that the *Uniform Rule* would also apply to remedial measures taken after the sale of a product to a user or consumer.

Two grounds have been advanced in support of the rule excluding evidence of subsequent remedial measures. Initially, Wigmore argued that the evidence was irrelevant on the issue of prior negligence or culpable conduct, namely, that the supposed inference of negligence is not the most probable one that can be drawn from the subsequent repair or improvement. But, even assuming that the inference was a reasonable inference to draw from the subsequent repair, Wigmore went on to advance the argument that public policy supported the exclusionary rule on the ground that it encouraged all owners to improve the place or thing that had caused the injury.[123]

Under the more modern liberal approach to relevancy under Rule 401 of the *Federal Rules of Evidence*, a strong argument can be made that the circumstantial evidence of repair has a tendency to make the fact of negligence more probable than it would be without the evidence. This preference for the admission of evidence as opposed to its exclusion has led to the more generally

---

[119] M.W. Orfield, 'The Exclusionary Rule and Deterence: An Empirical Study of Chicago Narcotics Officers', 54 *Univ. of Chic.L.Rev.* 1016 (1987); J.E. Spiotto, 'Search and Seizure: an Empirical Study of the Exclusionary Rule and Its Alternatives', 2 *J.Legal Studies* 243 (1973).

[120] F.C. Zacharias, 'Rethinking Confidentiality', 74 *Iowa L.Rev.* 351 (1989).

[121] T.M. Mengler, 'The Theory of Discretion in the *Federal Rules of Evidence*', 74 *Iowa L.Rev.* 413 (1989).

[122] L.E. Teitelbaum *et al.*, 'Evaluating the Prejudicial Effect of Evidence: Can Judges Identify the Impact of Improper Evidence on Juries?', 1983 *Wis.L.Rev.* 1147.

[123] 2 J.H. Wigmore, *Evidence* § 283, at 174-175 (Chadbourn rev. 1979).

accepted ground for exclusion as one of encouraging persons to take safety precautions.

At the same time, there are strong arguments which challenge this justification for the rule. As expressed by Weinstein, "[n]ot every defendant will be aware of the possibility that subsequent remedial measures might constitute an admission. Of those who would know of the rule, it is unlikely that a responsible insured defendant would refrain deliberately from taking action to prevent the recurrence of subsequent serious injuries, because in any subsequent case, evidence of the earlier accident would be admissible to show that defendant knew of the dangerous condition. Even if the defendant is as cold-blooded as the rule suggests, his awareness of the many exceptions to the general exclusionary rule would make it risky to refrain from making the needed repairs. Rule 407 could have been eliminated with no great loss."[124]

This reasoning is persuasive. At the same time, there is no empirical data yet available to reinforce the reasoning of Weinstein and refute the preferred premise upon which the rule is based that subsequent remedial measures would be discouraged if they were admissible to prove negligence, culpable conduct or a defect in a product.[125] But even if the data were available would this lead to a change in the rule?

Consider the excited utterance exception to the hearsay rule. Persuasive doctrinal scholarship[126] supported by substantial empirical data[127] that the excited utterance exception to the hearsay rule cannot be defended on the ground of declarant reliability has not resulted in the abolition of the exception. Indeed, the Advisory Committee on the *Federal Rules of Evidence* elected to retain the rule in 1975 in spite of its recognition of the criticism of the exception as early as 1928 on the ground that excitement impairs accuracy of observation even though it eliminates conscious fabrication.[128] The Committee justified its retention in that "it finds support in cases without number".[129] As recently observed, "[s]canning the wealth of information describing how stressful, traumatic events negatively affect human functioning, it is disturbing

---

[124] Weinstein's Evidence, 407[02] at 407-15.
[125] V.E. Schwartz, 'The Exclusionary Rule on Subsequent Repairs – A Rule in Need of Repair', 7 *The Forum* 1 (1971).
[126] *See* J.D. Moorehead, 'Compromising the Hearsay Rule: the Fallacy of Res Gestae Reliability', 29 *Loy. of L.A.L.Rev.* 203 (1995), for reference to doctrinal scholarship in this area.
[127] Y. Shaham *et al.*, 'Stabiliity/Instability of Cognitive Strategies Across Tasks Determine Whether Stress Will Affect Judgmental Processes', 22 *J.App.Soc.Psychol.* 691 1992); H.M. Schrider *et al.*, *Human Information Processing: Individuals and Groups Functioning in Complex Social Situations* 99 (1967); R.J. Ursano & C.S. Fullerton, 'Cognitive and Behavioral Responses to Trauma', 20 *J.App.Soc.Psychol.* 1766, 1772 (1990).
[128] The Committee acknowledged the criticism of R.M. Hutchins & D. Slesinger, 'Some Observations on the Law of Evidence', 28 *Colum.L.Rev.* 432, 439 (1928).
[129] Advisory Committee's Note, Rule 803(2).

to discover that judges regularly rely upon the excited utterance exception for no better reason than its 'firm entrenchment' in the law of evidence."[130]

## Formulating the Black Letter of Rules of Evidence

One of the basic questions confronting the American Law Institute in the drafting of the *Model Code of Evidence of 1942* was with method and style. For this purpose, Professor Wigmore submitted six postulates that the Institute should agree upon in the drafting of the rules.[131] With one exception, agreement was reached generally on all of the postulates, although there was some disagreement as to whether the *Model Code* as finally written manifested the spirit of them.[132]

The postulate upon which agreement could not be reached was that the rules should not deal with abstraction, but with all of the specific rules exemplifying the abstraction. Its importance in the drafting of the *Model Code* is evident by the degree of attention that was drawn to it in debate by the members of the Institute.[133] Should the *Model Code* be drafted in detail and embody all of the concrete rules exemplifying the application of an abstraction? Should the *Model Code* be stated in generalities as then exemplified by the *Federal Rules of Civil Procedure*? Or, should a compromise position be adopted?

The first – or Wigmore – view was directed toward providing a code of detailed directory provisions for the guidance of the bench and bar.[134] The second – or Clark view – can be characterized as the other extreme. Judge Clark argued that every detailed statement would result in an additional opportunity for litigation, necessitate judicial construction of all the language used and impede further development in the law of evidence.[135] However, the Clark view was, and is, not entirely free of difficulties. Generality in treatment often necessitates judicial elaboration, a problem recognized by Judge Clark that could only be overcome by frequent revision based upon experience in

---

[130] *See*, for example, J.D. Moorehead, 'Compromising the Hearsay Rule: The Fallacy of Res Gestae Reliability', 29 *Loy. of L.A.L.Rev.* 203 (1995), citing *US* v. *Moore*, 791 *F.2d* 566 (7th Cir. 1986), at p. 239.

[131] These were (1) the rules of evidence should be stated as they ought to be and might practically be made; (2) the rules should furnish a complete code; (3) the rules should not contain scientific generalizations in terms of expression which were complex, novel and unfamiliar to the bench and bar; (4) the rules should not deal with abstraction, but with all the specific rules exemplifying the abstraction; (5) any changes in an existing rule should be expressly stated and not left to implication; and (6) the comments should not contain any statement amounting to a rule of practice additional to the text of the rule. 17 *Proc.Am.Law Inst.* 66-87 (1940).

[132] J.H. Wigmore, 'The American Law Institute Code of Evidence Rules: A Dissent', 28 *A.B.A.J.* 23 (1941).

[133] 17 *Proc.Am.Law Inst.* 70-87 (1940).

[134] For example, *see* J.H. Wigmore, *Code of Evidence* (2nd ed. 1935).

[135] *See* note 3, *supra*, at 81-84.

working with the rules.[136] The problem in drafting rules of evidence is then twofold. First, it is one of devising a system rigid enough to reach accurate results in fact finding, secure equality in the treatment of litigants and systematize the disposition of litigation. Second, yet at the same time, the system must be flexible enough to provide for individuality in the application of the rules of evidence and give due regard to the substantive rights of the parties in specific cases.[137]

The American Law Institute resolved this basic problem in drafting, wisely I believe, by accepting the view of the Reporter, Professor Morgan, which represented a compromise between the two extremes. It was "to draw a series of rules in general terms covering the larger divisions and subdivisions of the subject without attempting to frame rules of thumb for specific situations and to make the trial judge's rulings reviewable for abuse of discretion."[138] This is essentially the approach followed in the drafting of the *Federal Rules of Evidence* of 1975 and the *Uniform Rules of Evidence* of 1974 based on the *Proposed Federal Rules of Evidence* prior to their adoption by the Congress of the US. How do the rules as drafted measure up to the approach first followed in the drafting of the *Model Code*?

There are two models in the current *Federal Rules* that are useful in illustrating this approach. These are Rules 401, 402 and 403 dealing with relevancy and unfair prejudice and Rule 803(3) providing for an exception to the hearsay rule to admit statements of existing mental, emotional, or physical condition of non-testifying declarants. Rule 401 provides: "'Relevant evidence' means evidence have any tendency to make the existence of any fact that is of consequence to the determination of the action more probable or less probable than it would be without the evidence."

Rule 402 provides, in part: "All relevant evidence is admissible (...). Evidence which is not relevant is not admissible." Rule 403 provides: "Although relevant, evidence may be excluded if its probative value is substantially outweighed by the danger of unfair prejudice, confusion of the issues, or misleading the jury, or by considerations of undue delay, waste of time, or needless presentation of issues."

Rule 402, with exceptions, providing that all relevant evidence is admissible and that evidence which is not relevant is not admissible is "a presupposition involved in the very conception of a rational system of

---

[136] C.E. Clark, 'Special Problems in Drafting and Interpreting Procedural Codes', 3 *Van.L.Rev.* 493, 507 (1950).
[137] 2 Holdsworth, *History of English Law* 251 (3rd ed. 1923); C.E. Clark, 'The Handmaid of Justice', 23 *Wash.U.L.Q.*. 297, 300 (1938).
[138] E.M. Morgan, 'Foreword', *Model Code of Evidence* 13 (1942).

evidence."[139] As such, the rule constitutes the foundation upon which rests the structure for the admission and exclusion of evidence.[140]

However, relevancy is not an inherent characteristic of any item of evidence. Rather, relevancy exists as a relation between an item of evidence and a fact of consequence sought to be proved. The existence of the relationship depends upon principles arising through experience or science that is applied logically to the facts at issue in the case.[141] As such, factual issues involving relevancy do not fall into a set pattern and, wisely, the drafters of the accompanying Rule 401 crafted only a general standard for handling them. Does the evidence have "any tendency to make the existence of a fact of consequence (...) more probable or less probable than it would be without the evidence?" The broad spectrum in which issues of relevancy arise do not lend themselves to the crafting of rules of thumb to govern specific situations.

Rule 403 also recognizes that in some circumstances evidence of unquestioned relevance requires its exclusion. At the same time, in drafting similar to Rule 401, Rule 403 states only general grounds for the exclusion of evidence through balancing the probative value of the evidence against harms likely to result from its admission. Accordingly, while unfair prejudice, confusion of the issues, misleading the jury, considerations of undue delay, waste of time and cumulative evidence are set forth as grounds for exclusion, the drafters wisely left their application in specific factual settings to the trial judge.

Now, compare the foregoing approach to relevancy with the somewhat more specific statements of the then existing mental, emotional, or physical condition exception to the hearsay rule. Rule 803(3) provides: "A statement of the declarant's then existing state of mind, emotion, sensation, or physical condition (such as intent, plan, motive, design, mental feeling, pain and bodily health), but not including a statement of memory or belief to prove the fact remembered or believed unless it relates to the execution, revocation, identification, or terms of declarant's will."

The underlying rationale for this exception is that the contemporaneity of the mental or physical condition and the statement relating to that condition negative the likelihood of deliberate or conscious misrepresentation. However, an examination of the black letter of the exception discloses, with one exception, that statements of memory or belief to prove the fact remembered or believed are not included within the exception.[142]

---

[139] J.B. Thayer, *Preliminary Treatise on Evidence* 264 (1898).

[140] Advisory Committee's Note, *Federal Rules of Evidence*, 56 *F.R.D.* 183, 216.

[141] G.F. James, 'Relevancy, Probability and the Law', 29 *Cal.L.Rev.* 689, 696, n. 15 (1941).

[142] The exclusion of these statements from the exception is justified, first, because they may be the product of improper perception, faulty memory, or deliberate misrepresentation, particularly when the statement is directed toward the past act of a third party. Second, to admit them would result in the virtual destruction of the hearsay rule since state of mind provable by a hearsay statement (to be continued)

If only statements of memory or belief to prove the fact remembered or believed are excluded by the black letter of the rule, does this mean that statements of mental state to prove the performance of a future act are admissible? The future act of the declarant only? The future act of the declarant participated in by a third person? The future act only of the third person? None of these issues are addressed in the black letter of Rule 803(3)? Should they be? The reliability of statements to prove future conduct is somewhat less in situations of this type since it is significantly less likely that a declared intention will be carried out than that a declared state of mind actually exists. The reliability then decreases proportionately when the issue involves participation or action of a third person.

What does the rule itself tell us as to the admissibility of statements to prove future conduct? First, by excluding only statements of a declarant's memory or belief to prove the fact remembered or believed a strong argument can be made that the exception can be interpreted to admit statements of a declarant as to the declarant's future conduct. This would conform to the interpretation placed on the rule by the House Committee on the Judiciary when the *Federal Rules of Evidence* were submitted to Congress for approval.[143] It is less clear whether the black letter of Rule 803(3) would permit statements of a declarant's belief to prove the future act of the declarant participated in by another person or the future act only of the third person. The issue grows out of a late 19th century decision of the Supreme Court of the US in which the Court held that a declarant's statement of belief to prove the cooperative action of a third person was admissible.[144] Nevertheless, it is clear from the legislative history that the House Committee on the Judiciary intended that the rule be interpreted to admit statements of the declarant only as to the declarant's future conduct.[145]

In spite of this legislative history, the ambiguity in Rule 803(3) has led to a split in Federal[146] and State[147] judicial authority as to whether the statement of

---

would serve as a basis for the inference of the happening of the event which produced the state of mind. *See Shepard* v. *US*, 290 *U.S.* 96, 54 *S.Ct.* 22, 78 *L.Ed.* 196 (1933). In contrast, permitting statements relating to the execution, revocation, identification, or terms of a declarants will are justified on the practical grounds of necessity and expediency. Advisory Committee's Note, *Federal Rules of Evidence*, 56 *F.R.D.* 183, 303.

[143] *See* House Comm. On Judiciary, *Federal Rules of Evidence*, H.R. Rep. No 650, *93rd Cong. & Ad. News*, 7075, 7087.

[144] *Mutual Life Insurance Company v. Hillmon*, 145 *U.S.* 285, 12 *S.Ct.* 909, 36 *L.Ed.* 706 (1892).

[145] *See* note 143, *supra*.

[146] The Second and Fourth Circuits hold that such statements are admissible only when they are linked with independent evidence that corroborates the statement. *See US* v. *Nersesian*, 824 *F.2d* 1294 (2d Cir. 1987) and *US* v. *Jenkins*, 579 *F.2d* 840 (4th Cir. 1978). In contrast, the Ninth Circuit has held that such statements are admissible without corroborating evidence. *See US* v. *Pheaster*, 544 *F.2d* 353 (9th Cir. 1976).

[147] A majority of the states hold that such statements are inadmissible. *See* Reporter's Note to *Uniform Rule 803* (3) of the *Uniform Rules of Evidence (1999)*.

the declarant is admissible to prove the future conduct of a third person. In the Court of Appeals for the Ninth Circuit the Court concluded that the early Supreme Court decision holding such statements admissible remained undisturbed after the adoption of Rule 803(3). It reasoned that such statements are admissible because (1) the text of the rule does not expressly prohibit their admission and (2) the legislative history surrounding the adoption of the rule is contradictory. The Advisory Committee on the *Federal Rules of Evidence* has apparently not considered resolving the interpretive problem. The problem was considered by the Drafting Committee of the National Conference of Commissioners on Uniform State Laws to revise the *Uniform Rules of Evidence (1999)*, but it chose not to recommend any change in the black letter of *Uniform Rule* 803(3).

Interestingly, this uncertainty has been resolved in five states by an express statutory or rule provision excluding statements of intent as to the conduct of third persons.[148] This may or may not be the policy choice which should be made regarding the admissibility of statements of a declarant's belief as to the conduct of third parties. Nevertheless, the issue is easily resolved by amending the black letter to embrace either the exclusion or admission of such statements and resolve the confusion currently existing among the courts in interpreting the rule. Unlike the essential generality of Rules 401 and 403, this issue regarding the interpretation of Rule 803(3) presents a relatively narrow fact specific issue which could be resolved easily through clarification in the black letter of the Rule.

### Evaluating the Appellate Interpretation of Rules of Evidence

In the adoption of the *Federal Rules of Evidence* in 1975 Congress approved of the inclusion of two identical residual exceptions to the hearsay rule, one in Rule 803(24) to apply where the availability of the declarant to testify was immaterial and one in Rule 804(b)(5) to apply where the unavailability of the declarant was required,[149] although the black letter of the exceptions was narrowed considerably over those proposed by the Supreme Court of the US.[150] In 1997 the two residual exceptions were combined in the *Federal*

---

[148] These are: Alaska, *Alaska R.Evid.* 803(3); California, *Ann.Cal.Evid. Code* § 1250; Florida, *Fla.Stat.Ann.* § 90.803(3); Louisiana, *La.R.Evid.* 803(3); and Maryland, *Maryland R.Evid.* 5-803(b)(3).

[149] These were Rules 803(24) and 804(b)(5), respectively.

[150] Proposed Rules 803(24) and 804(b)(6) provided: "A statement not specifically covered by any of the foregoing exceptions but having comparable circumstantial guarantees of trustworthiness." In contrast, Rules 803(24) and 804(b)(5), as adopted, required that a statement not falling within one of the specific exceptions (1) possess "equivalent circumstantial guarantees of trustworthiness", (2) be "offered as evidence of a material fact", (3) be "more probative on the point for which it is offered than any other evidence which the proponent can procure through (to be continued)

*Rules* into a single Rule 807 without any significant opposition.[151] It provides: "A statement not specifically covered by Rule 803 or 804 but having equivalent circumstantial guarantees of trustworthiness, is not excluded by the hearsay rule, if the court determines that (A) the statement is offered as evidence of a material fact; (B) the statement is more probative on the point for which it is offered than any other evidence which the proponent can procure through reasonable efforts; and (C) the general purposes of these rules and the interests of justice will best be served by admission of the statement into evidence. However, a statement may not be admitted under this exception unless the proponent of it makes known to the adverse party sufficiently in advance of the trial or hearing to provide the adverse party with a fair opportunity to prepare to meet it, the proponent's intention to offer the statement and the particulars of it, including the name and address of the declarant." The exception has been adopted in a majority of the American states.[152]

The rationale for the rule was explained in the Advisory Committee's Note to the predecessor Rules 803(24) and 804(b)(5) as follows: "It would (...) be presumptuous to assume that all possible exceptions to the hearsay rule have been catalogued and to pass the hearsay rule to oncoming generations as a closed system. Exception (24) and its companion provision in Rule 804(b) (...) (5) are accordingly included. They do not contemplate an unfettered exercise of judicial discretion, but they do provide for treating new and presently unanticipated situations which demonstrate a trustworthiness within the spirit of the specifically stated exceptions."[153]

Without questioning this rationale for establishing the exception, there are two difficult and recurring issues that arise in both the federal and state jurisdictions in determining the admissibility of statements under the residual exception. The first arises out of the language in the rule "[a] statement not specifically covered by Rule 803 or 804" and the second out of the language "having equivalent circumstantial guarantees of trustworthiness."

---

reasonable efforts" and (4) "the general purposes of these rules and the interests of justice will best be served by admission of the statement into evidence."

[151] The Committee Note states as follows: "The contents of Rule 803(24) and Rule 804(b)(5) have been combined and transferred to a new Rule 807. This was done to facilitate additions to Rules 803 and 804. No change in meaning is intended." Actually, the two residual exceptions, one where availability of the declarant is immaterial and one where the unavailability of the declarant is required, were superfluous. The foundational requirement in former Rules 803(24) and 804(b)(5) that "the statement must be more probative on the point for which it is offered than any other evidence which the proponent can procure through reasonable efforts" moots the requirement of the availability of the declarant to testify. If the declarant is available to testify the hearsay statement is not more probative on the point than evidence which can be procured through reasonable efforts. *See*, in this connection, *US* v. *Mathis*, 559 *F.2d* 294 (5th Cir. 1977).

[152] *See* Reporter's Note to *Uniform Rule* 808 of the *Uniform Rules of Evidence (1999)*.

[153] *See Dallas County* v. *Commercial Union Assur. Co.*, 286 *F.2d* 388 (5th Cir. 1961).

As to the first, may a statement which almost, but fails to meet the requisite foundational requirements of one of the specific exceptions in Rules 803 or 804(b) be admitted under the residual exception of Rule 807. At the time of the enactment of the *Federal Rules of Evidence*, Congressional concerns were expressed that hearsay statements which failed to meet the foundational requirements for admissibility under a potentially applicable specific exception would nevertheless be admitted under the then two residual exceptions of Rules 803(24) and 804(b)(5).[154] At the federal level, Congressional concerns have been found to be warranted. See, for example, *US* v. *Furst*, [155] in which the court concluded that "[r]ule 803(24)is not limited in availability as to types of evidence not addressed in the other exceptions; (...) [it] is also available when the proponent fails to meet the standards set forth in other exceptions."

More recently, this 'near miss' doctrine has been applied by the Ninth Circuit to admit under Rule 803(24) a prior inconsistent statement not under oath which was inadmissible for its substance under Rule 801(d)(1)(a). In *US* v. *Valdez-Soto*,[156] the court, rejecting the defendant's reliance on legislative history, easily dismissed Congressional concern as follows: "Relying on legislative history, defendants claim this hearsay exception must be interpreted narrowly. We decline the defendants' invitation to go skipping down the yellow brick road of legislative history. Rule 803(24) exists to provide courts with flexibility in admitting statements traditionally regarded as hearsay but not falling within any of the conventional exceptions."

At the state level, both a restrictive and liberal interpretation has been given to the expanded use of the residual exception. For example, in Alaska, in *Shakespeare* v. *State*,[157] the Court reasoned as follows in holding that a statement determined to be inadmissible under the State's statement against interest exception was not admissible under its residual exception.

This residual exception, however, is one of rare application and is not meant to be used as a catch-all for the admission of statements falling just outside the borders of recognized exceptions. Under *A.R.E.* 804(b)(5) an independent analysis must be undertaken to see if the case involves "exceptional circumstances where the court finds guarantees of trustworthiness equivalent to or exceeding the guarantees reflected in the present exceptions to the hearsay rule."

---

[154] *See* 120 *Cong.Rec.* H12255-57 (December 18, 1974).
[155] 886 *F.2d* 558 (3rd Cir. 1989).
[156] 31 *F.3d* 1467, 1471 (9th Cir. 1994). This has also presented a problem at the federal level with respect to the admissibility of grand jury statements under the residual exception. Compare *US* v. *Fernandez*, 892 *F.2d* 976 (11th Cir. 1989), with the concurring opinion of Judge Easterbrook in *US* v. *Dent*, 984 *F.2d* 1453 (7th Cir. 1993).
[157] 827 *P.2d* 454, 460 (Alaska App. 1992).

In contrast, in Wisconsin, in *Mitchell* v. *State*,[158] the issue involved the admissibility of police reports that did not meet the foundational requirements for admissibility under the business records exception to the hearsay rule. The Supreme Court rejected the defendant's argument "that to admit these reports under the residual exception is to circumvent the requirements of the business records exception." As in two previous cases, the Court reasoned that "that the drafters did not intend to restrict the use of the residual exception to situations which are completely different from those covered by the specifically enumerated exceptions." All that is required, the Court concluded, is that the statements have circumstantial guarantees of trustworthiness comparable to the enumerated exceptions.

How should this first issue, the so-called 'near miss' issue, be resolved? Initially, the question is whether interference with the appellate interpretations through rule modification is warranted. If not, then the residual exception should not be tampered with and the courts left free to determine on a case by case basis the admissibility of statements not falling within a specific exception to the hearsay rule.

Secondarily, there is the policy question of whether the hearsay rule and its exceptions as presently structured should afford an indirect abrogation of the hearsay rule in particular cases through a liberal interpretation of the residual exception. If so, drafting with greater specificity would not seem to be needed. If not, then it should be made clear in the black letter of the residual exception that only statements which do not fall within any of the enumerated exceptions are admissible under the residual exception. As in the case of our earlier discussion of Rule 803(3), this is a relatively narrow fact specific issue that does not require generality in treatment and is susceptible to correction through drafting.

As of the present time, the Advisory Committee on the *Federal Rules of Evidence* has elected not to attempt any clarifying amendments to Rule 807. In contrast, the National Conference of Commissioners on Uniform State Laws has approved the amendment of Rule 808(a) of the *Uniform Rules of Evidence (1999)*, that combines the former residual exceptions of former Rules 803(24) and 804(b)(5), as follows: "(a) Exception. In exceptional circumstances a statement not ~~specifically~~ covered by ~~any of the foregoing exceptions~~ Rule 803, 804, or 807 but ~~having~~ possessing equivalent, though not identical, circumstantial guarantees of trustworthiness, is not excluded by the hearsay rule if the court determines that:" Is this amendment a wise policy choice? Does it effectively circumvent the 'near miss' doctrine?

The second issue relates to the question of whether, under Rule 807 of the *Federal Rules of Evidence* the statement has "equivalent circumstantial guarantees of trustworthiness", or under Rule 808 of the *Uniform Rules of*

---

[158] 84 *Wis.2nd* 325, 267 *N.W.2nd* 349 (1978).

*Evidence (1999)* the statement "possesses equivalent, though not identical, circumstantial guarantees of trustworthiness". In either case this involves a fact-intensive inquiry and is not the type of issue that is susceptible to elaboration in the black letter of the rule. However, as in the case of the amendment to *Uniform Rule* 808(a), it is possible to circumvent the 'near miss' doctrine through a black letter amendment to the rule.

### Assessing the Degree of Congruence between Rules of Evidence and Their Efficiency in producing a Desired Result

In a recent Working Paper, Chief Judge Richard A. Posner of the Seventh Circuit, in addition to proposing and elaborating on an economic model of evidence and examining the structure of the evidence-gathering process, makes a compelling case for evaluating the rules of evidence from an economic point of view.[159] Posner analyzes many of the exclusionary rules of the *Federal Rules of Evidence* in terms of their cost benefit, including relevancy and unfair prejudice, the subsequent remedial measures rule, the character ban, privileges, expert testimony and hearsay. Two of his models are useful for illustrative purposes.

First, in a discussion of Rules 401, 402 and 403, Judge Posner concludes that "[t]hese rules make economic sense".[160] Of these areas of analysis, he focuses on Rule 403 to conclude that the rule "in requiring an explicit comparison of benefit and cost is central to an economic analysis of the law of evidence (...)."[161] The emotionality factor, as in the case of unfair prejudice, permits the exclusion of evidence which would otherwise require greater mental efforts by the jurors in reaching a correct decision without any reduction in costs and thereby increase the value of their verdict.

Similarly, those aspects of Rule 403 permitting the exclusion of evidence which confuses or misleads the jury, or wastes time, including undue delay or the needless presentation of cumulative evidence, carry with them a cost benefit by ameliorating the necessity for additional evidence and shortening the length of the trial.[162]

Judge Posner concludes his analysis of the cost benefits of Rules 401, 402 and 403 as follows: "By excluding irrelevant and also relevant but on balance unhelpful, evidence, Rules 402 and 403 counteract the incentive of the parties in some cases to overinvest in evidence from a social standpoint. We should expect these rules to be invoked most often in big money cases, for it is in such

---

[159] R.A. Posner, 'An Economic Approach to the Law of Evidence', J.M. Olin Law & Economics Working Paper No. 66 (2d Series), reprinted, 51 *Stan.L.Rev.* 1477 (1999).
[160] *Id.*, at 1522.
[161] *Id.*, at 1522.
[162] *Id.*, at 1523-1524.

cases that the risk of over investment is greatest. This suggests a possible direction for empirical research."[163]

Similarly, Judge Posner argues that the hearsay rule can be justified on a basis of the costs of the trial process just as the exclusion of evidence on the grounds of "waste of time" in rule 403 can be justified through cost-benefit analysis. The jury, he points out, cannot terminate the evidentiary process, but the hearsay rule aids the jury in this respect by excluding "an indefinite mass of generally dubious evidence".[164] Also, he suggests that the hearsay rule, as in the case of Rules 402 and 403, can be understood to counteract the incentive that may exist to overinvest in evidence.[165]

Second, in contrast to these foregoing models of cost-efficient rules of evidence, Judge Posner points to Rule 103(a) providing that a trial court's ruling on the admissibility of evidence cannot be overturned on appeal "unless a substantial right of a party is affected."[166] If this standard is not met the error of the trial court is a harmless error and will not constitute a ground for reversal. He argues from an economic perspective that the principle of harmless error is essential to prevent the reversal and remand of cases which would result in additional costs of litigation with no benefits.

At the same time, the harmless error principle "may often confer an undeserved, or at least unintended, advantage on prosecutors."[167] If the prosecutor knows that the particular jury before whom the defendant is being tried is prone to acquit, he may risk introducing otherwise inadmissible evidence to secure a conviction. Since the appellate court did not witness the trial, it will be difficult for the court to assess the likelihood that the errors affected that outcome. In consequence, an error may look harmless to the appellate court, yet may have been harmful in affecting the outcome. Although it is uncertain how great the incentive might be for prosecutors to use deliberate errors to convict a defendant, Posner concludes, to be on the safe side, that the doctrine of harmless error should be modified to exclude from its operation deliberate errors committed or induced by prosecutors and make them a ground for automatic reversal.[168]

---

[163] *Id.*, at 1524. *See* the discussion, *supra*, regarding the value of empirical studies in determining the efficacy of the exclusionary rules of evidence.

[164] *Id.*, at 1533. *But see*, for a contrary view, L. Kaplow, 'Note, The Theoretical Foundation of the Hearsay Rules', 93 *Harv.L.Rev.* 1786, 1794-1804.

[165] *Id.*, at 1530.

[166] Rule 103 (a) provides: "Error may not be predicated upon a ruling which admits or excludes evidence unless a substantial right of a party is affected (...)."

[167] *Supra*, note 159, at 1518.

[168] *Supra*, note 159, at 1519-1520.

## D. The Influence of Precedent, the Adversary System, Trial by Jury and Judicial Discretion in the Rational Development of Rules of Evidence

I firmly believe that reforms in the rules of evidence should be governed by the criteria I have outlined and illustrated. They could be broad based. For example, in the hearsay context, through deliberation, the development of a rational hypothesis and careful drafting we might implement the proposal of Roger Park to admit more hearsay in civil cases. The standard exceptions would remain, but a rule of preference coupled with a notice – and – counter notice would apply. The proponent would give notice of intent to offer hearsay whereupon by counter notice the opponent could instead demand production of the declarant. The proponent would then be required to produce the declarant or demonstrate the declarant's unavailability. In either case the hearsay statement would be admissible regardless of its reliability.[169]

Or, a more dramatic reform might be hypothesized, debated and drafted by implementing the proposal of Eleanor Swift who challenges the process of determining reliability by class exceptions to propose the admission of hearsay if the proponent presents 'foundation facts' sufficient to enable a jury to evaluate the reliability of the statement intelligently.[170]

As impressive as these proposals might be, I do not believe that these, or other similarly broad based reforms in the exclusionary rules, will be forthcoming in the near future. Rather, I believe that reform efforts will focus more narrowly on particular rules and the problematic evidentiary issues that have been raised in their application.

There are at least four characteristics of the American evidentiary system in the resolution of issues of fact that lead me to this conclusion. These are precedent, the adversary system, jury trial and restrictions on judicial discretion.

### Precedent

As to precedent, I would again allude to the excited utterance exception to the hearsay rule.[171] It is at least 200 years old and is recognized in every jurisdiction of the US, federal and state.[172] Moreover, it retains its vitality even in the face of impressive doctrinal scholarship and persuasive empirical

---

[169] *See* R.C. Park, 'A Subject Matter Approach to Hearsay Reform', 86 *Mich.L.Rev.* 51 (1987).

[170] E. Swift, 'Abolishing the Hearsay Rule', 75 *U.Cal.L.Rev.* 495 (1987).

[171] *See* the text at footnotes 126 to 130.

[172] *See*, for example, *White* v. *Illinois*, 502 *U.S.* 346, 112 *S.Ct.* 736, 116 *L.Ed.2d* 848 (1992), at n. 8.

research that the exception has outlived its usefulness.[173] These and other similarly recognized evidentiary rules are powerful forces against change.

### The Adversary System

Second, to what extent does the adversary system affect reforms in the law of evidence? In an adversary system of adjudication the parties control the procedural resolution of disputes, while the adjudicator, judge or jury, remains essentially passive. From this premise the question has been asked "[t]o what degree (…) do factual inquiries propelled by partisan self-interest spawn deviations from an ideal model of inquiry that aspires to objective knowledge?"[174] And, to what extent are reforms in the law of evidence affected by this partisan self-interest stemming from the adversary system?

In the *Uniform Rules of Evidence (1999)*, unlike recent proposals for amending the *Federal Rules of Evidence*, *Uniform Rule* 404(b) was amended to provide for procedural guidelines for the admissibility of other crimes, wrongs or acts evidence when offered for a permissible purpose under Rule 404(b). As a general rule other crimes, wrongs or acts evidence is not admissible to prove action in conformity therewith on a particular occasion. The evidence may be admissible for other purposes, such as, to prove motive, opportunity, intent, preparation, plan, knowledge, identity or absence of mistake or accident.[175] The apparent abuse of admitting other crimes, wrongs or acts evidence under these exceptions in the several states caused the National Conference to amend the rule this past year to provide procedural guidelines in determining the admissibility of other crimes, wrongs or acts evidence under these exceptions. These include the giving of notice, proving the commission of the other crime, wrong or act by clear and convincing evidence, establishing that the evidence is relevant, that its relevancy outweighs the danger of unfair prejudice and, upon the request of a party, giving an instruction to the jury as to the limited admissibility of the evidence.[176]

This amendment is not revolutionary at all since it incorporates in the rule black letter decisional law recognized in a significant number of state jurisdictions.[177] However, in spite of these decisional precedents, one may wonder how influential the amendment will be insofar as its enactment in the several states is concerned. Defense lawyers will in all probability speak

---

[173] *See* J.D. Moorehead, 'Compromising the Hearsay Rule: The Fallacy of Res Gestae Reliability', 29 *Loy. of L.A.L.Rev.* 203 (1995).
[174] M.R. Damaška, *Evidence Law Adrift* 75 (1997).
[175] *Uniform Rules of Evidence*, Rule 404(b). *See also* Rule 404(b) of the *Federal Rules of Evidence* which is the same as *Uniform Rule* 404(b).
[176] *Uniform Rules of Evidence (1999)*, Rule 404(c).
[177] *See* Reporter's Note to Rule 404, *Uniform Rules of Evidence* (1999).

approvingly of the amendment because it brings to bear black letter procedural requirements that must be observed by prosecutors in offering other crimes, wrongs or acts evidence under one of the permissible purposes. Conversely, prosecutors will resist enactment of the amendment because the black letter focuses on stricter control in the admissibility of the evidence. In short, the amendment focuses on greater objectivity in the application of Rule 404(b), but it directly impacts on the partisan self-interests of the parties.

## Trial by Jury

It has been observed that there is a dramatic decline in trial by jury and, with it, the *raison d'être* for the exclusionary rules, notably hearsay, is diminishing.[178] This includes the elimination or reduction of jury trials in civil litigation, the waiver of the right to jury trial in criminal litigation, the proliferation of administrative agency hearings where the triers of fact are administrative judges rather than jurors[179] and the increasing reliance upon alternative dispute resolution mechanisms in determining issues of fact.[180]

At the same time, it is less than clear whether this marginalization of jury trials will abate the claims of the proponents of the value of the exclusionary rules. Jury trials continue to be employed in both civil and criminal cases and they thereby serve as a medium for continuing to shape the evidentiary system in America.[181] This, together with the 'post-modern' justification for the exclusionary rules, hearsay in particular, suggest that trial by jury is still a significant influence insofar as reforming the law of evidence is concerned.[182]

## Restrictions on Judicial Discretion

Finally, among trial lawyers, there is a strong belief that rules provide protection against unlimited judicial discretion. This was certainly at the center of the objections to the *Model Code of Evidence* approved by the American Law Institute in 1942 which liberally modified the exclusionary rules and correspondingly enlarged the discretion of the trial judge.[183] As observed previously by one commentator, "[t]rial judges may need rules of some sort to deal wisely with hearsay". Even though a judge "who is both a scholar and an

---

[178] M.R. Damaška, *Evidence Law Adrift* 127 (1997).

[179] *Id.*, at 126-127.

[180] L.C. Kirkpatrick, 'Scholarly and Institutional Challenges to the Law of Evidence: From Bentham to the ADR Movement', 25 *Loy. of L.A.L.Rev.* 837 (1992).

[181] *Supra*, note 178, at 128.

[182] *See*, in this connection, a thoughtful analysis of the conventional modern account of hearsay, its defenders and its reformers, in C.B. Mueller, 'Post-Modern Hearsay Reform: The Importance of Complexity', 76 *Minn.L.Rev.* 367 (1992).

[183] *See* the text, *supra*, at notes 21-26.

extraordinary jurist" may work well without rules, it is "quite another to suppose most judges can do so".[184] In short, without the constraints of rules, trial judges may unwittingly favor one party's or another's cause, or one lawyer's or another's forensic talents, without a principled justification for doing so.[185]

## Conclusion

These forgoing forces of precedent, the adversary system, trial by jury and restricting judicial discretion suggest that dramatic proposals for reform in the American version of the rules of evidence in the early years of the coming millenium will have little chance of adoption. In the context of the hearsay rule, the reforms may be "too simple, too much attuned to the academic vision of rationality and too little attuned to the complexity of concerns underlying the doctrine."[186] However, this ought not to foreclose refining the hearsay rule or abolishing exceptions to the rule that rest on questionable theoretical premises.[187] In a broader context, useful reforms can be made in this and other troublesome areas if the suggested criteria for developing, evaluating and improving the rules of evidence are considered and applied.

---

[184] *See* Mueller, *supra*, note 182, at 397.
[185] *See* Mueller, *supra*, note 182, at 397.
[186] *See* Mueller, *supra*, note 182, at 368-369.
[187] J.D. Moorehead, 'Compromising the Hearsay Rule: The Fallacy of *Res Gestae* Reliability', 29 *Loy. at L.A.L.Rev.* 203, 223 (1995).

# Scientific Evidence in Polish Judicial Proceedings

*J. Wójcikiewicz*

## Introduction

"The examination of handwriting authenticity is carried out with or without the participation of experts, specifically through a comparison of the handwriting in question with that deriving from the same person as in authentic documents. If necessary, the court may summon the author to write down some dictated words."[1] Only French lawyers will probably recognise in the above text a rule from *The Napoleonic Code* of 1806. Almost 200 years later this provision, a real legal fossil, is still in effect as Article 254 § 1 of the *Polish Code of Civil Procedure* from 1964. Nevertheless, it can serve as a clear subjective and objective criterion of scientific evidence definition. Namely, it is obvious that an 'opinion' provided by a judge himself/herself, in a field not regarded as a branch of science[2] should not be treated as scientific evidence. On the contrary, as scientific evidence we can define an expert opinion based on science, and prepared in accordance to scientific methodology.[3]

The fundamental US Supreme Court's judgement in *Daubert* v. *Merrel Dow Pharmaceuticals* (1993) has had much farther reaching consequences than those affecting federal cases in the US. More than a few basic principles of well established forensic disciplines, like fingerprint identification, have begun to be questioned, as in *United States* v. *Mitchell* (1998).[4] Within other criminal justice systems as well, like Poland's, the need for the existence of some criteria for the scientific evaluation of evidence has also been expressed.[5]

## Scientific Evidence in Civil Proceedings

According to Article 233 § 1 of the *Code of Civil Procedure*, the court appraises the reliability and strength of the evidence according to its own convictions, based on comprehensive consideration of the material gathered. No doubt, "comprehensive consideration" refers also to the application of knowledge. This is an important aspect of the free appraisal of evidence. One of the vital sources of the court's knowledge is an expert opinion. In cases which demand specialised knowledge the court, after hearing the litigants' requests concerning the number and choice of expert witnesses, may call upon

---

[1] Ustawa z dnia 17 listopada, 1964.
[2] Cf. *United States* v. *Starzecpyzel* (1995); Majamaa (1998).
[3] Cf. Gruza (1995).
[4] Moenssens (1999); Grieve (1999).
[5] Waltoś (1998).

one or several experts in order to obtain their opinions (Article 278 § 1 *Code of Civil Procedure*).

The Code also provides the legal basis for other types of evidence other than documents, witness testimony, expert opinions, search, and interrogation of the parties. Namely, Section 7 contains provisions for blood testing, film, TV, photocopies, photographs, blueprints, drawings, records, tapes and other similar media. Moreover, Article 309 is the legal basis for so-called 'uncalled evidence'. This tendency to enumerate all possible forms of evidence is typical for civil proceedings, more conservative in this area than criminal proceedings.

Paradoxically, civil proceedings seem to be much more progressive in the terms of the status of scientific evidence, at least as concerns the views of the judiciary. Let us note that out of four fundamental American judgements on scientific evidence, that is *Frye* v. *United States* (1923), *Daubert* v. *Merrel Dow Pharmaceuticals* (1993), *General Electric* v. *Joiner* (1997), and *Kumho Tire Co.* v. *Carmichael* (1999), all but the first are the civil cases! Is it due to the fact that in criminal cases, where a person's freedom or even life is at stake, courts should be more reluctant to admit evidence based on new, unproven techniques?[6] On the other hand, they are criminal courts that ought to be more eager to establish some general criteria for the evaluation of admissibility and/or reliability of scientific evidence. A similar situation occurs in Polish judicial proceedings. To tell the truth, no general rulings on scientific evidence exist in civil and criminal procedures. Only in one civil case, the Supreme Court had an exceptional opportunity to establish some general criteria for the scientific evaluation of evidence.

Namely, in June, 1985 the Łódź Provincial Court asked the Supreme Court whether it was admissible to call as an expert witness a practitioner of a discipline which "did not fulfil contemporary criteria of science (for example a diviner)"[7] The plaintiff demanded a new flat from a lessor because the one he was leased turned out to be unsuitable for living. A diviner had found that the plaintiff's room was totally irradiated with negative energy created by underground streams that cause destructive vibrations. Spheres of such 'geopathic radiation' allegedly cause tiredness, nervousness, and sleeplessness.

The defendant claimed that the district court's verdict was based on unscientific statements. The Supreme Court, nevertheless, approved the diviner as an expert. It rightly ruled that, according to Article 278 § 1 in the *Code of Civil Procedure*, the need for 'specialised knowledge', which demands the calling up an expert, is not limited to scientific knowledge, but also extends into such areas as technology, art, craft, etc. The Court stated that the existence of dowsing and the guild of diviners justified an expert witness of that kind. The judgement was approved by a prominent professor of civil procedure.[8]

---

[6] Moenssens (1993).
[7] Uchwała SN (1986), p. 308.
[8] Siedlecki (1986).

However, the Supreme Court missed a very good opportunity to establish some criteria for the evaluation of scientific (or unscientific) evidence. They would be all the more desirable, as dowsing has turned out to be an artefact; two Polish physicists, after 20 years of intensive research, failed to find any scientific foundation for such a discipline.[9]

One can, however, notice some fragmentary criteria for scientific evidence in other (unpublished!) judgements. They are the following:

- the use of the results of the newest research provided they are reliable enough;[10]
- the acceptation of DNA analysis results if they were obtained in a laboratory within a scientific department or in an accredited laboratory;[11]
- the need for clarifying whether or not the anthropological method in a paternity case is based on a uniform and generally accepted research methodology.[12]

## Scientific Evidence in Criminal Proceedings

Article 7 of the new *Polish Code of Criminal Procedure* of 1997 contains the principle of the free appraisal of evidence: "The procedural organs determine their position based on all of the evidence, appraised independently according to the rules of correct reasoning, as well as on the basis of knowledge and life experience."[13] Knowledge is regarded as an objective condition for judicial free appraisal of evidence.[14]

Świda-Łagiewska (1983) distinguishes two kinds of judicial knowledge: internal and external. Internal knowledge is the subjective knowledge of a particular judge. External knowledge is that obtained from experts. According to Article 193 § 1 of the *Code of Criminal Procedure*, if a determination of significant importance to the solving of a case requires specialised knowledge, one consults an expert or experts. The Supreme Court, in its judgements of 1977[15] and 1983,[16] obliged the courts to apply the criterion of contemporary science requirements, especially during the evaluation of an expert opinion. Having a basic modicum of knowledge is therefore the duty of the court.[17]

In November 1999 the Supreme Court passed a judgement in a theft case, in which a dog scent line-up was the only piece of evidence against the accused. The Court confirmed the possibility of the conviction on the basis of

---

[9] Kiszkowski & Szydłowski (1999).
[10] Wyrok SN (1975).
[11] Wyrok SN (1996).
[12] Wyrok SN (1974).
[13] Ustawa z dnia 6 czerwca, 1997.
[14] Uzasadnienie (1997).
[15] Postanowienie SN (1977b).
[16] Wyrok SN (1983).
[17] Doda & Gaberle (1995).

one piece of evidence. However, it established the 'irreproachable methodology' criterion for such evidence evaluation. The Court formulated also six conditions for admitting an osmological opinion, based on a 'novel and unverified forensic method', as aggravating evidence.[18]

No definition of scientific evidence exists in Polish criminal procedure. Nevertheless, sometimes the opponents' arguments against a controversial method, like for example the polygraph examination, are based on the assumption that the method is inadmissible because it does not display the qualities of scientific evidence![19] Such a situation additionally emphasises the urgent need for consideration by the Supreme Court and/or Courts of Appeals the issue of the treatment of scientific evidence.

**Judges' Opinions on Scientific Evidence**

In May and October 1999, the author carried out some preliminary research on judges' opinions on scientific evidence. The respondents – 62 judges ruling in criminal trials – were asked about which forensic method out of 13 given could be regarded as 'scientific evidence', and on the basis of which method as 'the only piece of evidence' they would be apt to convict the accused.

The first question on the 'scientific evidence label' was answered as follows:

| Method | Percent of Positive Answers |
|---|---|
| DNA Analysis | 100 |
| Toxicological examination | 89 |
| Fingerprint examination | 87 |
| Fibre examination | 87 |
| Handwriting examination | 87 |
| Road accident reconstruction | 71 |
| Glass examination | 65 |
| Dog scent line-up | 56 |
| Polygraph examination | 23 |
| Identification parade | 13 |
| Forensic hypnosis | 8 |
| Dowsing | 3 |
| Clairvoyance | 0 |

The second question on 'the only piece of evidence as the basis for conviction' was answered as follows:

---

[18] Ordyński (1999), p. C2.
[19] Czapigo (1999).

| Method | Percent of Positive Answers |
|---|---|
| DNA Analysis | 100 |
| Fingerprint examination | 92 |
| Handwriting examination | 79 |
| Road accident reconstruction | 73 |
| Toxicological examination | 61 |
| Identification parade | 48 |
| Fibre examination | 44 |
| Dog scent line-up | 27 |
| Glass examination | 21 |
| Polygraph examination | 2 |
| Dowsing | 2 |
| Forensic hypnosis | 0 |
| Clairvoyance | 0 |

The respondents' answers are generally consistent with the state of knowledge in forensic science. However, some their preferences, even more than prejudices, are worthy of a more detailed analysis.

First of all, the respondents' unanimity concerning the DNA analysis has to be stressed. Its highest position in both rankings should not be a surprise taking into consideration the sophistication, and popularity of the method. However, this kind of attitude of the judiciary could threaten the principle of free appraisal of evidence. The Polish Supreme Court has warned the courts against such preferences. Already, over 20 years ago, it stated that an expert opinion must not be the only basis of the judgement.[20] Recently the Court passed two judgements on the status of DNA analysis in (once again!) civil proceedings, rightly stressing the necessity of the evaluation of other kinds of evidence existing in the case as well.[21]

As concerns other 'scientific' methods, the very high position of handwriting analysis contradicts the views expressed in *United States* v. *Starzecpyzel*.[22] Similarly, over half of the respondents considered dog scent line-ups to be scientific evidence, regardless of the fact that canine identification of human scent does not yet have a proper scientific foundation. Specifically, the method has not been standardised, its diagnostic value is rather low, it is not generally accepted, and therefore it would hardly fulfil the *Daubert* criteria.[23]

We should take into account that the second question, and the situation described by it, could appear somewhat contrived for the respondents (perhaps this was the reason the majority overlooked the fact that toxicological examinations never lead to perpetrator's identification). Regarding this question as the one concerning the diagnostic value of the methods, one comes to the conclusion that the responses reflect, though with some exceptions, the

---

[20] Postanowienie SN (1977a).
[21] Wyrok SN (1994); Wójcikiewicz (1995); Wyrok SN (1998).
[22] Majamaa (1998).
[23] Wójcikiewicz (1999).

actual hierarchy of forensic methods, arranged according to their diagnostic value.[24] The high rankings of DNA analysis and fingerprint examination seem justifiable, unlike those of eyewitness identification – every second judge was apt to convict the accused solely on the basis of identification parade results – and that of dog scent identification – approved as a sole basis of conviction by one fourth of the respondents! Such readiness to convict on such a basis could be the source of miscarriages of justice.

## Conclusions

The development of forensic science makes greater and greater demands on judges concerning evidence evaluation. An expert witness as a source of specialised knowledge, though indispensable, is insufficient. The growing number of 'superopinions', especially in fields of novel evidence like canine human scent identification paradoxically seems to confirm this statement. In this situation, a systematic forensic education of the judges becomes very important. To meet that need, the Forensic Science Education Centre in Cracow organises a five-day seminar entitled "Scientific evidence in judicial proceedings" for judges ruling in criminal trials. Nevertheless, some general indigenous criteria for the scientific evaluation of evidence formulated by the Supreme Court would be of inestimable value to the judiciary.

## References

**Czapigo, A.** (1999), 'Dowody w nowym kodeksie postępowania karnego (Evidence in the new Code of Criminal Procedure)', in: P. Kruszyński (ed.), *Nowe uregulowania prawne w kodeksie postępowania karnego z 1997 r. (New legal regulations in the Code of Criminal Procedure of 1997)*, Warszawa: Dom Wydawniczy ABC, pp. 165-219.
*Daubert v. Merell Dow Pharmaceuticals* (1993).
**Doda, Z. & Gaberle, A.** (1995), *Dowody w procesie karnym (Evidence in Criminal Proceedings)*, Warszawa: Dom Wydawniczy ABC.
*Frye v. United States*, 1923.
*General Electric v. Joiner* (1997).
**Grieve, D.L.** (1999), 'Daubert and fingerprints: The United States of America v. Bryan C. Mitchell', *The Print* 15, 4, 3-5.
**Gruza, E.** (1995), 'Przyczynek do zagadnienia dopuszczalności i wykorzystywania "dowodów naukowych" w procesie karnym (Contribution to the problem of admissibility and use of "scientific evidence" in criminal proceedings)', *Przegląd Sądowy*, 7-8, pp. 83-92.
**Kiszkowski, P. & Szydłowski, H.** (1999), 'Radiestezja a nauka (Dowsing and science)', *Wiedza i Życie* 2, pp. 34-37.
**Kleinmuntz, B. & Szucko, J.J.** (1984) 'A field study of the fallibility of polygraphic lie detection', *Nature* 308, 449-450.
*Kumho Tire Co. v. Carmichael* (1999).
**Majamaa, H.** (1998), *Working Group Marks, Paper presented at the 9ᵗʰ ENFSI Meeting*, Lisbon, 23-25 April, 1-4.

---

[24] Cf. Schoon (1998); Kleinmuntz & Szucko (1984); Siuta & Wójcikiewicz (1999).

**Moenssens, A.A.** (1993), 'Novel scientific evidence in criminal cases: Some words of caution', *The Journal of Criminal Law & Criminology*, 84, 1, 1-21.

Moenssens A.A. (1999). Is fingerprint identification a "science"? *The Print*, 15, 4, 1-2.

**Ordyński, J.** (1999), 'Wartość badań zapachowych (Reliability of scent examination)', *Rzeczpospolita*, 279, C2.

**Postanowienie SN.** (1977a), (Decision of the Supreme Court) II CR 44/77, from 28 February (unpublished).

**Postanowienie SN.** (1977b), (Decision of the Supreme Court) V KZ 54/77, from 20 July, *OSNKW*, 9, item 108, 44-47.

**Schoon, G.A.A.** (1998), 'A first assessment of the reliability of an improved scent identification line-up', *Journal of Forensic Sciences*, 43, 1, 70-75.

**Siedlecki, W.** (1986), 'Glosa (Gloss)', *OSPiKA*, 7-8, 309-310.

**Siuta, J. & Wójcikiewicz, J.** (1999), *Hipnoza kryminalna (Forensic Hypnosis)*, Kraków: Wydawnictwo Instytutu Ekspertyz Sądowych.

**Świda - Łagiewska Z.** (1983), *Zasada swobodnej oceny dowodów w polskim procesie karnym (The Principle of Free Appraisal of Evidence in the Polish Criminal Proceedings)*, Wrocław: Wydawnictwo Uniwersytetu Wrocławskiego.

**Uchwała SN.** (1986), (Resolution of the Supreme Court) z dnia 30 października 1985 r., III CZP 59/85, *OSPiKA*, 7-8, item 139, 308-309.

*United States v. Mitchell* (1998).

*United States v. Starzecpyzel* (1995).

Ustawa z dnia 17 listopada 1964 r., kodeks postępowania cywilnego (Act from 17 November, 1964, *Code of Civil Procedure*), Dz. U. 43, item 296.

Ustawa z dnia 6 czerwca 1997 r., kodeks postępowania karnego (Act from 7 June, 1997, *Code of Criminal Procedure*), Dz. U. 89, item 555.

**Uzasadnienie** (1997), Kodeks postępowania karnego (Reasoning of the Code of Criminal Procedure).

**Waltoś, S.** (1998), *Proces karny. Zarys systemu (Criminal Procedure. An Outline of the System)*, Warszawa: Wydawnictwa Prawnicze PWN.

**Wójcikiewicz, J.** (1995), 'Glosa do wyroku Sądu Najwyższego z 16 lutego 1994 r. (Gloss to the Supreme Court's judgement from 16 February, 1994)', *Palestra*, 3-4, 269-271.

**Wójcikiewicz, J.** (1999), 'Dog scent lineup as scientific evidence', Paper presented at the IAFS 15th Triennial Meeting, Los Angeles, 22-28 August, 1-8.

**Wyrok SN** (1974), (Judgement of the Supreme Court) III CRN 305/74, from 12 December (unpublished).

**Wyrok SN** (1975), (Judgement of the Supreme Court) II CR 898/74, from 25 February (unpublished).

**Wyrok SN** (1983), (Judgement of the Supreme Court) IV KR 74/83, from 6 May, *OSNKW*, 12, item 102, 22-26.

**Wyrok SN** (1994), (Judgement of the Supreme Court) II CRN 176/93, from 16 February, *OSNCP*, 10, item 197, 76-82.

**Wyrok SN** (1996), (Judgement of the Supreme Court) I CKU 27/96, from 27 November (unpublished).

**Wyrok SN** (1998), (Judgement of the Supreme Court) I CKU 13/98, from 6 April, *Orzecznictwo Prokuratury i Prawa*, 10, item 29, 17.

777